Software Reengineering

Robert S. Arnold

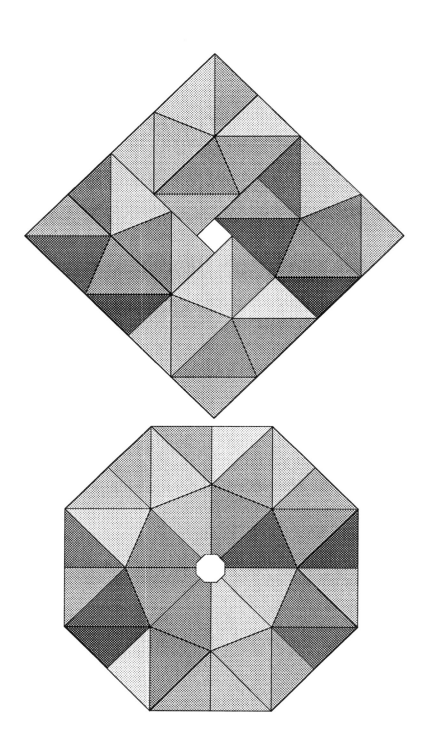

Software Reengineering

Robert S. Arnold

IEEE Computer Society Press
Los Alamitos, California

Washington • Brussels • Tokyo

IEEE COMPUTER SOCIETY PRESS TUTORIAL

Library of Congress Cataloging-in-Publication Data

Arnold, Robert S.
    Software reengineering / Robert S. Arnold.
        p.   cm.
    Includes bibliographical references.
    ISBN 0-8186-3272-0
    1. Software engineering.   2. Computer software–Development.
    I. Title.
    QA76.758.A76   1993
    005.1 ' 6—dc20   92-41597
                                                                      CIP

Published by the
IEEE Computer Society Press
10662 Los Vaqueros Circle
P.O. Box 3014
Los Alamitos, CA 90720-1264

IEEE Computer Society Press Order Number BP03272
Library of Congress Number 92-41597
ISBN 0-8186-3272-0

Additional copies can be ordered from

IEEE Computer Society Press	IEEE Service Center	IEEE Computer Society	IEEE Computer Society
Customer Service Center	445 Hoes Lane	13, avenue de l'Aquilon	Ooshima Building
10662 Los Vaqueros Circle	P.O. Box 1331	B-1200 Brussels	2-19-1 Minami-Aoyama
P.O. Box 3014	Piscataway, NJ 08855-1331	BELGIUM	Minato-ku, Tokyo 107
Los Alamitos, CA 90720-1264	Tel: (908) 981-1393	Tel: +32-2-770-2198	JAPAN
Tel: (714) 821-8380	Fax: (908) 981-9667	Fax: +32-2-770-8505	Tel: +81-3-3408-3118
Fax: (714) 821-4641	mis.custserv@computer.org	euro.ofc@computer.org	Fax: +81-3-3408-3553
Email: cs.books@computer.org			tokyo.ofc@computer.org

Technical Editor: Pradip K. Srimani
Production Editor: Catherine Harris
Cover Artist: Alex Torres
Printed in the United States of America by Braun-Brumfield, Inc.

99 98 97   5   4   3

The Institute of Electrical and Electronics Engineers, Inc.

Preface

Software reengineering is important for putting high software maintenance costs under control, recovering existing software assets, and establishing a base for future software evolution. The idea is to improve, or transform, existing software so one can understand, control, and use it anew. Software reengineering is integral for achieving many goals in software maintenance and for planning for change in existing systems.

Software reengineering is any activity designed to

(1) improve one's understanding of software, or
(2) improve the software itself, usually for increased maintainability, reusability, or evolvability.

Reverse engineering pertains to part 1 of the reengineering definition. Reverse engineering generates information about a software representation (such as source code) to help one understand it or to facilitate its processing.

Why this book?

The popularity of software reengineering from the mid-1980s until the present has increased greatly. People are trying to get as much value as possible from existing systems. There has also been a need to extend 1980s-vintage software restructuring techniques to resolve maintenance problems that could not be fixed by modifying source code control flow alone.

This collection of papers is a sound basis for understanding software reengineering technology. This book stems from my perception that people interested in reengineering need a handy, one-volume source of information about software reengineering technology, and a guide to its literature.

A wide variety of software reengineering approaches are presented, including approaches that do not modify software at all, approaches that perform mainly manual software changes, approaches that use commercially available reengineering tools, approaches that use computer graphics for discovering structure, and approaches that use automatic, rule-based transformation systems.

The book's goals are to acquaint the reader with software reengineering

- concepts,
- tools and techniques,
- case studies,
- risks and benefits, and
- research possibilities.

Intended audience

This book is intended for software engineering practitioners and researchers. Among practitioners, software managers will find a range of options and relative costs for planning and performing software reengineering. Programmers maintaining existing systems will find techniques and ideas designed to make their job easier. Even software developers will find software reengineering techniques useful for improving software during development.

For researchers, this book collects a substantial body of software reengineering literature. This book does not contain all known software reengineering work, but it does contain many seminal works in a handy, one-volume source.

Organization

The Introduction, **A Road Map Guide to Software Reengineering Technology**, describes software reengineering definitions, themes, technology, strategies, and risks. It helps the nonexpert in reengineering get quickly acquainted with reengineering technology, and also features a way to specify the meaning of software reengineering and related terms. **Chapter 1, Software Reengineering: Context and Definitions**, introduces the reader to terms, ideas, and examples of reengineering technology. It will give the reader a good understanding of reengineering ideas and some of the technology's capabilities and limitations.

The papers in **Chapter 2, Business Process Reengineering**, introduce the reader to the concepts of business process reengineering. Business process reengineering is often a prelude to software reengineering. Software reengineering in the past has often started with source code. Ways were sought to improve it, remodularize it, and render it reusable. Today it is frequently profitable first to revise the basic business (or other) processes supported by information technology. This can provide much bigger payoffs than by just improving the software itself.

Chapter 3, Reengineering Strategies and Economics, describes the processes, risks, and costs of reengineering and presents the "big picture" behind large reengineering efforts. **Chapter 4, Reengineering Experience**, provides several examples of real-life reengineering projects that give the reader valuable insight into applying reengineering technology today. **Chapter 5, Reengineering Evaluation**, presents evaluations of reengineering tools and the effectiveness of reengineering itself. Should the reader be faced with a reengineering tools evaluation or reengineering effectiveness evaluation, reading these papers will be helpful.

Chapter 6, Technology for Reengineering, will help the reader understand the technology behind reengineering tools. Users of reengineering and reverse engineering tools often take these details for granted. The papers discuss CASE tools, view-based systems, remodularization issues, and transformations for software reengineering. **Chapter 7, Data Reengineering and Migration,** helps the reader understand what data reengineering is, and provides approaches for reengineering data, improving data bases, and migrating data from one DBMS to another DBMS.

Decomposing software is fundamental to many reengineering tools. **Chapter 8, Source Code Analysis**, discusses tools and approaches for decomposing programs into objects and relationships, for creating program "slices," and for formal dependency modeling. **Chapter 9, Software Restructuring and Translation,** discusses restructuring and the technology and ideas behind it. It also examines techniques for translating source code from one language to another. These techniques are often fundamental to reverse engineering approaches.

Chapter 10, Annotating and Documenting Existing Programs, discusses annotating and documenting source code. The term "documentation" is used broadly here. It can mean graphical diagrams and mathematical descriptions, as well as textual documentation. Understanding and documenting assembly code is featured because assembly code is a kind of "worst case" for understanding and documentation. If assembly code can be successfully documented, then similar ideas, suitably modified, may apply to understanding code in higher level languages.

A major reengineering goal is reusing software. An important subtheme is salvaging software parts for reuse. **Chapter 11, Reengineering for Reuse**, discusses processes for finding candidate reusable parts, metrics for measuring source code to discover candidate reusable parts, and issues in transforming the parts into a more reusable form. **Chapter 12, Reverse Engineering and Design Recovery,** will give the reader a good understanding of the ideas and techniques of reverse engineering and design recovery. Reverse engineering commonly occurs in today's CASE toolsets. Full-fledged design recovery (such as large-scale, automatic generation of design rationales for existing code) is not considered practically feasible yet.[1] Nevertheless, the reader will find very interesting ideas here for approaching the design recovery problem on a small scale.

Chapter 13, Object Recovery, discusses reverse engineering of "object-oriented" objects from source code. Such objects typically feature the concepts of encapsulation, inheritance, and abstract data types, and are often programmed with languages such as C++. An object-oriented program structure may offer more program understanding and migration possibilities. **Chapter 14, Program Understanding**, discusses techniques for understanding code and creating models of its operation. The techniques vary from manual code reading to research systems that create models of program behavior based on knowledge of programming patterns.

Chapter 15, Knowledge-Based Program Analysis, discusses knowledge bases and architectures for supporting software reengineering and reverse engineering. Knowledge bases contain information that can support many activities. The technology offers flexibility that is attractive to reengineering and reverse engineering toolmakers.

The **Annotated Bibliography** of software reengineering literature concludes the book. The reader will find the references annotated there useful for further reading.

Robert S. Arnold
February 1993

---

[1]T. Corbi, "Program Understanding: Challenge for the 1990s," *IBM Systems J.,* Vol. 28, No. 2, 1989, pp. 294-306.

Acknowledgments

Many people helped with this book, both directly and indirectly. It is with great pleasure and gratitude that I acknowledge here their important influence on this book. I thank Henry Ayling and Pradip Srimani of the IEEE Computer Society for patiently and persistently encouraging completion of this book. I also thank Rao Vemuri, Editor-in-Chief of the Computer Society, for approving its publication. Catherine Harris, Production Editor, was essential in seeing the book smoothly through production, and in polishing the final manuscript.

Shawn Bohner provided helpful comments to improve "Road Map Guide to Software Reengineering Technology," a paper prepared for this book. H.E. Dunsmore and anonymous reviewers provided excellent suggestions for improving the paper selections, writing, and technical content of the book.

I would also like to thank the following people who made me aware of reengineering papers that I had not previously seen: Ted Biggerstaff, Ronald Brisebois, Frank Calliss, Yih-Farn Chen, Elliot Chikofsky, Aniello Cimitile, Don Coleman, Marshall Crawford, Ugo De Carlini, Prem Devanbu, Gene Forte, William Frakes, Judy Grass, John Hartman, James Haugh, Howard Haughton, H. Husmann, Dragos Luchian, Takis Katsoulakos, Hausi Müller, Malcolm Munro, Paul Oman, Peter Pfann, Herbert Ritsch, Peter Selfridge, Chris Sittenauer, Harry Sneed, Joel Sturman, Wui Gee Tan, William Ulrich, Peter Van Opens, Larry Van Sickle, David Workman, Ed Yourdon, and Don Yu. Other people who contributed important information to this book are Al Kortesoja, Vaclav Rajlich, and Tom Smith.

I thank the many publishers for kindly allowing publication of their papers in this volume. I thank all the authors, including those of papers not published here, for their efforts that have made software reengineering such a fast-growing field.

Contents

Introduction
A Road Map Guide to
Software Reengineering Technology

A Road Map Guide to Software Reengineering Technology

Robert S. Arnold

Purpose and Structure

This paper introduces the reader to software reengineering definitions and technology. Software reengineering technology supports three major themes: (1) understanding software, (2) improving software, and (3) capturing, preserving, and extending knowledge about software. This paper will help the reader see the boundaries of reengineering technology and appreciate some of its risks.

The reader is assumed to be interested in the maintenance, improvement, or understanding of existing source code. This interest may be of itself, or part of a larger task, such as converting software from one operating system to another. This paper will help reengineering nonexperts appreciate reengineering issues. Experts will see a fresh contemporary viewpoint.

The paper is structured as follows: "Reengineering Definitions" defines reengineering terms and places them in context. "The Significance of Reengineering" discusses why reengineering is significant and worthy of the reader's time and study. "Reengineering Technology" discusses reengineering technology themes and connects technology areas with the themes. It briefly discusses the importance and significance of the technology areas. "Reengineering Strategies and Risk Mitigation" discusses risks and cautions in using reengineering technology. "Future Advances" discusses future research issues for reengineering. Appendix A provides a procedure for classifying a software transformation consistent with the reengineering definition used here.

Reengineering Definitions

Software reengineering is any activity that

(1) improves one's understanding of software, or
(2) prepares or improves the software itself, usually for increased maintainability, reusability, or evolvability.

In this definition, the term "software" includes — in addition to source code — documentation, graphical pictures, and analyses. The analyses are about source code, designs, specifications, test data, and other documents directly supporting software development or maintenance.

3

Part 1 of this definition includes activities such as browsing, measuring, drawing pictures of software, documenting, and analyzing. Part 2 includes activities designed to improve static qualities of software, usually so the software is easier for people to work with.

Part 2 tends to exclude modifications whose purpose is not for maintainability, reusability, evolvability, or improving one's understanding of the software. For example, optimizing code or restructuring it purely for performance is not commonly thought of as reengineering.[1]

Reverse engineering pertains to part 1 of the reengineering definition. Reverse engineering generates information about a software representation (such as source code) to help one understand it or to facilitate its processing.

Other reengineering definitions

Different people or groups seem to have different meanings for reengineering. For example, GUIDE defines reengineering as

> the process of modifying the internal mechanisms of a system or program or the data structures of a system or program without changing its functionality [GUIDE89].

Chikofsky and Cross define reengineering as

> the examination and alteration of a subject system to reconstitute it in a new form and subsequent implementation of that form [Chikofsky90].

For reference in this discussion, the reengineering definition described in the previous section, the GUIDE definition, and the Chikofsky and Cross definition will be called definitions A, G, and C, respectively. Both definitions G and C are valuable and useful. The reengineering definition one uses depends on one's perspective. Reengineering definition A is used in this paper for several reasons.

First, definition A centers on the purpose of reengineering activities, rather than on their means or processes. This recognizes that reengineering activities can use technology that, in other contexts, may not be called "reengineering." For example, impact analysis and software testing are used in software maintenance, but not always in the context of reengineering.

Second, on close examination, definitions G and C allow different activities to be called "reengineering." Definition A is more inclusive. For example, under definition C one might classify a software functionality change as reengineering. But under definition G one would not. Under definition A one could classify a functionality change as reengineering, provided it was for the purposes mentioned.

As another example, definition G does not consider creating information about software as reengineering, unless the information is used to support modification. Definition C does define creating information about software as reengineering,[2] but only if it is on the path to reimplementation. Definition A allows the creation of information as an end in itself as part of reengineering. For example, definition A considers as reengineering the creation of information about software to facilitate understanding or to promote maintainability, reusability, or evolvability.

---

[1]The context of reengineering is expanding so rapidly, however, that some people include even these as reengineering — improving suitability for use — of the code.

[2]If we equate the information with "a new form" in definition C.

Third, definition G tends to focus on changes to source code. Improvements of non-source code items, such as documentation and specifications, may also be considered as reengineering. Such activities are allowed in definition A, and may be allowed in definition C.

This discussion should not be taken to imply that one reengineering definition is better than another. The definitions capture different perspectives. Perspective change is common in a rapidly evolving field such as reengineering. Because of the proliferation of reengineering definitions, the reader should ask people what they mean by reengineering when more than a general understanding is important.[3]

The discussion in this paper embodies an approach to classifying reengineering and similar activities, relative to reengineering definition A. In this approach, a written definition of reengineering is created. (This was done in the "Reengineering Definitions" section.) Then the context of reengineering and related terms is diagrammed. The diagram features various views of information and the transitions among the views. (Figure 1 is such a diagram, and is discussed in "The Context of Reengineering.") The transitions in the diagram are classified in a table. Finally, a decision procedure is created for classifying an activity using the table. (Table A2 and the decision procedure appear in Appendix A.)

Reengineering spellings and related terms

Just as there are no universally accepted reengineering definitions, there are no universally accepted spellings for reengineering. The most common spellings are reengineering and re-engineering. "Reengineering" is used in this paper.

Synonyms for reengineering abound, often with nuances reflecting a specific reengineering purpose:

- improvement
- renewal
- renovation
- refurbishing
- modernization
- redevelopment engineering
- reclamation
- reuse engineering

The terms *improvement, renewal, renovation, refurbishing, and redevelopment engineering* all have similar meaning: improving software for evolvability and further use. *Modernization* includes improvement of software, but may go beyond by improving software development and maintenance activities surrounding the software. *Reclamation* and *reuse engineering* refer to reengineering to make source code more reusable.

The context of reengineering

Figure 1 illustrates a framework for understanding reengineering and related terms. The figure, an update to a similar one in [Chikofsky90], reflects evolving connotations of terms. Five ideas are shown in Figure 1:

- (1) views of software,
- (2) information base,
- (3) decomposition,
- (4) composition, and
- (5) transformation.

---

[3]As in negotiating contracts for reengineering work.

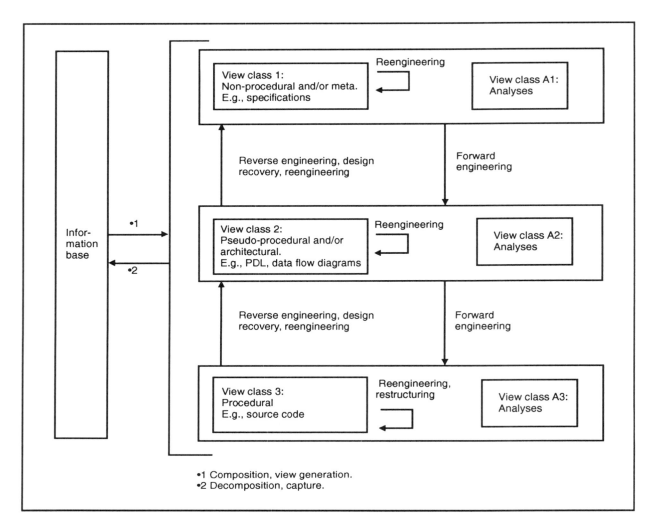

Figure 1. Reengineering and related terms. Reengineering and related technology may be viewed as transforming information in one software view to information in another software view. The transformation may move information into and out of the information base.

Understanding these ideas helps distinguish the terms presented in Figure 1.

A software *view* is a representation of software or a report about software. A software view may be for human viewing or not, but it typically is a significant interim representation of software that humans may want to see. In this discussion, the word view refers to the type of view (e.g., a data flow diagram). *View information* means the specific information in a view (e.g., a specific data flow diagram D), or the information base of knowledge decomposed from information in the view.

Examples of software views are specifications, source code, measurements, reports derived from static source code analysis, and test data used to characterize software behavior. Figure 2 has several sample views, with possible view information shown as pictures. When a view is supported by a tool, it nearly always comes with a view editor, to support entering, browsing, and changing view information.

As implied by Figure 1, views can be grouped into four classes:

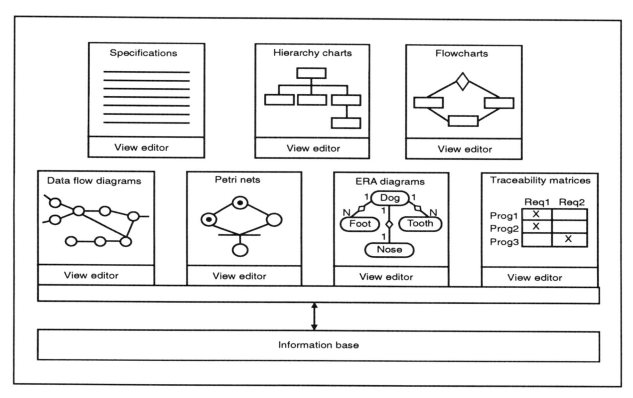

Figure 2. Multiple software views. Many reengineering tools, especially CASE toolsets, support several different views of software. No tool as yet supports all the views above, but this gives an idea of what can be found in a view.

Class 1:   Nonprocedural- and/or meta-oriented views.
Class 2:   Pseudoprocedural- and/or architectural-oriented views.
Class 3:   Highly procedural views, or close derivatives.
Class A: Analysis views that may accompany any other view.

Class 1 contains views that are nonprocedural and/or *meta*.[4] Software specifications and conceptual schemas fall into Class 1. Class 2 contains views that are pseudo-procedural or architectural. Designs, program design language descriptions, and software architecture diagrams (such as calling hierarchies or data flow diagrams) fall into this class. Class 3 contains highly procedural information, information closely associated or derived from this information, or direct information about representations. Source code, program slices, data, data definitions in source code, objects and relationships decomposed from views, and syntax trees are in this class.

Class A contains analysis views derived from any of the other views. For example, software metrics are derived by analyzing software. An analysis view can appear with information in any of the other views. Class A can be divided as follows:

Class A1:   Analyses pertaining to Class 1 views.
             Example: Fog index of specification text.

_____

[4]A "meta" view is a view *about* something. The intent here is *nonprocedural* meta views, such as data schemas or decision tables.

Class A2: Analyses pertaining to Class 2 views.
Example: Coupling levels of source modules.

Class A3: Analyses pertaining to Class 3 views.
Example: Number of modules in source code.

In practice, view classes 1, 2, 3, and A are not disjoint. For example, some people may place a program design language (PDL) description in Class 3, others in Class 2. However, it is assumed for the rest of the discussion that it is possible for an individual to create disjoint classes for himself or herself, if needed. For the rest of the paper, it is assumed that the classes are disjoint.

The *information base* is the repository of information about the software. It is loaded in three ways:

(1) Decomposing software into objects and relationships,
(2) Incrementally building up objects and relationships through tools that build on or add to knowledge in the information base, and
(3) Importing information from other information bases.

Decomposition is the process of transforming a view into objects and relationships stored in the information base. For example, compilers commonly decompose programs into abstract syntax tree representations.

Composition generates view information from information in the information base. The *composer* (the tool or person that does the composition) assembles view information by finding relevant objects and relationships in the information base, then adding view formatting as needed to display the view information. For example, the back end of a compiler commonly generates code by traversing a semantic graph of the program, or some equivalent.

The notion of *transformation* is central. In Figure 1, reengineering transforms, in effect, information from one software view into information in another view, at the same or earlier view class.[5]

Examples of reengineering transformations are transformations from source code (Class 3) to restructured source code (Class 3), updated designs (Class 2), corrected specifications (Class 1), or computed static measurements (Class A3). The reengineering transformation usually "improves" the information in the view according to some criterion.[6] Software restructuring is reengineering centered on transforming the source code's structure (syntax and semantics).

Transformation also underlies reverse engineering and design recovery. Reverse engineering is like reengineering, except the origin and target views are different, the target view normally being in an earlier view class. Transforming source code, for example, into structure charts may be either reengineering or reverse engineering. But transforming source code to restructured source code is reengineering or restructuring, not reverse engineering. Updating embedded source code comments is reengineering.

Reverse engineering has other meanings, though these are not used here. For example, it can mean to analyze a detailed representation to discover its inherent design. One sometimes hears that people perform reverse engineering to determine source code from object code. For other meanings of reverse engineering, see [Rekoff85].

Design recovery, a subset of reverse engineering, generates information about software. Often the information is

---

[5]Even though some reengineering tasks, such as purely manual inspection and improvement of source code, do not involve an online information base, they can still fit this model. Just substitute information in the person's head for information in the information base.

[6]A frequent criterion is that reengineering should change form but not function. For example, restructuring code to improve readability is also reengineering.

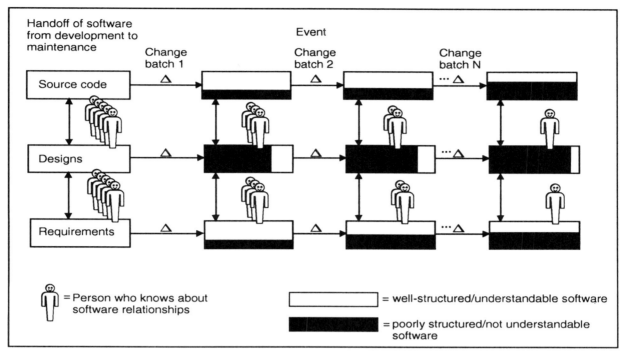

Figure 3. Dynamics of maintenance and information loss. Maintenance tends to make software harder to change through loss of information about how to modify it. Fewer and fewer people know less and less about the software. This happens because people leave who understand the software, and because the software itself becomes harder for new programmers to understand. Mental connections are lost.

not easily extractable from the software and associated documentation, and requires considerable effort to deduce. Three examples are generating rationales describing why the software is in its current form, generating specifications from source code, and generating black box test data sets for software without documentation that is current. Appendix A gives another interpretation of design recovery in terms of views.

Forward engineering is a transformation, usually from an earlier to a later view class. For example, generating source code from a data flow diagram is usually a forward engineering activity.

Reengineering can be considered in other ways besides transformations of view. The following section discusses the purposes behind reengineering.

Significance of Reengineering

Reengineering is important for several reasons:

(1) Reengineering can help reduce an organization's evolution risk.

To extend software capabilities, organizations can build new software, evolve existing software, reengineer and evolve existing software, use application generators, or obtain software parts or packages. When the latter two options are not available, organizations are faced with building new software or evolving existing software. Simply manually evolving existing source code tends, in current practice, to make the software harder to change, or less reliable when changed (see Figure 3). Building software from scratch can be expensive and uncertain. Reengineering software and evolving it sometimes offers less change risk. It can help safeguard an organization's software investment better than building software from scratch or simply evolving it through traditional maintenance.

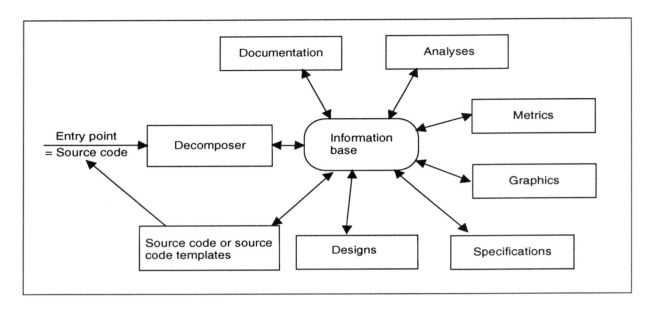

Figure 4. Reengineering and CASE toolsets. Most CASE toolsets started as forward engineering tools. For added value, CASE toolmakers have added reengineering and reverse engineering capabilities. Most entry points to these capabilities currently depend on source code only.

(2) Reengineering can help an organization recoup its investment in software.

Companies have spent hundreds of thousands of dollars building software. The software industry has spent billions. Rather than ignore existing software, companies can use reengineering to partially recoup their software investment. Reengineering helps organizations build on existing software.

(3) Reengineering can make software easier to change.

Improving software can pay rich dividends. It speeds productivity of the maintenance programmer by making code easier to understand or work with. It gives an organization more flexibility because its software can be modified more quickly to accommodate business changes. Reengineering extends an organization's options.

(4) Reengineering is big business.

The 1990's market for reengineering services and tools has been estimated to be in the billions. As reported in [*Computerworld* 91], the estimated expenditures allocated to reengineering *services* in 1990 was $4.6 billion. For 1995 the estimate is $11.9 billion. The estimated expenditures allocated to reengineering *products,* including back-end CASE tools, was $.8 billion in 1990. For 1995 the estimate is $2.7 billion. Many software systems, and system parts, need updating. Software contractors and service companies are pursuing work in this area. Many organizations are looking for reengineering techniques, tools, and processes to use.

(5) Reengineering capability extends CASE toolsets.

Reengineering helps new techniques and tools to be applied to old software. This has several benefits. For maintainers, it allows newer and more powerful tools to help them maintain software. Reengineering may be seen as a kind of technology transfer vehicle, allowing old systems to be brought into frameworks of new, more powerful tools. For CASE tool vendors, adding reengineering tools to their toolsets opens new markets of existing software. It also gives important added value to their previously forward-engineering-only toolsets (see Figure 4).

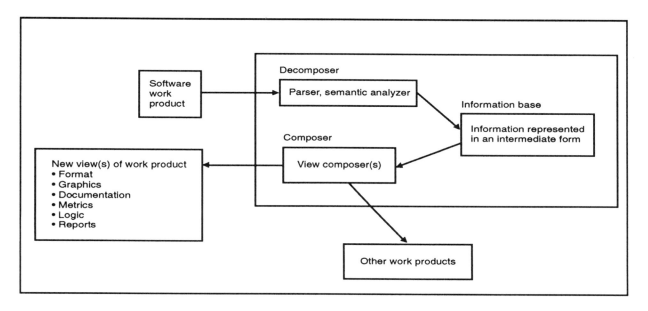

Figure 5. Automatic reengineering process. Reengineering tools tend to follow a common framework. They parse information into an information base. Views are then generated from the information base to reflect different information about software.

(6)   Reengineering is a catalyst for automating software maintenance.

Most reengineering tools follow the pattern of Figure 5. They are essentially repositories, with specialized ways to get information into and out of them. An important part of this is parsed information stored in the information base. The parsed information is valuable for analysis, automation, and research in software maintenance. The framework in Figure 5 also provides clear points of evolution within any of its parts.

(7)   Reengineering is a catalyst for applying artificial intelligence (AI) techniques to solve software reengineering problems.

As discussed earlier, reengineering has a basis in transformations. Historically, the field of automated transformations is an outgrowth of work in AI, such as the rule-based production systems [Davis76] and language processing. Earlier, transformations grew out of formal logic and mathematical rewrite systems. Reengineering is supplying AI workers with a fruitful field in which to apply their work (e.g., [Rich90], [Hartman91]).

For the preceding reasons, reengineering has been significant and likely will remain so during the next 5 – 15 years. Experience with reengineering will provide ways to improve software development and maintenance. Ideally, progress in reengineering, development, and maintenance will lessen the need to reengineer in the first place.

Reengineering Technology

There are several themes underlying software reengineering technology: improving software, understanding software, and capturing, preserving, and extending knowledge about software. Table 1 shows these themes and their associated technology. The following sections discuss these technology areas. They briefly describe each technical area and its significance, and list two or more references for further study. The reader will find the discussion useful for quickly appreciating reengineering technology. This discussion, being brief, is not comprehensive of all reengineering technology or all relevant work.

Table 1. Reengineering Technology	
Reengineering theme	Associated technology
Improving software	Restructuring Redocumenting, annotating, updating documentation Reuse engineering Remodularization Data reengineering Business process reengineering Maintainability analysis, portfolio analysis, economic analysis
Understanding software	Browsing Analyzing, measuring Reverse engineering, design recovery
Capturing, preserving, and extending knowledge about software	Decomposition Reverse engineering, design recovery Object recovery Program understanding Knowledge bases and transformations

Technology for improving software

Software restructuring. Software restructuring is the modification of software to make it easier to understand or easier to maintain [Arnold89b]. Nowadays the term connotes changing the source code control structure. Restructuring is significant because it is one of the oldest (e.g., [Bohm66]) and most refined reengineering techniques. Restructuring was one of the first reengineering tasks to be fully automated. Developing automated restructurers has led the way to other reengineering tools [Arnold90b]. Informative references on restructuring are [Arnold89b], [Miller87], and [Calliss88].

Redocumenting, annotating, and updating documentation. Redocumenting software is the creation of updated, correct information about software. Redocumenting code is a transformation from code (and other documents and programmer knowledge) into new or updated documentation about code. Normally this documentation is textual (e.g., embedded comments), but it can be graphical as well. Software improvement by updating documentation (embedded comments, designs, and specifications) is one of the older reengineering techniques ([Heninger78], [Sneed84]). Redocumentation is important because maintainers tend to depend on good inline comments [Glass81] as guideposts to what the code is doing.

Annotating connotes adding documentation to source code when there is little useful documentation to begin with. Annotating is particularly important for understanding assembly code. [Landis88] is an informative work on redocumentation. Success in redocumentation depends heavily on automated tools. [Philips84] tells a horror story about trying to perform redocumentation without tools.

Reuse engineering. Reuse engineering is the modification of software to make it more reusable, usually aiming to find software parts and rebuild them so that they can be put into a reuse library. Several authors describe processes for finding and reusing parts ([Arnold91b], [Caldiera88]). Prospecting metrics and heuristics are described in [Arnold90a], [Reynolds90], and [Caldiera91]. Specific techniques for making existing software reusable are described in [Bailey90]. Reengineering code into more object-oriented forms is related to reuse engineering, and is discussed below.

Legacy systems is a subfield of reuse engineering that decomposes existing systems into objects and relationships that may be reassembled (reused) in new systems. [Theby91] discusses finding and storing objects and relationships for legacy systems. The term "legacy system" may also refer to a system of enduring value.

Remodularization. Software remodularization is the changing of the module structure of a system. Often this depends on cluster analysis of system component characteristics and coupling measures. Recent work in this area is [Schwanke91] and [Sneed88]. Criteria for modularization are discussed in [Card85].

Data reengineering. Data reengineering improves a system's data. Schemas may be reorganized and updated, multiple schemas may be consolidated into one schema, data dictionary entries may be made semantically consistent, and invalid data may be removed. Data reengineering is often a prelude to other tasks, such as migrating data to another data base management system. Informative references on data reengineering are [Ricketts89] and [Hevner89].

Business process reengineering. With today's newer, flexible software architectures and information technology automation possibilities, there is a trend to make software fit the business, rather than business fit the software. Experience has shown that powerful productivity improvements can sometimes come from rethinking the business processes automated by software ([Hammer90], [Davenport90]). This rethinking may result in new software designs that can become the basis for reengineering, migrating, or evolving a software system.

Maintainability analysis, portfolio analysis, economic analysis. Software maintainability analysis is important for discovering what parts of a system should be reengineered. Typically the majority of maintenance work is centered on a relatively few modules in a system. Maintainability analysis helps to locate the high maintenance system parts. These parts have the biggest initial impact on maintenance costs.

[Peercy81] defines a methodology for determining program maintainability. More recently, [Oman92a] and [Oman92b] describe what maintainability is and metrics for assessing it. To decide when and where to reengineer, [Husmann90] discusses the use of portfolio analysis, [Sneed91] discusses the use of cost-benefit models, and [Connell87] describes reengineering criteria.

Technology for understanding software

Browsing. Browsing of software, such as with a text editor, is perhaps the oldest means for understanding it. Recently browsing has become more advanced, with the use of hypertext [Conklin87] to make connections between related parts and multiple view systems [Cleveland89] to provide different views at the click of a mouse (see Figure 2). Cross-reference tools are another important part of browsing.

Analyzing, measuring. Analysis and measurement are also important technologies for understanding program properties such as complexity. A large literature on metrics has accumulated (such as [Cote88]). Relevant techniques for reengineering are program slicing [Weiser81], control flow complexity measurement [McCabe76], coupling measures [Myers75], and many others (for example, [Harrison82], [Rombach89]).

Reverse engineering, design recovery. As indicated above, reverse engineering and design recovery generate new information about software, usually in a different view. This technology has become popular, but determining some kinds of design information (like design rationales) is still quite risky [Corbi90].

More commonly, reverse engineering generates structure charts or data flow diagrams from source code. These tools rely heavily on information readily available or analyzable from the code itself. The January 1990 issue of *IEEE Software* has a good collection of papers on reverse engineering and design recovery.

Capturing, preserving, and extending knowledge about software

Decomposition. Program decomposition takes a program and makes objects and relationships out of it. These objects and relationships are stored in an information base. The objects and relationships facilitate analysis, measurement, and transformation and extraction of further information. Working on a decomposition rather than directly on the source code saves the work of having to parse the program and create objects and relationships for use by a tool. This task, though straightforward for most languages, is time-consuming to solve from scratch. For

13

most languages it is easier to rely on off-the-shelf decomposers, or decomposer generators such as lex and yacc on Unix.

Decomposition is not confined to reengineering. It is used in integrated programming support environments and structured editors. Good references on decomposition are [Chen90], [Lyle88], and [Gopal88] — and there are many more.

Object recovery. Object recovery obtains objects from source code. This allows one to view previously nonobject-oriented source code in an object-oriented way. The object-orientation (classes, inheritance, methods, abstract data types, etc.) may be partial or complete.

Migrating source code to object-oriented form has been receiving attention. An object-oriented program structure may offer more program understanding, migration, and impact reduction possibilities than nonobject-oriented code. There has been previous experience with object orientation when converting systems from C to C++. [Breuer91], [Dietrich91], [Jacobson91], [Dunn91], and [Byrne91] describe recent experience and ideas for discovering objects in source code.

Program understanding. Program understanding takes several forms. One is manual or automated techniques for programmers to gain a better understanding of the software. The other is a body of work that stores information about programming and uses this information to find instances of programming knowledge in the code. Understanding is evidenced by the extent to which the software is matched with the tool's base of programming knowledge. [Robson91] gives a quick overview of both forms of program understanding. Instances of the latter work are [Hartman91], [Rich90], and [Harandi90].

Knowledge bases and transformations. Knowledge bases (for example, [Harandi90]) and program transformations (e.g., [Burson90]) are foundational to much reengineering technology today. The information base, associated transformation engine, and programmed transformations drive the power of the reengineering tool. The transformations work on program graphs and object graphs stored in the knowledge base. Object-based, transformational architectures for reengineering tools (e.g., [Burson90]) are attractive for building new reengineering tools (for example, see [Kozaczynski89]).

Reengineering Strategies and Risk Mitigation

Being able to apply reengineering technology is as important as knowing what it is and what it can do. Much experience has been accumulated.

Reengineering process

The reengineering process takes many forms, depending on its objectives. Sample objectives are code cleanup, redocumentation, migration, capture of information in an information base, and reengineering code for reuse.

Case studies are frequent sources of reengineering processes. For example, [Slovin91] describes the improvement of the modular structure and maintainability of a system having high maintenance costs. [Britcher90] describes a reengineering feasibility project in which a Federal Aviation Administration terminal approach control system was reengineered to operate on more modern hardware and in Pascal (instead of assembly code).

Others have tried to systematize the reengineering process. Such an approach has been described in [Ulrich90 – 91]. The major process steps here are inventory/analysis, positioning, and transformation. The inventory and analysis phase establishes a software components base and evaluates reengineering options based on this inventory. Positioning improves software quality without necessarily affecting existing functionality or architecture. Positioning improves the software to facilitate change, or analysis to support change. The transformation phase creates a new architecture from the existing one.

Reengineering evaluation

There is concern about the empirical effectiveness of reengineering. The evidence for reengineering falls into anecdotes, case studies, lessons learned, and experiments. A good discussion of cost-benefit analysis issues for reengineering can be found in [Sneed91]. Experiments such as [FSMSC87] and [Sneed90] imply that software restructuring and reengineering, respectively, can be helpful. An early case study ([Sneed84]) showed mixed cost-benefit results, but this is not unusual for major work being done for the first time. Later case studies (i.e., [Slovin91] and [Britcher90]) showed positive reengineering results.

Reengineering risk analysis and mitigation

Reengineering is not something that one simply "does." It is easy to waste time and dollars on ineffective approaches. As pointed out in [Ulrich90], one should approach reengineering with a plan. The plan can then be evaluated and risks assessed.

[Arnold91a] cataloged several typical reengineering risk areas, associated risks, and mitigations. Table 2 shows some of these areas and their associated risks.

Table 2. Reengineering Risks (from [Arnold91a])	
Risk Area	**Risks**
Process Risks	Extremely high manual reengineering costs. Cost benefits not realized in required time frame. Cannot economically justify the reengineering effort. Reengineering effort drifts. Lack of management commitment to ongoing reengineering solution [Ulrich90a].
Personnel Risks	Programmers inhibiting the start of reengineering. Programmers performing less effectively to make an unpopular reengineering project look less effective.
Application Risks	Reengineering with no local application experts available. Existing business knowledge embedded in source code is lost ([Koka91], [Ulrich90a]). Reengineered system does not perform adequately [Koka91].
Technology Risks	Recovered information is not useful or not used [Chikofsky91]. Masses of (expensive) documentation produced. Reverse engineering to representations that cannot be shared. Reengineering technology inadequate to accomplish reengineering goals. Reengineering where there is little reengineering technology support.
Tools Risks	Dependence on tools that do not perform as advertised. Not using installed tools.
Strategy Risks	Premature commitment to a reengineering solution for an entire system. Failure to have a long-term vision with interim goals [Ulrich90a]. Lack of global view: code, data, process reengineering. No plan for using reengineering tools [Ulrich90a].

The message here is to respect reengineering and have contingencies for mitigating risk. In many cases mitigation means trying reengineering on a small scale (e.g., a small subset of programs) and assessing risks before committing to a wholesale reengineering effort.

Future Advances

Several advances in reengineering technology can be expected, and are discussed briefly below. Some of the areas are already supported, and are being extended with CASE tools. Often CASE tool vendors are leading the way in (internal) research because of the product infrastructure that they own.[7]

Software maintainability measurement

There is interest in developing suites of metrics for finding hard-to-maintain code. This code could be a prime candidate for reengineering. Several maintainability metrics and frameworks exist (e.g., [Arnold83], [Arnold82], [Peercy81]). However, more recently, newer maintainability frameworks have emerged ([Oman92a], [Oman92b]).

Reengineering cost benefit models

A medium or large reengineering effort often requires cost-benefit justification. There is a need for organizations to input their maintenance parameters and get a reasonable estimate of the costs, benefits, and timeframe for payoff. More work is needed in making these estimation tools available ([Arnold89], [Sneed91], [Sittenauer92]).

Expert systems for reengineering tasks

Much expertise now exists about reengineering. A logical next step is to capture this expertise in an expert system rules base. The rules base can then be embedded into an existing CASE tool to enhance the value of the tool for users. Example areas where expert systems can be useful are prospecting for reusable parts in source code [Knight92], finding objects in source code, and remodularizing systems.

Reverse engineering into models

Model-based maintenance deals mainly with nonprocedural diagrams that together model an application. The source code is generated, usually with a CASE tool, from the diagrams. Maintenance of source code is done through the diagrams, not directly on the source code. This maintenance paradigm holds great promise for reducing maintenance costs and facilitating software evolution.

CASE tools already exist for model-based maintenance. Methodologies have been developed and are being refined for migrating existing systems into model-based systems. There is room for extending and automating parts of this work.

Software process instrumentation for maintenance

The software process needs to be instrumented to capture software change. This will allow change histories for software to be animated and "played back" to maintainers. This goes beyond configuration management. The change histories must be captured in ways that semantically make sense to maintainers that are browsing them.

---

[7]Trying to create a CASE tool infrastructure from scratch, without tool-building tools, can be time-consuming and expensive. However, powerful tool-building technology and off-the-shelf tools are now available that can speed the creation of a tool infrastructure.

Summary

The major points made here are

(1)   Software reengineering is any activity designed

- to improve one's understanding of software, or
- to improve the software itself, usually for increased maintainability, reusability, or evolvability.

(2)   There is no universally accepted definition of reengineering. Several definitions exist that reflect different perspectives on what reengineering is. The approach embodied in the section titled, "The Context of Reengineering," and Appendix A can be used to more precisely characterize definitions of reengineering, reverse engineering, and other terms.

(3)   Transformation is central to reengineering and related terms. Key elements of transformations are views of software, an information base, decomposition of software information into objects and relationships in an information base, and composition of views from information in the information base.

(4)   There are several reasons why reengineering is significant:

- Reengineering can help reduce an organization's evolution risk.
- Reengineering can help an organization recoup its investment in software.
- Reengineering can make software easier to change.
- Reengineering is big business.
- Reengineering capability amplifies CASE toolsets.
- Reengineering is a catalyst for automating software maintenance.
- Reengineering is a catalyst for applying artificial intelligence (AI) techniques to solve software reengineering problems.

(5)   Reengineering technology has three basic themes:

- Improving software,
- Understanding software, and
- Capturing, preserving, and extending knowledge about software.

(6)   Reengineering risks exist, but they can be planned for and mitigated.

Appendix A

A decision procedure for classifying a software transformation

To decide if a given transformation (or procedure), transforming information in view D into information in view C, is reengineering, reverse engineering, design recovery, or forward engineering, do the following:

1. Put view D and view C into one of the view classes (1, 2, 3, A1, A2, A3). (See Figure 1 and the discussion of it in the section titled, "The Context of Reengineering".) If D and C cannot be classified, then this decision procedure cannot be used.[8]

2. Classify the transformation according to the following table. A label of "open" in the table means the transformation is not classified. (A transformation not listed in the table is also "open.") It may or may not be an instance of the other terms. More information is needed.

Example

Each example is assumed to meet the necessary conditions of Table A2.

Table A1. Example Transformation Classifications			
Transformation	**View D, Class**	**View C, Class**	**Classification from Table**
Source code--> Decision table	Source code, 3	Decision table, 1	Reverse engineering, design recovery, reengineering
Data flow diagram --> Textual specifications	Data flow diagram, 2	Textual specifications, 1	Reverse engineering, design recovery, reengineering
Source code --> Lines of code measurement	Source code, 3	Lines of code measurement, A3	Open
Source code --> Pretty printed source code	Source code, 3	Pretty printed source code (same program and language), 3	Restructuring, reengineering
Source code inline comments --> Revised source code inline comments	Source code inline comments, 3	Revised source code inline comments, 3	Reengineering
Raw data in database --> Logical data schema	Raw data in database, 3	Logical data schema, 1	Reverse engineering, design recovery, reengineering

---

[8] It is also assumed that the classification has intuitive validity. For example, source code is not placed view class 1, nonprocedural specifications.

Table A2. Classification of Transformations in Figure 1.			
Classification	**View class of D**	**View class of C**	**Other conditions***
Forward engineering	1	2, A2, 3, or A3	
Open	1 or A1	A1	
Reengineering	1	1	V
Forward engineering	A1	1, 2, A2, 3, or A3	
Reverse engineering, design recovery, reengineering	2	1 or A1	V
Reengineering	2	2	V
Open	2 or A2	A2	
Forward engineering	2	3 or A3	
Reverse engineering	A2	1	V
Open	A2	A1	
Forward engineering	A2	2, 3, or A3	
Reverse engineering, design recovery, reengineering	3	1, 2, A1, or A2	V
Reengineering	3	3	V
Restructuring	3	3	V, and both D and C are source code in the same language for the same program.
Open	3 or A3	A3	
Forward engineering	A3	3	
Reverse engineering, design recovery, reengineering	A3	2 or A2	V

*Note: V means that the transformation meets the following conditions:
    (1) Improves one's understanding of software, or
    (2) Prepares or improves the software itself, usually for increased maintainability, reusability, or evolvability.
    The "or" is an inclusive "or."

References

The papers reprinted in this book are marked with an asterisk (*). Papers marked with a pound sign (#) were reprinted in [Arnold86].

#[Arnold82] R.S. Arnold, and D.A. Parker, "The Dimensions of Healthy Maintenance," *Proc. Sixth Int'l. Conf. on Software Eng.,* IEEE Computer Society Press, Los Alamitos, Calif., Sept. 1982, pp. 10-27.

[Arnold83] R.S. Arnold, *On the Generation and Use of Quantitative Criteria for Assessing Software Maintenance Quality,* doctoral dissertation, Univ. of Maryland, College Park, Md., 1983.

[Arnold86] R.S. Arnold, *Software Restructuring,* IEEE Computer Society Press, Los Alamitos, Calif., 1986.

[Arnold89a] R.S. Arnold, "Software Reengineering," private seminar notes, Herndon, Va., 1989.

*[Arnold89b] R.S. Arnold, "Software Restructuring," *Proc. IEEE,* Vol. 77, No. 4, Apr. 1989.

[Arnold90a] R.S. Arnold, "Heuristics for Salvaging Reusable Parts from Ada Source Code," Tech. Report: Ada Reuse Heuristics-90011-N, Software Productivity Consortium, Herndon, Va., Mar. 1990.

[Arnold90b] R.S. Arnold, "Software Restructuring: Foundation for Reengineering," *Proc. Reverse Eng. Forum,* St. Louis, Mo., Apr. 1990.

[Arnold90c] R.S. Arnold, "Tools for Static Analysis of Ada Source Code," Tech. Report: Ada Static Tools Survey-90015-N, Software Productivity Consortium, Herndon, Va., June 1990.

[Arnold91a] R.S. Arnold, "Risks of Reengineering," *Proc. Reverse Eng. Forum,* St. Louis, Mo., Apr. 1991.

*[Arnold91b] R.S. Arnold and W.F. Frakes, "Reuse and Reengineering," Final draft (1991) of a paper appearing under the same title in *CASE Trends,* Feb. 1992.

[Arnold92] R.S. Arnold, "Software Reengineering," seminar notes, Software Evolution Technology, Herndon, Va., 1992.

*[Bailey90] J.W. Bailey and V.R. Basili, "Software Reclamation: Improving Post-Development Reusability," *Proc. Eighth Ann. Nat'l. Conf. on Ada Technology,* U.S. Army Communications - Electronics Command, Fort Monmouth, N.J., 1990, pp. 477-498.

[Bohm66] C. Bohm and G. Jacopini, "Flow Diagrams, Turing Machines, and Languages with Only Two Formation Rules." *Comm. ACM,* Vol. 9, No. 5, May 1966, pp. 366-371.

*[Breuer91] P.T. Breuer and K. Lano, "Creating Specifications from Code: Reverse Engineering Techniques," *J. Software Maintenance: Research and Practice,* Vol. 3, 1991, pp. 145-162.

*[Britcher90] R.N. Britcher, "Re-engineering Software: A Case Study," *IBM Systems J.,* Vol. 29, No. 4, 1990, pp. 551-567.

*[Burson90] S. Burson, G.B. Kotik, and L.Z. Markosian, "A Program Transformation Approach to Automating Software Re-engineering," *Proc. COMPSAC,* IEEE Computer Society Press, Los Alamitos, Calif., 1990, pp. 314-322.

*[Byrne91] E.J. Byrne, "Software Reverse Engineering: A Case Study," *Software—Practice and Experience,* Vol. 21, No. 12, Dec. 1991, pp. 1349-1364.

[Caldiera88] G. Caldiera, and V.R. Basili, "Reusing Existing Software," Tech. Report CS-TR-2116, Computer Science Dept., Univ. of Maryland, College Park, Md., Oct. 1988.

*[Caldiera91] G. Caldiera and V.R. Basili, "Identifying and Qualifying Reusable Software Components," *IEEE Computer,* Vol. 24, No. 2, Feb. 1991, pp. 61-70.

[Calliss88] F.W. Calliss, "Problems with Automatic Restructurers," *SIGPLAN Notices,* Vol. 23, No. 3, Mar. 1988, pp. 13-21.

[Card85] D.N. Card, G.T. Page, and F.E. McGarry, "Criteria for Software Modularization," *Proc. Eighth Int'l Conf. Software Eng.,* IEEE Computer Society Press, Los Alamitos, Calif., 1985, pp. 372-377.

*[Chen90] Y.-F. Chen, M. Nishimoto, and C.V. Ramamoorthy, "The C Information Abstraction System," *IEEE Trans. Software Eng.,* Vol. 16, No. 3, Mar. 1990, pp. 325-334.

*[Chikofsky90] E. Chikofsky and J.H. Cross, "Reverse Engineering and Design Recovery: A Taxonomy," *IEEE Software,* Jan. 1990, pp. 13-17.

[Chikofsky91] E. Chikofsky, lecture notes on reverse engineering and design recovery, Feb. 1991.

*[Cleveland89] L. Cleveland, "A Program Understanding Support Environment," *IBM Systems J.,* Vol. 28, No. 2, 1989, pp. 324-344.

[*Computerworld* 91] *Computerworld,* Vol. XXV, No. 12, Mar. 25, 1991, p. 68.

[Conklin87] J. Conklin, "A Survey of Hypertext," *IEEE Computer,* Vol. 20, No. 9, Sept. 1987, pp. 17-41.

[Connell87] J. Connell and L. Brice, *The Professional User's Guide to Acquiring Software,* "Identifying Systems that Need Rework", Ch. 2, Van Nostrand, N.Y., 1987.

*[Corbi89] T. Corbi, "Program Understanding: Challenge for the 1990s," *IBM Systems J.,* Vol. 28, No. 2, 1989, pp. 294-306.

[Cote88] V. Cote, P. Bourque, S. Oligny, and N. Rivard, "Software Metrics: An Overview of Recent Results," *J. Systems and Software,* Vol. 8, 1988, pp. 121-131.

*[Davenport90] T.H. Davenport, and J.E. Short, "The New Industrial Engineering: Information Technology and Business Process Redesign," *Sloan Management Rev.,* Summer, 1990, pp. 11-27.

[Davis76] R. Davis, and J. King, "An Overview of Production Systems." In E.W. Elcock and D. Michie, eds. *Machine Intelligence,* 1976, Wiley, N.Y., pp. 300-332.

*[Dietrich89] W.C. Dietrich, Jr., L.R. Nackman, and F. Gracer, "Saving a Legacy with Objects," *Proc. OOPSLA,* Association for Computing Machinery, N.Y., 1989, pp. 77-83.

*[Dunn91] M.F. Dunn and J.C. Knight, "Software Reuse in an Industrial Setting: A Case Study," *Proc. 13th Int'l. Conf. on Software Eng.,* IEEE Computer Society Press, Los Alamitos, Calif., 1991, pp. 329-338.

*[FSMSC87] Fed. Software Management Support Center, "Parallel Test and Evaluation of a Cobol Restructuring Tool," *Office of Software Development and Information Technology,* Falls Church, Va., Sept. 1987.

[Glass81] R.L. Glass and R.A. Noiseux, *Software Maintenance Guidebook,* Prentice-Hall, N.J., 1981.

*[Gopal88] R. Gopal and S. Schach, "Using Automatic Program Decomposition Techniques in Software Maintenance Tools," *Proc. Conf. on Software Maintenance,* IEEE Computer Society Press, Los Alamitos, Calif., 1988, pp. 132-141.

[GUIDE89] "Application Reengineering," Guide Pub. GPP-208, Guide Int'l Corp., Chicago, 1989.

*[Hammer90] M. Hammer, "Reengineering Work: Don't Automate, Obliterate," *Harvard Business Rev.,* July-Aug. 1990, pp. 104-112.

*[Harandi90] M.T. Harandi and J.Q. Ning, "Knowledge-Based Program Analysis," *IEEE Software,* Vol. 7, No. 1, Jan. 1990, pp. 74-81.

[Hartman91] J. Hartman, "Understanding Natural Programs Using Proper Decomposition," *Proc. 13th Int'l Conf. on Software Eng.,* IEEE Computer Society Press, Los Alamitos, Calif., May 1991, pp. 62-73.

#[Harrison82] W. Harrison, K. Magel, R. Kluczny, and A. DeKock, "Applying Software Complexity Metrics to Software Maintenance," *Computer,* Vol. 15, No. 9, Sept. 1982, pp. 65-79.

[Heninger78] K. Heninger, J. Kallander, D. Parnas, and J. Shore, "Software Requirements for the A-7E Aircraft," NRL Memorandum Report 3876, Nov. 1978.

#[Hevner89] A.R. Hevner and R.C. Linger, "A Method for Data Re-engineering in Structured Programs," *Proc. 22nd. Hawaii Int'l Conf. on System Sciences,* IEEE Computer Society Press, Los Alamitos, Calif., Jan. 1989, Vol. 2, pp. 1024-1034.

[Husmann90] H.H. Husmann, "Re-Engineering Economics," Eden Systems Corp., Carmel, Ind., 1990. Also appeared in *System Development,* Feb. 1991.

*[Jacobson91] I. Jacobson, "Re-Engineering of Old Systems to an Object-Oriented Architecture," *Proc. OOPSLA,* Association for Computing Machinery, N.Y., 1991, pp. 340-350.

[Knight92] J. Knight, personal communication, telephone conversation between John Knight and Robert Arnold, June 1992.

[Koka91] R. Koka, "Mainframe Realities," *Software Magazine,* Jan. 10, 1991.

*[Kozaczynski89] W. Kozaczynski and J.Q. Ning, "SRE: A Knowledge-Based Environment for Large-Scale Software Reengineering Activities," *Proc. 11th Int'l Conf. on Software Eng.,* IEEE Computer Society Press, Los Alamitos, Calif., 1989, pp. 113-121.

*[Landis88] L.D. Landis, P.M. Highland, A.L. Gilbert, and A.J. Fine, "Documentation in a Software Maintenance Environment," *Proc. Conf. on Software Maintenance,* IEEE Computer Society Press, Los Alamitos, Calif., 1988.

*[Lyle88] J.R. Lyle and K.B. Gallagher, "Using Program Decomposition to Guide Modifications," *Proc. Conf. on Software Maintenance,* IEEE Computer Society Press, Los Alamitos, Calif., 1988, pp. 265-269.

[McCabe76] T. McCabe, "A Complexity Metric," *IEEE Trans. on Software Eng.,* Vol. SE-2, No. 2, Dec. 1976.

[Miller87] J.C. Miller, and B.M. Strauss, "Implications of Automatic Restructuring of Cobol," *SIGPLAN Notices,* Vol. 22, No. 6, June 1987, pp. 76-82.

[Myers75] G.J. Myers, *Reliable Software through Composite Design,* Van Nostrand Reinhold Co., N.Y., 1975.

[Oman92a] P. Oman, J. Hagemeister, and D. Ash, "A Definition and Taxonomy for Software Maintainability," Tech. Report #91-08 (revised version), Software Eng. Lab., Univ. of Idaho, Jan. 1992.

[Oman92b] P. Oman and J. Hagemeister, "Metrics for Assessing Software Maintainability," Tech. Report #92-01, Software Eng. Lab., Univ. of Idaho, Mar. 1992.

#[Peercy81] D.A. Peercy, "A Software Maintainability Evaluation Methodology," *IEEE Trans. on Software Eng.,* Vol. SE-7, No. 4, July 1981, pp. 343-352.

#[Philips84] J.C. Philips, "Creating a Baseline for an Undocumented System — Or What Do You Do with Someone Else's Code?" in *Record of the 1983 Software Maintenance Workshop,* R.S. Arnold, ed., IEEE Computer Society Press, Los Alamitos, Calif., 1984, pp. 63-64.

[Rekoff85] M.G. Rekoff, Jr., "On Reverse Engineering," *IEEE Trans. Systems, Man, and Cybernetics,* Mar.-Apr. 1985, pp. 244-252.

[Reynolds90] R.G. Reynolds and J.C. Esteva, "Learning to Recognize Reusable Software by Induction," White paper, Wayne State Univ., Detroit, Mich., 1990.

*[Rich90] C. Rich, and L.M. Wills, "Recognizing a Program's Design: A Graph-Parsing Approach," *IEEE Software,* Vol. 7, No. 1, Jan. 1990, pp. 82-89.

*[Ricketts89] J.A. Ricketts, J.C. DelMonaco, and M.W. Weeks, "Data Reengineering for Application Systems," *Proc. Conf. on Software Maintenance,* IEEE Computer Society Press, Los Alamitos, Calif., 1989, pp. 174-179.

*[Robson91] D.J. Robson, K.H. Bennett, B.J. Cornelius, and M. Munro, "Approaches to Program Comprehension," *J. Systems and Software,* Vol. 14, Feb. 1991, pp. 79-84.

[Rombach89] D.H. Rombach and B.T. Ulery, "Improving Software Maintenance through Measurement," *Proc. IEEE,* Vol. 77, No. 4, Apr. 1989, pp. 581-595.

*[Schwanke91] R.W. Schwanke, "An Intelligent Tool for Re-engineering Software Modularity," *Proc. 13th Int'l. Conf. on Software Eng.,* IEEE Computer Society Press, Los Alamitos, Calif., May 1991, pp. 83-92.

[Sittenauer92] C. Sittenauer, M. Olsem, and D. Murdock, "Software Re-engineering Tools Report," Software Technology Support Center (STSC), Hill Air Force Base, Utah, Apr. 1992.

*[Slovin91] M. Slovin and S. Malik, "Reengineering to Reduce System Maintenance: A Case Study," *Software Eng.,* July/Aug. 1991, pp. 14-24.

#[Sneed84] H.M. Sneed, "Software Renewal: A Case Study," *IEEE Software,* Vol. 1, No. 3, July 1984, pp. 56-63.

[Sneed88] H.M. Sneed and G. Jandrasics, "Inverse Transformation of Software from Code to Specification," *Proc. Conf. on Software Maintenance,* IEEE Computer Society Press, Los Alamitos, Calif., 1988, pp. 102-109.

*[Sneed90] H.M. Sneed and A. Kaposi, "A Study of the Effect of Reengineering upon Software Maintainability," *Proc. Conf. on Software Maintenance,* IEEE Computer Society Press, Los Alamitos, Calif., 1990, pp. 91-99.

*[Sneed91] H.M. Sneed, "Economics of Software Re-engineering," *J. Software Maintenance: Research and Practice,* Vol. 3, No. 3, Sept. 1991, pp. 163-182.

*[Ulrich90a] W.M. Ulrich, "The Evolutionary Growth of Software Reengineering and the Decade Ahead," *Am. Programmer,* Vol. 3, No. 10, Oct. 1990, pp. 14-20.

*[Ulrich90-91] W.M. Ulrich, "Reengineering: Defining an Integrated Migration Framework," *CASE Trends,* 4-part series, Nov./Dec. 1990; Jan./Feb. 1991; Mar./Spr. 1991; Summer, 1991.

[Theby91] S. Theby, "Mapping Cobol to Objects," *Proc. Reverse Eng. Forum,* St. Louis, Mo., Apr. 1991.

[Weiser81] M. Weiser, "Program Slicing," *Proc. Int'l. Conf. on Software Eng.,* IEEE Computer Society Press, Los Alamitos, Calif., Mar. 1981.

Chapter 1
Software Reengineering:
Context and Definitions

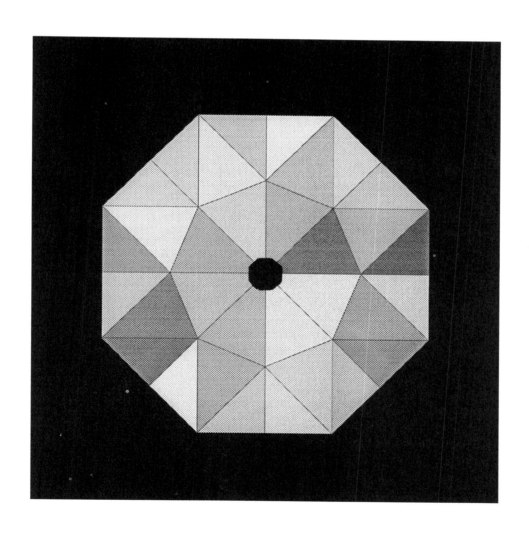

Chapter 1

Software Reengineering:
Context and Definitions

Purpose

This chapter introduces the reader to the terms, concepts, and examples of reengineering technology. Reading these papers will familiarize the reader with reengineering uses and some of reengineering technology's capabilities and limitations.

Papers

In the first paper, "Re-3, Part 1: Re-engineering, Restructuring, and Reverse Engineering," Ed Yourdon gives a good conceptual introduction to reengineering. After reading this paper, the reader will have a sense for the origin of the term "reengineering," some of the strengths and weaknesses of reengineering, and why reengineering is significant.

Many vendors are listed in the paper's references, but the reader is warned that there are many more reengineering tools available today. Reengineering technology is changing fast. For more comprehensive and contemporary information, the reader should consult published surveys[1] and call vendors for the latest product capabilities.

In the next paper, "The Evolutionary Growth of Software Reengineering and the Decade Ahead," William Ulrich points out that the role of reengineering is often to prepare a system for reverse engineering. Reverse engineering is then used to salvage business intelligence. The paper describes reengineering success stories, risks and realities of reengineering technology, and why strategic planning for reengineering is so important.

The next paper, "Re-engineering Existing Systems," edited by J.B. Rochester and D.P. Douglass, describes several short reengineering case studies. These will introduce the reader to reengineering in daily life. The paper describes the typical realities and results of reengineering.

In the next paper, "Reverse Engineering and Design Recovery: A Taxonomy," Elliot Chikofsky and James H. Cross, II, provide definitions of basic software reengineering and reverse engineering terms. The paper's conceptual framework for reengineering is well worth understanding. The definitions in this paper are frequently cited. However, the reader should be aware that these definitions are not universally held. The reader should ask people what they mean by reengineering and reverse engineering. This is especially important in contracting for reengineering work. The Introduction to this book provides a more recent view of what constitutes software reengineering and related terms.

In the final paper, "Automated Support of Software Maintenance," Keith Bennett gives another good conceptual introduction that illustrates its concepts with the work of several European reengineering and reverse engineering research projects. The paper provides a glimpse of European software maintenance and reengineering research activities.

---

[1]C. Sittenauer, M. Olsem, and D. Murdock, "Software Re-engineering Tools Report," Software Technology Support Center (STSC), Hill Air Force Base, Utah, April 1992.

RE-3

part 1

by Ed Yourdon

Soothsayers and prophets will tell you re-engineering, re-structuring, and reverse engineering can turn bad programs into good, cut software maintenance costs by a factor of ten, and improve the sex lives of your maintenance programmers. Naysayers and skeptics will tell you it's all bullshit and there simply is no mechanical way to derive a program's functional specification from the source code. I say: *it doesn't matter*.

The RE-3 technologies, as I call them, are less miraculous than claimed by soothsayers, yet more valuable than skeptics will admit. But the technology issues are far less important than the managerial and cultural issues involved in putting RE-3 to use. This is a two-part article. In the first part, we discuss the technology issues and summarize the management issues; next month, we'll discuss the management issue in more depth and cri-

tique some of the more popular RE-3 products.

We first need to differentiate between the three 'R' words, which software people often use interchangeably. The term "restructuring" has been around for at least 15 years and arguably more than 20. Quite simply, it means reorganizing the procedural logic of a computer program so that it conforms to the rules of structured programming. Or, as most programmers

RE-ENGINEERING
RESTRUCTURING
REVERSE ENGINEERING

3

Reprinted with permission from *American Programmer*, Vol. 2, No. 4, Apr. 1989, pp. 3–10.

would describe it, restructuring a program means changing "spaghetti bowl" or "rat's nest" programs—programs whose flowcharts resemble the New York City subway map—into programs that are easy to read and comprehend. Automatic restructuring is the mechanical translation of an arbitrary (unstructured) program into a functionally equivalent structured program. Language Technology's RECODER, available since the mid-eighties, is a good example of a commercial product that automatically restructures COBOL programs. Other well-known products include SUPER-STRUCTURE, now marketed by Computer Data Systems; IBM's Structuring Facility, Version 2; and Peat Marwick's Retrofit.

The concept of restructuring was used by Böhm and Jacopini [26] as the basis for the original proof that any program could be written in a structured form, using only three constructs: **SEQUENCE**, **IF-THEN-ELSE**, and **DO-WHILE**. In 1971, Ashcroft and Manna [27] demonstrated that unstructured programs containing **GOTO** statements could be translated easily into an equivalent structured form. And an early example of automatic restructuring, a so-called "structuring engine," was presented by Balbine [28] in

1975. As late as 1985, vendors such as Language Technology still referred to the process as "restructuring" in technical papers [29].

But now it has become fashionable to use the term "re-engineering" instead of restructuring. Part of this, I'm convinced, is pure marketing hype: a word that contains "engineer" sounds more impressive than a "techie" term like restructuring. But it also reflects the fact that it takes more than reorganizing program logic to really improve and rejuvenate an old program. As William Ulrich [5] points out,

Re-engineering and reverse engineering are two distinct functions, even though systems development professionals sometimes confuse the terms. Re-engineering changes the underlying technology of a system without affecting the overall function, while reverse engineering is the backward engineering of a system to the specification stage. A system which has been reverse engineered can be regenerated more economically and productively. Re-engineering reduces the skill set required to modify the system, reduces the likelihood of errors introduced during maintenance, and is the first step toward reverse engineering.

Several vendors in the re-engineering marketplace are capitalizing on the fact that a maintenance programmer has to have a solid understanding of the behavior and structure of his program before he can attempt to improve it. Language Technology has a product called INSPECTOR which shows the structure and com-

plexity of individual programs, or entire portfolios of programs. Similarly, Phoenix-based Viasoft offers an interactive code analyzer called VIA/Insight, which provides online information about a program's logic flow and data flow.

The term "reverse engineering" is a relatively recent addition to the software engineer's vocabulary, though the concept has been around almost as long as restructuring. Originally it meant discovering, or recreating, the design from which an existing computer program was developed. Thus, flowcharting programs like Autoflow—which can read a COBOL source program and generate a flowchart of its logic—represent a simple form of reverse engineering. (Incidentally, if you thought flowcharting programs disappeared in the sixties, you'll be surprised to learn there's a whole new generation: Cupertino-based Quantum Software has a product called ASMFLOW which produces flowcharts from IBM PC assembler code.)

When structured design became popular in the mid-seventies, a few organizations applied the concept of reverse engineering at a higher level: scanning the source code of a program in order to generate structure charts, or "module organization" charts. Software Products & Services, for exam-

4

ple, markets a product called RE-SPEC, which generates design documents directly from Fortran or Pascal source code; Heartland Systems markets SOURCEVIEW, which can generate Warnier-Orr diagrams from C, Pascal, or COBOL code.

Similarly, when entity-relationship diagrams and other data modeling tools became popular several years ago, some software engineers thought it might be useful to produce such diagrams automatically from, say, the DATA DIVISION of a COBOL program. Bachman Information Systems, for example, has a product called the Bachman Re-Engineering Product Set, which converts IDMS and DB2 database descriptions into graphical representations of the logical and physical database design. After the systems designer makes the desired changes and improvements to the graphical models, the Bachman system can "forward engineer" the new design into the code for a new database.

Today there is great interest in the next higher level of reverse engineering: deriving the specification, or user requirements, directly from the code. Meta Systems and AS-TEC market products that translate source code into PSL statements (which can be used by PSL/PSA CASE products

to "forward engineer" a new system).

WHY DOES ANY OF THIS MATTER?

The answer should be obvious—but let's restate the obvious. Software maintenance consumes more than 50 percent of the budget in most DP shops; in the larger shops, the number is typically 70 to 80 percent. And it's getting worse: the U.S. Air Force estimates that unless it does something about the "maintenance iceberg," it will require 25 percent of the country's 18- to 25-year-olds to maintain its software by the year 2000.

Part of the problem is that the applications portfolio in many large organizations is 10, 15, or even 20 years old—and obviously growing older each day. Even if the original programs had been perfectly designed and coded, 20 years of patching and modifying is almost certain to lead to a maintenance nightmare. But in fact, most programs developed in the sixties and seventies were *not* "perfect" in any sense of the word; they were difficult to maintain from the day they were put into operation. Along the way, the documentation for these old programs has become obsolete—if it ever existed in the first place!

The net result is that many organizations now find they have third-generation maintenance programmers talking to third-generation users about these ancient systems. The

current users and maintainers were not around when the system was developed, and they have little or no idea *what* the system does, *why* it does it, or *how* it manages to do it.

Hence the attractiveness of the RE-3 technologies.

TECHNICAL ISSUES

Here are the basic technical issues:

☆ *The RE-3 technologies* do *work as long as your expectations are modest.* As I noted, restructuring products are based on a firm theoretical foundation; mechanical translation of unstructured code to structured code is neither magic nor snake oil. And re-engineering products that produce diagrams—for example, flowcharts, structure charts, entity-relationship diagrams—from source code are also based on a firm foundation. The question is whether restructuring and/or re-engineering can really turn a bad system into a good system, and whether automated reverse engineering products really uncover "true" designs and specifications from existing code.

☆ *There is no form of "software alchemy" that can turn bad code into good code, or bad designs into good designs, or bad systems into good systems.*

5

There is no question that re-engineering and restructuring products can improve the typical program; Language Technology, for example, claims that use of its RECODER product can cut maintenance costs by 50 percent or more, and I think this is quite realistic. But if the underlying design of a system is fundamentally rotten, or if it has deteriorated over a period of 20 years, RE-3 technologies can only bring about a cosmetic improvement.

For example, what if we are trying to re-engineer a program whose data names and procedure names are cryptic abbreviations invented by an anti-social programmer years ago? How can a re-engineering program create meaning out of a name like RIPLVB—a name actually assigned by a programmer who noticed he was dealing with the number 1827, which happens to be the year Ludwig van Beethoven died? How can a re-engineering program cope with a system where a parameter such as "Social Security withholding rate" has been hard-coded as a numerical constant in dozens of places? How can a restructuring program convert a vintage-seventies assembler batch program into a vintage-nineties online, distributed transaction-processing system? Answer: It can't.

REFLECTIONS

If It Ain't Broke, Fix It!
by John Boddie

Conventional wisdom calls for introducing a new methodology on a virgin project, where its benefits will be obvious to everyone. I believe this approach is counterproductive, and it is one factor that has inhibited wider acceptance of CASE tools and the methodologies which serve as their foundation.

It is a bedrock truth in this business that a programmer who has just completed a successful program will be intensely aware of things that could be done to make it better. It is at this point that fresh tools and methods can be introduced most effectively. What better time to let programmers experiment with techniques than when they have a keen interest in improving an already successful product?

Why not introduce a new methodology by using it to redo a program or system that is already working well? It is usually possible to improve existing programs so that they will run better or be easier to modify in the future. Again, programmers can experience personally the improvements associated with their new working environment. It is the direct experience of doing things differently and watching them turn out better that moves programmers (an opinionated breed) to adopt new techniques and tools.

If the goal is to introduce an improved methodology, the enterprise is making a long-term investment and it must be treated as such. The payoff is expected to be improved productivity for years to come—not just on the next project in the queue. New tools and procedures must be introduced in a situation where they can be the focus of attention, and where the people who will use them can get empirical evidence that they work well.

In introducing new practices, don't focus on the next project—focus on the last one.

John Boddie is a consultant based in Landenberg, PA and author of **Crunch Mode** *(Yourdon Press/Prentice Hall, 1987).* ☆

6

☆ *There are some profound technical difficulties associated with reverse engineering because the mapping from analysis to design, and from design to code, is not a one-to-one mapping.* As a software developer moves forward from analysis to design, and from design to code, he is faced with a "one-to-many" mapping: countless potential designs can satisfactorily implement a system specification; and there are numerous ways of organizing procedural logic (code) to implement a design. This makes going *backward* in the process all the more difficult. Vaughan Merlyn expressed this eloquently in the March 1989 *Software Maintenance News:* "Re-engineering is like looking at a Picasso and trying to come up with a photograph of the subject." One of the most difficult problems is uncovering the *essential* (technology-independent) *requirements* and the *user implementation model* of the system (technology/implementation issues about which the users feel so strongly that they are imposed during the analysis stage), when the only information at hand is one arbitrary *physical/implementation model* of those requirements—that is, the code.

Suppose, for example, a maintenance programmer discovers the system he is maintaining consists of two programs which communicate through an intermediate disk file. Is that intermediate disk file part of the physical/implementation model? Probably. There could be many other ways of implementing the communication of data between the two programs, and the intermediate file was just one arbitrary solution.

But could it be part of the user implementation model? Maybe. Perhaps it was imposed by the auditors, or maybe the users insisted on it because of their own fears about backup/recovery problems. Could the intermediate file be part of the essential requirements of the system? Doubtful . . . though it is possible the essential system requirements involve asynchronous execution of the two programs, thus requiring *some* kind of time-delay "buffer" to hold the data that moves from one program to another.

MANAGEMENT ISSUES

The major management issues and questions associated with the RE-3 technologies are summarized below. We'll explore them in more depth in the next issue of *AP*.

☆ What are the potential savings an MIS organization could realize from RE-3 technologies? How much could its maintenance budget realistically be expected to decrease? *Some vendors have claimed fac-* *tor-of-ten savings; a 50 percent maintenance improvement is a good target to aim for.*

☆ How should an organization start? Should it consider a pilot project? Should it begin with its oldest system or its "buggiest" system? *As with all new technology, a pilot project is a must. After that, look for the systems where you'll get the biggest payback—but beware the cultural resistance.*

☆ What are the biggest obstacles and problems facing an organization that wants to carry out reverse engineering on some of its systems? *One of the biggest obstacles in some organizations is the inertia of the maintenance staff: they have grown comfortable maintaining rotten old systems and have no incentive to re-engineer them and put themselves out of a job.*

☆ Is there resistance to the RE-3 technologies? If so, what form does it take? Why should there be any resistance? *Of course there will be resistance! People resist change and can find all kinds of reasons why RE-3 won't work . . .*

☆ Is it possible for RE-3 to fail? What are the dangers and pitfalls? *Look out for snake oil salesmen. Beware promises of order-of-magnitude savings.*

7

☆ Are there any success stories—names, addresses, phone numbers of people who can describe fabulous results? *We think so . . . and we're in the process of interviewing them now. We'll have some references for you next month.*

☆ What's most important to concentrate on: reverse engineering and re-engineering of code? data? design? specification? All of the above? *Short term: restructure and re-engineer the code, for that's what the programmers work with every day. Long term: re-engineer the data; information is the fundamental asset of the organization.*

☆ How much reverse engineering has to be done manually, and how much can be automated? *Code restructuring can be automated 100 percent today; re-engineering and reverse engineering are, at best, 50 percent manual labor and 50 percent automated translation.*

☆ What is the future of RE-3? Will it get more important? Is it a "one-shot" activity for organizations that want to fix up their old systems but will be developing perfect new systems from now on? *Organizations have only three choices: (a) They can continue allowing their systems to deteriorate until they go out of business; (b) they can throw out their old systems and replace them with brand-new systems; or (c) they can turn to re-engineering and reverse engineering. Choice (a) is suicide; choice (b) is too expensive and too risky for most organizations. That leaves choice (c)— so, yes, the RE-3 technologies are going to be key technologies for the nineties.*

RESOURCES

Bachman Information
  Systems, Inc.
Four Cambridge Center
Cambridge, MA 02142
617-354-1414
contact: Ms. Pauli Uzzle

Catalyst division of
  Peat Marwick
303 E. Wacker Drive
Chicago, IL 60601

800-323-3059
contact: Ms. Mary Eichhorn

Quantum Software
19855 Stevens Creek Blvd.
Suite 154
Cupertino, CA 95014
408-244-6826
contact: Mr. Mike Schmit

Computer Data Systems, Inc.
One Curie Court
Rockville, MD 20850
contact: Ms. Jennifer
  Grossman

Heartland Systems
1611 St. Andrews
Lawrence, KS 66046
913-749-2626
contact: Mr. Paul Rasmussen

Language Technology, Inc.
27 Congress St.
Salem, MA 01970

8

508-741-1507
contact: Ms. Louise Waitkus

Software Engineering
  Service GmbH
Pappelstrasse 6,
8014 Neubiberg,
West Germany
+49-89-601-53-97
contact: Mr. Harry Sneed

Mentor Graphics Corp.
8500 SW Creekside
Beaverton, OR 97005
503-626-4757
contact: Ms. Amy Rivero

Advanced Systems Technology
  Corp. (ASTEC)
9111 Edmonston Road
Suite 404
Greenbelt, MD 20770
301-441-9036
contact: Dr. Hasan Sayani

Meta Systems
315 Eisenhower Parkway
Suite 200
Ann Arbor, MI 48104
313-663-6027
contact: Ms. Sherry Marci

On Line Software
  International
Fort Lee Executive Park
Fort Lee, NJ 07024
201-592-0009
contact: Ms. Cynthia
  Richmond

Promod, Inc.
23685 Birtcher Drive
Lake Forest, CA 92630

714-855-3046
contact: Mr. Norm Denton

Sage Software, Inc.
3200 Tower Oaks Road
Rockville, MD 20852
301-230-3200
contact: Mr. Dave Parker

Softlab, Inc.
188 The Embarcadero
San Francisco, CA 94105
415-957-9175
contact: Mr. Robert Coolidge

Software Products &
  Services, Inc.
14 East 38th Street
New York, NY 10016
212-686-3790
contact: Ms. Shellen Keohane

Viasoft, Inc.
3033 North 44th Street
Phoenix, AZ 85018
602-952-0050
contact: Mr. Robert Lindsey

REFERENCES

1   Michael Broddle, "CASE for more and better," *Computer Weekly*, Nov. 10, 1988, p. 34.

2   Robert Moran, "Pacbase performs reverse engineering," *Computerworld*, Nov. 14, 1988, pp. 33-34.

3   James Martin, "Modeling technology: trends for the late 1980s," *PC Week*, Oct. 24, 1988, p. 35.

4   Martin B. Azarnoff, "The CASE payback: nothing ventured, nothing gained," *Computerworld*, Oct. 5, 1988, pp. 15-18.

5   William Ulrich, "Re-engineering vs. reverse engineering," *Software Magazine*, Sept. 1988, pp. 8-9.

6   Melinda-Carol Ballou, "CASE package picks up tools for management, DBMS design," *Digital Review*, Sept. 12, 1988, pp. 33-34.

7   William Cutler, "Creating foundation for easy-care code," *Computerworld*, July 25, 1988, pp. 56-57.

8   Charles Bachman, "A CASE for reverse engineering," *Datamation*, July 1, 1988, pp. 49-53.

9   Roger Philips, "The neglected wasteland," *Computerworld Extra: Productivity*, June 20, 1988, pp. C42-C43.

10   Nell Margolis, "CASE system handles reverse engineering," *Computerworld*, Aug. 29, 1988, p. 8.

9

11 Steven Pfrenzinger, "Re-engineer with CASE," *Computerworld*, April 18, 1988, pp. 27-28.

12 Chris Terry, "Customer training and reverse engineering promise to escalate the acceptance of CASE," *Electronic Daily News*, March 17, 1988, pp. 73-76.

13 Mike Feuche, "New CASE reshapes software," *MIS Week*, Feb. 1, 1988, p. 35.

14 Nell Margolis, "CASE firms ask what's new; AI, shakeout seen impacting technology's growth in near future," *Computerworld*, Feb. 1, 1988, pp. 23-24.

15 John Desmond, "Martin on maintenance: 'rewrite': the sage's advice amplifies CASE clash," *Software News*, Nov. 1, 1987, pp. 20-21.

16 Chris Terry, "CASE tools," *Electronic Daily News*, Apr. 28, 1988, pp. 111-117.

17 Mike Feuche, "Attention is being generated by complexity metrics tools," *MIS Week*, Feb. 29, 1988, pp. 27-28.

18 Gary McWilliams, "Users see a CASE advance in reverse engineering tools," *Datamation*, Feb. 1, 1988, pp. 30-32.

19 David Kull, "One step forward, two steps back," *Computer & Communications Decisions*, Feb. 1988, pp. 100-101.

20 Colin Johnson, "CASE: the next major change in software," *Electronic Engineering Times*, Jan. 11, 1988, pp. 46-48.

21 Charles Babcock, "IDMS-R tool hooks into DB2; well-heeled start-up company devises reverse engineering system," *Computerworld*, Jan. 25, 1988, p. 101.

22 Karen Gullo, "Automating COBOL support is the cause celebre in IS shops," *Datamation*, Jan. 1, 1988, pp. 19-20.

23 Betty Y. Forman, "CAP tools make reverse engineering easier," *Digital Review*, Jan. 11, 1988, p. 38.

24 Mike Feuche, "Promod releases CAP tools," *MIS Week*, Oct. 26, 1987, p. 49.

25 J. Vaughn, "CASE world discovers all the possibilities" *ESD: The Electronic System Design Magazine*, Oct. 1987, pp. 31-32.

26 C. Böhm and G. Jacopini, "Flow diagrams, Turing machines, and languages with only two formation rules," *Communications of the ACM*, May 1966, pp. 366-371.

27 E. Ashcroft and Z. Manna, "The translation of 'go to' programs to 'while' programs," *Proceedings of the 1971 IFIP Congress*, Vol. 1, pp. 250-255.

28 Guy de Balbine, "Better manpower utilization through automatic restructuring," *Proceedings of the 1975 National Computer Conference*.

29 Eric Bush, "The automatic restructuring of COBOL," *Proceedings of the Conference on Software Maintenance—1985*, pp. 35-41. ★

10

The Evolutionary Growth of Software Reengineering and the Decade Ahead

by William M. Ulrich

They say that one good way to predict the future is to study the past. This is not due so much to nostalgia, but rather to the legacy of confusion passed down from previous generations of technicians. Most of us are aware that, long ago, programmers coded for efficiency, not maintainability. Knowing this does not make the job of deciphering aging, undocumented systems any easier. Adapting today's information systems to deregulation, global economies, increased competition, emerging technologies, and an increasingly dynamic business climate is becoming ever more difficult. Some organizations have turned to software reengineering as an answer. Many have been disappointed.

On this 10th anniversary of the reengineering industry, it is time to take a close look at why we have not achieved more reengineering successes. It is time to examine the future of a technology whose promises remain unfulfilled. The industry must assess the effective deployment of reengineering and other emerging technologies by examining, and not repeating, the mistakes of the past.

TERMINOLOGY—OBSTACLE NUMBER ONE

Before moving on, it is important to clarify some terms. Reengineering, as used in this article, reflects the definition penned in the 1988 GUIDE paper, "Application Reengineering." Specifically, reengineering involves improving the physical aspects of application systems or changing form without changing function. Reengineering's goal is to make systems more amenable to change. There is no specification-level abstraction available as an end product from reengineering, just better code. Examples of reengineering include data name rationalization, code restructuring, code splitting, code reaggregation, and language-level upgrades.

The term "reverse engineering" means going from existing systems to varying levels of specification. The term "forward engineering" implies going from specifications to operational systems. The global terminology encompassing this interlinked set of software engineering activities is called "redevelopment engineering." The need to redefine these terms prior to discussing their organizational impact exemplifies the industry's general lack of understanding and overall lack of acceptance of these various software engineering disciplines.

REENGINEERING: AN HISTORICAL PERSPECTIVE

Ten years have passed since the first commercially available restructuring tool and the first source code analyzer com-

Reprinted with permission from *American Programmer*, Vol. 3, No. 10, Oct. 1990, pp. 14–20.

pleted their respective alpha-test phases. At the time, few industry watchers and even fewer participants could conceive of a use for these tools. Little was said about existing maintenance problems, and most people believed that complete rewrites were still a cost-effective solution. Reengineering tools were indeed a solution looking for a problem.

As the years passed, large-scale MIS shops, riding the "bleeding" edge of technology, began using these tools. The earliest reengineering tool to emerge was the COBOL restructuring product. At first, organizations sent their source code to vendors; vendors restructured the code and then returned it to the customer for testing. Since this was very expensive, the MIS community demanded that vendors create products that they could install on site for use by their own people. This evolutionary process occurred between 1984 and 1986.

Next, the MIS community demanded an increase in the automated capabilities of these tools. At least two of the vendors at the time promoted a philosophy of reviewing program anomalies prior to restructuring based on input from static code analyzers. The rationale was that restructuring tools should not be allowed to "work their magic" on program logic that was clearly errant. Demand for "full automation" persisted, however, and the vendors complied.

As feature after feature was added to these tools and their scope of automation increased, the MIS community began to lose sight of the original objectives for restructuring code. The purpose of applying restructuring technology to old programs was to ease the effort required to modify source code and, it was hoped, to position systems for more significant transformations in the future. Evaluation criteria for these tools were dictated by "technocrats" searching for the ultimate technological weapon. Implementation strategies were rarely developed, clear and measurable objectives were seldom defined, and the restructuring products quickly fell into disuse. This situation was not, by any means, isolated to restructuring products; other reengineering tools suffered a similar fate. MIS management was treating the reengineering function with benign neglect.

SUCCESS OR FAILURE?

Let us continue our restructuring tool example a little further. The relatively low number of installations (between 400 and 500) compared to the the number of IBM MVS sites (over 6000 in North America) gives us a quick overview of the success, or failure, of restructuring technology. The fact that restructuring at most installed sites has never been used, has been applied in a limited or sporadic manner, or has been used without measured or quantifiable success further demonstrates that these tools have had limited industry impact.

The use of COBOL restructuring tools, as discussed here, is relevant because they represent the most mature, most widely installed, and most widely accepted reengineering products in the industry. If we judge the impact of restructuring technology as mediocre, then we can view the success of reengineering tools, in general, as a major disaster.

All of this would not be much of a problem if reengineering were just a passing fad that was being replaced by more mature technology. It would also be of little concern if people were applying other tools to accomplish similar goals. Reengineering would most certainly be a footnote in MIS history if organizations had clearly defined migration paths to meet changing business needs, integrate emerging technologies, and migrate to improved architectures. The sad fact, however, is that the industry's pattern of deployment for these tools mirrors MIS readiness to accept and embrace new technology in general.

REENGINEERING'S STRATEGIC IMPORTANCE

Before examining some reengineering case histories, it is important to recognize the strategic importance of this technology, particularly in relation to the emerging field of reverse engineering. Tool builders and early users envisioned reengineering as tactical, providing, at best, maintenance improvements. This narrow view of reengineering perpetuated a lack of senior management involvement and a general lack of focus. Over the years, our understanding has evolved dramatically and now encompasses a much broader view of how reengineering supports both short-term and long-term MIS requirements.

Reengineering is becoming recognized as a way to begin preparing systems for reverse engineering. Reverse engineering is an emerging technology, viewed by many as a way to migrate old systems toward new technology and improved architectures. The reasoning runs along the following lines: There is an estimated 120 billion lines of source code in the world today, mostly COBOL. The data and business rule representations embedded in these programs embody the collective intelligence poured into information systems over the last 30 years. While awkward to enhance and frustrating to interpret, these systems dictate how information systems automate and, therefore, control organizations today. Recreating these systems tends to be cost and time prohibitive; but that is usually not the main obstacle to the new development scenario. The main roadblock to

the scrap-and-replace movement is risk.

SALVAGING BUSINESS INTELLIGENCE—REVERSE ENGINEERING

A quick example of the risk-inherent problems associated with the scrap-and-replace approach helps support the case for reverse engineering and, as we will see later, reengineering.

A number of compensation systems—including payroll, personnel, pension, and insurance—have reached a point of technical and architectural obsolescence. The systems cost too much to actually run, information stores are redundant, and information delivery is ill timed. The systems must be redeveloped under a new architecture that reflects a restructured work flow. Regulatory requirements and special-case handling must be maintained identically in the new system or thousands of people will no longer receive accurate disbursements. The only way to accomplish this is to reuse the data and business rules that already exist. The time and cost to replace this system, while significant, are secondary to the risk of lost functionality.

Reverse engineering presents a hopeful scenario for the thousands of organizations with large investments in information systems, investments in collective business intelligence as well as in time and money.

This new concept has, however, introduced more questions than answers. Reverse engineering tools, particularly in the procedural area, are in their infancy. Even more important, methods and strategies for applying reverse engineering are limited at best. As this technology continues to improve, the need for planning and preparation becomes significantly more important than under the reengineering scenario. As mentioned earlier, reengineering was less than successful due to management neglect and a lack of planning. Since the industry is still in the early stages of reverse engineering maturation, there is a window of opportunity to integrate reengineering and reverse engineering under a single, integrated strategy. Reengineering plays an integral role in this strategy.

STRATEGIC POSITIONING— REENGINEERING AS AN INTERIM SYSTEMS APPROACH

Managing risk by capturing and reusing embedded data and process rules may be viewed as a long-term goal. The overall, phased redevelopment strategy is geared to this end. This same approach also delivers interim improvements to existing software portfolios, supporting the need for constant functional upgrades. Reengineering, as defined at the outset, provides this tactical interim environment under a long-term redevelopment strategy. In other words, MIS organizations can continue working toward long-term goals while delivering phased improvements to the existing portfolio. Reengineering helps accomplish these objectives concurrently.

The application of reengineering technologies can be modified based on the end objective or objectives. The restructuring tools tend to have immediate impact in the maintenance area while preparing code for medium-term reaggregation and long-term functional extraction. Data definition reengineering tools tend to have more medium-term impact for conversions or migrations, and significant impact on the bottom-up population of repositories and design tools. Knowing MIS goals in advance can support project justification efforts, tool/parameter establishment, and staff preparation.

It is actually somewhat ironic that it took the introduction of reverse engineering, a relatively new and unfamiliar field of study, to clarify and solidify reengineering's position within the industry. In providing upgraded, interim systems under a broad-scale strategy, reengineering also delivers the short-term maintenance benefits originally envisioned 5 to 10 years ago. But if the industry's experience is so limited in

these various software engineering disciplines, how can we be sure that these claims hold true?

REENGINEERING SUCCESS STORIES

Quite a few examples of productivity and quality improvements directly attributable to reengineering exist within the industry today. These particular cases were gleaned either from trade publications or from conference or seminar presentations by members of the organizations involved.

Pacific Bell, an early user of reengineering technology, has maintained or controlled support costs in major systems through the use of COBOL restructuring technology. It is also exploring the use of data name rationalization tools to leverage migration efforts. At Dunlop Tire and Rubber, programming activities were focused on fixing system failures. After language translation and restructuring, system failures dropped dramatically, and technicians refocused their efforts on adding new business functionality.

There are numerous other reengineering success stories that include large field expansion projects and a variety of nonstandard or customized activities. Trade journals have documented these and other stories over the years, but most organizations tend to view

other organizations' successes with more than a little skepticism.

One reason for this skepticism is that each organization views its situation as unique. To a great degree this is true, and there is no such thing as a canned formula for applying short-term improvements to existing systems. A second, and probably overriding, reason stems from not understanding where reengineering belongs strategically within most organizations. Certainly, if there is no canned formula for success for short-term improvements, long-term transformation strategies must be developed with much planning and forethought and must be based on the current and future needs of the organization involved. There is, however, a thread of similarity that runs through most large-scale IBM environments, signaling the need for a redevelopment framework to drive reusability strategies.

The last case study example demonstrates the viewpoint that reengineering provides short-term benefits while feeding long-term objectives. A large system at Ætna Life & Casualty evolved through a series of reengineering improvements that included code restructuring and data name rationalization. While these activities were intent on positioning the system for long-term goals—such as online access, DB2, and general architectural changes—the staff supporting ongoing maintenance changes to the system was reduced by 50 percent over a three-year period. System change requests continued to be met at the same rate or better during this time frame, while key staff members were diverted to redesign efforts. This example reflects continuous activity on a single system over a longer period of time than most of the other reengineering case studies. It also demonstrates how tactical improvements can be implemented while driving toward a long-term goal.

REFOCUSING TOWARD A STRATEGIC VIEWPOINT

There are several reasons to perform reengineering activities on existing systems. The original purpose for reengineering was to simplify the maintenance effort required on aging systems. The tasks under this scenario include language translation, code restructuring, data name rationalization, code splitting, and code reaggregation. Maintenance support personnel benefit from all these tasks but, in general, the more difficult a reengineering task, the more difficult it is to justify based solely on maintenance improvement. This has tended to be a large barrier to procuring tools and establishing a reengineering function within most organizations. Adopting a strategic view of reengineer-

ing can help in the cost justification equation.

If an organization establishes short-, medium-, and long-term business and information objectives, reengineering can be implanted within this framework. MIS goals may include

☆ *Short term*: maintaining head count in three main systems areas

☆ *Medium term*: migrating two key systems to an online environment while integrating DBMS structures

☆ *Long term*: moving to DB2 and a specification-level support environment

If reengineering is viewed under this scenario, certain activities support dual-advantage outcomes. For example, code restructuring not only improves understandability of old code, leveraging the maintenance group, but also prepares for and assists in code splitting, a prerequisite for moving functions online. Data name rationalization supports the merging of disparate DBMS, but it is also a prerequisite to populating a specification repository to support the DB2 and specification migration effort.

The key point here is to stop thinking of reengineering with preconceived notions that limit the application of a given tool to a single, short-term benefit. These attitudes are a

holdover from a time when the industry had a much narrower view of how to apply this technology. Even vendors have been guilty of not understanding the strategic position of their own reengineering tools within a larger framework. All this will take some time, but industry's mind-set is slowly beginning to change.

REENGINEERING AS AN EVOLVING TECHNOLOGY

Reengineering tools are still evolving and increasing in capacity, function, and number. The reasons for this include a larger maintenance demand than ever, industry disappointment with failed rewrite efforts, and the changing view of reengineering's strategic importance. Examples of this tool evolution are

☆ a growth in similarity of function in the major restructuring products.

☆ an increase in the functionality and number of system and code analyzers.

☆ an awareness of the need to link these tools to a repository capability.

Industry observers might say that the maturation of the reengineering toolsets has moved much too slowly. Ask any analyst who waited most of the last decade to have a reasonable CICS restructuring capability. The converse of this, however, is that the industry has been very slow in realizing the breadth and scope of the application for these tools; this has driven some of the vendors, and their financial backers, into a "slow down and wait" mode. The products will continue to evolve as the MIS industry becomes more aware of how these tools fit in the larger picture.

REENGINEERING RECOMMENDATIONS— LESSONS LEARNED

Based on the experience of the last 10 years and the industry's often-rocky relationship with code restructurers, the following points should be considered when evaluating reengineering tools and techniques in an MIS organization:

☆ Reengineering is not a panacea and can never compensate for a lack of planning, a lack of management, or a lack of commitment to solve the real problem.

☆ Buying tools without a plan to implement them and evaluate their success is a good way to waste MIS budget.

☆ Lack of senior management interest and commitment will doom reengineering projects from the start.

☆ The tools are the least costly item in a reengineer-

ing endeavor; the cost of planning, training, execution, testing, and internal marketing are the real reengineering costs.

☆ Readjustment of the MIS culture is a normal and required phenomenon when one is changing existing systems, although it is probably much easier than moving an organization to, say, an information engineering environment.

☆ Certain tools work better in conjunction with certain other tools, even though they may not be the best or most rigorous in their individual category. The key here is to examine a given vendor's entire offering.

☆ If there is an analyzer that supports a reengineering tool and related techniques, use it! Some analyzers are embedded within the reengineering tool itself; this is true with most of the data definition reengineering tools.

☆ Know why you are applying a tool before establishing the project; for example, certain restructuring parameters work to the detriment of trying to reverse engineer those same systems later.

☆ A focus on techniques, with proper training, is essential. As we said, the re-

structuring tools have been heavily automated; there are certain constructs that should be reviewed prior to applying restructuring tools to aging systems.

☆ A task force, or reengineering central coordination point, should be established to

★ serve an advisory function for planning support.

★ promote and support advanced reengineering techniques.

★ establish and monitor an evaluation and measurement function.

★ monitor successes and failures to improve subsequent projects.

★ serve as a link to senior management so reengineering and MIS goals remain synchronized.

☆ Do not expect miracles: many small gains can eventually add up to one large gain.

SUMMARY

The MIS industry has an opportunity today that is unique. While this is a time where demand for MIS responsiveness is at an all-time high, there is a significant amount of technology at hand to help. The industry is also at a very dangerous crossroads. If we continue to expect technology to solve all our problems without proper planning and management attention, we will be dooming this same technology to failure. Conversely, if the industry rejects new technology because it does not present a 100 percent solution, valuable technology will never have a chance to flourish.

It is time to learn from the pitfalls that reengineering encountered in the last decade. The recommendations we listed could all have been pulled from one haphazard experience with a failed restructuring implementation effort. They are actually this author's observations, based on working with hundreds of organizations in this area, of ways to avoid future, and certainly more costly, mistakes. The reverse engineering technology quickly becoming available is much more complex than any previous MIS offerings. For this reason, repeating the mistakes made over the last decade with reengineering could serve up much more serious consequences. Let us look to the future and learn from the past.

William M. Ulrich is a principal at the Tactical Strategy Group, a consulting firm specializing in reengineering and reverse engineering strategy development and deployment. Formerly director of product marketing at XA Systems and director of reengineering product strategies at KPMG Peat Marwick Advanced Technology, Ulrich has spent over 10 years in the software reengineering products and consulting arena.

A forerunner in the industry, he was a member of the alpha-test team for the first commercially available restructuring tool, RETROFIT. Ulrich has authored dozens of articles for major trade publications and technical journals and is sought after by industry conference coordinators to speak on redevelopment strategies and trends. His reputation as an expert in the field has led to his appointment to presenters' panels, advisory boards, and as keynote speaker for major industry conferences.

Mr. Ulrich can be reached at the Tactical Strategy Group (408/662-3165). ★

I/S ANALYZER

(formerly EDP ANALYZER)

© 1991 by United Communications Group

VOL. 29, NO. 10

For information systems management

Editors:
Jack B. Rochester
David P. Douglass

I/S ANALYZER

RE-ENGINEERING EXISTING SYSTEMS

Reverse engineering is the process of recapturing the essential design, structure, and content of a complex computer system which has proven useful in running the business. When the system is understood and defined, re-engineering is the process of rewriting the system to take advantage of new technology, such as relational databases or communications, while maintaining all the functions and features that were proven to be useful in the original system. These two processes are intertwined--there is no re-engineering of systems without first reverse engineering their content. In the last three years, this "software recycling" has progressed to the point where there are now many proven methods available for the various phases of the re-engineering process. This month we examine the rationale behind re-engineering, how companies are using reverse engineering as the first step in re-engineering old Cobol systems, and the benefits they are reaping from their efforts. (An Executive Summary is on page 16.)

DST Systems of Kansas City, Missouri is an industry leader in the processing of shareholder accounting and recordkeeping services for mutual funds. DST retains 40% of this industry, processing 23 million mutual fund accounts, with about $400 billion in assets, and well over 100 mutual funds.

In 1988, DST identified a need by clients for expanded field sizes for data items such as fund account numbers, dollar amounts, number of shares, price amounts, rates, address information, and several others.

Michael Waterford, group vice president, was chartered with the responsibility of adapting the

system to meet these needs. He has a development staff of 100 mainframe systems analysts, programmers, business analysts, and test specialists.

Field length specifications had begun to impede the business. DST could only have a maximum of 99 funds on one system, so they were running 23 copies of the system to handle the volume of accounts. Waterford pointed out that they also had a limitation of 99 million shares per account, and that they also had quite a few customers, particularly large institutions, that required more than that. In addition, the maximum redemption DST could handle was $10 million. This may sound like a sufficient amount, but in peak periods they moved more than a billion dollars a day through the Federal wires alone.

They also had some accounts that were doing 100 transactions a day, and their system would only allow them to keep 999 histories on a single account. This limited their ability to keep track of records efficiently.

No Alternative to Re-engineering

In 1986, DST decided to focus on this problem. Waterford noted that it was not a very complicated problem. They had three choices: buy another system, build a new system, or re-engineer the system they had. DST discarded the first option when they discovered they could not buy a system that was capable of processing the volumes of information and had the degree of functionality they required.

They also discarded the option of redesigning and rewriting the system when they estimated the cost to be approximately $50 million and that it would require more than three years to complete. Waterford decided to re-engineer the system despite the fact that re-engineering is a difficult task that nobody volunteers to do. It was the lesser of evils.

DST's re-engineering project was estimated to cost approximately $10 million and allow DST to implement the renovated system during 1990.

At the start, they tried to get control of the data in the system. They were a Datacom-DB shop, so they chose to use the Datacom data dictionary. They chartered a data management group and started to get control of the data definitions, and to populate the dictionary.

The data management project continued on through 1987 and 1988. But in 1988 the competitive pressure began to build. There were very large pieces of business on which they were actively bidding that would have been very difficult for their system to handle.

Two Re-engineering Approaches

DST came up with two alternative approaches to re-engineering--the "Big Bang" and the "Trickle Down" approaches.

In the 'Big Bang', the system is shut down while re-engineering is performed as quickly as possible.

Then the re-engineered system is installed, and everybody is brought up and the system is re-opened for business. In the 'Trickle Down', re-engineering is done incrementally--groups of programs at a time. Waterford felt that the pros and cons of these two approaches were fairly clear. The 'Big Bang' gets the job done relatively quickly, but it is much riskier. The 'Trickle Down' will take a long time, but quality checks can be done more easily. It is essentially a trade-off of time versus risk.

DST continued their data management work through most of 1988, and in the last quarter of 1988 put a team together to specifically decide on the re-engineering approach. They initially decided to try the 'Trickle Down' approach, but as 1989 unfolded, the competitive situation intensified. So they decided to go for the 'Big Bang', and put together their plan.

In March of 1989 Waterford went to the GUIDE meeting in Anaheim. In a re-engineering talk, William Ulrich, president of Tactical Strategy Group, a re-engineering consulting firm (Reference 1), mentioned a capability for data standardization and field expansion. Subsequent discussions with Ulrich led to the discovery of the DATATEC product from XA Systems Corporation (Reference 2). At that time the product was in a beta version. Since DST had a very large problem, Waterford was willing to look at a beta version. They bought the tool and began working in the 3rd quarter of 1989. They also engaged some consultants from Peat Marwick Advanced Technology to help them with the process.

Changing the Engines
on a 747 While in Flight

The re-engineering project was named FLEX (Field Length Expansion). The size of the project consisted of:
- 5,000 programs
- 350 resident files--either database or VSAM
- more than 3,000 work files
- 2,500 reports
- 800 screens

They developed a customized DATATEC process, and it became a key component of their overall FLEX project strategy. They used it to analyze the relationship of physical data structures and to change Cobol source code in more than 300 on-line data

2

structures and 4,000 batch programs.

DATATEC identified the relationship of physical data structures, and DST used this information to identify all programs which referenced a common logical data structure. Then its existing data definitions were automatically replaced by DATATEC with one common copy member containing the standardized data names with expanded fields. The movement or "tracing" of data names with expanded fields was important both to identify work fields requiring expansion and to audit the FLEX project.

The customized DATATEC process used by DST provided not only an automated approach to changing a large volume of Cobol applications, but also a method of providing centralized control of changing programs to meet new Cobol coding standards. The benefits they observed of using DATATEC for the FLEX project included reducing both the programming labor required to expand data fields and the number of modifications required during the unit testing process. The main FLEX project began in July of 1989, and continued through the first quarter of 1990. At the end of the first quarter, DST began running systems tests.

The pressure to implement the new system quickly was so great, Waterford felt that FLEX was "the moral equivalent of war." On Memorial Day weekend, 1990, they cut over their first client. To everybody's surprise the new system ran--and it ran pretty well. They rolled out the remaining 23 systems between the 25th of May and the 11th of November. Now they are just winding down on the final cleanup.

The whole of FLEX project took 100 man years-- 200,000 hours. It cost DST approximately $12 million. Of that, close to $1 million was spent on re-synchronizing the existing system. (Note that this eliminated the need for a $50 million rewrite over three years.)

In this effort, they had their share of problems, but the core system--the ability to buy and sell shares, and keep track of all of the shares, had very, very few problems. They never ever really shut down during FLEX. They managed that re-engineering project while they were still working on the system in the 'real world'. Waterford noted that this is a trick similar to changing the engines on a 747 while it is flying.

The Realities and Directions of Software Recycling

One of the biggest problems facing CEOs today is the inability to make corporate changes quickly. Organizations are positioning themselves to change faster, but the software layer is not positioned to change fast.

Stephen Errico, partner-in-charge of the Price Waterhouse RE/Cycle program (Reference 3), points out that the old strategy to remove this barrier was to perfect new development capability; the existing system problems would then disappear. But the barrier of success for a lot of companies is not new software development; it is the installed layer of software. The newer tactic is to move existing systems to new development technologies. Business wants to replace and enhance the existing systems. Technologists must salvage these systems through the employment of reusable components as they move to the new technical challenges. These include: cooperative processing, a common programming interface, common user access, and, in the IBM world, SAA compliance, AD/Cycle, repository, and DB2.

Errico notes that the lesson learned in this effort is that the key is process-driven tool support. We are now using specific tools that can accomplish parts of the job. The possibility of full automation is in the future.

According to David Sharon, President of CASE Associates, Inc. (Reference 4), as we move to more promising technologies, we should focus on prolonging the life of existing systems. This will reduce software maintenance budgets, help to recover the original costs of R&D, and reduce the risks that are inherent to the rewriting of systems. These new processes help us to understand existing systems and to better evaluate the alternatives.

Over the next two years, Sharon predicts there will be a proliferation of re-engineering services, together with a tight coupling of reverse-engineering to forward-engineering tools. There will be a discrete positioning of the tools on the market, but CASE integration frameworks will include re-engineering tools. We are heading to the era of the "software factory" for both data structures and process logic, where the work will be done by defined sets of methods, controlled, interlocked, and managed.

Why Reverse Engineering is Needed

Peter J. Van Opens, a systems coordinator at Northwestern Mutual Life Insurance Company in Milwaukee, Wisconsin, notes that reverse engineering is needed for software flexibility, increased productivity, cost reduction and system documentation. Its use clearly helps to understand the business process that is buried in the code, and helps to understand the data and process relationships, says Van Opens, who is active in systems re-engineering. It gives an opportunity to improve the quality of the system at the same time it corrects existing errors. It requires skillful systems people, but it is a challenge to them and is morale building. One of its biggest advantages is that the users are forced to get involved in the systems development process, greatly improving the product.

Dr. Hasan H. Sayani, President of Advanced Systems Technology Corporation in Greenbelt, Maryland (Reference 5), warns that reverse engineering must be carefully fit into the development cycle. This means that it is most effective when you have a well-defined forward engineering process and can match the reverse engineering output with the code generator. The final re-engineering then becomes a component of an integrated project support environment. The three best uses of reverse engineering are to provide a better methodology for maintenance, to allow rapid adaptation to changed requirements with traceability between requirements and implementation, and to take advantage of changed technologies and architectures.

Sayani emphasizes the need for re-engineering of our "legacy systems", our portfolio of operational systems, which are functioning, but are out-of-date, poorly documented, and full of technology constraints. The needs for handling our legacy in the organization are met, not with what he calls "CASE islands" of multiple, independent CASE tools, however, but with an integrated project support environment where vendor tools have an open architecture and use the same central repository.

The Place for Re-Engineering in Your Business

Reverse engineering has a very specific place in the overall scheme of system development. It extracts data definitions and process rules from existing systems, and represents them at the specification level. This information can be used for at least three purposes. First, it accurately documents current systems, simplifying changes and providing program modules as input to forward development analysis. Second, it can be used to "clean up" old systems, removing dead wood, and making the old logic understandable, and much more readily maintained. Third, it can clarify the old system specifications, giving the information necessary to forward engineer new systems from the current base of existing systems.

The Center for the Study of Data Processing at Washington University in St. Louis, Missouri (Reference 6), holds a regular series of forums on current I/S concerns and new approaches to the improvement of data processing performance. At a recent forum entitled "Reverse Engineering: Capturing Value," an impressive number of papers were presented on successes in the use of re-engineering methods. Reverse engineering was no longer approached as a future probability, but was demonstrated to be an available, profitable possibility today. The speakers mainly described reverse engineering techniques, but at least six profitable, re-engineering success stories were described.

There was a consistent refrain in many of the presentations at the forum--maintenance costs are out of control and vital production systems are very old. There was general agreement that there are now re-engineering techniques that can pull maintenance costs back into control and extend the life of a production system.

CASE--The Potential and the Pitfalls (QED Information Sciences, Inc. (Reference 7) sums up the concept and advantages of COBOL re-engineering technology very well. It states:

> The concept of reverse engineering is to begin the development life cycle with existing systems, or with parts of existing systems, at the abstraction specification level of the original system rather than at the strategic planning, requirements specification, and analysis levels. The idea is to recover the original design specification, as it has been modified over the years, from the current physical implementation, the databases, and the program

4

code in those existing systems or system parts. One of the problems in this process is to determine whether the existing systems really are an accurate reflection of the original design specifications that management requested, and whether it is worth enhancing rather than rewriting. If six generations of programmers have maintained the average system, as has been estimated, and if several different managers have requested modifications or enhancements, is it a good system that is worth saving?

Many consultants have expressed concern about COBOL reverse engineering because it may simply perpetuate the problems of the past. If the system was built the wrong way, for the wrong reasons, it is hardly worth saving. The gospel of [forward] information engineering is that old systems are too riddled with error to save, and are too inefficient in their mode of operation. So do away with them and start from scratch. This is certainly a worthy idea from a technical person's viewpoint. The reality, however, is that many large, operating COBOL systems are quite satisfactory in design and general structure, but are exceedingly difficult and expensive to maintain. It is well worth re-engineering them if the overall effort is markedly less than starting from scratch again.

Many of the comments at the St. Louis Reverse Engineering Forum agreed with those remarks. There are some COBOL systems that need a complete rewrite, but there are many, many large COBOL systems that are doing the job that is wanted, and a large set of their elements can be profitably saved for the new systems as we move to new technologies of operation.

The Concept of Logic Modeling

Reverse engineering is reasonably obvious in concept, but the layers on layers of old, maintained code that resides in our legacy systems, in a variety of languages, makes it highly complex technically. It is not necessary to understand the technicalities to appreciate the uses of reverse engineering, but there are two fairly new concepts that are worth a brief description: logic modeling and slicing.

Charles Bachman, chairman of Bachman Information Systems, Inc. in Burlington, Massachusetts (Reference 8), is well known for his significant information sciences contributions, including making the public aware of maintenance reverse engineering. He emphasizes that logic modeling is the keystone of the application development process. He describes logic models as that part of the specification layer in programs that joins with the data structure models (in the data dictionary) and the data flow models (the process) to define the sending and receiving of messages, the storing and retrieving of information, and the controlling of business decisions.

Data models and process models are important, but they are not new. What is new is the production of enterprise models that are understandable by business managers, and can be used as a source for generating code. The enterprise model pulls together data models (such as customer, order, product), the process model (such as order-entry-desk, shipping-dock), and the logic model (such as credit-approval, invoice-preparation). The logic models focus on business transactions as indivisible units of work. They are concerned with business procedures (e.g. credit approval), program statements (e.g. RETRIEVE customer), program iterators (e.g. FOR-EACH purchase-order), methods (e.g. add-customer), and events (e.g. order-received). The logic models integrate the methods and structures of the program, and can bring graphics to defining and reviewing business rules. They can be reviewed in English, or other natural languages, by managers.

Bachman reiterates that reverse engineering can be used to provide a cost-effective means to extract a machine-independent Enterprise Model from existing source code. The process is imperative to capitalize on the 70 billion lines of old, machine-dependent, COBOL source code that exist today. We need to move to the new object-oriented methods by integrating them with the old entity-relationship structures. Using these methods, we can provide the basis for access-based design of efficient, responsive databases.

Bachman points out that reverse engineering can be used to enhance systems by supporting the modification of the old Enterprise Model to take advantage of new business opportunities. It can be tied to forward engineering to rapidly and efficiently convert the enhanced Enterprise Model into source code for your new, selected information technologies. And it can be used to optimize by specializing new source code to user-specific configuration and performance requirements.

Bachman Information Systems, Inc., like the Price Waterhouse Re-Engineering Center, and a number of the other prominent vendors of re-engineering systems, have joined IBM under their AD/Cycle program umbrella. This will greatly assist the migration to IBM's AD/Cycle and SAA environments. Most companies will find it important to assure that their re-engineering work will be compatible with IBM's Information Model. IBM has said that it is willing to move the Enterprise Model outside the IBM world and open it to the ANSI and ISO standardization processes.

The Concept of Slicing

Anyone familiar with the piles of paper printouts on the computer room floor that represent Cobol programs will wonder how any programs or programmers can navigate adequately through the old "sphagetti code" that has built up over the years. It would seem to be nearly impossible to sort out the useful parts of the code from the changed and useless parts. The fact is, when we re-engineer we really want to save only part of the old code, and not waste time with the rest of it. One of the answers to this dilemma is the use of the technique called "slicing." It has become an important analytical technique for looking at programs.

Michael A. Wolf, Vice President for Development of VIASOFT, Inc. in Phoenix, Arizona (Reference 9), believes that we must get proven engineering principles into software engineering. One of these principles, ascribed to Henry Ford, is the reusability of pieces of design and components. One-of-a-kind production is too slow in delivery. We need to have tools that will automate the isolation of components of a program, to help understand, extract, re-use, and manage them. In essence, this is the extraction of business functions from a complex system.

Slicing, or code isolation, is thus a method for pulling out from a program those parts that are concerned with a specified behavior or interest, such as a particular business rule or transaction. It means locating the minimum amount of data and code that is required to derive a desired data item at a particular point in a program.

Slicing is conceptually easy. We simply accrue all data definitions and control flow which contribute to the desired data element values at the slice points. We discard anything that does not contribute to those values. After all, this is the way that good maintenance programmers have always approached problems. They have worked back in the code from the element that concerned them.

Slicing is technically very difficult to automate, however. It requires specific, or "expert", knowledge about data flows, control flows, dependencies, statements that modify the data, and the existence of "dead" code. It is of little use unless it is complete in its extraction. If it can be done, however, it automates time-consuming, tedious, and error-prone activities. It applies expert knowledge about semantics and dependencies, and can make a junior programmer more effective than a veteran working manually. Done correctly, it computes the minimal subset of code required for a function.

The VIA/Renaissance program from VIASOFT uses slice technology to re-engineer functions. It identifies and isolates components and business rules, by finding, describing, and regenerating functions that are buried in existing Cobol applications. This program uses the "analytical engine" approach to automate the extraction and generation of the desired functions.

Effective software production requires engineering approaches. One such approach is the use of isolation strategies to pull out effective, reusable program components. This is particularly true if you want to move to an object oriented strategy. You locate and pull out reusable objects, then insert them into the forward engineering packages.

This type of approach will become increasingly popular for supporting reusability strategies, because it will help feed into other CASE tools for forward engineering with a minimum of baggage. Only those objects and procedures that are desired to be taken forward will be presented to the forward strategy. There will be automatic removal of a large amount of code in the old system that is no longer wanted. In the near future we will see such types of extraction linked automatically to the forward engineering CASE systems.

Software slicing would also appear to offer great promise as a computer audit technique. It has the

6

advantage of discovering all the code that is related to a particular accounting function in a single, automated process. If your data processing auditors are not familiar with the new software slicing technique, it should be drawn to their attention.

Cost Justification of Re-Engineering

Re-engineering is rapidly being accepted, but it is still a technology that is little understood. Considering its proven possibilities of delivering savings with the rapid production of new systems, it is exceedingly underutilized. This is partly because many managers have the view that re-engineering is an alternative to new development or package purchase, rather than an integral subset of either one, or both.

Consultant Ulrich argues that there is great value in planning future architecture by "positioning" existing architecture before starting on a major transformation effort. The inventory and analysis of existing systems is not sufficient to find the best approach to future development. Positioning means first using tools and techniques to improve the quality of existing systems without affecting the functions or the basic architecture upon which those systems were built.

Ulrich notes that a key result of the positioning strategy is that improved systems can be used as a foundation upon which realistic plans and cost estimates may be made for future new systems. Pure technological change is never the best answer. If there is to be system replacement, the system must be put into the best condition as a source of viable information to temper new designs. If there is to be package purchase and implementation, structures must be rationalized and reconciled across disparate systems, and there is a necessity to know the data structures in the in-house systems.

Rapid growth, mergers and acquisitions all drive systems capacities beyond intended levels. If these capacities are understood in detail, before any decisions are made, there may be great savings available. A very good example of intelligent positioning was described earlier in the DST Systems case study. Instead of paying $50 million for a new system, which would have taken several years to complete, they accurately analyzed their existing system, and decided to make changes on it that cost $12 million, and were completed rapidly.

Thus, positioning of the existing system, the cleaning up and understanding of it, is fundamental to accurate cost analysis and justification of any major change, including re-engineering. Good planning and cost analysis can only be done if there is a solid base from which to figure.

Migration to new systems should be a multi-step approach, and planning is essential. Start with an inventory and analysis of existing systems so you know what base you are working from. Use positioning, before any transformation, so you can accurately determine the most cost-effective change to make. Insist on interim payback under any long-term strategy. Build a plan with solid cost figures.

When you consider that it is estimated that 5% to 15% of the current third generation language systems in operation contain 80% to 85% of the functionality, it becomes all the more important to understand the existing systems in detail as a base for any planning. It is imperative to talk to the maintenance people about any plans, know the current costs in detail, and go to the users for their opinions.

Ulrich notes that, although re-engineering may be less costly than writing all the new code from scratch, it is still expensive. It is a costly proposition, but its costs can be justified if the effort is handled step by step. The cost justification must be accomplished in stages as the re-development work proceeds--first the positioning, then the transformation.

Costing and justifying the positioning should be done first, says Ulrich. Based on the life expectancy of the system, positioning can generally be cost justified as a standalone effort. The justification calculations for positioning should include all the re-engineering conversion activities. Such tangible advantages should be included as integration with short-term system initiatives, phased re-allocation of key support personnel, and the use of the re-allocated staff, fully costed, for the system life. Include intangible advantages such as support of the physical data conversion efforts, confirmation of the new top-down analysis and design, and extension of the old system life as a safety net.

In any cost analysis, Ulrich has found that the problem with getting good information about the advantages of positioning is that you are usually going against old, faulty information on the system development costs with cost overruns. It is hard to agree on savings in reduction in current implementation complexity, for example. But it is possible to get metric measures on the reduced research efforts needed in facilitating major and minor fixes and enhancements. It is also possible to estimate general quality and productivity improvements through the advantage of failure rate reduction. The reduction of system skill level support requirements becomes a self-fulfilling prophecy.

After you learn more about the current system, and have done some top-down conceptual design for the new system, you can justify the phase for transformation to a new system. Transformation cost assessment is driven by functional mapping analysis from the earlier phase of inventory and analysis of the existing systems.

You can estimate the percent of savings of the new system cost obtained through reuse of parts of the old system, says Ulrich. Compare this to the cost of developing the reuse component. The direct savings that will be obtained by the new system can then be ascribed partly to the reuse component, and partly to the transformation to the new system.

A believable cost justification is always difficult to accomplish for large system development. Ulrich's phased approach, with incremental change, can add some credence to the numbers. Even then, he says that re-engineering is a sweeping cultural change for computer professionals, and it is only believable after considerable effort has been expended on education.

Elliot J. Chikofsky, Director of CASE Development at Progress Software Corp. (Reference 10), has noted that the cost of "understanding" existing software, while rarely seen as a direct cost, is nonetheless very real. It is manifested in the time required to comprehend software, which includes the time lost to misunderstanding. By reducing the time required to grasp the essence of software artifacts in each life-cycle phase, reverse engineering may greatly reduce the overall cost of software. For more of Chikofsky's views, see this month's Commentary.

Walt Scacchi of the University of Southern California has observed that: "Many claim that conventional software maintenance practices account for 50 to 90 percent of total life-cycle costs. Software

reverse engineering technologies are targeted to the problems that give rise to such a disproportionate distribution of software costs. Thus, if reverse engineering succeeds, the total system expense may be reduced/mitigated, or greater value may be added to current efforts, both of which represent desirable outcomes, especially if one quantifies the level of dollars spent. Reverse engineering may need to only realize a small impact to generate sizable savings."

Le Groupe Rona-Dismat

Rona-Dismat is a hardware retailer located in Quebec, Canada. The company owns 560 stores in the province of Quebec, selling everything from power tools to hammers and nails.

According to Marc Mazerole, Systems Coordinator, Rona-Dismat is using InterCASE, from InterPort Software Corporation, Fairfax, Virginia (Reference 11), to "get to know their applications better." The company has developed more than 5,000 Cobol programs during the past 15 years. The programmers who developed the programs no longer work for the company and many of their programs were never put into production or are no longer functioning.

These old programs were taking up valuable computer memory and are difficult, if not impossible, to upgrade. Therefore, the company needs a tool that provides a snapshot of the old applications in order to make them run more efficiently. InterPort's InterCASE Workbench provides Rona-Dismat with a clear look at their existing COBOL programs and gives them the tools to upgrade these applications.

InterCASE's "parser" capability allows Rona-Dismat to identify and eliminate "dead" code or ineffective programs and determine how others are being used. "The InterCASE parser capability has decreased the number of programs from over 5,000 to 4,500, and the company expects to reduce the number further to 4,000," Mazerole said.

The company is using InterCASE on a Novell network of 30 PCs and uploading the reverse-engineered applications to an IBM model 4381 mainframe. By editing on the PCs with InterCASE, the programmers are able to increase their productivity by 25% to 30%, according to Mazerole.

Another InterCASE feature important to Rona-

8

Dismat is its configuration management capabilities, which allow the company to develop and test code while controlling who has access to the code. This prevents programmers from overwriting code previously changed by another programmer. It also prevents two developers from working on the same program.

Configuration management also provides the programmer with a list of all the lines of code that were changed or that need to be changed. This allows the new code to be reviewed before it is incorporated into the program.

Rona-Dismat's original dilemma was that maintenance lead times had been increasing, yet management had told them to reduce the MIS budget. Portions of their two million lines of code were 15 years old, yet conversion to real-time inventory control was in progress.

They were able to install InterCASE in one month, including training, and change 33% of their programs in six months. On the first day of installation, they were able to eliminate three maintenance procedure errors, where programmers were prevented from overwriting updates. Initial opposition by some programmers disappeared rapidly, and now the entire staff uses the program. Maintenance now occurs entirely on PC workstations, and updates are sent to the mainframe via an automated process.

Rona-Dismat's maintenance lead time has decreased markedly, and maintenance costs have been reduced to an acceptable level. Development projects can now receive priority. The result has been satisfied clients, and higher staff morale.

Mellon Bank Corporation

With assets of $31.7 billion as of June 30, 1990, Mellon Bank Corporation is one of the nation's largest bank holding companies. Through its subsidiaries, Mellon provides a comprehensive range of banking services and quality products.

Mellon Bank, with over 21.5 million lines of code, feels it must preserve the value of its software investments through re-engineering. In fact, the bank's executive vice president for information management and research felt that it was a matter of survival.

Mellon has a trust application (InfoServ) that is used internally for client bank servicing and also is sold as a software product to outside customers. To achieve the productivity gains that high level languages deliver, Mellon wanted to convert the programs to an application generation tool. As a first step, the on-line programs were converted from assembler code manually, but the remaining challenge was to convert more than 400 batch Cobol programs.

Unfortunately, the existing Cobol programs were not accepted by the generator tool which, like many code generation products, required structured language syntax. To achieve the application consistency they were looking for, Mellon needed to solve this problem.

Mellon Bank was a long-time user of Language Technology Inc.'s Recoder system. They saw the trust conversion effort as another opportunity to take advantage of Recoder's capabilities. By structuring the existing programs, Recoder could produce valid input for the application generation tool.

The conversion process involved structuring the programs with Recoder, then sending them through a parser into the application generation product. This enabled Mellon to provide the structured, consistent syntax that the application generation product required. Mike DeLecce, assistant vice president, noted that the Recoder options enabled them to set a predefined format which was crucial to the conversion. All of the 400+ batch programs were recoded and fully converted within two weeks.

Code reusability is not the only benefit Mellon Bank has seen from Recoder. DeLecce recalls previous Recoder projects where structuring also paid off. One particular situation involved a complex module and a new, inexperienced programming team. With 89 recursive paths, the program was a nightmare. After recoding, the staff was very pleased with the results. Recoder had taken something that essentially was "totally beyond understanding" and turned it into something that could be easily understood.

The bottom line was that, by using Recoder, it was possible to automate the trust system conversion process, making the entire effort feasible. Structuring afforded Mellon the opportunity to reuse existing code and take advantage of additional CASE technology. Although past Recoder successes had helped save Mellon time and money on existing projects, the implementation of the product for the trust conversion project actually made the project possible.

The Risk Involved

There is risk involved, of course, in any new methodology, such as re-engineering. This requires some risk management planning. In most of the cases with which we are familiar, this was principally done by bringing in outside consultants, partly to assuage the fears of higher management, but mainly to be assured that someone with experience was on the team for this new approach. Such consultants will also do much of the training that is required if they are on board. This is particularly true if the consultants come from the vendor of the re-engineering software package. Such people have a very strong interest in the success of the project.

Robert S. Arnold, of the Software Productivity Consortium (Reference 12), has examined the re-engineering risks and the strategies for mitigating them. He emphasizes the need for management attention and the problems of justification of the effort. Too often, technical people put in too much manual effort, and the project drifts. Too much manual work is expensive. It is not uncommon for programmers to oppose the effort, and push it to failure. Competent technologists often work on the wrong things and head for the wrong goals. Arnold emphasizes that management must realistically fit re-engineering into a planned, long-range process, and manage their personnel accordingly. Do not overestimate the capabilities of modern technology.

You might ask why you should even consider spending such time, with these risks and problems. The reason is right under your nose in any organization with massive files of Cobol programs. Those programs are old. The need for more maintenance is growing every day, yet experienced Cobol maintainers are getting more and more difficult to hold or to find.

Over the years, maintenance has been far more than taking bugs, or errors, out of the original system. The programs have been added to, modified, and re-arranged, in response to user requests. Large sections may have been put in, and other large sections may have cut out from the data flow in the

program, but left in place in computer memory. The applications have been ported to new operating systems, with the old ports often left in place, and many new programs have been appended to any well-used application system. That is why the need for maintenance has been growing every day, and why the costs of maintenance have become a major item in any I/S budget.

Most of the companies that we talked to found that the principal advantage of re-engineering has been in cleaning up their old Cobol systems, sometimes quite dramatically, and in markedly reducing the maintenance effort that was then required. In fact, some companies had so much success with the clean-up of their old systems that they did not have to start heavy, new, system development work. Surely, this alone should be enough for managers to pay attention to re-engineering as one of their viable alternatives today.

Management Attention Needed

The reuse of software is not primarily a technical problem, but a management issue for information systems executives. We found that the technical problems are considerable, but they are being solved by many companies, and the I/S technical staff usually becomes enthusiastic about reuse after they have become immersed in it and have seen the results. There are quite adequate packages available today to re-engineer large pieces of software, and to introduce these pieces into forward CASE development systems.

In many instances, I/S management has become so involved in selling large system development projects, that they have overlooked the possibilities of markedly reducing the time and total costs of the projects by paying more attention to cleaning up the older systems and reusing some of their programs.

Many people we spoke to think of re-engineering as a major "cultural change," or a "paradigm shift" for their staffs that they are not ready to address. Yet the benefits that can be derived from reverse- and re-engineering systems will push more and more organizations to embrace the pursuit, we believe.

Such staff problems are only handled by detailed management attention. Changes like this probably will be neither rapid nor smooth, so you have to prepare detailed transition plans, and appoint people to be in charge of making the plans succeed. In two specific cases where we heard of failures in re-engineering projects, the idea had come up solely from the technical ranks, they had been given permission to go ahead, but management gave little attention to the work.

Perhaps getting management's attention is difficult because many re-engineering projects are not large, but are simply one part of much larger system development projects. This is unfortunate, because for some we looked at, re-engineering was fundamental to the success of the overall, larger project. This is because the re-engineering effort was the principle way in which the requirements for the big, new system were discovered and proven. A great deal of the real-world experience with the old system, over the years, can be recaptured, and held onto with confidence.

So what must management do besides learning about re-engineering and "paying attention to" the project? You must make transition plans, principally in both education of all concerned with the system, and training for the technical staff, and offer incentives for success to the technical people who are betting their jobs that they have a very worthwhile thing going.

Summary

Our research shows that the process of re-engineering existing systems is still rapidly evolving, but there are now enough capabilities on the market for organizations to do significant re-engineering. It is a tool-assisted process, and most of the tools marketed today do what their vendors say that the tools should do. The solutions available may still not meet all your needs in restoring old Cobol programs, but they are clearly useful and cost-effective. They should be employed, at the very least, so that your staff can learn this critical new area of CASE

technology. Re-engineering has now been proven useful, and should soon have widespread acceptance.

The place of re-engineering should be clearly understood. In the spectrum of management attention, it fits in between maintenance of old application systems and the building of new systems, preferrably with CASE forward engineering methods. This means, on the one hand, that re-engineering has been proven useful in the "clean-up" of massive, old Cobol systems to create leaner, better systems that are far easier to maintain. It also means that re-engineering can be used to accurately extract desired parts of the old Cobol systems so that they can be used in new systems, with new technologies, such as databases and fourth-generation languages, and inserted into the forward engineering process.

Reverse engineering assures that all the old management and clerical rules that have been put into the old system will be retained. There is never a complete record of all those old rules, and there is never anyone around who remembers all the "blood, sweat, and tears" that went into establishing them. No systems analyst today can sit down and create a completely new system, on new technology, that will not cause much future difficulty unless those old rules are recovered, documented, and used.

In addition, it should be emphasized that a number of reverse engineering methods, particularly software slicing, can offer considerable advantage to computer auditors, and the capabilities of these systems should be investigated by your computer audit team.

Reverse engineering does not produce a new program. It simply analyzes and displays the parts of the old program. Its great strength will be realized when it is tightly coupled to forward engineering, in the re-engineering process. We will see this integration happening in the next two years. In the next five years, we will see all phases of re-engineering as a component part of integrated CASE tool packages, and it will be generally accepted in all Cobol program maintenance work.

References

1. William Ulrich is president of Tactical Strategy Group, 1716 Cheryl Way, Aptos, CA 95003; tel. (408) 662-3165.

2. XA Systems Corp., 303 West Erie Street, Chicago, Illinois 60610; tel. (312) 280-4355. John Faulkenberry is consulting operations manager.

3. Steve Errico is partner-in-charge of the Price Waterhouse Re-Engineering Center, 1410 North Westshore Boulevard, Tampa, Florida 33607; tel. (813) 287-9296.

4. David Sharon is president of CASE Associates Inc., 15686 South Bradley Road, Oregon City, Oregon 97045; tel. (503) 656-0986.

5. Hasan Sayani is president of ASTEC, Advanced Systems Technology Corp., 9111 Edmonston Road, Suite 404, Greenbelt, Maryland 20770; tel. (301) 441-9036.

6. The Center for the Study of Data Processing, at Washington University in St. Louis, provided sources for much of the information in this report at their Reverse Engineering Forum: Capturing Value, held in St. Louis in April 1991. CSDP performs related professional studies, together with their series of professional development programs. Their address is Campus Box 1141, One Brookings Drive, St. Louis, Missouri 63130. For further information about their forums, or CSDP activities, contact Dee Toroian, (314) 889-5599.

7. CASE, The Potentials and the Pitfalls, is published by QED Information Sciences, Inc., P.O. Box 181, Wellesley, Massachusetts 02181. Hardcover 1989; ISBN 0-89435-282-7. Price $49.95. It discusses the position of re-engineering within the CASE life cycle, and explains how to evaluate and select CASE products.

8. Bachman Information Systems, Inc. is located at 8 New England Executive Park, Burlington, Massachusetts 01803; tel. (617) 273-9003.

9. Michael Wolf is vice president of development at VIASOFT, Inc., 3033 North 44th Street, Phoenix, Arizona 85018; tel. (602) 952-0050.

10. Elliot Chikofsky, director of CASE development at Progress Software Corp., 5 Oak Park, Bedford, Massachusetts, 01730; tel. (617) 275-4500.

11. InterPort Software Corp., 12150 East Monument Drive, Suite 700, Fairfax, Virginia 22033; tel. (703) 385-1515.

12. Robert Arnold is at the Software Productivity Consortium, 2214 Rock Hill Road, Herndon, Virginia 22070; tel. (703) 742-7149.

Executive Summary

RE-ENGINEERING EXISTING SYSTEMS

The re-engineering of existing systems is yet another aspect of CASE that could profitably be investigated by management. The methods available have now evolved to the point where thay can be used with assurance.

Re-engineering starts by using packaged programs to pull out all the management and procedural rules that have been embedded in, and encrusted on, some of your most critical operational systems that you may be considering upgrading to newer technology. This is called "reverse engineering." The new techniques help assure that all the key elements that have been incorporated in the system's operation over the years can be clearly recovered and documented.

The re-engineering process then moves forward, with CASE techniques, taking massive, old, operational COBOL programs and cleaning them up to markedly reduce maintenance workload and cost. Such an effort has the added advantage of providing more detailed control over the operation of the streamlined application.

Many people have told us that the biggest payback in re-engineering systems occurs when they must update their massive Cobol "legacy" systems. They are satisfied that the economics have been proven for bringing the maintenance of complex systems under control in this way. They insist that a decision to do nothing about re-engineering at this time will be much more expensive than starting now to learn the re-engineering process. It is too valuable an approach not to be employed in the near future.

The concept of the reusability of proven pieces of operational systems, as new programs are being written, is the key to understanding the process. With re-engineering, you are not translating old, batch systems into new, on-line systems. Rather, you are using reverse engineering to accurately capture the tested and desired business rules, and the operational experiences of many years, that are an integral part of the old programs. You are then using them in your new system, possibly on new technology platforms. We have heard of many success stories in this use of the time-tested procedures and rules in the new systems, using CASE forward engineering methods.

Of course, there is a down side to the use of re-engineering methods. Your staff will need oversight to assure that they do not spend their time on interesting technical excursions that are not pertinent to your long-range plan. To avoid anyone overestimating the capability of the re-engineering tools, it is important to move forward one step at a time, within your system development plan, and ask for cost-effective results at each step.

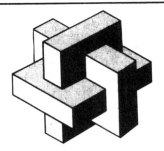

Reverse Engineering and Design Recovery: A Taxonomy

Elliot J. Chikofsky, Index Technology Corp. and Northeastern University
James H. Cross II, Auburn University

Reverse engineering is evolving as a major link in the software life cycle, but its growth is hampered by confusion over terminology. This article defines key terms.

The availability of computer-aided systems-engineering environments has redefined how many organizations approach system development. To meet their true potential, CASE environments are being applied to the problems of maintaining and enhancing existing systems. The key lies in applying reverse-engineering approaches to software systems. However, an impediment to success is the considerable confusion over the terminology used in both technical and marketplace discussions.

It is in the reverse-engineering arena, where the software maintenance and development communities meet, that various terms for technologies to analyze and understand existing systems have been frequently misused or applied in conflicting ways.

In this article, we define and relate six terms: forward engineering, reverse engineering, redocumentation, design recovery, restructuring, and reengineering. Our objective is not to create new terms but to rationalize the terms already in use. The resulting definitions apply to the underlying engineering processes, regardless of the degree of automation applied.

Hardware origins

The term "reverse engineering" has its origin in the analysis of hardware — where the practice of deciphering designs from finished products is commonplace. Reverse engineering is regularly applied to improve your own products, as well as to analyze a competitor's products or those of an adversary in a military or national-security situation.

In a landmark paper on the topic, M.G. Rekoff defines reverse engineering as "the process of developing a set of specifications for a complex hardware system by an orderly examination of specimens of that system."[1] He describes such a process

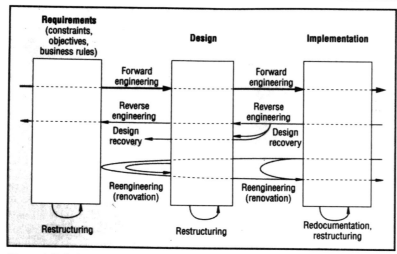

Figure 1. Relationship between terms. Reverse engineering and related processes are transformations between or within abstraction levels, represented here in terms of life-cycle phases.

as being conducted by someone other than the developer, "without the benefit of any of the original drawings ... for the purpose of making a clone of the original hardware system...."

In applying these concepts to software systems, we find that many of these approaches apply to gaining a basic understanding of a system and its structure. However, while the hardware objective traditionally is to duplicate the system, the software objective is most often to gain a sufficient design-level understanding to aid maintenance, strengthen enhancement, or support replacement.

Software maintenance

The ANSI definition of software maintenance is the "modification of a software product after delivery to correct faults, to improve performance or other attributes, or to adapt the product to a changed environment," according to ANSI/IEEE Std 729-1983.

Usually, the system's maintainers were not its designers, so they must expend many resources to examine and learn about the system. Reverse-engineering tools can facilitate this practice. In this context, reverse engineering is the part of the maintenance process that helps you understand the system so you can make appropriate changes. Restructuring and reverse engineering also fall within the global definition of software maintenance. However, each of these three processes also has a place within the contexts of building new systems and evolutionary development.

Life cycles and abstractions

To adequately describe the notion of software forward and reverse engineering, we must first clarify three dependent concepts: the existence of a life-cycle model, the presence of a subject system, and the identification of abstraction levels.

We assume that an orderly life-cycle model exists for the software-development process. The model may be represented as the traditional waterfall, as a spiral, or in some other form that generally can be represented as a directed graph. While we expect there to be iteration within stages of the life cycle, and perhaps even recursion, its general directed-graph nature lets us sensibly define forward (downward) and backward (upward) activities.

The subject system may be a single program or code fragment, or it may be a complex set of interacting programs, job-control instructions, signal interfaces, and data files. In forward engineering, the subject system is the result of the development process. It may not yet exist, or its existing components may not yet be united to form a system. In reverse engineering, the subject system is generally the starting point of the exercise.

In a life-cycle model, the early stages deal with more general, implementation-independent concepts; later stages emphasize implementation details. The transition of increasing detail through the forward progress of the life cycle maps

well to the concept of abstraction levels. Earlier stages of systems planning and requirements definition involve expressing higher level abstractions of the system being designed when compared to the implementation itself.

These abstractions are more closely related to the business rules of the enterprise. They are often expressed in user terminology that has a one-to-many relationship to specific features of the finished system. In the same sense, a blueprint is a higher level abstraction of the building it represents, and it may document only one of the many models (electrical, water, heating/ventilation/air conditioning, and egress) that must come together.

It is important to distinguish between *levels* of abstraction, a concept that crosses conceptual stages of design, and *degrees* of abstraction within a single stage. Spanning life-cycle phases involves a transition from higher abstraction levels in early stages to lower abstraction levels in later stages. While you can represent information in any life-cycle stage in detailed form (lower degree of abstraction) or in more summarized or global forms (higher degree of abstraction), these definitions emphasize the concept of *levels* of abstraction between life-cycle phases.

Definitions

For simplicity, we describe key terms using only three identified life-cycle stages with clearly different abstraction levels, as Figure 1 shows:

• requirements (specification of the problem being solved, including objectives, constraints, and business rules),

• design (specification of the solution), and

• implementation (coding, testing, and delivery of the operational system).

Forward engineering. Forward engineering is the traditional process of moving from high-level abstractions and logical, implementation-independent designs to the physical implementation of a system.

While it may seem unnecessary — in view of the long-standing use of design and development terminology — to introduce a new term, the adjective "forward" has come to be used where it is necessary to distinguish this process from reverse engineering. Forward engineering follows a sequence of going from requirements through designing its implementation.

Reverse engineering. Reverse engineering is the process of analyzing a subject system to
• identify the system's components and their interrelationships and
• create representations of the system in another form or at a higher level of abstraction.

Reverse engineering generally involves extracting design artifacts and building or synthesizing abstractions that are less implementation-dependent. While reverse engineering often involves an existing functional system as its subject, this is *not* a requirement. You can perform reverse engineering starting from any level of abstraction or at any stage of the life cycle.

Reverse engineering in and of itself does *not* involve changing the subject system or creating a new system based on the reverse-engineered subject system. It is a process of *examination*, not a process of change or replication.

In spanning the life-cycle stages, reverse engineering covers a broad range starting from the existing implementation, recapturing or recreating the design, and deciphering the requirements actually implemented by the subject system.

There are many subareas of reverse engineering. Two subareas that are widely referred to are redocumentation and design recovery.

Redocumentation. Redocumentation is the creation or revision of a semantically equivalent representation within the same relative abstraction level. The resulting forms of representation are usually considered alternate views (for example, dataflow, data structure, and control flow) intended for a human audience.

Redocumentation is the simplest and oldest form of reverse engineering, and many consider it to be an unintrusive, weak form of restructuring. The "re-" prefix implies that the intent is to recover documentation about the subject system that existed or should have existed.

Some common tools used to perform redocumentation are pretty printers (which display a code listing in an improved form), diagram generators (which create diagrams directly from code, reflecting control flow or code structure), and cross-reference listing generators. A key goal of these tools is to provide easier ways to visualize relationships among program components so you can recognize and follow paths clearly.

Design recovery. Design recovery is a subset of reverse engineering in which do-

> **Reverse engineering in and of itself does not involve changing the subject system. It is a process of examination, not change or replication.**

main knowledge, external information, and deduction or fuzzy reasoning are added to the observations of the subject system to identify meaningful higher level abstractions beyond those obtained directly by examining the system itself.

Design recovery is distinguished by the sources and span of information it should handle. According to Ted Biggerstaff: "Design recovery recreates design abstractions from a combination of code, existing design documentation (if available), personal experience, and general knowledge about problem and application domains ... Design recovery must reproduce all of the information required for a person to fully understand what a program does, how it does it, why it does it, and so forth. Thus, it deals with a far wider range of information than found in conventional software-engineering representations or code."[2]

Restructuring. Restructuring is the transformation from one representation form to another at the same relative abstraction level, while preserving the sub-

ject system's external behavior (functionality and semantics).

A restructuring transformation is often one of appearance, such as altering code to improve its structure in the traditional sense of structured design. The term "restructuring" came into popular use from the code-to-code transform that recasts a program from an unstructured ("spaghetti") form to a structured (goto-less) form. However, the term has a broader meaning that recognizes the application of similar transformations and recasting techniques in reshaping data models, design plans, and requirements structures. Data normalization, for example, is a data-to-data restructuring transform to improve a logical data model in the database design process.

Many types of restructuring can be performed with a knowledge of structural form but without an understanding of meaning. For example, you can convert a set of If statements into a Case structure, or vice versa, without knowing the program's purpose or anything about its problem domain.

While restructuring creates new versions that implement or propose change to the subject system, it does not normally involve modifications because of new requirements. However, it may lead to better observations of the subject system that suggest changes that would improve aspects of the system. Restructuring is often used as a form of preventive maintenance to improve the physical state of the subject system with respect to some preferred standard. It may also involve adjusting the subject system to meet new environmental constraints that do not involve reassessment at higher abstraction levels.

Reengineering. Reengineering, also known as both renovation and reclamation, is the examination and alteration of a subject system to reconstitute it in a new form and the subsequent implementation of the new form.

Reengineering generally includes some form of reverse engineering (to achieve a more abstract description) followed by some form of forward engineering or restructuring. This may include modifications with respect to new requirements not met by the original system. For exam-

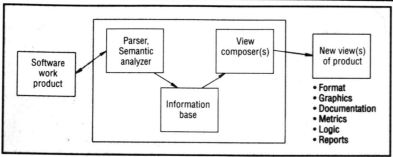

Figure 2. Model of tools architecture. Most tools for reverse engineering, restructuring, and reengineering use the same basic architecture. The new views on the right may themselves be software work products, which are shown on the left. (Model provided by Robert Arnold of the Software Productivity Consortium.)

ple, during the reengineering of information-management systems, an organization generally reassesses how the system implements high-level business rules and makes modifications to conform to changes in the business for the future.

There is some confusion of terms, particularly between reengineering and restructuring. The IBM user group Guide, for example, defines "application reengineering" as "the process of modifying the internal mechanisms of a system or program or the data structures of a system without changing the functionality (system capabilities as perceived by the user). In other words, it is altering the *how* without affecting the *what*."[3] This is closest to our definition of restructuring. How-

ever, two paragraphs later, the same publication says, "It is rare that an application is reengineered without additional functionality being added." This supports our more general definition of reengineering.

While reengineering involves both forward engineering and reverse engineering, it is *not* a supertype of the two. Reengineering uses the forward- and reverse-engineering technologies available, but to date it has not been the principal driver of their progress. Both technologies are evolving rapidly, independent of their application within reengineering.

Objectives

What are we trying to accomplish with reverse engineering? The primary purpose of reverse engineering a software system is to increase the overall comprehensibility of the system for both maintenance and new development. Beyond the definitions above, there are six key objectives that will guide its direction as the technology matures:

• Cope with complexity. We must develop methods to better deal with the shear volume and complexity of systems. A key to controlling these attributes is automated support. Reverse-engineering methods and tools, combined with CASE environments, will provide a way to extract relevant information so decision makers can control the process and the product in systems evolution. Figure 2 shows a model of the structure of most tools for reverse engineering, reengineering, and restructuring.

• Generate alternate views. Graphical representations have long been accepted as comprehension aids. However, creating and maintaining them continues to be a bottleneck in the process. Reverse-engi-

neering tools facilitate the generation or regeneration of graphical representations from other forms. While many designers work from a single, primary perspective (like dataflow diagrams), reverse-engineering tools can generate additional views from other perspectives (like control-flow diagrams, structure charts, and entity-relationship diagrams) to aid the review and verification process. You can also create alternate forms of nongraphical representations with reverse-engineering tools to form an important part of system documentation.

• Recover lost information. The continuing evolution of large, long-lived systems leads to lost information about the system design. Modifications are frequently not reflected in documentation, particularly at a higher level than the code itself. While it is no substitute for preserving design history in the first place, reverse engineering — particularly design recovery — is our way to salvage whatever we can from the existing systems. It lets us get a handle on systems when we don't understand what they do or how their individual programs interact as a system.

• Detect side effects. Both haphazard initial design and successive modifications can lead to unintended ramifications and side effects that impede a system's performance in subtle ways. As Figure 3 shows, reverse engineering can provide observations beyond those we can obtain with a forward-engineering perspective, and it can help detect anomalies and problems before users report them as bugs.

• Synthesize higher abstractions. Reverse engineering requires methods and techniques for creating alternate views that transcend to higher abstraction levels. There is debate in the software community as to how completely the process can be automated. Clearly, expert-system technology will play a major role in achieving the full potential of generating high-level abstractions.

• Facilitate reuse. A significant issue in the movement toward software reusability is the large body of existing software assets. Reverse engineering can help detect candidates for reusable software components from present systems.

Figure 3. Differences between viewpoints. Although reverse engineering can help capture lost information, some types of information are not shared between forward- and reverse-engineering processes. However, reverse engineering can provide observations that are unobtainable in forward engineering.

Forward engineering

Design Issues

Alternatives rejected

Ramifications of decisions

Existing design

Code

Reverse engineering

Unplanned ramifications (side effects)

16

IEEE Software

Economics

The cost of understanding software, while rarely seen as a direct cost, is nonetheless very real. It is manifested in the time required to comprehend software, which includes the time lost to misunderstanding. By reducing the time required to grasp the essence of software artifacts in each life-cycle phase, reverse engineering may greatly reduce the overall cost of software.

In commenting on this article, Walt Scacchi of the University of Southern California made the following important observations: "Many claim that conventional software maintenance practices account for 50 to 90 percent of total life-cycle costs. Software reverse-engineering techniques are targeted to the problems that give rise to such a disproportionate distribution of software costs. Thus, if reverse engineering succeeds, the total system expense may be reduced/mitigated, or greater value may be added to current efforts, both of which represent desirable outcomes, especially if one quantifies the level of dollars spent. Reverse engineering may need to only realize a small impact to generate sizable savings."

Scacchi also pointed out that "software forward engineering and reverse engineering are *not* separate concerns, and thus should be viewed as opportunity for convergence and complement, as well as an expansion of the repertoire of tools and techniques that should be available to the modern software engineer. I, for one, believe that the next generation of software-engineering technologies will be applicable in both the forward and reverse directions. Such a view also may therefore imply yet another channel for getting advanced software-environment/CASE technologies into more people's hands — sell them on reverse engineering (based on current software-maintenance cost patterns) as a way to then introduce better forward engineering tools and techniques."

We have tried to provide a framework for examining reverse-engineering technologies by synthesizing the basic definitions of related terms and identifying common objectives.

Reverse engineering is rapidly becoming a recognized and important component of future CASE environments. Because the entire life cycle is naturally an iterative activity, reverse-engineering tools can provide a major link in the overall process of development and maintenance. As these tools mature, they will be applied to artifacts in all phases of the life cycle. They will be a permanent part of the process, ultimately used to verify all completed systems against their intended designs, even with fully automated generation.

Reverse engineering, used with evolving software development technologies, will provide significant incremental enhancements to our productivity. ❖

Acknowledgments

We acknowledge the special contributions of these individuals to the synthesis of this taxonomy and the rationalization of conflicting terminology: Walt Scacchi of the University of Southern California, Norm Schneidewind of the Naval Postgraduate School, Jim Fulton of Boeing Computer Services, Bob Arnold of the Software Productivity Consortium, Shawn Bohner of Contel Technology Center, Philip Hausler and Mark Pleszkoch of IBM and the University of Maryland at Baltimore County, Linore Cleveland of IBM, Diane Mularz of Mitre, Paul Oman of University of Idaho, John Munson and Norman Wilde of the University of West Florida, and the participants in directed discussions at the 1989 Conference on Software Maintenance and the 1988 and 1989 International Workshops on CASE.

References

1. M.G. Rekoff Jr., "On Reverse Engineering," *IEEE Trans. Systems, Man, and Cybernetics,* March-April 1985, pp. 244-252.
2. T.J. Biggerstaff, "Design Recovery for Maintenance and Reuse," *Computer,* July 1989, pp. 36-49.
3. "Application Reengineering," Guide Pub. GPP-208, Guide Int'l Corp., Chicago, 1989.

Elliot J. Chikofsky is director of research and technology at Index Technology Corp. and a lecturer in industrial engineering and information systems at Northeastern University.

Chikofsky is an associate editor-in-chief of *IEEE Software,* vice chairman for membership of the Computer Society's Technical Committee on Software Engineering, president of the International Workshop on CASE, and author of a book on CASE in the Technology Series for IEEE Computer Society Press. He is a senior member of the IEEE.

James H. Cross II is an assistant professor of computer science and engineering at Auburn University. His research interests include design methodology, development environments, reverse engineering, visualization, and testing. He is secretary of the IEEE Computer Society Publications Board.

Cross received a BS in mathematics from the University of Houston, an MS in mathematics from Sam Houston State University, and a PhD in computer science from Texas A&M University. He is a member of the ACM and IEEE Computer Society.

Address questions about this article to Chikofsky at Index Technology, 1 Main St., Cambridge, MA 02142 or to Cross at Computer Science and Engineering Dept., 107 Dunstan Hall, Auburn University, Auburn, AL 36849.

Automated support of software maintenance

K H Bennett

Software maintenance is the general name given to the set of activities undertaken on a software system following its release for operational use. Surveys have shown that for many projects, software maintenance consumes the majority of the overall software life-cycle costs, and there are indications that the proportion is increasing. Inability to cope with software maintenance can also result in a backlog of application modifications. Despite the importance of software maintenance, it has acquired the reputation of being a second-class area in which to work.

The paper defines in more detail the term software maintenance, and then addresses the issues of maintaining existing code, and producing maintainable systems, stressing the role of reengineering. Three projects that focus on software maintenance are then summarized. All three aim to provide automated assistance to the software maintainer, but in contrasting ways. The ReForm project is based on a formal method to extract specifications from code using transformations. MACS and REDO are both transnational European projects funded by the Esprit collaborative programme of research; the former uses expert system technology to assist the maintainer, while REDO aims to provide a set of integratable tools within a single environment, to support the reverse engineering process.

software maintenance, reengineering, reverse engineering, software process, tools

The development of a software system is complete when the product is delivered to the customer or client, and the software installed and released for operational use. The term 'software maintenance' will be used to encompass the activities (technical and managerial) that are undertaken on the software subsequently. It is recognised that some organizations use terms such as 'enhancement' or 'system redevelopment' to express activities here classified as software maintenance. Some professionals use software maintenance to refer only to the correction of defects. The broader definition of the term is justified because the management approach, the methods, and the tool support are similar, yet differ substantially from those used in initial development. This interpretation is also consistent with the IEEE definition[1].

It is argued that there is a key difference between software development and software maintenance as defined here. In the former, the project is undertaken within a timescale, and to a budget. An identifiable product, meeting the original customer requirement, is the deliverable. In contrast, software maintenance is usually open ended, continuing for many years, and this is seen as a revenue item. It is often the objective to extend the life of the software system for as long as economically possible.

SOFTWARE MAINTENANCE

Four types of maintenance activity

Software maintenance is required for three principal reasons[2-4]. First, there may be a fault in the software, so that its behaviour does not conform to its specification. This fault may contradict the specification, or it may demonstrate that the specification is incomplete (or possibly inconsistent), so that the user's assumed specification is not sustained. Typically, the fault will have manifested itself in the form of an error when the program has been run, and the fault must be removed. This is termed 'corrective maintenance', though colloquially it is often called 'bug-fixing'. The computing profession abounds with anecdotes of emergency repairs (patching)—these can cause great difficulties for subsequent maintenance work.

Even if a software system is fault-free, the environment in which it operates will often be subject to change. The manufacturer may introduce new versions of the operating system, or remove support for existing facilities. The software may be ported to a new environment, or to different hardware. Modifications performed as a result of changes to the external environment are categorized as 'adaptive maintenance'.

The third category of maintenance is called 'perfective maintenance'. This is undertaken as a consequence of a change in user requirements of the software. For example, a payroll suite may need to be altered to reflect new taxation laws; a real-time power station control system may need upgrading to meet new safety standards. A 'rule of thumb' often used in industry is that around 10% of a software system will change each year because of modifications to the user requirements.

Finally, preventive maintenance may be undertaken on a system to anticipate future problems and make subsequent maintenance easier. For example, a particular part of a large suite may have been found to require sustained corrective maintenance over a period of time. It could be sensible to re-implement this part, using modern software engineering technology, in the expectation that subsequent errors will be much reduced.

Centre for Software Maintenance, University of Durham, Durham DH1 3LE, UK

"Automated Support of Software Maintenance," *Information and Software Technology*, Vol. 33, No. 1, Jan./Feb. 1991, pp. 74–85. Reprinted by permission of the publisher: Butterworth-Heinemann, Ltd©.

74

Cost of software maintenance

It is generally recognised that software maintenance consumes a large part of the life-cycle costs of a software product, and hence the total cost of maintenance is huge. At a workshop on maintenance[5] it was reported that in the UK £1 billion is spent annually on software maintenance. Only one major survey has been undertaken to try to quantify the cost; this was carried out by Lientz and Swanson[2] in the late 1970s, and produced a number of results of interest. The mean distribution of effort expended on maintenance in 487 data-processing (DP) organizations was:

- Perfective   50%
- Adaptive   25%
- Corrective   21%
- Preventive   4%

This suggests that corrective maintenance is a relatively small proportion of software maintenance. Clearly, preventive maintenance is not undertaken to any significant degree in the computing industry.

Lientz and Swanson also found that many organizations were spending 20%–70% of their computing (electronic DP (EDP)) effort on maintenance. The proportion was influenced by the type of organization; for example, consultancies spend only a small revenue on maintenance, while EDP organizations spend a substantial part of their budget. Results described by Ditri[6] and Hoskyns Ltd[7] provide support for these figures, though it is difficult directly to compare results as costs may be measured in different ways.

So far, attention has been directed at the direct costs of maintenance, but there are indirect costs that are more difficult to quantify. Many organizations rely on information technology to maintain a competitive edge, and hence their software systems must be modified quickly and reliably. Unfortunately, serious delays are incurred because perfective maintenance cannot achieve these goals. The problem is known as the applications backlog. One management approach divides modifications into essential and desirable to attempt to alleviate the backlog, but the basic difficulty remains. It is also a powerful stimulus for computing to be taken on by the end-user, who finally runs out of patience with the EDP department for taking so long to make what is considered a simple change.

Much of the technological development in software engineering has been focused on the early, development phases. This has been based on the assumption that high software quality is an end-product of the initial development. However, quality must be sustained, perhaps over many years, in an evolving system. While development is clearly of great importance, all surveys confirm the general result that it is software maintenance that is costly and lacks research and development input.

MAINTENANCE OF EXISTING CODE

There is an enormous financial investment in existing software that has been produced through conventional or *ad hoc* software engineering methods. Most of the software that is currently being written falls into this category. It is economically infeasible simply to discard this software and replace it by either off-the-shelf packages (if they exist), or by a rewritten system using modern engineering approaches. Much of this software will be required for many years yet. Furthermore, such software represents the accumulation of years of experience and refinement, and, however imperfect, it is a valuable asset. In many organizations, the software captures business rules, business goals, and business decisions that no longer exist explicitly elsewhere. The software is thus critical to the functioning of the organization. Originally, systems analysis involved the investigation of manual practices to automate them. Now that many business activities have been automated, systems analysis often demands an understanding of the organization that can only be acquired from source codes.

OVERVIEW OF REENGINEERING

Reengineering (in various flavours) is being promoted as the answer to many of the problems of maintaining existing software systems. The basic idea underlying reengineering is that design and specification information is extracted from the source codes, so that this may be used to gain insight into the purpose of the system, or to replace part or all of the system with modern software technology. The hope is that the software is then much more maintainable.

The need to find solutions to the problems of software maintenance has never been greater. This is only to be expected: the overall software inventory is continually being expanded and this software must be maintained. In addition, much of the software that is doing useful work today was originally written many years ago. Military software is a typical example, where systems may be 20 years old and may be expected to be viable for a further 15 or 20 years yet. The problem with such geriatric software is that it is just too valuable to throw away, yet it was written at a time when the main quality attribute of a program was its speed and its main memory requirements; issues such as design quality, adoption of standards and structured methods, etc. were not of major importance. Typically, any original structure possessed by the program has probably been lost in the face of years of modification and upgrade[8].

Nevertheless, such software represents the accumulation of years of experience and refinement, and, however imperfect, it is a valuable corporate asset. The major problems of maintaining such old software are[9]:

- Most existing software is unstructured, and thus difficult to understand, and much was produced before the introduction of structured programming methods. Source codes may be written in assembler or even machine code.

75

- Maintenance programmers have not been involved in the development of a product and find it difficult to map program actions to program source codes.
- The documentation of software is often nonexistent, or incomplete or out of date. Even if it is available, the documentation may not actually help the maintenance staff in an effective way.
- The ripple effect of changes to source codes is difficult to predict[10]. A major concern of maintenance programmers is the avoidance of introducing more problems than are solved by modification.
- Multiple concurrent changes are difficult to manage.

The basis of all approaches to reengineering is to try to make the existing system easier to maintain; usually, the starting point is the source code, because it is the only trustworthy representation of the system. Unfortunately, reengineering lacks a standard terminology and there is much confusion about the use of terms such as reverse engineering, inverse engineering, restructuring, and redocumentation. A recent paper by Chikofsky and Cross[11] has attempted to clarify the different forms of reengineering, and their definitions will be used here.

Reverse engineering is the process of analysing a subject system to identify the system's components and their interrelationships, and to create representations of the system in another form or at a higher level of abstraction.

Thus reverse engineering is a process of examination, and a subsequent forward engineering stage may be required to reimplement parts or all of the system if this is required. However, reverse engineering can play an important role in increasing the understandability of the system, without any subsequent forward engineering.

Restructuring is the transformation from one representation form to another at the same relative abstraction level, while preserving the subject system's external behaviour (functionality and semantics).

Because reverse engineering activities involve abstraction and understanding, these are creative activities in much the same way as normal systems analysis and design. However, just as forward engineering is greatly assisted by computer-aided software engineering (CASE) tools, so reverse engineering can be assisted by appropriate tools and techniques. There is currently much interest in software reconstruction tools for the following reasons:

- System understanding is a prerequisite for all software maintenance activities, and it has been argued that understanding occupies a major proportion of the time involved in software maintenance. Many older systems exist only in the form of their source codes, and if higher-level documentation does exist, it is typically out of date or not helpful. Typically, reverse engineering is currently performed manually, and the maintenance programmer reads the code and gets to know the system. The results are rarely documented properly, and are thus volatile and difficult to communicate.

- It is often the case that systems become more difficult to maintain as they age. Lehman[8] has argued that code becomes more complex under an accumulation of changes, and the original design is obscured. Thus both the cost and the time taken to implement change requests increase with time.
- It is recognised that many maintenance tasks could be made easier if the system was to be brought under the control of a structured method. Changes to functionality, for example, would be implemented by modifying the functional specification and rippling the resulting changes through the code under the guidance of a tool. Many lower-level changes can be implemented automatically by code generators or physical database schema generators. Some CASE tool vendors are introducing configuration management facilities to support this model. However, for existing systems that have not been developed using structured methods, reverse engineering is required to bring them under the control of modern methods.
- One large-scale maintenance activity commonly contemplated is the migration of systems between environments (for example from Cobol files to a relational database management system). Such a migration demands design documentation.
- The analysis of the current system is an early stage of many structured methods, and is required even if complete replacement of the current system is anticipated. Systems analysis used to mean the examining of the manual processes and data stores (usually filing cabinets) that a new system would automate. Nowadays, the current system is generally a computer-based system and current system analysis involves reverse engineering.

Many static analysers, control flow restructurers, and similar tools are currently available. They reengineer code, usually at the program level, and it is claimed that this goes some way to making source code more understandable. However, there is clearly a limit to how human readable low-level code can ever be. In addition, the reverse engineering tools becoming available concentrate on the redesign of DP systems by examining Cobol data divisions or IMS schemas and assisting the production of DB2 schemas. Currently, there are some tools that allow the description of the dynamics of the data in database systems, and few tools that support the real-time and the engineering and scientific applications domain.

All three projects described in this paper (ReForm, MACS, and REDO) have the objectives of supporting methods and tools for reverse engineering, rather than simple restructuring operations. However, the approaches being adopted in the projects differ significantly. To begin with, the ReForm project being undertaken in the Centre for Software Maintenance at Durham University in collaboration with IBM (UK) Ltd is described. The objective of this project is to extract specification requirements in the form of first-order logic from existing source codes using a formal mathematical

76

SOFTWARE REENGINEERING: CONTEXT AND DEFINITIONS

method. The MACS and REDO projects are both large research and development projects funded under the Esprit II programme of collaborative research. The Esprit II programme has the objective of advancing information technology research and development in the European community by sponsoring projects with partners drawn from a number of European countries. Both the above projects aim to provide method and tool support for reverse engineering, and both place considerable emphasis on a single integrated representation of the original system in a system database. This paper will describe the similarities and differences between the two projects and compare them to the inverse engineering project at Durham.

REFORM PROJECT

Overview

The ReForm project is researching a code analysis tool and method aimed at helping the maintenance programmer to understand and modify a given program (the name ReForm was suggested by the importance in the project of both reverse engineering and formal methods). Mathematical program transformation techniques are also employed by the system both to derive a specification from a section of code and to transform a section of code into a logically equivalent form. The basis for the ReForm project is a proof theory for program refinement and equivalence established by Martin Ward, who is currently working at Durham[12,13]. The theoretical underpinning for the project is summarized briefly in the section 'Theoretical foundation'.

Ward's formal system is independent of any particular programming language and allows the inclusion of arbitrary specifications, expressed in first-order logic, as statements in a program. This approach offers a possibility therefore of proving that a program is equivalent to a given specification. Within the context of this system, Ward has proved a number of transformations that in the implementation are stored in a transformation library. Thus a catalogue of proven transformations can be provided in the form of a toolkit that the programmer can use without needing to understand the theory behind them. The transformations may be used in several ways. First, local and global restructuring can be performed using the transformations. Second, parts or all of the program can be expressed in a higher-level notation, including in the form of a specification in first-order logic, which is more concise and closer to the problem domain. The program can also be expressed in terms of different data structures, for example, using the data structures in which the problem is represented, rather than those in which the program is written. An example of this is where two or more data structures in the specification are represented by a single data structure in the program. This makes the program more efficient but more difficult to understand. For program comprehension purposes, therefore, it may be better to express the program in the equivalent form using two data structures.

Wide spectrum language

To use the Durham ReForm system, it is necessary to convert the source code into an internal representation on which the transformations are performed. The transformation is automatic, using standard compiler writing techniques, but it is worth exploring why it has been necessary to develop a new language rather than use an existing language.

- A language was needed with simple semantics that are easy to reason about. None of the languages in general use at the moment were designed with semantics as a priority.
- A wide spectrum language was needed that could express low-level operations and high-level specifications with equal ease. This included nonexecutable specifications. Naturally enough, no programming language is suitable as the notation for expressing nonexecutable specifications. Also the currently popular specification languages such as Z[14] and VDM[15] would need radical changes to allow them to express low-level operations and constructs, and this would amount to developing a new language anyway.
- By translating programs in different programming languages into a common language and applying transformations it is possible to transform programs written in one programming language into equivalent programs written in a different language. This is especially useful for maintaining systems whose different versions run on different platforms or in different environments.
- Languages such as Cobol would present major difficulties if the transformations were attempted directly on Cobol programs. For example, many programs cause problems with aliasing of identifiers; the same name can be used in many different ways in different contexts and there are complicated rules governing the meaning of identifiers.
- Each programming language has its own problems and limitations—constructs that are difficult or impossible to express easily. Thus the language fundamentally has five constructs (a specification, statement, a guard statement, a nondeterministic construct, and a simple form of recursive procedure) common to all programming languages. This kernel language is extended using definitional transformations, to include the constructs required for the translation and transformation of programs expressed in typical modern programming languages.

Overview of ReForm tool set

The production of a specification from source code via a formal method is in the general case undecidable, and human assistance will always be required. Thus at the outset an interactive system was envisaged that offers

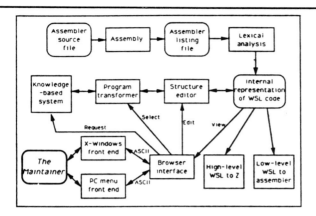

Figure 1. ReForm system architecture overview
WSL wide spectrum language

suggestions as to where the maintenance programmer should be directing attention in the mass of code available. It should present the code in a way that is easy to read, and this will involve automatic indentation, appropriate highlighting and use of colour, and local restructuring. To analyse the higher-level structure of the program, a summarizer is needed that collapses a section of code into a high-level specificational statement. The system must also be flexible: it should be able to cope with all kinds of programs developed using a variety of techniques and methods and not be restricted to a particular development method. Finally, the system must be able to construct transformation histories that provide a verification link between the programs and specifications. Figure 1 shows a diagrammatic representation of the architecture of the system (where WSL represents the Wide Spectrum Language representation). Here how the system is implemented currently is described. The representation of the code in the ReForm system is the actual WSL code in the form of a parse tree, plus some extra information that is needed by the transformations. A translator has been written to convert IBM assembler code into WSL, and initial experiments have been carried out in producing a Cobol to WSL translator.

Once in WSL form, a series of transformations is then applied to generate the specification of the system. As already noted, an interactive system is essential for this application. Each program has many different representations as a specification, and the choice of the correct representation depends on the problem domain, that is, on the way the program is being used. This information is not available from within the program but is available to the maintenance programmer. Therefore he or she is needed to guide the transformation process if a useful specification is to be generated. Since an aim of the project is to increase the programmer's understanding of this program, for the system alone to understand the program (even if that was possible) would not be so useful. A secondary aim is to enable the programmer to reexpress the program in terms that match the problem being solved, so that the form of the program reflects its function as far as this is possible. Finally, there are often

relationships among data structures in a program that are obviously true given the problem domain but that would be difficult to discover and prove from the source code (an example is the representation of data structures in flat files). The programmer can assist the system in proving that these relationships hold, and the relationships can then be used to develop further transformations, for example, to make the program more efficient. The reader is referred to Ward[13] for an example. Using the ReForm tool set, a maintenance programmer can do one of two things with a piece of code: examine it or modify it. All modifications of the program (in its WSL representation) are performed by the structure editor, while all examinations of the code are done via the browser. The following subsections describe the different ways in which the tool allows the maintenance programmer to view and manipulate the program.

Browser

The browser is used by the maintenance programmer to read the program in WSL form; the output of the browser is displayed on the screen. In its simplest form, the browser displays the WSL text, but it can also be used to help the maintenance programmer understand that piece of text. To do this, the programmer sends the browser a scaling instruction, which is a command either to replace some program text by a specification (contract instruction) or to replace a specification with the appropriate program text (an expand instruction). The browser takes care of indentation and other details, so that as the program undergoes transformation and editing, its structure is always immediately apparent from the display. Ward has shown transformations that are capable of deriving a specification from a piece of program text. The browser automates part of this transformation process; hence the maintenance programmer can be sure that he or she is looking at an up-to-date specification as it derives from the actual code. The theory of program equivalence established by Ward ensures that the specification received by the maintenance programmer is an accurate portrayal of the code that it represents.

The maintainer's tool set allows a maintenance programmer to manipulate the source code in three ways:

- By directly modifying the source in WSL form using editing commands.
- By selecting a particular transformation from the library of transformations.
- By requesting the knowledge-base system to search for a sequence of transformations that will achieve a given effect.

The editing commands form of program manipulation is the only method that allows a program to be transformed into a program that is not logically equivalent to the original, whereas the other two methods transform a program into a structurally different, but semantically equivalent program. Thus the editing commands may well have special access permissions on them. The follow-

78

ing three subsections describe the different program manipulation methods, starting with the knowledge-base system.

Knowledge base

The maintenance programmer sends request instructions to the knowledge base to transform a given piece of program text into a logically equivalent piece. The program is analysed by the tool and a suitable set of transformations are automatically suggested. Select transformation instructions are then sent to the transformation library, which translates each transformation into a sequence of editing operations, which are sent to the editor. The knowledge-base system is not yet implemented.

Transformation library

Some transformations are too complicated to be derived automatically. In these circumstances, the maintenance programmer can explicitly select suitable transformations, and this is done by sending a select transformation to the transformation library. When the transformation library receives a select transformation instruction, the appropriate transformation is recalled from the library together with the applicability conditions (the conditions on the program that must be satisfied for the transformation to guarantee equivalence). These conditions may range from trivial restrictions on the type of statement (for example, a transformation that can only be applied to a statement) to more complex requirements. Some applicability conditions may not be automatically derivable; for example, they could depend on the structure of the data to which the program will be applied. The system will ask the programmer for an assurance that the condition does indeed hold in this case, and the correctness of the transformation application will then depend on the correctness of this assertion. This fact will be recorded in documentation accompanying the program. Once the system is satisfied, or has been assured, that the transformation is applicable, the transformation is applied to the selected piece of the program text by sending the sequence of edit commands to the structure editor.

Structure editor

The structure editor is a syntax-based editor and is the only means that the tool set provides for manipulating source codes in WSL representation. Commands are entered, and the program text is modified in accordance with the instructions. The editor records the history of operation carried out on the program; when the maintainer directly edits the structure of the program this fact is recorded so that future users of the system will know which operations were transformations that are guaranteed not to change the effect of the program, and which operations may have changed the program's operations. The structure editor supplies the transformation library with details of the source code, for example, to check the applicability conditions for each transformation.

Theoretical foundation

The system is based on a formal system developed by Ward in which it is possible to prove that two versions of a program are equivalent. This section gives a brief overview of the theoretical aspects of the work. The theory is based on a simple imperative kernel language which has a clear denotational semantics. For each program, the semantics give the corresponding mathematical function that expresses the external behaviour of the program. For each possible initial state of the program, this function will return either a set of possible final states for the program or a special element indicating that the program does not terminate (or terminates in an error state). Programs may be nondeterministic, so a single initial state is associated with a range of possible final states. Programs are defined to be equivalent if they have the same semantic function; hence equivalent programs are identical in terms of their input-output behaviour, although they may have different running times and use different internal data structures. A refinement to the program or specification is another program that will terminate on each initial state for which the first program terminates, and will terminate in one of the possible final states for the first program. In other words, a refinement of a specification is an acceptable implementation of the specification and a refinement of a program is an acceptable substitute for that program. A transformation is a function that takes any program written in a particular form and returns an equivalent program.

Program transformations are used in program development. However, these methods cannot cope with general specifications nor with transforming programs into specifications. The theoretical results are derived using Dijkstra's weakest preconditions[16]; if there are two programs, and it can be proved that the corresponding weakest preconditions are equivalent formulas, then it is known that the programs are equivalent. This means that proving the transformation of the program to a different form amounts to proving the equivalence of two formulas, and for this all the apparatus of mathematical logic is available. Mathematics can also be used to write specifications, which are included in programs in the system. The problem of proving that a particular program is a correct implementation of the specification reduces to proving that one program is a refinement of the other. The success of this technique may be judged by the large number of useful transformations that have been proved and the wide range of problems to which they can be applied.

Implementation

The initial version of the system is used with programs written in IBM assembler language. This creates special problems with aliasing (common and overlapping data areas, pointers and indices used in an *ad hoc* way, etc.). The solution is to represent the whole store of the machine as a single array, with another array used to represent the registers. With other program analysis

79

techniques this would cause insurmountable problems since the most that could be said about any operation is that the store has changed in some way. However, special transformations have been developed for dealing with arrays that make this approach practical. It has been possible to transform the assembler to a high-level language representation, replace the areas of store by the data structures they implement (using transformations which change the data representation of a program), and then transform this high-level language version to a specification. Currently, this is all being done by hand, but the demonstrator stage has now been reached, in which many of the more tedious operations can be carried out automatically, making this a practical option for the maintenance of large assembly language programs. The tool set is written in Lisp and is implemented on an IBM 6150 workstation and on a Sun 3 workstation. The major components that have been implemented are: the translator from IBM assembler to WSL, the structure editor and browser; a front-end implemented on X windows; a transformation library of about 120 transformations; and a system database to provide central integrated storage for all system objects.

Summary

Proponents of program transformation systems have seen their value largely as an aid to program development. However, the Ward theory of program transformations has proved valuable in attacking the problem faced by maintenance programmers as well as development programmers. This has led to the development of the ReForm system as an interactive system for maintaining programs which is based on program transformations. The transformations derive the specification of a section of a program, present the program in different but equivalent form as an aid to program analysis and for general restructuring functions. The system also includes powerful editing functions and a mechanism for recording the editing history.

The author feels that this system is a substantial advance in reengineering technology. The ability to take well used, reliable, and important software components and derive a specification for them which is provably related to that implementation means that such components can be brought into a modern software engineering environment. The ReForm tool set has been demonstrated in terms of nontrivial examples, and performs as designed. Note that in the design of the tool itself, formal specifications describe the important data structures and components, and the transformations themselves have been described in a meta WSL, thereby allowing transformations to be applied to them.

REDO PROJECT

The REDO project is broadly concerned with the development of techniques and tools for the improved maintenance of software. It is characterized by the fact that in the intended product, to be developed beyond the termination of the project itself, there is a coherent integrated toolkit for software maintenance operating on a single shared representation of an application.

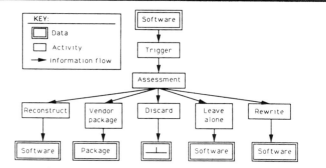

Figure 2. REDO decision-making model

The REDO project comprises 11 partners from seven European countries; the project manager is Dr T Katsoulakos from Lloyd's Register of Shipping.

Reconstruction and software life-cycle

Lehman[8] has argued that the evolution of the software system conforms to five laws, which he derived from empirical observation of several large software systems. Of these five laws, the first two are relevant to this paper.

- Continuing change: a program that is used in a real-world environment must change or become less and less useful in that environment.
- Increasing complexity: as an evolving program changes, its structure becomes more complex unless active methods are used to avoid this phenomenon.

Thus successful software will inevitably evolve, but the process of evolution will lead to degraded structure and increasing complexity unless remedial action is taken. The complexity has then become unacceptable and remedial action must be taken, resulting in an improvement in maintainability. Evolution continues until complexity again has degraded to such an extent that remedial action is required.

At certain points, therefore, in the life of a software system, major reconstruction will take place, with the objective of making the software system more maintainable. The REDO model of the reconstruction decision process is shown in Figure 2, which starts with the existing software application system. This is used by the triggering activity to determine when an assessment of the software system should be undertaken. When the assessment is initiated by the trigger, a range of outcomes is possible, as shown in the diagram. Of these, the reconstruction activity is provided by REDO. This results in a reconstructed software system, which is more maintainable than the original. The contents of each of the above activities are now addressed in more detail.

In REDO, it became clear that the definition of a reverse engineering process was central to the project. Tools to support the process would then be imple-

80

mented. Process modelling terminology will be summarized and then the REDO model itself described.

Process modelling in REDO

Much of the current research work in the area of software process models has been reported on in a series of four workshops, sponsored by the ACM and IEEE[17]. A fifth workshop was due to be held in October 1989, but the proceedings for this are not yet available.

Tully[17] provides a succinct rationale for the field of software process modelling. He argues that it is essential to be concerned with the processes by which software products are produced if one is concerned with the quality of that software. Product is determined by process. There is therefore a strong incentive to understand and formalize the software process so that processes can be compared and evaluated and reasoning about them made; in particular there would be potential to reuse evidently successful software processes. This is a view echoed in the Alvey ISF Study[18], and also in IPSE 2.5[19].

This has led to a strong emphasis on process programming within the field. This is based on the hypothesis that software process models should be developed through formalisms that allow them to be interpreted and executed (or in Tully's terms enactable). Clearly, it is not possible to automate totally the production of software, and humans must be involved in some of the processes. The word enactable is meant to designate a combined contribution of computer and human, with the whole process being described by process programs.

Two approaches to process modelling (and process programming) are advocated. In the descriptive approach, existing software engineering practices are observed, and abstraction is used to create a model of the practice. In the prescriptive approach, a model is created from theoretical or abstract considerations and is imposed on the software development process. In practice (at the current state of the art), research is likely to move forward by a combination of these approaches, and this reflects the description of maintenance models given for REDO.

REDO and reconstruction

It is not envisaged that the iterative approach to software maintenance will change, once a software system is brought within the REDO environment. The objective of REDO is to reengineer the software so that the iterative process can be undertaken:

- more cheaply
- more quickly
- to higher quality standards
- embodying emerging standards more

than before. In other words, the software will be more maintainable.

The technical procedure to achieve this is to bring the software system or parts of it in one or more standard

representations in REDO (i.e., in the system database as original source code, its translation to a common intermediate language (called UNIFORM), its transformation to a graph representation and the representation of the documentation). The representations in the central database are thus available for the REDO integratable tool set. In particular, program analysis (usually the most time-consuming and difficult part of software maintenance) should be considerably speeded up because of the use of a single representation stored in a single coherent database, with a single browser tool to view it.

However, software will need to be brought into the REDO environment. As explained previously in this paper, this will be triggered by management action, e.g., following a major change request that cannot be sensibly accomplished on the software in its existing state. This could be incremental or total.

Subsequently, the software (or parts of it) may again need reconstructing, even though it is within the REDO environment. This will be a much simpler and cheaper step than the initial loading, however.

To summarize, it is not envisaged that REDO will alter fundamentally the type of software maintenance life-cycle used by many organizations. Rather, it will lead to the more efficient execution of that model. Management action is needed to decide when to bring a software system into the REDO environment, so that it may be restructured and represented in a single coherent way.

Trigger activity

The objective of the trigger activity is to judge when in time an assessment of the software system should be undertaken. The following is a nonexhaustive list of events that could stimulate the triggering activity:

- A major change request could be received from a user. The change requested is so large that it is infeasible or too expensive to undertake it on the existing software system. An example of this might be the need to modify a batch system to an interactive system.
- The software may be under a continuous review process by management. Thus management statistics, such as the number of fault reports, the actual or estimated cost of maintenance, etc., could motivate an assessment of the software.
- The trigger could be stimulated by an external organization wishing to sell software maintenance services.
- A review of management practices. Hence it is not simply technology and technical aspects of the software that could trigger an assessment; it may be appropriate to do this if the practices of software maintenance management require updating.
- The strategic importance of the software for the organization may change. For example, a software suite may have a new lease of life (and profits) if it is reimplemented on a highly parallel machine.

The process of triggering may be less rational: it may be due to management's unhappiness with the general state of the software system.

81

Assessment activity

The assessment activity is fired off by the triggering activity. There are three major subactivities within the assessment activity, and these are:

- identification of the software system
- decision of the assessment criteria
- assessment based on above criteria

The first activity may appear obvious, but in some organizations the information on the software inventory is far from clear. Furthermore, software shared among several projects needs to be identified carefully. The assessment criteria may include both technical issues, such as the customer reported error rate, and the general level of customer satisfaction of the software, and also management criteria, such as the long-term strategic importance to the company, the training implications, etc. Information available on such criteria may be highly incomplete, and the assessment criteria may be less sophisticated.

Finally, the assessment of the software is undertaken on the basis of the criteria identified. This may lead to several outcomes, including the following:

- replace with vendor package
- rebuild from scratch
- discard software and discontinue
- leave well alone
- reconstruct using REDO

In this paper only the final alternative will be discussed.

Reconstruction process

As noted above, the major focus and contribution of the REDO project is to provide a tool set and environment for the reconstruction of software. The reconstruction activity takes the software in its initial state S1, and produces a more maintainable equivalent S2. The usual definition of reconstruction insists that the functionality of the original application is unchanged after reconstruction; it is the internal design that is modified to enhance maintainability. It shall be seen that this definition is too rigid if reconstruction is required simultaneously with a major change request. For example, the reconstruction may have been triggered by the need to move a software application system from a batch to an interactive mode of operation. It would not be appropriate to reconstruct the original batch application and then modify it to an interactive style.

The reconstruction process supported by REDO is thus stimulated by an assessment of the software system according to defined criteria. The assessment activity is itself triggered by one or more events, which are generated either internally or externally to the process. This three-step process is also known as inventory management. Figure 2 shows that the interfaces among the major activities are relatively simple. In practice, advan-

tage can be taken of data and expertise common to the three stages. For example, the assessment activity may call upon a technical evaluation of the software system in terms of its complexity, so that maintenance costs may be estimated. The reconstruction activity itself will need to do a technical appraisal, for example, to analyse which parts of the system require which type of reconstruction. Clearly, such an assessment would not be repeated, but the merit of Figure 2 is that the three activities are clearly separated.

Note that the above process model has not been acquired by the analysis of current practice, because there is little existing practice in software reconstruction that may be analysed. Rather, it is a conceptual model of a recommended procedure, and it is expected that case studies in the project will provide feedback on the validity of the model.

It is assumed that the assessment activity has resolved that the software system should be reconstructed. The objective of this part of the paper is to describe in more detail the model for software reconstruction. Currently, no adequate, widely accepted, quantitative definition of 'maintainability' is available. Maintainability could be judged in terms of the effort or time required to perform given modifications arising from adaptive, perfective, corrective, or preventive maintenance on the software system. An alternative approach is to assess maintainability indirectly in terms of attributes of the software itself, e.g., modularity, cohesion, or coupling. The two approaches should be related in some way, though the topic lacks theoretical insight. This report will assume that software A is more maintainable than software B if a given team in identical environments can undertake modifications more quickly on A. Pfleeger and Bohner[20] suggest what the component aspects of maintainability are.

The purpose of reconstruction is to take the software as it stands, and produce a more maintainable version. For this purpose, the software includes not only the source codes, but also documentation, design information, specification information, test suites, and any other information, including possibly local knowledge and expertise, that is available. The overall model is shown in Figure 3 (where IL refers to the UNIFORM intermediate representation). The first stage of the activity is to undertake a technical appraisal of the software according to the objectives and constraints set by the assessment activity. The output of the technical appraisal is a collection of what will be termed activity/object pairs. An object is a subcomponent of the software system, and an activity is the required reconstruction that it is necessary to perform on that subcomponent. This recognises that, in a software system, different subcomponents may require different degrees of reconstruction. Foster[21] has observed in maintaining the software for a telephone exchange system that over many years, large parts of the system are changed little, and maintenance is concentrated on a number of hot spots. In this sort of circumstance, it may make sense to perform cheap (or even no) reconstruction on the majority

82

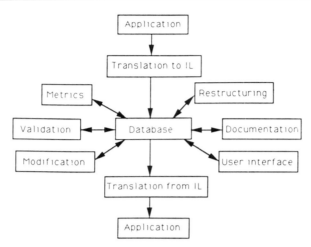

Figure 3. REDO architecture
IL refers to UNIFORM intermediate representation

of the software, but perform drastic reconstruction on the hot spots.

REDO architecture

In the REDO architecture the central component is the system database, which stores all software objects in the REDO world. This is being implemented using the Eclipse object-oriented database system (OODBS) (Eclipse is a commercially available OODBS produced by Ipsys in the UK). The source language program is loaded into the database using a translator that converts the source into the equivalent in the UNIFORM intermediate language. Currently, translators for Cobol and Fortran 77 are being implemented. To reimplement the application program, translators from UNIFORM to source language are being provided.

The REDO tools access the central database to perform redocumentation, application modification, and validation of the reimplemented system. Metrics of maintainability will be available, and there will be a common user interface.

MACS PROJECT

The MACS project comprises a consortium of five industrial organizations and two universities, from six different countries. The project leader is Dr Mari Georges from CAP Gemini (France). The objective of MACS is to support maintenance of existing systems and new applications programs. It is envisaged that it will be used by software maintainers from software development houses, user organizations, and within manufacturers. The strategy is to provide a maintainance assistance system, in the form of a tool set that comprises expert system tools to provide the assistance to a maintainer. The application domain that is chosen for the first evaluation is graphics interfacing software, written in the C language and developed using the HOOD object-oriented design method. It is the eventual intention to

experiment in another applications domain, namely, business data-processing software written in Cobol.

As in REDO, MACS provides a reengineering capability. It is intended to recover design specifications, given only source codes, so that functional specifications of the software can be recreated. From these, a new implementation of the application program can be achieved using modern software engineering methods. It is recognised that the main problem of software maintenance is an understanding of the existing system, and documentation alone can be dangerous for this purpose, as it may be out of date or it may have lacked adequate quality assurance procedures. In addition, nonfunctional information such as the rationale behind design decisions is important to capture and represent within the MACS world. Thus reverse engineering is seen as help in formulating mental models of the system, and design and decision recovery is a key part of the MACS project. As in REDO and ReForm, automatic reverse engineering is not seen as realistic, but assistance in the process is feasible and is likely to be helpful, so one of the objectives of MACS is indeed to provide such assistance by expert system tools.

The MACS approach to software maintenance has three main characteristics. First, the design and structure of an existing system is extracted using reengineering and is represented in a language-independent formalism called dimensional design. This is a graphical representation of the structure of both the code and the data in the system, and it has gained some popularity in Europe as a design diagramming technique.

Second, the way in which software maintenance is undertaken is addressed by integrated front-end tools holding knowledge about the maintenance process and expert maintainer behaviour. The design of the user interface to the software maintainer is being influenced strongly by human factors analysis.

Finally, the MACS system will also attempt to capture design decisions and their rationale.

MACS architecture

The MACS architecture is designed internally in four layers (see Figure 4). In the bottom layer, called the object layer, all objects in the MACS world are stored. The system used to implement the object layer is known as Eclipse (the same system is being used in REDO), and is an OODBS also containing a number of tool-building tools. Eclipse permits representation of fine grain and coarse grain objects and is a central repository for all data and knowledge used by MACS.

The level above the object layer is the tool box; this comprises a comprehensive configuration management system (CMS) together with other tools such as abstraction recovery support (ABR) and operations on the design state graph (DSG, see below) and reasoning world representation (RW). At the top layer is the context layer, which holds knowledge about different kinds of maintenance, about maintenance tasks, and about the context in which the maintenance is being done, for

83

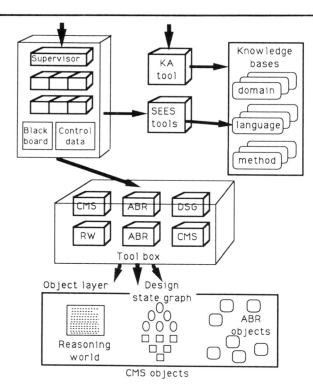

Figure 4. MACS architecture

CMS configuration management system; ABR abstraction recovery support; DSG design state graph; RW reasoning world; KA knowledge acquisition; SEES software engineering expert system

example, the nature of the application domain, the design methods, and the programming language. When the maintainer has a problem, the context layer will suggest strategies to answer it. A representation based on problem, decision, and solution is being used. (In the diagram, KA stands for knowledge acquisition, and SEES for software engineering expert system). The final layer is termed the domain and method layer. Based on the analysis and results of using the context layer, tools can identify a method layer that addresses specific application domains, specific languages, and specific methods. For example, if Jackson structured design has been used in the program, the context layer will allow selection of a particular knowledge base which is concerned with JSD. Thus it can be seen that MACS is an assistant, not an expert system as such.

The key data structure that provides access to various MACS objects is known as the design state graph. This provides an index into the CMS, into the knowledge bases and various reasoning worlds in MACS, and to the design diagrams obtained by extraction. Thus all references and dependencies among components are represented through the DSG. The only way to access information in MACS is to locate the appropriate mode in the DSG, and from it to retrieve the information. This navigation and design state graph itself is expected to be as transparent as possible for the user.

SUMMARY

All three projects use a common approach of a single repository in which all software items are stored, and where they are accessed for manipulation by the tools. ReForm uses Lisp, while MACS and REDO both use Eclipse.

In ReForm, the theoretical foundation existed at the start of the project. The construction of a formal derivation from source code back to design and specification suggests that the system will help to support reuse of both code and process activities. In maintenance, it is frequently desired to modify only a small part of the system, leaving the remainder unchanged (i.e., reused). If it can be ascertained that the system can be reused at a high level of abstraction, then all the work that is needed to generate an implementation from that design is not repeated.

ReForm is envisaged to be most useful in applications in which the stress is on very high quality (for example, safety-critical systems). There will be a substantial training need for many users, although they do not need expertise in formal verification methods. Finally, ReForm will need to be supported by additional conventional program analysis tools, such as cross reference listers, call graph generators, etc.

REDO takes a top-down approach to reverse engineering, by focusing on the process and method, and then implementing an environment and tool set to support the method. Its key contribution is the integration of the tool set through the central repository.

The MACS project provides automation through an expert system approach, and aims to provide an assistant instead of a fully automatic tool set. It encapsulates knowledge about both the application domain and implementation, and the expertise of software maintainers.

All three projects are still in progress, and it is not possible yet to report on their use. All three share a common approach that a completely automatic approach to reverse engineering is impossible, though simple automatic tools can help at the tactical level. This is realistic, because there is no control over the system that is to be reverse engineered.

It is often claimed that the largest proportion of time in software maintenance is spent on system understanding, so it is logical to try to provide automated assistance to this first. It is also reported that testing and regression testing form an increasingly expensive activity (especially when software quality receives increasing attention), and further research is urgently required in this field. Even so, it seems optimistic to hope that software maintenance productivity can be improved by a factor of 10 in the next decade, when there are still huge quantities of unmaintainable software being written. It would be helpful to see the emergence of some industry standard methods for software maintenance, which could then be supported by integrated tools of increasing sophistication. Currently, there are increasing numbers of tools, but

84

these do not support any method and are not designed to be integrated.

ACKNOWLEDGEMENTS

The financial support of the Centre for Software Maintenance by IBM (UK) Ltd and The Alvey Directorate is gratefully acknowledged. The following made major contributions to the REDO work described in this paper: Henk van Zuylen, Rob Martil, and Charles Hornsby. The permission of Dr T Katsoulakos (REDO) and Dr M Georges (MACS) to publish material on these two projects is gratefully acknowledged. The provision by Dr Georges of the slides prepared by the MACS software team is gratefully acknowledged.

REFERENCES

1 **IEEE** 'IEEE standard glossary of software engineering terminology' *ANSI/IEEE Standard 729* IEEE (1983)
2 **Lientz, B and Swanson, E B** *Software maintenance management* Addison-Wesley (1980)
3 **Lientz, B, Swanson, E B and Tompkins, G E** 'Characteristics of application software maintenance' *Commun. ACM* Vol 21 No 6 (1978)
4 **Swanson, E B** 'The dimension of maintenance' in *Proc. 2nd Int. Conf. Software Engineering* IEEE (1976) pp 492–497
5 **Munro, M and Callis, F** *Workshop on software maintenance* University of Durham, UK (1987)
6 **Ditri, A E, Shaw, J C and Atkins, W** *Managing the EDP function* McGraw-Hill (1971)
7 **Hoskyns Ltd** *Implications of using modular programming* Hoskyns Systems Research, London, UK (1973)
8 **Lehman, M M** 'Programs, life cycles, and laws of software evolution' *Proc. IEEE* Vol 68 No 9 (1980) pp 1060–1076
9 **Schneidewind, N F** 'The state of software maintenance' *IEEE Trans. Soft. Eng.* Vol 13 No 3 (1987) pp 303–310
10 **Yau, S, Collofello, J S and MacGregor, T** 'Ripple effect analysis of software maintenance' in *Proc. IEEE COM-PSAC 78* (1978) pp 492–497
11 **Chikofsky, E J and Cross, J H** 'Reverse engineering and design recovery: a taxonomy' *IEEE Software* Vol 7 No 1 (January 1990) pp 13–17
12 **Ward, M, Munro, M and Calliss, F W** 'The maintainer's assistant' *IEEE Conf. Software Maintenance* Miami, FL, USA (1989)
13 **Ward, M** 'Transforming a program into a specification' *Centre for Software Maintenance Report 88/1* University of Durham, UK (1988)
14 **McMorran, M A and Nicholls, J E** 'Z user's manual' *IBM Hursley Park Technical Report TR12.274* IBM Laboratories, Hursley Park, UK (July 1987)
15 **Jones, C B** *Systematic software development using VDM* Prentice Hall (1986)
16 **Dijkstra, E W** *A discipline of programming* Prentice Hall (1976)
17 **Tully, C J (ed)** 'Proc. 4th Int. Software Process Workshop' *Soft. Eng. Notes* Vol 14 No 4 (June 1989)
18 **Oddy, G C and Tully, C J** *Information systems factory study* UK Dept of Trade and Industry, London, UK (1988)
19 **Bennett, K H** *Software engineering environments: research and practice* Ellis-Horwood (1989)
20 **Pfleeger, S L and Bohner, S A** 'A framework for software metrics' in *Proc. IEEE Conf. Software Maintenance* (November 1990)
21 **Foster, J R and Munro, M** 'A documentation method based on cross referencing' in *Proc. IEEE Conf. Software Maintenance* Austin, TX, USA (1987)

85

Chapter 2
Business Process
Reengineering

Chapter 2
Business Process Reengineering

Purpose

The papers in this chapter introduce the reader to business process reengineering, which is often a prelude to software reengineering. Software reengineering in the past has often started with source code. Ways were sought to improve it, remodularize it, and render it reusable. Today, it is frequently useful first to consider and revise the basic business — or other — processes supported by source code. Much bigger payoffs are expected by revising the basic nature of the work performed rather than by just improving the software itself. Business process reengineering challenges us to rethink what we are doing in productive ways, often better leveraging current software and hardware technology.

Papers

In the first paper, "Reengineering Work: Don't Automate, Obliterate," Michael Hammer discusses the motivations and benefits of business process redesign. He gives a striking example of how Ford Motor Company used business reengineering and information technology to reduce by 75 percent the number of people needed to support its accounts payable process.

In the next paper, "The New Industrial Engineering: Information Technology and Business Process Redesign," Thomas Davenport and James Short discuss many of the issues for performing business process redesign. They discuss and provide examples for five major steps:

(1) develop business vision and process objectives,
(2) identify processes to be redesigned,
(3) understand and measure existing processes,
(4) identify information technology levers, and
(5) design and build a prototype of the process.

In the final paper, "Building a Better Mousetrap," Peter Krass discusses some experiences with business process reengineering in real companies. The paper explores the benefits and cautions of applying business process reengineering in a company.

Managers can release the real power of computers by challenging centuries-old notions about work.

Reengineering Work: Don't Automate, Obliterate

by Michael Hammer

Despite a decade or more of restructuring and downsizing, many U.S. companies are still unprepared to operate in the 1990s. In a time of rapidly changing technologies and ever-shorter product life cycles, product development often proceeds at a glacial pace. In an age of the customer, order fulfillment has high error rates and customer inquiries go unanswered for weeks. In a period when asset utilization is critical, inventory levels exceed many months of demand.

The usual methods for boosting performance—process rationalization and automation—haven't

 Use computers to redesign — not just automate — existing business processes.

yielded the dramatic improvements companies need. In particular, heavy investments in information technology have delivered disappointing results—largely because companies tend to use technology to mechanize old ways of doing business. They leave the existing processes intact and use computers simply to speed them up.

But speeding up those processes cannot address their fundamental performance deficiencies. Many of our job designs, work flows, control mechanisms, and organizational structures came of age in a different competitive environment and before the advent of the computer. They are geared toward efficiency and control. Yet the watchwords of the new decade are innovation and speed, service and quality.

It is time to stop paving the cow paths. Instead of embedding outdated processes in silicon and software, we should obliterate them and start over. We should "reengineer" our businesses: use the power of modern information technology to radically redesign our business processes in order to achieve dramatic improvements in their performance.

Every company operates according to a great many unarticulated rules. "Credit decisions are made by the credit department." "Local inventory is needed for good customer service." "Forms must be filled in completely and in order." Reengineering strives to break away from the old rules about how we organize

Michael Hammer is president of Hammer and Company, an information technology consulting firm in Cambridge, Massachusetts. This article is based in part on work performed in association with the Index Group, also a Cambridge-based consultancy.

104

and conduct business. It involves recognizing and rejecting some of them and then finding imaginative new ways to accomplish work. From our redesigned processes, new rules will emerge that fit the times. Only then can we hope to achieve quantum leaps in performance.

Reengineering cannot be planned meticulously and accomplished in small and cautious steps. It's an all-or-nothing proposition with an uncertain result. Still, most companies have no choice but to muster the courage to do it. For many, reengineering is the only hope for breaking away from the antiquated processes that threaten to drag them down. Fortunately, managers are not without help. Enough businesses have successfully reengineered their processes to provide some rules of thumb for others.

What Ford and MBL Did

Japanese competitors and young entrepreneurial ventures prove every day that drastically better levels of process performance are possible. They develop products twice as fast, utilize assets eight times more productively, respond to customers ten times faster. Some large, established companies also show what can be done. Businesses like Ford Motor Company and Mutual Benefit Life Insurance have reengineered their processes and achieved competitive leadership as a result. Ford has reengineered its accounts payable processes, and Mutual Benefit Life, its processing of applications for insurance.

In the early 1980s, when the American automotive industry was in a depression, Ford's top management put accounts payable—along with many other departments—under the microscope in search of ways to cut costs. Accounts payable in North America alone employed more than 500 people. Management thought that by rationalizing processes and installing new computer systems, it could reduce the head count by some 20%.

Ford was enthusiastic about its plan to tighten accounts payable—until it looked at Mazda. While Ford was aspiring to a 400-person department, Mazda's accounts payable organization consisted of a total of 5 people. The difference in absolute numbers was astounding, and even after adjusting for Mazda's smaller size, Ford figured that its accounts payable organization was five times the size it should be. The Ford team knew better than to attribute the discrepancy to calisthenics, company songs, or low interest rates.

Ford managers ratcheted up their goal: accounts payable would perform with not just a hundred

but many hundreds fewer clerks. It then set out to achieve it. First, managers analyzed the existing system. When Ford's purchasing department wrote a purchase order, it sent a copy to accounts payable. Later, when material control received the goods, it sent a copy of the receiving document to accounts payable. Meanwhile, the vendor sent an invoice to accounts payable. It was up to accounts payable, then, to match the purchase order against the receiving document and the invoice. If they matched, the department issued payment.

The department spent most of its time on mismatches, instances where the purchase order, receiving document, and invoice disagreed. In these cases, an accounts payable clerk would investigate the discrepancy, hold up payment, generate documents, and all in all gum up the works.

One way to improve things might have been to help the accounts payable clerk investigate more efficiently, but a better choice was to prevent the mismatches in the first place. To this end, Ford instituted "invoiceless processing." Now when the purchasing department initiates an order, it enters the information into an on-line database. It doesn't send a copy of the purchase order to anyone. When the goods arrive at the receiving dock, the receiving clerk checks the database to see if they correspond to an outstanding purchase order. If so, he or she accepts them and enters the transaction into the computer system. (If receiving can't find a database entry for the received goods, it simply returns the order.)

Under the old procedures, the accounting department had to match 14 data items between the re-

> ▌Why did Ford need
> 400 accounts payable clerks
> when Mazda had just 5?

ceipt record, the purchase order, and the invoice before it could issue payment to the vendor. The new approach requires matching only three items—part number, unit of measure, and supplier code—between the purchase order and the receipt record. The matching is done automatically, and the computer prepares the check, which accounts payable sends to the vendor. There are no invoices to worry about since Ford has asked its vendors not to send them. (See the diagram, "Ford's Accounts Payable Process...," for illustrations of the old and new payables processes.)

Ford didn't settle for the modest increases it first envisioned. It opted for radical change—and achieved dramatic improvement. Where it has instituted this new process, Ford has achieved a 75% reduction in head count, not the 20% it would have gotten with a conventional program. And since there are no discrepancies between the financial record and the physical record, material control is simpler and financial information is more accurate.

Mutual Benefit Life, the country's eighteenth largest life carrier, has reengineered its processing of insurance applications. Prior to this, MBL handled customers' applications much as its competitors did. The long, multistep process involved credit checking, quoting, rating, underwriting, and so on. An application would have to go through as many as 30 discrete steps, spanning 5 departments and involving 19 people. At the very best, MBL could process an application in 24 hours, but more typical turnarounds ranged from 5 to 25 days—most of the time spent passing information from one department to the next. (Another insurer estimated that while an application spent 22 days in process, it was actually worked on for just 17 minutes.)

MBL's rigid, sequential process led to many complications. For instance, when a customer wanted to cash in an existing policy and purchase a new one, the old business department first had to authorize the treasury department to issue a check made payable to MBL. The check would then accompany the paperwork to the new business department.

The president of MBL, intent on improving customer service, decided that this nonsense had to stop

and demanded a 60% improvement in productivity. It was clear that such an ambitious goal would require more than tinkering with the existing process. Strong measures were in order, and the management team assigned to the task looked to technology as a means of achieving them. The team realized that shared databases and computer networks could make many different kinds of information available to a single person, while expert systems could help people with limited experience make sound decisions. Applying these insights led to a new approach to the application-handling process, one with wide organizational implications and little resemblance to the old way of doing business.

MBL swept away existing job definitions and departmental boundaries and created a new position called a case manager. Case managers have total responsibility for an application from the time it is received to the time a policy is issued. Unlike clerks, who performed a fixed task repeatedly under the watchful gaze of a supervisor, case managers work autonomously. No more handoffs of files and responsibility, no more shuffling of customer inquiries.

Case managers are able to perform all the tasks associated with an insurance application because they are supported by powerful PC-based workstations that run an expert system and connect to a range of automated systems on a mainframe. In particularly tough cases, the case manager calls for assistance from a senior underwriter or physician, but these spe-

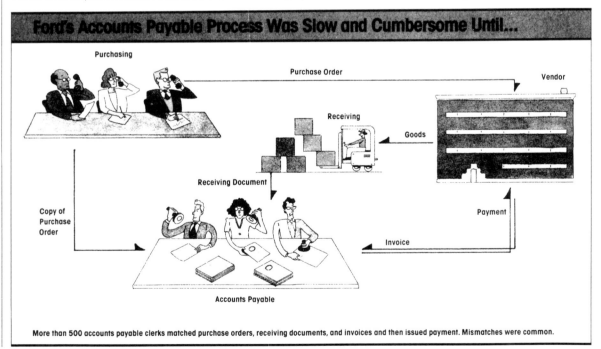

Ford's Accounts Payable Process Was Slow and Cumbersome Until...

Purchasing

Purchase Order

Vendor

Receiving

Goods

Receiving Document

Copy of Purchase Order

Payment

Invoice

Accounts Payable

More than 500 accounts payable clerks matched purchase orders, receiving documents, and invoices and then issued payment. Mismatches were common.

106

DRAWINGS BY GARISON WEILAND

cialists work only as consultants and advisers to the case manager, who never relinquishes control.

Empowering individuals to process entire applications has had a tremendous impact on operations. MBL can now complete an application in as little as four hours, and average turnaround takes only two to five days. The company has eliminated 100 field office positions, and case managers can handle more than twice the volume of new applications the company previously could process.

The Essence of Reengineering

At the heart of reengineering is the notion of discontinuous thinking – of recognizing and breaking away from the outdated rules and fundamental assumptions that underlie operations. Unless we change these rules, we are merely rearranging the deck chairs on the Titanic. We cannot achieve breakthroughs in performance by cutting fat or automating existing processes. Rather, we must challenge old assumptions and shed the old rules that made the business underperform in the first place.

Every business is replete with implicit rules left over from earlier decades. "Customers don't repair their own equipment." "Local warehouses are necessary for good service." "Merchandising decisions are made at headquarters." These rules of work design are based on assumptions about technology, people, and organizational goals that no longer hold. The contemporary repertoire of available information technologies is vast and quickly expanding. Quality, innovation, and service are now more important than cost, growth, and control. A large portion of the population is educated and capable of assuming responsibility, and workers cherish their autonomy and expect to have a say in how the business is run.

It should come as no surprise that our business processes and structures are outmoded and obsolete: our work structures and processes have not kept pace with the changes in technology, demographics, and business objectives. For the most part, we have organized work as a sequence of separate tasks and employed complex mechanisms to track its progress. This arrangement can be traced to the Industrial Revolution, when specialization of labor and economies of scale promised to overcome the inefficiencies of cottage industries. Businesses disaggregated work into narrowly defined tasks, reaggregated the people performing those tasks into departments, and installed managers to administer them.

Our elaborate systems for imposing control and discipline on those who actually do the work stem from the postwar period. In that halcyon period of expansion, the main concern was growing fast without going broke, so businesses focused on cost, growth, and control. And since literate, entry-level people were abundant but well-educated professionals hard

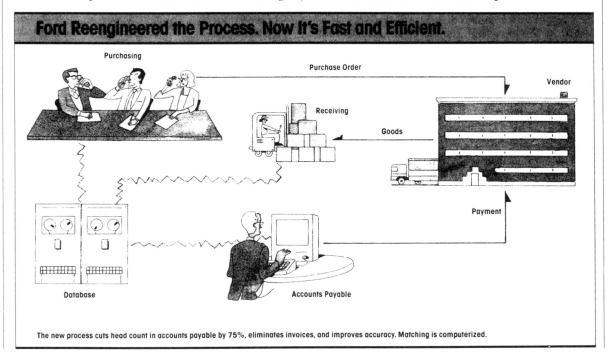

Ford Reengineered the Process. Now It's Fast and Efficient.

Purchasing

Purchase Order

Vendor

Receiving

Goods

Database

Accounts Payable

Payment

The new process cuts head count in accounts payable by 75%, eliminates invoices, and improves accuracy. Matching is computerized.

to come by, the control systems funneled information up the hierarchy to the few who presumably knew what to do with it.

These patterns of organizing work have become so ingrained that, despite their serious drawbacks, it's hard to conceive of work being accomplished any other way. Conventional process structures are fragmented and piecemeal, and they lack the integration necessary to maintain quality and service. They are breeding grounds for tunnel vision, as people tend to substitute the narrow goals of their particular

> **Ford's old rule: we pay when we get the invoice.**
> **Ford's new rule: we pay when we get the goods.**

department for the larger goals of the process as a whole. When work is handed off from person to person and unit to unit, delays and errors are inevitable. Accountability blurs, and critical issues fall between the cracks. Moreover, no one sees enough of the big picture to be able to respond quickly to new situations. Managers desperately try, like all the king's horses and all the king's men, to piece together the fragmented pieces of business processes.

Managers have tried to adapt their processes to new circumstances, but usually in ways that just create more problems. If, say, customer service is poor, they create a mechanism to deliver service but overlay it on the existing organization. Bureaucracy thickens, costs rise, and enterprising competitors gain market share.

In reengineering, managers break loose from outmoded business processes and the design principles underlying them and create new ones. Ford had operated under the old rule that "We pay when we receive the invoice." While no one had ever articulated or recorded it, that rule determined how the accounts payable process was organized. Ford's reengineering effort challenged and ultimately replaced the rule with a new one: "We pay when we receive the *goods.*"

Reengineering requires looking at the fundamental processes of the business from a cross-functional perspective. Ford discovered that reengineering only the accounts payable department was futile. The appropriate focus of the effort was what might be called the goods acquisition process, which included purchasing and receiving as well as accounts payable.

One way to ensure that reengineering has a cross-functional perspective is to assemble a team that rep-resents the functional units involved in the process being reengineered and all the units that depend on it. The team must analyze and scrutinize the existing process until it really understands what the process is trying to accomplish. The point is not to learn what happens to form 73B in its peregrinations through the company but to understand the purpose of having form 73B in the first place. Rather than looking for opportunities to improve the current process, the team should determine which of its steps really add value and search for new ways to achieve the result.

The reengineering team must keep asking Why? and What if? Why do we need to get a manager's signature on a requisition? Is it a control mechanism or a decision point? What if the manager reviews only requisitions above $500? What if he or she doesn't see them at all? Raising and resolving heretical questions can separate what is fundamental to the process from what is superficial. The regional offices of an East Coast insurance company had long produced a series of reports that they regularly sent to the home office. No one in the field realized that these reports were simply filed and never used. The process outlasted the circumstances that had created the need for it. The reengineering study team should push to discover situations like this.

In short, a reengineering effort strives for dramatic levels of improvement. It must break away from conventional wisdom and the constraints of organizational boundaries and should be broad and cross-functional in scope. It should use information technology not to automate an existing process but to enable a new one.

Principles of Reengineering

Creating new rules tailored to the modern environment ultimately requires a new conceptualization of the business process—which comes down to someone having a great idea. But reengineering need not be haphazard. In fact, some of the principles that companies have already discovered while reengineering their business processes can help jump start the effort for others.

Organize around outcomes, not tasks. This principle says to have one person perform all the steps in a process. Design that person's job around an objective or outcome instead of a single task. The redesign at Mutual Benefit Life, where individual case managers perform the entire application approval process, is the quintessential example of this.

The redesign of an electronics company is another example. It had separate organizations performing each of the five steps between selling and installing the equipment. One group determined customer requirements, another translated those requirements into internal product codes, a third conveyed that information to various plants and warehouses, a fourth received and assembled the components, and a fifth delivered and installed the equipment. The process was based on the centuries-old notion of specialized labor and on the limitations inherent in paper files. The departments each possessed a specific set of skills, and only one department at a time could do its work.

The customer order moved systematically from step to step. But this sequential processing caused problems. The people getting the information from the customer in step one had to get all the data anyone would need throughout the process, even if it wasn't needed until step five. In addition, the many handoffs were responsible for numerous errors and misunderstandings. Finally, any questions about customer requirements that arose late in the process had to be referred back to the people doing step one, resulting in delay and rework.

When the company reengineered, it eliminated the assembly-line approach. It compressed responsibility for the various steps and assigned it to one person, the "customer service representative." That person now oversees the whole process – taking the order, translating it into product codes, getting the components assembled, and seeing the product delivered and installed. The customer service rep expedites and coordinates the process, much like a general contractor. And the customer has just one contact, who always knows the status of the order.

Have those who use the output of the process perform the process. In an effort to capitalize on the benefits of specialization and scale, many organizations established specialized departments to handle specialized processes. Each department does only one type of work and is a "customer" of other groups' processes. Accounting does only accounting. If it needs new pencils, it goes to the purchasing department, the group specially equipped with the information and expertise to perform that role. Purchasing finds vendors, negotiates price, places the order, inspects the goods, and pays the invoice – and eventually the accountants get their pencils. The process works (after a fashion), but it's slow and bureaucratic.

Now that computer-based data and expertise are more readily available, departments, units, and individuals can do more for themselves. Opportunities exist to reengineer processes so that the individuals who need the result of a process can do it themselves. For example, by using expert systems and data-

bases, departments can make their own purchases without sacrificing the benefits of specialized purchasers. One manufacturer has reengineered its purchasing process along just these lines. The company's old system, whereby the operating departments submitted requisitions and let purchasing do the rest, worked well for controlling expensive and important items like raw materials and capital equipment. But for inexpensive and nonstrategic purchases, which constituted some 35% of total orders, the system was slow and cumbersome; it was not uncommon for the cost of the purchasing process to exceed the cost of the goods being purchased.

The new process compresses the purchase of sundry items and pushes it on to the customers of the process. Using a database of approved vendors, an operating unit can directly place an order with a vendor and charge it on a bank credit card. At the end of the month, the bank gives the manufacturer a tape of all credit card transactions, which the company runs against its internal accounting system.

When an electronics equipment manufacturer reengineered its field service process, it pushed some

Must technicians make repairs? Or can computers help customers make their own?

of the steps of the process on to its customers. The manufacturer's field service had been plagued by the usual problems: technicians were often unable to do a particular repair because the right part wasn't on the van, response to customer calls was slow, and spare-parts inventory was excessive.

Now customers make simple repairs themselves. Spare parts are stored at each customer's site and managed through a computerized inventory-management system. When a problem arises, the customer calls the manufacturer's field-service hot line and describes the symptoms to a diagnostician, who accesses a diagnosis support system. If the problem appears to be something the customer can fix, the diagnostician tells the customer what part to replace and how to install it. The old part is picked up and a new part left in its place at a later time. Only for complex problems is a service technician dispatched to the site, this time without having to make a stop at the warehouse to pick up parts.

When the people closest to the process perform it, there is little need for the overhead associated with managing it. Interfaces and liaisons can be eliminated, as can the mechanisms used to coordinate those who perform the process with those who use it.

Why Did We Design Inefficient Processes?

In a way, we didn't. Many of our procedures were not designed at all; they just happened. The company founder one day recognized that he didn't have time to handle a chore, so he delegated it to Smith. Smith improvised. Time passed, the business grew, and Smith hired his entire clan to help him cope with the work volume. They all improvised. Each day brought new challenges and special cases, and the staff adjusted its work accordingly. The hodgepodge of special cases and quick fixes was passed from one generation of workers to the next.

We have institutionalized the ad hoc and enshrined the temporary. Why do we send foreign accounts to the corner desk? Because 20 years ago, Mary spoke French and Mary had the corner desk. Today Mary is long gone, and we no longer do business in France, but we still send foreign accounts to the corner desk. Why does an electronics company spend $10 million a year to manage a field inventory worth $20 million? Once upon a time, the inventory was worth $200 million, and managing it cost $5 million. Since then, warehousing costs have escalated, components have become less expensive, and better forecasting techniques have minimized units in inventory. But the inventory procedures, alas, are the same as always.

Of the business processes that *were* designed, most took their present forms in the 1950s. The goal then was to check overambitious growth – much as the typewriter keyboard was designed to slow typists who would otherwise jam the keys. It is no accident that organizations stifle innovation and creativity. That's what they were *designed* to do.

Nearly all of our processes originated before the advent of modern computer and communications technology. They are replete with mechanisms designed to compensate for "information poverty." Although we are now information affluent, we still use those mechanisms, which are now deeply embedded in automated systems.

Moreover, the problem of capacity planning for the process performers is greatly reduced.

Subsume information-processing work into the real work that produces the information. The previous two principles say to compress linear processes. This principle suggests moving work from one person or department to another. Why doesn't an organization that produces information also process it? In the past, people didn't have the time or weren't trusted to do both. Most companies estab-

lished units to do nothing but collect and process information that other departments created. This arrangement reflects the old rule about specialized labor and the belief that people at lower organizational levels are incapable of acting on information they generate. An accounts payable department collects information from purchasing and receiving and reconciles it with data that the vendor provides. Quality assurance gathers and analyzes information it gets from production.

Ford's redesigned accounts payable process embodies the new rule. With the new system, receiving, which produces the information about the goods received, processes this information instead of sending it to accounts payable. The new computer system can easily compare the delivery with the order and trigger the appropriate action.

Treat geographically dispersed resources as though they were centralized. The conflict between centralization and decentralization is a classic one. Decentralizing a resource (whether people, equipment, or inventory) gives better service to those who use it, but at the cost of redundancy, bureaucracy, and missed economies of scale. Companies no longer have to make such trade-offs. They can use databases, telecommunications networks, and standardized processing systems to get the benefits of scale and coordination while maintaining the benefits of flexibility and service.

At Hewlett-Packard, for instance, each of the more than 50 manufacturing units had its own separate purchasing department. While this arrangement provided excellent responsiveness and service to the plants, it prevented H-P from realizing the benefits of its scale, particularly with regard to quantity discounts. H-P's solution is to maintain the divisional purchasing organizations and to introduce a corporate unit to coordinate them. Each purchasing unit has access to a shared database on vendors and their performance and issues its own purchase orders. Corporate purchasing maintains this database and uses it to negotiate contracts for the corporation and to monitor the units. The payoffs have come in a 150% improvement in on-time deliveries, 50% reduction in lead times, 75% reduction in failure rates, and a significantly lower cost of goods purchased.

Link parallel activities instead of integrating their results. H-P's decentralized purchasing operations represent one kind of parallel processing in which separate units perform the same function. Another common kind of parallel processing is when separate units perform different activities that must eventually come together. Product development typically operates this way. In the development of a photocopier, for example, independent units develop the various subsystems of the copier. One group works on the optics, another on the mechanical paper-handling device, another on the power supply, and so on. Having people do development work simultaneously saves time, but at the dreaded integration and testing phase, the pieces often fail to work together. Then the costly redesign begins.

Or consider a bank that sells different kinds of credit – loans, letters of credit, asset-based financing – through separate units. These groups may have no way of knowing whether another group has already

Coordinate parallel functions *during* the process – not after it's completed.

extended credit to a particular customer. Each unit could extend the full $10 million credit limit.

The new principle says to forge links between parallel functions and to coordinate them while their activities are in process rather than after they are completed. Communications networks, shared databases, and teleconferencing can bring the independent groups together so that coordination is ongoing. One large electronics company has cut its product

development cycle by more than 50% by implementing this principle.

Put the decision point where the work is performed, and build control into the process. In most organizations, those who do the work are distinguished from those who monitor the work and make decisions about it. The tacit assumption is that the people actually doing the work have neither the time nor the inclination to monitor and control it and that they lack the knowledge and scope to make decisions about it. The entire hierarchical management structure is built on this assumption. Accountants, auditors, and supervisors check, record, and monitor work. Managers handle any exceptions.

The new principle suggests that the people who do the work should make the decisions and that the process itself can have built-in controls. Pyramidal management layers can therefore be compressed and the organization flattened.

Information technology can capture and process data, and expert systems can to some extent supply knowledge, enabling people to make their own decisions. As the doers become self-managing and self-controlling, hierarchy – and the slowness and bureaucracy associated with it – disappears.

When Mutual Benefit Life reengineered the insurance application process, it not only compressed the linear sequence but also eliminated the need for lay-

GEOMETRIC DUDS

GOOFBALL

BLOCKHEAD

DUNCE

CLOD

CARTOON BY H. MARTIN

111

ers of managers. These two kinds of compression – vertical and horizontal – often go together; the very fact that a worker sees only one piece of the process calls for a manager with a broader vision. The case managers at MBL provide end-to-end management of the process, reducing the need for traditional managers. The managerial role is changing from one of controller and supervisor to one of supporter and facilitator.

Capture information once and at the source. This last rule is simple. When information was difficult to transmit, it made sense to collect information repeatedly. Each person, department, or unit had its own requirements and forms. Companies simply had to live with the associated delays, entry errors, and costly overhead. But why do we have to live with those problems now? Today when we collect a piece of information, we can store it in an on-line database for all who need it. Bar coding, relational databases, and electronic data interchange (EDI) make it easy to collect, store, and transmit information. One insurance company found that its application review process required that certain items be entered into "stovepipe" computer systems supporting different functions as many as five times. By integrating and connecting these systems, the company was able to eliminate this redundant data entry along with the attendant checking functions and inevitable errors.

Think Big

Reengineering triggers changes of many kinds, not just of the business process itself. Job designs, organizational structures, management systems – anything associated with the process – must be refashioned in an integrated way. In other words, reengineering is a tremendous effort that mandates change in many areas of the organization.

When Ford reengineered its payables, receiving clerks on the dock had to learn to use computer terminals to check shipments, and they had to make decisions about whether to accept the goods. Purchasing agents also had to assume new responsibilities – like making sure the purchase orders they entered into the database had the correct information about where to send the check. Attitudes toward vendors also had to change: vendors could no longer be seen as adversaries; they had to become partners in a shared business process. Vendors too had to adjust. In many cases, invoices formed the basis of their accounting systems. At least one Ford

supplier adapted by continuing to print invoices, but instead of sending them to Ford threw them away, reconciling cash received against invoices never sent.

The changes at Mutual Benefit Life were also widespread. The company's job-rating scheme could not accommodate the case manager position, which had a lot of responsibility but no direct reports. MBL had to devise new job-rating schemes and compensation policies. It also had to develop a culture in which people doing work are perceived as more important than those supervising work. Career paths, recruitment and training programs, promotion policies – these and many other management systems are being revised to support the new process design.

The extent of these changes suggests one factor that is necessary for reengineering to succeed: executive leadership with real vision. No one in an organization wants reengineering. It is confusing and disruptive and affects everything people have grown accustomed to. Only if top-level managers back the effort and outlast the company cynics will people take reengineering seriously. As one wag at an electronics equipment manufacturer has commented, "Every few months, our senior managers find a new religion. One time it was quality, another it was customer service, another it was flattening the organization. We just hold our breath until they get over it and things get back to normal." Commitment, consistency – maybe even a touch of fanaticism – are needed to enlist those who would prefer the status quo.

Considering the inertia of old processes and structures, the strain of implementing a reengineering plan can hardly be overestimated. But by the same token, it is hard to overestimate the opportunities, especially for established companies. Big, traditional organizations aren't necessarily dinosaurs doomed to extinction, but they are burdened with layers of unproductive overhead and armies of unproductive workers. Shedding them a layer at a time will not be good enough to stand up against sleek startups or streamlined Japanese companies. U.S. companies need fast change and dramatic improvements.

We have the tools to do what we need to do. Information technology offers many options for reorganizing work. But our imaginations must guide our decisions about technology – not the other way around. We must have the boldness to imagine taking 78 days out of an 80-day turnaround time, cutting 75% of overhead, and eliminating 80% of errors. These are not unrealistic goals. If managers have the vision, reengineering will provide a way. ⊌

Reprint 90406

The New Industrial Engineering:
Information Technology and Business Process Redesign

Thomas H. Davenport
James E. Short

Ernst and Young
MIT Sloan School of Management

THOSE ASPIRING TO IMPROVE the way work is done must begin to apply the capabilities of information technology to redesign business processes. Business process design and information technology are natural partners, yet industrial engineers have never fully exploited their relationship. The authors argue, in fact, that it has barely been exploited at all. But the organizations that *have* used IT to redesign boundary-crossing, customer-driven processes have benefited enormously. This article explains why.

Sloan
Management
Review

11

Summer 1990

A T THE TURN of the century, Frederick Taylor revolutionized the workplace with his ideas on work organization, task decomposition, and job measurement. Taylor's basic aim was to increase organizational productivity by applying to human labor the same engineering principles that had proven so successful in solving the technical problems in the work environment. The same approaches that had transformed mechanical activity could also be used to structure jobs performed by people. Taylor came to symbolize the practical realizations in industry that we now call industrial engineering (IE), or the scientific school of management.[1] In fact, though work design remains a contemporary IE concern, no subsequent concept or tool has rivaled the power of Taylor's mechanizing vision.

As we enter the 1990s, however, two newer tools are transforming organizations to the degree that Taylorism once did. These are *information technology*—the capabilities offered by computers, software applications, and telecommunications—and *business process redesign*—the analysis and design of work flows and processes within and between organizations. Working together, these tools have the potential to create a new type of industrial engineering, changing the way the discipline is practiced and the skills necessary to practice it.

This article explores the relationship between information technology (IT) and business process redesign (BPR). We report on research conducted at MIT, Harvard, and several consulting organizations on nineteen companies, including detailed studies of five firms engaged in substantial process redesign. After defining business processes, we extract from the experience of the companies studied a generic five-step approach to redesigning processes with IT. We then define the major types of processes, along with the primary role of IT in each type of process. Finally, we consider management issues that arise when IT is used to redesign business processes.

IT in Business Process Redesign

The importance of both information technology and business process redesign is well known to industrial engineers, albeit as largely separate tools for use in specific, limited environments.[2] IT is used in industrial engineering as an analysis and modeling tool, and IEs have often taken the lead in applying information technology to manufacturing environments. Well-known uses of IT in manufacturing include process modeling, production scheduling and control, materials management information systems, and logistics. In most cases where IT has been used to redesign work, the redesign has most likely been in the manufacturing function, and industrial engineers are the most likely individuals to have carried it out.

IEs have begun to analyze work activities in nonmanufacturing environments, but their penetration into offices has been far less than in factories. IT has certainly penetrated the office and services environments—in 1987 *Business Week* reported that almost 40 percent of all U.S. capital spending went

New IE

12

Davenport
& Short

to information systems, some $97 billion a year—but IT has been used in most cases to hasten office work rather than to transform it.[3] With few exceptions, IT's role in the redesign of nonmanufacturing work has been disappointing; few firms have achieved major productivity gains.[4] Aggregate productivity figures for the United States have shown no increase since 1973.[5]

Given the growing dominance of service industries and office work in the Western economies, this type of work is as much in need of analysis and redesign as the manufacturing environments to which IT has already been applied. Many firms have found that this analysis requires taking a broader view of both IT and business activity, and of the relationships between them. Information technology should be viewed as more than an automating or mechanizing force; it can fundamentally reshape the way business is done. Business activities should be viewed as more than a collection of individual or even functional tasks; they should be broken down into processes that can be designed for maximum effectiveness, in both manufacturing and service environments.

Our research suggests that IT can be more than a useful tool in business process redesign. In leading edge practice, information technology and BPR

have a recursive relationship, as Figure 1 illustrates. Each is the key to thinking about the other. Thinking about information technology should be in terms of how it supports new or redesigned business processes, rather than business functions or other organizational entities. And business processes and process improvements should be considered in terms of the capabilities information technology can provide. *We refer to this broadened, recursive view of IT and BPR as the new industrial engineering.*

Taylor could focus on workplace rationalization and individual task efficiency because he confronted a largely stable business environment; today's corporations do not have the luxury of such stability.[6] Individual tasks and jobs change faster than they can be redesigned. Today, responsibility for an outcome is more often spread over a group, rather than assigned to an individual as in the past. Companies increasingly find it necessary to develop more flexible, team-oriented, coordinative, and communication-based work capability. In short, rather than maximizing the performance of particular individuals or business functions, companies must maximize interdependent activities within and across the entire organization. Such business processes are a new approach to coordination across the firm; information technology's promise—and perhaps its ultimate impact—is to be the most powerful tool in the twentieth century for reducing the costs of this coordination.[7]

What Are Business Processes?

We define business processes as a set of logically related tasks performed to achieve a defined business outcome. This definition is similar to Pall's: "The logical organization of people, materials, energy, equipment, and procedures into work activities designed to produce a specified end result (work product)."[8]

A set of processes forms a business system—the way in which a business unit, or a collection of units, carries out its business. Processes have two important characteristics:
• They have customers; that is, processes have defined business outcomes, and there are recipients of the outcomes. Customers may be either internal or external to the firm.
• They cross organizational boundaries; that is, they normally occur across or between organizational subunits. Processes are generally indepen-

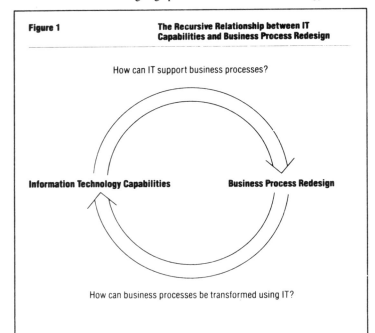

Figure 1   **The Recursive Relationship between IT Capabilities and Business Process Redesign**

How can IT support business processes?

Information Technology Capabilities → Business Process Redesign

How can business processes be transformed using IT?

dent of formal organizational structure.

Common examples of processes meeting these criteria include:

- developing a new product;
- ordering goods from a supplier;
- creating a marketing plan;
- processing and paying an insurance claim; and
- writing a proposal for a government contract.

Ordering goods from a supplier, for example, typically involves multiple organizations and functions. The end user, purchasing, receiving, accounts payable, etc., and the supplier organization are all participants. The user could be viewed as the process's customer. The process outcome could be either the creation of the order, or, perhaps more usefully, the actual receipt of the goods by the user.

Our examples so far are of large-scale processes that affect whole organizations or groups. There are more detailed processes that meet the definitional criteria above. These might include installing a windshield in an automobile factory, or completing a monthly departmental expense report. IT-driven process redesign can be applied to these processes, but the implications of redesigning them may be important only in the aggregate. In many of the firms studied, analyzing processes in great detail was highly appropriate for some purposes, for example, the detailed design of an information system or data model to support a specific work process. However, the firms that were truly beginning to redesign their business functions took a broader view of processes.

A Brief History of Process Thinking

Process thinking has become widespread in recent years, due largely to the quality movement. Industrial engineers and others who wish to improve the quality of operations are urged to look at an entire process, rather than a particular task or business function. At IBM, for example, "process management will be the principal IBM quality focus in the coming years."[9] But process discussions in the quality movement's literature rarely mention information technology. Rather, the focus is usually on improving process control systems in a manufacturing context; when IT is discussed, it is in the context of factory floor automation. Recent IE literature also borders on process thinking when advocating cross-functional analysis,[10] al-

though, as we will discuss, cross-functional processes are only one possible type of process.

Other than quality-oriented manufacturing process redesign, most processes in major corporations have not been subject to rigorous analysis and redesign. Indeed, many of our current processes result from a series of ad hoc decisions made by functional units, with little attention to effectiveness across the entire process. Many processes have never even been measured. In one manufacturing company studied, for example, no one had ever analyzed the elapsed time from a customer's order to delivery. Each department (sales, credit checking, shipping, and so on) felt that it had optimized its own performance, but in fact the overall process was quite lengthy and unwieldy.

Even fewer business processes have been analyzed with the capabilities of IT in mind. Most business processes were developed before modern computers and communications even existed. When technology has been applied, it is usually to automate or speed up isolated components of an existing process. This creates communication problems within processes and impediments to process redesign and enhancement. For example, in a second manufacturing firm studied, the procurement process involved a vendor database, a materials management planning system, and accounts payable and receivable systems, all running on different hardware platforms with different data structures. Again, each organizational subunit within the process had optimized its own IT application, but no single subunit had looked at (or was responsible for) the entire process. We believe the problems this firm experienced are very common.

Redesigning Business Processes with IT: Five Steps

Assuming that a company has decided its processes are inefficient or ineffective, and therefore in need of redesign, how should it proceed? This is a straightforward activity, but five major steps are involved: develop the business vision and process objectives, identify the processes to be redesigned, understand and measure the existing process, identify IT levers, and design and build a prototype of the new process (see Figure 2). We observed most or all of these steps being performed in companies that were succeeding with BPR. Each step is described in greater detail below.

Sloan Management Review

13

Summer 1990

Thomas H. Davenport is a partner at Ernst and Young's Center for Information Technology and Strategy in Boston, where he directs research and multiclient programs. He has consulted at McKinsey & Company, Inc., and the Index Group, and has taught at Harvard Business School and the University of Chicago. He holds the B.A. degree from Trinity University, and the M.A. and Ph.D. degrees from Harvard University. His current interests include the relationship between information technology and organization, and the development of IT infrastructures.

*Develop Business Vision
and Process Objectives*

In the past, process redesign was typically intended simply to "rationalize" the process, in other words, to eliminate obvious bottlenecks and inefficiencies. It did not involve any particular business vision or context. This was the approach of the "work simplification" aspect of industrial engineering, an important legacy of Taylorism. An example of the rationalization approach appears in a 1961 "Reference Note on Work Simplification" from the Harvard Business School:

New IE

14

Davenport
& Short

> A good manager asks himself *why* things are done as they are, extending his inquiry to every aspect of the job and the surroundings in which it is performed, from the flow of paper work to the daily functioning of his subordinates. . . . He is expected to supply the stimulus and show that job improvement or simplification of work is not only important but also is based on common-sense questioning aimed at uncovering the easiest, most economical way of performing a job.[11]

Our research suggests strongly that rationalization is not an end in itself, and is thus insufficient as a process redesign objective. Furthermore, rationalization of highly decomposed tasks may lead to a less efficient overall process. Instead of task ra-

tionalization, redesign of entire processes should be undertaken with a specific business vision and related objectives in mind.

In most successful redesign examples we studied, the company's senior management had developed a broad strategic vision into which the process redesign activity fit.[12] At Xerox, for example, this vision involved taking the perspective of the customer and developing systems rather than stand-alone products; both required cross-functional integration. At Westinghouse, the vision consisted largely of improving product quality. Ford's involved adopting the best practices of Japanese automobile manufacturers, including those of Mazda, of which it is a partial owner.

Each of these visions implied specific objectives for process redesign. The most likely objectives are the following:

• **Cost Reduction.** This objective was implicit in the "rationalization" approach. Cost is an important redesign objective in combination with others, but insufficient in itself. Excessive attention to cost reduction results in tradeoffs that are usually unacceptable to process stakeholders. While optimizing on other objectives seems to bring costs into line, optimizing on cost rarely brings about other objectives.

• **Time Reduction.** Time reduction has been only a secondary objective of traditional industrial engineering. Increasing numbers of companies, however, are beginning to compete on the basis of time.[13] Processes, as we have defined them, are the ideal unit for a focused time reduction analysis. One common approach to cutting time from product design is to make the steps begin simultaneously, rather than sequentially, using IT to coordinate design directions among the various functional participants. This approach has been taken in the design of computers, telephone equipment, automobiles, and copiers (by Digital Equipment, AT&T Bell Labs, Ford, and Xerox, respectively).

• **Output Quality.** All processes have outputs, be they physical—such as in manufacturing a tangible product—or informational—such as in adding data to a customer file. Output quality is frequently the focus of process improvement in manufacturing environments; it is just as important in service industries. The specific measure of output quality may be uniformity, variability, or freedom from defects; this should be defined by the customer of the process.

• **Quality of Worklife (QWL)/Learning/Em-**

| Figure 2 | Five Steps in Process Redesign |

Develop Business Vision and Process Objectives
• Prioritize objectives and set stretch targets

↓

Identify Processes to Be Redesigned
• Identify critical or bottleneck processes

↓

Understand and Measure Existing Processes
• Identify current problems and set baseline

↓

Identify IT Levers
• Brainstorm new process approaches

↓

Design and Build a Prototype of the Process
• Implement organizational and technical aspects

powerment. IT can lead either to greater empowerment of individuals, or to greater control over their output. Zuboff points out that IT-intensive processes are often simply automated, and that the "informating" or learning potential of IT in processes is often ignored.[14] Moreover, Schein notes that organizations often do not provide a supportive context for individuals to introduce or innovate with IT.[15] Of course, it is rarely possible to optimize all objectives simultaneously, and in most firms, the strongest pressures are to produce tangible benefits. Yet managers who ignore this dimension risk failure of redesigned processes for organizational and motivational factors.

Some firms have been able to achieve multiple objectives in redesigning processes with IT. American Express, for example, set out to improve the cost, time, and quality of its credit authorization process by embedding the knowledge of its best authorizers in an "Authorizer's Assistant" expert system. This successful redesign led to a $7 million annual reduction in costs due to credit losses, a 25 percent reduction in the average time for each authorization, and a 30 percent reduction in improper credit denials.

Finally, all firms found it was important to set specific objectives, even to the point of quantification. Though it is difficult to know how much improvement is possible in advance of a redesign, "reach should exceed grasp." Setting goals that will stretch the organization will also provide inspiration and stimulate creative thinking. For example, a company might decide to reduce the time to bring new products to market by 80 percent. In the accounts payable process at Ford, the "stretch" goal was to eliminate invoices—to pay suppliers upon receipt of their products or services. This goal has been achieved with help from an information system to confirm expected deliveries at the loading dock. As a result, Ford has eliminated three-quarters of the jobs in accounts payable.

Identify Processes to Be Redesigned

Most organizations could benefit from IT-enabled redesign of critical (if not *all*) business processes. However, the amount of effort involved creates practical limitations. Even when total redesign was the ultimate objective, the companies we studied selected a few key processes for initial efforts. Moreover, when there was insufficient commitment to total redesign, a few successful examples

of IT-enhanced processes became a powerful selling tool.

The means by which processes to be redesigned are identified and prioritized is a key issue. This is often difficult because most managers do not think about their business operations in terms of processes. There are two major approaches. The *exhaustive* approach attempts to identify all processes within an organization and then prioritize them in order of redesign urgency. The *high-impact* approach attempts to identify only the most important processes or those most in conflict with the business vision and process objectives.

The exhaustive approach is often associated with "information engineering" (developed by James Martin in the early 1980s), in which an organization's use of data dictates the processes to be redesigned.[16] For example, one information engineering method, employed at several divisions of Xerox, involves identifying business activities and the data they require using a data-activity matrix. The clusters of data activity interactions in the cells of the matrix are the organization's major business processes. Once processes are identified, Xerox managers prioritize them in the order in which new IT applications support should be provided. Although process identification in some Xerox divisions has taken as little as three months, many companies find this approach very time consuming.

The alternative is to focus quickly on high-impact processes. Most organizations have some sense of which business areas or processes are most crucial to their success, and those most "broken" or inconsistent with the business vision. If not, these can normally be identified using senior management workshops, or through extensive interviewing.[17] At IBM, the salesforce was surveyed to determine the relative importance of various customer support processes; the generation of special bids emerged as the highest priority and was the first process to be redesigned.

Companies that employed the high-impact approach generally considered it sufficient. Companies taking the exhaustive approach, on the other hand, have not had the resources to address all the identified processes; why identify them if they cannot be addressed? As a rough rule of thumb, most companies we studied were unable to redesign and support more than ten to fifteen major processes per year (i.e., one to three per major business unit); there was simply not enough management attention to do more. And some organizations have

Sloan
Management
Review

15

Summer 1990

James E. Short is Research Associate at the Center for Information Systems Research at the MIT Sloan School of Management. He is also Lecturer in Management Information Systems at Boston University's School of Management. Dr. Short holds the S.B., S.M., and Ph.D. degrees from MIT. His research interests include how information technology enables organizations to execute differential strategies and improve performance through enhanced integration and flexible, problem-focused teams and task forces.

New IE
16
Davenport
& Short

abandoned the exhaustive approach.[18]

Whichever approach is used, companies have found it useful to classify each redesigned process in terms of beginning and end points, interfaces, and organization units (functions or departments) involved, particularly including the customer unit. Thinking in these terms usually broadens the perceived scope of the process. For example, a sales manager may be aware that there are inefficiencies in customer order entry. A skilled process consultant might decide that the whole process—negotiating, receiving, and fulfilling orders—needs to be redesigned. Whether the problem is broken down into three processes or viewed as one is not important; expanding the *scope* of the process analysis is the key issue.

High-impact processes should also have owners.[19] In virtually all the process redesigns we studied, an important step was getting owners to buy in to both the idea and the scope of process redesign at an early stage. In several companies, managers felt that the process owner's job should be either above the level of the functions and units involved, or, if on the same level, that the owner should be willing—and able—to change the status quo. The difficulty, however, is that some processes only come together at the CEO level. In this situation, the CEO should designate a senior manager as owner and invest him or her with full authority. Processes that are fully contained within a single function or department can normally be owned by the manager of that area.

Understand and Measure Existing Processes

There are two primary reasons for understanding and measuring processes before redesigning them. First, problems must be understood so that they are not repeated. Second, accurate measurement can serve as a baseline for future improvements. If the objective is to cut time and cost, the time and cost consumed by the untouched process must be measured accurately. Westinghouse Productivity and Quality Center consultants found that simply graphing the incremental cost and time consumed by process tasks can often suggest initial areas for redesign. These graphs look like "step functions" showing the incremental contribution of each major task.

This step can easily be overemphasized, however. In several firms, the "stretch" goal was less to elimi-

nate problems or bottlenecks than to create radical improvements. Designers should be informed by past process problems and errors, but they should work with a clean slate. Similarly, the process should not be measured for measurement's sake. Only the specific objectives of the redesign should be measured. As with the high-impact process identification approach, an 80-20 philosophy is usually appropriate.

Identify IT Levers

Until recently, even the most sophisticated industrial engineering approaches did not consider IT capabilities until after a process had been designed. The conventional wisdom in IT usage has always been to first determine the business requirements of a function, process, or other business entity, and then to develop a system. The problem is that an awareness of IT capabilities can—and should—influence process design. Knowing that product development teams can exchange computer-aided designs over large distances, for example, might affect the structure of a product development process. The role of IT in a process should be considered in the early stages of its redesign.[20]

Several firms accomplished this using brainstorming sessions, with the process redesign objectives and existing process measures in hand. It was also useful to have a list of IT's generic capabilities in improving business processes. In the broadest sense, *all* of IT's capabilities involve improving coordination and information access across organizational units, thereby allowing for more effective management of task interdependence. More specifically, however, it is useful to think about IT capabilities and their organizational impacts in eight different ways (see Table 1).

There are undoubtedly other important IT capabilities that can reshape processes. Organizations may want to develop their own lists of capabilities that are specific to the types of processes they employ. The point is twofold: IT is so powerful a tool that it deserves its own step in process redesign, and IT can actually create new process design options, rather than simply support them.

Design and Build a Prototype of the Process

For most firms, the final step is to design the process. This is usually done by the same team that performed the previous steps, getting input from constituencies and using brainstorming workshops. A key point is that the actual design is not the end of the process. Rather, it should be viewed as a prototype, with successive iterations expected and managed. Key factors and tactics to consider in process design and prototype creation include using IT as a design tool, understanding generic design criteria, and creating organizational prototypes.

• **IT as a Design Tool.** Designing a business process is largely a matter of diligence and creativity. Emerging IT technologies, however, are beginning to facilitate the "process" of process design. Some computer-aided systems engineering (CASE) products are designed primarily to draw process models. The ability to draw models rapidly and make changes suggested by process owners speeds redesign and facilitates owner buy-in. Some CASE products can actually generate computer code for the information systems application that will support a modeled business process.

Several Xerox divisions, for example, are moving directly from process modeling to automated generation of computer code for high-priority processes. They report improved productivity and high user satisfaction with the resulting systems. A further benefit is that when the business process changes, the IS organization can rapidly modify the affected system. Use of code generation products generally presumes that process designers will use the exhaustive approach to process identification.

• **Generic Design Criteria.** Companies used various criteria for evaluating alternative designs. Most important, of course, is the likelihood that a design will satisfy the chosen design objectives. Others mentioned in interviews included the simplicity of the design, the lack of buffers or intermediaries, the degree of control by a single individual or department (or an effective, decentralized coordinative mechanism), the balance of process resources, and the generalization of process tasks (so that they can be performed by more than one person).

• **Organizational Prototypes.** Mutual Benefit Life's (MBL) redesign of its individual life insurance underwriting process illustrates a final, important point about process design. At MBL, underwriting a life insurance policy involved 40 steps with over 100 people in 12 functional areas and 80 separate jobs. To streamline this lengthy and complex process, MBL undertook a pilot project with the goal of improving productivity by 40 per-

cent. To integrate the process, MBL created a new role, the case manager. This role was designed to perform and coordinate all underwriting tasks centrally, utilizing a workstation-based computer system capable of pulling data from all over the company. After a brief start-up period, the firm learned that two additional roles were necessary on some underwriting cases: specialists such as lawyers or medical directors in knowledge-intensive fields, and clerical assistance. With the new role and redesigned process, senior managers at MBL are confident of reaching the 40 percent goal in a few months. This example illustrates the value of creating organizational prototypes in IT-driven process redesign.

Creating prototypes of IT applications has already gained widespread acceptance. Advocates argue that building a prototype of an IT change usually achieves results faster than conventional "life cycle" development, and, more important, that the result is much more likely to satisfy the customer. Building prototypes of business process changes and organizational redesign initiatives can yield similar benefits.[21] The implications of this extension are that process designs, after agreement by owners and stakeholders, would be implemented on a pilot basis (perhaps in parallel with existing processes), examined regularly for problems and objective achievement, and modified as necessary. As the process approached final acceptance, it would be phased into full implementation.

Sloan Management Review

17

Summer 1990

Table 1	IT Capabilities and Their Organizational Impacts
Capability	**Organizational Impact/Benefit**
Transactional	IT can transform unstructured processes into routinized transactions
Geographical	IT can transfer information with rapidity and ease across large distances, making processes independent of geography
Automational	IT can replace or reduce human labor in a process
Analytical	IT can bring complex analytical methods to bear on a process
Informational	IT can bring vast amounts of detailed information into a process
Sequential	IT can enable changes in the sequence of tasks in a process, often allowing multiple tasks to be worked on simultaneously
Knowledge Management	IT allows the capture and dissemination of knowledge and expertise to improve the process
Tracking	IT allows the detailed tracking of task status, inputs, and outputs
Disintermediation	IT can be used to connect two parties within a process that would otherwise communicate through an intermediary (internal or external)

Figure 3	Types of Processes	
Process Dimension and Type	**Typical Example**	**Typical IT Role**
Entities		
Interorganizational	Order from a supplier	Lower transaction costs; eliminate intermediaries
Interfunctional	Develop a new product	Work across geography; greater simultaneity
Interpersonal	Approve a bank loan	Role and task integration
Objects		
Physical	Manufacture a product	Increased outcome flexibility; process control
Informational	Create a proposal	Routinizing complex decisions
Activities		
Operational	Fill a customer order	Reduce time and costs; increase output quality
Managerial	Develop a budget	Improve analysis; increase participation

Defining Process Types

The five steps described above are sufficiently general to apply to most organizations and processes. Yet the specifics of redesign vary considerably according to the type of process under examination. Different types require different levels of management attention and ownership, need different forms of IT support, and have different business consequences. In this section, we present three different dimensions within which processes vary.

Understanding and classifying the different types of processes is important because an organization can appear to be a seamless web of interconnected processes. With various process *types* in mind, a manager can begin to isolate particular processes for analysis and redesign, including activities that, without process thinking, might otherwise be overlooked.

Three major dimensions can be used to define processes (see Figure 3). These are the organizational entities or subunits involved in the process, the type of objects manipulated, and the type of activities taking place. We describe each dimension and resulting process type below.

Defining Process Entities

Processes take place between types of organizational entities. Each type has different implications for IT benefits.

Interorganizational processes are those taking place between two or more business organizations. Increasingly, companies are concerned with coordinating activities that extend into the next (or previous) company along the value-added chain.[22] Several U.S. retail, apparel, and textile companies, for example, have linked their business processes to speed up reordering of apparel. When Dillard's (department store) inventory of a particular pants style falls below a specified level, Haggar (apparel manufacturer) is notified electronically. If Haggar does not have the cloth to manufacture the pants, Burlington Industries (textile manufacturer) is notified electronically. As this example of electronic data interchange (EDI) illustrates, information technology is the major vehicle by which this interorganizational linkage is executed.

For most companies, simple market relationships are the most common source of interorganizational processes. All the tasks involved in a selling-buying transaction form a critical process for sellers, and an increasingly important one for buyers seeking higher quality, cost efficiency, and responsiveness. Yet much of the focus has been on a simple transaction level, rather than on an interorganizational business process level. Again, how EDI is used illustrates this point.

Buyers and sellers have used EDI largely to speed up routine purchasing transactions, such as invoices or bills of materials. Few companies have attempted to redesign the broader procurement process—from the awareness that a product is needed, to the development of approved vendor lists, or even to the delivery and use of the purchased product. In the future, sellers will need to look at all buyer processes in which their products are involved.

Moreover, many firms will need to help the buyer improve those processes. Du Pont's concept of "effectiveness in use" as the major criterion of customer satisfaction is one leading approach to measuring the effectiveness of interorganizational processes. Du Pont is motivated not simply to sell a product, but to link its internal processes for creating value in a product, to its customer's processes for using the product. This concept led Du Pont to furnish EDI-provided Material Safety Data Sheets along with the chemicals it sells to its customers to ensure their safe use.

Westinghouse used an interorganizational process approach in dealing with Portland General Electric (PGE), a major customer of power generation equipment. PGE managers called upon Westinghouse's Productivity and Quality Center, a national leader in process improvement, to help them implement EDI, but the Westinghouse team asked if it could analyze the entire process by which PGE procured equipment from Westinghouse and other suppliers. They found that, while implementing EDI could yield efficiencies on the order of 10 percent, changing the overall procurement process, including using EDI and bypassing the purchasing department altogether for most routine purchase orders, could lead to much greater savings. In one case, the time to execute a standard purchase order, for example, could be reduced from fifteen days to half a day; the cost could be reduced from almost $90 to $10.

A second major type of business process is *interfunctional*. These processes exist within the organization, but cross several functional or divisional boundaries. Interfunctional processes achieve major operational objectives, such as new product realization, asset management, or production scheduling. Most management processes—for example, planning, budgeting, and human resource management—are interfunctional.

Many manufacturing companies that focused on quality improvement found that producing quality products and services required addressing difficult interfunctional issues. Yet most firms have never even listed their key interfunctional processes, let alone analyzed or redesigned them, with or without the aid of IT.

Two companies that recently analyzed their key interfunctional business processes are Baxter Healthcare Corporation and US Sprint Communications Company. Baxter's 1985 merger with American Hospital Supply provided the context for a major analysis of key business strategies, and the alignment of the IT infrastructure with those strategies.[23] As part of a seven-month IT planning effort, the company defined twenty-nine major interfunctional processes and analyzed the current and future role of IT in supporting them. For example, in the distribution area, the company identified order entry, inventory, warehouse management, purchasing, transportation, and equipment tracking as key processes. The success of this IT planning effort led Baxter to incorporate the process definition approach into its annual corporate planning process.

At US Sprint, well-publicized problems with the customer billing system prompted the company's IT function to develop a model of information flows for the entire business as part of a comprehensive systems improvement program. This model defined the critical information and key interfunctional processes necessary to run the business. Sprint is now assigning ownership to key processes and continuing to identify improvements—and ways to measure them—in each process. The systems improvement program raised the IT organization's composite internal quality index by more than 50 percent in one year.[24]

A major problem in redesigning interfunctional processes is that most information systems of the past were built to automate specific functional areas or parts of functions. Few third-party application software packages have been developed to support a full business process. Very few organizations have modeled existing interfunctional processes or redesigned them, and companies will run into substantial problems in building interfunctional systems without such models.

Interpersonal processes involve tasks within and across small work groups, typically within a function or department. Examples include a commercial loan group approving a loan, or an airline flight crew preparing for takeoff. This type of process is becoming more important as companies shift to self-managing teams as the lowest unit of organization. Information technology is increasingly capable of supporting interpersonal processes; hardware and communications companies have developed new networking-oriented products, and software companies have begun to flesh out the concept of "groupware" (e.g., local area network-based mail, conferencing, and brainstorming tools).[25]

Several companies, including GM's Electronic Data Systems (EDS), are exploring tools to facilitate the effectiveness of meetings and small group interactions. At EDS, the primary focus is on enhancing the interpersonal processes involved in automobile product development. The company's Center for Machine Intelligence has developed a computer-supported meeting room, and is studying its implications for group decision making and cooperative work.[26]

We should point out that IT can make it possible for employees scattered around the world to work as a team. As an example, Ford now creates

Sloan
Management
Review

19

Summer 1990

new car designs using teams that have members in Europe, Central America, and the United States. Because Ford has standardized computer-aided design systems and created common data structures for the design process, engineers can share complex three-dimensional designs across the Atlantic. Similarly, a small team at Digital Equipment used the company's electronic mail and conferencing capabilities to build the core of a new systems integration business. The team was scattered around the United States and Europe and only rarely met in person.

Defining Process Objects

Processes can also be categorized by the types of objects manipulated. The two primary object types are physical and informational. In physical object processes, real, tangible things are either created or manipulated; manufacturing is the obvious example. Informational object processes create or manipulate information. Processes for making a decision, preparing a marketing plan, or designing a new product are examples.

Many processes involve the combination of physical and informational objects. Indeed, adding information to a physical object as it moves through a process is a common way of adding value. Most logistical activities, for example, combine the movement of physical objects with the manipulation of information concerning their whereabouts. Success in the logistics industry is often dependent on the close integration of physical and informational outcomes; both UPS and Federal Express, for example, track package movement closely.

The potential for using IT to improve physical processes is well known. It allows greater flexibility and variety of outcomes, more precise control of the process itself, reductions in throughput time, and elimination of human labor. These benefits have been pursued for the past three decades. Still, manufacturing process flows are often the result of historical circumstance and should usually be redesigned before further automation is applied. This is particularly true in low volume, job shop manufacturing environments.[27] Redesigners of physical processes should also consider the role of IT in providing information to improve processes; Shoshana Zuboff has described this "informating" effect in detail for the paper industry.[28]

Strangely, the proportion of informational processes already transformed by IT is probably lower

than that of physical processes. True, legions of clerks have become unemployed because of computers. But the majority of information processes to which IT has been applied are those involving high volume and low complexity. Now that these processes are well known even if not fully conquered, the emphasis needs to shift to processes that incorporate semistructured and unstructured tasks and are performed by high-skill knowledge workers. Relevant IT capabilities include the storage and retrieval of unstructured and multimedia information, the capturing and routinizing of decision logic, and the application of far-flung and complex data resources. A computer vendor's advertising videotape, for example, illustrates how artificial intelligence and "hypertext," or mixed-media databases, combine to lead a manager through the process of developing a departmental budget. The IT capabilities in the video are available today, but they are rarely applied to such information-intensive yet unstructured processes.

Defining Process Activities

Our examples of business processes have involved two types of activities: operational and managerial. Operational processes involve the day-to-day carrying out of the organization's basic business purpose. Managerial processes help to control, plan, or provide resources for operational processes. Past uses of IT to improve processes, limited as they are, have been largely operational. We will therefore focus almost entirely on managerial processes in this section.[29]

Applying IT to management *tasks* is not a new idea. The potential of decision support systems, executive support systems, and other managerial tools has been discussed for over twenty years. We believe, however, that the benefits have not been realized because of the absence of systematic process thinking. Few companies have rigorously analyzed managerial activities as processes subject to redesign. Even the notion of managerial activities involving defined outcomes (a central aspect of our definition of business processes) is somewhat foreign. How would such managerial processes as deciding on an acquisition or developing the agenda for the quarterly board meeting be improved if they were treated as processes—in other words, measured, brainstormed, and redesigned with IT capabilities?

The generic capabilities of IT for reshaping

IT-Driven Process Redesign at Rank Xerox U.K.

Rank Xerox U.K. (RXUK), a national operating company of Xerox Corporation, has undertaken the most comprehensive IT-driven process redesign we have studied. The process was led by David O'Brien, the division's managing director, who arrived at the company in 1985. O'Brien quickly came to two realizations: first, the company needed to focus on marketing "office systems" in addition to its traditional reprographics products; and second, the company's strong functional culture and inefficient business processes would greatly inhibit its growth. He began to see his own organization as a place to test integrated office systems that support integrated business processes; if successful, he could use RXUK as a model for customers.

The company began to redesign its business in 1987. In a series of offsite meetings, the senior management team reappraised its external environment and mission, then identified the key business processes needed if the company was to achieve its mission. The group began to restructure the organization around cross-functional processes, identifying high-level objectives and creating task forces to define information and other resource requirements for each process. It created career systems revolving around facilitation skills and cross-functional management, rather than hierarchical authority. O'Brien decided to keep a somewhat functional formal structure, because functional skills would still be needed in a process organization and because the level of organizational change might have been too great with a wholly new structure.

The level of change was still very high. Several senior managers departed because they could not or would not manage in the new environment. Two new cross-functional senior positions, called "facilitating directors," were created, one for organizational and business development, the other for process management, information systems, and qual-

ity. O'Brien took great advantage of the honeymoon period accorded to new CEOs, but managing the change still required intense personal attention:

> Of course, this new thinking was in sharp contrast to some of the skills and attitudes of the company. We were introducing a change in management philosophy in a company that, in many ways, was very skillful and effective, but in a different product-market environment. We faced all the issues of attitudinal change and retraining that any such change implies. We were moving to a much more integrated view of the world and had to encourage a major shift in many patterns of the existing culture. This meant a very hard, tough program of selling the new ideas within the organization as well as an extensive and personal effort to get the new messages and thinking to our potential customers.*

As the key processes were identified and their objectives determined, the company began to think about how information technology (its own and from other providers) could enable and support the processes. The facilitating director of processes and systems, Paul Chapman, decided that the firm needed a new approach to developing information systems around processes. His organization used the information engineering approach discussed earlier and worked with an external consultant to refine and confirm process identification. They uncovered 18 "macro" business processes (e.g., logistics) and 145 "micro" processes (e.g., fleet management).

The senior management team reconvened to prioritize the identified processes and decided that seven macro processes had particular importance: customer order life cycle, customer satisfaction, installed equipment management, integrated planning, logistics, financial management, and personnel man-

*David O'Brien, quoted in B. Denning and B. Taylor, "Rank Xerox U.K., Office Systems Strategy (C): Developing the Systems Strategy," (Henley on Thames, England: Henley–The Management College case study, September 1988). Other Rank Xerox U.K. information comes from personal interviews.

Sloan
Management
Review

21

Summer 1990

agement. It selected personnel management as the first process to be redesigned because this was viewed as relatively easy to attack and because personnel systems were crucial in tracking the development of new skills. The personnel system has now been successfully redesigned, using automated code generation capabilities, in substantially less time than if normal methods had been used.

RXUK's financial situation began to improve as it redesigned its business processes. The company emerged from a long period of stagnation into a period of 20 percent revenue growth. Jobs not directly involved with customer contact were reduced from 1,100 to 800. Order delivery time was, on aver-age, reduced from thirty-three days to six days. Though many other market factors were changing during this time, O'Brien credits the process redesign for much of the improvement.

Other Xerox divisions heard of RXUK's success with process redesign and began efforts of their own. Xerox's U.S. product development and marketing divisions now have major cross-functional teams performing process redesign. Paul Chapman has been loaned to Xerox corporate headquarters, where he is heading a cross-functional team looking at corporate business processes. Commitment to IT-driven process redesign by Xerox senior corporate management is also growing.

management processes include improving analytic accuracy, enabling broader management participation across wider geographical boundaries, generating feedback on actions taken (the managerial version of "informating" a process), and streamlining the time and resources a specific process consumes. Texas Instruments and Xerox's corporate headquarters provide excellent examples.

Texas Instruments has developed an expert system to facilitate the capital budgeting process. Managers in a fast-growing and capital-intensive TI division were concerned that the time and experience necessary to prepare capital budget request packages would become an obstacle to the division's growth. The packages were very complex and time consuming, and few employees had the requisite knowledge to complete them accurately. The expert system was developed by two industrial engineers with expertise in both the technology and the budget process.

TI's system has radically improved the capital budget request process. Requests prepared with the system require far less time than the manual approach and conform better to the company's guidelines. One experienced employee reported a reduction in package preparation time from nine hours to forty minutes; of the first fifty packages prepared with the system, only three did not conform to guidelines, compared to an average of ten using a manual approach.[30]

At Xerox Corporation headquarters, IT has been used to improve the review of division strategic plans. Prior to the development of the company's Executive Information System (EIS), the planning process was somewhat haphazard; each division prepared its planning documents in a different format and furnished different types of information to corporate headquarters. Plans often came in too late for the corporate management committee to review them before the quarterly or annual review meeting. The EIS was developed to include standard information formats and a user friendly graphical interface enabling fast comprehension. Divisional plans are now developed on the EIS and delivered instantaneously over Xerox's network to all corporate management committee members. These members can now read and discuss the plans beforehand and can move directly to decisions at the review meetings. The workstations are even used in the meetings themselves, allowing revisions to be made and agreed upon before adjournment. As one manager put it, ". . . [the system] lets us communicate at higher speed and in greater depth."[31]

Management Issues in IT-Enabled Redesign

Companies have found that once a process has been redesigned, several key issues remain. These include the management role in redesigned activity, implications for organization structure, new skill requirements, creating a function to perform IT-enabled BPR, the proper direction for the IT infrastruc-

Management Roles

Perhaps the greatest difficulty in IT-driven redesign is getting and keeping management commitment. Because processes cut across various parts of the organization, a process redesign effort driven by a single business function or unit will probably encounter resistance from other parts of the organization. Both high-level and broad support for change are necessary.

To perform the five redesign steps described above, several companies created a cross-functional task force headed by a senior executive. These task forces included representatives from key staff and line groups likely to be affected by the changes, including IT and human resources. It was particularly important that the customer of the process be represented on the team, even when the customer was external. The team composition was ideal if some members had some record of process or operations innovation involving IT.

As the redesign teams selected processes and developed objectives, they needed to work closely with the managers and staff of the affected units. Managing process change is similar to managing other types of change, except that its cross-functional nature increases the number of stakeholders, thereby increasing the complexity of the effort.

It was also important to have strong, visible commitment from senior management. Employees throughout the organization needed to understand that redesign was critical, that differences of opinion would be resolved in favor of the customer of a process, and that IT would play an important role. In many cases, the CEO communicated any structural implications of the redesign effort.

An example of the importance of the CEO's role is found at GUS Home Shopping, the largest home shopping company in Europe. GUS undertook a $90 million project to redesign its logistical processes with IT. Redesign objectives involved both cost and time: to be able to sell a product within five minutes of its arrival on the loading dock, and to be able to deliver a product to the customer's door at an average cost of sixty cents. The company's managing director commented on his role in meeting these objectives:

To change our business to the degree we have [done] demands integration. How involved should the managing director get in designing computer systems? My view is totally, because he's the one who can integrate across the entire organization.[32]

Process Redesign and Organizational Structure

A second key issue is the relationship between process orientation and organizational structure. Certainly someone must be in charge of implementing a process change, and of managing the redesigned process thereafter. But process responsibilities are likely to cut across existing organizational structures. How can process organization and traditional functional organization be reconciled?

One possible solution is to create a new organization structure along process lines, in effect abandoning altogether other structural dimensions, such as function, product, or geography. This approach presents risks, however; as business needs change, new processes will be created that cut across the previous process-based organization. This does not mean that a process-based structure cannot be useful, but only that it will have to be changed frequently.

While no firm we studied has converted wholly to a process-based structure, a few organizations have moved in this direction. For example, Apple Computer recently moved away from a functional structure to what executives describe as an IT-oriented, process-based, customer satisfaction-driven structure called "New Enterprise." The company relishes its lack of formal hierarchy; Apple managers describe their roles as highly diffuse, and team and project based.

A more conservative approach would be to create a matrix of functional and process responsibilities. However, because of the cross-functional nature of most processes, the functional manager who should have responsibility for a given process is not always easy to identify. The company may also wish to avoid traditional functional thinking in assigning process responsibilities. For example, it may be wiser to give responsibility for redesigning supplies acquisition to a manager who uses those supplies (i.e., the customer of the process), rather than to the head of purchasing.

Sloan
Management
Review

23

Summer 1990

New Skill Requirements

For process management to succeed, managers must develop facilitation and influence skills. Traditional sources of authority may be of little use when process changes cut across organizational units. Managers will find themselves trying to change the behavior of employees who do not work for them. In these cases, they must learn to persuade rather than to instruct, to convince rather than to dictate. Of course, these recommendations are consistent with many other organizational maxims of the past several years; they just happen to be useful in process management as well.[33]

Several organizations that are moving toward IT-driven process management are conducting programs intended to develop facilitation skills. These programs encourage less reliance on hierarchy, more cross-functional communication and cooperation, and more decision making by middle- and lower-level managers. Such a program at American Airlines is being used to build an organizational infrastructure at the same time a new IT infrastructure is being built.

An Ongoing Organization

Organizations that redesign key processes must oversee continuing redesign and organizational "tuning," as well as ensure that information systems support process flows. In most companies, the appropriate analytical skills are most likely to be found in the IT function. However, these individuals will also require a high degree of interpersonal skills to be successful as the "new industrial engineers." The ideal group would represent multiple functional areas, for example, information systems, industrial engineering, quality, process control, finance, and human resources.

There are already some examples of such process change groups. Silicon Graphics has created a specific process consulting group for ongoing process management; it is headed by a director-level manager. At United Parcel Service, process redesign is traditionally concentrated in the industrial engineering function. The UPS group is incorporating IT skills in the IE function at a rapid rate, and creating task forces with IT and IE representation for process redesign projects. Federal Express has gone even further, renaming its IE organization the "Strategic Integrated Systems Group," placing it within the Information Systems function, and giving it responsibility for designing and implementing major IT-driven business changes.

Process Redesign and the IT Organization

Just as information technology is a powerful force in redesigning business processes, process thinking has important implications for the IT organization and for the technology infrastructure it builds. Though few IT groups have the power and influence to spearhead process redesign, they can play several important roles. First of all, the IT group may need to play a behind-the-scenes advocacy role, convincing senior management of the power offered by information technology and process redesign. Second, as demand builds for process redesign expertise, the IT group can begin to incorporate the IE-oriented skills of process measurement, analysis, and redesign, perhaps merging with the IE function if there is one. It can also develop an approach or methodology for IT-enabled redesign, perhaps using the five steps described above as a starting point.

What must the information systems function do technologically to prepare for process redesign? IT professionals must recognize that they will have to build most systems needed to support (or enable) processes, rather than buy them from software package vendors, because most application packages are designed with particular functions in mind. IT professionals will need to build robust technology platforms on which process-specific applications can be quickly constructed. This implies a standardized architecture with extensive communications capability between computing nodes, and the development of shared databases. However, like the organizational strategies for process management described above, these are appropriate technology strategies for most companies, whether or not they are redesigning processes with IT.

Continuous Process Improvement

The concept of process improvement, which developed in the quality movement, requires first that the existing process be stabilized. It then becomes predictable, and its capabilities become accessible to analysis and improvement.[34] Continuous process improvement occurs when the cycle of stabilizing, assessing, and improving a given process becomes institutionalized.

IT-enabled business process redesign must generally be dynamic. Those responsible for a process should constantly investigate whether new information technologies make it possible to carry out a process in new ways. IT is continuing to evolve, and forthcoming technologies will have a substantial impact on the processes of the next decade. The IT infrastructure must be robust enough to support the new applications appropriate to a particular process.

Summary

We believe that the industrial engineers of the future, regardless of their formal title or the organizational unit that employs them, will focus increasingly on IT-enabled redesign of business processes. We have only begun to explore the implications and implementation of this concept, and only a few companies have ventured into the area. Many companies that have used IT to redesign particular business processes have done so without any conscious approach or philosophy. In short, the actual experience base with IT-enabled process redesign is limited.

Yet managing by customer-driven processes that cross organizational boundaries is an intuitively appealing idea that has worked well in the companies that have experimented with it. And few would question that information technology is a powerful tool for reshaping business processes. The individuals and companies that can master redesigning processes around IT will be well equipped to succeed in the new decade — and the new century. ■

References

The authors wish to acknowledge the support of the Center for Information Systems Research at the MIT Sloan School, Harvard Business School's Division of Research, and McKinsey & Company. They are also grateful for the comments of Lynda Applegate, James Cash, Warren McFarlan, John Rockart, Edgar Schein, and Michael S. Scott Morton.

1
L. Gulick, "Notes on the Theory of Organization," in L. Gulick and L. Urwick, eds., *Papers on the Science of Administration* (New York: Institute of Public Administration, 1937), p. 9.

2
S. Sakamoto, "Process Design Concept: A New Approach to IE," *Industrial Engineering*, March 1989, p. 31.

3
"Office Automation: Making It Pay Off," *Business Week*, 12 October 1987, pp. 134–146. For an alternative perspective, see
R.E. Kraut, ed., *Technology and the Transformation of White-Collar Work* (Hillsdale, New Jersey: Lawrence Erlbaum Associates, 1987).

4
G.W. Loveman, "An Assessment of the Productivity Impact of Information Technologies" (Cambridge, Massachusetts: MIT Sloan School of Management, Management in the 1990s, Working Paper 90s:88-054, July 1988). Loveman studied microeconomic data from manufacturing firms to estimate econometrically the productivity impact of IT in the late 1970s and early 1980s. In finding no significant positive productivity impact from IT, he argues that his findings in manufacturing raise serious questions about impacts in nonmanufacturing firms as well.
Baily and Chakrabarti (1988) studied white-collar productivity and IT as one part of a broader inquiry into poor productivity growth. They found no evidence of significant productivity gain. See M.N. Baily and A. Chakrabarti, *Innovation and the Productivity Crisis* (Washington, D.C.: Brookings Institution, 1988).

5
Loveman (1988);
Baily and Chakrabarti (1988).
See also L.C. Thurow, "Toward a High-Wage, High-Productivity Service Sector" (Washington, D.C.: Economic Policy Institute, 1989).

6
Robert Horton, who became chairman and chief executive of British Petroleum in March 1990, argues that his major concern in setting BP's course in the next decade is "managing surprise." Horton's belief is that the external business environment is so unpredictable that surprise, rather than managed change, is inevitable. See R. Horton, "Future Challenges to Management," *MIT Management*, Winter 1989, pp. 3–6.

7
T. Malone, "What is Coordination Theory?" (Cambridge, Massachusetts: MIT Sloan School of Management, Center for Coordination Science, Working Paper No. 2051-88, February 1988);
K. Crowston and T. Malone, "Information Technology and Work Organization" (Cambridge, Massachusetts: MIT Sloan School of Management, Center for Information Systems Research, Working Paper No. 165, December 1987).

8
G.A. Pall, *Quality Process Management* (Englewood Cliffs, New Jersey: Prentice-Hall, 1987). Our definition also complements that of Schein, who focuses on human processes in organizations — e.g., building and maintaining groups, group problem solving and decision making, leading and influencing, etc.
See E.H. Schein, *Process Consultation: Its Role in Organization Development*, Vol. 1, 2d ed. (Reading, Massachusetts: Addison-Wesley, 1988).

9
E.J. Kane, "IBM's Total Quality Improvement System" (Pur-

Sloan Management Review

25

Summer 1990

chase, New York: IBM Corporation, unpublished manuscript), p. 5.

10

See, for example, M.F. Morris and G.W. Vining, "The IE's Future Role in Improving Knowledge Worker Productivity," *Industrial Engineering*, July 1987, p. 28.

11

"Reference Note on Work Simplification" (Boston: Harvard Business School, HBS Case Services #9-609-0601961, 1961).

12

The relationship between business vision and IT has been explored by several researchers under the auspices of the MIT Sloan School's five-year "Management in the 1990s" research program. An overview volume is scheduled for publication by Oxford University Press in August 1990.

13

See, for example, G. Stalk, Jr., "Time—The Next Source of Strategic Advantage," *Harvard Business Review*, July-August 1988, pp. 41–51.

14

S. Zuboff, *In the Age of the Smart Machine* (New York: Basic Books, 1988).

15

E.H. Schein, "Innovative Cultures and Organizations" (Cambridge, Massachusetts: MIT Sloan School of Management, Management in the 1990s, Working Paper 90s:88-064, November 1988).

16

Information engineering and other redesign approaches based on data modeling are necessarily limited in scope. More than data is exchanged in many process relationships. Note too that many companies have used information engineering methods *without* a specific process orientation.

17

Examples of IT planning approaches where high-impact objectives and/or goals are defined include critical success factors (CSFs) and business systems planning (BSP). See J.F. Rockart, "Chief Executives Define Their Own Data Needs," *Harvard Business Review*, March-April 1979, pp. 81–93; and IBM, *Information Systems Planning Guide*, 3d ed. (Business Systems Planning Report No. GE20-05527-2, July 1981).

18

D. Goodhue, J. Quillard, and J. Rockart, "Managing the Data Resource: A Contingency Perspective" (Cambridge, Massachusetts: MIT Sloan School of Management, Center for Information Systems Research, Working Paper No. 150, January 1987).

19

J.F. Rockart, "The Line Takes the Leadership—IS Management in a Wired Society," *Sloan Management Review*, Summer 1988, pp. 57–64.

20

J.C. Henderson and N. Venkatraman, "Strategic Alignment: A Process Model for Integrating Information Technology and Business Strategies" (Cambridge, Massachusetts: MIT Sloan School of Management, Center for Information Systems Research, Working Paper No. 196, October 1989).

21

Dorothy Leonard-Barton introduced the concept of organizational prototyping with regard to the implementation of new information technologies. See D. Leonard-Barton, "The Case for Integrative Innovation: An Expert System at Digital," *Sloan Management Review*, Fall 1987, pp. 7–19.

22

R. Johnston and P.R. Lawrence, "Beyond Vertical Integration—The Rise of the Value-Adding Partnership," *Harvard Business Review*, July-August 1988, pp. 94–101.
See also N. Venkatraman, "IT-Induced Business Reconfiguration: The New Strategic Management Challenge" (Cambridge, Massachusetts: Paper presented at the annual conference of the MIT Center for Information Systems Research, June 1989).

23

T.J. Main and J.E. Short, "Managing the Merger: Building Partnership through IT Planning at the New Baxter," *Management Information Systems Quarterly*, December 1989, pp. 469–486.

24

C.R. Hall, M.E. Friesen, and J.E. Short, "The Turnaround at US Sprint: The Role of Improved Partnership between Business and Information Management," in progress.

25

R.R. Johansen, *Groupware: Computer Support for Business Teams* (New York: The Free Press, 1988).
Also see C.V. Bullen and R.R. Johansen, "Groupware: A Key to Managing Business Teams?" (Cambridge, Massachusetts: MIT Sloan School of Management, Center for Information Systems Research, Working Paper No. 169, May 1988).

26

See L.M. Applegate, "The Center for Machine Intelligence: Computer Support for Cooperative Work" (Boston: Harvard Business School Case Study No. 189-135, 1988, rev. 1989).

27

J.E. Ashton and F.X. Cook, "Time to Reform Job Shop Manufacturing," *Harvard Business Review*, March-April 1989, pp. 106–111.

28

See cases on "Tiger Creek," "Piney Wood," and "Cedar Bluff" in S. Zuboff (1988); other industries discussed by Zuboff primarily involve informational processes.

29

One might consider managerial processes synonymous with informational processes. Certainly the vast majority of managerial processes, such as budgeting, planning, and human resource development, involve informational objects. Yet it is important to remember that informational processes can be either operational or managerial, so we believe that this separate dimension of process types is warranted.

30

A case study describes the process and the creation of the expert system. See "Texas Instruments Capital Investment Expert System" (Boston: Harvard Business School Case Study No. 188-050, 1988).

31

Some aspects of this process improvement are described in

New IE

26

Davenport & Short

L.M. Applegate and C.S. Osborne, "Xerox Corporation: Executive Support Systems" (Boston: Harvard Business School Case Study No. 189-134, 1988, rev. 1989).

32
R.H.C. Pugh, address to McKinsey & Co. information technology practice leaders, Munich, Germany, June 1989.

33
See, for example, A.R. Cohen and D.L. Bradford, "Influence without Authority: The Use of Alliances, Reciprocity, and Exchange to Accomplish Work," *Organizational Dynamics*, Winter 1989, pp. 4–17.

34
See G.A. Pall (1987).

Reprint 3141

Sloan
Management
Review

27

Summer 1990

BUILDING A BETTER MOUSETRAP

What role do MIS executives play in business reengineeering projects?

by Peter Krass

When Bruce Ryan, VP and corporate controller at Digital Equipment Corp., began to rework the way the computer maker handles its internal finances several years ago, he challenged company tradition. In the past, DEC executives changing business practices would review available technologies, pick one, and then build solutions, even whole organizations, around it. But this time, Ryan told colleagues, "Let's ignore the technology."

Instead, what Ryan and his team did was redesign DEC's finance function with a tight focus on the business issues. Though one senior IS official helped with the early stages of the project, the larger IS organization did not get involved until Ryan's initial team had finished its finance blueprint.

DEC's ongoing machinations are just one example of the latest corporate rage: business reengineering. Used to describe efforts aimed at redesigning internal work processes in order to boost productivity and competitiveness, business reengineering projects have been launched at many corporations, including Ford Motor Co., Mutual Benefit Life Insurance Co., and AT&T. They have typically reported an increase in productivity and a decrease in staff by roughly 80%. At DEC, Ryan's team converted 20 incompatible accounts-payable systems to a VAX standard and consolidated 55 accounting groups down to five, eliminating 450 jobs in the process.

Business reengineering (also known as business process rede-

At Tupperware International, the IS group 'planted the seed' of business reengineering, says Richard Duchaine, VP of MIS. But the final decision 'came from the top down.'

sign) also promises to finally make information technology pay off. Despite the massive investments companies have made in IT—which now represents as much as 40% of total U.S. capital spending, according to some estimates—national productivity figures have not improved since 1973. In fact, both national and industry figures show that as IT spending grows, productivity gains actually decline. This in turn has led a growing number of consultants and academics to the idea that different forms of organization are needed to fully exploit IT.

But for IS managers, business reengineering is beginning to look like another case of "so near and yet so far." Only a select few IS executives have led their companies' business reengineering efforts. In an overwhelming number of cases, CIOs have acted as reengineering "evangelists, supporters, and peers," says Tom Davenport, an analyst with Ernst & Young. These IS executives begin by convincing colleagues from other parts of their companies to take an interest in reengineering. Then, after business processes have been redesigned, the IS executives are called on to provide enabling systems. Their role is certainly important, consultants and CIOs stress, but it's not a primary one.

DOWNPLAYING IT

But in virtually every company that has reengineered business processes, the managers involved needed IS support. This alone marks a turning point. "In the past, technology automated existing processes," says Michael Hammer, president of consultants Hammer & Co. and the author of an influential *Harvard Business Review* article on business reengineering. "Now, IT enables totally new processes." Adds James Champy, chairman and CEO of Cambridge, Mass.-based Index Group Inc., "From thinking about IS, one logically moves to reengineering discussions."

Yet despite the importance of IT to reengineering—and vice versa—IS executives rarely lead reengineering efforts. Usually, "IS plays an important role but isn't at the center of reengineering," says Hammer. States DEC's Ryan: "You shouldn't start with an IS bias."

In fact, some managers involved in business reengineering downplay IT's transformative powers altogether. While reengineering does require a change in how information is collected and distributed, "just changing your IS won't change the way you do business," says Michael Kalashian, a senior consultant in Hewlett-Packard Co.'s manufacturing applications group.

That lesson was learned the hard way by Xerox Corp. The company last summer brought over a Rank Xerox U.K. colleague, who was experienced in the field, to form an eight-person team to define cross-functional processes ripe for reengineering. Xerox managers started with high hopes for the role IS would play in the work. But now, with four major groups in various stages of reengineering, those same managers believe they overestimated the importance of IS. ''Originally, our vision was more IS-focused,'' admits Judy Campbell, director of corporate business process. ''We began by thinking about the information flow. But we quickly found that the steps that come before automating are more critical. You've got to understand the strategic vision.''

Similarly, Bath Iron Works Corp. in Bath, Maine, plans to enlist IS to help ongoing business reengineering projects only at the final stage. ''We don't want to jump to a systems or software solution,'' says Paul Mayotte, the privately held shipbuilder's director of material management systems.

The company has identified six business processes that go into building a ship, and in December it formed two 10-person groups, called Pipeline Teams, to streamline them. Though both teams include IS executives among their members, ''there will be nothing about automating until we first develop, then test, the new processes,'' Mayotte insists. He expects that reengineering the first two processes to be examined—ship piping and hull outfitting—will take about six months and a year, respectively. After the new procedures are developed and tested, Bath Iron Works' data adminis-

MARCH 25, 1991

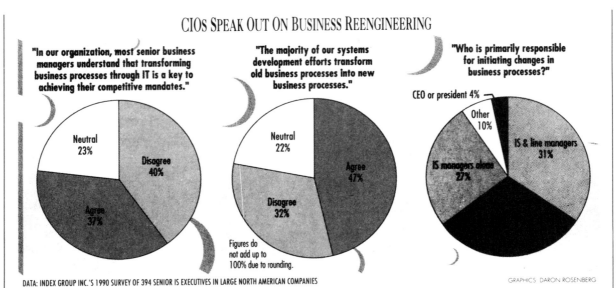

CIOS SPEAK OUT ON BUSINESS REENGINEERING

"In our organization, most senior business managers understand that transforming business processes through IT is a key to achieving their competitive mandates."

- Neutral 23%
- Disagree 40%
- Agree 37%

"The majority of our systems development efforts transform old business processes into new business processes."

- Neutral 22%
- Agree 47%
- Disagree 32%

Figures do not add up to 100% due to rounding.

"Who is primarily responsible for initiating changes in business processes?"

- CEO or president 4%
- Other 10%
- IS & line managers 31%
- IS managers alone 27%

DATA: INDEX GROUP INC.'S 1990 SURVEY OF 394 SENIOR IS EXECUTIVES IN LARGE NORTH AMERICAN COMPANIES

GRAPHICS: DARON ROSENBERG

tration group will help to integrate systems and create companywide databases.

IS is playing a more active role in the reengineering efforts of Westinghouse Electric Corp. The company's electronic systems group, which manufactures radar and missile systems under government contracts, is now testing a computer and communications system that will allow employees to create, store, and distribute information anywhere the group has offices. Although the system, called Westinghouse Integrated System for the Enterprise (WISE), was developed by a team from the design engineering group, the IS group is acting as a central coordinator for the integration of various systems that feed into WISE, according to John Teixeira, manager of advanced development and operations.

TECHNOLOGY PARTY AT TUPPERWARE

Westinghouse is not an isolated case. At many companies, IS helped get the ball rolling on reengineering by prompting senior and line managers to take action. For instance, at Tupperware International in Orlando, Fla., the IS group "planted the seed," says Richard Duchaine, VP of MIS and international administration. But, he adds, the final decision "came from the top down."

To ensure ongoing dialogue between the IS team and senior management, Duchaine's boss, executive VP of international administration Bill Phillips, attends a monthly meeting of the Tupperware executive committee. Duchaine often speaks before the group, too. Tupperware also convenes a committee of its worldwide IS leaders three times a year, and this body periodically meets with the executive committee as well.

But there's more than just talk going on. Tupperware has built a computer system to process customer orders and shipping requests that has reportedly saved eight times its cost in its first year of operation alone. The

company is also building a global manufacturing and distribution system that will track demand, inventory, manufacturing capability, and local costs. The system will run EDI (electronic data interchange) transactions over a public data network. Next, Duchaine wants to develop an automated decision-making system, based on expert systems software, linked to the EDI network. Tupperware sales managers would use the smart system to help them forecast sales for new products or new markets.

Some IS groups that have dreamed up reengineering projects for their companies report that internal politics prevent them from taking the lead. The IS group of New York Life Insurance Co. instigated such a project, known internally as the Individual Operations Support Plan. But leadership for the project has been passed on to line managers. "The person responsible for that function must carry the ball," says Tom Pettibone, the insurer's senior VP of IS.

New York Life is now about one year into the project, which involves nothing less than a complete rethinking of the way the company serves its customers. For his part, Pettibone hopes to move the company from a predominantly IBM mainframe environment to one made up of distributed Unix workstations, local area networks, radio-linked hand-held computers, image processing systems, and client/server software. But while Pettibone is sold on the benefits of new technology, he believes only 20% to 25% of the gains from the project will come from automation; the rest will be the effect of eliminated processes and other direct results of reengineering.

One factor behind the New York Life IS group's inability to lead the project, Pettibone explains, is the delicate matter of

Reengineering: What You Can Do

Want to help your company reengineer business processes but don't know where to start? Gary Gulden, executive VP of the Index Group consultancy, offers this action checklist:

▶ Gain an in-depth understanding of what reengineering is. Appreciate its ambition and scope, as well as IT's central role.

▶ Detect latent opportunities. Consider especially these two: intensive quality programs that have no IT connection and large IS replacement projects that are reengineering opportunities disguised. Also, be alert to a lack of alignment between the expectations of senior line managers and IS people.

▶ Find ways to expose leading executives to the reengineering idea. Introduce the work of other organizations that have tried reengineering.

▶ Sensitize IS people. Are they pouring cement around the old ways? What can they do to look for new ways?

▶ Develop a scheme for rapid systems deployment. Build quickly and interactively. Deliver systems fast. Construct prototypes. Work on a try-and-fix basis. **IW**

layoffs. Business reengineering often helps companies dramatically reduce the number of people needed to handle a function, and while that looks good on paper, the people who lose their jobs see things differently. "There's pain involved," Pettibone admits, "and IS can't do that." That leaves the information chief assuming the role of internal consultant, "looking in from the outside," Pettibone says. Otherwise, he adds, "It's tough for a person to look at his own job and say, 'We can do this differently.' "

At the far end of the spectrum, some very IT-intensive reengineering projects have had very little input from the IS department. The Dallas-based diagnostics division of Abbott Laboratories is now engaged in two reengineering projects, both with plenty of IT. One will create nine self-directed work teams in a

group that makes analyzers and monitors for hospitals, laboratories, and physicians' offices. It will use databases on computers linked by local area networks, a move that will eliminate certain data-gathering chores and enable the 15-person teams to shrink to 11, says production manager Steven Robertson. The other will link manufacturing employees of the diagnostics division with engineering research and development. Yet in both cases, says Peter Storti, the division's operations support manager, "MIS is on the periphery."

In fact, the involvement of Abbott's IS group is limited to representation on a cross-functional council overseeing the two projects. One reason for that, Storti explains, is that the reengineering projects will make use of Unix-based systems, with which the IS group has no experience. In addition, while Abbott's corporate IS group focuses on accounting, payroll, and other back-office jobs, the reengineering efforts involve engineering and other specialized systems. "It's a whole different environment," says Storti.

The eventual role of IS managers in reengineering could be even more negligible. Jeffrey Miller, a professor of operations at Boston University's School of Management, recently wrote a letter to the *Harvard Business Review* arguing that the drive for reengineering will come not from IS managers but from operating managers, teams of workers, and manufacturing and process engineers with some knowledge of MIS capabilities. "MIS executives can be effective, given the right experiences," he notes, "but I'm not looking for the revolution to be led from there."

Another naysayer is Bruce Johnson, director of Andersen Consulting's Center for Strategic Technology Research in Chicago. "IS assumes that if we share information, we'll get business integration, and that if we give information to top management, they'll make rational decisions. But passively moving information is insufficient for business integration," he says, adding, "IS needs to rise above its analytical and procedural thinking."

Even consultant Hammer admits that IS executives often underestimate the complexity of human relations in organizations. "IS tends to be logical—Mr. Spock is the model," he says. "They fail to realize that feelings, politics, and resistance can torpedo the finest process design."

That said, Hammer still believes IS executives possess a problem-solving, multidimensional way of thinking that makes them the strongest candidates for the role of corporate reengineer. In fact, he predicts that at some future time, CIO will come to stand for Chief *Innovation* Officer. —*Peter Krass*

> **'IS** assumes that if we share information, we'll get business integration,' says Andersen Consulting's Bruce Johnson. 'But passively moving information is insufficient.'

Chapter 3
Software Reengineering
Strategies and Economics

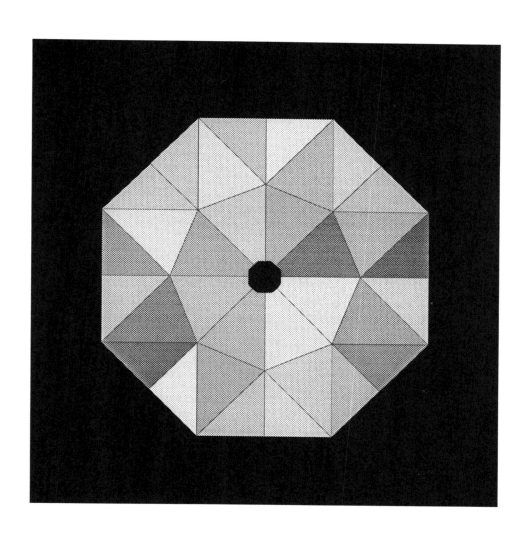

Chapter 3
Software Reengineering Strategies and Economics

Purpose

This chapter introduces the reader to the strategies, processes, and economics of reengineering. Reading these papers will help the reader understand issues affecting planning for reengineering.

Papers

The first paper, "Re-engineering: Defining An Integrated Migration Framework," by William Ulrich, describes a customizable three-phase framework for reengineering.[1] The major phases are: (1) inventory and analysis, (2) positioning, and (3) transformation. The inventory and analysis phase allows "MIS [Management Information System] management to objectively evaluate various investment alternatives based on business and technical criteria — and select the best course of action available." It looks at existing software parts and does preliminary planning for migrating to a future architecture. The positioning phase uses tools and techniques to "improve the quality of existing systems without affecting the functions or the basic architecture upon which those systems were built." The postioning phase focuses on near-term objectives. The transformation phase focuses on longer-term objectives. The transformation phase accomplishes the steps of changing software to migrate to a target architecture.

In the next paper, "Common Risks of Reengineering," Robert Arnold briefly describes several potential pitfalls in applying reengineering. He cautions, for example, about overestimating the capabilities of current reengineering technology, about being unable to demonstrate a cost benefit for the reengineering work, and about not reengineering the process along with the product.

In the final paper, "Economics of Software Reengineering," Harry Sneed discusses economic factors and models of reengineering. He describes maintenance cost drivers, and maintenance and reengineering cost models. He also describes a framework for deciding when reengineering activities are cost-effective.

---

[1] This paper combines a series of four papers into one paper. The original papers, all by William Ulrich, were, "Re-engineering: Defining An Integrated Migration Framework," *CASE Trends,* November/December 1990; "The Re-development Framework: Inventory Analysis," *CASE Trends,* January/February 1991; "The Re-development Framework: The Positioning Stage," *CASE Trends,* March/April 1991; "The Re-development Framework: The Transformation Stage," *CASE Trends,* May/June 1991.

CASE ⋮ TRENDS

THE MAGAZINE FOR COMPUTER-AIDED SOFTWARE ENGINEERING

Re-engineering: Defining an Integrated Migration Framework

This article was published in a four-part series in CASE Trends magazine from Nov/Dec 1990 to May/June 1991. It describes a methodological framework to support the software re-engineering process.

by William M. Ulrich

R e-engineering has received widespread attention as of late. Unfortunately, not all the coverage has been favorable. Re-engineering successes, and failures, have been exaggerated beyond reasonable proportion leading to two potentially serious problems. First, certain organizations have written off re-engineering as a build/buy alternative without clearly investigating how it can help. Others view re-engineering as a panacea for solving every MIS problem. Somewhere between these two views lies a realistic approach for systematically changing current information systems to meet ever changing business needs.

The opposing views expressed above stem from the lack of a well defined framework to drive the transition of aging information systems towards effective utilization of new technologies. Simply stated, MIS lacks a sound frame of reference to help them understand how re-engineering can help. This issue, effective technology transfer, needs to be resolved quickly so the industry can readily identify potential re-engineering opportunities.

This article describes a basic framework that MIS can use for developing a customized re-engineering strategy. Using this framework as a point of reference, we will examine the role of software tools and discuss arguments for and against re-engineering. The goal of this discussion is to help MIS managers both evaluate the value of re-engineering and understand how to best apply it. First however, we must address the definition problem.

What Is Re-engineering?

Re-engineering has two, widely held definitions. The *GUIDE Project on Application Re-engineering* defines re-engineering as a means to improve current systems without impacting current functions, technology platforms or architectures. The *GUIDE Project on Reverse Engineering* reiterated this belief adding that re-engineering may be viewed as a way to prepare systems for reverse engineering.

The IEEE however, views re-engineering as an umbrella technology, encompassing restructuring, reverse engineering and eventual system regeneration through forward engineering. While terminology need not concern most MIS professionals, they should be aware that there are differences. In this article, the IEEE definition of re-engineering will be used since it meets most organizations' broad use of the term. The term re-development will be used to include both re-engineering, and all the necessary ancillary analysis activities.

The Re-development Framework

The purpose of a re-development framework is to clearly define a set of individual activities. These are comprised of methods and tools that collectively serve to analyze, position and transform existing information systems into the desired systems of the future. This conceptual framework provides MIS professionals with:

Author: William Ulrich, Tactical Strategy Group, Aptos, CA. This article has been reprinted from the Nov./Dec. 1990 to May/June 1991 issues of *CASE Trends* magazine, © 1992, Software Productivity Group, Inc. *CASE Trends* magazine reports on the use of advanced information and software technology. Address: PO Box 294-MO, Shrewsbury, MA 01545-0294. 508/393-7100, fax 508/393-3388.

- A common point of reference for diverse re-development activities.

- An integrated structure defining points of interchange and flow between apparently disparate technologies.

- A clear statement of short and long-term benefits for each re-development activity to support later cost justification.

- A guide for reconciling re-development activities with accepted, top-down development methodologies.

- A foundation that, when coupled with an organization's unique business and technical needs, serves as a basis for a customized re-development strategy.

The overriding philosophy permeating the re-development framework is that each activity within the framework has value in and of itself. Thus, cost benefit should be derived from individual re-development activities while positioning the organization to pro-

ceed to a subsequent stage. Secondly, this framework must be reconciled with traditional, top-down development methodologies. Re-development supports planning, analysis and design. It is not meant to replace these activities, nor is it meant to displace careful business analysis of a given situation. The concluding deployment decision for any re-development activity must be driven by evaluating alternatives and taking the most judicious course of action. Lastly, employing a re-development alternative demands attention from senior level management. Without a "guiding light" at senior levels, re-development attempts will fall short of expectations.

Re-development Framework: A Three Stage Approach

The re-development framework supports many activities that MIS organizations are already performing. The three main components of this framework are:

- Inventory/Analysis
- Positioning
- Transformation.

Since individual re-development activities can be cost justified on their own merit, only those components of value to a particular organization need be applied. MIS organizations should have a clear understanding of the entire framework at the outset, since implementation decisions in early stages may impact the timing and approach used during later stages. The three stages of the re-development framework and typical activities are shown in Figure 1.

Taken in its entirety, these activities would require extensive effort for any but the most trivial of systems. The point is, that while many organizations cannot currently take systems into the Transformation stage, they can gain significant and immediate benefit from Inventory/Analysis and Positioning activities. This can be accomplished with an eye towards final transformation to new technologies and integrated architectures. Note that in our discussion, the Transformation stage implies populating current data and functions into newly designed architectures, whereas simple language, hardware or DBMS conversions are considered Positioning activities.

INVENTORY/ANALYSIS

Technical Assessment

- Environmental Analysis
- Process Analysis
- Data Definition Analysis
- Architecture Analysis

Functional Assessment

- Bottom-up Data Modeling
- Bottom-up Functional Mapping
- Current to New Data Mapping
- Current to New Functional Mapping

Re-development Feasibility Assessment

- System Weighting Factor Analysis
- Re-development Strategy Creation
- Interim System Support
- Re-development Plan
- Cost Assessment
- Data Migration

POSITIONING

- Language Translation/Upgrade
- Source Code Restructuring
- Data Definition Rationalization and Standardization
- Code Splitting/Code Re-aggregation
- Data/Process Rule Externalization
- Redundancy Consolidation & Elimination

TRANSFORMATION

- Architecture Reconciliation
- Logical Data & Process Mapping
- Physical Data & Process Mapping
- System/Sub-system Migration
- System Regeneration
- Data/DBMS Migration

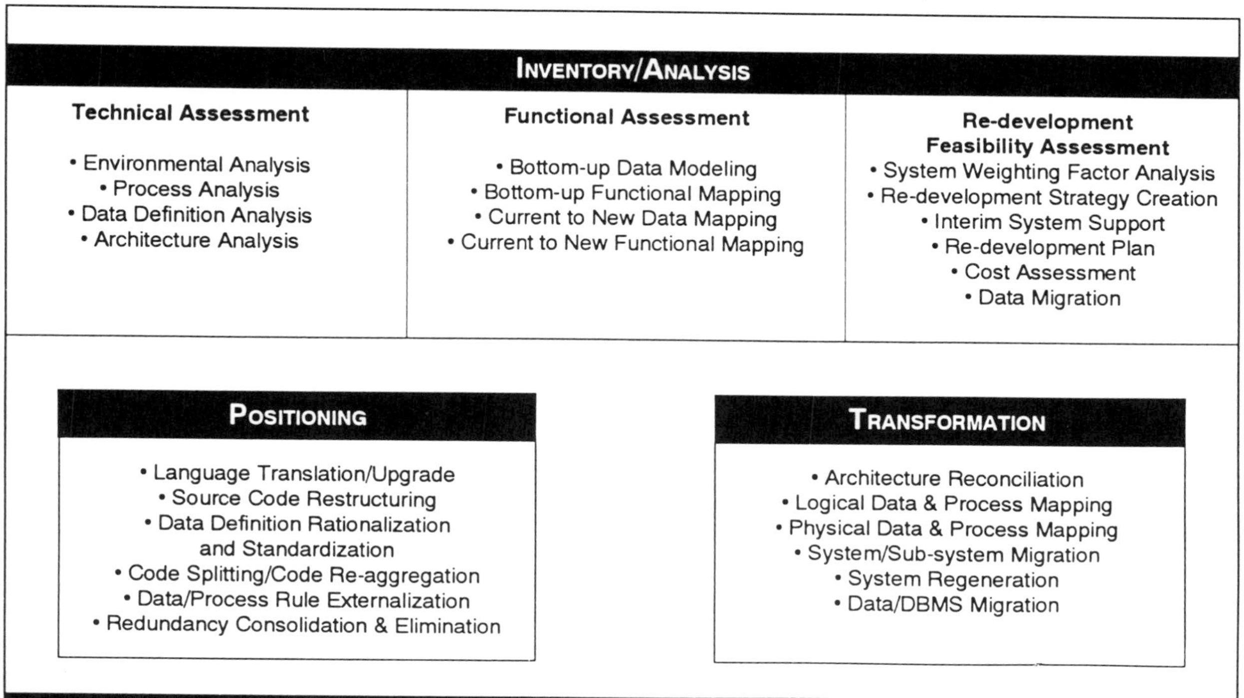

Figure 1. Re-development Framework—A Three Stage Approach

Within a given sub-category, certain activities provide significant payback to an organization. For example, Process Analysis, under the Technical Assessment class of the Inventory/Analysis stage, delivers physical documentation to technicians while providing management with planning and quality metrics for the application portfolio. Deliverables derived from Process Analysis simplify short-term maintenance efforts while feeding into the longer term planning process. Similarly, Source Code Restructuring under the Positioning stage delivers short-term improvements in code understandability while stabilizing code for eventual reuse in the Transformation stage.

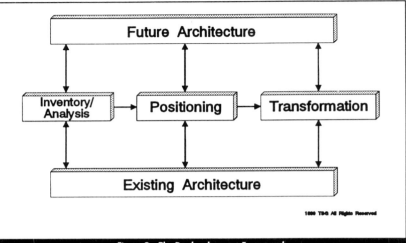

Figure 2. The Re-development Framework

Defining the Problem

Most MIS organizations typically select and obtain re-development tools before clearly defining the short-term and long-term benefits to be derived from these tools. Often as a consequence, organizations find themselves inundated with a library full of *"productivity tool shelfware."* Defining a high-level strategy first, and then concentrating on mission critical components, allows an organization to select the right tools and maximize benefit once implemented. This is not to imply that an entire, three-stage strategy must be in place before procuring tools. In fact, it would be difficult or impossible to identify a concise Positioning and Transformation strategy before completing certain Inventory/Analysis activities. Indeed, these activities require certain tools.

Although this discussion is primarily focused on framework and strategy, we should point out a few important product related issues. Tools being marketed as analyzers tend to be useful in all three stages, not just the Inventory/Analysis stage. Tools that 'discover' or abstract information about the current system and transform this information into a reusable, abstract format are typically called reverse engineering tools. While reverse engineering is a key component of Transformation, the discovery components of these tools

support planning during Inventory/Analysis. Finally, certain tools may cross all three stages of the re-development framework. This should be considered when building a case for software acquisition.

Why Re-engineer?

Why even bother investigating the possibility of reusing or extending the life of the current system when evaluating new development or package purchase options? One view is that the information derived from the Inventory/Analysis stage of the re-development framework can also serve as input to making a build or buy decision, particularly when preliminary information and process models have been developed for the new system. Mapping data and process models derived from current systems to models derived from user-driven requirements can provide a "hybrid architecture." This would be useful in assessing the choice to build, buy or re-engineering. At a minimum, top-down models will be validated against existing systems, and will most likely uncover inaccuracies early in the design cycle.

While conceding that the Inventory/Analysis stage has value, some argue that the Positioning stage is an extraneous activity. Positioning activities tend to be cost justifiable regardless of the decision to proceed with Transformation activities. Since restructuring and

data definition rationalization make a system more amenable to change, these activities may be justified based on reduced system support costs, manpower realignment and prolonged life of the current system. Some organizations view this as a safety net, extending the life of the current system in case the new development effort or package acquisition encounters problems. In the interim, current systems continue to support user requirements while being positioned for potential transformation.

The typical argument against full-scale Transformation is that old systems represent dated methods and do not support new business requirements. This is true to the degree that data access, presentation interfaces and functional execution flow do change under new architectures. However, key business rules tend to remain unchanged. The decision not to take a system through the Transformation stage is one of economics and measured risk reduction, since core data and business rules typically remain intact.

Where To Begin

As evidenced by the re-development framework, and the numerous activities underlying this framework, the question of whether or not to re-engineer is a complex one. Organizations should perform in-depth Inventory/Analysis work, and even certain Positioning activities, before making a Transformation decision. This effectively allows organizations to develop input to major replacement decisions while improving current systems and positioning them for the future. Re-engineering, as defined under the re-development framework, can be successful if various activities are evaluated for their short-term value, as well as their value under a broader strategy. Ignoring basic business and economic justification, acquiring tools before mapping out a strategy and arguing against re-engineering on groundless points are not an effective way to begin. Outlining clear and economically feasible alternatives to evolve current systems to meet long-term organizational demands clearly is.

PART II

A recent Index Group survey identified re-engineering as the "number one critical issue" in the minds of over 400 top MIS executives. With senior MIS personnel targeting this relatively new discipline as a number one priority, the industry will see an increased emphasis on planning, cost/benefit analysis, asset management and increased support for rapid organizational change. The demand to objectively assess a broad range of MIS alternatives will increase while the blind application of new technology, no matter how promising, will become a thing of the past. This emphasis on planning and analysis is critical not only in achieving re-engineering success, but in avoiding bad MIS investments in general. Stage one of the Re-development Framework (Figure 2), focuses on these key planning issues. Part One of the series established basic migration requirements and an overview of the "Re-development Framework." This section outlines how inventory, analysis and planning activities support the development of an integrated MIS migration strategy.

Why Inventory/Analysis?

To gain a proper perspective on the Inventory/Analysis stage of the Re-development Framework, let us exam-

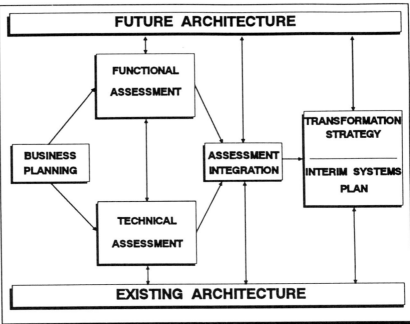

Figure 3. *Inventory / Analysis*

ine management's historical motivation behind decisions driving large scale MIS initiatives. When faced with mounting pressure to enact significant change requests, MIS has typically turned to either a 'build' or 'buy' scenario. These requests typically involve non-trivial architectural changes to one or more major systems, shifting the focus from simple maintenance to a major capital expenditure. Many organizations admit that past decisions have resulted in less than optimal returns on their investment. Now, with re-engineering as a third alternative, this decision process has been complicated even further.

Knowledgeable advocates of re-engineering view it as a hybrid solution, typically coupled with a build/buy scenario. This drives the decision process well beyond the perceived three-way matrix to an infinite myriad of solutions depending on numerous business and technical variables. MIS executives might be confused by this new and complex set of options. However, re-engineering presents significant opportunities to leverage current software assets. Inventory/Analysis allows MIS management to objectively evalu-

ate various investment alternatives based on current business and technical criteria - and select the best course of action available.

Leveraging Existing Software Assets

Inventory/Analysis is designed to augment, not replace, established analytical methods. Most development methodologies provide only cursory analysis of existing environments. The re-development approach assumes there is value to be gained by analyzing current production systems. Minimally, high-level models representing replacement systems may be validated against today's systems. At the other end of the spectrum, components salvaged from existing environments can help minimize the time, cost and risk involved in building new systems. Inventory/Analysis therefore supplements traditional business planning activities by providing another dimension of analysis: that of interrogating existing MIS environments.

The Integrated Assessment

Inventory/Analysis concurrently examines future information requirements and the existing software base.

Findings from these dual assessments provide the basis required to develop an integrated migration plan; a plan that supports both short-term and long-term information requirements. Key tasks include functional analysis, technical analysis and the creation of a comprehensive plan that outlines both tactical and strategic information alternatives. Each analysis phase, as shown in Figure 3, incorporates findings from a top-down (the way things should be) and a bottom-up (the way things are) view of the information systems architecture. A plan derived from this level of analysis reflects an accurate, objective and integrated view of reality; something not always available to the MIS executive.

The Functional Assessment

The functional assessment identifies future information requirements, captures and categorizes the existing system's functional capabilities and maps the level of conformance between these two views. The goal is to identify specific similarities and variances between planned systems and existing systems to determine opportunities for software reuse. Some organizations have a framework established to support top-down / bottom-up mapping. Many do not. To address functional mapping requirements, the Re-development Framework uses John Zachman's Information Systems Architecture Framework. Based on the Zachman Framework, an organization establishes a business plan, builds a business model and develops an information systems model. These top-down models, once completed, become the mapping target for information captured from the existing environment.

Bottom-up analysis is a relatively immature discipline. It is a key factor, however, in determining what role current systems play in the evolution of the strategic information architecture. Bottom-up analysis captures information about the data and functions active in today's systems. Data, the more static of the two, is captured and analyzed first. This is accomplished through Subject Matter Expert (SME)

interviews and automated analysis described in the next section. Captured data definitions are rationalized and imported to a data modeling tool. Entity Relationship (E/R) models derived from the current system are compared to models built during top-down analysis. Data element conformance is measured on a percentage basis. Assuming that current definitions represent a significant majority of key primary elements, functional analysis may begin.

Functions, for purposes of this analysis, are considered major system transformations. This definition may be adjusted as long as it is consistent for current/future mapping purposes. There are several methods for identifying specific functions within a system. While tools cannot specifically identify a business function, this is clearly a tools-assisted process. The Technical Assessment, defined below, supports system-level inventory and cross-reference as well as program process analysis. Cross-references and verb counts are used to classify and scope physical objects containing processing functions. This physical inventory, combined with a manual review of system and user documentation, establishes a basis for further analysis. The key to validating bottom-up functional analysis relies on interviews with user and technical SMEs.

Functional mappings between the current system and future designs are completed using a mapping chart that identifies planned function, current function, program name or names, system name and various physical attributes such as verb counts. Where no mapping exists in the old system, this must be clearly indicated. Results are summarized by assigning a reusability factor for each module, sub-system and system component.

The Technical/Architectural Assessment

The Technical/Architectural component of Inventory/Analysis provides an inventory of physical system objects, cross-reference analysis, quantitative and qualitative software metrics and an overview of the existing architecture. This information is collected

by various static analysis tools in order to facilitate the collection process. The goal of the technical assessment is to support the functional assessment defined above, drive software reusability cost analysis and provide input to an interim systems support plan.

Automated analyzers are available for major languages such as COBOL, PL/I or even Assembler as well as data definition languages, online monitors and job control languages. More obscure languages may require direct manual review to determine potential reuse. Basic tools include system-wide inventory and cross-reference analyzers, cross-module data definition analyzers, process analyzers, data modeling tools and, depending on the depth of analysis desired, data/functional reverse engineering facilities. While not always available, each tool category should be supported by a relational repository, graphical representation, cross-reference facilities and metrics analysis capabilities. Deliverables from this phase include qualitative reusability factors coupled with the functional analysis outlined above.

Building an Integrated MIS Plan

Any migration plan must obviously accommodate strategic MIS initiatives. It is equally important that such a plan support transitional activities that address immediate maintenance needs and other near-term MIS requirements. Components of the integrated MIS plan include a reusability assessment, a detailed positioning and transformation strategy, cost analysis and a supporting implementation plan. Long-term plans typically contain elements of reuse, new functions, architecture reconciliation activities and new technology. Interim support plans typically include restructuring, streamlining of maintenance functions, reallocation of key support personnel and support for major changes that cannot wait for a replacement system.

Large scale initiatives are generally driven by costs. Compromises are not unusual in today's environments. Specific migration scenarios, once various assessments are completed, may be recast and costs recalculated. Management will be able to execute decisions based on economic data supported by objective risk analysis. Cost analysis is a critical factor in most MIS decisions and an integral component in an integrated information migration plan.

If You Don't Know Where You Are

Watts Humphrey stated in his most recent book, "if you don't know where you are, a map won't help." When building an integrated information strategy, organizations must clearly define an end target through top-down planning. This is the map. Today, organizations are beginning to realize the need to add another dimension to this analysis. Formal, bottom-up analysis provides this added dimension. The results obtained from Inventory/Analysis allows organizations to determine "where they are." This vital component of the information planning process must not only be recognized by senior management - it must be demanded from the outset.

PART III

The term 'Positioning' may seem to imply that activities in this stage of the Re-development Framework provide little or no immediate organizational benefit. In fact, benefits accrued with the use of positioning tools and techniques include maintenance productivity improvement, system failure rate reduction and the realization of a wide range of short-term priorities. Positioning, stage two of the Re-development Framework shown in Figure 2, supports a variety of tactical requirements while concurrently moving systems and organizations towards their strategic goals. This discussion centers on Positioning motivational factors, pertinent tools and techniques, and the fostering of management understanding and support.

Positioning: Strategic and Tactical Impact

An information strategy aimed at meeting the business and technical demands facing today's MIS executive must address both short-term and long-term requirements concurrently. Posi-

tioning activities, such as restructuring or data definition rationalization, were largely dismissed because many of the systems that could benefit were targeted for replacement. As the industry matured, these technologies evolved to become key components under long-term migration strategies. However, economic realities dictate that the procurement and deployment of technological solutions deliver rapid and quantifiable investment returns. One main benefit of the Positioning approach is the ability to satisfy these more immediate needs while supporting longer range goals.

A major difficulty in introducing Positioning to an organization is that of posturing this technology as a solution to legitimate business concerns. Senior management personnel generally have a limited understanding of technology and have been misled by past claims of "quick fix" solutions. MIS should recast specific technical requirements in business terms that management understands. These requirements typically have both immediate and long range implications. For example, system replacement efforts typically last several years. Existing systems must continue to support user requests in the interim. Positioning improvements help simplify maintenance efforts and free MIS personnel to support new design activities. The improved system may also serve as a basis for design verification. MIS plans must therefore identify business and technical initiatives, the strategies to accomplish these initiatives and the tactics to both implement and augment long-term strategies.

Defining Positioning Activities

Before discussing the motivational forces behind Positioning, it is important to overview this stage of the framework. A common thread links the various Positioning technologies. Positioning tools and techniques improve the quality of existing systems without affecting the functions or the basic architecture upon which those systems were built. Activities include language change, program restructuring, data

definition rationalization, data migration and externalization and the re-aggregation of system components. These are source code to source code transformations. Figure Four highlights these Positioning activities and a common sequence of events. Based on specific system requirements, one or more of these activities may be applied.

Once these various transformations are completed, systems are easier to understand and easier to change. Case studies support this fact. A second, and key component of the Positioning strategy is that improved systems serve as a foundation from which new systems may be spawned. Motivating factors behind this technology begin with real business limitations and concerns.

Business and Technical Motivating Factors

An insurance company is downsizing a major system to put workstation technology into regional offices. A telecommunications company has multiple billing systems as a result of operations consolidation. A financial institution's order entry system no longer supports huge increases in business volume. A mission critical manufacturing system relies on obsolete and dangerously aging technology. When MIS management is confronted with these issues, the options seem quite limiting.

The typical MIS response to these widely varying demands reflects dated thinking that no longer serves the best interests of the organization. Admittedly, many new systems are being built with integrated methodologies and CASE technology. Also, packages are still a viable solution in certain cases. Nevertheless, decisions as to how and when these solutions are implemented are often made in haste and without considering recent technological breakthroughs. Today, with the facilities available under the Re-development Framework, management is obligated to investigate a broader range of information alternatives. The process of assessing these alternatives involves probing beyond claims that "we must shift more resources from maintenance to new development" or "we need a replacement system in two years." To accomplish this goal, MIS must categorically analyze MIS demands, pursue the in-depth analysis outlined under the Inventory/Analysis stage and consider the practical applications for the Positioning capabilities outlined.

Practical Applications for Positioning Technology

A number of scenarios exemplify how Positioning technology supports benefit oriented solutions. These scenarios include system replacement, package implementation, wide-spread growth, technological obsolescence and system consolidation or integration. Positioning can augment or supplant traditional "scrap and replace" or package purchase options while supporting many other needs.

System replacement is driven by a variety of needs. Close examination usually reveals that pure technological change does not justify total replacement. Assuming a replacement scenario, Positioning technology leverages development efforts in several ways. Program restructuring and data definition rationalization stabilize and standardize existing systems so experienced personnel can be diverted to new development. Existing systems are also an excellent source of information to temper new designs, ensuring that critical data and functions are included in the new system. An organization may wish to reuse system components ranging from screen layouts to complex calculations. Elimination of system redundancies and inconsistencies prepares systems for reverse engineering analysis and component reuse. Finally, data conversions require analysis of current data structures. This is greatly simplified after record level rationalization.

Package implementation efforts tend to stall during the customization and integration stages. Analyzers defined in the Inventory/Analysis stage are useful in identifying data structures within packages and within in-house systems being integrated with those packages. Once identified, structural inconsistencies may be rationalized and recon-

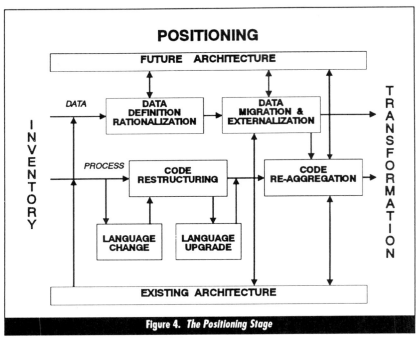

Figure 4. The Positioning Stage

ciled across disparate systems, supporting the goal of shared data between and among in-house systems and purchased packages.

Rapid growth, mergers and acquisitions all drive system capacities beyond intended levels. Field and record size expansion, a rationalization subactivity, alleviated a $50 million rewrite at one mutual funds company. Another common concern, technological obsolescence, tends to prompt rewrite initiatives. Unless obsolescence forces an architectural change, activities including COBOL to COBOL II, CICS Macro to Command or file access upgrades provide interim solutions. Interim solutions can be delivered faster than complete rewrites while establishing a baseline for eventual replacement. Another major issue, system consolidation, is supported by in-depth analysis and standardization techniques. Data definition rationalization, restructuring and various re-aggregation techniques simplify the identification of reusable or redundant components, creating the foundation for an integrated system. Under these scenarios, positioning can avert expensive, time consuming and risk prone

replacement alternatives typically embraced by MIS traditionalists.

Positioning Tools and Techniques

Each Positioning category shown in Figure Four includes a mix of software tools and human engineering techniques. Each category relies on a diverse mix, depending on the maturity of the tool and the task at hand. Positioning tools tend to be the most mature in the re-engineering technology set. The Positioning activity, tools, techniques and benefits are discussed below. Analyzer support, defined in the Inventory/Analysis stage, is inherent in the various tasks.

Language change is a starting point for many organizations. Reasons include lack of an application package, the cost and complexity of creating a new system, SAA compliance, lack of support personnel or preparing a system for respecification and reuse. Most tools convert a given language to COBOL. Systems targeted for production should undergo further standardization since converted source code is quite cryptic. Full-scale conversion is an expensive proposition, suggesting that other avenues be fully explored before proceeding. A second language change objective, that of recapturing 'lost' data or functions, converts a system as a prelude to applying industry standard analyzers or reverse engineering tools. This is useful when system documentation is unavailable. Since full-scale conversion involves multiple QA checkpoints and a myriad of complex tools and techniques, organizations should proceed only after developing an integrated conversion plan with help from experienced professionals. Language to specification 'conversion' involves architectural changes and is addressed under the Transformation stage.

Program restructuring is perhaps the most widely known and widely used Positioning technology. COBOL restructuring first emerged in the early 1980s. Initial infatuation with restructuring tools had the unfortunate effect of forcing vendors to automate the handling of code constructs that tend to degrade, not improve, program quality. Organizations blindly applying these tools lack the understanding and techniques to fully leverage them. On the other hand, restructuring tools have been tremendously successful in effecting maintenance productivity improvement, defect reduction, personnel reallocation and in positioning code for subsequent analysis and enhancement. These tools, used by knowledgeable personnel equipped with the appropriate analyzers, will continue to play a key role in preparing systems for eventual design recovery and reuse.

Data definition rationalization is an established, yet relatively unused, Positioning capability. This may be attributed to the fact that motivating factors behind rationalization and standardization generally fall into the long range category. This includes dictionary/repository migration, re-documentation, elimination of error prone redundancies and preparation for redesign efforts. Since data definition changes include the consolidation of redundant records and global renam-ing, entire systems are affected. These are generally large scale projects that are difficult to justify solely on maintenance productivity improvement – although this is a documented benefit.

A subset facility of the rationalization category is field and record size expansion. The requirement for field and record size expansion is self explanatory. Both the rationalization and the field expansion process follow a similar methodological approach using the same basic tools. Human engineering skills are critical in this area since much of the work requires human decision making interface support. Demand for rationalization and field/record size expansion will increase as more organizations attempt bottom-up analysis of existing data structures and as system capacities continue to be exceeded.

Code re-aggregation is a largely unexplored Positioning category due to the relative immaturity of the tools and techniques. Re-aggregation is the repositioning of system components to more adequately reflect functional requirements. Activities include code splitting, recombining functions, table externalization and logic redundancy reconciliation. Motivating factors include improving user responsiveness and preparing systems for respecification and reuse. In the case of table externalization, updates previously made by MIS can be externalized for direct user access. Re-aggregation projects are motivated by immediate MIS needs but should consider long-term issues as well. For example, code splitting divides monolithic modules, streamlining enhancement efforts. Moreover, split points should be selected based on functional realignment requirements.

Re-aggregation requires program analysis and logic tracing tools, McCabe metrics and cross-system analysis capabilities. Automated assistance is available to pinpoint split points, identify embedded data structures and suggest logic redundancies. In contrast, human engineering abilities are critical to re-aggregation success and must evolve further before widespread deployment occurs.

Validating Systems

Positioning, by our earlier definition, changes form not function. This does not mean that a project utilizing these techniques would not include functional upgrades or even architectural changes. It does mean that correctness should be proven at the end of each self-contained phase. This ensures that audit trails are established and system integrity is maintained. As improved systems return to production, a key benefit of the phased Positioning approach, maintenance personnel can apply functional upgrades with impunity from a given Positioning change. This approach assumes that systems work identically before and after Positioning activities are completed. Proving equivalence is called validation and accomplished by running before and after comparisons. Variations on this approach can be taken by experienced professionals but not suggested for the novice re-developer.

Justification - Where to Begin

A solid business case must be developed prior to initiating a Positioning project. The motivating factors outlined in this article serve as the basis for some of the more common scenarios. Historically, organizations have attempted to build cost justification around a specific tool. This is a backwards approach. Organizations should rather identify business goals for a given area, reduce these goals to a series of interim and long-term objectives, outline an action plan to meet these multi-level objectives and define the tools and techniques to accomplish each action item. In following this approach, MIS will avoid many of the pitfalls associated with bottom-up tool/project cost analysis and begin to function more strategically. Finally, Positioning is not designed to replace business analysis, system replacement initiatives or package implementation efforts. It is specifically designed to support and augment these traditional endeavors and allow organizations to more effectively leverage existing information assets in the process.

PART IV

As MIS pressures mount, organizations continue to pursue three traditional alternatives; build a new system, buy a package or just maintain. While any one decision may be correct under a given scenario, two points are clear. The way decisions are made must be refined and, once made, the process used to implement a given decision must improve. Inventory/Analysis supports this decision making process while Positioning and Transformation drive various implementation scenarios. While Positioning focuses on near-term requirements, Transformation supports strategic objectives. Regardless of a decision to build, buy or maintain, migration to strategic architectures, integration of 'island' systems, deployment of new technology and implementation of new functionality are all common MIS goals supported by Transformation.

Why Transformation?

As MIS executives crystallize a strategic vision, the question of how this vision will be realized typically remains unanswered. Under the Inventory/Analysis stage, current and future architectures play a key role in near-term and long-term planning.

In other words, the state of the information infrastructure today will, at least to some degree, dictate how and when strategic architectures are achieved. Positioning addresses short-term maintenance needs while concurrently preparing systems for potential reuse under new architectures. Transformation is a natural outgrowth of the planning and positioning process. Unfortunately, many organizations take this step prematurely. Assuming an organization conforms to the guidelines in stages one and two of the Re-development Framework, Transformation is the vehicle driving the implementation of new technologies, new functionality and strategic architectures.

One important point in achieving this vision is the use of a development model as a mapping target for re-engineering activities. This is required because the Re-development model supplements, rather than supplants, various analysis, design and development activities. The Inventory/Analysis discussion utilized the Zachman Model to map re-engineering activities to planning and high-level designs. Since Transformation focuses at the implementation level, a more rigorous paradigm is required.

For this reason, re-engineering activities defined under the Transformation stage are mapped to the Information Engineering methodology. If an organization uses a different methodology, this should be the target of Re-development mapping. If an organization has no development methodology, one should be established before proceeding.

Transformation Scenarios - Driving the Process

Component reuse in the development of new systems has been in use for decades by programmers who understand the value of not reinventing key functionality. Formalization of this process under the Re-development Framework recognizes the value of reuse early in the planning, analysis and design cycle. By doing so, reuse becomes a strategy driven by management, not by programmers. Transformation supports reuse under Information Engineering's Design and Construction phases. Figure Five identifies various Transformation activities and assumes that replacement systems are to be created using an integrated CASE tool. The application of various Transformation activities is driven by specific organizational requirements. Transformation scenarios, developed during Inventory/Analysis and refined during Positioning, ultimately drive the Design and Construction process.

For example, an organization may wish to implement cooperative processing, consolidate corporate data under a relational data base, integrate stand-alone functions under a single system and significantly change how a given component of the business functions. Management may initially assume that there is no element of reuse under this scenario. However, Inventory/Analysis ultimately determines if component reuse is of value and if it is cost beneficial in a given situation. If it is not, Transformation may not be applicable. If the target has changed, the Inventory/Analysis process must be repeated. The point being that, each case is different and implementation scenarios must be adjusted accordingly. The following discussion views Transformation generically, facilitating a broad view of the process and its application.

Establishing a Baseline & Technology Support

After completion of Inventory/Analysis, organizations have established a software inventory, a conceptual data model representing a merger of current and future entities and a high-level mapping of current and future functions. They should also have a Transformation plan and an analysis, outlining the cost of component reuse versus 'from scratch' development. Since systems are in flux, organizations must establish a systems baseline and manage change between that baseline and the image being re-engineered. Changes that may have occurred since the planning stage include functional upgrades, maintenance changes and Positioning changes such as restructuring, data definition rationalization or related activities. If a change control process has not been established, this would be the time.

Tool support varies depending on the particular undertaking but, in general, most of the following technology of use. In order to view the entire system at the meta-model level, organizations should use a reverse engineering tool that can analyze, store and cross-reference as many physical objects as possible from the current system. The supporting repository should allow relational cross-reference, extensions for non-standard object types and impact analysis reflecting object

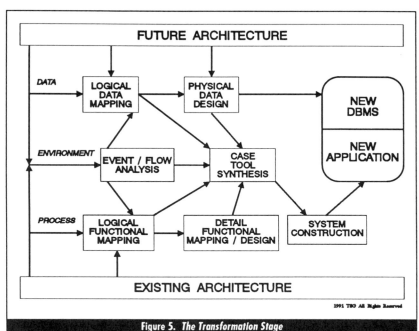

Figure 5. The Transformation Stage

changes. The lower the level of object granularity and cross-reference capability the better. A related facility allows for cross-reference reporting on these objects and, if available, metric analysis.

Organizations must be able to capture, refine and merge current and future data definitions using formal modeling processes. This requires a data definition reverse engineering tool to load a refinement repository, create a first-cut E/R model, further normalize the model using rationalized data definitions and integrate bottom-up objects with top-down models. One additional tool examines physical data from existing file structures and supports further refinement of logical and physical data models utilizing AI techniques.

Tools required on the functional side capture information from the current system, store this information in a relational repository and allow analysts to run inquiries against the repository to verify certain functional assertions about the existing system. Unfortunately, functional analysis of the current system is clearly the weakest area in terms of tool support. Much analysis requires the use of component

documentors for screen maps, JCL flows, report layouts and other information analysts could use to intuitively decipher system functionality. Finally, a facility to export captured physical objects from the reverse engineering repository into various levels of an I-CASE repository/encyclopedia supports the Transformation activities below.

Transformation Activities

Three general categories of physical system objects may be reused in the development of strategic systems. Environmental objects controlling screen I/O, execution flow, file access, data base definitions and related objects support event analysis and subsequent data and functional analysis. Data definition analysis supports the development of a global data model that is initiated in the Inventory/Analysis stage and refined during the Transformation stage. Procedural reuse focuses on key business functions that prove too time consuming, costly or risky to recreate from scratch. A function is defined based on the organization's development methodology. For example, Information Engineering defines a

function as a group of processes under a business segment. There is no need to redefine terminology for re-engineering purposes when terms already are defined under the accepted development paradigm.

Environmental Objects: Analysis & Reuse

Many believe that the only information required for component reuse is derived from source code data and/or process definitions. In contrast, physical objects, including JCL, Sorts, CICS Tables, Data Definition Language, screen maps and connectors such as Copy and Call structures, all have value. These components represent processing controls that serve as input to design efforts or that may be reused in the new system. System objects are loaded into the relational repository using an environmental reverse engineering tool during Inventory/Analysis. This information must be updated frequently as the production system evolves. Reverse engineering tools can transverse various control objects, such as JCL, into a form useful to certain I-CASE tools, assuming conformance to the new design.

Data Architecture Reconciliation

Under the Inventory/Analysis stage, organizations build a strategic information plan resulting in the development of conceptual information models. These models form the mapping target for data captured from the existing environment. Bottom-up analysis captures and categorizes existing data and maps this data to top-down, strategic models. The objective is to temper top-down conceptual designs with entities derived from existing systems. These first cut Entity Relationship (E/R) models serve as the basis for a multilevel, data architecture.

First cut E/R data models, initiated during Inventory/Analysis, are normalized and attributed during Transformation, utilizing data definitions rationalized during Positioning. This provides 'clean' data as input to the bottom-up component of the model. The process utilizes a modeling tool capable of merging top-down and bottom-up entities based on input from skilled data analysts. Physical data base designs are an outgrowth of this model. Information from the environmental analysis is available to locate and further identify physical data structures as required. Data migration and purification planning begins at this stage as well. Upon completion and refinement, these models are imported into various levels of the I-CASE repository/ encyclopedia.

Functional Reuse

Tools cannot specifically identify a concise business function. It is very much, however, a tools-assisted process. Functional reuse, under the Information Engineering model, occurs at the Design and Construction level. Four general approaches are considered, depending on the objectives of a given situation. The first approach relies on manual analysis of structured source code while building detail designs, typically in the form of action diagrams. This approach is useful if the code is structured and a knowledgeable analyst identifies specific functions or algorithms for reuse. On a large scale, however, this approach is impractical.

Remaining approaches utilize automated reverse engineering tools, capable of capturing existing process logic, storing it in an intermediate repository and transversing existing representations into those used by the CASE tool. In the case of Information Engineering, this would be an action diagram. The first of these automated approaches involves capturing and moving all procedural logic from the existing system into an Action Diagram format. While technically possible, it tends to propagate old processes, including potential problems and unnecessary logic, into design level representations. Unnecessary logic includes hierarchical data base manipulations, screen handling routines or other logic that must be recreated under new designs and architectures. This facility has merit if the objective is current design understanding and not actual reuse.

The second automated approach utilizes selective transversal, moving only those procedural blocks useful in duplicating complex business functions. This requires a skilled business analyst with knowledge of the action diagraming process. This approach effectively uses what is required and allows mechanical I/O and data access logic to be generated through the CASE tool. The CASE tool is allowed to function as intended while reusing key functions in selected areas. This is the most difficult approach but tends to yield the most desirable results since it retains key functions under a new architecture.

The last of the automated approaches allows manipulation of all system objects within the intermediate repository, loading the CASE design tool after component refinement. The benefit of this approach is that captured logic has been refined under the system as a unit. One concern is that the new system will retain the weaknesses and inadequacies of the old architecture, nullifying the goals of designing a new system in the first place. In each of the four procedural re-engineering approaches, the focus remains on the human factor. Tools are meant to assist, not replace, analysts. In spite of the complexity, the benefit of reusing critical or complex functions in the development of new systems cannot be understated.

Once the I-CASE tool has imported relevant designs, event flows and reusable functions, work is still required to create a cohesive, functioning system. As stated earlier, Transformation augments the development of new systems, it does not supersede the process. However, in light of the industry's recent track record of failed development projects, this is probably an alternative worth reviewing.

Cost Justifying the Transformation Approach

Cost justification for Transformation is a matter of assessing the feasibility and practicality of reusing components from the current system in the design and construction of replace-ment systems. Assuming various Positioning activities are justified under an interim support plan and that component reuse can reduce design and construction efforts, the cost of reuse should be weighed against the cost of from scratch development. This makes the decision of reuse one of economics. One intangible that can justify reuse in and of itself is risk reduction. Occasionally, certain capabilities must be retained and cannot be recreated accurately from scratch. In these cases, reuse is mandated since from scratch development may not deliver the required functionality.

The Transformation stage of the Re-development Framework utilizes powerful re-engineering technology. The technology exists and continues to evolve. The challenge is to harness its power to improve the way organizations develop systems. Undirected use of this technology may propagate errors or unneeded logic into integrated CASE tools and strategic architectures, causing more harm than good. Thorough planning, good management and careful analysis will prevent this from occurring and benefit organizations tremendously.   ✳

William Ulrich is principal of the Tactical Strategy Group, (Aptos, CA), a consulting firm specializing in re-development engineering strategies, and deployment.

CASE TRENDS® *is published nine times a year by Software Productivity Group, Inc., PO Box 294-MO, Shrewsbury, MA 01545-0294, 508/842-4500. Annual subscription rate is $37.00. CASE TRENDS magazine reports on the use of advanced information technology for the development of software systems.*

Reverse Engineering Newsletter

Subcommittee on Reverse Engineering
Technical Committee on Software Engineering IEEE Computer Society

© 1992 IEEE Computer Society / TCSE   no. 2   April 1992   Editor: Jon Clark

Message from the Chair
James H. Cross II
Auburn University

One year ago, meeting at the Reverse Engineering Forum at St. Louis, this subcommittee was formed. We adopted as our purpose:

"• To increase the awareness of technologies for the understanding of existing systems; and,

"• To encourage the advancement of reverse engineering, reengineering, design recovery, and related approaches."

In only our first year of operation, we are making good headway. We now have 370 members. Our newsletter's premier was well-received. Projects that members have suggested are taking shape.

The subcommittee will hold its next general meeting as part of the 3rd Reverse Engineering Forum, to be held September 15-17, 1992 in Burlington, Mass. (Boston area), hosted by Northeastern University. The Forum will again be a combined industry / university review of the state of the art and the state of the practice in reverse engineering and reengineering. Forum registration information will be mailed directly to all subcommittee members by mid-June. If you would like to propose making a presentation on your experience, research, or tool, promptly contact the subcommittee secretary, Elliot Chikofsky, at e.chikofsky@compmail.com or (617)280-4560.

The subcommittee will also sponsor a research working conference in May 1993 in conjunction with the International Conference on Software Engineering (ICSE-15 Baltimore). This limited attendance working meeting, to be co-sponsored with us by ACM Sigsoft, is being co-chaired by Dick Waters (Mitsubishi Electric Research Lab) and Elliot Chikofsky (Northeastern Univ).

We are open to suggestions for new projects. The possibilities are limitless. Please feel free to contact me, even if it is only to discuss the first glimmer of an idea. We're a new field. There are a lot of opportunities, and we have the interested people to pursue them.

James Cross, (205)844-4330
cross@eng.auburn.edu

Send submissions to:
Reverse Engineering Newsletter
c/o Jon D. Clark, editor
CIS Department, C115 Clark Bldg.
College of Business
Colorado State University
Fort Collins, CO 80523 USA
303-491-6203; jclark@vines.colostate.edu

Common Risks of Reengineering
Robert S. Arnold
Software Evolution Technology

© 1992 Robert S. Arnold

Problems in planning and performing software reengineering can be reduced by anticipating risks, making plans to avoid them, and mitigating their effect should they occur. This article will give several reengineering risks and ideas for mitigating them. For space reasons, this article can only scratch the surface of this topic. The article is for those planning or managing reengineering or reverse engineering work.

Several assumptions are made. First, you have decided or determined that reengineering is needed in your environment. This may seem obvious, but one risk is applying software reengineering to solve the symptoms of a problem rather than determining what the problem cause(s) are and applying software reengineering IF APPROPRIATE. For example, if code is hard to understand, the problem could be high maintainer turnover rather than problems inherent in the code. (Maintainers may not be staying long enough to understand the software and pass this understanding on.) High maintainer turnover may be due to non-software factors, such as an impending corporate downsizing causing staff to scurry for secure jobs. Software reengineering alone would not ease staff worries.

A second assumption is that these are risks in general. They may appear in slightly different forms in your environment. Finally, each environment has its own special risks. The list of risks below is not exhaustive.

[Arnold91a] classified reengineering risks into six areas--process, personnel, applications, technology, tools, and strategy--and gave several examples of risks in each area. The rest of this article summarizes six common reengineering risks. Each risk is described, its significance is discussed, and a possible mitigation strategy is suggested.

Risk 1. Overestimating the capabilities of current reengineering technology.

Sometimes people plan to do reengineering because a tool exists to help them. For some reengineering areas, such as COBOL restructuring, technology is fairly mature and much value has been added to the tools. In other areas, such as generating specifications or business rules from source code, the technology is less mature and is still advancing. The risk here is that a tool's capabilities are overestimated and (1) the tool does not support a reengineering task, or (2) effective ways to use the tool are not anticipated or understood.

To avoid this trap, tool capabilities need to be properly appreciated and tool expectations managed. You should ask others about their experience in solving, with the contemplated tool, a reengineering problem related to yours. To better assure that the tool adequately supports a step in your reengineering process or plan, you should (1) try the tool with the people who will use the tool in their reengineering work and (2) use realistic sample problems. You should ensure that previous reengineering steps provide the inputs needed for using the tool on the current step and that the outputs of the tool truly meet the information needs of succeeding reengineering steps. Naturally this should be done BEFORE a tool is purchased or leased.

A mitigation strategy for this risk is, if a tool does not support what is intended, then plans for doing the reengineering supported by the tool will likely have to be revised and workarounds created. The extent of the possible revisions and workarounds should be determined to be workable before the tool is adopted.

Risk 2. Failure to take personnel concerns into account in adopting reengineering technology.

At the current state of technology, reengineering frequently involves people in addition to tools. Often the people deciding that reengineering should be done are not the people who will actually DO the reengineering. People like to participate in decisions that affect them. The risk here is that if

---

Rev-1

the people asked to perform the reengineering tasks feel like pawns in a reengineering chess game, the reengineering task may end up checkmated (i.e., lengthened, done differently than intended, not done at all, done with resentment that leads to long term residual task difficulties, etc.). A mitigation strategy is to meet with your maintainers, listen and understand their views on the problem, ask them their opinions in solving problems, and use this information to design a solution that takes their observations and concerns into account. Involving people in the decision-making process will help them "buy into" the reengineering solution.

Risk 3. Failure to be able to demonstrate cost benefit.

Doing reengineering has costs and can be costly. It is worth getting some estimate of the up front tool purchase and staff training costs, per seat tool and hardware costs, return on investment, time frame for the return, amount of programming training needed, tool learning curve times, application learning curve times for new maintainers, costs of staff turnover and retraining of new staff, residual benefits such as value of reusable code obtained through software salvaging, and the value of increased software maintainability due to reengineering. The risks here are threefold: by not doing a cost benefit analysis based on detailed reengineering activities, you can underestimate the actual costs, run over budget, and be more susceptible to costly unanticipated activities. Another less obvious risk is that of being unprepared to account for maintenance or reengineering costs. At one site that was having maintenance cost problems, upper management demanded that the maintenance manager supply his top 10 cost drivers. The maintenance manager, not having collected maintenance cost data and fearing for his job scrambled to get together the drivers AND their justifications based on local data. If he had already collected such data, his trauma would have been reduced.

A mitigation for this risk is to turn to maintenance/reengineering cost and activity models, customize these for your environment, collect (or estimate) maintenance cost data, create immediate reports as needed, and begin to regularly assess, as part of ongoing maintenance management, activity costs and effectiveness.

Risk 4. Lack of a long range view.

Reengineering should be part of a long range program of software improvement or quality maintenance. Ideally, reengineering should only be done zero or once. Zero means reengineering is not needed at all. Once means reengineering is done and then there is no further need for reengineering. The risk here is that if reengineering is not part of a long range view for software improvement, reengineering may have to be redone by future maintainers. An implication is that reengineering is not addressing all the causes of software obsolescence. A mitigation strategy is to apply incremental reengineering [Arnold91b]. This strategy allows you to reengineer those parts of your software at your own pace and budget, while avoiding software obsolescence as software is maintained. The strategy starts with finding and reengineering only those software parts that are causing serious maintenance problems. Thereafter, the system is selectively improved in small increments based on modules modified during normal maintenance, while preserving previous quality instilled in the software.

Risk 5. Not reengineering the process in addition to the product.

This is related to the previous risk. The risk here is that reengineering may be focusing on the product, when in fact it is the maintenance process that is causing the problems. For example, if code is hard to maintain because documentation is out of date, you can reengineer the documentation to make it consistent with the software. However, if maintainers do not update documentation as part of their maintenance practice, then the documentation will soon be out of date. Reengineering in this case did not resolve the source of the problem, leaving you open to recurrences. If this risk happens to you, you should try to determine the source of your maintenance problems, determine if reengineering is appropriate for resolving the problem, and apply reengineering to do so when appropriate. Be prepared to apply non-reengineering solutions to resolve the problems.

Risk 6. Persisting in using high maintenance representations of software and documentation.

Maintaining software at the pure source code level is costly. We know that. The risk here is reengineering within maintenance paradigms that are known to be inherently costly. Reengineer as much as you want, but there are maintenance economies you cannot gain because you are sticking with a costly maintenance approach. For example, one of the ideas about repository-based software maintenance is to use the repository as the source of information about the system. In theory, if a maintainer leaves, the loss of knowledge is not as serious as without a repository. If the repository has been managed productively, much valuable information should remain in the repository. (One tool that promotes a repository-centered maintenance approach is InterCycle from InterPort Software Corporation, Fairfax, Virginia.) Another approach that is gaining popularity is model-based maintenance. In this approach, models are maintained and source code is automatically generated from the models. Much end source code maintenance is avoided. (IEF, from Texas Instruments, Plano, Texas, is an example of a tool supporting this approach.)

A mitigation, if you are caught in this risk, is to identify more productive maintenance approaches, and incrementally move toward them. Try to migrate to environments where maintenance tasks are better automated and the system maintains knowledge about the software. If you cannot do so now or feel that technology is not mature enough, then developing a migration plan will be helpful.

Notes
Robert Arnold may be contacted at Software Evolution Technology (SEVTEC), 12613 Rock Ridge Road, Herndon, Virginia 22070; 703-450-6791; r.arnold@compmail.com. Robert Arnold also works with the Software Productivity Consortium, 703-742-7149, arnold@software.org. Views presented here are the author's only.

Shawn Bohner provided many helpful comments for improving the content and readability of this article.

References
[Arnold91a] Arnold, R.S. Risks of Reengineering, Reverse Engineering Forum, April 1991.
[Arnold91b] Arnold, R.S. Software Reengineering (seminar notes), 1991.

Related Readings
[Boehm89] Boehm, B. W. Tutorial: Software Risk Management, IEEE CS Press, 1989.
[Charette89] Charette, R.N. Software Engineering Risk Analysis and Management, McGraw-Hill, 1989.

SOFTWARE MAINTENANCE: RESEARCH AND PRACTICE. VOL. 3, 163–182 (1991)

Economics of Software Re-engineering

HARRY M. SNEED

Software Engineering Service, Rosenheimer Landstrasse 37, 8012 Ottobrunn, Munchen, Germany

SUMMARY

There is a pressing need to be able to calculate and to justify the costs of software re-engineering. The purpose of the paper is to address that need by establishing a framework for the economics of re-engineering. The objective of re-engineering is to reduce maintenance costs. This objective is served by increasing quality and reducing complexity. Both of these goals are examined here in the light of software maintainability metrics. The costs of re-engineering are driven by the size and interdependency of the software as well as by the degree of automation available. The paper presents a method of estimating the costs of re-engineering, and presents some figures acquired through practical experience. Finally, a method is defined for weighing estimated costs against expected benefits in order to support decisions on whether to renovate existing software or replace it by a new development. This is a major decision faced by many industrial managers today.

KEY WORDS   Software economics   Re-engineering   Software-maintenance   Conversion

1. REVIEW OF MAINTENANCE ECONOMICS

The economics of software re-engineering should be viewed as a subdiscipline of software maintenance economics and this in turn as a subdiscipline of software engineering economics. The economic objectives of software engineering are outlined in the classic book of Barry Boehm on that subject (1981). The economic issues of software maintenance are dealt with in the landmark book of Lientz and Swanson (1980) as well as in Boehm's paper on the 'Economics of software maintenance' (1983).

The general position on maintenance economics is stated by Linda Brice (1981) that for every dollar spent on quality in development a dollar is saved in maintenance. There has been a series of studies in the past years to demonstrate the relationship between software quality and maintenance costs, but the evidence is still not conclusive. Nevertheless, the assumption persists and is the driving motive in the work of maintainability metrics.

There are, however, other factors which drive maintenance costs no less than the product quality (Nosek and Palvia, 1990). These are (see Figure 1):

—environment quality,
—personnel quality, and
—organizational quality.

164   H. M. SNEED

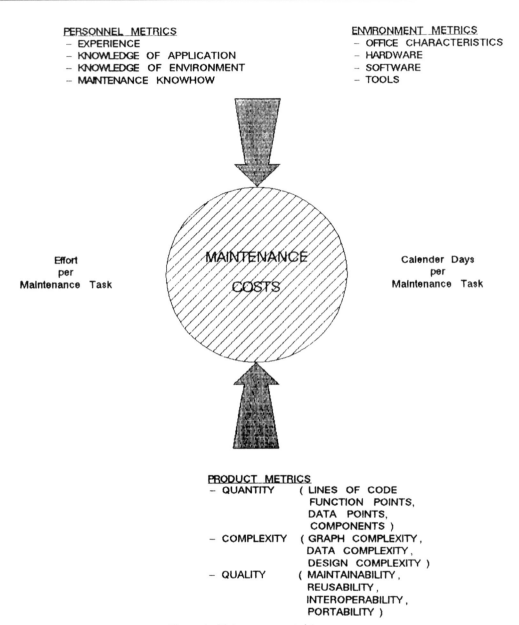

PERSONNEL METRICS
- EXPERIENCE
- KNOWLEDGE OF APPLICATION
- KNOWLEDGE OF ENVIRONMENT
- MAINTENANCE KNOWHOW

ENVIRONMENT METRICS
- OFFICE CHARACTERISTICS
- HARDWARE
- SOFTWARE
- TOOLS

Effort
per
Maintenance Task

MAINTENANCE COSTS

Calender Days
per
Maintenance Task

PRODUCT METRICS
- QUANTITY   (LINES OF CODE
                  FUNCTION POINTS,
                  DATA POINTS,
                  COMPONENTS)
- COMPLEXITY   (GRAPH COMPLEXITY,
                  DATA COMPLEXITY,
                  DESIGN COMPLEXITY)
- QUALITY   (MAINTAINABILITY,
                  REUSABILITY,
                  INTEROPERABILITY,
                  PORTABILITY)

Figure 1. Maintenance cost drivers

Even more than developers, software maintainers are dependent on the environment in which they work. Their productivity is determined by their workstation, their editor, their library system and their analysis tools. A maintenance programmer working on a highly automated graphical maintenance workbench is much more productive than one working on a conventional terminal with an antiquated editor and library system. Evidence to support this assertion was provided by a study at the Union Bank of Switzerland (Marty, 1990).

Personnel quality is, according to Boehm (1987), the most influential factor in driving development costs. There is no reason why this should not also apply to maintenance costs. Familiarity with the problem domain and the language are just as important in maintenance as in developments. In addition, the maintenance programmer must be familiar with the solution space itself. It takes someone who is familiar with the program only a fraction of the time to locate an error compared with someone to whom the program is absolutely unfamiliar. An otherwise highly gifted technician can be less effective than a less gifted person, depending on their domain knowledge. Thus, in dealing with the effect of personnel quality, the degree of familiarity plays a particularly important role in maintenance. This is why maintenance managers are so reluctant to part with their personnel.

Finally, there is the factor of maintenance organization. A well-organized, highly structured maintenance organization with change and configuration management is much more effective than an ad hoc maintenance shop, regardless of the quality of the product. If there are no control mechanisms for the maintenance process, the process will inevitably go out of control (Vallabhaneni, 1987). Uncontrolled processes produce a lot of entropy and are, therefore, less effective than well-controlled processes where the energy is directed. This is particularly true of software maintenance, where it is so easy to lose one's direction in the mass of details.

The maintenance cost factors listed above must all be considered when estimating maintenance costs. To some degree, this has been done by Boehm (1984) with his COCOMO equation for predicting maintenance effort (E_m) on the basis of (see Figure 2):

ANNUAL
MAINT – EFFORT = 1.2 ((ACT) (DEV – EFFORT)) (1.5 = QUAL)

ACT (ANNUAL CHANGE RATE) = Percent of Software deleted, altered and inserted

DEV – EFFORT = Man Months of Development Effort

QUALITY = Quality Factor 0.00 : 1.00

When ACT = 15 %
and DEV – EFFORT = 125 MM
and : QUAL = 0.3 BEFORE REENGINEERING

ANNUAL = 1.2 ((0.15) (125)) (1.5 – 0.3)
MAINT – EFFORT = 27 Man Months

IF QUAL = 0.6 AFTER REENGINEERING

ANNUAL = 1.2 (0.15) (125) (1.5 – 0.6)
MAINT – EFFORT = 20 Man Months
SAVINGS = 7 Man Months per annum

Figure 2. Estimating software maintenance costs (see Boehm, 1981)

—system type for which there is a given multiplication factor (MF),
—development costs in man-months (E_{d}),
—annual change rate, i.e. the number of changed and inserted lines of code (ACT),
—product quality (PQF)

$$E_{\mathrm{m}} = MF\,(ACT^{*}E_{\mathrm{d}})^{*}PQF$$

Product quality, product size and the product type are all accounted for in this equation, but the environment and the personnel are not. Maintenance costs are viewed as an extension of development costs, which may or may not be what they are. Therefore, Boehm's equation must be applied with caution. It can, however, serve to justify the higher costs of quality assurance and, as will be pointed out later, to justify the costs of re-engineering the product.

In summarizing maintenance economics, it must be stated that there is little established evidence to support the prediction of maintenance costs and that there is even less evidence on the benefits of maintenance. This makes it particularly difficult to justify software re-engineering projects on the basis of reduced maintenance costs and increased maintenance benefits. Most organizations have no means of measuring their maintenance productivity, but without that, there is no way to measure the benefits of re-engineering.

2. MEASURING SOFTWARE MAINTAINABILITY

Software maintenance is not one of the most popular jobs among software engineers. According to Yourdon (1988), maintaining a computer program is one of life's dreariest jobs, perhaps on the same level as picking cotton or digging ditches. It is not that programmers are afraid of maintenance, but rather that they look upon it as demeaning work. To be called a maintenance programmer is akin to being termed a second-class citizen.

Yourdon goes on to say that there are two ways of dealing with this problem. One is to eliminate maintenance as a job performed by human beings, as was done with cotton picking and ditch digging, both of which have been automated. The other way is to make the job more attractive, as was done with garbage collection and typing. The garbage collector becomes an environmental protection agent and the typist becomes a data processor. Reverse-engineering will not eliminate maintenance, but it can elevate the maintenance job by moving the software onto a more modern platform, where the maintenance programmer can use sophisticated tools to perform his job. The new environment will contribute to a better image of maintenance work which will, in turn, attract better-qualified people to the job.

Maintenance effort can be measured in different ways. One way is to observe how many person-hours are required to perform corrections, enhancements, and alterations. This is the common approach taken by many attempting to quantify maintainability. The problem with this approach is that it measures not only maintainability, but also the person doing the maintenance, as well as the environment in which the person is working and the tools the person is using. In fact, there are so many dependencies involved in measuring person-hours that, unless the measurements are applied to a statistically relevant number of maintenance programmers working in various maintenance environments with a cross sample of maintenance tools, the measurements are not valid (see Figure 3).

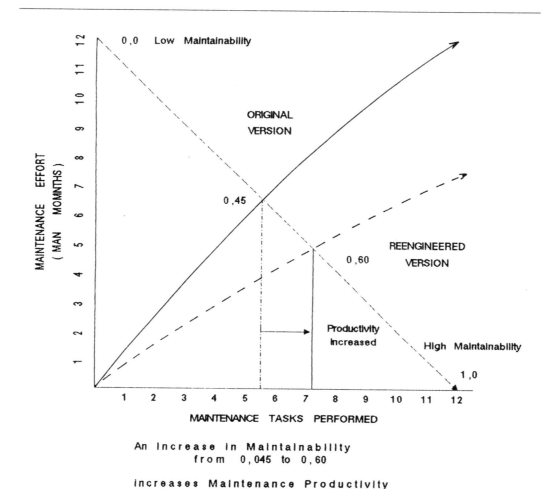

Figure 3. Increasing software maintenance productivity

Nevertheless, most measurements of maintainability are done in this way. As long as the people, the environment, and the tools involved remain constant, there is some validity to the observations. One such observation is that of Linda Brice (1981) of the Los Alamos National Laboratory. She studied a FORTRAN application which cost nine person-years to maintain over a 13-month period. This added up to 3.8 full-time employees or $31 000 per month. To this sum is added the hardware cost of approximately $7000 per month. Both staff and hardware maintenance costs were plotted as a function of time:

$$T_1 = t^*(C+P)$$

where T_1 = total maintenance costs without renewal, t = elapsed time in months, C = computer costs per month, and P = personnel costs per month.

By renovating the application, it was possible to reduce the maintenance effort from 3.8 to 2 people per month. Considering the hardware costs as remaining constant, this resulted in a net saving of $12 400 per month.

On the other hand, the renovating of a system also has its price. In the first case described by Brice, it took 3 people 9 months to renovate the system. It took another 15 months following the completion of the renewal project to recover the renewal costs. After that, each additional month resulted in a saving of $12 400. In the second case, it took 2 people 6 months to renovate the software. In this case, it took less than 6 months to break even. By the 24th month it was possible to save $160 000.

The rewrite or renewal costs are calculated by Brice as follows:

$$R = N_r{}^*A^*t$$

where N_r = number of people required for renewal, A = average monthly cost per person, and t = elapsed time in months for rewrite.

The costs of maintenance in the case of a renewal project are calculated as:

$$T_2 = t^*(C+P/p) + R$$

where t = elapsed time in months, C = monthly computer costs, P = monthly personnel costs, and p = personnel reduction factor as a result of the improved maintainability.

Costs should start to decline following completion of the renewal and the payoff period begins at some point after the renewal project is completed, namely at that point where the renewal costs are amortized.

The costing model proposed by Brice is a way of justifying software renewal based on maintenance effort in person-months. The problem with it is that it assumes maintenance effort to be constant over time and independent of the people involved. Unfortunately, many managers will take issue with this assumption, since most managers expect maintenance effort to decline over time as the system becomes more stable and the maintenance personnel become more familiar with it. There is a much more intricate relationship between the maintainer and the maintained programs than the conclusions of Brice would lead us to believe. Knowledge of the programs is the most critical factor in maintenance productivity. Re-engineering a program is a way to regain that knowledge, once it has been lost.

3. INCREASING MAINTAINABILITY THROUGH RE-ENGINEERING

Software re-engineering is an attempt to increase the quality of the software product so as to decrease maintenance costs. In an experiment conducted within the framework of the Software Metrics Project 'METKIT' of the European ESPRIT Programme it was demonstrated how maintainability and reliability could be increased through restructuring and re-engineering measures (Sneed and Kaposi, 1990).

By restructuring a COBOL program it was possible to reduce the effort to adapt it by 18% and to enhance it by 21%. The impact domain of adaptation was 24% and that of enhancement 29% less for the restructured variant than for the original unstructured variant. The number of second-level defects, i.e. errors introduced through the maintenance process, was 36% less for the restructured program. Only in the case of corrective maintenance did the restructured variant prove more costly, in terms of effort as well as impact domain.

By re-engineering the same program, maintainability and reliability were increased even more. Re-engineering entailed here a conversion into COBOL-85 as well as the restructuring and cleaning up of the code. In this case, adaptation effort was reduced by 42% and the enhancement effort by 32%. The impact domain of adaptation was 34% less for the re-engineered variant and that of enhancement 23% less. The second-level defects rate was reduced by 45% through re-engineering. The effort for correction remained approximately the same.

The more maintenance actions performed on the subject program, the greater the savings through restructuring and re-engineering. This was underscored by the fact that the cyclomatic complexity of the unstructured program rose from 29 to 37 within the course of the experiment, while that of the re-engineered variant rose only from 19 to 24 (McCabe, 1976). At the same time, the data complexity according to Chapin's (1979) 'Q' metric grew from 1.87 to 1.98 for the unstructured program, whereas that of the re-engineered variant went from 1.66 to 1.79. These figures reveal the effect that re-engineering has upon the structure of the program. The re-engineered program variant could be maintained with approximately 33% less effort than the original variant (see Figure 4).

A similar study reported on by Gibson and Senn (1989) in the *Communications of the ACM* came to the same conclusion. By re-engineering a suite of COBOL programs it was possible to reduce both the error rate and the maintenance effort.

Other studies which have analysed the relationship between product characteristics and maintenance effort are those of Yau and Collofello (1980), Peercy (1981), Vessey and Weber (1983), Berns (1984), Gremillion (1984), and Rombach (1987). In all of these reports, maintenance effort was related in some way to some inherent program characteristics, implying that an improvement to the program would increase maintainability.

There is still too little evidence to conclude that re-engineering will in all cases increase maintainability. However, the studies made so far would indicate that there is a strong relationship between the structure of a software product and the effort required to maintain it. Definitely more work is needed to prove this relationship.

4. RATIONALE FOR RE-ENGINEERING

The decision to re-engineer a software system is a difficult decision to make. It must be based on sound economic considerations. Ideally, before a re-engineering project is launched, one should be aware of the underlying maintenance problem, how much the re-engineering effort will cost, how much can be saved on maintenance, and when this return on investment will be visible.

One of the first guidelines to making such a decision was the Guideline on Software Maintenance published by the National Bureau of Standards (NBS, 1983). There, eleven criteria are given to help in deciding, when to revise an existing system. They are:

(1) when frequent system failures occur,

(2) when the code is over seven years old,

Mean of three program variants

Metric	Original version	Corrected version	Adapted version	Enhanced version
(K2) Module complexity	0.86	0.86	0.68	0.88
(K2) Graph complexity	29	29	34	37
(K3) Data complexity	1.87	1.87	1.87	1.98
(K4) Difficulty degree	0.033	0.032	0.032	0.026
(K5) Test complexity	0.409	0.409	0.422	0.437

Unstructured program metrics

Metric	Original version	Corrected version	Adapted version	Enhanced version
(K2) Module complexity	0.33	0.39	0.39	0.42
(K2) Graph complexity	25	26	26	31
(K3) Data complexity	1.83	1.84	1.86	1.88
(K4) Difficulty degree	0.031	0.030	0.029	0.024
(K5) Test complexity	0.360	0.369	0.371	0.368

Restructured program metrics

Metric	Original version	Corrected version	Adapted version	Enhanced version
(K2) Module complexity	0.38	0.40	0.43	0.44
(K2) Graph complexity	19	21	23	24
(K3) Data complexity	1.66	1.66	1.70	1.79
(K4) Difficulty degree	0.044	0.042	0.039	0.031
(K5) Test complexity	0.354	0.339	0.333	0.353

Re-engineered program metrics

Figure 4. Effect of re-engineering upon maintainability

(3) when the program structure and logic flow have become overly complex,

(4) when the programs were written for a previous generation of hardware,

(5) when the programs are running in emulation mode,

(6) when the modules or unit subroutines have grown excessively large,

(7) when excessive resources are required to run the system,

(8) when hard-coded parameters are subject to change,

(9) when it becomes difficult to retain the maintainers,

(10) when the documentation has become out of date,

(11) when the design specifications are missing, incomplete or obsolete.

These are important points to consider when deciding whether to re-engineer or not, but they represent an oversimplification of the problem and need to be handled with caution. A thorough cost-benefit analysis is unavoidable.

The most-often-cited reason for re-engineering software is, of course, to reduce maintenance costs, but there are other reasons as well. One reason is to decrease the error rate. Another is to convert the software to a better platform. A third is to lengthen the life of a system. A fourth is to enable business change within the company. In any case one must calculate the expected lifetime of the target system and compare the costs of re-engineering with the costs of redevelopment starting from scratch. Re-engineering is often only considered a viable alternative, when the re-engineering effort is no more than 50% of the redevelopment effort. It may also be too expensive to re-engineer an entire system. It is here where the Pareto law comes into effect. It states that 80% of the problems are caused by 20% of the software. So, it may be advisable to re-engineer only that 20% and leave the rest as it is.

The author has been called upon many times by some of the leading companies in Europe to perform a re-engineering task. In all cases one of the four situations mentioned above has prevailed.

Three times a re-engineering task was necessary because a system which had just been released was so bad that it could not be maintained. The error rate was high, the documentation was incomplete, and the design architecture was inadequate to allow system evolution.

Five times the author was called upon to re-engineer programs because the responsible programmer had left, had suffered a nervous breakdown (twice), had died prematurely, or had retired.

Twice the author was asked to re-engineer a system because it had to be functionally overhauled and the customer felt this would be a good time to renew the programs.

Finally, the author has been asked seven times to re-engineer a system in conjunction with system migration. The most common migration projects in which re-engineering is required are:

—in moving from one language to another, such as from COBOL-74 to COBOL-85,
—in moving from one database system to another, such as from IMS to DB-2,
—in moving from one teleprocessing monitor to another, such as from SHADOW to CICS,
—in moving from one computer to another, such as from UNISYS to IBM.

Migration is by far the most common cause of a re-engineering project, since the software has to be changed anyway and it might as well be upgraded. It is here where the greatest market potential exists for re-engineering vendors.

5. ESTIMATING THE COSTS OF RE-ENGINEERING

Estimating the costs of a software re-engineering project presupposes knowledge on the size and complexity of the system to be re-engineered. The target system must be analysed and broken down into its component parts. For a typical business application these may be:

—programs
—subroutines
—job procedures
—utilities
—maps/reports
—files
—data structures
—parameters

The size of the software can be expressed by the number of program components, e.g. programs, subroutines, jobs, etc., or by the number of lines of code. The size of the data is determined by the number of data objects, e.g. maps/reports, files, records, parameters, etc., or by the number of elementary data items.

Just as in estimating development effort it is also necessary here to weight the size by the complexity. At the system level size is determined by the number of relationships between the component parts, e.g. subroutine calls, file accesses, input/output operations. This number should be used as an adjustment factor to take account of the number of relationships relative to the number of components (see Figure 5).

To estimate the re-engineering effort the weighted number of units to be re-engineered needs to be multiplied by the effort required for each unit type. This effort per unit type is the re-engineering productivity which is derived from an empirical analysis of past experience. A sample re-engineering productivity table used by the author is displayed in Figure 6. There, it states, for instance, that the re-engineering of a 2000-statement COBOL program requires 0.5 person-days, a figure derived from the experience at the Union Bank of Switzerland using the tool SOFT-REORG.

To calculate the total effort of re-engineering one should weight the effort for each unit type by the complexity factor as shown in Figure 7, and sum them up for the system as a whole. At the Union Bank approximately 50% of the costs accrued after the programs were converted and transferred to the new environment. Most of these costs were a result of testing and debugging. This leads to the conclusion that conversion costs are matched by testing costs. Since testing requires at least as much as the conversion effort, the sum of the conversion costs should be multiplied by 2 to give the total effort involved including testing. This figure for the total effort can, of course, be adjusted by a multiplication factor to take account of the particular environment in which the re-engineering is to take place.

A sample calculation with a system of

—500 programs with 2000 file accesses,
—100 subroutines with 400 CALLs,
—50 job procedures using 200 files,
—200 files with 2000 accesses,
—300 COPYs with 300 references, and
—200 maps with 2000 fields

is shown in Figure 8.

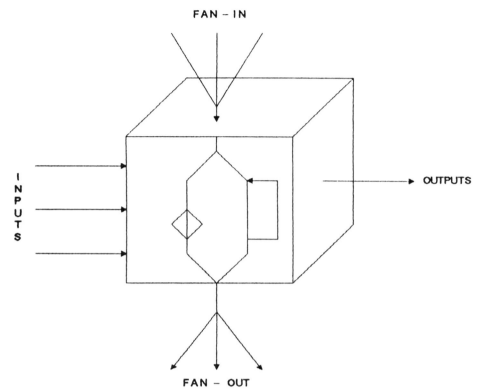

Figure 5. Program maintainability metrics

The sample illustrates that the greatest cost of a renovation project is the cost of retesting and reintegrating all of the components once they have gone through the re-engineering process. This is the major deterrent to a wider use of automated re-engineering, which is in itself relatively cheap. The high costs of retesting and reintegration can only be offset by correspondingly high benefits, for instance, the higher performance of a new operating environment. That is the reason why re-engineering is used primarily in connection with conversion.

Of course, the amount of effort necessary to convert a system is highly dependent upon the degree of automation. Thus, whereas a person can convert only one COBOL-74 program per day to COBOL-85, the same person with the use of automated tools might be able to convert four programs per day.

The costs of conversion are comparable to those of redesign and reprogramming. According to a study done by Walston and Felix (1977) on a database of 60 software development projects with delivered source lines ranging from 4000 to 467 000 the redesign of an existing system requires an effort comparable to the development of a new system of the same size, whereas the reprogramming of an existing system requires an effort equal to one half the effort required for redesign. A study of the Rome Air Development Center database seemed to verify this linear relationship.

Component	Manual	Automatic
Program (2000 LOC)	5	1 PD
Subroutine (100 LOC)	2	0.5 PD
Job	4	2 PD
Utility	2	0.5 PD
Database	8	4 PD
File	4	2 PD
Copy/include	1	0.5 PD
Parameter	1	1 PD
Panel	1	0.5 PD
	28	12 PD

50% cost reduction through automation

Figure 6. Re-engineering costs

E_1 = (Number of programs × Program effort) ×
(1 + (Number IOs/Number of programs + Number IOs))

E_2 = (Number of subroutines × Subroutine effort) ×
(1 + (Number CALLs/Number of subroutines + Number CALLs))

E_3 = (Number jobs × Job effort) ×
(1 + (Number files/Number jobs + Number files))

E_4 = (Number files × File effort) ×
(1 + (Number IOs/Number files + Number IOs))

E_5 = (Number copys × Copy effort) ×
(1 + (Number ref/Number copys + Number ref))

E_6 = (Number panels × Panel effort) ×
(1 + (Number fields/Number panels + Number fields))

E = $(E_1 + E_2 + E_3 + E_4 + E_5 + E_6)$ × 2 [Test effort]

E = Total re-engineering effort

Figure 7. Weighting of renovation costs

Similar results were reported by the author (Sneed, 1984) in his case study of software renewal at the Bertelsmann AG. There, it took 17 person-months to respecify and reprogram 232 PL/1 programs with 24 000 statements. This meant some 72 statements per day. Considering the test of the reused programs, the total effort came to 84% of the original development effort. This was deemed to be too expensive by Bertelsmann, which then discontinued the re-engineering effort. This would also confirm the contention of Walston and Felix, 'that the redesign of an existing system requires an effort comparable to the development of a new system'.

However, three years later, at a similar project done for BMW in Munich, the reprogramming productivity could be raised to 350 statements per day through the use of more automation. This was a fivefold productivity increase over the Bertelsmann project. Considering 50 statements per day as the average productivity of a COBOL programmer when developing a new system, this meant now that a software system could be reprogrammed for one-seventh the cost of programming it. At this time the cost of software restructuring sank to $2 per procedural statement and $1 per data statement.

Sample-system
500 Programs with 2000 accesses
100 Subroutines with 400 CALLs
50 Jobs with 200 files
200 Files with 2000 accesses
300 COPYs with 3000 references
200 Panels with 2000 fields

$$
\begin{aligned}
E_1 &= (500 \times 1) \times (1 + 2000/2500) &&= 900 \text{ PD} \\
E_2 &= (100 \times 0.5) \times (1 + 400/500) &&= 90 \text{ PD} \\
E_3 &= (50 \times 2) \times (1 + 200/250) &&= 180 \text{ PD} \\
E_4 &= (200 \times 2) \times (1 + 2500/2700) &&= 760 \text{ PD} \\
E_5 &= (300 \times 0.5) \times (1 + 3000/3300) &&= 285 \text{ PD} \\
E_6 &= (200 \times 0.5) \times (1 + 2000/2200) &&= 190 \text{ PD}
\end{aligned}
$$

$$
\begin{aligned}
&\overline{\quad\quad 2405 \text{ PD}} \\
&\quad\quad\quad \times 2 \\
\end{aligned}
$$

PD = Person-days
PM = Person-months

$$
\begin{aligned}
&\overline{\quad 4810 \text{ PD}} \\
&\quad\quad \downarrow \\
&\quad 240 \text{ PM}
\end{aligned}
$$

Figure 8. Sample estimation of re-engineering effort

But for most users even this was too much to pay for the refurbishment of old software.

Four years later at the Union Bank of Switzerland in Zurich the author's team was able to restructure, refurbish, redocument, and convert COBOL programs at the rate of 2000 statements per day. This meant a fourfold increase over the BMW performance, and a thirty fold increase over the Bertelsmann renewal project. The price of re-engineering had sunk to less than $0.50 per procedural instruction, and $0.25 per data declaration (Sneed, 1990).

This example goes to show how automation can increase productivity and reduce costs. It also goes to show that refurbishment is easier to automate than development once the objectives of re-engineering are well defined.

The price of $1200 for a 2500 statement program to be remodularized, restructured, and freed of numeric constants and literals with encapsulized and normalized data structures together with a graphical program documentation is a price any company should be willing to pay. Similar cost reductions have been cited by Peat Marwick and Language Technology in the USA (Bush, 1985). So, from the viewpoint of costs, re-engineering no longer seems to present a problem. The problem now seems to lie more on the side of the expected benefits. It has to be demonstrated that re-engineering measures will really increase the quality and reduce the complexity of software.

6. ASSESSING THE BENEFITS OF RE-ENGINEERING

In assessing the benefits of re-engineering one must first define the context of the problem. There are basically three types of situation:

—A, when the existing application system has become technically obsolete, and must be replaced,

—B, when there are severe technical problems with the existing system,

—C, when it might be expedient to upgrade the existing system.

In the A case, there is only a choice between redevelopment and re-engineering. If the functions of the system are stable and only the technical implementation is obsolete, it is definitely cheaper to re-engineer. If, however, the functionality of the system or the user interfaces are obsolete, it may be necessary to redevelop. It may happen that one is still forced to retain the old functionality, if the experts required for a new development are not available. In this instance, there is no need to justify re-engineering in terms of benefits, since the existing system must be either replaced or renovated. Here it is only a question of the added functionality minus the costs and risks of a new development versus the costs and risks of renovation. In arithmetic terms it would appear as follows:

$$\text{Re-engineering Benefit} = [\text{Old-Value} - (\text{Re-eng.Cost} * \text{Re-eng.Risk})]$$
$$- [\text{New-Value} - (\text{Dev.Cost} * \text{Dev.Risk})]$$

If the new value of the newly developed system is high relative to its cost and risk, the re-engineering benefit will be negative. The same is true if the value of the old system is low. However, if there is not much difference between the new value and the old value, and the cost and risk of re-engineering are significantly lower than that of a new development, as is often the case, then re-engineering becomes an economic alternative.

Replacing a technically obsolete system may not be an all-or-nothing proposition. There may be many parts of the system, whose functionality is still adequate. Here, it would be necessary to apply the re-engineering benefit formula to subsystems or components. Re-engineering may also be a prerequisite to adding new functions to overcome obsolescence.

In the B case, the user is not being forced to act. He could go on living with the existing system, albeit at a high cost of maintenance. Therefore, here he is faced with four possibilities.

—replacing the system with a standard package,

—redeveloping the system,

—re-engineering the system,

—continuing to pay the high costs of maintaining the present system.

Replacing one's own customized system with a standard package is an attractive alternative which, if possible, should always be chosen, especially if the supplier of the standard package is responsible for maintaining it. However, more than often it is not possible and then the user is left with only three choices.

In examining the benefits of re-engineering in this case, one must consider the difference in maintenance costs of the old system, the re-engineered system, and the new system.

$$\text{Re-engineering Benefit} = [\text{Old-Maint.Cost} - \text{Re-eng.Maint.Cost}]$$
$$+ [\text{Old-Value} - (\text{Re-eng.Cost} * \text{Re-eng.Risk})]$$
$$- [\text{New-Value} - (\text{Dev.Cost} * \text{Dev.Risk})]$$

If there is no significant difference between the old maintenance costs and the re-engineered maintenance cost, or the re-engineering costs are too high, it will be more economical to remain with the old system. On the other hand, if maintenance costs can be significantly reduced, and the costs of re-engineering are low, then it will be more economical to re-engineer the system, provided it is not even more economical to redevelop the system. This depends again upon the added value of a new system and its costs of development as compared to the costs of re-engineering (see Figure 9).

In the C case, there is no immediate need to do anything. The performance of the application system is adequate, but the maintenance costs are higher than they should be, and the morale of the maintenance programmers is low. The user has a high personnel turnover and it takes too long to get maintenance tasks completed. In other words, the situation is not critical but a nuisance.

It is here that the benefits presented by Robert Figliolo (1989) at the Software Maintenance Association Conference in Atlanta can be used. Figliolo calculates the following cost reductions through renovation:

—lower maintenance costs in saved time and effort per maintenance task,
—lower maintenance costs through the replacement of senior personnel through junior personnel,
—lower costs through a reduction of failure time,

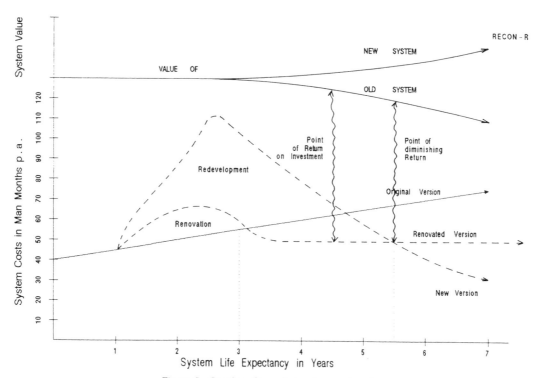

Figure 9. Cost/benefit analysis of re-engineering

—lower costs of hiring and training new personnel,
—lower lost opportunity costs by freeing capacity from maintenance.

Together these savings add up to the benefit of re-engineering an existing system which is neither obsolete nor in a critical state where the user is under pressure to act. If the sum of the biannual saving is higher than the costs of re-engineering weighted by the risk, it is worth re-engineering the system even though there is no immediate need.

Re-engineering Benefit = 2 × (Ann.Cost-Reduction of Figliolo)
                          − (Re-eng.Costs * Re-eng.Risk)

In all of the above expressions, the risk factor is used to weight the estimated costs. A list of possible risk factors is given by Charette (1989) in his book on software engineering risk analysis. They are as given in Table 1.

One of the most significant benefits of software re-engineering projects is the fact that the risk factor is low when automated tools are available. This is not true of development projects, where a high risk rating may exist even when CASE tools are available. A study at the Union Bank of Switzerland concluded that the risk factor of a new development is two to three times higher than the risk factor of a renovation project, provided the data structures are not altered. Since the costs of re-engineering should only be at the most one-quarter of the costs of a new development, this makes re-engineering a viable alternative wherever functionality remains relatively constant. This is particularly true for conversions where the application is transferred from one technical environment to another (Wolberg, 1983).

7. SELECTING PROGRAMS FOR RE-ENGINEERING

Application software systems may not have a uniform quality standard. Some programs may become obsolete before others, some may have a higher error rate, and others may be particularly difficult to maintain. Therefore, it will not always be possible to pass judgement on a system as a whole. In deciding whether to replace, renovate, or leave alone, it will be necessary to assess the individual components rather than the system as a whole. In this case, one will need selection criteria for judging each program, e.g. each online transaction, each batch job step, and each report generation.

Table 1.

Risk rating	Probability of failure	Risk factor
Extremely high	0.99–0.81	3
Very high	0.80–0.61	2.5
High	0.60–0.50	2
Moderate	0.49–0.25	1.5
Low	0.24–0.10	1.25
None	0.09–0.01	1

There are many theoretical approaches to ranking programs based on their static and dynamic properties. Statically one can measure their size, their graph complexity, their data complexity, their modularity factor, etc. However, these metric-based approaches fail to give the whole picture.

A practical approach to selecting programs for re-engineering has been developed by Nolan Norton & Co. and is called 'portfolio analysis' (Verdugo, 1988). According to this method all of the programs of a given organization should be placed in one of four quadrants produced by crossing the two axes (see Figure 10):

—technical quality and
—user satisfaction.

In this manner, programs are ranked both by technical quality and by their importance to the organization. Technical quality can be measured automatically by a static analyser using software metrics. Importance to the organization, i.e. user satisfaction, is measured by surveys or interviews.

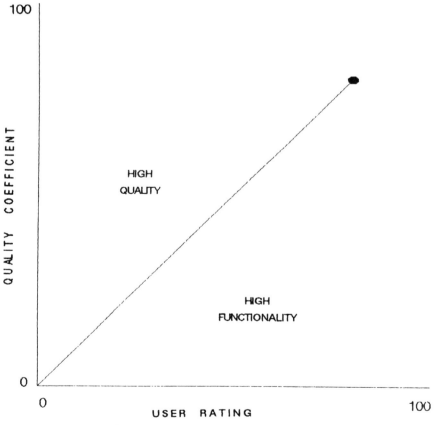

Figure 10. Selection criteria for re-engineering

Those programs which rate high, both in user appreciation, and in technical quality, should be further maintained. Those which rate high in technical quality, but are of little importance to the organization, need not be maintained but should be left to their fate. Those which rate low, both in technical quality and in user appreciation, should be combined. It is those programs in the remaining quadrant which are interesting, that is those programs which are considered relatively important to the organization, but which have a lower than average technical quality. These programs perform vital functions, but they are error-prone and difficult to maintain. Therefore, they should be considered first for re-engineering.

When considering programs for re-engineering some other factors should be considered as well. These are:

—What is the strategic importance of the program?
—What is the mean time to failure rate of the program?
—What is the frequency of maintenance activities?
—What future is foreseen for that program?

Finally, once programs have been selected as candidates for re-engineering, it is important to choose the right moment for the re-engineering effort. This may be,

—when a program has to be converted to another environment,
—when a program has to be functionally altered or enhanced,
—when the responsible programmer has left, or
—when the system is out of control.

8. COSTS AND BENEFITS OF RE-ENGINEERING

This treatise has attempted to provide a framework for the cost/benefit analysis of software re-engineering projects. It has pointed out that the economics of re-engineering must be viewed in the context of the economics of software maintenance and that the economics of software maintenance must be viewed within the context of system life-cycle economics. It is misleading to view only the costs and benefits of renovation without considering the costs, benefits, and risks of developing a new system as well as the costs and risks of maintaining an old system. Software re-engineering is only one of several options the manager has to fulfil his user needs. These options have to be weighed against one another.

Four factors are important to consider in deciding whether to

—re-engineer,
—redevelop, or
—maintain as is.

They are:

(1) Costs of re-engineering relative to the costs of redevelopment and the costs of maintenance.

(2) Added value of re-engineering relative to the value of a new system and the value of the present system.

(3) Risk of re-engineering relative to the risk of a new development and the risk of doing nothing.

(4) Life-expectancy in time of the existing system relative to the time required to re-engineer it and the time required to redevelop it.

Finally, the decision maker must have a means of assessing the quality and the functional significance of software components and ranking them relative to one another.

The more accurately the decision maker is able to quantify effort, benefits, risk, and calendar time, and the better able he is to rank his software according to quality and functionality, the better will be his decisions. There will be many cases where re-engineering is an economically sound compromise between doing nothing and starting over again from scratch.

References

Berns, G. M. (1984) 'Assessing software maintainability', *Communications of the ACM*, **27**, No. 7, p. 14.

Boehm, B. W. (1981) *Software Engineering Economics*, Prentice-Hall, Englewood Cliffs, NJ, p. 207.

Boehm, B. W. (1983) 'Economics of software maintenance', in Proceedings of IEEE Software Maintenance Workshop, Monterey, CA, Dec. 1983, p. 9.

Boehm, B. (1984) 'Software engineering economics', *IEEE Transactions on Software Engineering* **SE-10**.

Boehm, B. (1987) 'Improving software productivity', *IEEE Computer*, Sept.

Brice, L. (1981) 'Existing computer applications—maintain or redesign', in Proceedings of Computer Measurement Group, Dec. 1981, pp. 20–28, IEEE, Washington, D.C.

Bush, E. (1985) 'Automatic restructuring of COBOL', in Proceedings of IEEE Conference on Software Maintenance, R. J. Martin (ed.) Washington, DC, Nov. 1985, p. 52.

Chapin, N. (1979) 'A measure of software complexity', in *Proceedings of National Computer Conference*, AFIPS Press, Arlington, VA, p. 103.

Charette, R. N. (1989) *Software Engineering Risk Analysis and Management*, McGraw-Hill, New York.

Figliolo, R. (1989) 'Benefits of software re-engineering', in Proceedings of Software Maintenance Association Conference, N. Zwetginzor (ed.) Atlanta, May 1989.

Gibson, V. R. and Senn, J. A. (1989) 'System structure and software maintenance performance', *Communications of the ACM*, **32**, No. 3, p. 347.

Gremillion, L. (1984) 'Determinants of program repair maintenance', *Communications of the ACM*, **27**, No. 8, p. 826.

Lientz, B. P. and Swanson, E. B. (1980) *Software Maintenance Management*, Addison-Wesley, Reading, MA, p. 34.

Marty, R. (1990) 'Reengineering of user interfaces—connecting modern dialogue interfaces to conventional batch applications at the UBS', in *Reengineering—An Integral Maintenance Concept for Preserving Software Investments*, R. Thorner (Ed.), AIT Verlag, Halbergmoos, Germany.

McCabe, T. J. (1976) 'A complexity measure', *IEEE Transactions on Software Engineering*, **SE-2**.

NBS (1983) 'Guidance on software maintenance', Special Publication No. 500–106, US National Bureau of Standards, Washington, DC.

Nosek, J. T. and Palvia, P. (1990) 'Software maintenance management: changes in the last decade', *Journal of Software Maintenance*, **2**.

Peercy, D. E. (1981) 'A software maintainability evaluation methodology', *IEEE Transactions on Software Engineering*, **SE-7**, p. 343.

Rombach, H. D. (1987) 'A controlled experiment on the impact of software structure on maintainability', *IEEE Transactions on Software Engineering*, **SE-13**, No. 3, p. 344.

Sneed, H. (1984) 'Software renewal—a case study', *IEEE Software*, **1**, No. 3, p. 56.

Sneed, H. (1990) 'Program reengineering at the UBS', in *Migration Strategies*, Handbuch moderner Datenverarbeitung, Heft 156, Forkel Verlag, Stuttgart, p. 11.

Sneed, H. and Kaposi, A. (1990) 'An experiment on the effect of reengineering upon program maintainability', in *Proceedings of Conference on Software Maintenance*, J. C. Minson (ed.) IEEE Press, San Diego, p. 91.

Vallabhaneni, S. R.(1987) *Auditing the Maintenance of Software*, Prentice-Hall, Englewood Cliffs, NJ, p. 61.

Verdugo, G. G. (1988) 'Portfolio analysis—managing software as an asset', in Proceedings of 6th International Conference on Software Maintenance Management, 1988, S.M.A., New York.

Vessey, I. and Weber, R. (1983) 'Some factors affecting program repair maintenance—an empirical study', *Communications of the ACM*, **26**, No. 2, p. 128.

Walston, C. E. and Felix, C. P. (1977) 'A method of programming measurement and estimation', *IBM Systems Journal*, **17**, No. 1, p. 54.

Wolberg, J. (1983) 'Software conversion economics', in *Conversion of Computer Software*, Prentice-Hall, Englewood Cliffs, NJ, p. 92.

Yau, S. S. and Collofello, J. S. (1980) 'Some stability measures for software maintenance', in *IEEE Transactions on Software Engineering*, **SE-6**, No. 6, p. 545.

Yourdon, E. (1988) 'Software maintenance', in *American Programmer*, **1**, p. 5.

Chapter 4
Reengineering Experience

Chapter 4
Reengineering Experience

Purpose

In this chapter the reader will find several real-life reengineering case studies. The case studies encompass reengineering a very old system, reengineering to reduce the number of emergency maintenance problems in a system, and migrating a network data base system to a relational data base system in a more open environment.

Papers

In the first paper, "Re-engineering Software: A Case Study," Robert Britcher discusses the successful reengineering of the New York terminal approach control and tower facilities software. The Federal Aviation Administration, for whom this work was performed, wanted to determine "if a 20-year-old, real-time system could be cost-effectively reengineered to a commercial platform — including commercial hardware, commercial tools and languages, and commercial operating system software — while retaining the behavior of the applications." The reengineering project was to move the existing code to a new hardware platform so that the new code was functionally identical to the previous code, and the new code was traceable to the previous code. This paper details how this challenging task was successfully accomplished in a safety-critical system.

In the next paper, "Reengineering to Reduce System Maintenance: A Case Study," Malcolm Slovin and Silas Malik describe how a large insurance system was reengineered. This system was over ten years old and had passed through the hands of several maintenance contractors. The result was a system that was difficult to change. The authors describe many practical issues in performing the reengineeering. They demonstrate with measurements that the reengineering proved worthwhile.

In the final paper, an extract of the Executive Summary, Chapter 3, and Chapter 4 from the report, "Software Reengineering: A Case Study and Lessons Learned," Mary Ruhl and Mary Gunn discuss experience with reengineering the IRS Centralized Scheduling Program (CSP) system. The reengineering goals were to move CSP to a more open environment, and convert the network data base to a relational data base in third normal form.[1] The results of the work indicated that reengineering can be cost-effective for extending an application system's lifetime.

---

[1]A relational data model definition in third normal form can reduce impacts on the data model definition when certain kinds of definition changes are made. A definition in third normal form can also reduce the number of data base record updates needed when data records are changed. Third normal form is frequently discussed in data base textbooks. For more information, see "Further Normalization of the Data Base Relational Model," by E.F. Codd in *Courant Computer Science Symposia, 6: Data-Base Systems*, R. Rustin, ed., Prentice-Hall, Englewood Cliffs, N.J., 1972.

Re-engineering software: A case study

by R. N. Britcher

In 1986, the Federal Aviation Administration formed a contract with three companies to re-engineer a major portion of the New York terminal approach control (TRACON) application software—the software that supports air traffic control in the New York City and Newark, New Jersey, area. This paper discusses the techniques used to successfully re-engineer the software to run on an IBM System/370™, illustrating that real-time software can be logically converted from one computer to another, reliably and cost-effectively.

In 1981, the Federal Aviation Administration (FAA) issued a plan to upgrade the national airspace system. An overview of the system is depicted in Figure 1. The new plan included the host computer system that would replace the existing IBM 9020 computers (derivatives of the IBM System/360™) in the en route air traffic control centers, and the advanced automation system that would upgrade the host computer system and the terminal approach control (TRACON) and tower facilities.

In 1986, during the host computer system acquisition and two years prior to the start of the advanced automation system acquisition, the FAA awarded a small contract, of approximately $2.5 million, to Data Transformation Corporation, International Business Machines Corporation, and Pailen-Johnson Associates to re-engineer[1] part of the New York TRACON software in a high-order language, to run on an IBM System/370™ Model 3083.

This paper describes the scope of that project and the tools and methods the contractors used to re-engineer the software. The results and conclusions indicate that re-engineering the software of an existing system may be preferable to reinventing it. Table 1 is provided to assist the reader in identifying the terms and abbreviations used frequently in this paper.

The scope of the project

The project was officially entitled "New York TRACON Demonstration of Program Recoding" and was aimed at recording the methods used to re-engineer the (then) current New York TRACON application software and verify the equivalence of the re-engineered version to its source.[2] The FAA's statement of work required the contract team to demonstrate and document a logical conversion of the existing New York TRACON operational software assembler source code (ULTRA™ from UNIVAC™) into a compiler language. The newly generated software had to be functionally identical and directly traceable to the existing code. The work was to be completed in nine months and culminate in two demonstrations: the first demonstration in early

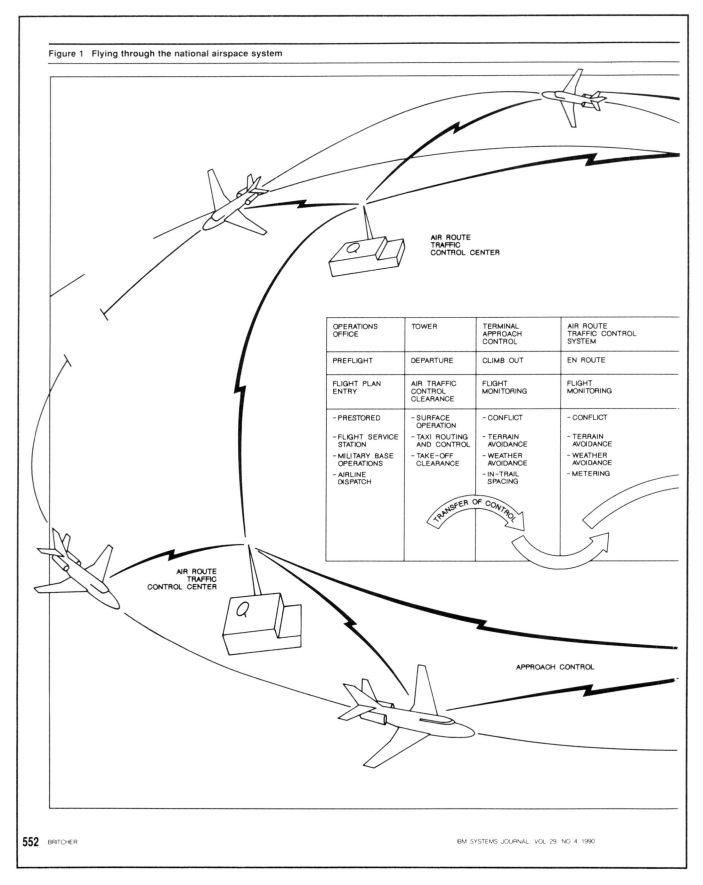

Figure 1   Flying through the national airspace system

OPERATIONS OFFICE	TOWER	TERMINAL APPROACH CONTROL	AIR ROUTE TRAFFIC CONTROL SYSTEM
PREFLIGHT	DEPARTURE	CLIMB OUT	EN ROUTE
FLIGHT PLAN ENTRY	AIR TRAFFIC CONTROL CLEARANCE	FLIGHT MONITORING	FLIGHT MONITORING
- PRESTORED - FLIGHT SERVICE STATION - MILITARY BASE OPERATIONS - AIRLINE DISPATCH	- SURFACE OPERATION - TAXI ROUTING AND CONTROL - TAKE-OFF CLEARANCE	- CONFLICT - TERRAIN AVOIDANCE - WEATHER AVOIDANCE - IN-TRAIL SPACING	- CONFLICT - TERRAIN AVOIDANCE - WEATHER AVOIDANCE - METERING

TRANSFER OF CONTROL

AIR ROUTE TRAFFIC CONTROL CENTER

AIR ROUTE TRAFFIC CONTROL CENTER

APPROACH CONTROL

146

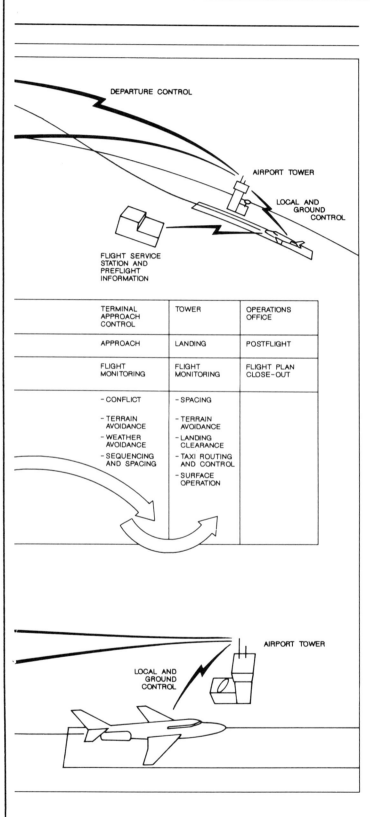

TERMINAL APPROACH CONTROL	TOWER	OPERATIONS OFFICE
APPROACH	LANDING	POSTFLIGHT
FLIGHT MONITORING	FLIGHT MONITORING	FLIGHT PLAN CLOSE-OUT
- CONFLICT - TERRAIN AVOIDANCE - WEATHER AVOIDANCE - SEQUENCING AND SPACING	- SPACING - TERRAIN AVOIDANCE - LANDING CLEARANCE - TAXI ROUTING AND CONTROL - SURFACE OPERATION	

April of 1987, the second in mid-May, the ninth month. If it were successful, the project would bolster the idea of improving systems through planned evolution.

The objective in re-engineering. The FAA wanted to determine if a 20-year-old, real-time system could be cost-effectively re-engineered onto a commercial platform—including commercial hardware, commercial tools and languages, and commercial operating system software—while retaining the behavior of the applications. As a by-product of the re-engineering, the architecture of the applications and their database would be simplified to eliminate unnecessary dependencies, while creating a visible architecture. This is in keeping with the long-range objective of the FAA (and other United States government agencies) to eliminate customized system components and to develop and use application programs that are reliable and easy to modify and extend. Customized components typically require specialized training and maintenance and are vulnerable to changes in a product line or technology. The National Bureau of Standards publication in Reference 3 lists characteristics of systems that are candidates for redesign. Among them are code over seven years old, overly complex structure, code written for a previous generation of hardware, hard-coded parameters, and very large modules. All of these characteristics applied to the New York TRACON system.

It is essential that all parties involved in a particular application of re-engineering clarify its meaning and scope, and define their rationale for doing it. Does it include designing, coding, specifying, testing? Houtz,[4] in writing about how much software improvement differs from conventional system development, argues convincingly for a precisely documented software improvement program that would record which software would be affected; a strategy for each case such as purging, conversion, or replacing; a cost benefit assessment; and the detailed plan for implementing each strategy.

It was only after beginning the New York TRACON demonstration that the FAA and the contract team clearly understood the extent and type of re-engineering that would be applied to the TRACON software. For example, a recently completed project[5] moved the applications of the national airspace en route system from an IBM 9020 to an IBM System/370

Table 1 Terms used frequently in this paper

Term	Definition
FAA	
ARTS	automated radar terminal system
CDR	continuous data recording
FAA	Federal Aviation Administration
PSRAP	preliminary sensor receiver and processor
RETRACK	replay radar and controller data
TRACON	terminal approach control
UNIVAC	
ARTS IIIA	ARTS system coded in ULTRA
UNIVAC IOP	(input/output) multiprocessor (operational system)
MPE	multiprocessor executive for ARTS IIIA
Sperry 1100	development and support system
ULTRA	UNIVAC assembler source
IBM	
IBM 3083	demonstration (and target), development system
VM/SP-HPO	virtual machine control program for 3083

host computer system. Isolated portions of the software were respecified and redesigned, then coded in the original source language. The re-engineered system was tested by verifying its functional equivalence to the original IBM 9020 version. The New York TRACON demonstration, on the other hand, moved the applications from a UNIVAC host computer to an IBM System/370 host, replaced the platform software (the operating system), redesigned the software architecture and top-level design of the applications, specified the design (but not the system functions), re-engineered the software in a new target language, and tested it by verifying functional equivalence.

In both projects the results justified the cost. But without a well-defined rationale and plan, re-engineering could be at best too expensive, and at worst the wrong thing to do. For example, Sneed,[6] describing work performed for the Bertelsmann Publishing Corporation in West Germany, reported that the work of specifying and retesting, without re-engineering, 232 PL/I programs was grossly underestimated, and that only the judicious use of tools—such as a static analyzer—made the job feasible: the cost being two-thirds of the cost of developing the original software. Sneed also reported that the effort to find out whether software systems could be economically renovated resulted in no new software, only better documentation and a testbed for future testing.

The applications to be re-engineered. The New York TRACON is the largest terminal and approach control area in the United States, supporting five major airports in and around New York City. The automated radar terminal system that supports TRACONs around the country (ARTS IIIA), was developed in the early 1970s. The heart of the application software is the ARTS IIIA tracking algorithm. Because it is central to all air traffic automation, the FAA required that the contract team re-engineer the tracker as faithfully as possible. Tracking enables an air traffic controller to observe an aircraft's position and speed (and other important information, such as its transponder code) at the controller's workstation, by continually correlating the computer-modeled vector with the digitized radar return, every sweep of the radar. Tracking is supported by 1) an application program that buffers the digital radar returns, 2) an application that enables the TRACON to communicate with other facilities, and 3) an application that supports the controller workstation.

Of the ARTS IIIA applications, the FAA and the contract team agreed to re-engineer the tracker, the radar input program, or PSRAP (for preliminary sensor receiver and processor), a small portion of the interfacility support, and the controller workstation support. The PSRAP and tracking algorithms were coded virtually line for line, so that the FAA and the contract team could evaluate in some detail the results of re-engineering a real-time system. Although there were accommodations to the change in structure of the applications (the design process is described below) and to the lexical differences between source and target languages, the re-engineered software was traceable to its source without much difficulty. Because the target hardware and the operating environment differed from the source system, the other applications were re-engineered—with FAA approval—to achieve functional equivalence, but not necessarily algorithmic equivalence. In particular, because the prototype situation display used in the demonstration system was not equivalent to the TRACON workstation, the applications that support the data entry and display system were not re-engineered line for line.

Two support programs developed for the ARTS were key to the demonstration, because of their role in testing and verifying functional equivalence. The continuous data recording (CDR) editor reduces the data recorded by the operational software so that programmers and analysts can evaluate the functional performance of the system. A simulator,

RETRACK, uses the CDR data recorded from a previous run to feed the operational software, so that testing need not depend on the availability of live radar and controller inputs.

The contract team developed one new program: a CDR conversion program to translate the FAA-provided CDR file from ULTRA-compatible format to Pascal/VS records that could be processed by an IBM System/370.

The support programs and the conversion program provided a coherent thread of automation that connected airplanes to the controller monitoring them. It was enough to give the demonstration the characteristics of a complete system.

The software to build and execute the applications was provided by the contract team. The estimated number of lines of source code (in ULTRA) to be re-engineered was 8000 for the tracker and PSRAP, 7000 lines to support the workstation, 3000 lines for the operational database, and about 13 000 lines of support software, to drive the system and to record and reduce its outputs. (The actual number of lines converted exceeded the estimate by 66 percent: the contract team converted 53 000 lines of source code; the bulk of the 22 000 lines excluded from the estimate was taken up by the database specifications and the site (such as the location of the radar sensors) database.

The FAA provided the New York TRACON source code and listings, specifications and design data, database definitions, and files containing recorded radar and air traffic controller inputs that would be used to drive the system. In addition to providing contract team members, IBM also provided the laboratory and equipment to develop and demonstrate the converted software.

The current system architecture

The New York TRACON development and support system runs on a commercial Sperry™ 1100 processor under a commercial operating system, but uses specially-built software to build and reduce data generated by the operational system. The operational software can be assembled and linked on either the Sperry 1100 or on the operational system, UNIVAC's Input Output (IOP) multiprocessor. Data are reduced only on the IOP.

The operational system runs on the IOP, a multiprocessor developed for the automated radar terminal system (ARTS), and a derivative of the UNIVAC 8300. It drives the data entry and display subsystem, a configuration of Texas Instrument's workstations, containing neither software nor microcode.

The ARTS IIIA is coded in ULTRA, a 16-bit assembler developed in the 1960s for the UNIVAC processors. Like the assemblers of its generation, it was developed to get the most out of the target processor. The version of ULTRA in use now is not much different from the original, in that it offers no macro facility and no structured programming control structures.

The operational software is supervised by a customized multiprocessor executive (MPE) written for the ARTS. The rules for concurrent and sequential execution of the applications are encoded in a lattice and carried out and enforced by the MPE. Because the IOP is a multiprocessor, the MPE assigns work—radar to be buffered and sorted, tracks to be correlated—to the applications in a strict time-sequenced order. The MPE allocates each work-application pair to an available processor, the object being to keep the processors busy.

The application software is organized as tasks. The application tasks, in general, correspond to the applications: PSRAP, which processes incoming radar data; the tracker, consisting of the applications to support the controller workstation data entry and display; and the support for interfacility communications.

The small global database, comprising predominantly radar returns and tracks and the information describing the current state of each workstation, is organized in tables accessible by the applications without executive supervision.

The target system architecture

The contract team developed and demonstrated the re-engineered New York TRACON software on an IBM System/370 Model 3083. Unlike the UNIVAC IOP, the IBM 3083 is a uniprocessor. It executes at roughly four times the cycle speed of the IOP and contains 16 megabytes of primary storage. Its channels operate at about three megabytes per second. Each of its attached storage devices, both direct and sequential access, holds gigabytes of data.

The IBM 3083 drove a prototype situation display enabling the FAA to observe the display outputs. The situation display supports a 2048 by 2048 pixel color

Figure 2 Demonstration system hardware configuration

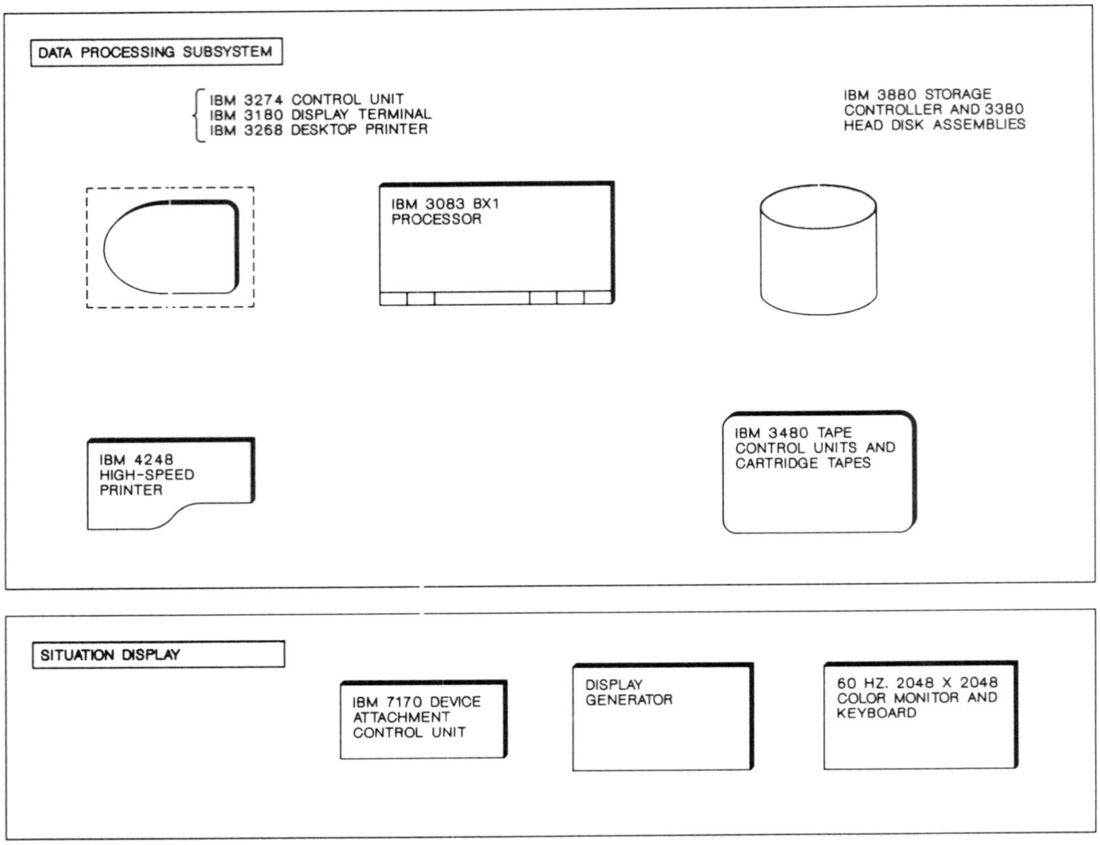

DATA PROCESSING SUBSYSTEM

IBM 3274 CONTROL UNIT
IBM 3180 DISPLAY TERMINAL
IBM 3268 DESKTOP PRINTER

IBM 3880 STORAGE
CONTROLLER AND 3380
HEAD DISK ASSEMBLIES

IBM 3083 BX1
PROCESSOR

IBM 4248
HIGH-SPEED
PRINTER

IBM 3480 TAPE
CONTROL UNITS AND
CARTRIDGE TAPES

SITUATION DISPLAY

IBM 7170 DEVICE
ATTACHMENT
CONTROL UNIT

DISPLAY
GENERATOR

60 HZ. 2048 X 2048
COLOR MONITOR AND
KEYBOARD

raster presentation driven by a state-of-the-art display generator, and it embeds a workstation processor. For the demonstration, it was used in a mode that emulated the current ARTS IIIA situation displays as closely as possible. Figure 2 describes the configuration.

The development processor and the demonstration processor were one unit. IBM's virtual machine operating system, VM/SP-HPO, made this possible. It allows users to run different systems and different kinds of systems, such as batch systems, interactive systems, and real-time systems, on a single processor.

The contract team chose Pascal/VS as the target compiler. The compiler and the operational system were controlled by Multiple Virtual Storage (MVS), whereas the development system was run under the Conversational Monitoring System (CMS). Both MVS and CMS can run concurrently under VM/SP-HPO. (Although the same processor supported both the development and the demonstration system, the customer demonstrations were given with the demonstration system running in native mode, that is, MVS interacting directly with the IBM 3083, without VM/SP-HPO and the development software, CMS, configured. The intent was to present the re-engineered system in an environment as close to operational as possible.) Figure 3 shows the commercial platform under which the re-engineered applications were developed and executed.

Figure 3 Development and demonstration system software architecture

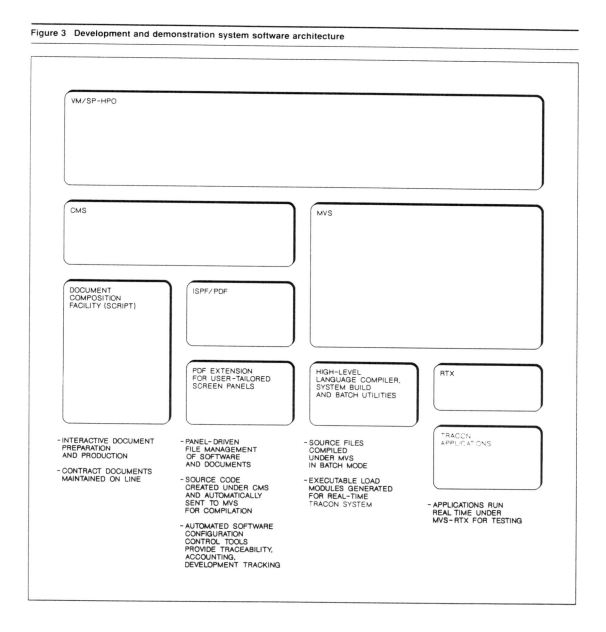

Demonstration environment and data flow

The demonstration was run in test mode; no live inputs were permitted. It lasted about 20 minutes. The FAA-supplied CDR file, containing recorded radar, interfacility, and workstation inputs from a live New York TRACON operation, was read by RETRACK. RETRACK primed the input buffers of the radar input program PSRAP, the workstation keyboard and interfacility input programs; tracking was executed; and the resulting data were written to the display. The applications ran in real time—as if the inputs were

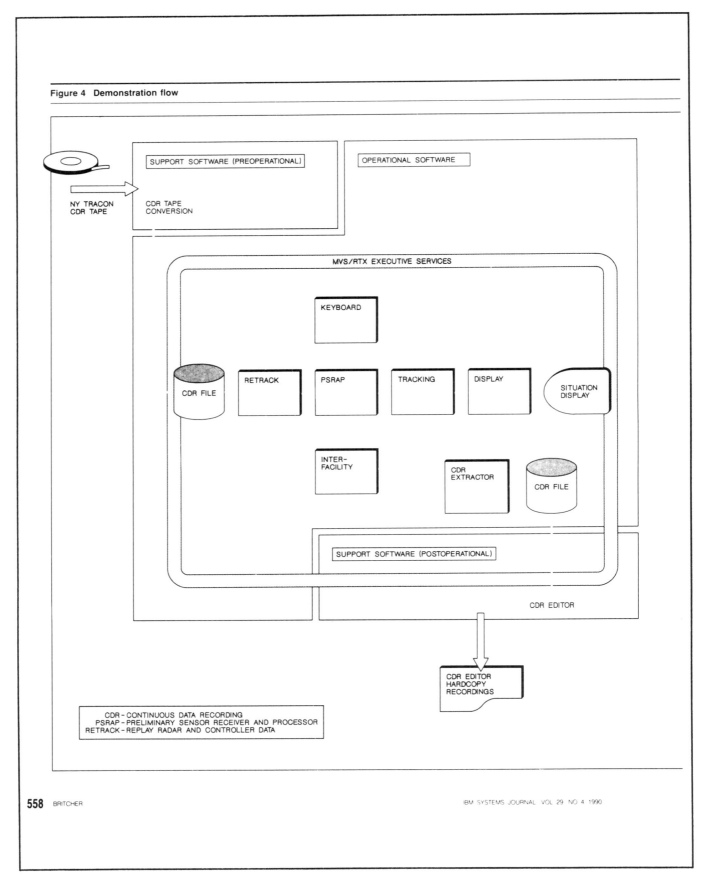

Figure 4 Demonstration flow

152

live—and recorded their CDR data. After the run was complete, the newly-generated CDR file was reduced by the CDR editor and the listing compared with a New York TRACON test run made using the identical CDR inputs. (See Figure 4.)

Tools

The tools were critical to the success of the demonstration. The development tools were similar to those IBM used in re-engineering the IBM 9020 en route system into the IBM System/370 host computer system.[5] They consisted of interactive programming and management tools, built on IBM commercial products, executing under CMS. The products included an interactive editor and library manager (ISPF/PDF), an interpretive language that enables programmers to take advantage of the ISPF/PDF dialog manager by developing their own panels and executive software (REXX), a relational database management system (SQL/DS), and an automated document preparation package (Document Composition Facility). For the host computer system IBM developed an automated software development plan to track the completion of all software and testing milestones from the level of the module to that of the system; an automated design issues and trouble report system; and an automated software configuration control and accounting system. These were changed slightly for the New York TRACON project.

The unifying architecture of the target system increased productivity significantly over that of the source system. (Growth in productivity might be one of the factors that would encourage a customer to re-engineer an old system, if the life span of the system were long enough.) Because the development system ran on the same processor as the demonstration system, a programmer could develop a schedule for a module, design, code, compile, unit test, repair, promote, and transmit it—through VM/SP-HPO—to the demonstration system for integration testing in a single session from the programmer's interactive terminal.

A tool that was central to the success of the demonstration was a PC-based relational database, hosted under dBASE III™, because it contained a data dictionary identifying every variable and constant in the source system, with the following attributes:

- the company responsible for coding the identifier
- the identifier

- the name of the table, if any, in which the identifier resides (in the source system)
- the page number in the New York TRACON coding specifications where the identifier is described
- the names of the procedures that reference the identifier
- with each procedure, a value—given here in parentheses—indicates whether the procedure sets the variable (1), uses it (2), both (3), or that data are not yet known (0)
- the type of identifier (e.g., character, Boolean, array, real)
- the new name of the identifier in Ada and Pascal/VS
- the name of the new design package that would own the identifier (the re-engineered system was designed to eliminate global data)
- the page number in the new database design document where the identifier is described

Figure 5 illustrates a page of the data dictionary.

The target language, Pascal/VS, and the target operating system, Multiple Virtual Storage/Extended Architecture (MVS/XA™), although they were part of the demonstration system architecture, were also tools, in that their characteristics facilitate and encourage certain methods. Pascal/VS was chosen because all of the programmers had experience with some form of Pascal, which is lexically similar to Ada used to develop the design, and because Pascal/VS runs under MVS. The FAA had requested that the demonstration system be coded in Ada. Because the contract team was not experienced in writing Ada and the schedule was quite short, all parties agreed on an Ada design (described in the section on methods) and a Pascal/VS implementation.

Lexically, the source system and the target system differed markedly. ULTRA is a 16-bit assembler that provides very little built-in support for development (e.g., no macro facility), for execution (no distinction is made between instruction space and the data space), or for testing. Because it is almost entirely a specification for the computer, its nature is lexical—and mechanical. Pascal/VS, because it is a specification for the programmer, provides not only a lexicon, but an emphasis; one that is mathematical rather than procedural. For example, variables and data types are specifications, and are distinguished from the instructions, which are fabricated of single-entry, single-exit control structures. Of equal importance, Pascal/VS implies rules for the development of programs, and it promotes the decomposition of

Figure 5 Data dictionary sample records

Record#	COMPANY	DATANAME	DATABASE	PAGENUMBR	P1	S1	P2	S2	P3	S3	P4	S4	P5	S5	P6
14		BOTIT9	BOT	4	TPUR	3		0		0		0		0	
15		ABEAT1	CTS	7		0	CRIT	0	DBATM	0	IFI	2	KOF	3	
16		ABEAT1	CTS	7	TEDC	3		0	TINIT	3		0	TPUR	3	TPRED
17		ABEAT1	CTS	7	PSBLD	0	RETRACK	1	SMOTH	0	TEDCRS	0	TI	0	TPSEC
18		ABEAT2	CTS	7	TPSEC	3	TCRSS	2	TINIT	3	IFI	3	TPUR	3	TPRED
19		ABEAT3	CTS	7	TEDC	3	TCRSS	2	TINIT	3	IFI	3	TPUR	3	TPRED
20		ABEAT4	CTS	7	TPSEC	3	COMA	3	TINIT	1		0	TPUR	3	
21		ABEAT5	CTS	7	TEDC	3	TCRSS	2	TINIT	3	DOP	3	TPUR	3	SLINK
22		ACTYPT	CTS	18	TPRED	0	TPSEC	3	TPUR	3	KOF	3	IFI	3	
23		ACTYPT2	CTS	18	TFI	3		0	KOF	3		0		0	
24		ALT1	CTS	17	TINIT	3	AUT	2	TPUR	1	ALTRKR	0	CDR	2	COMA

abstract programs into smaller, less abstract programs. It also imparts structure to a program and, to the advantage of large software products, among programs.

The choice of MVS to be the host for the ARTS applications was in keeping with the overall approach: providing a commercial platform for the re-engineered applications. MVS, unlike the specially-built supervisor developed for the ARTS IIIA (MPE), is a general-purpose operating system. It supports a wide range of applications, including both batch and interactive development, database management systems, network systems, production systems, and real-time systems. For example, the contract team used MVS to support batch compilations, to perform interactive reduction of CDR data using the CDR editor, and to run the ARTS applications. The last, because the ARTS executes in real time, required the presence of a real-time control program. The real-time control program used was RTX, developed by IBM to support the real-time applications for the National Aeronautics and Space Administration (NASA) and United States Air Force ground control space programs. Although the demonstration was carried out in a test environment using simulated inputs, the re-engineered system was designed and implemented as if it would be run in real time.

Methods

Within the contract team there were three teams, totaling 25 people, roughly aligned with the three companies. The first team was responsible for implementing the tools and the new software architecture. The second team concentrated on re-engineering the on-line applications. The third team coded RETRACK, the CDR editor, and the database constants, and

conducted system testing. The teams were directed by a software architect, who developed the program plan, including the methods and the standards by which the software would be developed, and the software architecture. The teams met two or three days a week to discuss both methods and architecture. Every developer knew the approach, and frequent and formal communication marked the project. All project data, plans, standards, design, and code were on line and easily accessible through a hierarchy of directories.

A software development plan defined the software build plan and the standards for designing and developing the software, for software configuration control, and for software quality control. The standards contained templates, such as the gateway program that enabled each application to interface with the application control programs using one standard protocol. Every rule the developers might need was defined and in most cases examples were provided.

A formal life cycle, based on the traditional waterfall life cycle, was strictly adhered to. It was:

• Requirements analysis, methods, and architecture
• Level-1 software design (in Ada)
• Level-2 software design (in Ada)
• Coding, in three increments (in Pascal/VS)
• Software integration and testing
• Demonstrations and delivery of documentation

Figure 6 describes the contract team's approach to re-engineering. Although no software improvement program[4] was formally documented, the methods were defined in detail in the team's proposal to the FAA.

154

S6 P7	S7 P8	S8 P9	S9 P10	S10	TYPE	VARNAME	DBNAME	NEWPGNUM
0	0	0	0	0	E	bot_time_of_last_correl	TRACK	0
0	0 MSAW	0 MTGCT	0	0	L	last_correl_on_radar_only_trk	TRACK	0
0 ALTRKR	0 CDR	2 COMA	3 COMB	2	L	last_correl_on_radar_only_trk	TRACK	0
3 TSUB0	0 TSUB1	0	0	0	L	last_correl_on_radar_only_trk	TRACK	0
2 COMA	3	0	0	0	L	initial_correl_proc_enabled_trk	TRACK	0
2 SLINK	2 TPSEC	3 RETRACK	2 KOF	3	E	assigned_beacon_code_trk	TRACK	0
0	0	0	0	0	I	constant_zero_trk	TRACK	0
3 IFI	3 TPSEC	1 KOF	3 TPRED	2	I	beac_code_status_code_trk	TRACK	0
0 SCTME	2 TINIT	3 SLINK	0 TEDC	2	I	aircraft_type_code_trk	TRACK	0
0	0	0	0	0	C	sp_amen_site_ad_alphy	TRACK	0
3 COMB	2 KOFB	0 KOFC	0 MSAW	0	I	rep_altitude_trk	TRACK	0

The project began in September 1986. Within a month, two critical milestones were met: the development tools were adapted (from the host computer system) to suit the demonstration. For example, interactive panels that invoked the Jovial compiler on the host computer system were modified to invoke Pascal/VS, and a set of macros were developed that enabled RTX and the Pascal/VS run-time software to work together in a real-time environment (Pascal/VS was developed for a batch and interactive environment and its built-in storage management and error processing had to be modified).

The contract team did not reinvent the system. The source system requirements, an English description of its expected behavior, on the whole were not changed. To complete the requirements analysis, the team recorded their intent in the *New York TRACON Demonstration of Program Recoding Requirements Analysis Document.*

Re-engineering the software architecture. The official name given to the project, "New York TRACON Demonstration of Program Recoding," is somewhat misleading. A new architectural platform had to be designed before the applications could be re-engineered. The architecture of the source system is profoundly different from that of the target. (This would be the case in re-engineering many old systems.) Although both are von Neumann machines, the UNIVAC IOP is a multiprocessor, its storage shared among processors; the IBM 3083 is a uniprocessor. In the IOP, work is distributed among the processors to meet the system's demand for service in real time. The system was designed to get the most out of all the data processing elements, processors, channels, storage, and devices. In the IOP system, *the work is moved to the machine.* The supervisory software

(MPE), schedules tasks from a prefabricated two-dimensional lattice, a directed graph that specifies the interdependency, priority, and, in some cases, the expendability of each unit of work. PSRAP must run before tracking, tracking must run before display, and so on. In the IOP system, the application is aware of its processing constraints. For example, tracking must execute within a fixed period of time, or work is flushed from the input queues.

The IBM System/370 architecture is the inverse where *the machine is moved to the work,* at least in the abstract. The System/370 computer family, of which the IBM System/370 Model 3083 is representative, is event-driven. Work is defined and allocated dynamically. MVS dispatches applications when they are available, not according to a predefined sequence. The rules of concurrency, of data coherency, and of application communications are left to the designer.

The new software architecture centralized the control program services within its run-time system (that included MVS, RTX, and Pascal/VS) and a layer of applications control programs, thereby decoupling the applications from their processing environment, and insulating them so that they could be re-engineered free of operating system dependencies. A single gateway package enabled all the applications to interface with the control program services.

The architecture was developed as a set of rules and formally documented as part of a requirements analysis document. It contained the following:

- Definitions to include names of methods, attributes of behavior, objects (e.g., Ada package, application work, conversation, pipeline, process)

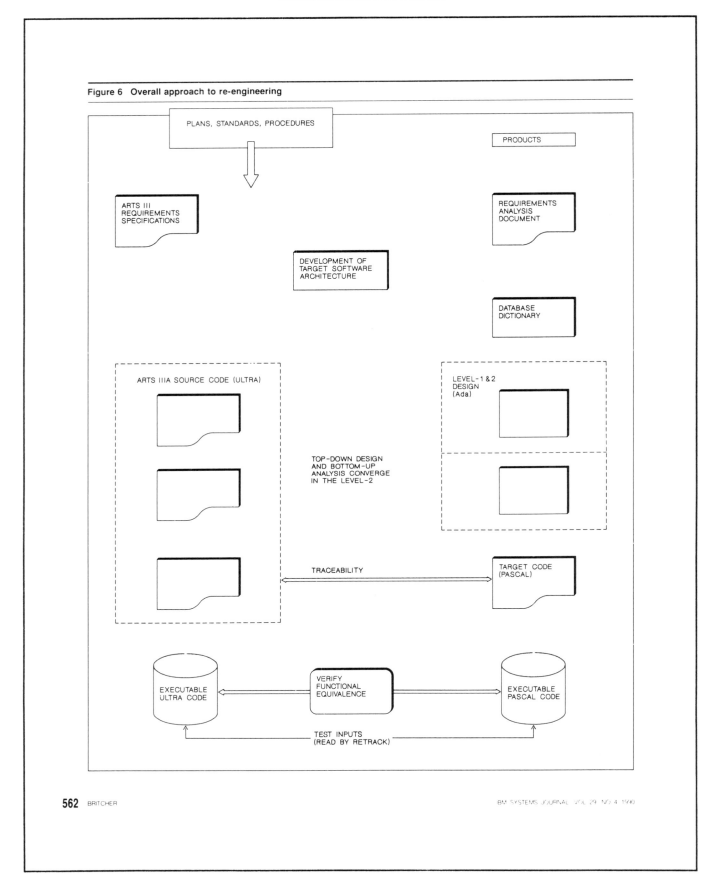

Figure 6 Overall approach to re-engineering

156

- Rules for packages and their attributes to define the five classes of applications and identification of the applications that fell within each: off line (O), control (C), interactive (I), pipeline (P), and data (D), and definition of the rules of behavior (e.g., pipeline packages shall not converse with each other)
- Rules for system work to define the units of work (e.g., radar targets, tracks) and their relationship to each other
- Rules for system parts and their work to describe the behavior of the packages with respect to their attributes (e.g., pipeline)
- Rules for the decomposition of parts to define the design levels (there were two) and their relationship to one another (e.g., the relationship between a Level-1 package and its Level-2 packages can be one-to-one or one-to-many)
- Rules for tasks and concurrency to define the behavior of the applications as real-time programs
- Rules for the communications between subtasks to define a message control system that would enable applications to operate independently, and send and receive messages to and from one another
- Rules for database and data coherency to define the rules for data aggregation and acquisition (data were defined as records in the demonstration system, rather than as tables in the source system, and, because the applications were redesigned as state machines, there were no global data)

The abstract rules provided a natural specification for the applications control packages, shown in the upper left of Figure 7.

Figure 7 describes one dimension of the software architecture, the Level-1 Ada packages, the attributes of each, and their interfaces.

Re-engineering the database. The new software architecture gave the applications independence, and as a result, it gave the teams coding them independence. The data dictionary progressed in parallel. As the architecture unfolded, developers studied the source system code and coding specifications of the applications, without having to worry about the environment in which they would run. The developers identified the variables and constants that are set and used by each application (e.g., PSRAP). By identifying the data space of the source system and mapping it to the target system, and recording both the domain (source) and range (target), the developers reduced the re-engineering of the applications to a simple

mathematical function. The function is the set of ordered pairs (s,t), where s is the set of identifiers that define the potential states of the source system and t is the set of identifiers that define the potential states of the target system. In many cases the domain mapped to an empty set: variables were not needed because the target system excluded capabilities, for example, the live interface to the PSRAP.

Formally defining the on-line software architecture and the data space, before elaborating the design of programs, was central to producing a target system that met the design and performance constraints within the short schedule.

Re-engineering the design of the applications. The design of the applications was re-engineered and recorded in two levels. The design was predicated on the methods used by IBM on all its major software development projects. The methods treat (computer) programs as mathematical objects, either functions or state machines.[7] A function maps inputs to outputs; a state machine is a function with a memory. Most modules or collections of modules behave as state machines. Designing a program as a state machine promotes the use of abstraction, where interfaces are specified before modules are fully elaborated, and data hiding. For example, a state machine implemented as an Ada package would specify the inputs, outputs, and a private set of state data, accessible to users of the package only by invoking one of its collection of procedures. In summary then, the contract team re-engineered the design of the applications as a set of communicating state machines.

The team used an Ada process design language to record the design. Using Ada as a design language turned out to have several advantages. Ada encourages both the use of abstraction and data hiding, so it is a good fit for using the concept of state machines; both the FAA and the contract team learned Ada and its characteristics, at least as a tool for design; the FAA is committed to using Ada on its large projects, and this project increased their confidence; Ada provided a common vernacular for talking about the design and the design process.

Three months after the project began, the Level-1 Ada packages were completely specified. All state machine interfaces, state data (the data owned by the Level-1 package), and CDR records were classified by type. The gateway package was specified. The successor packages, the Level-2 Ada packages that

Figure 7 Level-1 Ada packages and their relationships

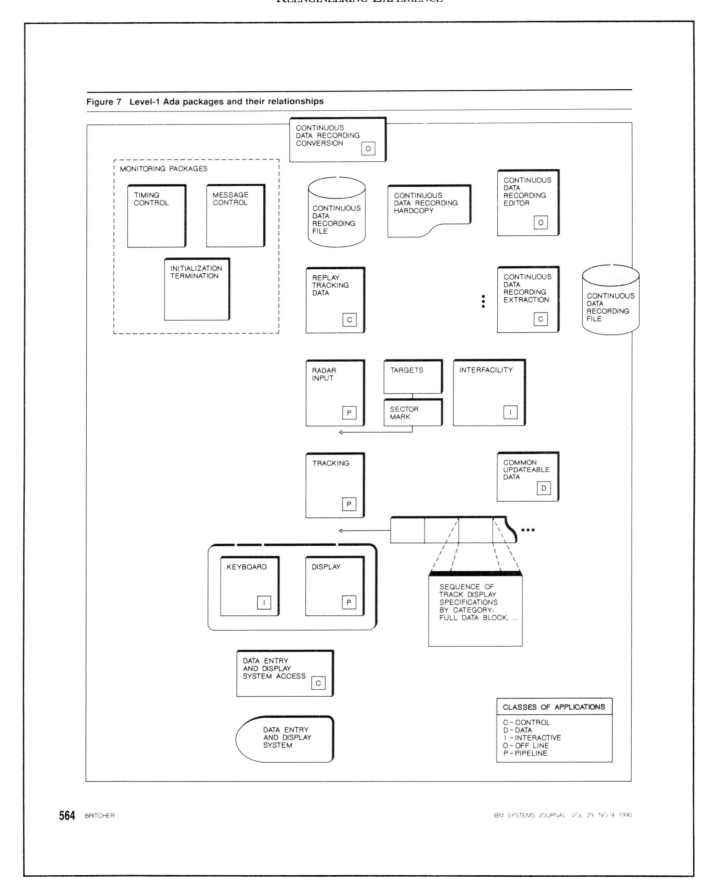

158

would decompose from Level-1, were identified. All recording was inspected.

Incremental implementation. About a month later, the first of three software builds was completed and running. It included the support software, the CDR conversion program and the CDR editor, the on-line platform (including MVS, RTX, the Pascal/VS run-time support), the application control services (initialization/termination, timing control, message control), and the application gateways. The complete system structure was in place. The first build verified that records could be read from the converted CDR file and that messages (internal work) could be transmitted between tasks.

The Level-2 design (the full elaboration of the applications in the Ada design language) and the conversion of Ada to Pascal/VS proceeded in step with the build plan. The second build contained all the applications except tracking and parts of keyboard processing, both of which were completed in the third build.

Each Level-2 Ada package was inspected after it was completed and then converted to Pascal/VS. In writing the Pascal/VS code, the application programmer would use the Ada, the ULTRA, the ULTRA coding specifications, and the database dictionary to ensure that the re-engineering resulted in a functionally equivalent system.

The second and third builds were elaborations of the first. No structural changes were made to the system after the first build. The applications were laid into the system as they became available, and then verified by the software integration and test team.

Testing. During software integration and testing, formal error reporting and correction procedures and configuration control procedures were practiced, just as they would be on a large-scale development project.

Each build was tested at the unit and system level. Pascal/VS provided excellent debugging facilities; most modules ran in the system environment without error. System testing was performed under VM/SP-HPO and then natively, with MVS running directly on the processor. Not allowing enough time to test natively was a difficulty uncovered in the first demonstration. Errors were masked in the virtual machine environment. One of the advantages of transporting software, over inventing it, is the cost-effectiveness of testing by comparison. Because the source

system and re-engineered system were functionally equivalent (with predetermined allowances), testing proved to be inexpensive and incisive. The outputs of the re-engineered system were compared with the outputs of the source system. Since both were driven by the same inputs, errors showed up as markers (discrepancies) rather than as the object of human evaluation and judgment, the reliability of which depends on many complex factors such as interpreting requirements, training, and experience.

The results

The contract team completed the re-engineering of the New York TRACON applications software and successfully demonstrated its functional equivalence in nine months. The budget was met. The team gave a final presentation and demonstration in May 1987. The demonstration was given using an FAA-provided input file, containing the recorded output of a then current run of the New York TRACON system. The FAA and the contractors compared the output recorded from the demonstration run with the New York TRACON generated output and found no unanticipated discrepancies. The analysis showed that the re-engineered tracker was functionally equivalent to the source original. The digitized radar and track data blocks stepping across the projected airspace on the modern situation display gave impressive visual evidence that the system worked.

The team converted over 53 000 lines of ULTRA to 83 000 lines of Pascal/VS (62 percent comments). The team developed 340 Pascal procedures. One-hundred-and-fifty-six (156) procedures, mostly in tracking, were implemented with no deviations from the original ULTRA. The Pascal/VS was converted from 47 000 lines of Ada process design language, including Level-1, Level-2, and commentary. The source code ratio of ULTRA to Pascal/VS, without commentary, was 1.6:1. The team identified and documented 58 design issues; all were resolved within a week. There were 78 errors found and corrected during software integration and testing.

Conclusions

The authorized logical conversion and demonstration of more than a third of the New York TRACON software, from an UNIVAC IOP ULTRA architecture to an IBM System/370 architecture, coded in Pascal/VS, is sound evidence that real-time software is transportable, even if the environments of the source and target system are markedly different.

In the final report delivered to the FAA the following factors were identified as key contributors to the success of the project:

- The software development environment, including the laboratory and software tools, was available shortly after the project started and was easy to learn and use.
- The team used a consistent and proven set of development methods and followed the standard software development life cycle, including require-ments analysis and architecture, two levels of design, incremental software builds, design and code inspections, and an independent software integration and test team.
- The software architecture was formally recorded.
- A complete data dictionary mapped ULTRA variables to the re-engineered system.
- The on-line applications were designed as independent items, with no global data, with precisely-defined interfaces, and without embedding information about their operating environment.
- Early in the project, the system inputs were converted to System/370 format; the input records were defined as Ada data types to ensure consistency throughout the entire software system (the CDR editor, for example, used the same data types as RETRACK).
- The software was re-engineered in Pascal/VS, which made the transition from the Ada process design language easy, and, because of its rules for data typing and program construction, Pascal/VS code proved to be reliable.

The most significant problem, because of the tight schedule, was the short time allotted to test the system, in its final demonstration environment. This was overcome by working considerable overtime. At that, there were latent faults and errors, discovered after the final demonstration.

The advantages of re-engineering a software product or system, over reinventing it, are significant. Re-engineering avoids 1) the effort of, and the errors that accrue from, developing new engineering requirements and functional specifications, and 2) the effort of full-scale verification and validation, the very activities Sneed[6] found so expensive. In short, re-engineering takes advantage of the profound effects of evolution. It preserves the functional behavior of a system that had been specified, designed, implemented, repaired, enhanced, verified, validated, and most importantly, used over years, while improving its quality. The cost, as demonstrated by this project, need not be prohibitive.

Acknowledgments

The performance of the contract team was outstanding, as was the commitment and cooperation of the FAA and their system integration contractor Martin-Marietta. The FAA program manager, Dick Bock, deserves special recognition for his support and encouragement throughout the project. Art Smock from Martin-Marietta was particularly helpful in providing information about the New York TRACON system. The work of each member of the team was critical; in that sense every participant made an outstanding contribution to the success of the project: from Data Transformation Corporation—Bob Bosworth, Marie Brown, Annette Cabbell, Wai Cheung, Ben Dennis, Bill Earley, Hussein-Khomassi, Eugene Liberman, Stan Mead, Andre Small; from IBM—Dick Allardyce, Larry Boulia, Stuart Cramer, Jeff Dollyhite, Austin Gallow, Connie Hayes, Stephan Landau, Michielle Looser, Michele Ichniowski, Lana Massung, Margaret McCandless, Barb Morten, Bob Scheuble, Richard Wei; and from Pailen-Johnson Associates—Tom Baxter, Lalitha Bhat, Clarke Thomason, Stephen Hall, Michael Gandee, James Atkinson, Marvin Sendrow.

Cited references and note

1. In this paper, *re-engineering* means the authorized logical conversion of a customized architecture (implemented in assembler source code) to a commercial architecture (implemented in a compiler source language). Re-engineering does not include unauthorized reverse compilation of object code to form source code as the basis for the derivation of a substitute product, generally referred to as "reverse engineering."
2. *New York TRACON Demonstration of Program Recoding Software Translation and Verification Methodology Document*, DOT/FAA/CT-87/33, Federal Aviation Administration, U.S. Department of Transportation (August 1987); available through the National Technical Information Service, Springfield, VA 22161.
3. *Guideline on Software Maintenance*, Section 5, Federal Information Processing Standards Publication 106, National Bureau of Standards (June 15, 1984), pp. 14–17.
4. C. A. Houtz, "Software Improvement Program: A Treatment for Software Senility," *Proceedings of the 19th Computer Performance Evaluation Users Group*, National Bureau of Standards Special Publication 500-104 (October 1983), pp. 92–107.
5. R. N. Britcher and J. J. Craig, "Using Modern Design Practices to Upgrade Aging Software Systems," *IEEE Software* **3**, No. 3, 16–24 (May 1986).
6. H. M. Sneed, "Software Renewal: A Case Study," *IEEE Software* **1**, No. 3, 53–56 (July 1984).
7. A. B. Ferrentino and H. D. Mills, "State Machines and Their Semantics in Software Engineering," *Proceedings, IEEE Com-

puter Society First International Computer Software and Applications Conference COMPSAC (1977), pp. 242–251.

Robert N. Britcher *IBM Federal Sector Division, 9231 Corporate Boulevard, Rockville, Maryland 20850.* Mr. Britcher received a B.A. in chemistry from Gettysburg College in 1968, and joined IBM in 1969. He has worked primarily on the automation of air traffic control systems and is currently assigned to the FAA advanced automation system (AAS). He has written about several aspects of software, including design, standards, correctness, size estimation and metrics, maintenance, and software systems engineering. His articles have appeared in a number of journals and magazines, including *IEEE Software* and (IEEE) *Computer.* Mr. Britcher's research interests include program correctness and verification, and the development and evolution of software systems. He is a member of the IEEE Computer Society.

Reprint Order No. G321-5418.

161

Reengineering to Reduce System Maintenance: A Case Study

Malcolm Slovin and Silas Malik

This article is a case study of how a large insurance company reduced the maintenance of its aging, COBOL-based system and made the system more adaptable to change through reengineering and CASE technology. Before the system was revitalized, data had been collected on maintenance work performed, and users as well as the IS staff were interviewed about their experience with the system. Tom Gilb's evolutionary method for systems development was used to formally define system requirements, the ends to meet those requirements, and the metrics to measure fulfillment of those requirements. A CASE environment was implemented for the reengineering effort and future development and maintenance work. An analysis of the project's results shows up to a 50% reduction in some types of maintenance work.

In recent years, many IS departments have begun to concentrate on revitalizing instead of replacing large systems that have been functioning for more than a decade. Typically, these systems have been meeting users' needs but have needed an increasing amount of maintenance work to continue to meet users' demands. Rising costs for developing new software have made the replacement of these systems exceedingly expensive and have forced IS managers to investigate other options. One of these options, reengineering, offers a cost-effective alternative to system redevelopment. This article describes the reengineering techniques and management approaches that were used along with other standard software engineering methods to revitalize a large, COBOL-based insurance system that was requiring an increasing amount of maintenance. The same reengineering techniques with the addition of CASE technology were also used to integrate the system with newer technologies.

The system's development history

Under study is a large insurance system that was the product of two outside contractors. It was developed in stages as need demanded and resources permitted. The first and major portion of the system produced was the policy subsystem. This subsystem originally operated in batch mode and processed data collected from 42 servicing companies. It was later converted to an online operation and was administered by a single agent.

To compound the problems produced by the company's unstable development environment, the dynamic nature of the insurance industry demanded that the system be constantly updated. The system underwent numerous updates and revisions since it was implemented. Because there was no mechanism in place to monitor possible side effects of changes made to the system, updates and revisions in one area frequently caused problems in other areas.

The system was developed between 10 and 14 years ago in COBOL with a few Assembler utilities. Before, the revitalizing effort con-

Malcolm Slovin is director of the advanced technology center at Computer Sciences Corp. Lanham MD.

Silas Malik, formerly a systems analyst at Computer Sciences Corp, is currently with the engineering department of the Washington Suburban Sanitary Commission, Laurel MD.

sisted of approximately 1,600 programs totaling more than two million lines of code. The system sustained during its life more than 1,000 changes, several of which required major restructuring. Approaches in implementing the system changed many times, resulting in a patchy system that was well integrated in some areas and functionally disparate in others. The system's documentation was like the system's integration: excellent in some areas and completely lacking in others. Moreover, the documentation was not readily available to support an active maintenance program.

A data base environment had been implemented to support the informational needs of various user segments. Two major subsystems were built using Information Builders Inc's Focus to provide statistical and historical data from a variety of sources. Although integration was technically possible, these subsystems were not integrated with the policy subsystem, and intersystem communication was provided only when business needs dictated. In addition, many data elements were duplicated within all three systems.

The reporting subsystem reflected the entire system's history. The lack of a central data dictionary led to the production of reports that gave conflicting information. The reasons for this problem were many, but in general it was because of the use of the same term for different concepts, different terms for the same concept, and the lack of a systematic method for report development and integration.

Despite its problems, the system met the functional requirements of the business. In addition, the user community had developed procedures and processing flows that were based on the system's operation. Therefore, implementing a new system would not only have caused a major impact within the data processing area; it would have disrupted the current business flow and required extensive changes from the user community.

The system's maintenance history

During the last several years, a minimum of data was collected on the maintenance work performed. Although the type of data and the definitions of the type of work changed, the data indicates the problems encountered. Exhibit 1 categorizes the type of maintenance work requested as adaptive enhancement, or corrective. Both enhancement and corrective maintenance remained at significant levels through 1988. However, little adaptive maintenance was ever performed. The exhibit indicates that the level of corrective maintenance, as compared to other work, remained constant during the past few years.

A second class of data that was only recently collected is on trouble reports, which were issued when emergency maintenance was needed. This temporary or permanent maintenance work was necessary for the system's nightly batch operations. These repairs were usually followed up with corrective maintenance if the emergency repair was not permanent. Exhibit 2 shows the number of emergency corrections performed in 1987 and 1988 and in the last three months of 1986. A second statistic in this class of data—reruns and restarts—indicates the number of times a program abended and had to be rerun or the number of times the system needed to be restarted at a particular point in its operation. The exhibit also contains the number of system change requests received per year as compared to the number of trouble reports and reruns and restarts. Not only is the number of trouble reports many times the number of maintenance items completed each year, but this figure, as well as the number of reruns, increased for the past two years.

Exhibit 3 lists the subsystems that required the most emergency maintenance. An examination of this list reveals that a few subsystems required a very high level of emergency repairs. The remaining trouble reports were issued for program areas spread throughout the entire system. In 1987, the most troubled program areas accounted for approximately 23% of the total number of trouble reports filed. In 1988, these program areas accounted for approximately 21% of the trouble reports filed. However, frequent-problem program areas tended to be the modules that were most frequently enhanced, were most often executed, and contained the largest portions of code.

Analysis of the maintenance data

The data indicates several maintenance problems, which are: a lack of adaptive mainte-

SOFTWARE ENGINEERING

Exhibit 1. *Volumes and Types of System Maintenance*

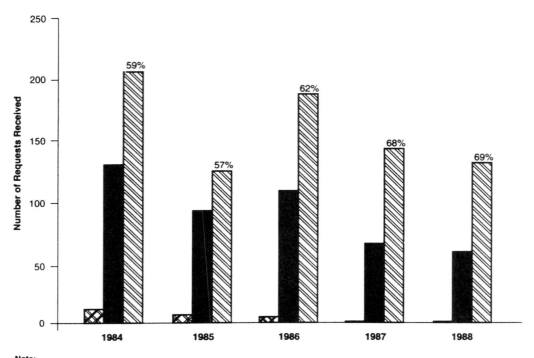

Note:
The percent figures are the percentage of total maintenance that is corrective.

Key:
- Adaptive maintenance
- Enhancement maintenance
- Corrective maintenance

nance, a large amount of corrective maintenance, incomplete and inadequate system data, and a large number of enhancements suggesting either poor planning in the initial systems development stages or a highly dynamic business environment. As the volume of system demands grew, the lack of adaptive maintenance (i.e., integration of new technology to accommodate new demands) certainly caused a significant amount of corrective maintenance. The high level of corrective maintenance is also symptomatic of a system that exhibits a significant number of side effects when enhanced.

The emergency maintenance data was separated from the other types of maintenance data because only partial data on emergency maintenance was available. If added to the original matrix, this data would have skewed the five-year totals and given a distorted view of the maintenance work. However, a high level of emergency maintenance compared to the amount of corrective maintenance can be seen in Exhibit 2.

In addition, although the data is incomplete, the amount of emergency maintenance has apparently increased, and the actual number of corrections in the same years decreased slightly. This implies that more corrective maintenance was being done in an emergency mode rather than through more formal channels. Reruns and restarts generally resulted from side effects caused by emergency corrections to the system and indicate problems that include the system complexity, inadequate understanding of system components, and

Reengineering Case Study

Exhibit 2. **Work Hours Spent on Emergency Maintenance per Category**

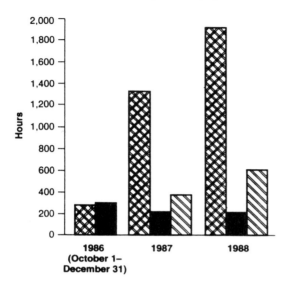

Note:
Data on reruns and restarts was not available for 1986.

Key:
- Trouble reports
- Change requests
- Reruns and restarts

lack of comprehensive testing, test systems, and tools.

The system revitalization strategy

In general, the goal of the revitalization effort was to decrease the amount of changes to the system, particularly those made during corrective maintenance. As part of the strategy to reach this goal, many hours were spent interviewing both system users and technical staff members. The conclusion drawn from these interviews was that a technical solution (i.e., only reengineering the system software) was not sufficient. Therefore, to realize the project's goal, it was determined that the system also had to become robust enough to accommodate future technology. The software support environment as well as the technical and management techniques used in both the software development and support environments were also targeted for restructuring. Given the cost benefit inherent in the system's functional capability and the high cost of developing a new system, the approach selected was

to reengineer the main COBOL system and to integrate it with a statistical reporting system that uses a data base.

Although the system was continually enhanced to reflect changes in the business environment, the aim of revitalization was to restructure the technical portion of the system rather than the business environment. Therefore, screens, transaction flow, and functional capabilities were not altered, and system users did not notice any changes to the automated interface. However, functional enhancements were designed to meet with changing business requirements and implemented according to technical standards developed during reengineering. After completion of reengineering, the entire system also complied with these standards.

Another objective of the reengineering project was to produce a more modular system architecture. The operational boundaries between subsystems were indistinct, and it was determined that greater modularity would be accomplished by separating processes. An example of these indistinct boundaries was in the file management used by the transaction processing subsystem to generate reports as well as process transactions. Files were managed by either IBM's VSAM filing system or a statistical data base running under Focus. The two file management systems exchanged data as needed, but there did exist some data duplication.

Exhibit 3. **Most Frequently Troubled Program Areas**

Program	Percentage of Maintenance That Is Corrective	
	1987	1988
Policy update	5.18%	5.18%
Policy reports	5.87%	4.60%
Claims update	2.57%	1.37%
Document catalogue update	0.85%	2.40%
Batch monitor	1.02%	2.07%
Transaction update	0.50%	1.55%
Zone rating processor	0.35%	1.35%
Zone extract	1.20%	1.20%
Policy administration	1.20%	0.85%
Special action report	1.55%	0.50%

Note:
Of the approximately 1,600 programs in the system, the above programs required nearly a quarter of all corrective maintenance performed in 1987 and 1988

To produce the more modular environment, several actions were determined necessary. Under the new, modular architecture, the transaction processing subsystem had to perform those functions relevant to the processing of transactions and produce only those control reports used to balance the system's operations. All data files had to be maintained and processed only by the data base storage and retrieval subsystem. All ad hoc, canned, and special reports had to be generated by the reporting subsystem through interfaces to the data base storage and retrieval subsystem.

A technical planning team was formed to consider several techniques for the reengineering effort; the final decision was to combine various facets of several methods. Tom Gilb's evolutionary method of systems development was used in the initial stages of the project to develop direction and objectives.

In addition, a mini analysis was developed and used as a front-end diagnostic to determine the feasibility of reaching the project's goals. The mini analysis was also devised to document both system problems and the maintenance used to correct these problems. This analysis established the following set of procedures:
- Formally defining the problem and its solution.
- Defining the system parameters involved in both the problem and its solution.
- Determining the number of system components affected by both the problem and its solution.
- Documenting the results of the mini analysis as well as the maintenance work performed as a result of the mini analysis.

The results of the mini analysis were also used to garner the support of a steering committee, which was composed of various department managers and was responsible for approving all user requests for system changes.

Applying the evolutionary method

The evolutionary method is based on the idea of establishing and completing intermediate deliverables within the life cycle of a project, measuring the added value of the deliverable to the user, and adjusting both the design and objectives to correspond with the changing

nature of user requirements. Instead of planning toward one delivery date, the project evolves and is completed in stages. Each stage represents a deliverable that involves complete analysis, design, coding, and testing. Each stage advances the project toward its goals.

When completed, each stage was evaluated by determining how well it met the needs of the data processing staff. After a favorable evaluation, the project's design and objectives were reevaluated to determine whether changes in either the business or systems environment required changes in the design and objectives. As implemented in this project, the evolutionary method had one disadvantage: because the reengineering was done in stages, different areas of the system were in various states of restructuring. However, once completed, all portions of the system were reengineered.

The implementation of the evolutionary method for the project involved identifying and listing system functions that meet technical and user requirements. These functions were selected through an iterative process, which categorized the entire insurance system into four major areas: policy, claims, finance, and edit and input. Within each of these areas, a list of descriptive functions was generated. The first list was a very general listing of all system functions, both global and specific. Through several iterations, this list was condensed and modified to yield the high-level functions addressed by the reengineering project. These included maintainability, adaptability, reliability, and performance.

Once the high-level functions had been identified, the next step established a set of metrics to measure the results of reengineering. A list of measurable attributes for each of these functions was then compiled. Through a similar iterative process and use of the mini analysis, each list was refined to yield a list of attributes associated with each function. These attributes provided workable measures of improvement. A sample list of functions and attributes appears in Exhibit 4.

The final step in the planning stage provided a set of solutions for improving the functions and attributes. The application of these solutions to the functions and attributes was the complete plan for reengineering the system. A

Reengineering Case Study

Exhibit 4. *System Function Requirements and Attributes*

Maintainability

Attribute: Correction implementation
Definition: The design and implementation of a system correction
Test: Time required by completion of maintenance correction cycle
Success Rating: According to mini analysis time estimates
Failure Rating: 50% greater than mini analysis time estimates
Before Reengineering: 150% greater than mini analysis time estimates

Reliability

Attribute: Error evolution
Definition: Those errors that become visible and have a system impact over time
Test: Number of requests for corrective maintenance received
Success Rating: 25% of all situation bulletins received
Failure Rating: 30% of all situation bulletins received
Before Reengineering: 50% greater than all situation bulletins received

Adaptability

Attribute: Modularity
Definition: The logical separation of functions within a system
Test: Number of functions per program
Success Rating: Each program is designed to support a single function
Failure Rating: 90% support a single function
Before Reengineering: Data not collected

Performance

Attribute: Online storage
Definition: The amount of disk space required to maintain system programs and data
Test: Total number of gigabytes of disk space on direct-access storage devices
Success Rating: Maintain current level
Failure Rating: 10% increase
Before Reengineering: 42G bytes available

sampling of solutions with corresponding functions and attributes appears in Exhibit 5.

Implementing the solutions

The solutions were divided into three categories: transaction processing, data management, and data modeling. Accordingly, three teams were defined to simultaneously implement these solution areas.

The transaction processing team was given responsibility to optimize and standardize the batch and online processing system. In addition, it built a test facility that became available to the entire programming staff after the reengineering effort was completed. As part of the evolutionary development strategy, the

team began with a review of the batch processing system, which included an analysis of its critical path (i.e., the sequence in which the system's programs were executed). Next, system processing was optimized by removing or realigning processes originally a part of the transaction processing critical path. Processes that could be realigned were run in parallel with the critical processing path. Finally, the various programs within the processing system were evaluated and restructured.

The data management team was responsible for the definition and integration of data elements into a data base environment. This required a review of all existing reports to eliminate redundancy and provide integrated reporting across several systems.

The data modeling team began by implementing a CASE environment that included automated tools. It then worked with the other solution teams to configure the tools and train the members on each team. With the aid of a data dictionary, the data modeling team analyzed and pinpointed data anomalies (e.g., data elements with multiple definitions) and resolved them. Once all errors were resolved,

Exhibit 5. *Design Solutions to Implement User Requirements*

Maintainability

Correction Implementation:
• Implement more measurable maintenance life cycle standards.
• Establish a full test system.

Reliability

Error Evolution:
• Involve quality assurance with all phases of projects.
• Install automated tools for program analysis.
• Have formal walkthroughs to examine software designs and code, documentation, and test plans.
• Establish quality metrics for program modules.
• Monitor and record the effects of system changes.

Performance

Batch and Online Processing:
• Reduce the number of tape mounts required.
• Refine the CICS processing structure.
• Isolate critical processing and run at the beginning of the cycle.
• Restructure bottleneck programs.
• Tune VSAM files.
• Reassign data from tape to disk.
• Remove unused software code.
• Reformat and restructure software for readability.
• Reduce logic complexity.
• Reduce the use of hard-coded data.

the data dictionary was used as the basis for the modeling effort, which required the development of CASE data flow diagrams. The CASE tools were then made available for the analysis of future system enhancements and for the development of documentation.

The role of CASE tools

During the redevelopment effort, automated tools aided in effecting changes and in ensuring that the system's quality could be maintained through future changes. These tools included Retrofit, a source code restructuring and reformatting tool by Catalyst Inc; Analyzer, a test coverage monitor from Alden Computer System Corp; and Eden Systems Corp's Q/Auditor, a quality assurance tool that measures program complexity. These tools were part of a more comprehensive CASE environment.

During reengineering, the CASE environment was involved in modeling the system. Afterward, it was implemented to provide ongoing modeling of the restructured system, thereby enabling maintainers and developers to better monitor potential ripple effects of proposed modifications and enhancements. In addition, a data dictionary was created to serve as a central repository of information on the system. In general, the CASE environment provided a shell to support the tools and techniques necessary for the redevelopment and integration. It currently supports the ongoing software engineering environment needed to ensure that future changes to the system are well integrated and of high quality.

The major mainframe tools—Retrofit, Analyzer, and Q/Auditor—were selected on the basis of an analysis of system data and the need for tools that are capable of maintaining software throughout the entire life of the system. The standards established with Q/Auditor became standards for future maintenance and enhancement projects and were found to be more easily implemented with the aid of Retrofit. The test monitor, Analyzer, was chosen to monitor and analyze the test environment throughout the system's life.

The results of using CASE tools

More than 90% of all requests for corrective maintenance were for problems concerning the batch portion of the system. The major

goal during the one-year project was to decrease the amount of maintenance that was needed to support the system. However, it was necessary to show short-term results to users and technical staff to make sure reengineering was meeting their expectations. To accomplish this task, the system was divided into four parts: transaction processing, policy, claims, and other. The transaction processing group concentrated on streamlining the processing flow, reducing the critical path, modernizing the use of data storage, and replacing non-COBOL vendor utilities with ones either written in COBOL or from IBM. Exhibit 6 shows the effects of the group's efforts on the daily processing subsystem and weekly processing subsystem.

> *During the redevelopment effort, automated tools aided in effecting changes and in ensuring that the system's quality could be maintained through future changes.*

Programs were reviewed using both automated methods and manual inspection before they were submitted for actual code restructuring. The tool used for automated inspection, Q/Auditor, rated each program in terms of its complexity. The criteria to which each program was subjected were grouped into several categories: verb (e.g., goto and do statements) counts, verb statistics, size analysis, comment analysis, data division analysis, formatting analysis, standards analysis, and structure analysis. Q/Auditor totals data gathered in each category to give a program a grade that could range from A for excellent to F for failure. For example, a program must have one exit for an A, three or fewer exits for a B, and five or fewer exits for a C. Initially, all programs failed the Q/Auditor inspection. However, programs failed for different reasons, each of which needed to be reviewed before being restructured. During inspection, many small changes were able to be made that allowed the program to pass the Q/Auditor inspection. All programs were required to pass before being put into the production environment.

Reengineering Case Study

Exhibit 6. *Effects of Reengineering on Daily and Weekly Transaction Processing Systems*

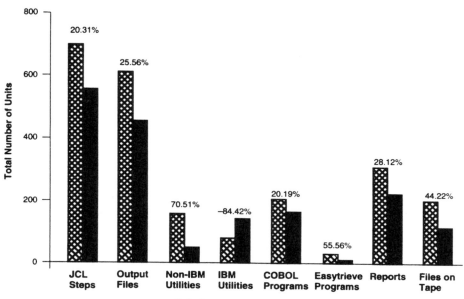

a. Daily Processing Subsystem

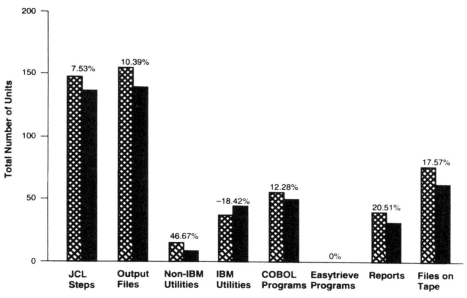

b. Weekly Processing Subsystem

Note:
Percentages denote the decreases in units.

Key:
⬚⬚⬚ Before reengineering
■ After reengineering

July/August 1991 **21**

SOFTWARE ENGINEERING

The restructuring tool, Retrofit, was used for three purposes: to increase the readability of the code, to standardize naming conventions throughout the system, and to restructure code. For most of the programs, readability was increased and naming standardized. However, only a few programs had code restructured by Retrofit. There were several reasons for this. First, the programs that had been optimized after the initial Q/Auditor inspection were found to be better structured and more maintainable than originally believed possible by optimization alone. The small changes required by Q/Auditor were sufficient to clean up the code. Second, the restructuring tool did not have the degree of flexibility needed. This was particularly true for programs in which the I/O sections had been specifically placed for ease of maintenance. Finally, there was reluctance to restructure a program that was working well. The amount of time and resources required to test totally restructured programs was also a concern and therefore played a part in the decision not to restructure a program.

The actual effects of the restructured code on the transaction processing system are not easily defined or measured. Exhibit 1 indicates that the number of requests for corrections decreased considerably although requests for enhancements remained at a constant level. The amount of adaptive maintenance had to be calculated separately because the reengineering effort composed this entire category. This calculation was based on the average amount of time required to complete a request for maintenance divided by the number of staff hours spent on reengineering. The percentage of requests for corrective maintenance has been reduced from previous years. The number of trouble reports issued from January through July of 1989 decreased approximately 35% from 1988.

Exhibit 7 provides information on another metric that was collected for two separate time periods. The first three-month period (October through December) was a time when few of the changes to the transaction processing system were implemented. This is in contrast to the period when most of the optimized and restructured system had been implemented. The number of hours spent on emergency maintenance was reduced by almost 50%.

The results from two other areas—data management and data modeling—are not currently available. The data management work was put on hold and has not yet been rescheduled. The data modeling work requires several major software bridges that have to be built and tested between the mainframe and local area network.

Analysis of the revitalization project

Several factors contributed to the project's accomplishments. First, the project was conceived on the basis of knowledge of what was possible. In this case, the problem was extensively examined and understood by both the technical staff and the users. Second, there was an excellent understanding of the system and its problems. The technical team members were selected on the basis of both their technical abilities and their knowledge of the system. Third, the tools were reviewed before being used on the project and then were reevaluated during the initial stages of the project.

Fourth, the technical planning team provided a fresh look at the problem, a second level of detail for the actual work, and a more realistic estimate of time and staffing needed to

Exhibit 7. *Hours Spent on Emergency Maintenance Before and After Reengineering*

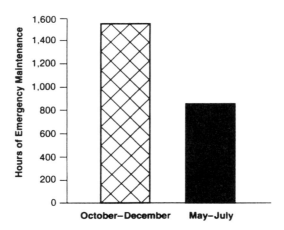

Key:
▨ Before reengineering
■ After reengineering

complete the project. Central to their recommendations was the adoption of the evolutionary development approach and the formation of project groups. The first task of each project group was to reevaluate the planning group's estimates and plans and produce a more detailed work and staffing plan (to the task level) and schedule. Finally, the project group leaders were selected for their technical expertise and communication skills.

As the project progressed, several problems surfaced. A major concern was the changing client priorities that required reassignment of many of the project staff members. Some of the scheduled tasks were not completed and had to be rescheduled. In addition, because the project affected a large portion of the system, there was a tendency to add work to the reengineering effort that would typically be part of another project. Finally, a larger portion of the system had to be manually restructured than expected; this was due not only to the inflexibility of the restructuring tool but in some cases to the desire to maintain particular portions of the system in the original development format.

It is envisioned that a set of tools and techniques will be used to support a more maintainable system as well as a more flexible network of documentation.

Overall, the project was effective as a reengineering effort but was not as successful as it could have been. There were several reasons for this. For example, the client's project planning cycle prohibited acquiring support from all levels of management. Therefore, overviews of the work were still being presented many months after the actual work had begun. This frequently forced reevaluation and change of both focus and staffing. In addition, staff members needed to be shifted to higher-priority projects even while additional work was being added to the reengineering project.

Another reason the project was not as successful as it could have been is that long-range planning was not completed as early in the project as needed to allow a gradual introduction of the new standards, tools, and techniques, which are necessary to maintain the system at its new technical level. Although the tools are in use, there now exists an uneven distribution of knowledge of the new tools and the standards needed to maintain the system.

Conclusion

Overall, many of the goals that were set for the project have been met by restructuring. In particular, the system has been restructured to sustain the needs of the maintenance staff in their daily efforts to support the system and, at the same time, provide a reasonable structure at a higher level to define the system and assist in its management. Restructuring has been especially beneficial to the system's reliability and performance.

Data collected shows that most planned measures in these areas have been met or exceeded. The results include the following:

- The number of situation bulletins received for corrective maintenance has decreased by 50%.
- The number of hours spent on emergency maintenance has been reduced by 50%.
- The number of trouble reports received has been reduced by more than 60%.
- Online storage has been reduced slightly.
- Tape storage has been reduced.
- The batch processing time has been cut almost in half.

Maintainability and adaptability measures will need to be judged by future results and will depend on the completion of the remaining parts of the project, which include integration with the data base system and full implementation of the CASE system. In addition, the tools and techniques used throughout the project will need to be incorporated and enforced in the current technical environment before some of the other planned measures of performance can be obtained.

When work by the data management and data modeling teams is completed, it is envisioned that a set of tools and techniques will be used to support a more maintainable system as well as a more flexible network of documentation. This documentation will be divided into two sections bound together by a com-

SOFTWARE ENGINEERING

mon cross-referencing organization. Programming documentation will be maintained online on the mainframe system and will include procedure languages and the comments they contain, program source code with header and paragraph comments, and object code. All comments from either procedure languages or programs will be extractable for maintenance in a paper library as well as online. A microcomputer-based CASE system will consist of subsystem and system documentation in the form of narrative, data flow diagrams, process specifications, and structure charts. The mainframe and microcomputer documentation will be bound together by a comprehensive data dictionary, resident on the microcomputer system. The data dictionary will include all field-level data as extracted from the mainframe source code and files, cross-referenced to both the microcomputer documentation and mainframe programs and files.

The system revitalization addressed software shortcomings as well as the system changes necessary to prevent future problems. The project's approach was holistic because it addressed not only the software problems but the environmental problems that increased the need for software maintenance. ▲

Recommended Reading

Boehm, B.W. "Improving Software Productivity." *Computer* 20 (September 1987), pp 43–57.

Card, D.N. "The Role of Measurement in Software Engineering." *Proceedings: Second IEEE/BCS Software Engineering Conference* (July 1988).

Card, D.N.; Cotnoir, D.V.; and Goorevich, C.E. "Managing Software Maintenance Cost and Quality." *Proceedings: IEEE Second Conference on Software Maintenance* (September 1987). pp 145–152.

Card, D.N.; McGarry, F.E.; and Page, G.T. "Evaluating Software Engineering Technologies." *IEEE Transactions on Software Engineering* 13 (July 1987), pp 845–851.

Gilb, T. *Principles of Software Engineering Management.* Reading MA: Addison-Wesley, 1988.

NIST Special Publication 500-193

Software Reengineering:
A Case Study and Lessons Learned

Mary K. Ruhl and Mary T. Gunn

Computer Systems Laboratory
National Institute of Standards and Technology
Gaithersburg, MD 20899

September 1991

U.S. DEPARTMENT OF COMMERCE
Robert A. Mosbacher, Secretary

NATIONAL INSTITUTE OF STANDARDS
AND TECHNOLOGY
John W. Lyons, Director

Executive Summary

Software reengineering involves the use of existing software and documentation to specify requirements, design, documentation, and to produce software for a target platform. Many Federal government agencies and other organizations are evaluating the migration of older software to more powerful, more open computing environments. Additional system concerns include the high cost of software maintenance, the need to gain a better understanding of existing systems, and the impact of reduced computer systems budgets. Federal agencies are looking to software reengineering as a solution to these problems.

A case study conducted by the National Institute of Standards and Technology (NIST) and the Internal Revenue Service (IRS) indicates that software reengineering can be a cost-effective, viable solution for extending the lifetime of an application system. The degree to which it is cost-effective depends on the goals for reengineering, the condition of the original application system and documentation, available automated tool support, and the involved personnel.

The context for reengineering should be established in terms of the corporate goals for the organization before undertaking the task of reengineering. It is also important to clearly define the system goals and motivations for reengineering. Clearly defined goals are needed to determine a suitable approach for reengineering.

A variety of approaches can be employed to gain the benefits of reengineering. These approaches differ by the amount of design that is to be retained from the original system, the organization's reengineering goals, the condition of the current system, and the resources to be allocated to the project. Before determining a reengineering approach, the application system should undergo a thorough evaluation to determine what is worth retaining for future use and what is not. During the evaluation, data definitions and usage, code, documentation, maintenance history, and appropriate metrics should be analyzed to determine the current condition of the system.

The case study indicates that full support for software reengineering from CASE tools is currently lacking in several aspects. Most currently available CASE tools are directed at one particular aspect of software reengineering and are targeted for a certain environment. Therefore, expectations for automated support from CASE tools must be realistic. Provisions in terms of personnel, effort and tools must be made to compensate for the lack of full support of the reengineering process by currently available off-the-shelf tools.

Performing reengineering requires a highly trained staff with experience in the current and target system, the automated tools, and the specific programming languages involved. Application system experts must be involved throughout the reengineering process; they are essential for design recovery.

Software reengineering is a complex and difficult process. The success of an organization's application of this technology will be determined by the level of commitment made by the organization.

iv

3. A Government Case Study

3.1 Background and Goals

In order to investigate the feasibility and cost-effectiveness of reengineering existing code, a case study was performed in which a structured COBOL application system was reengineered and migrated to a more disciplined, more open environment. The application system was provided by the Internal Revenue Service (IRS). The purpose of the case study was to evaluate the applicability of reengineering technology for use in the Federal Government. NIST conducted a competitive procurement to award a Labor Hours contract for performance of the case study. The ceiling price for the contract was set at $250,000.

It is important to note that this is only one case study conducted on one application system, using a particular set of tools and reengineering methodology. Also, the approach was based on a certain set of goals for the study. Additionally, this case study focused on a business oriented application. Reengineering military applications with demanding real-time constraints and embedded assembly code would require different tools than those used in this study. Different goals, application systems, CASE tool selections, and methodologies may have very different results. Thus, the results documented in this publication neither recommend nor condemn the CASE tools or employed practices of the contractor selected. Our hope is that, despite such differences, other organizations can apply lessons from this case study to aid in determining an appropriate approach for their organization.

The reengineering project was conducted on the IRS Centralized Scheduling Program (CSP) system. This system was written in 1983 using structured COBOL 74 for Unisys 1100 hardware. It includes batch jobs, database queries and updates, and on-line processing. The application system is made up of 37 source programs consisting of approximately 50,000 lines of COBOL code, along with 53 subroutines of MASM assembly language, consisting of 2,738 lines. The database is a DMS 1100 network database. The application system is currently in use at the IRS and is one of several currently operating on the Unisys 1100 which serves approximately 1000 users. Documentation for the original application system that was provided to the contractor included Data Flow Diagrams (DFDs), Functional Specification Packages (FSPs — in a structured English format), Computer Programmer Books (CPBs), relevant schema definitions from the DMS 1100 database, and Nassi-Schneiderman diagrams. All relevant documentation that was available within IRS was provided.

The contractor was to examine the effort needed and issues by attempting to reengineer the CSP system to a more open target environment and convert the network data base to a relational database, normalized to Third Normal Form (3NF). The target environment and reengineering tools were to be chosen by the contractor. Selections were to address the Government's interest in the extent to which Federal Information Processing Standards (FIPS) are included or considered. Particular standards of interests for this study included SQL (FIPS PUB 127), Portable Operating System Interface (POSIX, FIPS PUB 151), Government

7

Open Systems Interconnection Profile (GOSIP, FIPS PUB 146) and IRDS (FIPS PUB 156). It was realized that implementations do not currently exist for some of these standards. Therefore, an evolutionary path to these standards was to be shown for the proposed target environment. Additionally, the use of custom tools was to be limited — off-the-shelf tools were preferred. The contractor was required to demonstrate that the reengineered system was equivalent to or better than the original in behavior, outputs, and performance. Application system experts for the current system were on-site throughout the project to provide expertise on system operation. IRS and NIST personnel were on-site to receive training in the methodology and tools.

It was assumed that for software reengineering to be considered cost-effective, the process should, in principle, be achievable in a fairly short period of time. Accordingly, an aggressive 17 week time schedule was set for the project. Following a competitive procurement, the contract was awarded to Booz, Allen & Hamilton Inc. of Bethesda, Maryland.

3.2 Technical Approach

Two major off-the-shelf tools were selected for this project, one to support reengineering the data side of the application system, and the other to support reengineering the process side. Each of these tools has high visibility for its functionality and a fairly large market base (as compared to other tools). Additional tools (some proprietary) were used to analyze COBOL procedure division code, develop higher-level design documentation, and produce metrics data from the COBOL source programs. The need for some of the additional tools was not apparent at the start of the project. As the project progressed and difficulties were encountered with some off-the-shelf tools, on-hand, proprietary tools were utilized as a solution.

The reengineering methodology was broken down into the five steps listed below:

Step 1: baseline the original system;

Step 2: extract/analyze data, code functionality and documentation;

Step 3: produce documentation;

Step 4: generate new code;

Step 5: execute and test code.

In the context of the defined terms of section 2.1 of this document, reverse engineering is accomplished in Steps 1 through 3 while forward engineering is completed in Step 4.

8

Portions of the system were identified and prioritized for reengineering. Programs were categorized by level of complexity and the interfaces between programs. The categories, in order of increasing complexity, were:

- batch programs not accessing the database, not using COBOL's Report Writer or Sort;

- batch programs accessing the database;

- batch programs using Report Writer;

- interactive programs (included database access and screen interface).

3.3 Issues

Difficulties were encountered during the reengineering process. It was discovered that the original DFDs were out-of-date. In order to gain a consistent understanding of the system and to obtain a dependable set of documentation, the DFDs were analyzed and corrected. These analyses and corrections were based on information collected from the application system experts and the documentation, particularly the FSP.

It was concluded that any database redesign can have a significant impact on the manner in which application software accesses and processes data. Thus, any database redesign will force changes to the code that performs these functions. For example, in order to normalize the database to First Normal Form (1NF), it was necessary to eliminate repeating groups in each record definition. The original database definition was cluttered with repeating groups, making frequent use of the "OCCURS" clause in the DMS 1100 definition. Eliminating the redundancy forced changes to the application code that accessed the database and processed the data. In addition, redesign of some application code was necessary because of the change in navigation strategy. For example, one program sequentially processed database records by traversing the network structure of the database (i.e., get one record, process it, get next, and so on). This is perfectly suitable for hierarchical and network model databases, but not for relational databases in which record selection is based on the satisfaction of some criteria.

Once a relational database design that met our normalization requirements was developed, it was observed that the normalized design was not an optimum one. A more optimal design would have required a major redesign of the application code. It was realized that many design solutions were possible, and in order to adhere to the goals of the case study and time constraints, an optimal design was not necessary. Therefore, a database design solution that met the goal of 3NF was devised in which the impact on the application code was minimal.

The database conversion stressed to the members of the project team the importance of data reengineering and the essential coordination of the data side and process side of an application system during reengineering. When reengineering a system, it was felt that

9

emphasis should be placed on data reengineering because it will drive the reengineering of the data processing code. This suggests that perpetuation of the data will be more useful than preservation of the original application process.

3.4 Findings

3.4.1 Process

It was determined that the complexity of the reengineering process increased in relation to the complexity of the programs. The most complex programs required the most manual effort. The program groups are listed below in order from the easiest (highly automated process overall) to the most difficult (much manual process required), with the breakdown of the required automated and manual effort provided as percentages. Note that the calculations below reflect the effort on the part of Booz, Allen only. The time dedicated by NIST and the IRS personnel is not included in these computations because the focus for the Government employees' time was on training and providing application system expertise to the contractor.

Program Group	Automated	Manual
Batch	96%	4%
Batch with SORT	90%	10%
Batch with DBMS access	88%	12%
Batch with SORT and DBMS access	82%	18%
Interactive	50%	50%

The majority of interactive programs were written in assembly language and therefore, this category required the most manual effort. Much time was spent determining the functionality of the assembler code and whether that functionality was still necessary in the target environment. It was calculated that overall 20% of the reengineering process was performed manually and 80% was performed automatically.

The following chart identifies the level of effort that was required to reengineer the system for each step in the methodology.

Step	Percentage of Total Effort	Total Hours
Step 1 Baseline current system	19.76%	780
Step 2 Extract/analyze ...	43.26%	1,708
Step 3 Produce documentation	4.05%	160
Step 4 Generate new code	26.34%	1,040
Step 5 Execute and test new code	6.59%	260

10

Some of the CASE tools did not perform as advertised and required a greater than expected amount of manual intervention. On-hand, proprietary tools were modified to produce high-level design documentation. Some steps in the reengineering process seemed cumbersome and time-consuming. It was possible to automate some steps, but human effort was needed for analysis and tool operation. As a result of these difficulties, reengineering of the entire application system was not completed. Approximately 56% of the CSP system was reverse engineered to a design level and approximately 38% of the CSP system was reengineered (source code produced). Reengineering was completed on a representative sample of programs from each group. During an extended 18 week period, 24.7 staff months were expended. After accounting for the learning curve and problem resolutions, it was estimated that an additional 10 staff months would be necessary to complete the reengineering process.

Realizing the existence of other approaches for extending software lifetime, estimations were made in order to compare the effort required for reengineering with the effort for other approaches. The effort needed to convert the CSP system was calculated using the Office of Technical Assistance (OTA) Conversion Cost Model Version 4 and assuming the utilization of CASE tools. It was determined that approximately 30 staff months would be necessary to convert the CSP system. Possible reasons for this low number could be attributed to the large degree of automation of the conversion effort and that analysis would not be performed to gain higher-level design documentation.

The effort to redesign and redevelop the CSP system was calculated using the Constructive Cost Model (COCOMO) [BOEH81] for system development. It was assumed that CASE tools and 4GLs would be employed in this effort. Approximately 151.9 staff months would be necessary to redesign and redevelop a new system to meet the CSP requirements. The estimate of 34.7 staff months for reengineering compares favorably with these estimates.

The case study indicated that intimate knowledge of the original and target system platforms, the automated tools, and the implementation language is essential to carry out the reengineering process.

3.4.2 Metrics Analysis

In order to relate productivity and the quality achieved through the reengineering process, two analyses were performed on the accumulated measurements. Function point analysis was used to formulate indicators of productivity. Result metrics (metric counts before and after reengineering process) were analyzed to evaluate the degree to which the reengineering process affected maintainability and code flexibility. Caution must be used when evaluating the relevance of these calculations. Proper consolidation of function point measurements requires a significant sample size of similar reengineering projects that were all performed under the same conditions. Accordingly, this single project sample should not be regarded as sufficient for proper calibration. The metrics analysis is discussed in detail in Appendices A and B.

11

Through function point analysis on the reengineered programs, the following productivity measurements for the CSP system were derived:

- 164 function points per staff-year;

- 11.68 staff hours per function point;

- 1,516 executable statements per staff-year;

- 6,387 COBOL statements per staff-year.

As the sample size for this project is insufficient for drawing conclusions on the productivity of reengineering, the measurements above are presented for the purpose of information only.

Result metrics indicate that the reengineered programs are more complex than the original programs. This is evident in the increased number of logical NOT and GOTO statements. Also, the decision density is alarmingly high. Reasons for the increased complexity could be attributed to certain practices of the forward engineering tool. While the forward engineering tool has certainly eased the task of code generation, it has increased code complexity. It is important to note that increasing the code complexity may have a direct effect on the complexity of testing the code. The additional complexity could be justified if the code, hereafter, will be maintained at the design level and then forward engineered with the forward engineering tool. If maintenance returns to manual practices, then the task has been made more complex.

3.4.3 Reengineering Tools

The study indicated that the off-the-shelf tools used in this case study do not fully support the entire reengineering process. It was necessary to augment the off-the-shelf tools with modifications to available, proprietary tools. Most reverse engineering tools are analyzers, based on the recognition of certain structures, and are oriented towards a particular set of machines or environments (e.g., mainframe COBOL applications). However, this case study indicates the ability to maintain programs at a higher level of abstraction than at the source code level. Also, the code that was produced by the tool contained functions that can be time-consuming to code manually (i.e., record counting, file status checking, cleanup and housekeeping functions). This case study indicates that present CASE tools provide some efficiency and productivity gains, but further development of the reengineering technology is necessary. Human effort for design recovery and analysis is essential and can not be overlooked.

12

4. Conclusions and Recommendations

4.1 General

The following conclusions and recommendations are largely based on findings of this case study. Experience gained from other NIST projects involving reengineering also contributed to these recommendations. During the case study, only one application system was reengineered using a particular set of tools and a particular methodology. Accordingly, it would be incorrect to infer from this study absolute rules for when to reengineer and when to redesign. It must also be noted that the approach taken to reengineering was based on a certain set of goals for the study. Other reengineering approaches could be employed to achieve a different set of goals.

By comparing the efforts required to reengineer, convert, and redesign and develop the CSP system, it was concluded that software reengineering can be a cost-effective and viable solution to extending the lifetime of an application system. The cost-effectiveness and feasibility for reengineering a particular software system will be dependent on a number of variables that are specific to that system and the approach taken. These variables are: the goals for reengineering, condition of current application system and documentation, tool(s) support, and involvement of knowledgeable personnel.

NIST experience indicates that there is a spectrum of approaches that could be applied to extend the lifetime of a software application system as illustrated in figure 1. At one end of the spectrum is straight code conversion and at the opposite end is total redesign and development. In the middle of the spectrum are varying approaches of reengineering. These approaches are positioned between the endpoints in correspondence to the degree the original design and implementation is to be retained. The placement and separation between approaches on the spectrum is not clear cut. In each approach across the spectrum, higher-level abstractions of the system, in the form of analysis and design documentation, are derived. Reengineering approaches that are positioned on the spectrum include:

- reengineering with no change in design or functionality — design of original implementation is fully retained;

- reengineering with minimal change to design — only modifications necessary for target environment;

- reengineering with modifications to optimize the functionality and performance.

This case study focused on maintaining the functionality of the original system. Some redesign was necessary in order to convert the network database to a relational database structure that is normalized to 3NF. By positioning the approach for this case study around

13

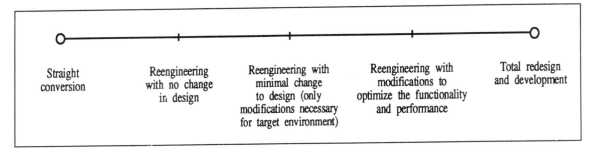

Figure 1. Spectrum of Reengineering Approaches.

the center of the spectrum a set of guidelines for various reengineering approaches across the spectrum can be inferred.

The effectiveness of a reengineering approach is dependent on the variables of:

- corporate and system goals;

- condition of current application system and documentation;

- available resources (automated tool(s) support and personnel).

When determining if reengineering is an appropriate alternative for a particular application system and a given organization, the condition of these variables must be determined. The reason behind the success of this case study could be attributed to the strong correlation between the approach taken and these variables. This case study was supported by the following factors:

- well-defined focus and goals for this case study;

- original CSP system recently designed and implemented (1983);

- majority of original CSP code was well-structured (modularized with a minimum number of GOTOs);

- CSP was fairly well-documented — the primary documentation, the FSP, was up-to-date and complete;

- CASE tool support automated a majority of reengineering tasks;

- operations people who had excellent understanding of the original CSP system were involved throughout this project.

14

Reengineering can help an enterprise change its business functionality to meet its corporate goals. Through reengineering, changes to the way current business is done can be put into place. In order to be effective, upper management support is imperative. The degree of success of reengineering will be determined by the level of commitment made by the organization.

4.2 Corporate, System, and Reengineering Goals

■ When considering reengineering, one of the first tasks is to set the context for reengineering in terms of the corporate goals of the organization and the dependencies between application systems. For example, some Federal agencies (e.g., DoD) wish to implement some "corporate information management" policy in which the information used across the organization is effectively and efficiently controlled to eliminate inconsistencies, redundancies, and duplication of effort. The organization need not be global in scope, but could be at a local scope. Software reengineering is applicable in this context and would be most effective if directed at the information and its usage. A suitable approach for reengineering in the context of a corporate information management policy may be to reengineer the data and redesign the application processes. The various groups and application systems that use the same information should be identified along with their dependencies (i.e., what system creates the information, and what others display it or use it for further computations). Some redesign of the data and its usage may be necessary to implement a corporate information management policy. The processing of data in the original system is highly likely to change based on the redesign of data usage. Therefore the processing in the original system should not be a major influence on redesign or reengineering decisions. Organizations may have different corporate goals that will influence the effectiveness of software reengineering. These corporate goals and system dependencies must be considered to establish a context for reengineering.

Recommendation: **Establish the context for reengineering by considering the corporate goals of the organization and how reengineering could be applied to achieve the mission. Information dependencies between application systems must be identified.**

■ When examining the functional aspects of the current system, it is crucial to investigate the possibility of new solutions. Perhaps, using new technology, there is a better way to do business. The business may have been constrained, in the past, by technology. Indeed, the old manual methods, before computers, constrained the way business functions could be carried out. It was a mistake then to carry the manual methods into automation. Today it may be incorrect to carry current methods to newer architectures and approaches. If the current environment is driving the business approach, then it would be wise to reevaluate the technology currently being applied, the current business approach, and the business goals.

Recommendation: **Analyze system requirements from a functional viewpoint and consider new technology to improve current business practices.**

15

■ When determining a target computing architecture, conformance to government and industry standards should be considered. Because of the history of a computing environment, an organization may feel tied to a particular vendor for future purchases in order to achieve system compatibility. However, this argument is no longer accepted by the Government Accounting Office (GAO) in procurements for Federal agencies. Requiring equipment (hardware and software) to conform to appropriate standards (e.g., FIPS) can eliminate incompatibility problems, provide buyers with more flexibility when selecting equipment, and ease future migrations. Increasingly, Federal agencies are being mandated to procure equipment that conforms to FIPS, in particular the FIPS for POSIX, GOSIP, and SQL.

Recommendation: **When procuring equipment, require conformance to applicable standards (e.g., FIPS) to achieve flexibility and ease future migrations.**

■ It is important to have clearly defined motivations in order to determine a suitable reengineering approach. There are a number of factors to be considered. They include: current problems, the functional requirements and how they are currently met, new technology and how it can be exploited to improve satisfaction of the functional requirements, and an appropriate target environment. During the investigation of these factors, various motivations for reengineering will become clear. Because of the complexity of the reengineering process, the goals an organization expects to accomplish should be clearly stated before attempting to reengineer an application system. As discussed earlier, there are numerous reasons to consider reengineering such as:

- migrate to a new target environment;

- reduce maintenance costs;

- gain understanding of the current system's complexity;

- improve system performance;

- reduce software errors;

- recover information.

The selection of what is to be achieved by reengineering will assist in determining a suitable reengineering approach.

Recommendation: **Identify motivations and what is to be achieved by reengineering.**

16

4.3 Condition of Original System and Documentation

■ It is essential that the current condition of an application system be examined to determine if reengineering is practical, and if it is, how much redesign is required. Analysis of the dependencies between an application system and others that it may impact, in terms of information creation and usage, and functionality is needed. This calls for the system to undergo a thorough evaluation. In actuality, reverse engineering — gathering information about the system — is a large part of the system evaluation. The evaluation should be approached with the intent of discovering what is worth retaining for future use and what is not. Determining the extent to which modification is needed will narrow the field of choices of reengineering approaches. The system evaluation will determine if reengineering is practical and if it is, will identify the parts of the original design that should be retained, and necessary steps in the process. It is important to budget plenty of time for system analysis (reverse engineering) — it is a complex task and there are numerous aspects to consider.

Recommendation: **Evaluate application system with the intent of discovering what is worth retaining for future use and what is not.**

■ This case study stressed the importance of data and its usage in driving the application system. During evaluation, emphasis should be placed on the data side of the application rather than the process side. A functional perspective of data usage should be taken, and the system should be analyzed as to whether redesign of the data is needed. Redesign may be necessary because of poor original design, continual enhancements that have obscured the original design, inconsistent naming conventions, inconsistent data definitions, migration to a database of a different structure or the need to improve data management. Data redesign forces redesign of the processing code because of the change in definitions, access, and processing functionality. In some cases, data redesign will facilitate the removal of data processing code.

Considering the influence that the data side has on the application code, it would be practical to first evaluate the original data design and determine how much redesign is needed. Then an impact analysis should be performed to determine what programs are impacted and how. It may be that only the data access code will be effected, which is a minimal change. If the database is converted to a database of different structure, the functionality of how the application processes data may need to be modified. This evaluation strategy will narrow the choices of reengineering approaches.

Recommendation: **Stress data design because it will force modifications to the process design.**

■ Maintenance data and appropriate metrics should be analyzed for information concerning the system's history and performance. It should be determined whether the system conforms

17

to software standards and the degree to which it conforms. To be reengineered the software should be in an extractable state — modularized software components with well-defined interfaces. Restructuring of the system may be necessary in order to prepare it for further reengineering. One possible reengineering approach is based directly on the application system's maintenance history. In this incremental strategy, the code that has the highest maintenance cost is reengineered first and work progresses on code segments that have decreasing maintenance costs.

Many organizations are currently operating application systems that are older than the CSP system and the code and documentation are in poor condition. Many older programs contain programming "tricks" for purposes of avoiding constraints of the environment or optimizing performance, such as saving memory or processing cycles. Reverse engineering from such code is dependent on an analyst's ability to recognize such sections of code.

It is possible that the results from the reverse engineering will indicate that the system is so error-prone and complex that perpetuation of the system is not practical. This conclusion eliminates the applicability of reengineering and narrows the choices to continue the use of the existing system or redesign and develop a new system. Another possibility is that the evaluation may indicate the need for some redesign. In those cases where a large percentage of redesign is required, it is better to scrap the system and redesign from scratch. A study of maintenance costs at IBM suggested that if 12% of a system has to be changed, then it is cheaper to redevelop [MART90a]; the study was too limited to support 12% as a generally applicable threshold.

Determining what parts of the system merit future use may also uncover redundant code segments. These segments do not have to be exactly the same, but may still be redundant even though they have slight differences. It may be possible to eliminate the redundancy by combining the redundant segments into one reusable part. Creating a reusable part from several redundant parts depends on whether the component can be extracted without significant effort. A redundant component that can be extracted as a distinct module with well-defined interfaces will be easiest to combine with other similar components. It may be valuable to create a library of reusable parts for use across application systems.

During system evaluation, asking the following types of questions will assist in determining if reengineering of an application system is suitable:

1. Does the original system's design and implementation merit reuse in a future system?

2. Are new technologies or methodologies exploitable that would improve satisfaction of the system requirements over the original application system?

3. Is the target environment vastly different from the original environment and if so, how?

18

4. Is redesign of the data necessary? If so, what parts on the process side will be impacted?

5. What parts of the system require redesign for operation in the target environment?

6. Is the system well-structured (modules with 1 entrance, 1 exit; no GOTOs)? If not, could it be improved by restructuring?

7. Is the system well-maintained?

8. Is the current performance of the system acceptable?

9. Is the documentation consistent and accurate with current system functionality?

Recommendation: **Evaluate the code, documentation, maintenance history, and appropriate metrics to determine the current condition of the application system.**

■ One motivation for reengineering is to gain a better understanding of the application system. The DFDs for the application system used in this study were out-of-date. In order to gain a more complete knowledge of the system and make the documentation consistent with the code, the documentation was analyzed, the application system experts were consulted and the DFDs were corrected. This was a long and difficult process because some information was recorded in other documentation forms while some was not recorded at all. This design recovery process served two purposes: to recover lost information and to assist the contractor personnel in gaining insight into the functionality of the application system.

Recommendation: **While design recovery is difficult, time-consuming, and essentially a manual process, it is vital for recovering lost information and information transfer.**

■ That information which is the most critical for understanding the system should be identified for preservation. All documentation forms should be analyzed to determine what information is stored and how important it is to understanding the system. For example, the application system experts relied most heavily on the FSP for functional information of the system — hence it represented the most up-to-date documentation. The focus here is not on documentation form, but on the content. It is important not to be strongly tied to a certain set of documentation forms. It is useful to have standards for documentation, but it is critical to be open for better ways of representing and maintaining information. Current documentation practices are quite limited in the types of information that are maintained. While it may be necessary to restrict information in a documentation form to ensure consistency and completeness, it is important to analyze other perspectives of the system to gain as complete

19

an understanding of the system as possible. Currently formal description techniques, such as SDL [CCITTRB], SPEC [BERZ90], Estelle [ISO9074], LOTOS [ISO8807], are being utilized for design and documentation of systems. Some of these techniques may be more appropriate for documentation and maintenance than the current practices.

In addition, current document practices should be analyzed as to how useful each is for various purposes. For example, DFDs are useful in the software design phase for identifying processes and the data needed by each process. However, DFDs can quickly become overly complex. This was evident in this study — the highest level DFD looked like the physical layout of a micro-chip, despite consolidation of the data streams and process bubbles. This complexity might well be the reason why reliance during maintenance is placed on the FSPs, rather than the DFDs.

Recommendation: **Identify critical system information. Do not be tightly tied to a certain set of documentation forms; focus on information content and usage.**

4.4 Resources

It became apparent during this study that resources (automated tools support and personnel) are a critical factor in the successful completion of a reengineering project. The selection of a software engineering methodology and the associated CASE tools is of paramount importance because of their impact on the future operation and maintenance of the reengineered system. The reengineering process can add additional overhead to the system (i.e., more documentation, increased complexity of the generated code). This additional overhead is justifiable if the system will be maintained at the design level and then forward engineered with the methodology used in the reengineering process. If maintenance returns to manual practices or employs different tools that do not use the information recorded in the repository, then much of the gains from the reengineering effort will be lost.

4.4.1 Automated Tool Support

■ This case study indicates that the support for software reengineering from currently available off-the-shelf CASE tools is far from the ideal situation of totally automated reengineering — building high-level design and analysis information based on low-level descriptions (code) and then forward engineering to an environment of choice. Although present CASE tools do provide much efficiency and productivity gains, the technology needs further development to provide a complete set of needed functions. CASE tools do not always perform as advertised, may require manual intervention, and some steps may be cumbersome and time-consuming. It was necessary to augment the CASE tools used in this study with on-hand proprietary tools. In many cases, modifications were made to the proprietary tools to resolve problems encountered or lack of support from off-the-shelf tools.

20

Recommendation: **Provisions in terms of personnel and effort must be made to compensate for the lack of full support of the reengineering process by currently available off-the-shelf tools.**

■ Most currently available CASE tools are directed at one particular aspect of software engineering (and reengineering) and are targeted for a certain environment. Application systems within an organization may differ drastically in terms of environment and methodology. Because of the differences across applications and the targeting of tools, it should not be assumed that a single toolset will apply uniformly well across all application systems. It may be suitable to utilize a number of tools, each being used for its particular strength in the reengineering process and supported environment.

Recommendation: **Considering the focus of most CASE tools for a particular computing environment, one set of CASE tools should not be depended on for uniform applicability to all needs across an organization.**

■ It is essential that the hardware that supports the reengineering process have adequate storage capacity and processor speed. With the methodology and tools used in this study, large files were generated during the reengineering process. If sufficient processor speed is not used, the reengineering process could be inhibited.

Recommendation: **Adequate storage capacity and processor speed in equipment supporting the reengineering tools are essential to facilitate the reengineering process.**

■ Before reengineering a system, decision makers should consider if the tools chosen to handle this procedure follows any particular methodology. The current methodologies utilized by an organization may change drastically once an application system is reengineered. These changes may cause frustration for individuals working with the system.

Recommendation: **Consider CASE reengineering tools that provide methodologies which are compatible to the requirements of the particular enterprise.**

■ When reengineering an application, it may be necessary to use multiple tools from different vendors. This may cause problems with the interchange and integration of data and data models across different tools. A data model provides a method for representing the data structures used in a software engineering toolset or repository. Different tools may not

21

support the same data models and methodologies resulting in the need for data model integration.

There are additional CASE tool features that are worthy of consideration, such as export/import and appropriate metrics analysis. This, of course, is dependent on the functional requirements of the CASE tools. For example, in order to accomplish data model integration when using different software engineering tools, the user organization must be able to recognize the similarities and differences between the different data models in use. One means of achieving data model integration is by identifying the differences between the data models and building a target data model that will be sufficiently robust so as to be capable of capturing both data models. When toolsets or tool dictionaries have fixed, non-extensible data models, then data model integration becomes difficult or even impossible to accomplish. An export/import interchange facility can provide some support for interchange of data models and data. Also, it is beneficial to utilize CASE tools that support data collection and appropriate metrics analysis. Having an automated means for data collection is superior to manual methods because of savings in time and labor. Also, automated methods ensure that the data are collected and measurements are made in a consistent manner.

Recommendation: **Additional features that merit consideration include a data interchange facility and appropriate metric analysis utility.**

4.4.2 Personnel

■ Reengineering requires a highly trained staff that has experience in the current and target system, the automated tools, and the specific programming languages. It is not necessary that all the reengineering team members have all of these skills, but these skills must be present across the team. If it is desired to automate the reengineering process as much as possible, team members who are able to write additional software to bridge the gaps between the CASE tools and/or provide special support for the tools may be required.

Recommendation: **Reengineering requires a highly trained staff that has experience in the current and target system, the automated tools, and the specific programming languages.**

■ Human knowledge and understanding of the application system to be reengineered is extremely important. Without the involvement of the application system experts, this study could not have been completed. While the documentation was helpful, some sections were out-of-date and the application system was quite complex. With their knowledge and experience, the human experts were able to supply complete information of the system that could not have been gained from the documentation alone. However, shifting application system experts from maintenance to reengineering implies that considerable staff hours may need to be diverted from operational work.

22

Recommendation: **It is critical that the application system experts be involved throughout the reengineering process. They are essential for design recovery.**

5. Final Remarks

This document discusses software reengineering (and related terminology) and how reengineering can be used to extend the lifetime of existing software. The use of CASE tools for the support of reengineering and various tool considerations have been examined. Through the completion of a case study directed at evaluating the feasibility and cost-effectiveness of software reengineering, some preliminary results have been determined. Software reengineering can be a cost-effective and viable solution for extending the lifetime of an application system. The degree to which it is cost-effective is dependent on the goals for reengineering, the condition of the original application system and documentation, available automated tool support, and the involved personnel. These variables must be thoroughly analyzed before selecting a reengineering approach. This approach determination analysis is essential and must not be overlooked. Factors to be considered when determining a reengineering approach were addressed. These factors range from corporate goals to the condition of the original system and resource support.

23

6. References

[ARAN85] Arango, G., Baxter, I., Freeman, P., and Pidgeon, C., "Maintenance and Porting of Software by Design Recovery," Proceedings from Conference on Software Maintenance 1985.

[ARNO90] Arnold, R., Notes from Seminar on Software Reengineering.

[BACH88] Bachman, C., "A CASE for Reverse Engineering," Datamation, July 1, 1988.

[BASI90] Basili, V., "Viewing Maintenance as Reuse-Oriented Software Development," IEEE Software, January 1990.

[BERZ90] Berzins, V., et al, "An Introduction to the Specification Language Spec," IEEE Software, March 1990.

[BIGG89] Biggerstaff, T., "Design Recovery for Maintenance and Reuse," COMPUTER, July 1989.

[BOEH81] Boehm, B.W., Software Engineering Economics, Prentice-Hall, Inc., 1981.

[BOOZ91] Booz, Allen & Hamilton, Reverse Engineering Evaluation Process Report, January 15, 1991. This is an internal, restricted report.

[CCITTRB] CCITT Red Book Volume VI-Fascicle V1.10, "Functional Specification and Description Language (SDL)."

[CHIK90] Chikofsky, E., and Cross, J., "Reverse Engineering and Design Recovery: A Taxonomy," IEEE Software, January 1990.

[CHOI90] Choi, S., and Scacchi, W., "Extracting and Restructuring the Design of Large Systems," IEEE Software, January 1990.

[DIEH89] Diehl S., et al, "Making a Case for CASE," BYTE, December 1989.

[FAIR85] Fairley, R., Software Engineering Concepts, McGraw-Hill Book Co., 1985.

[GANE90] Gane, C., Computer-aided Software Engineering the methodologies, the products, and the future, Prentice-Hall, Inc., 1990.

[HAUG91] Haugh, J., "A Survey of Technology Related to Software Reengineering," Proceedings from Systems Reengineering Workshop, Naval Surface Warfare Center, Silver Spring, Maryland, March 25-27, 1991

[IFPUG90] Sprouls, J., (ed.), IFPUG Function Point Counting Practices Manual, Release 3.0, 1990.

25

[ISO8807] International Organization for Standardization, "Information processing systems — Open systems interconnection — LOTOS — A Formal description technique based on the temporal ordering of observational behavior," 1988.

[ISO9074] International Organization for Standardization, "Information processing systems — Open Systems Interconnection — Estelle — A formal description technique based on an extended state transition model," 1989.

[JONE88] Jones, Capers, "A Short History of Function Points and Feature Points," Software Productivity Research, Inc., Version 2.0, Feb. 20, 1988.

[KOZA91] Kozacynski, W., "A Suzuki Class in Software Reengineering," IEEE Software January, 1991.

[MART90a] Martin, J., "The Beauty of Re-Engineering: Continual Enhancements," PC Week, April 30, 1990.

[MART90b] Martin, J., "Restructuring Code Is a Sound Investment in the Future," PC Week, May 7, 1990.

[RICK89] Ricketts, J.A., DelMonaco, J.C., Weeks, M.W., "Data Reengineering for Application Systems," Proceedings from Conference on Software Maintenance, 1988.

[ROSE89] Rosen, Bruce K., and Law, Margaret H., "Information Resource Dictionary System (IRDS) and Modeling Tools," Proceedings of 3Rs of Software Automation, Re-engineering, Reusability, Repositories, An Extended Intelligence, Inc. Conference and Tool Exhibition, 1989.

[RUHL91] Ruhl, M., IRS Software Reengineering Report and Strategy Plan, January 30, 1991. This is an internal, restricted report.

[SHAR91] Sharon, D. "CASE Standards: Is Anyone Listening?," CASE Trends, March/April 1991.

[SNEE87] Sneed, H., and Jandrasics, G., "Software Recycling," Proceedings from Conference on Software Maintenance, 1987.

[WEIN91] Weinman, E., "The Promise of Software Reengineering," InformationWeek, April 22, 1991.

26

Appendix A: Function Point Analysis

Function point analysis was chosen to measure the productivity achieved in the reengineering process, as well as to measure the degree of functionality of the original CSP system. Function point analysis has, in many cases, been proven to be superior to conventional metrics based on lines of code (LOC) count. Such conventional metrics would have posed several problems in this reengineering study since:

- CSP consisted of COBOL, assembly language code, and DBMS commands, making a reduction to normalized LOC difficult;

- LOC is usually a meaningless measure for systems making significant use of DBMS;

- there are no standard scope of effort guidelines [BOOZ91].

Function point analysis is based on measurements of inputs, outputs, inquiries, master files, and interfaces, each of which is appropriately weighted. The impacts of possible influential factors are analyzed to determine the level of system complexity. This provides a dimensionless number as an indicator of functionality. The International Function Point Users Group (IFPUG) publishes counting rules and guidelines to ensure consistent definitions and counting methodology [IFPUG90]. As the sample size for this project is insufficient for drawing conclusions on the productivity of reengineering, the measurements below are presented for the purpose of information only.

Function point analysis was first performed on the CSP system before reengineering in order to gain some idea of its condition. Function point analysis was also performed on the 14 programs that were reengineered.

A final function point count of 1,192 for the entire CSP system before reengineering was derived. Considering the size of the reengineered program inventory (approximately 50,000 total COBOL source statements), the function point total is high. Most published reports associate 100 COBOL source statements per function point. Following this estimate, less than half the function points found would be expected for this application system. The main conclusion that can be drawn from this is that it is incorrect to expect a high correlation between function points and lines of code count. Secondly, the analysis of the original inventory indicated that the original code was well-structured with a high degree of functionality. It is not improbable to derive a high function point count to code ratio for well-structured, highly functional programs.

Reengineering was completed on 14 programs. The measurements for these programs before the reengineering process are as follows:

- 13,131 COBOL source statements,

27

- 3,116 executable statements,

- 338 function points.

The following measurements were obtained for the sample programs after reengineering:

- 21,480 COBOL source statements,

- 4,062 executable statements.

The reengineering process required a total of 3,948 staff hours. Assuming 1,920 staff-hours per work year, 2.056 staff years were expended. Because the goal was to reengineer without any changes to the functionality and the high level of automation of the reengineering process, the productivity measurements were based on the measurements before reengineering. The productivity measurements are listed below:

- 164 function points per staff-year,

- 11.68 staff hours per function point,

- 1,516 executable statements per staff-year,

- 6,387 COBOL statements per staff-year.

Because of the significant use of DBMS in this application system, the statements per staff-year measurements should not be considered highly meaningful. Rather, the 164 function points per staff-year is the key parameter [BOOZ91].

28

Appendix B: Result Metrics Analysis

The result analysis focused on how the reengineering process affected maintainability and code flexibility. The classifications chosen for the totals reflect this focus. The measurements were made using an automated tool which collects and categorizes statement counts.

The following counts were used as a basis for comparison:

- ELOC: Executable lines of code;

- CLOC: ELOC divided by 100;

- Size: $CLOC^{**}2$ (Note: the choice of power 2 was arbitrary; the intent was to penalize programs exceeding 100 ELOC by a significant margin);

- Decision count: Count of all decision statements (if, do-while, do-until, etc.);

- Decision density: Number of decision statements per CLOC;

- Function count: Number of COBOL functional statements (call, perform, compute, sort, merge, etc.);

- Number of COBOL I/O statements;

- Entry/Exit Ratio (EER): Number of ENTRY statements per program exit (EXIT, GOBACK, and STOP RUN statements).

Computed values were normalized to a base of 100 executable lines of code (CLOC). This was done to allow meaningful analysis between before and after measurements and so that structured code would not be penalized — structured code typically results in more lines of code than equivalent unstructured code, although the number of executable lines of code is no higher. Additionally, these derived metrics were divided by the number of reengineered programs in order to provide an averaged measurement.

Decision counts are closely related to complexity and testability. A decision density (decisions per CLOC) of 10 or less is desirable. When decision density exceeds 20-25, it is likely that maintenance problems will be experienced. The number of functional statements in a program is an indicator of a module's function strength. A function density of over 20% is a good indicator of a highly functional, and therefore easily maintainable, module. Conversely, a GOTO count of over 10 will cause maintenance problems — a count of 2-3 is desirable. Additionally, a large number of NOT logical statements will cause problems since NOT statements test what is not and give no indication of what is. Well-modularized

29

programs will contain balanced counts of ENTRY/EXIT statements. A comment density of 10% or more is desirable for COBOL code [BOOZ91].

Table 1 displays the key result metrics counts before and after the reengineering process.

Table 1. Key Result Metrics Counts

Metric	Before Reengineering	After Reengineering
Total Executable Lines of Code	3116.00	4062.00
Number of Programs	14.00	14.00
CLOC	2.23	2.90
Total Decision Count	710.00	1376.00
Decision Density	22.74	33.89
Total Function Count (COBOL)	537.00	1407.00
Total I/O Count	384.00	335.00
Entry/Exit Ratio (EER)	0.50	0.66
Size	4.95	8.41
GOTO Density	0.25	6.67
NOT Clauses	159.00	466.00
Functions/Programs	38.36	100.50
Function Density	17.20	34.66
Total Number of Files	46.00	57.00
Total Number of Calls	42.00	8.00
Comments Density	118.87	318.04

The metrics before reengineering present a mixed picture. The size is relatively small (1 is ideal). The GOTO density is very small, but there are a large number of NOT clauses. Function density is high, which is good, but decision density is also high. A high decision density is indicative of complex code. The relatively high I/O count also indicates a high level of complexity. These sample programs could be characterized as well-written, highly structured and modular, overly documented, and somewhat complex.

30

The result metrics indicate that the reengineered programs are more complex then the original programs. This is evident from the increase in the number of logical NOT and GOTO statements. Also, the decision density is alarmingly high. Size has increased while the I/O count has decreased slightly. Function density is nearly doubled (mostly due to PERFORMs) [BOOZ91].

Reasons for this added complexity could be attributed to certain practices of the forward engineering tool. While the forward engineering tool has certainly eased the task of code generation, it has increased code complexity. It is important to note that increasing the code complexity may have a direct effect on the complexity of testing the code. The additional complexity could be justified if the code, hereafter, will be maintained at the design level and then forward engineered with the forward engineering tool. If maintenance returns to manual practices, then the task of maintaining the program has been complicated.

31

Chapter 5
Reengineering Evaluation

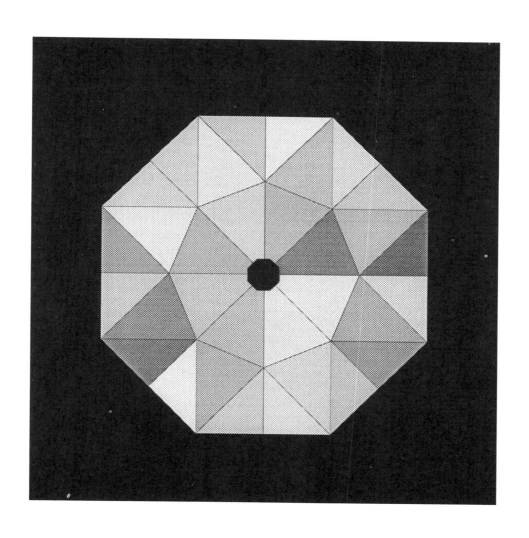

Chapter 5
Reengineering Evaluation

Purpose
In this chapter the reader will find evaluations of reengineering tools and of the effectiveness of reengineering itself. Should the reader be faced with a reengineering tools evaluation or reengineering effectiveness evaluation, reading these papers will be helpful.

Papers
In the first paper, an extract of the Executive Summary, Chapter 1, and Chapter 2 from the much larger report, "Parallel Test and Productivity Evaluation of a Commercially Supplied Cobol Restructuring Tool," Mel Colter documents the evaluation of an early version of Recoder, a Cobol restructuring tool. The goal of the study was to determine if programmers found restructured code easier to maintain. Programmers were asked to make changes to original and restructured versions of Cobol code. Then the resulting changes were compared.[1] The restructured code showed decreased time to change and more coding style consistency. However, the programmers needed to adjust to the new coding style caused by automatic restructuring.

The next paper, "CASE Tools Supporting Ada Reverse Engineering: State of the Practice" by M. Cassandra Smith, Diane E. Mularz, and Thomas J. Smith, presents a valuable framework for evaluating a set of related reengineering or reverse engineering tools. The authors define a tool evaluation process and apply it to evaluate four reverse engineering tools for Ada source code. Though applied to reverse engineering tools for Ada, their evaluation process is useful for evaluating reverse engineering tools for other languages.

In the final paper, "A Study of the Effect of Reengineering upon Software Maintainability," Harry Sneed and Agnes Kaposi describe an experiment that studied the effect of reengineering on code maintainability. In their experiment, programmers made changes to original, restructured, and reengineered versions of the code. They found that reengineering reduced code complexity and increased maintainability, and that restructuring had a minor positive effect on code maintainability. The study is interesting for its experimental design, procedure, and measurements.[2]

---

[1] In this report extract, the study's results are summarized in the Executive Summary.

[2] From a statistical viewpoint, the study's results are more illustrative of the advantages of reengineering, rather than definitive, due to the small sample size of tasks and the small number of programmers who participated.

PARALLEL TEST AND PRODUCTIVITY EVALUATION OF A COMMERCIALLY SUPPLIED COBOL RESTRUCTURING TOOL

Prepared By:

FEDERAL SOFTWARE MANAGEMENT SUPPORT CENTER

In Conjunction With:

THE DEFENSE LOGISTICS AGENCY

SEPTEMBER 1987

Office of Software Development
and Information Technology

5203 Leesburg Pike, Suite 1100
Falls Church, VA 22041-3467

Excerpts from "Parallel Test and Productivity Evaluation of a Commercially Supplied Cobol Restructuring Tool," by the Federal Software Management Support Center, reprinted from *Office of Software Development and Information Technology*, Sept. 1987.

EXECUTIVE SUMMARY

INTRODUCTION

This document reports the results of a study of the Language Technology Incorporated (LTI) product, "Recoder", conducted at and by the Defense Logistics Agency's (DLA) Defense Systems Automation Center (DSAC), Columbus, Ohio. This evaluation of Recoder was undertaken in parallel with a study of a Programmer's Workbench supplied by Rand Information Systems, Inc., in conjunction with the General Services Administration's Federal Software Management Support Center.

LTI provided the product for evaluation, along with training necessary for its use. The Federal Software Management Support Center (FSMC) at the GSA, provided tasking and general project support. Dr. Mel A. Colter, of Colter Enterprises, Inc., assembled and analyzed the data collected by DSAC. The final report was prepared by Dr. Colter under the combined direction of DSAC and the FSMC.

THE PROJECT PLAN

As a part of the planning process, a set of programs was selected for the project and the evaluation procedures were determined. For each program in the evaluation, a baseline version was established. That baseline version was used to create two program versions upon which maintenance tasks were performed, one in the original form, and the other in a restructured form. To control experimental variability, the same maintenance changes were applied to each version of each program.

A series of measurements was made on each version of the program. These measurements involved metric analysis before and after each change and studies of time required to make and test the change. Detailed subjective evaluations were also obtained from study participants.

RESULTS AND CONCLUSIONS

There were both positive and negative results from this study. On the positive side:

- *The recoded versions demonstrated a 44% reduction in maintenance and test time. Since this is the primary purpose of the product, it may be the most important result of the study.*

- *The recoded versions demonstrated a consistency of style and documentation which was not present in the original code.*

vi

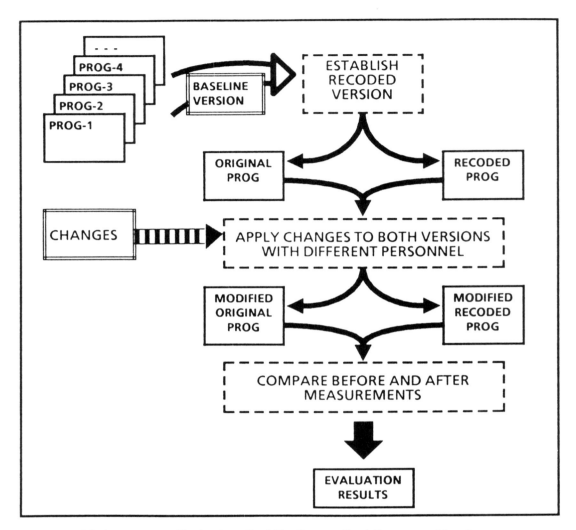

Maintenance Tasks Applied To Controlled Program Versions

- *The recoded versions produced significant reductions in local standards violations and structure violations.*

- *There are strong indications that the programmers who worked with the recoded programs acquired increased knowledge levels and skills over those who worked with the unstructured versions.*

vii

- *The study participants showed strong positive responses to the documentation provided by Recoder. There was general consensus that this output was very helpful in understanding program control structures and relationships between program components.*

On the negative side:

- *A significant number of the target programs failed to run through Recoder on the first pass, and several were never successfully reprocessed during the study time period.*

- *A great deal of concern was expressed by the participating professionals about the style and structure of the programs after they were run through Recoder.*

- *The recoded programs exhibited significant increases in resource utilization. This included compile time and resources, Load module size, and CPU resources necessary to run the program.*

- *The restructured program generally requires some human intervention after the fact to provide meaningful names for paragraphs and variables which have been added by Recoder.*

- *Some particularly poor quality programs may require an initial step in which programmers clean up certain aspects of the code to make it acceptable to Recoder.*

These results are fully documented in the body of the report. They support the following conclusions:

Evaluation of the RECODER product at DSAC has proven, within the limitations of the methodology used, that this restructuring tool can improve productivity in the maintenance process by reducing the amount of time necessary to implement and test maintenance changes. Further examination of this process could greatly reduce the cost of software management within government agencies, particularly if the test and evaluation methods are tightened to ensure more reliable outcomes.

The Federal Software Management Support Center should continue to pursue its interest in automated restructuring products. The productivity gains and other observed benefits are too great to ignore this opportunity to reduce maintenance costs. The issues of resource utilization and subjective concerns, however, may warrant further study, particularly in light of the obvious conflict between the subjective and objective portions of this evaluation.

viii

1. INTRODUCTION

1.1 Project Background

Increasing software maintenance expenditures have received growing attention over the past decade. However, with the rapid introduction of tools directed at increasing maintenance productivity, some of this interest has become more focused. Some industry experts have questioned the efficacy and cost effectiveness of maintenance productivity tools. As a result, there is serious interest in the evaluation of maintenance tools in actual working environments.

This document reports the results of a study of the Language Technology Incorporated (LTI) product, "RECODER", conducted at and by the Defense Logistics Agency's (DLA) Defense Systems Automation Center (DSAC), Columbus, Ohio. This evaluation of RECODER was undertaken in parallel with a study of a Programmer's Workbench supplied by Rand Information Systems, Inc., in conjunction with the General Services Administration's Federal Software Management Support Center.

Initially, the study was to have received support from independent industry experts on software maintenance. However, time considerations and other issues resulted in the design, performance, and collection of the raw data being conducted almost entirely by DSAC. LTI provided the product for evaluation, along with training necessary for its use. The Federal Software Management Support Center (FSMC) at the GSA, provided tasking and general project support. Dr. Mel A. Colter, of Colter Enterprises, Inc., assembled and analyzed the data collected by DSAC. The final report was prepared by Dr. Colter under the combined direction of DSAC and the FSMC. The comments, opinions, and recommendations contained in the report and not directly attributed to study participants are the consensus views of the entire study management.

1.2 The Target Project

The product under evaluation (RECODER) is advertised as a software tool which inputs an unstructured COBOL program and produces an equivalent program (referred to as "recoded") in structured format. This process is fully automated, accepting any valid ANSI COBOL program. The recoded program which is the product of the process is advertised as being functionally equivalent and executable without any programmer effort required. Furthermore, the recoded version is claimed to produce significant increases in maintenance productivity.

This study, while not extremely formal from a research perspective, was planned to investigate these claims and evaluate the effects of the restructuring process on production code managed by the DLA. The current DLA/DSAC COBOL inventory

- 1 -

includes roughly 9600 programs consisting of about 14 million lines of code. The majority of this code was originally designed and produced more than ten years ago. It has been subject to significant change during maintenance and thus represents an excellent base for testing an automated restructuring tool.

2. PROJECT ORGANIZATION AND METHODOLOGY

2.1 The Project Plan

The RECODER evaluation project was initiated through a tasking statement in March, 1986. At that time, a project plan was constructed. That plan, with some delays and modifications, was followed throughout the project It involved evaluation planning, installation of RECODER, training, the evaluation process, and the reporting of results, as shown in Exhibit 2-1. The steps from the installation on will be discussed in the Evaluation Results Section.

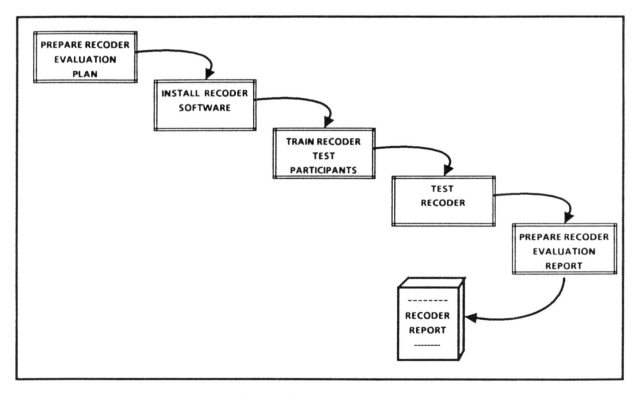

Recoder Evaluation Project Plan

Exhibit 2-1

- 3 -

As a part of the planning process, a set of programs was selected for the project and the evaluation procedures were determined. The program selection criteria will be discussed in the relevant section. The actual procedures for running the programs through the recoding and evaluation process are detailed below.

2.2 The Project Methodology

For each program in the evaluation, a baseline version was established. As shown in Exhibit 2-2, that baseline version was used to create two program versions upon which maintenance tasks were performed. To control experimental variability, the same maintenance changes were applied to each version of each program. Also, DSAC assigned different maintenance programmers to the different versions to minimize learning curve effects. Furthermore, the project plan required that no maintenance programmer in the study be allowed to work on a program of his or her authorship.

A series of measurements was made on each version of the program. These measurements involved metric analysis before and after each change and studies of time required to make and test the change.

The evaluation methodology was intended to maximize the research validity of the project while remaining manageable in a production shop under a modest budget. In an early document on the project, the following major directions were established to set and maintain this direction.

- *Objective measures will be applied (line counts, execution times, response times, etc.) but the most important part of the evaluation will be subjective.*
- *Questionnaires will address usability, adequacy, and productivity impacts of the software included in the evaluation.*
- *The final report document will describe all the observed effects of the software restructuring tool as tested at DSAC and make recommendations as to the appropriateness and usefulness of that software product, both within the DLA and in other government installations.*

2.3 Program Selection

At the start of the project, a set of seven programs was selected as targets for the study. These programs were chosen to reflect the style and structure of programs within the DSAC production library. Most of the programs were, of course, considered to be unstructured, reflecting an interest in the operation of RECODER on the type of program for which it is targeted. All programs were currently running in a standard compiler environment. In addition, they reflected the style and standards of the organization.

In reality, as with most organizations, the programs reflected more organization style than standards. Though a formal set of standards exists and can be monitored through a local source library and preprocessor routine (SLAP), many SLAP violations have been allowed to exist in the code due to urgency issues during historical change processes. In

- 4 -

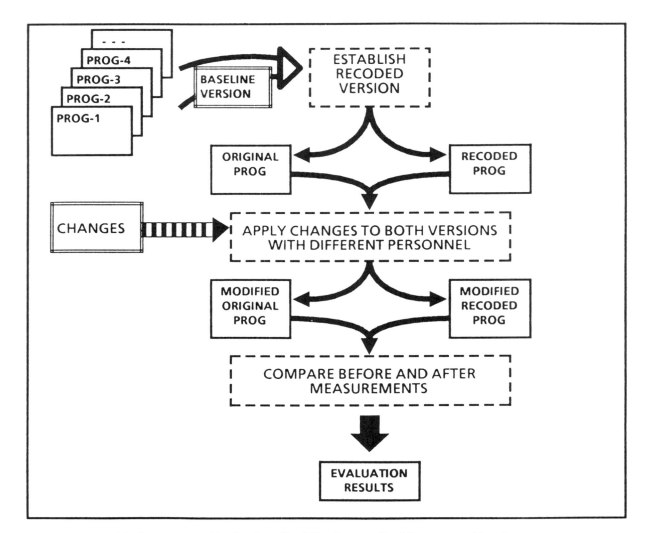

Maintenance Tasks Applied To Controlled Program Versions

Exhibit 2-2

addition, some violations of internal structure standards exist for the same reasons. Finally, the programs exhibited some style characteristics which are variations of the interpretation of the ANSI COBOL standard. This is also common in production shops.

The set of programs selected should have provided a reasonable test of the RECODER product. The product is claimed to accept any acceptable program under ANSI COBOL compilers. However, as discussed in the section, "Implementing The Study," some

- 5 -

problems were encountered in actually processing the original program set through RECODER.

2.4 The Evaluation Process

The formal evaluation process was carefully planned to provide a structure for each participant in the study. The evaluation steps were defined and specific measures were selected for the programs.

2.4.1 Evaluation Structure

The following paragraphs summarize the detailed plans for the test and evaluation phase of the project.

A. *Training*
Each programmer/analyst participated in the training provided by Language Technology Incorporated. The following parameters were used in the evaluation of the training exercise:

1. *Complexity*
The participants evaluated the degree of understanding and comprehension of the RECODER product resulting from the vendor's training. This included the amount of follow-up training required to fully utilize the product.

2. *Completeness*
Participants evaluated the degree that the training exercise covered the total product capabilities.

3. *Applicability*
The ability of the programmer/analyst to apply the product in the work environment after the training was completed by the vendor was evaluated by each individual.

B. *RECODER Execution*
Each selected program was input to RECODER for test and evaluation. The two versions (original and recoded) were then tested against the same test base in a stand alone environment to collect statistics on program performance. Specific items reviewed included the following:

1. *Structure*
Junior level programmers reviewed RECODER output and baseline programs to determine the degree of structure and ease of following program flow and logic. The overall structure of each program version was evaluated using SLAP to identify non-structured characteristics such as backward GOTO's, PERFORM THRU's, etc.

- 6 -

2. **Completeness**
Recoded programs were evaluated for functional equivalency to the baseline. Output reports and listings were compared as well as intermediate and working files created by both versions of the code.

3. **Performance**
Recoded and baseline programs were tested against the same test base to collect performance statistics. Those test statistics are summarized in the next section.

C. **Maintenance Evaluation**
After testing the recoded version of the program, junior level programmers were given changes to evaluate maintenance capabilities with and without the use of RECODER. Here, each programmer reported two factors:

1. **Revision Time**
Revision time was the time necessary to identify the problem in a program and make the necessary change. This was recorded for changes to both versions of the program.

2. **Test Time**
Here, participants reported the time required to test the change and evaluate the correctness of the change for both versions.

D. **Documentation**
Programmers and analysts evaluated the documentation capabilities of RECODER. This included three primary factors:

1. **Control Flow Documentation**
This factor dealt with the ability of RECODER to document the program's control flow in a hierarchical, top down structure.

2. **Ease of Interpretation**
This factor related to the ability of the programmer/analyst to comprehend what the program does and how it works. Recoded programs and baseline versions were given to junior and senior level programmers for this evaluation. As noted before, the evaluation methodology called for the avoidance of this evaluation being performed by the original author of the program under test.

3. **Program Format**
Here, individuals evaluated the degree of readability of each RECODER program version and the ability of the programmer to identify procedures and modules within the code.

E. **RECODER Survey**
Participants in the study were required to document his/her evaluation of the LTI training, ease of product use, value to the job, support, and overall lessons learned from working with the product.

- 7 -

This list of evaluative factors was designed to provide a broad spectrum evaluation of the LTI product. As a part of the collection of data on these factors, both subjective and empirical data were collected. The actual measurements made on the code versions and included in this report are detailed below.

2.4.2 Empirical Measurements

Within the general evaluation structure, a number of actual measurements were made on the versions of the code. While the intent of the study was to stress subjective evaluation, these measures are of value in making comparative statements about the original and recoded versions. The factors subjected to formal measurement included:

- **Number of source lines** before and after applying RECODER to the target programs.
- **Number of statements** before and after applying RECODER to the programs.
- **Number of standards violations** before and after applying RECODER. (Note that the standards violations measured here reflect the standards at DSAC and not those implied by the LTI product. Other shops' standards sets may result in different counts.)
- **Compile service units** before and after recoding, without optimization.
- **Compile service units** before and after recoding, with optimization.
- **Load module size** before and after recoding, without optimization.
- **Load module size** before and after recoding, with optimization.
- **Execution time** (CPU time) before and after recoding.

2.5 Comments On The Methodology

As with all studies, and particularly studies which take place within production environments, considerations of practicality and budget result in research methodologies which can be criticized from a pure research perspective. In this case, some specific strengths and weaknesses of the methodology may be noted as discussed below.

- *The study provides reasonable controls in the creation of baseline programs and the application of identical changes to the two versions of the software.*

- *The study also provides good controls through the use of different personnel on the two versions of the code. This avoids problems with the learning curve affecting the time required to make the change from version to version.*

- *The study also standardized the collection of measurements on the code versions by allocating this effort to a group different than the one making the changes.*

- *The study provided for programmer preparation of evaluative reports on the subjective components of the study. These reports are enclosed in this document as appendices. Their content is summarized in the evaluation sections of the document.*

- 8 -

- *The evaluation involved too few programs and too few maintenance changes to be statistically significant. This is the reason for the extensive use of subjective evaluations in addition to objective measures of program size, etc.*

- *Because of the limited number of maintenance changes investigated, the evaluation did not allow sufficient time to investigate the learning curve effects associated with the original and restructured programs. The vendor claims of the benefits of restructuring would lead one to a hypothesis of reduced learning time on restructured code. However, since the restructured code reflects different standards and style than the code in the DSAC library, one would expect that a learning curve would be exhibited as maintenance programmers become familiar with the different style. This study did not attempt to investigate a sufficient number of programs and changes to consider these effects. As a result, subjective evaluations and comments must be carefully considered. Subjective comments, both positive and negative may shift as the maintenance programmer becomes more familiar with the output of the product.*

- *The operational characteristics of the RECODER product, along with characteristics of the restructured output of the product, appear to be sensitive to a set of characteristics of the input code. This issue is treated mostly subjectively in this study, with some data on structure characteristics of the input programs. The combination of empirical and subjective information on this topic provides some insight into this issue.*

In summary, the study provides a good amount of experimental control, given the demands of time, budget, and practicality of running such a test in a production shop. While certain research design questions exist, the results can, if carefully interpreted, yield insights into the performance and effects of the product under examination. Furthermore, the subjective comments provided by the study participants help us to understand the product from the practicing professional's point of view.

- 9 -

CASE TOOLS SUPPORTING Ada REVERSE ENGINEERING: STATE OF THE PRACTICE

M. Cassandra Smith   Diane E. Mularz   Thomas J. Smith

The MITRE Corporation, McLean, VA

Abstract

The purpose of this paper is to discuss the methodology and results of a study of Computer-Aided Software Engineering (CASE) tools that reverse engineer Ada programs. The paper discusses a list of features that support reverse engineering with Ada, criteria for interpreting vendor information on tools to identify candidates for further assessment, the results of exercising four candidate tools with sample Ada programs, and observations on the state of the practice of reverse engineering Ada in the CASE tools industry. The predominant finding is that the tools are in their infancy--they are primarily graphics-based and weak in scaling up.

Introduction

CASE technology is being used to increase programmer productivity and reduce software life cycle costs. Ada is being used increasingly for software development. There is a growing body of code that already has been written and could be targeted for reuse and revitalization. Given these considerations, a project was undertaken to evaluate commercially-available CASE tools claiming to support reverse engineering of Ada.

This paper discusses a list of features that support Ada reverse engineering, criteria for interpreting vendor information to find candidates for further assessment, the results of exercising four candidate tools with sample Ada systems, and recommendations for new features that CASE vendors should consider for future enhancement of their products. The purpose of this study has not been to identify the best tool but rather to identify what capabilities exist in CASE tools to support reverse engineering; to assess the extent to which these capabilities exist now in CASE products; and finally, based on the exercising of CASE tools with both real and textbook applications and the knowledge of what is needed for reverse engineering, to assess the state of the practice of Ada reverse engineering in the CASE tools industry.

Study Approach

Figure 1 gives an overview of the study approach. First, a working definition of reverse engineering was formulated. Second, based on the working definition, selection criteria were defined. Third, using the selection criteria and vendor literature on tools, four tools were selected on which to perform experiments. Next, experiments were performed using the tools. Finally, using the experiment results and a set of evaluation criteria, the four tools were evaluated and the current capabilities of the tools and recommendations were reported. The following sections discuss the major elements of the study.

Definition of Reverse Engineering

Bachman,[2] CASE Outlook,[8] and Wilde and Thebaut[24] offer alternative definitions of reverse engineering. Wilde and Thebaut,[24] for example, consider the recovery of program requirements to be a goal of reverse engineering. We feel that currently this is not achievable. Ideas from the three above-mentioned sources have been used to synthesize our working definition of reverse engineering, which follows:

Reverse engineering is the process of analyzing an existing program to obtain an understanding of that program. This is accomplished by producing representations of the program in forms different from the implementation language. These representations may take a graphical form, such as structure charts or structure diagrams, or they may be a subset of the information that presents a particular view of the software system, such as compilation dependencies.

This definition is assumed throughout the following discussions.

As a point of clarification, we distinguished re-engineering and reverse engineering: It is often advantageous for a reverse engineered program to be enhanced further. The product of reverse engineering might be refined by a human and entered into the forward engineering process of a tool. This process--reverse engineering followed by forward engineering of the product--is considered re-engineering.

Reprinted from *Proc. Eighth Nat'l Conf. on Ada Technology*, U.S. Army Communications-Electronics Command, Fort Monmouth, N.J., 1990, pp. 157-164. Reprinted with authors' permission.

157

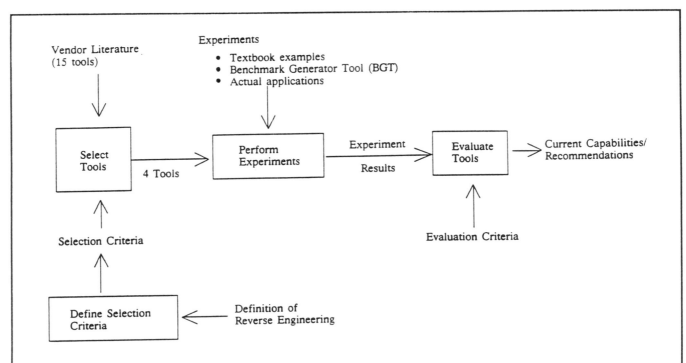

Vendor Literature
(15 tools)

Experiments
- Textbook examples
- Benchmark Generator Tool (BGT)
- Actual applications

Select Tools → 4 Tools → Perform Experiments → Experiment Results → Evaluate Tools → Current Capabilities/Recommendations

Selection Criteria

Evaluation Criteria

Define Selection Criteria ← Definition of Reverse Engineering

FIGURE 1
STUDY APPROACH

Reverse Engineering Tools Selection

We formulated a set of criteria for selecting Ada-oriented reverse engineering tools using Bachman,[1] Bush,[5] Campbell, et al.,[7] Roman,[17] Scarborough,[20] Schneidewind,[21] Wilde and Nejmeh,[23] and Wilde and Thebaut.[24] A reverse engineering tool:

1. Accepts general Ada code that was not necessarily generated by the tool (some tools require that the program input to reverse engineering be the output from the forward engineering of the tool).

2. Provides calling tree structure, structure charts, structure/Buhr/Booch graphs, or detailed design specifications (e.g., graphical program design language (PDL)).

3. Recognizes Ada structures (control, data, input/output)--tool should indicate hierarchy of modules and data, and indicate concurrent and sequential processes.

4. Presents compilation dependencies.

5. Provides batch analysis--the tool should allow the entire set of code to be analyzed without interruption.

6. Runs on common hardware platform--the tool may be used on generally available hardware, preferably multiple platforms.

7. Is available commercially.

A list of fifteen potential reverse engineering tools was compiled and checked against the reverse engineering selection criteria. This list was compiled from CASE Outlook,[8] Mimno,[14] Kerner,[11] and vendor presentations at the MITRE-Washington CASE Symposium.[6] When early information indicated that a tool did not currently support Ada or was not currently available, additional information was not pursued vigorously.

After the evaluation of the fifteen tools based on the selection criteria, four tools were selected to be subjected to the experiments described in the following section.

Reverse Engineering Experiments

A set of experiments was conducted with selected CASE reverse engineering tools as the second stage of the tool evaluation process. Reverse engineering, according to our definition, is the "process of analyzing an existing program to obtain an understanding of that program". Therefore, these experiments were conducted to determine the ability of a given tool to accurately import various Ada source programs into an internal tool representation, and the tool's ability to present various views of the program to promote an understanding of the original source code. The experiments were intended to provide comparative data regarding the capabilities of several reverse engineering tools that cannot be evaluated without actual usage of the tool. As a secondary objective, the experiments were used to validate the information obtained about each tool in the first stage of the evaluation process.

Experiments A description of each experiment, the method used for evaluation of each, and the methods used to generate or acquire programs that meet the purpose of each experiment are described in this section. Given the previously stated objectives, the following experiments were performed:

- Capacity check--the tool was exercised with various capacity values to determine the upper bounds of tool-dependent parameters such as number of statements, number of units, level of unit dependencies, etc.

- Well-formed, known application--the tool was exercised with a small application that is easily understandable, but complex enough to use a variety of Ada constructs and include a level of interdependence among compilation units.

- Ill-formed application--the tool was exercised with a small application that had both syntactic and semantic errors to determine the tool's ability to process an ill-formed program.

- Unknown, real application--the tool was exercised with a large application by an experimenter who had limited knowledge of the application to determine if the available information views contribute to understanding the intent of the program.

- Partial system model--a portion of an application was used to see if the tool allows for import and analysis of a partially implemented application.

- Re-engineer--using the well-formed application, the program was reverse engineered. Then, using the forward engineering capabilities of the tool, if available, the program was re-engineered into source code as a way of verifying the tool's ability to capture and retain a complete model of the original source code internally.

Sources for Experiment Programs The experiments exercised the tools using actual Ada source code. The source code used for each experiment was one of the following: generated code, small programs taken from Ada texts, and code developed for an actual application.

- Generated Code--The generated code was constructed using the Benchmark Generator Tool (BGT).[16] This tool was designed to test the limits of an Ada compilation system in two areas: library capacity and recompilation efficiency based on various dependency structures. Although the BGT's orientation is toward compiler benchmarking, its generated Ada structures are useful for evaluating the CASE tools in two ways. Simple well-defined program structures can be generated for exercising the tool in a minimal way. More elaborate structures can be produced for evaluating the actual limits of the CASE tool in terms of number of compilation units, number of statements per unit, levels of nesting, total source lines, number and variety of dependencies. The BGT assists in generating a variety of Ada program structures whose representation in the CASE tool under evaluation can be easily verified since the generated program structures are known a priori and are well formed. The two sets of code used for the experiment contain 436 and 86 semicolons respectively. (The number of semicolons is a frequently used size measure of Ada projects.)

- Well-formed Applications--Given the BGT's focus, it does not generate compilation units with complex internal structures. If a context dependency is established between two packages, there is no actual usage of the exported declarations included in the generated structure. Therefore, another level of source code is needed. This level still needs to be well-formed, but should represent an actual application where unit dependencies are present and used. Various Ada texts[3,15] present such programs and their corresponding designs. Some of these textbook examples are not fully implemented, thereby providing partially implemented programs for the experiments. The availability of both source code and design provides a good validation mechanism for the reverse engineered graphical notations produced by the CASE tools. A selected set of these programs was used for a portion of the experiments. The two programs (Booch's[3] Concordance and Nielsen and Shumate's[15] Remote Temperature Sensor) used in the experiment contain 308 and 368 semicolons respectively.

- Actual Applications--Finally, actual applications were imported into the tools. These applications were used to evaluate the tools given large line of code counts and architectures produced for real-world applications. The two programs used in the experiment contain 3,058 and 53,756 semicolons respectively.

Method of Evaluation Each experiment was performed on each of the candidate tools. Comparative data was gathered for each tool's performance in each experiment. The following evaluation criteria were defined:

- Accuracy of internal model--determine if there is consistency between the internal representation and original source input into the tool. The accuracy of this internal representation can only be evaluated in terms of the support functions provided by the CASE tool for viewing the internal model. Therefore, the variety of information presented via the analysis, graphical, and reporting functions was used as the primary method of evaluation.

- Retention of information for re-engineering--determine if information is lost in the reverse engineering process. If a tool does not retain all the information from the original source code, then modification and re-engineering of the tool's internal representation will result in a new source program that does not contain the detail of the original program.

- User views--determine what subsets of information are made visible to the user. A variety of views that focus on different aspects of the program (e.g., compilation dependencies, calling trees, cross reference reports) will aid in understanding the program. The types of views and their usefulness for understandability were determined.

- Analysis support--determine if analysis functions can be executed against the internal model to derive additional program information. Such an analysis might include finding all compilation units that are dependent on a given package.

- Error handling and recovery--determine the tool's ability to reverse engineer programs with compile and/or run-time errors that are imported into the tool as well as recover from errors during normal user interaction and batch processing.

- Performance statistics--determine the times required to perform the tool's functions such as the reverse engineering process, display of a given graphics notation, etc. These times will be gathered as by-products of performing the experiments.

Table 1 provides a summary of the application of the first five of these criteria to the four tools on which the experiments were performed. Table 2 summarizes the application of the sixth criterion (performance statistics) to the four tools. In Table 2 process time is the time required to generate the internal representation for the tool. Note that the tools were weak in scaling up. As Table 2 indicates, none of the tools was successful in handling both the real applications.

TABLE 1

TOOL EVALUATION SUMMARY

Evaluation Criteria	Tool 1	Tool 2
Internal Model	• Complete and accurate compilation dependencies • Accurate overviews of program unit declarations • No library support	• No abstraction takes place. No information is lost. • No library support
Re-engineering	• Incomplete—Object, type and exception declarations omitted.	• Source code, generated PDL, and regenerated code are same.
User Views	• Compilation dependencies • Program unit declarations • Some compilation dependency diagrams overcrowed	• Program design language on a program unit, code block, and declarative region basis.
Analytic Capability	None	None
Error Handling and Recovery	• Good syntax recognition • Minimal semantic error recognition	• Very good syntax recognition • Minimal semantic error recognition

TABLE 1

TOOL EVALUATION SUMMARY

(Continued)

Evaluation Criteria	Tool 3	Tool 4
Internal Model	• Complete Ada syntax, incomplete Ada static semantics • Lack of simple mechanism to import implementation-dependent environment • No support for hierarchy of program libraries of units • Incorrect name visibility and scoping semantics implemented	• Complete Ada syntax and fairly complete Ada static semantics • Support for implementation-dependent environment for host on which tool executes • Support for hierarchies of program libraries of units • Unable to generate most forms of cross reference information • Unable to identify calling structures for nested units
Re-engineering	• Support for re-engineering of source code units via resubmission and "make" capabilities	• Support for re-engineering of source code units via resubmission and notification of obsolete dependencies
Analytic Capability	• Static set of metrics calculated and presented as part of reports	• Over 100 source code counts based on Ada structure usage

TABLE 1

TOOL EVALUATION SUMMARY

(Concluded)

Evaluation Criteria	Tool 3	Tool 4
User Views	• Support for multiple views via diagrams including compilation dependencies, call trees, declaration structures, and diagrams • Support for name cross reference reports and exception propagation • Some diagrams overcrowded, missing information • Ambiguities in name overloading and in declaration structure presentation • Limit on compilation dependency nesting • User selectable units for generation of views and reports	• Support for multiple views via reports including unit dependencies, call trees, exception propagation, name cross reference, and control flow • Tailorable standards checker • User selectable units for generation of views
Error Handling and Recovery	• Very good syntax recognition • Minimal semantic error recognition • Error reporting of syntax and some semantic errors • Inconsistent libraries caused by lack of semantic recognition • No access protection against modification of graphical information	• Very good syntax recognition • Good semantic recognition • Detailed error reporting of syntax and semantic errors • Weak error reporting at run time • Corruption of library during unit deletion • No access protection against modification of library information

TABLE 2

PERFORMANCE STATISTICS APPLIED TO TOOLS

Performance Statistics				
Experiment	Tool 1	Tool 2	Tool 3	Tool 4
Capacity Check (Minimal Sizing):				
Process Time (minutes)	35	(6)	4.5	26.3
Data Storage (Kbytes)	13		751 (1)	1609 (3)
Reports (Kbytes)	35		272	1129
Capacity Check (Minimal Dependency):				
Process Time (minutes)	6		3.4	14.3
Data Storage (Kbytes)	3	(6)	522 (1)	1052 (3)
Reports (Kbytes)	7		80	455
Well-Formed:				
Process Time (minutes)	7	18	4.75	5.5
Data Storage (Kbytes)	18	18	1042 (1)	826 (3)
Reports (Kbytes)	10	15	214	(4)
Partially Implemented:				
Process Time (minutes)	11	32	8.8	12.3
Data Storage (Kbytes)	25	25	1166 (1)	606 (3)
Reports (Kbytes)	13	39	246	(4)
Unknown Real Application 1:				
Process Time (minutes)	256 (5)	5 (6)	69.3	(2)
Data Storage (Kbytes)	342	342	8883 (1)	(2)
Reports (Kbytes)	62	11	2786	(2)
Unknown Real Application 2:				
Process Time (minutes)	1 (2)		(2)	(2)
Data Storage (Kbytes)	5064	(6)	(2)	(2)
Reports (Kbytes)	0		(2)	(2)

Notes:

(1) The storage requirements identified here represent storage for the application-specific code. In addition, storage is required for all of the predefined Ada units. These units required an additional 143 Kbytes of storage that was allocated for each experiment.

(2) Information not available since application was not successfully imported.

(3) The storage requirements identified here represent storage for the application-specific code. In addition, storage is required for all of the predefined Ada units and the run-time library. These units require an additional 16400 Kbytes of storage that was allocated once for all experiments.

(4) All reports could not be generated.

(5) Program failure before completion.

(6) Tediousness of input and predicatability of results precluded performing all experiments.

Kbytes = thousands of bytes

Summary of Findings

The hands-on experiments were extremely useful in providing information on the capabilities of the tool that could not be acquired through vendor literature or demonstration copies. Results indicate that the tools generate useful compilation dependency diagrams of an overall program system and various diagrams of individual program units. The information subsets generated are primarily graphics based and weak in scaling up. These information subsets also are primarily based on the Ada syntactical structures with very weak capture of semantic information.

We found that the tools are in their infancy. They have difficulty analyzing production-level applications. In certain cases, modest-sized applications (approximately 40,000 lines of code) could not be imported into the tool due to inefficient resource utilization. Most tools also require that the imported code be compilable. In one tool this compilation must occur on the compilation system associated with the tool's execution environment. This tool cannot process an application that makes use of implementation-dependent features that differ from the capabilities of the tool's host compilation system. Input of the application to a tool is unique per tool. In some cases it is extremely cumbersome requiring the separation of multiple compilation units in a single file into distinct physical files. This becomes burdensome for any reasonably sized application. It also adds to the burden of using different vendor tools to examine and develop the code since each tool has its own unique form of importation. Iteration between forward and reverse engineering in a single tool is not generally supported. In one case, the reverse engineering process actually loses information that would have to be re-entered in the forward engineering step. This eliminates support for iterative development in the context of a tool.

The tools, in general, recognize and flag syntactic errors in programs. One tool even permits the interactive correction of syntactic errors with a continuation of the reverse engineering process from that point. Semantic errors, on the other hand, are not readily detected. To summarize, the tools provide limited information that would help in understanding a program.

Recommendations

We conclude with the following recommendations for Ada reverse engineering tools. The tools on the whole capture the properties of a program that can be inferred from the structure of the Ada language. The tools in general do not capture the meaning of programs which might be discernible from the dynamic or runtime semantics. The tools also should capture the error model of a program via exception recognition and understanding. Understanding the behavior of a program could be enhanced by the analysis of data structures and their use throughout a program. To provide for these capabilities, the next generation reverse engineering tools should include a query capability supported by a database that stores dynamic, structural, and context information required for understanding a program. Without such a capability ad hoc analysis support will continue to be lacking. Some commercially available products appear to provide such capabilities for other languages. The tools also should provide the capability to identify the implementation-dependent features of the Ada language in the source code. For instance, the specification of the packages STANDARD and SYSTEM should be profiled and recognized by the tool, and available to the user depending upon the compilation system used for development. The user would define an environment for an application via these packages.

REFERENCES

1. Bachman, C. July 1988. *A CASE for Reverse Engineering*, Datamation.

2. Bachman, C. 1988. *Reverse Engineering: The Key to Success*, CASE Outlook 1988, Vol. 2, No. 2.

3. Booch, G. 1986. *Software Engineering with Ada*. Menlo Park, CA: The Benjamin Cummings Publishing Company, Inc.

4. Buhr, R. J. A. 1984. *System Design with Ada*. Englewood Cliffs, NJ: Prentice Hall, Inc.

5. Bush, E. 1988. *CASE for Existing Systems*, CASE Outlook 1988, Vol. 2, No. 2.

6. Byron, D. and R. Fuss, eds. 1989. *Proceedings of the Computer-Aided Software Engineering Symposium*, 23 January 1989, MP89W00010. McLean, VA: The MITRE Corporation.

7. Campbell, K. et al. 1987. *Evaluation of Computer-Aided System Design Tools for SDI Battle Management/C3 Architecture Development*. Alexandria, VA: Institute for Defense Analysis.

8. CASE Outlook. 1988. *CASE Tools for Reverse Engineering*, CASE Outlook 1988, Vol. 2, No. 2.

9. Department of Defense. 1983. *Reference Manual for the Ada Programming Language*, ANSI/MIL-STD-1815A.

10. Firth, Robert et al. August 1987. *A Guide to the Classification and Assessment of Software Engineering Tools,*" Technical Report CMU/SEI-87-TRIO, ESD-TR-87-111. Pittsburgh, PA: Software Engineering Institute Carnegie Mellon University.

11. Kerner, J. November/December 1988. *Ada Design Language Developers Matrix*, Ada Letters, VIII: 6.

12. Lempp, P. and R. J. Torick. March 1988. *Software Reverse Engineering: An Approach to Recapturing Reliable Software*, Fourth Annual Joint Conference on Software Quality and Productivity.

13. Lempp, R. and A. Zeh. May 1988. *Interfacing a Development Support Environment to a MAPSE through Ada Code Generation and Code Feedback: A Step Towards an APSE*, National Aerospace and Electronics Conference (NAECON '88).

14. Mimno, P. R. May 1988. *James Martin Productivity Series: CASE Tools Comparison and Review*, CASE Expo Spring Infomart. Dallas, TX.

15. Nielson, K. and K. Shumate. 1988. *Designing Large Real-Time Systems with Ada*. New York, NY: McGraw-Hill Book Company.

16. Rainier, S. R. and T. P. Reagan. 1988. *User's Manual for the Ada Compilation Benchmark Generator Tool*, MTR-87W00192-01, Volume 1. McLean, VA: The MITRE Corporation.

17. Roman, D. June 1986. *Classifying Maintenance Tools*, Computer Decisions.

18. Rosenblat, G. D. and H. Fischer. 1989. *Reverse Engineering and the Ada Software Development Cycle.*

19. Scandura, J. M. 1987. *A Cognitive Approach to Software Development: The PRODOC Environment and Associated Methodology,* Journal of PASCAL, Ada, Modula-2, Vol. 6, No. 5. pp. 10-25.

20. Scarborough, K. 1988. *Tool Evaluation Report.* Reston, VA: Software Productivity Consortium.

21. Schneidewind, N. F. March 1987. *The State of Software Maintenance,* IEEE Transactions on Software Engineering, Vol. SE-13, No. 3.

22. Seviora, R. May 1987. *Knowledge-Based Program Development Systems,* IEEE Software.

23. Wilde, N. and B. Nejmeh. September 1987. *Dependency Analysis: An Aid for Software Maintenance.* Gainesville, FL: Software Engineering Research Center.

24. Wilde, N and S. Thebaut. October 1987. *The Maintenance Assistant: Work in Progress,* Post Deployment Software Support Symposium.

Authors' Address   MITRE Corporation
7525 Colshire Drive
McLean, VA 22102

M. Cassandra Smith received the B.A. degree in mathematical and statistical economics from Howard University and the M.S. and Ph.D. degrees in computational linguistics from Georgetown University. Her current interests include CASE technology, software metrics, and database technology. Dr. Smith is currently employed by the MITRE Corporation as a member of the technical staff in the Washington Software Center. She is a member of ACM, ACM SIGMOD and Association for Computational Linguistics (ACL).

Diane E. Mularz received the B.S. degree in mathematics from Indiana University of Pennsylvania and the M.S. degree in computer science from Johns Hopkins University. Ms. Mularz has over 15 years experience in the field. Her current interests include software engineering environments and design quality assessment. Ms. Mularz is currently employed by the MITRE Corporation as a lead scientist in the Washington Software Center. She is a member of the ACM, ACM SIGAda and the IEEE Computer Society.

Thomas J. Smith received the B.Sc. degree in mathematics from the University of Manitoba, the Ph.D. degree in mathematics from the University of Iowa and the M.S. degree in computer science from Georgia Institute of Technology. Dr. Smith has 20 years of experience in the fields of mathematical and computer sciences. During the past 10 years he has concentrated particularly in parallel and distributed computing, programming languages, software tools, and programming environments. Dr. Smith is presently a lead scientist at the MITRE Corporation in Washington, DC. He is a member of the ACM, ACM SIGAda, and the IEEE.

A study on the Effect of Reengineering upon Software Maintainability

Harry M. Sneed & Agnes Kaposi

Software Engineering Service
Rosenheimer Landstrasse 37, D-8012 Ottobrunn

The report presented here on the effect of re-engineering upon software maintainability stems from a laboratory experiment conducted within the METKIT research project of the European ESPRIT program for the study and promotion of the use of metrics in Software-Engineering. The experiment was conducted as a case study in measuring software complexity and maintainability. However, the results also serve to assess the benefits of reengineering old programs. Maintainability is defined as the effort to perform maintenance tasks, the impact domain of the maintenance actions and the errror rate caused by those actions. Complexity is defined as a combination of code, data, data flow, structure, and control flow metrics. From the data collected it demonstrates that reengineering can decrease complexity and increase maintainability, but that restructuring has only a minor effect on maintainability.

1. INTRODUCTION TO METKIT EXPERIMENT

The need to find better measures of software quantity, quality and complexity is essential to the discipline of software engineering. Without accurate measurements it is impossible to justify increased costs for software development methods, tools or testing effort. Business managers are unwilling to invest in software engineering, unless someone can quantify their reduction in development costs or increased quality. The same applies to software maintenance. Everyone is aware of the high cost of maintenance, but no one is in a position to prove how these costs can be reduced without adequate quantitative data.

In recent years software reengineering has been advocated as a means of reducing maintenance costs. Yet there is very little data, if any, to substantiate this claim. Managers want to know how much they will save in maintenance effort by reengineering their software. To answer this question one must either collect data on a reengineered system over several years and compare it with the data on the original system as was done by Linda Brice at the Los Alamos Laboratory (1), or one must conduct laboratory experiments on representative objects using representative subjects applying software maintainability metrics to collect data which can be scaled upwards to predict larger systems.

Due to the difficulty in obtaining useful data from industry, the ESPRIT METKIT project for promoting the study of software metrics in the European Community has chosen to follow the second path to obtain data on software maintainability. The laboratory experiment reported on here is one in a long series of such experiments reported on throughout the world, all of which have the purpose of measuring, explaining and predicting software maintenance effort. The emergence of software reengineering, renewal, and renovation techniques have only increased the demand for better metrics to justify their costs.

2. OBJECTIVES OF METKIT EXPERIMENT

The objectives of the METKIT experiment in maintainability measurement were threefold:

- first, to test various maintainability measures, i.e. to investigate the relationship between the static properties of a program on one side and the effort required to maintain it as well as the number of data items and procedural statements affected on the other side, i.e. the impact domain;

- second, to study the effect of restructuring and reengineering upon program maintainability as defined by maintenance effort and impact domain;

- third, to demonstrate how software-metrics might be applied to estimate maintenance effort and impact domain.

Maintenance has been defined by Lientz and Swanson as

- corrective maintenance
- adaptive maintenance, and
- perfective maintenance (2).

91

Reprinted from *Proc. Conf. on Software Maintenance*, 1990, pp. 91 – 99. ©1990 by The Institute of Electrical and Electronics Engineers, Inc. All rights reserved.

Corrective maintenance entails the repair of errors, so that the program meets its original specification.

Adaptive maintenance entails the changing of the program, so as to coincide with changes in its environment. Perfective maintenance entails the functional enhancement or internal renovation, i.e. optimization of the program to make it functionally or qualitatively better. To measure maintainability, it was necessary to perform all three types of maintenance.

Furthermore, maintainability has to be defined. In the literature cited above, maintainability has been defined as effort in personnel hours, errors caused by maintenance actions, scope of effect of the maintenance actions and program comprehension as viewed by the maintenance programmer. Since program comprehensibility is subject to the programmer's experience and preferences, it was decided to restrict maintainability in this experiment to the factors:

- effort in minutes required to perform maintenance
- impact domain of the maintenance actions
- errors caused directly or indirectly by the maintenance actions.

The impact domain was defined as the number of data declarations and procedural lines added, deleted or changed as a result of each maintenance task. In all cases, maintainability increases inverse to the decrease of the maintenance factors - effort, impact and error rate (3).

3. OBJECT OF METKIT EXPERIMENT

The object of the case study was a typical commercial application program written in COBOL. The program in question was designed for order entry processing in batch modus. It reads the order file, searches a customer file, updates an article file, writes a dispatch file or an open order file, and writes an order report for each order item. The basic logic is one of multiple file handling, master file, updating, information dispatching, report generating, and error handling. It includes such typical commercial data processing algorithms as merging, sorting and control group changing. There are two loops - an outer loop for each order and an inner loop for each order item.

The original program was monolithic and unstructured. It contained 377 lines of code with 137 procedural statements and 101 data declarations. It processed 5 files and wrote one report. In addition, it displayed messages in the system log.

The restructured version of the original program was modular and structured in terms of the three basic control structures - sequence, selection

and repetition. It contained 546 lines of code with 163 procedural statements in 11 modules and 129 data declarations. The increased size came about by the restructuring process, by replacing all literals and numeric constants with symbolic names, and, in particular, by grouping all input/output operations in subroutines at the end of the program.

The reengineered version of the original program was not only modular and structured, but also converted into COBOL-85. It contained 548 lines of code with 160 procedural statements in 10 modules, and 129 data declarations. It used no GOTO's, no literals, and no numeric constants. All file operations were grouped into an interface subroutine.

4. SUBJECTS OF METKIT EXPERIMENT

Three experienced programmers with at least 3 years of programming experience were used to conduct the experiment parallel to one another. Programmer A had only elementary knowledge of COBOL (3 years) and no knowledge of the application. Programmer B had a working knowledge of COBOL (5 years), but good knowledge of the application. Programmer C had a very good knowledge of COBOL (8 years), but no knowledge of the application.

5. METKIT EXPERIMENT

The experiment on maintainability was carried through in a 5 day period. On the first day the original unstructured COBOL-74 program was submitted to the SOFT-REORG restructuring tool. The result was the structured COBOL-74 version of the original program. On the same day the structured COBOL-74 program was manually reengineered and converted to COBOL-85. Thus the experiment began by creating three versions of the same COBOL batch order entry program:

- an unstructured COBOL-74 version (the original)
- a restructured COBOL-74 version
- a reengineered COBOL-85 version.

On the second day of the experiment three different programmers - A, B and C - were given the task of making the same two corrections in all three versions of the original program:

- a loop error in which the processing loop was terminated too soon;
- an off by 1 counting error due to a logic problem.

On the third day of the experiment the three programmers were given the task of making the same four alterations in all 3 versions of the corrected program:

- a change in the report page layout
- a change in the report structure
- a change in the error handling
- a change of all messages from English to German.

92

224

On the fourth day of the experiment the three programmers were given the task of making the same two enhancements in all three versions of the corrected and altered program

- a separation of the order entry file into
  2 files to be processed in parallel,
- a separation of the order report into
  2 reports to be printed in parallel.

On the fifth and final day, the 3 original versions, the 3 corrected versions, the 3 altered versions and the 3 enhanced versions, altogether 12 variants of the same program, were statically analyzed by the tool SOFTDOC to postdocument them and to collect automatically the elementary measurements d_1 thru d_{20} displayed in the table. The computed metrics K_1 thru K_5 were derived from these elementary measures. Later the programs were submitted to a source comparison tool to determine the differences in data declarations and source statements between the three mutants of the original three versions. Finally, all nine variants were dynamically analyzed by the tool SOFTEST to determine the number of errors caused by the mutations.

6. PROCESS DATA

The data collected in the METKIT project can be divided into two types

- process measurements, and
- product measurements.

The process measurements were similar to those observed by Gibson and Senn - maintenance effort in minutes to perform each maintenance task, impact domain in percentage of lines changed, and the second level error rate caused by the maintenance actions (4).

The exact maintenance tasks for

- correction,
- adaptation, and
- enhancement

to each of the three program versions

- unstructured COBOL-74 (COBOLD)
- restructured COBOL-74 (COBNEW)
- reengineered COBOL-85 (COB2NEW)

are described in Glossary I. The maintenance effort involved by each of the three maintenance types on each of the three program versions is depicted in Table-A. The effort curve is illustrated in Figure-1. It is interesting to note that for the corrective maintenance all of the subjects required more effort for the mechanically restructured program. For the reengineered program the effort was roughly equivalent to that of the original unstructured program. This would seem to indicate that a mechanically restructured program is less assessable to minor changes. However, for the

adaptive and enhancive maintenance the effort is less for the restructured program and significantly less for the reengineered program. The effort to adapt and enhance the restructured program is approximately 16% and for the reengineered program circa 32% less than for the original unstructured program.

```
1. CORRECTION TASKS

   There are the same 2 errors in each of the three
   programs:
                  - COBOLD
                  - COBNEW
                  - COB2NEW.

   a) The last (9th) order item of an order is not
      processed but is skipped over.

   b) The number of items ordered for each customer
      is always one too many.

2. ADAPTATION TASKS

   There are the same 4 changes to be made to the three
   programs.

   a) There should be 60 lines per page instead of 50.

   b) Each customer should be printed on a separate page.

   c) There should be a new error type - if there are no
      order items in the order file. I.e. if first item-no 0.

   d) All messages should be changed from English to
      German.

3. ENHANCEMENT TASKS

   There are the same 2 enhancements to be made to the three
   programs.

   a) The order file should be divided into two files, the
      orders and order items, which are both sorted by the
      order-no.

   b) The report should be divided into two reports - one
      for the order items which are rejected and one for the
      order-items accepted.
```

GLOSSARY I

TASK	PROGRAM VARIANT	PROGRAM VERSION	SUBJECT A	SUBJECT B	SUBJECT C	AVERAGE
			EFFORT IN MINUTES			
1. CORRECTION	COBOLD	1	45	30	43	39
	COBNEW	1	90	36	75	67
	COB2NEW	1	50	24	45	39
2. ADAPTION	COBOLD	2	78	45	70	64
	COBNEW	2	50	55	54	53
	COB2NEW	2	35	37	40	37
3. ENHANCEMENT	COBOLD	3	127	65	85	92
	COBNEW	3	92	58	70	73
	COB2NEW	3	74	47	70	63
TOTAL EFFORT			641	397	552	530

TABLE A: MAINTENANCE EFFORT TABLE

93

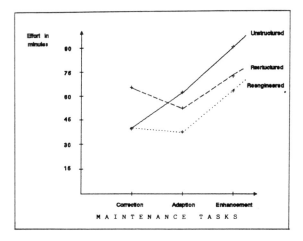

Figure 1: Maintenance Effort Rate

TASK	PROGRAM VARIANT	PROGRAM VERSION	CHANGE RATE % LINES CHANGED			
			SUBJECT A	SUBJECT B	SUBJECT C	AVERAGE
1. CORRECTION	COBOLD	1	1,8	3,4	2,9	2,7
	COBNEW	1	7,7	3,5	2,2	4,5
	COB2NEW	1	6,0	2,7	2,9	3,9
2. ADAPTION	COBOLD	2	18,5	10,1	18,4	15,7
	COBNEW	2	12,2	11,3	12,2	11,9
	COB2NEW	2	12,0	12,2	6,6	10,3
3. ENHANCEMENT	COBOLD	3	30,7	15,2	30,7	25,5
	COBNEW	3	24,5	12,0	17,4	18,0
	COB2NEW	3	26,8	13,5	18,7	19,6
	TOTAL % CHANGE		140,2	83,9	112,0	112,1

TABLE B: MAINTENANCE IMPACT TABLE

The impact domain, displayed in Table-B and illustrated by the curve in Figure-2, demonstrates a similar pattern to the maintenance effort. The impact domain as defined here is the percentage of lines affected by the maintenance action, computed as follows:

$$\frac{\text{Total-New-Lines} - \text{Unaltered-New-Lines}}{\text{Total-Old-Lines}}$$

For the correction of the restructured program the average impact domain increases from 2.7 % to 4.5 %. Even in the case of the reengineered program it is still 1.2 % greater than for the original unstructured program, which reinforces the conclusion that for minor corrective maintenance restructuring and reengineering are counterproductive. However, for the adaptive maintenance the average impact domain of the restructured program and the impact domain of the reengineered program is 1/3 less than that of the original program. This indicates a major savings in maintenance costs. For the enhansive maintenance the average impact domain of the restructured program is 30% less, whereas the impact domain of the reengineered program is only 24% less than that of the original program. This apparent anomaly is explained by the fact that the reengineered variant has a different data structure than that of the restructured variant, which is closer to that of the original program. In any case, the experiment demonstrates that the impact domain is a useful indicator of maintenance cost, independent of the maintenance subjects.

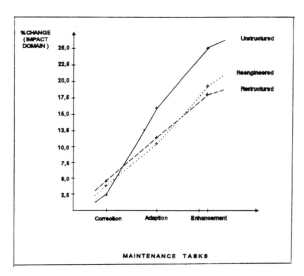

Figure 2: Maintenance Impact Rate

The second level error rate is shown in Table-C and analyzed by the graph in Figure-3. From the data gathered in this experiment, it would appear that the longer an unstructured program is maintained the greater is the propensity to introduce new errors. The total number of second level errors made through the maintenance actions on the original unstructured program is twice that of the number of errors introduced by maintenance actions on the reengineered variant, whereas the error rate in the restructured variant is slightly more than that of the reengineered program. From this, one can conclude that reliability can be improved by restructuring, and improved even more by

94

reengineering. However, one should be careful to draw conclusions on reliability from such a small sample. The errors detected here were, of course, only logic and other errors which can occur within a single module. By limiting the experiment to one module, a number of other error types which plague the maintenance process, such as interface and interaction errors, are excluded. To draw definite conclusions on reliability the experiment would have to be expanded to an entire system.

TASK	PROGRAM VARIANT	PROGRAM VERSION	2ND LEVEL ERRORS FOUND			
			SUBJECT A	SUBJECT B	SUBJECT C	TOTAL
1. CORRECTION	COBOLD	1	0	1	1	2
	COBNEH	1	0	1	0	1
	COB2NEH	1	0	1	0	1
2. ADAPTION	COBOLD	2	1	1	1	3
	COBNEH	2	0	1	1	2
	COB2NEH	2	0	1	1	2
3. ENHANCEMENT	COBOLD	3	1	3	2	6
	COBNEH	3	1	1	2	4
	COB2NEH	3	1	1	1	3
	TOTAL ERRORS		4	11	9	24

TABLE C: MAINTENANCE ERROR TABLE

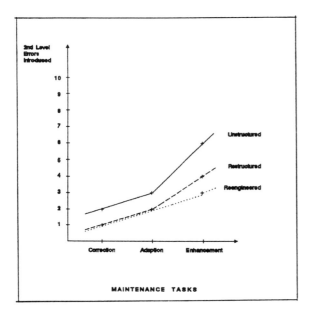

Figure 3: Maintenance Error Rate

7. PRODUCT DATA

The product measurements include selected quantitative program properties, which could be automatically derived from the program as well as various metrics computed from the basic program properties. The basic program properties d_1 thru d_{20} are explained in the Glossary II. The computed metrics are defined in the Glossary III. Five different metrics were examined in the METKIT project:

- Gilb's modularity metric (5),
- McCabe's graph complexity metric (6),
- Chapin's data complexity metric (7),
- Halstead's effort metric (8),
- Sneed's test effort metric (9).

The 20 elementary program measurements are displayed in

- Table-D for the unstructured COBOL-74 program
- Table-E for the restructured COBOL-74 variant
- Table-F for the reengineered COBOL-85 variant.

The program properties d_1 thru d_{20} are as follows:

(d_1) External Inputs — Arguments read by the program from an external input file

(d_2) Procedures — Number of modules or subgraphs contained in the program

(d_3) External Outputs — Results written by the program onto an external output file

(d_4) Interfaces — Input and output operations

(d_5) Predicates — Data items used as conditional operands, i.e. arguments controlling the program flow

(d_6) Inputs — Data items used within the program to generate results, i.e. arguments

(d_7) Outputs — Data items generated within the program, i.e. results

(d_8) Data used — Total number of data items referenced

(d_9) GOTO's — GOTO control flow branches

(d_{10}) PERFORM's — Internal subroutine invocations

(d_{11}) UNTIL's — Repetition commands

(d_{12}) IF's — Selection commands

(d_{13}) ON's — Exception condition commands

(d_{14}) Branches — Corners of the program control flow graph

(d_{15}) Path's — Sequence of branches through the control flow graph from entry to exit (here the minimum number of paths to traverse each branch at least once.)

(d_{16}) Lines of Code — Number of lines in the program including comment lines

(d_{17}) Statements — Number of executable procedural statements

(d_{18}) Statement Types — Number of distinct statement types such as MOVE, COMPUTE, IF, READ, etc. used by the program

(d_{19}) Data References — Total number of references to the data items declared in the program

(d_{20}) Files — Number of files or data streams flowing into and out of the program (fan in/fan out)

GLOSSARY II

95

The maintainability metrics K_1 thru K_5 are as follows:

(K_1) Gilb Module Complexity = Inverted relationship of procedural statements to internal modules expressed on a relational scale from 0.00 to 1.00 of increasing complexity

$$K_1 = 1.00 - (d_2/d_{17})$$

(K_2) McCabe Graph Complexity = Branches - Control Nodes + 1

$$K_2 = d_{14} - (d_9 + d_{10} + d_{11} + d_{12} + d_{13}) + 1$$

(K_3) Chapin Data Complexity = Average weight of data items weighted by their usage as predicate, input or output on an ordinal scale

$$K_3 = \frac{(d_5 \cdot 3) + (d_7 \cdot 2) + (d_6 \cdot 1)}{d_8}$$

(K_4) Halstead Difficulty Measure = Product of the program length and the program vocabulary

$$K_4 = (2/d_{17}) \cdot (d_8/d_{19})$$

(K_5) Sneed Test Effort = Effort required to test a program expressed on a relational scale of 0.00 to 1.00 of increasing effort

$$K_5 = d_{15}/d_{14}$$

GLOSSARY III

MEAN OF 3 SUBJECT PROGRAMS

MEASURE	ORIGINAL VERSION	CORRECTED VERSION	ADAPTED VERSION	ENHANCED VERSION
D1) EXTERNAL INPUTS	18	18	18	20
D2) PROCEDURES	11	11	11	11
D3) EXTERNAL OUTPUTS	23	23	23	24
D4) INTERFACES	20	20	20	23
D5) PREDICATES	18	18	21	23
D6) TOTAL INPUTS	78	78	81	84
D7) TOTAL OUTPUTS	52	53	53	56
D8) DATA USED	129	130	134	138
D9) GOTO'S	1	1	1	1
D10) PERFORM'S	16	18	19	22
D11) UNTIL LOOPS	2	2	2	3
D12) IF'S	16	17	19	19
D13) ON'S	4	4	4	5
D14) BRANCHES	61	65	70	76
D15) PATHS	22	24	26	28
D16) LOC	546	558	585	623
D17) STATEMENTS	163	169	178	187
D18) STATEMENT TYPES	18	18	18	18
D19) DATA REFERENCES	426	434	449	484
D20) FILES	7	7	7	9

TABLE E: RESTRUCTURED PROGRAM DATA

MEAN OF 3 SUBJECT PROGRAMS

MEASURE	ORIGINAL VERSION	CORRECTED VERSION	ADAPTED VERSION	ENHANCED VERSION
D1) EXTERNAL INPUTS	19	19	19	21
D2) PROCEDURES	1	1	1	1
D3) EXTERNAL OUTPUTS	25	25	25	26
D4) INTERFACES	20	20	21	22
D5) PREDICATES	8	8	8	11
D6) TOTAL INPUTS	61	61	61	63
D7) TOTAL OUTPUTS	52	52	52	55
D8) DATA USED	101	101	101	106
D9) GOTO'S	13	13	14	15
D10) PERFORM'S	0	0	0	0
D11) UNTIL LOOPS	0	0	0	0
D12) IF'S	14	14	15	16
D13) ON'S	3	3	3	4
D14) BRANCHES	44	44	45	48
D15) PATHS	18	18	19	21
D16) LOC	377	385	401	439
D17) STATEMENTS	137	139	149	158
D18) STATEMENT TYPES	16	16	16	17
D19) DATA REFERENCES	348	348	352	389
D20) FILES	7	7	7	9

TABLE D: UNSTRUCTURED PROGRAM DATA

MEAN OF 3 SUBJECT PROGRAMS

MEASURE	ORIGINAL VERSION	CORRECTED VERSION	ADAPTED VERSION	ENHANCED VERSION
D1) EXTERNAL INPUTS	13	13	14	20
D2) PROCEDURES	10	10	10	11
D3) EXTERNAL OUTPUTS	19	19	19	20
D4) INTERFACES	16	16	16	20
D5) PREDICATES	15	15	19	21
D6) TOTAL INPUTS	76	76	78	83
D7) TOTAL OUTPUTS	47	47	47	50
D8) DATA USED	129	129	133	138
D9) GOTO'S	0	0	0	0
D10) PERFORM'S	18	18	18	21
D11) UNTIL LOOPS	2	2	2	3
D12) IF'S	11	12	15	16
D13) ON'S	4	4	4	5
D14) BRANCHES	48	53	60	65
D15) PATHS	17	18	20	23
D16) LOC	548	558	578	634
D17) STATEMENTS	160	166	175	196
D18) STATEMENT TYPES	20	20	20	20
D19) DATA REFERENCES	341	346	352	424
D20) FILES	7	7	7	9

TABLE F: REENGINEERED PROGRAM DATA

96

Notable on the elementary measurement is the uniformity of the external inputs and outputs as well as the interfaces. This reflects the fact that the external behavior of all program variants remains constant except for the enhanced version, where the number of inputs and outputs increase. Internally the three variants of the program differ considerably. Both the restructured and the reengineered variants use almost 30% more data internally. This reflects the fact that the program control flow behavior has been mapped into internal data states. The size of the program is also increased significantly, by 31% through restructuring and by 32% through reengineering. The original unstructured program contains only 137 procedural statements as opposed to 163 for the restructured variant and 160 for the reengineered variant. This reflects the fact that unstructured programs are by nature smaller. The original unstructured program also has only 44 branches and 18 paths compared to the restructured variant, which has 61 branches and 22 paths. This would tend to disclaim the fact that mechanical restructuring reduces absolute control flow complexity. In this instance, the control flow complexity has been increased through mechanical restructuring by some 26%. On the other hand, the reengineered program has about the same control flow complexity in terms of branches and paths as the original unstructured program. The predicates used to control the program logic also increase from 8 in the unstructured variant to 18 in the restructured variant. Thus, in absolute terms, both the size and the complexity of the program increased through restructuring and to a slightly lesser degree through reengineering as depicted in Figure-4.

The 5 computed program complexity metrics are displayed in

- Table-G for the unstructured COBOL-74 program,
- Table-H for the restructured COBOL-74 program,
- Table-I for the reengineered COBOL-85 program.

These metrics depict program complexity in relative terms. The test effort decreases from 0.409 in the unstructured program to 0.360 in the restructured and 0.394 in the reengineered variants, a decrease of 13%. Module complexity decreases by restructuring from 0.86 in the original unstructured program to 0.33. If the GOTO's are indicative of structuredness, then the reengineered variant includes none and the restructured variant includes only one as compared to 13 in the original unstructured program. McCabe's cyclomatic complexity measure, considered by many to be the best indicator of control flow complexity, is reduced from 29 to 25 by mechanical restructuring and from 29 to 19 by reengineering – a reduction of 35%. Chapin's data complexity measure is reduced from 1.87 to 1.83 through restructuring and from 1.87 to 1.66 through reengineering – a reduction of 12%. Halstead's difficulty measure is effected negatively by reengineering, and somewhat positively by restructuring. This is due to the

fact that Halstead measures vocabulary. In the reengineered variants, the number of variables and operators increased, thus increasing the difficulty of comprehension.

The growth in program complexity through maintenance work is reflected in all of the program variants by all of the metrics except for that of Halstead. Module complexity was increased only marginally by the maintenance tasks in this example. However, McCabe's graph complexity measure increases in the unstructured variant from 29 in the original version to 37 in the enhanced version, in the restructured variant from 25 to 31, and in the reengineered variant from 19 to 25, an increase of 20 - 24%. A slighter but significant increase can also been seen in the data complexity. The test effort increases most for the unstructured variant, only marginally for the restructured variant, and even decreases for the reengineered variant. Only Halstead's difficulty metric denotes a decrease in the effort required to comprehend all program variants, since the number of operator and operand types remains approximately the same, while the numer of their usages increases. Thus, all of the computed metrics, with the exception of the Halstead metric, indicate a growth in program complexity as a result of the successive maintenance activities. This would confirm Belady and Lehman's law of structural degradation through program evolution. (10)

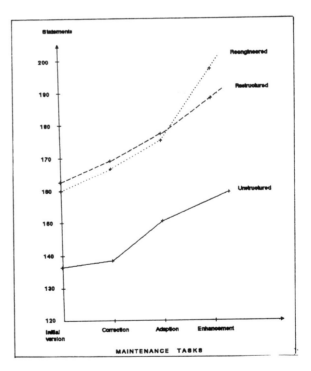

Figure 4: Growth in Program Size

97

MEAN OF 3 SUBJECT PROGRAMS

METRIC	ORIGINAL VERSION	CORRECTED VERSION	ADAPTED VERSION	ENHANCED VERSION
K1) MODULE COMPLEXITY	0,86	0,86	0,87	0,88
K2) GRAPH COMPLEXITY	29	29	34	37
K3) DATA COMPLEXITY	1,87	1,87	1,87	1,98
K4) DIFFICULTY	0,033	0,032	0,032	0,026
K5) TEST COMPLEXITY	0,409	0,409	0,422	0,437

TABLE G: UNSTRUCTURED PROGRAM METRICS

MEAN OF 3 SUBJECT PROGRAMS

METRIC	ORIGINAL VERSION	CORRECTED VERSION	ADAPTED VERSION	ENHANCED VERSION
K1) MODULE COMPLEXITY	0,33	0,39	0,39	0,42
K2) GRAPH COMPLEXITY	25	26	26	31
K3) DATA COMPLEXITY	1,83	1,84	1,86	1,88
K4) DIFFICULTY	0,031	0,030	0,029	0,024
K5) TEST COMPLEXITY	0,360	0,369	0,371	0,368

TABLE H: RESTRUCTURED PROGRAM METRICS

MEAN OF 3 SUBJECT PROGRAMS

METRIC	ORIGINAL VERSION	CORRECTED VERSION	ADAPTED VERSION	ENHANCED VERSION
K1) MODULE COMPLEXITY	0,38	0,40	0,43	0,44
K2) GRAPH COMPLEXITY	19	21	23	24
K3) DATA COMPLEXITY	1,66	1,66	1,70	1,79
K4) DIFFICULTY	0,044	0,042	0,039	0,031
K5) TEST COMPLEXITY	0,354	0,339	0,333	0,353

TABLE I: REENGINEERED PROGRAM METRICS

8. RELATIONSHIP BETWEEN PRODUCT AND PROCESS METRICS

As pointed out in the review of the previous research on software maintainability, the ultimate goal of maintainability measurement is to establish a relationship between the static properties of programs and maintenance effort, i.e. to predict process costs based on product data. This being the case, no experiment in maintainability would be complete without a reference to correlations between product and process data.

The total maintenance effort expended on the original unstructured program including correction, adaptation and enhancement amounted to 195 minutes, for the restructured variant 193 minutes, and for the reengineered variant 142 minutes. The average impact domain of the unstructured program for all maintenance actions amounted to 14.6 %, that of the restructured variant to 11.5 %, and that of the reengineered variant to 11.2 %. It is interesting to note that the effort required to maintain the unstructured variant and its domain of impact was 27% less. The effort required to maintain the restructured variant was only 1% less than the effort required

to maintain the unstructured variant, although its domain of impact was 22% less. This discrepancy can only be explained by the unfamiliarity of the subjects with mechanically derived program structure requiring more time for them to understand. Given more time to understand the restructuring algorithms the subjects would certainly have performed better. In this respect, the impact domain appears to be a more objective measure of maintainability.

On the side of the product, the test complexity for the restructured variant is 5% less than that of the original unstructured program, whereas the same metric for the reengineered variant is 6% less. Chapin's data complexity metric for the restructured variant is only 3% less than for the original program, but 11% less for the reengineered variant. McCabe's cyclomatic complexity is 14% less for the restructured variant and 24% less for the reengineered variant. Halstead's effort measure was decreased by 2% through restructuring, but was increased 11% through reengineering. Finally, module complexity was decreased by 53% through restructuring and 48% through reengineering.

From these metrics it can be concluded that none of them correlate to either the maintenance effort expended or the domain of impact. The best indicator of impact domain was the McCabe metric and the best indicator of actual maintenance effort was the Chapin metric. Yet, both of them display significant deviations from the actual impact domain and maintenance effort.

9. SUMMARY

The conclusion of this experiment on maintainability is that neither the elementary program properties nor the computed metrics examined here could be used to precisely predict maintenance costs. However, they can indicate tendencies to the better or to the worse. In general, the experiment came to the same conclusions as that of Gibson and Senn in their study of COBOL program maintainability, that simply restructuring programs to adhere to the rules of Boehm and Jacobini may reduce the probability of second level errors, but it does not make the program significantly more maintainable. Their restructured variant produced only a 5% reduction in maintenance cost, whereas the reengineered variant produced a 17% reduction. They conclude that "structural differences do impact maintenance performance". Specifically, improving a system by eliminating GOTO's and eliminating redundancies through reorganization appears to decrease the time required to perform maintenance, and to decrease the number of second level defects.

The same results can be drawn from this experiment. Restructuring the program reduced the maintenance effort and decreased the impact domain slightly. Reengineering the program reduced both the maintenance effort and the

98

impact domain significantly. Even more noticeable is the trend of the original unstructured program to become progressively less reliable and less maintainable through continued maintenance as compared to the restructured and reengineered variants. This trend could also be indicated by certain metrics such as McCabe's cyclomatic complexity measure, Chapin's data complexity measure, and Sneed's test effort measure. So is hoped that through further research better metrics can be found, which will relate more accurately to actual maintenance costs. Also, as pointed out by Senn and Gibson, further research is needed in the programmer's subjective view of complexity, which was a definite effect upon his or her performance.

REFERENCES

(1) Brice, L.: "Existing Computer Applications, Maintain or Redesign: How to decide" in Proc. of Computer Measurement Group IEEE Press, Dec. 1981, p. 20-28

(2) Lientz, B. / Swanson, E.: "Problems in Application Software Maintenance", Comm. of ACM, Vol. 24, No. 11, Nov. 1981

(3) Kearney, J. / Sedlmeyer, R. / Thompson, W. / Gray, M. / Adler, M.: "Software Complexity Measurement", Comm. of ACM, Vol. 29, No. 11, Nov. 1986

(4) Gibson, V. / Senn, J.: "System Structure and Software Maintenance Performance", Comm. of ACM, Vol. 32, No. 3, March 1989

(5) Gilb, T.: "Software Metrics", Studentlitteratur, Stockholm, 1976

(6) McCabe, T.: "A Complexity Measure", IEEE Trans on S.E., Vol. 2, No. 12, Dec. 1976

(7) Chapin, N.: "Input-Output Tables in Structured Design", in Tutorial on Structured Analysis & Design, Vol. 2, Infotech Ltd., Maidenhead, UK, 1978, p. 43-55

(8) Halstead, M.: "Elements of Software Science", Elsevier North-Holland, New York, 1977

(9) Sneed, H.: "Automated Software Quality Assurance", IEEE Trans on S.E., Vol. 11, No. 9, Sept. 1985

(10) Belady, L. / Lehman, M.: "Software Evolution" Academic Press, London, 1985

99

Chapter 6
Technology for Reengineering

Chapter 6
Technology for Reengineering

Purpose

This chapter will help the reader understand software reengineering tools and some of the technology behind the tools. The papers discuss CASE tools, view-based systems, repositories, code remodularization, and program transformation technology.

Papers

In the first paper, "Getting Back to Requirements Proving to Be a Difficult Task," Mary Alice Hanna discusses CASE tools and concepts for reengineering. The article also lists several of the people prominent in the CASE reengineering world.

In the next paper, "A Program Understanding Support Environment," Linore Cleveland discusses a typical reengineering or reverse engineering support system. It consists of a repository component and a user interface component. The repository component stores and maintains the system's representation of the program under study. The user interface component allows the user to see information about the program through views and analyses available from the system. The system was developed to allow users to view assembly code, but the foundations of the system apply to reengineering for other languages as well.

In the next paper, "An Intelligent Tool for Re-Engineering Software Modularity," Robert Schwanke discusses a tool that provides advice for remodularizing a software system. The paper discusses two remodularization techniques, clustering and maverick analysis. In clustering, procedures are found that "share enough information that they belong together in the same module." In maverick analysis, individual procedures are found that appear to be in the wrong module because "they share more information with procedures in other modules than with procedures in their own module." The paper is a good introduction to software remodularization issues and techniques.

In the final paper, "A Program Transformation Approach to Automating Software Re-engineering," Scott Burson, Gordon Kotik, and Lawrence Markosian present transformation-based technology for manipulating information in an object-based repository. Transformation is at the core of reengineering technology. They show how transformation technology can be used, in common reengineering problems, to specify concise analyses of objects and to transform programs.

GETTING BACK TO REQUIREMENTS PROVING TO BE A DIFFICULT TASK

Science of software archeology busy being born; McCabe: "Reengineering is not one big mess"

By Mary Alice Hanna

The black sheep of the Case world may well be the stubborn and often perverse discipline of reengineering. It is frequently purported to be the light at the end of the software maintenance tunnel, and more frequently, the focus of despair for software vendors and customers alike.

Today's customers want tools that will help them "fix" their older systems, as well as capture the information contained in these older systems to use in future development projects. The vehicle designated to accomplish this is the repository.

But how realistic is this? Are there any reengineering tools available that even approach this goal of feeding the repository automatically?

To start, an understanding of the term is required. Just about everyone agrees that reengineering is the examination and alteration of existing code for the purpose of recasting it into a new form. This definition, including the concepts of renovation and reclamation, is taken from "Reverse Engineering and Design Recovery: A Taxonomy," by Eliot Chikofsky and James H. Cross, *IEEE Software Magazine*, January 1990.

Today, MIS shops are utilizing a variety of reengineering tools. These tools may well represent the best hope for legacy systems.

The problems with legacy systems, as the older systems are often called,

Hanna is a freelance writer based in Poughkeepsie, N.Y. She has over 20 years experience in programming and systems management.

EXTRACTING REUSABLE CODE. VIA/Renaissance, from Viasoft, extracts a function from an existing Cobol program and creates a new Cobol program that performs a specific business function.

are many and varied. The difficulties revolve around three of the major reasons for trying to alter existing code:

■ correction of existing errors;

■ accommodation of new business requirements; and

■ upgrading to take advantage of a new technology.

Dave Sharon, president of Case Associates, Inc., Oregon City, Ore., said the problems are multiplied by the number of people touching the code. "It is practically impossible to get back to original requirements," he said. "The task requires automation along with intensive human work."

He continued, "It is an absolute requirement among users that reengineering solutions be part of the Case toolset. They must be able to migrate existing systems to the new environments."

One of the most popular notions of what Case will provide is the ability to create "pictures" of what the code does. "By allowing the programmer to see graphical representations of a program," said Sharon, "Case tools help the programmer understand more quickly and thoroughly what is happening in the program."

Implementing software complexity metrics and analysis tools are usually the first steps in any reengineering project. "Customers must define what their reengineering difficulty is. It could be any number of things, such as rehosting, reuse or translation," said Thomas McCabe, president of McCabe and Associates, Inc., Columbia, Md., which supplies metrics and analysis tools. "Reengineering is not just one big, jumbled mess. There are subproblems within reengineering and each one can be handled separately."

SHARON

Among several offerings in the McCabe Toolset is the Battlemap Analysis Tool, which graphically displays the structure of any system or subsystem, while also indicating complexity levels. Battlemap allows a user to visualize more than 20,000 lines of code on a workstation screen where it can be analyzed and manipulated as needed. "Visualization tools can turn a large-scale, complex system into a modularized and more easily understood set of functions," McCabe said.

Jerry Chappell, vice president of marketing at Intersolv Corp., Rockville, Md., said his company is marketing an updated version of Design Recovery. The product, available on DOS, scans the code and places paragraph names onto a structure chart with the code stored beneath it.

Peggy Ledvina, Intersolv marketing programs manager, said, "The product thus provides a rapid way of laying out a program so someone can look at it and understand it." Chappell added, "A large portion of maintenance is impact analysis. Design Recovery greatly reduces the time to do this; it gives a roadmap to the existing system."

WHEN TO REENGINEER

Not all systems are candidates for reengineering. Stephen Errico, partner at Price Waterhouse's RE/Center in Tampa, Fla., explained that the typical MIS shop has several groups of applications, each with separate characteristics. He believes the code found in each group is different, since it reflects the different programming methods and styles a company has used as the data processing industry has evolved.

Errico defines four possible approaches to reengineering a company's application systems, depending on the programs' characteristics. The approaches are: replacement, enhancement, endurance and salvage.

"It is critical to develop multiple approaches to reengineering and apply them selectively, according to well-developed criteria," he said.

The move to repository-based technology is governed by four approaches, according to Errico. They are:

■ Creation of colorful graphic boxes or pictures of the application's processing in order to populate one of the more abstract layers of the repository.

■ Development of a lower level of the repository by translating the application code into External Source Format (ESF); the idea is that, some day, it will be possible to build from there toward a higher level of abstraction.

■ Proceeding with "endurance" activity, recognizing that the code is too expensive to move or that the business whose functions were performed by the code has changed direction; the intent is to keep the system alive and the maintenance costs under control.

■ Selective rewriting of those older

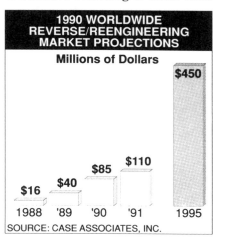

1990 WORLDWIDE REVERSE/REENGINEERING MARKET PROJECTIONS

Millions of Dollars

1988	'89	'90	'91	1995
$16	$40	$85	$110	$450

SOURCE: CASE ASSOCIATES, INC.

CONTINUING GROWTH. According to Case Associates, Inc., the MIS market for reverse/reengineering products between 1990 and 1995 is expected to increase at a compond annual growth of 40%.

systems whose modernization would not be cost-effective.

"It is dangerous to let customers believe that reengineering can take a system and create pictures or graphics. That is just one strategy and even then, it most likely will not reach a company's economic goals," said Errico. PW's RE/Center suggests that customers need to establish, onsite, a centrally located suite of tools and capabilities that supports the reengi-

neering process.

And yet, most customers are very interested in the idea of moving their code to that "higher level of abstraction" so appealingly described by most reengineering vendors. How a piece of code can be moved up to that higher level is one of the main puzzles of the repository technology.

Arrae, the tool Errico developed, is an attempt to perform at least part of the magic needed to get to that "higher level of abstraction." It scans Cobol programs, identifying up to 14 categories of logic. It then identifies the parameters being applied to the categories and stores it all in an "Active Component Dictionary," which then contains all the data objects, screens, reports and processing logic—in effect, the program. The programmer can access screens that show summaries of the categories (or program steps) and the various parameters used in the particular functions.

With Arrae's algorithmic parsing capability, existing programs can be read and then represented at that "higher level."

The next step in the process is to manipulate the abstraction, creating an ESF-like layer, by means of tools developed by PW or by its associates in the Companion Technology Vendor Program. This program offers the tools and products of many vendors to help a customer migrate existing applications into IBM's Application Development Cycle (AD/Cycle) and Systems Application Architecture (SAA) environments.

A somewhat different perspective on reengineering is offered by Stephen Unterberger, senior manager with PW's West Coast RE/Center at Santa Monica, Calif. According to Unterberger, the objective of moving to the repository is not as big an opportunity as some others, especially since the technology is not yet really in place.

"Here, right now, is the need to reengineer systems to provide more of what the users want, for example, *ad hoc* reports from new database platforms, distributed applications and easier enhancements," he said.

"PW has a major interest in making the application more reflective of where the business is going." He sees

PW's role as "a reengineering services integrator whose tool side is subordinate to the methodological basis of approach and training."

THE REENGINEERING CYCLE

Another piece of realism pertinent to any discussion of reengineering is that it is not something anyone ever finishes. Charles Bachman, founder and chairman of Bachman Information Systems, Inc., Burlington, Mass., describes six steps that constitute the software reengineering cycle:

■ Capture: takes in source code and categorizes it into data definitions, data-flow definitions and data processing definitions.

■ Reverse Engineering: changes the information from one level of code to the next higher level. This is not a simple one-for-one transformation—it moves the system from a Technology Model Representation to an Enterprise Model Representation, producing a unified description of the business rules.

■ Enhancement: takes the output of the Reverse Engineering step and updates the business rules to meet new requirements.

■ Forward Engineering: takes the business rules of an enterprise and adds the technological details. It is the inverse of the Reverse Engineering step.

■ Optimization: using metrics obtained about the system (such as data transaction rates), applies the appropriate processing methods.

■ Generation: takes the internal format and creates compiler-legible code. This step is the inverse of the Capture step. At this point, the system is open again for reengineering.

Bachman believes that although the entire process is not yet automated, "a good number of the individual pieces of the puzzle have solutions." For example, Bachman/Analyst and Bachman/Designer, part of the Bachman/Reengineering Product Set, handle the enhancement and forward engineering parts of the cycle. "IBM's CSP [Cross System Product] performs the optimization and generation," said Bachman. And capture is being addressed by products like Arrae.

It is a given that the successful use of

REPRESENTATIVE REENGINEERING TOOLS

For more information about a particular product, circle the corresponding reader service number on the reader service card located at the back of this issue. Compiled by Products Editor Deborah Melewski.

VENDOR	PRODUCT/ CIRCLE NO.	OPERATING SYSTEM REQUIREMENTS	COMMENTS
Adpac Corp. San Francisco, CA	PM/SS Circle No. 200	MVS	Data name standardization, code analysis for Cobol, PL/1, JCL
Advanced Technology International New York, NY	superCase Circle No. 201	VAX/VMS	Integrated development tool; reverse engineering
AdvantEdge Systems Group San Diego, CA	Database Migration Tools Circle No. 202	MVS	DBMS migration
Aldon Computer Oakland, CA	Analyzer Circle No. 203	HP-3000	Code analyzer
Andersen Consulting Chicago, IL	Foundation Circle No. 204	MVS, PC-DOS, OS/2, VAX/VMS	Integrated, full life-cycle Case, reengineering
Application Programming Moorestown, NJ	LogicChain Circle No. 205		Documentation and metric analyzer
AutoCASE Technology Cupertino, CA	AutoFlow-C Circle No. 206	PC-DOS, OS/2	Generates structure charts and flowcharts from existing C source code
Bachman Information Systems Burlington, MA	Bachman Reengineering Product Set Circle No. 207	PC-DOS	Reengineering, re-usability of database descriptions and code
Cadre Technologies Providence, RI	Teamwork Circle No. 208 PathMap Circle No. 209 Teamwork/C Rev Circle No. 210	VAX/VMS; Unix; PC-DOS, OS/2 VAX/VMS; Unix; PC-DOS VAX/VMS; Unix	Integrated full life-cycle Case toolset Runtime reverse engineering, design-level analysis Builds structure charts from C source files
Carleton Corp. Burlington, MA	CQS Circle No. 211	MVS	Data analysis, conversion and migration tools
CGI Systems Inc. Pearl River, NY	PacBase Circle No. 212 PacLAN Circle No. 213	MVS, DOS/VSE PC-DOS, OS/2	Full life-cycle Case, specifications dictionary, change control Team development across multiple workstations; multiaccess repository
Computer Associates Int'l. Garden City, NY	CA-Librarian Circle No. 214	DOS/VSE, MVS, VM	Source code management
Computer Data Systems, Inc. Rockville, MD	The Re-engineering Platform Circle No. 215	MVS	Reengineering methodology for Cobol
Computer Task Group Buffalo, NY	Data Conversion Tools Circle No. 216	MVS, DOS/VSE, PC/DOS	Migration, analysis, conversion tools/ services
Compuware Corp. Farmington Hills, MI	Retrofit Circle No. 217 Pathvu Circle No. 218 Navigator/MF Circle No. 219	MVS, PC-DOS MVS, PC-DOS MVS	Cobol restructuring, reengineering Cobol quality assurance, static analysis Interactive Cobol source code analysis

REPRESENTATIVE REENGINEERING TOOLS

VENDOR	PRODUCT/ CIRCLE NO.	OPERATING SYSTEM REQUIREMENTS	FUNCTIONS
D. Appleton Co. Manhattan Beach, CA	IDEF/Leverage Circle No. 220	MVS; VAX/VMS	Design of reusable systems; based on IDEF methodology
Digital Equipment Corp. Maynard, MA	VAX DEC/CMS Circle No. 221	VAX/VMS	Library system; tracks changes
	VAX Source Code Analyzer Circle No. 222	VAX/VMS	Source code cross-reference, static analysis
Eden Systems Corp. Carmel, IN	Q/Auditor Circle No. 223	MVS, PC-DOS	Quality measurement of Cobol or PL/1, at code, program, or system level
	Q/Artisan Circle No. 224	MVS, PC-DOS	Rules-based reengineering for Cobol or PL/1 code
EDP Management La Mesa, CA	Reformat Circle No. 225		Reformatting tool
FWM Digitech New York, NY	COBXREF Circle No. 226	Wang VS	Documentation and metric analyzer
Global Software Duxbury, MA	Olga Circle No. 227	MVS	Captures, maintains JCL in data dictionary
	Urma Circle No. 228	MVS	Captures, maintains program documentation in data dictionary
Group Operations Washington, DC	Scan/Cobol Circle No. 229	MVS, DOS/VSE	Documents logic, data relationships; identifies potential problems
	Superstructure Circle No. 230	MVS, DOS/VSE, PC-DOS	Cobol structuring tool
Hewlett-Packard Cupertino, CA	HP C++/Softbench Circle No. 231	HP-UX	Object-oriented development; static analyzer for source-based analysis
Hypersoft Corp. Cambridge, MA	Application Browser Circle No. 232	VAX/VMS	Reverse engineering for Cobol applications; prographic map from source files
InfoSpan Corp. Edina, MN	InfoSpan Repository Management System (IRMS) Circle No. 233	PC-DOS, OS/2; Unix	Supports Case, reengineering, data dictionary tools
Integrated Systems Santa Clara, CA	AutoCode Circle No. 234	PC-DOS	Case workbench, reusable engineering blocks
InterPort Software Burke, VA	InterCase Circle No. 235	VAX/VMS; Unix; Xenix; PC-DOS, OS/2	Object-oriented, knowledge-based rules repository for Cobol reverse engineering
InterSolv Rockville, MD	APS Development Center Circle No. 236	MVS, PC-DOS, OS/2	Integrated Case tools for Cobol development, reengineering
	Design Recovery Circle No. 237	PC-DOS, OS/2	Integrated reverse engineering; analyzes, documents, revises Cobol code

Case will ultimately depend on the successful implementation of the repository. It is the medium in which all the other Case products will operate, following its protocols and adhering to its interface regulations. The long-awaited completion of the repository's definition from IBM and its inner-circle business partners may be available in the very near future.

"Once the Logic Model section of the Enterprise Model has been defined, and significant progress has been made on this," Bachman said, "the three areas of a system will be present in the repository specification: data structure, data flows and processing rules."

Mark Crego, president of InterPort Software Corp., Fairfax, Va., said, "The repository should be an active place because elements in a repository must be changeable. After all, if a system can no longer be changed, it really is dead."

InterCase, the product offered by InterPort, uses a repository-based technology to store design specification information extracted from mainframe Cobol programs—including both data and process models. Once the Structure Database repository is populated, programmers can analyze, inventory, change and reassemble the application code at a higher level of abstraction, through use of products such as Atlanta-based KnowledgeWare's Information Engineering Workbench (IEW) or Application Development Workbench (ADW) toolset.

Rona-Dismat, a hardware retailer in Quebec, Canada, used InterCase to get a handle on the 5,000 Cobol programs it had developed over the years. Marc Mazerolle, project manager, said that through the use of this toolset, "programmers have experienced a 25 percent increase in productivity, and among the analysts that use the package, the specifications are almost error-free."

Mazerolle did caution users that "the repository is difficult to change once it has been built." He recommended careful planning and a lot of prototyping to ensure that the configuration of the repository meets an organization's needs.

Reusability of code is quickly gaining popularity among MIS departments as the means to salvage part of their legacy systems. Viasoft's VIA/Renaissance product is breaking ground in this area, according to Frank Hill, Renaissance product manager at Viasoft, Inc. in Phoenix. He said, "Renaissance is the only product that extracts a function from an existing Cobol program and creates a new Cobol program that now performs that specific business function."

Viasoft's direction is to take pieces of code and populate a repository with them, thereby enabling their reuse in other programs.

WHAT'S NEEDED IS COMMITMENT

The biggest problem software reengineering advocates face is convincing management that it can be cost-effective to embark on this effort, and that it is the right thing to do.

Al Smith, executive vice president of Bell Atlantic, Systems Integration Corp., Arlington, Va., said, "Very few clients have a commitment to change the way they build systems. Very few have and are using Case tools." He added, "In the software reengineering market, tools will not be mature enough for the average programmer to be using them for another couple of years, with the best estimates suggesting sometime in the mid-'90s."

Pacific Bell of San Ramon, Calif., is convinced that the time to start is now. Karin Giardina, systems analyst with the Systems Renewal Group, describes the effort to start moving the embedded base of systems into the repository. "At this time, we are concentrating on restructuring and cleaning up the architecture of the systems, but that does not work with multifunctional, complex programs," she said.

Viasoft's Renaissance tool (just out of beta testing) is being used to extract certain functions from the code and split large modules into several smaller ones. Giardina said, "Once the modules are smaller, they are much easier to put into Case." This extraction capability provides several benefits, she said. For example, it:

■ Permits the reassigning of responsibility for code maintenance to the

REPRESENTATIVE REENGINEERING TOOLS

VENDOR	PRODUCT/ CIRCLE NO.	OPERATING SYSTEM REQUIREMENTS	FUNCTIONS
K-C Computer Svcs. Dallas, TX	K-C Enable/DB2 Circle No. 238	MVS	Reengineering tools, consulting services for conversion to DB2
KnowledgeWare Atlanta, GA	ADW Circle No. 239	MVS, OS/2	Supports data analysis, data capture; automates reverse engineering
	Recoder Circle No. 240	MVS	Cobol restructurer
	Inspector Circle No. 241	MVS, DOS/VSE	Code analyzer; evaluates program quality
LBMS Inc. Houston, TX	LBMS Systems Engineer Circle No. 242	PC-DOS, Windows	Repository-based, multiuser development, reverse engineering
Legent Corp. Vienna, VA	Endevor Circle No. 243	MVS, VM, PC-DOS, OS/2	Source and file comparison, change management
Marble Computer Martinsburg, WV	CSA Circle No. 244	MVS	Data name standardization
	DCD II Circle No. 245	MVS	Cross reference, documentation; metric analyzer
McCabe & Associates Columbia, MD	McCabe Toolset Circle No. 246	MVS, PC-DOS	Includes Battlemap analysis tool, for visual analysis of code
Mentor Graphics Beaverton, OR	CodeLink Workstation Circle No. 247	Unix	Structure Map tool generates structure charts from source code
Meta Systems Ann Arbor, MI	PSL/PSA Circle No. 248	MVS, VM, PC-DOS; VAX/VMS	Reverse engineering; parses existing source code, produces specs in Case repository
Micro Focus Palo Alto, CA	Animator Circle No. 249	PC-DOS	Displays source code by statement
	Micro Focus Cobol/2 Workbench Circle No. 250	PC-DOS, OS/2	Includes source code analyzer; identifies unused/unreferenced code
National Database Software W. Bloomfield, MI	X-Ref Circle No. 251	MVS, VS, DOS/VSE	Cross-reference tool
Netron Downsview, Ontario	Netron/CAP Development Center Circle No. 252	MVS, PC-DOS; VAX/VMS; Wang VS	Frame-based Case; reusable Cobol components; development and maintenance
Price Waterhouse Tampa, FL	Arrae Circle No. 253	MVS, PC-DOS	Scans Cobol programs, identifies logic and parameters, creates abstract
	Re/Cycle Circle No. 254	MVS, PC-DOS	Reengineering tools for data conversion
ProCase Corp. Santa Clara, CA	Smartsystem Circle No. 255	Unix	Reengineering for C programs

REPRESENTATIVE REENGINEERING TOOLS

VENDOR	PRODUCT/ CIRCLE NO.	OPERATING SYSTEM REQUIREMENTS	FUNCTIONS
Programmed Solutions Marietta, GA	Struct Circle No. 256		Restructurer; reformatter
Quibus Enterprises Champaign, IL	Forwarn Circle No. 257	PC-DOS; Unix	Static analyzer for Fortran programs
Scandura Intelligent Systems Narberth, PA	Prodoc re/NuSys Workbench Circle No. 258	PC-DOS	Reverse engineering; converts C, C++, Cobol, Ada, Fortran, or Pascal code into Flow-Forms
Seec Inc. Pittsburgh, PA	Seec/Care Circle No. 259	PC-DOS, Windows, OS/2	Interactive analysis for Cobol/IMS; reverses business rules/data model to PDL, to forward engineer to DB2
	IMS-DB2 Migration Toolkit Circle No. 260	PC-DOS, Windows, OS/2	Converts IMS schema to DB2 tables; Cobol with DL/1 calls to Cobol with DB2 ESQL
Seer Technologies New York, NY	HPS Case Circle No. 261	PC-DOS, OS/2	Object-oriented analysis, design, development
Softool Corp. Goleta, CA	CCC/Enterprise Life Cycle Management Circle No. 262	MVS, VM, PC-DOS; VAX/VMS/Ultrix	Code management, change and configuration control
Software Maintenance & Development Systems Concord, MA	Aide-de-Camp Circle No. 263	VAX/VMS/ Ultrix; Unix; Xenix; PC-DOS	Manages code, documentation, historical records
Software Products & Services Inc. New York, NY	Re-Spec Circle No. 264	PC-DOS; VAX/VMS; Unix	Regenerates design specs from source code for reuse
	Epos Circle No. 265	PC-DOS; VAX/VMS	Integrated Case; development
Sterling Software Systems Software Marketing Div. Rancho Cordova, CA	Comparex Circle No. 266	MVS, DOS/VSE, VM/CMS	Source and file comparison; maintenance debugging, quality assurance
Syncsort Woodcliff Lake, NJ	Sydoc Circle No. 267	MVS, VS, VS1	Documentation and metrics analyzer
SysCorp Int'l. Austin, TX	MicroStep Circle No. 268	PC-DOS	Copies, stores design specs in dictionary for reuse
Texas Instruments Plano, TX	Information Engineering Facility (IEF) Circle No. 269	MVS, OS/2, PC-DOS	Integrated, full lifecycle Case; repository; data reengineering
Transform Logic Corp. Scottsdale, AZ	Transform Circle No. 270	MVS	Applications maintenance, reengineering
Unisys Blue Bell, PA	Linc Circle No. 271	Unisys	4GL for Case reengineering
Viasoft, Inc. Phoenix, AZ	VIA/Insight Circle No. 272	MVS	Interactive source code analysis for Cobol
	VIA/SmartEdit Circle No. 273	MVS	Cobol-intelligent extensions to ISPF; analysis, documentation, edit, test/debug
	VIA/Renaissance Circle No. 274	MVS	Code extraction

proper group.

■ Enables the removal of redundant functions from the various programs where they reside, and facilitates the creation of the business function in a single module.

■ Moves a function from one program to another.

■ Provides a benchmark with which to compare new software, thus ensuring that the replacing system performs the functions that the old system did.

The Systems Renewal Group is spearheading reengineering at Pacific Bell. The group, which assists in the reengineering effort throughout the company, operates by proposing methods and implementing solutions through the use of various tools. These tools include Pathvu and Retrofit from XA Systems, Inc., Los Gatos, Calif. (lately acquired by Compuware Corp., Farmington Hills, Mich.) and IBM's Repository/MVS, among others. The work of the group is to determine if a system should be reengineered and, if so, what method and tools should be used. Initiating change in the corporate environment is the major problem the group faces.

TAKING A PRAGMATIC APPROACH

Computer Task Group Inc., headquartered in Buffalo, N.Y., concentrates on reconditioning, or upgrading the technology, rather than on redesigning it. Deidra Barron, manager of Applications Outsourcing, said, "The reason we took the reconditioning approach was that the older systems require a more pragmatic approach, and one at a lower technological level."

One of the difficulties facing many MIS shops is how to manage their data. "Customers are overwhelmed with data inventory questions," said Ilmara Mazeika, principal consultant, Information Engineering Services for On-Line Software International Inc., operating out of Marina del Ray, Calif. (On-Line, headquartered in Fort Lee, N.J., has recently agreed to be purchased by Computer Associates, Garden City, N.Y.) She explained, "They have been operating without standards and have often been bypassing the use of dictionaries. They are now

MCCABE

faced with trying to define their data."

Mazeika's clients are starting to find their way clear with tools such as PM/SS, from AdPac Consulting Languages Corp., San Francisco, and the Bachman toolset.

Two other tools that address the more basic issues are Olga and Urma, from Global Software, Duxbury, Mass. Olga captures and maintains Job Control Language (JCL) in a data dictionary, while Urma does the same for program documentation. Urma's record processing feature is useful in determining the impact of proposed software changes since it enters, standardizes and intelligently interprets data structures.

Carleton Corp., Burlington, Mass., has developed a reengineering tool that assists in the conversion of applications to DB2, the database model designated by IBM to support the database requirements in SAA. Carleton's CQS toolset not only handles the conversion of the databases and the migration of data to the new file structures, but also assists the user in analyzing and scrubbing the data before it is moved.

Reengineering often presents an opportunity to achieve more than the essentials by providing improved documentation or staff training, for example. As a newly hired manager of corporate information of North Carolina Electric Membership Corp. in Raleigh, N.C., Ben Moore needed to collect and organize his programmers' knowledge about the systems with which they were working. Moore's task was to rehost a large utility billing application from an IBM 4361 under MVS/Vsam to an AS/400 computer. He chose the Design and Analysis tools of KnowledgeWare's ADW. Moore said, "KnowledgeWare was brought in so that it could help automate the migration as well as capture the staff's knowledge of the application."

AdvantEdge Systems Group of San Diego, Calif., presents products that concentrate on database migrations such as IDMS-DC to CICS or to DB2. Being closely allied with several service companies, such as Price Waterhouse, allows AdvantEdge to leverage its strengths, providing conversion tools and supporting its customer's professional staffs.

VARIETY IN MULTIVENDOR SOLUTIONS

In an industry like data processing, and especially in a relatively new, socalled fix-it-all solution like Case, one of the few solid truths is that reengineering will provide no "silver bullet." It is equally true that no one product can provide all the solutions to the embedded systems that constitute and indeed operate a company's business. Too many lines of code with vastly different programming styles and wildly varying levels of technology prevent any one tool from being able to reengineer these older systems back into a state of health.

Pete Privateer, staff vice president of strategic product planning for KnowledgeWare, agrees. "The industry hasn't yet been able to find a 'one size fits all' reengineering tool," he said. "Reengineering expectations need to be set correctly. If a system is not doing what it should, there is no reason to reengineer it."

Peter Harris, president of AdPac, sees the role of the AdPac toolset, PM/SS, as "a necessary front end to other products. It analyzes Cobol, PL/1 and JCL, extracts information from them, draws structure models and provides a good high-level view of the system." As part of IBM's Vtap, Vendor Technical Assistance Program, AdPac is becoming more coupled to the repository.

Harris added that most software vendors are not equipped to do major reengineering projects; they can only provide the tools. Service is supplied by larger consortiums that can supply a trained professional staff.

Texas Instruments, Inc. of Dallas is an example of a company marketing tools as well as services. The Applications Development (APD) Services organization markets the software tools (included in their Information Engi-

neering Facility) and the professional expertise to assist their clients in their reengineering efforts.

Another such full-service company is Learmonth & Burchett Management Systems Plc of London, England. LBMS offers a toolset whose core is its Information Manager repository. Tony Eaves, supervisory consultant at LBMS, said, "We are currently assisting a large brewery client to migrate its Cobol code into Linc [a 4GL from Unisys].

LBMS's System Engineer product, in conjunction with Information Manager, provides support for managing the Cobol environment data, the Linc environment data as well as the overall project."

Unisys Corp., Bluebell, Pa., is approaching the reengineering puzzle with Linc. Mory Bahar, director of the Corporate Case Center in Malvern, Pa., said, "The approach that Unisys is taking is to lower the design level representation to where the code sits. The plan is to make code generators do more."

ERRICO

George Germann, national director of Management Information Systems for Ernst and Young, headquartered in New York City, said, "Reengineering, by which I mean, taking Cobol code and going to a 4GL, doesn't quite exist today."

Germann said that his people use Pathvu to ensure that standards are being followed and Retrofit to restructure the code. (The Unisys-compatible versions of these two products are offered by Unisys Corp. XA Systems, now part of Compuware, continues to offer and support the products for other platforms.)

Germann added, "Using 4GLs can often make you lose functionality, but since Linc is very powerful, we haven't had to give up any functionality."

For companies using VAX/VMS equipment, SmartStar Corp., Goleta, Calif., offers a means of reducing the lines of 3GL code that must be maintained. Reynolds Electrical & Engineering Co., Inc. of Las Vegas embarked on such a project, according to Charlie Auer, systems and programming section chief. "The goal was to cut the time it takes to write new applications and make them simpler to modify and maintain."

Using SmartStar's Consulting Services Organization, the company successfully completed the project. The key was to leave Cobol in as the language where it made sense and to use a 4GL where it could save time and effort, without decreasing functionality. SmartStar's methodology requires the strong central repository provided by Digital Equipment Corp., Maynard, Mass. DEC's CDD/Repository (Common Data Dictionary) can be populated with SmartStar's data definitions by using CDD/Plus.

Another aid for VAX/VMS users comes from Cadre Technologies, Inc., Beaverton, Ore. Cadre offers the Teamwork family of products for VAX/VMS-based applications. Specifically, reverse engineering products that exist for C (C Rev), are extended to handle Fortran, Pascal, Basic and other languages. The toolset generates structured design charts and allows the user to browse the source code associated with that section of the structure chart.

For Unix platforms, Procase Corp., Santa Clara, Calif., offers Smartsystem, a set of tools that assists programmers in reengineering software written in C. It operates under the X Window System.

Language Technology, Inc., Salem, Mass., markets tools called Inspector that evaluate program quality; Pinpoint, which charts the control flow of a program and prepares instream documentation; and Recoder, which restructures Cobol code. Claude Barbour, supervisor of Central System Support for Blue Cross and Blue Shield of Maryland, located in Baltimore, said, "These tools are quite helpful in decreasing the cost of maintaining these systems, as well as in positioning them for reverse engineering. They are ready to be moved into front-end Case tools where they can be maintained at a higher level of abstraction."

Sara Lee, the hosiery distributor located in Atlanta, decided to change its computer platform from Bull equipment to a DB2 database running on IBM equipment. Describing the magnitude of

BACHMAN

the task, Craig Guinn, manager of Data Administration, said, "A million lines of code had to be moved to IBM by programmers who had no IBM background."

The company used a twofold approach incorporating Joint Application Development (JAD) sessions to develop the enterprise model along with the reverse engineering capabilities of Bachman's tools. The online programs are being converted via a 4GL product called Ideal, from Computer Associates International, Garden City, N.Y.; the batch programs are being rewritten in Cobol 2.

Sara Lee hired consultants to help with the overall project plan and with some technical issues, but, said Guinn, "The consultants were not really involved in the choice of tools; Sara Lee did that for themselves." The project is well over 50 percent completed, with 90 percent of the data moved successfully.

With so many varieties of products and methods, reengineering can be a process that complicates matters before it facilitates them. The advice, universally given and frequently ignored, is to plan, plan, plan. After that, training of staff is essential. Too many times, the new productivity aids brought into a shop end up on the shelf, or worse, worked around by the in-house staff.

It is important to teach the new techniques to both the technical staff and the business people associated with MIS. Because it does finally come down to people, people doing the right things and doing them for the right reasons. As Smith of Bell Atlantic said, "A lot is having the right people, and having the right organization that can empower the right people." ■

A program understanding support environment

by L. Cleveland

Software maintenance represents the largest cost element in the life of a software system, and the process of understanding the software system utilizes 50 percent of the time spent on software maintenance. Thus there is a need for tools to aid the program understanding task. The tool described in this paper—Program UNderstanding Support environment (PUNS)—provides the needed environment. Here the program understanding task is supported with multiple views of the program and a simple strategy for moving between views and exploring a particular view in depth. PUNS consists of a repository component that loads and manages a repository of information about the program to be understood and a user interface component that presents the information in the repository, utilizing graphics to emphasize the relationships and allowing the user to move among the pieces of information quickly and easily.

Software maintenance is broadly defined as any work done on an operational programming system at any time, for any reason.[1] Maintenance begins when the initial development effort ends and the system is put into production. Recent surveys show that expenditures for such software maintenance (including improvements) account for between 50 and 90 percent of the total life-cycle expenditures on the programming system.[2,3]

Many of the activities of a person who maintains software—in adapting the system to new environments or enhancing the system by adding or improving function—are very similar to activities of a software developer during the initial creation of the system. However, there is a difference in that software maintainers are constrained by the framework of the system being maintained. They must work within this framework in developing adaptations or enhancements. A software maintainer must be very familiar with the current system and must fully understand the framework of the particular system.

Studies of the activities of software maintainers have shown that approximately 50 percent of their time is spent in the process of understanding the code they are to maintain.[4,5] This is particularly true for code that was not developed using modern software engineering principles (e.g., data abstraction and structured programming).

As a programming system ages, the code for the system becomes increasingly the only true definition of the system, and ancillary specifications for the system become out of sync with the system. A software maintainer must read the code in order to determine the framework for the system. Brooks[6] defines the essence of a software system as a complex construct of interlocking concepts: data sets, relationships among data items, algorithms, and the invocation of functions. The software maintainer must understand these concepts and how they interlock in order to fit an adaptation or enhancement into the framework.

In determining the framework, a programmer is attempting to determine the relationships that exist within the program: where the variables are defined and where these definitions are used; what the interface of a piece of code is to other pieces; which data items are imported and which are exported; what data items are defined globally; where a function is used; what are the interfaces of the function; what is the scope of the definition of a particular piece of data; which internal procedures assign the data a value; which procedures reference the value; where is a file referenced; where is an entity in a database updated. By acquiring this information, the maintainer can begin to define the concepts that are used within the programming system and determine how the concepts have been interwoven to structure the programming system.

Program elements (e.g., functions, subprograms, and procedures) are still being written using a linear-language paradigm and then stored in files. Relationships among these files are understood only by analyzing the statements within the program elements. These relationships that are defined within the program are multidimensional. For example, a procedure E might be called by procedure C, E might also call procedure G and define data used by procedure H, and then E might update data defined in procedure B. Thus procedure E is related in various ways to four additional procedures. The programmer, in the task of understanding, must attempt to superimpose these multidimensional relationships on the linear text for the program. A tool that allows the programmer to easily view the multidimensional relationships that exist within the program would make easier the task of understanding.

The tool discussed in this paper, a Program UNderstanding Support environment, supports the program understanding task by organizing and presenting the program from many different viewpoints (e.g., a call graph for a collection of procedures, a control flow graph for a single procedure, a graph that relates a file to the procedures that use it, a data-flow graph, a use-def chain for a variable). The tool detects the low-level relationships that exist within the program using static analysis techniques, and it consolidates and organizes these relationships and presents them in a user-friendly environment. The user interrogates various pieces of information presented by the tool using a point-and-click mouse interface to point at a piece of information (an object) and click the mouse. The tool responds by providing more information about the object at

which the user was pointing, including the object's relationships to other objects. The user can follow relationships between objects, easily moving between high-level and low-level objects.

There are two components to the Program UNderstanding Support environment tool (hereafter known simply as PUNS): (1) a repository and the associated routines to load the repository and respond to high-level queries to the repository and (2) a user interface that presents program information obtained from the repository in a user-friendly manner and supports the programmer during the exploration of the program. The repository component of PUNS must be established prior to utilizing the user interface component.

The two components are designed to be distributed. The repository component resides on a host machine (i.e., a powerful shared machine), able to use the power of the host for efficient repository loading and query response. The user interface component of PUNS resides on a workstation, utilizing the graphical strengths of the workstation in the presentation of information to the user. The components are connected via a communications link. The user interface component sends queries to the repository component over the communication link, and the repository component responds using the communication link.

A research prototype for the PUNS tool supports IBM System/370 Assembler Language. The repository component exists on an IBM System/370 30XX host and runs under the EAS-E Application Development System, which supports an Entity-Relationship data model and provides a language in which to write programs to create and access a database developed using this model.[7] The user interface exists on a workstation (either an IBM PC/AT or PS/2) and uses Microsoft Windows* to support the multiwindow point-click interface.

Several research vehicles have been developed that investigate the presentation of multiple views of a program.[8,9] However, these systems have focused on the initial development cycle and develop the views as the program is developed. A few maintenance environments have been explored,[10-13] most of which have used a database to maintain information about the program. However, to obtain information about the program, the maintainer has been forced to use a query language rather than a point-click interface. Also, it has not been easy to move between views in these environments.

In the first section of this paper, the user interface component for PUNS is described from a user point of view. The second section provides a general description of the PUNS repository and the routines to support the repository. The third section discusses the current research. The concluding section suggests adjunct areas of research.

The PUNS user interface

The PUNS user interface is organized around the notion of a set of objects that are of interest to the programmer who is using PUNS. Examples of objects include a module, a node in a control flow graph, a statement in an assembly unit, a database, a global data structure, and a symbol. Each of the objects is supported in the interface by a separate window. All information that PUNS knows about the object appears in the window for the object. Certain information about the object may appear when the window for the object is first created in response to the user's having pointed at a representation for the object and clicked the mouse. Other information is indicated as being available by its appearing on a menu bar, and it may be obtained by the selection of the item on the menu bar. Objects exist in the context of other objects. For example, a node of the control flow graph for a module has meaning only in the context of the module. The presentation of the windows maintains this context. An object that is known within the context of another object has its window appear within the window of the contextual object.

It is assumed that the maintainer using the PUNS user interface has previously used the PUNS repository component to structure a database for support of the user interface. The scenario described next also assumes that the communication link between the two components has been established and that the PUNS user interface component can talk to the PUNS repository component.

Sample scenario. The program being explored in the sample scenario is one that allows the user to maintain and explore a database of bibliographic information. In this discussion, the program is known as the *biblio* program. The series of events that led to the use of PUNS were: (1) a user of the *biblio* program has requested information about a particular reference represented in the database that the *biblio* program manages; (2) the *biblio* program was run and produced a document that contained the citation information for the reference as requested by the

user; (3) the user has found that the page numbers given for the reference in the document are incorrect; the page number specification should be 1024–1035 and is given as 1024–10; (4) the programmer who is responsible for the *biblio* program, who has recently assumed responsibility for the program and is not familiar with all its parts, is attempting to determine how incorrect page numbers were established.

A repository for the *biblio* program has previously been created using the PUNS repository component. The programmer invokes the PUNS user interface component and establishes the communication link to the PUNS repository component. The sample scenario details the programmer's exploration of the *biblio* program.

The programmer is first presented with a window that represents any component object. The only option available for selection on the menu bar is the component name. The programmer selects this option and enters the name of the component, *biblio*. This name is sent to the PUNS repository component, which selects the repository for the *biblio* program. The component window is updated to reflect the name of the component to be explored, and the following options become available on the menu bar: high-level structure, global data relations, and intermodule data sharing. The programmer is interested in determining how a piece of information that exists in the database is created, updated, and displayed, and selects the global-data-relations option on the menu bar. This is accomplished by pointing the mouse at the menu item and single-clicking the left mouse button. Within the component window appears a window that displays a graph showing the relationships between the global data elements used in the program (databases, files, screen definitions, and global data structures) and the individual modules of the program. Figure 1 shows the window that is displayed. Each module in the current PUNS context that references a global data element is represented in the graph by an ellipse that contains the name of the module. Each global data element is represented by a rectangle that contains the name and type of the global data element. The arcs (or lines) that connect modules and global data elements represent relationships among the modules and the global data elements. In the current PUNS prototype, the arcs as seen in Figure 1 are undirected. However, each arc should be directed to show the flow of data between a module and a global data element. If a module references data that exist within a global data element, the arc is directed from the global data

Figure 1 Global data relations window

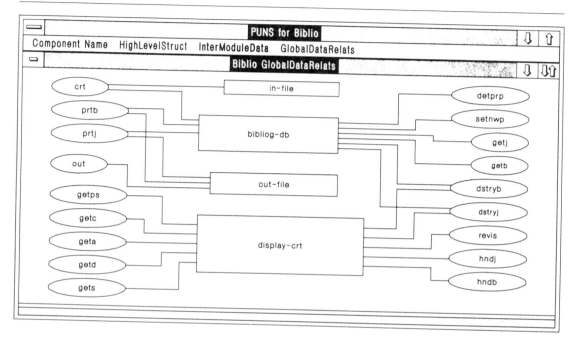

element to the module. If the module supplies (updates or creates) data for the global data element, the arc is directed from the module to the global data element. In cases where the module both references and supplies data, a doubly-directed arc exists between the module and the data element.

To provide another context in which to view the modules, the programmer also decides to look at the high-level structure chart by selecting this piece of information through the menu bar of the component window. Figure 2 shows the high-level structure chart for the *biblio* program. As in the global-data-element graph, an ellipse represents a module, and an arc in the structure chart represents a call-return relationship between two modules. Again, in the current research prototype, the arcs are undirected. The caller in the diagram is placed at a higher level than the callee.

Figure 3 shows the two graphs within the context of the component window. Microsoft Windows supports a feature that allows any window to be maximized to the size of the window in which it is contained. The PUNS user interface uses this facility

to allow the programmer to concentrate on the details of a specific window. In Figures 1 and 2, maximized versions of the two graphs are shown. Figure 3 shows the graphs as they exist within the context of the component window.

The relationships provided by the two charts show overall organizational information about the *biblio* program. The programmer uses this information to delve further into the way that the *biblio* program utilizes the database it maintains and points to the database object on the global data relations chart and double-clicks the left mouse button. A new window, one representing the database, now appears. The menu options on this window are: *dbDef* (database definition), *relGraph* (graph of database usage by program modules), *dbObject* (objects defined in the database), *objAttribute* (attributes of the objects defined in the database). Because the programmer is specifically interested in the page numbers for a journal article but is not sure whether the page numbers are represented in the database as a separate object or simply as an attribute of an object, the next step is to select the *dbDef* option on the menu bar. This selection brings up a window showing the da-

Figure 2   High-level structure window

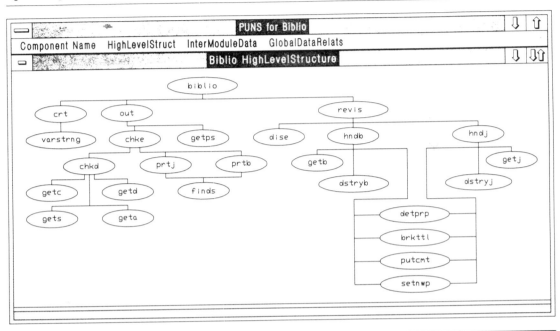

Figure 3   PUNS component window

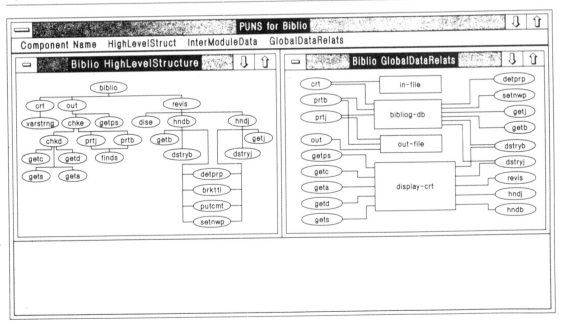

Figure 4   Bibliog database with dbDef window

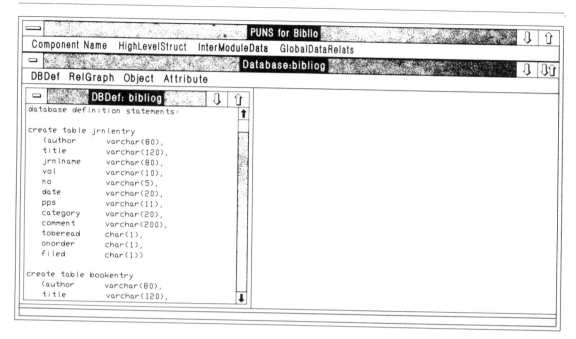

tabase definition statements. The programmer scrolls through the definition and finds the page numbers as an attribute of the journal entry (*jrnlentry*) object. Figure 4 shows the *dbDef* window within the database object window. The programmer finds that the page number attribute seems to be defined to handle a sufficiently large page number specification and thus concludes that the problem of an incorrect page number specification is not the result of any truncation of data within the database. By pointing the mouse at the page number specification attribute (*pps*) and double-clicking, the programmer can bring up two windows contained one within another. The windows represent the object (*jrnlentry*) and the specific attribute (*pps*) associated with the object. The menu bar for the attribute window shows the attribute-specific information that can be obtained: description, references by, updates by. Because the programmer is interested in who updates the page number attribute, the *updates by* option is selected. Figure 5 shows the window that results from this selection.

Had the programmer known the specific attribute specification for the page number specification and

the fact that it is an attribute of the journal object, the object and attribute windows presented in Figure 5 could have been obtained more directly. Rather than having to select the *dbDef* option and find the page number specification attribute therein, the programmer could have selected the attribute option on the database object window menu bar and provided the attribute and object specification. The windows shown in Figure 5 would have appeared directly. If the programmer had known the specific attribute specification, but not the object specification, the attribute option could also have been selected. The programmer could then have provided the attribute name, and the user interface would have presented a list of objects in which attributes with the specified name appeared. The programmer would then have selected the appropriate object, and the object and attribute windows shown in Figure 5 would have appeared.

In Figure 5, the *updates by* window indicates that the page number specification field in the journal object is updated in two modules, the *crt* module and the *setnwp* module. For each module, the specific statement(s) that accomplishes the update is

Figure 5 Database object and attribute windows

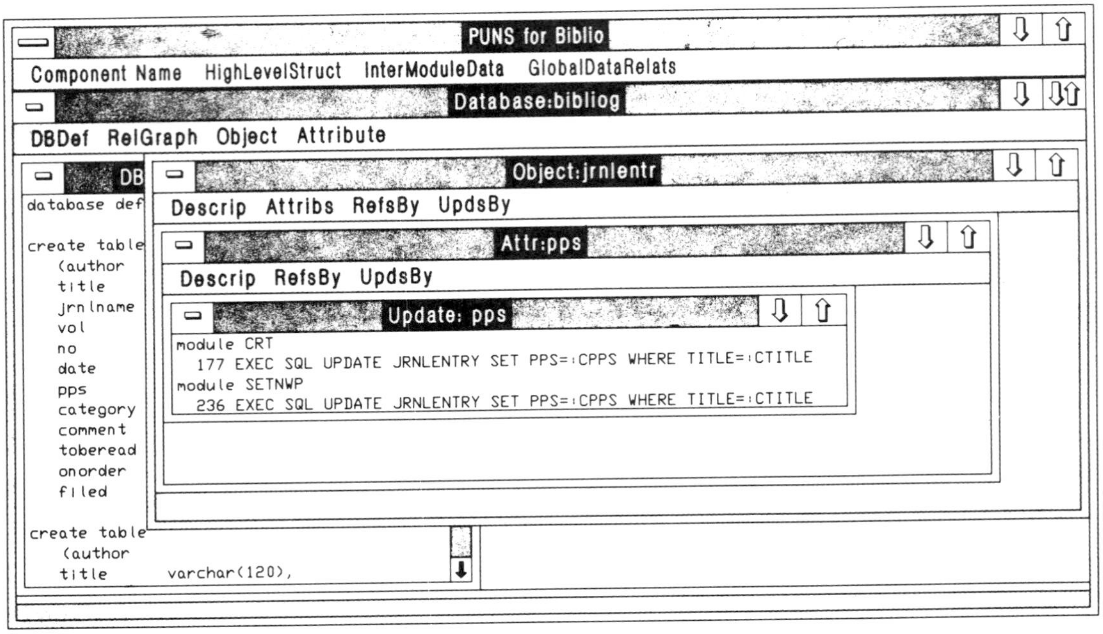

also shown, but the context in which the update is done is not shown. There are two aspects to context, the context in which the module exists and the context within the module. To see the context in which the module exists, the programmer need only look again at the structure chart shown in Figure 2. To see the context within the module, the programmer points to a statement that updates the page number specification and double-clicks the mouse. Two new windows appear, a window that represents the module object and a window within this window that represents the statement object within the module.

The programmer first chooses to explore the *crt* module and the statement that updates the field within this module. Figure 6 shows the windows that appear when the programmer selects the statement within the *crt* module. The updating statement shows that the page specification attribute (*pps*) is updated using the value in the variable CPPS, which is defined within the program. By pointing to the CPPS symbol and double-clicking the right mouse button, the programmer selects the symbol CPPS as an object of interest, and a window with information about the

symbol CPPS appears within the module window. Figure 7 shows this window in its maximized format. The definition for CPPS provides for eleven characters in the variable-length-character-string portion of CPPS. When using SQL with variable-length character strings, the storage for a symbol to supply the value of the variable length character string is defined as a half-word that contains the length of the actual character string followed by a set of bytes that contain the actual character string data. In the current version of PUNS, data-flow analysis is done only for registers; thus the information about the symbol CPPS is cross-reference information only. Data-flow analysis for symbols is a planned extension to PUNS and, when done, the window for the symbol CPPS will provide data-flow relationships for the references to and sets of the symbol.

In this example, the other statements that reference the symbol CPPS appear immediately to precede the statement that uses the value in CPPS to update the database. The programmer brings up the source for the *crt* module, scrolls to the first statement specified in the cross reference and studies the code. Figure 8 shows the windows that the programmer studies,

Figure 6   Module and statement windows

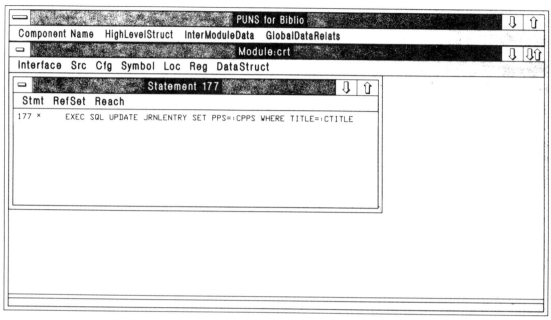

Figure 7   Symbol CPPS window

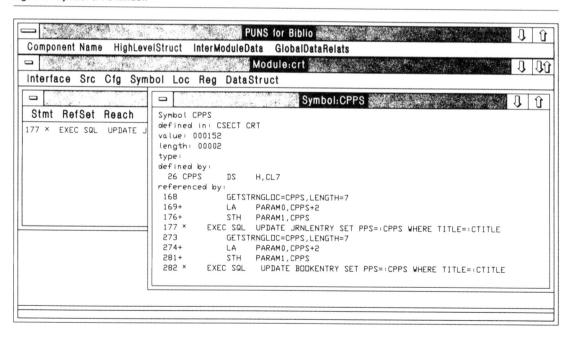

Figure 8   CRT module window

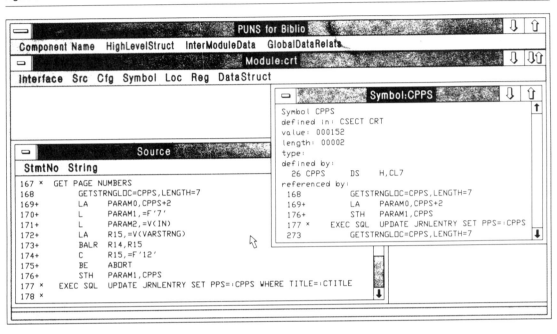

where the symbol CPPS is referenced in a macroinstruction as the operand of the keyword parameter LOC. The expansion of this macroinstruction causes the following actions: (1) it loads the address of the symbol CPPS into a register; (2) a constant value, specified as the operand of the other keyword LENGTH is loaded into another register; and (3) control passes to a subprogram VARSTRNG. When the subprogram returns, the value in the other register is stored into the first half word associated with the symbol CPPS. The programmer thinks that this macro invokes a subroutine that reads a variable-length character string (which is terminated by a special character) from a file and places the character string into the specified location, providing only as many characters as requested. The length specification given is 7. If the length specification indicates a maximum number of characters to be read, the page specification for the reference in which the user is interested would have been truncated. However, if the length specification indicates a minimum number of characters to be provided (including padding with blanks, if fewer are available from the input stream), the page specification has probably been processed properly here, and the problem lies else-where. To determine which is the case, the programmer must look at the subprogram VARSTRNG.

On the high-level structure chart for the *biblio* program, the programmer points the mouse at the module VARSTRNG and double-clicks the left button. A window for the module VARSTRNG appears. The programmer first explores the interface of this module to other modules by selecting the interface option on the menu bar of the module window. An interface window appears with menu options: Prologue, ESD, EntryData, ExitData. The programmer selects the *Prologue* option, and a window containing the comments that appear in the program prior to the first storage allocating statement appears. The interface and prologue windows are shown in Figure 9. The prologue seems to indicate that the length parameter specifies a maximum length. However, the programmer decides to investigate the logic of the VARSTRNG subprogram to be sure that the comment accurately reflects what the module does. The programmer displays the control flow graph for the subprogram by selecting the *Cfg* option on the menu bar for the module and displays the source for the module by selecting the *Src* option on the menu bar for the

Figure 9 VARSTRNG interface and prologue windows

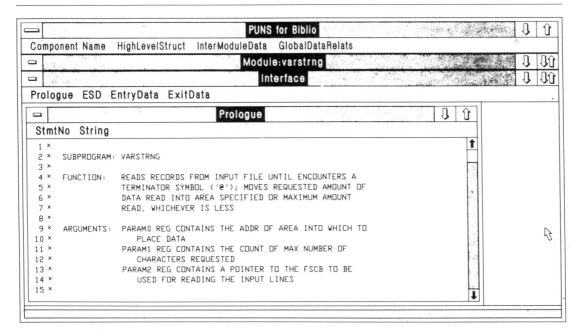

Figure 10 VARSTRNG module window

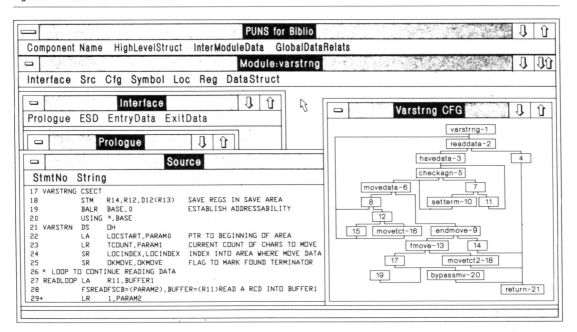

module. Figure 10 shows the module window and contained windows at this point. The programmer is particularly interested in the use of the length parameter and selects the *EntryData* option on the menu bar of the interface window to see how the parameter register (register 1, in this case) is used initially within the module. Figure 11 shows the contents of the interface window at this point.

The *EntryData* window shows that register 1 is used to set register 5 (TCOUNT) in the subprogram. Thus register 5 is now an alias for register 1, and the programmer explores how register 5 is used in the

---

The schema captures many of the low-level relationships that exist within a program.

---

module. By pointing the mouse at statement 23 in the *EntryData* window (which is the statement that assigns the value in register 1 to register 5) and by double-clicking the left button, the programmer indicates an interest in statement 23 as an object. A window appears for statement 23. The particular concern of the programmer is in how register 5 is used in the module. Thus the *RefSet* option is selected on the menu bar for the statement window for statement 23. A window containing information about where the value placed in register 5 is referenced in the program appears. Figure 12 shows the contents of this window. Using the statement number and node information given in this window, along with the control flow graph and source for the module, the programmer explores the subprogram. From the prologue, one finds that the initial impression that the length parameter specifies a maximum is correct.

At this point, the programmer may wish to explore the other updating of the database to ensure that no truncation occurs there. Once the error(s) in the *biblio* program have been found, the programmer can correct them and test the program.

User interface summary. The sample scenario just described is intended to provide a feeling for the functions available in the user interface. This sample scenario illustrates the two governing principles followed in the development of the user interface: (1) organizing information about the program around the notion of sets of objects and (2) supporting the point-click technique for exploring an object and moving between objects. In the sample scenario, several of the types of objects supported by the user interface have been illustrated (the component object, the database object, the database object object, the database attribute object, the module object, the module symbol object, the module statement object, and the module interface object). Windows to support these objects and to support information about these objects are also illustrated. The point-click technique for navigation is used extensively.

PUNS repository component

There are three elements of the PUNS repository component: (1) a schema for the repository, (2) a set of routines to load the repository with data, and (3) a set of routines to pull from the repository the appropriate information to satisfy high-level queries from the user interface component. The schema uses an entity-attribute-relationship (EAR) model. The schema captures many of the low-level relationships that exist within a program. The set of routines that load the repository are of three types: (1) a set of routines that scan assembler listings (outputs from the assembler) and load a portion of the repository with information directly discernable from the listing information, (2) a set of routines that are environment-specific (the environment in which the code runs, with a knowledge of ways in which services provided by the environment are invoked) which extract/update information about global objects associated with each assembler listing, and (3) a set of routines that do control flow and data-flow analysis on the information available in the repository. The routines that respond to queries from the workstation interpret each query to determine what data are needed from the repository to satisfy the query. These routines may need to analyze some of the extracted information to determine additional data to extract from the repository. Each of these elements of the repository component is now described in greater detail.

Schema for the repository. The model used for PUNS is an entity-attribute-relationship model. The schema can be depicted using a graph in which each

Figure 11 VARSTRNG interface window

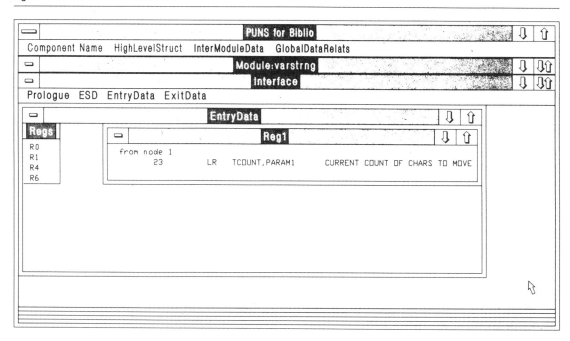

Figure 12 VARSTRNG statement window

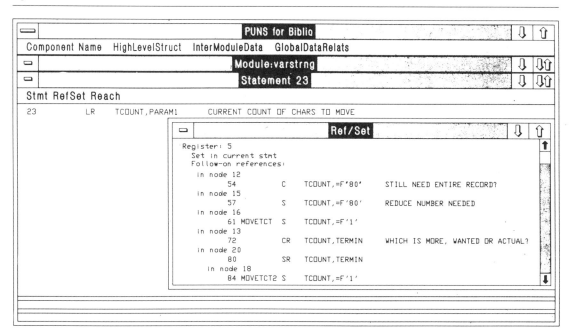

255

node represents an entity that may have attributes associated with it. The directed arcs in the graph represent the relationships between entities. A *relationship* exists between an entity that is a member of a set owned and the entity that owns the set. The owner of the set is shown at the tail of the directed arc, and the member of the set is shown at the head of the directed arc. Each one of the nodes represents a class, and there may be many entity instances each of which will belong to the class. As an example, consider an entity that represents a statement in a higher-level language. In a particular program, there would exist many statements. Each of these statements would be represented in the database by an entity instance as defined by the entity *statement* in the schema. The entity instances would differ in their associated attributes. Each unique statement would have at least one unique attribute (where *attribute* may include the sets owned by the entity instance). In the specific EAR model used by PUNS, the relationships are restricted to one-to-many relationships.

The simplified schema for the repository component of PUNS is shown in Figure 13. Different colors are used to represent different entities. The coloring indicates the routine that created each entity (and thus when and how the information represented by the entity has been derived). The arcs are labeled to specify the relationships which are specified for the schema. The arcs are also colored to indicate which routine established the relationship indicated by the arc. The schema is simplified to remove details that are unimportant to the understanding of the functioning of the tool but necessary to handle idiosyncrasies in the language supported. Discussed next are the entities shown in the schema.

The *component* entity serves as the consolidating entity for all component-wide information. If the repository is established to represent exactly one component, there will be only a single instance of the entity in the repository. The *component* entity owns collections of entity instances that represent the basic objects which make up the component: modules, databases, files, screen definitions, and global data structures. For ease of reference, each type of object, as represented by an instance of an entity for that object, is owned by the *component* entity via a unique set. The *component* entity itself would contain the name of the component and might contain functional or ownership information that is solicited from humans at the time the database is established. The sets that the *component* entity owns are: *files_are* with an entity representing a file

as the member, *dbs_are* with an entity representing a database as the member, *sub_units_are* with an entity representing a module (generally an assembly unit) as the member, *screens_are* with an entity representing a screen definition as the member, and *glblds_are* with an entity representing a global data structure as the member.

The *module* entity represents a unifying entity for a particular assembly that results in a single module to consider. The only attribute is file name for the source for the assembly. This entity owns a number of sets, many of which relate the module to objects within the module as described later in this paper. The *module* entity is connected to the global domain of the *component* entity. It belongs to the *sub_units_are* set, which is owned directly by the *component* entity. Also defined at the component level are entities that represent objects that may be used globally, i.e., in more than one module. Because a global object may be used by many modules and a module may use many global objects of a particular type, a set of *connector* entities are shown in the graph to resolve the many-to-many relationships. The *module* entity owns a *connector* entity via a set relationship, and the entity representing the global object owns the *connector* entity via a different set relationship. This allows the many-to-many relationships to be established. The sets owned by the *module* entity in this context are: *uses_glbl* to relate a module to a global data structure (connector entity is *mod_glblds*), *uses_screens* to relate a module to a screen definition (connector entity is *mod_scrdef*), *uses_db* to relate a module to a database (connector entity is *mod_db*), and *uses_file* to relate a module to a file used by the module (connector entity is *mod_file*).

In this version of the schema, the only connection between the global objects and the modules that act upon the global objects is via the sets that relate the *module* entity to each of the entities for these global objects. Certainly there are finer relationships that could be expressed in the schema for any of the objects: the information specifying where within the module the object is referenced, the type of reference, and whether the module in fact defines the object. In the schema, we opted to walk through the repository (i.e., knowing the module, find the references to the global object through the local symbol table and determine the reference types and definitions) to determine this information as it was needed, rather than capturing it in the database at the time the database is established. The schema also shows

Figure 13 PUNS repository schema

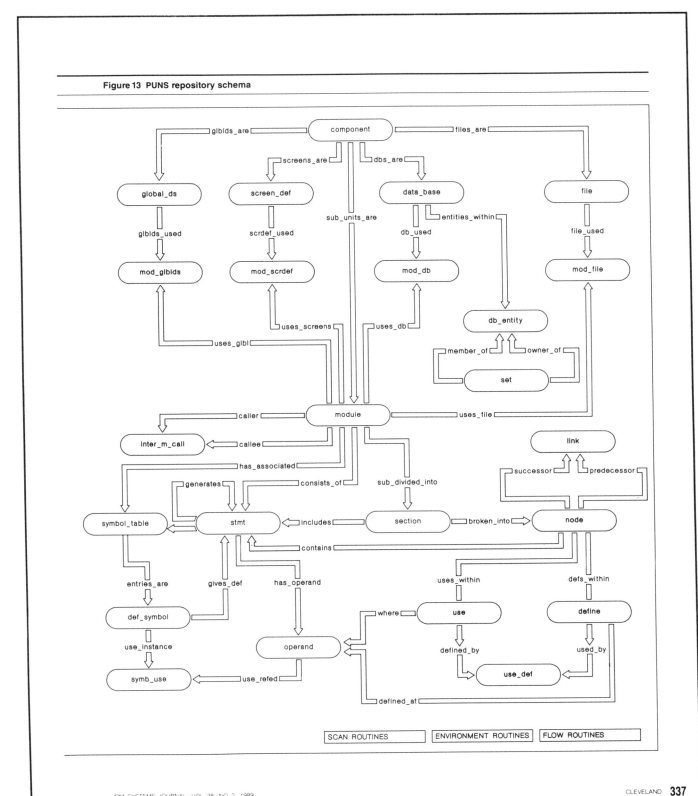

257

the *module* entity owning two sets (*caller* and *callee*) that both have as a member the *inter_m_call* entity. This structure captures the use of one *module* entity instance by another *module* entity instance. The *inter_m_call* entity contains a pointer to a *stmt* entity instance representing the point at which the call is made. The *global_ds, screen_def,* and *file* entities are handled in a similar fashion in the schema.

The *data_base* entity, which represents a global database is connected in a similar fashion to the modules that reference the database. However, as elements within the database are distinguishable and may serve as focus points for an exploration session, they have been abstracted from the schema definition of the database and exist as separate entities. The *data_base* entity has a textual specification of its schema as an attribute. It owns the *db_used* set for connection to modules (via the *mod_db* entity). The *data_base* entity also owns an *entities_within* set, whose members are the *db_entity* entity. In order to capture the relationships between *db_entity* entities, the *db_entity* entity owns two sets, the *owner_of* set and the *member_of* set. The member of each of these sets is the *set* entity. Such an organization resolves the many-to-many relationships that may exist between entities in the database. In representing a referenced database in the PUNS repository, the EAR model has been selected to describe the referenced database. For a referenced relational database, each *db_entity* entity represents a table, each *set* entity represents a key used to move from table to table. For a referenced hierarchical database, each *db_entity* entity represents a record, each *set* entity represents a parent-child relationship.

The *module* entity is described above in terms of its interconnection with other global objects. As the unifying element for an assembly unit, the *module* entity owns several sets: (1) the *sub_divided_into* set, which associates entities representing individual section definitions within the assembly, i.e., the *section* entity, with the *module* entity; (2) the *consists_of* set, which associates entities representing individual statements in the assembly, i.e., the *stmt* entity, to the *module* entity; and (3) the *has_associated* set, which links the entity representing the local symbol table, i.e., the *symbol_table* entity, with the *module* entity.

The *symbol_table* entity represents the local symbol table for the module. It owns an *entries_are* set which has as a member the *def_symbol* entity which rep-

resents the individual symbols defined in the local symbol table. Each *def_symbol* entity is a member of a *gives_def* set owned by the *stmt* entity, which defines the symbol represented. The *def_symbol* entity also owns the *use_instance* set whose member is the *symb_use* entity, which represents a particular use of the symbol (and resolves an otherwise many-to-many relationship).

The *section* entity represents a control section or a dummy section within the assembly. The *section* entity owns two sets and serves as an organizing vehicle for each defined control or dummy section. The sets are the following: (1) *includes* set, which has as member the *stmt* entity and connects those statements defined within the section with the *section* entity and (2) *broken_into* set, which connects the *section* entity to the *node* entity, which represents the set of statements to be treated as a single node in the control flow graph for a control section.

The *operand* entity represents a single operand. It is singled out, as it is the operand that provides the reference to a symbol and also the use or definition of a variable in the data flow. The *operand* entity owns one set, the *use_refed* set, which associates the *operand* entity with its use of a symbol (and resolves a many-to-many relationship). The *operand* entity also participates as member in three set relationships: (1) *has_operand* set owned by the *stmt* entity, (2) *where* set owned by the *use* entity and relating a use of the variable represented by the operand to the operand, and (3) *defined_at* set, which relates the definition of a variable represented by the operand to the *operand* entity.

The *node* entity represents a division of the module according to control flow. Each *node* entity is connected to other *node* entities (to show the flow of control) via the *predecessor* and *successor* sets and the *link* entity which is a member of both sets. This structure reduces the many-to-many relationship of the flow of control among nodes into one-to-many relationships. The *node* entity is also a member of the *broken_into* set that is owned by the *section* entity. It is an owner of the *contains* set that shows the statements within the node and the owner of two sets, the *uses_within* and *defs_within* sets, which relate specific definitions and uses of variables (for data flow) that occur within the node. The definition of a variable is represented by the *define* entity, which is connected to uses of the variable via the *used_by* set, and to the *operand* entity which provides the definition via the *defined_at* set. The use of a variable within a node is represented by the *use* entity. The *use* entity is connected to definitions for the variable it represents via the *defined_by* set and to the *operand* entity that represents the use via the *where* set. The *use_def* entity connects uses of variables to definitions and is needed to resolve a many-to-many relationship.

Load routines. There are three types of routines that are used to load the PUNS repository: (1) routines to scan the input statements for the modules that make up the component to be described in the PUNS repository, (2) routines to deal with the environmental services used by the modules, and (3) routines to deal with representing the control and data-flow aspects of the modules. These three types of routines are now presented under the headings scan, environment, and flow.

Scan. The routines that scan the individual assembler listings for the component for which the repository is being established do the following: set up the *module* entity instance; set up the *symbol_table* entity instance; set up *section* entity instances for each control or dummy section encountered; set up a *stmt* entity instance for each statement encountered (from macro expansion information contained within the assembly listing also establishing the *generates* set); establish a *def_symbol* entity instance for each symbol defined in a statement; identify operands for each statement that has such and creates appropriate *operand* entity instances; and set up the appropriate *symb_use* entity instance for each operand reference.

As each of the entity instances is created it is placed in the proper set(s) to express the relationship of the entity instance to other entity instances that exist within the repository. In certain cases (for example with the *generates, consists_of, includes,* and *has_operands* relationships), it is necessary for the routines to establish a context for the processing of information so that as new entity instances are created, the necessary information to connect them to existing entity instances is available.

Attributes are established for each of the entity instances as the instance is created. The collection of attributes for a particular entity instance may not be complete at this time. The scan routines are written to utilize only information about the syntax of the language in which the module is expressed. These routines do not utilize semantic information about the statements of the language used. The semantic

information provided by the statements is captured in the repository by the flow routines. For example, the *operand* entity instance contains an attribute that identifies where the operand represents a use or redefinition of the variable represented by the operand. In order to determine how the operand is used,

> **When dealing with an assembler language, the use of services provided in the environment is evidenced in the assembly listing by the use of macros.**

the meaning of the operation on the operand must be established. The scan routines do not deal with this type of information and thus the use/redef attribute information is not established at this time.

Environment. When dealing with an assembler language, the use of services provided in the environment (e.g., linking, use of files, and use of databases) is evidenced in the assembly listing by the use of macros. The environment routines are aware of the macros supported within the environments in which the code is to run. By locating the macro calls that have been used (by inspecting the created *stmt* entity instances) and evaluating the paramaters specified on each macro call, these environment routines can create the global objects associated with the component and establish the relationships between these global objects and the particular *module* entity instances that reference the global objects. There may exist several sets of environmental routines that must be run, one set for each of the support subsystems called upon by the modules within the component.

Flow. The routines that establish the control and data-flow entity instances within the PUNS repository must be written to deal with the semantic information associated with each executable statement. This information can either be encoded into the routines or the routines can be written to operate on a separate body of knowledge that provides the semantic information for each executable statement. The second option was utilized in setting up the PUNS repository. A database—the semantic database—was built that contained an entity instance for each executable statement type. The entities were subdivided into those representing data manipulation opera-

---

In an assembler setting, it may be impossible to resolve completely the control flow and branch-link relationships.

---

tions, those representing conditional or unconditional branch operations, and those representing branch-link operations.

The first task for the flow routines is to identify the executable statements and classify each according to the types specified by the entity instances in the semantic database. Once the branch operations are identified, the basic blocks (nodes) for each module can be established, and by examining branch targets the control flow can be represented by using link-entity instances to interconnect the basic blocks (nodes). The possible entry points for each control section (each represented by a *node* entity instance) can be identified and represented in the repository as can the exit points for each control section.

The next task for the flow routines is to determine the data flow within each node. The semantic database provides the necessary information to classify operands as to use or redefinition. The appropriate *use* and *define* entity instances can be created and associated with the *node* entity instances. These entity instances can be associated with the appropriate operands. Where the use of a data item is satisfied by a prior redefine within the block, a *use_def_connect* entity instance can also be created. Once intrablock data flow is established, interblock data flow can also be established, and the appropriate *use_def_connect* entity instances can be created. In the PUNS context, all data-flow analysis should be optimistic. That is, if it appears that a particular data-flow assertion may be true, it should be captured. In doing this, a weighting can be used to indicate that the assertion is probably true, although not necessarily exact.

The final task for the flow routines is to deal with the branch-link operations and, where possible, to resolve these branch-links within or across the modules and build the appropriate entity instances to express these interconnections.

In an assembler setting, it may be impossible to resolve completely the control flow and branch-link relationships. Inasmuch as the interblock data flow depends on the established control flow, the data flow may also be incompletely determined. Although the current PUNS implementation accepts this incomplete resolution, a better solution is to involve a human expert during the running of the flow routines to achieve a more complete resolution. For branch and branch-link types, where the flow routines are unable to detect a target, the human expert can be queried to provide a target. The information from the expert can be treated using a weighting factor so that the future user of PUNS knows that the information is a best guess.

Query-response routines. The PUNS user interface queries the PUNS repository component to obtain information necessary for developing the windows that are presented to the user via the user interface. These queries may require interrogation of many of the repository-entity instances and the following of many relationships or may be able to be satisfied by attention to only one or a few entity instances. The repository schema should be developed to allow those queries that will be issued frequently by the user interface to be satisfied by accessing only one or a few entity instances. Queries that will be issued more infrequently or at points at which user activities can be overlapped with a wait for response from the query can require interrogation of many repository-entity instances. The current implementation of the PUNS repository has not been optimized to minimize the time for queries that are frequently issued by the PUNS user interface component.

We now discuss a few of the queries that are issued by the PUNS user interface component and then sketch the method used to develop the appropriate information to respond to each query. Our intention is to give a flavor for the types of queries and show how the repository component can navigate the repository schema to provide the requested information.

High-level structure chart query. To satisfy the query to provide a high-level structure chart for the component, each one of the *module* entity instances existing in the subunits relationship to the *component* entity instance must be enumerated. The caller-callee relationship between the modules is captured by the *inter_m_call* entity and the caller and callee relationships. For each caller module, the appropriate callees must be specified.

Global data relations query. To satisfy the query to provide a graph description showing the use of the global data elements by modules, each one of the global data element entity instances must be enumerated. For each global data element entity instance (*global_ds, screen_def, file, data_base*) the modules to which it is connected via the *xxx_used* and *uses_xxx* sets and the connector entity instances must also be enumerated. If a relationship is defined for the use of a global data element and a separate relationship for the definition of a global data element, the enumeration of modules can specify a direction for the arcs.

Prologue for interface query. To satisfy this query, it is necessary to specify which statements within a module are part of the prologue for the module. Currently, the prologue is interpreted to mean those statements in a module that precede the first storage-allocating statement within the module. Because the statements forming the prologue are contiguous, a specification of the first and last statement numbers and a count of the number of statements in the prologue suffices. The *module* entity for the module for which the information is desired must be located. Then each of the *stmt* entities in the set *consists_of* owned by the *module* entity must be checked until an entity representing a storage-allocating statement is encountered. All checked entities prior to that representing a storage-allocating statement are part of the prologue. The data representation to satisfy the query is then the statement number attribute for the first and last of these entities and a count of the number of entities.

RefSet query for registers within a statement within a module. This query provides reference and set information for registers used within a statement in a particular module. For each register used in the statement, the query identifies the use of the register (reference or set). For a reference register, the query supplies all statements (and nodes within which the statements exist) that previously set the register in the module. For a set register, the query supplies all statements (and nodes within which the statements exist) that reference the register following the set.

The entity representing the module (*module* entity) and the entity representing the statement (*stmt* entity) within the module must be located. Then each of the operands of the statement (*operand* entity) must be inspected to see whether it represents a register. If the *operand* entity represents a register, then the membership of the *operand* entity in either the *where* or *defined_at* sets indicates whether the register is set or referenced in the statement. For purposes of illustration, assume that the operand is set (defined) in the statement under consideration. The *operand* entity then belongs to a *defined_at* set owned by a *define* entity. By looking at each *use_def* entity that is owned by the *define* entity in the *used_by* set, one can find the *use* entity that owns the *use_def* entity in its *defined_by* set. Then tracing back to the *operand* entity associated with the *use* entity, the *stmt* entity that owns the *operand* entity via the *has_operand* set can be determined. To find the node in which the statement exists, one must find the owner of the *contains* set to which the *stmt* belongs. This owner will be the *node* entity representing the node in which the statement exists. Repeating this procedure for each of the *use* entities linked to the *define* entity via the *use_def* entity, all the necessary information for an operand that is set in a statement can be found. For an operand that is referenced in a statement, one begins with the *use* entity and finds the *define* entity linked to the *use* entity via the *use_def* entity. From the *define* entity, one can determine the statement and node information needed to satisfy this query.

Current research

There are many directions that extensions to the current work on PUNS might take. These include performance issues, dynamic information updating, a logging of explorations with a replay option, a checkpoint/restart facility, a notebook facility for recording discoveries, and experimentation with the current prototype.

Performance. To achieve reasonable performance for a system such as PUNS requires an analysis of frequently issued queries and of the expectations of the user as to response for different query types. The repository can be organized so that those queries that are frequently issued or have a user expectation for immediate response can be quickly satisfied. That is, all the analysis to answer the query is done during the loading of the repository. Queries that are less frequently issued or are perceived by the user either to take time to answer or to be capable of being overlapped with other user activities can be satisfied by analysis on the fly by using the current data in the repository as the source for analysis routines to isolate what is actually needed to satisfy the query.

At one extreme is a repository whose schema allows immediate satisfaction of all queries. A repository built using such a schema would—for even a very small component—be enormous in size. However, the response time would be very short, even on a moderately powerful host. At the other extreme is a

---

If a high-performance host is available, a minimal schema can be used, saving disk space for repository storage and allowing the repository to be more quickly loaded.

---

repository schema that captures only the most significant relationships; all other relationships must be dynamically derived. A repository built using such a schema would be compact and not require a significant amount of space. However, the number of instructions that would have to be executed to satisfy any but the most basic query would be very large. Only if a very high performance computer were used as host, would the resulting response time be acceptable. Thus a compromise between these extremes in terms of space is indicated.

One interesting point about the design of PUNS is that different repository components can be used, depending on the availability of resources. If a high-performance host is available, a minimal schema can be used, saving disk space for repository storage and allowing the repository to be more quickly loaded. On the other hand, if a low-performance host, such as a workstation with sufficient storage is used, a more comprehensive schema can be used. It takes more disk space and a longer set-up time, but performance during a use of the PUNS user interface component would be acceptable. The intended users

for PUNS and the types of available hardware need to be taken into account in the research to produce a tool that will satisfy the performance needs of the users.

Dynamic information updating. The PUNS tool as described does not allow for the dynamic updating of information. The PUNS repository is set up prior to a user session using the current versions of modules of the component and not changed during the user session.

However, there is much to be gained by allowing the user to update incomplete information on the component during an exploratory session. There will always be relationships that cannot be determined via the static analysis done in setting up the repository. Allowing the user to add information to the repository raises the question of the accuracy of the information provided, particularly if more than one user has access to the PUNS repository for a particular component. Should the added information be held as user-specific information and not shared with others using the repository? Should the information have a probability associated with it, so that if it is presented to a user it is flagged as only being a possible truth? What if the information presented by a user affects relationships previously determined by static analysis on the basis of incomplete information?

The question of the need to update the PUNS repository also arises in the case of allowing the user to investigate the impact of changes in the module versions during an exploratory session. Each change would have an impact on the relationships represented in the repository, and there would be a need for incremental updating of the repository. The extent of such incremental updating would be a function of the number of relationships explicitly expressed in the repository. If most of the relationships are derived dynamically from a minimal set of relationships expressed in the repository, the updating would be minimal. However, if almost all relationships were expressed in the repository, a significant amount of reanalysis and updating would be necessary prior to continuing to use the repository.

Logging of an exploration. The current prototype for PUNS has no facility to record the use of the PUNS user interface for a particular exploration. Such a recording could prove to be very beneficial. A programmer using the system who is interrupted during a task could quickly replay the recording of that prior exploration upon returning to the task to set the context for continuing the task. Even more beneficial would be a facility to allow a replay of an exploration session with interruption to alter the exploration at a point where it went astray or where more information is needed that was not gathered in the initial exploration.

Checkpoint and restart. Not as extensive as logging, the ability to checkpoint the PUNS user interface during an exploration session and then restart at a later point is also a needed extension and subject for further study. Given this facility, the system could be checkpointed at predetermined or user-selected points so that, in case of interruption—a loss of machine facility or a hopeless deadend in an exploration—the user could restart without the need to repeat the entire exploration.

Notebook facility. A user working through any exploration of a system usually takes notes of the significant issues uncovered or needing to be resolved. These notes generally include information about the current point in the exploration and how the information available at that point has led to a particular conclusion. The PUNS user interface provides support for the exploration phase of a system, and the user also needs support for the notetaking activity. It should be possible for the user to select certain pieces of information currently available on the screen, place them into an on-line notebook (probably represented as a viewable, scrollable window), indicate relationships between the items of information, and add comments. What is placed in the notebook may be fairly static information. However, it may also be quite dynamic, thereby allowing a sequence of windows to be captured as the notebook is written and replayed when the notebook is read. The notebook need not be simply a linear text. Rather, it could encompass many of the aspects of hypertext.[14]

Experimentation. The PUNS prototype described in this paper has been demonstrated extensively. However, it has not been used in a production programming environment. There is a need to define, conduct, and analyze experiments for using the tool in such a realistic environment. Such experiments can provide much feedback to the research team from which would come an understanding of such things as relationships that have been ignored, performance, extensions to the tool, and areas of the tool that are not user friendly. Such experiments are contemplated and we hope they will be carried out.

Concluding remarks

PUNS is a tool to support programmers in their effort to understand a program. The PUNS user interface presents many views of a program under consideration and allows the programmer to gain an overview of the program and to explore any aspect of the program in depth. The interface is so structured that the user can move between the overview type information and the detailed levels using a simple point-click interaction with the PUNS tool. The PUNS repository component is designed to provide the necessary information to the user interface component, so that the many views can be made available when requested.

With continuing development and extension the PUNS tool described in this paper should allow programmers to reduce the proportion of time they spend on the program understanding task while increasing their level of comprehension of the program. As such, it should be a valuable tool in any software maintainer's toolbox.

It is interesting to speculate on potential adjacent areas of research. The availability of a tool such as PUNS should prove useful to the community of scientists attempting to understand how people comprehend programs. By recording exploration sessions using PUNS, a machine readable, nonintrusively obtained set of data on sequences of actions taken by an individual trying to comprehend a portion of a program to accomplish a particular task is available for analysis. If the scope of the PUNS tool is sufficient, any desired set of relationships can be explored in any logical sequence, and the tool will not constrain the explorer. The data obtained by recording tool exploration will not be contaminated by the facilities provided by the tool.

Not only can the recording of exploratory sessions provide detailed input for the study of how people go about certain tasks involving comprehension, but also the tool can provide a vehicle for exploring whether a certain set of steps are necessary and sufficient for a particular task. By adding on top of PUNS a component that constrains the user of the tool to following certain relationships at any particular point in the exploration only, the tool could be programmed to force the user into following a certain task structure. Experiments using different task structures could yield valuable information about task content.

A third area of associated research in which a tool such as PUNS could prove useful is that of reverse engineering, that is, the attempt to capture design information from existing code. The PUNS repository component provides much of the relationship information necessary to begin a reverse engineering task. The user interface could be modified (or extended) to maximize user input for cases in which there is insufficient information to make the reverse-engineering decisions. Thus, human guided reverse engineering could be done easily and interactively.

Acknowledgments

I want to thank Don Pazel and Ashok Malhotra for their technical assistance in this work. I thank Tom Corbi for his vision of what PUNS could be and for his continuing enthusiasm and support for the work as it has progressed.

Microsoft Windows is a registered trademark of Microsoft Corporation.

Cited references

1. G. Parikh, *Handbook of Software Maintenance*, John Wiley & Sons, Inc., New York (1986), p. 14.
2. B. P. Lientz, E. B. Swanson, and G. E. Tomkins, "Characteristics of application software maintenance," *Communications of the ACM* **21**, No. 6, 466–471 (June 1978).
3. E. B. Swanson, "The dimension of maintenance," *Proceedings of the Second International Conference on Software Engineering*, San Francisco (October 1976), pp. 492–497.
4. R. K. Fjeldstad and W. T. Hamlen, "Application program maintenance-report to our respondents," in G. Parikh and N. Zvegintzov, Editors, *Tutorial on Software Maintenance*, IEEE Computer Society Press, Silver Springs, MD (1983), pp. 13–27.
5. T. A. Standish, "An essay on software reuse," *IEEE Transactions on Software Engineering* **SE-10**, No. 5, 494–497 (September 1984).
6. F. P. Brooks, Jr., "No silver bullet: Essence and accidents of software engineering," *IEEE Computer* **20**, No. 4, 10–19 (April 1987).
7. A. Malhotra, H. M. Markowitz, and D. P. Pazel, "EAS-E: An integrated approach to application development," *ACM Transactions on Database Systems* **8**, No. 4, 515–542 (December 1983).
8. M. Moriconi and D. F. Hare, "The PegaSys System: Pictures as formal documentation of large," *ACM Transactions on Programming Languages and Systems* **8**, No. 4, 524–546 (October 1986).
9. S. Reiss, "PECAN: Program development systems that support multiple views," *IEEE Transactions on Software Engineering* **SE-11**, No. 3, 30–41 (March 1985).
10. J. Ambras and V. O'Day, "Microscope: A program analysis system," *Proceedings of Hawaii International Conference on System Sciences-20* (January 1987), pp. 71–81.
11. Y. Chen and C. V. Ramamoorthy, "The C information abstractor," *COMPSAC 86*, Chicago (October 1986), pp. 291–298.
12. J. S. Collofello and J. W. Blaylock, "Syntactic information useful for software maintenance," *National Computer Conference 85*, Chicago (July 1985), pp. 547–553.
13. W. Teitelman, *Interlisp Reference Manual*, Xerox PARC, Palo Alto, CA (1978).
14. J. Conklin, "Hypertext," *IEEE Computer* **20**, No. 9, 17–41 (September 1987).

Linore Cleveland *IBM Research Division, T. J. Watson Research Center, P.O. Box 704, Yorktown Heights, New York 10598.* Ms. Cleveland worked for IBM from 1963–1969, teaching in and managing an internal programmer education group in Poughkeepsie, New York. After leaving IBM, she taught at Vassar College in Poughkeepsie and Polytechnic University in Brooklyn, New York, and served as chairman of Vassar's Computer Science Studies Program. She also spent two years as a guest researcher at the Tokyo Research Laboratory of IBM Japan. She rejoined IBM in late 1986. She has been working in a program understanding group developing demonstration vehicles and prototypes of a tool to assist programmers in understanding programs written in old code. Ms. Cleveland has a B.S. in mathematics from Michigan State University, East Lansing, Michigan, an M.S. in computer science from Polytechnic University, and is currently a candidate for the Ph.D. in computer science at Polytechnic University.

Reprint Order No. G321-5362.

An Intelligent Tool For Re-engineering Software Modularity

Robert W. Schwanke

Siemens Corporate Research, Inc.
755 College Rd. East
Princeton, NJ 08540

This paper describes a software tool that provides heuristic modularization advice for improving existing code. A heuristic design similarity measure is defined, based on Parnas's information hiding principle. The measure supports two services: clustering, which identifies groups of related procedures, and maverick analysis, which identifies individual procedures that appear to be in the wrong module. The tool has already provided useful advice in several real programming projects. The tool will soon incorporate an automatic tuning method, which allows the tool to "learn" from its "mistakes", adapting its advice to the architect's preferences. A preliminary experiment demonstrates that the automatically tuned similarity function can assign procedures to modules very accurately.

1. Introduction

A medium or large scale software project's success depends heavily on how well the software is organized, because the organization affects understandability, modifiability, integratability, and testability. Unfortunately, because software changes rapidly, even during maintenance, its organization often deteriorates. Each time that a programmer adds a new procedure to the system, he must decide which existing module he should place it in. Sometimes, he should form a new module, containing this object and objects drawn from existing modules, but the mental and administrative effort involved often deters him. Either way, the programmer often has only a worm's eye view of the system, from the corner where he is working, and makes his organizational decisions accordingly.

This problem is exacerbated by the fact that most widely-used programming languages still have inadequate scope-control facilities, so that modularity is a matter of programer self-discipline, and is not normally enforced by the language support tools.

Sooner or later, someone on the project usually notices that the organization has deteriorated. Then, a small team of experts is appointed as "architects", to analyze and reorganize the system. However, their task is even more formidable than the programmer's, because they must understand many more system-wide interrelationships, and must carry out widespread changes without causing the system to break. Furthermore, because the programming language and tools do not support modularity adequately, they must analyze actual cross-reference information to deduce the scopes of many program units, rather than relying on specifications.

The goal of the Arch project is to help rescue the architects from their predicament, by providing them with intelligent tools for analyzing the system's structure, reorganizing it, documenting the new structure, and monitoring compliance with it, so that significant structural changes can be detected and evaluated early, before they become irreversible.

Arch is a graphical and textual "structure chart editor" for maintaining large software systems. It extracts cross reference data from the code itself and, using the current subsystem tree as a guide, creates several kinds of graphical and textual views of the cross reference data, at varying levels of detail. In order to help create subsystem trees where none existed before, Arch provides a clustering algorithm that groups related procedures into modules. In order to improve the quality of existing modules, Arch provides a "critic", which identifies individual procedures that apparently violate good information hiding principles.

Overview of the paper

This paper describes a set of methods for providing heuristic advice on modularity, including an adaptation mechanism that automatically tunes the heuristic to the preferences of the software architects.

We begin by discussing the *information hiding principle* [1], and then describe a heuristic measure of information sharing. Next we describe two services that provide heuristic advice for modularizing existing code, and the results we have achieved with these services. One service, *clustering*, identifies clusters of procedures that share enough design information that they belong together in the same module. The other service, *maverick analysis*, identifies individual

83

Reprinted from *Proc. 13th Int'l. Conference on Software Engineering*, pp. 83-92. ©1991 by The Institute of Electrical and Electronics Engineers, Inc. All rights reserved.

procedures that appear to be in the wrong module, because they share more information with procedures in other modules than with procedures in their own module.

Both services present lists of suggestions, which the architect can accept or reject. The lists are long enough that they must be prioritized, so that the architect can tackle the problems "worst first". As she does so, she sometimes finds that she disagrees with Arch's recommendations, because (for example) she believes that encapsulating one data type is more important than encapsulating another. Since the similarity measure incorporates a weight representing the importance of each non-local identifier in the system, it can be adapted to the architect's preferences by increasing the weights of some identifiers and decreasing others. Informal experiments on real, production code show that heuristic analysis provides useful information to practicing maintainers, and that hand-tuning a few of the weights can make Arch and the maintainer agree most of the time.

However, the tuning process is too tedious and demanding to expect an architect to do it. Instead, we have developed an automatic tuning method. It is essentially a curve-fitting method, which takes a set of approved modules and their approved members, and finds coefficients for the similarity measure that minimizes the number of apparently misplaced procedures. The method is a gradient descent method that combines and extends several neural network design and training methods. Although the implementation details are beyond the scope of this paper, we describe the results of our experiments, which show that an automatically-tuned similarity function can assign a new procedure to the correct existing module with very high accuracy.

One potential problem with automatic tuning is that, if the measure is tuned too closely to the data, then Arch will have no suggestions to make, because the fitting process assumes that the given modules are correct. To prevent this, we give the weight coefficients initial values based based on objective information measures of the code itself, without any architect's input, and create an initial list of suspect procedures. The weights are changed only when the architect rejects a suggestion, and are only changed "just enough" to make Arch agree with the architect.

By this adaptation method, the architect is freed from laborious hand-tuning. She only needs to say "yes" or "no" to specific suggestions, and can expect the tool to adapt to her preferences.

2. Information Hiding

One of the most influential writers on the subject of modularity has been David L. Parnas. In 1971, he wrote of the information distribution aspects of software design (italics his):

"The connections between modules are the assumptions which the modules make about each other. In most systems we find that these connections are much more extensive than the calling sequences and control block formats usually shown in system structure descriptions." [1]

The same year he formulated the "information hiding" criterion, advocating that a module should be

"... characterized by a design decision which it hides from all others. Its interface or definition [is] chosen to reveal as little as possible about its inner workings." [2]

According to Parnas, the design choices to hide are those that are most likely to change later on. Good examples are data formats, user interface (I/O formats, window vs. typescript, choice of window management system), hardware (processor, peripheral devices), and operating system.

2.1. An Example

In practice, the information hiding principle works in the following way. First, the designers identify the role or service that the module will provide to the rest of the system. At the same time, they identify the design decisions that will be hidden inside the module. For example, the module might provide an associative memory for use by higher-level modules, and conceal whether the memory is unsorted or sorted, all in memory or partly on disk, and whether it uses assembly code to achieve extra-fast key hashing.

The module description is then refined into a set of procedures and data types that other modules may use when interacting with the associative memory. For example, the associative memory might provide operations to insert, retrieve, modify, and remove records. These four operations would need parameters specifying records and keys, and some way to determine when the memory is full. It would declare and make public the data types "Key" and "Record", and the procedures "Insert", "Retrieve", "Modify", and "Remove".

Next, the associative memory module is implemented as a set of procedures, types, variables, and macros that together make, for example, a large in-core hash table. The implementation can involve additional procedures and types beyond the ones specified in the interface; only the procedures belonging to that module are permitted to use these "private" declarations. Many design decisions are represented by specific declarations, such as

84

```
HashRecord array
        HashTable[TableSize]
```
which embodies the decision to store hash records in a fixed-size table rather than, say, a linked list or tree. Procedures that depend on such design decisions normally use the corresponding declarations, for example,

```
proc Retrieve(KeyWanted: Key)
    Index = Hash(KeyWanted)
    if HashTable[Index].Key
            equals KeyWanted
        return HashTable.Record
    else return FAILURE
```

Procedures outside the associative memory module cannot, for example, determine which order the records are stored in, because they cannot use the name HashTable. Later, if the implementer should decide to replace the hashing algorithm, or even to use a sorted tree, all of the code that he would need to change would be in the associative memory module.

2.2. A Heuristic

The example above leads us to a simple *information sharing heuristic* for detecting when two procedures share a design decision:

> If two procedures use several of the same unit-names, they are likely to be sharing significant design information, and are good candidates for placing in the same module.

2.3. Coupling: Control, Data, or Design?

A unique aspect of our research is that we measure design coupling, rather than data or control coupling. A simple example will illustrate the difference:

This diagram contains four procedures, A, B, C, and D and a table, T. Procedure A calls procedure B to write information into table T, and calls D to read information from the table. Procedure C also writes information into table T. Procedures A and B have a *control link* between them, because A calls B. Procedures B and D have a *data link* between them, because data passes from B to D through the table. Likewise, A and B are data-linked through parameters, and C and D are data-linked through T. However, B and C are **not** data-linked, because because both of them put data into T, but neither one takes data out. Finally, B, C, and D have a **design link** among them, because all three share assumptions about the format and interpretation of table T. If one of the procedures ever needs to be rewritten in a way that affects the table T, the other two should be examined to see if they require analogous changes.

Before Parnas's work, it was commonplace to divide a system into modules that each represented a major computational step of the program. For example, a compiler would be divided into a lexical analyzer, a syntax analyzer, a semantic analyzer, and an optimizer. The lexical analyzer would include a procedure for inserting symbols into the symbol table; the other modules would contain routines for retrieving information from the symbol table. The format of the symbol table itself would be exposed to all of the modules, so that a change in its format required the programmer to review every module to see what the impact would be. Nowadays, programmers generally agree that it is more important to group together procedures that share data, than to group procedures that call one another.

2.4. Real Life Is Not So Simple

It would be nice if the clear, simple concepts contained in a system's original design were faithfully adhered to throughout the software's lifetime. However, the implementation process always uncovers technical problems that lead to changes in the design. Furthermore, design decisions are almost never so clearly separable that they can be neatly divided into subsystems and sub-subsystems. Each decision interlocks with other decisions, so that inevitably there are some decisions that cannot be concealed within modules, even though they are likely to change. These typically show up as public variables and unprotected data types.

Private declarations are not the only design decisions that may be shared among procedures. Module interface specifications also represent design decisions, although the designers hope that they will change less often. Even so, in many cases a certain interface procedure is only used in one or two other modules in a system, and represents a design decision on which all of the using procedures depend.

In the final analysis, good modularity is highly subjective. Not only must the designers select good abstract roles for the modules to implement, but they must try to predict what kinds of changes are likely to happen to the system in the future. Then they must determine which design decisions can be hidden within modules, and which ones must be shared. Finally, they must adapt the module specifications to the project team that is building them, incorporating both technical and non-technical influences.

Therefore, modularization as a reverse-engineering process must be treated heuristically, rather than by a formal set of rules. The information hiding heuristic suggests that "belonging together" is proportional to "shared declarations". Arch uses a similarity function that measures information sharing based on shared declarations, and uses it to give the architect advice on how to modularize or remodularize a system.

85

3. Measuring Information Sharing

To turn the information sharing heuristic into an actual similarity function, Arch profits from research on human similarity judgment, in the field of cognitive science. One particular model, Tversky's Ratio Model [3], corresponds to our intuitive notion of how humans judge that two procedures share design information. In this section we outline that model, and describe how we have adapted it to our problem domain. First, however, we define the software features on which the similarity function is based.

3.1. Features of Software

The information sharing heuristic is based on the non-local names that procedures use. More formally, a non-local name is any name whose scope includes two or more procedure bodies. Arch assigns a unique identifier to each such name, to distinguish multiple declarations of the same identifier (in different scopes). Every non-local name is a potential feature name. Every non-local name appearing in the body of a procedure is a feature of that procedure.

Sometimes, two or more procedures are placed together in the same module because they are called from the same other procedures. Therefore, whenever procedure A calls procedure B, not only does A receive the feature "B", but B receives the feature "called-by-A".

For the C language, we are using a cross-reference extractor based on cxref that collects all occurrences of non-local names, including the names of procedures, macros, typedefs, variables, and even the individual field names of structured types and variables.

3.2. Requirements on a Software Similarity Measure

In agreement with Tversky's work, we have identified the following requirements for a software similarity measure:

- *Matching*: Similarity must be a function of the features common to the two procedures, or distinctive to one or the other. It should not be a function of how many possible features are missing from both procedures.

- *Monotonicity*: Adding a common feature to two procedures must increase their similarity. Adding a distinctive feature to one of them must decrease similarity.

- The relative significance of two features must be independent of whether they are common or distinctive. As a whole, common features may be more or less significant than distinctive features, but individual variations are not permitted.

- The similarity between two procedures with no common features must be zero.

- **Exception**: Arch's actual similarity measure has an additional term representing whether or not one of the procedures calls the other. This term is ignored in the requirements above.

The following mathematical development, derived from Tversky's work, is not essential to understanding Arch. The uninterested reader may skip to section 4 without loss of continuity.

3.3. Matching and Monotonicity

Let $A,B,C,...$ be objects described by sets of features $a,b,c,...$, respectively. Each member of a feature set is the name of a characteristic that is true of the corresponding object. Then common and distinctive features are defined as:

$a \cap b$ The set of features that are common to A and B.

$a - b, b - a$ The sets of features that are distinctive to A or B, respectively.

A similarity function, SIM, has the *matching* property if there exists functions F and f such that

$$SIM(X,Y) = F(f(x \cap y), f(x - y), f(y - x))$$

This assures that the significance of a set of features occurring in one or both of the compared objects is computed without reference to whether the features are common or distinctive. It also assures that similarity is independent of any other features.

A similarity function, SIM has the *monotonicity* property if

$$SIM(A,B) \geq SIM(A,C)$$

whenever

$a \cap b \supseteq a \cap c,$
$a - c \supseteq a - b,$ and
$c - a \supseteq b - a$

and, furthermore, the inequality is strict whenever at least one of the set inclusions is proper.

Note that monotonicity is based only on the set inclusion ordering, and not on the number or weight of the features. Thus, mononicity does not by itself ensure that the more-similar-than relation is a total ordering.

3.4. Arch's Similarity Function

Tversky proposed two similarity functions that were intuitive, easy to compute, and satisfied the matching and monotonicity properties. One of them, the Ratio Model, seems well suited to comparing procedures, because its value is zero in the absence of shared features. Arch's similarity function, although developed independently, has a nearly identical form. First we describe its components:

86

268

$$w_x > 0 \qquad \textit{weight of feature } x$$

$$W(X) = \sum_{x \in X} w_x \qquad \textit{Weight of } X$$

$$Linked(S,N) = \begin{cases} 1, & \textit{if A calls B or B calls A} \\ 0, & \textit{otherwise} \end{cases}$$

The weight of a feature is a positive, real number representing its importance, relative to other features. The weight used is the same whether the feature is common or distinctive. Although Tversky's theory permits other aggregate weight functions, we have found the linear sum to be sufficient. The predicate *Linked* is needed because caller-callee relationships must be considered in module formation, in addition to information sharing. Observations of real software confirm that small procedures with few non-local identifiers in them are frequently grouped with their callers.

The similarity function used in Arch is defined as follows:

$$Sim(A,B) =$$

$$\frac{W(a \cap b) + k \times Linked(S,B)}{n + W(a \cap b) + d \times (W(a-b) + W(b-a))}$$

Notes:

- All coefficients are non-negative.

- Only shared and distinctive features count. The similarity of two procedures is not affected by adding unrelated declarations (features) to the program.

- Similarity increases with shared features and decreases with distinctive features. The constant d controls the relative importance of common and distinctive features.

- If there are no common features, and neither procedure calls the other, similarity is zero.

- The constant n controls normalization. For example, if n is 0, then all similarities are normalized between 0 and 1 (ignoring the *Linked* term). However, if n is large, then similarities are not normalized. The similarity of two objects with identical feature sets X would then be

$$\frac{W(X) + k \times Linked(X,X)}{n + W(X)}$$

showing that objects with large numbers of features could be more similar to other objects than could objects with few features.

- $Sim(A,B) = Sim(B,A)$

We are still left with the problem of how to assign weights to the features, and values to k, n and d. Ideally, the heavily-weighted features would be the names corresponding to hidden design decisions.

However, we have no direct way of determining which identifiers should be hidden. Our early attempts gave all features the same weight, but found that frequently-occurring features dominated our classifier's performance, and rare features were ignored. More recently, we have been estimating the significance of a feature by its Shannon information content:

$$Weight(f) = -log(Probability(f))$$

where the probability of f is the fraction of all procedures that have feature f. This gives rarely-used indentifiers higher weights than frequently-used identifiers, in keeping with the idea that rare names are more likely to be hidden in modules than frequently-used ones.

To date, we have selected values for k, n, and d by trial and error. In a later section we will describe how we will compute them automatically in the future.

4. Re-Engineering Software Modularity

Re-engineering modularity includes both discovering the latent structure of existing code, and changing that structure to obtain better modularity. Arch supports three different (although overlapping) styles of re-engineering work:

- Incremental change: the software is already organized into high-quality modules. The architect wishes to identify individual weak points in the architecture, and repair them by making small changes.

- Moderate reorganization: although the sofware is already organized into modules, their quality is suspect. The architect wishes to reorganize the code into new modules, but with an eye to preserving whatever is still good from the old modularity.

- Radical (re)organization: Either the software has never been modularized, or the existing modules are useless. The architect wishes to organize the software without reference to any previous organization.

Arch supports these activities with two kinds of intelligent advice: *clustering* and *maverick analysis*. To simplify their description, we first introduce some terminology.

4.1. Clustering and Reclustering

These services organize procedures into a subsystem hierarchy, by hierarchical agglomerative clustering. They can be run in batch or interactively, and can use a pre-existing modularization to reduce the amount of human interaction needed. The architect uses the resulting categories as proposals for new modules.

87

The basic clustering algorithm is called *hierarchical, agglomerative clustering* [4]. It proceeds as follows:

Place each procedure in a group by itself
Repeat
    Identify the two most similar groups
    Combine them
until
    the existing groups are satisfactory

The resulting groups are then used to define the memberships of modules.

Similarity between groups is defined by a *group similarity measure*, of which we are experimenting with several. Termination may be based on computed criteria or on the architect's judgment.

Arch supports three variations on this algorithm:

- Batch clustering: the algorithm runs without supervision. Each *combine* operator makes a supergroup out of the two groups it is combining, creating a completely binary tree of groups. Then it heuristically eliminates "useless" groups to create a wider, shallower tree. (Cf. [5]) This variation has the weakness that mistakes early in the clustering process cause the final results to diverge widely from what the architect would like.

- Interactive, radical clustering: this algorithm repeatedly selects pairs of groups to combine but asks for confirmation from the architect before combining them. When accepting a pair to combine, the architect can either merge the two groups, or make a supergroup out of them. When the architect disagrees, the tool notes the pair of groups that was rejected, and never again tries to combine exactly that pair. Instead, it selects the next-most-similar pair of groups.

- Interactive reclustering: this method uses a previous classification to guide the clustering. It starts by noting the original module in which each procedure was located. Then, when it has selected two new groups to merge, it first checks whether their members were all in the same module previously. If so, it combines them without asking the architect. If they originated from different modules, the tool asks the architect, who can accept or reject the proposal, or set aside one or both of the groups for classification later.

4.2. Group Similarity Measures

An earlier version of the Arch clustering algorithm used a similarity measure based on information loss [5]. The same measure was used for individual procedures and for groups. However, it relied on

characteristic properties of the group as a whole. This strategy is not always appropriate for combining groups that represent software modules. For example, sometimes only a handful of the procedures in a module share design information with the procedures in another module. Furthermore, the similarity measure we are using cannot be directly generalized to groups without computing group centroids, which would not be appropriate because of wide variation among the features of group members. Therefore, we are using aggregate measures based on pairwise comparisons of all members of two groups. The most promising of these is:

Single-link group similarity: The similarity between two groups is the maximum similarity between any pair of group members (one from each group).

4.3. Good and Bad Neighbors

The following definitions, although not profound, are very useful for discussing comparisons among procedures and across module boundaries:

Subject: A procedure that is being compared to several other procedures, for purposes of clustering or classification.

Neighbor: A neighbor of a subject is any procedures with which it has at least one common feature.

Good Neighbor: A subject's good neighbors are those neighbors that belong to the same module as it does.

Bad Neighbor: A subject's bad neighbors are those that belong to different modules than it does.

4.4. Maverick Analysis

A *maverick* is a misplaced procedure. Arch detects potential mavericks by finding each procedure's most similar neighbors, and noticing which modules they belong to.

More formally,

Maverick: A procedure for which the majority of its k nearest neighbors are bad neighbors.

We found that simply looking at the nearest neighbor was not sufficient, because sometimes it is the neighbor that is the maverick and not the subject itself. In this case, the second and third nearest neighbors will likely be in the same module, so setting k to 3 has proved satisfactory. However, there is nothing magic about the three nearest neighbors; one could also examine a larger neighborhood.

Since a maverick list can potentially be quite large, Arch prioritizes each mavericks by its similarity to its nearest bad neighbor, and presents them "worst first".

88

4.5. Tuning and User-Defined Features

When the architect disagrees with Arch's findings, she can tune the similarity function to remove the disagreement. One way of doing so is to "bias" some of the feature weights, supplying a multiplier to factor into the Shannon-derived weight. She can also provide biases for feature types, such as macronames, type-names, "called-by" features, and so on.

Sometimes, the available features simply cannot adequately explain the architect's decision. The architect could, for example, put together two procedures that have no common features, because they use the same algorithm. In this case the architect can define a new feature name representing the abstract property that the procedures share, and assign that feature to all the procedures known to have that property.

5. Practical Results

We have used Arch to critique the modularity of five software systems. These informal experiments have taken place over an 18-month period, and so each used Arch at a somewhat different level of ability. However, together they show that Arch gives valuable advice in real maintenance situations.

5.1. Systems Studied

The systems were all written in C, ranging in size from 64-1100 procedures, spanning 7-75 modules. Types of systems studied included experimental code, rapid prototype, carefully crafted product, and old, heavily abused code. Some of the code was still undergoing maintenance, while other code was abandoned. In every case we were able to consult code experts to assess the value of Arch's analysis.

5.2. Maverick Experiments

Experiments on four systems, without tuning, flagged 10-30% of the procedures as mavericks. Of these, 20-50% were symptoms of real modularization errors in the code. Types of errors encountered included:

- A module that had been split into two without regard to information hiding.

- Modules that were "temporarily" split during development, and never put back together.

- Procedures that combined two very different kinds of functionality, each belonging to a different module. (These procedures were all written by the same rogue programmer!)

- An "unformed module": functionality scattered throughout the system that should have been collected into a single, new module.

- Pairs of procedures, in different modules, that performed exactly the same function on slightly different data structures.

- Programming bugs such as using the wrong global variable, or omitting a required procedure call.

- Code fragments that had been copied many times rather than making a procedure or macro out of them.

- A data abstraction that was violated by outside procedures accessing record fields directly.

- An incomplete data abstraction, missing some the access procedures needed to hide its implementation.

- Mistakes left over from a previous reorganization.

- Three small, closely related modules that should have been merged.

- Unused procedures.

5.3. Clustering

Clustering experiments have been more limited, because clustering systems containing large numbers of undetected mavericks is laborious. However, we have run the batch clustering algorithm on its own code. It contained 64 procedures, in seven modules. The clustering process required 56 choices (to reduce 64 groups to 7). We convened a panel of three architects, all familiar with the code, to review the outcome.

Forty of the choices the algorithm made combined groups whose members had originally been in the same module. Sixteen choices combined procedures originating in different modules. *However*, the panel agreed that 10 of the 16 decisions were correct! That is, when Arch disagreed with the original modularity, it was correct more often than not.

Next, we tried to determine how much improvement could be obtained by hand tuning. The experimenter made modest adjustment to 8 of the feature weights (there were 80 features), such that rerunning the clustering algorithm achieved complete agreement between the tool and the panel of experts.

5.4. Hand Tuning

For one of the systems we studied, the architect investigated each maverick that Arch reported, and decided whether a code change to eliminate the maverick would be appropriate. He then took his analysis to the system's maintainer, who validated the results. Next, he hand-tuned Arch's similarity measure, by biasing the weights of some features, and adding some user-defined features, so as to minimize the number of mavericks that were not symptoms of harmful information sharing between modules. The results are summarized in the following table. The full study is reported separately [6].

89

Modules	27		
Procedures	300		
Mavericks	51		
	Before	After	Tuning
Legitimate	18	13	
False Alarm	33	10	

Hand tuning consisted essentially of biasing 8 features, adding 5 user-defined features, and removing two anomalous procedures from the analysis.

5.5. Discussion

In every case, maverick analysis turned up significant problems with the modularity of existing software. Although one might question the ratio of identified mavericks to real problems, enough real problems were detected to justify further research and development. The clustering experiment, although limited, indicated that clustering is a viable means for proposing a substantial reorganization of a subsystem. Hand-tuning the similarity measure, and adding a few user-defined features, significantly improved agreement between Arch and the architect. However, the tuning process is difficult and unenlightening. The next section describes the automatic tuning method we are developing to replace hand-tuning.

6. Automatic Tuning

The automatic tuning method is based on the expectation that a procedure will be more similar to other procedures in the same module than to procedures in different modules. For each procedure in the system, it identifies the five (more generally, k) nearest good neighbors, and compares each of them to each of the procedure's bad neighbors. Its goal is to minimize the frequency with which a bad neighbor is more similar to a subject procedure than one of the subject's five nearest good neighbors. It achieves this goal by repeatedly examining each of the possible combinations of a subject, a good neighbor, and a bad neighbor, and adjusting the weights (by gradient descent) to bring the good neighbor closer and push the bad neighbor farther away. Implementation details are described in a companion paper [7].

6.1. Learning Performance

Although we eventually hope to solve maintenance problems on the grand scale described earlier, we have been using a rather modest-sized problem for our early experiments. The code is real: it is an early version of Arch's batch clustering tool. It comprises 64 procedures, grouped into seven modules. Membership in the modules is distributed as follows:

```
# module

12 outputmgt
14 simwgts
10 attr
12 hac
 7 node
 4 objects
 5 massage
```

The sample problem has two parts:

1. Identify classification errors in the given data, and remove the offending procedures for reclassification later.

2. Learn a similarity measure, by training on the remaining procedures, that can be used to classify the procedures by the nearest-neighbor rule.

The software is written in C. Extracting cross-references produced 152 distinct feature names. However, many of these features occurred in only one procedure each, and were therefore greatly increasing the size of the problem without ever contributing to the similarity of two procedures. Therefore, we eliminated all such singly-occurring features, leaving 95.

We expected the code to contain modularization errors, being a rapid prototype. However, we wanted to create a "clean" data set for test purposes. Therefore, by a combination of logical and heuristic methods we identified and examined several possible errors. However, we did not remove a procedure from the data set unless we were convinced that it was *both* a true modularization error *and* an object that our method would not be able to adapt to. Twelve procedures were thus removed, leaving 52.

When trained on the remaining 52 procedures, the gradient descent algorithm successfully found weights for which every procedure was in the same module as its nearest neighbor. Therefore, we say that Arch "learned" a similarity measure that was adequate to explain the module membership of every procedure in the training data. The computation took about 10 minutes on a Sun Microsystems SPARCstation 1+.

6.2. Generalization Performance

Learning performance, by itself, is not the primary goal. Instead, the objective is to use the tuned similarity measure to check the module assignment of procedures that were not in the training data.

To test the network's generalization, we constructed a jacknife test, in which the 52 procedures were divided into a training set and a test set, to determine how well the tuned similarity measure would predict the module membership of procedures that were not in the training data. The test consisted of 13 experi-

90

ments, each using 48 procedures for training and 4 for testing, such that each procedure was used for testing exactly once. Each procedure was tested by using the similarity function to identify its nearest neighbor, and predicting that the tested procedure belonged to that neighbor's module.

The results of the jacknife test are shown in the table below. Each row gives the number of procedures that were in that module, and how many of them were classified into each module during the jacknife test.

```
actual     predicted
module   A  B   C  D   E  F
A 11    11
B 11        10  1
C  9             9
D  8                   8
E  7                      7
F  2                         2
```

Out of the 52 procedures in the data set, only one was misclassified!

Naturally, we will conduct more experiments, on other data sets, to better evaluate the usefulness of the tuned similarity measure If further experiments confirm these results, we will conclude that Arch's similarity function adequately measures similarity between procedures for the purpose of grouping procedures into modules.

6.3. Incremental Adaptation To The Architect

Next, we need a way to incorporate the automatic tuning method into the maverick analysis and clustering services. The difficulty lies in fitting the data too well. If Arch tunes the measure to precisely fit an existing system, the services will not suggest any changes!

Arch will overcome this problem by using only qualified data to tune the similarity function. The complete process will proceed something like this:

1. Arch identifies procedures that have no good neighbors at all, and presents them as mavericks. The architect must either agree that they are mavericks, set them aside for later analysis, or supply user-defined features that they share with other procedures in the same module.

2. Arch estimates the feature weights, without training, based on Shannon information content.

3. Arch creates an initial maverick list. Any procedure not appearing on the list is marked "qualified". Mavericks are marked "deferred".

4. Arch presents the mavericks to the architect, who may then either move a

maverick, defer deciding about it, or mark it as qualified to remain in its present module.

5. Each time the architect qualifies a maverick to remain where it is, Arch retrains its similarity measure, as described below.

Retraining:

1. Construct the training set using only qualified procedures as subjects and neighbors. Deferred procedures are excluded.

2. Bias the training toward subjects that are architect-approved as opposed to machine-approved, reflecting the higher level of confidence placed on them.

3. Use the Shannon-based feature weights as the starting point for training.

4. Stop the training when all the procedures are correctly classified.

5. Update the maverick list, rechecking all the deferred mavericks, and highlighting any additions.

6. If, after a reasonable time, training does not achieve completely correct classification, Arch will report the failure to the architect and request a user-defined feature to resolve the problem.

The net effect of this incremental learning process will be that Arch starts with a naive view of similarity based on the information hiding principle and Shannon information content, then gradually modifies this view to fit the architect's judgements, bending "just enough" to agree with the architect. The architect will not have to manually approve the procedures that the tool already agrees are classified correctly; she only needs to examine those that seem to be mavericks. Whenever she rejects a maverick, Arch revises its own maverick criteria, by tuning weights, and removes from the list any procedures that are no longer mavericks by the revised criteria.

7. Conclusions

From experiments with the basic advisory services and with the training system, we conclude that Arch's similarity measure is a useful model for the way that programmers judge similarity between procedures during modularization, and that the advisory services are promising tools for re-engineering software modularity.

8. Acknowledgements

Monica Hutchins designed and implemented the current Arch prototype, including inventing some graphical browsing capabilities that are very helpful for investigating mavericks. Ronald Lange contributed many implementation ideas, as well as thoroughly testing Arch and using it for a thorough case study. H. G. Tempel and Shuyuan Chen also explored significant design and implementation issues.

References

1. David L. Parnas, "Information Distribution Aspects of Design Methodology", *Information Processing 71*, North-Holland Publishing Company, 1972.

2. David L. Parnas, "On the Criteria To Be Used In Decomposing Systems Into Modules", Tech. report, Computer Science Department, Carnegie-Mellon University, August 1971.

3. Amos Tversky, "Features of Similarity", *Psychological Review*, Vol. 84, No. 4, July 1977.

4. Yoelle S. Maarek, *Using Structural Information for Managing Very Large Software Systems*, PhD dissertation, Technion -- Israel Institute of Technology, January 1989.

5. Robert W. Schwanke and Michael A. Platoff, "Cross References Are Features", *Second International Workshop on Software Configuration Management*, ACM Press, November 1989, also available as SigPlan Notices, November 1989

6. Ronald Lange and Robert W. Schwanke, "Software Architeture Analysis: A Case Study", *Third International Workshop on Software Configuration Management*, ACM Press, June 1991.

7. Robert W. Schwanke and Stephen José Hanson, "Using Neural Networks to Modularize Software", Tech. report, Siemens Corporate Research, Inc., September 1990, Submitted to *Machine Learning*

92

A Program Transformation Approach to Automating Software Re-engineering

Scott Burson, Gordon B. Kotik and Lawrence Z. Markosian

Reasoning Systems, Inc.
3260 Hillview Avenue
Palo Alto, CA 94304

Abstract

We describe a new approach to software re-engineering that combines several technologies: object-oriented databases integrated with parsers for capturing the software to be re-engineered; specification and pattern languages for querying and analyzing a database of software; and transformation rules for automatically generating re-engineered code. We present a program transformation system, REFINE™, that incorporates these and other technologies within an integrated environment for software re-engineering. Finally, we present examples of how our approach has been applied to re-engineering software in a variety of languages.

1   Overview

Eighty percent of programming resources are allocated to maintaining and re-engineering existing code, not to developing new applications [3]. The need for specialized re-engineering and maintenance tools is driven by the need to analyze and understand a large body of existing code and then modify it so that it conforms to new requirements. The existing code may be written in old languages or dialects, may run on obsolete hardware, or may use an old database management system instead of a modern relational one that may be more appropriate.

Development of new software requires traditional CASE tools such as incremental compilers, interpreters, diagrammers, simulators and code generators. Re-engineering, on the other hand, requires tools that capture, analyze and transform existing code. This paper describes a CASE approach to automating maintenance and re-engineering that applies, in a novel way, new and traditional computer science technologies to these problems. Our approach uses

- object-oriented databases integrated with LALR parsing technology to capture and represent software as annotated abstract syntax trees stored in a database;

- a program specification and pattern matching capability to describe and analyze software once it is in the database; and

- program transformation rules to automatically perform large-scale modifications to the software.

Typical analysis and transformation tasks might include the following:

- Analysis: What parts of my C program might behave differently when ported to a new platform? What datasets are input or output by which COBOL programs in my JCL code?

- Transformation: Make the necessary changes to parts of my C program so it will compile on a small computer. Change a program so that I can use the new X window system instead of OldWindows.

Programmers currently store software in text files and and apply text-oriented tools to these files in order to address analysis and transformation problems. Examples of these text-oriented tools are editors and string search and replace utilities [2]. The string search utilities generally pattern-match text strings against regular expressions that define the target pattern.

While the string-based facilities provide an improvement over visual search and manual replacement, they do not directly support analysis based on the syntax and semantics of the programming language. In addition, they do not support automatic transformation of complete programs.

This paper presents an approach to machine capture, analysis and transformation that significantly extends the opportunity for automating maintenance and re-engineering. This approach is centered on:

1. an object-oriented database instead of text files to capture existing software;

2. data definition and query languages that support program analysis;

3. syntactic pattern-matching against program templates expressed largely in the target language (instead of matching text strings against regular expressions);

4. program transformation rules that automatically modify existing code or generate new code.

To integrate this approach with existing file-based storage of software, tools are needed for parsing source files into the database and printing the database back to source files. To facilitate program analysis, the data definition and query languages should support the mathematical abstractions used in high-level descriptions of programs (set notation, first order logic, tree comparison). Pattern matching and transformation are actually performed on the (annotated) abstract syntax of the software, which reflects program structure. Thus the purpose of the object-oriented database is to represent the abstract syntax of the programs, together with any additional information needed for analysis. Sophisticated analysis and code generation tools such as compilers must create their own abstract syntax trees (ASTs) from the text file representation of programs. Our approach facilitates development of comparably sophisticated program analysis and manipulation tools for re-engineering by using an object-oriented database to represent ASTs. The approach is implemented in RE-FINE, a toolset for software re-engineering.

The approach described in this paper builds on the experience of other systems. Lisp programming environments have been built around a representation for Lisp programs as list structures stored in virtual memory. The prime example is the Interlisp programming environment [8]. Interlisp provided software analysis tools, including Masterscope, an interactive query system. Language-based environments introduced the idea of building general programming environments that could be customized to a particular programming language [7]. Smalltalk-80 compilers represent parse trees using instances of Smalltalk objects [4, 5].

Section 2 examines the REFINE-based approach to re-engineering. Section 3 considers actual applications of the approach. Section 4 provides a summary and conclusion.

2 The REFINE toolset for software re-engineering

The objective of the REFINE [1] toolset is to provide a foundation for rapid development of automated, language-specific and even application-specific re-engineering capabilities. Language-specific tools are needed because there are many tasks common to representing and analyzing software in a particular language. Such tasks include parsing, control and data flow analysis, pattern-matching and printing. Therefore language-specific tools are likely to be used regardless of the goals or details of the re-engineering task.

Language-specific tools alone cannot achieve a high level of automation in re-engineering, as large-scale re-engineering tasks require application-specific tools. For example, converting a C application containing one vendor's embedded SQL to another SQL may require analysis and modification of both the C and embedded SQL code to implement optimizations appropriate to the target dialect. The extent of the required optimizations will depend on the run-time characteristics of the SQL implementations and the C application, which may not be adequately understood until well into the project.

REFINE provides basic capabilities for representing software, together with generic tools and tool generators. The principal components of the REFINE toolset are:

- a very high level, executable specification language for describing and transforming software;

- an object-oriented database that provides the necessary abstractions for representing software and software-related objects; and

- a language processing system that accepts definitions of programming languages and produces language-specific tools.

Additionally, REFINE provides an X Windows-based graphics package that supports interactive displays of the contents of its database and the results of code analysis.

Programs are converted between source files and the object-oriented database using the parsers and printers created by the language processing system. The database is thereby integrated with conventional file-based systems and tools. The REFINE object system and other high-level data types in the specification language (sets, sequences, maps, etc.), support a data model for software objects that captures the standard conceptual view of annotated abstract syntax trees.

315

Tools that analyze and transform software in the database are written in the REFINE specification language, which provides mechanisms for template-based program description and rule-based program transformation.

Figure 1 indicates how REFINE components can be used in software maintenance.

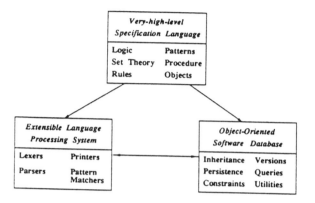

Figure 1: REFINE Components

2.1 The REFINE specification language

The REFINE language supports a variety of specification techniques including set theory, first order logic, rules, object-oriented and procedural programming. The specification language is also used as the query/update language for the database. The compiler for the specification language is implemented as a rule-based program transformation system. The compiler and most of the rest of REFINE are written in this specification language.

Use of the specification language shortens and simplifies program analysis functions. Examples are provided in Section 3.

2.2 Object-oriented database

The REFINE database provides persistent storage of software and software-related objects. It provides mechanisms for version control, concurrency control for multiple users, computed attributes, and constraint maintenance. The database is integrated with the language

processing system (described below) and is used to store software in the form of annotated abstract syntax trees. It is customizable by the user for specific languages and applications. In a typical software re-engineering application, the developer will use an existing domain model or define one for the language of the source code to be re-engineered and for the target language if different from the source. The example in Figure 2 shows the definition of a domain model for a simple numerical expression language.

```
class EXPR
    subclass-of USER-OBJECT
    attributes
        TEST-SUCCEEDED?: boolean

class NUMERAL-EXPR
    subclass-of EXPR
    attributes
        MAGNITUDE: integer

class SUBTRACTION-EXPR
    subclass-of EXPR
    attributes
        MINUEND: EXPR SUBTRAHEND: EXPR

class MULTIPLICATION-EXPR
    subclass-of EXPR
    attributes
        FACTORS: seq(EXPR)
```

Figure 2: Domain model for Numerical Expression Language (NEL)

Object classes have been defined to model the non-terminals of the language such as expressions. The slots (called attributes in REFINE) model those properties of the non-terminals that are of interest, for example, for parsing, printing, and analysis. The REFINE database is customizable: the user can define domain models for the languages of interest or extend existing language domain models (for example, by adding attributes that annotate the abstract syntax tree). REFINE provides utilities for traversing abstract syntax trees stored in the database.

2.3 Language processing system

The REFINE language processing system takes as input a description of a language in the form of a grammar. It produces a parser, printer, pattern-matcher and mouse-sensitive text browser for the language. Figure 3 is a grammar for the numerical expression language whose domain model was specified in the previous section.

316

```
grammar NEL-GRAMMAR
  productions
    SUBTRACTION-EXPR ::=
      [ MINUEND "-" SUBTRAHEND ]
      builds SUBTRACTION-EXPR,
    TIMES-EXPR ::=
      [ FACTORS ++ "*" ]
      builds TIMES-EXPR,
    NUMERAL-EXPR ::= [MAGNITUDE]
      builds NUMERAL-EXPR
  precedence
    for EXPR brackets "(" matching ")"
      (same-level "-" associativity left),
      (same-level "*" associativity left)
  end
```

Figure 3: Grammar for NEL

Grammars are written using a high-level syntax description language that includes

- regular right-part operators for productions;

- precedence tables;

- semantic actions for productions; and

- a mechanism for specifying lexical analyzers.

These capabilities reduce the need for recursive productions and shorten and increase the readability of the grammar specification. A key component of the language processing sysetm is an LALR(1) parser generator. In addition, REFINE provides a capability for defining program templates. These templates can be used:

- in pattern matching, to test whether an existing program is an instance of a template, and

- in pattern instantiation, to build a new program that is an instance of the template.

Typically pattern matching is done during analysis — for example, to detect code that must be altered; pattern instantiation is then performed to generate the modified code. Usually pattern matching is combined with semantic program analyses that exercise the full REFINE specification capability.

The additional production rules needed for parsing program templates are added automatically to the user-specified grammar by the language processing system. Compiling the NEL grammar shown in Figure 3 allows examples of program templates from the example language NEL in Figure 4 to be parsed into abstract syntax

trees, and allows the trees to be printed as text. Figure 4 also shows examples of program templates from the example language NEL that are accepted by the parser. Templates are delimited by single quotes.

NEL expressions	Templates for NEL expressions
(a) 2 * 3 - 4 * 5	'@x - @y' matches (a, c)
(b) 2 * (3 - 4) * 5 * 12	'.. * 5' matches (b)
(c) 2 * 3 - (4 * 5)	'@@ - 4 * 5' matches (c)

Figure 4: Examples

The language processing system has been used to build software management and re-engineering tools for a number of languages, including REFINE itself, Ada, C, COBOL, IBM JCL, SQL, NATURAL and SDL. These tools have in turn been used for applications including automated software maintenance, re-engineering, code generation and program verification.

3 Examples

Several examples have been selected to illustrate the application of the database/transformational approach to software re-engineering. Each of these example applications was developed quickly once the required language was modeled and its syntax defined. The syntax definitions were generally derived from a standard published language grammar. The primary technical reason for the speed of development is that we used the very high level language features of REFINE, which allowed us to express concepts about software declaratively. The RE-FINE compiler then automatically generated code that implemented analysis tools based on these concepts.

3.1 Analysis Examples

An abstract syntax-based representation of software for analysis is commonly used in modern approaches to software engineering. Most software analysis tools build such a model as a preliminary phase to the actual analysis phase. Perry summarizes some of the important uses of abstract syntax trees analysis in software development in [6]. The analysis capabilities and applications described here can be regarded as extensions of

317

these common analyses in that they take advantage of the novel features of the database model of software.

The analysis problem addressed in this example is portability of a C program. The C language does not specify the order of evaluation of arguments in function calls. Thus, if a function call has two or more arguments, one of which is a side-effecting expression, the program behavior may differ with different C compilers. Our objective was to analyze programs for this potential portability problem. Our approach was to use a complete language model and syntax for ANSI C that had already been defined in REFINE, and to write program specifications that would identify suspect function calls.

The rule **Analyze-Function-Call** applies the test to an object in the database and if the test succeeds, puts the function call in a set of program expressions for later examination by the user or for further automated analysis.

```
Rule Analyze-Function-Call (node)
  node = '#E @@($args)' &
  num-args = size(args) &
  num-args > 1 &
  se1 in [1 .. num-args] &
  ~ Pure(args(se1))
-->
  node in *suspect-nodes*
```

The function **Pure** returns **True** if its argument is a non-side-effecting expression. It is defined recursively with a number of base cases, several of which are shown in the following partial definition:

```
Pure function(expr: expression) : boolean
  computed-using
    Literal(expr) or
    Identifier-reference(expr) or
    (expr = '#E @base[@offset]' &
       Pure(base) & Pure(offset)) or
    (expr = '#E @func($args)' &
       Pure(func) &
       for-all(arg)(arg in args =>
         Pure(arg))) or ...
```

We note several points about these analysis functions. First, they are largely declarative specifications, using set-theoretic data types (sequences and sets) and first order logic, including quantifiers. The functions contain no implementation details. Second, where appropriate, they use program templates for pattern matching and pattern variable binding.

For example, the template '#E @func($args)' is used to test whether **expr** is an expression that is a function

call. **#E** is part of the pattern syntax that asserts that what follows is an expression.

If the pattern match succeeds, the pattern variables **func** and **args** are appropriately bound and further tests are made to determine whether they are non-side-effecting.

3.2 Dataflow analysis of IBM JCL

The motivation for this example was the need to maintain applications controlled by IBM Job Control Language (JCL). Both the applications and the JCL code itself were undocumented and the authors unavailable. The initial problem faced by anyone maintaining or modifying such code is to understand dataflow among the programs and datasets referenced by the JCL. This section discusses a REFINE application that provides a facility for parsing and analyzing programs written in JCL under the VM and MVS operating systems on a wide range of IBM mainframes. The complete application includes the following components:

- a domain model that specifies the classes of syntactic objects in JCL source code and the relations among them;

- a grammar for parsing and printing JCL source files;

- a data flow analysis tool; and

- code to display, using the REFINE user interface tools, the abstract syntax and surface syntax of a JCL source file as well as the results of the data flow analysis.

The remainder of this section focuses on the REFINE code for the first three of these components. A screen dump is included to illustrate the use of the fourth.

Domain model: The domain model includes an object class for each non-terminal of the JCL language. The model forms a hierarchy under the **subclass** relation. At the top of the hierarchy is **JCL-OBJECT**. Part of the hierarchy is shown in Figure 5.

Each class in the hierarchy has one or more attributes (slots), which are expressed as mappings in REFINE. The domain of an attribute map is the object class for which it is defined, and the range is either an object class or data type. The attributes of the **DD-STATEMENT** class are inherited from **STATEMENT**, of which it is a subclass:

```
stmnt-name:  map(statement,
general-identifier)
```

318

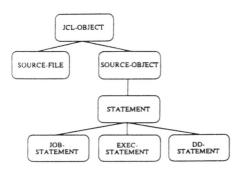

Figure 5: JCL Hierarchy

```
stmnt-parameters: map(statement,
seq(non-null-parameter))
```

REFINE allows an object class to have attributes that are not used for parsing or printing. Such attributes can be used by analysis functions. For example, following parsing, the JCL code might be analyzed to determine, for each statement, the number of parameters it contains. This value could be held in the attribute parameter-count:

```
parameter-count: map(statement, integer)
```

Those attributes of an object class that are used to define the abstract syntax tree are asserted to be **tree attributes**, as in the following example:

```
define-tree-attributes(DD-statement,
{'stmnt-name, 'stmnt-parameters})
```

REFINE provides database utility functions that traverse and otherwise manipulate database structures for which a tree structure is defined.

Grammar: Once the abstract syntax for a language has been captured in a domain model, a surface syntax can be defined. REFINE provides several tools for defining the surface syntax. For JCL, a customized lexical analyzer was necessary. The lexical analyzer returns the token "˜statement˜" whenever it detects a statement number. A parser for JCL was also necessary. REFINE provides a regular right-part production language for defining LALR(1) grammars. The following production defines the surface syntax for the JCL DD statement:

```
DD-statement ::= [ "˜statement˜" { stmnt-name }
"DD"stmnt-parameters*"," ]
```

```
// acc008   JOB  (acc001,nwdata),prty=8
//step1    exec pgm=demo010,region=1024k,time=2
//steplib  dd   dsn=demo1.scott.prodlib,disp=shr
//in1      dd   dsn=demo1.scott.data1,disp=shr
//out1     dd   dsn=demo1.scott.data2,disp=(new,catlg,catlg),dcb=(lrecl=80,blksiz
//out2     dd   dsn=demo1.scott.data3,disp=(new,catlg,catlg),dcb=(lrecl=80,blksiz
//step2    exec pgm=demo020,region=512k,time=1
//steplib  dd   dsn=demo1.scott.prodlib,disp=shr
//in1      dd   dsn=demo1.scott.data2,disp=shr
//in2      dd   dsn=demo1.scott.data1,disp=(shr,delete)
//out1     dd   dsn=demo1.scott.data4,disp=(new,catlg,catlg),dcb=(lrecl=80,blksiz
```

Figure 6: JCL Example

This production says that a DD-statement is of the following form: the keyword "˜statement˜" (returned by the lexical analyzer) optionally followed by the name of the statement followed by the keyword "DD" followed by the statement parameters. If there are more than one statement parameter, they are separated by commas. Since **stmnt-parameters** is defined in the domain model as a sequence of non-null-parameter objects, a (separate) production rule must be included in the grammar for printing instances of the non-null-parameter class. The "[" and "]" that enclose the right part of the production rule for the DD-statement require that each of the items within the square brackets must appear (except for the optional items), and they must appear in the order indicated. The "{" and "}" notation indicates that the enclosed item(s) are optional and may appear in any order.

REFINE also provides mechanisms for defining operator precedence and non-standard semantics for a language. Use of these mechanisms, plus the "*" and related notation used in other rules, simplifies the grammar definition and avoids the need for most recursive productions.

When the grammar definition is compiled, REFINE generates a parser, printer and pattern matcher for the language. Figure 6 contains an example of JCL code that can be read into the REFINE object-oriented database, together with a diagram of the abstract syntax of the sample.

Data flow analysis: The data flow analyzer uses both the REFINE language and the pattern-matching capability. For example, one analysis step to be performed is to determine whether a particular JCL statement is a DD statement. This condition can be expressed as follows:

```
stmnt = '//@ddnameDDdsn=@dsname, .. ,
disp=@displst, ..'
```

The above expression can be used to test, or pattern-match, the value of stmnt against the program template on the right side of the equality. The match succeeds if the following conditions are met:

- stmnt is a statement
- stmnt is a DD statement

319

- **stmnt** has a **DSN** and

- **stmnt** has a **DISP**.

If the match succeeds, the REFINE pattern variable **DDNAME** is bound to the name of the statement, **DSNAME** is bound to the DSN parameter list, and **DISPLST** is bound to the **DISP** parameter list. The program template is written primarily using the syntax of JCL, with the addition of the syntax for REFINE pattern variables (the @ followed by the name of a REFINE variable).

3.3 Program Transformation Examples

These examples focus on perhaps the most novel capability of the REFINE system, specifying and automatically executing transformation rules that perform complex modifications to software. This is the heart of providing automation for software maintenance and re-engineering activities. The analysis activities discussed earlier are performed with the goal of determining where or how subsequent modifications to the software should be made.

3.3.1 Porting C Applications to a Microcomputer

One common instance of non-portability in programs written in *portable* languages is the syntax of identifiers. For example, in the C language, newer implementations for engineering workstations usually allow identifiers to be more than eight characters long, but implementations for smaller machines often require identifiers to be eight characters or less. Therefore porting a C program to run on a small machine may require renaming all identifiers longer than eight characters to be shorter than eight characters.

This transformation is simple to describe and formalize, complicated to implement correctly using a text-based approach, but easy to implement using a transformation-rule based approach. In fact, a REFINE program that performs this program transformation correctly is about twenty lines long and easy to understand.

It is instructive to examine some of the complications that arise in performing this transformation using a text-based approach, because they are typical of problems that arise in performing non-trivial program manipulations on text strings.

- Lexical analysis: the text-based approach requires performing the equivalent of lexical analysis to de-termine which character string in the input file define tokens in the C language. The lexical analyzer must parse comments and string constants correctly so that they are not mis-identified as tokens.

- Identifying identifiers: the text-based approach requires that tokens that are identifiers be known, so that keywords in the language are not inadvertently renamed.

- Avoiding conflicts: the text-based approach requires keeping track of which identifiers (both original and shortened) have been encountered so far, to avoid creating a name conflict arising from C's scoping rules.

Getting all the details correct using this approach will take time and experimentation. The program will duplicate many of the analyses performed by a C compiler during parsing, breaking the input into tokens, performing lexical scope analysis, etc. On the other hand, the REFINE program that performs the same task has none of these problems. The C program stored in the database embodies the results of syntactic and static semantic analysis.

Here is the REFINE rule that forms the heart of the required program transformation:

```
rule rename-long-identifier (id)      % The input to
  % the rule is an object "id"

identifier(id) &                      % If id is an
  % instance of the class "identifier"

length(name(id)) > *max-id-length*    % and id's
  % name is longer than the limit

  -->                                 % then

new-name = make-new-name(id) &        % generate a
  % new name called "new-name"

name(id) = new-name &                 % rename the
  % identifier id to new-name, and

(ref in identifier-references(id)     % for each
   % occurrence of the id in the program

  --> name(ref) = new-name)           % rename it
  % to preserve consistency.
```

The REFINE code that applies this transformation to an entire C program is:

```
preorder-transform(my-program,
['rename-long-identifier])
```

320

which can be read as "traverse the tree rooted at the object **my-program**, applying the rule rename-long-identifier at each object in the tree".

A similar approach can be used to solve related problems that arise in software maintenance, such as the problem of merging two large programs written in a language that does not support any scoping mechanism for functions.

3.3.2 Converting between incompatible versions of a programming language

Two of the advantages of high-level languages over assembler and machine languages are portability and ease of integration. In theory, porting a program written in a high-level language to a different machine is easy if there exists a compiler for same language on the target machine; one simply recompiles the source code. Also, in theory, high-level languages make it easy to combine programs using mechanisms such as external subroutines.

In practice it is not that simple because popular high-level languages (e.g., FORTRAN and COBOL) have a maddening variety of dialects and versions that at least partially (and sometimes completely) remove the advantages mentioned above. Programs written in one dialect cannot be compiled with a compiler written for another dialect, and programs written in different dialects cannot necessarily call each others' routines. These incompatibilities between dialects introduce the need to convert programs among dialects in order to combine them and run them on different machines. Program transformation is often the most effective technology for automating these conversion processes, because the necessary changes are structural (rather than textual) in nature, and must be made pervasively across large bodies of application source code.

An example of such a conversion task arises in connection with the language NATURAL. NATURAL is a COBOL-like language used primarily for MIS applications. There are several versions of NATURAL on different machines with varying degrees of compatibility. In particular, there is a recent version (NATURAL 2.0) that runs almost identically on IBM mainframes and DEC equipment. The older and most widely used version for IBM mainframes is NATURAL 1.2, which is substantially incompatible with NATURAL 2.0. Thus customers must convert NATURAL 1.2 applications to NATURAL 2.0 and then recompile them in order to run them on DEC equipment.

A fully automated NATURAL 1.2 ⟶ 2.0 converter is currently under development using REFINE. Be-

Figure 7: NATURAL Conversion/Re-compilation Cycle

fore choosing REFINE, the customer investigated several strategies for conversion tools, including text-based approaches and approaches using YACC and C. The customer and Reasoning Systems jointly developed a prototype converter using REFINE in two weeks. The prototype included parser/printers for subsets of both NATURAL 1.2 and NATURAL 2.0, and transformation rules that handled several key incompatibilities between the two language versions. The prototype was able to completely convert several examples.

Below is an example conversion rule used in the NATURAL 1.2 ⟶ 2.0 prototype converter. This rule makes a conversion that is necessary because NATURAL 1.2 allows variables to be defined anywhere within a program, whereas NATURAL 2.0 requires that all variable definitions occur within a single **data definition** clause at the beginning of the program.

```
rule hoist-variable-definition (node)
variable(node) &
var-fmt = variable-format(node) &
*data-def-clause* = 'DEFINE DATA LOCAL
$old-defs END-DEFINE'

   -->

variable-format(node) = undefined &
new-var = make-variable(var-name, var-fmt) &
*data-def-clause* =
   'DEFINE DATA LOCAL $old-defs, @new-var END-DEFINE'
```

In this rule, the input node is first tested to see if it is an in-line variable declaration. If so, then **var-fmt** is set to the format of the inline declaration. Then (on the right hand side of the arrow), a new variable declaration **new-var** is created and added to the "data definition" clause *data-def-clause*. Also, the variable format of node is erased, effectively deleting node from the program.

4 Summary and conclusion

Software maintenance and re-engineering is characterized by an emphasis on analyzing and transforming existing software. This emphasis distinguishes re-engineering from forward engineering and demands a correspondingly different set of CASE tools.

321

We have described an approach to software maintenance and re-engineering based on object-oriented databases integrated with LALR parsing technology. Software is captured and represented as annotated abstract syntax trees that are stored in a database. Program specification and pattern matching capabilities are used to describe and analyze software once it is in the database. Program transformation rules automatically perform extensive modifications to the software.

We have described REFINE, an environment for program representation, analysis and transformation that provides the tools needed to implement the automation of software maintenance and re-engineering. The transformational approach has been illustrated with examples taken from actual experience in re-engineering software in C, JCL and NATURAL.

The ability to support automation in modifying large software systems by using rule-based program transformation is a key innovation of our approach that distinguishes it from tools that focus only on automation of program analysis. The approach has been validated by applications to software in a wide variety of languages .

References

[1] REFINE *User's Guide*. Reasoning Systems, Palo Alto, CA, 1985.

[2] AHO, A. V., KERNIGHAN, B. W., AND WEINBERGER, P. J. *The AWK Programming Language*. Addison-Wesley, Reading, MA, 1988.

[3] BOEHM, B. *Software Engineering Economics*. Prentice-Hall, Englewood Cliffs, N.J., 1981.

[4] GOLDBERG, A., AND ROBSON, D. *Smalltalk-80: The Language and its Implementation*. Addison-Wesley, 1983.

[5] GRAVER, R. J. J., AND ZURASKI, L. RTS: An optimizing compiler for Smalltalk. In *Proceedings of OOPSLA-88* (September, 1988), p. .

[6] PERRY, D. Software interconnection models. In *9th International Conference on Software Engineering* (Monterey, CA, March 30–April 2, 1987), pp. 106–116.

[7] REPS, T. W. *Generating Language-Based Environments*. MIT Press, 1984.

[8] TEITELMAN, W., AND MASINTER, L. The Interlisp programming environment. In *Interactive Programming Environments*, D. R. Barstow, H. E. Shrobe, and E. Sandewall, Eds., McGraw-Hill, 1984.

322

Chapter 7
Data Reengineering and Migration

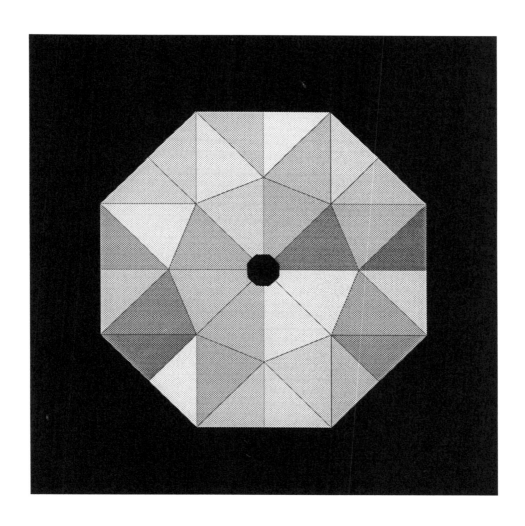

Chapter 7

Data Reengineering and Migration

Purpose

Data reengineering is one of the most important parts of reengineering. This chapter will help the reader understand

- Approaches for reengineering data and improving data bases,
- Experiences in using CASE tools to extract data models from source code,
- Approaches for migrating data on one DBMS to another DBMS, and
- Specific tools for helping perform data reengineering and migration.

Papers

The first paper, "Data Reengineering for Application Systems," by J. Ricketts, J. DelMonaco, and M. Weeks, is useful for those interested in the process of data reengineering. The authors discuss the data reengineering phases of code analysis, data analysis, metadata synthesis, redesign, revision, and definition exportation. They also discuss the differences between data reengineering and data engineering, and the types of data problems expected in reengineering.

In the next paper, "A Method for Data Re-Engineering in Structured Programs," A.R. Hevner and R.C. Linger describe a "box structure" approach to data engineering. In this approach, systems are described with box structures, and data is described with regular expressions. The results of the reengineering are the elimination of data flow anomalies, the reduction of data scope, and the construction of reusable data objects.

In the last paper, "From IMS or Non-IBM, the Move is on to DB2," B. Francett discusses data base migration, conversion, and bridging. She discusses the migration process and how some specific tools are used to assist the migration effort. Even though her discussion is in the context of migrating to IBM's DB2 data base management system, the discussion is still valuable for illustrating the ideas involved with data base migration in general.

Data Reengineering for Application Systems

J.A. Ricketts   J.C. DelMonaco   M.W. Weeks

Peat Marwick Advanced Technology
303 E. Wacker Drive
Chicago, IL 60601

Abstract

Reengineering of the data component of existing application systems can now be done with the aid of methods and software tools. Data reengineering extends the life of existing systems by standardizing data definitions and facilitating source code simplification. It also can provide an accurate data model for use as a starting point in data modeling, database technology migration, and as a preparation step for reverse engineering.

Introduction

Many information system departments are mired in maintenance of old application systems that are too important to discard, too costly to redevelop, and too fragile to ignore. When purchase of replacement packaged software is not appropriate, reengineering of existing systems improves the technical quality of old systems at a cost far below that of redevelopment. This can provide a sound, non-disruptive platform on which to base functional enhancements. Furthermore, the scope of reengineering continues to expand. Procedure reengineering has been automated for several years, and it is still evolving. Data reengineering is more recent, and it extends reengineering in another direction.

Data reengineering is important because data problems are widespread across installations and deeply rooted within systems. The development and maintenance history of data definitions for typical application systems is painfully familiar:

o Data elements, records, and files were created separately for each system, if not each program, and then integrated by force
o Data validation rules were embedded in non-shared procedures
o Naming conventions were non-existent or non-enforceable
o Dozens of programmers modified programs without knowing with certainty which other programs and files were affected

Consequently, the extent of data problems is staggering. Typical application portfolios contain hundreds of programs -- many of them over fifteen years old. Those programs contain thousands of data elements -- some redundant, inconsistent, or incomprehensible -- and millions of lines of code -- some obsolete, others erroneous.

Using computer-aided software engineering (CASE) tools can avoid data problems in new systems, but most tools are powerless to detect or correct data problems in old systems. Relocating poorly formed data definitions from source code to data dictionaries or data modeling tools may facilitate some manual corrections, but it also will perpetuate unrecognized problems.

Data reengineering can improve the maintainability of existing systems. Sankar, for example, reduced by 82% the data required for a government system by eliminating redundancy [14]. Bastani and Iyengar found that programs with fewer data structures were easier to comprehend [3]. Dunsmore and Gannon found that programs with fewer variables per statement were easier to modify [4].

This paper discusses data reengineering methods and tools, with emphasis on data definition reengineering. Comparisons are made between procedure and data reengineering, between data definition and data value reengineering, and between data reengineering and data engineering. Several cases of data definition reengineering are described.

Overview of Application Reengineering

Since it has been practiced longer, procedure reengineering is more familiar than data reengineering, but they are complementary. Today they differ in scope and degree of automation. Procedure reengineering is a program-level process that restructures control flows. Data reengineering is a system-level process that purifies data definitions and values. Procedure reengineering can be fully automated, whereas data reengineering can be partly automated [2].

Procedure reengineering establishes an overall architecture at the program level, transforms undesirable constructs (e.g., GOTOs and ALTERs) into desirable constructs (e.g., PERFORMs), and documents the source code for easier understanding of program control flow. Thus, when applied to COBOL, procedure reengineering affects mostly the PROCEDURE DIVISION. This process is also known as code restructuring, even though there may be little structure evident in the old program. (For a deeper discussion of this topic see [13].)

Data reengineering establishes meaningful, nonredundant data definitions and valid, consistent data values. To do this, data definitions and flows must be tracked through chains of programs and files. Analyses of Job Control Language (JCL) and source code (ENVIRONMENT, DATA, and PROCEDURE DIVISIONs) are always required. Sometimes, analysis of the actual contents of files is required, too. (For other discussions of this topic see [10] and [12].)

Data Problems

Data problems can be divided into two broad classes: data definition problems and data value problems. Though problems from one class rarely occur without problems from the other, the solutions are different enough to justify making the distinction. The focus of this paper is data definition reengineering because relevant software tools are now available. Data value reengineering is included for completeness, and as an indication of future research.

174

Data Definition Problems

Typical data definition problems include the following:

o Cryptic, inconsistent names. One program can have many names for the same element. A system can have even more. A classic example is ACCOUNT-NUMBER, ACCT-NUM, ACCT-NO, A-N, ACCT-ID, etc. Other elements may have the same name, but in fact be different elements. Furthermore, element names may not be descriptive of the actual contents of the elements.

o Inconsistent field lengths. Zip codes may be 5 digits in some instances, 9 in others. Dates may be 6 or 8 digits, depending on whether programmers anticipated the turn of the century.

o Inflexible field lengths. Critical fields need to be expandable as organizations grow. Total fields be should expandable with inflation. Yet neither happens often or easily when definitions are hard-coded in many places.

o Inconsistent record layouts. Named fields in one record may be FILLER in another. Some record definitions may be longer than others for the same record type. Some records define a series of bytes as a single field, while others define those bytes as several fields.

o Hard-coded literals. Literal values sprinkled through PROCEDURE DIVISIONs are difficult to change correctly and impossible to audit. Declaring named constants and condition names in the DATA DIVISION can solve both problems.

o Non-existent, incomplete, or inaccurate data dictionary. When no data dictionary exists, examination of source code is necessary, but laborious and error-prone. When data dictionaries are incomplete or inaccurate (as they often are when manually loaded from old systems), data problems are relocated, but not solved.

Another way to view data definition problems is by their effects on development and maintenance:

o Adding a new field or expanding the size of an existing one can require updating hundreds of programs and converting dozens of files. Identifying those programs and files is difficult, but implementing the changes can be a multi-year, multi-million dollar project. Part of the difficulty arises from hidden data flows. Aliases, synonyms, and homonyms mask data flows within and between programs.

o Lack of auditability causes risk for the organization, its employees, and its customers or clients. Improper alteration or disclosure of data, whether unauthorized or inadvertent, exposes these parties to potential harm.

o When new systems have been developed with CASE tools, but old systems exhibit data problems, the value of those CASE tools is diminished unless the new and old systems can be maintained separately. However, separate maintenance is often undesirable, even when technically feasible.

Data Value Problems

Typical data value problems include the following:

o Inconsistent default values. The default value of a field may be spaces in one program, zeros in another, and low values in yet another. Record selection based on one of these values will not select the others. Likewise, tallying all of them will create multiple subtotals where there should be only one.

o Lack of distinction between valid and missing values. When zero is both a valid value and the missing-value indicator, two conditions that ought to be distinguishable are not. The same situation arises with spaces.

o Negative values in fields that should always be non-negative. Issuing invoices or credit memos for negative amounts is wasteful and embarrassing.

o Negative values become positive values when signs are omitted. Reflecting negative values into the positive domain grossly distorts true distributions. Of course, incrementing a field when it should be decremented leads to ever-increasing values.

o Truncation of most-significant digits. Undetected overflow can create spuriously low values.

o Inconsistent units. Confusing dollars and pounds, or ounces and pounds, leads to nonsense results that may be overlooked if they seldom occur or are in masses of data.

o Text values stored in mixed case, but tests presume upper case. Valid records may be erroneously rejected or may inappropriately receive default processing.

o Changes to data validation rules are not propagated to static or historical files. Since these file types are not updated routinely, they are easy to overlook.

Data Reengineering versus Data Engineering

Data reengineering and data engineering are related, but different. Table 1 compares them in general terms. While data reengineering is concerned more with existing systems, and data engineering more with prospective systems, harmony between existing and prospective systems is achievable. Data engineering can be based on information gathered

TABLE 1.

	Data Reengineering	Data Engineering
Orientation	Old systems	New systems
Frequency	Once for each system	Continuous process
Coverage	Data definitions Data values	Data definitions
Approaches	Fully manual Semi-automatic	Cold start Warm start
Effects	Old systems become more maintainable and more compatible with new ones	New systems provide better data initially and are more maintainable

175

during data reengineering, then the transformed data model can be propagated throughout the old systems. Thereafter, a unified data model is shared by old and new systems, and the old versus new dichotomy is much less significant.

Data reengineering normally gets done just once for each system, but data engineering should be an on-going process. Data reengineering covers both definitions and actual values (because the two are seldom in agreement), while data engineering covers just definitions (because actual values are enforced in systems developed with the revised definitions).

The manual approach to data reengineering is typically limited to a few critical master files. In contrast, the semi-automated approach can address entire systems, faster and more thoroughly than the manual approach. Thoroughness is a critical success factor since overlooked data definitions are a major cause of data problems.

Although each can be done by itself, data reengineering is a desirable precursor to data engineering. A cold start to data engineering occurs when data administrators must develop their models from scratch, without benefit of reengineering. In contrast, a warm start occurs when the results of data reengineering are fed into data engineering so that data administrators have an accurate model of existing systems from which to begin their work. A warm start prevents old systems from becoming more isolated and obsolete as new ones are built. At the same time, it usually provides a better foundation for data engineering than a cold start does.

Data Reengineering Phases and Tools

Table 2 continues the comparison of data reengineering and data engineering. The phases of each are shown side-by-side to emphasize that they really are different processes. However, to illustrate that both are viable, some commercially available software tools are also listed.

Since the phases of data engineering are widely discussed elsewhere (e.g., [8] and [9]) and should be familiar to most readers, this discussion will not be repeated here. The phases of data reengineering, however, are not as well known, so they are discussed at length below.

Code Analysis

Code analysis is the discovery of data definitions, flows and rules, wherever they exist in source code and JCL. For example, in a COBOL program, file and record declarations are found in the ENVIRONMENT and DATA DIVISIONs. Data flows within programs and between files are found in the PROCEDURE DIVISION. Data flows between programs are found in the LINKAGE SECTION and in JCL DD statements. Validation rules are much more difficult to discover because they are woven throughout the PROCEDURE DIVISION.

Data flow analysis for the COBOL language is more difficult than for many other languages because (1) actions on elementary data elements affect group items, (2) actions on group items affect elementary elements [7], and (3) multiple, conflicting definitions for the same physical storage locations are common. Since COBOL is not a strongly typed language and all data definitions are global, unintended side effects are often inherent in old systems.

As code is analyzed, a meta-data repository is populated. (Meta-data is data about data [9].) The level of analysis must be deeper than the level at which programmers usually think about systems. For instance, programmers usually think in terms of programs affecting data, but what actually happens is a particular entry point in a load module is executed by a job step, and thereby affects data. Knowing which programs affect a given file requires knowing precisely the associations between programs and entry points, between entry points and load modules, between load modules and jobs, and between jobs and the file in question. Furthermore, the chain of associations is less apparent when aliases are involved.

TABLE 2.

	Data Reengineering	Data Engineering
Phases	Code analysis Data analysis Meta-data synthesis Redesign Revision Definition exportation	Enterprise modeling Conceptual modeling Logical modeling Physical modeling Procedure specification Code generation
Tools	DataTec o Environment Analyzer o Definition Standardizer o Metric Analyzer o Definition Exporter	SilverRun o Entity-Relationship Modeler o Logical Data Modeler o Data Flow Diagrammer o Specification Exporter GoldRun o Code Generator

Note: DataTec, SilverRun, and GoldRun are trademarks of Peat Marwick Advanced Technology.

176

Data Analysis

Data analysis is the discovery of data properties by examination of actual data and comparison of those properties to data definitions. In the course of data analysis, however, it sometimes becomes apparent that the definitions themselves are incorrect or imprecise. Hence, data definitions or values or both can be incorrect.

For instance, if a definition permits negative numeric values, but only non-negative values have meaning in the context of the application, the definition should be revised. The values in the file, however, might already satisfy the revised definition. The converse is also possible. Even though all programs currently prohibit negative values, such values may have been placed in the file by a program no longer in existence or by a person who circumvented controls.

Just as troublesome, and no more unusual, are multiple definitions that contradict one another. If one program initializes a field to zeros and another program initializes the same field to spaces, a third program that depends on that field may produce erratic results, depending on which of its predecessors executed most recently.

Comparing definitions and actual values reveals missing, imprecise, and contradictory definitions. Though a system may continue to operate under such conditions, subsequent reengineering steps should not tolerate the disparities. Like code analysis results, data analysis results are stored in the meta-data repository.

Meta-data Synthesis

Meta-data synthesis brings together the pieces of information collected during the preceding phases. The objective is to make hidden data models visible. This is accomplished by inferring relationships among data and programs that are evident only when systems are examined in their entirety. For instance, when the same physical data has 18 different record definitions over as many programs and is stored in 7 different files, tracing data flows from beginning to end cannot be done by examining programs, JCL, or files separately.

After synthesis, the revised meta-data repository provides an inventory of data sources, flows, and sinks. It also provides cross-references between programs, load modules, entry points, jobs, job steps, and files.

Redesign

Redesign converts data definitions from one form to another. Most often the objective is to purify data definitions without changing the underlying data model. Some redesign activities clarify data definitions, yet may require little or no change to existing data. Others require substantial changes [2].

The simplest redesign, data record standardization, is the creation of composite record definitions which include (1) the lowest level of detail from all the old, different definitions and (2) useful data aggregates. Standardization reconciles physical formats that are different (but should be the same) and creates shared copy books in their place.

Design of composite records is best done by people who know both the organization and its data, but the information needed to accomplish this task is best provided by data reengineering tools that have examined the whole system thoroughly.

A more complex kind of redesign, data name rationalization, is the creation of consistent names across all copy books. To rationalize data names, data flows must be traced from sources to sinks -- both within and between programs. Though rational names can be assigned automatically, human judgment is usually preferable. Sometimes it is simply a matter of choosing the best name from among the old ones. This may be the case when old naming conventions are being enforced, but it is less often the case when new naming conventions are being established. Since standardization precedes rationalization, both definitions and names are made consistent by these processes.

The most complex kind of redesign, data restructuring, has significant implications for existing data because it changes the underlying physical data model [6]. For instance, repeating groups may be converted into tables during the normalization process. This process should be a familiar one to most readers since it also occurs during data engineering. Of course, when the ultimate objective is migration to relational database technology, normalization is essential. Yet data restructuring is not limited to relational databases: It can be applied to hierarchical data models, too [11]. Whether redesigns are done during data reengineering or data engineering depends on factors such as urgency, availability of tools or people, or the extent of expected changes.

Revision

Revision implements the redesign in source code, and sometimes in existing files [1]. The goal, obviously, is to make existing systems conform to the redesign. Less obvious is that few tools for data definition reengineering actually revise source code. Most, but not all, leave source code revision as a manual, unassisted process.

Source code revision includes at least the following:
o Replace old definitions with standardized and rationalized copy books, thereby externalizing these definitions from the code
o Change old references in the code to the new names
o Replace literals with named constants, creating copy books when those constants are common across programs
o Change procedures to conform to the new data definitions (e.g., a series of MOVEs may become a single group MOVE)

Optional source code revisions include the following:
o Extract I/O handling routines into copy books. Thereafter, all the I/O routines are reusable code that is maintained in copy books rather than individual programs. Furthermore, with I/O isolated, changes in access methods are easier.
o Simplify the code. Replicated procedures that operate on different data elements can be consolidated into a single procedure once the data in question is redefined. For example, one program that had been in production for years was found to contain essentially the same 14 lines of code in over 50 places.

177

Data value revision (also called data conversion [1]) may or may not be required for two reasons. First, name standardization, by itself, has no effect on data values. Second, the extent of data value revision required can be so large, or the value of that revision so small, that organizations choose to begin anew with the revised definitions rather than revise old data values. When data value revision is done, it includes physical format conversion [5] and data validation. The latter is difficult to do thoroughly because there presently is no way to extract validation rules from old systems and reconcile them automatically. However, this is an area of active research.

Definition Exportation

Definition exportation makes reengineered data definitions available to other CASE tools such as data dictionaries, data modelers, design workbenches, and application generators. Although most CASE tools today employ proprietary repository formats and processing algorithms, the trend is toward provision of public interfaces that can receive data definitions created elsewhere [5]. This allows users of data reengineering tools to export their results to other tools and proceed with data engineering.

Data Definition Reengineering Cases

DataTec is a set of software tools and a methodology for carrying out data definition reengineering. It has been used in several projects with a variety of objectives, methods, and deliverables. Three diverse cases are described below. One characteristic common to all these cases is that the scope of the reengineering effort was so large that only the semi-automated approach was feasible.

Data Name Rationalization

After conversion from autocoder, 5 COBOL programs were restructured and a huge one was split into 4 smaller programs. Since the original data names were not sufficiently meaningful, they were rationalized and placed into copy books.

Field Expansion & Record Standardization

An organization with extensive historical records had outgrown the size of one of its primary keys. The objective was to expand this field in 120 VSAM files and 440 CICS/COBOL programs by creating standard copy books.

Data Modeling

The objectives of this project were to (1) create a data model by deriving data definitions from existing systems, (2) create a work plan for moving to a new data architecture, and (3) disaggregate certain compound codes into separate data elements. The existing systems included 1600 COBOL programs, 60 VSAM files, 80 record types, and 5000 data elements. The target data model was relational.

Conclusions

Methods and tools for data definition reengineering are available today. They have been used to solve a variety of data definition problems in commercial and government application systems. Several conclusions can be drawn from those experiences.

First, some data definition reengineering tools available today can change source code, not just produce documentation. The revised source code then reflects current reality, rather than a catalog of problems or a vision of the ideal system. When pursued to completion, data definition reengineering leads to working systems, but not all tools support the revision step as well as the analysis and synthesis steps.

Second, reengineered data definitions can increase the maintainability of existing systems (e.g., [3], [5], [14]). Adoption of data reengineering tools is not yet as widespread as other CASE tools because data tools are a more-recent development and because data reengineering is not a fully automatable process [2]. Nevertheless, awareness of data reengineering technology is equal to that of procedure reengineering at a comparable stage in its evolution.

Third, data definition reengineering is a desirable precursor to data engineering. In the short run, exporting reengineered data definitions to data modeling tools creates representative models quickly. In the long run, systems developed from those models will be more compatible with existing systems than otherwise might be the case.

Finally, data definition reengineering, along with procedure reengineering and data value reengineering, prepares an organization for reverse engineering. Though reverse engineering technology is not yet mature, it will eventually extract specifications from existing systems so that those systems can be maintained at the specification level rather than the code level. However, data reengineering itself takes time (because data engineers and users learn more about the organization's data than they have ever known before). Organizations that reengineer their data now can earn immediate maintenance gains as they position themselves for additional gains when reverse engineering arrives in force.

178

References

[1] "Conversion Technology: An Assessment," *Data Base*, vol. 12&13, no. 4&1, Summer-Fall, 1981, pp. 39-61.

[2] C. Bachman, "A CASE for Reverse Engineering," *Datamation*, vol. 34, no. 13, July 1, 1988, pp. 49-56.

[3] F.B. Bastani and S.S. Iyengar, "The Effect of Data Structures on the Logical Complexity of Programs," *Communications of the ACM*, vol. 30, no. 3, March 1987, pp. 250-259.

[4] H.E. Dunsmore and J.D. Gannon, "Data Referencing: An Empirical Investigation," *Computer*, vol. 12, no. 12, December 1979, pp. 50-59.

[5] L.J. Gallagher, "Data Base Conversions Demand Common Standards for Data Structure," *Data Management*, vol. 23, no. 1, January 1985, pp. 22-28.

[6] J.L. Hursch, "Methods of Normalizing Databases," *Database Programming and Design*, vol. 1, no. 9, September 1988, pp. 52-58.

[7] H. Kao and T.Y. Chen, "Data Flow Analysis for COBOL," *SIGPLAN Notices*, vol. 19, no. 7, July 1984, pp. 18-21.

[8] J. Martin, *Strategic Data-Planning Methodologies*, Prentice Hall, London, 1982.

[9] F.R. McFadden and J.A. Hoffer, *Data Base Management*, 2nd edition, Benjamin/Cummings, Menlo Park, CA, 1988.

[10] J. Nelipovich, Jr., "When to Retrofit Your Data Dictionary," *Database Programming & Design*, vol. 1, no. 8, August 1988, pp. 26-32.

[11] T. Niemi, "Specification of Data Restructuring Software Based on the Attribute Method," *International Journal of Computer and Information Sciences*, vol. 13, no. 6, 1984, pp. 425-460.

[12] D.G. Rice and S. Laufer, "Putting Top-Down and Bottom-Up Analysis Together," *Database Programming & Design*, vol. 1, no. 12, December 1988, pp. 46-53.

[13] J.A. Ricketts and J.C. DelMonaco, "Software Reengineering with RETROFIT," *Computer Programming Management*, September 1988, pp. 1-21.

[14] C.S. Sankar, "Analysis of Names and Relationships Among Data Elements," *Management Science*, vol. 31, no. 7, July 1985, pp. 888-899.

A METHOD FOR DATA RE-ENGINEERING IN STRUCTURED PROGRAMS

Alan R. Hevner
Information Systems
University of Maryland
College Park, MD 20742
(301) 454-3260

Richard C. Linger
Systems Integration Division
IBM Corporation
Bethesda, MD 20817
(301) 493-1491

ABSTRACT

The poor performance and maintainability of unstructured software is creating a software crisis in many business organizations. There is a great need for effective methods to re-engineer existing software inventories to acquire the benefits of structured design. While the problem of restructuring control flow in software is fairly well understood, few methods exist for understanding and restructuring the data flow of software. We propose a method of data re-engineering that combines the theories of data usage abstractions with box structure abstractions for system redesign. The principal results of this re-engineering process are the elimination of data flow anomalies, the reduction of data scope, and the construction of reusable data objects as common services.

1. Software Re-engineering

The quality and performance of information systems are of strategic importance to business organizations. Many businesses are in crisis because their information systems have poor performance and cannot be maintained and evolved to meet changing business needs. In large measure, these problems are due to the unstructured software on which the information systems are based. Years ago, when the software was created, the benefits of program structure and software engineering were largely unknown. The software was written, debugged, optimized, and placed into production. It may have satisfied original requirements, however, new requirements for modification, increased function, and integration with other software inevitably arose. As the software evolved through unstructured patches and bridges, performance and maintainability decreased dramatically. In addition, system documentation quickly became out of date. As a result, many businesses today are faced with a large inventory of poor quality software that impacts their ability to grow, adapt, and even survive.

Principles of software engineering which emphasize mathematical approaches to design and correctness verification provide a rigorous basis for creating and maintaining high quality software [Linger et al. 1979, Mills 1986]. It is infeasible, however, for business enterprises to scrap millions of lines of unstructured software and develop new structured programs from scratch. The time, money, and human resources are normally not available to undertake such an immense effort. Thus, there is a great need for effective methods to embed software engineering principles and structures into existing software. This process is known as software re-engineering.

The primary objectives of software re-engineering are to regain control of program logic by restructuring control flows and data flows, and, thus, make the program understandable to all who use, maintain, and evolve it. The lifetime of the software is extended and opportunities for software reuse can be identified. While re-engineering often improves performance, the principal benefits come from improved ability to understand, maintain, and evolve the software.

Most of the research and practice in software re-engineering has concentrated on restructuring control flow in programs. (See [Arnold 1986] for an excellent tutorial.) It is a difficult problem to re-engineer complex, unstructured logic into functionally equivalent structured form. Many heuristic methods have been proposed, however, and deterministic, theory-based techniques are available. In particular, one proven technique is based on a Structure Theorem that guarantees any flowchartable, unstructured program has a structured counterpart [Linger et al. 1979, Linger 1988]. The result of this process is logic with no arbitrary jumps in control flow that displays top-down referential transparency in program modules. The Structure Theorem proof is constructive, and forms the basis for an automatic program re-engineering system [COBOL/SF 1988].

The restructuring of control flow may have

1025

Reprinted from *Proc. 22nd Annual Hawaii Int'l. Conference on System Sciences (HICSS)*, pp. 1025-1034. ©1989 by The Institute of Electrical and Electronics Engineers, Inc. All rights reserved.

little impact on improving poor data design and data flow in a program. While understandability is greatly increased by control structuring, additional benefits are achievable by addressing poor data flow characteristics. For many years, attention has been given to data flow analysis for program improvement [Fosdick 1976, Kam and Ullman 1976, Agarwal and Jachner 1984]. Most of this research deals specifically with code optimization and does not address the more general issues of improving program understanding, maintainability, and evolution. In more closely related research, Maher and Sleeman have developed a programming restructuring system (Leeds Transformation System) that includes some aspects of data flow re-engineering [Maher and Sleeman 1983]. Their method uses a bottom-up abstraction procedure to discover and remedy redundant variables, redundant assignments of variables, and inefficient placement of variable assignments.

One of the principal difficulties in data re-engineering is that few measures of data flow quality in software exist. In [Harrison et al. 1982], three data flow metrics are described and discussed:

- A **data reference span** measures the distance in lines of code between successive references to the same data item.

- The **segment-global usage pair** [Basili 1980] quantifies the likelihood that a code segment will reference a global variable.

- The **Q measure** [Chapin 1979] calculates a complexity measure, Q, for each program segment based upon how data is used in that segment. These values are then used to calculate the complexity of higher level segments and eventually the complete program.

Harrison points out that these measures are not widely applicable and have not been used to validate data re-engineering in realistic studies.

We present a new method of data re-engineering that combines the theories of data usage abstractions with box structure abstractions for software redesign. For this paper, we apply the method to the flow of data items in a structured program. More complex forms of data, i.e., data structures, file organizations, and data-bases, can be handled as natural extensions to this research. In Section 2, we use a box structure hierarchy to present the control structure decomposition of a structured program. In Section 3, the data usage of the program is described formally in regular expressions. In Section 4, we

present a data re-engineering method based on these two abstractions. Research extensions to the method are discussed in Section 5.

2. Describing Structured Programs in Box Structures

Structured programs are described naturally as a uses hierarchy of referentially transparent program parts. That is, any structured program can be decomposed into nested and sequenced control structures (sequence, alternation, iteration), from the top down to individual statements. This ability to analyze and design programs by stepwise abstraction and refinement, respectively, with referential transparency is the essence of mathematics-based structured programming [Linger et al. 1979].

For analyzing data flow in structured programs, we first describe a structured program in a box structure hierarchy form. Box structures are a theory and methodology for analyzing and designing information systems [Mills et al. 1986, Mills et al. 1987]. Basically, any system or software part can be described in three data abstractions. A black box defines a data abstraction entirely in terms of external behavior, in transitions from stimulus histories to responses. A state box defines a data abstraction in terms of transitions from a stimulus and internal state to a response and new internal state (with necessary stimulus histories encapsulated in the state). A clear box defines the procedure that accesses the internal state and possibly calls on other black boxes at the next level of decomposition. Figure 1 shows the graphic representation of the three box structures. The recursion of black boxes in a clear box defines a usage hierarchy of box structures that can be extended to any level of system detail. Common service box structures can be defined at any level in the hierarchy. Common services have been popularized as so-called objects, but are defined within box structures as part of a rigorous methodology, rather than as heuristic acts of invention [Mills 1988].

Box structure theory provides a set of analysis and design principles for system and software development. By describing a structured program as a box structure hierarchy, we can take advantage of these principles to analyze and restructure program data flow.

Since the structured program is available as input to our data re-engineering method, we can describe it's control structure decomposition as a usage hierarchy of clear boxes. The decomposition of a structured

1026

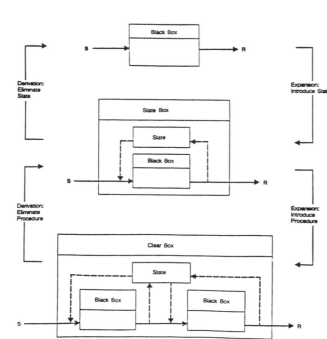

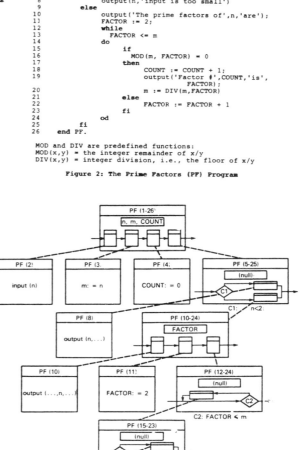

Figure 1: Graphic Representation of Box Structures

```
statement number
     1      begin PF
     2          input(n);
     3          m := n;
     4          COUNT := 0;
     5          if
     6              n < 2
     7          then
     8              output(n,'input is too small')
     9          else
    10              output('The prime factors of',n,'are');
    11              FACTOR := 2;
    12              while
    13                  FACTOR <= m
    14              do
    15                  if
    16                      MOD(m, FACTOR) = 0
    17                  then
    18                      COUNT := COUNT + 1;
    19                      output('Factor #',COUNT,'is',
                                    FACTOR);
    20                      m := DIV(m,FACTOR)
    21                  else
    22                      FACTOR := FACTOR + 1
    23                  fi
    24              od
    25          fi
    26      end PF.

MOD and DIV are predefined functions:
MOD(x,y) = the integer remainder of x/y
DIV(x,y) = integer division, i.e., the floor of x/y
```

Figure 2: The Prime Factors (PF) Program

Figure 3: The Box Structure Hierarchy of Program PF

program is defined in [Linger et. al. 1979] as a program hierarchy in which every control structure defines a new level of refinement. Four control structures can be described in clear boxes; sequence (do-od), alternation (if-then-else-fi), iteration (while-do-od), and concurrency (con-noc). These structures are shown graphically in standard flowchart notation within a clear box.

To illustrate the prime decomposition of a simple structured program in a box structure hierarchy, consider the Prime Factors (PF) program shown in Figure 2. The program accepts as input an integer value n, greater than or equal to 2, and produces as output a list of the prime factors of n. The control structure decomposition of this program is shown graphically in Figure 3 as a usage hierarchy of clear boxes. The leaves of the hierarchy are statements in the program that cannot be further decomposed. We will use this program as an example in the remainder of the paper.

3. Using Regular Expressions for Data Usage Abstraction

In any program, data are assigned and referenced during execution. In a structured program, data usage can be formulated as regular expressions for better understanding of the program, to improve reada-

bility, and to verify correctness. Regular expressions for data usage are compact and precise abstractions of all data references in a structured program. They are derived by syntactic analysis, a

1027

process which can be automated, since it is purely mechanical with no human judgment required. Automatically generated usage expressions will support the intellectual management of data in large, complex systems.

The definition of regular expressions is based on how data is used in the control structure decomposition of a structured program as described in the box structure hierarchy. In assignments, a data item on the right side is read, a data item on the left side is written. In conditional tests, data items can only be read. In input statements, data items are written; and in output statements, data items are read. We adopt the usage categories of "read" (R) and "written" (W), and, for convenience, an additional category, "not used" (N).

Control structure decomposition defines the structure of the regular expression for each data item. For the sequence structure, the data usages are concatenated. For the alternation structure, the binary branching data usages are separated by an 'or' bar, |. For iteration, the * (star) operator is used to prefix the data usage in the loop. For concurrency, a parallel operator, ||, will separate the concurrent data uses. Figure 4 summarizes the rules for constructing regular expressions for each of the primary control structures.

For each data item, then, a regular expression of its use is constructed from bottom-up in the box structure hierarchy. First, the use(s) of the data item in each program statement is recorded. A regular expression is built by combining the data uses in the structured hierarchy through application of the regular expression construction rules. For example, Table 1 contains a complete data usage analysis of the Prime Factors program found in Figure

2. For ease of comparison, we have included the statement and control structure types in the second column. The final row contains the regular expression for the usage of each data item throughout the complete program.

4. A Method for Data Re-engineering

With the rigor and expressive power of box structures and regular expressions at our disposal, we outline next a comprehensive method for data re-engineering in structured programs. The description applies the method to restructuring based on data usage characteristics of element variables in our miniature program, but is readily generalized to deal with more complex data structures and their operations.

Develop a Box Structure Hierarchy of the Control Structure Decomposition

The input to data re-engineering is a structured program of arbitrary size and complexity, that perhaps existed in unstructured form and has been subjected to a rigorous control structuring process. It is a mechanical operation, amenable to automation, to derive the uses hierarchy of clear boxes for the program based on stepwise control structure decomposition, as shown in Figure 3.

Construct Data Usage Regular Expressions

Next, the regular expressions for data usage can be defined bottom up in the box structure hierarchy. This construction can be automated because it is a syntactic process. Each clear box in the hierarchy will be associated with a list of regular expressions which record the usage patterns of all data items referenced in the control structure represented by the clear box. The rows of Table 1 are the data usage

---

sequence structure	sequence regular expression
expl; exp2; exp3	exp1 exp2 exp3

alternation structure	alternation regular expression

if
  expl
then
    exp2
else
    exp3
fi
	exp1 (exp2 | exp3)

iteration structure	iteration regular expression

while
  expl
do
    exp2
od
	exp1 *(exp2)

concurrent structure	concurrent regular expression

con
  exp1,
  exp2
noc
	(exp1 || exp2)

Figure 4: Rules for Forming Regular Expressions

Table 1: Regular Expressions for Data Usage in Program PF

statement number	type	n	m	FACTOR	COUNT
2	input	W			
3	assignment	R	W		
4	assignment				W
6	iftest	R			
8	output	R			
10	output	R			
11	assignment			W	
13	whiletest		R	R	
16	iftest	R	R		
18	assignment				RW
19	output			R	R
20	assignment		RW	R	
22	assignment			RW	

control structure range	type	n	m	FACTOR	COUNT
18-20	sequence		RW	RR	RWR
15-23	alternation		R(RW|N)	R(RR|RW)	(RWR|N)
12-24	iteration		R*(R(RW|N))	R*(R(RR|RW))	*(RWR|N)
10-24	sequence	R	R*(R(RW|N))	WR*(R(RR|RW))	*(RWR|N)
5-25	alternation	R(R|R)	(N|R*(R(RW|N)))	(N|WR*(R(RR|RW)))	(N|*(RWR|N))
1-26	sequence	WRR(R|R)	W(N|R*(R(RW|N)))	(N|WR*(R(RR|RW)))	W(N|*(RWR|N))

lists for the corresponding clear boxes of the hierarchy in Figure 3.

Recognize and Eliminate Data Flow Anomalies

The first active step of data re-engineering recognizes and eliminates various types of data flow anomalies that occur frequently in programs. An analysis of the data usage regular expressions allows a rapid means of recognizing data anomalies. This detection process can be automated efficiently via finite state automata that recognize anomalous patterns in data usage regular expressions [Hausler 1985]. These anomalies can then be eliminated by modifying the data design and referencing control structures as required. Techniques for recognizing and eliminating several types of data anomalies are discussed below.

Uninitialized Data Reads. When a data item is read without a previous write operation, the value read is undefined. The usage pattern of this anomaly is any occurrence of an R before a W is encountered. For example, RR(N|WR) indicates an anomalous data usage. This anomaly is corrected by adding a write operation (an assignment or an input) before the data item is first read.

Unused Data Writes. This anomaly occurs when a data item is written and the new value is not read before another value is written. In this case, the usage pattern would contain consecutive W's, perhaps separated by null operations, N. Thus, WNWR indicates an unused data write anomaly. This usage anomaly often indicates a subtle program error, and is corrected by removing the first write operation or adding code that reads the result of the first write.

Overloaded Data Items. When a data item is repeatedly written between reads, such usage may indicate the overloading of a data item. Often a programmer, for efficiency or convenience, uses a single data item for different functional duties in a program. This type of reuse complicates the understanding of a program and creates difficulties for program maintenance and evolution. Consider the following code segment:

```
1    if
2        x > y
3    then
4            t := x;
5            x := y;
6            y := t;
7    fi
8    t := x + y;
9    z := t;
```

The data item t has a usage pattern of (WR|N)WR. By recognizing this pattern and looking at the code, we can discover that, when the iftest is true, t is being used in two functionally distinct roles. This anomaly can be corrected by defining a new data item, say, sum, to replace t in lines 8 and 9. Another advantage of having distinct data items is that the program scope of each can be made smaller. The benefits of reduced data scope are discussed below.

Other Data Flow Anomalies. The power and flexibility of regular expressions are such that any pattern of anomalous data usage can be easily recognized. Also, if data usages must conform to certain patterns, then automatic recognizers can be built to check the legality of all data flows. For example, if certain sections of a program are not allowed to write a data item, a recognizer could be developed to detect such illegal data uses. In this way, our data re-engineering method can be adapted to the specific needs of a program environment.

Recognize and Reduce Data Scope

The scope of a data item in a structured program is the lowest level clear box (i.e., control structure) that contains all references to the data item. Analysis of data usage regular expressions provides an efficient means of recognizing and reducing the scope of data items for improved understandability. The required scope of a data item is defined by the regular expression of the lowest level clear box that contains all references to it. The scope of each data item in the Prime Factors (PF) program is shown in Figure 3. Each data item becomes part of the state in the scoping box structure.

Our objective in this step for data re-engineering is to reduce the scope of each data item. There are important reasons to limit data scope:

- Program understanding: Tracing the logic of a program is simplified when references to individual data items are contained in a well defined range of code.

- Maintenance and evolution: The impact of program changes on data can be better managed when data scopes are limited. A data item does not exist outside its scope, and thus cannot cause side effects in other parts of a program.

- Discovering data objects: By consciously limiting data scope, we discover data whose use is required by large sections of the program, i.e.,

1029

data that has a high-level scope. Such data are promising candidates for encapsulation as data objects with well defined common services. This data re-engineering step is described in the next section.

After the scope of each data item has been discovered in the box structure hierarchy, we invoke a procedure that reduces the scope of a data item where possible. Again, data usage regular expressions are used to support the discovery of such opportunities. The procedure is summarized as follows:

Procedure Reduce Scope

1. Select each data item in a top-down order based on its scope in the box structure hierarchy of the program. Perform steps 2 through 5 on the selected data item, x.

2. Data item x is contained in the state of a clear box. Consider the clear boxes at the next level in the box structure hierarchy. Compare the data usage regular expressions for x in each of these child clear boxes.

3. If only one clear child box has a long expression of data usage (i.e., a complex data usage pattern) then consider modifying the program code to move all uses of data item x into that clear box. (While programmer intervention is required to make the required modifications, the data usage regular expressions provide important guidance.) Migrating the data item reduces the scope of x by one level.

4. If two or more child clear boxes have long expressions of data usage, then x should be left at the current scope.

5. Select the next data item to analyze. If the current data item was moved down in the hierarchy, it will be reconsidered in its new location for further reduction in scope.

End of Procedure Reduce Scope

For example, we can apply this procedure to the Prime Factors program. The current data item scopes are shown in Figure 3 with data usage regular expressions in Table 1. Consider the reduction of scope for data item m. Data item m is contained in the state of the top-level clear box, PF(1-26). By inspecting the four child clear boxes at the next level, we find that m has data usage regular expressions in two of them; in PF(3), W, and in PF(5-25), (N|R*(R(RW|N))). Clearly, we should consider moving the write of data item m in statement 3 into the alternation structure of PF(5-25). The analysis of the data usage of m in the alternation shows that m is not used in the **then** branch, therefore, the write statement can be migrated into the sequence structure of the **else** branch, PF(10-24). (This demonstrates the expert guidance that can be gained from the data usage regular expressions.) Thus, the scope of m can be reduced by two levels in the box structure hierarchy. Similarly, we can migrate the scope of data item COUNT down two levels in the hierarchy. After performing this algorithm on the PF program, the modified program, PF', is shown in Figure 5, with its new box structure hierarchy shown in Figure 6 and the new set of data usage regular expressions presented in Table 2.

statement number

```
 1   begin PF'
 2       input(n);
 3       if
 4           n < 2
 5       then
 6           output(n,'input is too small')
 7       else
 8           output('The prime factors of',n,'are');
 9           m := n;
10           COUNT := 0;
11           FACTOR := 2;
12           while
13               FACTOR <= m
14           do
15               if
16                   MOD(m,FACTOR) = 0
17               then
18                   COUNT := COUNT + 1;
19                   output('Factor #',COUNT,'is',
                                      FACTOR);
20                   m := DIV(m,FACTOR)
21               else
22                   FACTOR := FACTOR + 1
23               fi
24           od
25       fi
26   end PF'.
```

MOD and DIV are predefined functions:
MOD(x,y) = the integer remainder of x/y
DIV(x,y) = integer division, i.e., the floor of x/y

Figure 5: The Modified Prime Factors (PF') Program

Table 2: Regular Expressions for Data Usage in Program PF'

statement number	type	n	m	FACTOR	COUNT
2	input	W			
3	iftest	R			
6	output	R			
8	output	R			
9	assignment	R	W		
10	assignment				W
11	assignment			W	
13	whiletest		R	R	
16	iftest		R	R	
18	assignment				RW
19	output			R	R
20	assignment		RW	R	
22	assignment			RW	

control structure range	type	n	m	FACTOR	COUNT
18-20	sequence		RW	RR	RWR
15-23	alternation		R(RW|N)	R(RR|RW)	(RWR|N)
12-24	iteration		R*(R(RW|N))	R*(R(RR|RW))	*(RWR|N)
8-24	sequence	RR	WR*(R(RW|N))	WR*(R(RR|RW))	W*(RWR|N)
3-25	alternation	R(R|RR)	(N|WR*(R(RW|N)))	(N|WR*(R(RR|RW)))	(N|W*(RWR|N))
1-26	sequence	WR(R|R)	(N|WR*(R(RW|N)))	(N|WR*(R(RR|RW)))	(N|W*(RWR|N))

1030

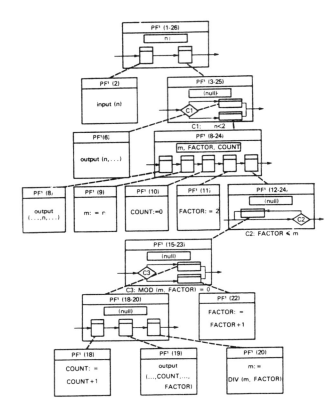

Figure 6: The Box Structure Hierarchy of Program PF'

Discover and Form Data Objects

Data objects are abstractions that encapsulate data and the services on that data. The final step of our data re-engineering method is to discover opportunities for the formation of data objects in a program. The use of data objects is receiving much attention in the research and practice of software engineering. Object-oriented design and object-oriented programming have become widely used methodologies for software development. The benefits of using objects include object reuse within and among programs, controlled access to data, shared object use, and enhanced maintenance and evolution characteristics; for example, new services can be added to an object without affecting the use of the object in current programs. Our objective, then, is to re-engineer the use of data objects into existing programs.

The principle of **common services** in the box structure methodology embodies the object concept [Mills et al. 1987, Mills 1988]. By analyzing the box structure hierarchy of

a structured program and the data usage therein, opportunities for forming data objects and using them as common services can be discovered. The actual data objects are designed as state boxes, expanded into clear boxes, and implemented. The objects are then available for use as common services in the box structure hierarchies of application programs. Note that the data within the object no longer have a scope within the application program, they can only be referenced by using the data object as a common service.

We now sketch a procedure for identifying data items in a program that have potential for forming data objects. Typically, data objects are formed to encapsulate more complex data structures than simple data items, for example, files and databases. For the purposes of this paper, however, we will limit our discussion to data items, with a view toward extending the procedure to handle complex data structures. We also take into account that data objects may already exist in the business information system for reuse. Thus, the first step of the procedure assumes that a repository of reusable data objects is available.

Procedure Form Data Objects

1. For each data item x in the structured program, check for existing data objects in the information system that encapsulate x. Evaluate the use of the selected data objects in the program. If appropriate, modify the program to use the data object that contains data item x. It may also be necessary to modify the data object by adding required services.

2. For each data item x remaining in the program, an analysis is performed to determine its potential for forming a new data object. A number of characteristics must be considered:

   - Scope. If the data item has a high level scope in the hierarchy, then by forming a data object, global access to the data item is removed from the program. Controlled access can only be obtained by using the data object.

   - Data Usage. If the data item has a usage pattern that repeats itself in several distinct places in the program, then a data object can be used at those places.

   - Services. By analyzing the use of the data item in the program code, a set of services (e.g., input, output, read, write) used with the data item can be defined. These services would need to be defined in the data object.

1031

The above data characteristics can be studied with the information found in the data re-engineering method for a particular structured program. The following characteristics require outside knowledge of the business information system in which the program resides.

- **Retention.** If the data item is permanent data that is retained outside of the application program being studied, then the defined data object can be used throughout the information system.

- **Control.** Control requirements, such as security and integrity controls, are very appropriate for placement into a data object. No access to the data is allowed outside of the data object, thus, these controls can be enforced with each access.

- **Reuse.** If the data item is shared among several programs, then a data object is recommended. Data objects support the objective of software reuse.

- **Changes.** If the data item is likely to change over time based on new requirements, then, such changes can be isolated in the data object. For example, a change in data structure or the addition of new services can be made transparent to the use of the data object in application programs.

Based upon these characteristics a decision is made to encapsulate data item x in a data object. If not, return to step 1 and consider another data item.

3. Before forming a data object for x by itself, consideration should be given to beneficial groupings of x with other data items in the program. There may exist a natural grouping of data items and services among them. The resulting data object presents a higher level data abstraction for use in the program.

Data item groupings are found by analyzing how data are used with one another in the program. We define the following data structures for this analysis:

USE(x) = the number of uses of data item x in the program.

LINK(x, y) = the number of times that data item x is used with data item y in the same statement, each appearance of a data item in a statement is counted separately. This is a symmetric matrix.

GROUP(x, y) = LINK(x, y) / USE(x).

The matrix GROUP(x, y) provides information on how data items are used with one another in the program. Note that this matrix is not symmetric. GROUP(x, y) tells how often given the appearance of x that you also find y; while GROUP(y, x) tells how often given the appearance of y that you also find x. Both values are relevant in the decision of whether to group data items x and y in the same data object. For example, if data item x is selected to form a data object, then the decision of whether to include data item y also in the object could be based on having a large (e.g., 0.5) value for GROUP(y, x).

If data items x and y present a natural grouping based on their use in the program, then data item y must be analyzed in terms of the characteristics of step 2. If appropriate for inclusion in a data object, y will be grouped with x.

4. The selected data item, or group of data items, is formed into a data object by designing a state box, and subsequent box structure hierarchy, for the encapsulated data and accompanying services. Services will include the standard actions on individual data items (i.e., input, output, read, write) as well as the set of operations performed among the data in the object. For example, if data items x and y are in the same data object and the operation x+y is used frequently in programs, then the object could contain a service that returns the value x+y upon request. In this way, higher level data abstractions are defined via data objects.

Place the newly formed data object into the system repository of data objects for potential reuse.

5. If further data items remain to be considered, return to step 1.

Once all data items have been analyzed, the structured program must be modified to use the newly defined data objects. The box structure hierarchy supports an efficient re-design of the program based on the inherent referential transparency of the structured program. Each use of the data object simply becomes a black box within a clear box in the hierarchy. In fact, the pattern of use of the data object will be identical to the data usage regular expression of the encapsulated data

1032

301

items. This fact provides a method of verifying the correctness of the program modification.

End of Procedure Form Data Objects

The disciplined practice of forming reusable data objects will aid not only future software re-engineering projects, but also new software development can make effective use of the available data objects.

5. Conclusions and Research Extensions

We have proposed a new method of re-engineering data flow in existing structured programs. We believe that the method provides a comprehensive strategy to restructure the use of data in programs. The strength of the method is based on theories of box structures and regular expressions. We view the structured program in a referentially transparent hierarchy of modules, decomposed via control structures. The usage of each data item is defined in regular expressions and mapped onto the hierarchy. Based on these abstractions, the program data flow is re-engineered to eliminate data use anomalies, reduce data scope, and form data objects. The significant advantages brought about by data re-engineering include increased program understand-ability, improved maintenance and evolution characteristics, and, in many programs, better performance.

We plan to pursue several extensions of this research in data re-engineering. The use of box structures and regular expressions provides a rigorous foundation for automation of the data flow analysis tasks. We also recognize the requirement for an intelligent programmer interface and the potential for automated knowledge-based guidance to be used with the method.

As discussed in section 1, there currently exists no valid measure of data flow quality for software. In our method, effective use of data is measured by number of anomalies, range of data scope, and use of data objects. These are largely qualitative measures that are open to programmer interpretation. More research is needed to study and develop a software metric to measure data flow quality in structured programs. Then, this metric must be validated in realistic data re-engineering experiments.

The data re-engineering method will be extended to include the re-engineering of more complex data, such as records, stacks, queues, arrays, files, and databases. In particular, we believe the value of

recognizing and forming data objects that encapsulate large, persistent data organizations will be significant. In addition, we plan to study the use of program execution-time information in data re-engineering decisions. Such information may provide important guidance in identifying the most critical data flows for analysis and restructuring.

References

[Agarwal and Jachner 1984] V. Agrawal and J. Jachner "Data Flow Anomaly Detection," **IEEE Transactions on Software Engineering**, Vol. SE-10, No. 4, July 1984, pp. 432-437.

[Arnold 1986] R. Arnold, editor, **Tutorial on Software Restructuring**, IEEE Computer Society Press, 1986.

[Basili 1980] V. Basili "Product Metrics," in **Tutorial on Models and Metrics for Software Management and Engineering**, IEEE Computer Society Press, 1980, pp. 214-217.

[Chapin 1979] N. Chapin "A Measure of Software Complexity," **Proceedings of the National Computer Conference**, 1979, pp. 995-1002.

[COBOL/SF 1988] IBM COBOL Structuring Facility (COBOL/SF), Version 2.0, **COBOL Structuring Facility Reengineering Concepts**, IBM Publication CS34-4079, 1988.

[Fosdick 1976] L. Fosdick "Data Flow Analysis in Software Reliability," **ACM Computer Surveys**, Vol. 8, No. 3, September 1976, pp. 305-330.

[Harrison et al. 1982] W. Harrison, K. Magel, R. Kluczny, and A. DeKock "Applying Software Complexity Metrics to Program Maintenance," **IEEE Computer**, Vol. 15, No. 9, September 1982, pp. 65-79.

[Hausler 1985] P. Hausler "Data Usage Abstraction in Structured Programs," Master's Thesis, Department of Computer Science, Univ. of Maryland, 1985.

[Kam and Ullman 1976] J. Kam and J. Ullman "Global Data Flow Analysis and Iterative Algorithms," **Journal of the ACM**, Vol. 23, No. 1, January 1976, pp. 158-171.

[Linger et al. 1979] R. Linger, H. Mills, B. Witt **Structured Programming: Theory and Practice**, Addison-Wesley, 1979.

[Linger 1988] R. Linger "Software Maintenance as an Engineering Discipline," Proceedings of the Conference on Software Maintenance-88, Phoenix, Arizona, October 24-27, 1988.

1033

[Maher and Sleeman 1983] B. Maher and D. Sleeman "Automatic Program Improvement: Variable Usage Transformations," **ACM Transactions on Programming Languages and Systems**, Vol. 5, No. 2, April 1983, pp. 236-264.

[Mills 1986] H. Mills "Structured Programming: Retrospect and Prospect," **IEEE Software**, November 1986, pp. 58-66.

[Mills et al. 1986] H. Mills, R. Linger, and A. Hevner **Principles of Information Systems Analysis and Design**, Academic Press, 1986.

[Mills et al. 1987] H. Mills, R. Linger, and A. Hevner "Box Structured Information Systems," **IBM Systems Journal**, Vol. 26, No. 4, December 1987, pp. 395-413.

[Mills 1988] H. Mills "Stepwise Refinement and Verification in Box-Structured Systems," **IEEE Computer**, Vol. 21, No. 6, June 1988, pp. 23-36.

1034

FROM IMS OR NON-IBM, THE MOVE IS ON TO DB2

Help from tools varies: some normalize data, others build bridge to new while running old

By Barbara Francett

Along with the move to relational database management systems in commercial data processing has come the need to convert from older DBMS and file structures.

The move to a relational database in many cases may drive an operating system conversion, such as from IBM's DOS/VSE to MVS. That has been the case for many such conversions recently, according to a spokesman for the Computer Task Group, Orchard Park, New York, which specializes in systems integration work.

Terry Warren, manager of the Cortex operating system conversion tool at CTG, said, "DOS/VSE people migrating to MVS are establishing a foundation for database conversion. They're looking at relational futures. Basically, we're positioning clients for database conversions."

Users contemplating database conversions generally find them-

Francett is a freelance writer based in Bloomfield, N.J.

selves in one of two situations. Some try to get from sequential or flat file systems to a database manager of some type. Most, however, are moving from an existing database manager, especially older hierarchical or network systems, to a RDBMS.

Most conversions in the latter category can be further subdivided into two groups: users moving from non-IBM systems to DB2, IBM's relational database; and users moving from IMS, IBM's hierarchical database, to DB2.

Business needs are driving the trend to convert to relational systems. Partly, the notion results from a belief that an enterprise-wide view of a corporation's data, considered

essential today, may sit on a relational database foundation.

"People have to get their arms around the data," says Dean Mohlstrom, president and CEO of Information Engineering Systems Corp., a Dallas-based consultant.

"They need to get a handle on the company's information resources. They need to structure their data so they can obtain the information they need to run the business."

Taking a five-year view, businesses should convert now to be in good shape for the future, Mohlstrom says.

Increasingly, users are embracing relational database technology, with its extensibility, ease of use and ease of maintenance, as the means to achieve that goal.

"Users are looking to take advantage of new technology, like SQL (Structured Query Language)," says Dick Manasseri, DB2 product manager at Bachman Information Systems, Inc., Cambridge, Mass. "The only way they'll be able to take advantage of that technology is on top of a relational system."

For example, as many corporations

try to distribute their businesses to get closer to their customers, they'll also need to distribute their databases. "They won't be able to do that without moving to a relational system first," Manasseri maintains.

For IBM shops, another concern pushing conversions to relational systems, specifically DB2, is the ability to participate in IBM's Systems Application Architecture. "To take advantage of SAA—running the same applications on multiple platforms, from mainframes down to PCs, and participating in cooperative processing—the underlying assumption is that you're on a relational system," Manasseri says.

But database conversions of any type, especially conversions to a relational system, are far from easy.

"Conversion can be very tough, depending on the structure of the database," says Matt Dombrowski, marketing manger, Interactive Systems, Inc., Lowell, Mass., maker of Clone, a syntax translator.

Moving a heavily networked, hierarchical system to a relational system is difficult because hierarchical systems tie "child" records to "parent" records, whereas relational systems' tabular structure relates records by values in fields, Dombroski explained.

"The difficulty in database conversion is that it revolves around the database design and existing technology," says Mike Niemann, specialty group manager for DB2 support services at Computer Task Group. "The existing database design may be inelegant, having evolved over 10 or 12 years. Migration represents an opportunity to start over and do it right." Most conversions he sees are from non-IBM databases to IBM's DB2.

There are generally two extremes to database migration, Niemann says. "Either customers say, 'Take what we've got and reproduce it exactly in the new environment,' or 'Here's our current . . . portfolio and

database design. Help us decide what it should be to support our needs for the next five years.' "

APPROACHES TO CONVERSIONS

There are several approaches to database conversions. These include rewriting, re-engineering, reverse engineering and the use of bridging technologies. Rewriting applications to the new database, the most time-consuming approach, is generally chosen only when no other alternative is feasible, or when business needs demand it.

Re-engineering refers to work done to an existing system to improve its structure, such as eliminating redundancies and standard-

izing data definitions. Reverse engineering refers to the extraction of design specifications from an existing application.

"If we're going to do a database conversion from a flat file to IMS, or more typically today, go from a hierarchical to a relational system, such as IMS to DB2, we apply logical data modeling techniques to get a normalized data model—how the data should be implemented and accessed," says William Ulrich.

Ulrich is director of re-engineering products at Peat Marwick Advanced

Technology, Chicago, whose software division was acquired by XA Systems of Los Gatos, Calif., in June.

"We also glean data definitions from the current system. These definitions contain information about how the data is used and accessed as well as defined. We call this a 'bottom-up' approach. If the data definitions are wrong, they must be adjusted, but if they're right, we save a lot of time," Ulrich said.

Peat Marwick offers several automated tools to aid in conversion efforts. DataTEC-EA (Environmental Analyzer) is used to capture a picture of the existing database's source code and file relationships. The next step is to capture Cobol code. DataTEC-DS (Data Definition Standardization) captures all record or file layouts and arranges them into logical groupings.

As a next step, PMAT offers Silverrun, which creates entity-relationship data models. Silverrun takes those Cobol record definitions as input into the entity relationship model and bring them down to the data model. "Then you'd go through the process of normalizing the data and finalizing the data model," Ulrich said.

Peat Marwick is also developing a reverse engineering repository. The repository will be a logical representation of an existing database. Both data definitions and process rules would be fed into the representation, and then ported into forward engineering tools like Case products. The repository is about a year away from availability.

The Personal Financial Security Division of Aetna Life & Casualty in Hartford, Conn., is using DataTEC-DS to help it convert from a 20-year-old tape sequential database system to a relational system. The database, called Claim Data File (CDF), runs on an Amdahl 5890 mainframe and comprises 100 million records of automobile, homeowner and personal claims. The system processes

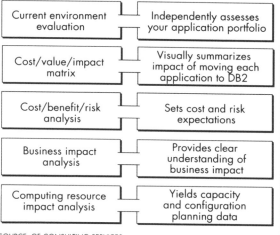

DATABASE MIGRATION STRATEGY PLAN

An evaluation of your application portfolio, charting a course for migration, quantifying impacts on computer and people resources, and highlighting pitfalls and opportunities.

Current environment evaluation	Independently assesses your application portfolio
Cost/value/impact matrix	Visually summarizes impact of moving each application to DB2
Cost/benefit/risk analysis	Sets cost and risk expectations
Business impact analysis	Provides clear understanding of business impact
Computing resource impact analysis	Yields capacity and configuration planning data

SOURCE: GE CONSULTING SERVICES
IDMS MIGRATION SERVICES

750,000 to 1 million transactions per month.

"It's a very good, functional system, but we need to take that system into the next century," says Bruce Skivington, director of home office claim processing systems. "And when it comes to defining data sources in different ways for different uses, relational is the future."

Aetna began using DataTEC-DS in August 1988 to go through CDF's source code and identify key record structures. "DataTEC-DS assembles different local views of a given record to form a composite view," says Thomas Wheeler, senior systems engineer. "It allows you to standardize data names through all different key records. This would be a mammoth undertaking if we had to do it manually."

Skivington says, "Using DataTEC-DS to normalize our data, we've cut the number of data elements from 15,000 to 4,000. It allows us to do the data modeling necessary to move toward relational."

Aetna plans to use DataTEC-EA to create its data dictionaries and is evaluating relational databases.

"We could have rebuilt the system the traditional way—writing new specifications, redesigning and then rebuilding—but we couldn't afford it in terms of people, time or money," Skivington said. "This approach allows us to integrate systems and data at a price we can afford."

Bachman Information Systems, Inc., Cambridge, Mass., offers several re-engineering and reverse engineering products that do database and data modeling design, which can also be used in database conversions. The flagship product is Bachman/Database Administrator (DB2), a database design tool

REPRESENTATIVE CONVERSION TOOLS

Products listed here are data center tools which support conversion between languages, operating systems or DBMSs. For more information about a particular product, circle the number on the reader service card located at the back of this issue. Compiled by Products Editor Deborah Melewski.

VENDOR	PRODUCT/ CIRCLE NO.	OPERATING SYSTEM REQUIREMENTS	LANGUAGE/OPERATING SYSTEM CONVERSION	DBMS CONVERSION
ABC Development Systems Minneapolis, MN	Convert/36 275	IBM PC-DOS, Unix, Xenix	Converts S/36 Basic code to Workstation Basic code	
Advanced Systems Concepts Hoboken, NJ	CICS Liberator 276	DEC VAX/VMS	Automates migration of IBM CICS applications to DEC VAX in DECintact environment	
Bachman Information Systems Cambridge, MA	Bachman Re-engineering Product Set Toolset 277	IBM PC		Database re-engineering, for MVS, DB2, IMS
California Interactive Computing N. Hollywood, CA	CIC/MVS Conversion 278	IBM MVS	Pick, Primos, Reality Data/ Basic to IBM Assembler	
CGI Systems Pearl River, NY	PacBase 296	IBM		Case product; automates re-use of design specifications to generate applications
CompAct Data Systems Inc. Canoga Park, CA	CDS Conversion 279	IBM DOS to MVS	Conversion services; includes planning, implementation, training	
Computer Assoc. International Garden City, NY	CA-Convertor 280	IBM MVS	IBM DOS/VSE to MVS, MVS/XA; Cobol, Assembler, JCL converters; includes CA Accuchek verification	
	CA-Datacom/DB 281	IBM MVS, DOS/VSE		Automated migration software allows conversion from from Vsam, IMS, Total to Datacom/DB
	CA-Duo 282	IBM MVS	Interface allows DOS/VSE programs to run under MVS	
	CA-Transit 283	IBM MVS	Unisys, DEC VAX, HP, Honeywell, Prime Cobol to IBM MVS translation system	
Computer Task Group Orchard Park, NY	Dataware 284	Supports most platforms	Tools/services for a wide variety of conversions	
	Cortex 285	IBM MVS	IBM DOS to MVS	
	Cobol to Cobol Converter 286	IBM DOS, OS/MVS	Cobol to Cobol	
Desktop AI Fairfield, CT	dBx/Express 287	IBM PC		dBase programs to C
Diversified Data Services Inc. Providence, RI	Go-Between 288	IBM PC-/MS-DOS, Unix, RMS	Datapoint RPGII batch source code to Databus source code	
Evansville Data Processing Evansville, IN	CBLAID 289	DEC VAX/VMS	Cobol programs to DEC VAX/VMS	

geared to DB2. A version is also available for IDMS.

Using the Database Administrator, existing physical files or designs can be reverse-engineered for use within Bachman's Data Analyst product. That product is used to create a data model, which can then be used to "forward-engineer" the data model into a DB2 design.

The vendor also offers DA Capture (Files) for migrating Vsam and sequential files to IDMS or DB2, and DA Capture (IMS), which performs the same function for IMS.

Another conversion option is to bridge technologies, to create what some call "transparencies." These allow users to run existing applications against their old database system, while migrating data into the new database structure.

Essentially, the bridges translate the old system's calls to those of the new system. The old applications run unchanged under the new system, without rewriting.

Software AG of North America, Inc., Reston, Va., maker of Adabas, offers three bridges to its database: DL1/IMS, Vsam and Total.

Bridges can be either permanent or interim solutions, says Doug Henrich, product manager for the Natural 4GL, also a Software AG product, and bridging technologies. "Half of our customers use them as long-term, production-oriented tools, and never rewrite their applications. The other half rewrite their applications for a relational system, especially those moving away from IMS."

Why use a bridge? "For static applications that are just fine the way they are, why rewrite?" asks Henrich.

Bridge products allow users to

REPRESENTATIVE CONVERSION TOOLS

VENDOR	PRODUCT/ CIRCLE NO.	OPERATING SYSTEM REQUIREMENTS	LANGUAGE/OPERATING SYSTEM CONVERSION	DBMS CONVERSION
Interactive Systems Inc. Lowell, MA	Clone 290	DEC VAX/VMS	Cobol to Cobol, from HP, Unisys DECsystems to DEC VAX/VMS	
Language Technology Inc. Salem, MA	Recoder/CICS 291	IBM MVS	Automated re-engineering tool for online Cobol applications	
MHT Services River Edge, NJ	MHTran-1 293	IBM MVS	IBM DOS/VSE to MVS migration	
	MHTran-2 294	IBM MVS	Cobol to Cobol translator	
Michaels, Ross & Cole Glen Ellyn, IL	mrc-Productivity Series 295	IBM AS/400, S/38	Streamlines conversion to native on IBM AS/400 and S/38	
Pennington Systems Pennington, NJ	Conpax 297	DEC VAX/VMS	Assembler conversion utility; Macro-11 to VAX-11	
Rand Information Systems Alameda, CA	Rand Development Center 298	IBM MVS	Supports several types of conversions	
	Cobol to Cobol Translator 299	IBM MVS	Cobol to Cobol	
Rapitech Systems Suffern, NY	Fortrix-C 300	DEC VAX/VMS, Unix, MS-DOS	Fortran to C source language converter	
	Fortrix Ada 301	DEC VAX/VMS, Unix	Fortran to Ada translator	
	Coblix C 302	C environments	Cobol to C source language translator	
Seed Software Alexandria, VA	Migration Master 303	IBM MVS, VM, DOS, DEC VAX/ VMS, Prime, Unix, Unisys	Migration tool for Cobol, Fortran, C; code functions identically across multiple hosts	
Softool Corp. Goleta, CA	Fact 304	DEC VAX/VMS, DG, IBM PC	Fortran to Fortran, DEC to IBM PC, PC to DG, DG to DG	
Software Translations Newburyport, MA	B-Tran 305	IBM PC	Quick Basic to C source code translator	
STARx Technology Bakersfield, CA	Business Basic Translator 306	DG	Data General Basic to C	
Tom Software Seattle, WA	Lexigen 307	Wang VS, Cobol	Cobol to Speed II 4GL	
Viasoft Inc. Phoenix, AZ	Via/Insight 308	IBM MVS, MVS/XA		Code analyzer
XA Systems Los Gatos, CA	DataXpert 309	IBM MVS, MVS/XA		Restructuring tool; file extracts and conversions
	ReAct 310	IBM MVS, Unisys	Assembler to structured Cobol	

maintain their investments in existing technology. However, strategic applications warrant the time and trouble to redesign and rewrite, Henrich notes.

The use of transparencies may result in a performance trade-off, but this is frequently offset by the advantages of moving to the new database, said Henrich.

Leroy Jones, director of data processing for Tulsa County, Okla., uses Software AG's Vsam Bridge to link three county offices—the treasurer, assessor and county clerk. The county runs two IBM 4341s and one 4381, all tied together under DOS/VSE.

Three years ago, Jones brought in Adabas. "Each office wanted access to the other's data," Jones explains, "but it would have taken five man-years to convert our Vsam files."

The solution is still workable today, Jones says. "Access time isn't degraded at all, even though we added overhead."

Cost is also a factor. Vsam Bridge costs about $40,000, Jones says, but a total conversion project would cost $750,000, he estimates.

Computer Associates International, Inc., Garden City, N.Y., offers three products—Vsam Transparency, DL1 Transparency and Total Transparency—for its Datacom/DB database. "Transparencies lay a foundation for using data more intelligently," says Orrin Stevens, product analyst for CA/Datacom.

"Earlier data access methods were marked by a high level of difficulty. By moving it into a table-oriented relational environment, data becomes part of the corporate information resource," Stevens said.

Bruce Conforto, director of information services at American Olean Tile Co., a wholly owned subsidiary of Armstrong Industries in Lansdale, Pa., uses both DL1 Transparency and Vsam Transparency. The company runs an IBM 3090 120 E under VM and DOS/VSE SP 3.2.

"When it comes to databases, it's clear that relational technology is superior to any other," Conforto says. "It's far easier to add a new column or field. In the old days, to describe a larger field in a flat file or Vsam file, we'd have to recompile all the pro-

grams using that file. With a relational system, we can have different views of different tables without writing new programs.

"Rewriting applications is a good thing to do, but we can't necessarily afford to do that," Conforto continues. "We have to spend our time working on things that add value to the business. Recreating a database doesn't do that."

The transparencies allow Conforto to convert the system to native Datacom/DB over time. "We can redesign the system and replace existing applications at our leisure," he says. Without the license fees of the old system, the new solution can be cost-effective as well, he added.

For many users, the big question is not just how to get to a relational system, but how to get to a specific relational system: IBM's DB2. To help them, IBM has recently introduced three conversion guides, for converting from IDMS, Adabas, and Datacom/DB to DB2.

USER INTEREST IN DB2

IBM has received thousands of requests for the guides, according to Russell Donovan, database market support manager at IBM's application enabling marketing center in San Jose, Calif.

User acceptance of relational database technology and SQL, as well as improved relational productivity, are sparking this newfound interest in DB2, Donovan says. "People aren't going to buy non-relational systems they know they'll have trouble maintaining and will have to rewrite into relational in just a few years. They want to protect their investments by investing in relational systems and SQL now."

SAA, too, has been a "real boost" for relational technology, Donovan says. "SAA is based on a relational database. Customers want to be able to move applications across hardware platforms and access data transparently. The acceptance of SAA has accelerated the acceptance of SQL and relational technology."

Despite his conviction that users no longer want to invest in non-relational technology, Donovan does not recommend wholesale conver-

sion efforts. "When major changes have to be made, that's a good time to think about moving over. But if there's no reason to change, don't convert," he advises.

Donovan recommended the following steps for converting to DB2: First, optimize the existing database for a relational system, to gain full performance advantages.

Second, minimize code changes. "Call-to-call conversions won't perform well," Donovan says. For instance, five or six IDMS calls can be replaced by one call to DB2.

Then, automate testing—one of the most time-consuming aspects of any database conversion; and finally, hold end-user requests for changes until after the conversion is completed.

IBM recommends several tools to aid in the DB2 conversion effort. "Bachman's tools do a nice job of analyzing the existing data dictionary and coming up with an optimized design," Donovan said.

Another product, DBLink/IDMS from San Francisco-based Forecross, actually runs through application code and converts it to DB2, Donovan says. The product creates DB2 tables from IDMS records, migrates the data over to DB2—generating a series of Cobol programs for each record that is converted—and finally converts the source code to DB2 calls.

In addition to the Cross System Product (CSP) fourth-generation language and Query Management Facility, IBM offers several other tools to aid in conversions to DB2.

DBMaui is a migration aid that allows users to move tables from one system to another. DXT accesses data from IMS, Vsam or other relational systems and moves it to DB2. Additional tools are DBEdit, a screen editor; DB2PM, a performance monitor; and DBRad, a dictionary product.

As for IMS conversions to DB2, IBM is promoting co-existence as the best solution—for now. IBM is looking at putting SQL interfaces to IMS, Donovan says. But eventually, a conversion guide for IMS will come, because IMS is not—and never will be—part of SAA.

Consultants are also available to help in DB2 conversions.

Carl Fitch, corporate director of database consulting at New York-based Cap Gemini America, said sources at the IBM Application Enabling Marketing Center in Cary, N.C., told him that of all companies that installed DB2 last year, 42% used a consultant or vendor to help them get started.

GOOD DESIGN IS IMPORTANT

Cap Gemini has developed a series of Prolog-based expert systems programs that it uses as part of its services to aid the conversion effort. The expert system ''pulls apart'' calls in the source database, analyzes them, and breaks down the Cobol syntax.

Converting from other relational systems to DB2 is a straightforward process, says Fitch, if—and it's a big if—both databases use Ansi standard SQL calls. But converting hierarchical or network databases, such as

IMS or IDMS, to DB2 is ''at the other end of the spectrum,'' Fitch says.

''In a hierarchical system, you have to write all your programs around the database's structure. You have to write navigational code that tells the system how to go get what you want.

''That means squat to a relational system. You just tell it what you want, not how to go get it, and you get a set of data back, rather than record by record,'' Fitch says.

The job of Cap Gemini's expert system tool is to follow the old database's programming logic, analyze what the process is doing, and determine which calls are really necessary in designing the new database.

''The most important piece of a DB2 conversion is doing a good job of designing the DB2 tables,'' Fitch says. ''After you do your logical data modeling and normalize the data, then you can do physical database design and look at your processes.

The idea is to set up a quality platform for DB2 and figure out the best way to get there from where you are now, whether that means re-engineering, rewriting or converting source code.''

Niemann of Computer Task Group, another DB2 conversion consultant, sees the shift to DB2 and other relational systems as preparation for the future of information systems. ''Migration to DB2 is going to be more common,'' he says.

''As SAA matures, we'll see another revolution in terms of process distribution between workstations and the mainframe, and distributed databases working together,'' Niemann continued.

''Lots of companies are rethinking the way they do applications, and such issues as managing networks of workstations and distributing software. The changes will be even more radical than database conversion. It's a fun area to watch,'' he said. ∎

Chapter 8
Source Code Analysis

Chapter 8
Source Code Analysis

Purpose

Source code analysis is fundamental to many reengineering tools. This chapter discusses tools and approaches for decomposing programs into objects and relationships that can be further used, studied or transformed. This will help the reader understand what reengineering and reverse engineering can do with program decompositions. The papers presented here also discuss why program decompositions are so valuable.

Papers

In the first paper, "The C Information Abstraction System," Yih-Farn Chen, Michael Nishimoto, and C.V. Ramamoorthy discuss a system for decomposing C programs into a relational database containing information about the programs. To get information about a program, the database is queried. This approach makes it much easier for users to get program information. The steps of parsing a program, storing the results, and making the information easily accessible, without the need for programmed queries, are built into the tool.

In the next paper, "Using Program Slicing in Software Maintenance," Keith Gallagher and James Lyle discuss program slicing and its use in software maintenance, particularly in understanding code and in impact analysis. Program slicing[1] captures subsets of program code according to "slice criteria." For example, if one wanted to find all the code that could conceivably affect the value of a variable X in a given statement, a slice could be used to determine this code. The authors show how slicing can be used to reduce regression testing. This is significant because retesting reengineered code often consumes much time in practice.

In the last paper, "Using Automatic Program Decomposition Techniques in Software Maintenance Tools," Rajeev Gopal and Stephen R. Schach formally characterize a program decomposition. A formal program decomposition characterization — especially characterizing program semantics — helps determine the "power" or limitations of a chosen program decomposition scheme, and of the tools that use the decomposition. This is important when using decomposition for impact analysis and regeneration of source code.

---

[1]Mark Weiser, *Program Slicing: Formal Psychological Investigations of an Automatic Program Abstraction Method,* PhD thesis, University of Michigan, Ann Arbor, Michigan, 1979.

325

The C Information Abstraction System

YIH-FARN CHEN, MEMBER, IEEE, MICHAEL Y. NISHIMOTO, AND
C. V. RAMAMOORTHY, FELLOW, IEEE

Abstract—This paper describes a system for analyzing program structures. The system extracts relational information from C programs according to a conceptual model and stores the information in a database. We show how several interesting software tasks can be performed by using the relational views. These tasks include generation of graphical views, subsystem extraction, program layering, dead code elimination, and binding analysis.

Index Terms—Entity-relationship model, hierarchy, hypertext, modularization, multiple views, program database, software maintenance, software metrics, software restructuring, software reusability.

I. INTRODUCTION

ANALYZING the structure of large programs is one of the most frustrating and time-consuming parts of software maintenance. This paper describes a program abstraction system designed to provide different levels of abstractions that can aid the discovery process during software maintenance. The system summarizes the structure information of programs in a relational database. Programmers can invoke relational queries to analyze various aspects of their software. Sophisticated tools have been built on top of the relational views to automate many software development and maintenance functions.

The construction of a program abstraction system involves three steps:

• *Form a Conceptual Model:* A conceptual model for the target programming language defines the software objects and relationships at a selected level of abstraction. It serves as a requirements specification for the information abstractor and determines the extent of knowledge available in the database. A conceptual model must be *complete*, i.e., all object and relationship kinds at the selected level of abstraction must be present in the model. Completeness guarantees that software tools working at that level of abstraction will perform correctly without missing information.

Manuscript received December 10, 1987; revised September 10, 1989. Recommended by F. B. Bastani.

Y.-F. Chen was with the Computer Science Division, Department of Electrical Engineering and Computer Science, University of California, Berkeley, CA 94720. He is now with AT&T Bell Laboratories, 600 Mountain Avenue, Murray Hill, NJ 07974.

M. Nishimoto was with the Computer Science Division, Department of Electrical Engineering and Computer Science, University of California, Berkeley, CA 94720. He is now with MIPS Computer Systems, Inc., 928 Arques Avenue, Sunnyvale, CA 94086.

C. V. Ramamoorthy is with the Computer Science Division, Department of Electrical Engineering and Computer Science, University of California, Berkeley, CA 94720.

IEEE Log Number 8933201.

• *Extract Relational Views:* A parser is then built to analyze the program text and extract relational information according to the conceptual model. At this stage, the textual representation of programs is converted to a relational database.

• *Construct Abstract Views:* A set of tools is then built to process the relational views and provide different levels of abstract views. An abstract view shows one aspect of the program structure and hides unnecessary details.

This approach can be applied to most programming languages and structured documents. For an initial application, we selected C [14] as our target language because it is in wide use. A large pool of production C programs are available for analysis and they need automated tools to improve their maintainability.

We decided to store the program structure information in a relational form because it allows us to use the sophisticated query power of relational database systems. Joining the program database with relational databases for other forms of software documents will be a natural extension in the future.

We built the C Information Abstraction system (CIA)[1] used to analyze many production programs at the University of California, Berkeley. This paper discusses the rationale behind the design of CIA and shows how CIA can be used to study the following aspects of program structures:

• *Subsystem:* Identify self-contained components in a large system.

• *Layering:* Topologically sort different combinations of reference relationships.

• *Dead code:* Detect unused code in a software system.

• *Coupling:* Analyze the binding strength between pairs of software objects.

Section II discusses some related work in program abstraction systems. Section III gives an overview of CIA. Section IV describes the CIA conceptual model, which defines the objects and relationships to be extracted by CIA. It also compares a set of program databases. Section V gives a few examples of relational queries. Section VI demonstrates the use of CIA in exploring several aspects of program structures. Finally, Section VII gives our retrospection and describes the current status and future work on CIA.

[1]In this paper, we use the lower case italic word *cia* to denote the C Information Abstractor, and the word CIA in capital letters to denote the C Information Abstraction System.

Reprinted from *IEEE Transactions on Software Engineering,* Vol. 16, No. 3, March 1990, pp. 325-334. ©1990 by The Institute of Electrical and Electronics Engineers, Inc. All rights reserved.

II. Related Work

Several program abstraction systems have been proposed and reported in the literature. In the following, we give a brief description of a selective set of systems that were actually implemented. We then summarize the lessons we learned from these implementations.

A. MasterScope

MasterScope is used in the Interlisp environment [24] to analyze and cross-reference user programs. MasterScope originated from a simple program, PrintStructure, which analyzed function definitions and printed out the tree structure of their calls.[2] Later, to eliminate the difficulty of extracting specific information from the massive output generated by PrintStructure, a separation between program analysis and interrogation was introduced.

MasterScope is integrated with the file and editor packages in Interlisp. It can automatically reanalyze changed pieces of a program to maintain its database. Users communicate with MasterScope by using an English-like command language. The Common Lisp Framework programming environment (CLF) [13] also has a static analysis tool similar to MasterScope.

B. FAST

FAST (Fortran Analysis System) [2] provides a set of analysis capabilities for Fortran programs. Unlike MasterScope, FAST uses a general database management system, System 2000, which is based on a hierarchical data model, to manage its program information. This approach allows FAST to avoid duplicating the functions of a database system. The conceptual model of FAST consists of attributes of modules, statements, and names, and relationships between these language objects. FAST also uses a command language, instead of a fixed set of commands, to perform query and analysis functions.

C. OMEGA

The idea of storing program information in a database was also implemented in the experimental system OMEGA [16], which incorporated the design of a relational schema for a Pascal-like language called *Model*. Unlike FAST, OMEGA used INGRES [22] for database management and thus could apply all relational operators on its program database. One of the goals of OMEGA was to allow reconstruction of software objects from the program database. Therefore, detailed information about variables, expressions, statements, and relationships among them were stored in the database. A total of 58 relations were used in the database schema. This information took significant time to process and required the manipulation of a large database even for a small project. According to [16], the prototype implementation of OMEGA had poor response time in retrieving the body of a procedure. Different objects within the procedure had to be retrieved, and each retrieval required a separate database query.

[2] *Cflow* [15] does a similar job for C programs.

D. Cscope

Cscope [21] is a screen-oriented C program browser that allows one to examine C symbol usages and locate or modify function definitions and macros. Cscope creates a cross-reference file that essentially stores all the compressed source text. Every line is tagged with information about references to symbols. The size of the cross-reference file is usually close to that of the source files.

E. Lessons

From examination of these systems, we infer certain desirable properties of a program abstraction system:

• *Separation of Extraction and Presentation:* The information extraction process should be separate from the presentation process. Such an approach allows greater flexibility for information presentation. The shift from PrintStructure to MasterScope in Interlisp is an example of this effort. OMEGA, FAST, and CLF also followed this principle. However, several existing systems still merge these two processes together, e.g., *Cflow*. Cscope has two execution phases: extraction and presentation, but the two phases are merged in a single tool.

• *A Concise Conceptual Model:* A conceptual model defines what information should be stored in the database. We found the entity-relationship model [3] suitable for modeling C programs. Using this model, programmers view their programs as a collection of software objects and a set of relationships between objects. Each object has a set of attributes. This abstraction is essential for understanding large programs. Unlike OMEGA, however, we believe that only *global* objects, i.e., objects that can be referred to across function boundaries, and their interrelationships need to be stored in the program database. Details of interactions between local objects are ignored because they are only interesting in a small context. This approach not only helps reduce the size of the program database but also speeds up information retrieval.

• *Separation of Database and Source:* If a database consisted of all the information required to make the correct executable code, then theoretically the source code could be thrown away. Unfortunately, to represent a complete program in a relational form can cause a retrieval of a complex object to be extremely slow, as experienced in the OMEGA system. On the other hand, the database of Cscope is a file that compresses and stores the program text. This approach allows efficient search of strings and symbols for small or medium-sized programs, but might not scale up for large programs. Our decision was to store only pointers to the source text in the database. A database query operation and a source file access operation are sufficient to retrieve the full text of any software object.

• *Incremental Database Cosntruction:* Since a program may consist of hundreds of modules, it is crucial that the program database be constructed incrementally. A separate database should be kept for each module or collection of modules, and it should be possible to link a set of databases together to construct a large one. Both

327

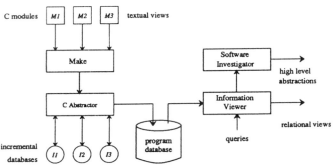

Fig. 1. The C information abstraction system.

MasterScope and CLF provide an incremental abstraction facility at a finer granularity. For our system, we decided to combine the dependency checking mechanism of the UNIX[3] *Make* [6], [7] command with our incremental abstraction facility. This approach avoids duplicating the task of checking timestamps for related files and allows a database to be reconstructed efficiently when a subset of the source files is modified.

The above discussion outlines the design rationale of the CIA system. In the following, we give a brief description of the CIA components and the conceptual model.

III. SYSTEM OVERVIEW

The CIA system consists of three major components: the C Abstractor, the Information Viewer (InfoView) and Software Investigator, as shown in Fig. 1. The C Abstractor uses a conceptual model to convert the textual description of a set of C source modules (files) into a set of objects and relationships. Make checks the timestamps of each file and invokes the C Abstractor on a file only if that file has been modified since the creation of the last program database. The relational information of each source file is recorded in an incremental database. The incremental databases are then linked together to construct a large program database, which can be processed by a variety of database management systems and tools, including Awk [1], INGRES and our InfoView system. A collection of tools has been built to process the relational views to provide graphical views and some interesting information about program structures. These tools are collectively called the Software Investigator.

IV. THE CIA CONCEPTUAL MODEL

Fig. 2 shows the conceptual model of the C program database as viewed by the CIA tools and users. Each box represents an object kind, while each connection between two boxes represents a reference relationship. Object kinds, attributes of objects, and relationships between objects are defined in the following sections.

A. Object Kinds and Domains

A C program is viewed as a collection of *global* objects. A global object is a software object definition whose

[1]UNIX is a registered trademark of AT&T Bell Laboratories.

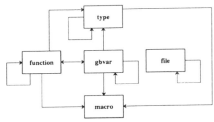

Fig. 2. The conceptual model of the C program database.

identifier can be referred to across function boundaries in C programs. Only five kinds of global objects exist in C programs: files, macros, global variables, data types, and functions. An object *domain* is a collection of objects of a particular kind.

For example, Fig. 3 shows a simple C program that consists of ten global objects in the five object domains:

file domain:	**main.c, coor.h, until.c**
macro domain:	**DELTA**
data type domain:	**struct coor, COOR**
global variable domain:	**org**
function domain:	**main, rotate, shift**

B. Attributes

Each object has a set of attributes. For example, the *nonstatic* function[4] **main** shown in Fig. 3 resides in **main.c** and returns an integer. Its text starts at line 7 and ends at line 12. Therefore, the attribute list of **main** is as follows:

file:	**main.c**
datatype:	**int**
name:	**main**
static:	**no**
bline:	**7**
eline:	**12**

Similarly, there is a different set of attributes for macros, types, global variables, and files. The CIA conceptual model does not explicitly define the order of attri-

[4]A function in C is *static* if its scope is limited to the source file in which it is defined.

```
<main.c>                  <coor.h>                 <util.c>
1  #include "coor.h"      1  struct coor {        1  #include "coor.h"
2  #define  DELTA 5        2      int x;           2
3                         3      int y;           3  rotate(degree, point)
4  COOR org =             4  };                   4  int degree;
5  {DELTA, 2*DELTA};      5                       5  COOR point;
6                         6  typedef              6  { /* rotate */ }
7  main(angle)            7  struct coor COOR;    7
8  int angle;                                     8  shift(distance, point)
9  {                                              9  int distance;
10   rotate(angle, org);                          10 COOR point;
11   shift(DELTA, org);                           11 { /* shift */ }
12 }
```

Fig. 3. A textual view.

butes or their storage format in the database. These details are specified in the relational database schema.

C. Relationships

In the CIA conceptual model, a *reference* relationship exists between objects *A* and *B* if the definition of *A* refers to *B*. In other words, *A* refers to *B* if *A* cannot be compiled and executed without the definition of *B*.

Table I lists all the meaningful reference relationships among the five object kinds in C programs. As an example, in Fig. 3, the following reference relationships can be identified:

object 1	relationship	object 2	comment
main.c	includes	coor.h	file to file
until.c	includes	coor.h	file to file
org	refers to	DELTA	gbvar to macro
org	refers to	COOR	gbvar to type
main	refers to	rotate	function to function
main	refers to	shift	function to function
main	refers to	org	function to gbvar
main	refers to	DELTA	function to maco
COOR	refers to	struct coor	type to type
struct coor	refers to	COOR	type to type
rotate	refers to	COOR	function to type
shift	refers to	COOR	function to type

Note that there is a *defined-in* relationship between any object (other than a file) and the file in which it resides. However, this relationship is modeled as the *file* attribute of each object because an object definition can only reside in a single file.

Relationships can also have attributes, as was done in MasterScope, FAST, and OMEGA. Moreover, attribute grammars can be used to support and augment the relational model in an editing environment [10]. However, our simplified model proves to be adequate for studying most applications (shown in Section VI) in structure analysis.

D. A Comparison of Several Program Databases

Our initial implementation of the C Information Abstractor collects the attributes of all object definitions and the first four relationships shown in Table I.[5]

The program database consists of nine files in two categories. The files in the first category include **file.data**,

TABLE I
REFERENCE RELATIONSHIPS IN C PROGRAMS

num	objkind1	objkind2	definition
1	file	file	file1 includes file2
2	function	function	function1 refers to function2
3	function	gbvar	function refers to gbvar
4	function	macro	function refers to macro
5	function	type	function refers to type
6	gbvar	function	gbvar refers to function
7	gbvar	gbvar	gbvar1 refers to gbvar2
8	gbvar	macro	gbvar refers to macro
9	gbvar	type	gbvar refers to type
10	type	type	type1 refers to type2
11	type	macro	type refers to macro

function.data, gbvar. data, macro.data, and **type.data.** They store the attribute of each object domain. The files in the second category include **filefile.data** (file-to-file), **funcfunc.data** (function-to-function), **macrofunc.data** (function-to-macro), and **gbvrfunc.data** (function-to-global). They store information about the four relationships. Additional files can be generated to record function call arguments.

Table II compares some metrics obtained from the database of four programs in different application areas.[6] They include a database tool, a language parser (*cia* itself), a distributed server, and a graphics editor.

The first six rows in Table II show the number of different kinds of objects in each program. The next five rows compare the number of various relationships. The last four rows give the size of databases and source files. Note that the program database is normally between 25% and 50% of the size of source files. Both the execution time for building an incremental database (see Section III) and the time to link all incremental databases to build the final program database are normally half that of corresponding parts in a C compiler. For example, it took 301 cpu seconds to compile the graphics editor on a SUN 3/60 workstation, but only 167 cpu seconds to build its program database. This is because *cia* does not generate actual code, and it assumes that all the input source files are syntactically correct.[7] The storage requirement and abstrac-

---

[5]A new implementation at AT&T Bell Laboratories collects all relationships shown in Table I.

[6]Large databases have also been built for proprietary programs on the order of five hundred thousand lines of code.

[7]Merging compilation and information abstraction in a single task would perform more quickly than compilation followed by abstraction; in practice, however, one would like to update a database only after several compilations to remove all syntactic and most semantic errors.

TABLE II
COMPARING FOUR PROGRAM DATABASES

metric	meaning	dbtool	parser	server	gfxed
nfile	number of files	50	42	51	25
ngbvar	number of global variables	39	141	205	279
ntype	number of data types	12	33	64	11
nmacro	number of macros	144	203	330	226
nfunction	number of functions	60	125	155	437
objtot	total number of objects	305	544	978	832
nfifi	file to file relationships	128	152	240	157
nfufu	function to function relationships	168	191	229	955
nfugb	function to gbvar relationships	76	606	418	1178
nfuma	function to macro relationships	292	486	505	1699
reltot	total number of relationships	664	1435	2197	3999
enttot	total number of database entries	969	1979	2197	4967
dbsize	database size in bytes	29073	67770	57323	157648
srcline	total number of source lines	3526	8350	9580	13996
srcsize	source size in bytes	95001	251638	227779	330756

tion speed of *cia* make it a practical tool for building program databases.

Additional software metrics can be derived from the metrics shown in Table II. We name a few here:

- $AvgFunction\_File = nfunction/nfile$: Average number of functions per file.
- $AvgFunction\_Gbvar = nfugb/ngbvar$: Average number of functions referring to a global variable.
- $AvgGbvar\_Function = nfugb/nfunction$: Average number of global variables referred to by a function.

These size metrics give us some preliminary ideas on how complex the interconnections between components are in these programs. For example, a program with a large value of $AvgFunction\_Gbvar$ often indicates that most functions in that program are tightly coupled through references to the same global variables. Additional interesting metrics derivable from the program database are described in the next section and in Section VI.

V. RELATIONAL VIEWS AND TEXTUAL VIEWS

The program database created by *cia* can be loaded and processed by any relational database system. This section shows what relational and textual views can be created by retrieving and processing information in the database. Examples of three major types of information retrieval are provided:

- info: retrieval of attribute information
- rel: retrieval of relationships between two object domains
- view: view the definition of an object.

For each kind of information retrieval, we give examples for queries in InfoView, a collection of tools specifically designed for accessing the program database, and QUEL, the relational query language of INGRES, to show the kind of information that can be retrieved from the program database.

A user only has to understand the CIA conceptual model to use the InfoView commands. They operate on the database in the local directory or the one specified by a UNIX environment variable. Knowledge of the underlying relational database schema or a complex query language is not required. In the following, we use a program database built from the example shown in Fig. 3 to illustrate the use of the InfoView and QUEL queries.

A. Info

The InfoView command *info* gives information about an object's attributes. An object is specified by its object domain and name. For example, to see the attributes of the function main, one would type the following:

$ info function main

file	type	function	static	bline	eline
main.c	int	main	no	7	12

Info is especially useful for finding the data type and location of an object. The *view* command introduced below uses the **file, bline,** and **eline** information to retrieve the definition of an object.

An option is provided for all InfoView commands to output the information in an unformatted form (fields separated by colons). This allows the data to be easily processed by other commands through UNIX pipes.

With a complete relational query language, one can ask the following queries:

- What is the average size of a function?
- What is the number of static functions in the program?
- Which file has the most number of functions?
- Which functions in **main.c** return a pointer to **COOR?**

For example, the last query expressed in QUEL would be

range of p is function
retrieve (p.function) where p.file = ''main.c'' and
p.type = ''COOR *''

These queries can also be implemented by UNIX shell scripts or C programs that use the InfoView commands or libraries.

B. Rel

The InfoView command *Rel* retrieves the relational information between two object domains. The relational information is especially useful for constructing graphical views and studying program structures.

The basic syntax of *rel* is

$ rel obj_kind1 obj_kind2 obj_name1 obj_name2

The first two arguments specify the kind of relationship. The next two arguments are optional and they specify a parent (an object that makes a reference) and a child (an object that is referred to). For example, to print out all the functions called by **main,** one would type the following:

$ rel function function main −

file1	function1	file2	function2
main.c	main	until.c	rotate
main.c	main	until.c	shift

The wildcard ``−`` matches anything and can be used for the parent, the child, or both.[8] To print out all the files

---

[8] Ideally, the wildcard should also be allowed for object kinds.

that include **coor.h,** one would type:

```
$ rel file file − coor.h
```

filename	include
main.c	coor.h
until.c	coor.h

The database can answer many interesting queries:
- Which function defined in **until.c** are referred to by functions in **main.c?**
- Which functions refer to the global variable **org** and the data type **COOR?**
- Which function has the largest fan-in?
- Which static functions refer to the macro **DELTA?**

The first query expressed in QUEL would be

```
range of p is funcfunc
retrieve (p. function1, p.function2)
where p.file1 = "main.c" and p.file2 = "until.c"
```

The last query expressed in QUEL would be

```
range of p is function
range of q if funcmacr
retrieve (p.function)
where p.static = "yes"
and p.function = q.function
and q.macro = "DELTA"
```

C. View

View retrieves the definition of a specified object. It obtains the location information of an object from the program database and then extracts the text out of the source file that contains the object definition. For example, to see the definition of the global variable **org,** one would type:

```
$ view gbvar org
COOR org =
{DELTA, 2*DELTA};
```

At this point, the definition of the data type **COOR** and the marco **DELTA** would be of interest and this information can be obtained by typing the following:

```
$ view type COOR
typedef
struct coor COOR;

$ view marco DELTA
#define DELTA 5
```

Note that a programmer can easily trace the definitions of various objects along any reference path without memorizing the locations of any object definitions.

D. Performance of the InfoView Queries

The three commands *info, ref,* and *view* provide information that most programmers would need during the development and maintenance of software. With a proper user interface, the database information might effectively turn the C program text into Hypertext [5].

Table III shows the performance of three most frequently used InfoView queries:

TABLE III
PERFORMANCE OF THE INFOVIEW QUERIES (UNIT: SECOND)

metric	info	rel	view
real time	0.80	1.26	1.40
user time	0.16	0.25	0.16
system time	0.25	0.35	0.25

- info function main
- rel function function main
- view function main.

We ran the queries on the program database for the graphics editor shown in Table II on a SUN 3/60 workstation. The **info** command retrieves one function record from 437 records. The **rel** command retrieves fourteen function-to-function records from 955 records. The **view** command first retrieves one function record to obtain the **file, bline,** and **eline** attributes of the specified function and then retrieves the text from the source file. Three metrics are compared: the real time elapsed, the time spent on user programs, and the time spent on system calls. These metrics were collected by the UNIX *time* command. We found the response time of these queries adequate for most applications.

Our implementation of the InfoView commands perform only linear scans on the database files. For large programs, the query performance can be improved by introducing index files or by simply using a relational database system.

VI. The Software Investigator

The program database provides a basis to build software tools that uncover interesting aspects of program structures. In this section, we briefly discuss CIA-based software tools in five areas: graphical views, subsystem extraction, program Layering, dead code elimination and binding analysis. These tools are collectively called the Software Investigator.

A. Graphical Views

The program database can be used to generate graphical information that shows the internal structure of C programs. For example, Fig. 4 shows the function call graph of a system called *MiniInfo.* The graph was automatically drawn by DAG [8] using the function-to-function relationship information. The picture reveals the fan-ins and fan-outs of each function, and the layering structure of function calls.

Fig. 5 shows the file dependency structure of some header files used on SUN workstations. This information is obtained from the file-to-file relationships in a program database. The picture shows that thirteen header files have to be processed when the header file **window_hs.h** is included by any source file. File dependency information can be used to generate make dependencies automatically [26].

Similarly, other relationships in the program database can be displayed. The graphical views provide users with

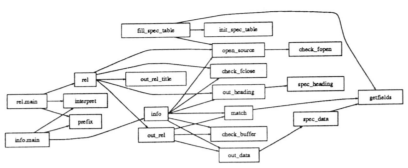

Fig. 4. The functional call structure of *MiniInfo*.

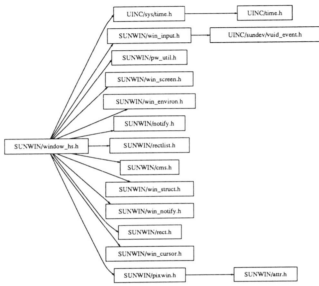

Fig. 5. A file dependency map.

helpful structural information that is usually hidden in the program text. Below, we use graphical views to illustrate some useful abstractions.

B. Subsystem Extraction

Suppose one would like to reuse the function **out_rel** in *MiniInfo* (shown in Fig. 4) in a different system *MaxInfo*. Furthermore, due to practical considerations, the source code of *MiniInfo* cannot be shared directly with *MaxInfo*. Note that **out_rel** cannot simply be copied over to *MaxInfo*. It will not compile because there will be missing references. In order to get a minimal *compilable slice* (in contrary to *executable slice* in [27]), all objects referred to directly or indirectly by **out_rel** have to be extracted and carried over to *MaxInfo*. The reachable set (closure) of an object can be computed by tracing all the reference relationships. We call the reachable set a *subsystem* of that function. For example, all objects in the subsystem of the function **out_rel** are listed here.

object_kind	in_file	object_name
macro	/usr/include/stdio.h	FILE
macro	Infoview.h	MAXBUFLEN
macro	Infoview.h	MAXLINE
macro	Infoview.h	TRUE
macro	error.h	BUFFER_OVERFLOW
macro	Infoview.h	MAXFIELD
macro	Infoview.h	NUMFIELD
type	relation.h	struct relation
gbvar	info.c	FORMAT
gbvar	info.c	MAXBUFFER
gbvar	dbschema.c	schema
function	xrel.c	out_rel
function	buffer.c	check_buffer
function	match.c	match
function	field.c	getfields
function	format.c	out_data
function	spec.c	spec_data

The list shows that at least six macros, one data type definition, three global variable definitions, and six function definitions, and six function definitions must be brought over to *MaxInfo* in order for the function **out_rel** to compile in the new system. Note that these objects are spread over different files, and it is not very effective use of programmer's time to extract these objects without the assistance of an automated tool.

The definitions of all objects in a reachable set can be assembled into a self-contained package to be reused in any other system. Subsystem extraction is useful for constructing a family of systems or for understanding portions of a large system by ignoring unrelated parts.

C. Program Layering

The function layering structure of a program can be obtained by using *topological sorting* on the function call relationships. Functions that are not called will appear at level 0,[9] functions that are called only by level 0 functions will appear at level 1, functions that are called only by level 0 and level 1 functions will appear at level 2, and so forth. In addition, strongly connected components (recursive functions) can be collapsed into a single node before the topological sorting algorithm is applied.

As an example, the layering structure of *MiniInfo* (shown in Fig. 4) can be shown in the following (including the fan-ins and fan-outs of each function):

in_file	func_name	level	fan-out	fan-in
info.c	main	0	3	0
rel.c	main	0	3	0
spec.c	fill_spec_table	0	3	0
xinfo.c	info	1	6	1
xrel.c	rel	1	5	1
interp.c	interpret	1	0	2
prefix.c	prefix	1	0	2
spec.c	init_spec_table	1	0	1
file.c	open_source	2	1	3
xrel.c	out_rel_title	2	0	1
xrel.c	out_rel	2	3	1
format.c	out_heading	2	1	2
file.c	check_fclose	2	0	2
match.c	match	3	1	2
format.c	out_data	3	1	2
file.c	check_fopen	3	0	1
spec.c	spec_heading	3	0	1
buffer.c	check_buffer	3	0	2
spec.c	spec_data	4	1	1
field.c	getfields	5	0	3

```
$ bind rel info
```

in_file1	func_name1	in_file2	func_name2	fun	mac	gbv	tot
xrel.c	rel	xinfo.c	info	3	8	1	12

```
$ bind interpret info
```

in_file1	func_name1	in_file2	func_name2	fun	mac	gbv	tot
interp.c	interpret	xinfo.c	info	0	2	0	2

A program can be layered in many ways. A type layering structure and a file layering structure can be obtained through the type-to-type and file-to-file relationships. A *complete* layering of all program objects will include all kinds of reference relationships.

The layering idea is similar to the implementation aspect of the *users hierarchy* proposed by Parnas [19], the functional hierarchy discussed in the FAMOS paper [9] and *Grids* proposed by Ossher [18]. The advantage provided by the program database is that the layering structure can be obtained automatically from the implementation and checked against the original design.

D. Deadcode Elimination

Only the **main** functions should appear at level 0 in C programs. However, in the case of *MiniInfo* shown in Fig. 4, we see one extra function **fill_spec_table** at level 0. This suggests that **fill_spec_table** is probably not used in the program and is a candidate for deletion.[10]

Before deleting **fill_spec_table**, we need to determine its *delete set*. The delete set of a function f is the set of objects in its subsystem that do not belong to the subsystem of any objects *outside* the subsystem of f. Each object in the delete set should be deleted to completely eliminate the dead code. For example, in Fig. 4, the subsystem of **fill_spec_table** includes five functions: itself, **init_spec_table, open_source, check_fopen,** and **getfields**. Both **fill_spec_table** and **init_spec_table** do not belong to the subsystem of any object outside the subsystem **fill_spec_table** and, therefore, are candidates for deletion.

E. Binding Analysis

We consider two functions to be strongly coupled if they share many references to the same objects. This is termed *used data bindings* by Hutchens and Basili [11]. For example, if function A and B share three function references, two macro references, and three global variable references, we might say that the binding strength between A and B is eight. Numbers like these may be obtained by analyzing the program database. For example, the following output shows the binding strength between two pairs of functions:

It shows that the two functions **rel** and **info** are tightly coupled (twelve shared references). On the other hand, **interpret** and **info** are loosely coupled (two shared references). In general, the binding strength values can be

---

[9]Parnas uses level 0 for the set of all programs that use no other program [19].

[10]The topological sorting should be applied to all relationships to make sure that **fill_spec_table** is not referenced by other kinds of objects, e.g., global variables.

333

used to cluster functions to reduce the cross coupling between modules. This approach has the advantage of localizing the impact of each change in the software. However, more research needs to be performed in assigning weights to different types of shared references. The closures of shared references should also be considered.

The layering analysis and the binding analysis allow us to recover the design decisions made on modularization and hierarchy in existing systems. An interesting discussion about the interactions between these two abstraction techniques can be found in [9].

VII. RETROSPECTION, CURRENT STATUS, AND FUTURE WORK

Users of CIA have found the system helpful in discovering various aspects of their programs. However, we also learned a few lessons from building CIA:

• A partial implementation of the complete conceptual model limits our ability to perform several analysis jobs accurately, e.g., the subsystem computation and the detection of unnecessary include files.

• Some InfoView commands require the user to specify the object kind of an object to retrieve its information. Unfortunately, when the user is viewing a program, the kind of an object is usually not obvious. For example, macro calls and function calls look the same in C programs.

• A C program can be built in various ways from the same source files simply by changing the compilation flags. Unfortunately, our program database does not keep any information about the compilation flags used and, therefore, only represents one of many possibilities. This problem can be partially corrected by applying the same information abstraction approach to the UNIX makefiles. The extracted information can supplement the program database and describe accurately how the database was built.

Both the C Information Abstractor and the InfoView system have been rewritten at AT&T Bell Laboratories to eliminate early design deficiencies and portability problems. The new C Information Abstractor implements the full conceptual model, and it conforms to the draft proposed ANSI C standard [12]. The new InfoView system has expanded the query capabilities to allow selection operations and regular expressions.

CIA is currently being widely used within AT&T for analyzing a variety of programs. Besides providing relational views that help software maintainers understand their code, the CIA tools also reveal various weaknesses in the programs analyzed.

Our future plans include the following.

• Integrate CIA tools with a source code control system, such as SCCS [20] or RCS [25]. The integration will allow a programmer to view objects from different versions and study the evolution of their software.

• Develop tools to automatically restructure C programs to reduce compilation cost and improve maintain-

ability. The restructuring tools will use the program database to guarantee the consistency of the result after program transformation.

• Perform controlled experiments to study the usage pattern of database queries. The results can be used to improve the query performance and user interface.

• Apply the same information abstraction approach to C++ [23] programs. The focus would be on the applicability of the relational model on object oriented programs.

We believe that with the program database and a set of application tools, the development and maintenance cost of most software systems can be greatly reduced.

ACKNOWLEDGMENT

We would like to thank L. Eng, W.-L. Chen, B. Chang, S. Nishimoto, A. Hung, and J.-S. Song for their contribution to the phototype of the CIA tools. The design of the original CIA system was affected by the ideas from many colleagues at the University of California, Berkeley, and AT&T Bell Laboratories, including A. Prakash, V. Garg, W.-T. Tsai, Y. Usuda, I. Brohard, and B. Wachlin. A draft of this paper was reviewed by D. Belanger, D. Korn, J. Grass, C. Hayden, S. Nishimoto, S. North, J. Schwarz, K.-P. Vo, A. Wolf, and other anonymous reviewers. Their comments improved the quality of this paper. Finally, we would also like to thank AT&T Bell Laboratories for the use of the excellent tool DAG to draw graphical views of program structures shown in this paper.

REFERENCES

[1] A. V. Aho, B. W. Kernighan, and P. J. Weinberger. *The AWK Programming Language.* Reading, MA: Addison-Wesley, 1988.

[2] J. C. Browne and David B. Johnson, "FAST: A second generation program analysis system," in *Proc. Second Int. Conf. Software Engineering,* 1977, pp. 142–148.

[3] P. S. Chen, *The Entity-Relationship Approach to Software Engineering.* New York: Elsevier Science, 1983.

[4] Y.-F. Chen and C. V. Ramamoorthy, "The C information abstractor," in *Proc. Tenth Int. Computer Software and Applications Conf. (COMPAC),* Oct. 1986, pp. 291–298.

[5] J. Conklin, "Hypertext: An introduction and survey," *IEEE Computer,* vol. 20, no. 9, pp. 17–41, Sept. 1987.

[6] S. I. Feldman, "Make—A program for maintaining computer programs," *Software—Practice and Experience,* vol. 9, no. 4, pp. 256–265, Apr. 1979.

[7] G. S. Fowler, "The fourth generation Make," in *Proc. USENIX Portland 1985 Summer Conf.,* 1985, pp. 159–174.

[8] E. R. Gansner, S. C. North, and K. P. Vo, "DAG—A program that draws directed graphs," *Software—Practice and Experience,* vol. 18, no. 11, Nov. 1988.

[9] A. N. Habermann, L. Flon, and L. Cooprider, "Modularization and hierarchy in a family of operating systems," *Commun. ACM,* vol. 19, no. 5, pp. 266–272, May 1976.

[10] S. Horwitz and T. Teitelbaum, "Generating editing environments based on relations and attributes," *ACM Trans. Program. Lang. Syst.,* vol. 8, no. 4, pp. 577–608, Oct. 1986.

[11] D. H. Hutchens and V. R. Basili, "System structure analysis: Clustering with data bindings," *IEEE Trans. Software Eng.,* vol. 11, no. 8, pp. 749–757, Aug. 1985.

[12] American National Standards Inst., *Draft Proposed American National Standard for Information Systems—Programming Language C.* Document X3J11/88-090, May 1988.

[13] USC Inform. Sci. Inst., *Introduction to the CLF Environment*, Mar. 1986.

[14] B. W. Kernighan and D. M. Ritchie, *The C. Programming Language*. Englewood Cliffs, Prentice-Hall, 1978.

[15] AT&T Bell Laboratories, *Unix System V Programmer's Manual*, 1985.

[16] M. A. Linton, "Implementing relational views of programs," in *Proc. ACM SIGSOFT/SIGPLAN Software Engineering Symp. Practical Software Development Environment*, May 1984.

[17] M. Nishimoto and Y. F. Chen, "Tutorial on the C information abstraction system," Comput. Sci. Division, Univ. California, Berkeley, Tech. Rep. UCB/CSD 327, 1987.

[18] H. L. Ossher, "A new program structuring mechanism based on layered graphs," in *Conf. Rec. Tenth Annu. ACM Symp. Principles of Programming Languages*, Jan. 1984, pp. 11-22.

[19] D. Parnas, "Designing software for ease of extension and contraction," *IEEE Trans. Software Eng.*, pp. 128-137, Mar. 1979.

[20] M. J. Rochkind, "The source code control system," *IEEE Trans. Software Eng.*, vol. 5, no. 2, pp. 364-370, Dec. 1975.

[21] J. L. Steffen, "Interactive examination of a C program with Cscope," In *Proc. USENIX Assoc. Winter Conf.*, Jan. 1985, pp. 170-175.

[22] M. Stonebraker, E. Wong, R. Kreps, and G. Held, "The design and implementation of INGRES," *ACM Trans. Database Syst.*, vol. 1, no. 3, pp. 189-222, Sept. 1976.

[23] B. Stroutsrup, *The C++ Programming Language*. Reading, MA: Addison-Wesley, 1987.

[24] W. Teitelman and L. Masinter, "The Interlisp programming environment," *Computer*, vol. 14, no. 4, pp. 25-34, Apr. 1981.

[25] W. F. Tichy, "Design, implementation, and evaluation of a revision control system," in *Proc. Sixth Int. Conf. Software Engineering*, Sept. 1982.

[26] K. Walden, "Automatic generation of Make dependencies," *Software—Practice and Experience*, vol. 14, no. 6, pp. 575-585, June 1984.

[27] M. Weiser, "Program slicing," *IEEE Trans. Software Eng.*, vol. SE-10, no. 4, pp. 352-357, July 1984.

Yih-Farn Chen (S'83-M'86) received the B.S. degree in electrical engineering from National Taiwan University, Taiwan, in 1980, the M.S. degree in computer science from University of Wisconsin, Madison, in 1983, and the Ph.D. degree in computer science from the University of California, Berkeley, in 1987.

He is currently a Member of Technical Staff at AT&T Bell Laboratories in Murray Hill, NJ. His research interests include the modeling and integration of software databases, programming languages and environments, and network management.

Dr. Chen is member of the IEEE Computer Society and the Association for Computing Machinery.

Michael Y. Nishimoto received the B.S. degree in electrical engineering/computer science from the University of California, Berkeley, in 1987, and the M.S. degree from Stanford University, Palo Alto, CA, in 1989.

He is currently working in the operating systems group at MIPS Computer Systems, Inc., Sunnyvale, CA, which designs, manufactures, and markets high-performance computer systems, workstations, and software based on RISC technology. Prior to joining MIPS Computers, he worked on the V Distributed Operating System at Stanford University, concentrating on improvements to the distributed file server and development of better process migration heuristics. At UC Berkeley he worked in a research group where he developed the C Information Abstractor, a system which determined relationships between software objects of large programs. His current research interests include distributed systems, programming environments, and multiprocessor architectures.

C. V. Ramamoorthy (M'57-SM'76-F'78) received the M.S. and Ph.D. degrees in applied math from Harvard University, Cambridge, MA, and the M.S. degree in mechanical engineering from the University of California, Berkeley.

Since 1972 he has been a Professor in the Department of Electrical Engineering and Computer Science at the University of California, Berkeley. Previously, from 1967 to 1972, he was a Professor of Electrical Engineering and Computer Science at the University of Texas, Austin. From 1956 to 1971 he was associated with Honeywell's Computer Division (now Honeywell Bull), Waltham, MA, where he last held the position of Senior Staff Scientist. He also held the Grace Hopper Chair and C.D.C. Distinguished Visiting Professorships at the Navy Post Graduate School and the University of Minnesota, respectively.

Dr. Ramamoorthy served as First Vice President of the IEEE Computer Society, Editor-in-Chief of the IEEE TRANSACTIONS ON SOFTWARE ENGINEERING from 1983 to 1987, and is currently Editor-in-Chief of the IEEE TRANSACTIONS ON KNOWLEDGE AND DATA ENGINEERING. He is presently a participant in the Distributed Intelligent Networking Group of the U.S. Army Strategic Defense Command. In 1989 he received the Taylor Booth Education Award for "outstanding contributions to computer science and engineering education" from the IEEE Computer Society.

IEEE TRANSACTIONS ON SOFTWARE ENGINEERING, VOL. 17, NO. 8, AUGUST 1991

751

Using Program Slicing in Software Maintenance

Keith Brian Gallagher and James R. Lyle, *Member, IEEE*

Abstract—Program slicing, introduced by Weiser, is known to help programmers in understanding foreign code and in debugging. We apply program slicing to the maintenance problem by extending the notion of a program slice (that originally required both a variable and line number) to a *decomposition slice*, one that captures all computation on a given variable; i.e., is independent of line numbers. Using the lattice of single variable decomposition slices ordered by set inclusion, we demonstrate how to form a slice-based decomposition for programs. We are then able to delineate the effects of a proposed change by isolating those effects in a single component of the decomposition. This gives maintainers a straightforward technique for determining those statements and variables which may be modified in a component and those which may not. Using the decomposition, we provide a set of principles to prohibit changes which will interfere with unmodified components. These semantically consistent changes can then be merged back into the original program in linear time. Moreover, the maintainer can test the changes in the component with the assurance that there are no linkages into other components. Thus decomposition slicing induces a new software maintenance process model which eliminates the need for regression testing.

Index Terms—Software maintenance, program slicing, decompostion slicing, software process models, software testing, software tools, impact analysis.

I. INTRODUCTION

IN "Kill that Code!" [32], G. Weinberg alludes to his private list of the world's most expensive program errors. The top 'hree disasters were caused by a change to exactly one line of code: "Each one involved the change of a *single digit* in a previously correct program." The argument goes that since the change was to only one line, the usual mechanisms for change control could be circumvented. And, of course, the results were catastrophic. Weinberg offers a partial explanation: "Unexpected linkages," i.e., the value of the modified variable was used in some other place in the program. The top three of this list of ignominy are attributed to linkage. More recently, Schneidewind [30] notes that one of the reasons that maintenance is difficult is that it is hard to determine when a code change will affect some other piece of code. We present herein a method for maintainers to use that addresses this issue.

While some may view software maintenance as a less intellectually demanding activity than development, the central premise of this work is that software maintenance is *more* demanding. The added difficulty is due in large part to the semantic constraints that are placed on the maintainer. These

Manuscript received March 17, 1989; revised April 5, 1991. Recommended by R. A. DeMille.
K. B. Gallagher is with the Computer Science Department, Loyola College in Maryland, 4501 N. Charles Street, Baltimore, MD 21210.
J. R. Lyle is with the University of Maryland, Baltimore Campus, 5401 Wilkens Avenue, Baltimore, MD 21228.
IEEE Log Number 9101139.

constraints can be loosely characterized as the attempt to avoid unexpected linkages. Some [4], [14] have addressed this problem by attempting to eliminate these semantic constraints and then providing the maintainer with a tool which will pinpoint potential inconsistencies after changes have been implemented. This makes maintenance appear to be more like development, since the programmer does not need to worry about linkages: Once the change is made, the tool is invoked and the inconsistencies (if any) are located. One would expect that the tool would proceed to resolve these inconsistencies, but it has been shown that this problem is NP-hard [14]. Thus the maintainer can be presented with a problem which is more difficult to resolve than the original change.

We take the opposite view: Present the maintainer with a semantically constrained problem and let him construct the solution which implements the change within these constraints. The semantic context with which we propose to constrain the maintainer is one that will *prohibit* linkages into the portions of the code that the maintainer does not want to change. This approach uncovers potential problems earlier than the aforementioned methods, and, we believe, is worth any inconvenience that may be encountered due to the imposition of the constraints.

Our program slicing-based techniques give an assessment of the impact of proposed modifications, ease the problems associated with revalidation, and reduce the resources required for maintenance activities. They work on unstructured programs, so they are usable on older systems. They may be used for white-box, spare-parts, and backbone maintenance without regard to whether the maintenance is corrective, adaptive, perfective, or preventive.

II. BACKGROUND

Program slicing, introduced by Weiser [33], [36], is a technique for restricting the behavior of a program to some specified subset of interest. A slice $S(v, n)$ (of program P) on variable v, or set of variables, at statement n yields the portions of the program that contributed to the value of v just before statement n is executed. $S(v, n)$ is called a *slicing criteria*. Slices can be computed automatically on source programs by analyzing data flow and control flow. A program slice has the added advantage of being an executable program. Slicing is done implicitly by programmers while debugging [33], [35]; slices can be combined to isolate sections of code likely to contain program faults and significantly reduce debugging times [23]–[25].

There has been a flurry of recent activities where slicing plays a significant role. Horwitz *et al.* [15], [16], [28] use slices in integrating programs. Their results are built on the seminal

752   IEEE TRANSACTIONS ON SOFTWARE ENGINEERING, VOL. 17, NO. 8, AUGUST 1991

work of Ottenstein and Ottenstein [7], [27], combining slicing with the robust representation afforded by program dependence graphs. Korel and Laski [20]–[22] use slices combined with execution traces for program debugging and testing. Choi *et al.* [6] use slices and traces in debugging parallel programs. Reps and Wang [29] have investigated termination conditions for program slices. Hausler [13] has developed a denotational approach to program slicing. Gallagher [8] has improved Lyle's [23] algorithm for slicing in the presence of GOTO's and developed techniques for capturing arbitrarily placed output statements. We will not discuss slicing techniques in this paper and instead refer the interested reader to these works.

Since we want to avoid getting bogged down in the details of a particular language, we will identify a program with its flowgraph. Each node in the graph will correspond to a single-source language statement. Henceforth the term statement will mean a node in the flowgraph. Using a common representation scheme makes the presentation clear, although it is clear that any tool based on these techniques will need to account for the nuances of the particular language. In this paper we also ignore problems introduced by having dead code in the source program, and declare that the programs under consideration will not have any dead code. See [8] for slicing-based techniques to eliminate dead code.

Figs. 2–6 illustrate slicing on the program of Fig. 1, a bare bones version of the Unix utility **wc**, word count, taken from [19]. The program counts the number of characters, words, and lines in a text file. It has been slightly modified to illustrate more clearly the slicing principles. The slices of Figs. 2–4 are complete programs which compute a restriction of the specification. The slice on **nw** (Fig. 2) will output the number of words in a file; the slice on **nc** (Fig. 3) will count the number of characters in the input text file; and the slice on **nl** (Fig. 4) will count the number of lines in the file.

III. USING SLICES FOR DECOMPOSITION

This section presents a method for using slices to obtain a decomposition of the program. Our objective is to use slicing to decompose a program "directly" into two (or more) components. A program slice will be one of the components. The construction is a two step process. The first step is to build, for one variable, a *decomposition slice,* which is the union of certain slices taken at certain line numbers on the given variable. Then the other component of the decomposition, called the *complement,* will also be obtained from the original program. The complement is constructed in such a way that when certain statements of the decomposition slice are removed from the original program, the program that remains is the slice that corresponds to the *complement* (in a sense to be defined) of the given criteria with respect to the variables defined in the program. Thus the complement is also a program slice.

The decomposition slice is used to guide the removal of statements in a systematic fashion to construct the complement. It is insufficient to merely remove the slice statements from the original program. Since we require that a slice be executable, there will be certain crucial statements that are necessary in both the slice and its complement. For example,

```
1   #define YES 1
2   #define NO 0
3   main()
4   {
5       int c, nl, nw, nc, inword ;
6       inword = NO ;
7       nl = 0;
8       nw = 0;
9       nc = 0;
10      c = getchar();
11      while ( c != EOF ) {
12          nc = nc + 1;
13          if ( c == '\n')
14              nl = nl + 1;
15          if ( c == ' ' || c == '\n' || c == '\t')
16              inword = NO;
17          else if (inword == NO) {
18              inword = YES ;
19              nw = nw + 1;
20          }
21          c = getchar();
22      }
23      printf("%d \n",nl);
24      printf("%d \n",nw);
25      printf("%d \n",nc);
26  }
```

Fig. 1. Program to be sliced.

```
1   #define YES 1
2   #define NO 0
3   main()
4   {
5       int c, nw, inword ;
6       inword = NO ;
8       nw = 0;
10      c = getchar();
11      while ( c != EOF ) {
15          if ( c == ' ' || c == '\n' || c == '\t')
16              inword = NO;
17          else if (inword == NO) {
18              inword = YES ;
19              nw = nw + 1;
20          }
21          c = getchar();
22      }
24      printf("%d \n",nw);
26  }
```

Fig. 2. Slice on **nw**: word counter.

```
3       main()
4       {
5           int c, nc ;
9           nc = 0;
10          c = getchar();
11          while ( c != EOF ) {
12              nc = nc + 1;
21              c = getchar();
22          }
25          printf("%d \n",nc);
26      }
```

Fig. 3. Slice on **nc**: character counter.

if we start with the slice of Fig. 2 and remove *all* its statements from the original program, the resulting object will not even compile!

```
3      main()
4      {
5          int c, nl, ;
7          nl = 0;
10         c = getchar();
11         while ( c != EOF ) {
13             if ( c == '\n')
14                 nl = nl + 1;
21             c = getchar();
22         }
23         printf("%d \n",nl);
26     }
```

Fig. 4. Slice on **nl**: line counter.

```
1      #define YES 1
2      #define NO 0
3      main()
4      {
5          int c, inword ;
6          inword = NO ;
10         c = getchar();
11         while ( c != EOF ) {
15             if ( c == ' ' || c == '\n' || c == '\t')
16                 inword = NO;
17             else if (inword == NO) {
18                 inword = YES ;
20             }
21             c = getchar();
22         }
26     }
```

Fig. 5. Slice on **inword**.

```
3      main()
4      {
5          int c ;
10         c = getchar();
11         while ( c != EOF ) {
21             c = getchar();
22         }
26     }
```

Fig. 6. Slice on **c**.

We use this decomposition to break the program into manageable pieces and automatically assist the maintainer in guaranteeing that there are no ripple effects induced by modifications in a component. We use the complement to provide a semantic context for modifications in the decomposition slice; the complement must remain fixed after any change.

The decomposition ideas presented in this section are independent of a particular slicing method. Once a slice is obtained by any slicing algorithm, a program decomposition may be computed. Clearly, the quality of the decomposition will be affected by the quality of the slice, in the sense that more refined slices give a finer granularity and also deliver more semantic information to the maintainer.

A program slice is dependent on a variable and a statement number. A *decomposition slice* does not depend on statement numbers. The motivation for this concept is easily explained using the example of Fig. 7. The slice $S(t, 4)$ is statements 1, 2, 3, 4, while the slice $S(t, 6)$ is statements 1, 2, 5, 6. Slicing at statement *last* (in this case 6) of a program is insufficient to get all computations involving the slice variable

```
1      input a
2      input b
3      t = a + b
4      print t
5      t = a - b
6      print t
```

Fig. 7. Requires a decomposition slice.

t. A decomposition slice captures all relevant computations involving a given variable.

To construct a decomposition slice, we borrow the concept of *critical instructions* from an algorithm for dead code elimination as presented in Kennedy [18]. A brief reprise follows. The usual method for dead code elimination is to first locate all instructions that are useful in some sense. These are declared to be the critical instructions. Typically, dead code elimination algorithms start by marking output instructions to be critical. Then the *use-definition* [18] chains are traced to mark the instructions which impact the output statements. Any code that is left unmarked is useless to the given computation.

Definition 1: Let $Output(P, v)$ be the set of statements in program P that output variable v, let $last$ be the last statement of P, and let $N = Output(P, v) \cup \{last\}$. The statements in $\bigcup_{n \in N} S(v)$ form the decomposition slice on v, denoted $S(v)$.

The decomposition slice is the union of a collection of slices, which is still a program slice [36]. We include statement *last* so that a variable which is not output may still be used as a decomposition criteria; this will also capture any defining computation on the decomposition variable after the last statement that displays its value. To successfully take a slice at statement last, we invoke one of the crucial differences between the slicing definitions of Reps [29], with those of Weiser [36], Lyle [23], and this work. A Reps slice must be taken at a point p with respect to a variable which is defined or referenced at p. Weiser's slices can be taken at an arbitrary variable at an arbitrary line number. This difference prohibits Reps's slicing techniques from being applicable in the current context, since we want to slice on every variable in the program at the last statement.

We now begin to examine the relationship between decomposition slices. Once we have this in place, we can use the decomposition slices to perform the actual decompositions. To determine the relationships, we take the decomposition slice for each variable in the program and form a lattice of these decomposition slices, ordered by set inclusion. It is easier to gain a clear understanding of the relationship between decomposition slices if we regard them *without* output statements. This may seem unusual in light of the above definition, since we used output statements in obtaining relevant computations. We view output statements as windows into the current state of computation, which do not contribute to the realization of the state. This coincides with the informal definition of a slice: the statements which yield the portions of the program that contributed to the value of v just before statement n is executed. Assuming that output statements do not contribute to the value of a variable precludes from our discussion output statements (and therefore programs) in which the output values are reused, as is the case with random access files or output to files which are later reopened for input. Moreover, we are describing a decomposition technique which is not dependent on any particular slicing technique; we have no way of knowing whether or not the slicing technique includes output statements or not. We say a slice is *output-restricted* if all its output statements are removed.

Definition 2: Output restricted decomposition slices $S(v)$ and $S(w)$ are *independent* if $S(v) \cap S(w) = \varnothing$.

It would be a peculiar program that had independent decomposition slices; they would share neither control flow or data flow. In effect, there would be two programs with nonintersecting computations on disjoint domains that were merged together. The lattice would have two components. In Ott's slice metric terminology [26], independence corresponds to low (coincidental or temporal) cohesion.

Output-restricted decomposition slices that are not independent are said to be *(weakly) dependent*. Subsequently, when we speak of independence and dependence *of slices*, it will always be in the context of output-restricted decomposition slices.

Definition 3: Let $S(v)$ and $S(w)$ be output-restricted decomposition slices, $w \neq v$, and let $S(v) \subset S(w)$. $S(v)$ is said to be *strongly dependent* on $S(w)$.

Thus output-restricted decomposition slices strongly dependent on independent slices are independent. The definitions of independence and dependence presented herein are themselves dependent on the notion of a slice. The analogous definitions are used by Bergeretti and Carré [3] to *define* slices. In Ott's metric terminology [26], strong dependence corresponds to high (sequential or functional) cohesion.

Strong dependence of decomposition slices is a binary relation; in most cases, however, we will not always need an explicit reference to the containing slice. Henceforth we will write "$S(v)$ is strongly dependent" as a shorthand for "$S(v)$ is strongly dependent on some other slice $S(w)$" when the context permits it.

Definition 4: An output-restricted slice $S(v)$ that is *not* strongly dependent on any other slice is said to be *maximal*.

Maximal decomposition slices are at the "ends" of the lattice. This definition gives the motivation for output restriction; we do not want to be concerned with the possible effects of output statements on the maximality of slices or decomposition slices. This can be observed by considering the decomposition slices on **nw** and **inword**, of Figs. 2 and 5. If we regarded output statements in defining maximal, we could force the slice on **inword** to be maximal by the addition of a *print* statement referencing **inword** along with the others at the end of the program. Such a statement would not be collected into the slice on **nw**. Since this added statement is not in any other slice, the slice on **inword** would be maximal and it should not be.

Fig. 8 gives the lattice we desire. $S(nc), S(nl)$, and $S(nw)$ are the maximal decomposition slices. $S(inword)$ is strongly dependent on $S(nw)$; $S(c)$ is strongly dependent on all the other decomposition slices. The decomposition slices on $S(nw), S(nc)$, and $S(nl)$ (Figs. 2–4) are weakly dependent and maximal when the output statements are removed. There

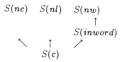

Fig. 8.　Lattice of decomposition slices.

are no independent decomposition slices in the example. Recall that independent decomposition slices cannot share any control flow: the surrounding control statements would make them dependent.

We now begin to classify the individual statements in decomposition slices.

Definition 5: Let $S(v)$ and $S(w)$ be output-restricted decomposition slices of program P. Statements in $S(v) \cap S(w)$ are called *slice dependent statements.*

Slice independent statements are statements which are not slice dependent. We will refer to slice dependent statements and slice independent statements as *dependent statements* and *independent statements*. Dependent statements are those contained in decomposition slices which are interior points of the lattice; independent statements are those in a maximal decomposition slice which are not in the union of the decomposition slices which are properly contained in the maximal slice. The terms arise from the fact that two or more slices *depend* on the computation performed by dependent statements. Independent statements do not contribute to the computation of any other slice. When modifying a program, dependent statements cannot be changed or the effect will ripple out of the focus of interest.

For example, statement 12 of the slice on **nc** (Fig. 3) is a slice independent statement with respect to any other decomposition slice. Statements 13 and 14 of the slice on **nl** (Fig. 4) are also slice independent statements with respect to any other decomposition slice. The decomposition slice on **c** (Fig. 6) is strongly dependent on all the other slices; thus all its statements are slice dependent statements with respect to any other decomposition slice. Statements 6 and 15–20 of the slice on **nw** (Fig. 2) are slice independent statements with respect to decomposition slices $S(nc), S(nl)$, and $S(c)$; only statement 19 is slice independent when compared with $S(inword)$. Statements 6, 15–18, and 20 of the decomposition slice on **inword** (Fig. 5) are slice independent statements with respect to decomposition slices $S(nc), S(nl)$, and $S(c)$; no statements are slice independent when compared with $S(nw)$.

We have a relationship between maximal slices and independent statements. This proposition permits us to apply the terms "(slice) independent statement" and "(slice) dependent statement" in a sensible way to a particular statement in a given maximal decomposition slice without reference to the binary relation between decomposition slices which is required in definition 5.

Proposition 1: Let 1) Varset(P) be the set of variables in program P; 2) $S(v)$ be an output-restricted decomposition slice of P; 3) Let $M = \{m \in \text{Varset}(P)|S(m) \text{ is maximal}\}$; 4) Let $U = M - \{v\}$. The statements in $S(v) - \bigcup_{u \in U} S(u)$ are independent.

Proof: Let $U = \{u_1, \ldots, u_m\}$. $S(v) - \bigcup_{u \in U} S(u) = S(v) - S(u_1) \ldots - S(u_m)$. ◇

There is a relationship between the maximal slices and program. (Recall that dead code has been excluded from our discussions.)

Proposition 2: Let $M = \{m \in \text{Varset}(P) | S(m)$ is maximal. Then $\bigcup_{m \in M} S(m) = P$.

Proof: Since $S(m) \in P$, $\bigcup_{m \in M} S(m) \subset P$. If $P \nsubseteq \bigcup_{m \in M} S(m)$, then the statements in P that are not in $\bigcup_{m \in M} S(m)$ are dead code. ◇

Maximal slices capture the computation performed by the program. Maximal slices and their respective independent statements also are related.

Proposition 3: An output-restricted decomposition slice is maximal if it has at least one independent statement.

Proof: Suppose $S(v)$ is maximal. By definition, $S(v)$ has at least one statement that no other slice has. This statement is an independent statement.

Now suppose that $S(v)$ has an independent statement s. Then s is not in any other slice, and the slice that contains s is maximal. ◇

Conversely, a slice with no independent statements is strongly dependent.

We also have another characterization of strongly dependent slices.

Proposition 4: Let 1) $\text{Varset}(P)$ be the set of variables in program P; 2) $S(v)$ be an output-restricted decomposition slice of P; 3) Let $D = \{w \in \text{Varset}(P) | S(v)$ is strongly dependent on $S(w)\}$; 4) Let $M = \{m \in \text{Varset}(P) | S(m)$ is maximal$\}$; 5) Let $U = M - \{v\}$. An output-restricted decomposition slice $S(v)$ is strongly dependent (on some $S(d)$) if $\bigcup_{u \in U} S(u) = P$.

Proof: Suppose $S(v)$ is strongly dependent. We need to show that D has a maximal slice. Partially order D by set inclusion. Let d be one of the maximal elements of D. The element d is maximal; if it is not, then it is properly contained in another slice d_1, which is in D and contains $S(v)$. Then $d \in M, d \neq v$, and $S(v)$ makes no contribution to the union.

Suppose $\bigcup_{u \in U} S(u) = P$. Since $U \subseteq M, S(v)$ makes no contribution to the union. By proposition 3, $S(v)$ is strongly dependent. ◇

We are now in a position to state the decomposition principles. Given a maximal output-restricted decomposition slice $S(v)$ of program P, delete the independent and output statements of S and P. We will denote this program $\sum (v)$ and call it the *complement of decomposition slice $S(v)$* (with respect to P). Henceforth, when we speak of complements, it will always be in the context of decomposition slices. The decomposition slice is the subset of the program that computes a subset of the specification; the complement computes the rest of the specification.

Figs. 9–11 give the complements of the slices on **nw**, **nc**, and **nl** of Figs. 2–4. Using proposition 4, we obtain that the complement of both the slice on **inword** and the slice on **c** is the entire program.

This yields the approximation of a direct sum decomposition of a program which preserves the computational integrity

```
3    main()
4    {
5        int c, nl, nw, nc, inword ;
7        nl = 0;
9        nc = 0;
10       c = getchar();
11       while ( c != EOF ) {
12           nc = nc + 1;
13           if ( c == '\n')
14               nl = nl + 1;
21           c = getchar();
22       }
23       printf("%d \n",nl);
25       printf("%d \n",nc);
26   }
```

Fig. 9. $\sum(nw)$. Complement of slice on **nw**: computes line count and character count.

```
1    #define YES 1
2    #define NO 0
3    main()
4    {
5        int c, nl, nw, nc, inword ;
6        inword = NO ;
7        nl = 0;
8        nw = 0;
9        nc = 0;
10       c = getchar();
11       while ( c != EOF ) {
12           nc = nc + 1;
13           if ( c == '\n')
14               nl = nl + 1;
15           if ( c == ' ' || c == '\n' || c == '\t')
16               inword = NO;
17           else if (inword == NO) {
18               inword = YES ;
19               nw = nw + 1;
20           }
21           c = getchar();
22       }
23       printf("%d \n",nl);
24       printf("%d \n",nw);
26   }
```

Fig. 10. $\sum(nc)$. Complement of slice on **nc**: computes word count and line count.

of the constituent parts. This also indicates that the only useful decompositions are done with maximal decomposition slices. A complement $\sum$ of a maximal slice can be further decomposed, so the decomposition may be continued until all slices with independent statements (i.e., the maximal ones) are obtained.

In practice, a maintainer may find a strongly dependent slice as a starting point for a proposed change. Our method will permit such changes. Such a change may be viewed as properly *extending* the domain of the partial function that the program computes, while preserving the partial function on its original domain.

IV. APPLICATION TO MODIFICATION AND TESTING

Statement independence can be used to build a set of guidelines for software modification. To do this, we need to make one more set of definitions regarding variables which appear in independent and dependent statements. With these

```
1     #define YES 1
2     #define NO 0
3     main()
4     {
5          int c, nl, nw, nc, inword ;
6          inword = NO ;
8          nw = 0;
9          nc = 0;
10         c = getchar();
11         while ( c != EOF ) {
12              nc = nc + 1;
15              if ( c == ' ' || c == '\n' || c == '\t')
16                   inword = NO;
17              else if (inword == NO) {
18                   inword = YES ;
19                   nw = nw + 1;
20              }
21              c = getchar();
22         }
24         printf("%d \n",nw);
25         printf("%d \n",nc);
26    }
```

Fig. 11. $\sum(nl)$. Complement of slice on **nl**: computes character count and word count.

```
1     main()
2     {
3          int a, b, c, d, e, f;
4          c = 4;
5          b = c;
6          a = b + c;
7          d = a + c;
8          f = d + b;
9          e = d + 8;
10         b = 30 + f;
11         a = b + c;
12    }
```

Fig. 12. Dependent variable sample program.

```
1     main()
2     {
3          int a, b, c, d, e, f;
4          c = 4;
5          b = c;
6          a = b + c;
7          d = a + c;
8          f = d + b;
10         b = 30 + f;
11         a = b + c;
12    }
```

Fig. 13. Slice on **a**.

```
1     main()
2     {
3          int a, b, c, d, e, f;
4          c = 4;
5          b = c;
6          a = b + c;
7          d = a + c;
9          e = d + 8;
12    }
```

Fig. 14. Slice on **e**.

```
1     main()
2     {
3          int a, b, c, d, e, f;
4          c = 4;
5          b = c;
6          a = b + c;
7          d = a + c;
8          f = d + b;
10         b = 30 + f;
12    }
```

Fig. 15. Slice on **b**.

definitions we give a set of rules which maintainers must obey in order to make modifications without ripple effects and unexpected linkages. When these rules are obeyed, we have an algorithm to merge the modified slice back into the complement and effect a change. The driving motivation for the following development is: "What restrictions must be placed on modifications in a decomposition slice so that the *complement* remains intact?"

Definition 6: A *variable* that is the target of a dependent assignment statement is called a *dependent variable*. Alternatively and equivalently, if *all* assignments to a variable are in independent statements, then the variable is called an *independent variable*.

An assignment statement can be an independent statement while its target is not an independent variable. In the program of Fig. 12, the two maximal decomposition slices are $S(a)$ and $S(e)$ (Figs. 13 and 14). Slice $S(b)$ (Fig. 15) is strongly dependent on $S(a)$, and $S(f)$ (Fig. 16) is strongly dependent on $S(b)$ and $S(a)$. $S(d)$ and $S(c)$ (not shown) are strongly dependent on both maximal slices. In $S(a)$, statements 8, 10, and 11 are independent, by the proposition. But *variables* **a** and **b** are targets of assignment statements 6 and 5, respectively. So, in the decomposition slice $S(a)$, only variable **f** is an independent variable.

A similar argument applies for independent control flow statements which reference dependent variables. A dependent variable in an independent statement corresponds to the situation where the *variable* in question is required for the compilation of the complement, but the *statement* in question does not contribute to complement. If a variable is referenced in a dependent statement, it is necessary to the complement and cannot be independent.

If a decomposing on a single variable yields a strongly dependent slice, we are able to construct a slice where the original slice *variable* is an independent variable.

Proposition 5: Let 1) Varset(P) be the set of variables in program P; 2) $S(v)$ be a strongly dependent output restricted decomposition slice of P; 3) Let $D = \{w \in \text{Varset}(P) | S(v) \text{ is strongly dependent on } S(w)\}$; 4) Let $M = \{m \in \text{Varset}(P) | S(m) \text{ is maximal}\}$; 5) Let $U = D \cap M$; 6) Let $T = \bigcup_{u \in U} S(u)$. The variable v is an independent variable in T.

In other words, when $S(v)$ is a strongly dependent slice and T is the union of all the maximal slices upon which $S(v)$ is strongly dependent, then v is an independent variable in T.

Proof: We show that the complement of T, $P-T$ has no references to v: if variable v is in the complement of T, then there is a maximal slice in the complement upon which

```
1   main()
2   {
3     int a, b, c, d, e, f;
4     c = 4;
5     b = c;
6     a = b + c;
7     d = a + c;
8     f = d + b;
12  }
```

Fig. 16. Slice on **f**.

$S(v)$ is strongly dependent. This contradicts the hypotheses, so the complement if T has no references to v and the variable v is independent in T. ◇

This can be interpreted as the variable version of Proposition 1, which refers to statements.

This has not addressed the problem that is presented when the decomposition slice on variable is maximal, but the variable itself remains dependent. This is the situation that occurred in the example at the beginning of the chapter; the slice on variable a (Fig. 13) is maximal, but the variable is dependent. The solution is straightforward: we construct the slice that is the union of all slices in which the variable is dependent.

Proposition 6: Let 1) Varset(P) be the set of variables in program P; 2) $S(v)$ be an output-restricted decomposition slice of P; 3) Let $E = \{w \in \text{Varset}(P)|v$ is a dependent variable in $S(w)\}$; 4) Let $T = \bigcup_{e \in E} S(e)$.

We have two cases: 1) $E = \varnothing$ (and thus T is empty also), in which case v is an independent variable; 2) $E \neq \varnothing$, so T is not empty and the variable v is an independent variable in T.

Proof:
Case 1: $E = \varnothing$
$S(v)$ contains all references to v. In particular, $S(v)$ contains all assignments to v. So v is an independent variable in $S(v)$.
End Case 1
Case 2: $E \neq \varnothing$
T contains references to v. In particular, T contains all assignments to v. So v is an independent variable in T. *End Case 2* ◇

This proposition is about *variables*.

A. Modifying Decomposition Slices

We are now in a position to answer the question posed at the beginning of this section. We present the restrictions as a collection of rules with justifications.

Modifications take three forms: additions, deletions, and changes. A change may be viewed as a deletion followed by an addition. We will use this second approach and determine only those statements in a decomposition slice that can be deleted, and the forms of statements that can be added. Again, we must rely on the fact that the union of decomposition slices is a slice, since the complementary criteria will usually involve more than one maximal variable. We also assume that the maintainer has kept the modified program compilable and has obtained the decomposition slice of the portion of the software that needs to be changed. (Locating the code may be a highly

nontrivial activity; for the sake of the current discussion, we assume its completion.)

Since independent statements do not affect data flow or control flow in the complement, we have:

Rule 1: Independent statements may be deleted from a decomposition slice.

Reason: Independent statements do not affect the computations of the complement. Deleting an independent statement from a slice will have no impact on the complement. ◇

This result applies to control flow statements and assignment statements. The statement may be deleted, even if it is an assignment statement which targets a dependent variable or a control statement which references a dependent variable. The point to keep in mind is that if the statement is independent, it does *not* affect the complement. If an independent statement is deleted, there will certainly be an effect in the slice. But the purpose of this methodology is to keep the complement intact.

There are a number of situations to consider when statements are to be added. We progress from simple to complex. Also note that for additions, new variables may be introduced *as long as the variable name does not clash with any name in the complement*. In this instance the new variable is independent in the decomposition slice. In the following, *independent variable* means an independent variable or a new variable.

Rule 2: Assignment statements that target independent variables may be added anywhere in a decomposition slice.

Reason: Independent variables are unknown to the complement. Thus changes to them cannot affect the computations of the complement. ◇

This type of change is permissible even if the changed value flows into a dependent variable. In Fig. 13, changes are permitted to the assignment statement at line 8, which targets **f**. A change here would propagate into the values of dependent variables **a** and **b** at lines 10 and 11. The maintainer would then be responsible for the changes which would occur to these variables. If lines 10 and 11 were dependent (i.e., contained in another decomposition slice), line 8 would also be contained in this slice and variable **f** would be dependent.

Adding control flow statements requires a little more care. This is required because control statements have two parts: the logical expression, which determines the flow of control, and the *actions* taken for each value of the expression. (We assume no side effects in the evaluation of logical expressions.) We discuss only the addition of **if-then-else** and **while** statements, since all other language constructs can be realized by them [5].

Rule 3: Logical expressions (and output statements) may be added anywhere in a decomposition slice.

Reason: We can inspect the state of the computation anywhere. Evaluation of logical expressions (or the inclusion of an output statement) will not even affect the computation of the slice. Thus the complement remains intact. ◇

We must guarantee that the statements which are controlled by newly added control flow do not interfere with the complement.

Rule 4: New control statements that surround (i.e., control) any dependent statement will cause the complement to change.

758   IEEE TRANSACTIONS ON SOFTWARE ENGINEERING, VOL. 17, NO. 8, AUGUST 1991

Reason: Suppose that newly added code controls a dependent statement.

Let C be the criteria which yield the complement. When using this criteria on the modified program, the newly added control code will be included in this complementary slice. This is due to the fact that the dependent statements are in both the slice and the complement. Thus any control statements which control dependent statements will also be in the slice and the complement.   ◊

By making such a change we have violated the principle that the complement remain fixed. Thus new control statements may not surround any dependent statement.

This short list is necessary and sufficient to keep the slice complement intact. This also has an impact on testing the change that will be discussed later.

Changes may be required to computations involving a dependent variable v in the extracted slice. the maintainer can choose one of the following two approaches:

1) Use the techniques of the previous section to extend the slice so that v is independent in the slice.
2) Add a new local variable (to the slice), copy the value to the new variable, and manipulate the new name only. Of course, the new name must not clash with any name in the complement. This technique may also be used if the slice has no independent statements; i.e., it is strongly dependent.

B. Merging the Modifications into the Complement

Merging the modified slice back into the complement is straightforward. A key to understanding the merge operation comes from the observation that through the technique, the maintainer is editing the *entire program*. The method gives a view of the program with the unneeded statements deleted and with the dependent statements restricted from modification. The slice gives a smaller piece of code for the maintainer to focus on, while the rules of the previous subsection provide the means by which the deleted and restricted parts cannot be changed accidentally.

We now present the merge algorithm.

1) Order the statements in the original program. (In the following examples we have one statement per line, so that the ordering is merely the line numbering.) A program slice and its complement can now be identified with the subsequence of statement numbers from the original program. We call the sequence numbering from the slice the *slice sequence,* and the numbering of the complement, the *complement sequence.* We now view the editing process as the addition and deletion of the associated sequence numbers.
2) For deleted statements, delete the sequence number from the slice sequence. Observe that since only independent statements are deleted, this number is not in the complement sequence.
3) For statements inserted into the slice, a new sequence number needs to be generated. Let P be the sequence number of the statement preceding the statement to be inserted. Let M be the least value in the slice sequence

greater than P. Let $F = \min(\text{int}(P+1), M)$. Insert the new statement at sequence number $(F+P)/2$. (Although this works in principle, in practice, more care needs to be taken in the generation of the insertion sequence numbers to avoid floating point errors after 10 inserts.)
4) The merged program is obtained by merging the modified slice sequence values (i.e., statements) into the complement sequence.

Thus the unchanged dependent statements are used to guide the reconstruction of the modified program. The placement of the changed statements within a given control flow is arbitrary. Again, this becomes clearer when the editing process is viewed as a modification to the entire program. The following example will help clarify this.

C. Testing the Change

Since the maintainer must restrict all changes to independent or newly created variables, testing is reduced to testing the modified slice. Thus the need for regression testing in the complement is eliminated. There are two alternative approaches to verifying that only the change needs testing. The first is to slice on the original criteria, plus any new variables, minus any eliminated variables, and compare its complement with the complement of the original: they should match exactly. The second approach is to preserve the criteria which produced the original complement. Slicing out on this must produce the modified slice exactly.

An axiomatic consideration illumines this idea. The slice and its complement perform a subset of the computation; where the computations meet are the dependencies. Modifying the code in the independent part of the slice leaves the independent part of the complement as an invariant of the slice (and vice versa).

If the required change is "merely" a module replacement, the preceding techniques are still applicable. The slice will provide a harness for the replaced module. A complete independent program supporting the module is obtained. One of the principal benefits of slicing is highlighted in this context: any side effects of the module to be replaced will also be in the slice. Thus the full impact of change is brought to the attention of the modifier.

As an example, we make some changes to $S(nw)$, the slice on **nw**, the word counter of Fig. 2. The changed slice is shown in Fig. 17. The original program determined a word to be any string of "nonwhite" symbols terminated by a "white" symbol (space, tab, or newline). The modification changes this to the requirement to be alphabetical characters terminated by white space. (The example is illustrating a change, not advocating it.) Note the changes. We have deleted the independent "variables" YES and NO; added a new, totally independent variable **ch**; and revamped the independent statements. The addition of the C macros **isspace** and **isalpha** is safe, since the results are only referenced. We test this program independently of the complement. Fig. 18 shows the reconstructed, modified program. Taking the decomposition slice on **nw** generates the program of Fig. 17. Its complement is already given in Fig. 9.

```
 3      main()
 4      {
 *          int ch;
 5          int c, nw ;
 *          ch = 0;
 8          nw = 0;
10          c = getchar();
11          while ( c != EOF ) {
 *              if (isspace(c) && isalpha(ch))
 *                  nw = nw + 1;
 *              ch = c ;
21              c = getchar();
22          }
24          printf("%d \n",nw);
26      }
```

Fig. 17.   Modified slice on **nw**, the word counter.

```
 3      main()
 4      {
 *          int ch;
 5          int c, nl, nw, nc ;
 *          ch = 0;
 7          nl = 0;
 8          nw = 0;
 9          nc = 0;
10          c = getchar();
11          while ( c != EOF ) {
 *              if (isspace(c) && isalpha(ch))
 *                  nw = nw + 1;
 *              ch = c ;
12              nc = nc + 1;
13              if ( c == '\n')
14                  nl = nl + 1;
21              c = getchar();
22          }
23          printf("%d \n",nl);
24          printf("%d \n",nw);
25          printf("%d \n",nc);
26      }
```

Fig. 18.   Modified program.

the starred ($*$) statements indicate where the new statements would be placed using the line-number-generation technique above.

V. A NEW SOFTWARE MAINTENANCE PROCESS MODEL

The usual Software Maintenance Process Model is depicted in Fig. 19. A request for change arrives. It may be adaptive, perfective, corrective, or preventive. In making the change, we wish to minimize defects, effort, and cost, while maximizing customer satisfaction [12]. The software is changed, subject to pending priorities. The change is composed of two parts: Understanding the code, which may require documentation, code reading, and execution. Then the program is modified. The maintainer must first design the change (which may be subject to peer review), then alter the code itself, while trying to minimize side effects. The change is then validated. The altered code itself is verified to assure conformance with the specification. Then the new code is integrated with the existing system to insure conformance with the system specifications. This task involves regression testing.

The new model is depicted in Fig. 20. The software is changed, subject to pending priorities. The change is com-

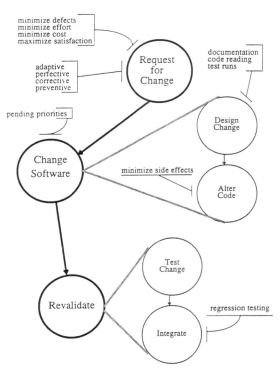

Fig. 19.   A software maintenance process model.

posed of two parts: Understanding the code will now require documentation, code reading, execution, and the use of decomposition slices. The decomposition slices may be read and executed (a decided advantage of having executable program slices). The code is then modified, subject to the strictures outlined. Using those guidelines, no side effects or unintended linkages can be induced in the code, even by accident. This lifts a substantial burden from the maintainer.

The change is tested in the decomposition slice. Since the change cannot ripple out into other modules, regression testing is unnecessary. The maintainer need only verify that the change is correct. After applying the merge algorithm, the change (of the code) is complete.

VI. FUTURE DIRECTIONS

The underlying method and the tool based on it [9] need to be empirically evaluated. This is underway using the Goal-Question-Metric paradigm of Basili *et al.* [2]. Naturally, we are also addressing questions of scale, to determine if existing software systems decompose sufficiently via these techniques, in order to effect a technology transfer. We are also evaluating decomposition slices as candidates for components in a reuse library.

Although they seem to do well in practice, the slicing algorithms have relatively bad worst-case running times of $O(n\ e\ \log(e))$, where n is the number of variables and e is the number of edges in the flowgraph. To obtain all the slices, this running time becomes $O(n^2 e\ \log(e))$. These worst-case times would seem to make an interactive slicer

760   IEEE TRANSACTIONS ON SOFTWARE ENGINEERING, VOL. 17, NO. 8, AUGUST 1991

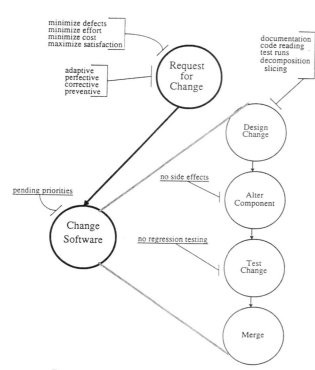

Fig. 20. A new software maintenance process model.

for large (i.e., real) programs impractical. This difficulty can be assuaged by making the data-flow analysis one component of the deliverable products which are handed off from the development team to the maintenance team. An interactive tool could then be built using these products. Then as changes are made by the maintainers, the data flow data can be updated, using the incremental techniques of Keables [17].

Interprocedural slices can be attacked using the techniques in Weiser [36] and Barth [1]. The interprocedural slicing algorithms of Horwitz *et al.* [16] cannot be used, since they require that the slice be taken at a point where the slice variable id **def**ed or **ref**ed; we require that all slices be taken at the last statement of the program. For separate compilation, a worst-case assumption must be made about the external variables if the source is not available. If the source is available, one proceeds as with procedures.

Berzins [4] has attacked the problem of software merges for *extensions* of programs. To quote him:

"An extension extends the domain of the partial function without altering any of the initially defined values, while a modification redefines values that were defined initially."

We have addressed the modification problem by first *restricting* the domain of the partial function to the slice complement, modifying the function on the values defined by the independent variables in the slice, then merging these two disjoint domains.

Horwitz *et al.* [15] have addressed the modification problem. They start with a *base* program and two modifications it, *A* and *B*:

"Whenever the changes made to *base* to create *A* and *B* do not 'interfere' (in a sense defined in the paper), the algorithm produces a program *M* that integrates *A* and *B*. The algorithm is predicated on the assumption that differences in the *behavior* of the variant programs from that of *base*, rather than the differences in *text*, are significant and must be preserved in *M*."

Horwitz *et al.* do not restrict the changes that can be made to *base*; thus their algorithm produces an approximation to the undecidable problem of determining whether or not the behaviors interfere. We have side-stepped this unsolvable problem by constraining the modifications that are made. Our technique is more akin to the limits placed on software maintainers. Changes must be done in a context: independence and dependence provides the context. It is interesting to note, however, that their work uses program slicing to determine potential interferences in the merge.

They do note that program *variants*, as they name them, are easily embedded in the change control system, such as RCS [31]. Moreover, the direct sum nature of the components can be exploited to build related families of software. That is, components can be "summed" as long as their dependent code sections match exactly, and there is no intersection of the independent domains. We also follow this approach for component construction.

Weiser [34] discusses some slice-based metrics. *Overlap* is a measure of how many statements in a slice are found only in that slice, measured as a mean ratio of nonunique-to-unique statements in each slice. *Parallelism* is the number of slices that has few statements in common, computed as the number of slices that have pairwise overlap below a certain threshold. *Tightness* is the number of statements in every slice, expressed as a ratio over program length. Programs with high overlap and parallelism but with low tightness would decompose nicely: the lattice would not get too deep or too tangled.

We have shown how a data flow technique, program slicing, can be used to form a decomposition for software systems. The decomposition yields a method for maintainers to use. The maintainer is able to modify existing code cleanly, in the sense that the changes can be assured to be completely contained in the modules under consideration and that no unseen linkages with the modified code is infecting other modules.

REFERENCES

[1] J. M. Barth, "A practical interprocedural dataflow analysis algorithm," *Comm. Assoc. Computing Machinery*, vol. 21, no. 9, pp. 724–726, Sept. 1978.

[2] V. Basili, R. Selby, and D. Hutchens, "Experimentation in software engineering," *IEEE Trans. Software Eng.*, vol. 12, pp. 352–357, July 1984.

[3] J.-F. Bergeretti and B. Carré, "Information-flow and data-flow analysis of **while**-programs," *ACM Trans. Programming Languages and Systems*, vol. 7, no. 1, pp. 37–61, Jan. 1985.

[4] V. Berzins, "On merging software extensions," *Acta Informatica*, vol. 23, pp. 607–619, 1985.

[5] C. Bohm and G. Jacopini, "Flow diagrams and languages with only two formation rules," *CACM*, vol. 9, no. 5, pp. 366–371, May 1966.

[6] J.-D. Choi, B. Miller, and P. Netzer, "Techniques for debugging parallel programs with flowback analysis," Univ. Wisconsin–Madison, Tech. Rep. 786, Aug. 1988.

[7] J. Ferrante, K. Ottenstein, and J. Warren, "The program dependence graph and its use in optimization," *ACM Trans. Programming Languages*

and Systems. vol. 9, no. 3, pp. 319–349, July 1987.

[8] K. B. Gallagher, "Using program slicing in software maintenance," Ph.D. thesis, Univ. Maryland, Baltimore. Dec. 1989.

[9] K. B. Gallagher, "Surgeon's assistant limits side effects." IEEE Software, vol. 7, p. 64, May 1990.

[10] K. B. Gallagher and J. R. Lyle, "Using program decomposition to guide modifications." in Proc. Conf. Software Maintenance—1988, Oct. 1988, pp. 265–268.

[11] K. B. Gallagher and J. R. Lyle, "A program decomposition scheme with applications to software modification and testing." in Proc. 22nd Int. Conf. System Sciences (Hawaii). Jan. 1989, vol. II, pp. 479–485.

[12] R. Grady, "Measuring and managing software maintenance," IEEE Software, vol. 4, Sept. 1987.

[13] P. Hausler, "Denotational program slicing," in Proc. 22nd Hawaii Int. Conf. System Sciences, Jan. 1989, vol. II (Software Track), pp. 486–494.

[14] S. Horwitz, J. Prins, and T. Reps, "Integrating non-interfering versions of programs," in Proc. SIGPLAN'88 Symp. Principles of Programming Languages. Jan. 1988.

[15] S. Horwitz, J. Prins, and T. Reps. "Integrating non-interfering versions of programs," ACM Trans. Programming Languages and Systems, vol. 11, no. 3, pp. 345–387, July 1989.

[16] S. Horwitz, T. Reps, and D. Binkley, "Interprocedural slicing using dependence graphs," ACM Trans. Programming Languages and Systems, vol. 12, no. 1, pp. 35–46, Jan. 1990.

[17] J. Keables, K. Robertson, and A. von Mayrhauser, "Data flow analysis and its application to software maintenance," in Proc. Conf. Software Maintenance—1988, Oct. 1988, pp. 335–347.

[18] K. Kennedy, "A survey of data flow analysis techniques," in Program Flow Analysis: Theory and Applications, S. S. Muchnick and N. D. Jones, Eds. Englewood Cliffs, NJ: Prentice-Hall, 1981.

[19] B. Kernighan and D. Ritchie, The C Programming Language. Englewood Cliffs, NJ: Prentice-Hall, 1978.

[20] B. Korel and J. Laski, "Dynamic program slicing," Inform. Process. Lett., vol. 29. no. 3, pp. 155–163, Oct. 1988.

[21] B. Korel and J. Laski, "STAD—a system for testing and debugging: User perspective." in Proc. 2nd Workshop on Software Testing, Verification and Analysis (Banff, Alberta, Can.), July 1988, pp. 13–20.

[22] J. Laski, "Data flow testing in STAD" Systems and Software, to be published.

[23] J. R. Lyle, "Evaluating variations of program slicing for debugging." Ph.D. thesis, Univ. of Maryland, College Park, Dec. 1984.

[24] J. R. Lyle and M. D. Weiser, "Experiments in slicing-based debugging aids," in Empirical Studies of Programmers, E. Soloway and S. Iyengar, Eds. Norwood, NJ: Ablex, 1986.

[25] J. R. Lyle and M. D. Weiser, "Automatic program bug location by program slicing." in Proc. 2nd Int. Conf. Computers and Applications (Peking, China), June 1987, pp. 877–882.

[26] L. Ott and J. Thuss, "The relationship between slices and module cohesion." in Proc. 11th Int. Conf. Software Eng., May 1989, pp. 198–204.

[27] K. Ottenstein and L. Ottenstein, "The program dependence graph in software development environments," ACM SIGPLAN Notices, vol. 19, no. 5, pp. 177–184, May 1984; see also, Proc. ACM SIGSOFT/SIGPLAN Software Eng. Symp. Practical Software Development Environments.

[28] T. Reps and S. Horwitz, "Semantics-based program integration," in Proc. 2nd European Symp. Programming (ESOP '88) (Nancy, France). Mar. 1988, pp. 133–145.

[29] T. Reps and W. Yang. "The semantics of program slicing," Univ. Wisconsin–Madison, Tech. Rep. 777, June 1988.

[30] N. Schneidewind, "The state of software maintenance," IEEE Trans. Software Eng., vol. SE-13, pp. 303–310, Mar. 1987.

[31] W. Tichy, "RCS: A system for version control," Software—Practice and Experience, vol. 15. no. 7, pp. 637–654, July 1985.

[32] G. Weinberg. "Kill that code!." Infosystems, pp. 48–49, Aug. 1983.

[33] M. Weiser. "Program slicing: Formal, psychological and practical investigations of an automatic program abstraction method," Ph.D. thesis, Univ. Michigan, Ann Arbor, 1979.

[34] M. Weiser, "Program slicing," in Proc. 5th Int. Conf. Software Eng., May 1981, pp. 439–449.

[35] M. Weiser, "Programmers use slicing when debugging," CACM, vol. 25, no. 7, pp. 446–452, July 1982.

[36] M. Weiser, "Program slicing," IEEE Trans. Software Eng., vol. SE-10, pp. 352–357, July 1984.

Keith Brian Gallagher received the B.A. degree in mathematics from Bucknell University, the M.S. degrees in both mathematics and computer and communication sciences from the University of Michigan, and the Ph.D. degree from the University of Maryland Graduate School in Baltimore.

He is an Assistant Professor of Computer Science at Loyola College in Baltimore, MD, where his research interests are in the software maintenance process and practice and computing for the disabled.

Dr. Gallagher is a member of the IEEE Computer Society and the Association for Computing Machinery. He has received a Research Initiation Award from the National Science Foundation to continue exploring issues in software maintenance.

James R. Lyle (S'80–M'84) received the B.S. and M.S. degrees in mathematics from East Tennessee State University, and the M.S. and Ph.D. degrees in computer science from the University of Maryland. College Park.

He is an Assistant Professor in the Department of Computer Science at the University of Maryland, Baltimore. and a Faculty Researcher at the National Institute of Standards and Technology Computer Systems Laboratory in Gaithersburg, MD. His research area is in software tools for testing and debugging supported by graphics workstations.

Dr. Lyle is a member of the IEEE Computer Society and the Association for Computing Machinery.

Using Automatic Program Decomposition Techniques in Software Maintenance Tools

Rajeev Gopal and Stephen R. Schach
Department of Computer Science
Vanderbilt University
Box 70, Station B
Nashville, TN 37235
(615) 322-2924

Abstract

Program decomposition can assist maintenance programmers in all three phases of maintenance, namely comprehension, modification and debugging. Visibility flow graphs are introduced to represent the information about the static semantics of a program. Using static analysis of programs, it is possible to approximate their dynamic behavior. More precise analysis is possible if the program is monitored during its execution. For dynamic semantics, dependence relations are used that reflect the dependency of statements on the input value of variables and of the output value of variables on the statements. These relations are generated both at static analysis time, and also during program execution. Some sample sessions with a prototype program analyzer for a subset of Ada are also included.

1 Introduction

Software maintenance continues to be an intricate and costly aspect of software development. Although it has received less attention compared to the other phases of the software development process, it now accounts for more than half of software costs [10]. The most effective way of reducing the overall cost of software is therefore to reduce the maintenance cost. This calls for an improvement in software evolution models and maintenance methods, as well as the development of associated tools.

There has been considerable progress in the design of higher level specification languages and comprehensive programming environments to support program coding. The design of complex systems can be simplified with techniques such as stepwise refinement, modular decomposition, and structured programming. Despite these accomplishments, systems are still being implemented in procedural languages. Automatic translation of high level design specifications is either domain dependent or is too inefficient for practical purposes [8]. If programs are manually implemented, based on informal (or formal) design specifications, then maintenance will have to be performed on the actual implementation rather than the high level design.

This is necessary, as the original design may not correspond fully to the original implementation. Unless the program code is machine translated from the specifications, it remains the only correct representation of the system. There are further reasons as to why source code continues have a dominating position [13].

This implies that maintenance programmers have to understand the source code correctly before they can make modifications. This comprehension process can be assisted by providing the specifications documents, but only to some extent. If the documentation is missing or incomplete, or even incorrect, the situation worsens. Typically, the number of maintenance programmers is substantially smaller than the size of the original development team. Thus, fewer individuals are responsible for maintaining larger programs. Even though a modification may be small, the program has to be understood in its entirety to ensure correct maintenance.

Maintenance productivity can be improved in several ways [10]. Here we focus on the design and effectiveness of program decomposition techniques in the context of software maintenance. These techniques have been incorporated in an interactive program analyzer that can provide information about the static and dynamic semantics of programs.

Static Semantics The static semantics correspond to the information pertaining to the structure and syntax of the program. For example, a program can be decomposed into several modules. Depending on the language, each module can be a procedure or a collection of procedures such as an Ada **package**. A procedure itself can have nested *contexts* in the form of internal packages and procedures. Other items of interest include scalar and structured variables, and types. In this context, the decompositions correspond to the location and display of entities that are visible in a certain portion of the program. The following are some typical situations:

- *Display the body of the procedure that is invoked at the current statement.*

- *Show the declaration of the type that is used to declare a specific variable.*

132

0-8186-3272-0/93 $3.00 ©1989 IEEE

- *Find all variables that are visible in a procedure and are of the specified type.*

- *Identify the set of all procedures that are directly or indirectly invoked by the specified procedure.*

The above queries are trivial for small programs and do not require any automation. However, for large multi-module programs, an interactive tool is indispensable. Although traditional cross-reference generators can provide this kind of information, their effectiveness diminishes as programs become larger and the programmer has to deal with increasingly voluminous cross-reference information. An interactive tool is needed to maintain the information related to the declaration of entities in various contexts and the visibility rules that describe the availability of entities that are not declared locally.

Dynamic Semantics A program can be visualized as an abstract function that generates the output value of the variables based on the specified input values. The dynamic semantics of a program correspond to this functional behavior of the program. It is possible to analyze a program and determine its dynamic behavior, at least approximately, without actually executing the program. This has traditionally been done for program optimization at the compilation stage, and also for other applications like comprehension, verification, and documentation [6]. A program can also be monitored while it is executing and information can be collected. By using dynamic analysis, the actual program trace for a specific execution can be used to generate precise dependence relations. Thus, both static and dynamic analyses are useful when considering the dynamic semantics of programs. The following are some of the typical situations when program decompositions with respect to dynamic semantics can be useful.

- *Identify only those statements that are executed to produce the output value of a variable.* This can be helpful in locating the cause of an erroneous output value of a variable. Instead of analyzing the entire program, it may be possible to consider only those statements that are directly relevant.

- *Select all statements that may use the input value of a specific variable.* This can be of help while analyzing the effect of introducing a new variable during program modification. Again only a limited portion of the program needs checking rather than the entire program.

- *Find all variables whose input value is used in determining the output value of a specific variable.* This again is applicable to modification.

Our approach to dependence analysis is derived from the relation-based static information-flow analysis introduced in [1]. We provide a generalized framework that allows us to generate dependence relations by using either static or dynamic analysis of programs. In a recent paper [4], a technique is presented for generating dynamic program slices. A dynamic slice is similar to our program projection (see Section 4) generated from dynamic dependence relations. In [11] (static) program slices are defined and a method is presented to perform program slicing by using static analysis. It has been shown that slicing can be helpful during program debugging [12]. In [5] a program slicing-based method is used for determining the impact of program modification.

The paper is organized as follows. In Section 2 we introduce a formalism, called visibility flow graphs, that can be used as a framework for maintaining the visibility information in a program. This is a general scheme and is aimed at languages with strong typing, block structure, and language-supported features for multiple modules. This model can be used to elicit information about the static properties of programs. In Section 3 the dependence relations are defined. In Section 4 we introduce program projections. Some examples are also included. In Section 5 the salient features of a prototype program analyzer are presented along with some sample sessions. Finally, we address the current status of this project and provide some directions for future work.

2 Visibility Flow Graphs

A Visibility Flow Graph (*VFG*) displays the interconnection of the declarative contexts in a program. Depending on the programming language and the associated visibility constructs used, a declarative context may correspond to an entire program, a module, or part of a module. This representation is uniform across the inter- and intra-module visibility flow. This uniformity is in sharp contrast with the duality of "large" and "small" programs associated with the Module Interconnection Language (MIL) approach [7] towards large programs.

A *VFG* consists of structured nodes interconnected by edges. A node corresponds to a declarative context (*DC*) while the edges interlinking *DC*s depict visibility flow information. Within a declarative context, a sequential list

133

provides the skeletal structure connecting various units of declarative or requisitionary types. A unit may correspond to an atomic program construct such as a variable declaration (declarative) or a statement (requisitionary). A non-atomic unit is associated with a different declarative context that may participate in the visibility flow information of the current declarative context. Atomic units never exist on their own and are always contained within a DC. An entity may have several attributes but usually its name is sufficient for this discussion of the VFG model.

2.1 Declarative Contexts and Units

The declarative contexts constitute the nodes of the visibility graphs. A context is structured as a sequential list[1] of units corresponding to declarations and statements. A declarative unit may declare a new entity (e.g., a variable) and may require other entities (the type). A unit corresponding to a statement may require access to other entities such as variables or procedures. Thus, there are two attributes of each unit; the set δ_i includes the entities *declared* in unit i, and the set ρ_i corresponds to the set of entities that are *required* by unit i.

To accommodate linear elaboration, each unit is assigned an index number which denotes its position in the sequential unit-list associated with a declarative context. This ordering can readily be determined for the declarative part of a context because any non-atomic declaration is treated as a different declarative context. For the procedural part, it is necessary to provide an ordering function to accommodate compound statements like conditionals and loops.

2.2 Visibility Function for a Context

The visibility function V_i at the end of unit i of a declarative context can be defined as follows

$$\Psi_i = (\Psi_{i-1} \cup \psi_i - \delta_i) \cup \delta_i \qquad (1)$$

where δ_i corresponds to the entities provided by the ith unit. The term ψ_i denotes the visibility imported from other contexts and should be known before Ψ_i can be

---

[1] All programming languages employ this sequential juxtaposition of declarations and statements. Although for statements this sequential nature provides the control flow, its importance for visibility purposes is relevant only when linear elaboration is effective. Thus, for Modula-2 declarations the sequential aspect of this list is meaningless.

effectively determined. Subtracting δ_i takes care of visibility hiding due to a redeclaration of an entity at unit i that is already visible from some non-local context.

2.3 Importing and Exporting Visibility

In (1) the term ψ_i corresponds to the visibility imported from other contexts. To accommodate linear elaboration, ψ_i is defined for each unit.

In a VFG, an arc (S, D) corresponds to the flow of visibility from declarative context S (the source) to context D (the destination). With linear elaboration, the interpretation of visibility importation is dependent on the actual position of the flow arc within the destination context. Thus, the target of the arc (S, D) is qualified by an index I of the Ith unit. The following equation describes the imported visibility for a declarative context D.

$$\psi_I^D = \bigcup_{(S,D) \in VFG_{edges}} \theta_I^D \circ \chi_J^S \qquad (2)$$

Here, θ is a function defined at the targets of the VFG edges. Similarly, χ, defined at the source nodes, describes the export of entities from the declarative context S to D. The source S is qualified by index J.

2.4 Secondary Information from VFGs

The set ρ_i contains all entities that are required in unit i. The union of these sets over all units in a declarative context D corresponds to the *requirement* set corresponding to that declarative context; it is defined as

$$R^D = \cup_{i=1}^n \rho_i^D \qquad (3)$$

Similarly, $\Delta^D = \cup_{i=1}^n \delta_i$ describes the set of all local declarations. If the requirements of a context can be met locally then $R^D \subseteq \Delta^D$ and for linear elaboration, $\cup_{i=1}^k \rho_i \subseteq \cup_{i=1}^k \delta_i$, for $k = 1 \ldots n(D)$. Here $n(D)$ is the number of units in the declarative context D.

For a well formed program, it is essential that all required entities within a declarative context should be provided locally or imported. This is equivalent to saying that relation $R_i^D \subseteq \Psi_i^D$ must be true for all i.

The *provision* set Π, corresponding to an entity e, is defined as follows

$$\Pi(e) = \bigcup_{D \in VFG_{nodes}} \{(D, i) \mid e \in \rho_i^D, \ i \in 1 \ldots n(D)\} \qquad (4)$$

The information contained in provision sets is a generalization of traditional cross-referencing.

Using the concepts of requirement and provision sets, we define the *import* and the *export* sets for a declarative context:

$$\Gamma^D = \bigcup_{i=1}^{n(D)} (\rho_i^D - \Psi_i^D) \qquad (5)$$

$$\Omega^D = \bigcup_{D' \in VFG_{nodes}} \{e \in D \mid (D', i) \in \Pi(e),\ D' \neq D\} \qquad (6)$$

3 Dependence Relations

We define three relations that are useful in capturing the dynamic semantics of a program, namely S_V, V_S, and V_V.

- $(s, v) \in S_V$ if statement s depends on (uses) the input value of variable v.

- $(v, s) \in V_S$ if the output value of variable v depends on execution of statement s.

- $(v, u) \in V_V$ if the output value of v depends on the input value of u.

Variables u and v belong to Ψ, the set of all variables that are visible in the current part of the program. While considering the dependence relations of multiple programs (or multiple parts of the same program), a superscript is used to associate a program with its relations. Thus, V_S^P denotes the V_S relation of program P. For these relations, the input and output values correspond to the state before and after executing the program, or its parts. These dependence relations can easily be defined for simple statements. Other statements can be visualized as a sequence of smaller statements. The following definitions for the modification and preservation of variable v in a program P will be used later for generating these relations.

MOD = $\{v \mid v$ is modified by the program $P\}$

PRE = $\{v \mid v$ is preserved (not modified) in $P\}$

Relation V_V for a program P can be defined in terms of S_V and V_S as follows:

$$V_V = V_S \cdot S_V \cup P_V, \text{ where } P_V = \{(v, v) \mid v \in \text{PRE}\} \qquad (7)$$

3.1 Null statement

A program P that consists only of a single null statement does not modify any variable. For all $v \in \Psi$, the output value of v depends only on the input value of v. Thus, $(v, u) \in V_V$ if and only if $v = u$. This results in $V_V = \iota$. Other relations are obvious as there is no assignment in a null statement and all variables of the program P are preserved. Thus, MOD = ϕ, PRE = Ψ, $S_V = \phi$, and $V_S = \phi$.

3.2 Assignment Statement

For an assignment statement,

$$v := \text{RHS\_EXPR}; \quad -- s$$

Variable v is the only one that is modified. The new value of v depends on all variables appearing in the RHS_EXPR part of the statement. Therefore, PRE = $\Psi - \{v\}$, MOD = $\{v\}$, and relation $S_V = \{(s, u) \mid u \in \text{RHS}\}$. The output value of variable v depends on the execution of statement s, so $V_S = \{(v, s)\}$. The relation V_V can be obtained by using Equation (7).

$$V_V = \{(v, u) \mid u \in \text{RHS}\} \cup \{\iota - (v, v)\}$$

3.3 Sequence of Statements

Previously, relations were defined for programs containing a single assignment and a null statement. Definitions for loop and conditional statements are provided later. These basic definitions can be used to construct relations for programs containing multiple statements where the program is visualized as a finite sequence of statements. Since these relations satisfy the associativity rule, it is sufficient to show how to generate relations for a sequence of two programs. Using induction, a program of arbitrary size can be analyzed and relations can be constructed.

Consider the sequence P of two programs P_1 and P_2, where all three relations, V_V, S_V and V_S are known for each of P_1 and P_2. For the sequence, $\text{PRE}^P = \text{PRE}^{P_1} \cap \text{PRE}^{P_2}$ and $\text{MOD}^P = \text{MOD}^{P_1} \cup \text{MOD}^{P_2}$. It is assumed that both P_1 and P_2 have single entry and exit points. The relations for the sequence can readily be determined to be

$$S_V^P = S_V^{P_1} \cup S_V^{P_2} \cdot V_V^{P_1} \qquad (8)$$

$$V_S^P = V_S^{P_2} \cup V_V^{P_2} \cdot V_S^{P_1} \qquad (9)$$

$$V_V^P = V_V^{P_2} \cdot V_V^{P_1} \qquad (10)$$

135

Procedure calls can be accommodated by using dependence relations of the invoked procedure and performing a context-dependent elaboration in the invoking procedure's environment [2]. Another method is to visualize procedure calls as generalized assignment statements. Global variables that are visible in both the procedures are directly translated. Actual arguments corresponding to formal arguments of type **out** (by reference) can be modified due to a procedure call, while actual arguments of type **in** can supply input values for the statements of the invoked procedure.

3.4 Compound Statements

Dependence relations can also be determined for compound statements. However, unlike assignment and null statements, the definitions are different for static and dynamic contexts. For example, unless the program is executed for specific initial values for the input variables, it is not possible to determine whether the **then** part or the **else** part of a conditional will be executed.

Conditionals For a program P, composed of a single **if** statement, of the form

$$s : \textbf{if } expr \textbf{ then } P_1 \textbf{ else } P_2 \textbf{ end};$$

the following results can be derived:

$$MOD^P = MOD^{P_i},$$
$$PRE^P = PRE^{P_i},$$
$$V_S^P = MOD^{P_i} \otimes s \cup V_S^{P_i},$$
$$S_V^P = \{s\} \otimes COND \cup S_V^{P_i}, \text{ and}$$
$$V_V^P = V_V^{P_i} \cup (MOD^{P_i} \otimes COND)$$

Here COND denotes the set of variables in $expr$, $\otimes$ is the Cartesian product operator, and i is either 1 or 2 depending on whether $expr$ evaluates to TRUE or FALSE.

Loops Determination of dependence relations for loops is more intricate. During static analysis it is not possible to predict the number of times a loop will iterate. The relations are discussed later for both the static and dynamic cases.

3.5 Static Relations

In general, it is not possible to predict the actual path of computation using static analysis of a program. All control flow paths have to be considered—similar to flow insensitive dataflow analysis—while generating these dependence relations. Using static analysis alone, for $(v, s) \in V_S^P$ the final value of variable v after executing program P *may* depend on the execution of statement s. This relational approach to static analysis was introduced in [1]; the definition of our dependence relations is motivated by the λ, μ, and ρ relations of [1] and their usefulness in generating information about live variable analysis, redundant code elimination, expression movement and generation of partial statements (conceptually similar to *static* program projections).

For example, in the case of a loop, the relations reflect all possible numbers of iterations, ranging from 0 to infinity. Since the relations are defined on finite sets it is possible to get closed form results even with this assumption. Suppose the program P consists of the single loop statement

$$s : \textbf{while COND loop } b \textbf{ end};$$

The loop may not iterate even once so all the variables may be preserved. Therefore, $MOD^P = \phi$, and $PRE^P = \Psi$.

The dependence relations can be shown to be [2]

$$S_V^P = (\{s\} \otimes COND \cup S_V^b) \cdot V_V^{b^*},$$
$$V_V^P = (MOD^b \otimes COND \cup \iota) \cdot V_V^{b^*}, \text{ and}$$
$$V_S^P = MOD^b \otimes \{s\} \cup (MOD^b \otimes COND \cup \iota) \cdot V_V^{b^*} \cdot V_S^b.$$

Here $V_V^* = \iota \cup V_V \cup V_V \cdot V_V \cup \ldots$

3.6 Dynamic Relations

The dependence relations that were defined for static analysis are also useful during the dynamic execution of a program with actual values. Dynamic relations can be more precise since the actual trajectory of the program execution is also available to the analyzer. For a conditional statement, it is known whether the **then** (or **else**) part is executed or not. For a loop, the number of iterations is also known. For example, the following are the dynamic dependence relations for a loop that iterates $(n + 1)$ times. It is assumed that the body b of the loop has invariant relations for each iteration. We use lower case letters for denoting dynamic relations.

$$s_v^{P(n+1)} = (\{s\} \otimes COND \cup s_v^p) \cdot (\iota \cup v_v^p \cup \ldots \cup \underbrace{v_v^p \cdot \ldots \cdot v_v^p}_{n})$$

$$v_v^{P(n+1)} = (Mod^p \otimes COND) \cdot (\iota \cup v_v^p \cup \ldots \cup \underbrace{v_v^p \cdot \ldots \cdot v_v^p}_{n}) \cup$$

136

$$\underbrace{v_v^p \cdot \ldots \cdot v_v^p}_{(n+1)}$$

$$v_s^{P(n+1)} = \text{Mod}^P \otimes \{s\} \cup (\iota \cup v_v^p \cup \ldots \cup \underbrace{v_v^p \cdot \ldots \cdot v_v^p}_{n}) \cdot v_s^p \cup$$

$$(\text{Mod}^P \otimes \text{COND}) \cdot (\iota \cup v_v^p \cup v_v^p \cdot v_v^p \cup \underbrace{v_v^p \cdot \ldots \cdot v_v^p}_{(n-1)}) \cdot v_s^p$$

For the general case, when the body of the loop may have different dynamic dependence relations, we have developed an efficient method for generating dynamic dependence relations for a specific execution of the program. This method uses sets which are updated after each iteration, and it is not required to maintain relations for each iteration of the body of the loop [2].

3.7 Other Programming Constructs

In this paper we have discussed how to generate dependence relations for simple control structures. In addition, we have developed techniques extending this approach to the analysis of block statements, simple recursive procedures, **return** statements, and loops with multi-level exits [2]. Control flow associated with arbitrary **goto**s can pose a considerable challenge in any static analysis. However, many forms of **goto**s can easily be translated to loops with multi-level exits [9]. Nonscalar variables like **records** and **arrays** can also be accommodated.

4 Program Projections

In this section, we define program projections of two types: static and dynamic. We define a program projection to be a subset of all program statements, maintaining the original order and a part of the overall semantics. A projection $P_P(v)$ of program P is defined for a variable v, $v \in \Psi$, and with respect to the sequence of statements from S_1 to S_2. The aim is to construct $P_P(v)$ such that $P_P(v)$ consists of only those statements from the sequence S_1 to S_2 such that the value of v is same after executing $P_P(v)$ as it would be after statement S_2 when P is executed.

Static analysis has been used to generate useful information about programs for the purpose of optimization, testing, and understanding [3]. Projections can be defined based only on the static analysis of the program, similar to program slicing [11] or partial statements [1]. Such projections, however, have limited applicability while executing a program with actual values for testing and debugging purposes. Projections defined in dynamic

contexts are more precise compared to their static counterparts.

Program projections can be generated using dependence relation V_S. For a program P and variable v:

$$P_P(v) = \{s | (v, s) \in V_S^P\} \tag{11}$$

4.1 An Example

To illustrate the definition of a program projection, we present a session with the prototype program analyzer, *AdaAn*. The analyzer itself is described in the next section.

The source file *Fibonacci.a* contains a small program to generate Fibonacci numbers. First, the program analyzer is used to list the *Fibonacci* program.

```
AdaAn => Analyze Fibonacci.a
AdaAn => List FG
.........................................
--- FILE: FG.a    LINES: 1-29 ---
procedure FG is
    VALUE : integer;
    N : integer;
    procedure fi(FIRST, SECOND, N: in integer;
                     FIBO: out integer) is
        FN1, FN2, FN: integer;
        I: integer;
    begin
        if ( N > 0 ) then
            FN1 := FIRST;
            FN2 := SECOND;
            I := 1;
            while ( I <= N ) loop
                FN := FN1 + FN2;
                FN1 := FN2;
                FN2 := FN;
                I := I + 1;
            end loop;
        else
            FN := -1;
        end if;
        FIBO := FN;
    end fi;
begin
    get(N);
    fi(0,1,N, VALUE);
    put(VALUE);
end FG;
```

137

Next the static projection of procedure *fi* with respect to variable *I* is shown.

```
.........................................
AdaAn => Projection_static FG.fi I
.........................................
    if ( N > 0 ) then            -- FG.fi-1
        I := 1;                  -- FG.fi-4
        while ( I <= N ) loop    -- FG.fi-5
            I := I + 1           -- FG.fi-9
        end loop;
    end if;
```

Now the static projection of procedure *fi* is generated with respect to variable *FIBO*.

```
.........................................
AdaAn => Projection_static FG.fi FIBO
.........................................
    if ( N > 0 ) then            -- FG.fi-1
        FN1 := FIRST;            -- FG.fi-2
        FN2 := SECOND;           -- FG.fi-3
        I := 1;                  -- FG.fi-4
        while ( I <= N ) loop    -- FG.fi-5
            FN := FN1 + FN2;     -- FG.fi-6
            FN1 := FN2;          -- FG.fi-7
            FN2 := FN;           -- FG.fi-8
            I := I + 1;          -- FG.fi-9
        end loop;
    else
        FN := -1;                -- FG.fi-10
    end if;
    FIBO := FN;                  -- FG.fi-11
.........................................
```

The following are the dynamic projections for the *Fibonacci* program when it is executed for (1) $N = 1$ and (2) $N = 2$. The program is executed under the control of the analyzer and the execution trajectory is also analyzed to determine more precise projections.

(1) N = 1

```
.........................................
AdaAn => projection_Dynamic FG VALUE
.........................................
    get ( N );                   -- FG-1
    if ( N > 0 ) then            -- FG.fi-1
        FN1 := FIRST;            -- FG.fi-2
        FN2 := SECOND;           -- FG.fi-3
        I := 1;                  -- FG.fi-4
        while ( I <= N ) loop    -- FG.fi-5
            FN := FN1 + FN2;     -- FG.fi-6
```

```
        end loop;
    end if;
    FIBO := FN;                  -- FG.fi-11
.........................................
```

(2) N = 2

```
AdaAn => projection_Dynamic FG VALUE
.........................................
    get ( N );                   -- FG-1
    if ( N > 0 ) then            -- FG.fi-1
        FN1 := FIRST;            -- FG.fi-2
        FN2 := SECOND;           -- FG.fi-3
        I := 1;                  -- FG.fi-4
        while ( I <= N ) loop    -- FG.fi-5
            FN := FN1 + FN2;     -- FG.fi-6
            FN1 := FN2;          -- FG.fi-7
            FN2 := FN;           -- FG.fi-8
            I := I + 1;          -- FG.fi-9
        end loop;
    end if;
    FIBO := FN;                  -- FG.fi-11
.........................................
```

5 A Prototype Program Analyzer

We have implemented an interactive tool, called *AdaAn*, for analyzing programs written in an Ada subset. Here the design of *AdaAn* is outlined, and the functionality of its main components is discussed. A schematic representation of the system is displayed in Figure 1. The system is implemented on a Sun workstation using a UNIX[2]/C platform and tools like *lex*, a lexical analyzer generator and *yacc*, an LALR parser generator.

5.1 VFG Generator

The *VFG* for a program is generated in a bottom-up fashion. The grammar of Ada is described in *yacc* notation. Currently only a representative subset of Ada has been targeted. Real and integer types along with single dimensional arrays are included. Statements can be of the following types: null, assignment, conditional, loop, block, procedure call. *AdaAn* supports separately compiled units and packages.

The *VFG-GEN* component takes a program, generates the *VFG*, and when all the programs have been

---

[2]UNIX is a trademark of AT&T

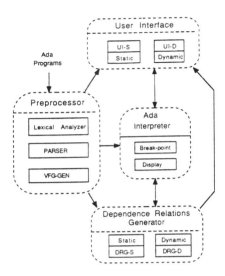

Figure 1: *AdaAn*: Ada Program Analyzer

This is performed by the *Preprocessor*, and its output is used to generate relations in both static and dynamic contexts. In the static situation, *DRG-S* (Dependence Relations Generator in Static Context) requires information from only the preprocessor. However, for *DRG-D* (Dynamic Relations Generator in Dynamic Context), information from the Ada interpreter is also needed so that the actual program trajectory can be utilized for generating dependence relations.

5.3 User Interface

The functionality of the user interface is divided into two parts dealing with the static and dynamic aspects of the program semantics, respectively. *UI-S* (User Interface for Static Semantics) is a browsing tool supporting cross-referencing, visibility, and scoping properties in terms of the requirement, provision, import, and export sets. The *UI-D* component handles the dynamic semantics of programs based on static and dynamic dependence relations. Traditional debugging can be supported by supplementing the interpreter with a breakpoint and display facility. This debugging process is improved by using the dependence relations.

5.4 A Session with *AdaAn*

Here we display the capabilities of *AdaAn* with respect to the analysis of dynamic semantics of a simple program called SUMPROD. This program reads in an array and determines the sum and the product of its items. Program projections are generated for both the static case, and the actual execution with specific input values.

```
AdaAn => Analyze sumprod.a
AdaAn => resolve_all_requirements
AdaAn => List SUMPROD
.............................................
--- FILE: Sumprod.a   LINES: 1-31 ---
procedure sp is
    i, j: integer;
    type INT_ARRAY is array(1..100) of integer;
    ITEMS : INT_ARRAY;
    SUM, PRODUCT : integer;
    MAX: integer;
begin
    get(MAX);
    if (MAX > 0 ) then
        i := 1;
```

transformed, links the individual *VFG*s together. The linking phase provides resolution for all the unresolved names in **is separate** and **with** clauses. An **is separate** clause requires a corresponding **separate** clause in a subunit. Similarly, the **with** clause needs a package that is implemented as a separate compilation unit. If the package specification and the corresponding body are implemented as different compilation units (the specification as a library unit and the body as a secondary unit), then they are also linked together by a *VFG* arc.

After the linking phase, there are two types of *VFG* arc. An arc of type *A_NEST* corresponds to traditional nesting in block structured languages and signifies a unidirectional flow of visibility from the parent to its child. To accommodate packages, an arc of type *A_PACK* links a package to another declarative context describing the visibility of the package name, and eventually the non-private declarations of that package.

5.2 Dependence Relations Generator

The dependence relations generator consists of three units. Dependence relations for assignment statements can be generated directly from the syntax tree of a program. For compound statements, information about the statement type and structure of expressions can be prepackaged.

139

```
        SUM := 0;
        while ( i <= MAX) loop
            get(ITEMS(i));
            SUM := SUM + ITEMS(i);
            i := i + 1;
        end loop;
        j := 1;
        PRODUCT := 1;
        while (j <= MAX) loop
            PRODUCT := PRODUCT*ITEMS(j);
            j := j + 1;
        end loop;
        put(SUM);
        put(PRODUCT);
    end if;
end sp;
```

Now the static relations are determined for the procedure *sp*. Once the relations are ready, projections can be generated with respect to any variable visible in *sp*. Here we show the static projection with respect to *SUM*.

```
. . . . . . . . . . . . . . . . . . . . . . . . . . . . . . . . . . .
AdaAn => Generate_static_relations sp
AdaAn => Projection_static sp SUM
. . . . . . . . . . . . . . . . . . . . . . . . . . . . . . . . . . .
 get ( MAX );                        -- sp-1
 if ( MAX > 0 ) then                 -- sp-2
    i := 1;                          -- sp-3
    SUM := 0;                        -- sp-4
    while ( i <= MAX ) loop          -- sp-5
        get ( ITEMS ( i ) );         -- sp-6
        SUM := SUM + ITEMS ( i );    -- sp-7
        i := i + 1;                  -- sp-8
    end loop;
 end if;
```

In the next session, the program *sp* is executed under the control of *AdaAn*. The user types 0 for the value of *MAX*. For this value, program tests the first **if** statement and then terminates. This dynamic behavior is reflected by the dynamic relations generated for this execution.

```
. . . . . . . . . . . . . . . . . . . . . . . . . . . . . . . . . . .
AdaAn => generate_Dynamic_relations sp
. . . . . . . . . . . . . . . . . . . . . . . . . . . . . . . . . . .
Executing the Program sp
Control Passed to the Program
0
Program Completed, Control Back to the Analyzer
```

```
. . . . . . . . . . . . . . . . . . . . . . . . . . . . . . . . . . .
AdaAn => projection_dynamic sp SUM
. . . . . . . . . . . . . . . . . . . . . . . . . . . . . . . . . . .
    -- EMPTY
. . . . . . . . . . . . . . . . . . . . . . . . . . . . . . . . . . .
AdaAn => show_dynamic_relations sp
. . . . . . . . . . . . . . . . . . . . . . . . . . . . . . . . . . .
Mod = {sp.MAX}
Pre = {sp.i, sp.j, sp.ITEMS, sp.SUM, sp.PRODUCT}
vv  = {(sp.i, sp.i), (sp.j, sp.j),
        (sp.ITEMS, sp.ITEMS), (sp.SUM, sp.SUM),
        (sp.PRODUCT, sp.PRODUCT)}
vs  = {(sp.MAX,sp-1)}
sv  = {}
```

6 Concluding Remarks

The design of decomposition techniques is aimed at providing support for maintenance activities. It is possible to implement these techniques in an interactive fashion. The visibility flow graphs serve as an intermediate representation form for static and dynamic analysis of programs. Dependence relations are used to capture the dependencies among the variables and statements of a program in both static and dynamic contexts. Projections are obtained when the dependence relations are used for defining program decompositions with respect to dynamic semantics.

The visibility flow graphs facilitate an efficient representation of the static semantics of multi-module programs. The static and dynamic relations can store dependence information within a monolithic program and also for programs with multiple procedures. This ensures the applicability of *AdaAn* for analyzing large programs that typically have multiple procedures implemented in several modules.

We have also presented the major features of the prototype program analyzer, *AdaAn*. It can assist maintenance programmers by automatically providing decompositions for Ada programs. It supports both the projections generated by only static analysis, and those generated based on specific program execution trajectories. We are currently formalizing the applicability of automatic program decomposition techniques for supporting program testing and verification. With this additional functionality, *AdaAn* will support all major programming activities related to software maintenance.

Although there have been empirical studies support-

140

ing the usefulness of program slicing for debugging purposes [12], it will be worthwhile to study the scope and effectiveness of various types of program decompositions in a more comprehensive fashion. Another line of future work will be to use these techniques in restructuring existing code for better future maintenance.

References

[1] J. F. Bergeretti and B. A. Carre. Information-flow and data-flow analysis of while-programs. *ACM Transactions on Programming Languages and Systems*, 7(1):37–61, January 1985.

[2] R. Gopal. On supporting software evolution—decomposition schemes for static and dynamic analyses of programs. *In preparation*. 1989.

[3] K. Kennedy. A survey of data flow analysis. In: Stevens S. Muchnick and Neil D. Jones, Editors, *Program Flow Analysis*, Prentice Hall, Englewood Cliffs, New Jersey, 1981.

[4] B. Korel and J. Laski. Dynamic program slicing. *Information Processing Letters*, 29:155–163, October 1988.

[5] J. R. Lyle and K. B. Gallagher. Using program decomposition to guide modifications. *Proceedings of Conference on Software Maintenance-1988*, Phoenix, Arizona, 265–269, October 1988.

[6] L. Osterweil. Using data flow tools in software engineering. In: S. S. Muchnick and N. D. Jones, Editors, *Program Flow Analysis*, Prentice Hall, Englewood Cliffs, New Jersey, 1981.

[7] R. Prieto-Diaz and J. M. Neighbors. Module interconnection languages. *The Journal of Systems and Software*, 6:307–334, 1986.

[8] C. V. Ramamoorthy, V. Garg, and A. Prakash. Programming in the large. *IEEE Transactions on Software Engineering*, SE-12(7):769–783, July 1986.

[9] L. Ramshaw. Eliminating goto's while preserving program structure. *Journal of the ACM*, 35(4):893–920, October 1988.

[10] N. F. Schneidewind. The state of software maintenance. *IEEE Transactions on Software Engineering*, SE-13(3):303–310, March 1987.

[11] M. Weiser. Program slicing. *IEEE Transactions on Software Engineering*, SE-10(4):352–357, July 1984.

[12] M. Weiser. Programmers use slices when debugging. *Communications of the ACM*, 25(7):446–452, July 1982.

[13] M. Weiser. Source code. *IEEE Computer*, 20(11):66–74, October 1987.

141

Chapter 9
Software Restructuring and Translation

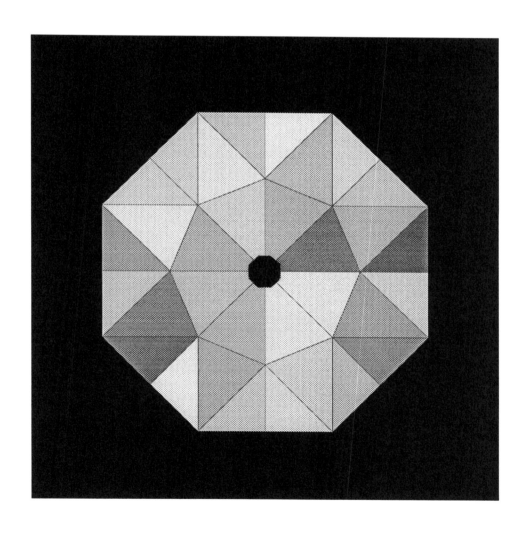

Chapter 9
Software Restructuring
and Translation

Purpose

This chapter discusses software restructuring techniques for improving the logical structure and understandability of source code. It discusses what restructuring is, its capabilities and limitations, and how it is incorporated into reengineering processes. The chapter also discusses techniques for translating source code, since these techniques often share the same underlying technology as restructuring techniques.

Papers

In the first paper, "Software Restructuring," Robert Arnold gives a tutorial on software restructuring technology. He discusses many aspects of restructuring: what restructuring is, its advantages and disadvantages, and case studies.

In the next paper, "Software Recycling," Harry Sneed and Gábor Jandrasics describe a tool-supported process for reengineering old software. The process involves static analysis, modularization, restructuring, backwards translation, design tuning, and code regeneration. The paper is a good example of how restructuring often fits within a broader reengineering plan, rather than just as an end in itself.

The next three papers discuss ideas applicable to the internal operations of restructuring and translation tools. In the paper, "Software Maintenance as an Engineering Discipline," Richard Linger discusses the theory and practical steps behind a reengineering process. One of the results of this process is restructuring. The major reengineering steps are to (1) reengineer the code into a structured form, (2) create a hierarchy of program functions that describe what the code is doing, and (3) selectively reprogram the code using the program function hierarchy as a guide.

In the next paper, "Software Reverse Engineering: A Case Study," Eric Byrne discusses how he used reverse engineering to aid in translating a program from Fortran into Ada. He distinguishes between program documentation and design documentation. Program documentation reflects implementation details (like data item names, basic data types, system interfaces, and optimized code sections). Design documentation reflects, at a higher level, how a program functions. Byrne's approach recovers a design and uses this to guide translation into Ada. This avoids the problem of "Adatran" — Ada source code whose coding style mimics that of the Fortran source code.

In the final paper, "Program Translation via Abstraction and Reimplementation," Richard Waters describes technology fundamental to many reengineering tools: translation, transformation, and refinement. Though this paper discusses the more general problem of conversion, restructuring may be a by-product of conversion when the source and target languages are the same.

607

Software Restructuring

ROBERT S. ARNOLD

Invited Paper

Perhaps the most common of all software engineering activities is the modification of software. Unfortunately, software modification—especially during software maintenance—often leaves behind software that is difficult to understand for those other than its author. The result is software that is harder to change, less reliable when it is changed, and progressively less likely to be changed. Software restructuring is a field that seeks to reverse these effects on software.

This paper is a brief tutorial on software restructuring. The paper discusses what restructuring is, advantages and disadvantages of restructuring, tools and case studies, and future possibilities. The reader is assumed to have a general appreciation for building and maintaining software systems. After reading this paper, the reader should have a feel for the strengths, weaknesses, and capabilities of software restructuring technology.

I. INTRODUCTION

A. The Concept of Software Restructuring

Software restructuring is the modification of software to make the software easier to understand and to change, or less susceptible to error when future changes are made. "Software" includes external and internal documentation concerning source code, as well as the source code itself.

This definition of software restructuring excludes software changes for other purposes, such as code optimization. Code optimization does imply "restructuring" in a sense, but normally does not concern the key element—for this paper—of improving software maintainability.

Some examples of software restructuring are pretty printing (spaces and aligns software statements so that they are easier to comprehend as logical units); manual restructuring according to coding style standards (infuses software with standard, recognizable structure); editing documentation for readability (makes the documentation easier to read, possibly improving software maintainability); creating an index for some software documentation (makes it easier to locate information about software); and so on.

Fig. 1 illustrates software restructuring. The original program is hard to maintain. Its purpose is apparently to edit

Manuscript received August 8, 1988; revised October 18, 1988. In preparing this paper, the author has reused and updated much of the material in [5]. All views are the author's only, and do not necessarily reflect those of the Software Productivity Consortium.

The author is with the Software Productivity Consortium, Herndon, VA 22070 USA.

IEEE Log Number 8926704.

ORIGINAL PROGRAM FRAGMENT:

```
000100  EDIT-COST-INDICATORS.
000110    IF C NOT EQUAL TO "A" OR "B" MOVE "X" TO COST-INDICATOR
000120       GO TO EDIT-COST-INDICATORS-EXIT.
000130       IF C EQUAL TO "A" AND CS EQUAL TO 1 MOVE 0 TO
000140          PGNT ADD1 TO PGNT MOVE "007" TO SPAG.
000150  MOVE ALL NINES TO ZCOD ADD 1 TO NLCNT
000160  ADD SPC TO CUM-SPC PERFORM OK-RECD-PRINT THROUGH
000170     OK-RECD-SUB-PRINT GO TO EDIT-COST-INDICATORS-EXIT.
000180  IF C EQUAL TO "B" AND CS EQUAL TO 1 MOVE 0 TO PGNT ADD 1
000190     TO PGNT MOVE "007" TO SPAG    MOVE "99999" TO ZCOD.
000200        ADD 1 TO NLCNT            ADD SPC TO CUM-SPC
000210  PERFORM OK-RECD-PRINT THROUGH OK-RECD-SUB-PRINT
000220  GO TO EDIT-COST-INDICATORS-EXIT.
000230        IF C EQUAL TO "A" OR "B" AND CS NOT EQUAL TO 1 ADD 1
000240     TO PGNT MOVE "010" TO SPAG    ADD 2 TO NLCNT
000250     ADD SPC TO CUM-SPC PERFORM NOT-OK-RECD-PRINT.
000260  EDIT-COST-INDICATORS-EXIT.
000270    EXIT.
```

RESTRUCTURED PROGRAM FRAGMENT:

```
000100  EDIT-COST-INDICATORS-1080.
000110    IF COST-INDICATOR = "A" OR "B".
000120       IF SUB-COST-INDICATOR = 1.
000130          MOVE 0 TO PAGE-COUNT.
000140          ADD 1 TO PAGE-COUNT.
000150          MOVE "007" TO SPECIAL-AGENT.
000160          MOVE "99999" TO ZIP-CODE.
000170          ADD 1 TO NEW-LINE-COUNT.
000180          ADD SPECIAL-COST TO CUMULATIVE-COST.
000190          PERFORM OK-RECD-PRINT-1470 THROUGH
000200             OK-RECD-PRINT-1580.
000210       ELSE
000220          ADD 1 TO PAGE-COUNT.
000230          MOVE "010" TO SPECIAL-AGENT.
000240          ADD 2 TO NEW-LINE-COUNT.
000250          ADD SPECIAL-COST TO CUMULATIVE-COST.
000260          PERFORM NOT-OK-RECD-PRINT-1780.
000270    ELSE
000280       MOVE "X" TO COST-INDICATOR.
000290  EDIT-COST-INDICATORS-EXIT-1260.
000300    EXIT.
```

Fig. 1. Software restructuring of a COBOL program. (From [25], p. 129.)

some cost indicators (see line 100), but other details, such as the meaning of the cost indicators being edited, are unclear. Its variables are not mnemonic. (What does "SPAG" mean in line 140?) More than one statement per line, lack of consistent indentation, and splitting of statements across physical lines makes following the control flow difficult. The program has literal constants (e.g., "007"), instead of symbolic constants (e.g., SPECIAL-AGENT with a constant value of "007"), which makes the program harder to change.

The restructured program has fixed many of these problems. From quick inspection, the purpose of the program has something to do with accumulating costs related to special agents. (James Bond's—agent 007's—expense accounting program?) Statements appear on one line. The control flow has been simplified and indentation makes the control flow easy to follow. Variables have more meaningful names (e.g., SPECIAL-AGENT instead of SPAG). Literal constants like "007" still remain, but their purpose is easier to fathom (e.g., since "007" is assigned to SPECIAL-AGENT, 007 appears to be the number of a special agent).

Several terms related to software restructuring have appeared. Software reengineering, software renewal [51], software renovation, software rejuvenation [16], [17], software improvement [25], [26], software recycling [52], and so on, have approximately the same intent as software restructuring: modifying or adding to software to make it easier to understand and to change.

Reverse engineering is the recovery of information about software to make the software easier to understand and to change. For example, creating design diagrams for a system whose design diagrams are out of date is a reverse engineering technique.

Reverse engineering and software restructuring are related. Reverse engineering connotes adding new information to software where such information previously did not exist, or was hopelessly inaccurate. Software restructuring connotes taking existing information and refashioning it so it can be more easily understood. However, since the process of refashioning information often incorporates new insights about software, for this paper we consider reverse engineering a part of software restructuring.

B. Why Be Concerned About Software Restructuring?

With continued change, software tends to become less "structured" [31]. This is manifested by out-of-date documentation, code which does not conform to standards, increased time for programmers to understand code, increased ripple effect of changes, and so on. These can—and usually do—imply higher software maintenance costs.

Software restructuring is an important option for putting high software maintenance costs under control. The idea is to modify software—or programmer's perceptions of software structure—so one can understand and control it anew.

There are many other reasons why software engineers should be aware of software restructuring:

- Regaining understanding of software by instilling software with known, easily traceable structure. This has the side benefits of
  - easier documentation,
  - easier testing,
  - easier auditing,
  - potentially reduced software complexity,
  - potentially greater programmer productivity,
  - reduced dependence on individuals who alone understand poorly structure software,
  - increased interchangeability of people maintaining software, and
  - greater programmer job satisfaction due to decreased frustration in working with poorly structured software.
- Creating software whose structure more closely resembles the structure taught to newer generations of programmers
- Reducing the amount of time needed for maintenance programmers to become familiar with a system

- Upgrading software along with upgrading software engineering practices
- Implementing standards for software structure
- Making bugs easier to locate
- Extending system lifetime by retaining a system's flexibility through good structure
- Preparing software as input for software analysis tools
- Preparing software for conversion
- Preparing to add new features to software
- Preserving software's asset value to an organization

Software restructuring is an integral part of achieving many goals in software maintenance and in corporate planning for software change.

C. What "Structure" is the Target of Restructuring?

Software restructuring is not just concerned with objectively observable/measurable aspects of software structure. It is also concerned with people's perceptions of software structure. When asked about the understandability of a piece of software, most software engineers will not base their answer exclusively on measurements of objective software aspects; they also look at at least part of the software.

The point here is that in considering restructuring, one needs to consider that the structure (ideas about the software) in people's heads matters as much as the objective structure of software itself. For software restructuring, "structure" is determined by at least two things: the software and the perceiver. Thus anything that can influence the software's state or the perceiver's state might influence software structure. The succeeding discussion will use the term "software structure" with both these aspects of structure in mind.

Fig. 2 presents some of the factors influencing people's perceptions of software structure. The clearest influence

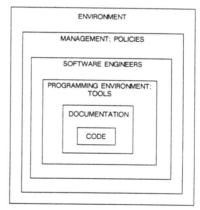

Fig. 2. Factors influencing perceptions of software structure.

on software structure comes from the software code itself, at the core of Fig. 2. Next, the in-line software documentation—often the primary documentation programmers depend on [22]—can have a strong influence on a programmer's perception of structure. Other documentation, when available, up-to-date, easily referenced, clearly written, and so on, can also influence a programmer's perception of structure. Next come the set of available software

609

tools (or programming environment) which can illuminate different views of the software for the programmer. For example, program traces can show dynamic execution behavior, algorithm animation can help programmers understand the dynamic strategy behind an algorithm, global variable cross referencers can help programmers understand the interactions between modules, and pretty printers can make reading code much more appealing.

In the middle layer of Fig. 2 is the programmer, the "other side" of software structure. If the programmer is not trained to look for certain aspects of structure, his or her perception of structure will be influenced.

Because programmers' perceptions differ (even in the same programmer at different times[1]), the notion of software structure is not constant, but *dynamic*. In fact, failure to have written notions of structure (such as structural standards) which programmers are aware of, or failure to allow programmers to refresh their notions of structure by viewing software in various ways, can lead to a net *loss* of structure. For example, program patches are insidious structure-reducers because the reason for the patch is often lost when the patch's author leaves. In effect, the programmer has promoted in the software his or her structural view without telling others of this view, resulting in a net loss of software structure for others.

At the next higher layer of Fig. 2 is the management layer, which can sensitize a programmer to aspects of software structure. For example, management can emphasize software quality as embodied in a set of standards. If a programmer's performance review is tied to how well these standards are met, then the programmers' perceptions of software will likely be influenced!

The highest layer of Fig. 2 is the environment surrounding the lower levels. This includes physical facilities, degree of influence on software maintenance tasks by computer users, lack of availability of hardware, and so on. All can influence a programmer's attitude, which in turn can influence his or her perception of software structure.

By changing the state of items at any of the levels in Fig. 2, "software structure" can be influenced. Thus, approaches that influence any layer(s) of Fig. 2 are all candidate software restructuring approaches.

For example, reducing programmer turnover—a problem of the management layer of Fig. 2—may be viewed as a structure-preserving technique. Since programmers have invaluable insight into the behavior of software, high turnover of programmers can lead to information loss about the software. High turnover does not allow enough time to pass on this information before a person leaves. The result is a progressive net loss in software structure, which is typically manifested by software changes becoming harder to implement. The basic problem of preserving information among programmers may be ameliorated by decreasing programmer turnover.

Unfortunately, few authors—anywhere—define their notions of software structure in their papers or books. The reader should realize the "structure" in restructuring is often implicit, with the discussion context hinting at what structure is intended.

---

[1]For example, if a programmer returns to software he (or she) has written years earlier, it may initially appear strange and difficult to understand.

D. Software Restructuring is a Means to an End

Software restructuring should not be an end in itself. Restructuring should be related to locally defined goals, and achieving goals should be related to perceived software value. If restructuring cannot be justified in terms of higher goals, then these goals should be rethought, or more information collected, before the decision to restructure is made.

For example, if the problem is slow performance of user-requested changes in a software maintenance shop then maintenance management's higher goal of satisfactory software service is affected. The reason for the slow performance could be hard-to-modify software (in which case software restructuring may be advisable), or unrestrained user requests for change (in which case software restructuring may not be advisable), among other reasons. Further information is needed before one decides to restructure. But if restructuring is selected, it is because of the goal of satisfactory software service and not restructuring for its own sake.

A major goal of software restructuring is to preserve or increase software value. Software value can be measured externally or internally:

• External software value is the cost savings the software provides to the user community, relative to other, non-software means of satisfying user needs. For users, successful software maintenance is typified by few—preferably no—visible bugs in the software and rapid response to, and implementation of, user requests for system change. As noted earlier, systems undergoing maintenance often become progressively more difficult to change. If this progressive software ossification ever begins affecting the user's expectation of delivered software capability, the external value of the software may decrease.

• Internal software value involves at least three kinds of cost savings: 1) the maintenance cost savings that the software form provides relative to some other software form, 2) the cost savings incurred by reusing parts of the software in other systems, and 3) the cost savings due to an extended software lifetime (which delays the introduction of a replacement system). If software restructuring reduces maintenance costs, increases the software's potential for reuse in other software, and extends the software's lifetime, the internal value of the current software should increase!

There is little reason to believe that the same definition of value is used by all maintenance environments. Software value can be measured in other ways, such as savings in calendar time to implement software changes, increase in maintainer morale, increase in management respect for software maintenance, and so on.

But having *some* definition of software value can materially affect decisions to restructure. Any decision to use a software restructuring approach should try to quantify the added software value, as locally defined, which the approach will provide.

E. Software Restructuring and Software Maintenance

Software restructuring is most often applied to software undergoing maintenance, for this is where the lack of software structure becomes most evident (and expensive). Throughout this paper, software restructuring will be considered in the context of software maintenance.

However, software restructuring is also applicable during software development. This occurs especially when development activities are undertaken in an environment resembling "traditional" software maintenance (i.e., no quality assurance, deadline-driven, little if any testing, no code reviews, etc.). This can result in software becoming less and less structured.

To take a plausible example, in a large software project that has little reused code that takes several calendar years to build, and has little quality assurance, the potential for unstructured software toward project end can increase. The development activities prior to delivery could center on corrections to errors uncovered by tests and on enhancements requested by users due to changed needs since the system was contracted. If development is deadline-driven, the changes may be hurried and resemble patches, which can lead to worse software structure. In this situation, software restructuring might be advisable before the system is accepted for maintenance.

II. State of the Art in Software Restructuring Technology

As noted earlier, by changing the state of items at any of the levels in Fig. 2, "software structure" can be influenced. We can study restructuring approaches by the levels of Fig. 2 addressed by each approach.

This section briefly describes restructuring approaches. The approaches are divided into techniques, methodologies, and reverse engineering. Techniques (Section II-A) pertain to making changes at one (or a few) of the levels in Fig. 2. Methodologies (Section II-B) can pertain to all levels. Reverse engineering (Section II-C) pertains to repopulating, or bringing up-to-date, information in any of the levels.

Two caveats: this section is not intended to be exhaustive. It is intended to give the reader a feel for a wide range of restructuring approaches. Also, the classifications are not exclusive; some approaches could be placed in more than one section.

A. Techniques

A "technique" for this list is a restructuring approach that pertains to one (or a few) levels of Fig. 2. The restructuring techniques presented here correspond to the innermost five levels: code, documentation, programming environment/tools, software engineers, and management/policies.

1) Code: Code-oriented restructuring techniques pertain to modifying code directly, mostly without relying on information in the other levels. In the following sections they are divided into techniques based on coding style, packages and reusable code, control flow, and data.

a) Coding style: These restructuring approaches modify code to make it easier to understand, often without altering control structure or data structure.

• *Pretty printing and code formatting:* This restructuring technique textually restructures code by applying spacing between logical subparts, indentation of nested statements, one statement per line, and so on. This often can be done totally automatically and may be available as a compiler option for output listings.

• *Coding style standardization:* This restructuring technique textually restructures code by modifying code to conform to coding standard style guidelines. For example, a style manual may require that certain coding structures be avoided (e.g., ALTER statements in COBOL) and that standard keywords be used. This approach is mostly manual, but is often used with automated tools such as pretty printers and control flow restructurers. Some COBOL restructurers (see below) allow their output code to be tailored to better conform to local style guidelines.

• *Restructuring with a preprocessor* ([29] and others): The idea here is to replace sections of code with statements in another, presumably easier-to-understand, language. The new statements can be automatically expanded into statements of the original language. This approach has the advantage of allowing software to be selectively restructured, with statements recognized by the preprocessor, while leaving the remaining software unchanged. This is important because some people are leery of restructuring approaches that restructure more than is apparently necessary.

(b) Packages/reusable code: These approaches use software packages, or reusable code, to replace poorly structured software, or add to software.

• *Restructuring code for reusability [30]:* This technique takes existing code and puts it in a form for reuse. This often involves "cleaning up" software interfaces (e.g., removing superfluous parameters, reducing procedural side effects, and so on). Another aspect of this technique is changing a system to accept reusable code. Several examples of this follow.

• *Buy a package to replace an old system [16]:* Sometimes the best way to "restructure" a system is to replace it with a system with known structure. Restructuring is not the only way to solve problems with a system that is hard to understand, hard to change, and unreliable when changed. Since most packages do not make their source code available to users for modification, modifications to the packages must be done—at potentially substantial cost and on the vendor's timetable—through the package vendor.

• *Buy a software package to replace an old system; then extend the package [16]:* If it is risky or expensive to modify a system, a package may exist that both does the system's function and can be extended for new use. This is a straightforward approach, provided a suitable, adequately documented package can be found. Again, getting the package supplier's source code for the package can be a problem. Getting information on how the package works can be a bigger problem.

• *Buy a package to replace part of an old system [16]:* As the title implies, this approach replaces a software part that is particularly in need of restructuring. The approach depends on being able to find a suitable replacement package. The concerns raised above about vendor packages still apply.

• *System sandwich approach [16]:* This is an ingenious approach for retaining the benefits of code that is so badly structured it must be treated as a black box. The idea is to sandwich the old system between a new front-end interface (e.g., written in a fourth generation language) and a new back-end data base. The front-end interacts with the user. It also issues calls to the black box to compute information not currently available from the back-end data base. The black box system computes its outputs and directs it to the back-end database. The front-end and back-end can directly

611

communicate for report generation purposes. The old system is used primarily for its outputs to the back-end database.

c) Control flow: Much of the concern for software restructuring began with a concern for making a program's control flow easier to follow. This category contains algorithms and procedures for restructuring program control flow graphs, and tools for restructuring programs. The restructuring tools are mostly oriented to COBOL, for this is where most commercial interest in restructuring has been. The tools typically offer much more than just the ability to restructure code. For example, many tools offer style standardization, measurements of the code before and after restructuring (e.g., number of goto's), and/or automatically generated documentation (e.g., depicting control flow relationships among program elements) about the code. Since competition is motivating constant improvements the tool marketers should be consulted for latest information. No evaluation is implied by the presence or absence of a tool/approach in this list.

• *Early goto-less approach [11]:* This approach is famous for showing "goto's" are not theoretically necessary to create a computer program. The proof is by construction and contains a way to restructure software.

• *Giant case statement approach [7]:* This is another constructive way to remove goto's. The resulting program looks like a giant case statement.

• *Boolean flag approach [58]:* This is a procedure for creating a "structured" flowgraph by introducing Boolean variable(s).

• *Duplication of coding approach [58]:* This approach eliminates goto's to shared sections of code by duplicating the shared code and eliminating the sharing. This approach will not work for some looping programs.

• *Baker's graph-theoretic approach [8]:* This is the algorithm behind the tool "struct" for restructuring FORTRAN programs. Goto's are allowed on a limited basis.

• *Refined case statement approach [33]:* This approach introduces some procedures and heuristics to make the program resulting from the giant case statement approach easier to read and understand. This approach has some mathematical foundations in the work in [37].

• *RETROFIT (tm) [35]:* A tool for restructuring COBOL programs. Marketed by the Catalyst Group of Peat Marwick Main & Co., Chicago, Illinois.

• *SUPERSTRUCTURE (tm) [38]:* A tool for restructuring COBOL programs. Marketed by the Software Productivity Tools Division of Computer Data Systems, Inc., of Rockville, Maryland, through a recent acquisition of the previous marketer, Group Operations, Washington, D.C.

• *RECORDER (tm) [15]:* A tool for restructuring COBOL programs. Marketed by Language Technology, Salem, Massachusetts.

• *Cobol Structuring Facility (tm) [34]:* A tool for restructuring COBOL programs. Marketed by IBM, Bethesda, Maryland.

• *Delta/STRUCTURIZER (tm):* A tool for restructuring COBOL programs. Marketed by Delta Software Technologie AG, Switzerland.

• *Double conversion:* This approach takes a program in language A, uses an automated conversion tool to translate the program into language B, then uses another automated conversion tool to reconvert the program into language A.

The result of this will usually be a program with different structure from the original.

d) Data: Historically, restructuring of software tends to connote restructuring of its control structure. But possibilities for restructuring data are important too. One example is putting the relations of a relational data base into third normal form. This has the advantage of reducing the need to propagate updates in a data base when data records are updated. Another example crops up in multidatabase environments. In such environments each database can have its own schema. Often, there are data items that mean approximately the same thing, but are named differently in each schema. To reduce the dependence of programs on the idiosyncrasies of data names with each database, the schemas might be restructured into a master schema that can hide lower level schema naming conventions. Programs can then be restructured to make queries using the master schema. This increases program understandability because programmers only have to know what data items in the master schema mean, rather than having to know the semantic nuances for each database.

2) Documentation: Documentation is often the first place programmers turn to before modifying code. Documentation helps the programmer understand code, plan and perform modifications, and perform testing. Unfortunately, documentation often goes out-of-date and then is never referred to. Missing or inconsistent documentation seems to be a constant complaint from maintenance programmers.

• *Upgrade documentation:* Examples of this are adding in-line code comments, making comments more accurate, expanding on cryptic commentary, and so on. Upgrading documentation and reverse engineering (discussed below) can overlap. The loose distinction we make is that upgrading documentation takes existing documentation and updates it, often without creating new forms of documentation. Reverse engineering may create new forms of documentation as well.

• *System modularization:* System modularization concerns how to decompose a proposed system into logically meaningful modules, or re-decompose an existing system into modules. System modularization currently requires much human judgment. Principles for manually performing modularization are available [41]–[43]. Some work on automating the modularization of systems has recently been reported [52].

3) Programming Environments/Tools: A programming environment provides a set of tools to assist the programmer in building, browsing and modifying software. Often the environment is used not just for programming, but for designing and creating requirements. In some environments the tools are integrated, where the environment provides support for sharing data among the tools.

• *Upgrade the programming environment:* Examples of this are adding windows to the programming interface, improving interaction of tools, replacing hard-to-use operating system command languages, and so on. These measures do not directly restructure target software, but they can increase the ability of a programmer to deal with software.

• *Programming environments/workstations ([9], [57] and others):* Programming environments offer more comprehensive support for programming needs than do tool collections. For example, the programming environment may allow tools to be easily combined in a control procedure to create new tools. The programming workstation offers increased computing power to the programmer, along with new programming interfaces (e.g., windows).

• *Software metrics ([10], [23], [39], [47], and others):* The restructuring idea here is: 1) measure the software with a software metric (or a set of software metrics); 2) from the metric's value, answer the question, "Is the software property measured by the metric satisfactory?"; 3) if not, restructure the software and go to step 1); 4) if so, you are done.

• *Standards checkers and other aids:* These are tools that take a program and automatically report which software standards the program does and does not meet. Based on the reported violations, the code may be modified (restructured) to remove the violations.

• *Tool collections ([56] and others):* There is a growing number of tool collections that may be used to illuminate aspects of software structure. For example, MAP [56] will display the structure chart for a COBOL system, display a unit interface chart, highlight procedures in the structure chart that contain selected statements, display possible references of modifications to selected variables, and so on. MAP is now available as VIA/INSIGHT from VIASOFT, Phoenix, Arizona.

• *Program transformation systems [44]:* These systems involve automatic changes to software. The changes are accomplished with rules called transformations. This approach is related to the rule-based systems of artificial intelligence.

• *Fourth generation languages ([24] and others):* Though not generally thought of as restructuring tools, fourth generation languages offer significant benefits to the set of applications that may be rewritten in them. These benefits include ease of change, usability by end users, and quick development of small systems.

4) Software Engineers: The benefits of software structure must be perceived before they can be practically realized. Software problems (such as difficulty in modifying source code)—problems that normally suggest software modification-oriented restructuring solutions—may only be symptomatic of nonsoftware problems that impair or lose programmer's perceptions about software structure. Software restructuring is, in a very real sense, concerned with improving programmer's perceptions about software.

• *Train programmers:* Some common examples of this are the training courses in "structured programming" adopted by some companies, instruction on how to use existing tools to accomplish tasks, and advice from fellow programmers on how software works.

• *Hire new programmers, more experienced with the existing software application:* This is a most direct way to gain fresh insight into software structure. For example, if existing programmers are having difficulties modifying a windowing package to run on a new operating system, hiring a system programmer already experienced with the windowing package and with installing it might be advised. Even if the windowing package and the operating system are poorly documented so that they are difficult to understand, the new programmer's experience could compensate for these disadvantages. Of course, this may be only a short-term solution because the problem of the software being

hard to understand by the general programming community may persist.

• *Reduce turnover:* When a person leaves an organization, a wealth of perceptions about software walks out the door. Steps to reduce turnover can help keep strong the group's consciousness about software structure.

5) Management and Policies: Management and policies can have a great impact on what people do with software, and therefore how software is perceived.

• *Programming standards and style guidelines ([28] and others):* This idea seems widely accepted, but surprisingly may not be put widely into practice [59].

• *Inspections and walkthroughs ([18], [20] and others):* This is one of the most effective practices for making software understandable and structure more recognizable.

B. Methodologies

A methodology is typically a set of steps for improving software at several of the levels shown in Fig. 2. A methodology helps direct the use of other, more specific, restructuring techniques.

• *System rejuvenation [16]:* System rejuvenation is defined as "using an existing system as the basis for a new strategic system." This is a methodology that involves cleaning up the existing system, making it more efficient (sometimes restructuring introduces a performance overhead), and putting the rejuvenated system into use.

• *Software Improvement Program [26], [27]:* This is an ambitious, management-intensive way to both restructure software and upgrade the software engineering practices of a maintenance environment. It consists of detailed technical guidance for planning the restructuring of software and improving the programming environment in which software is built.

Incremental restructuring [4]: Incremental restructuring is a restructuring approach without as much management overhead as the Software Improvement Program. The approach allows "structure" to be defined by users (rather than being built into the restructuring approach); restructuring is done in small, manageable parts. Also, a system can have the benefits of restructuring without having to be totally restructured. The approach is specifically designed to avoid introducing poor structure as a result of maintenance.

• *Software renewal [51]:* Software renewal is an approach not so much for modifying code as for upgrading system documentation, system specifications, and system tests.

C. Reverse Engineering

The reverse engineering techniques here emphasize recovering design information about existing code. Recreating complete documentation (including requirements documents) on existing code is often exorbitantly expensive and tends not to be done (e.g., see [45]).

• *Strategies for understanding software [19], [32]:* This approach suggests several heuristics for programmers to apply in trying to understand software that lacks up to date documentation. The steps in [19] are to learn the structure and organization of the program, determine what the program is doing, and document the program.

• *Design recovery [1], [2], [13], [40]:* These approaches suggest specific forms for recreated design information. In

613

some cases, automated tools are used to recreate the documentation.

• *Conversion [52]:* This approach creates information about a system as the system is being converted. The new information is used to assist the programmer in converting the system and in documenting the new system.

III. A SOFTWARE RESTRUCTURING CASE STUDY

Whenever one considers a restructuring technique, one is naturally curious about what results others have achieved. Supposing that the technique is a code restructuring tool, one can go to the tool vendor and inquire about the tool. Naturally one expects to get glowing praises and referrals to the most satisfied customers. The next source of information might be a users' group for the tool. Here one can expect more realistic appraisals of a tool's practical value. But the appraisals, though valuable, are very subjective. Other users gained experience with the tools in *their* environments with *their* programs; whether similar results will happen in one's own environment is unclear, given that environments and programs can differ dramatically.

Recently an attempt was made to compare the usefulness of maintaining restructured code with original code. Though methodological problems (discussed below) can be found in the study, the approach and results represent a noteworthy contribution to the measurement of restructuring efficacy.

The study, conducted by the Defense Logistics Agency[2] (DLA) of Columbus, Ohio, was an evaluation of a particular COBOL restructuring tool, RECODER (tm), from Language Technology[3], Salem, Massachusetts [21]. The goal of the study was to investigate claims made by the vendor about the restructuring abilities of the tool and to "evaluate the effects of the restructuring process on production code managed by DLA."

Fig. 3 presents the study plan. Six programs were selected by DLA to be restructured. Most of these programs were considered "unstructured." (See Table 1.) The programs were then restructured using RECODER. Programmers who were to work on the restructured code were given a training course taught by Language Technology. A set of measurements of recoded versus original programs was taken. The same set of changes were applied to both recoded and original programs. Different programmers were used to perform the changes. (No programmer was allowed to modify a program he or she wrote originally.) Measurements of the recoded and original software were taken again. (See Table 2.) Programmers were interviewed to get feedback about using the restructuring tool and about modifying the restructured programs.

The study resulted in several assessments. On the positive side, restructuring was generally beneficial: The recoded programs were easier to modify. (See Table 3.) The time to test the modified restructured programs was about the same as for the original programs. (See Table 4.) The recoded versions had better consistency in the coding style and documentation than the original versions. The recoded versions had significantly reduced violations in local stan-

---

[2]Dr. M. Colter analyzed the study results and wrote the final report.
[3]Language Technology is to be commended for taking the risk of exposing their tool for such scrutiny.

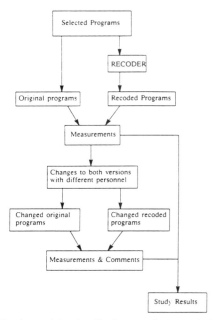

Fig. 3. Plan for studying the effectiveness of a restructuring tool [21].

Table 1 Programs Selected to Be Restructured

Program ID for Study	Program Name	Structured?*
PROG1	Policy Tables	No
PROG2	Prog. Data Ref. File Update	No
PROG3	Family & Cat. Chgs. to SCF	No
PROG4	Defense Inactive Item Prog.	No
PROG5	Stratification	No
PROG6	NON-NSN Demand Hist. Update	Yes

*Based on internal DLA assessment.

dards and structure conventions. Programmers using the recoded versions "acquired increased knowledge levels and skills over those who worked with the unstructured versions." Programmers generally felt that the documentation generated by RECODER was helpful in understanding the recoded versions.

There were several negative observations: Several programs could not be restructured on the first attempt with RECODER.[4] The programmers expressed concern about the documentation style of programs produced by RECODER. The recoded programs had significant increases in resource utilization, such as compile time, load module size, and CPU resources. Programmers generally had to change paragraph names in the recoded versions to more meaningful names. Programs of poor quality to begin with were not considerably improved by restructuring. Some clean up of these programs prior to restructuring resulted in improvements in the code.

---

[4]This ostensibly denied the vendor's claim that an ANSI standard COBOL could be restructured totally automatically. The problem lay with the standard, rather than the vendor, as the ANSI standard leaves room for interpretation and an instance of differing interpretations was uncovered here. Language Technology has since made changes so that the given programs can be restructured automatically.

Table 2 Sample Measurements Taken on Programs and Programmers

Measure	When Taken
Number of source lines	Before/after recoding
Number of statements	Before/after recoding
Number of standards violations	Before/after recoding
Compile service units, without optimization	Before/after recoding
Compile service units, with optimization	Before/after recoding
Load module size, without optimization	Before/after recoding
Load module size, with optimization	Before/after recoding
Execution (CPU) time	Before/after recoding
Revision time	After performing a modification on original and recoded programs
Test time	After performing a test on modified original and recoded programs

Table 3 Time to Modify Original and Recoded Programs*

Program ID for Study	Original Program	Recoded Program
PROG1	8	4
PROG2	1	1
PROG3	3	3
PROG4	1	1
PROG5	8	3
PROG6	2	1

*All times are in man-hours.

Table 4 Time to Test Original and Recoded Programs*

Program ID for Study	Original Program	Recoded Program
PROG1	1	1
PROG2	.5	1
PROG3	1	1
PROG4	2	.5
PROG5	1	1
PROG6	1	1

*All times are in man-hours.

As the report points out, several experimental methodology improvements are possible. Due to the study's design, it is not clear how much of these results are attributable to RECODER in particular, versus restructuring tools in general. No other restructuring tools were tried. Apparently the ability of the programmers was not made clear; the effect of programmer ability—a significant experimental variable to control—on the results is not clear. Not enough programs were selected to provide statistically significant results. Nevertheless, the study is a worthwhile start for the more rigorous investigation of the pros and cons of software restructuring.

IV. SOFTWARE RESTRUCTURING LESSONS LEARNED

A. Restructured Code Takes Some Getting Used To

When code is restructured, it is unfamiliar to programmers until they get used to its style. This depends on the style and supporting documentation created in the restructuring process. Often programmers react negatively at first to restructured code, but later like the code because its style is regular and predictable. Depending on the restructuring algorithm, the coding style of the restructured program may reflect modern programming practices—something which is a plus when hiring programmers recently graduated from curricula that stressed such program structuring principles. Older programmers not used to such principles can find the restructured code uncomfortable to deal with.

B. Restructuring Code for Large Systems is Often not Enough

For software many thousands of lines long, restructuring code to impart regularity and predictability in coding style is helpful, but modularization to further increase system comprehensibility is desirable. As noted earlier, modularization of code as part of its restructuring is still largely manual.

C. We Need Restructured Documentation Too

When code is automatically restructured, the in-line documentation can lose its relevance because the restructured code does not pose the same documentation referents. Since in poorly structured code the in-line documentation is often the final documentation (apart from the code itself) that the programmer depends on, the in-line documentation can be valuable to retain. Few restructuring tools attempt to modify inline code documentation so it can be transferred to restructured code.

D. The Programming Environment Affects How We Perceive Software Structure

Collections of tools, such as MAP mentioned above, allow different views of a program to be displayed one at a time. When a programmer moves from one view to the next, however, he or she is confronted with two problems: 1) retaining the information presented by each view, and 2) maintaining *relationships* between the views.

In terms of programmer understanding of software structure, the mental context switching needed as one moves from view to view can interfere with the gradual build-up of understanding about software. For example, a serial view of programming—e.g., view through an editor, view of compiler output, view of program output, view of debugger output—may have a high context switching overhead in the programmer's head. This could impair the programmer's ability to integrate the multiple views when solving restructuring problems.

Allowing programmers to see many software structure dimensions at once [54], with multiple windows or screens, may be more effective in restructuring than the typical serial views of software structure [50]. This ability ought to be "standard equipment" in programming environments.

615

E. Payoff of Restructuring can be Quantified and Predicted

Restructuring software alone does not assure a payoff. If the software is never modified, inspected, or reused again, then there is little opportunity to realize the potential gains of restructuring.

When selecting a restructuring approach for practical use, it is important to determine the approach's leverage—the ability of an approach to deliver effective results given the dollars invested. There are at least four factors that determine the leverage of a restructuring approach:

- The dollars invested to set up the approach
- The staff and facilities needed to support the approach
- The expected return of the approach
- The time frame for the return

The idea is, if the expected time frame for the return is satisfactory (e.g., does not exceed the expected remaining lifetime of the software), and the expected return (possibly including nonquantifiable benefits such as staff morale) significantly exceeds the return on the way maintenance is currently performed, then consider applying the restructuring approach. For some quantified models of this, see [12] and [4].

The time frame for the *quantifiable* return for most restructuring approaches is on the order of months to years. True, the effects of restructuring may appear immediately in the software itself, but the residual effects on maintenance economics can take much longer to appear, and even then must be considered with other factors before one can be sure improvements were due primarily to restructuring.

F. Systematically Decide How to Solve Problems With Restructuring

The software restructuring action plan in Table 5 outlines a way to select, apply, and evaluate a restructuring approach. The idea is first to discover the local, real maintenance problems. From these problems, one decides whether restructuring is the right approach at all. If so, then knowledge about the maintenance problems can be used to select from Section II a set of candidate restructuring approaches. According to the target level of software, local maintenance goals, and so on, candidate restructuring approaches may be selected. These approaches are then

Table 5 An Action Plan for Software Restructuring

1) Talk to maintainers about their perceptions of maintenance problems.
2) Identify current tasks where restructuring software might save staff time, reduce the maintenance budget, or achieve some other significant benefit.
3) Match an appropriate restructuring approach to the most pressing maintenance problems. A restructuring approach should be selected to have most impact on the tasks identified in step 2).
4) Do a feasibility analysis and a technology transfer analysis of the intended restructuring approach. A technology transfer analysis examines the social and psychological issues affecting acceptance and use of the restructuring approach in the workplace.
5) Select a restructuring technique, plan its use, and use it.
6) Monitor the restructuring effort, preferably by collecting data and applying measures of structure and of maintenance performance, and evaluate the results.

evaluated as to leverage, suitability in the local environment, and so on. Finally, a restructuring approach is used and evaluated.

G. Take Steps to Preserve Software Structure After Restructuring

Software restructuring should be viewed as part of a more comprehensive solution to poor software structure. Once software is structured, presumably one would like it to stay structured with each software change. Here is where practices that foster good software structure come in—practices like defining and using software standards, giving programmers tools for checking conformance to software standards, performing code reviews, performing software tests with known degree of test coverage, quality assurance, and so on.

Quality assurance and restructuring are more related than one might think. Quality assurance applied from the beginning of maintenance can reduce the need for restructuring later on. If restructuring is required, quality assurance can help keep the software structured.

V. FUTURE WORK

Many software restructuring advances remain to be found. Here are some interesting topics for future research:
- *Deciding when and where to restructure:* Restructuring tools often go hand-in-hand with software metrics tools. The software metrics tools gather metrics that can help decide where and when to restructure. Despite research on systematic interpretation of metrics values and how to turn these interpretations into justifiable management actions (e.g., see [3]), there is still much work in guiding people in making restructuring decisions. What is needed are quantitative restructuring criteria based on validated metrics, along with practical results demonstrating efficacy.
- *Using restructuring for standardizing:* An important application of restructuring tools is to impose coding style standards. Tools are becoming increasingly parameterized to allow users more control in the style of programs produced. More work is needed to increase the tool's ability to accommodate many different standards.
- *Restructuring of documentation:* One problem with automated restructuring techniques that modify code is they don't restructure in-line documentation (i.e., rewrite program comments) along with the code. This means that manual labor to restructure documentation is nearly always needed after applying a restructuring approach. Automating the restructuring of documentation is important for making restructuring more cost-effective.
- *Modularization and design level information:* Design level information in the past was often not on-line, and hence not readily available for analysis and restructuring. Some CASE tools produce design information in the course of building software, and this information is available to restructuring tools. Relatively little work has been done in using this information for restructuring purposes.

Automatically restructuring systems by modularization is nearly uncharted territory. A Ph.D dissertation by Sobrinho [53] has started work in this area. More recently, [52] has discussed another approach for remodularization. It is unclear how effective these approaches are compared to manual remodularization. More work on new automatic (or semi-automatic) modularization approaches is needed, along with studies demonstrating their effectiveness.

• *Graphical programming:* Graphical programming (e.g., [48]) offers a relatively new way to visualize, specify, and build software. Graphical programming may help alleviate some lower-level problems such as hard-to-understand control flow, and so change concern for software structure to other dimensions. Graphical programs could become a target output for reverse engineering tools.

• *Making available parts of restructuring tools:* Software restructuring tools are often highly proprietary. Users can adjust the restructuring process by using only the options made available in the tool's interface. Sometimes users may want to build their own special-purpose restructuring tools. Users might benefit from reusing parts used to build a proprietary tool. The idea here is that it may be profitable for both vendor and tool user to have "open architecture restructuring" tools. Users would have the option of using the complete package (i.e., the original tool), or using parts of the tool to accomplish restructuring. How to repackage tools into reusable parts useful to other restructuring tool builders is an open question.

• *Displaying software evolution:* One reason programmers have little clues about hard-to-understand software is that programmers have few tools for conveniently tracing how the software evolved to its current form. True, one can examine configuration management records, but a lot of detective work is often needed to recreate the programmer's mindset about the software that was changed. Evolution replay tools deserve consideration as ways to enhance understanding of software structure.

VI. SUMMARY

Software restructuring is a tool for meeting maintenance goals and for increasing and preserving software structure. Software restructuring is part of a larger solution for maintaining the value of software as the software evolves.

Because software structure depends on programmer perceptions as well as the software state, software structure is dynamic. Steps must be taken to preserve structure in the minds of programmers, otherwise structure will be lost with programmer turnover.

There is a wide variety of restructuring approaches, ranging from approaches that do not modify software at all, but modify programmer perceptions of software, to those approaches that do modify software. The limit to what is a software restructuring approach is a gray area.

There is a lack of quantitative information about software restructuring. What we do know suggests restructuring leverage (the ability of a restructuring approach to "deliver" given the dollars invested) tends to come in the medium to long term (months to years). Even then, the effort to maintain software structure must be diligent, which may translate to higher quality assurance costs per maintenance change. Later, these costs are hoped to be justified through increased software flexibility (able to perform enhancements faster), reliability (fewer introduced bugs with each fix), lifetime (through extended usefulness to the enterprise), and reusability (due to the known software structure instilled in the software).

Software restructuring presents a very interesting research area. Besides the need for quantitative studies of restructuring effectiveness, work is needed in areas such as restructuring of documentation to correspond with restructured code, design restructuring, automatic application of software standards, automatic system modularization, and tools to reveal new aspects of software structure, such as graphical programming and software evolution animation.

ACKNOWLEDGMENTS

The author wishes to thank Language Technology, Peat Marwick Main & Co., Group Operations (now part of Computer Data Systems, Inc.), IBM Corporation, Adpac, and Lexeme Corporation for information on the current status of their restructuring and restructuring-related tools. The author also thanks N. Schneidewind, D. Nettles, and B. Nejmeh, and an anonymous referee for their comments for improving the paper.

The following are Registered Trademarks: RECODER (of Language Technology, Inc.), RETROFIT (of Peat Marwick Main & Co.), Delta/STRUCTURIZER (of Delta Software Technologie AG), COBOL Structuring Facility (of IBM Corp.), VIA/INSIGHT (of Viasoft, Inc.), and SUPERSTRUCTURE (of Computer Data Systems, Inc.)

REFERENCES

[1] P. Antonini, P. Benedusi, G. Cantone, and A. Cimitile "Maintenance and reverse engineering: low-level design documents production and improvement," in *Proc. Conference on Software Maintenance—1987*, IEEE Computer Society, 1987.

[2] G. Arango, I. Baxter, P. Freeman, and C. Pidgeon, "TMM: Software maintenance by transformation," *IEEE Software*, vol. 3, no. 3, May 1986.

[3] R. S. Arnold, "On the generation and use of quantitative criteria for assessing software maintenance quality," Ph.D. Dissertation, Computer Science Department, University of Maryland, College Park, 1983.

[4] ——, "Techniques and strategies for restructuring software," Notes for a software restructuring seminar conducted by R. S. Arnold, May 1985.

[5] ——, "An introduction to software restructuring," in *Tutorial on Software Restructuring*. Washington, DC: IEEE Computer Society, 1986.

[6] ——, *Tutorial on Software Restructuring*. New York, NY: IEEE Computer Society, 1986.

[7] E. Ashcroft and Z. Manna, "The translation of 'goto' programs in 'while' programs," in *Proceedings of the 1971 IFIP Congress*. Amsterdam, The Netherlands: North-Holland, 1971, pp. 250–260.

[8] B. Baker, "An algorithm for structuring flowgraphs," *J. ACM*, vol. 24, no. 1, pp. 98–120, Jan. 1977.

[9] D. R. Barstow, H. E. Shrobe, and E. Sandewall, *Interactive Programming Environments*. New York, NY: McGraw-Hill, 1984.

[10] V. Basili, *Tutorial on Models and Metrics for Software Management and Engineering*. Washington, DC: IEEE Computer Society, 1980.

[11] C. Bohm and G. Jacopini, "Flow diagrams, Turing machines, and languages with only two formation rules," *Commun. ACM*, vol. 9, no. 5, pp. 366–371, May 1966.

[12] L. Brice, "Existing computer applications. Maintain or redesign: How to decide?" in *Proc. of the Computer Measurement Group*, Dec. 1981. Reprinted in [6].

[13] R. N. Britcher and J. J. Craig, "Using modern design practices to upgrade aging software systems," *IEEE Software*, vol. 3, no. 3, May 1986.

[14] M. H. Brown and R. Sedgewick, "Techniques for algorithm animation," *IEEE Software*, vol. 2, no. 1, pp. 28–39, Jan. 1985.

[15] E. Bush, "The automatic restructuring of COBOL," in *Proceedings of the Conf. on Software Maintenance—1985* (Washington, DC), IEEE Computer Society, pp. 35–41, 1985.

617

[16] R. Canning, Ed., "Rejuvenate your old systems," *EDP Analyzer*, vol. 22, no. 3, pp. 1–16, Mar. 1984.

[17] ——, "Tools to rejuvenate your old systems," *EDP Analyzer*, vol. 22, no. 4, pp. 1–16, Apr. 1984.

[18] M. Fagan, "Design and code inspection to reduce errors in program development," *IBM Sys. J.*, vol. 15, no. 3, pp. 182–212, 1976.

[19] S. D. Fay, D. G. Holmes, "Help! I have to update an undocumented program," in *Proc. Conf. on Software Maintenance—1985*, IEEE Computer Society, 1985.

[20] D. Freedman G. Weinberg, *Handbook of Walkthroughs, Inspections, and Technical Reviews* (3rd ed.). Boston, MA: Little, Brown, 1982.

[21] Federal Software Management Support Center. "Parallel test and evaluation of a Cobol restructuring tool," Federal Software Management Support Center, 5203 Leesburg Pike, Suite 1100, Falls Church, VA 22041-3467, Sept. 1987.

[22] R. L. Glass and R. A. Noiseux, *Software Maintenance Guidebook*. Englewood Cliffs, NJ: Prentice-Hall, 1981.

[23] W. Harrison, K. Magel, R. Kluczny, and A. DeKock, "Applying software complexity metrics to software maintenance," *Computer*, vol. 15, no. 9, pp. 65–79, Sept. 1982.

[24] P. R. Hessinger, "Strategies for implementing fourth generation software," *Computerworld* (In Depth section), vol. VXIII, no. 8, pp. ID/1–ID/11, Feb. 20, 1984.

[25] C. Houtz, "Guidelines for planning and implementing a software improvement program (SIP)," Rep. OSD/FCSC-83/004, May 1983. Available from the Federal Software Management Support Center, 5203 Leesburg Pike, Falls Church, Virginia 22041-3467.

[26] ——, "Software improvement program (SIP): A treatment for software senility," in *Proceedings of the 19th Computer Performance Evaluation Users Group* (National Bureau of Standards Special Publ. 500-104), pp. 92–107, Oct. 1983.

[27] Special issue of *Computer* devoted to visual programming. *Computer*, vol. 18, no. 8, Aug. 1985.

[28] B. W. Kernighan, and P. J. Plauger, *Elements of Programming Style*. New York, NY: McGraw-Hill, 1974.

[29] ——, *Software Tools*. Reading, MA: Addison-Wesley, 1976.

[30] R. G. Lanergan and C. A. Grasso, "Software engineering with reusable designs and code," *IEEE Trans. Software Eng.*, vol. SE-10, no. 5, pp. 498–501, Nov. 1984.

[31] M. M. Lehman, "Programs, life cycles, and laws of software evolution," *Proc. IEEE*, vol. 68, no. 9, pp. 1060–1076, Sept. 1980.

[32] S. Letovsky and E. Soloway, "Delocalized plans and program comprehension," *IEEE Software*, vol. 3, no. 3, May 1986.

[33] R. C. Linger, H. D. Mills, and R. J. Witt, *Structured Programming: Theory and Practice*. Reading, MA: Addison-Wesley, 1979.

[34] R. C. Linger and H. D. Mills, "A case study in cleanroom software engineering: the IBM COBOL Structuring Facility," in *Proc. COMPSAC 1988*, IEEE Computer Society, 1988.

[35] M. J. Lyons, "Salvaging your software asset (tools based maintenance)," in *Proceedings of the National Computer Conf. 1981*. Arlington, VA: AFIPS Press, 1981, pp. 337–341.

[36] J. Martin and C. McClure, *Software Maintenance: The Problem and Its Solution*. Englewood Cliffs, NJ: Prentice-Hall, 1983.

[37] H. D. Mills, *Mathematical Foundations for Structured Programming*. First written in 1972; reprinted in *Software Productivity*. Boston, MA: Little, Brown, 1983.

[38] H. W. Morgan, "Evolution of a software maintenance tool," in *Proceedings of the 2nd National Conf. on EDP Software Maintenance*. Silver Spring, MD: U.S. Professional Development Institute, 1984, pp. 268–278.

[39] B. Nejmeh, "NPATH; A measure of execution path complexity and its applications," *Commun. ACM*, vol. 31, no. 2, pp. 188–200, Feb. 1988.

[40] G. Parikh, "Logical retrofit may save millions of dollars in software maintenance," in *Proceedings of the 2nd National Conf. on EDP Software Maintenance*. Silver Spring, MD: U.S. Professional Development Institute, 1984, pp. 427–429.

[41] D. L. Parnas, "On the criteria to be used in decomposing systems into modules," *Commun. ACM*, vol. 15, no. 12, pp. 1053–1058, Dec. 1972.

[42] ——, "Designing software for ease of extension and contraction," *IEEE Trans. Software Eng.*, vol. SE-5, no. 2, pp. 128–138, Mar. 1979.

[43] D. L. Parnas, P. C. Clements, and D. M. Weiss, "The modular structure of complex systems," in *Proceedings of the 7th International Conf. on Software Engineering*. Washington, DC: IEEE Computer Society, 1984, pp. 408–417.

[44] H. Partsch and R. Steinbruggen, "Program transformation systems," *Computing Surveys*, vol. 15, no. 3, pp. 199–236, Sept. 1983.

[45] J. C. Phillips, "Creating a baseline for an undocumented system—or what to you do with someone else's code," in *Record of the Software Maintenance Workshop*, Monterey, CA, Dec. 6–8, 1983, R. S. Arnold, Ed. Washington, DC: IEEE Computer Society, 1984.

[46] S. P. Reiss, "PECAN: program development systems that support multiple views," *IEEE Trans. Software Eng.*, vol. SE-11, no. 3, pp. 285–302, Mar. 1985.

[47] H. D. Rombach, "Impact of software structure on maintenance," in *Proc. Conf. on Software Maintenance—1985*, IEEE Computer Society, 1985.

[48] R. V. Rubin, E. J. Golin, and S. P. Reiss, "Thinkpad: a graphical system for programming by demonstration," *IEEE Software*, vol. 2, no. 2, pp. 73–79, Mar. 1985.

[49] B. Shneiderman and G. Thomas, "An architecture for automatic relational database system conversion," *ACM Trans. Database Systems*, vol. 7, no. 2, pp. 235–257, June 1982.

[50] B. Shneiderman, P. Shafer, R. Simon, L. Weldon, "Display strategies for program browsing," in *Proceedings of the Conf. on Software Maintenance—1985*. Washington, DC: IEEE Computer Society, 1985, pp. 136–143.

[51] H. Sneed, "Software renewal—a case study," *IEEE Software*, vol. 1, no. 3, July 1984.

[52] H. Sneed and G. Jandrasics, "Software recycling," in *Proc. Conf. on Software Maintenance—1987*, IEEE Computer Society, 1987.

[53] F. G. Sobrinho, "Structural complexity: A basis for systematic software evolution," Ph.D Dissertation, Dept. of Computer Science and College of Business and Management, University of Maryland, College Park, 1984.

[54] W. Teitelman, "A tour through Cedar," *IEEE Trans. Software Eng.*, vol. SE-11, no. 3, pp. 285–302, Mar. 1985.

[55] J.-D. Warnier, *Program Modification*. Boston, MA: Martinus Nijhoff, 1978.

[56] S. Warren, "MAP: A tool for understanding software," in *Proceedings of the 6th International Conf. on Software Engineering*. Washington, DC: IEEE Computer Society, 1982, pp. 28–37.

[57] A. I. Wasserman, *Tutorial: Software Development Environments*. Washington, DC: IEEE Computer Society, 1981.

[58] E. Yourdon, *Techniques of Program Structure and Design*. Englewood Cliffs, NJ: Prentice-Hall, 1975.

[59] M. V., Zelkowitz, R. T. Yeh, R. G. Hamlet, J. D. Gannon, V. R. Basili, "Software engineering practices in the U.S. and Japan," *Computer*, vol. 17, no. 6, pp. 57–66, June 1984.

Robert S. Arnold received the B.A. degree (Hons.) from Northwestern University, Evanston, IL, and the M.S. and Ph.D. Degrees in computer science from Carnegie-Mellon University, Pittsburgh, PA, and the University of Maryland, College Park, respectively.

He is a member of the technical staff at the Software Productivity Consortium, Herndon, VA, where his interests are in software ripple effect analysis and software maintenance. Before joining the Consortium, he worked at the MITRE Corporation, EVB Consulting, Sperry Corporation, and IBM/San Jose Research Laboratory.

Dr. Arnold is a member of Phi Beta Kappa and Phi Kappa Phi. He is author of *Tutorial on Software Restructuring*, and has been program Chair and General Chair of the Conference on Software Maintenance.

SOFTWARE RECYCLING

Harry M. Sneed & Gabor Jandrasics

Software Engineering Service
Pappelstr. 6, 8014 Neubiberg, West-Germany

This contribution describes a set of software tools developed to recycle old software by the methods of static analysis, modularization, restructuring, backwards translation, design tuning, and code regeneration. The tools are a static analyzer, a syntax driven PDL editor, and a code generator. The source language is COBOL-74, the target language is COBOL-85. The purpose of the system is to reuse as much as possible of the old code while creating a new software architecture based on the principles of modular and structured programming. To this end the source programs are submitted to an extensive static analysis of their data and control structures. Then the remodularization and restructuring occurs by retranslating the original source back into an intermediate higher level design language. From there new programs are generated.
Keywords: Static Analysis, Modular Programming, Structured Programming, Software-Restructuring.

1. The status Quo

The issue of software reusability has been addressed in the technical literature by many autors (1-3). In the main, they have been concerned with the use of existing software components by transporting them from one system onto another. This, however, presupposes that the components which are to be reused can be extracted from their present environment without significant effort. This again requires that the components to be extracted are distinct modules with well defined interfaces as forseen by Parnas in his outstanding contribution to developing software for reusability (4). His point is that, reusability has to be developed into the software.

This is a prerequisite which does not exist in the commercial data processing environment. The great majority of business COBOL programs are neither modular nor structured (5). In a survey of 100 representative COBOL programs from the German commercial market it was discovered that 82 programs consisted of only one module (defined here as a separately compatible and testable unit), that all of the sections were connected via COMMON data in the Data Division and could not be extracted without taking the Data Division with them and that only 28 programs could be considered well structured in the sense of structured programming. Furthermore, 93 programs contained data which were not used at all, many of which contained whole data structures which were not used. The average number of data definitions was 1104, the average size of the Procedure Division 2255 lines. In less then 10% of the programs analyzed, would it have been possible to extract portions of the code without taking a significant amount of the environment with them. The program sample contained both batch and online programs. The online programs all consisted of one module and were generally less structured than the batch ones.

The conclusion of this analysis is that less then 20 % of the existing COBOL code is reusable. Despite the fact that structured and modular programming techniques have been advocated since the late 1960's, less then 30 % of the existing COBOL programs can be considered structured and modular. Yet this nonreusable, unstructured and nonmodular code represents a significant investment of the business users. The maintenance of these old programs costs more than 60 % of the software budget in the companies from which the sample programs were taken (6).

In light of this situation which has been confirmed by Brown(7), Swanson (8), Mc Clure (9) and many others, the greatest need of the business data processing market is the renewal and recycling of substandard software. Just as scrap metal or glass is melted down to its basic components and recycled, old programs need to be broken down into their basic building blocks and reassembled. Without this melting down and reassembling process only a small portion of the existing code can be reused. Not only that, the existing code can also not be susceptible to modern analysis and testing techniques, which is

82

Reprinted from *Proc. Conf. on Software Maintenance*, 1987, pp. 82-90. ©1987 by The Institute of Electrical and Electronics Engineers, Inc. All rights reserved.

the main reason why these techniques are rejected. In order to document existing programs with the aid of a static analyzer, the programs must possess a minimum of structure and modularity. If not, the static analyzer can only document how badly constructed the programs are. The same applies to dynamic analysis. Modules which contain more then 500 branches or more than 200 input/output variables, cannot be tested systematically (10). Of the 100 COBOL programs mentioned earlier only 36 could be considered systematically testable. The majority were either too large or too complex.

This problem has not gone unrecognized by the software community. In the last years, not only has there been a surge of literature on the subject of software restructuring, there also been a number of restructuring tools developed such as Superstructure, Structuring Facility and Restructurizer (11). Hovever, the issue of remodularizing has not been addressed, neither by the methodology nor by the tools. Yet, it would appear that this is the main issue. Restructuring code by replacing GOTO's with PERFORM's and creating additional code blocks may help to make a code more readable, but it fails to make the code more modular or testable, both of which are prerequisites to reusability (12).

The main problem, as addressed by this paper, is the decomposition of existing programs into separate modules which can be compiled and tested separately and which can be connected to other modules through a parameter interface, in the case of COBOL by a LINKAGE SECTION. Only then can reusability be really attained. For this reason, the methodology described here is referred to as software recycling as opposed to software restructuring which is only a part of the recycling process.

2. The recycling process

The general strategy of the recycling process described here is to retranslate COBOL-74 programs back into a higher level design language, to modify them there and then to generate equivalent modular and structured COBOL-85 programs from the design language (see Fig. 1). This process involves five distinct steps:

- Step 1 is the static analysis of the existing COBOL-74 program and the creation of the necessary data and data command.

- Step 2 is the modularization of the program using the data and command tables

together with the modularization criteria.

- Step 3 is the internal restructuring of the new modules in the design language.

- Step 4 is the manual optimization and adjustment of the new modules in the design language.

- Step 5 is the generation of structured COBOL-85 modules from the design language modules.

The steps 1, 2, 3 and 5 are fully automated. Step 4 is a manual intervention on the part of the maintenance programmer using a syntax driven editor to correct the regenerated design language modules. Thus, there are also 5 tools involved in the recycling process:

- a static analyzer
- a modularizer
- a restructurizer
- a syntax driven editor and
- a code generator (see fig. 2).

Static Analysis

The task of the static analyzer is to analyze the code structure, the data structure, the control flow, the data flow and the module interfaces. Not only does it produce a series of reports to document these features of the programs, it also creates externally stored tables which can be used by the modularizer and restructurizer (13).

For the data structure a table is created with an entry for each data item defined, describing its name, base, position, type, length, dimension and picture. In addition, its usage is also recorded, i.e. whether it is a predicate, an input or an output to the program (see Fig. 3).

For the data flow a table is created with an entry for each reference to each defined data item. The data item is identified by an index to the data table. The reference is identified by the statement number and the reference type-predicate, input, output, transit, init (see Fig. 4).

For the control flow a connectivity table is created with an entry for each procedural statement and a reference to the successor statement. A statement with more than one successor will have an entry for each successor in which the statement number of the COME FROM statement points to the statement number of the GO TO statement.

83

From this table, a directed graph and a path documentation are derived (see Fig. 5).

For the module interfaces, an interface table is created with an entry for each ENTRY, CALL, IO, database and data communication command with the interface type, objectname and parameters as well as the statement number of the interface (see Fig. 6).

Finally, the PERFORM table is generated for all SECTION labels and all internal invocations of these sections (see Fig. 7).

The tables are all stored in direct access files by module name and entry number. The reports are printed out to assist the maintenance programmer in understanding the existing program.

Modularization

The task of the modularizer is to break large monolitic programs down into several modules which can be compiled, analyzed, maintained and tested separately. Any program with more than 1000 procedural statements is considered as a candidate for modularization.

The modularization criteria are as follows:

- any COBOL Section which contains more than 200 statements becomes a separate module,

- any COBOL Section which is invoked by a PERFORM and which itself invokes another Section is placed together with all of its subsections into a separate module,

- any loop terminated by a backward GO TO which contains more than 200 statements becomes a separate module,

- any block of code beginning with a label which exceeds 500 statements and into which there are no GO TO branches coming into it either from before or from behind, is made into a separate module,

- all IO and database operations are placed into a separate input/output module with a standard parameter list and a function code to invoke each IO operation. The IO and database commands in the inline code are replaced by statements which set the parameters, call the IO module and query the resulting return-code,

- finally, any remaining code block which

exceeds 800 statements is broken off at the last graph node and made into a separate module. All GO TO branches passing the entry and exit nodes are capped here. This, of course, will lead to some unsatisfied references, but it is a problem the programmer must solve.

Once the procedural code of the modules has been determined, the data flow table is examined to see what data items are referenced by the statements in each module. For all data items referenced, COPY statements are included in the module for the data structures in which they are embedded. In this way the modules are assigned only those data structures which they use.

The data structure itself is modularized by creating a datamacro or COPY segment for each data structure beginning with level 1 and storing it in the data design table.

The modularized procedural code is stored in the design language tables, where the statement types are marked, e.g. MOVE, COMPUTE, PERFORM, GOTO, PERFORM, CALL, IO, etc. (14).

Thus, at the end of the modularization step the design data base contains a file of data structures and a file of COBOL statements divided up into modules of 800 or less statements with COPY references to the data structures. In addition, there is a file description file with a standard file or database definition for each file and database referenced by the IO-module.

Restructuring

The task of the restructurizer is to restructure the flow of control within COBOL modules. This is done in the following manner:

- first, all backward branching GO TO's are located and converted to ENDDO satements. A WHILE-DO statement is inserted behind the label to which the GO TO refers to. If the GO TO is marked by an IF statement, the negated IF condition is placed in the WHILE-DO statement. If the GO TO is the only statement marked by the IF, the IF statement is deleted. All the statements within the loop are nested by one.

- Secondly, all forward branching conditional GO TO's are deleted, the IF condition negated and all the statements up to the label referenced are nested by one.

84

- Thirdly, all forward branching unconditional GO TO's are converted to EXIT-Section commands and the code block in which they are embedded is made into a section.

- Fourthly, all GO TO DEPENDING ON statements are deleted and replaced by an IF statement behind each label refered to by the GO TO.

- Fifthly, all IF statements which contain an ELSE clause are terminated by an ENDIF prior to the ELSE and the ELSE converted to an IF NOT original condition.

- Sixthly, all IF statements are terminated by an ENDIF and all Sections by an ENDSECT.

- Finally, all PERFORM UNTIL statements are converted to WHILE DO satements, the performed code nested behind the WHILE DO and terminated by an ENDDO.

After completing the 7 steps the code is now in the form of a structured design language with only sequence, selection and repetition control structures. The design language only allows the following control statements:

- IF ... ENDIF
- WHILE DO ... ENDDO
- SECTION ... ENDSECT
- EXIT
- PERFORM
- CALL.

All of the other COBOL statements are now nested within these control structures. So, not only has the original program been broken down into a set of modules less than 1000 statements, but it has also been converted into a pure structured version of the original code as depicted in figure 8 (see Fig. 8).

Adaptation

The task of adaptation is one that the maintenance programmer has to make with the aid of the design language and a syntax driven editor. It could be that some of the code has become superfluous and should be removed. It may also be necessary or appropriate to insert additional statements or to change existing ones. It is also possible that the modularization and restructuring of the program has caused some errors, such as the case when GO TO branches beyond the borders of a module are capped. In this case, the programmer must solve the problem by changing the logic. There is no

guarantee that the new program version will perform exactly as the old one did. Therefore, an interaction with the programmer is absolutely necessary to handle these exceptions which are not automatically resolvable.

At this point, the program could also be extensively revised if so desired by the user. Then this is the time to insert new functions or change existing ones as well as to optimize the code in view of the new COBOL-85 features.

Regeneration

Once the design language version of the program has been adapted to meet the current user requirements, it is inputed to a COBOL-85 generator (15). From the data description tables COBOL COPY segments are generated. From the file description tables the FILE-CONTROL and FD sections are generated. The DATA DIVISION only contains COPY references to the data structures referenced by the module. The PROCEDURE DIVISION is generated from the design language module. WHILE DO statements are converted into PERFORM UNTIL WITH TEST BEFORE statements. EXIT statements are realized by GO TO Section-end statements. The control statements - IF, PERFORM and CALL - are transformed on a 1:1 basis. The remaining COBOL statements are carried over unchanged into the new COBOL version (see Fig.9).

The new COBOL-85 modules are systematically testable, reusable and maintainable with less effort then the previous ones. Not only are they smaller and less complex, but better structured and free of IO operations, since these have been removed in accordance with the principle of portability. These new modules can be easily tested in a test harness such as SOFTEST in order to verify their correctness and they can be easily analyzed by a static analyzer such as SOFTDOC in order to document them (16).

Summary

This paper has described a method for recycling old software using COBOL as a case study. The process itself proceeds by first statically analyzing existing COBOL-74 programs, then modularizing, and adapting them before converting them into COBOL-85 modules. A key factor in the recycling process is the presence of an intermediate design language to which the COBOL-74 code is first converted before being regene-

85

ràted as COBOL-85 code.

The purpose of recycling is to reuse as much as possible of the existing code to create new programs which are well structured, and modularized so as to improve testability and maintainability. Large, unstructured programs which were previously untestable and unmaintainable become more manageable once they are broken up into several small modules with a limited number of paths and input/output variables (17).

The special merit of the process described here is that it not only restructures the code but that it also modularizes the programs. This modularization has proven to be of far greater significance to the ease of testing and maintaining than the sole restructuring of the control flow which makes programs more readable but not necessarily more testable and maintainable (18).

References

(1) Wegner, P.: "Capital-Intensive Software Technology-Reusability of Software Components" in IEEE Software, Vol. 1, No. 3, July 1984

(2) Horowitz, E./Munson, I.: "An Expansive View of Reusable Software" in IEEE Trans. on S.E., Vol. 10, No. 5, Sept. 1984

(3) Jones, T.C.: "Reusability in Programming - A Survey of the State of the Art" in IEEE Trans. on S.E., Vol. 10, No. 5, Sept. 1984

(4) Parnas, D.: "Designing Software for Ease of Extension and Contraction" in IEEE Trans. on S.E., Vol. 5, No. 2, March 1979

(5) Parikh, G.: Techniques of Program and System Maintenance, Winthrop Pub., Cambridge, 1982, p. 183-191

(6) Sneed, H.: "Statische Analyse von COBOL Programmen mit dem System SOFTDOC" in ONLINE? Zeitschrift für Datenverarbeitung, Nov. 1985

(7) Brown, P.: "Why does Software die" in IEEE Tutorial on Software Maintenance, Ed. G. Parikh, Computer Society Press, New York 1983, p. 279-286

(8) Lientz, b./Swanson, E.: "Problems in Application Software Maintenance" in Comm. of ACM, Vol. 24, No. 11, Nov.1981

(9) Martin, J./McClure, c.: Software Maintenance - The Problem and it's Solution, Prentice Hall, Englweood Cliffs, 1983

(10) Sneed, H.: "Software Renewal - a case study" in IEEE Software, Vol. 1, No.3, July 1984

(11) Arnold, R.: "An Introduction to Software Restructuring, Ed. R. Arnold, Computer Society Press, New York 1986, p. 1-10

(12) Berns, G.: "Assessing Software Maintainability" in Comm. of ACM, Vol. 27, No. 1, Jan. 1984

(13) Sneed, H.: SOFTDOC Static Analyzer, System Docdumentation, Vers. 5, Munich, 1985

(14) Sneed, H.: SOFTCON Design Language, System Documentation, Vers. 3, Munich 1986

(15) Sneed, H.: SOFTGEN COBOL-85 Generator, System Documentation, Vers. 3, Munich 1987

(16) Majoros M./Sneed, H.: "Testing programs against a formal Specification" in Proc. of COMPSAC Conference, 1983, IEEE Computer Society Press, New York 1983

(17) Sneed,H./Kirchhof, K.: Prüfstand - a system for testing Software Components" in Proc. of IEEE Workshop on Software Maintenance, Monterey 1983

(18) Gilb, T.: "Design by Objectives - Maintaintainability" in IEEE Tutorial on Software Maintenance Ed. G. Parikh, Computer Society Press, New York 1983, p- 167-182

86

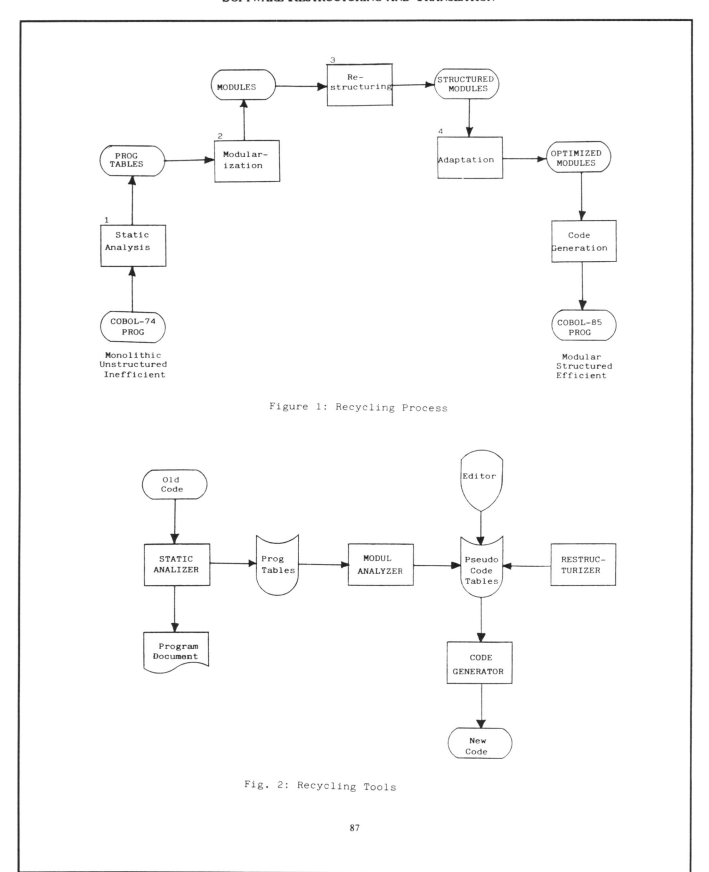

Figure 1: Recycling Process

Fig. 2: Recycling Tools

87

```
              S O F T D O C   M O D U L D O K U M E N T - 4
                        MODUL DATENVERZEICHNIS                              SEIT
MODUL:  LAGERERF            Fig.3: SOFTDOC Data Table
                                                                          DATUM: 13
NUTZUNG                        SPEICHER ADDRESSIERUNG         FELD  FELD  FELD
P E A I T ST DATEN NAME        KLASSE  BASIS                  POS.  TYP  LAENGE DIMENSION    MASKE
*******************************************************************************************************
  E A   T  3 LIEF-NR          STATIC  LAGERERF               272  ZONED    6  1            S9(6)
  E A   T  3 ARTIKELBEZEICHNUNG STATIC LAGERERF              278  CHAR    40  1            X(40)
  E A   T  3 LAGERMENGE        STATIC  LAGERERF               318  PACK     6  1            S9(11)
  E A   T  3 MINDESTMENGE      STATIC  LAGERERF               324  PACK     6  1            S9(11)
  E A   T  3 MAXIMALMENGE      STATIC  LAGERERF               330  PACK     6  1            S9(11)
  E A   T  3 BESTELLMENGE      STATIC  LAGERERF               336  PACK     6  1            S9(11)
  E A   T  3 ARTIKELPREIS      STATIO  LAGERERF               342  PACK     5  1            S9(7)V9(2)

  E A   T  1 ARTIKEL          STATIC  LAGERERF               352  STRUC   81  1
  E A   T  2 ARTIKELDATEN     STATIC  LAGERERF               352  STRUC   81  1
  E A   T  3 ART-NR           STATIC  LAGERERF               352  ZONED    6  1            S9(6)
  E A   T  3 LIEF-NR          STATIC  LAGERERF               358  ZONED    6  1            S9(6)
  E A   T  3 ARTIKELBEZEICHNUNG STATIC LAGERERF              364  CHAR    40  1            X(40)
  E A   T  3 LAGERMENGE       STATIC  LAGERERF               404  PACK     6  1            S9(11)
  E A   T  3 MINDESTMENGE     STATIC  LAGERERF               410  PACK     6  1            S9(11)
  E A   T  3 MAXIMALMENGE     STATIC  LAGERERF               416  PACK     6  1            S9(11)
  E A   T  3 BESTELLMENGE     STATIC  LAGERERF               422  PACK     6  1            S9(11)
  E A   T  3 ARTIKELPREIS     STATIC  LAGERERF               428  PACK     5  1            S9(7)V9(2)

        T  1 XDC-SS           PARAM   XDC-SS                   0  STRUC 2051  1
P   A   T  2 XDC-ZUSTAND      PARAM   XDC-SS                   0  PACK     3  1            S9(4)
        T  2 XDC-MAP          PARAM   XDC-SS                   3  CHAR  2048  1            X(2048)

        T  1 LAGERBEWEGUNG    PARAM   LAGERBEWEGUNG            0  STRUC  220  1
        T  2 ZEILE-004        PARAM   LAGERBEWEGUNG           12  STRUC    9  1
        T  3 TAGESDATUM-L     PARAM   LAGERBEWEGUNG           12  BIN      2  1            S9999
        T  3 TAGESDATUM-A     PARAM   LAGERBEWEGUNG           14  CHAR     1  1            X
        T  3 TAGESDATUM       PARAM   LAGERBEWEGUNG           15  ZONED    6  1            Z(5)9
        T  2 ZEILE-009        PARAM   LAGERBEWEGUNG           21  STRUC    4  1
        T  3 BEWEGUNGSART-L   PARAM   LAGERBEWEGUNG           21  BIN      2  1            S9999
        T  3 BEWEGUNGSART-A   PARAM   LAGERBEWEGUNG           23  CHAR     1  1            X

              S O F T D O C   M O D U L D O K U M E N T - 8
                        DATENVERWENDUNGSTABELLE                             SEIT
MODUL: LAGERERF            Fig.4: SOFTDOC Data Usage Table
  DATENNAME                                                                DATUM: 13
                                   VERWENDET IN          ANGESPROCHEN IN ANWEISUNG
***************************************************************************************************
                                  SENDE-LAGERBEWEGUNG    196(P)

                                  PRUEFE-LAGERBEWEGUNG   209(P),210(P)

                                  GENSECT-01             263(P),264(T),267(P),268(T)
LAGERBEWEGUNG.ART-NR-L            LAGERERF               146(T)

                                  GENSECT-01             264(T),268(T)
LAGERBEWEGUNG.ART-NR-A            LAGERERF               146(T)

                                  GENSECT-01             264(T),268(T)
LAGERBEWEGUNG.ART-NR              LAGERERF               146(T)

                                  PRUEFE-LAGERBEWEGUNG   205(P),205(P)

                                  GET-ARTIKEL            223(E)
```

Fig.5: SOFTDOC Control Flow Graph

```
                         158   000340 X-INITIALISIERE-ERFASSUNG.
                         159   000350     EXIT.
                         160   000360 EMPFANGE-LAGERBEWEGUNG SECTION.
                         161   000370     IF  (BEWEGUNGSART IN LAGERBEWEGUNG = XENDE) THEN
  <----------------------< 162 193 000380   GO TO X-EMPFANGE-LAGERBEWEGUNG.
                         163   000390     MOVE ' ' TO  MELDUNG IN LAGERBEWEGUNG.
                         164   000400     MOVE ' ' TO  MELDUNG-1 IN LAGERBEWEGUNG.
                         165   000410     MOVE ' ' TO  MELDUNG-2 IN LAGERBEWEGUNG.
                         166   000420     MOVE ' ' TO  MELDUNG-3 IN LAGERBEWEGUNG.
                         167   000430     MOVE 0 TO  FEHLERART (1).
                         168   000440     MOVE 0 TO  FEHLERART (2).
                         169   000450     MOVE 0 TO  FEHLERART (3).
                         170   000460     MOVE 0 TO  FEHLERART (4).
                         171   000470     MOVE 0 TO  FEHLERART (5).
  <-+--------------------< 172 000480     PERFORM PRUEFE-LAGERBEWEGUNG.
                         173   000490 MELDE-ART-NR.
                         174   000500     IF  (FEHLERART (1) = XEIN) THEN
                         175   000510       MOVE 'LAGERBEWEGUNG NICHT VERARBEITET' TO  MELDUNG
                         176   000520       IN LAGERBEWEGUNG
                         177   000530       MOVE 'ART-NR UNGUELTIG' TO  MELDUNG-1 IN LAGERBEWEGU
                         178   000540 MELDE-BEWEGUNGSART.
                         179   000550     IF  (FEHLERART (2) = XEIN) THEN
                         180   000560       MOVE 'LAGERBEWEGUNG NICHT VERARBEITET' TO  MELDUNG
                         181   000570       IN LAGERBEWEGUNG
                         182   000580       MOVE 'BEWEGUNGSART UNGUELTIG' TO  MELDUNG-2
                         183   000590       IN LAGERBEWEGUNG.
                         184   000600 MELDE-BEWEGUNGSMENGE.
                         185   000610     IF  (FEHLERART (3) = XEIN) THEN
                         186   000620       MOVE 'LAGERBEWEGUNG NICHT VERARBEITET' TO  MELDUNG
                         187   000630       IN LAGERBEWEGUNG
                         188   000640       MOVE 'BEWEGUNGSMENGE UNGUELTIG' TO  MELDUNG-3
                         189   000650       IN LAGERBEWEGUNG.
                         190   000660 STEUERE-ZUGANG-ABGANG.
                         191   000670     IF  (FEHLERART (1) = 0 AND FEHLERART (2) = 0 AND FEHLER
  <-+--------------------< 192 000680       (3) = 0) THEN PERFORM GENSECT-01.
  >----------------------> 193 000690 X-EMPFANGE-LAGERBEWEGUNG.
```

88

365

```
                  S O F T D O C   M O D U L D O K U M E N T - 2
                             MODUL EVA DIAGRAMM                            SEITE : 1
```

MODUL: LAGERERF   DATUM: 13

EINGABEN	ABSCHNITTE	AUSGABEN
	LAGERERF	
XDC-SS XDC-ZUSTAND	INITIALISIERE-ERFASSUNG	

LAGERBEWEGUNG
  BEWEGUNGSART
	EMPFANGE-LAGERBEWEGUNG	LAGERBEWEGUNG
		  MELDUNG
		  MELDUNG-1
		  MELDUNG-2
		  MELDUNG-3

LAGERBEWEGUNG
  BEWEGUNGSART
	SENDE-LAGERBEWEGUNG	XDC-SS
		  XDC-ZUSTAND

LAGERBEWEGUNG
  BEWEGUNGSART
  ART-NR
  BEWEGUNGSMENGE
	PRUEFE-LAGERBEWEGUNG	

XDB-SS
  XOBJEKT
  ART-NR
  LIEF-NR
  ARTIKELBEZEICHNUNG
  LAGERMENGE
  MINDESTMENGE
  MAXIMALMENGE
  BESTELLMENGE
  ARTIKELPREIS
LAGERBEWEGUNG
  ART-NR
	GET-ARTIKEL	XDB-SS
		  XOBJEKTNAME
		  XFUNKTION
		  XRETCODE
		  XSUCHBEGRIFF
		ARTIKEL
		  ART-NR
		  LIEF-NR
		  ARTIKELBEZEICHNUNG
		  LAGERMENGE
		  MINDESTMENGE
		  MAXIMALMENGE
		  BESTELLMENGE
		  ARTIKELPREIS

Fig.6: SOFTDOC Data Flow Diagram

```
                  S O F T D O C   M O D U L D O K U M E N T - 1
                             MODULBAUM                                     SEI
```

MODUL: LAGERERF   DATUM: 1

```
STUFE STMNT   MODULORGANISATION
**********************************************************************************
  1   146    PROC LAGERERF
  2   155      SEC  INITIALISIERE-ERFASSUNG
  3   157        |--->  OPEN-ARTIKEL   (237)
  2   159      END  INITIALISIERE-ERFASSUNG
  2   160      SEC  EMPFANGE-LAGERBEWEGUNG
  3   172        |--->  PRUEFE-LAGERBEWEGUNG  (203)
  3   192        |--->  GENSECT-01    (253)
  2   194      END  EMPFANGE-LAGERBEWEGUNG
  2   195      SEC  SENDE-LAGERBEWEGUNG
  3   197        |--->  CLOSE-ARTIKEL  (244)
  2   202      END  SENDE-LAGERBEWEGUNG
  2   203      SEC  PRUEFE-LAGERBEWEGUNG
  2   218      END  PRUEFE-LAGERBEWEGUNG
  2   219      SEC  GET-ARTIKEL
  2   227      END  GET-ARTIKEL
  2   228      SEC  REWRITE-ARTIKEL
  2   236      END  REWRITE-ARTIKEL
  2   237      SEC  OPEN-ARTIKEL
  2   243      END  OPEN-ARTIKEL
  2   244      SEC  CLOSE-ARTIKEL
  2   252      END  CLOSE-ARTIKEL
  2   253      SEC  GENSECT-01
  3   255        |--->  GET-ARTIKEL   (219)
  3   270        |--->  REWRITE-ARTIKEL  (228)
  2   272      END  GENSECT-01
  1   272    END  LAGERERF

           ANZAHL MODULABSCHNITTE = 10
```

Fig. 7: SOFTDOC Function Tree

89

```
LABEL        2   38  |  |  LABEL     MELDE-ART-NR
IF           2   39  |  |  IF        (FEHLERART (1) = XEIN)
             3   40  |  |    MOVE    LAGERBEWEGUNG.MELDUNG = 'LAGERBEWEGUNG NICHT VERARBEITET'
             3   41  |  |    MOVE    LAGERBEWEGUNG.MELDUNG-1 = 'ART-NR UNGUELTIG'
ENDIF        2   42  |  |  ENDIF
LABEL        2   43  |  |  LABEL     MELDE-BEWEGUNGSART
IF           2   44  |  |  IF        (FEHLERART (2) = XEIN)
             3   45  |  |    MOVE    LAGERBEWEGUNG.MELDUNG = 'LAGERBEWEGUNG NICHT VERARBEITET'
             3   46  |  |    MOVE    LAGERBEWEGUNG.MELDUNG-2 = 'BEWEGUNGSART UNGUELTIG'
ENDIF        2   47  |  |  ENDIF
LABEL        2   48  |  |  LABEL     MELDE-BEWEGUNGSMENGE
IF           2   49  |  |  IF        (FEHLERART (3) = XEIN)
             3   50  |  |    MOVE    LAGERBEWEGUNG.MELDUNG = 'LAGERBEWEGUNG NICHT VERARBEITET'
             3   51  |  |    MOVE    LAGERBEWEGUNG.MELDUNG-3 = 'BEWEGUNGSMENGE UNGUELTIG'
ENDIF        2   52  |  |  ENDIF
LABEL        2   53  |  |  LABEL     STEUERE-ZUGANG-ABGANG
IF           2   54  |  |  IF        (FEHLERART (1) = 0 AND FEHLERART (2) = 0 AND FEHLERART
             3   55  |  |            (3) = 0)
             3   56  |  |    COM     LESE ARTIKEL , SUCHBEGRIFF = ART-NR
             3   57  |  |    PERFORM GET-ARTIKEL
LABEL        3   58  |  |    LABEL   MELDE-ART-FEHLT
IF           3   59  |  |    IF      (XRETCODE = XDBKEY)
             4   60  |  |      MOVE  LAGERBEWEGUNG.MELDUNG = 'LAGERBEWEGUNG NICHT VERARBEITET'
             4   61  |  |      MOVE  LAGERBEWEGUNG.MELDUNG-1 = 'ARTIKEL NICHT IM BESTAND'
ENDIF        3   62  |  |    ENDIF
LABEL        3   63  |  |    LABEL   VERARBEITE-LAGERZUGANG
IF           3   64  |  |    IF      (XRETCODE = XDBOK AND BEWEGUNGSART =XZUGANG)
CALL         4   65  |  |      CALL  VERARBEITE-LAGERZUGANG (LAGERBEWEGUNG, ARTIKEL)
ENDIF        3   66  |  |    ENDIF
LABEL        3   67  |  |    LABEL   VERARBEITE-LAGERABGANG
IF           3   68  |  |    IF      (XRETCODE = XDBOK AND BEWEGUNGSART = XABGANG)
CALL         4   69  |  |      CALL  VERARBEITE-LAGERABGANG (LAGERBEWEGUNG, ARTIKEL)
ENDIF        3   70  |  |    ENDIF
             3   71  |  |    PERFORM REWRITE-ARTIKEL
ENDIF        2   72  |  |  ENDIF
ENDSECT      1   73  |  ENDSECT     EMPFANGE-LAGERBEWEGUNG
LABEL        1   74  |  SECTION     SENDE-LAGERBEWEGUNG
IF           2   75  |  |  IF        (BEWEGUNGSART = XENDE)
             3   76  |  |    PERFORM CLOSE-ARTIKEL
             3   77  |  |    STMT    CLOSE BESTELLPOSTEN
ENDIF        2   78  |  |  ENDIF
             2   79  |  MOVE        XDC-ZUSTAND = XAKTIV
RETURN       2   80  |  RETURN
ENDSECT      1   81  ENDSECT       SENDE-LAGERBEWEGUNG
```

Fig. 8: Program Design Language

```
000650 MELDE-ART-NR.                                                       00000650
000660     IF  (FEHLERART (1) = XEIN) THEN                                 00000660
000670         MOVE  "LAGERBEWEGUNG NICHT VERARBEITET" TO   MELDUNG        00000670
000680            IN LAGERBEWEGUNG
000690         MOVE  "ART-NR UNGUELTIG" TO  MELDUNG-1 IN LAGERBEWEGUNG     00000680
000700     END-IF.                                                         00000690
000710 MELDE-BEWEGUNGSART.                                                 00000700
000720     IF  (FEHLERART (2) = XEIN) THEN                                 00000710
000730         MOVE  "LAGERBEWEGUNG NICHT VERARBEITET" TO   MELDUNG        00000720
000740            IN LAGERBEWEGUNG                                         00000730
000750         MOVE  "BEWEGUNGSART UNGUELTIG" TO   MELDUNG-2               00000740
000760            IN LAGERBEWEGUNG                                         00000750
000770     END-IF.                                                         00000760
000780 MELDE-BEWEGUNGSMENGE.                                               00000770
000790     IF  (FEHLERART (3) = XEIN) THEN                                 00000780
000800         MOVE  "LAGERBEWEGUNG NICHT VERARBEITET" TO   MELDUNG        00000790
000810            IN LAGERBEWEGUNG                                         00000800
000820         MOVE  "BEWEGUNGSMENGE UNGUELTIG" TO   MELDUNG-3             00000810
000830            IN LAGERBEWEGUNG                                         00000820
000840     END-IF.                                                         00000830
000850 STEUERE-ZUGANG-ABGANG.                                             00000840
000860     IF  (FEHLERART (1) = 0 AND FEHLERART (2) = 0 AND FEHLERART     00000850
000870         (3) = 0) THEN                                               00000860
000880*    LESE ARTIKEL , SUCHBEGRIFF = ART-NR                             00000870
000890     PERFORM GET-ARTIKEL.                                            00000880
000900 MELDE-ART-FEHLT.                                                    00000890
000910     IF  (XRETCODE = XDBKEY) THEN                                    00000900
000920         MOVE  "LAGERBEWEGUNG NICHT VERARBEITET" TO   MELDUNG        00000910
000930            IN LAGERBEWEGUNG                                         00000920
000940         MOVE  "ARTIKEL NICHT IM BESTAND" TO   MELDUNG-1             00000930
000950            IN LAGERBEWEGUNG                                         00000940
000960     END-IF.                                                         00000950
000970 VERARBEITE-LAGERZUGANG.                                             00000960
000980     IF  (XRETCODE = XDBOK AND BEWEGUNGSART = XZUGANG) THEN          00000970
000990?    CALL "VERARBEI" USING  LAGERBEWEGUNG, ARTIKEL                   00000980
001000     END-IF.                                                         00000990
001010 VERARBEITE-LAGERABGANG.                                             00001000
001020     IF  (XRETCODE = XDBOK AND BEWEGUNGSART = XABGANG) THEN          00001010
001030?    CALL "VERARBAB" USING  LAGERBEWEGUNG, ARTIKEL                   00001020
                                                                           00001030
```

Fig. 9: COBOL-85 Program

90

Software Maintenance as an Engineering Discipline

Richard C. Linger

IBM Corporation
Systems Integration Division
Bethesda, Maryland

Abstract

Software maintenance can be transformed from the unmanageable, cut-and-try activity of today into a systematic engineering discipline through application of mathematics-based principles and practices that have wrought a similar transformation in software engineering. The mathematics provide rigorous techniques for converting unstructured programs into structured form, recovering program design documentation, and modifying and verifying programs. While these principles and practices are technical, the ultimate benefits are managerial, in a new level of predictability and control of maintenance operations to meet business needs.

Software Maintenance Today and Tomorrow

Software maintenance today is a large-scale, multi-billion dollar corporate necessity with no theoretical foundations for its practice. It has emerged from the obscure, backroom activity of 25 years ago into the corporate limelight, and today is a critical component of business growth and survival. But software maintenance is practiced today much as it was 25 years ago, as a collection of ad hoc techniques in a black art that is virtually impossible to reliably manage and control. As a result, software maintenance consumes most of the human resources in information systems, and sharply limits new software development and evolution to meet changing business conditions [Boehm 1981].

But while this experience has seemed inevitable in the past, it need not be so in the future. Software maintenance can be carried out as a systematic engineering discipline based on rigorous theoretical foundations [Osborne 1987]. This evolution to rigor will recapitulate and capitalize on the experience of software engineering over the past 25 years, in moving from a hodge-podge of personal styles and techniques to a systematic, mathematics based discipline [Mills 1986, Linger 1988]. And it will occur for the same reason, namely, the need for management predictability and control in responding to business needs for information processing.

It is indeed fortunate that theoretical foundations for software maintenance already exist, in the mathematics that underlie the practice of rigorous software engineering. We invoke here not the superficial prescriptions of buzz word software engineering, in avoiding goto's where convenient, but rather the deeper, semantic understanding of programs as mathematical objects [Mills 1975], as summarized next.

These mathematical foundations provide a theory for transforming unstructured programs into structured form, recovering program design documentation, and designing and verifying program modifications.

Theoretical Foundations for Software Maintenance

Proper and Prime Programs

We consider a restricted class of flowchart programs, namely single-entry, single-exit programs composed of binary branching predicate nodes (i.e., IF A LESS THAN B in COBOL) and single-entry, single-exit function nodes (i.e., MOVE A TO B in COBOL), and that contain no dead code or endless loops. Such programs are known as **proper programs**, and can be of any size and internal complexity, but always with a single entry point and a single exit point.

Prime programs are proper programs that are irreducible in that they contain no proper subparts other than themselves and function nodes. While prime programs can also be of any size and complexity, of special interest for programming purposes are the zero- and one-predicate prime programs (referred to here as the small primes), namely, sequence, ifthen, ifthenelse, whiledo, dountil, and dowhiledo, that is, the primes of structured programming. Programs composed of nested and sequenced small primes define a natural decomposition hierarchy formed by abstracting visible primes to single-entry, single-exit

Reprinted from *Proc. Conference on Software Maintenance—1988*, pp. 292-297. ©1988 by The Institute of Electrical and Electronics Engineers, Inc. All rights reserved.

function nodes, to reveal new primes for abstraction, continuing until the entire program has been abstracted to a single function node, as illustrated in Figure 1.

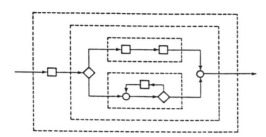

Figure 1. Nested Prime Programs Form a Decomposition Hierarchy

The Structure Theorem

The Structure Theorem [Linger 1979] guarantees that any proper program, of any complexity whatsoever, can be represented by an execution-equivalent program expressed solely in zero- and one-predicate prime programs (in fact, just sequence, ifthenelse, and whiledo are sufficient). The proof of the theorem is constructive, and defines a transformation process from arbitrary, unstructured programs to equivalent structured programs that works in all possible circumstances, in contrast to heuristic methods of structuring that can fail in unusual situations. This constructive proof is the basis for automatic structuring algorithms in a COBOL program re-engineering system [COBOL/SF 1988].

While the Structure Theorem states a technical result, its ultimate implications are managerial, in guaranteeing the sufficiency of a structured programming standard for program development and maintenance.

Program Functions

In execution, prime programs simply transform data from an initial state at their entry line to a final state at their exit line, with no side effects in control flow possible, say from arbitrary branching with gotos. In their effect on data, prime programs correspond to mathematical functions, as mappings from domains to ranges. That is, specifications for prime programs are mathematical functions, and prime programs are themselves rules for the functions. In illustration, the specification

    exchange the values of x and y

written in natural language, or as an equivalent concurrent assignment

    x, y := y, x

defines a mathematical function that can be expanded into the sequence prime program (introducing incidental variable T)

```
*      EXCHANGE THE VALUES OF X AND Y
       PERFORM
           MOVE X TO T
           MOVE Y TO X
           MOVE T TO Y
       END-PERFORM
```

where the specification becomes a **function comment** to document the prime, and the keywords PERFORM, END-PERFORM delimit the scope of the comment. In short, every prime program computes a mathematical function, whether that function is written down or not. This function is known as the **program function** of the prime, and describes its effect on data in all possible circumstances.

Consider next the COBOL fragment on the left of Figure 2. This sequence structure is composed of two ifthenelse primes. Because the ifthenelses are self-contained with no control flow side effects, they can be read and understood independently, and their branch-free program functions recorded as shown in the center of Figure 2. The original program has now been abstracted to a sequence prime in the center, which can in turn be read and abstracted to the sequence-free program function shown on the right. Each abstraction step results in a function-equivalent program at successively higher levels of abstraction. This substitution process is summarized as an **axiom of replacement** between a prime program and its program function.

The axiom of replacement motivates an **algebra of functions** in prime programs,

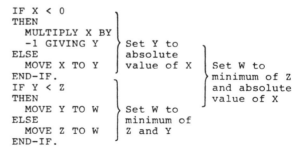

Figure 2. Abstracting Program Functions of Prime Programs

whereby program functions and their primes can be freely substituted. In this case, **function abstraction** was carried out to recover design documentation. The reverse process of **function expansion**, moving from right to left in Figure 2, is important in software design. Note also that the process of **function comparison** is critical in verifying the correctness of designed expansions, for example, in deciding whether or not the sequence in the center does the function specified on the right. Functional correctness requirements for the small primes are defined in [Linger 1979], and are illustrated in Figure 3 for the primes of Figure 2.

```
Whenever X < 0 is true,
     does MULTIPLY X BY -1 GIVING Y
     do Set Y to the absolute value of X,
and whenever X < 0 is false,
     does MOVE X TO Y
     do Set Y to the absolute value of X?

Whenever Y < Z is true,
     does MOVE Y TO W
     do Set W to the minimum of Z and Y,
and whenever Y < Z is false
     does MOVE Z TO W
     do Set W to the minimum of Z and Y?

Does
     Set Y to the absolute value of X
followed by
     Set W to the minimum of Z and Y
do
     Set W to the minimum of Z and the
     absolute value of X?
```

Figure 3. Correctness Questions for the Prime Programs of Figure 2

Software Maintenance Engineering

The function-theoretic foundations briefly sketched above provide a ready-made basis for software maintenance as an engineering discipline in three major steps:

    Step 1: Re-engineering to Structured
            Form
            Done once, to get programs in
            shape for understanding.

    Step 2: Design Recovery
            Done once, to understand and
            document program designs.

    Step 3: Design Modification and
            Verification
            Repeated as necessary, while
            preserving programs in
            structured, documented form.

These steps are described in more detail below.

Step 1: Re-engineering to Structured Form

The first step in software maintenance engineering is to re-engineer programs under maintenance that contain large, arbitrary primes, that is, programs that are unstructured, into equivalent programs expressed in nested and sequenced small primes that can be systematically read and understood. When restated in small primes, the physical and logical structure of the programs will correspond, and a stepwise process of design recovery through derivation and recording of program functions will be possible.

In illustration, consider the miniature COBOL program fragment, perhaps part of a banking application, depicted in Figure 4. It contains code that has been commented out (lines 3-5, 23), and has just one small prime. The program is in fact an arbitrary prime whose control flow is a complex jumble of iftests and gotos that can only be read and understood as a unit, with no stepwise abstraction process possible. That is, the fragment can only be understood by tracing and remembering the effect of every possible execution path.

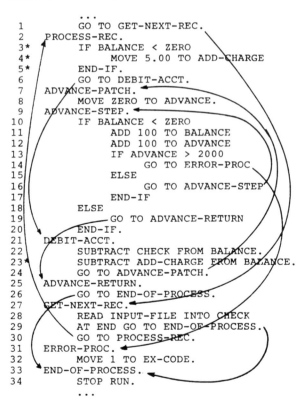

```
    ...
 1         GO TO GET-NEXT-REC.
 2    PROCESS-REC.
 3*        IF BALANCE < ZERO
 4*            MOVE 5.00 TO ADD-CHARGE
 5*        END-IF.
 6         GO TO DEBIT-ACCT.
 7    ADVANCE-PATCH.
 8         MOVE ZERO TO ADVANCE.
 9    ADVANCE-STEP.
10        IF BALANCE < ZERO
11            ADD 100 TO BALANCE
12            ADD 100 TO ADVANCE
13            IF ADVANCE > 2000
14                GO TO ERROR-PROC
15            ELSE
16                GO TO ADVANCE-STEP
17            END-IF
18        ELSE
19            GO TO ADVANCE-RETURN
20        END-IF.
21    DEBIT-ACCT.
22        SUBTRACT CHECK FROM BALANCE.
23*       SUBTRACT ADD-CHARGE FROM BALANCE.
24        GO TO ADVANCE-PATCH.
25    ADVANCE-RETURN.
26        GO TO END-OF-PROCESS.
27    GET-NEXT-REC.
28        READ INPUT-FILE INTO CHECK
29        AT END GO TO END-OF-PROCESS.
30        GO TO PROCESS-REC.
31    ERROR-PROC.
32        MOVE 1 TO EX-CODE.
33    END-OF-PROCESS.
34        STOP RUN.
    ...
```

Figure 4. An Unstructured COBOL Program Fragment

294

These tracings must then be combined to describe the overall effect on data in all possible circumstances, clearly a non-trivial task even for this miniature illustration.

Application of an automatic structuring process based on the Structure Theorem proof construction results in the functionally equivalent structured version of Figure 5 (shown in VS COBOL II with local terminators END-IF, END-PERFORM). The logic is now expressed in small primes and all gotos have been eliminated. A new data item named NEXTSTMT was created in the structuring process to help control the logic flow.

```
    ...
1    MOVE "F" TO CSF-AT-END
2    READ INPUT-FILE INTO CHECK
3    AT END
4        MOVE "T" TO CSF-AT-END
5    END-READ
6    IF NOT (CSF-AT-END = "T")
7        SUBTRACT CHECK FROM BALANCE
8        MOVE ZERO TO ADVANCE
9        MOVE 2 TO NEXTSTMT
10       PERFORM
11           UNTIL NEXTSTMT = 0
12           IF BALANCE < ZERO
13               ADD 100 TO BALANCE
14               ADD 100 TO ADVANCE
15               IF ADVANCE > 2000
16                   MOVE 1 TO EX-CODE
17                   MOVE 0 TO NEXTSTMT
18               ELSE
19                   MOVE 2 TO NEXTSTMT
20               END-IF
21           ELSE
22               MOVE 0 TO NEXTSTMT
23           END-IF
24       END-PERFORM
25   END-IF
26 CSF-TERMINATION.
27   STOP RUN.
    ...
```

Figure 5. The COBOL Fragment of Figure 4 After Automatic Structuring

Step 2: Design Recovery

Although in structured form the logic of this miniature fragment is self explanatory and understanding could be quickly refreshed whenever required, the program is hard for its size, and it is instructive to proceed with formal design recovery and documentation as if it were a larger program. In fact, these methods scale up to programs of any size; abstracting program functions may require more effort in larger programs, but they are still just program functions!

Reading can begin with the most deeply nested primes which, when abstracted to their program functions, will reveal new primes for abstraction, continuing in this fashion until the entire program has been abstracted. Not every program function need be documented; judgement is required to select documentation anchor points that effectively capture and convey the design.

The whiledo (perform loop) of Figure 5 has a body at lines 12-23 composed of nested ifthenelses. One action of the body is to set NEXTSTMT to either zero (to exit the loop) or 2 (to repeat the loop). With a little thought, the program function of the loop body (named PF1) can be documented as shown in Figure 6.

```
PF1:

1    if BALANCE is not less than zero
2    then
3        set NEXTSTMT to 0,
4    otherwise
5        if ADVANCE + 100 > 2000
6        then
7            add 100 to BALANCE and to ADVANCE,
8            set EX-CODE to 1, and set NEXTSTMT
9            to 0,
10       otherwise
11           add 100 to BALANCE and to ADVANCE,
12           and set NEXTSTMT to 2
```

Figure 6. Program Function of Lines 12-23 of Figure 5

Structured English with indentation is used here to guide the eye and mind in understanding the function. Note also that care has been taken to ensure that the function description is non-procedural. That is, the operations on lines 7-9 of PF1 are concurrent, as are those on lines 11-12, and could be carried out in any order. Conditions in program functions should refer to initial state values to ensure non-procedurality, as, for example, the condition on ADVANCE + 100 on line 5. This program function reveals the actual effect on data of the loop body that was obscured in the unstructured version, but is it the right function for the bank? For example, it shows that the maximum advance is actually \$2100, not \$2000 as might be intended.

Next, the program function of the whiledo on lines 10-24 of Figure 5 and its NEXTSTMT initialization on line 9 can be determined, as depicted in Figure 7. This loop-free program function correctly describes the effect of the initialized loop (note that NEXTSTMT is regarded as incidental and is not mentioned), but again, is it the right

295

function for the bank? For example, if the advance limit is exceeded, all available advance funds will have already been added to BALANCE, even though it may still end up negative. It may seem surprising that such a small unit of code could represent so much possible behavior, all the more reason to know for sure what that behavior actually is.

PF2:

```
1    if BALANCE is non-negative
2    then
3      do nothing,
4    otherwise
5      if number of $100 increments to make
6      BALANCE non-negative does not exceed
7      number of $100 increments left up to
8      $2000
9      then
10       set BALANCE to BALANCE +
11       sufficient $100 increments to
12       make it non-negative, and set
13       ADVANCE to ADVANCE + sufficient
14       $100 increments to make BALANCE
15       non-negative,
16     otherwise
17       set BALANCE to BALANCE + all $100
18       increments left up to $2100, set
19       ADVANCE to ADVANCE + all $100
20       increments left up to $2100, and
21       set EX-CODE to 1
```

Figure 7. Program Function of Lines 9-24 of Figure 5.

Continuing, the program function of the ifthen thenpart on lines 7-25 of Figure 5 can be derived as shown in Figure 8. This program function defines the effect on data of most of the program. PF3 shows that three actions (each concurrent) are possible, at lines 3-4, 10-15, and 17-19. Two conditions at lines 1 and 6-8 determine the action to be carried out.

Finally, the program function of the entire fragment of Figure 5 can be described as depicted in Figure 9 (treating CSF-AT-END as incidental and abbreviating to save space).

These four program functions could be written as comments directly in the structured code, or referenced by name from the code as shown in Figure 10. The complex logic of the original unstructured program of Figure 4 has now been systematically structured and abstracted to a precise definition of its program function. It would be difficult indeed to develop this level of understanding from the unstructured version. These techniques

PF3:

```
1    if BALANCE - CHECK is non-negative
2    then
3      set BALANCE to BALANCE - CHECK and
4      set ADVANCE to 0,
5    otherwise
6      if number of $100 increments to make
7      BALANCE - CHECK non-negative does
8      not exceed $2000
9      then
10       set BALANCE to BALANCE - CHECK +
11       sufficient $100 increments to make
12       BALANCE - CHECK non-negative, and
13       set ADVANCE to sufficient $100
14       increments to make BALANCE -
15       CHECK non-negative,
16     otherwise
17       set BALANCE to BALANCE - CHECK +
18       $2100, set ADVANCE to $2100, and
19       set EX-CODE to 1
```

Figure 8. Program Function of Lines 7-25 of Figure 5

PF4:

```
1    if INPUT-FILE is empty
2    then
3      do nothing,
4    otherwise
5      do PF3 with "next record in
6      input-file" substituted for
7      CHECK and position INPUT-FILE to
8      next record, if any
```

Figure 9. Program Function of Entire Program Fragment of Figure 5

make the difference between a cut-and-try maintenance process and a process based on intellectual control.

Step 3: Design Modification and Verification

Once a structured program has been abstracted into a hierarchy of program functions, understanding is sufficient to begin maintenance operations. Given an understanding of a maintenance requirement, modification and verification is carried out in the function-theoretic approach as follows:

Program Analysis

Identify the program function in the hierarchy that encompasses all parts of the program that will require modification.

296

```
      ...
  *   PF4
1     MOVE "F" TO CSF-AT-END
2     READ INPUT-FILE INTO CHECK
3     AT END
4         MOVE "T" TO CSF-AT-END
5     END-READ
  *   PF3
6     IF NOT (CSF-AT-END = "T")
7         SUBTRACT CHECK FROM BALANCE
8         MOVE ZERO TO ADVANCE
  *       PF2
9         MOVE 2 TO NEXTSTMT
10        PERFORM
11            UNTIL NEXTSTMT = 0
  *           PF1
12            IF BALANCE < ZERO
13                ADD 100 TO BALANCE
14                ADD 100 TO ADVANCE
15                IF ADVANCE > 2000
16                    MOVE 1 TO EX-CODE
17                    MOVE 0 TO NEXTSTMT
18                ELSE
19                    MOVE 2 TO NEXTSTMT
20                END-IF
21            ELSE
22                MOVE 0 TO NEXTSTMT
23            END-IF
24        END-PERFORM
25    END-IF
26 CSF-TERMINATION.
27    STOP RUN.
      ...
```

Figure 10. The Structured Fragment of Figure 5 With Function Comments Referencing Named Functions

Program Modification

Reprogram top down by stepwise refinement in small primes from the identified program function, preserving existing program functions and code where possible and modifying them where necessary, while preserving structured form.

Correctness Verification

At each refinement step, verify the expansion according to functional correctness techniques [Linger 1979].

Managing Software Maintenance Engineering

Rigorous software maintenance techniques of re-engineering to structured form, design recovery, and modification and verification are the basis for a new level of effectiveness in managing maintenance activities. In illustration, imagine a large program inventory with many outstanding maintenance requests. Complexity metrics can be used to identify the least structured, most complex programs as the best candidates for re-engineering

into structured form. Analysis of the re-engineered programs may reveal particular islands of complexity that should be read and abstracted to program functions first for maximum benefit in processing maintenance requests. Other parts of the programs can be abstracted later if required in preparation for maintenance work that will affect them. Modification work can be assigned to persons who have done the abstraction and are most familiar with the program functions.

All of these tasks are discrete work assignments with definite beginning and ending criteria and work products. The management benefits are obvious. It is far easier to assign and monitor systematic tasks to abstract, modify, and verify a given re-engineered program part of known size and complexity under full intellectual control than it is to assign indefinite code modification tasks against unstructured logic that no one can ever fully understand.

Acknowledgements

It is a pleasure to acknowledge the excellent comments of Mark Pleszkoch and the reviewers of this paper.

References

[Boehm 1981] Boehm, B. W., **Software Engineering Economics**, Prentice-Hall, Englewood Cliffs, NJ, 1981.

[COBOL/SF 1988] **COBOL Structuring Facility Re-engineering Concepts**, IBM Publication SC34-4079, 1988.

[Osborne 1987] Osborne, W. M., Building and Sustaining Software Maintainability, **Proceedings of Conference on Software Maintenance**, Austin, Texas, September, 1987, pp. 13-23.

[Linger 1979] Linger, R. C., Mills, H. D., and Witt, B. I., **Structured Programming: Theory and Practice**, Addison-Wesley, Cambridge, Mass., 1979.

[Linger 1988] Linger. R. C., A Case Study in Cleanroom Software Engineering: The IBM COBOL Structuring Facility, **Proceedings of COMPSAC '88**, Chicago, Ill., October, 1988.

[Mills 1975] Mills, H. D., The New Math of Computer Programming, **Communications of the ACM**, Vol. 18, No. 1, January, 1975, pp.43-48.

[Mills 1986] Mills, H. D., Structured Programming: Retrospect and Prospect, **IEEE Software**, November 1986, pp. 58-66.

297

SOFTWARE—PRACTICE AND EXPERIENCE, VOL. 21(12), 1349–1364 (DECEMBER 1991)

1349

Software Reverse Engineering: A Case Study

ERIC J. BYRNE

Department of Computing and Information Science, Kansas State University, Nichols Hall, Manhattan, Kansas 66506, U.S.A.

SUMMARY

This paper presents lessons learned from an experiment to reverse engineer a program. A reverse engineering process was used as part of a project to develop an Ada implementation of a Fortran program and upgrade the existing documentation. To accomplish this, design information was extracted from the Fortran source code and entered into a software development environment. The extracted design information was used to implement a new version of the program written in Ada. This experiment revealed issues about recovering design information, such as, separating design details from implementation details, dealing with incomplete or erroneous information, traceability of information between implementation and recovered design, and re-engineering. The reverse engineering process used to recover the design, and the experience gained during the study are reported.

KEY WORDS   Design recovery   Reverse engineering   Structured design   Re-implementation   Re-engineering   Language translation

INTRODUCTION

For the problem of reimplementing an old Fortran program in Ada and providing new documentation, a typical solution is to translate the Fortran source code directly into Ada and document the new program. This paper describes the author's experience with an alternative solution. This alternative applies software reverse engineering techniques to Fortran source code. Design information is recovered from the source code and any existing documentation. This recovered design information is then used to implement a new version of the program written in Ada and to generate up-to-date documentation. The process of recovering a program's design is called design recovery and is an element of software reverse engineering.

Software reverse engineering[1] is defined as the process of analysing a system to identify the system's components and their interrelationships, and to create representations of the system in another form or at a higher level of abstraction. There are many types of program information that can be abstracted and examined.[2–5] With an older software system it is particularly useful to abstract and record its design. A design is recovered by piecing together information from the source code, existing documents, personnel experienced with the system and application domain knowledge. Design recovery differs from reverse engineering by emphasizing the recovery of application domain knowledge that helps achieve informative higher level abstractions beyond those created by examining only the source code. Ted Biggerstaff in his article[6] on design recovery stated that:

1350   E. J. BYRNE

The recovered design abstractions must include conventional software engineering representations such as formal specifications, module breakdowns, data abstractions, data-flows, and program description language. ... design recovery must reproduce all the information required for a person to fully understand what a program does, how it does it, why it does it, ...

Modern software designers and developers have useful techniques and methodologies derived from years of experience and observations to guide them in their work.[7] Automated tools have been collected into environments that support the development of software. These tools embody software engineering techniques that assist with the development of software that is well structured, understandable, easier to maintain, contains fewer errors and is properly documented.[8] By recovering the design of an older system, these modern techniques can be applied to transform the design, and to produce a better implementation. This is software re-engineering.

This paper reports on an experiment with reverse engineering conducted at the U.S. Air Force's Avionics Laboratory, System Avionics Division, Avionics Logistics Branch at Wright-Patterson AFB. A Fortran program was selected that is used in a simulation environment for the real-time testing and analysis of the Fire Control Computer used on F-16 aircraft. This simulation environment simulates the subsystems of an F-16 aircraft in an operational environment, including models for the aircraft's aerodynamics, on-board computers, avionics sensors, weapon systems and targets. The simulation environment is composed of separate programs that execute in a distributed environment. The programs execute concurrently and communicate via shared memory. In the autumn of 1988 a project was started to rewrite the existing Fortran code in Ada. The source code is manually translated using source-to-source techniques. Documentation for the translated programs is produced separately by a different group.

The selected program for this experiment was a software model of the Air Data Computer (ADC) used in F-16 aircraft. This is a small program, only several hundred lines of code. The goal of this experiment was to gain experience with software reverse engineering and identify possible problems. A secondary goal was to use a software development environment to record the recovered design information so that the suitability of the environment for supporting reverse engineering could be evaluated. The reverse engineering process began with the existing Fortran source code and documentation for the ADC model, extracted the software design and recorded the recovered design using the software development environment tool. The recovered design was used to generate new documents and to create a new implementation of the ADC model in Ada. Figure 1 shows an abstract representation of the experiment.

WHY USE REVERSE ENGINEERING?

The motivation for this experiment derived from a single problem: given an existing software system written in Fortran, how can an equivalent system, written in Ada, be developed? The problem of reimplementing an existing system in a different programming language has been around for years and three general approaches have emerged:[9]

1. Manually rewrite the existing system.

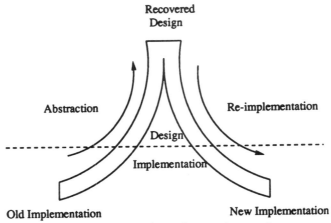

Figure 1. Reverse engineering and re-implementation process

2. Use an automatic language translator.
3. Redesign and reimplement the system.

In the first approach, manually rewriting the existing software system means manually translating from the source language to the target language. With this approach no new software tools are required. There is flexibility in terms of translating the system and changing the system structure. However, there are several disadvantages as well. Manually translated source code often retains the style and flavour of the original implementation. Chances to change the system are often not planned. Individual programmers tend to redo as they work, instead of planning the changes in advance. This approach is time consuming. The number of lines of code that can be translated manually per programmer per day is small. Finally, this is an error-prone approach. Humans make mistakes. There is no means to guarantee that the rewritten system is functionally equivalent to the original. The new system must be thoroughly tested to achieve confidence in it.

The second approach, automatic translation, relies on the use of a tool that accepts software written in the source programming language and generates new source code written in the target language. It is possible for the translation process to be done with little or no human intervention, thereby avoiding many of the problems with the manual rewrite approach. This approach generates new code quickly. However, this approach has several disadvantages. The source language may not yield itself to simple translation into the chosen target language. Some automated translator tools only do the easy part of the translation and leave difficult portions for a human. Automatic translation tends to focus solely on language transformation and does not address the issue of program structure modifications.[10] The most commonly recognized problem with literal translation is summed up as: garbage in, garbage out. If the existing system is not well-structured, both in terms of its architecture and control-flow, then the resulting system will be of the same poor quality. Automatically generated code may be terribly inefficient. The code produced by translation may also be difficult to understand, greatly increasing its future maintenance costs.[11]

1352

E. J. BYRNE

Thus, automatic language conversion may not provide an easy route to a complete conversion to a new system.

The third approach is to redesign and reimplement the system. This approach starts with the requirements for the current system and builds a completely new system in the target language. This new system is required to be functionally equivalent to the original system even though it is not derived from it. Of the three approaches, this approach has the greatest chance of producing the best possible new system. Redesigning and reimplementing the system in the new language provides the most power and the greatest flexibility in terms of creating the end product. The resultant system may have significantly lower maintenance costs than systems generated by the other approaches. Finally, redesigning the existing system for implementation in the target language allows for better use of the features of that language. However, this approach also has several disadvantages. It is more difficult than doing an initial design, because of the requirement to emulate the existing system interfaces. This approach has the highest initial cost. It is equivalent to building a new system. The most serious disadvantage is that for many systems it is not possible to redesign from the system requirements, since the requirements may not exist. For many older systems the only accurate statement of the system's capabilities and functionality is often the source code itself. There often is no valid requirement specification for the system.

Reverse engineering provides a new approach. If there is no requirement specification for a system, reverse engineering the system can produce a reconstructed design that captures the functionality of the system. The design should be represented at an abstraction level that removes implementation language dependencies. This makes it possible to reimplement the system in a new language. In addition, the reconstructed design can be transformed to modernize it, restructure it, incorporate new requirements, etc. This is software re-engineering. Thus re-engineering based on a reverse engineering process offers many of the advantages of the redesign and reimplement approach. This approach is always feasible if the source code for a system exists.

Is this a cost-effective solution? It is commonly stated that tool support is necessary to be able to effectively reverse engineer large systems. One project reverse engineered a 24,000 LOC (lines of code) system to respecify and redocument the system.[12] With tool support it was possible to statically analyse and document the system in one week. It was estimated that it would have taken three man years to document the system manually at the same level of detail. The generated information was used to respecify the system. Respecification took 17 man-months to complete. This amounted to one man-month of specification per 1400 lines of code. In another project, 100,000 LOC comprising over 60 programs were redesigned by manually reconstructing a design representation of the original source code.[13] In addition, 52,000 LOC of new software was written. The original system totalled 1·5 million LOC. This project was completed in 21 months.

Considering these approaches with respect to the work at the U.S. Air Force's Avionics Laboratory, the programs forming the F-16 simulation environment are currently translated manually into Ada. Several automatic translators were reviewed, but no suitable translator was found. No requirement specification for the selected program, the Air Data Computer (ADC) model, was available. Thus reverse engineering was selected as the alternative method to explore. The purpose of the experiment reported in this paper was to examine the use of reverse engineering to generate a language-independent design and to create valid documentation for the program. The goal was to produce a design that could be used to implement an Ada program that was free of Fortran characteristics. This paper describes the reverse engineering process used and the problems encountered. The emphasis is on the application of the reverse engineering technique. The issue of cost effectiveness was not explored.

REVERSE ENGINEERING PROCEDURE

The reverse engineering process begins by extracting detailed design information, and from that extracting a high-level design abstraction. Detailed (low-level) design information is extracted from the source code and existing design documents. This information includes structure charts, data descriptions and PDL to describe processing details. A similar approach, but automated, is described elsewhere to recover Jackson and Warnier/Orr documents from code.[14] The high-level design representation is extracted from the recovered detailed design and expressed using data-flow and control-flow diagrams. Throughout this paper the term 'recovered design' will be used to denote the extracted design. The procedure steps are discussed below. Figure 2 summarizes the procedure.

1. *Collect information.* Collect all possible information about the program. Sources of information include source code, design documents and documentation for system calls and external routines. Personnel experienced with the software should also be identified.
2. *Examine information.* Review the collected information. This step allows the person(s) doing the recovery to become familiar with the system and its components. A plan for dissecting the program and recording the recovered information can be formulated during this stage.
3. *Extract the structure.* Identify the structure of the program and use this to create a set of structure charts. Each node in the structure chart corresponds to a routine called in the program. Thus the chart records the calling hierarchy of the program. For each edge in the chart, the data passed to a node and returned by that node must be recorded.
4. *Record functionality.* For each node in the structure chart, record the processing done in the program routine corresponding to that node. A PDL can be used to express the functionality of program routines. For system and library routines the functionality can be described in English or in a more formal notation.
5. *Record data-flow.* The recovered program structure and PDL can be analysed to identify data transformations in the software. These transformation steps show the data processing done in the program. This information is used to develop a set of hierarchical data flow diagrams that model the software.
6. *Record control-flow.* Identify the high-level control structure of the program and record it using control-flow diagrams. This refers to high-level control that affects the overall operation of the software, not to low-level processing control.
7. *Review recovered design.* Review the recovered design for consistency with available information and correctness. Identify any missing items of information and attempt to locate them. Review the design to verify that it correctly represents the program.

1354   E. J. BYRNE

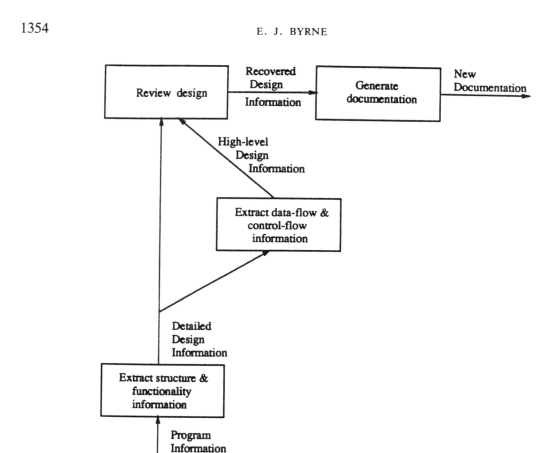

Figure 2. Reverse engineering procedure

8. *Generate documentation.* The final step is to generate design documentation. Information explaining the purpose of the program, program overview, history, etc, will need to be recorded. This information will most probably not be contained in the source code and must be recovered from other sources.

SUPPORTING TOOLS

The only computer-based tool used during this experiment was a commercial software development environment. There are several commercial tools that claim to provide reverse engineering capabilities. In truth, such tools typically provide only program analysis capabilities that produce program-level documentation. These tools are unable to generate higher-level abstractions such as source code to PDL transformations. Most tools can generate structure charts automatically. This capability would have been useful; unfortunately, a tool with this capability was not available in-house.

A commercially produced software development environment was used to record the recovered design information. This environment provided an integrated collection of editors for data-flow diagrams, control-flow diagrams, structure charts, data structure diagrams, E-R diagrams, state transition diagrams and others, with an on-line data dictionary, and a document preparation system. This environment is designed to support software forward engineering. It does not enforce a particular development methodology, yet it is oriented towards structured design[15] with extensions for expressing the design of real-time systems.[16]

A goal of this experiment was to evaluate the usefulness of this environment during reverse engineering. The needs of reverse engineering differ from those of forward engineering, but both processes need to record a design. Could an environment designed to support forward engineering be used when the work is done in reverse, i.e. starting at the most detailed level of representation with higher-level representations created later?

EXPERIENCE

During the reverse engineering effort several problems arose. Many problems concerned how to conduct the reconstruction of the design. However, the most serious problem was not detected until the design was used to create an Ada version of the program. At that point it was discovered that the design was heavily biased by the original Fortran implementation. This problem is discussed in the next section.

Collecting information

The first step was to collect information about the program and the system in general. Sources of information consisted of the program source code, one design document, a document containing an overview of the simulation system architecture, and several programmers experienced with the overall system. The reverse engineering effort was handled by the author, who had no previous exposure to this system.

Several items of information were not found. One type of missing information was data descriptions involving shared memory. The software models use signals and shared memory to communicate between themselves. Descriptions of the data passed in the shared memory areas, ranges of values and significance were not documented completely. Shared memory data items referenced by the Air Data Computer (ADC) model were briefly explained in the available design document, but other items in the shared memory were not. This meant that the recovered design, though it needed to document the structure of the shared memory area, could not document the purpose of most of the data elements. A second type of missing information was application domain information. The origin of the ADC model was not available and equations used in the software were not commented. The recovered design could list equations found in the code but could not explain their significance. Domain knowledge was needed to provide this information. Because domain knowledge was not available 'design recovery' as defined in Reference 1 was not achieved. Design information was recovered but the design could not be completely documented and explained in terms of the application domain.

1356

E. J. BYRNE

Examining information sources

The second step was to become familiar with the program. its structure and how it worked. This step permitted a plan to be created for dissecting the program and entering its information into the development environment.

Unfortunately, this familiarization with the Fortran implementation also biased the reverse engineering effort. Familiarity with the details of the implementation influenced the perspective of what should be recovered and how it should be expressed.

Extracting the structure

The third step was to begin recovering the detailed design from the source code. This step involved two tasks: extracting the calling hierarchy and expressing it as a structure chart, and recording information about data exchanged between nodes in the chart. The recovered information was recorded using the structure chart editor and data structure editor in the software development environment.

To create the structure chart the main program routine became the top node in the chart. Routines called by the main routine were represented by the second layer of nodes in the structure chart. Thus. each node in the structure chart corresponded to a subroutine, function or library routine used in the program. For each node, subnodes were added if the corresponding routine contained calls to other routines. This was done until leaf nodes were reached. Leaf nodes correspond to routines that call no other routines or are library routines.

Creating structure charts from source code is easily automated. There are commercially available tools that do this. The structure charts capture the calling hierarchy of the program routines and to show their interaction. The intent was to capture this information at an implementation language independent level. Several problems were encountered while trying to achieve this language independence.

Each node in the structure chart was given the name of its corresponding routine. This allowed easy recognition between viewing the structure chart and reading the code. Unfortunately it placed a language dependency in the recovered design. Fortran restricts a routine name to a maximum of seven characters. Most names are abbreviations of more meaningful terms. Meaningful names for the structure chart nodes should have been used instead. Ideally the name selected should convey the functionality expressed by the node. This is also important when dealing with nodes that correspond to system routines. These are implementation level details. Using a more abstract and generic name in the design helps ensure that the design is free of such low-level details. For example, the name WAIT-FOR-RESPONSE is less implementation oriented than SYS$WAIT(...).

Associating structure chart nodes with source code routines raises the issue of traceability. In reverse engineering it is desirable to record the links between the recovered design and the original source code or documentation. In this specific case it would be desirable to give a node a meaningful name and record the name of the implemented function to which it corresponds.

As the structure chart was recorded the data items passed between nodes (routines) were also recorded. Structure charts show the direction that data items are passed between nodes. Data item usage had to be analysed to determine whether data items served to carry input data, output data or both. Information about data items, such as purpose, data type, range of values, etc, were recorded in data structure diagrams.

The names recorded for data items were the names of the data items as given in the source code. The language dependency issue discussed for routine names applies here as well. More meaningful names should have been used in the recovered design.

Another problem with data items was expressing their data type in the recovered design. In an effort to have the design be language independent the Fortran data types were mapped to generic types. For example the Fortran type int2 was recorded as '2-byte-integer' in the design. A better approach would be to analyse the purpose of the variable and give it a meaningful type name. For example, a Fortran variable that contained an error number has an integer data type. When expressed in the design, a more meaningful type name would be ERROR-VALUE, where this would be an enumerated type in the design. Using meaningful design data types would have aided the clarity of the recovered design.

Common blocks posed a problem. Source routines did not use parameters to pass information. All information was exchanged via common blocks. The question was how to express this in the recovered design? A study of the common blocks and their usage revealed that there were two types of common blocks in the program. The first type of common block was used as a map to shared memory. The second type was used to pass information internally in the program.

Common blocks that mapped to shared memory had to be kept intact. The order of definitions in the common block declaration was important. This ordering was certainly an implementation detail but it placed a constraint on the recovered design since the program interacted with other programs via these shared memory areas. The recovered design had to represent the structure of these memory areas accurately. The solution was to represent these common blocks as data sources and sinks in the structure chart. The name of a common block became the name of the source/sink, and data was shown to be exchanged between the source/sink and the nodes. The data structure editor was used to record the information about these common blocks. That they were implemented as common blocks in Fortran was not recorded.

The other type of common block was used to pass data between routines in the program. It was decided that this was an implementation detail. These common blocks were broken up and their data items represented as data passed directly between routines. This would leave an implementer free to implement these items as parameters, global variables, or again as common blocks. That these data items had been collected together in common blocks was not recorded.

Recording functionality

Once the structure chart was created the next step was to record the processing associated with each node. For nodes that corresponded to system or library routines an English explanation of the routine was recorded. For source routines the processing steps were recorded using a pseudo-English PDL. This involved manually translating from Fortran to PDL.

One problem was what to do about debugging statements? The source code contained debugging statements that were guarded by conditional compilation directives. Were these part of the design? Probably not, but they were part of the operational capabilities of the software. Talks with the maintenance staff revealed that debugging statements were never used. Therefore, these statements were not recovered.

This raised the issue about how to handle conditional compilation code. Generally, such code is selected based on the operating system, machine, etc. The conditional compilation code used here referred to differences between PDP-11 systems and MicroVaxes. The maintenance staff was again consulted and it was learned that the software would not be used on PDP-11 systems, so the conditional code was not recovered. This solved the problem for this case, but leaves the general question unsolved.

A possible solution to the conditional compilation problem is to consider the purpose of the conditional compilation code. One use of such code is to handle functionality that must be implemented differently on different computer systems. Here, the functionality can be recovered and the system differences ignored as an implementation detail. A more difficult case occurs when conditional compilation code is used to hold functionality that is implemented on one computer system and not on others, i.e. system-dependent capabilities. Here, the design of the program differs depending on the intended implementation system.

Another issue that arose is where does detailed design stop and implementation begin. There is a wealth of information in the source code that would not normally be recorded in a design. The problem is realizing what should not be recovered. For example, the source code contains a system routine that requires a parameter to hold a returned status value. In the code the variable used for this parameter is of type integer. Should the system routine be included in the detailed design? Should its calling interface be recovered exactly as given in the code? Should the detailed design declare the variable as an integer or as a design level type name? In this experiment the system routines were recovered into the detailed design. Later this information was determined to be too implementation specific. A generic processing step should have been given instead.

Recovering the detailed design forced a hard look at the source code and software documentation. One error in the source code was discovered. Comments that were incorrect or outdated were also detected. The documentation was found to be badly outdated and incomplete. A total of 44 errors were located in the documentation. These errors consisted of mistakes in the documentation itself and discrepancies between the documentation and the source code. Because of these errors some information contained in the documentation could not be trusted. These errors eliminated one source of information about the software.

Recording data-flow

The fifth step was to develop a data-flow model. Structured design[15] gives guidelines for transforming data-flow diagrams into structure charts. To some extent, these guidelines can be reversed. The idea is to identify transformations on data expressed in the detailed design and use these transformations to create processes in a data-flow model. The order of transformations in the detailed design determines the order in the data-flow model.

The data-flow model consists of a hierarchy of data-flow diagrams. The top level diagram shows a single process representing the program and its input sources and output destinations. The process in the top-level diagram is then expanded in a separate diagram. This second level diagram shows processes that together do the transformation attributed to the top-level process. Each of these processes can be expanded into lower level diagrams that show even more detailed transformations. Processes can be expanded into more detailed data-flow diagrams until atomic processes are reached.

Data-flow diagrams were constructed from the recovered detailed design using a procedure presented in Reference 17. In this procedure, data transformations in the detailed design are identified using a two-step process. In the first step, each node in the structure chart becomes a process in a data-flow diagram. The names given to processes were not the names from the structure chart nodes. Instead, descriptive process names that suggested the task of a process were used. This step creates a hierarchy of data-flow diagrams. In the second step, the PDL associated with each structure chart node is examined and data transformations are identified. Such transformations are then added to the appropriate data-flow diagram as new processes with descriptive names. In this fashion all data transformations present in the detail design are captured in the data-flow model.

Each process in a data-flow diagram had an associated process specification (pspec). A pspec gave an English description of the purpose of a process. Equations in the PDL were copied into pspecs because they showed the necessary calculation. Each data-flow diagram was also annotated. These annotations explained the significance of the data.

Recovery of the data-flow diagrams forced an analysis of the data items exchanged between nodes in the structure chart. Individual data items carry either data information or control information, or in a poorly designed system both. A data-flow model is concerned with modelling transformations on data and does not express control information. Data items used solely to carry control information were extraneous to the model and therefore were not recovered.

The higher-level abstraction of the data-flow diagrams brought out important details that were obscured in the structure charts and PDL. Two context diagrams were produced. One showed the logical environment of the ADC model and the data exchanged with other models. The second context diagram showed the actual environment of the ADC model and the data exchanged with the simulation driver program and shared memory area. The data-flow model of the ADC clearly revealed the processing structure of the program with respect to collecting data, performing calculations and communicating the results to other models. For example, a node in the structure chart that corresponded to a routine that did calculations showed calls to routines such as sqrt(), and log(). Whereas the data-flow diagram corresponding to that node clearly expressed the calculations as subprocesses with descriptive names. The data-flow diagrams emphasized what happened to the data as it flowed through the system, as opposed to the PDL where this information, while present, is buried with other details.

Creating control-flow diagrams

The sixth step was to identify the control structure of the software. The task of uncovering this structure occurred while creating the data-flow diagram. What remained was to record the control structure and explain its purpose. The control structure was recorded using control-flow diagrams, which were overlaid on the data-

1360   E. J. BYRNE

flow diagrams. This step allowed both data and control-flow to be visible on the same diagram. In addition, a state control model was defined and recorded using a state diagram.

The control structure of interest for the ADC program concerned co-ordinating the actions of this program with other programs executing concurrently. This control governed access to the shared memory areas, when to read and write to them, and the exchange of signals between this program and other programs.

A problem during this step was distinguishing between low-level control structures that involved the implementation of a routine and high-level control structures that served to control the software operation. The former should be included as part of the processing described in the detailed design, the latter needs to be recorded in a control flow diagram and its control specification. The temptation is to recover too much of the control structure.

Constructing the control-flow diagram for the ADC model brought out information that was obscured in the structure charts and PDL. In addition to the control-flow diagram a state-transition diagram for the ADC model was constructed. These two diagrams clearly showed the execution control flow of the ADC program. Of course this same information was present in the structure charts and PDL, but it is not as visible in the detailed design representations.

Reviewing recovered design

At this point the recovered design was reviewed for completeness and accuracy. Reviewing for accuracy means verifying that the recovered design does describe the program, that no functionality of the program has been omitted and that no extraneous information has been recorded. The point to keep in mind is that this effort was to document the recovered design, not the program.

Reviewing for completeness involves determining what information is missing and whether it can be recovered. It was not possible to recover the design completely. The most difficult information to recover was the reason behind a processing step. Other information that could not be recovered was:

1. Equations used in the code were not documented. The significance of these equations could not be determined without knowledge of the application domain.
2. The meaning of the information held by some data items was not documented. Possible significance could only be guessed at.
3. The range of possible values for some data items was not known and could not be determined.

Document generation

The final step was to prepare the recovered information and format it into a design document. Information not recovered in earlier steps was collected at this point. This included an overview of the system, an overview of the program, its intended purpose, history, related documents, etc. The software development environment used provided a document generation system. This system was used to generate a design document for the recovered design.

GENERATING AN ADA IMPLEMENTATION

The recovered design was used to develop an Ada implementation of the ADC program. Because the design had been recovered from a Fortran program, using a different language to reimplement the program served to test the adequacy of the recovered design. This step revealed many of the shortcomings of the recovered design that were discussed in the previous section.

The software development environment used to record the design was used to generate Ada data declarations from the data structure diagrams. The shared memory area data structure chart was converted into Ada data declarations and then placed in a package declaration. Structure chart nodes were converted into Ada procedure declarations using an Ada procedure declaration template. The associated PDL was inserted into the procedure body. The PDL was then manually translated into Ada.

It was during the translation of the PDL into Ada that the Fortran implementation dependencies were noticed. A fundamental property of software designs, as they are normally created in forward engineering, is that a design should be free of constraints imposed by an implementation language or the implementation phase. An important problem in reverse engineering is recognizing effects of implementation phase decisions on the program. Such decisions are imposed on an implementor by the implementation language, the operating system, the machine architecture, etc. However, the effects of these decisions should not be recovered in the design. Identifying or unravelling such effects proved to be difficult.

For example, the Fortran code contained a call to a system function that returned a status value when completed. The calling interface of this system function was recovered. The data type of the status variable was integer; this plus the purpose of the variable was recovered. In Ada, the same system function had a different name and interface. It was no longer a function but a procedure, and the status variable was passed as a parameter. The status variable no longer had a type of integer. Its Ada type was COND_VALUE_TYPE. In addition, the value of the status variable was checked in several IF statements. In Fortran the condition tests had the form if (variable) then.... Because the Ada version of the variable was not of type boolean the condition tests in Ada had to be rewritten to check against a specific value.

This example points out that data type information should be represented in an abstract way that emphasizes the purpose of the data as much as its range of values. During the implementation phase the decision can be made about which language-supported data type will be most suitable to express a design-specified data type.

The strong Fortran bias in the recovered PDL could have been reduced by creating a new structure chart and PDL from the recovered data-flow and control-flow models. These models were further removed from the original source code and were less biased by the implementation than the recovered detailed design. By recreating the detailed design from the recovered high-level design, a new language-independent detailed design could have been produced. However, this is equivalent to redesigning the program, which may not be desirable. It is more desirable to do a better job of recognizing implementation details and not recovering them.

Another issue raised by the recovered design was the effect of efficiency concerns during the implementation phase. Programmers often write complicated code sections to achieve better run-time performance. During design recovery these complicated code sections affect the recovered design. The problem is to identify such code

E. J. BYRNE

sections. One solution is to restructure these code sections to be cleaner and easier to understand. The question is when should this be done? Should it be before recovery, during recovery, i.e. not changing the current implementation, but recovering a cleaner design, or after the recovery process has been completed? The issue was not resolved.

CONCLUSIONS

This paper has presented a procedure for reconstructing the design of an existing software system. This procedure was used to reconstruct and document the design of a program. The recovered design was recorded in a software development environment and used to develop a new implementation of the program. The experiences and observations gained during this work have been described in the preceding sections. Several issues have been identified and these are summarized in the following paragraphs.

1. *Implementation bias.* Perhaps the most important issue in recovering a design is to separate design information from implementation information. At the implementation level it can be difficult to recognize what information should not be recorded in the recovered design. It can be difficult to 'throw away' information during the abstraction process, particularly, when the goal is to reimplement the system. It is necessary to realize that the design does not serve as program documentation. Program documentation reflects the implementation details of the source code. Design documentation reflects a higher-level view of 'how' a program functions. Implementation details that need to be watched for are data item names, basic data types, data structuring, system interfaces, code sections written to be efficient, code that is biased by the underlying computer architecture and code whose expression was biased by the original implementation language.

2. *Traceability.* A recovered design should record links between recovered information and the original sources. This permits traceability between the recovered design and the original implementation. This experiment has shown that an existing software development environment can be used to record a recovered design. However, such a tool must provide the flexibility to record information not envisioned when the tool was created.

3. *Domain information.* The information recorded in a program is sufficient to explain 'what' is being done, but not 'why'. To understand the significance of a processing step, deeper information is often required. This information is often not recorded in the source code or existing documentation. An understanding of the application domain can aid the recovery of information about the purpose of a function and its significance.

4. *Re-engineering.* Reverse engineering will most often be done on older software systems whose documentation is out-of-date or non-existent. Such systems will often be candidates for re-engineering: rewriting the system to improve its understandability, ease maintenance, remove dead code, etc. It is easier to change a design than source code. When should design changes occur: as the design is recovered or afterwards? It seems reasonable to change the recovered design. This way the recovered design describes the current system. The recovered high-level design will be updated and a new detailed design generated.

A new version of the system generated from this design can be developed using modern techniques and programming languages. This will result in a system that is better structured, documented, and more easily maintained than the previous version. Thus, reverse engineering as a part of re-engineering will prove to be useful in extending the life of older programs.

5. *Existing documentation.* One last issue is the use of comments and existing documentation. These sources of information may be out-dated or incorrect. They must be used carefully. They can provide useful information about a program, but they can also be misleading or wrong. The source code is the final statement about what the program actually does.

In summary, this experiment was successful in identifying several issues in software reverse engineering. It is hoped that further investigation into these issues will result in a methodology for software reverse engineering and aid in the development of tools to support this task.

ACKNOWLEDGEMENTS

Research sponsored by the Air Force Office of Scientific Research/AFSC, United States Air Force, under Contract F49620-88-C-0053. The United States Government is authorized to reproduce and distribute reprints for governmental purposes notwithstanding any copyright notation here on.

REFERENCES

1. E. J. Chikofsky and J. H. Cross II, 'Reverse engineering and design recovery: a taxonomy', *IEEE Software*, **7** (1), 13–17 (1990).
2. S. C. Choi and W. Scacchi, 'Extracting and restructuring the design of large systems', *IEEE Software*, **7**(1), 66–71 (1990).
3. Y. F. Chen, M. Y. Nishimoto and C. V. Ramamoorthy, 'The C information abstraction system', *IEEE Trans. Software Engineering*, **SE-16**, (3), 325–334 (1990).
4. J. R. Cordy, N. L. Eliot and M. G. Robertson, 'Turing Tool: a user interface to aid in the software maintenance task', *IEEE Trans. Software Engineering*, **SE-16**,(3), 294–301 (1990).
5. J. A. Ricketts, J. C. DelMonaco and M. W. Weeks, 'Data reengineering for application systems', *Conference on Software Maintenance*, Miami Florida, 16–19 October 1989, pp. 174–179.
6. T. J. Biggerstaff, 'Design recovery for maintenance and reuse', *Computer*, **22**(7), 36–49 (1989).
7. I. Sommerville, *Software Engineering*, 3rd edn, Addison Wesley, 1989.
8. R. N. Charette, *Software Engineering Environments: Concepts and Technology*, Intertext Publications, Inc, New York, 1986.
9. R. A. Converse and M. J. Bassman, 'Conversion to Ada: does it really make sense?', *Avionics Panel Symposium: Software Engineering and Its Application to Avionics*, AGARD-NATO, Cesme Turkey, 25–29 April 1988, paper 8.
10. R. C. Waters, 'Program translation via abstraction and reimplementation', *IEEE Trans. Software Engineering*, **14**(8), 1207–1228, (1988).
11. P. J. L. Wallis, 'Automatic language conversion and its place in the transition to Ada', *ACM Ada Letters (Proceedings of the Ada International Conference, Paris France, 1985)*, **V**(2), 275–284, (1985).
12. H. M. Sneed, 'Software renewal: a case study', *IEEE Software*, **1**(3), 56–63 (1984).
13. R. N. Britcher and J. J. Craig, 'Using modern design practices to upgrade aging software systems', *IEEE Software*, **3**(3), 16–24 (1986).
14. P. Antonini, P. Benedusi, G. Cantone and A. Cimitile, 'Maintenance and reverse engineering: low-level design documents production and improvement', *Conference on Software Maintenance*, Austin Texas, 21–24 September 1987, pp. 91–100.
15. E. Yourdon and L. L. Constantine, *Structured Design: Fundamentals of a Discipline of Computer Program and Systems Design*, Prentice-Hall, 1979.

1364

16. D. J. Hatley and I. A. Pirbhai, *Strategies for Real-Time System Specification*, Dorset House Publishing, 1987.
17. P. Benedusi, A. Cimitile and U. De Carlini, 'A reverse engineering methodology to reconstruct hierarchical data flow diagrams for software maintenance', *Conference on Software Maintenance*, 16–19 October 1989, pp. 180–189.

IEEE TRANSACTIONS ON SOFTWARE ENGINEERING, VOL. 14, NO. 8, AUGUST 1988

Program Translation via Abstraction and Reimplementation

RICHARD C. WATERS, SENIOR MEMBER, IEEE

Abstract—Essentially all program translators (both source-to-source translators and compilers) operate via transliteration and refinement. The source program is first transliterated into the target language on a statement-by-statement basis. Various refinements are then applied in order to improve the quality of the output. Although acceptable in many situations, this approach is fundamentally limited in the quality of the output it can produce. In particular, it tends to be insufficiently sensitive to global features of the source program and too sensitive to irrelevant local details.

This paper presents an alternate translation paradigm—abstraction and reimplementation. Using this paradigm, the source program is first analyzed in order to obtain a programming-language-independent abstract understanding of the computation performed by the program as a whole. The program is then reimplemented in the target language based on this understanding. The key to this approach is the abstract understanding obtained. It allows the translator to see the forest for the trees, benefiting from an appreciation of the global features of the source program without being distracted by irrelevant details.

Translation via abstraction and reimplementation is one of the goals of the Programmer's Apprentice project. A translator which translates Cobol programs into Hibol (a very-high-level business data processing language) has been constructed. A compiler which generates extremely efficient PDP-11 object code for Pascal programs has been designed. Currently, work is proceeding toward the implementation of a general-purpose, knowledge-based translator.

Index Terms—Artificial intelligence, compilation, program analysis, Programmer's Apprentice, program translation.

I. INTRODUCTION

THE goal of this paper is to present the idea of translation via abstraction and reimplementation and to compare it to the standard approach of translation via transliteration and refinement. In the main, this is done through a discussion of the basic ideas behind the two approaches and a discussion of the designs for two translators based on abstraction and reimplementation. In addition, the paper presents a detailed description of an implemented prototype translator which demonstrates the efficacy of the abstraction and reimplementation approach. In order to emphasize the fact that translation via abstraction and reimplementation applies equally well to source-to-source translation and to compilation, examples of both are shown.

The process of program translation takes a program written in some source language and creates an equivalent program in some target language. The primary goal of translation is to create a syntactically correct program in the target language which computes the same thing as the source program in more or less the same way. For a wide variety of source and target languages, satisfying this goal is relatively straightforward.

In addition to the primary goal of correctness, translation typically has one or more subsidiary goals such as efficiency or readability of the target program. In general, the most difficult aspect of translation is not producing correct output, but rather attempting to satisfy these subsidiary goals. The main problem is that typically the subsidiary goals of translation are at best orthogonal to, and at worst in conflict with, the goals of the original authors of the source program.

Translations vary widely in quality. An optimal translation would produce the program which the original authors would have produced had they been writing in the target language in the first place and had they had the desired subsidiary goals in mind.

An important application of program translation is source-to-source program translation. In this situation, a program is translated from a language which may be in some way obsolete into another language where it can be more easily maintained. In source-to-source translation, the key subsidiary goal is achieving readability (and hence maintainability) of the target program. The use of automatic translation during maintenance has been severely limited by the fact that readability of the target program is very difficult to achieve.

An even more common example of program tanslation is compilation, the translation of a program written in a high-level language into machine language. In compilation, the key subsidiary goal is achieving efficiency in the target program. The work on compilers has demonstrated that acceptable efficiency can be obtained. However, there is still a long way to go. Even the best optimizing compilers fall short of the efficiency which programmers can achieve writing directly in machine language.

Most current program translators operate by a process which could be called translation via *transliteration and refinement*. In this process, the source program is first

Manuscript received November 29, 1985; revised January 31, 1986. This work was supported in part by the Advanced Research Projects Agency of the Department of Defense under Office of Naval Research Contract N00014-80-C-0505, in part by the National Science Foundation under Grants MCS-7912179 and MCS-8117633, and in part by the International Business Machines Corporation.

The author is with the Artificial Intelligence Laboratory, Massachusetts Institute of Technology, Cambridge, MA 02139.

IEEE Log Number 8822011.

SoftWARE RESTRUCTURING AND TRANSLATION

1208　　　　　　　　　　IEEE TRANSACTIONS ON SOFTWARE ENGINEERING, VOL. 14, NO. 8, AUGUST 1988

transliterated into the target language on a line-by-line basis by translating each line in isolation. Various refinements are then applied in order to improve the target program produced. As discussed in Section II, this process
has a number of advantages. However, it is inherently
limited in the extent to which it can satisfy the subsidiary
goals of translation. In particular, translation via transliteration and refinement tends to be insufficiently sensitive
to global features of the source program and too sensitive
to irrelevant local details of the source program.

Section III presents an alternative approach to program
translation–translation via *abstraction and reimplementation*. In this process, the source program is first analyzed in order to obtain a programming-language-independent abstract description of the computation being
performed. The program is then reimplemented in the target language based on the abstract description. The central feature of this approach is the abstraction step. It allows the translator to benefit from a global understanding
of what the source program does. In addition, the abstraction step deliberately discards information about details
of the source program which are not relevant to the translation process. Although inherently more complex than
translation via transliteration and refinement, translation
via abstraction and reimplementation is capable of producing very-high-quality results.

Sections IV and V present examples of program translators which operate via abstraction and reimplementation. The first example translator (Satch [10]) is a prototype system which translates Cobol programs into Hibol.
(Hibol is a very-high-level, nonprocedural, business data
processing language.) Satch is notable because it produces extremely readable output. The second example
(Cobbler [9]) is a proposed compiler which translates Pascal programs into PDP-11 assembler language. Cobbler
is notable because it produces extremely efficient output.

Section VI describes efforts within the Programmer's
Apprentice project [29] toward the construction of a general-purpose knowledge-based translation system operating via abstraction and reimplementation. In order to support very-high-quality translation, this system will have
extensive knowledge of how algorithms can be expressed
in the source and target languages. In order to make the
system general purpose, this knowledge will be represented declaratively in a library of algorithm schemas.
Each schema will specify how a class of algorithms can
be rendered in the source or target language.

Section VII discusses other work which is relevant to
the idea of translation via abstraction and reimplementation. In particular, research on natural language translation has shown that obtaining a global understanding of
the source text is essential for producing high-quality
translations.

II. TRANSLATION VIA TRANSLITERATION AND REFINEMENT

As shown in Fig. 1, translation via transliteration and
refinement operates in two steps. The transliteration step

Fig. 1. Translation via transliteration and refinement.

translates the source program on an element-by-element
basis. (The word *transliteration* (as opposed to *translation*) is used to connote the idea of literal translation where
each element is translated in isolation without regard for
context). The output of the transliteration step is expressed either directly in the target language or in an intermediate language which is semantically similar to it.

The refinement step takes the output of the transliteration step and applies various correctness-preserving transformations in order to improve its quality. For example,
compilers apply optimizations in order to improve the efficiency of the code produced. If the intermediate language is not identical to the target language, the refinement step also performs the (typically trivial) translation
from intermediate to final form.

A. Example of Transliteration and Refinement

As an example of translation via transliteration and refinement, consider how this approach could be used to
translate Fortran [35] programs into Ada [38] programs.
Fig. 2 shows a Fortran program BOUND, which is taken
from the IBM Fortran Scientific Subroutine Package [36].
Fig. 3 shows the result of the transliteration step of the
translation process. Fig. 4 shows the final result after the
refinement step of the translation process.

The program BOUND has six input parameters and four
output parameters. The input parameter A is a matrix
which contains a set of observations of a number of variables presumably determined in some experiment. The integer input parameters NO and NV specify the number of
observations and the number of variables, respectively.
(As is generally the case in the programs in the Scientific
Subroutine Package, although A is logically a matrix, it is
declared to be a vector, and all of the index computations
are explicit in the program.)

The input parameter S is a vector of length NO. The
vector S selects the observations which should be considered by the program BOUND. An observation J is considered only if S(J) is nonzero.

The input parameters BLO and BHI are vectors of length
NV. For each variable, these vectors specify lower and
upper bounds, respectively, for the observation values.
The integer output parameter IER is used to return an error
code. If BLO(I) > BHI(I) for any I, then IER is set to one,
and computation is aborted; otherwise, IER is set to zero.

The output parameters UNDER, BETW, and OVER are also
vectors of length NV. For each variable I, the program
BOUND counts how many of the selected observations are
under BLO(I), how many are between BLO(I) and BHI(I) inclusive, and how many are over BHI(I). These counts are
stored in the variables UNDER, BETW, and OVER, respec-

```
      SUBROUTINE BOUND(A,S,BLO,BHI,UNDER,BETW,OVER,NO,NV,IER)
      DIMENSION A(1),S(1),BLO(1),BHI(1),UNDER(1),BETW(1),OVER(1)
      IER = 0
      DO 10 I = 1, NV
      IF (BLO(I)-BHI(I)) 10,10,11
   11 IER = 1
      GO TO 12
   10 CONTINUE
      DO 1 K = 1, NV
      UNDER(K) = 0.0
      BETW(K) = 0.0
    1 OVER(K) = 0.0
      DO 8 J = 1, NO
      IJ = J-NO
      IF (S(J)) 2,8,2
    2 DO 7 I = 1, NV
      IJ = IJ+NO
      IF (A(IJ)-BLO(I)) 5,3,3
    3 IF (A(IJ)-BHI(I)) 4,4,6
    4 BETW(I) = BETW(I)+1.0
      GO TO 7
    5 UNDER(I) = UNDER(I)+1.0
      GO TO 7
    6 OVER(I) = OVER(I)+1.0
    7 CONTINUE
    8 CONTINUE
   12 RETURN
      END
```

Fig. 2. The Fortran program BOUND.

```
type VECTOR is array (INTEGER range <>) of REAL;

procedure BOUND(A,S,BLO,BHI,UNDER,BETW,OVER: in out VECTOR;
                NO,NV,IER: in out INTEGER) is
      I,IJ,J,K: INTEGER;
begin
      IER := 0;
      I := 1;
      loop;
          if BLO(I)-BHI(I)<=0.0 then goto L10;
          else goto L11;
          end if;
  <<L11>> IER := 1;
          goto L12;
  <<L10>> null;
          I := I+1;
          exit when I>NV;
      end loop;
      K := 1;
      loop
          UNDER(K) := 0.0;
          BETW(K) := 0.0;
  <<L1>> OVER(K) := 0.0;
          K := K+1;
          exit when K>NV;
      end loop;
      J := 1;
      loop
          IJ := J-NO;
          if S(J)=0.0 then goto L8;
          else goto L2;
          end if;
  <<L2>> I := 1;
          loop
              IJ := IJ+NO;
              if A(IJ)-BLO(I)<0.0 then goto L5;
              else goto L3;
              end if;
  <<L3>>    if A(IJ)-BHI(I)<=0.0 then goto L4;
              else goto L6;
              end if;
  <<L4>>    BETW(I) := BETW(I)+1.0;
              goto L7;
  <<L5>>    UNDER(I) := UNDER(I)+1.0;
              goto L7;
  <<L6>>    OVER(I) := OVER(I)+1.0;
  <<L7>>    null;
              I := I+1;
              exit when I>NV;
          end loop;
  <<L8>> null;
          J := J+1;
          exit when J>NO;
      end loop;
  <<L12>> return;
end BOUND;
```

Fig. 3. A transliteration of Fig. 2 into Ada.

```
type VECTOR is array (INTEGER range <>) of REAL;

procedure BOUND(A,S,BLO,BHI: VECTOR;
                UNDER,BETW,OVER: in out VECTOR;
                NO,NV: INTEGER; IER: out INTEGER) is
      I,IJ,J,K: INTEGER;
begin
      IER := 0;
      I := 1;
      loop
          if BLO(I)-BHI(I)<=0.0 then goto L10; end if;
          IER := 1;
          return;
  <<L10>> I := I+1;
          exit when I>NV;
      end loop;
      K := 1;
      loop;
          UNDER(K) := 0.0;
          BETW(K) := 0.0;
          OVER(K) := 0.0;
          K := K+1;
          exit when K>NV;
      end loop;
      J := 1;
      loop;
          IJ := J-NO;
          if S(J)=0.0 then goto L8; end if;
          I := 1;
          loop;
              IJ := IJ+NO;
              if A(IJ)-BLO(I)<0.0 then goto L5; end if;
              if A(IJ)-BHI(I)>0.0 then goto L6; end if;
              BETW(I) := BETW(I)+1.0;
              goto L7;
  <<L5>>    UNDER(I) := UNDER(I)+1.0;
              goto L7;
  <<L6>>    OVER(I) := OVER(I)+1.0;
  <<L7>>    I := I+1;
              exit when I>NV;
          end loop;
  <<L8>> J := J+1;
          exit when J>NO;
      end loop;
end BOUND;
```

Fig. 4. A refined transliteration of Fig. 2 into Ada.

tively, which are the principal outputs of the program BOUND.

The transliteration process is illustrated by Fig. 3. Each part of the program is translated locally. The Fortran parameters are all turned into "in out" parameters of appropriate types in the Ada program. They are given the mode "in out" because every Fortran parameter can potentially be both an input value and an output value. The Fortran assignment statements are converted into equivalent Ada assignments. This requires very little change because Fortran is essentially a subset of Ada when it comes to arithmetic expressions and assignment statements. Fortran arithmetic IFS are expanded into equivalent Ada "if then else" statements branching to the appropriate labels. Arithmetic IFS where two of the labels are the same are treated as special cases in order to avoid the need for temporary variables. Each Fortran DO is expanded into an equivalent Ada "loop." The Ada "for" construct cannot be used because Ada "for" tests for termination at the top of the loop, while Fortran DO tests for termination at the bottom of the loop. Fortran CONTINUE, RETURN, and GO TO are turned into Ada "null," "return," and "goto" respectively. The only aspect of the transliteration which is not totally local is that the Fortran program has to be scanned in order to determine what variables are used in the program so that appropriate variable declarations can be inserted at the beginning of the Ada program.

1210   IEEE TRANSACTIONS ON SOFTWARE ENGINEERING, VOL. 14, NO. 8, AUGUST 1988

As is typically the case with transliteration, the program in Fig. 3, although correct, does not do a good job of satisfying the subsidiary goals of translation (in this case readability). Fig. 4 shows the final result after the refinement step of the translation process.

Fig. 4 is derived from Fig. 3 by applying a number of correctness-preserving transformations. Complex "if then else" statements, which have clauses which branch to the next statement, are simplified to remove these clauses. The branch to a "return" statement is replaced by a "return" statement. Unnecessary "null" statements, "return" statements, and labels are removed. Instead of giving all the parameters the mode "in out," some of the parameters are given just the mode "out" or "in" (the default in Ada). This is done in a purely syntactic way by noting that parameters which are never assigned cannot be "out" and parameters which are never read cannot be "in."

There are a number of transformations which could, in principle, have been applied to the program which have not been. For example, the computation involving UNDER, BETW, and OVER could be rearranged into one large "if then else." However, in keeping with the kinds of refinements typically supported by source-to-source translators (see Section VII), two criteria were used in order to decide which refinements to perform. First, no support was provided for transformations which require either control flow or data flow analysis of the program. This rules out transformations like the one suggested above.

Second, the main emphasis was placed on transformations which look only at an adjacent pair of statements. The only transformation which is more complicated than this is the one which refines the mode of the parameters. This transformation has to scan the program in order to determine which parameters are read and assigned. However, it does not do an actual data flow analysis. If it did, it would realized that UNDER, BETW, and OVER are actually "out" parameters and not "in out" parameters since they cannot be read until after they have been assigned.

Fig. 4 is readable, but still not as good as one would like. In particular, it falls far short of the goal of producing the program the programmers would have produced had they been writing in Ada—it is a Fortran-style Ada program instead of an Ada-style Ada program. As will be discussed in Section III, better translations of Fig. 2 can be achieved using translation via abstraction and reimplementation.

Figs. 3 and 4 are not the output of any particular translator. Rather, they are hypothetical examples intended to illustrate the process of transliteration and refinement. However, it is not clear that any existing source-to-source translator produces output which is significantly better than that in Fig. 4 (see Section VII).

B. Advantages of Transliteration and Refinement

Translation via transliteration and refinement has several advantages. Most importantly, it uses a divide-and-conquer strategy in order to satisfy the goals of translation. The basic goal of obtaining a correct translation is achieved by the transliteration step. The refinement step need only guarantee that it preserves this correctness. The subsidiary goals of the translation (e.g., efficiency or readability) are achieved by the refinement step. The transliteration step is greatly simplified by not having to worry about the subsidiary goals.

Another advantage is that the localized nature of the transliteration step makes it easy to encode the basic knowledge needed for translation. This knowledge is economically represented by stating how each of the constructs in the source language should be converted into equivalent constructs in the target language. The transliteration step need not have any knowledge about how special combinations of source constructs can be represented as special combinations of target constructs. (This latter kind of knowledge is the province of the refinement step, which presumably knows how to fine tune cumbersome combinations of target constructs.)

A final advantage of translation via transliteration and refinement is that it makes it easy to construct families of translators which either share the same transliteration step or share the same refinement step. For example, one might construct a family of compilers which compile various high-level languages into the same machine language and which share the same refinement step.

C. Transliteration Is Not Always Practical

Although it works satisfactorily in many situations, translation via transliteration and refinement has some fundamental disadvantages. To begin with, it assumes that transliteration is practical. This in turn depends on the assumption that each of the source language constructs can be individually translated into target language constructs in a practical way. Unfortunately, this is not always the case.

The main way in which transliteration can be blocked is that the source language may support a primitive construct which is not supported by the target language. For example, consider translating from a language which supports GOTOS into a language which does not, or from a language which supports multiple assignments to a variable into a functional language which does not. In the case of Fortran and Ada, consider the fact that Ada has nothing which is equivalent to the Fortran EQUIVALENCE statement.

The primary source of incompleteness in current translators is primitive constructs which cannot be transliterated. Current translators typically just ignore nontransliteratable constructs, either refusing to process source programs which contain them or copying them unchanged from the source to the target. Human intervention is required either to remove them from the source or to fix them up in the target.

A second way in which transliteration can be blocked is that the source and target languages may have constructs which, although they correspond closely, differ in significant semantic details. Most of the time these details may not matter for translation. However, when they matter, they are liable to matter a lot. For example, consider translating into a language which forces complex data structures to be copied when they are assigned to a variable from a language which does not, or between languages which differ in their variable scoping rules. In the case of Fortran and Ada, consider the fact that vector arguments to Fortran subroutines are passed by reference, while Ada specifies that it is undefined whether or not vector arguments will be copies or passed by reference.

The primary source of incorrectness in current translators is constructs which can be transliterated straightforwardly most of the time, but ony with great difficulty (or not at all) in certain hard-to-detect situations. Current translators typically just use the straightforward transliteration all of the time without giving any indication that there might be a problem. (For example, the transliteration in Fig. 3 blindly assumes that it does not matter how the vector parameters get passed.) Human intervention is required in order to correct any problems which arise in the target program produced.

D. Transliteration Complicates Refinement

The principal virtue of the transliteration and refinement approach is that it simplifies the problem of satisfying the primary goal of translation (i.e., correctness) by factoring out the problem of satisfying the subsidiary goals of translation. Unfortunately, this factoring typically complicates the task of satisfying the subsidiary goals. This is particularly unfortunate since the subsidiary goals are usually harder to satisfy than the primary goal.

The basic reason why translation via transliteration and refinement complicates the task of satisfying the subsidiary goals of translation is that typically the process of transliteration does not merely ignore the subsidiary goals, it works against them. Simply put, whether or not the original source program is *good* from the point of view of the subsidiary goals of the translation, the output of the transliteration step is almost always guaranteed to be *bad* from this point of view.

The most obvious way in which transliteration makes things difficult for later refinement is that, more often than not, the transliteration of a given construct in the source language requires the use of a circumlocution in the target language. The only time when this can be completely avoided is when the target language possesses a semantically identical construct. Examples of both of these cases can be seen in Fig. 3. The DO loops in the Fortran program are converted into cumbersome ''loop'' statements in the Ada program. In contrast, the assignment statements remain essentially unchanged.

A more subtle way in which transliteration makes things difficult for later refinement is that it tends to obscure the key features of the algorithm implemented by the program being translated. Transliteration does this through both camouflage and the creation of decoys. The mass of circumlocutions produced by transliteration acts as camouflage hiding the key features. Decoys (features which are prominent, but actually unimportant) are created because the code produced is sensitive to unimportant details of the source. For example, Fig. 3 would have looked quite different if the Fortran programmer had used logical IFs instead of arithmetic IFs. A kind of indirect camouflage is produced because the transliteration step is insensitive to global considerations. Transliteration typically renders a given construct in exactly the same way even if the context suggests that it should be translated differently. For example, all of the parameters are given the mode ''in out'' in Fig. 3 whether or not this is actually necessary given the way they are used.

A final way in which transliteration makes things difficult for later refinement is that useful information about the source program can get lost. As an example of this, consider translating from a language (such as Ada) where the order of evaluation of the arguments of a function call is undefined to a language where the order is defined. In this situation, straightforward transliteration will define an evaluation order and thereby discard the information that many evaluation orders are equally acceptable. This loss of information makes it hard for the refinement step to apply transformations which are not applicable to the chosen evaluation order, but which are applicable to one of the evaluation orders which was not chosen.

E. Applicability of Transliteration and Refinement

The primary requirement for the applicability of translation via transliteration and refinement is that transliteration must be practical. For this to be the case, the target language must support all of the primitive constructs supported by the source language. In general, this implies that the target language must be at a lower level than the source language, i.e., have a wider variety of primitive constructs. This is why the arrow in Fig. 1 between the source and the intermediate language is drawn pointing downward.

Translation via transliteration and refinement is perhaps most applicable to compilation because any primitive construct can be expressed in machine language. In constrast, source-to-source translators typically have to restrict the input language and/or admit possibly incorrect translations in order to make transliteration practical.

A second limitation on the applicability of translation via transliteration and refinement is that refinement is an inherently difficult task which transliteration makes more difficult. As a result, the transliteration and refinement approach is more applicable in situations where the subsidiary goals of translation are not too stringent.

Transliteration and refinement works well in a straightforward compiler where readability of the output is not an issue and only moderate efficiency is required in the out-

1212   IEEE TRANSACTIONS ON SOFTWARE ENGINEERING, VOL. 14, NO. 8, AUGUST 1988

put code. In order to achieve significantly higher levels of efficiency in the output code, optimizing compilers expend a large amount of effort on refinement.

III. TRANSLATION VIA ABSTRACTION AND REIMPLEMENTATION

As shown in Fig. 5, translation via abstraction and reimplementation operates in two steps. The abstraction step performs a global analysis of the source program. The goal of this analysis is to obtain an understanding of the algorithms being used by the program. In particular, it throws away language-specific syntactic information so that it can represent the essential semantic features of the program in a way which is independent of both the source and target languages.

The reimplementation step takes the abstract description produced by the abstraction step and creates a program in the target language which implements this description. In order to simplify this task, the abstract description is designed so that it contains exactly the right kind of information needed in order to guide the reimplementation process.

The basic difference between translation via transliteration and refinement and translation via abstraction and reimplementation can be seen by comparing the shapes of Figs. 1 and 5. The transliteration and refinement approach translates directly into the target language. In contrast, the abstraction and reimplementation approach first translates the source program up to a very-high-level programming-language-independent description and then translates this description down to the target language.

Like translation via transliteration and refinement, translation via abstraction and reimplementation uses a divide-and-conquer strategy to attack the translation task. However, it divides the translation task differently. The transliteration and refinement approach separates the problem of satisfying the primary goal of translation from the problem of satisfying the subsidiary goals of translation. In contrast, the abstraction and reimplementation approach separates knowledge of the source language from knowledge of the target language.

A. Example of Abstraction and Reimplementation

As an example of translation via abstraction and reimplementation, consider how this approach could be used to translate the Fortran program in Fig. 2 into Ada. The first step is to obtain an abstract description of the computation in Fig. 2. Fig. 6 shows the key elements of such an abstract description.

Fig. 6 is divided into three parts. The first part lists the parameters of the program BOUND and their types as specified in the original Fortran program. (By convention, the Scientific Subroutine Package uses the dimension specification v(1) to specify a vector of unknown length rather than a vector of length one.) A complete data flow analysis of the program is used in order to determine which parameters are "in" and which are "out." This analysis

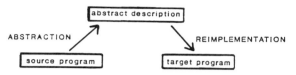

Fig. 5. Translation via abstraction and reimplementation.

reveals that UNDER, BETW, and OVER are never read before they are written and are therefore "out" parameters.

The second part of Fig. 6 lists a number of constraints which must be satisfied in order for the program BOUND to produce reasonable results. The first seven constraints state that the ranges of the various vector parameters must be large enough to prevent referencing memory locations outside of the vectors. These constraints are determined by looking at the largest values which the various index variables in the program can reach.

The last two constraints specify that the parameters NO and NV must be positive and therefore that the vector parameters must have a positive extent. These are particularly interesting constraints because they imply that Ada "for" loops can be used when translating the program. The constraints follow from the observation that a Fortran DO loop which enumerates the elements of an array does not operate correctly when given an array of zero extent. The problem is that the body of a Fortran DO loop is always executed at least once, even if the limits placed on the DO variable suggest that zero executions would be more appropriate. (This feature of DO is occasionally used in a constructive way by Fortran DO loops which do not enumerate the elements of arrays.)

The third part of Fig. 6 describes the computation performed by the program. The first two lines specify that the program checks to see that every element of BLO is less than or equal to the corresponding element of BHI. If this is true, then IER is set to zero. Otherwise, IER is set to one, and the program is terminated.

The remainder of Fig. 6 describes the main computation performed by the program BOUND in terms of recurrence equations. The main body of the program is a doubly nested loop iterating over the index variables J and I. The various evaluations of the body of the inner loop can be referred to in terms of the corresponding values of the index variables. The notation $x_{m,n}$ is used to refer to the value of the variable x at the end of the evaluation of the inner loop body, during which the outer loop index has the value m and the inner loop index has the value n. The recurrence equations specify how variable values corresponding to a given evaluation of the inner loop body are computed from values corresponding to earlier evaluations. The recurrence equations are derived by inspecting the data flow in the loops. As part of this process, the middle loop in the Fortran code is revealed to be part of the initialization for the main loop in the program.

The fact that Fig. 6 is shown in a textual form is not intended to imply that the abstract description would actually be represented textually. For example, it might take

```
PARAMETERS:
   in A,S,BLO,BHI: vector of real
   out UNDER,BETW,OVER: vector of real
   in NO,NV: integer
   out IER: integer
CONSTRAINTS:
   A'RANGE⊇1..NV*NO,   S'RANGE⊇1..NO,
   BLO'RANGE⊇1..NV,   BHI'RANGE⊇1..NV,
   UNDER'RANGE⊇1..NV,   BETW'RANGE⊇1..NV,   OVER'RANGE⊇1..NV,
   NO≥1,   NV≥1
COMPUTATION:
   if (∀ I∈1..NV BLO(I)≤BHI(I)) then IER=0
      else IER=1 ∧ computation is aborted
   The main computation is a doubly nested loop
      The outer index (first subscript) counts from 1 to NO
      The inner index (second subscript) counts from 1 to NV
      The variables assigned within the loops have the following values:
      ∀ j∈1..NO, i∈1..NV, K∈1..NV
```

$$IJ_{j,0} = j - NO$$
$$IJ_{j,i} = IJ_{j,i-1} + NO$$
$$UNDER(K)_{0,i} = 0.0$$

```
      if K=i ∧ S(j)≠0.0 ∧ A(IJ_{j,i}) < BLO(i)
```
$$then\ UNDER(K)_{j,i} = 1.0 + UNDER(K)_{j-1,i}$$
$$else\ UNDER(K)_{j,i} = UNDER(K)_{j-1,i}$$
$$BETW(K)_{0,i} = 0.0$$

```
      if K=i ∧ S(j)≠0.0 ∧ BLO(i) ≤ A(IJ_{j,i}) ≤ BHI(i)
```
$$then\ BETW(K)_{j,i} = 1.0 + BETW(K)_{j-1,i}$$
$$else\ BETW(K)_{j,i} = BETW(K)_{j-1,i}$$
$$OVER(K)_{0,i} = 0.0$$

```
      if K=i ∧ S(j)≠0.0 ∧ BHI(i) < A(IJ_{j,i})
```
$$then\ OVER(K)_{j,i} = 1.0 + OVER(K)_{j-1,i}$$
$$else\ OVER(K)_{j,i} = OVER(K)_{j-1,i}$$

Fig. 6. An abstract description of Fig. 2.

the form of logical expressions annotating a data flow graph representing the program.

· Based on the abstract description in Fig. 6, it is a straightforward matter to create a quality translation of the program BOUND into Ada as shown in Fig. 7. The parameters are made parameters in the code with the specified types. The recurrence equations map directly into a triply nested loop. Transformations similar to those used by an optimizing compiler can be used to get rid of the unnecessary innermost loop over K and to move the test S(J)/=0.0 out to the outermost loop since it is an invariant in the inner loop.

A comparison of Fig. 7 with Fig. 4 shows that the translation in Fig. 7 is superior in several respects. Most notably, the parameters have all been given the correct modes; labels and "goto" statements have been eliminated in favor of complex "if then else" statements, and "for" loops have been used.

Some of the improvements which are seen in Fig. 7 could have been achieved in Fig. 4 if local refinement had been applied more aggressively. For example, it is plausible that local transformations could have been used to combine the simple "if then else" statements in Fig. 4 with the statements following them in order to create the "if then else" statements shown in Fig. 7.

However, improvements such as determining the proper modes for the parameters and utilizing "for" loops depend critically on an understanding of the program as a whole. These changes cannot be made until after a global analysis of the program has determined that the changes are valid.

Although Fig. 7 is a good translation of Fig. 2 into Ada,

```
type VECTOR is array (INTEGER range <>) of REAL;
procedure BOUND(A,S,BLO,BHI: VECTOR;
                UNDER,BETW,OVER: out VECTOR;
                NO,NV: INTEGER; IER: out INTEGER) is
   I,IJ,J,K: INTEGER;
begin
   IER := 0;
   for I in 1..NV loop
      if BLO(I)>BHI(I) then IER := 1; return; end if;
   end loop;
   for K in 1..NV loop
      UNDER(K) := 0.0;
      BETW(K)  := 0.0;
      OVER(K)  := 0.0;
   end loop;
   for J in 1..NO loop
      if S(J)/=0.0 then
         IJ := J-NO;
         for I in 1..NV loop
            IJ := IJ+NO;
            if A(IJ)<BLO(I) then UNDER(I) := UNDER(I)+1.0;
            elsif BHI(I)<A(IJ) then OVER(I) := OVER(I)+1.0;
            else BETW(I) := BETW(I)+1.0;
            end if;
         end loop;
      end if;
   end loop;
end BOUND;
```

Fig. 7. A translation of Fig. 2 into Ada based on Fig. 6.

it is still far from optimal. Appropriate Ada-style constructs have been used; however, the result is still essentially a Fortran-style program. In particular, the fact that A is really a matrix, but is declared to be a vector, and the fact that the various vector parameters may have ranges which are larger than the ranges indicated by the parameters NO and NV is in the style of the Fortran Scientific Subroutine Package, but it is not in the style of Ada.

Fig. 7 is shown as it is because it is just about the best translation which can be achieved if the parameters and their types are required to remain the same as in the Fortran program. In addition, it illustrates the kind of translation which can be achieved by using an abstract representation which is only moderately abstract.

B. Example of Increased Abstraction

Figs. 8 and 9 show a translation of the program BOUND into Ada which is better than the one shown in Fig. 7 and the abstract description on which it is based. There are two fundamental ways in which the translation shown in these figures is different from the one shown in Figs. 6 and 7.

First, Figs. 8 and 9 assume that the program BOUND and all the programs which call it are being translated together. (This is an assumption which can often be made, but which also quite often cannot be made. It depends on the exact context of the translation task.)

When joint translation of a program and its callers is possible, it opens up two new avenues of attack on the translation problem. The programs which call BOUND can be inspected in order to obtain additional information about BOUND. The interface to the program BOUND can be altered in order to render the program more aesthetically in Ada.

In Fig. 8, it is assumed that an analysis of the programs which call BOUND shows that BOUND is called only with vectors which have the exact sizes indicated by the parameters NO and NV. This makes it possible to tighten up the constraints in the description and to eliminate all mention of the variables NO and NV in favor of using the Ada array attribute "RANGE" applied to the parameters.

The second fundamental difference between Figs. 8 and 9 and Figs. 6 and 7 is that Fig. 8 is significantly more abstract than Fig. 6. The computations being performed are described in terms of their net effects. The computations involving UNDER, BETW, and OVER are described as computing a count of elements of A which have certain properties. The variable S is described as a vector of flags which are tested. A is described directly as a matrix, and no mention is made of the variable IJ. The computation involving IER is summarized by stating that the computation is aborted and an error is signaled if the first constraint is violated. No mention is made of how this might be done.

The key to the increase in abstraction in Fig. 8 is the ability to *recognize* the net effects of a computation. This in turn depends on the abstraction component having a significant amount of knowledge about what kinds of computations can be performed. For example, it can presumably recognize that the recurrence equations in Fig. 6 compute counts and that the computation involving the variable IJ converts matrix indexes to vector indexes. Similarly, it can recognize that the computation involving the variable IER reflects the standard way that error conditions are signaled in the Fortran scientific subroutine library.

Based on Fig. 8, the reimplementation step can produce a much better program (see Fig. 9) than the one shown in Fig. 7 because it has fewer restrictions placed on it. It can

```
LOGICAL INPUTS:
   A matrix of real
   S vector of flag
   BLO,BHI vector of real
LOGICAL OUTPUTS:
   UNDER,BETW,OVER vector of count
   error signaled (and computation aborted) if constraint (1) is violated
CONSTRAINTS:
  (1) ∀ I∈BLO'RANGE BLO(I)≤BHI(I)
  (2) A'RANGE(1)=BLO'RANGE=BHI'RANGE=UNDER'RANGE=BETW'RANGE=OVER'RANGE
  (3) A'RANGE(2)=S'RANGE
COMPUTATION:
   ∀ I∈UNDER'RANGE
      UNDER(I) = count-of {J∈S'RANGE | S(J) ∧ A(I,J)<BLO(I)}
   ∀ I∈BETW'RANGE
      BETW(I) = count-of {J∈S'RANGE | S(J) ∧ BLO(I)≤A(I,J)≤BHI(I)}
   ∀ I∈OVER'RANGE
      OVER(I) = count-of {J∈S'RANGE | S(J) ∧ BHI(I)<A(I,J)}
```

Fig. 8. A more abstract description of Fig. 2.

```
type VECTOR is array (INTEGER range <>) of REAL;
type BOOLS is array (INTEGER range <>) of BOOLEAN;
type VECT is array (INTEGER range <>) of INTEGER;
type MATRIX is array (INTEGER range <>, INTEGER range <>) of REAL;
procedure BOUND(A: MATRIX; S: BOOLS; BLO,BHI: VECTOR;
                UNDER,BETW,OVER: out VECT) is
      I,J: INTEGER;
begin
      for I in BLO'RANGE loop
         if BLO(I)>BHI(I) then raise CONSTRAINT_ERROR; end if;
      end loop;
      UNDER := (UNDER'RANGE => 0);
      BETW  := (BETW'RANGE => 0);
      OVER  := (OVER'RANGE => 0);
      for J in A'RANGE(2) loop
         if S(J) then
            for I in A'RANGE(1) loop
               if A(I,J)<BLO(I) then UNDER(I) := UNDER(I)+1;
               elsif BHI(I)<A(I,J) then OVER(I) := OVER(I)+1;
               else BETW(I) := BETW(I)+1;
               end if;
            end loop;
         end if;
      end loop;
end BOUND;
```

Fig. 9. A translation of Fig. 2 into Ada based on Fig. 8.

choose better parameters and better types because the abstract description does not require that the parameters and types be the same as in the Fortran program. It is free to implement the error signaling using standard Ada methods, i.e., by raising an exception instead of returning an error value, which has to be explicitly checked by the caller. The parameter A can be operated on as a matrix instead of as a vector. Due to the stronger constraints on the length of the vectors, array literals can be used to initialize the vectors UNDER, BETW, and OVER instead of a loop.

In some situations, the added freedom does not cause any change in the translation. For example, the reimplementation step could have computed the counts in several different ways. However, none of these methods would have been any better than the one shown in Fig. 7, so the same method was used in Fig. 9.

There is a price which has to be paid in order to get the improved translation shown in Fig. 9. Analysis is made more complicated by the need to recognize the net effects of the computation being performed. In addition, reimplementation is made more complicated because there are more implementation decisions which have to be made.

Figs. 6–9 are not produced by an particular translator. Rather, they are hypothetical examples intended to illustrate the process of abstraction and reimplementation. In particular, they demonstrate that increased abstraction leads to improved translation. In the limit, it is possible to create a translation which compares favorably to the program the programmers would have written had they been writing in the target language.

C. Advantages of Abstraction and Reimplementation

The most important advantage of translation via abstraction and reimplementation is that, while translation via transliteration and refinement is, in essence, designed to facilitate achieving the primary goal of translation (i.e., correctness), translation via abstraction and reimplementation is specifically designed to facilitate achieving the subsidiary goals of translation. As discussed in Section II, transliteration creates many problems for later refinement. In contrast, the sole purpose of abstraction is to simplify later reimplementation. Sections IV and V give extended examples of the way in which abstraction and reimplementation can cooperate in order to produce high-quality translation.

A second important advantage of translation via abstraction and reimplementation is that it is not limited by the practicality of transliteration. As discussed in Section II, the local nature of transliteration can cause it to be blocked even though overall translation is possible. In constrast, there is no a priori reason for abstraction ever to be blocked since the result of abstraction is not constrained by the target language. Further, reimplementation need not be blocked as long as overall translation is possible.

A final virtue of translation via abstraction and reimplementation is that it lends itself to the construction of families of translators which share components at least as well as translation via transliteration and refinement, if not better. In this regard, note that designing an abstract representation which is compatible with a diverse set of target languages is easier than designing a target-like intermediate language which is compatible with them.

D. Disadvantages of Abstraction and Reimplementation

Like translation via transliteration and refinement, translation via abstraction and reimplementation has a fundamental problem of incompleteness. Unlike transliteration, abstraction and reimplementation is always possible as long as translation is possible. However, it would not be reasonable to assume that these processes will always be practical. When they are not, a translator will have to fall back on some other method of translation. For example, it might use transliteration (or ask for human assistance) in order to translate those parts of a program which could not be usefully abstracted and/or reimplemented.

A key issue then is the percentage of a typical source program that can be practically abstracted and reimplemented. This question can be answered only in the context of a particular application. However, two general statements can be made. First, any particular deficiency in abstraction or reimplementation can be rectified by adding more knowledge to the abstraction and reimplementation modules. Second, the limits of abstraction and reimplementation are essentially orthogonal to the limits of transliteration. Therefore, a translator which uses abstraction and reimplementation and which falls back on transliteration should always be more complete than one which uses transliteration alone.

Another disadvantage of the abstraction and reimplementation approach is that it is more complicated than transliteration and refinement. All in all, in situations where transliteration is practical and little refinement is necessary, translation via transliteration and refinement is probably the approach of choice. However, in situations where transliteration is not practical or where translation is subject to stringent subsidiary goals, translation via abstraction and reimplementation can succeed in producing high-quality output where translation via transliteration and refinement would fail.

IV. SATCH—TRANSLATING FROM COBOL TO HIBOL

Faust's Satch system [10] uses abstraction and reimplementation in order to attack a problem which is particularly difficult for translation by transliteration and refinement—translation from a low-level programming language to a high-level programming language. There are two key problems with this kind of translation. First, transliteration is usually not practical. Second, the subsidiary goal of such a translation is readability, which is an exceptionally difficult goal to satisfy well.

In the case of Satch, the source language is Cobol [37], and the target language is Hibol [20]. The motivation behind the translation performed by Satch is the desire to convert preexisting Cobol programs into a form where they can be more easily maintained. The benefits of the translation are illustrated by the fact that the resulting Hibol program can be as much as an order of magnitude shorter than the original Cobol program.

Hibol is a special-purpose business data processing language. It is a very-high-level, nonprocedural, single-assignment language based on the concept of a *flow*. A flow is a multidimensional aggregate of data values which are indexed by one or more keys. Each Hibol statement specifies how a flow is computed from other flows. This is done by specifying how a typical element of the output flow is computed from typical elements of the input flows. An important advantage of Hibol is that both file I/O and iteration over the elements of flows are implicit in a Hibol program and therefore do not have to be explicitly specified by the programmer. Fig. 11 (which will be discussed below) shows an example of a Hibol program.

A key aspect of the nonprocedural nature of Hibol is that there is no explicit control flow in a Hibol program. The statements in a Hibol program are unordered, and there are no flow-of-control constructs such as conditionals or loops. As a result of this, direct transliteration from a programming language such as Cobol, which has flow-of-control constructs, to Hibol is not practical.

1216   IEEE TRANSACTIONS ON SOFTWARE ENGINEERING, VOL. 14, NO. 8, AUGUST 1988

A. Example of Satch's Translation

Figs. 10 and 11 (adapted from [10]) show an example of a translation performed by Satch. Fig. 10 shows a Cobol program named PAYROLL. This program reads in a file of records which specify the wage rate for each member of a group of employees. The program computes the gross pay for each employee based on a 40 hour week along with a count of the employees and the total gross pay for all the employees.

Fig. 11 shows the Hibol translation which is produced by Satch. Like any Hibol program, this program is divided into two parts, which are closely analogous to the parts of a Cobol program. The data division of the Hibol program specifies the data types of the flows (introduced by the keyword FILE) used in the program and how these flows are indexed. The computation division specifies how the output flows are computed from the input flows. The first line of the computation division specifies that the elements of the flow GROSS-PAY are computed by multiplying the elements of the flow HOURLY-WAGE by 40. The second line of the computation division specifies how to compute the single-element flow TOTAL-GROSS-PAY. The operator SUM collapses a dimension of a flow by adding all of the elements in that dimension together. In an analogous way, the third line of the computation division specifies how to count the number of employees.

Without discussing Figs. 10 and 11 in any more detail, it can be seen that Satch is capable of creating quite good Hibol translations of Cobol programs. (More complex examples are given in [10].) However, the translations produced by Satch are still not optimal. For example, it would be better if Satch were capable of realizing that the flow TOTAL-GROSS-PAY in Fig. 11 could be computed using the more compact expression (SUM OF GROSS-PAY).

B. Implementation of Satch

Like the architecture of any translation system based on abstraction and reimplementation, Satch's architecture is divided into two basic parts (see Fig. 12). The five modules on the left-hand side of the figure operate together to create an abstract description of the Cobol program supplied to Satch. The Hibol reimplementation module creates a Hibol program based on the abstract description. Most of the burden of the translation is carried by the abstraction modules. This asymmetry is due to the fact that the very-high-level nature of Hibol allows the abstract description to be similar to the target language.

The parsing module (implemented by Burke) parses the Cobol program and transliterates it into pseudo-Lisp. (Lisp [25] was chosen as the output of this module in order to facilitate the use of a preexisting plan creation module.) The parsing module is implemented in essentially the same way that the transliteration component of a Cobol-to-Lisp translator operating via transliteration and refinement would be implemented.

For each file in the Cobol program, the key determination module determines which of the fields of the file

```
ENVIRONMENT DIVISION.
CONFIGURATION SECTION.
INPUT-OUTPUT SECTION.
FILE-CONTROL.
    SELECT HOURLY-WAGE-IN ASSIGN TO DA-2301-S-HWI.
    SELECT GROSS-PAY-OUT ASSIGN TO DA-2301-S-GPO.
    SELECT EMPLOYEE-COUNT-OUT ASSIGN TO DA-2301-S-ECO.
    SELECT TOTAL-GROSS-PAY-OUT ASSIGN TO DA-2301-S-TGPO.
DATA DIVISION.
FILE SECTION.
FD hourly-wage-in
    LABEL RECORD IS OMITTED
    DATA RECORD IS hourly-wage-rec.
01 hourly-wage-rec.
    02 employee-number                      PICTURE IS 9(9).
    02 hourly-wage                          PICTURE IS 999V99.
FD gross-pay-out
    LABEL RECORD IS OMITTED
    DATA RECORD IS gross-pay-rec.
01 gross-pay-rec.
    02 employee-number                      PICTURE IS 9(9).
    02 gross-pay                            PICTURE IS 999V99.
FD employee-count-out
    LABEL RECORD IS OMITTED
    DATA RECORD IS employee-count-rec.
01 employee-count-rec.
    02 employee-count                       PICTURE IS 9(6).
FD total-gross-pay-out
    LABEL RECORD IS OMITTED
    DATA RECORD IS total-gross-pay-rec.
01 total-gross-pay-rec.
    02 total-gross-pay                      PICTURE IS 9(7)V99.
PROCEDURE DIVISION.
initialization SECTION.
    MOVE ZERO TO total-gross-pay.
    MOVE ZERO TO employee-count.
    OPEN INPUT hourly-wage-in.
    OPEN OUTPUT gross-pay-out.
mainline SECTION.
    READ hourly-wage-in AT END GO TO end-of-job.
    MOVE employee-number OF hourly-wage-rec
        TO employee-number OF gross-pay-rec.
    MULTIPLY hourly-wage BY 40 GIVING gross-pay.
    ADD 1 TO employee-count.
    ADD gross-pay TO total-gross-pay.
    WRITE gross-pay-rec.
    GO TO mainline.
end-of-job SECTION.
    CLOSE hourly-wage-in.
    CLOSE gross-pay-out.
    OPEN OUTPUT employee-count-out.
    WRITE employee-count-rec.
    CLOSE employee-count-out.
    OPEN OUTPUT total-gross-pay-out.
    WRITE total-gross-pay-rec.
    CLOSE total-gross-pay-out.
    STOP RUN.
```

Fig. 10. The Cobol program PAYROLL.

```
DATA DIVISION
    KEY SECTION
        KEY EMPLOYEE-NUMBER  FIELD TYPE IS NUMBER  FIELD LENGTH IS 9
    INPUT SECTION
        FILE HOURLY-WAGE  KEY IS EMPLOYEE-NUMBER
    OUTPUT SECTION
        FILE GROSS-PAY  KEY IS EMPLOYEE-NUMBER
        FILE EMPLOYEE-COUNT
        FILE TOTAL-GROSS-PAY
COMPUTATION DIVISION
    GROSS-PAY IS (HOURLY-WAGE * 40.)
    TOTAL-GROSS-PAY IS (SUM OF (HOURLY-WAGE * 40.))
    EMPLOYEE-COUNT IS (COUNT OF HOURLY-WAGE)
```

Fig. 11. Satch's translation of Fig. 10 into Hibol.

act as keys. Various heuristics could be used to determine this information by looking at the Cobol program. However, Satch currently asks the user to specify which fields are key fields. In ordinary use, this would not lead to an excessive amount of user interaction because key determination has to be done only once for each file, even if a large number of programs which operate on the files are being translated.

The plan creation module converts the pseudo-Lisp out-

SOFTWARE RESTRUCTURING AND TRANSLATION

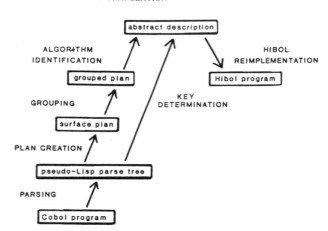

Fig. 12. The architecture of Satch.

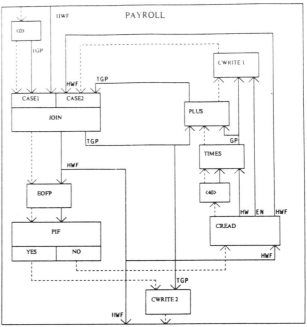

HWF => HOURLY-WAGE FILE-OBJECT   TGP => TOTAL-GROSS-PAY
HW => HOURLY-WAGE   GP => GROSS-PAY
EN => EMPLOYEE-NUMBER

Fig. 13. A simplified surface plan for PAYROLL.

put of the parsing module into a programming-language-independent internal respresentation called a *surface plan*. Fig. 13 (adapted from [10]) shows a simplified version of the surface plan which Satch creates when operating on the Cobol program PAYROLL shown in Fig. 10.

A plan is similar to a data flow diagram. Computations are represented by boxes (called segments). The segments are connected by solid arrows indicating data flow and dashed arrows indicating control flow. In the figure, many of the data flow arrows have annotations indicating the variables to which they correspond. The names of the segments represent the operations they perform. PLUS adds two numbers. CREAD reads a record from a file. EOFP determines whether the end of a file has been reached. PIF splits control flow based on whether or not its input is TRUE.

In the interest of brevity, the plan in Fig. 13 has been simplified in several ways. The computation of EM-PLOYEE-COUNT has been omitted. The file open and close functions have been removed. Except for the file HOURLY-WAGE, the data flow corresponding to the various file objects has been omitted. The data flow for the file HOURLY-WAGE was retained in order to make the EOFP test understandable.

Plan creation is performed using global data flow and control flow analysis, which is similar to the kind of analysis performed by an optimizing compiler.

The grouping module takes the surface plan generated by the plan creation module and converts it into a *grouped plan*. A grouped plan differs from a surface plan in two ways. First, the segments in the plan are grouped into a hierarchy of segments within segments in order to highlight the logical structure of the plan. Second, the loops in the plan are identified and broken down into their component parts.

Fig. 14 shows a simplified grouped plan for the program PAYROLL. As in Fig. 13, the grouped plan omits the file open and close functions and some of the other file operations. The figure is also simplified in that it does not show the computation which occurs within the various

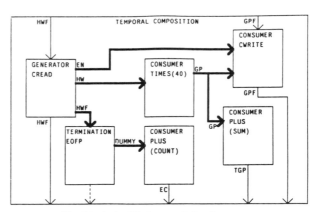

Fig. 14. A simplified grouped plan for PAYROLL.

segments. Unlike Fig. 13, the grouped plan shows the computation of EMPLOYEE-COUNT.

The key difference between Figs. 13 and 14 is the way the loop in the program PAYROLL is represented. In Fig. 14, the various parts of the loop are broken apart in segments connected by data flow rather than by control flow. This is done through a process called *temporal abstraction* [28].

Temporal abstraction treats sequences of values in the loop (e.g., the successive values of HOURLY-WAGE) as if they were single data objects. These *temporal sequences* are represented by bold data flow arrows in Fig. 14. Temporal abstraction analyzes a loop as a set of *generators* and *consumers*, which are sources and sinks for temporal sequences. For example, in Fig. 14, the generator CREAD creates a temporal sequence of HOURLY-WAGE values which are consumed by the segment TIMES (40). This segment in turn creates a temporal sequence of GROSS-PAY values which are summed up by the segment PLUS(SUM).

As discussed in detail in [28], the process of temporal abstraction is based on the data flow in a loop. Generators and consumers are located by identifying tightly interconnected subsections of the loop which can be understood in isolation.

Satch was implemented in the context of the Programmer's Apprentice project, and it shares many ideas with the rest of the project. In particular, the plan representation, the plan creation module, and the grouping module are borrowed directly from KBEmacs [29], which is the current demonstration system developed as part of the Programmer's Apprentice project.

The algorithm identification module inspects the grouped plan and determines the net effect of the computation being performed. In combination with the results of key determination, the results of algorithm identification form an abstract description of the program. Fig. 15 (adapted from [10]) shows the abstract description created for the program PAYROLL. The first part of Fig. 15 comes directly from the data division of the Cobol program annotated by the key determination module. The second part of Fig. 15 comes from algorithm identification.

Algorithm identification operates in two stages. The first stage identifies what kinds of looping computations are present in the program. This is done by special-purpose procedures which scan the grouped plan and recognize standard kinds of computation. In Fig. 14, these recognition procedures identify that the segments CREAD and EOFP enumerate the records in a file, while the segment CWRITE accumulates a sequence of records into a file. They also identify that the segment PLUS(SUM) computes a sum, while the segment PLUS(COUNT) computes a count. (The names of these segments in Fig. 14 reflect the fact that this recognition has been performed.) The recognition stage of the algorithm identification module makes it possible to use the terms "enumerate," "sum," and "count" in the abstract description to describe the computation in the loop instead of recurrence equations.

The second stage of algorithm identification computes summary descriptions of the computation performed by the program. This is done by means of a symbolic evaluator, which traverses the plan and accumulates algebraic equations which describe the computation. For example, the symbolic evaluator determines that the field GROSS-PAY has the value "CREAD-VALUE(HOURLY-WAGE-IN, HOURLY-WAGE)*40," i.e., 40 times the value of the HOURLY-WAGE field read from the file HOURLY-WAGE-IN. Similarly, it determines that the field TOTAL-GROSS-PAY accumulates the sum of the GROSS-PAY values. An algebraic simplifier is used in order to render the equations in as compact a form as possible.

```
FILES:
  HOURLY-WAGE-IN
    key-field EMPLOYEE-NUMBER-IN 9(9)
    data-field HOURLY-WAGE 999V99
  GROSS-PAY-OUT
    key-field EMPLOYEE-NUMBER-OUT 9(9)
    data-field GROSS-PAY 999V99
  EMPLOYEE-COUNT-OUT
    data-field EMPLOYEE-COUNT 9(6)
  TOTAL-GROSS-PAY-OUT
    data-field TOTAL-GROSS-PAY 9(7)V99
COMPUTATION:
  The main loop in the program enumerates the records in the file
  HOURLY-WAGE-IN.  It terminates when EOFP(HOURLY-WAGE-IN).
  fields written on each cycle of the main loop:
    EMPLOYEE-NUMBER-OUT = CREAD-VALUE(HOURLY-WAGE-IN, EMPLOYEE-NUMBER-IN)
    GROSS-PAY = CREAD-VALUE(HOURLY-WAGE-IN, HOURLY-WAGE)*40.
  fields written after the main loop:
    EMPLOYEE-COUNT = count(NOT(EOFP(HOURLY-WAGE-IN)))
    TOTAL-GROSS-PAY = sum(CREAD-VALUE(HOURLY-WAGE-IN, HOURLY-WAGE)*40.)
```

Fig. 15. An abstract description of PAYROLL.

The reimplemenation module of Satch produces a Hibol program based on the abstract description of the Cobol program. This is done by converting these equations into Hibol syntax. The only real complexity in this is checking that the program is expressible in Hibol. In particular, the reimplementation module has to check that each input file is processed in full and that the input keys map to the output keys in a way which is compatible with the implicit file reading and writing performed by Hibol.

C. Limits of Satch

Although it illustrates the efficacy of translation based on abstraction and reimplementation, there are several ways in which Satch is limited. First of all, Satch is only a demonstration system. It has been tested on only a few examples and therefore has not been fully debugged. In addition, it is quite slow.

A more fundamental problem with Satch is that it is applicable to only a narrow class of Cobol programs. Part of this is due to the fact that, since Hibol is a relatively special-purpose language, many Cobol programs cannot be reasonably translated into Hibol by any means. However, there are many Cobol programs which could in principle be translated into Hibol in a reasonable way which cannot be translated by Satch. The basic difficulty is that Satch does not have a generalized recognition facility. Rather, special-purpose procedures have to be written in order for Satch to be able to identify the kinds of looping computations present in a program. Overcoming this difficulty is a primary goal of the knowledge-based translation system discussed in Section VI.

V. COBBLER—TRANSLATING FROM PASCAL TO ASSEMBLER LANGUAGE

Duffey's proposed Cobbler system [9] uses translation via abstraction and reimplementation in order to compile Pascal [13] programs into PDP-11 assembler language [34]. Cobbler's goal is the creation of extremely efficient object code, code which is comparable in efficiency to the code which could be produced by an expert assembly language programmer. This is a level of efficiency which is beyond any existing compiler and is arguably beyond the abilities of any translator based on transliteration and refinement.

At first glance, it may seem surprising that Cobbler and Satch use the same approach to translation. After all, the problems associated with compiling Pascal do not seem to be very similar to the problems associated with translating Cobol to Hibol. In particular, the goal of the former is efficiency of low-level output, while the goal of the latter is readability of high-level output.

However, the two kinds of translation actually have a great deal in common. Stated generally, the key problem both systems face is that the quality criteria which govern the source are very different from the quality criteria which govern the target. In order to have the freedom to do a good job of satisfying the target criteria, the source must be analyzed and restated in an abstract way which frees it from the constraints of the source criteria.

A. Example of Cobbler's Compilation

Figs. 16 and 17 (adapted from [9]) show an example of how Cobbler is intended to operate. Fig. 16 shows a Pascal program which initializes a 4×4 array A of bytes to the identity matrix. The program does this a column at a time by setting each column element to zero and then changing the diagonal element to one. Fig. 17 shows the PDP-11 assembler code which would be produced by Cobbler.

The code in Fig. 17 is much more efficient than a simple literal translation of Fig. 16 into PDP-11 assembler. The optimizations introduced can be divided into two categories: algorithm-independent optimizations and changes to the algorithm.

The algorithm-independent optimizations are improvements which any good optimizing compiler might make. The inner loop is unrolled in order to eliminate the overhead engendered by having a loop. The matrix A is operated on as a one-dimensional vector in order to simplify address calculations. The outer loop is controlled by an auxiliary counter (R0), which counts down instead of up. This allows the code to take advantage of the fact that, on the PDP-11, comparison to zero is more efficient than comparison to other numbers. (After each arithmetic operation, condition codes are automatically set which specify whether the result is greater than, equal to, or less than zero.)

For the most part, the optimizations above are straightforward. The first simply involves duplicating the inner loop body, and the second is essentially a strength reduction. However, introducing an auxiliary loop counter is somewhat more complex. If a loop counts from n up to m by s, then a new loop counter can be introduced which counts from $(m-n)/s$ down to zero by one. Computation of the old counter is retained so that it can be used within the loop, while the new counter is used to control the loop. (In Fig. 17, no trace of this computation remains because the simplification of the addressing calculations has rendered it unnecessary.) The correctness of this transformation is supported by the fact that Pascal prohibits the body of a ''for'' loop from modifying the iteration variable or the bounds of the iteration.

```
var   I: 1..4; J: 1..4;
      A: array[1..4, 1..4] of 0..255;
begin
   for J := 1 to 4 do
      begin
         for I := 1 to 4 do A[I,J] := 0;
         A[J,J] := 1
      end
end
```

Fig. 16. The Pascal program INITIALIZE.

```
      MOV  #A,R3     ;Move address of A to R3.
      MOV  #3,R0     ;Move 3 to R0.
L1:   MOVB #1,(R3)+  ;Move 1 to location indexed by R3 incrementing R3.
      CLRB (R3)+     ;Move 0 to location indexed by R3 incrementing R3.
      CLRB (R3)+
      CLRB (R3)+
      CLRB (R3)+
      DEC  R0        ;Decrement R0.
      BGT  L1        ;Branch to L1 if result of decrement is positive.
      MOVB #1,(R3)   ;Move 1 to location indexed by R3.
```

Fig. 17. Cobbler's compilation of Fig. 16.

In order to highlight the algorithmic changes introduced by Cobbler, Fig. 18 shows a decompilation of Fig. 17 which undoes the effects of the algorithm-independent optimizations discussed above while leaving the algorithmic changes in place. It should be noted that the figure is merely intended as a presentational device. There are a number of reasons why Fig. 18 is not a valid Pascal program. (Most notably, the matrix A is declared to have different bounds from those which are presumably associated with other uses of the matrix.)

Comparison of Fig. 16 with Fig. 18 shows that the computation performed by the target code produced by Cobbler is startlingly different from the computation performed by the source code. In fact, it is probably not appropriate to say that the two pieces of code are using the same algorithm.

Three algorithmic changes have been introduced. The target code avoids redundantly setting the diagonal elements to zero before setting them to one. The target operates on A in row major order rather than column major order. The target treats A logically as a rectangular 3×5 matrix plus one additional element instead of as a square 4×4 matrix.

Perhaps the most important difference is the switch to row major order. For whatever reason, the programmer chose to use column major order in Fig. 16. This choice clashes with the fact that Pascal stores arrays in row major order. Switching to row major order changes the program so that it references the elements of A in memory storage order. This in turn makes it possible to use autoincrement mode PDP-11 instructions to support the address calculations required.

Undoubtedly, the most surprising change is the switch to operating on A as a 3×5 matrix. This makes it much easier to set the appropriate elements of A to one since all these elements are now in the same column.

As will be discussed in the next subsection, Cobbler is able to make the algorithmic changes outlined above because it creates an abstract description of the program which is not constrained by the order of iteration in the

1220   IEEE TRANSACTIONS ON SOFTWARE ENGINEERING, VOL. 14, NO. 8, AUGUST 1988

```
var   I: 1..3; J: 2..5;
      A: array[1..3, 1..5] of 0..255;
begin
  for I := 1 to 3 do
    begin
      A[I,1] := 1;
      for J := 2 to 5 do A[I,J] := 0
    end;
    A[4,1] := 1
end
```

Fig. 18. A decompilation of Fig. 17 into pseudo-Pascal.

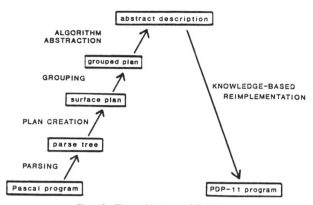

Fig. 19. The architecture of Cobbler.

loops or even by the fact that A is declared to be a 4 × 4 matrix. These changes are arguably beyond the scope of any current optimizing compiler because they require an understanding of what is being computed by the source program as a whole.

If the programmer had written the program as shown in Fig. 18, then any good optimizing compiler could have produced the code in Fig. 17. However, it is implausible that the programmer would have written the program in a form anything like that in Fig. 18. This is, of course, partly due to the fact that it is not technically possible to write the program shown in Fig. 18 in Pascal. However, much more importantly, it is not desirable to write programs like that in Fig. 18. The programmer should not have to worry about detailed efficiency in the source code. Rather, readability should be the primary concern. The source program in Fig. 16 is preferable to the one in Fig. 18 because it is more readable and therefore easier to test, verify, and maintain. (One might argue that Fig. 16 would be even more readable if it operated in row major order. However, the fact that it operates on A as a 4 × 4 matrix clearly makes the program easier to understand than the one in Fig. 18.)

D. Design of Cobbler

As shown in Fig. 19, the architecture of Cobbler is similar to the architecture of Satch (see Fig. 12). In particular, the first three stages of abstraction (parsing, plan creation, and grouping) are identical and are intended to make use of the same modules of KBEmacs. The difference between the lengths of the right-hand sides of Figs. 12 and 19 is intended to indicate that creating an efficient PDP-11 implementation of an abstract description is much harder than creating a Hibol implementation.

The final stage of abstraction used by Cobbler (algorithm abstraction) goes beyond the algorithm identification used by Satch. The goal of algorithm abstraction is to identify the various design decisions used when writing the Pascal program and then undo them. This leads to a hierarchy of abstract descriptions for the program which are constrained by fewer and fewer design decisions.

When analyzing the program in Fig. 16, the algorithm abstraction module first withdraws the decision to use loops when operating on A. This implicitly withdraws the decision to iterate in column major order as opposed to row major order. It then withdraws the decision to set the diagonal elements to zero before setting them to one. Fi-

nally, it withdraws the decision to implement A as a Pascal array as opposed to a noncontinuous group of variables. All of these steps could be performed by recognizing standard algorithms in a grouped plan for Fig. 16.

The left-hand side of Fig. 20 summarizes the last step of algorithm abstraction. The 4 × 4 description represents the net effect of the program in Fig. 16 on the Pascal array A. The abstract description represents the net effect of the program operating directly on the individual matrix elements. The significance of the abstract description is that it gives Cobbler the freedom to consider ways of accessing A other than as a 4 × 4 array.

The knowledge-based reimplementation module creates an efficient PDP-11 implementation corresponding to the abstract description. As one of the first parts of the reimplementation process, Cobbler looks for patterns in the abstract description in order to decide how to use loops in the output program. The recurring pattern ''1 0 0 0 0'' is discovered. This causes Cobbler to reorganize its understanding of the program into the 3 × 5 description shown on the right-hand side of Fig. 20.

Once the 3 × 5 description has been created, reimplementation proceeds by investigating a variety of implementation options and then choosing a consistent and efficient set of these options. Following standard Pascal practice, the array A is implemented as a row major order sequence of consecutive bytes in memory. (This decision has to take the other uses of the matrix A into consideration.) Elements of A are addressed by stepping a pointer through memory. Since the inner loop which zeros the nondiagonal elements of A is very small and only iterates four times, it is unrolled into a sequence of four separate instructions. Clear-byte instructions are used to zero elements of A.

The key difficulty in making the above design decisions (and the other decisions which are required) is controlling the search process which investigates the various options. Flexibly and efficiently controlling search was the major focus of Duffey's research. He proposed the following approach to the problem.

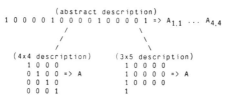

Fig. 20. Some descriptions of Fig. 16 used by Cobbler.

A database is used to represent Cobbler's evolving understanding of the implementation. Design decisions are represented in terms of transformations. Each transformation consists of a pattern and a procedural body. Transformations are triggered (causing their bodies to be executed) when their patterns match portions of the database. The effect of a transformation is to modify the information in the database or add new information to the database.

The key component of the knowledge-based reimplementation module is *conflict resolution monitor*, which controls the triggering of transformations. It exercises control principally by deactivating and activating groups of transformations. Associated with each group of transformations is a function which can create estimates of the costs in time and space associated with the design decision suggested by the group of transformations. (For a discussion of one way in which such estimates can be computed, see [14].) The conflict resolution monitor decides which groups of transformations to activate by comparing efficiency estimates.

An important feature of Cobbler is that it does not assume that it will always be able to make an informed choice between the design decisions with which it is faced. In order to deal with this problem. Cobbler keeps a record of the design decisions which were used in the source program. In situations where Cobbler is not able to make an informed choice, it uses the relevant source program decision. For example, if no pattern had been found in the abstract description, Cobbler would have used the 4×4 structure suggested by the source program.

It would also be possible for Cobbler to take advice on how to compile a program because Cobbler's processing is based on design decisions which are comprehensible to a programmer.

The discussion above shows how Cobbler is intended to operate. However, Cobbler is not a running system. With the exception of parts of the reimplementation component, no attempt has been made to implement Cobbler.

VI. THE KNOWLEDGE-BASED TRANSLATOR

Work is currently underway in the Programmer's Apprentice project on the components of a general-purpose knowledge-based translator operating via abstraction and reimplementation. An important virtue of this system is that much of its knowledge of translation will be represented as data rather than procedures. As a result, it will be possible to extend the system readily to cover a wide range of source and target languages.

In order to understand how the knowledge-based translator will operate, it is first necessary to discuss two of the key ideas which underlie the Programmer's Apprentice (see [29]). The first idea is the concept of a *cliché*. Programs are not constructed out of arbitrary combinations of primitive programming constructs. Rather, programs are built up by combining standard computational fragments and data structure fragments. These standard fragments are referred to as clichés and form the heart of the Programmer's Apprentice's understanding of programming, just as they form the heart of any person's understanding of programming.

As an example of clichés, consider the Cobol program PAYROLL in Fig. 10. This program contains a number of clichés which can be named and described as follows. The data cliché *keyed-sequential-Cobol-file* specifies how a sequence of records with keys can be combined into a file. The computational cliché *enumerate-keyed-sequential-Cobol-file* enumerates all of the records in a file taking care of opening and closing the file. The computational cliché *accumulate-keyed-sequential-Cobol-file* writes a sequence of records into a file taking care of opening and closing the file. The computational cliché *Cobol-sum* computes the sum of a sequence of numbers.

A crucial feature of clichés is that they can be arranged in multilevel specialization hierarchy as shown in Fig. 21. The descendents of a cliché in this hierarchy are more specialized clichés which specify how the cliché should be adapted in various specific situations. For example, there is an abstract cliché *enumerate* which has a set of descendents which specify how to enumerate various kinds of data structures (e.g., *enumerate-file* and *enumerate-vector*). Similarly, the middle-level cliché enumerate-file has a set of descendents which specify how to enumerate different types of files (e.g., *enumerate-indexed-file* and *enumerate-keyed-sequential-file*). Going one step further, each of these specific file enumeration clichés has a set of descendents which specify exactly what functions are used to open, close, and read files in various different programming language environments (e.g., *enumerate-indexed-Ada-file* and *enumerate-keyed-sequential-Cobol-file*).

A second key idea which underlies the Programmer's Apprentice is the plan representation which was discussed briefly in Section IV. The most important feature of a plan is that it is an abstract representation of a program which captures the key features of the computation while ignoring the syntactic details of particular programming languages. For example, data flow is represented by simple arcs in the plan for a program no matter how it is implemented in the program (e.g., via variables or parameter passing or nesting of expressions).

Both Satch and Cobbler make use of the version of the plan representation which is used by KBEmacs. Since the design of those systems, Rich [17], [18] has developed an extended plan representation, called the *Plan Calculus*, which is capable of representing much more information about a program. In particular, the plan calculus is capa-

1222   IEEE TRANSACTIONS ON SOFTWARE ENGINEERING, VOL. 14, NO. 8, AUGUST 1988

Fig. 21. Examples of specialization relationships between clichés.

ble of representing data clichés and the specialization relationships between clichés. In contrast, the plan representation used by KBEmacs is capable only of representing computational clichés and only in isolation from each other.

A. Design of the Knowledge-Based Translator

Fig. 22 shows the way in which plans and clichés can be used as the basis for a knowledge-based translator operating via abstraction and reimplementation. The modules on the left-hand side of the diagram support abstraction. The modules on the right-hand side of the diagram support reimplementation. The key component of the system is a library of clichés like the ones described above. Specialization relationships are used as the basis for the organization of the library.

The first two steps of abstraction (parsing and plan creation) are exactly the same as in Satch and Cobbler. The last two steps of abstraction (recognition and cliché abstraction) are similar to Cobbler's algorithm abstraction module. A key feature of these modules is that they are data driven, operating based on the clichés stored in the cliché library.

The recognition module scans the grouped plan and determines what source language clichés were used to construct the source program. (This recognition is performed directly on the surface plan and therefore subsumes the grouping performed by Satch and Cobbler.) When applied to the Cobol program in Fig. 10, recognition would reveal that the program was composed of clichés such as keyed-sequential-Cobol-file, enumerate-keyed-sequential-Cobol-file, accumulate-keyed-sequential-Cobol-file, Cobol-count, and Cobol-sum.

The cliché abstraction module creates an abstract plan by replacing specialized plans with the more abstract plans of which they are specializations. In the example above, this would yield a plan involving the abstract clichés keyed-sequence, enumerate, accumulate, count, and sum.

The abstract plan attempts not to force any design decisions. It simply states that there are certain sequences of values containing certain data values and keys and that various operations are performed on these values. The paramount feature of the abstract plan is that it is completely neutral between the Cobol program, which implements the sequences as files, and a Hibol program, which implements them as flows or, for that matter, a Lisp program, which implements them as lists.

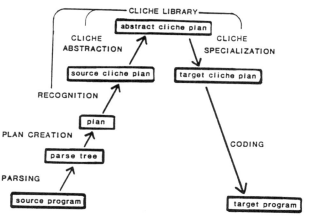

Fig. 22. Translation based on clichés and plans.

The reimplementation process in Fig. 22 operates in the reverse of the way in which abstraction operates. Cliché specialization selects clichés which specialize the clichés in the abstract plan in a way appropriate for the target language. Cliché specialization (which can be looked at as library-driven synthesis) is the inverse of cliché abstraction. However, it is more difficult than cliché abstraction because it is harder to make design decisions than to discard them.

Coding creates program text corresponding to the specialized clichés selected by cliché specialization. Coding is the inverse of parsing, plan creation, and recognition. Inverting recognition and parsing is trival. However, inverting plan creation is difficult, because information corresponding to the information thrown away by plan creation must be generated. For example, the coding module has to decide how to render data flow aesthetically in the target language using variables and nesting of expressions.

B. Implementing the Knowledge-Based Translator

Progress has been made toward implementing most of the components in Fig. 22. However, none of these components has yet been completed. Rich and Feldman are currently in the process of implementing the plan calculus together with a general-purpose automatic deduction system [19] to support reasoning in it. Extensive work has already been done on designing the library [17].

Given a particular source language, it is not difficult to implement a parsing module. As mentioned above, the plan creation module already exists as part of KBEmacs. This module has to be rewritten so that it operates in the domain of the Plan Calculus. However, there should be no particular difficulty in doing this.

KBEmacs also contains a coding module analogous to the one needed by the knowledge-based translator. Although there are many improvements which need to be made in this module, it should not be difficult to implement an adequate coding module which operates in the context of the Plan Calculus.

No attempt has yet been made to implement the cliché abstraction module. However, its implementation should be straightforward. Cliché abstraction is driven by the specialization links in the cliché library. Cliché abstraction is particularly easy because it follows these links in the many-to-one direction.

There has also been no attempt to implement the cliché specialization module. Like cliché abstraction, cliché specialization is driven by the specialization links in the cliché library. However, cliché specialization is harder than cliché abstraction because numerous design decisions have to be made when choosing a path through the specialization links in the one-to-many direction. It is expected that, like Cobbler, the cliché specialization module will use a variety of estimates and heuristics in order to make design decisions. Also like Cobbler, design decisions detected during cliché abstraction will be used to guide cliché specialization in situations where these heuristics fail to be applicable.

In many ways, the central module in Fig. 22 is the recognition module. Work on this module has been underway for several years. Recognition can be viewed as a parsing task. From this viewpoint, the cliché library is a grammar which can be used to derive plans for programs. In order to determine which clichés were used to construct a given plan, one needs to parse the plan. This would be a straightforwward task if it were not for the fact that the plan for a program is a graph rather than a string, and cliché instances correspond to subgraphs in the plan rather than substrings.

As a first step toward solving the recognition problem, Brotsky [6] implemented a parser which is able to efficiently parse flow graphs (a restricted form of acyclic directed graph) given a flow graph grammar. Currently, Zelinka [30] is implementing an experimental recognition module which utilizes this graph parser. Further research is required in order to develop effective methods whereby the knowledge-based translator can deal with incomplete recognition.

Once the implementation of the components described above has been completed, it will be possible to use them to construct a general-purpose knowledge-based translator. As mentioned above, a key feature of this system is that it will be data driven, with most of its knowledge embedded in the cliché library. Additional research will have to be performed in order to discover how best to represent the heuristics which are an essential part of the specialization component and to a lesser extent of the coder component.

VII. RELATED WORK

There are several areas where active work is in progress on translators. However, essentially all current translators operate via transliteration and refinement. Some translators (e.g., optimizing compilers) do a significant amount of global analysis of the source program. However, it is not clear that any program translator takes the step of attempting to obtain an abstract understanding of the computation being performed by the program as a whole.

A. Compilers

Compilers are the most common example of translators. They have been well developed over the years and work quite well. As described in textbooks on compiling (e.g., [1]), the prototypical compiler operates by transliteration and refinement. The source language is transliterated (via parsing and syntax-directed translation) into an intermediate language which is analogous to a machine language. Refinements (optimizations) are then applied to this intermediate representation. Finally, the intermediate language is translated into the actual target language. The current developments in compiler research [31] indicate that the basic appoach to compilation outlined above is still adhered to.

However, over the years, two trends in compiler research have been moving in the direction of abstraction and reimplementation. One trend is the development of intermediate representations which look more like data flow diagrams and less like particular machine languages. These more abstract representations facilitate the construction of families of compilers which produce output for a variety of target machines. They also facilitate the manipulation of the program when optimizations are being applied. In particular, they make it easier to keep track of the data flow in a program.

Another trend is toward more powerful optimizations which require a greater understanding of what is going on in a program. Classic peephole optimizations such as locating patterns of instructions for which a special target instruction is available operate in a very local way without any understanding of context. More powerful optimizations, such as removing an invariant expression from a loop, require a general understanding of the surrounding data flow and control flow. Optimizations such as strength reduction additionally require an understanding of the mathematical properties of the basic operators (e.g., "+" and "*").

The kind of analysis which underlies complex optimizations is a step toward creating an abstract summary of the program being compiled. However, it is only a small step in this direction because the information obtained by analysis is not very abstract. The only abstraction is away from particular data flow and control flow constructs. In addition, the analysis is narrow in scope, aiming only to gather enough information to answer a few specific questions about the program. No attempt is made to obtain a general understanding of the computation performed by the program.

B. Compiling for Parallel Machines

The problem of compiling a conventional programming language so that it runs efficiently on a parallel machine highlights the strengths and weaknesses of current ap-

1224   IEEE TRANSACTIONS ON SOFTWARE ENGINEERING. VOL. 14. NO. 8. AUGUST 1988

proaches to optimization. Consider compiling the Fortran program fragment in Fig. 23 for a vector machine. The fragment is a triply nested loop which computes the product of two N × N matrices.

The loops in Fig. 23 can be efficiently executed on a scalar machine. Unfortunately, they cannot be efficiently executed on the typical vector machine. The problem is that each cycle (after the first) of the innermost loop uses the value computed on the prior cycle, leaving little room for vectorization. However, if the loops are interchanged so that the κ loop is outermost, then they can be efficiently executed on a vector machine.

The discussion in [2] shows how a compiler for a vector machine can automatically interchange loops in order to improve the efficiency of the code produced. Interchanging two loops changes the order in which computations are performed. Many subcomputations which were performed in the order s1 s2 before the interchange will be performed in the order s2 s1 after the interchange. An interchange is correctness preserving as long as nothing in the original program either requires that s2 follow s1 or prohibits s2 from preceding s1.

A global analysis of the loops in question is a key part of the loop interchange optimization. The compiler must obtain an understanding of the data dependences between array elements in the loops. This requires an understanding of the data flow involving the arrays (i.e., A, B, and C). It also requires at least a partial understanding of the interaction between the loop iteration variables and the index expressions which select array elements.

In Fig. 23, the index expressions are very easy to understand. However, the index expression in a loop can be arbitarily complex. For example, they may be functions of the input data. The analysis of index expressions used by the loop interchange optimization described in [2] is limited to situations where the index expressions are linear functions of the loop iteration variables.

An interesting aspect of loop interchange in particular, and compiler optimizations in general, is that they are deliberately designed to be narrow in scope and independent of whatever computation is being performed. This has the advantage that the various optimizations can be applied in a wide variety of contexts without the need for any special knowledge about the particular algorithms being used. However, it has the disadvantage that the optimizations cannot utilize special knowledge about the particular algorithms being used.

Given the algorithm-independent nature of optimizations in general, the level of object code efficiency which can be achieved is very impressive. However, there are definite limits to the efficiency which can be achieved. For example, consider compiling Fig. 23 for a highly parallel machine which has many independent processors. For this kind of machine, optimizations such as loop interchange are not sufficient to produce efficient code. The problem is that for a multiple processor machine, the standard matrix multiplication algorithm is simply the wrong algorithm to use. Special algorithms for matrix multipli-

```
DO 100 J = 1. N
   DO 100 I = 1. N
      DO 100 K = 1. N
         C(I,J) = C(I,J)+A(I,K)*B(K,J)
100 CONTINUE
```

Fig. 23. Loops performing matrix multiplication.

cation have been developed which are much more efficient when run on a multiple processor machine.

In order to create really good code for a multiple processor machine, a compiler would have to recognize that matrix multiplication was being performed in Fig. 23 and then replace the standard algorithm with one of its multiple processor counterparts. At the current time, the lack of compilers which can make this kind of transformation significantly limits the usability of multiple processor machines. In order to make full use of these machines, programmers have to rewrite their programs in special languages using new algorithms.

C. Very-High-Level Language Compilers

A third category of compilers is compilers for general-purpose very-high-level languages. A number of such languages have been designed (e.g., Setl [22], Gist [3], and Refine [23]). These languages differ from high-level languages in that they are more abstract. A good example of this difference is the treatment of data structures. High level languages provide facilities so that the programmer can specify the exact details of how data structures should be implemented. In contrast, very-high-level languages typically support only a few universal data structures such as sets and mappings. All decisions about how to implement a given set or mapping efficiently are left up to the very-high-level language compiler. This simplifies what the programmer has to do by removing large parts of the programming task from consideration.

Unfortunately, constructing a compiler for a general-purpose very-high-level language which produces efficient object code has proved very difficult. Although these compilers are the subject of active research, it is not clear that such a compiler can be said to exist even in a research setting.

The Setl compiler [11] is implemented more or less along traditional lines, with the addition of a special component which selects data structure implementations. However, the key technique which is being pursued as a basis for very-high-level language compilers in *refinement through transformation* [3], [23]. In this approach, a very-high-level language source program is progressively refined into an efficient target program by applying a sequence of correctness-preserving transformations. The net effect of the transformations is to replace all of the abstract concepts (e.g., set) in the source with concrete concepts (e.g., record or array) in the target. The key problem (which has so far resisted solution) is that there are a vast number of ways in which a source program can be transformed, and it is very hard to decide which ones will lead to acceptably efficient results.

Refinement through transformation is basically an example of the transliteration and refinement approach, or rather, just refinement. Using transformations has several advantages. In particular, each transformation typically embodies a single implementation decision and is straightforward to understand in isolation. Further, since each transformation is correctness preserving, it is clear that the result produced will be correct.

What is lacking in the transformational approach is a general strategy for making overall design decisions. It is not clear that it is possible to make these decisions on a local basis as individual transformations are applied. One alternative approach would be to pursue all of the major choices, compiling a given program in many different ways, and then to pick the implementation which is best [14]. However, it is not clear that this approach can be practically applied to complex programs where large numbers of choices have to be made.

Another approach, which has not yet been tried, would be to use abstraction and reimplementation as the basis for choice. The goal would be to recognize patterns of computation in the source program which suggest that particular design choices should be used. A strategy would still be required for selecting between conflicting suggestions. However, this strategy could benefit from having a high-level description of the conflict.

D. Source-to-Source Translation

A number of source-to-source program translators exist. However, as a group, they are not as well developed as compilers, and relatively little has appeared in the literature about them. It seems that all current source-to-source translators operate via transliteration and refinement, doing relatively little refinement.

Unfortunately, source-to-source translators tend to be incomplete and incorrect. Most of them handle only part (around 90 percent) of the source language. Further, relatively few source-to-source translators correctly handle the sublanguage to which they are applicable.

As discussed in Section II, both of these problems stem from difficulties in transliteration. Source language constructs which cannot be reasonably transliterated are not supported. Further, transliteration methods which work most of the time, but not all of the time, are used as if they worked all of the time.

In addition to the problems above, when measured by the criterion of readability, the output of most translators is not particularly good. Although serviceable, the output produced seldom comes anywhere near the goal of being what the programmers would have written had they been writing in the target language.

Due to the difficulties above, it is not accurate to refer to typical source-to-source translation systems as *automatic* systems. It is more accurate to describe them as *human-assisted* translation systems. In order to obtain correct (let alone aesthetic) output, human intervention is usually required. The user has to edit the source program (to remove untranslatable constructs) and/or the target program (to correct errors and improve the translation).

As a straightforward example of a translator, consider the Lisp 1.6-to-Interlisp translator implemented by Samet [21]. This translator operates purely by transliteration. It does no refinement. Although reasonably efficient output is produced, the translator makes no attempt to create aesthetic output. In particular, there is no attempt to create Interlisp-style output. Rather, a set of functions is defined in Interlisp which, as much as possible, allows Interlisp to stimulate Lisp 1.6. For example, instead of translating the source program into Interlisp syntax, the Interlisp reader is modified so that it can read in a program in Lisp 1.6 syntax. In [21], Samet identifies a number of features of Lisp 1.6 which his translator cannot handle. The user is required to edit the source program in order to eliminate these features. Samet also describes several features of Lisp 1.6 which are translated in ways which are often, but not always, correct. The translation produced has to be carefully tested in order to check that these over-simple transliterations have not led to any problems.

At first glance, it might appear that translation between two dialects of Lisp should be easy. However, this is not the case. In fact, List supports a number of features which are spectacularly difficult to translate. For example, a Lisp program can construct a new Lisp program and then execute this new program. Consider a Lisp 1.6 program which constructs a Lisp 1.6 program and then calls it as a subroutine. The program would have to be translated into an Interlisp program which constructs an Interlisp program. It is very unlikely that this kind of translation could be performed without using abstraction and reimplementation of the most powerful kind.

Another straightforward translator is the Fortran-to-Lisp translator implemented by Pitman [16]. Like Samet's translator, this translator operates purely by transliteration, doing no refinement. The translator produces readable output. However, it deliberately attempts to create Fortran-style output as opposed to Lisp-style output. The translation is supported by a set of functions which allow Lisp to stimulate the Fortran run-time environment. This approach introduces a significant overhead, which causes a translated program to run several times slower than the Fortran source program. Pitman's translator is far superior to Samet's translator in that, except for one or two very obscure features, all of the features of Fortran are translated correctly all of the time.

A third translator in this vein is the Fortran-to-Jovial translator implemented by Boxer [4]. Like the translators above, it operates purely by transliteration. The output of the translator is not intended for human consumption, and no attempt is made to make it particularly readable or to render it in Jovial style. (The examples in [4] indicate that the output is similar in style to that of the Ada, shown in Fig. 3.) The translator handles only a subset of Fortran. It succeeds in translating from 90 to 100 percent of the typical input module. User intervention is required to complete the translation.

The Lisp-to-Fortran translator developed by Boyle [5] is interesting because it is based on the transformational

1226

IEEE TRANSACTIONS ON SOFTWARE ENGINEERING. VOL. 14. NO. 8. AUGUST 1988

approach discussed in the last subsection. The translator handles an applicative subset of Lisp which does not include such hard-to-translate features as the ability to create and execute new Lisp code. Readability is not a goal of the translation. Rather, readability of the output is abandoned in favor of producing reasonably efficient Fortran code. As discussed in [5], this translator is perhaps best thought of as a compiler of Lisp into Fortran rather than a source-to-source translator.

Boyle's translator operates by transliterating the Lisp source into an extension of Fortran and then transforming this extended Fortran into ordinary Fortran. The transformation process is controlled by dividing it into a number of phases. Each phase applies transformations selected from a small set. The transformations within each set are chosen so that conflicts between transformations will not arise.

Boyle's translator is successful not because it has solved the problems faced by very-high-level language compilers, but rather because it succeeds in avoiding them. First, compared to Setl, Gist, and Refine, Lisp is not very abstract. Therefore, there are fewer complex design decisions which have to be made. Second, the design decisions are small enough in number that it is possible to find a fixed set of choices which works reasonably well for all of the Lisp programs being translated. These fixed choices are embedded in the translator through the choice of phases and transformations. Lists are always implemented the same way. Recursion is always simulated in the same way. This leads to the production of Fortran programs which are reasonably efficient, but typically far from optimally efficient.

E. Commercially Available Source-to-Source Translators

In addition to the in-house translation systems described above, a number of translators are commercially available. One area where several translators are available is translating between assembler languages for various microprocessors. A detailed discussion of the particular problems associated with translating between various machine languages is given in [12]. It is interesting to note that this paper was written 20 years ago, and yet its comments are as applicable now as they were then. In particular, currently available assembler language translators do not appear to be appreciably better than the machine language translators of 20 years ago. This contrasts sharply with compilers, where vast improvements have been made.

The decision in [26] compares three translators between 8080 assembler and 8086 assembler, which are currently commercially available. An in-house attempt at a translator between Z80 assembler and MC6809 assembler is described in [24]. All four translators operate primarily by transliteration on an instruction-by-instruction basis and do little or no refinement. They all operate on only a subset of the source language and use simplistic transliterations which are not correct in all contexts. Human in-

tervention is often required in order to obtain correct output. The translations produced are also quite inefficient, consisting of from three to six times as many instructions as the source. One of the 8080-to-8086 translators (XLT86 from Digital Research Inc.) uses global data and control flow analysis in order to guide the choice of transliteration for instructions. It produces output which is significantly more efficient and more often correct than that of the other translators.

Another area where a number of translators are available is translating between various languages used for business data processing (e.g., Cobol, RPGII, and PL/I). Numerous translators exist (for example, see [32], [33]). Substantive information about the internal operation of these translators is hard to obtain; however, several things are clear from their external descriptions. They do not handle the whole source language. In general, they succeed in translating only 90–95 percent of typical source programs. They do not always produce correct output. (In [33], the user is specifically instructed to test and debug the translations produced.) Examples suggest that the output is not particularly readable and that the output was probably created primarily through transliteration.

F. Code Restructuring

An interesting subcategory of source-to-source translators is systems which translate a program from a language back into the same language. The goal of these systems is to create output which is more readable than the input. In particular, these systems typically seek to render unstructured source programs in a structured form. Given that the source and target languages are the same, it is a relatively straightforward matter to make sure that the entire source language is handled correctly. However, it is far from straightforward to produce output which really is significantly more readable than the input. Many of these systems are little more than pretty printers and are of marginal use. However, at least one system (Recoder [7]) is a true translator and creates highly structured output.

Recoder operates on Cobol programs in three stages. The first stage creates a flowchart-like graph representing the source program. The key feature of the graph representation is that all control flow is represented by explicit arcs which are independent of the Cobol constructs originally used to implement the control flow. The second stage applies correctness-preserving transformations to the graph in order to rearrange the graph into a structured form. The third stage creates a new Cobol program based on the rearranged graph.

Recoder represents a step toward the abstraction and reimplementation approach because the abstraction it uses is clearly the driving force behind the translation. However, the step is strictly limited by a number of factors. The graph representation used is not very abstract. The only abstraction is away from particular control flow constructs. No attempt is made to recognize the algorithms being used in the source program or to abstract away from them.

G. Natural Language Translation

An interesting area which is closely related to program translation is natural language translation. Work on natural language translation started by using transliteration and, in a quest for high-quality output, is now moving in the direction of translation via abstraction and reimplementation.

Almost all of the natural language translation systems which are in actual regular use today operate via transliteration and refinement (see [27]). In general, these systems produce output which is very rough, but which is readable to a person who is familiar with the subject area. A good example of such a system is the Paho system [27], which translates from Spanish to English.

Paho operates by transliterating the source text on a sentence-by-sentence basis. This transliteration is carried out for the most part on a word-by-word basis with a small amount of interword analysis to take care of issues such as providing correct translations for idioms and rearranging the adjectives in a noun phrase. (Adjectives follow nouns in Spanish, whereas they precede nouns in English.) The practicality of this kind of transliteration depends heavily on a number of convenient correspondences between the basic structure of Spanish and English (e.g., the near identicality of word order and the fact that Spanish pronouns are more heavily marked for gender than English pronouns rather than vice versa).

Paho is not capable of refining the English it produces. Manual postediting is required in order to generate an acceptable translation. The biggest weakness of Paho is that it knows very little about syntax and nothing about the meaning of the sentences being translated. Further, it has no knowledge of interactions between sentences.

In the quest for higher-quality tranlations than the ones generated by systems like Paho, translators are now being developed which operate more in the vein of abstraction and reimplementation. A good example of such a translator is the Eurotra system [15], which is currently being developed to translate between the major western European languages. Eurotra uses semantically annotated syntactic parse trees as an abstract representation for the sentences being translated. Analysis (abstraction) and synthesis (reimplementation) components convert source languages into parse trees and parse trees into target languages, respectively.

Eurotra is not a true abstraction and reimplementation system because the annotated parse trees are not independent of the source and target languages. Procedural *transfer components* are required in order to convert a source-language-specific tree into a target language parse tree.

It is expected that Eurotra will produce significantly better output than Paho. However, it is expected that Eurotra will still fall short of high-quality translation. In particular, although Eurotra has much more syntactic understanding than Paho, its semantic and intersentential understanding is still quite weak.

In order to achieve high-quality translation, natural language translation systems have to be able to obtain an in-depth understanding of the text being translated. One approach to this is the recent work on *knowledge-based machine translation* (see [8]). This work has succeeded in demonstrating natural language translation via abstraction and reimplementation. The abstract description used by this approach is a language-independent representation of the conceptual dependences in the text. Knowledge-based machine translation is intended to operate by first analyzing the entire source text in order to determine its meaning and then reexpressing this meaning in the target language using the syntactic structure of the source as a guide to what to say when.

Although knowledge-based machine translation holds the promise of generating very-high-quality output, more work has to be done before a translator following this approach will be practical. In particular, as with translation via abstraction and reimplementation in general, there is a significant problem with incompleteness. Considerable further research has to be done before it will be possible to achieve anywhere near a complete understanding of arbitrary passages of source text. However, perfection is not required. Human translators are unable to translate technical texts unless they understand the technical area being discussed.

VIII. CONCLUSION

Program translation in the form of both compilation and source-to-source translation is an important aspect of software engineering. Particularly in the guise of compilation, translation is very successfully applied in many situations. However, it is clear that there are significant limits to the quality of the output produced by current translators. This can be most clearly seen in source-to-source translation, where human intervention is typically required in order to produce acceptable output.

It is the thesis of this paper that translation via analysis and reimplementation is the key to providing a quantum improvement in the quality of translation. In contrast to the standard translation approach of transliteration and refinement, translation via analysis and reimplementation utilizes an in-depth understanding of the semantics of the source program. This understanding makes it possible for the translator to create target code without being constrained by irrelevant details of the source program.

Unfortunately, both in-depth analysis and reimplementation are difficult tasks. Considerable further research has to be done before either of these tasks becomes a well-understood process. As a result, the benefits of translation via analysis and reimplementation are currently more of a promise than a reality.

Fortunately, significant progress has already been made toward effective analysis and reimplementation. There is every reason to believe that this progress will continue in the future and that it will lead to the construction of very-high-quality translators.

ACKNOWLEDGMENT

Under the supervision of the author, G. Faust designed and implemented the Satch system and R. Duffey de-

1228   IEEE TRANSACTIONS ON SOFTWARE ENGINEERING, VOL. 14, NO. 8, AUGUST 1988

signed the Cobbler system. C. Rich (with the assistance of Y. Feldman) and L. Zelinka (building on the earlier work of D. Brotsky) are laying the foundations for a generalized translation system based on abstract and reimplementation. C. Rich made a number of suggestions which greatly improved both the form and content of this paper. Discussions with D. Chapman, R. Duffey, G. Faust, H. Reubenstein, G. Parker, and L. Zelinka helped clarify the ideas presented. Special thanks are due to C. Ciro for her assistance with the illustrations and to the reviewers for their helpful suggestions.

REFERENCES

[1] A. V. Aho, R. Sethi, and J. D. Ullman, *Compilers–Principles, Techniques, and Tools.* Reading, MA: Addison-Wesley, 1986.

[2] J. R. Allen and K. Kennedy, "Automatic loop interchange," in *Proc. ACM SIGPLAN Symp. Compiler Construction,* SIGPLAN Notices, vol. 19, no. 6, June 1984.

[3] R. Balzer, "Transformational implementation: An example," *IEEE Trans. Software Eng.,* vol. SE-7, no. 1, Jan. 1981.

[4] R. K. Boxer, "A translator from structured Fortran to Jovial/J73," in *Proc. IEEE Nat. Aerospace Electron. Conf. (NAECON-83), 1983.*

[5] J. M. Boyle and M. N. Muralidharan, "Program reusability through program transformation," *IEEE Trans. Software Eng.,* vol. SE-10, no. 5, September 1984.

[6] D. C. Brotsky, "An algorithm for parsing flow graphs," M.S. thesis, Mass. Inst. Technol., Cambridge, MA, MIT/AI/TR-704, Mar. 1984.

[7] E. Bush, "The automatic restructing of Cobol," in *Proc. IEEE Conf. Software Maintenance,* Nov. 1985.

[8] J. Carbonell, R. Cullingford, and A. Gershman, "Knowledge-based machine translation," *IEEE Trans. Pattern Anal. Mach. Intell.,* vol. PAMI-3, no. 4, 1981.

[9] R. D. Duffey II, "Formalizing the expertise of the assembler language programmer," Mass. Inst. Technol., Cambridge, MA, MIT/AI/WP-203, Sept. 1980.

[10] G. G. Faust, "Semiautomatic translation of Cobol into Hibol," M.S. thesis, Mass. Inst. Technol., Cambridge, MA, MIT/LCS/TR-256, Mar. 1981.

[11] S. M. Freudenberger, J. T. Schwartz, and M. Sharir, "Experience with the SETL optimizer," *ACM Trans. Programming Lang. Syst.,* vol. 5, no. 1, Jan. 1983.

[12] R. S. Gaines, "On the translation of machine language programs," *Commun. ACM,* vol. 8, no. 12, Dec. 1965.

[13] K. Jensen and N. Wirth, *Pascal User Manual and Report.* New York: Springer-Verlag, 1975.

[14] E. Kant, "On the efficient synthesis of efficient programs," *Artif. Intell.,* vol. 20, no. 3, May 1983.

[15] M. King, "Eurotra: A European system for machine translation," ISSCO, Univ. Geneva, Switzerland, 1980.

[16] K. M. Pitman, "A Fortran → Lisp translator," in *Proc. 1979 Macsyma Users' Conf.,* Washington, DC, June 1979.

[17] C. Rich, "Inspection methods in programming," Ph.D. dissertation, Mass. Inst. Technol., Cambridge, MA, MIT/AI/TR-604, June 1981.

[18] ——, "A formal representation for plans in the Programmer's Apprentice," in *Proc. 7th Int. Joint Conf. Artif. Intell.,* Vancouver, B.C., Canada, Aug. 1981.

[19] ——, The layered architecture of a system for reasoning about programs," in *Proc. 9th Int. Joint Conf. Artif. Intell.,* Los Angeles, CA, Aug. 1985.

[20] G. G. Ruth, S. Alter, and W. A. Martin, "A very high level language for business data processing," Mass. Inst. Technol., Cambridge, MA, MIT/LCS/TR-254, 1981.

[21] H. Samet, "Experience with software conversion," *Software—Practice Experience,* vol. 11, no. 10, 1981.

[22] J. T. Schwartz, "On programming," Interim Rep. SETL Project, Courant Inst. Math. Sci., New York Univ., New York, June 1975.

[23] D. R. Smith, G. B. Kotik, and S. J. Westfold, "Research on knowledge-based software engineering environments at Kestrel Institute," *IEEE Trans. Software Eng.,* vol. SE-11, no. 11, Nov. 1985.

[24] M. F. Smith and B. E. Luff, "Automatic assembler source translation from the Z80 to the MC6809," *IEEE Micro,* vol. 4, no. 2, Apr. 1984.

[25] G. L. Steele, Jr., *Common Lisp: The Language.* Maynard, MA: Digital Press, 1984.

[26] R. Taylor and P. Lemmons, "Upward migration part 1: Translators," *Byte,* vol. 7, no. 4, June 1983.

[27] A. B. Tucker, Jr., "A perspective on machine translation: Theory and practice," *Commun. ACM,* vol. 27, no. 4, Apr. 1984.

[28] R. C. Waters, "A method for analyzing loop programs," *IEEE Trans. Software Eng.,* vol. SE-5, no. 3, May 1979.

[29] ——, "The Programmer's Apprentice: A session with KBEmacs," *IEEE Trans. Software Eng.,* vol. SE-11, no. 11, Nov. 1985.

[30] L. M. Zelinka, "Automated program recognition," Mass. Inst. Technol., Cambridge, MA, MIT/AI/WP-279, Dec. 1985.

[31] *Proc. ACM SIGPLAN Symp. Compiler Construction,* SIGPLAN Notices, vol. 19, no. 4, June 1984.

[32] Brochures describing various translation products, Cap Gemini Dasd Inc., New York, 1985.

[33] Brochures describing various translation products, Dataware Inc., Orchard Park, NY, 1985.

[34] *PDP-11/34 Processor Handbook,* Digital Equipment Corp., Maynard, MA, 1976.

[35] *Fortran IV Language,* pub. C28-6515-6, IBM, White Plains, NY, 1966.

[36] *Scientific Subroutine Package Version III Programmer's Manual,* pub. GH20-0205-4, IBM, White Plains, NY, 1970.

[37] *American National Standard Cobol,* pub. GC28-6396-5, IBM, White Plains, NY, 1973.

[38] *Military Standard Ada Programming Language,* ANSI/MIL-STD-1815A, U.S. Dep. Defense, Washington, DC, Jan. 1983.

Richard C. Waters (M'78–SM'86) received the B.S. degree magna cum laude in applied mathematics (computer science) from Brown University, Providence, RI, in 1972, the M.S. degree in computer science from Harvard University, Cambridge, MA, in 1973, and the Ph.D. degree in computer science with a minor in linguistics from the Massachusetts Institute of Technology, Cambridge, in 1978.

Since then, he has worked in the Artificial Intelligence Laboratory at the Massachusetts Institute of Technology and is currently a Principal Research Scientist. He is working on the Programmer's Apprentice project. This project is developing a system which can assist programmers in developing and maintaining programs. His other interests include programming languages and engineering problem solving.

Dr. Waters is a member of the Association for Computing Machinery and the American Association for Artificial Intelligence as well as a senior member of the IEEE Computer Society.

Chapter 10
Annotating and Documenting Existing Programs

Chapter 10
Annotating and Documenting Existing Programs

Purpose

Papers in this chapter discuss creating information about source code by annotating and documenting the code. "Documentation" here is used broadly. It can mean graphical diagrams, mathematical descriptions, and rationales for why the code is in its current form, as well as the more usual textual documentation.

Papers

The first paper, "A Model for Assembly Program Maintenance" by S. Chen, K.G. Heisler, W.T. Tsai, X. Chen, and E. Leung, describes how a tool can aid in understanding assembly code. The authors describe a theory of program understanding and a tool built to support understanding according to the theory. Understanding will ultimately be evidenced in documentation.

Understanding and documenting assembly code is featured in this tutorial because assembly code is a kind of "worst case" for understanding and documentation. Assembly code tends not to supply as many clues to its purpose as does code in higher level languages. If assembly code can be successfully documented, then similar ideas —suitably modified — may well apply to understanding and documenting code in higher level languages.

The next paper, "Using Function Abstraction to Understand Program Behavior" by Philip Hausler, Mark Pleszkoch, Richard Linger, and Alan Hevner, discusses how to systematically derive a program function that describes the mathematical function that a program performs. The methodology used is called program-function abstraction. Program-function abstraction allows one to create precise functional specifications of existing programs.

In the next paper, "Documentation in a Software Maintenance Environment," L.D. Landis, P.M. Hyland, A.L. Gilbert, and A.J. Fine describe several ways and notations to document programs. They describe a tool, the parser/documenter, for generating Nassi-Shneiderman diagrams from Fortran source code. Their approach to documentation is interesting because their idea, to "take working source code, massage it in some way for representation purposes, and extract that massaged information for generation of documentation output," is typical of reverse engineering documentation tools.

In the final paper, "Recognizing Design Decisions in Programs," Spencer Rugaber, Stephen Ornburn, and Richard LeBlanc, Jr., discuss design decisions inherent in software. The authors note that to "effectively maintain an existing system, a maintenance programmer must be able to sustain design decisions made earlier unless the reasons for the decisions have also changed." They discuss the benefits of capturing design rationale for software maintenance, how to characterize design decisions, and how to find decisions in programs.

SOFTWARE MAINTENANCE: RESEARCH AND PRACTICE, VOL. 2, 3–32 (1990)

A Model for Assembly Program Maintenance

S. CHEN, K. G. HEISLER, W. T. TSAI, X. CHEN AND E. LEUNG
Department of Computer Science, University of Minnesota, Minneapolis, MN 55455, U.S.A.

SUMMARY

This paper presents a model for understanding assembly programs for software maintenance. It is based on the theory that explicit representation of various structural and functional elements of code and multiple relationships among them will aid program understanding and thus software maintenance. We present a parsing technique to extract all the required elements from assembly code to populate the model. The model is a reverse engineering technique. We use the term reverse engineering in its broad sense to include specification as well as design recovery. Most features of this model have been implemented in a tool named 'RETA' for Reverse Engineering Tool for Assembly programs.

The model is useful for software maintenance activities such as program understanding, ripple effect analysis, and program re-documentation. The ripple effect of a contemplated change is the parts of code that depend on the variable or a piece of code to be changed. Once the change is made, those parts need to be re-examined for possible modification. The model generates a functional menu for a given application. The menu describes the functionality of each routine. It is a hierarchical presentation of major program routines, the sub-routines supporting each major routine and so on. A routine at any level of detail consists of one or more paths through the code. Paths are presented as control flow sequences between code blocks. Code blocks, and hence functionalities, use and modify data.

The maintainer locates the routine to be modified at the lowest level of detail within the functional menu. This automatically slices out the set of paths, and hence the set of code blocks, that have a role in the functionality to be changed. The code blocks in the slice determine the data that are used and modified within the routine to be changed. Path analysis and associated data-used and data-modified information are used to determine which code blocks are to be changed and which data roles are to be modified. The same set of relations are applied in reverse to identify the ripple effect.

KEY WORDS   Software maintenance   Design recovery   Reverse engineering   Assembly language   Computer aided software engineering

The high cost of software maintenance and the importance of effective maintenance techniques are widely known (Heninger, 1980; Lehman, 1980; Martin, 1983; Ramamoorthy *et al.*, 1984; Pressman, 1987; Hazzah, 1989). Even a small percentage improvement in the maintenance process can result in significant savings to organizations using large applications. Major improvements in the maintenance process can have far-reaching effects by reducing the investment required to support software, extending the useful life of existing systems, and expanding the range of problems that can be realistically addressed by large software applications.

In general, the software maintenance process is:

(1) *Problem identification*: Identifying the specific functionality to be added or modified and understanding how the new functionality is different from the old functionality.

(2) *Program understanding*: Identifying which program elements are involved in the functionality to be changed and the role these elements play in that functionality. Also, understanding the roles affected program elements may play in other functionalities that are not to be changed. One cannot maintain a program unless one understands it. Program understanding can be a complex task for large applications. Program understanding often involves the specification, the design and the code as well as the interrelationships between them. The solution to this problem is to document, possibly automatically, the software so that it can be easily understood by the maintainer. Specific tools include: program understanding tools (Johnson and Soloway, 1985), reverse engineering tools (Arango *et al.*, 1985; Antonini *et al.*, 1987; Chen and Ramamoorthy, 1986; Waters, 1988; Yamamoto and Isoda, 1986; Bachman, 1989), interconnection language (Yau and Tsai, 1987) and configuration control tools (Rochkind, 1975; Shigo *et al.*, 1982; Tichy, 1982).

(3) *Program modification*: Designing and implementing changes to various code elements to bring about the required functionality changes without adversely affecting other functionalities. Once a modification of software is requested, the maintainer must identify and evaluate design alternatives. The maintainer also examines the impacts of the modification. The reason is that for each change strategy, the maintainer must determine the other routines and variables that might be affected by the contemplated change, i.e., ripple effect, and the maintainer must also decide which portions of the code and which variables have a role in the functionality to be added or changed, i.e., program slicing. Specific tools that are useful in this stage are: ripple effect analyser (Yau *et al.*, 1978) and program slicer (Weiser, 1982).

(4) *Program re-validation*: Testing that the new functionality performs as specified and that no other program functionality has been changed. It is necessary to re-validate a program once it has been changed to ensure its correctness. It is not only necessary to validate new features, but also to validate those unchanged functionalities. This is to ensure that changes do not distort the unchanged functionalities. Thus, previous test cases should be available to test these existing functionalities, but new test cases have to be generated for new features. Tools that are useful in this phase are test case generation tools and test result comparators.

(5) *Re-documentation*: Changing the related program documents including specification and design to reflect the program changes.

The specification and design often reflect a broad range of implementation possibility. The program is an instance drawn from the equivalence class of implementations allowed by the original specification. A maintainer is usually not interested in the broad interpretation, but rather the specific interpretation that applies to the code to be maintained. The derived specification and design information are more specific and more closely related to the actual code, therefore they are more directly applicable to specific program maintenance and evolution. In addition, the specification and design information provided for various program elements by reverse engineering are often more useful for reuse than their original counterparts.

Considerable research continues in this area. Examples include: the C information abstractor (Chen and Ramamoorthy, 1986); a model-based design recovery system (DESIRE) (Biggerstaff, 1989); the ASU software maintenance environment (Collofello and Orn, 1988); a system for inverse transformation of software from code to specification (Sneed and Jandrasics, 1988); the programmer's apprentice (Rich and Waters, 1988); extracting code into Jackson or Warnier/Orr documents (Antonini *et al.*, 1987); a software re-engineering environment (SRE) (Kozaczynski and Ning, 1989); maintenance and porting of software by design recovery (Arango *et al.*, 1985); PROUST (Johnson and Soloway, 1985), intelligent assistance for software development and maintenance (Kaiser, Feiler and Popovich, 1988); Microscope (Ambras and O'Day, 1988); an environment for understanding programs (Cleveland, 1988); a software maintenance support environment (Wild and Maly, 1988); an object-orientated database representation of code for maintenance (Ketabchi *et al.*, 1989); and many commercial companies are developing CASE tools for software maintenance (Hazzah, 1989).

Most reverse engineering tools concentrate on high-level languages such as C or COBOL. Some focus on certain aspects of programs, such as global variables (Chen and Ramamoorthy, 1986). This paper focuses instead on *assembly* programs. Currently, significant software, for a variety of reasons such as efficiency, real-time constraints and history, is written in assembly language or a combination of high-level and assembly languages. These assembly programs are considerably harder to maintain than their high-level counterparts since assembly languages do not support high-level data and control abstractions (Ghezzi and Jazayeri, 1987). It is also important to represent both high-level and assembly parts in a uniform and integrated way because many large applications are written in a combination of high-level and assembly languages.

This paper proposes a reverse engineering model for BAL-like assembly programs. It is based on the theory that explicit representation of various structural and functional elements of code and multiple relationships among them will aid software maintenance. The model interconnects the structural and functional elements of code. The model is useful for many software maintenance activities such as program understanding, ripple effect analysis, and program redocumentation. It aids program understanding, as it can explicitly show various relationships among software components. It is useful for performing ripple effect analysis and thus revalidation of software because it allows the program to trace via these relationships. It is also useful for program redocumentation because it automatically extracts these relationships from the code.

The model can be populated by using a parser-like process from the code. Specifically, we used a syntax tree to represent the code and designed algorithms to extract the required relationships from the syntax tree. Most features of this mode has been implemented in a tool called 'RETA', for Reverse Engineering Tool for Assembly programs in a UNIX (Trademark of AT&T) environment.

This paper is organized as follows: Section 1 states the underlying theory behind our approach and the model which includes structural and functional views. Section 2 describes the implementation of RETA. Our implementation extension is described in Section 3. Finally, this paper concludes in Section 4.

1. THEORY

Our approach to reverse engineering is based on the following theories:

(1) *Explicit representations of various structural and functional elements of the code and multiple relationships among them will aid program understanding and thus software maintenance.* According to Brooks, in his 'No Silver Bullet' article, many software problems exist due to the fact that software is invisible. He said, 'In spite of progress in restricting and simplifying the structures of software, they remain inherently unvisualizable, and thus do not permit the mind to use some of its most powerful conceptual tools. This lack not only impedes the process of design within one mind, it severely hinders communication among minds' (Brooks, 1987).

(2) *The required representations can be classified into two components: structural and functional.* The structural model is a collection of hierarchical entities of the structural elements such as routines and code blocks modelling the code. The functional view provides a hierarchical outline describing the functionalities and sub-functionalities carried out by the application.

(3) *The structural model consists of three important views: part-of, connected-to (which is data connection), and path (which is control connections).* These are necessary information. and they can be derived automatically from the code using parser-like techniques.

(4) *It is useful to associate a role or functionality with each of the elements in each structural view, i.e., part-of, connected-to and path.* According to many software studies, such as (Soloway *et al.*, 1988), programmers think of programs in terms of functionality, but not in terms of programming constructs. The rationale behind a particular element in the program is important as the specific programming syntax used to express the program element.

(5) *The functional hierarchy associated with the overall program is important during maintenance.* This functionality is most closely related to requirement specification and design. It is correlated with the functionality of each path of the software. Thus, the hierarchy of path functionality is an approximation to the application of functional hierarchy. A path represents the dynamic characteristics of an application and these dynamic characteristics are usually the functionality of the application.

Our approach to reverse engineering is based on a model that supports both structural and functional views. The functional view includes specification information (what is done) as well as design information (how it is done). The specification information is detailed in language understood by the maintainer and easy to access. The design information is easy to access and facilitates selective probing at all levels of detail.

It is important that the model should correspond to the actual code. The specification and design aspects of the functional view must be directly related to the structural view which in turn must faithfully represent the actual code. The model described in this paper meets these requirements.

Section 1.1 describes the model which consists of structural and functional views. Examples of these two views are given in Section 1.2. Section 1.3 presents the required mechanisms to support these two views. Section 1.4 presents a scenario of software maintenance using these two views.

1.1. Model Overview

1.1.1. Structural view

The structural view is presented as a hierarchy of code blocks. It contains various relations within a code block, data flow information such as data use and modify, and control flow information such as exists. The structural view can be derived using a parsing technique.

Code block hierarchy. The code block hierarchy consists of three layers:

(1) The application, which represents the overall software application.

(2) Routines within the application. An application contains multiple routines.

(3) Code blocks within a routine. A code block which is a contiguous sequence of instructions is defined below.

Assembly languages are flat in scope, i.e., all routines and variables within routines are global. Thus, the code block hierarchy consists of only three layers, the overall application, routines within the applications, and code blocks within a routine. The rules for blocking code blocks are as follows:

Rule 1: The instruction immediately preceding a label is the last instruction of a code block. Labels will be generated for blocks with no label.

Rule 2: The instruction associated with a label is the first instruction of a code block.

Rule 3: A branch instruction is the last instruction of a code block unless it is followed by another branch instruction.

Rule 4: If a block ends with a branch instruction (BAL and BALR excepted) then there is no implicit exit to the next code block; otherwise there is.

A code block is similar to a basic block in compiler theory. A basic block is a contiguous sequence of instructions that are always entered at the beginning and there is no branching within a basic block, i.e., any branching is always to some other basic blocks (Hecht, 1977). Furthermore, a call within a basic block is considered as an assignment statement. A code block, however, may allow multiple branches to be placed at the end.

Data and control flow information. We capture three kinds of information within each code block.

(1) Data flow:
variables defined within a code block;
variables referenced but not modified within a code block;
variables whose value may be modified within a code block.

(2) Exits from a code block:
   calls to a routine;
   returns;
   explicit branches to another code block;
   implicit exits to the next code block in sequence.

(3) Entry point:
   the entry point of a routine is the first code block to be executed within the routine.

Relations within a code block. Code blocks and their associated information establish a hierarchical structure and important relations as follows:

1. The code block hierarchy.

2. A set of relations as follows: (dn = variable; cbn = code block name)
   r1: <dn> defined-in <cbn>
   r2: <dn> referenced-by <cbn>
   r3: <dn> modified-by <cbn>
   r4: <cbn> part-of <cbn>
   r5: <cbn> includes <cbn>
   r6: <cbn> defines <dn>
   r7: <cbn> references <dn>
   r8: <cbn> modifies <dn>
   r9: <cbn> exits-to <cbn>
   r10: <cbn> entered-from <cbn>

The relation 'references' implies use but not modification of the variable within a code block. This hierarchical structure and its associated relations constitute the structural view of the model. A second hierarchy and associated set of relations make up the functional view of the model. This structure is called the functional hierarchy and is introduced in Section 1.1.2.

An automatic parsing process is used to decompose any program into code blocks within each routine. The decomposition depends on the implementation language and may be tuned to specific practices within an implementation environment.

1.1.2. Functional view

The functional view presents the user's view on the program. The functional view provides a hierarchical outline describing the functionalities and sub-functionalities carried out by the application. It can be used to slice out the appropriate code for software maintenance. Assembly language is flat, thus all routines are on the same level. Even though for any large application a conceptual hierarchy exists, this hierarchy is lost during coding. We introduce a functional block which can be nested to recapture this hierarchy.

Functional blocks. In addition to code blocks, we introduce functional blocks. A functional block is either a code block annotated with a functionality, or code blocks that work together to perform some functionality, or a combination of other functional blocks with a higher level functional meaning. Code blocks cannot be nested, but functional blocks can.

Since functional blocks are collections of code blocks, they automatically inherit the relations associated with code blocks. In particular, each functional block uses certain code blocks and references or modifies certain data. A given code block is used by certain functional blocks and a given variable is referenced by or modified by certain functional blocks. We analyse paths among functional blocks in the same way we analyse paths between code blocks. These paths among functional blocks, along with the specific details of the code blocks that make up a functional block, constitute the design-type information associated with functional view.

Functional hierarchy. The functional hierarchy is displayed as a functional menu. The functional menu is organized as illustrated in Figure 1. The menu is headed by the functionality associated with the overall application. Within the application, there are entry points to each routine. Within each routine, its functionality can be divided into sub-functionalities. This process can be repeated up to the routine call level. A call in the functional menu leads to the entry point of another routine.

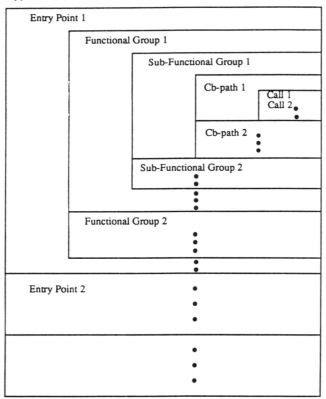

Figure 1. Functional menu format

Code-block-path (Cb-path) analysis is used to group code blocks into a hierarchy of functional groups. This formation of code blocks into functional groups leads to the formation of a functional menu, representing a hierarchical specification of what the code actually does. The exits from each code block form the basis for path tracing in the form of sequences of code blocks. Cb-paths analysis shows all possible sequences of code blocks through an application beginning with each entry point to the application.

A functional menu serves as a table of contents and index into the functionality of an application. The functional menu is most closely related to requirement specification. Design is correlated with paths. These may stand alone as reconstituted documentation when original documentation is inadequate or may be cross referenced to original specifications and design.

Relations within functional hierarchy. Each entry in the functional menu corresponds to a functional block which is a set of code blocks. Therefore all the relations which hold between code blocks apply equally to functional blocks. These include: (fn = functional block name; dn = variable; cbn = code block name)

r11. <fn> uses <cbn>
r12. <cbn> used-by <fn>
r13. <fn> exits-to <fn>
r14. <fn> entered-from <fn>

There are also the two relations that define the functional hierarchy.

r15. <fn> part-of <fn>
r16. <fn> contains <fn>

Functionality is most closely related to requirement specification and design, and is correlated with each path of the software. Thus, the hierarchy of path functionality is an approximation to the application of functionality hierarchy.

Slicing and ripple effect. The functional menu and its associated relations support many maintenance tasks. For example, given a maintenance requirement, the user can select those functional blocks from the functional menu that have a role in the functionality to be changed. An immediate list of variables and code blocks used by the selected functional blocks can be produced.

Conversely, when the user is contemplating a change to a code block or a variable, the list of functional blocks using that code block or variable can be produced to decide which competing options have the least ripple effect.

1.2. Example of Structural and Functional Views

Figure 2 shows an example routine. It is named 'RS' and controls the scheduling of various processes simultaneously within a large application. These processes use devices and channels. Each process is tracked by a status block.

The horizontal lines in Figure 2 delineate the code blocks. Each code block is assigned a unique number. These numbers are shown in the left column of Figure 2. Figure 3 shows the data and control flow of each code block.

0	1	RS	ST	R5,RSRET	RUN SCHEDULLER
	2		BAL	R5,CLOSEQ	CLOSE PHASE?
	3		B	RSCLOSE	IF TRUE
	4		B	RSSCH	CONTINUE IF FALSE
1	5	RSSCH	BAL	R5,TIMEQ	TIME EXPIRED?
	6		B	RSCLOSE	IF TRUE
	7		B	RSNEXT	CONTINUE IF FALSE
2	8	RSNEXT	BAL	R5,GETNEXT	GET NEXT ACTIVITY
	9		B	RSACT0	NOT READY FOR NEXT ACTIVITY
	10		B	RSACT1	TYPE1 ACTIVITY NEXT
	11		B	RSACT2	TYPE2 ACTIVITY NEXT
3	12	RSACT0	B	RSRET2	NOT READY FOR NEXT ACTIVITY
4	13	RSACT1	BAL	R5,TYPE1	PROCESS TYPE1 ACTIVITY
	14		B	RSSCH	IF RETURN IS "0"
	15		B	RSEND	END THE RUN IF RETURN IS "1"
5	16	RSACT2	BAL	R5,TYPE2	PROCESS TYPE2 ACTIVITY
	17		B	RSSCH	IF RETURN IS "0"
	18		B	RSEND	END THE RUN IF RETURN IS "1"
6	19	RSCLOSE	BAL	R5,SETCL	SET CLOSE FLAG TO TRUE
	20		BAL	R5,RESETQ	RESET PHASE?
	21		B	RSRESET	IF TRUE
	22		B	RSREL	IF FALSE
7	23	RSREL	BAL	R5,DEVYQ	DEVICE Y ATTACHED?
	24		B	RSRELY	IF TRUE
	25		B	RSREADY	CONTINUE IF FALSE
8	26	RSREADY	BAL	R5,MKRDY	RESET STATUS BLOCK
	27		B	RSRET1	
9	28	RSRELY	BAL	R5,RELY	RELEASE DEVICE Y
	29		B	RSREADY	
10	30	RSRESET	BAL	R5,INITQ	RUN INITIATION?
	31		B	RSREL	IF TRUE
	32		B	RSCHAN1	IF FALSE
11	33	RSCHAN1	BAL	R5,CHAN1Q	CHANNEL 1 IDLE?
	34		B	RSCHAN2	IF TRUE
	35		B	RSRET2	IF FALSE
12	36	RSCHAN2	BAL	R5,CHAN2Q	CHANNEL 2 IDLE
	37		B	RSREL	IF TRUE
	38		B	RSRST	CONTINUE IF FALSE
13	39	RSRST	BAL	R5,RESETX	RESET DEVICE X
	40		B	RSRET2	WAIT FOR X TO RESET
14	41	RSEND	BAL	R5,HIACTQ	HIGH ACTIVITY?
	42		B	RSHIGH	IF TRUE
	43		B	RSLOW	CONTINUE IF FALSE
15	44	RSLOW	BAL	R5,SETLOW	SET LOW PRIORITY
	45		B	RSCLOSE	
16	46	RSHIGH	BAL	R5,SETHI	SET HIGH PRIORITY
	47		B	RSCLOSE	
17	48	RSRET1	L	R5,RSRET	PROCESS COMPLETE
	49		BR	R5	RETURN 1
18	50	RSRET2	L	R5,RSRET+2	PROCESS WAITING
	51		BR	R5	RETURN 2
	52	RSRET	DSF	1	RETURN ADDRESS

Figure 2. Code blocks within sample routine

The sample routine has one entry point, which is block rs.0. Figure 4 shows the paths through this sample routine from its entry point. The boxes shown represent code blocks. The numbers in the boxes refer to the code block numbers in Figure 2. The circles represent path segment terminators. The numbers in the circles refer to the block to which control flows next. The letter R denotes a return from the routine.

```
Code Block 0                    Code Block 9
        modifies RSRET              call RELY
        call CLOSEQ                 exit to 8
        exit to 6               Code Block 10
        exit to 1                   call INITQ
Code Block 1                        exit to 7
        call TIMEQ                  exit to 11
        exit to 6               Code Block 11
        exit to 2                   call CHAN1Q
Code Block 2                        exit to 12
        call GETNEXT                exit to 18
        exit to 3               Code Block 12
        exit to 4                   call CHAN2Q
        exit to 5                   exit to 7
Code Block 3                        exit to 13
        exit to 18              Code Block 13
Code Block 4                        call RESETX
        call TYPE1                  exit to 18
        exit to 1               Code Block 14
        exit to 14                  call HIACTQ
Code Block 5                        exit to 16
        call TYPE2                  exit to 15
        exit to 1               Code Block 15
        exit to 14                  call SETLOW
Code Block 6                        exit to 6
        call SETCL              Code Block 16
        call RESETQ                 call SETHI
        exit to 10                  exit to 6
        exit to 7               Code Block 17
Code Block 7                        references RSRET
        call DEVYQ                  return +0
        exit to 9               Code Block 18
        exit to 8                   defines RSRET
Code Block 8                        references RSRET
        call MKRDY                  return +1
        exit to 17
```

Figure 3. Contents of each sample code block

In Figure 4, for example, the paths seem to group into those that emanate from code block rs.6 and those that emanate from code block rs.2. Code block rs.0 distributes control either to rs.6 or to rs.2. Within the group following rs.6, there are two sub-groups; those emanating from rs.10 and those emanating from rs.7. Finally, within the paths emanating from rs.2, there is an embedded functional block emanating from rs.14.

We return to Figure 2 with this analysis of paths in mind and look at the operations, names and comments within the code blocks associated with each path grouping. We can group code blocks to form functional blocks. This is an iterative process. Figure 5 shows a three-level hierarchy of functional blocks.

From the functional block grouping, we then document the code to the routine call level. This process forms a functional menu. Figure 6 shows the functional menu.

The numbers along the left side of Figure 6 are menu line numbers for easy reference. The numbers in parentheses are the code blocks that participate in a given functionality. If the code blocks are in a list (1,2,3, . . .) then more than one path is involved. If the code blocks form a sequence (1–2–3– . . .), the functionality represents the single code block path indicated.

A MODEL FOR ASSEMBLY PROGRAM MAINTENANCE   13

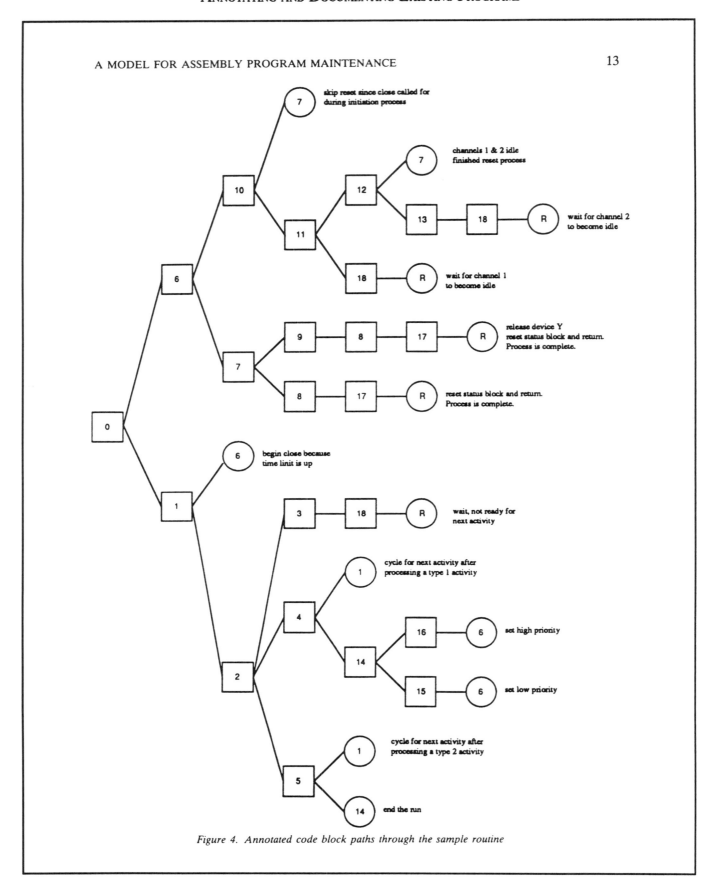

Figure 4. Annotated code block paths through the sample routine

RS: Run scheduling. (0, 1,2,3,4,5,6,7,8,9,10,11,12,13,14,15,16,17,18)
   ENTER: distributing control to the right part of RS
              depending on current state. (0)
   SCHEDULE: Scheduling activities. (1,2,3,4,5,18)
   CLOSE: Releasing devices and channels. (6,7,8,9,10,11,12,13,17,18)
       FINISH: Releasing device Y and resetting the status block. (7,8,9,17)
       RESET: Waiting for the channels to become idle and resetting device X.
              (6,10,11,12,13,18)
   END: Setting priorities before ending a session. (14,15,16)

Figure 5. Sample functional block groupings

1.3. Required Mechanisms

To support the above model, we need the following support mechanisms: structural abstraction, path information, functional menu, and data flow information. Section 2.2 describes the implementation of these features in RETA.

Structural abstraction. The tool should be able to recognize routines within an application, and all code blocks within a routine. The user should be able to group several code blocks to form a functional block.

Path information. The tool should recognize all exits from a code block and connect code blocks to form paths. It should be able to trace these paths and a user should be able to attach a functionality with paths.

Functional menu. The tool should be able to form a functional menu starting with entry points. The functional menu should correspond with the code and should be constructed automatically if the user supplied proper annotations. The functional menu should contain call information.

Data flow information. The tools should provide data use, data modify and data definition within a code block. This information is useful for ripple effect analysis.

1.4. Using the model for software maintenance

The model can be used to support maintenance tasks:

(a) Viewing the model from a requirements specification point-of-view (functionality) to enable focus on the areas in which corrections are to be made..The user can select those functional blocks from the functional menu that have a role in the functionality to be changed.

(b) Viewing the model from a design point-of-view, i.e., the structural view. Once the functional blocks have been identified for change, we can identify the related code blocks to be changes.

(c) Path tracing to interrelate the functional and structural views as an aid to determining which changes to make and where to make them.

(d) Ripple effect analysis to assess the potential side effects from contemplated changes.

(e) Repeating these four steps until the changes provide the required modifications without undesirable side effects.

```
1       RS: Run scheduling. (0,1,2,3,4,5,6,7,8,9,10,11,12,13,14,15,16,17,18)
2            ENTER: route to scheduling or close. (0)
3                 TOCLOSE: continue close phase. (0-6-)
4                      call CLOSEQ: In close phase? (0)
5                 TOSCHEDULE: begin or continue scheduling. (0-1-)
6                      call CLOSEQ: In close phase? (0)
7            SCHEDULE: Schedule run activities. (1,2,3,4,5,18)
8                 TIMEOUT: (-1-6-)
9                      call TIMEQ: Time expired? (1)
10                WAIT: not ready for next activity. (-1-2-3-18-R)
11                     call TIMEQ: Time expired? (1)
12                     call GETNEXT: get next activity. (2)
13                     RETURN (18)
14                TYPE1: schedule a type1 activity. (1,2,4)
15                     TYPE1S: short duration activity. (-1-2-4-1-)
16                          call TIMEQ: Time expired? (1)
17                          call GETNEXT: get next activity. (2)
18                          call TYPE1: schedule a type1 activity. (4)
19                     TYPE1L: long duration activity. (-1-2-4-14-)
20                          call TIMEQ: Time expired? (1)
21                          call GETNEXT: get next activity. (2)
22                          call TYPE1: schedule a type1 activity. (4)
23                TYPE2: schedule a type2 activity. (1,2,5)
24                     TYPE2S: short duration activity. (-1-2-5-1-)
25                          call TIMEQ: Time expired? (1)
26                          call GETNEXT: get next activity. (2)
27                          call TYPE2: schedule a type1 activity. (5)
28                     TYPE2L: long duration activity. (-1-2-5-14-)
29                          call TIMEQ: Time expired? (1)
30                          call GETNEXT: get next activity. (2)
31                          call TYPE2: schedule a type 2 activity. (5)
32           END: end current session. (14,15,16)
33                HIP: end with high priority for resumption. (-14-16-6-)
34                     call HIACTQ: high activity? (14)
35                     call SETHI: set high priority. (16)
36                LOWP: end with low priority for resumption. (-14-15-6-)
37                     call HIACTQ: hight activity? (14)
38                     call SETLOW: set low priority. (15)
39           CLOSE: release channels and devices. (6,7,8,9,10,11,12,13,17,18)
40                RESET: reset channels and devices. (6,10,11,12,13)
41                     SKIP: skip reset since close called during initiation. (-6-10-7-)
42                          call SETCL: set close flag to true. (6)
43                          call RESETQ: reset phase complete? (6)
44                          call INITQ: run initiation? (10)
45                     IDLE: chans 1 & 2 idle, finished reset. (-6-10-11-12-7-)
46                          call SETCL: set close flag to true. (6)
47                          call RESETQ: reset phase complete? (6)
48                          call INITQ: run initiation? (10)
49                          call CHAN1Q: channel 1 idle? (11)
50                          call CHAN2Q: çhannel 2 idle? (12)
51                     WAIT1: wait for chan 1 to become idle. (-6-10-11-18-R)
52                          call SETCL: set close flag to true. (6)
53                          call RESETQ: reset phase complete? (6)
54                          call INITQ: run initiation? (10)
55                          call CHAN1Q: channel 1 idle? (11)
56                          RETURN
57                     WAIT2: wait for chan 2 to become idle. (-6-10-11-12-13-18-R)
58                          call SETCL: set close flag to true. (6)
59                          call RESETQ: reset phase complete? (6)
60                          call INITQ: run initiation? (10)
61                          call CHAN1Q: channel 1 idle? (11)
62                          call CHAN2Q: çhannel 2 idle? (12)
63                          call RESETX: reset device X. (13)
64                          RETURN
65                FINISH: finish close process. (7,8,9,17)
66                     YACTIVE: release device Y, reset status block. (-7-9-8-17-R)
67                          call DEVYQ: device Y attached? (7)
68                          call RELY: release device Y. (9)
69                          call MKRDY: reset status block. (8)
70                          RETURN
71                     YINACTIVE: reset status block. (-7-8-17-R)
72                          call DEVYQ: device Y attached? (7)
73                          call MKRDY: reset status block. (8)
74                          RETURN
```

Figure 6. Sample functional menu

Figure 6 is used as an example. Recently, channel 2 was replaced with a faster channel. After this replacement the users discovered that sometimes device X did not reset. What is the problem? A probe of the functional menu reveals that the resetting of device X is only carried out within the RS run scheduling routine. Examination of the functional menu for RS (Figure 6) reveals that the resetting of device X takes place only in code block 13 and that code block 13 is only used along one path (line 57 on Figure 6). However, this path is never taken if channel 2 becomes idle before channel 1; the path at line 45 is taken instead. This had never happened until the new, faster channel 2 was installed. The answer is either to add the reset X command to the second path or move the reset command to a block that is common to the two paths, but not common to any other path. The only code block that is common to both paths and common with no other path is code block 12. This focuses attention on code blocks 12 and 13. The recommended change is to move the reset X command from block 13 (which in fact eliminates this block) into the beginning of code block 12.

Conversely, when the user is contemplating a change to a code block or a variable, the list of functional blocks using that code block or variable can be produced to decide which competing options are likely to have the least ripple effect. In the above example, the only use of the code blocks to be changed is within the original slice. However, as another example, code block 18 has different roles along three different paths: setting up a return to wait for channel 1 to idle; setting up a return to wait for channel 2 to idle; and setting up a return to wait until the system is ready for the next activity to be scheduled. Any change to code block 18 must be consistent with each of these three roles.

2. DESIGN AND IMPLEMENTATION

RETA is a prototype of the model described in Section 1. This section describes RETA with emphasis on the design issues.

RETA consists of the modules shown in Figure 7. Annotated code is used as input to the parser, the parser reads the input source and constructs a syntax-tree according to the rules specified in the grammar. The retrieval routine takes the syntax-tree as input and produces a display file. The user interface takes this display file, and generates the information needed for the display. Currently we use Sun View, a Sun workstation graphic tool, as the display for RETA. The display file is updated as code and code

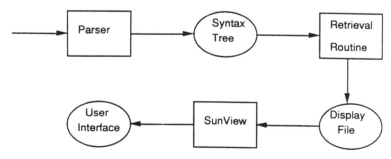

Figure 7. Structure of RETA

Figure 8. Cyclic process of annotation and reverse engineering

annotation changes by re-running the code through the parser, retrieval routines, and display routines in sequence.

Functionality information can be approximated by the comments in code. The quality of this approximation depends critically on the original comments and how well the comments have been maintained. Poorly maintained software does not have reliable comments. We view supplemental annotation as an important part of the program understanding and maintenance process. This is a cyclic process as shown in Figure 8. Initially, if the comments are not reliable, a maintainer can just parse the program to RETA. As the maintainer gains understanding of the code, annotation can begin and the annotated code can be parsed through RETA interactively. The annotator can be simply an editor such as **vi** or a syntax-directed editor.

Section 2.1 discusses design issues including classification of instruction statements and parsing techniques. Section 2.2 presents the difficulties encountered, including identification of macros, annotation, meaning of a label, local versus global variables and evaluation of pointers. Section 2.3 describes the syntax tree. It shows an example syntax tree, demonstrates how information can be retrieved from the syntax tree and describes how the tree supports ripple effect analysis.

2.1. Design issues

2.1.1. Input source code and classification

Each source line in an assembly code is one of the following types:

Macro call;
Comment line/annotation statement;
Data/memory storage definition;
Instruction line.

Macros are expanded only if the code has been assembled. A comment line which begins with a period has no instruction directives. Data/memory storage definitions are the directives that define a constant or reserve memory locations for data.

Each instruction line can be divided into four fields. They are label field, mnemonic code field, operand(s) field and comment field. All fields except the mnemonic code fields may not exist in an instruction line. The handling of a symbol in the label field is similar to the handling of symbols in the label field of data/storage definition lines.

2.1.2. The design

We considered two alternative ways to design RETA. One was to design individual tools to obtain the necessary information. This would require that a program be written and maintained for each tool. Also, there would be overlapping among these tools. Moreover, for each new language new tools need to be developed.

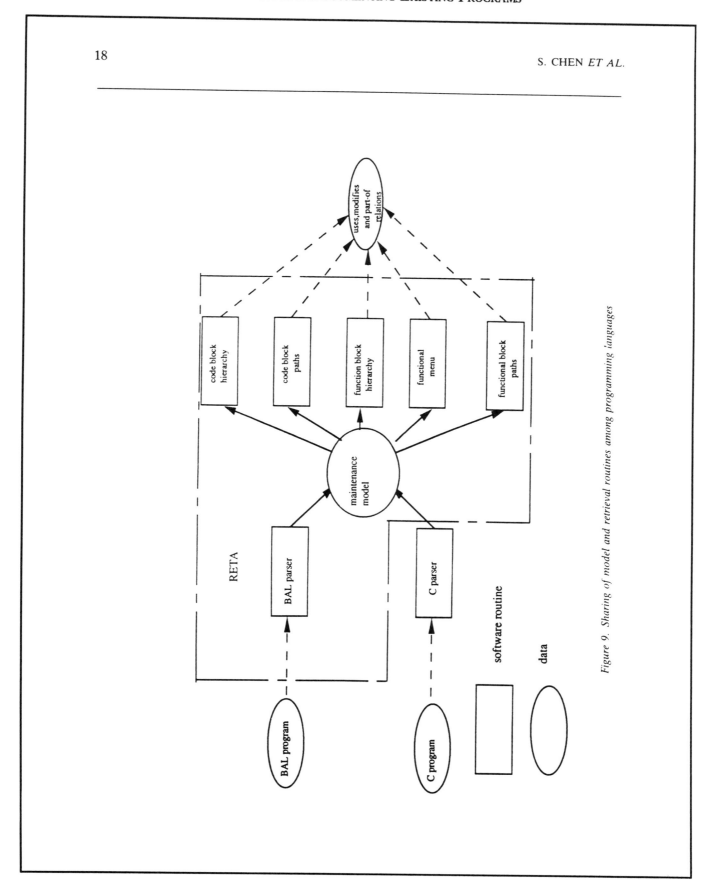

Figure 9. Sharing of model and retrieval routines among programming languages

The second alternative was to find an overall representation of the software that allows a uniform retrieval of information. We choose this latter alternative because no matter what the input language is, only the language dependent part of the model needs to be re-built. Thus, we can easily extend RETA to include other programming languages. A possible scenario is to have BAL and C programs as inputs, but sharing the same model and tools, see Figure 9.

We decided to employ high-level programming language parsing techniques. Specifically we use a parse-tree-like structure, i.e., syntax tree, to represent code. The syntax tree is hierarchical in structure and contains syntactic information from the code. It can also extract the relevant information from the comment statements.

Use of existing tools, such as YACC (Johnson, 1984), provides flexibility in building RETA. We tried to develop specialized programs without YACC but it did not work because the design was changing frequently. Thus, we were forced to use YACC and it has helped significantly. Often we need to change only the grammar to reflect a design change.

The existing parsing techniques used in compilers most likely generate an intermediate form that is useful for code generation. Since our goal is to obtain a hierarchical representation of the assembly code that is as complete as possible, we chose to generate a complete syntax tree instead.

2.1.3. The implementation

The inputs to RETA are CODEL (NCR COMTEN 1986) assembly programs, which are similar to BAL. There are two main sets of instructions. One is the sequential instructions, which do not change the execution sequence, such as load, store, compare, arithmetic and logical instructions. The other is the jump instructions. A label is always global and it can either be a variable or an address. A data label is where the variable is defined. Store instructions determine if a variable gets modified, and load instructions indicate the use of a variable. Jump instructions determine a path through the software.

Sequential instructions can range from zero-operand to three-operand instructions, jump instructions can be two or three operand instructions, and a routine call instruction is a two operand instruction. If a register is involved in the instruction, a trace of register contents is needed to determine where variables are used and modified.

To use YACC, we need to:

(1) Identify the syntax structure of the input source language.

(2) Identify the instruction fields.

(3) For each instruction, identify the type of instruction.

(4) Identify the syntactic structure of the language, the structure must be expressed as a set of grammar rules. Each of the grammar rules describes an acceptable structure within the language. The grammar for CODEL is given in Appendix A.

(5) After specifying the grammar rules, a set of semantic routines is built with respect to the set of grammar rules. Semantic routines specify what action to take when a

particular grammar rule is recognized by the parser. In other words, a semantic routine will be invoked only when its corresponding grammar rule is recognized.

(6) Use YACC to generate code for these grammar rules and their corresponding semantic routines.

Recall that there are two types of blocks: code blocks and functional blocks. A user can specify a functional block by placing the keyword **fb** at beginning of the block, and **fe** at the end. Code blocks are created automatically.

2.2. Difficulties encountered

Instruction format in assembly language varies a lot. Effort has been devoted to studying and clarifying the expressions used in the operand field. Macro expansion, functionality annotation, labels, local versus global variables and pointers are the major issues.

2.2.1. Identification of macros

If the source code has been macro-expanded, all statements contain regular instructions and RETA can process them. If the source code has not been macro-expanded, RETA will skip all the macro calls except HDNG (abbreviation for heading) which identifies the beginning of a routine. We introduce a lexical scope for an assembly routine based on this HDNG statement.

2.2.2. To what extent should comment statements be used?

Comment statements can be used as the functionality of code, but there is no standard placement or format for the comment statement. As a result, each programmer has his own commenting style. If all comments become the functionality, there might be redundant or incorrect information, because not all comments are up-to-date. Thus, RETA will not pick up any comments as functionality unless the maintainer formally annotates or selects them. RETA uses a formalized format for placing annotation statements:

'fb,r,name'   : marks the beginning of a routine name as indicated;
'fb,b,name'   : marks the beginning of a functional block with name as indicated;
'fe'   : marks the ending of a block.

2.2.3. Meaning of a label

Although assembly language is flat and all the labels are global, we physically create a local symbol table within the scope of a routine. This aids in deciding whether a particular jump instruction is within or outside of this scope.

A label can mean a piece of data, which is equivalent to variables in high level language, but, it can also mean an address, which is equivalent to a routine name or a branch address in high level language. Or, it can mean both. For example:

```
HINST     BAL    R8,HROUTE


LINST     BAL    R8,LROUTE


          CR     R1,R2          COMPARE REGISTER CONTENT
          BH     LOADH          R1>R2 ?
          L      R3,LINST       R1<R2, CHOOSE LOW ROUTE
          B      OVERWRT        STORE CODE IN INTRLA
LOADH     L      R3,HINST       R1>R2, CHOOSE HIGH ROUTE
OVERWRT   ST     R3,INTRLA      STORE CODE IN INTRLA
          B      INTRLA


INTRLA    DSF    1              INSTRUCTION IS A CALL TO
          B      MORE           EITHER HIGH OR LOW ROUTE
```

Figure 10 shows a part of this example. From the example, the instruction 'B INTRLA' has a pointer to the node labelled 'INTRLA' which is located in the symbol table. By traversing the link from the branch instruction node to 'INTRLA', we know that

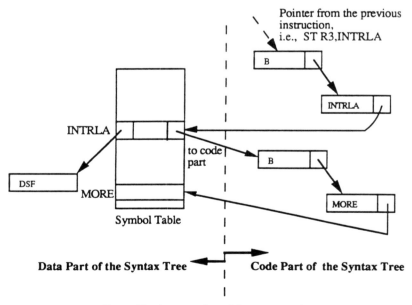

Figure 10. An example and its representation

'INTRLA' has been used as a branch address. Also, by the instruction 'ST R3,INTRLA', we know that 'INTRLA' has been used as a variable. Thus the label 'INTRLA' has both meanings. RETA shows that INTRLA has been used and also there is an exit to the block named INTRLA. This gives the maintainer an idea of the use of label INTRLA.

We identify data labels and address labels by analysing the code. For example, a label that is branched to is a branch address and a label that is the object of a load or stores instructions is a datum.

2.2.4. *Local versus global variables*

All variables are global in CODEL. But when an implementor writes code, he might have in mind what is global and what is local. A local variables may be declared with a routine, but when a variable is declared within a certain routine, we do not know if it is global unless we trace through the code to find out the usage of the variable. This is further complicated by the need to trace register contents.

```
THE FIRST ROUTINE
          ST    R1,STORR1        BEGIN OF A ROUTINE
          L     R1,GLOBALD       USE R1 IN THIS CONTEXT
          .                      PREVIOUS CONTENT OF
          .                      R1 IS NOT USED IN THIS
          .                      ROUTINE.

          L     R1, STORR1       RESORE VALUE OF R1
          .                      END OF ROUTINE
          .
          .
STORR1    DSF   1                TEMPORARY STORAGE: R1
GLOBALD   DF    2                GLOBAL DATA
          .
          .
          .
.END OF ROUTINE
          .
          .
          .
          L     R4,GLOBALD       GLOBALD DEFINED IN
                                 PREVIOUS UNIT
```

In this example, GLOBALD is being defined in the first routine. From the first routine, we might think that it is a local variable, but in fact, GLOBALD is shared by at least two routines. Thus, at the current stage we consider all variables as global.

2.2.5. *Evaluation of pointer type*

Registers are heavily used in the code. If registers are involved, it is impossible to tell if a certain variable gets used or modified by static analysis. This cannot be done unless we trace the contents and the meaning of the register.

```
        L     R1,INDRTAD    C(R1)=INDRTPTR
        .
        ALR   R1,R2         C(R1)=C(R1)+C(R2)
        .
        BR    R1            BRANCH TO INDRTPTR+C(R2)
        .
        .
INDRTAD DF    INDRTPTR      C(INDRTAD)=INDRTPTR
        .
        .
INDRTPTR.
        .
```

From the example above, INDRTPTR is being loaded into register R1. This is in fact equivalent to loading the address of label INDRTPTR into register R1. Static analysis can indicate that variable INDRTAD is being used, and the subsequent branch statement 'BR R1', which is a branch to INDRTPTR, is an indirect jump. However, the contents of R1 may have been changed before the branch instruction. Without tracing the contents of R1, there is no way of knowing to where 'BR R1' actually branches.

2.3. Syntax tree

We use the syntax tree to represent assembly programs because it can show many implicit relations within an assembly program. For example, routines, calls, data use, data modify, functional blocks, and code blocks need to be explicitly represented for easy retrieval. Figure 11 shows the syntax tree of the sample program in Section 2.3.1.

2.3.1. Example

The following is an example written in CODEL.

```
              HDGN SORT INTEGER ARRAY OF MAXIMUM SIZE 100
._fb,r,sorting: the following routine sorts elements in the array

._fb,b, sort:this routine sorts elements using bubble sort
SORT        LH    R3,FIRST            R3=I
._fb,b,loopi:this loop on index i, i.e., outer loop in C part
CMPNEXTI    LR    R4,R3               R4=J
            A     R4,ONE              R4=J+1
            LH    R2,FIRST            R2=INDEX
            LH    R1,ARRAY(R2)        R1=TEMP
._fb,b,loopj:this loop on index j, i.e., inner loop in C part
CMPNEXTJ    CH    R1,ARRAY(R4)        R1>ARRAY(R4)?
            BH    NEXT
            LH    R1,ARRAY(R4)        IF R1<ARRAY(R4)
            LR    R2,R4               TRACK INDEX AND VALUE
NEXT        A     R4,ONE              INCREMENT R4
            C     R4,N                END OF LIST?
            BNE   CMPNEXTJ
._fe:end loop on index j
._fb,b,swap:call swap to interchange two elements
            BAL   R5,SWAP             R5=RETURN ADDRESS
```

```
._fe:
                    A      R3,ONE              INCREMENT R3
                    C      R3,LAST             LAST TWO ELEMENTS?
                    BNE    CMPNEXTI
        ._fe:end loop on index i
        FIRST       DH     0
        LAST        DH     99
        N           DH     100
        ONE         DH     1
        ._fe:
        ._fe:
                    HDNG   SWAP TWO ELEMENTS
        ._fb,r,swap:this routine exchanges two elements in the array
        SWAP        R6,ARRAY(R3)               R6=FIRST
                    LH
                    LH     R7,ARRAY(R2)        R7=SECOND
                    STH    R6,ARRAY(R2)
                    STH    R7,ARRAY(R3)
                    BR     R5
        ARRAY       DSH    100
        ._fe:
```

Figure 11 shows the syntax tree of the CODEL example. Whenever the instruction is in register mode, the instruction is not evaluated, for example LR (load content of one register to another register) instruction, since a trace of the register content is required to know what variable gets used. Figure 12 shows the functional menu from the example.

2.3.2. Description of nodes in the syntax tree

The tree consists of a symbol table part and a code part. The symbol table stores the labels that appear in the code. The code part builds the structural hierarchy. A local symbol table is associated with each routine, and is used to determine if a branch address is within or outside of the routine. It contains all the labels in the routine. A global symbol table is used to check if a label has been defined. Since all labels are global within the application, the global symbol table contains all the labels within the application. Therefore, a label will appear in both local and global symbol tables.

The following is a brief description of the data structure used in RETA.

BAL_LET This node represents a routine or an application. If it represents an application, its BODY field points to the routines within it. If it is a routine, it points to the CODE_BLOCKs within it. The VAR (for variable) field of an application points to the global symbol table, and the *VAR* field of a routine points to the local symbol table.

FUNCTIONAL_BLOCK This node represents a functional block. It holds the content of the annotation, from the assembly source code, which identifies the functionality of the block. Its *BODY* field points to the blocks within the functional blocks.

CODE_BLOCK This node represents a code block. All the instructions that belong to this block are linked. Its *CHAIN* field points to the instructions and *NEXT* field points to the next block.

BAL_INSTR This node represents instructions of no interest currently. It contains the mnemonic code of the instruction and the corresponding operands (as a string of character). It also contains a pointer to its supercontext (its parent block node). Its *OPERAND* field points to the operands of the instruction.

TWO_OPERAND_INSTR This node represents a two-operand sequential instruction. It contains the mnemonic code of the instruction and two pointers to each of its

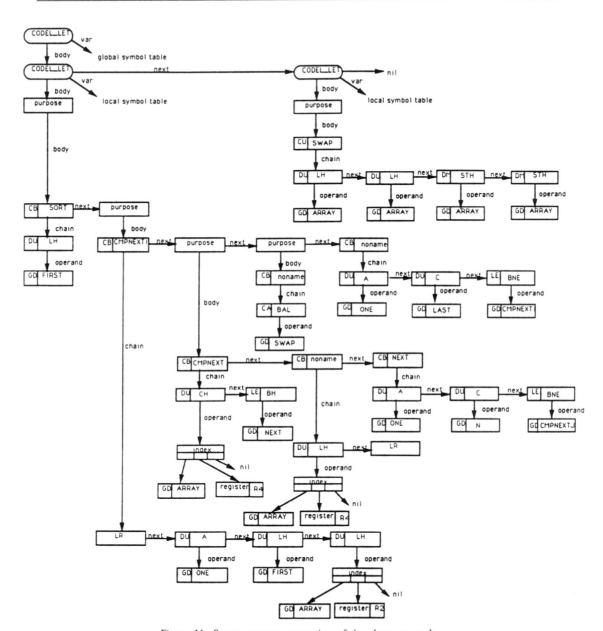

Figure 11. Syntax tree representation of the above example

operands. It also contains a pointer to its supercontext (its parent block node). Its *OPERAND* field points to the operand of the instruction.

THREE_OPERAND_INSTR   This node represents a three-operand sequential instruction. It is similar to TWO_OPERAND_INSTR. Its *OPERAND* field points to the operand of the instruction.

BAL_CALL. BAL_GOTO and BAL_COND_BRANCH   They are the same node type. This node contains the mnemonic code of the instruction, a pointer to the target

```
the following routines sorts elements in the array
    routine sorts elements using bubble sort
        loop on index i, i.e., outer loop in C part
            loop on index j, i.e., inner loop in C part
            swap to interchange two elements
                CALL SWAP
    this routine exchanges two elements in the array
```

Figure 12. Functional menu from example

destination, and a pointer to its supercontext (its parent code block node). Its *OPERAND* field points to the operands of the instruction.

BAL_DEST This node contains the destination address of the instructions of interest. The address is stored in the global symbol table.

BAL_EXPR This node represents any expression within the operand field.

BAL_DATA This node represents a data statement, storage reservation directive, program control, and so on.

BAL_REGISTER This node represents the use register in the operand field. The register number will be stored in this node.

BAL_INDEX This node represents the indexed reference. It is used for index mode in the operand field.

BAL_CONSTANT This node represents an integer constant used in the operand field of assembly code, i.e., immediate mode.

BAL_SYMBOL This node represents all labels, data symbols and branch labels used in assembly language. It contains a global pointer and a local pointer. The global pointer points to global symbols and the local pointer points to local symbols.

2.3.3. Description of tree construction
Description of the syntax tree construction from top down

(1) The topmost node of the syntax tree is a BAL_LET node, which represents the software application. This node is the root of the application. As the top of the syntax tree it has two pointers, VAR and BODY. These two pointers point to the global symbol table and the first block of the application respectively.

(2) The second level, pointed to by the BODY pointer of the topmost BAL_LET node, consists of one or more BAL_LET nodes, which represent routines. All these nodes are linked together by the NEXT pointer.

(3) The third level of the syntax tree is composed of one or more FUNCTIONAL-_BLOCK and/or CODE_BLOCK nodes. Nodes are chained together in the same manner as above.
  (3.1) The FUNCTIONAL_BLOCK node consists of two pointers, CONTEXT and BODY. The CONTEXT pointer points to the content, which is in text form. The BODY pointer points to the blocks that contribute to this functionality. The nodes pointed to by the BODY pointer are the same as the third level nodes. It consists of a combination of FUNCTIONAL_BLOCK or CODE_BLOCK nodes.

(3.2) The CODE_BLOCK node links to the first statement within it by a CHAIN pointer. Each CODE_BLOCK points to an entry in the global symbol, which is the name of the block. If it is a labelled block then the label is in the symbol table. Otherwise, a label is generated and entered into the symbol table.

(4) The lowest level of the syntax tree consists of a combination of one or more BAL_INSTR, TWO_OPERAND_INSTR, THREE_OPERAND_INSTR, BAL_CALL, BAL_GOTO, or BAL_BRANCH nodes. This list is chained together by the NEXT pointers.

(4.1) The BAL_INSTR node contains the instruction code and the operand for the instruction. This is a leaf node within this sub-tree.

(4.2) The BAL_CALL, BAL_GOTO and BAL_BRANCH nodes contain the branch instruction code and a pointer to operands. The structure of the operands can be one of the following: BAL_DEST, BAL_EXPR, BAL_REGISTER or BAL_INDEX. The information within these nodes was described in the previous sections.

(4.3) The TWO_OPERAND_INSTR and THREE_OPERAND_INSTR nodes contain the sequential instruction code and a pointer to operands. The structure is the same as (4.2).

Symbol table construction. The local symbol table is implemented as part of the global symbol table. When a label is found in a routine, a BAL_SYMBOL node is created. The global pointer of this newly created node is linked to the top of the global symbol table and the VAR pointer of the topmost BAL_LET node is then pointing to this node.

The local pointer of this node links to the top of the local symbol table which is pointed to by the VAR pointer of a routine and the VAR pointer of the routine is pointing to this node.

2.3.4. *Retrieving information from the syntax tree*

Routine—This information is obtained by retrieving the chain of BAL_LET nodes under the topmost BAL_LET node. (Refer to r4 and r5 in Section 1.1.1).

Blocks within a routine—From each of the first level BAL_LET nodes, retrieve the list of nodes pointed to by the BODY pointer followed by the NEXT pointer. This list contains top level (functional or code) blocks within the routine. The node is either a FUNCTIONAL_BLOCK (which forms a functional block) or CODE_BLOCK (which forms a code block) node. If it is a FUNCTIONAL_BLOCK node, search the tree for a CODE_BLOCK node. If it is a CODEL_BLOCK node, the name of this node is the name of the code block. (Refer to r4 and r5 in Section 1.1.1).

Functional block grouping—Code and functional blocks enclosed by the **fb** and **fe** pair are a sub-level of that functional block. Therefore, the functional block grouping information can be obtained by picking up FUNCTIONAL_BLOCK and CODE-_BLOCK nodes under each and every FUNCTIONAL_BLOCK node. (Refer to r11 and r12 in Section 1.1.2).

Identify exits—The exit of a block to the following block is implicit unless a code block ends with branch statements, i.e., BAL_BRANCH and BAL_GOTO nodes. For each CODE_BLOCK node, RETA identifies each branch instruction. For each JUMP (branch out of block) and BRANCH (branch within the block) statement, RETA determines the operand type. If the operand is of type register, no analysis can be done at the present time, since it involves the analysis of the register content. Otherwise, RETA determines if it is a branch within routine or a branch out of routine. A special case in CODEL is when calling a routine with BAL or BALR instruction, for example BAL R5, SWAP, the return address from routine SWAP is in register R5, the instruction BR R5 in routine SWAP is considered as RETURN (from a routine). (Refer to r9 and r10 in Section 1.1.1).

Path tracing—A path that leads to another routine is done by entering that routine, and tracing the path within that routine. Path tracing is done from the root of the application. To retrieve this information, start from a routine, blocks within routine, and the exits of blocks, trace sequence of possible paths from one block to another. (Refer to r9 and r10 in Section 1.1.1).

Associating a functionality with a path—From each FUNCTIONAL_BLOCK node, traverse the sub-tree in depth-first manner within the functional block. Paths are formed from the code blocks and the exits of code blocks within the functional block. Those paths are associated with the text description in FUNCTIONAL_BLOCK node. (Refer to r11 and r12 in Section 1.1.2).

Entry point—The entry point is the name, i.e., the label of the first code block of a routine, which is the second level BAL_LET node. (Refer to r10 in Section 1.1.1).

Each functional path from an entry point—From each entry point, traverse the sub-tree for FUNCTIONAL_BLOCK nodes in depth-first manner. (Refer to r13 and r14 in Section 1.1.2).

Calls—Routine call information is obtained from BAL_CALL nodes. From the operand field of the BAL_CALL node, the name of the routine that is called is identified. (Refer to r9 and r10 in Section 1.1.1).

Data use, data modify and data definition—Data use and modify information can be retrieved by tracing through the relevant operand field of TWO_OPERAND_INSTR and THREE_OPERAND_INSTR nodes. Data definition is obtained by traversing the global symbol table. (Refer to r1, r2, r3, r6, r7 and r8 in Section 1.1.1).

Functional menu—Functional menu is formed by searching all FUNCTIONAL_BLOCK and BAL_CALL nodes in a depth-first manner. (Refer to r15 and r16 in Section 1.1.2).

2.3.5. Support for ripple effect analysis

Two types of ripple effects are supported. They are namely variable and code ripple effects.

Variable ripple effect. When a change of variable occurs, the maintainer needs to know what code blocks use and modify the variable. From the data use and modify relations, we capture blocks that used the variables, i.e., r7 and r8 in Section 1.1.1, and conversely, the variables appear in which blocks, i.e., r2 and r3 in Section 1.1.1. Refer to Data Use, Data Modify in Section 2.3.4.

Code ripple effect. When a code block has been changed, the maintainer needs to know what functional blocks call this code block. One way this information can be found is:

(1) Through relation r4 find the routine name of this block;

(2) From r12, find the functional block that uses the affected block.

3. EXTENSIONS

Future plans include providing more flexibility in functional block analysis, providing automatic restructuring of code, register tracing, and improving the interactive user interface. Register tracing can give more insight than the current system does. For example, it gives the possible addresses that a branch statement can branch to if the address is stored in a register. The current path analysis capabilities are being extended to provide more flexibility in creating and reorganizing functional blocks interactively without depending on annotation within the code. The intent is to replace the current requirement to annotate the code before parsing with an ability to group code blocks into annotated functional blocks interactively. In the current system, restructuring and other changes must be carried out in the code and the code re-parsed to update the maintenance model. An extension is planned to allow automatic code regeneration when the model is changed. We plan to improve the current user interface with standard graphics such as X-windows.

4. CONCLUSION

We have presented a software maintenance model for assembly programs. It supports many maintenance activities such as ripple effect analysis, program slicing and re-documentation. We have also presented a parsing technique to populate the model. Specifically, we used a syntax tree to capture the required information from the code and explicitly stored it in the tree.

Most features of the model have been implemented in RETA. It is implemented in C and a UNIX environment. It is being revised as we gain more understanding of the model.

RETA aids in program understanding. From a routine, we can trace its functionality which is useful for program understanding.

RETA helps in performing ripple effect analysis. There are many kinds of ripple effect analysis. In RETA, we provide functional menu, global variable analysis, and jump/calling relations. When a change is made, RETA can provide the calls, called by jump information. The user can interactively trace and re-trace the connections at different routines.

Finally, since all information is stored in the model, a change of code will be updated in the model, and in turn automatically reflected on the documentation. This facilitates program re-documentation.

Many concepts and techniques discussed here can apply to other high-level and assembly languages. Similar data structures and the same parsing technique can be used to generate syntax trees for these languages. The information retrieval tool can be reused also. Currently, we are implementing this model for C programs.

Acknowledgements

The authors acknowledge the contributions of B. Chavez, Y. Kasho, C. Li and C. Ong.

APPENDIX

```
                        /* translation rules */

program    :units                      /* root of the syntax tree */    ;
units      : unit                      /* blocks beginning with HDNG or ._fb*/
           | units unit    ;
unit       : HEADER extdefs            /* block beginning with HDNG or ._fb*/
           | HEADER
           | FUNCTIONALITY units END_FUNCTIONALITY    ;

extdefs    : extdef                    /* statements under HDNG */
           | extdefs extdef    ;
extdef     : code_block                /* statement under HDNG */
           | data_block
           | FUNCTIONALITY extdefs END_FUNCTIONALITY
           | LABEL DATA_MNEMONIC statements    ;

data_block    : LABEL data_mnemonics   /* forming a data block */
              | LABEL
              | data_mnemonics    ;
data_mnemonics : DATA_MNEMONIC         /* statements in data blcok */
               | data_mnemonics DATA_MNEMONIC    ;

code_block    : LABEL statements       /* forming a code block */
              | statements    ;
statements    : sequential_stmts branch_stmts    /* statements in code block */
              | sequential_stmts
              | branch_stmts    ;
sequential_stmts : sequential_stmt     /* statements not changing the flow of control */
                 | sequential_stmts sequential_stmt    ;
sequential_stmt : SEQUENTIAL_INSTR     /* statement not changing the flow of control */
                | THREE_OPERAND_INSTR instr_field COMMA instr_field COMMA instr_field
                | TWO_OPERAND_INSTR instr_field COMMA instr_field    ;
instr_field   : expression             /* type of operand field in sequential statement */
              | OPEN_P expression CLOSE_P
              | expression OPEN_P expression CLOSE_P
              | expression opcode OPEN_P expression CLOSE_P
              | expression OPEN_P expression COMMA expression CLOSE_P
              | expression OPEN_P COMMA expression CLOSE_P    ;

branch_stmts  : branch_stmt            /* statements possible of changing flow of control */
              | branch_stmts branch_stmt    ;
branch_stmt   : BRANCH_INSTR operand_fields    /* statement possible of changing flow of control */;
operand_fields : operand_field         /* type of operand fields in branch statement */
               | operand_fields COMMA operand_field    ;
operand_field : operand1               /* type of operand field in branch statement */
              | operand1 OPEN_P operand CLOSE_P
              | operand1 OPEN_P operand COMMA operand CLOSE_P
              | operand1 OPEN_P COMMA operand CLOSE_P    ;
operand1      : expression             /* expression of operand field in branch statment */
              | OPEN_P expression CLOSE_P    ;

expression    : operand                /* expression of operand field in sequential statement */
              | expression opcode operand    ;

operand       : DEST_LABEL             /* basic operand type */
              | CONSTANT
              | REGISTER    ;

opcode        : PLUS                   /* opcode in operand field */
              | MINUS    ;
```

References

Ambras, J. and O'Day, V. (1988) 'MicroScope: a knowledge-based programming environment,' *IEEE Software*, **5**, 50–58.

Antonini, P., Benedusi, P., Cantone, G. and Cimitile, A. (1987) 'Maintenance and reverse engineering: low-level design documents production and improvement,' in *Proceedings of Conference on Software Maintenance*, 91–100.

Arango, G., Baxter, I., Freeman, P. and Pidgeon, C. (1985) 'Maintenance and porting of software by design recovery,' in *Proceedings of Conference on Software Maintenance*, 42–49.

Bachman, C. W. (1989) 'A personal chronicle: creating better information systems, with some guiding principles,' *IEEE Trans. on Knowledge and Data Engineering*, 1(1), 17–32.

Biggerstaff, T. (1989) 'Design RECOVERY for maintenance and reuse,' *IEEE Computer*, 22(7), 36–49.

Brooks, F. P. (1987) 'No silver bullet,' *IEEE Computer Magazine*, 20(4), 10–19.

Chen, Y. F. and Ramamoorthy, C. V. (1986) 'The C information abstractor,' in *Proceedings of IEEE COMPSAC*, 291–298.

Cleveland, L. (1988) 'An environment for understanding programs,' in *Proceedings of HICSS-21*, 2, 500–509.

Collofello, J. S. and Orn, M. (1988) 'A practical software maintenance environment,' in *Proceedings of IEEE Conference on Software Maintenance*, 45–51.

Ghezzi, C. and Jazayeri, M. (1987) *Programming Language Concepts*, second ed., John Wiley & Sons, Inc, New York.

Hazzah, A. (1989) 'Everything is in the names for coming "Capture" tools,' *Software Magazine*, 9(12), 40–50.

Hecht, M. S. (1977) *Flow Analysis of Computer Programs*, North-Holland, New York.

Heisler, K. G., Tsai, W. T. and Powell, P. A. (1989) 'An object-oriented maintenance oriented model for software,' in *Proceedings of COMPCON*, 248–253.

Heninger, K. L. (1980) 'Specifying software requirements for complex systems: new techniques and their applications,' *IEEE Trans. on Software Engineering*, SE-6(1), 2–13.

Johnson, S. C. (1984) 'Yacc: yet another compiler-compiler,' *Unix Programmer's Manual*, 2, 353–387.

Johnson, W. L. and Soloway, E. (1985) 'PROBUST: knowledge-based program understanding,' *IEEE Trans. on Software Engineering*, SE-11(3), 267–275.

Kaiser, G. E., Feiler, P. H. and Popovich, S. S. (1988) 'Intelligent assistance for software development and maintenance,' *IEEE Software*, 5(3), 40–49.

Ketabchi, M., Lewis, D., Dasananda, S., Lim, T., Roudsari, R., Shik, K. and Tan, J. (1989) 'Object-oriented database management support for software maintenance and reverse engineering,' in *Proceedings of IEEE COMPCON*, 257–260.

Kozaczynski, W. and Ning, J. Q. (1989) 'SRE: a knowledge-based environment for large-scale software re-engineering activities,' in *Proceedings of the 11th International Conference on Software Engineering*, 113–122.

Lehman, M. M. (1980) 'Program, life cycles, and laws of software evolution,' in *Proceedings of IEEE*, 68(9), 1060–1076.

Martin, J. (1983) *Software Maintenance*, Prentice-Hall, Englewood Cliffs, N.J.

NCR COMTEN (1986) *CODEL Communication Definition Language* Revision A.

Pressman, R. S. (1987) *Software Engineering, A Practitioner's Approach*, second edition, McGraw-Hill, New York.

Ramamoorthy, C. V., Prakash, A., Tsai W. T. and Usuda, Y. (1984) 'Software engineering: problems and perspectives,' *IEEE Computer*, 17(10), 191–209.

Rich, C. and Waters, R. (1988) 'The programmer's apprentice: a research overview,' *IEEE Computer*, 21(11), 10–25.

Rochkind, M. J. (1975) 'The source code control system,' *IEEE Trans. on Software Engineering*, SE-1(4), 364–370.

Shigo, O., Wada, Y., Terashima, Y., Iwamoto, K. and Nishimura, T. (1982) 'Configuration control for evolutionary software production,' in *Proceedings of the 6th International Conference on Software Engineering*, 68–75.

Sneed, H. M. and Jandrasics, G. (1988) 'Inverse transformation of software from code to specification,' in *Proceedings of IEEE Conference on Software Maintenance*, 102–109.

Soloway, E., Pinto, J., Letovsky, S., Littman, D. and Lampert, R. (1988) 'Designing documentation to compensate for delocalized plans,' *CACM*, 31(11), 1259–1267.

Tichy, W. F. (1982) 'Design, implementation, and evaluation of a revision control system,' in *Proceedings of International Conference on Software Engineering*, 58–67.

Waters, R. C. (1988) 'Program translation via abstraction and reimplementation,' *IEEE Trans. on*

Software Engineering, **SE-14**(8), 1207–1228.

Weiser, M. (1982) 'Programmers use slices when debugging,' *CACM,* **25**(7), 446–452.

Wild, C. and Maly, K. (1988) 'Towards a software maintenance support environment,' in *Proceedings of IEEE Conference on Software Maintenance,* 80–83.

Yamamoto, S. and Isoda, S. (1986) 'SOFTDA—A reuse-oriented software design system,' in *Proceedings of IEEE COMPSAC,* 284–290.

Yau, S. S., Collofello, J. S. and MacGregor, T. (1978) 'Ripple effect analysis of software maintenance,' in *Proceedings of IEEE COMPSAC,* 60–65.

Yau, S. S. and Tsai, J. (1987) 'Knowledge representation of software component inter-connection information for large-scale software modification,' *IEEE Trans. on Software Engineering,* **SE-13**(3), 355–361.

55

Using Function Abstraction to Understand Program Behavior

Philip A. Hausler and **Mark G. Pleszkoch**
IBM Systems Integration Division and University of Maryland at Baltimore County
Richard C. Linger, IBM Systems Integration Division
Alan R. Hevner, University of Maryland at College Park

You can understand programs by abstracting their functions. The potential exists for an automatic tool to take unstructured code and derive its function.

Because much of the complexity of programs arises from unstructured logic, the first step in improving the understandability of existing programs is to reengineer them into structured form so program logic and text correspond precisely. When there are no arbitrary jumps in control flow, you can understand structured programs through systematic reading and documentation recovery. This process results in full intellectual control over programs and permits reliable modification and evolution. In fact, by taking full advantage of the mathematical properties of structured programs, you can precisely abstract a program's logic to a higher level to understand its functions. Furthermore, there is evidence that this process can be automated.

The Linger/Mills/Witt structure theorem[1] summarizes the theoretical foundations for program structuring. This theorem guarantees that any flowchart can be transformed into a flowchart composed solely of sequence (like Begin-End), If-Then-Else, and While-Do control structures. The structure theorem has been embodied in a reengineering tool, the IBM Cobol Structuring Facility, that automatically transforms unstructured Cobol programs into structured form to improve maintainability.

This reengineering process eliminates such constructs as Alter and Goto statements and overlaps of performed procedures and fall-throughs, and it unravels mixed performed-procedure and goto logic to produce a top-down hierarchy of structured, single-entry, single-exit procedures.

To understand programs by abstracting program function, you determine the precise function of a program or program part, which explains exactly what it does to data in all possible circumstances. (The box on p. 59 describes the uses of program-function abstraction.) This abstrac-

0-8186-3272-0/93 $3.00 ©1990 IEEE

56

```
ID DIVISION.
PROGRAM-ID.  ADJUST-ACCOUNT.
ENVIRONMENT DIVISION.
  INPUT-OUTPUT SECTION.
    FILE-CONTROL.
      SELECT ACCOUNT-FILE         ASSIGN TO ACCOUNT.
      SELECT ADJUSTMENT-FILE      ASSIGN TO ADJUST.
DATA DIVISION.
  FILE SECTION.
    FD ACCOUNT-FILE
      LABEL RECORDS ARE STANDARD
      DATA RECORD IS ACCOUNT-REC.
    01 ACCOUNT-REC.
      05   ACCT-NUM   PIC 9(15).
      05   BALANCE    PIC 9(8)V99.
      05   LOAN-OUT   PIC 9(8)V99.
      05   LOAN-MAX   PIC 9(8)V99.
    FD ADJUSTMENT-FILE
      LABEL RECORDS ARE STANDARD
      DATA RECORD IS ADJUST-REC.
    01 ADJUST-REC.
      05   ACCT-NUM   PIC 9(15).
      05   BALANCE    PIC 9(8)V99.
      05   LOAN-OUT   PIC 9(8)V99.
      05   LOAN-MAX   PIC 9(8)V99.
      05   DEFAULT    PIC X(1).

PROCEDURE DIVISION.
MAIN.
  OPEN INPUT ACCOUNT-FILE
       OUTPUT ADJUSTMENT-FILE.
READ-NEXT-ACCT.
  READ ACCOUNT-FILE
    AT END GO TO DONE.
  MOVE CORRESPONDING ACCOUNT-REC TO ADJUST-REC.
  IF BALANCE OF ADJUST-REC < 0.00
    MOVE 'Y' TO DEFAULT
  ELSE
    MOVE 'N' TO DEFAULT.
MORE.
  IF (BALANCE OF ADJUST-REC NOT < 0.00) OR
     (LOAN-OUT OF ADJUST-REC + 100.00 > LOAN-MAX OF ADJUST-REC)
    GO TO WRAP-UP.
  ADD 100.00 TO LOAN-OUT OF ADJUST-REC.
  ADD 100.00 TO BALANCE OF ADJUST-REC.
  GO TO MORE.
WRAP-UP.
  WRITE ADJUST-REC.
  GO TO READ-NEXT-ACCT.
DONE.
  CLOSE    ACCOUNT-FILE
           ADJUSTMENT-FILE.
  STOP RUN.
```

Figure 1. An unstructured Cobol banking program. Lines indicate goto flow.

tion is made possible by the algebraic structure and mathematical properties of structured programs.[2] The high-level abstractions produced by this method represent business rules. Such rules are often invisible in a program, since they are distributed (buried) across hundreds or thousands of lines of code. However, when abstracted out of the code, they can be read and understood as a unit.

For example, a billing program may contain rules for applying discounts according to pricing policies based on customer type, inventory levels, size and frequency of orders, and shipping and handling costs. The objective of function abstraction is to extract such rules from the code and express them in compact, nonprocedural terms for inspection and analysis.

To a large extent, the abstraction of program functions can be automated. Although no tool to do so is available, the abstraction algorithms described here provide a firm basis for such a tool. In fact, many of the abstraction algorithms embody constructive proofs of theorems from Linger, Mills, and Witt's work, just as in the case of the structure theorem. Thus, these theorems have a firm founda-

57

tion in established mathematics. The abstraction examples presented in this article are manual applications of these algorithms. This article also explores what the goals of a program-abstraction tool should be.

Example program

Consider the miniature Cobol program for a banking application shown in Figure 1, which reads file Account-File and writes file Adjustment-File. The program is unstructured and complex for its size. The conditions under which records are processed and the contents of records written are not immediately obvious. In fact, the program embodies a surprising amount of possible behavior in its business rules.

Imagine a programmer trying to understand this program. The first step is to get the program in shape for understanding by transforming its control logic into structured form. Figure 2 shows the structured version produced by the IBM Cobol Structuring Facility. The program has now been reexpressed in terms of nested single-entry, single-exit control structures. The structured control flow reveals the two program loops that were implicit in the unstructured program and makes clear what conditions must be satisfied for the loops to terminate. Even without considering the additional benefit of function abstraction, the structured program is already much easier to read and maintain.

Given the procedure in Figure 2, you would like to be able to see directly the business rules that it embodies. Figure 3 shows these rules, which we derived by manually executing algorithmic processes described later. The abstractions are procedure-free and are stated in terms of the net functional effect of the program on two data objects: the files Account-File and Adjustment-File. (Working storage objects hold the program's local data and so are incidental to the overall function of the program — the abstractions capture net file-to-file effects that can be expressed without the use of working storage objects.)

As Figure 3 shows, Account-File's contents are guaranteed to be unchanged by the program, which in itself is important information for a maintenance programmer.

```
PROCEDURE DIVISION.
CSF-MAIN.
  OPEN  INPUT ACCOUNT-FILE
          OUTPUT ADJUSTMENT-FILE
  PERFORM READ-NEXT-ACCT
  PERFORM
    UNTIL CSF-AT-END = 'T'
    MOVE CORRESPONDING ACCOUNT-REC TO ADJUST-REC
    IF BALANCE OF ADJUST-REC < 0.00
      MOVE 'Y' TO DEFAULT
    ELSE
      MOVE 'N' TO DEFAULT
    END-IF
    PERFORM
      UNTIL  (BALANCE OF ADJUST-REC NOT < 0.00) OR
              (LOAN-OUT OF ADJUST-REC + 100.00 > LOAN-MAX OF
                ADJUST-REC)
      ADD 100.00 TO LOAN-OUT OF ADJUST-REC
      ADD 100.00 TO BALANCE OF ADJUST-REC
    END-PERFORM
    WRITE ADJUST-REC
    PERFORM READ-NEXT-ACCT
  END-PERFORM
  CLOSE      ACCOUNT-FILE
              ADJUSTMENT-FILE
  STOP RUN.

READ-NEXT-ACCT.
  MOVE 'F' TO CSF-AT-END
  READ ACCOUNT-FILE
    AT END
    MOVE 'T' TO CSF-AT-END
  END-READ.
```

Figure 2. The Procedure Division portion of the banking program in Figure 1 after being structured by the IBM Cobol Structuring Facility.

In reviewing the program abstraction, we found three cases of update criteria for the business rule for Adjustment-File, a fact not obvious from inspecting the code. Further inspection revealed that

• case 1 describes the business rule for dealing with an account whose balance is nonnegative and thus does not require an advance,

• case 2 describes the business rule for dealing with an account whose balance is negative and thus requires an advance but that cannot receive a further advance without exceeding the maximum advance allowed, and

• case 3 is the most difficult rule. It describes the net effect of the program in computing sufficient advances in $100 increments that do not exceed the maximum permissible outstanding loan amount. Both Balance and Loan-Out are augmented by 100 times the minimum of two terms: the first a multiplier for a sufficient advance to make the balance nonnegative and the second a multiplier for the maximum remaining advance.

These three cases together define precisely every possible effect of the program on Adjustment-File. Having the business rules available makes it possible to determine if they are indeed the right rules for the bank and its operations.

A further goal for an automatic program-abstraction tool would be to annotate the abstracted rules with cross-references to identify and isolate program parts corresponding to the functional effects defined. You would use these annotated rules in subsequent maintenance and evolution. The availability of precise function abstractions like those in Figure 3 could improve the conditions of maintenance, development, and verification. A significant part of the effort in maintenance today is getting such information through fallible processes with substantial variation in completeness and accuracy.

Function abstraction

The basis of function abstraction is an application of the function-theoretic concepts[1,3] combined with data analysis, pro-

1. ACCOUNT-FILE: File is unchanged.

2. ADJUSTMENT-FILE: For every record in ACCOUNT-FILE, a record is appended to ADJUSTMENT-FILE, the contents of which are described in three cases:

Case 1:
```
    if (acct-rec.balance >= 0.00)
    then
        adjust-rec.acct-num = acct-rec.acct-num
        adjust-rec.balance = acct-rec.balance
        adjust-rec.loan-out = acct-rec.loan-out
        adjust-rec.loan-max = acct-rec.loan-max
        adjust-rec.default = 'N'
```

Case 2:
```
    if (acct-rec.balance < 0.00) and
       (acct-rec.loan-out + 100.00 > acct-rec.loan-max)
    then
        adjust-rec.acct-num = acct-rec.acct-num
        adjust-rec.balance = acct-rec.balance
        adjust-rec.loan-out = acct-rec.loan-out
        adjust.rec.loan-max = acct-rec.loan max
        adjust-rec.default = 'Y'
```

Case 3:
```
    if (acct-rec.balance < 0.00) and
       (acct-rec.loan-out + 100.00 <= acct-rec.loan-max)
    then
        adjust-rec.acct-num = acct-rec.acct-num
        adjust-rec.balance = acct-rec.balance + (100.00 * term)
        adjust-rec.loan-out = acct-rec.loan-out + (100.00 * term)
        adjust-rec.loan-max = acct-rec.loan-max
        adjust-rec.default = 'Y'
    where
        term = min(term1, term2)
        term1 = ceiling((0.00 - acct-rec.balance)/100.00)
        term2 = 1 + floor((acct-rec.loan-max - 100.00 - acct-rec.loan-out)/100.00)
```

Figure 3. Business rules of the structured banking program in Figure 2, produced by manually applying the abstraction algorithms.

```
*   exchange values of x and y          *   exchange values of x and y
    PERFORM                                 PERFORM
        COMPUTE X = X + Y                       MOVE X TO T
        COMPUTE Y = X - Y                       MOVE Y TO X
        COMPUTE X = X - Y                       MOVE T TO Y
    END-PERFORM                             END-PERFORM
```

Figure 4. Two sequence programs with the same program function.

gram slicing, and pattern recognition, which are themselves based on function-theoretic ideas. While we show these ideas applied to Cobol here, they apply to all languages.

The input to program abstraction is a structured program: a single-entry, single-exit program whose flowchart is composed of single-entry, single-exit function nodes (like Move A To B and Perform X),

single-entry, binary-branching predicate nodes (like If $A < B$), and binary-entry, single-exit collector nodes (like End-If).

To explain the special property of structured programs that makes abstraction possible, we must first define two other classes of programs: proper and prime.

A proper program is a flowchart program that has a single entry and single exit

and a path through each node from the entry to the exit line.

A prime program is a proper program that is irreducible in that it contains no proper subprograms other than itself and single function nodes. Prime programs can be of any size and complexity; of special interest are the zero- and one-predicate prime programs (which we call small primes). We group small primes into three categories:

• sequence, like Begin-End,
• alternation, like If-Then and If-Then-Else, and
• iteration, like While-Do, Repeat-Until, and Do-While-Do.

These small primes are the basis of structured programming.

You can construct any proper program by function expansion: Starting with a single function node, you repeatedly replace function nodes with prime subprograms. If you use only small-prime subprograms at each step, the resulting proper program will be a structured program.

In execution, prime programs transform data from an initial state at their entry line to a final state at their exit line, with no side effects on control flow. We call this transformation from initial to final state the prime's program function; the program function describes the program's effects on data in all possible circumstances. Thus, specifications for prime programs are mathematical functions, and prime programs themselves are rules for functions.

For example, the specification for two integers

exchange the values of X and Y

written in natural language, or as a concurrent assignment statement

$X, Y := Y, X$

defines a mathematical function. You can then expand this function (or program specification) into Cobol code that accomplishes the desired behavior. Figure 4 gives two sequence primes that satisfy the function. In the second example in Figure 4, the variable T is assumed to be incidental (local in scope) to the function.

Because a structured program is formed by function expansion using small

59

primes, the problem of determining a structured program's function is reduced to determining the function of each category of small prime. The function of a sequence is a sequence-free summary of the effects of an ordered set of operations on data. Given a sequence-prime program, two of which Figure 4 shows, you can derive the program function by function composition of the individual statement functions. (The function composition of the functions f and g is the function that maps input value x to $f(g(x))$.)

For an alternation prime, like

P: IF b THEN g ELSE h END-IF

the program function is given by a case analysis in a conditional rule (which reads "where b is true, perform function g, otherwise, where b is false, perform function h"):

f = [P] = [IF b THEN g ELSE h END-IF]
   = ([b] = TRUE → [g] | [b] = FALSE → [h])

In this conditional rule, the brackets surrounding a program denote the function of the enclosed program; brackets surrounding an expression of a program denote the value of the enclosed expression. You can often simplify the conditional rule for an alternation prime:

```
*   z := max(x,y)
    IF X > Y
       MOVE X TO Z
    ELSE
       MOVE Y TO Z
    END-IF
```

For looping primes, the program function is given by function composition and case analysis in a recursive equation based on the equivalence of a looping program and a loop-free program. (Linger, Mills, and Witt showed this equivalence in their iteration-recursion lemma.[1]) For example, the analysis for the While-Do prime is

P: WHILE b DO g OD

where P is expressed in non-Cobol syntax for readability of the loop transformation and where

f = [P] = [WHILE b DO g OD]
   = [IF b THEN g; WHILE b DO g OD
      END-IF]
   = [IF b THEN g; f END-IF]

Function f is therefore given by the loop-free rule

Uses of program-function abstraction

Function abstraction can improve the practice of software maintenance, development, and verification by giving programmers mathematically precise definitions of the functions of programs. Example applications include:

• Maintenance. A programmer submits a program undergoing modification to a function-abstraction facility that defines at every level of abstraction the precise functional effect of the program. The programmer uses this information to evaluate where and how to make the required changes. Once the modifications are made, the programmer resubmits the program to the function-abstraction facility to derive the new functional effects. The new abstractions are reviewed to ensure that the changes embody the desired effects and no others.

• Development. A programmer periodically submits a program under development to a function-abstraction facility to determine if the function so far is indeed the function intended. Any discrepancies are dealt with before proceeding, so the programmer ultimately arrives at a program that has the intended behavior.

• Documentation. A programmer submits a completed program to a function-abstraction facility for a final abstraction process to produce precise functional documentation for delivery with the program. The abstractions are stored in a database with the program for subsequent reuse.

• Verification. A certification inspector submits a program to be verified to a function-abstraction facility to derive its functional effect on data. This function definition is reviewed for correctness with respect to external specifications of intended behavior.

• Reuse. A programmer queries the database of program abstractions for matches against a requirement. Responses are browsed to determine the closest match. Programs corresponding to the selected abstractions may be usable directly, but if not, they can be modified as required and stored with their rederived abstractions in the database for future reuse.

f = [P] = ([b] = TRUE → [f] ○ [g]
   | [b] = FALSE → I)

where I is the identity function and $○$ denotes function composition. The following While-Do Cobol prime with its corresponding function for the integer variable Z; it treats integers A and B as incidental variables.

```
*   ((a > 0) → z := z + a * b | (a <= 0) → z := z)
    PERFORM UNTIL NOT (A > 0)
       ADD B TO Z
       SUBTRACT 1 FROM A
    END-PERFORM
```

A prime program and its program function are interchangeable, as summarized in an axiom of replacement.[1] Because a structured program defines an expression in an algebra of functions, the program functions of constituent primes can be automatically derived in stepwise fashion through composition and case analysis. Programs composed of nested and sequenced small primes define a natural decomposition hierarchy formed by abstracting visible primes into single-entry, single-exit function nodes to reveal new primes for abstraction, continuing until

the entire program has been abstracted to a single program function.

The derived functions for sequence and alternation primes are directly usable, as described in the box above. However, the recursive functions derived for looping primes, while correct, generally do not characterize the loop functions in a form that aids understanding, so loop-function derivations require additional analysis.

Automating abstraction

To obtain the full benefit of program functions in software maintenance, you must be able to abstract them from existing code. Of course, maintenance programmers can manually do function abstraction when warranted, but it is a labor-intensive process. In automating the process, a straightforward solution is possible if the sole criteria is correctness of the resulting program functions. However, straightforward abstraction techniques may lead to program functions that are difficult to read and understand, especially for looping primes. While we have not implemented a system to auto-

Rule	Value of X	Value of Y
X := X + Y	X_0	Y_0
X := X − Y	$X_1 = X_0 + Y_0$	$Y_1 = Y_0$
X := X − Y	$X_2 = X_1 = X_0 + Y_0$	$Y_2 = X_1 − Y_1 = X_0$
	$X_3 = X_2 − Y_2 = Y_0$	$Y_3 = Y_2 = X_0$

Figure 5. Trace table for a simple sequence.

```
IF
    X < Y
THEN
    MOVE X TO T
    MOVE Y TO X
    MOVE T TO Y
END-IF
COMPUTE T = X − Y
MOVE T TO Z
```

mate abstraction, we have investigated the problem of generating useful, as well as functionally correct, abstractions.

The automatic-abstraction process has several steps. First, you must transform the program into a structured form using an existing tool like IBM's Cobol Structuring Facility. Second, you run the structured program through an automated abstraction facility. This facility would analyze the program data to localize the scope of each program variable and to split occurrences of overloaded data items. Third, the facility would compute the function of each prime during the function expansion of the structured program. For looping primes, this involves program slicing to allow the abstraction of loop-program functions one variable at a time. These last two steps are instrumental in yielding simpler abstractions. Moreover, program slicing makes possible a pattern-matching approach for recognizing loop patterns that appear again and again.

You apply data analysis to a structured program to improve its dataflow characteristics before functional abstraction is performed. Our techniques of data analysis are derived from data-reengineering methods.[4] The principal objective is to reduce the scope of data objects to simplify the abstraction process. As an added benefit, this also identifies and lets you reduce data-usage anomalies.

In any program, data are assigned and referenced during execution. In a structured program, data usage can be formulated in regular expressions as compact and precise abstractions of all data references, organized according to the program's prime-program hierarchy. You can derive regular expressions by syntactic analysis, a process that can be automated, since it is requires no human judgment.

The definition of regular expressions is based on how data are used in the prime decomposition of a structured program. In assignments, data on the right side are read (used) and data on the left side are written (set). In conditional tests, data can only be read. In input statements, data are written. And in output statements, data are read. This is what is commonly referred to as set-used information.

The scope of a data item in a structured program is the lowest-level prime that contains all references to the data item. Analysis of data-usage regular expressions provides an efficient way to recognize and reduce the scope of data items. After uncovering the scope of each data item in the program, an automated system following our approach would invoke a procedure (described elsewhere[4]) that reduces the scope of a data item where possible.

Analysis of data-usage regular expressions also permits the recognition of data anomalies. You can automate this detection efficiently by using finite-state automata that recognize anomalous patterns in data-usage regular expressions. You can then eliminate these anomalies by modifying the data-design and referencing-control structures. For example, a detection system could find anomalies like uninitialized data reads and unused data writes so you could correct them. It could also handle more complex data anomalies like detecting overloaded data items.

When a data item is repeatedly written between reads, such usage may indicate an overloaded data item. Often a programmer, for efficiency or convenience, uses a single data item for different functional purposes. This type of reuse complicates the understanding of a program and creates difficulties for program maintenance and evolution. Consider the following code segment:

By recognizing the usage pattern of data item T and looking at the code, you can see that, when the If test is true, T is being used in two functionally distinct roles. You can correct this anomaly by defining a new data item, like Sum, to replace T in the last two lines. Another advantage of distinct data items is that you can make the program scope of each smaller.

Prime programs

Automatic abstraction of program functions is done prime by prime. Each type of prime (sequence, alternation, and iteration) is handled differently. Because abstraction is bottom-up, all lower level primes will have been abstracted into program functions by the time any given prime is processed.

An automated system should conveniently record the abstracted program functions of prime programs as single statements in a closed specification language composed of a concurrent assignment statement, whose outer syntax is

<id>, <id>, ..., <id> := <expr>, <expr>, ..., <expr>

and a concurrent conditional assignment statement, whose outer syntax is

```
( <condition> → <concurrent assignment>
| <condition> → <concurrent assignment>
| ...
| <condition> → <concurrent assignment>
)
```

Sequence abstraction. To abstract program functions from sequences, we use our trace-table technique.[1] For example, consider the left-most sequence in Figure 4; Figure 5 shows the corresponding trace table. As each rule (which may be an abstraction of a lower level prime) is processed, the automated system would record its effect on the state space of all variables, using one column per variable. In our manual method, we use X_0 to denote the initial value of variable X, X_1 to

61

denote the value of X after the first statement has executed, and so on. Because, as you see from the trace table, the final value of X is the initial value of Y and the final value of Y is the initial value of X, you can conclude that the program function of the sequence is $[X, Y := Y, X]$.

If the rules in the sequence are conditional, you must do trace-table analysis on each possible combination of conditions. You can do this conveniently in a conditional trace table,[1] which tracks the conditions in an additional column.

Straightforward conditional trace-table analysis can result in case explosion, where the number of cases in an abstracted conditional rule can grow as an exponential function of the program size. There are several measures that you can take to prevent or limit case explosion.

First, you must recognize and discard impossible cases. For example, consider Figure 6. Simple case analysis will result in four cases (Figure 6c), including the impossible case

$$((x < 0) \text{ and } (x >= 1)) \rightarrow y, z := 2, 1$$

If this impossible case is not eliminated, it will cause additional impossible cases as higher level primes are abstracted, creating an unnecessary case explosion. The other three cases, although possible, have conditions that are needlessly complicated. If these conditions are not simplified, the higher level primes will also be unnecessarily complicated.

Even if you eliminate impossible cases, you can still have an exponential number of cases. In such situations, you can use single-valued functional abstractions to improve a program function's readability. A single-valued functional abstraction is an abbreviation created to represent part of the abstracted function.

For example, consider the following example:

```
PERFORM
    ((x >= y) → z := x | (x < y) → z := y)
    ((v >= z) → w := v | (v < z) → w := z)
END-PERFORM
```

Straightforward case analysis yields four cases. However, using the single-valued functional abstraction max(–,–), representing the maximum function on two inputs, you can express the entire program function in a single case (a concurrent assignment statement):

$$z, w := \max(x,y), \max(v,\max(x,y))$$

Often, single-valued functional abstractions will represent complex mathematical definitions involving several cases but will correspond to basic business concepts; for example, compute_federal_withholding(–). One essential advantage that single-valued functional abstractions have over English descriptions is that you can use them in trace tables and thus propagate them to higher level abstracted functions.

Alternation abstraction. Because the outer syntax for abstracted program functions includes conditions, abstracting alternations is straightforward. If the Then part of an alternation prime has p cases

and the Else part has q cases, the combined abstraction will have $p+q$ cases. As before, you can eliminate impossible cases to avoid unnecessary case explosion.

Iteration abstraction. Although you can handle loops several ways, including with an existentially quantified formula to represent the program function,[1] no single technique produces the best result on all loops. But a generalized table-lookup, pattern-matching approach is a useful strategy.

Program slicing. Programmers generally have simple patterns in mind when coding loops, for example, "increment until a condition is reached" or "process a file one record at a time." Using a generalized form of production rules, you can encode such human patterns into program patterns for machine processing and recognition. Some human patterns use other patterns in combinations; these become superpatterns at the program level.

The key to recognizing instances of program patterns in actual programs is using the technique of program slicing.[5] By slicing, you can consider in isolation the effect of a program loop in computing a single variable. After abstracting the program function for each variable, you can combine them into the program function for the loop.

Slices are formed by decomposing programs based on their control flow and dataflow. Given a program, a slice based on a specified subset of behavior is an exe-

```
PERFORM
    IF X >= 0 THEN
        MOVE 1 TO Y
    ELSE
        MOVE 2 TO Y
    END-IF
    IF X >= 1 THEN
        MOVE 1 TO Z
    END-IF
END-PERFORM

(a)
```

```
PERFORM
    ((x >= 0) → y := 1 | (x < 0) → y := 2)
    ((x >= 1) → z := 1 | (x < 1) → z := z)
END-PERFORM

(b)
```

```
( (x >= 0) and (x >= 1) → y, z := 1, 1
| (x >= 0) and (x < 1) → y, z := 1, z
| (x < 0) and (x >= 1) → y, z := 2, 1
| (x < 0) and (x < 1) → y, z := 2, z

(c)
```

Figure 6. A sequence of conditional rules arising from lower level alternation primes: **(a)** the original program, **(b)** the program after abstracting lower level alternations, and **(c)** the abstracted function of the entire sequence.

If the loop slice matches the superpattern
    PERFORM UNTIL PRED1(X) OR PRED2(Y)
        X, Y := EXPR1(X), EXPR2(Y)
    END-PERFORM
then the function abstraction for variables X and Y is
    X, Y := F1(X,N), F2(Y,N)
where F1(X,N) is the function of N iterations of the loop
    PERFORM UNTIL PRED1(X)
        X := EXPR1(X)
    END-PERFORM
where F2(Y,N) is the function of N iterations of the loop
    PERFORM UNTIL PRED2(Y)
        Y := EXPR2(Y)
    END-PERFORM
and where N is min($N1$,$N2$), where $N1$ and $N2$ are the total number of iterations of the previous two loops, respectively.

Figure 7. A superpattern for loop abstraction.

If the loop slice matches the pattern
    PERFORM UNTIL X >= EXPR3
        X := X + EXPR4
    END-PERFORM
then the function abstraction for variable X after N loop iterations is
    X := X + EXPR4*N
where the total number of loop iterations is
    $((X < EXPR3) \rightarrow N := ceiling((EXPR3 - X)/EXPR4) \mid (X >= EXPR3) \rightarrow N := 0)$

Figure 8. A pattern for loop abstraction.

If the loop slice matches the pattern
    PERFORM UNTIL X > EXPR3
        X := X + EXPR4
    END-PERFORM
then the function abstraction for variable X after N loop iterations is
    X := X + EXPR4*N
where the total number of loop iterations is
    $((X <= EXPR3) \rightarrow N := 1 + floor((EXPR3 - X)/EXPR4) \mid (X > EXPR3) \rightarrow N := 0)$

Figure 9. Another pattern for loop abstraction.

cutable program that reduces the program to a minimal form that still produces the wanted behavior. In other words, a slice of a program on X is an executable subset of the program required to compute just the value for X.

The sliced subprogram must execute identically to the original program in its effect on variable X. Consider the simple sequence

    MOVE 1 TO Z
    MOVE A TO T
    MOVE Z TO C

A slice of the sequence on variable C is a subset of the three statements that will have the same execution behavior for C. When the last Move is executed, C receives its value from Z. Clearly, the third statement must be in the slice. But, because C receives its value from Z, the statement that sets Z must also be included; thus, the first statement must also be added. As a result, the appropriate slice is

    MOVE 1 TO Z
    MOVE Z TO C

The second statement in the original sequence is not included here because it does not contribute to the function of the program for variable C. When the slice is executed, C will have the same value as the one computed by the original program.

An attractive property of slices is their well-defined and predictable relation to one another and to the original program. Slices have clear semantics based on the original program and the behavior of interest. Furthermore, you can efficiently automate the computation of slices by using algorithms described elsewhere.[5]

Pattern matching. For an example of the entire pattern-matching process, consider the inner loop of the banking program in Figure 2.

```
( (balance >= 0.00) or (loan-out + 100.00 > loan-max) →
  balance, loan-out := balance, loan-out
| (balance < 0.00) and (loan-out + 100.00 <= loan-max) →
  balance, loan-out :=
     balance + (100.00 * min(ceiling((0.00 - balance)/100.00), 1 + floor((loan-max - 100.00 - loan-out)/100.00)))
     loan-out + (100.00 * min(ceiling((0.00 - balance)/100.00), 1 + floor((loan-max - 100.00 - loan-out)/100.00)))   )
```

Figure 10. The final program function for the inner loop of Figure 2, after some simplification.

63

First, you slice on the loop-control variables (those variables in the loop predicate). Unfortunately in this case, the entire loop is required for the slice.

However, because the loop operates on variables Balance and Loan-Out somewhat independently, the loop matches the superpattern in Figure 7: Variable X of the superpattern is instantiated to become Balance, variable Y becomes Loan-Out, Pred1(X) becomes (Balance >= 0.00), Pred2(Y) becomes (Loan-Out > (Loan-Max − 100.00)), Expr1(X) becomes (Balance + 100.00), and Expr2(Y) becomes (Loan-Out + 100.00).

This superpattern lets you compute the function of two smaller loops:

```
PERFORM UNTIL BALANCE >= 0.00
    BALANCE := BALANCE + 100.00
END-PERFORM
```

and

```
PERFORM UNTIL LOAN-OUT >
    (LOAN-MAX − 100.00)
    LOAN-OUT := LOAN-OUT + 100.00
END-PERFORM
```

These smaller loops match patterns in Figures 8 and 9. Figure 10 shows the final program function for the inner loop of the program of Figure 2, after some simplification.

It is important to perform as much simplification as possible so subsequent abstractions are not unnecessarily complicated. In addition, simplification at the expression level, comparable to that done in computer algebra systems,[6] can improve the readability of the abstractions.

Once an automatic program-abstraction tool has abstracted the overall program function, it must apply human factors to translate the mathematical constructs into English text. Figure 3 shows the output of such a transformation. The simplification and presentation of the abstractions in a readable format is an essential aspect of a practical function abstraction tool.

Human factors analysis is required to understand how maintenance programmers can interact with the abstraction process. In addition, the loop-abstraction techniques must be extended to cover an even larger percentage of real-world program loops. ❖

References

1. R.C. Linger, H.D. Mills, and B.I. Witt, *Structured Programming: Theory and Practice*, Addison-Wesley, Cambridge, Mass., 1979.
2. R.C. Linger, "Software Maintenance as an Engineering Discipline," *Proc. Conf. Software Maintenance*, CS Press, Los Alamitos, Calif., 1988, pp. 292-297.
3. H.D. Mills, R.C. Linger, and A.R. Hevner, *Principles of Information Systems Analysis and Design*, Academic Press, Orlando, Fla., 1986.
4. A.R. Hevner and R.C. Linger, "A Method for Data Reengineering in Structured Programs," *Proc. Hawaii Int'l Conf. System Sciences*, Vol. 2, CS Press, Los Alamitos, Calif., 1989, pp. 1025-1034.
5. P.A. Hausler, "Denotational Program Slicing," *Proc. Hawaii Int'l Conf. System Sciences*, Vol. 2, CS Press, Los Alamitos, Calif., 1989, pp. 486-494.
6. B. Buchberger et al., eds., *Computer Algebra: Symbolic and Algebraic Computation*, second ed., Springer-Verlag, New York, 1982.

Philip A. Hausler is a project programming manager at IBM's System Integration Division and is on the computer-science faculty at the University of Maryland at Baltimore County. His research interests include software engineering, formal language theory, denotational semantics, and program slicing.

Hausler received a BS summa cum laude in computer science from the University of Maryland at Baltimore County and an MS in computer science from the University of Maryland at College Park. He is a member of the IEEE.

Richard C. Linger is a senior programming manager of software-engineering studies at IBM's Systems Integration Division. His research interests include box structures for system specification, Cleanroom software engineering, and zero-defect software.

Linger received a BS in electrical engineering from Duke University. He is a member of the IEEE and ACM.

Mark G. Pleszkoch is a staff programmer at IBM's System Integration Division and a computer-science instructor at the University of Maryland at Baltimore County. His research interests include program verification, denotational semantics, and recursion-theoretic inductive inference.

Pleszkoch received a BA and an MA in mathematics from the University of Virginia. He is a member of the Association for Symbolic Logic.

Alan R. Hevner is an associate professor and chairman of the Information Systems Dept. at the University of Maryland at College Park. His research interests include distributed database systems, information-system analysis and design, and software engineering.

Hevner received a PhD in computer science from Purdue University. He is a member of the IEEE Computer Society and ACM.

Address questions about this article to Hausler or Linger at IBM Systems Integration Div., Rm. 864/5A20, Dept. NF1, 100 Lake Forest Blvd., Gaithersburg, MD 20877.

DOCUMENTATION IN A SOFTWARE MAINTENANCE ENVIRONMENT

L.D. Landis   P.M. Hyland   A.L. Gilbert   A.J. Fine

Technical Solutions, Incorporated
P.O. Box 1148   Mesilla Park, N.M. 88047
(505) 524-2154

ABSTRACT:

A great many software tools exist to aid in design and development of software systems. However, very little success has been realized in developing cost-effective tools for the maintenance programmer. An approach has been defined, and a system developed, to aid the maintenance programmer by producing documentation from source code input. TSI has developed a system, the Parser/Documenter, which is designed to accept source code from a variety of third generation languages and outputs one of several documentation tools. This paper discusses current documentation methodologies, development of the Parser/Documenter and one application currently under development: expanded Nassi-Shneiderman charts.

I. INTRODUCTION

A. The Problem

When determining the true cost of a new software package, one important consideration is the estimation of the useful lifetime of the package. Of great importance in this estimation is the maintainability of the software. Maintainability determinations include three major factors:

- adequacy of the software in the first place,
- adequacy of the programmer documentation, and
- the skill level of the maintenance programmer(s).

Depending on the programming skills of the original implementors, a software system may be "good" code or not, where a measure of "goodness" might include the degree to which the code is self-documenting, the open-endedness of design, and the closeness of fit of the software and the user's needs. However, the quality of the original software is outside the scope of this paper.

Programmer documentation, or internal documentation, is generally the poor stepchild of any software development effort. This does not imply that programmers see no need for internal documentation, but rather that it is usually the

last priority in the development effort. Documentation is the effort that suffers as developers try to get a package out the door before it is obsolete; or before the competition beats them to the market; or as managers discover that their original time table is slipping; or that programmers need to be moved to some other project. Consequently, few assumptions are safe regarding the quality, or existence, of the original internal documentation for a given software system. As code is modified, the original documentation may or may not have been modified to keep it current with the code. Consequently, after a few modifications, the original documentation may be inaccurate.

The large, expensive software systems are those one least wants to replace. Maintenance of large systems is rarely tasked to a single person, and team maintenance efforts suffer from the same communication and coordination problems of a committee effort. Also, maintenance programming is considered fit only for beginners. As programmers gain experience and seniority they want to move on to development programming, leaving maintenance programming behind as a less-interesting effort.

In order to extend the useful lifetime of a software system, some way must be found to make aging software easier to maintain/modify. Enforcing documentation standards works for new development efforts but tends not to address the problem of the large amount of existing software with either non-existent documentation, or documentation that is suspected of being out-of-date. What is needed is some way of generating useful programmer documentation for existing software in an easy, demand-driven way. (Demand-driven implies that more than one documentation method is available, and that documentation can be updated as necessary with a small amount of effort.) Ease-of-use and demand-drivability leads to automatic documentation generation as the preferred approach.

B. Our Interest in the Problem

Our interest in the problem exists since we both develop large software projects internally and acquire large software systems from external sources. Our need is for both a robust maintenance tool, and for a training tool that allows programmers to familiarize themselves with

*This research was supported by the U.S. Army Research Office, contract #DAAG29-85-C-0026.

large software systems without having to read and study large pieces of code.

This need led to undertaking a three-year project for the Army Research Office examining the issue of automatic documentation generation. This project consisted of several steps. A study was undertaken on the issue of providing an automatic documentation generator, several documentation methodologies were examined, and one solution is being implemented at this time. This paper discusses the documentation methodologies examined, the proposed solution, progress made in implementing this solution, ways in which the project could evolve, and research topics spawned by the work.

C. Current Documentation Methodologies

Before beginning to automate the process of generating software documentation, it was necessary to determine which documentation methods would be most useful to the maintenance programmer. Several documentation methods were evaluated:

- Pretty Printing
- Warnier-Orr Diagrams
- Jackson Diagrams
- Flowcharts
- Pseudocode/Structured English
- Nassi-Shneiderman Diagrams
- Action Diagrams
- HOS Charts
- Cross References

Information about each of these methods can be found in the references, and results of the evaluatins are presented in the Appendix.

D. Tools Considered to Provide a Similar Functionality

There exist tools such as lint [5] and cxref that are considered to provide a similar functionality. (Lint is a Unix utility that imposes strict type-checking on C code; it warns the user about usages the C compiler typically allows. Cxref creates a listing of all identifiers by file name and line number.)

The authors consider lint especially, and cxref, to a certain extent, to be debugging tools. The need TSI is attempting to address is not provision of debugging tools, but rather of a tool that assists the programmer in developing a conceptual understanding of the software system to be maintained. It is possible that the tool we propose could also be used as a debugging tool, but that is not its primary purpose.

II. IMPLEMENTATIONS OF INTEREST

An initial step in building an automatic documentation generator was to decide upon documentation methodologies of interest and source languages for which a documentation tool was most useful.

A. Documentation Methodologies

It was decided that several documentation techniques were both feasibly automated and familiar to a large segment of the computing community. One should not infer that these techniques are going to solve all maintenance problems, but rather that a set of familiar tools can be provided to aid the maintenance programmer. A short description of the plan for using these techniques follows.

Nassi-Shneiderman Charts: Nassi-Shneiderman (N-S) charts provide a pictorial representation of a block of code. This is useful for programmers new to the language being used, or programmers new to a given piece of software. The N-S chart format was extended to allow for representation of inputs and outputs to a block of code, and also for constructs like the Ada* "tasks".

Figure A depicts a small N-S chart for a factorial computation. The original format for N-S charts has been modified to allow for subroutine representation, with parameters and variables explicitly represented.

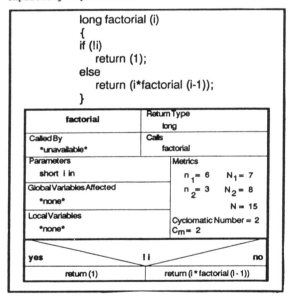

Figure A. A Nassi-Shneiderman Chart

Data Dictionary: Data dictionaries are of interest at two levels. At the simpler level, it would be useful to allow a programmer to check for mis-spelled identifiers in FORTRAN code or determination of types and evaluation for expressions in C. A more complex dictionary usage could support an interactive documentation manual, (using a technology such as hypertext), for the programmer.

Pictorial Representation of Complex Data Structures: Another useful tool would be an automated diagrammer for complicated data structures. Whether these data structures are FORTRAN equivalences, COBOL redefines (explicit or implicit), or a multi-layered struct and union definition from C, complex data manipulations could be comprehended (and many problems could be detected) more easily if a picture of the data structure was available.

This representation could be analogous to a FORTRAN "lint" utility, another useful tool.

Source Code Transliteration: Finally it would be a useful side-effect to have a simple code transliterator, that accepted source code from one language and generated pretty-printed code in another language.

B. Source Languages

It was necessary to determine which source languages are in great use or have that potential. After surveying the software systems in use today, it was decided that FORTRAN, COBOL, C, and eventually, Ada were of greatest interest.

FORTRAN: Many millions of lines of FORTRAN code are in use today, much of it belonging to the U.S. Government. This code is possibly the largest body of code in "maintenance mode" in the world. The government cannot simply replace all of its code base, and so it provides a great opportunity for development/evaluation of maintenance tools.

COBOL: The government's business software is mostly written in COBOL, a language that is outwardly different from the "computer science" languages, yet is strongly related. There is no real difference between

    add 1 to discount

in COBOL, and C's version of the same instruction

    discount += 1

COBOL has a good data-structuring ability and is a good target for the pictorial representations of a documentation generator.

C: C has become a popular language for production programming, and is unusual in its expressive power. Experienced C users may use constructions that are not obvious in their side-effects to the less experienced C user.

Ada: Since the DoD has mandated Ada as its language of choice, it is anticipated that a great demand for Ada maintenance tools will exist in the near future.

III. AN APPROACH

A. The Concept

A solution was envisioned, the Parser/Documenter (P/D), that would take working

*Ada is a registered trademark of the Ada Joint Program Office, U.S. Government.

source code, massage it in some way for representation purposes, and extract that massaged information for generation of documentation output. The solution system should be:

- modular, for ease of development and maintenance
- open-ended, to facilitate interchanging source languages or application outputs
- capable of retaining the full semantics of the source code when transforming to the target application
- general enough in nature to handle the third generation block structured languages
- able to handle large software systems
- interactive

The system chosen for implementation consists of three separate parts, or phases. The first phase is to transform the source code into equivalent code in an intermediate language named the Documentation Language (DL). This DL equivalent of the source code is then processed in the second phase. The second phase is actually the symbol table generation step found in production compilers. Finally relevant information is extracted from the symbol tables by the documentation post-processor to generate the desired documentation output. Figure B. contains a dataflow diagram for the implementation of P/D currently in development.

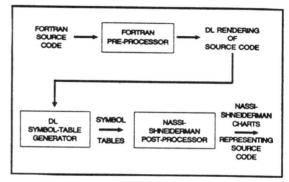

Figure B. P/D Dataflow Diagram

B. The Documentation Language Symbol-Table Generator

DL had to have a notation rich enough to handle features of several third generation languages: FORTRAN, Pascal, C, and eventually, Ada. These languages are all similar, (especially Pascal, C, and Ada), and all can support modern, structured programming techniques. Specific features deemed necessary for DL include:

- block structure
- standard types
- user defined types
- aliasing
- operator overloading
- overloading of function and procedure names
- nesting of subroutines

68

The X3J11 standard of C was used as a basis for DL. C was deemed a strong beginning because it is low level, powerful, flexible, abstract, and is generally machine independent. The X3J11 standard addresses some of the problems left unresolved by the Kernighan and Ritchie (1978) C. The expressiveness of X3J11 was expanded to encompass the necessary features from the other languages.

The parser for the DL symbol-table generator is Lex/Yacc based (Unix utilities), and generates the symbol tables that contain the complete semantics of the source program. (Retention of complete semantics implies that as information is stored in the symbol tables, nothing is changed, moved, optimized, or reduced.) Constant folding does occur but the constituent subexpressions are retained. Since P/D is designed to allow for different documentation applications, it cannot be known in advance what information will be relevant for the applications chosen. Therefore, ALL relationships found in the source code are stored in the symbol tables. (A production compiler stores only those relationships necessary to generate machine language instructions for a particular machine.) Also of interest is the caveat that the DL symbol-table generator expects working source code. P/D is not designed as a debugging aid for non-working code; the source program is expected to be operational code, or reliable documentation is not produced.

C. Pre-processor

The pre-processors are designed to take original source code, one file at a time, and transform it to DL code with equivalent functionality. The source languages to be handled, in order of implementation, are: FORTRAN, C, and Ada.

SUBROUTINE

<Name>		Return Type	
Called By		Calls	
Parameters		Metrics	
Global Variables Affected		$n_1 =$ $n_2 =$	$N_1 =$ $N_2 =$ $N =$
Local Variables		Cyclomatic Number = $C_m =$	
<Subroutine Statement>			

Figure C. Nassi-Shneiderman Chart Format for Subroutines

D. Post-processor

The post-processor is designed to search the symbol tables for information relevant to generating the desired documentation output. The

documentation outputs to be generated, (in order of implementation,) are: Nassi-Shneiderman charts, a data dictionary, pictorial representation of data structures, and pretty-printers for other languages.

One N-S chart format that is used is depicted in Figure C. Extra space is allocated for tracking of parameters and variables, and of course the <subroutine statement> can be any compound statement. When it is determined that the N-S chart would overflow a page (too long) or would become too cluttered to be readable (deeply nested code segments), the post-processor breaks to a new page, tying the charts across pages in a manner analogous to flowcharting's off-page connectors. Figure D depicts the N-S chart that might be generated for the following code segment:

```
subroutine dummy ( type_par par_1, par_2 ) : real
integer var_1, var_2,
begin
   if cond_1 then
      while cond_2
         repeat
            loop_statements;
         until cond_3
      statements_1
      loop
         statements_2
         exit cond_4
         statements_3
   else
      case gl_1 of
         val_1 : val_1_statements;
         val_2 : val_2_statements;
               break;
         val_3 : val_3_statements;
         else  : default_statements;
      else_statements;
   end_if;
   statements_4
end_subroutine;
```

In the example, all variables are identified by name and type, and parameters and global variables are identified by usage, where usage values are in, out, in-out, and unused. Usage values are defined as follows:

in	passed in and used
out	computed and passed out
in-out	passed in, used/changed, and passed out
unused	passed in and never accessed

The possible callers for the subroutine are identified as much as possible, and also any subroutines this subroutine can call. The final addition made to the format is to provide some software metrics for evaluation. These are the counts defined by Halstead, McCabe's Cyclomatic Number, and McClure's complexity measure. For a brief discussion of these metrics, see [7].

The N-S post-processor is implemented as two programs. The first stage searches the symbol tables for information needed to generate the N-S output, and creates a text file, written in an N-S

69

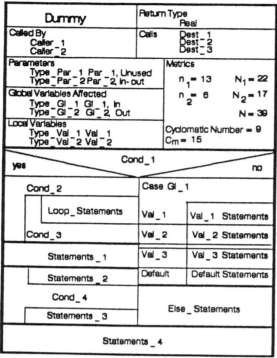

Dummy		Return Type Real		
Called By Caller_1 Caller_2		Calls Dest_1 Dest_2 Dest_3		
Parameters Type_Par_1 Par_1, Unused Type_Par_2 Par_2, In-out		Metrics $n_1 = 13$ $N_1 = 22$		
Global Variables Affected Type_GI_1 GI_1, In Type_GI_2 GI_2, Out		$n_2 = 6$ $N_2 = 17$ $N = 39$		
Local Variables Type_Val_1 Val_1 Type_Val_2 Val_2		Cyclomatic Number = 9 $Cm = 15$		

Figure D. Nassi-Shneiderman Example

"language", describing the source code structure. The N-S language describes the structure to be drawn, e.g. if-then-else, and its contents. The second stage processes the N-S language file, actually generating the N-S charts using a PostScript engine.

E. Work Accomplished

P/D is a three-year contract, begun in August 1985. At this time, TSI perceives the following progress to have been made, with P/D's strengths and limitations as given.

Progress: At this point in time the DL symbol-table generator is finished, and accepts the following features:

- external declarations, including types, void, subrange, complex, and double complex
- multiple blocks
- expressions with strong type checking, including complex data type operations
- handling of constant expressions inside array and subrange declarations, and case statements
- initialization for declared variables
- statements: if-then-else, switch/case, for-do-while, continue, break, return, labelled statements, compound statement blocks

Due to internal interests FORTRAN was chosen for the first source language pre-processor, and Nassi-Shneiderman charts for the first documentation tool post-processor. Work has begun

on both the pre- and post-processors and a working system is expected by the end of July of 1988.

Strengths: The following features are perceived to be design strengths of P/D:

- The transformation from source language to DL preserves the complete semantics of the source code, so no meaning is lost.
- Since no program semantics are lost, the transformation should be reversible. It would be possible to go backwards from the DL rendering of a piece of code to an equivalent rendering in the original language. The reconstituted code would be semantically equivalent, but not syntactically identical.
- P/D is open-ended in that a pre- or post-processor could be replaced without disturbing the rest of the system. Also the generator itself may be modified without disturbing the pre-/post-processors.

Implementation Limitations: At this time P/D has the following implementation limitations:

- It cannot process software projects that consist of several source files all at one time. They have to be processed one file at a time, so P/D does not track the interaction between files. This was a simplifying design decision that will be addressed in the near future.
- Overloading of operators and names is not complete.

The reader should not infer that the authors consider P/D useful in a real-world environment with these limitations. Before P/D could be considered a production tool, these limitations (and possibly others) would have to be addressed.

F. Possible Further Work

As supporting funding becomes available there are several extensions to the current state of P/D that are planned.

Upgrade to Multiple Source Files: As mentioned earlier, the task of expanding P/D to accept and track multiple-source-file projects at a single time is being examined. This is probably the most desirable feature to be implemented since literally no significant software system has been implemented as a single file for some time.

Add COBOL: COBOL should be added to the languages accepted by P/D. It was not addressed before since no COBOL is used in-house, but too large a COBOL code base exists for it to be ignored.

Upgrade to Ada: At this time P/D does not handle several features necessary to Ada, such as (generic) packages, tasks, and overloading of function and procedure names. The generator should be expanded to accept the full Ada specification. This is anticipated to be a two-to-three programmer-year effort due to Ada's non-trivial nature.

70

IV. OTHER RESEARCH AREAS

There are two areas of research spawned by the work on the Parser/Documenter: Knowledge-Based Translation Systems, and Software Metrics.

A. Knowledge-Based Translation Systems

As P/D was developed, the problem of using it to provide an acceptable source code translation became more interesting. Since what it now produces is transliteration, thought was given to the translation issue, and it was decided that in order to achieve a translator, knowledge had to be added to the P/D.

If the original source code were translated into a low level intermediate knowledge-based representation; and an "expert system" were used to achieve some level of "understanding" of the software system being translated; and finally target code was created from the knowledge-base, it should be possible to achieve good, idiomatic target code.

A target for such a system is the large amount of FORTRAN code owned by the government. This code serves as a potential source for translation to Ada. It is not clear at this time, however, whether it would be better, (for many reasons), to simply use the original code until it is scrapped, or to translate it to a much different language like Ada.

B. Software Metrics

Since complete symbol tables are built, P/D is well suited for providing a number of software metrics that provide a quantitative measure of module complexity. Three metrics which appear to be worth pursuing as an interesting extension the the P/D effort are Halstead's Software Science, McCabe's Cyclomatic Number, and McClure's Control Variable Complexity Measure. More information is available from [7].

V. CONCLUSION

In conclusion, we believe that P/D is a valuable tool for extending the lifetime of a software system in an easy, useful way. There are many software tools on the market but none directed specifically at providing the maintenance programmer a conceptual handle to the software to be maintained.

REFERENCES

[1] A.L. Gilbert, L.D. Landis, W.L. Hembree, A.J. Fine, P.M. Hyland, "Documentation In A Software Maintenance Environment", TSI Internal Report, August 1987.

[2] M. Hamilton and S. Zeldin, "Higher Order Software: A Methodology for Defining Software", IEEE Transactions on Software Engineering, SE-2, no 1, 1976.

[3] M.A. Jackson, Principles of Program Design, New York: Academic Press, 1975.

[4] M.A. Jackson, System Development, Englewood Cliffs, New Jersey: Prentice-Hall, 1983.

[5] S.C. Johnson, "Lint, a C Program Checker", Unix Programmer's Manual, Supplementary Documents 1 (PS1), 1986.

[6] J. Martin and C. McClure, Action Diagrams, Clearly Structured Program Design, Englewood Cliffs, N.J.: Prentice-Hall, 1985.

[7] J. Martin and C. McClure, Structured Techniques For Computing, Englewood Cliffs, N.J.: Prentice-Hall, 1985.

[8] K.T. Orr, Structured System Design, New York: Yourdon Press, 1978.

[9] J.D. Warnier, Logical Construction of Programs, New York: Van Nostrand, 1974.

[10] J.D. Warnier, Logical Construction of Systems, New York: Van Nostrand, 1981.

[11] R. Wiener and R. Sincovec, Software Engineering with Modula-2 and Ada, New York: John Wiley & Sons, 1984.

APPENDIX - DOCUMENTATION METHODOLOGIES

Pretty Printing: A pretty printer is a stylizer. By reformatting the original program into a "standard" format, it is possible that the correction of misleading indentation (in the original) can highlight errors. This technique may be quite useful with old, unsightly source code.

Strengths:
- Can be implemented for any language.
- Output style is consistent for a specific language.
- The style reveals essential elements and structure of the code.

Weaknesses:
- Every language has different dialects known as standards, as well as the standard for the original definition.

Warnier-Orr Diagrams: Warnier-Orr diagramming offers a single technique to show functional decomposition and hierarchical data structures. The technique's primary strength is in the design phase, not maintenance phase.

Strengths:
- The system is modular, allowing the user to specify a design over multiple levels of detail.

Weaknesses:
- More useful for small programs, or high levels of large programs.
- Do not help reveal the extent of coupling and cohesion between modules.
- Input/output paths for procedural components are not shown.

71

- Conditions and variables that control procedural flow are not shown.
- Relationships between procedure and data are not shown.

Jackson Diagrams: Jackson Diagrams show data coupling and cohesion. Logic is not represented in this technique, which is thus of limited value. During maintenance the depiction of data coupling and cohesion would be of some use.

Strengths:
- Similar to Warnier-Orr Diagrams, but with data-related coupling and cohesion shown.
- The pictorial relationships and structured text within the icons can be automated.

Weaknesses:
- Lowest levels of detail can degenerate into pseudocode, thus degrading comprehension.
- No provision for showing variables and conditions that control procedural flow.
- Easily overloaded with detail, thus degrading comprehension.
- Descriptive structures are more wordy that the program they represent.

Flowcharts: Flowcharts are an elementary technique easily understood by programmers and non-programmers. The method is fairly reasonable for maintenance, provided the flowchart is correct. Unless automated, (which has been done by others), it is very difficult to maintain accuracy.

Strengths:
- Simple, elegant, flexible.

Weaknesses:
- Perpetuate the "spaghetti code" approach to programming.
- Make it too easy to confuse high level and low level operations.
- Not easy to draw for large, complex programs.

Pseudocode/Structured English: Pseudocode, or Structured English, is a narrative form of program logic which is difficult to produce automatically, and suffers from many of the same problems of standard documentation, if manually generated. In the opinion of many programmers, a pseudocode or narrative description of the code could be the most useful of all documentation methods since it would allow for description of the programmer's thoughts, e.g., tricks employed to save time or space at run-time, or obscure side effects. This is difficult-to-impossible to generate automatically though.

Strengths:
- Narrative form is easy to read and comprehend.
- Helpful for depicting overall program structure and architecture.
- Facilitates the process of stepwise refinement, to achieve actual compilable code.

Weaknesses:
- Narratives can be lengthy, difficult, or convoluted.
- Narratives tend to not be updated, and so suffer the same end as initial internal documentation.

Nassi-Shneiderman Diagrams: Nassi-Shneiderman Diagrams are a relatively modern replacement for flowcharts, depicting structured programming constructs and are easily automated. They are useful in maintenance for depicting static control structure, and interaction of test conditions within multiply-nested constructs.

Strengths:
- Deliberately designed to be graphically appealing.
- Easy to read, learn, and teach.

Weaknesses:
- Time consuming to draw and change.
- Procedure oriented, not data oriented; no provision for organizing data structures, in general cannot be linked to data models.
- Extensions are needed to show input and output data paths between procedures.

Action Diagrams: Action Diagrams were designed specifically to overcome many of the disadvantages of older techniques. They are not dependent upon specialized output devices, and can be superimposed on many of the commonly available languages (especially when used in connection with a pretty printer). During maintenance they are overshadowed by N-S charts as depictors of static structure.

Strengths:
- Easily drawn, taught, and learned.
- Easily computerized, with no hardcopy output forms required.
- Well adapted to modern programming techniques.
- Are a good interface with actual programming languages.

Weaknesses:
- Relatively new and unknown; have not gained a wide acceptance in the field.

HOS Charts: HOS (Higher Order Software) charts guarantee provably correct programs when no modules external to their immediate control are used. They have a highly mathematical rule-based orientation, and need much patience to learn and use correctly. They are not considered an appropriate mechanism for maintenance since most (or all) code was developed "outside" of the HOS environment.

Strengths:
- Notation extends over multiple levels of program design
- Binds data and procedures to each other intrinsically.
- One of the most mathematically rigorous development methods ever devised.

Weaknesses:
- Requires a highly mathematical orientation to use correctly.
- Primarily a team-oriented tool.

Cross Reference Listings: An adequate cross reference listing with derived information can provide the programmer with a quick method of determining where to look for changes to variables of interest. Not of great use in determining overall structure of the code, or dataflow.

72

461

Strengths:
- Allow rapid identification of potential side-effect instances within functions.
- Offer some check on typographical errors in languages such as FORTRAN.
- Offer data dictionary-type services.

Weaknesses:
- Do not necessarily perform an adequate job of typographical-error detection.
- Do not address program semantics.
- Can be somewhat confusing if an identifier name occurs in different scopes.

73

46

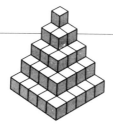

Recognizing Design Decisions in Programs

Spencer Rugaber, Stephen B. Ornburn, and **Richard J. LeBlanc, Jr.**
Georgia Institute of Technology

Recognizing design decisions is essential to maintaining and reverse-engineering code. But you first need a way to characterize these decisions and their underlying rationales.

Maintenance, reverse engineering, and reuse rely on being able to recognize, comprehend, and manipulate design decisions in source code. But what is a design decision? We have derived a characterization of design decisions based on the analysis of programming constructs. The characterization underlies a framework for documenting and manipulating design information to facilitate maintenance and reuse activities.

During program development, many decisions are made. Some address the problem domain and how it should be viewed and modeled. Others address constraints imposed by the solution space, including the target machine and language. Some decisions stand alone and have little effect on the rest of the program. Others are subtly interdependent. Sometimes decisions are explicitly documented along with their rationales, but more often the only indication of a decision is its resulting influence on the source code.

To effectively maintain an existing system, a maintenance programmer must be able to sustain decisions made earlier unless the reasons for the decisions have also changed. To accomplish this, he must recognize and understand the decisions.

Design process. Software design is the process of taking a functional specification and a set of nonfunctional constraints and producing a description of an implementation from which source code can be developed.

Whether formal or informal, functional specifications are primarily concerned with what the target system is supposed to do, not with how it is to do it. Source code is inherently formal. Although its primary purpose is to express solutions to problems, other concerns like target-machine characteristics intrude. The middle ground between specifications and code is more nebulous. Dallas Webster has sur-

0-8186-3272-0/93 $3.00 ©1990 IEEE

veyed the variety of notations and graphical representations used to handle this middle ground.[1]

You can describe the design process as a whole as repeatedly taking a description of intended behavior (whether specification, intermediate representation, or code) and refining it. Each refinement reflects an explicit design decision. Each limits the solution to a class of implementations within the universe of possibilities.

Rationale missing. Design involves making choices among alternatives. Too often, however, the alternatives considered and the rationale for making the final choice are lost.

One reason design information is lost is that commonly used design representations are not expressive enough. While they are adequate for describing the cumulative results of a set of decisions, particularly about the structure of components and how they interact, they do not try to represent the incremental changes that come with individual design decisions.

They also fail to describe the process by which decisions are reached, including the relevant problem requirements and the relative merits of the alternative choices.

The well-known tendency for system structure to deteriorate over time is accelerated when the original structure and design intent are not retained with the code.

Design decisions are not made in isolation. Often, a solution is best expressed through several interrelated decisions. Unless the interdependencies are explicitly documented, the unwary maintenance programmer will fail to notice all the implications of a proposed change. For example, if several pieces of source are interdependent and one piece is changed during maintenance, the others must be changed to sustain the design dependency and to preserve the program's correct functioning. Elliot Soloway and his colleagues have called these situations "delocalized plans" and described specific instances that are difficult for programmers to handle.[2]

Benefits of capturing rationale. If design decisions and their rationale were captured during initial program development, and if a suitable notational mechanism existed to describe their interdependencies, then several aspects of software engineering would profit:

• Initial development would benefit from the increased discipline and facilitated communication provided by the notation.

• Opportunities for reuse would be multiplied by the availability of design information that could be reused as is or transformed to meet new requirements.

• Maintenance would be vastly improved by the explicit recognition of dependencies and the availability of rationale.

Characterizing decisions

In studying various areas, computer science has revealed several categories of design decisions. Abstraction mechanisms

Languages and design decisions

There is a correspondence between the categories of design decisions and the variety of approaches to language design found in modern programming languages. This is not accidental but reflects the fact that languages are designed to make program development easier. They do this by providing a variety of abstraction mechanisms:

• Algol-60, Algol-68, and Pascal introduced and systematized control and data structures. They provided mechanisms to support decomposition of procedures into statements and data into its components. Of course, procedural abstraction has been with us since the early days of languages in the form of procedures and functions.

• Variables, too, have been part of programming since its beginning, but the explicit tradeoffs between data and procedures have become more prominent with the advent of functional languages. Programming in a functional language is difficult for a traditional programmer accustomed to using variables.

• Similarly, logic languages like Prolog highlight the function/relation dichotomy. The same kind of conceptual barriers confront a new Prolog programmer used to more traditional styles of programming or even used to a functional style.

• The issue of encapsulation is explicitly stressed in languages like Ada, Modula, and Clu. The programmer expresses the functional interface to a module in a separate construct from the implementation. The idea is to insulate the rest of the code from subsequent maintenance activities that alter the module's implementation while leaving the functional interface unchanged.

• Generalization/specialization is a primary consideration in Smalltalk. The class hierarchy expresses how subclasses specialize their parents. Dynamic binding invisibly delegates computation responsibility to the least general class able to handle it. Ada supports compile-time specialization of generic packages and procedures by data type and functional parameters.

• Representation is supported in most languages, but Clu emphasizes the distinction between representation and specialization by providing separate language constructs for expressing them. Gypsy has features to describe both ideal behavior and implementation details. It supports the proof of their equivalence via semiautomated means.

48

Encapsulation in Ada

The Ada package construct was designed to support encapsulation via information hiding. You achieve information hiding by separating the description of the facilities that a module provides (its functional specification) from the description of how it provides them (its body or implementation). But even with such a well-designed construct, there remains a range of ways to use encapsulation in Ada.

Imagine an application that requires lines of text to be read from an input file and broken up into words. The words will be statistically analyzed based on properties like their length and position. It is natural to think of a word as being a candidate for encapsulation within a package. This is not just a binary choice; there are a variety of ways that you might address the issue in Ada:

• No encapsulation at all. Read, parse, and analyze the words in the context of the controlling (client) code.

• Hide the reading and parsing in a subprogram (Get_Next_Word) that returns a string (array of characters) each time it is called.

• Define a new data type. Make word a new string type returned by Get_Next_Word. Its structure is visible, but the compiler will detect operations on words that should only be performed on strings and vice versa.

• Encapsulate the functionality for dealing with words in a package. The package will make visible (export) a data type (word) and one or more subprograms for obtaining and processing them. This approach has four further options.

1. Publish the representation for words by using an existing Ada data type like string.

2. Use the Ada Private keyword to hide the representation of the new type but allow assignment and equality tests on words. If you use an unconstrained array type as the representation, you must publish this fact in the public part of the package specification so package users can indicate the length of the words when they are declared.

3. Use the Ada Limited Private keywords to hide the representation and prevent even the use of assignment and equality tests.

4. Use an Access type (pointer) to hide even the knowledge that an array is holding the words.

• Completely hide the data type. No type is exported. The Get_Next_Word subprogram reads and parses the next word but returns nothing. Other subprograms in the package assume the existence of a current word and perform their analysis functions on it.

The design of Ada provides considerable freedom along this range of design decisions. Most languages allow only a more restricted set of choices, either because they do not support encapsulation at all or because they include features intended to support a particular style of encapsulation to the exclusion of others.

---

in languages provide evidence of the need to express design ideas in code. Semantic relationships from database theory support the modeling of information structures from a variety of fields. Examination of tools used for reverse engineering and maintenance indicate decisions that have been found useful in understanding existing programs. The box on p. 47 describes several mechanisms for implementing design decisions in current languages.

Composition and decomposition. Probably the most common design decision made when developing a program is to split it into pieces. You can do this, for example, by breaking a computation into steps or by defining a data structure in terms of its fields. Introducing a construct and then later decomposing it supports abstraction by letting you defer decisions and hide details. You manage complexity by using an appropriate name to stand for a collection of lower level details.

If you take a top-down approach to design, you decompose a program into pieces. If you take a bottom-up approach, you compose a program from available subcomponents. Regardless of the approach, the result is that a relationship has been established between an abstract element and several more detailed components.

Data and control structures are language features that support these decisions. For example, a loop is a mechanism for breaking a complex operation into a series of simpler steps. Likewise, arrays and record structures are ways to collect related data elements into a single item. Of course, building an expression from variables, constants, and operators is an example of composition. So too is building a system from a library of components.

Encapsulation and interleaving. Structuring a program involves drawing boundaries around related constructs. Well-defined boundaries or interfaces

limit access to implementation details while controlling clients' access to functionality. Encapsulation, abstract data types, and information hiding are all related to this concept.

Encapsulation is the decision to gather selected parts of a program into a component (variously called a package, cluster, or module.) You restrict the component's behavior by a protocol or interface so other parts of the system can interact with the component only in limited ways.

Encapsulation is a useful aid to both program comprehension and maintenance. A decision to encapsulate the implementation of a program component reflects the belief that the encapsulated construct can be thought of as a whole with a behavior that can be described by a specification that is much smaller than the amount of code in the component. If the component hides the details of a major design decision, side effects of the change are limited when that decision is altered during later maintenance. The box at left presents some alternative approaches to encapsulation in Ada.

The alternative to encapsulation is interleaving. It is sometimes useful, usually for efficiency, to intertwine two computations. For example, it is often useful to compute the maximum element of a vector as well as its position in the vector. These could be computed separately, but it is natural to save effort by doing them in a single loop. Interleaving thus makes the resulting code harder to understand and modify. Martin Feather has described how transformational programming can systematically perform interleaving.[3]

Generalization and specialization. One of the most powerful features of programming languages is their ability to describe a whole class of computations using a subprogram parameterized by arguments. Although programmers usually think of procedures and functions as abstractions of expressions, the ability to pass arguments to them is really an example of generalization. The decision of which aspects of the computation to parameterize is one of the key architectural decisions made during software design.

Generalization is a design decision in which you satisfy a program specification by relaxing some of its constraints. For example, you might require a program to compute the logarithm of a limited set of numbers. You could satisfy the requirement by providing access to a general-purpose library function for computing logarithms. The library function could compute logarithms of the complete set of required numbers as well as many others. The decision to use the library function is thus a generalization decision.

You can parameterize abstractions other than numerical computations. For example, Ada provides a generic facility that lets data types and functions parameterize packages and subprograms. Many languages provide macro capabilities that parameterize textual substitutions. For example, variant records in Pascal and Ada and type unions in C use a single, general construct to express a set of special cases, possibly depending on the value of a discriminant field.

Another example of generalization is the use of interpreters for virtual machines. It is often useful for a designer to introduce a layer of functionality controlled by a well-defined protocol. You can think of the protocol as the language for the virtual machine implemented by the layer. The decision to introduce the protocol reflects the desire to provide more generality than a set of disparate procedures would offer.

Specialization is a design decision related to generalization. It involves replacing a program specification with a more restricted one. You can often optimize an algorithm based on restrictions in the problem domain or in the language facilities. Although these optimizations can dramatically improve performance, they lengthen the program size and make it harder to understand.

Specialization also occurs in the early stages of design. Specifications are often expressed in terms of idealized objects like infinite sets and real numbers. But actual programs have space and precision limitations. Thus, a program is necessarily a special case of a more general computational entity.

In object-oriented languages like Smalltalk and C++, the designer is provided with a collection of class definitions. A class provides an implementation for

objects that belong to it. A new class inherits the common functionality from its more general predecessor. Knowledgeable developers can quickly implement new classes by specializing existing classes.

Generalization and specialization decisions have long-term implications on the program being developed. It is easier to reuse or adapt a generalized component than a restricted one. But generality has a cost: Generalized components may be less efficient than specially tuned versions. Moreover, it often takes more effort to test a component intended for wide application than to test its more specific counterpart.

> *It is easier to reuse or adapt a generalized component than a restricted one. But generality has a cost: Generalized components may be less efficient than specially tuned versions.*

Representation. The selection of a representation is a powerful and comprehensive design decision. You use representation when one abstraction or concept can better express a problem solution than another. It may be better because the target abstraction more ably captures the sense of the solution or because it can be more efficiently implemented on the target machine. For example, you may choose a linked list to implement a push-down stack. Or you may use bit vectors to represent finite sets. Representation is the decision to use one construct in place of another functionally equivalent one.

Representation must be carefully distinguished from specialization. If you implement a (possibly infinite) push-down stack with a fixed-length array, you have made two decisions. The first decision is that a bounded-length stack will work for this program. This is a specialization deci-

sion. The second is that the bounded stack can be readily implemented by a fixed-length array and an index variable. This is a representation choice.

When you keep in mind the distinction between specialization and representation, you can see representation to be a flexible and symmetrical decision. In one context, it may be appropriate to represent one construct by another. But you might use the inverse representation in a different context. For example, operations on vectors are usually implemented by a loop, but if using vector-processing hardware, the compiling system may invert the representation to reconstruct the vector operation.

Another example of representation comes from the early stages of design. Formal program specifications are often couched in terms of universal and existential quantification like "All employees who make more than $50,000 per year ... ." Programmers typically use loops and recursion to represent these specifications.

Data and procedures. Variables are not necessary to write programs, since you can always explicitly recompute values. Program variables have a cost: the amount of effort required to comprehend and modify a program. But they can improve the efficiency of the program and, by a judicious choice of names, clarify its intent.

You must be aware of the invariants relating the program variables when you insert statements into a program. For example, suppose a maintenance programmer is investigating a loop that reads records from a file and counts the number of records read. The programmer has been asked to make the loop disregard invalid records. Because the counter is used to satisfy design dependencies between this loop and other parts of the program, he must modify the semantics of the counter.

The programmer must choose from three alternatives: counting the total number of records, counting the number of valid records, or doing both. To make the correct choice, he must determine how the counter is used later in the program. In this case, he can replace references to variables with the computations that produced their most recent values. He can rearrange the resulting state-

50

ments to reconstruct the high-level operations applied to the file. Having done this, the programmer can confront the semantic problems raised by the distinction between valid and invalid records. Once he has solved those semantic problems, he can again interleave the components by reintroducing assignment statements.

The introduction of variables constrains the sequence in which computations may be made. This increases the possibility of errors when modifications made during maintenance accidently violate an implicit design dependency such as causing variables to be computed in the wrong order.

The alternative to introducing a variable is to recompute values when they are needed. This sometimes makes a program more readable, since a reader does not have to search the program for the declaration and assignments to a variable but can directly use local information. Optimizing compilers often reduce the cost of recomputation, particularly where constant expressions are involved.

The decision to repeat a computation or to save the result of the computation in a variable reflects the deeper concept of the duality of data and procedure. The implementation of a finite-state machine is an example of where the data/procedure decision is apparent.

In the data-oriented approach, possibilities for the machine's next state are recorded in a two-dimensional array, often called the next-state table. Alternatively, you can directly compute the next-state information in code for each of the states. Although this may seem unusual, it is exactly the same technique used to speed up lexical analyzers: Token classes are first represented as regular expressions and then as states in a state machine. The states are then compiled directly into case/switch statements in the target language. The reason to do this is efficiency: In the procedural version, it avoids the cost of indexing into the array.

Function and relation. Logic languages let you express programs as relations between sets of data. For example, sorting is described as the relationship of two sets, both of which contain the same members, one of which is ordered. In Prolog, this

might be described by the rule

sort(S1,S2) :-
    permutation(S1,S2),ordered(S2).

If S1 is given as input, a sorted version S2 is produced. But if, instead, an ordered version S2 is provided, unordered permutations are produced in S1. You can leave the decision about which variable is input and which is output to the user at runtime instead of to the developer at design time.

Formal functional specifications are often nondeterministic about the relation's direction of causality. If there is a preferred direction, the designer may use a function instead of a relation to express it. But this may reflect an implementation bias rather than a requirement.

Of course, more traditional languages do not support nondeterministic relationships. Even in Prolog it may be impossible, for any given problem, to write a set of rules that works equally well in both directions. Thus, the designer is usually responsible for selecting the preferred direction of causality — which variables are input and which are output.

An alternative approach is to provide separate functions that support both directions. For example, in a student-grading system it may be useful to provide a function that, when given a numeric grade, indicates the percentage of students making that grade or higher. It may also be valuable to provide the inverse function that, when given a percentage, returns the numeric grade that would separate that proportion of the students.

> *Even in Prolog it may be impossible, for any given problem, to write a set of rules that works equally well in both directions. Thus, the designer must select the preferred direction of causality - which variables are input and which are output.*

Finding decisions

Maintenance and reuse require the detection of design decisions in existing code, which is a part of reverse engineering. Because reverse engineering is the process of constructing a higher level description of a program from a lower level one, this typically means constructing a representation of a program's design from its source code. The process is bottom-up and incremental; you detect low-level constructs and replace them with their high-level counterparts. If you repeat this process, the overall architecture of the program gradually emerges from the language-dependent details.

The program in Figure 1 is taken from a paper by Victor Basili and Harlan Mills[4] in which they use flow analysis and techniques from program proving to guide the comprehension process and document the results. It is a realistic example of production software in which design decisions can be recognized. (Basili and Mills obtained the program from a book by George Forsythe and colleagues.[5])

The real function Zeroin finds the root of a function, F, by successively reducing the interval in which it must occur. It does this by using one of several approaches (bisection, linear interpolation, and inverse quadratic interpolation), and it is the interleaving of the approaches that complicates the program.

Interleaving program fragments. A casual examination of the program indicates that it contains two Write statements that provide diagnostic information when the program is run. In fact, these statements display the progress that the program makes in narrowing the interval containing the root. The execution of the Write statements is controlled by the variable IP. IP is one of the program's input parameters, and an examination of the program indicates that it is not altered by the program and has no other use.

This leads to the conclusion that you can decompose the overall program into two pieces: the root finder and the debugging printout. To make the analysis of the rest of the program simpler, you can remove the diagnostic portion from the text being considered. This means removing

51

```
001        REAL FUNCTION ZEROIN (AX,BX,F,TOL,IP)
002        REAL AX,BX,F,TOL
003  C
004. C
005        REAL A, B, C, D, E, EPS, FA, FB, FC, TOL1, XM, P, Q, R, S
006  C
007  C    Computer EPS, The RelativeMachine Precision
008  C
009        EPS = 1.0
010     10 EPS = EPS/2.0
011           TOL1 = 1.0 + EPS
012        IF (TOL1 .GT. 1.0) GO TO 10
013  C
014  C    Initialization
015  C
016        IF (IP .EQ. 1) WRITE (6,11)
017     11 FORMAT ('THE INTERVALS DETERMINED
                   BY ZEROIN ARE')
018        A = AX
019        B = BX
020        FA = F(A)
021        FB = F(B)
022  C
023  C    Begin Step
024  C
025     20 C = A
026        FC = FA
027        D = B - A
028        E = D
029     30 IF (IP .EQ. 1) WRITE (6,31) B, C
030     31 FORMAT (2E15.8)
031        IF (ABS(FC) .GE. ABS(FB)) GO TO 40
032        A = B
033        B = C
034        C = A
035        FA = FB
036        FB = FC
037        FC = FA
038  C
039  C    Convergence Test
040  C
041     40 TOL1 = 2.0*EPS*ABS(B) + 0.5*TOL
042        XM = .5*(C-B)
043        IF (ABS(XM) .LE. TOL1) GO TO 90
044        IF (FB .EQ. 0.0) GO TO 90
045  C
046  C    Is Bisection Necessary
047  C
048        IF (ABS(E) .LT. TOL1) GO TO 70
049        IF (ABS(FA) .LE. ABS(FB)) GO TO 70
050  C
051  C    Is Quadratic Interpolation Possible
052  C
053        IF (A .NE. C) GO TO 50
054  C
055  C    Linear Interpolation
056  C
057        S = FB/FA
058        P = 2.0*XM*S
059        Q = 1.0 - S
060        GO TO 60
061  C
062  C    Inverse Quadratic Interpolation
063  C
064     50 Q = FA/FC
065        R = FB/FC
066        S = FB/FA
067        P = S*(2.0*XM*Q*(Q-R) - (B-A) * (R-1.0))
068        Q = (Q-1.0)*(R-1.0)*(S-1.0)
069  C
070  C    Adjust Signs
071  C
072     60 IF (P .GT. 0.0) Q = -Q
073        P = ABS(P)
074  C
075  C    Is Interpolation Acceptable
076  C
077        IF ((2.0*P) .GE. (3.0*XM*Q - ABS(TOL1*Q)))
                   GO TO 70
078        IF (P .GE. ABS(0.5*E*Q)) GO TO 70
079        E = D
080        D = P/Q
081        GO TO 80
082  C
083  C    Bisection
084  C
085     70 D = XM
086        E = D
087  C
088  C    Complete Step
089  C
090     80 A = B
091        FA = FB
092        IF (ABS(D) .GT. TOL1) B = B + D
093        IF (ABS(D) .LE. TOL1) B = B + SIGN(TOL1,XM)
094        FB = F(B)
095        IF ((FB*(FC/ABS (FC))) .GT. 0.0) GO TO 20
096        GO TO 30
097  C
098  C    Done
099  C
100     90 ZEROIN = B
101        RETURN
102        END
```

Figure 1. Realistic example of production software in which you can recognize design decisions.

lines 016, 017, 029, and 030 and modifying line 001 to remove the reference to *IP*.

The removed lines may themselves be analyzed. In fact, the job of producing the debugging printout has been decomposed into two tasks. The first produces a header line, and the second prints a description of the interval on every iteration of the loop.

Representing structured control flow.

Basili and Mills begin their analysis by examining the program's control flow. In fact, the version of Fortran used in this program has a limited set of control structures that forces programmers to use Goto statements to simulate the full range of structured-programming constructs. In Zeroin, for example, lines 010-012 implement a Repeat-Until loop, lines 031-037 are an If-Then statement, and lines 050-068 are an If-Then-Else statement. These lines are the result of representation decisions by the original developer. You can detect them with straightforward analysis like that typically performed by a compiler's flow-analysis phase.

This program illustrates another technique to express control flow. In several cases (lines 043-044, 048-049, and 077-078), an elaborate branch condition is broken up into two consecutive If statements, both branching to the same place.

Each pair could easily be replaced by a single If with multiple conditions, thus further simplifying the program's control-flow structure at the expense of complicating the condition being tested.

Interleaving by code sharing. Further analysis of the control flow of the program indicates that lines 085 and 086 make up the Else part of an If-Then-Else statement. Moreover, these lines are branched into from lines 048 and 049 — the two assignment statements are really being shared by two parts of the program. Two execu-tion streams are interleaved because they share common code. Although this makes the program shorter and assures that both parts are updated if either one is, it makes understanding the program structure more difficult.

To express the control flow more cleanly, you must construct a structured version. This requires that the shared code be duplicated so each sharing segment has its own version. If the common statements were more elaborate, you could introduce a subroutine and call it from both sites. As it is, it is simple here to duplicate the two lines producing two properly formed conditional constructs.

Data interleaving by reusing variable names. An unfortunately common programming practice is to use the same variable name for two unrelated purposes. This naturally leads to confusion when trying to understand the program. You can think of it as a kind of interleaving where, instead of two separable segments of code being intertwined at one location in the program, two aspects of the program state share the use of the same identifier.

This occurs twice in Zeroin, with the identifiers Tol1 (in lines 011-012 and in the rest of the program) and Q (on line 064 through the right side of line 068 and in the rest of the program, including the left side of line 068). Compilers can detect instances of this practice with dataflow analysis.

Generalizing interpolation schemes. Zeroin has two sections of code that use alternative approaches to compute the values of the same set of variables. Both lines 057-059 and 064-068 compute the values of the variables P and Q. The determination of which approach to use is based on a test made on line 053. This is an example of specialization.

You can replace both computations and the test conceptually by a more general expression that computes P and Q based on the current values of the variables A, B, C, FA, FB, FC, and XM. This has the further benefit of localizing the uses of the variables S and R in the new expression.

There are really several design issues involved here. First, both code segments result from the decomposition of the problem into pieces expressed by a series of assignment statements. Then, the realization that both segments are specializations of a more general one lets the details of the individual cases be hidden. This, in turn, makes the code shorter and easier to understand.

Variable introduction. A common programming practice is to save the result of a computation to avoid having to recompute the same value later. If the computation is involved, this practice can result in

Design-decision projects

The design-decision concept plays a central role in several research efforts at Georgia Institute of Technology. These projects span a considerable range of applications, including specification-driven software reuse, a generalization of the application-generator concept, reverse engineering of Cobol programs, and transformation-based compiler construction.

These projects all depend (to varying degrees) on the existence of a program representation that expresses the link between specification, design, and code. This representation must also provide some way to record the rationale behind the transformations that create the design and code from the specification.

The specification-based reuse project is driven by the idea that reusing specification-level components makes it easier to customize components to facilitate their reuse. In this project, a component is considered to consist of a specification, one or more versions of code that implements the specification, and scripts that describe the transformations necessary to derive the code version(s) from the specification. You can immediately reuse a component whose specification matches a need if the set of implementation decisions captured by a script is suitable for the reuse context. If not, you might choose alternative decisions, thus creating a slightly modified script. One of this project's long-term goals is to build an environment to automatically replay a script of transformations.

The application-generator project uses this same technology. You can think of an application generator as an environment for producing variants of a program. The generator pre-defines the program's basic structure. The specification of the variants is, in effect, a specification of a set of decisions that determine certain implementation details. Each component of such a specification either chooses among alternatives or fills in blanks in the standard script that represents the application-generation process. The advantage of this approach is that it supports the construction of a wide variety of application generators by providing an underlying conceptual basis for their design.

The Cobol reverse-engineering project is an experiment in translating Cobol programs to Ada. The planned approach is to derive a functional description and a high-level design from examining the code and available documentation. The reverse-engineering process relies heavily on the design-decision recognition process described in the accompanying article. thus providing empirical validation of our model if it is successful. The project will also explore the representation issues in linking the new descriptions to the original code and representing the connections between them with design decisions.

The transformation-based compiler-construction project is exploring the derivation of software in this well-understood domain. You can think of the alternative design decisions, like the compiler's structure or the target machine's instruction set, as alternative transformation paths in the derivation of a compiler from its specification. This project's short-term goal is to guarantee the correctness of code generation, given a formal semantic specification for the source language and a suitable target-machine description.

```
001        Real Function Zeroin (AX,BX,F,TOL)
024   C
028        initialization
      C
           loop
               conditional adjustment 1
038   C
043            if (close enough to final answer)
                   return (B)
045   C
092            compute new value of B
      C
               conditional adjustment 2
096        endloop
```

Figure 2. Program architecture after analyzing its structure.

a significant savings at runtime with a modest cost.

Zeroin contains several instances of this practice. They made a concerted effort to save the results of calls to the user-supplied function, F, in the variables FA, FB, and FC. Because F may be arbitrarily complex, this practice may be the most important determinant of Zeroin's ultimate efficiency.

An examination of the program reveals that FA, FB, and FC always contain the results of applying F at the points A, B, and C, respectively. From the standpoint of understanding the algorithm, these three additional variables do not provide a significant abstraction — to the contrary, they require a nontrivial effort to understand and manipulate. Replacing them with their definitions makes the resulting program easier to understand.

When readability is the goal, there are two factors to be weighed in deciding whether to write the program with a variable name or to replace it with its value. One factor is that each new variable places a burden on the person trying to understand the program, since he must read the variable and understand and confirm its purpose. The other factor is that variables can be valuable abbreviations for the computation that they replace. It is easier to understand a variable with a carefully chosen name than the complex expression it represents.

In the case of Zeroin, the variables FA, FB, and FC provide little in the way of abstraction. P and Q, on the other hand, abbreviate significant computations, although without the benefits of mnemonic names. XM lies somewhere in the middle.

Generalizing interval computation. Now that the recognition of some intermediate decisions has clarified the program structure, you can make the same sort of observation about lines 048-086. They assign values to the variables D and E based on the values of the variables A, B, C, D, E, F, Tol1, and XM. The fact that the list of variables is so long indicates that this segment is highly interleaved with the rest of the program. Nevertheless, it is helpful to indicate that the only explicit effect of these lines is to set the two variables.

There are also several instances of spe-

cialization in these lines. Lines 079-080 and 085-086 are selected based on the tests on lines 077-078. Likewise, lines 082-086 and 050-081 are special cases selected on the basis of the tests on lines 048-049.

Program architecture. Once you have performed this analysis, you can appreciate the program's overall structure. Based on the test in line 044, you can see that the program uses the variable B to hold approximations of the root of the function. B is modified on lines 092-093 by either XM or D. The sections on lines 025-028 and 031-037 act as adjustments in special situations.

Another conclusion that is now apparent is that A gets its value only from B, while C gets its value only from A. Thus, A, C, and B serve as successively better approximations to the root. In fact, except under special circumstances, A and C have identical values. Likewise, E normally has the same value as D. Figure 2 shows the resulting program architecture.

Representing decisions

It is not sufficient to simply recognize design decisions in code. Once recognized, you must organize the decisions so maintenance programmers and reuse engineers can use them. The organization chosen serves as a representation for design information.

There are many methods for designing software and many representations for the intermediate results. Typically, you use several during program design, some during the architectural stages and others during low-level design. You may use still others during maintenance if there is a separate maintenance staff. It may thus be difficult to recreate and reuse the original representation.

A usable representation for design in-

formation must be easy to construct during development and easy to reconstruct during reverse engineering. Once constructed, it must facilitate queries and report generation to support maintenance. It must provide a way to attach available documentation. Also, it must support automation.

The representation must be formal enough that its components can be automatically manipulated. For example, it is desirable to be able to determine if a previously developed partial description of a software component can be reused in a new situation.

A representation for design information must let all types of design information be attached. This includes high-level specifications, architectural overviews, detailed interfaces, and the resulting source code. It is also desirable that the representation support requirements tracing, informal annotations, and version information.

Several approaches to organizing design information have been proposed.

Ted Biggerstaff's Desire system[6] is concerned with relating code fragments to information from the problem domain. Reuse will be facilitated if a new problem's requirements can be easily matched against a description of existing software.

Mark Blackburn's work[7] is also concerned with reuse. He proposes a network of design information where fragments are connected by one of two relationships, either "is-decomposed-into" (decomposition) or "is-a" (specialization).

Derek Coleman and Robin Gallimore have reported on FPD,[8] a framework for program development. Arcs in their network model correspond to refinements steps taken during the design. Each refinement engenders a proof obligation to guarantee the correctness of the step taken.

54

Maintenance and reuse require of their practitioners a deep understanding of the software being manipulated. That understanding is facilitated by the presence of design documentation. Effective documentation should include a description of the software's structure and details about the decisions that led to that structure.

Design decisions occur where the abstract models and theories of an application domain confront the realities of limited machines and imperfect languages. If the design decisions can be reconstructed, there is greater hope of being able to maintain and reuse the mountains of undocumented software confronting us all. ❖

References

1. D.E. Webster, "Mapping the Design Representation Terrain: A Survey," Tech. Report STP-093-87, Microelectronics and Computer Technology Corp., Austin, Texas, July 1987.

2. E. Soloway et al., "Designing Documentation to Compensate for Delocalized Plans," *Comm. ACM*, Nov. 1988, pp. 1,259-1,267.

3. M.S. Feather, "A Survey and Classification of Some Program-Transformation Approaches and Techniques," in *Program Specification and Transformation*, L.G.L.T. Meertens, ed., North Holland, Amsterdam, 1987, pp. 165-195.

4. V.R. Basili and H.D. Mills, "Understanding and Documenting Programs," *IEEE Trans. Software Eng.*, May 1982, pp. 270-283.

5. G. Forsythe, M. Malcolm, and M. Moler, *Computer Methods for Mathematical Computations*, Prentice-Hall, Englewood Cliffs, N.J., 1977.

6. T.J. Biggerstaff, "Design Recovery for Maintenance and Reuse," *Computer*, July 1989, pp. 36-49.

7. M.R. Blackburn, "Toward a Theory of Reuse Based on Formal Methods," Tech. Report SPC-TR-88-010, Version 1.0, Software Productivity Consortium, Herndon, Va., April 1988.

8. D. Coleman and R.M. Gallimore, "A Framework for Program Development," *Hewlett-Packard J.*, Oct. 1987, pp. 37-40.

Spencer Rugaber is a research scientist with the Software Engineering Research Center and the School of Information and Computer Science at Georgia Institute of Technology. His research interests include software maintenance and reverse engineering.

Rugaber received a BS in engineering and applied science and a PhD in computer science from Yale University and an MS from Harvard in applied math. He is a member of the ACM.

Stephen B. Ornburn is a PhD candidate and research assistant in Georgia Institute of Technology's School of Information and Computer Science. His dissertation research investigates the application of transformational programming techniques to problems in the reuse of software. Other research interests include the design of fault-tolerant software and the economic value of information systems. Before pursuing his PhD, he was an industrial engineer for General Foods.

Ornburn received a BS in industrial engineering and management science from Northwestern University and an MS in computer science from Georgia Institute of Technology. He is a member of the IEEE Computer Society and ACM.

Richard J. LeBlanc, Jr., is a professor in Georgia Institute of Technology's School of Information and Computer Science. His research interests include language design and implementation, programming environments, and software engineering. His research work involves applying these interests to distributed systems. He is also interested in specification-based development methodologies and tools.

LeBlanc received a BS in physics from Louisiana State University and an MS and a PhD in computer sciences from the University of Wisconsin at Madison. He is a member of the ACM, IEEE Computer Society, and Sigma Xi.

Address questions to the authors at Software Engineering Research Center, Georgia Institute of Technology, Atlanta, GA 30332-0280.

Chapter 11
Reengineering for Reuse

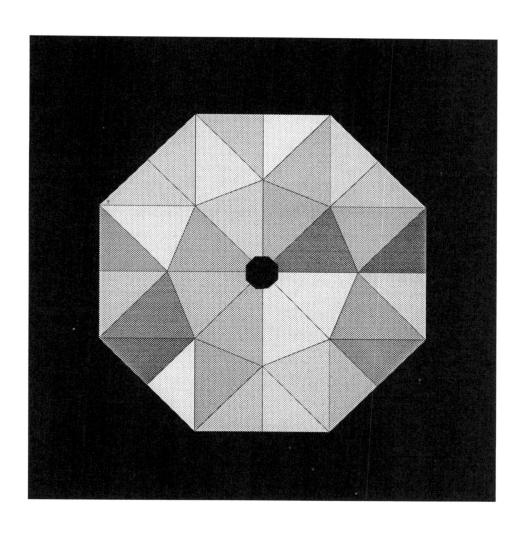

Chapter 11
Reengineering for Reuse

Purpose

A major reengineering goal is reusing software. An important sub-theme is finding software parts and rendering them more reusable. This chapter discusses processes for finding candidate reusable parts, metrics for measuring source code to discover candidate reusable parts, and issues in transforming the parts into a more reusable form.

Papers

In the first paper, "Software Reuse and Reengineering,"[1] Robert Arnold and William Frakes provide a brief conceptual overview of reengineering to recover source code for reuse. They discuss prospecting, transformation of parts, certification of parts, and measurement of part reuse. This paper is a good start for becoming familiar with reengineering for reuse.

The next paper, "Identifying and Qualifying Reusable Software Components," by Gianluigi Caldiera and Victor Basili, describes a process, model, and metrics for extracting candidate reusable parts from existing source code. The authors define a reusability attributes model featuring factors affecting software reusability, give metrics for measuring key concepts in the model, define a measure of reuse frequency, and give empirical measurements of reusability attributes.

In the next paper, "Software Reclamation: Improving Post-Development Reusability," John Bailey and Victor Basili discuss specific transformations of source code (here, in Ada) to improve its reusability. The paper well illustrates the many low-level issues facing someone trying to systematically make existing source code more reusable.

The last paper, "Software Reclamation" by E.S. Garnett and J.A. Mariani, discusses reengineering software for reuse, particularly for making the software more object-oriented. They discuss what the attributes of reusable code are in general. They then discuss a prototype tool for parameterizing source code for reuse.

---

[1]The final draft version of this paper is reproduced here. The paper was later published in the February 1992 issue of *CASE Trends*.

Software Reuse and Reengineering

Robert S. Arnold and William B. Frakes

Introduction

Software reuse and reengineering are receiving much attention as enterprises reclaim their tremendous software investment to support software evolution. Reusing assets may help a company evolve with less risk and cost than creating new systems from scratch. Part-based software reuse—the use of parts from previous systems to build new ones—is widely seen as a key technology for improving software flexibility, quality, and productivity. This article discusses approaches for recovering and reusing software assets.

Many problems—managerial, legal, economic, and technical—must be addressed for reuse to succeed. The most immediate problem in reuse today is how to acquire reusable assets [Frakes91a].

A software asset is any software-related, non-hardware item deemed valuable. Example software assets are software parts (e.g., systems, functions, procedures, packages, data type definitions, variable definitions, "objects"), designs (e.g., structure charts, data flow diagrams), specifications (e.g., business models and proposals for building software), test data, code templates, and notebooks of software documentation.

Reusable parts can be at different levels of granularity, from functions and subprograms to entire subsystems. They need not only be code. Indeed, larger payoffs might be obtained from reuse of other lifecycle objects such as test cases or design architectures.

Figure 1 illustrates a process for acquiring and reusing parts. There are three ways to get reusable parts, by purchasing them, designing them from scratch for reuse (including automatically generating parts), or reengineering them from previous systems. Once the parts are acquired, they should go through a certification process to ensure their quality and relevance. They then must be classified [Frakes90] and stored in a repository. Users may then search for them using a repository search tool. In time, parts from the repository are reused in systems. Based on actual use of parts, reuse levels are monitored. This information is used to refine the previous process steps through feedback. Constant improvement will help the reuse and reengineering process converge towards greater local effectiveness.

The rest of this article focuses on salvaging parts and reusing them. For brevity, the sections discuss only a very small fraction of the available information and experience.

Software Salvaging

Software salvaging is a reengineering specialty for recovering software assets for reuse. Software salvaging is part of the reuse cycle of Figure 1.

Sometimes software salvaging is done in the large, e.g, a payroll system is reengineered so new retirement benefit payments can be added more easily. Salvaging in the large extends a system's lifetime, allowing the entire system to be reused.

1

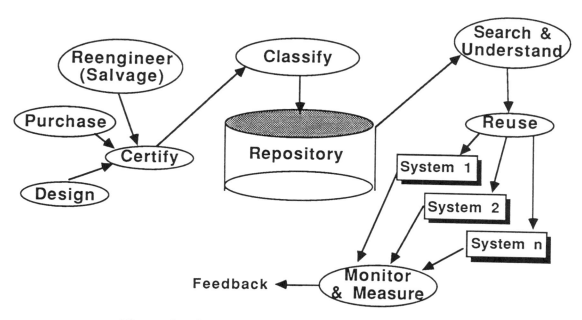

Figure 1: Overview of a Part Reuse Environment

Software salvaging in the small recovers parts for reuse. Software salvaging in the small may obtain software building blocks for reuse, help populate a repository with parts and relationships, or help recover object-oriented objects and classes from non-object-oriented software.

Figure 2 elaborates the Reengineering/salvaging process bubble in Figure 1, from the perspective of software salvaging in the small and parts-based reuse.

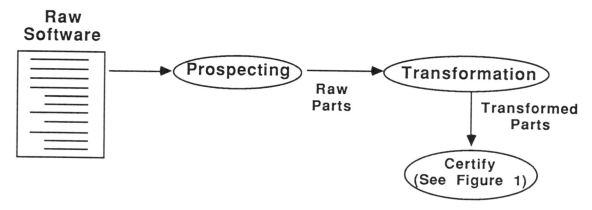

Figure 2. Software Salvaging Process

2

The parts of the process are:

• **Prospecting**. Looking at "raw" software to determine what looks interesting to reuse. Salvaging criteria are applied to determine what software "nuggets" (parts) are worth further attention.

• **Transformation**. A part is "refined" (modified and certified) so that it meets style and and quality criteria for insertion into the repository.

Customizing the prospecting process of Figure 2 results in different salvaging approaches. Three salvaging approaches are:

• Domain-independent software salvaging
• Domain-dependent software salvaging
• Object salvaging

Domain-independent software salvaging uses information readily obtained from the software itself (e.g., see [Arnold90a,b]) to find parts to salvage. A domain is a general area of interest. Domain-independent software salvaging means that relatively little information about the software's application area is used to find parts.

An example of domain-independent software salvaging is using software metrics to find redundant code. For example, McCabe and Associate's **CodeBreaker**™ is a tool that uses control flow metrics, such as essential and cyclomatic complexity, to find control flow (and code) redundancies. Another example is the plagiarism detection program a professor uses to detect student plagiarism (i.e., one student largely reuses another student's software solution.) Here salvaging is not the point, but detecting code redundancies—which in other contexts may the basis for software salvaging—is.

Domain-dependent software salvaging uses information about the software application or design history to find parts from code. An example of domain dependent software salvaging is the determining of common missile software parts in CAMP (Common Ada Missile Packages) by McDonnell Douglas.

Object salvaging tries to find object-oriented objects from non-object-oriented code.
An example of object salvaging is the work of Dunn and Knight [Dunn91], where C++ classes and object instances were salvaged from marine support software written in C.

Transforming a Part to Make it More Reusable

Transforming a part to make it more reusable presupposes that we know how to design for reuse, i.e. the attributes that a reusable part has. Reuse transformation ideas are still evolving.

One way to transform parts for reuse is to find several parts that have similar functionality and combine them into a single reusable part. A simple example might be several sort functions.

Sort-1	sorts integers in ascending order
Sort-2	sorts strings in descending order
Sort-3	sorts reals in descending order

3

In examining these functions, we see that they share a basic activity—sorting—but vary in the order of sort (ascending, descending) and in the data type they handle (integers, reals, strings). Having isolated the varying aspects, we move them to the interface. In C, for example, this is done by having a parameter that is used to indicate sort order, and by having parameters which point to functions that do the comparison and swap operations for the sort as in the following example.

```
/* sorts an array of objects in ascending or descending order */
void sort(array, order, comp, exch)
int *array;
int order;          /* 1-ascend, 2=descend */
int (*comp)();      /* user supplied comparison function */
int (*exch)();      /* user supplied exchange function */
{
    the sort routine
}
```

Often, one pays a price in making something reusable by simultaneously making it larger and slower. This problem can usually be minimized, however with optimization techniques.

The rest of this article discusses the remaining reuse steps of Figure 1.

Certification

Once reusable parts are obtained, it will generally be necessary to certify their quality. The experience of many organizations is that if parts in a repository are thought to be of poor quality, software engineers will avoid using the repository. Certification is the process of establishing properties about assets–for example their correctness or timing behavior.

Each organization will need to determine what sort of certification is right for them. Some suggested guidelines for C are [Frakes88]:

Support Documents:	References to design documents used to implement the module should be included in the module documentation.
Data:	There should be no dependency on data that appears external to the module.
Documentation Quality:	The comment-to-code ratio should be no less than 1.
Portability:	The module should have been demonstrated to run correctly on several different machines.
Programming Standards:	The module should adhere to existing coding standards.
Time in Use:	The module should have been used in one or more systems that have been released to the field for period of three months.
Reuse Statistics:	The extent to which the module has been successfully reused by others is perhaps the best indicator of module quality.

4

Reuse Reviews:	Favorable reviews from those that have used the module is a good indication that the module is of high quality.
Complexity:	Overly complex modules may not be easy to modify or maintain.
Inspection:	The module should have been inspected.
Testing :	The modules should have been thoroughly tested at the unit level with statement coverage of 100% and a branch coverage of at least 80%.

Classifying Assets

As Figure 1 illustrates, reusable assets are eventually put into a repository of some sort, and must be classified so that they can be found and understood. For small collections simple classification schemes are adequate. For larger collections, automated library systems with more elaborate classification methods may be required.

Frakes and Gandel [Frakes90], in an extensive survey of reuse library representation methods, identified three major classes of them:

- Library and Information Science Methods

- Hypertext

- Artificial Intelligence Methods

Most fielded systems use one or more of the library and information science part classification techniques. These fall into two major categories—controlled vocabulary methods and uncontrolled vocabulary methods.

Controlled vocabulary methods place constraints on the words that can be used to describe reusable assets and/or the way those words can be combined. Human indexers are required for controlled methods. Two of the most popular controlled methods are,

- Enumerated Classification -   The subject area is broken into mutually exclusive, usually hierarchical, classes.

- Faceted Classification -   The subject area is analyzed into basic terms which are organized as facets.

The most popular uncontrolled vocabulary method is free text keyword. In this method indexing terms are automatically extracted from textual descriptions of reusable assets or from the assets themselves. Since the process is automatic, no human indexer is required. This makes this method relatively less expensive than the controlled vocabulary methods.

Hypertext and AI classification methods for parts have only been used so far in experimental systems.

5

Measuring Reuse Effectiveness

The parts based approach to reuse assumes that systems are made up of parts which may be at different levels of abstraction. A C system, for example, is composed of C functions. C functions in turn are composed of lines of code.

To measure reuse, the levels of abstraction must be defined. Questions about the level of reuse must be asked in terms of a higher level of abstraction, and a lower level of abstraction. The reuse level of a C system, for example, could be expressed in terms of lines of code or in terms of functions (or indeed many other things such as files, tokens, etc.). Similarly, the reuse level of a function could be expressed in terms of lines, tokens, etc.

Given a higher level item composed of lower level items, certain fundamental quantities need to be calculated. These are:

L = the total number of lower level items in the higher level item.

E = the number of lower level items from an external repository in the higher level item. An external repository is a source of parts outside the system being measured. Some well known examples are the stdio.h library of C functions, and the Booch parts for Ada.

I = the number of lower level items in the higher level item which are not from an external repository.

M = the number of items not from an external repository which are used more than once. This criterion can be adjusted for more uses, and weighted to take the functionality of the reuse part into account.

The reuse level metrics are calculated from these quantities as follows.

External reuse level = E/L.   **Internal reuse level** = M/I.

To calculate these measures, the following information is needed. It will, in general, have to be supplied by the user of the metrics.

- The abstraction hierarchy,
- A definition of external repositories.
- A definition of the "uses" relationship (i.e., what parts use what other parts).

The following information will be needed for each part.

- Name of the part
- Source of the part (internal or external)
- Level of abstraction
- Usage - the number of times an item is used.

As an example of the use of reuse level, consider the systems in the C language. The table below shows an abstraction hierarchy for C. An "x" in the table means that the corresponding column item is considered more abstract than the corresponding row item. For example, reuse within systems can be at the subsystem, .c file, function, or line level. Reuse within subsystems can be at the .c file, function, and line levels and so on.

6

	System	Subsystem	.c File	Function
Subsystem	X			
.c file	X	X		
Function	X	X	X	
Line	X	X	X	X

As an example, we will select "system" as the higher level and "function" as the lower. To calculate reuse level, then we must,

- Break the C system into functions

- Distinguish internal from external functions.

This can be done with a tool called **cflow** that produces call hierarchies for C based systems [Frakes91b]) The process for deriving reuse level metrics using **cflow** is described in the diagram below. The 'analyze' process is implemented with a small **shell** and **awk** program.

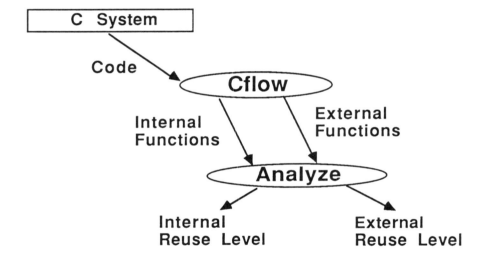

Having built the tool, called **rl**, we ran it on 29 C systems. The results are described in the table below.

7

	Internal Reuse	External Reuse	Total	NCSL*
Mean	.07	.51	.58	3837
Median	.04	.51	.60	802
Max	.20	.88	.88	35025
Min	0.00	.14	.29	102
Std Dev.	.07	.24	.18	8281

*Non-commentary source lines of code.

There are several interesting points about this data. First is that the reuse levels are much higher than is generally assumed. DeMarco, for example, estimated 5% reuse on an average project [DeMarco84]. The total average reuse for the C systems was 58%. This high figure can partially be explained by the design of the C language--that is a small language that requires the reuse of functions for such simple tasks as printing and I/O. Even so, these levels are much higher–internal reuse alone is larger at 7%.

Conclusion

Software salvaging is an important technology for acquiring reusable assets. It is part of the wider reuse process which is considered critical for improving software quality and productivity. We have discussed the major phases of salvaging and reuse.

References

[Arnold86]   Arnold, R.S. *Tutorial on Software Restructuring*, Washington, D.C.: IEEE Computer Society Press, 1986.

[Arnold90a]   Arnold, R.S. "Heuristics for Salvaging Reusable Parts from Ada Source Code," Tech. Rept. Ada_Reuse_Heuristics-90011-N, Software Productivity Consortium, March 1990.

[Arnold90b]   Arnold, R.S. "Salvaging Reusable Components from Ada Source Code: A Progress Report," Tech. Rept. Ada_Static_Tools_Survey-90015-N, Software Productivity Consortium, September 1990.

[DeMarco84]   DeMarco, T. "Controlling software projects: management, measurement, and evaluation," Seminar Notes, Atlantic Systems Guild, Inc., New York, New York, 1984.

[Dunn91]   Dunn, M.F. and Knight, J.C. Software Reuse In an Industrial Setting: A Case Study, *Proceedings of the 13th International Conference on Software Engineering*, IEEE Computer Society, May 1991, pp. 329-338.

[Frakes88]   Frakes, W. B. and Nejmeh, B. A., "An Information System for Software Reuse", in Tracz, W. (Ed.), *IEEE Tutorial: Software Reuse: Emerging Technology*, IEEE Computer Society, 1988.

8

[Frakes90]   Frakes, W.B. and P.B. Gandel, "Representing Reusable Software", *Information and Software Technology*, **32**(10):653-664, Butterworth-Heinemann Ltd., December, 1990.

[Frakes91b]   Frakes, W.B., Fox, C.J., Nejmeh, B.A., *Software Engineering in the UNIX/C Environment*, Prentice-Hall, 1991.

[Frakes91a]   Frakes, W. B. "Software Reuse: Payoff and Transfer", *Proceedings of AIAA 8*, Baltimore, 1991.

Authors

Dr. Robert Arnold is head of Software Evolution Technology, a firm specializing in software reengineering, reverse engineering, maintenance, impact analysis, and repository and bridge technology. Dr. Arnold wrote the *IEEE Tutorial on Software Restructuring* (IEEE Computer Society, 1986) and has tracked technology and events in software maintenance and reengineering since 1980. He headed the Reengineering Project at the Software Productivity Consortium. He may be reached at Software Evolution Technology, 12613 Rock Ridge Road, Herndon, Virginia 22070, 703-450-6791, r.arnold@compmail.com.

Dr. William Frakes is an independent consultant specializing in software reuse, measurement and experimental methods, UNIX/C software engineering, and information retrieval systems. Previously, he was supervisor of the Intelligent Systems Research Group at Bell Laboratories and manager of the Software Reuse Research Group at the Software Productivity Consortium. He is the author of *Software Engineering in the Unix/C Environment* (Prentice-Hall 1991) and editor of *Information Retrieval: Data Structures and Algorithms* (Prentice-Hall 1992). He can be reached at 400 Drew Ct., Sterling, Virginia 22170, 703-450-5954, 70761.1176@compuserve.com.

9

Identifying and Qualifying Reusable Software Components

Gianluigi Caldiera and Victor R. Basili

University of Maryland

Effective reuse of knowledge, processes, and products from previous software developments can increase productivity and quality in software projects by an order of magnitude. In fact, software production using reusable components will probably be crucial to the software industry's evolution to higher levels of maturity.

Software reuse is not new. McIlroy[1] proposed using modular software units in 1969, and reuse has been behind many software developments. However, the method has never acquired real momentum in industrial environments and software projects, despite its informal presence there.

The first problem we encounter in reusing software arises from the nature of the object to be reused. The concept is simple — use the same object more than once. But with software it is difficult to define what an object is apart from its context.[2] We have programs, parts of programs, specifications, requirements, architectures, test cases, and plans, all related to each other. The reuse of each software object implies the concurrent reuse of the objects associated with it, and informal information traveling with the objects. Thus, we must reuse more than code. Software objects and their relationships incorporate a large amount of experience from past development. We need to reuse this experience in the production of new software. The experience makes it possible to reuse software objects.[3]

A second major problem in code reuse is the lack of a set of reusable components,

Software metrics provide a way to automate the extraction of reusable software components from existing systems, reducing the amount of code that experts must analyze.

despite the large amount of software that already exists in the portfolios of many software producers. Reuse efficiency and cost effectiveness require a large catalog of available reusable objects.

In this article, we outline a way to reuse development experience along with the software objects it produces. Then, we focus on a problem in the development of a catalog of reusable components: how to analyze existing components and identify ones suitable for reuse. After they are identified, the parts could be extracted, packaged in a way appropriate for reuse, and stored in a component repository. This catalog of heterogeneous objects would

have to be designed for efficient retrieval of individual components, but that topic is beyond our scope.

Our model for reusing software components splits the traditional life-cycle models into two parts: one part, the project, delivers software systems, while the other part, the factory, supplies reusable software objects to the project. The factory's primary concerns are the extraction and packaging of reusable components, but it must, of course, work with a detailed knowledge of the application domain from which a component is extracted.

Our approach to identification and qualification of reusable software is based on software models and metrics. Because software metrics take into account the large volume of source code that must be analyzed to find reusable parts, they provide a way to automate the first steps of the analysis. Besides, models and metrics permit feedback and improvement to make the extraction process fit a variety of environments.

The extracted candidates are analyzed more carefully in the context of the semantics of the source application in a process we call "qualification."

In this article, we describe some case studies to validate our experimental approach. They deal with only the identification phase and use a very simple model of a reusable code component, but our results show that automated techniques can reduce the amount of code that a domain expert needs to evaluate to identify reusable parts.

February 1991

61

0-8186-3272-0/93 $3.00 ©1991 IEEE

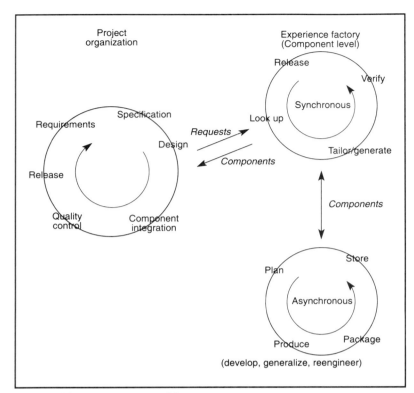

Figure 1. The reuse process model.

Reuse framework and organization

In many software engineering projects, reuse is as common as in everyday life: It is an informal sharing of techniques and products among people working on the same or similar projects. Transforming informal reuse concepts into a technology of reuse would provide the basis for the future software factory, improving quality and increasing productivity, as well as making production more manageable. To achieve higher levels of reuse, we must recognize the experience appropriate for reuse, package experience in a readily available way, and formally integrate reuse into software development.

Currently, all reuse occurs in the project development, where reuse is difficult because a project's focus is system delivery. Packaging reusable experience is at best a secondary concern. Besides, project personnel cannot recognize the pieces of experience appropriate for other projects.

Existing process models, which tend to be rigidly deterministic, are not defined to

take advantage of reuse, much less to create reusable experience. To create packaged experience and then reuse it, multiple process models are necessary.

Figure 1 shows an organizational framework that separates project- specific activities from the reuse-packaging activities, with process models that support each activity.[4] The framework defines two separate organizations: a project organization and an experience factory.

The project organization develops the product, taking advantage of all forms of packaged experience from prior and current developments. In turn, the project offers its own experiences to be packaged for other projects. The experience factory recognizes potentially reusable experience and packages it so it is easy for the project organization to use.

Within the experience factory, an organization we call the component factory develops and packages software components. It supplies code components to the project upon demand, and creates and maintains a repository of components for future use. As a subdivision of the experience factory, the experience that the com-

ponent factory manipulates is programming and application experience as embodied in programs and their documentation. Because the experience factory gathers all kinds of experience from the project, the component factory understands the project context and can deliver components that fit.

The project organization performs activities specific to implementation of the system to which it is dedicated. It analyzes the requirements and produces the specifications and the high-level system design. Its process models are like those used by today's software engineering projects (for instance, it may use the waterfall model or iterative enhancement model). Software engineers generate specifications from requirements and design a system to satisfy those requirements. However, when the engineers have identified the system components, usually after the so-called preliminary design, they request components from the component factory and integrate them into the programs and the system they have designed. The project organization engineers may also request a list of components that satisfy a given specification. Then, from several design options, they can choose the one for which more reusable components are already available.

After component integration, the project organization process model continues as usual with product quality control (system test, reliability analysis) and release.

The component factory's process model is twofold:[3] it satisfies requests for components coming from the project organization, but it also prepares itself for answering those requests. This mix of synchronous and asynchronous activities is typical of the process model of the experience factory in general.[4]

Synchronous activity. When the component factory receives a request from the project organization, it searches its catalog of components to find a software component that satisfies that request with or without tailoring. Two kinds of tailoring can be applied to a software component: instantiation and modification. To an extent, the component's designer has anticipated instantiation by associating with the component some parameters to make it suit different contexts. A generic unit in Ada is an example of such a parametric component and of the instantiation process. Modification is an unanticipated tailoring process in which statements are changed, added, or deleted to adapt the component to a request.

If no component that approximates the

request can be found in the catalog of the available components or if the necessary modification is too expensive, the component factory develops the requested component from scratch or generates it from more elementary components. After verification, the component is released to the project organization that requested it.

Asynchronous activity. The component factory's ability to efficiently answer requests from the project organization is critical for the successful application of the reuse technology. Therefore, the factory's catalog must contain enough components to reduce the chances that the factory will have to develop a component from scratch. Moreover, looking up components must be easy. This is why the component factory's process model has an asynchronous part.

To produce some software components without specific requests from the project organization, the component factory develops a component production plan — it extracts reusable components from existing systems or generalizes components previously produced on request from the project organization. The Booch components[5] are an example of a component production plan: The most common data structures and the main operations on them have been implemented as Ada packages.

A component factory can develop an application-oriented component production plan by analyzing an application domain to identify the most common functions. Then it can implement these functions into reusable components to be used by the developers. Or the factory can generalize a preexisting component into a new one by adding more functionality or parameterizing it.

To ensure that the generated components are well packaged and easily retrieved, a process called component qualification provides components with functional specifications and test cases, and classifies them according to a component taxonomy.[6] Software components are then stored in a repository.

Extracting components

In the short term, developing reusable components is generally more expensive than developing specialized code, because of the overhead of maintaining the component factory. A rich and well-organized catalog of reusable components is the key to a successful component factory and a long-term economic gain. But at first such a catalog will not be available to an organiza-

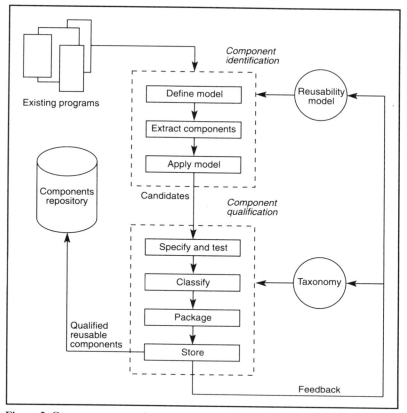

Figure 2. Component extraction.

tion, unless it can reuse code that it developed in the past without reuse in mind.

Mature application domains, where most of the functions that need to be used already exist in some form in earlier systems, should provide enough components for code reuse. In such cases, the earlier systems were probably designed and implemented by reusing code informally. For example, Lanergan and Grasso found rates of reuse of about 60 percent in business applications.[7]

To package such code for reuse, the component factory analyzes existing programs in the two phases shown in Figure 2. First, it chooses some candidates and packages them for possible independent use. Next, an engineer with knowledge of the application domain where the component was developed analyzes each component to determine the service it can provide. Then, components are stored in the repository with all information that has been obtained about them.

The first phase can be fully automated. The necessary human intervention in the

second phase is the main reason for splitting the process in two steps, instead of searching through existing programs looking for "useful" components first. The first phase reduces the amount of expensive human analysis needed in the second phase by limiting analysis to components that really look worth considering.

In the component identification phase, program units are automatically extracted, made independent, and measured according to observable properties related to their potential for reuse. There has been much discussion about these properties. According to Prieto-Diaz and Freeman,[6] a software component is reusable if the effort required to reuse it is remarkably smaller than the effort required to implement a component with the same functions. Thus, we need a quantitative measure of the distance of the component from its potential reuse. In the section below on component identification, we give details about a family of such measures that we call the reusability attributes model.

The identification phase consists of three steps:

(1) *Definition (or refinement) of the reusability attributes model.* Using our current understanding of the characteristics of a potentially reusable component in our environment, we define a set of automatable measures that capture these characteristics and an acceptable range of values for these metrics. We verify the metrics and their value ranges using the outcomes in the next steps and continually modify them until we have a reusability attributes model that maximizes our chances of selecting candidate components for reuse.

(2) *Extraction of components.* We extract modular units from existing systems, and complete them so they have all the external references needed to reuse them independently (for example, to compile them). By "modular unit" we mean a syntactic unit such as a C function, an Ada subprogram or block, or a Fortran subroutine.

(3) *Application of the model.* The current reusability attributes model is applied to the extracted, completed components. Components whose measurements are within the model's range of acceptable values become candidate reusable components to be analyzed by the domain expert in the qualification phase.

During the component qualification phase, a domain expert analyzes the candidate reusable components to understand and record each component's meaning while evaluating its potential for reuse in future systems. The expert also repackages the component by associating with it a reuse specification,[8] a significant set of test cases, a set of attributes based on a reuse classification schema, and a set of procedures for reusing the component.

The reuse classification schema, called a taxonomy, is very important for storing and retrieving reusable components efficiently. The definition and the domain of the attributes that implement the taxonomy can be improved each time an expert performs component qualification and analyzes the problems encountered.

The qualification phase consists of six steps:

(1) *Generation of the functional specification.* A domain expert extracts the functional specification of each candidate reusable component from its source code and documentation. This step provides insight into the correctness of the component in relationship to the new specification.

Components that are not relevant or not correct, or whose functional specification is not easy to extract, are discarded. The expert reports reasons for discarding candidates and other insights so they can be used to improve the reusability attributes model.

(2) *Generation of the test cases.* Using the functional specification, the expert generates, executes, and associates with the component a set of test cases. Components that do not satisfy the tests are discarded. Again, the reasons for discarding candidates are recorded and used to improve the reusability attributes model, and possibly the process for extracting the functional specification and assessing its correctness (step 1). This is most likely the last step at which a component will be discarded.

(3) *Classification of the component.* To distinguish it from the other components and assist in its identification and retrieval, the expert associates each reusable component with a classification according to a set of attributes identified in the domain analysis. Problems with the taxonomy are recorded for further analysis.

(4) *Development of the reuser's manual.* Information for the future reuser is provided in a manual that contains a description of the component's functions and interfaces as identified during generation of its functional specification (step 1), directions on how to install and use it, information about its procurement and support, and an appendix with structure diagrams and information for component maintenance.

(5) *Storage.* Reusable software components are stored in the repository together with their functional specifications, test cases, classification attributes, and reuser's manuals.

(6) *Feedback.* The reusability attributes model is updated by drawing on information from the qualification phase to add more measures, modify and remove measures that proved ineffective, or alter the ranges of acceptable values. This step requires analysis and possibly even further experimentation. The taxonomy is updated by adding new attributes or modifying the existing ones according to problems reported by the experts who classified the components (step 3).

This sketch illustrates the main concepts behind our approach: the use of a quantitative model for identification of components and a qualitative, partially subjective model for their qualification, with continuous improvement of both models using

feedback from their application. The reusability attributes model is the key to automating the first phase.

Component identification

According to Booch, a software component "is simply a container for expressing abstractions of data structures and algorithms."[5] The attributes that make a component reusable as a building block of other, maybe radically different, systems are functional usefulness in the context of the application domain, low reuse cost, and quality.

The reusability attributes model attempts to characterize those attributes directly through measures of an attribute, or indirectly through measures of evidence of an attribute's existence. These measures must be automatable.

We define a set of acceptable values for each of the metrics. These values can be either simple ranges of values (measure α is acceptable between α_1 and α_2) or more sophisticated relationships among different metrics (measure α is acceptable between α_1 and α_2, provided that measure β is less than β_0).

Figure 3 shows a "fishbone diagram" that represents the reusability factors. With each factor in the diagram, we associate metrics directly measuring the factor or indirectly predicting the likelihood of its presence.

Costs. Reuse costs include the costs of extracting the component from the old system, packaging it into a reusable component, finding and modifying the component, and integrating it into the new system. We can measure these costs directly during the process or use metrics to predict them.

To define the *basic reusability attributes model,* the entry-level model that the component factory starts with and later improves through feedback from the qualification phase, we divide reuse costs into two groups: costs to perform the extraction and costs to use the component in a new context. To minimize the costs of finding the component and extracting it, we need code fragments that are small and simple. Measures of volume and complexity also provide a partial indication of how easy qualification will be. The costs to reuse the component can be influenced by the readability of a code fragment, a characteristic that can again be partially evaluated using volume and complexity measures, as well as measures of the nonredundancy and structuredness of the component's implementation.

Usefulness. Functional usefulness is affected by both the commonality and the variety of the functions performed by the component. The commonality of a component for reuse can be divided into three parts: its commonality within a system or a single application, its commonality across different systems in the same application domain, and its overall commonality. It is hard to associate metrics with these factors. Experience with the application domain might provide subjective insight into whether the function is primitive to the domain and occurs commonly. An indirect automatable measure of functional usefulness might be the number of times the function occurs within the analyzed system (if we assume that an often-reused component is probably highly reusable). The variety of functions performed by the component is even more difficult to measure: An indirect metric could be component complexity. However, for a component's complexity to reflect its ability to perform more functions, we would have to assume that the component was developed in a nonredundant way.

The basic reusability attributes model measures a component's functional usefulness, derived from the commonality of the functions performed by the component, by comparing the number of times the component is invoked in the system with the number of times a component known to be useful is invoked. Components known to be useful can usually be found in the standard libraries of a programming environment. The basic reusability attributes model measures the commonality of a function by the ratio between the number of its invocations and the invocations of standard components.

The basic reusability attributes model assesses functional usefulness derived from the number and the variety of functions incorporated in a component by measuring its complexity and the nonredundancy of its implementation. This last feature can be translated into volume measures comparing the component's actual volume with its expected volume, which is computed from the number of tokens (operators and operands) that the component processes. When these values are close, we say the implementation of the component is regular. High regularity suggests that the component's complexity indicates the "amount" of function it performs.

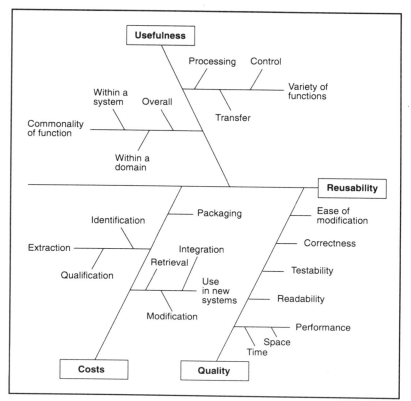

Figure 3. Factors affecting reusability.

Quality. Several qualities important for component reuse are correctness, readability, testability, ease of modification, and performance. Most are impossible to measure or predict directly. The domain expert who extracts the functional specification handles correctness and testing (steps 1 and 2 of the qualification phase). For the reusability attributes model, we are interested in qualities we can predict based upon automated measures. Therefore, we might consider such indirect metrics as small size and readability as predictors of correctness, and the number of independent paths as a measure of testability.

The basic reusability attributes model attempts to predict a component's correctness and testability using volume and complexity measures. It assumes that a large and complex component is more error prone and harder to test. Ease of modification is reflected in a component's readability.

Four metrics. Synthesizing these considerations, the basic reusability attributes model for identifying candidate reusable components characterizes a component's reusability using the four metrics shown in Figure 4.

Volume. A component's volume can be measured using the Halstead Software Science Indicators,[9] which are based on the way a program uses the programming language. First, we define the operators and the operands.

The *operators* represent the active elements of the program: arithmetic operators, decisional operators, assignment operators, functions, etc. Some operators are provided by the programming language, and some are defined by the user according to the rules of the language. The total number of these operators used in the program is denoted by η_1, and the total count of all usage of operators is denoted by N_1.

The *operands* represent the passive elements of the program: constants, variables, etc. The total number of unique operands defined and used in the program is denoted by η_2, and the total count of all usage of operands is denoted by N_2.

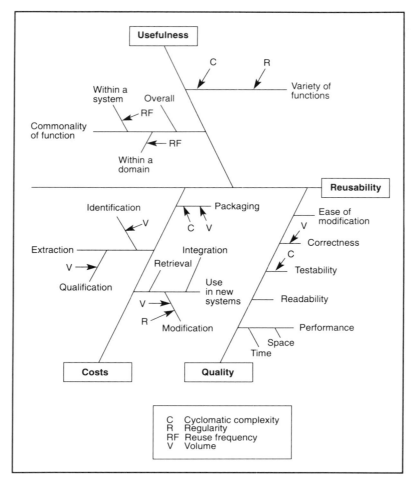

Figure 4. The basic reusability attributes model.

Legend within figure:
C   Cyclomatic complexity
R   Regularity
RF Reuse frequency
V   Volume

the use of correct programming practices, by seeing how well we can predict its length based on some regularity assumptions. Again using the Halstead Software Science Indicators, we have the actual length of the component

$$N = N_1 + N_2$$

and the estimated length

$$\dot{N} = \eta_1 \log_2 \eta_1 + \eta_2 \log_2 \eta_2$$

The closeness of the estimate is a measure of the regularity of the component's coding:

$$r = 1 - \frac{N - \dot{N}}{N} = \frac{\dot{N}}{N}$$

Component regularity measures the readability and the nonredundancy of a component's implementation. Therefore, we select components whose regularity is in the neighborhood of 1.

Reuse frequency. If we compare the number of static calls addressed to a component with the number of calls addressed to a class of components that we assume are reusable, we can estimate a given component's frequency of reuse. Let's suppose our system is composed of user-defined components $X_1, ..., X_N$ and of components $S_1, ..., S_M$ defined in the standard environment (such as printf in C or text_io.put in Ada). For a given component X, let $n(X)$ be the number of calls addressed to X in the system. We associate with each user-defined component a static measure of its reuse throughout the system: the ratio between the number of calls addressed to the component C and the average number of calls addressed to a standard component:

$$v_\sigma (C) = \frac{n(C)}{\frac{1}{M} \sum_{i=0}^{M} n(S_i)}$$

The reuse-specific frequency is an indirect measure of the functional usefulness of a component, if we assume that the application domain uses some naming convention, so components with different names are not functionally the same and vice versa. Therefore, in the basic model we have only a lower limit for this metric.

Criteria. To complete the basic model we need some criteria to select the candidate reusable components on the basis of

Using the operators and operands, we define the Halstead volume by the formula

$$V = (N_1 + N_2) \log_2 (\eta_1 + \eta_2)$$

The component volume affects both reuse cost and quality. If a component is too small, the combined costs of extraction, retrieval, and integration exceed its intrinsic value, making reuse very impractical. If it is too large, the component is more error prone and has lower quality. Therefore, in the basic reusability attributes model, we need both an upper and a lower bound for this measure.

Cyclomatic complexity. We can measure the complexity of a program's control organization with the McCabe measure,[9] defined as the cyclomatic number of the control-flow graph of the program:

$$v(G) = e - n + 2$$

where e is the number of edges in the graph G, and n is the number of nodes.

The component complexity affects reuse cost and quality, taking into account the characteristics of the component's control flow. As with volume, reuse of a component with very low complexity may not repay the cost, whereas high component complexity may indicate poor quality — low readability, poor testability, and a higher possibility of errors. On the other hand, high complexity with high regularity of implementation suggests high functional usefulness. Therefore, for this measure we need both an upper and a lower bound in the basic model.

Regularity. We can measure the economy of a component's implementation, or the values of the four measures we have defined. The extremes of each measure depend on the application, the environment; the programming and design method, the programming language, and many other factors not easily quantified. We determine therefore the ranges of acceptability for the measures in the basic reusability attributes model experimentally, through a series of case studies described in the section titled "Case studies."

The basic model is elementary, but it is a reasonable starting point that captures important characteristics affecting software component reusability. Moreover, it probably contains features that will be common to every other reusability attributes model.

Care system

To support component factory activities, we have designed a computer-based system that performs static and dynamic analysis on existing code and helps a domain expert extract and qualify reusable components. We call the system Care, for computer-aided reuse engineering.

Figure 5 shows the parts of the Care system.

Component identifier. The component identifier supports source code analysis to extract the candidate reusable components according to a given reusability attributes model. The system stores candidates in the components repository for processing in the qualification phase. The identifier has two segments:

- *Model editor.* The user either defines a model, selecting metrics from a metrics library and assigning to each metric a range of acceptable values, or updates an old model from a models library, adding and deleting metrics or changing the adopted ranges of values.
- *Component extractor.* Once a reusability attributes model has been defined, the user can apply it to a family of programs to extract the candidate reusable components. The user can work interactively or extraction can be fully automated, provided that the system can automatically solve problems associated with the naming of the components.

Component qualifier. The component qualifier supports interactive qualification of the candidate reusable components according to the process model outlined ear-

lier. For the qualifier to be effective, the candidate components must be small and simple. The qualifier has three segments:

- *Specifier.* The specifier supports the construction — through code reading and program analysis — of a formal specification to be associated with the component. The interactive tool controls as much as possible the correctness of the specification a domain expert extracts from a component. If the domain expert generates specifications, they are stored in the component repository together with the expert's measure (a subjective evaluation) of the component's practical usefulness.
- *Tester.* The tester uses the formal specification produced by the specifier to generate or to support user generation of a set of test cases for a component. If, as is likely, the component needs a "wrapping" to be executed, the tester supports the generation of this wrapping. It then executes the generated tests, reporting their outcomes and coverages. Test cases, wrapping, and coverage data are stored in the component repository with the expert's test report recommending retention or rejection of the component.
- *Classifier.* The classifier directs the user across the taxonomy of an application domain to find an appropriate classification for the component. Users with special authorization can modify the taxonomy, adding or deleting facets or altering the range of values available for each facet. The classifier and the taxonomy are directly related to the query used to retrieve the components from the repository.[6]

The current version of the Care system supports ANSI C and Ada on a Sun workstation with Unix and 8 Mbytes of memory. In the prototype, we have implemented three parts of the system:

- A component extractor for C programs based on the basic reusability attributes model described earlier. We used this part of the Care system for the case studies described in the next section. We have enriched the basic model with the data bindings metric[10] to take into account a static analysis of the flow of information between components of the same program. We have also developed a measurement tool and a data bindings analyzer for Ada programs.

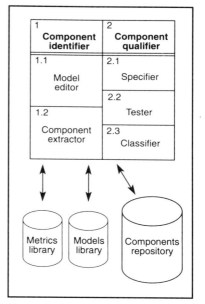

Figure 5. Care system architecture.

- A coverage analyzer for C programs (part of the tester in the component qualifier). An equivalent analyzer for Ada programs is under development.
- A prototype specifier to help the user build the Mills specification for programs written in a subset of Pascal. We plan to develop a version to process components written in C.

Case studies

In this section, we describe experiments with the current version of the Care system and the basic reusability attributes model, analyzing existing systems to identify reusable components. Some goals of the case studies were to

- evaluate the concept of extracting reusable candidates from existing programs using a model based on software metrics,
- complete the basic reusability attributes model with experimentally determined extremes for the metrics given earlier,
- study the application of the basic reusability attributes model to different environments and observe its selective power,
- analyze the interdependence of the metrics used in the basic model, and

Table 1. Characteristics of the analyzed systems.

Case	Application	Lines of Code (in thousands)	User-Defined Components
A	Data processing	4.04	83
B	File management	17.41	349
C	Communication	67.02	730
D	Data processing	17.63	156
E	Data processing	6.50	53
F	Language processing	58.55	1,235
G	File management	3.32	57
H	Communication	7.70	232
I	Language processing	4.63	87

Table 2. Average values for measures of the basic reusability attributes model.

Case	Volume	Complexity	Regularity	Reuse-Specific Frequency
A	8,967	21.1	0.76	0.05
B	7,856	23.6	0.74	0.08
C	45,707	153.7	0.66	0.10
D	11,877	32.1	0.64	0.11
E	4,054	16.8	0.76	0.18
F	82,671	198.7	0.33	0.13
G	7,277	25.5	0.65	0.24
H	12,044	40.7	0.77	0.23
I	20,131	44.7	0.79	0.41

Table 3. Measurement data for components whose reuse-specific frequency is greater than 5.0.

Case	Average Volume	Average Complexity	Average Regularity	Reuse-Specific Frequency
A	2,249	7.0	0.89	>0.50
B	2,831	4.8	0.77	>0.50
C	13,476	43.8	0.68	>0.50
D	4,444	8.5	0.80	>0.50
E	1,980	10.7	0.87	>0.50
F	156,199	384.3	0.40	>0.50
G	1,904	5.4	0.70	>0.50
H	8,884	31.1	0.75	>0.50
I	6,237	9.6	0.85	>0.50

- identify candidate reusable components to use with research and experimentation on the qualification phase.

The data we discuss here originated from the analysis of nine systems totalling 187,000 lines of ANSI C. The systems analyzed ranged from file management to communication applications, including data processing and system software. Table 1 outlines their characteristics.

Because of the characteristics of C, the natural "component" is the C function. But a function is not self-contained: It references variables, data types, and functions that are not part of its definition. To have an independent component, we had to complete the definition of the function with all the necessary external references. Therefore, in the context of the case studies, a component is the smallest translation unit containing a function. We per-

formed each case study according to these steps:

(1) Acquire and install the system, making sure all the necessary sources are available.

(2) Build the components from the functions, adding to each function its external references and making it independently compilable.

(3) Compute the four metrics of the basic reusability attributes model for the components.

(4) Analyze the results.

Table 2 shows the average values for the measures of the basic model obtained from the case studies.

The case studies show volume, regularity, and reuse-specific frequency to have a high degree of independence. Volume and complexity show some correlation related to the "size" of the component, but it is not significant enough to make the two measures equivalent. Thus, the basic reusability attributes model is not redundant.

The data in the last column of Table 2 are below 0.5. Therefore, we can assume that a component whose specific reuse frequency is higher than 0.5 is a highly reused one. This choice is rather arbitrary, but it is useful for setting a reference point for the case studies. Accordingly, Table 3 presents the measurement data for high-reuse components whose reuse-specific frequency is more than 0.5.

Comparing Tables 2 and 3 we see, with a few exceptions, a very regular pattern. The highly reused components have volume and complexity lower than the average — about one fourth of the average. Their regularity is slightly higher than the average, generally above 0.70. The only exception is case F, a compiler with a very peculiar design, where the function calls are mostly addressed to high-level and complex modules. These results confirm, in different environments, the results obtained for Fortran programs in NASA's Software Engineering Laboratory.[11]

The regularity result is very important by itself. Because the length equation used in the regularity measure has such a good fix on the reusable components, we can use it to estimate the size of the components. Recall that the Halstead length equation ($\dot{N} = \eta_1 \log_2 \eta_1 + \eta_2 \log_2 \eta_2$) is a function of the two indicators η_1 and η_2. The first, the number of operators, is more or less fixed in the programming environment. The second, the number of operands, corresponds to the number of data items the system deals with. The value of η_2 can be rather precisely estimated in the detailed design phase of a project. The high regularity of the reusable components implies, therefore, that we can estimate the total effort for their development with an accuracy often higher than 80 percent. This is better than the estimate we get from components that are not as reusable.

The case studies show that, in most cases, we can obtain satisfactory results using the values in Table 4 as extremes for the ranges of acceptable values. Table 5 compares the number of user-defined functions in each system with the number of candidate reusable components extracted with the settings of Table 4.

Table 5 shows that, in general, 5 to 10 percent of the existing code should be analyzed for possible reuse. This is a cost-effective rate of reduction of the amount of code needing human analysis in the qualification phase. It is also a satisfactory figure for future reuse. In absolute terms, this 5 to 10 percent of the existing code accounts for a large part of a system's functionality.

The number of those candidates that the qualification phase will actually find to be reusable is hard to determine without a series of controlled experiments. On the basis of a cursory analysis, we think that the extracted components perform useful functions in the context of the application domain they come from. A complete and rigorous evaluation of the model is an immediate goal of our project.

These case studies show that reusable components have measurable properties that can be synthesized in a simple quantitative model. Now, we need to bring experimentation to the qualification activities, to verify how good the basic model is in practice, and to study how we can process the feedback from the qualification phase to improve the reusability attributes model. A possibility is a mechanism associated with the model editor for manipulating the reusability attributes model. We also need to broaden our analysis to different programming environments for broader verification of our hypotheses.

We foresee two major developments in the architecture of the Care system. The first is the design of a prototype for the components repository, supporting component retrieval both by queries to the classification system and by browsing on the basis of the specification.

Table 4. Extremes for ranges of acceptable values in the basic reusability attributes model.

Measure	Minimum	Maximum
Volume	2,000	10,000
Complexity	5.00	15.00
Regularity	0.70	1.30
Reuse frequency	0.30	

Table 5. User-defined system components compared with extracted candidates for reuse.

Case	User-Defined Components	Extracted Candidates	Percentage of User-Defined Components Extracted
A	83	4	5
B	349	17	5
C	730	36	5
D	156	16	10
E	53	4	8
F	1,235	81	7
G	57	10	18
H	232	24	10
I	87	11	13

The second development will be an integration with the Tame system for tailoring a measurement environment.[12] In the version of Care we outlined here, the metrics library is a static object from which users can only retrieve measures. The Tame system allows users to create a measurement environment tailored to the goals of their activities and to their model. This environment will provide a more elastic metrics library for defining measures in the reusability attributes model. ∎

Acknowledgments

We are indebted to Daniele Fantasia, Bruno Macchini, and Daniela Scalabrin of Italsiel S.p.A., Rome, for developing the programs that made possible the case studies, and for many useful discussions.

This work was supported by Italsiel S.p.A. with a grant given to the Industrial Associates Program of the Department of Computer Science at the University of Maryland. Computer support was provided in part through the facilities of the Computer Science Center at the University of Maryland.

References

1. M. McIlroy, "Mass Produced Software Components," *Proc. NATO Conf. Software Eng.*, Petrocelli/Charter, New York, 1969, pp. 88-98.

2. P. Freeman, "Reusable Software Engineering Concepts and Research Directions," *ITT Proc. Workshop on Reusability in Programming*, ITT, Stamford, Conn., 1983, pp. 129-137.

3. V.R. Basili and H.D. Rombach, "Towards a Comprehensive Framework for Reuse: A Reuse-Enabling Software Evolution Environment," Tech. Report CS-TR-2158 (UMIACS-TR-88-92), Computer Science Dept., Univ. of Maryland, College Park, Md., 1988.

4. V.R. Basili, "Software Development: A Paradigm for the Future," *Proc. Compsac 89*, IEEE Computer Soc. Press, Los Alamitos, Calif., Order No. 1964, pp. 471-485.

5. G. Booch, *Software Components with Ada*, Benjamin/Cummings, Menlo Park, Calif., 1987.

6. R. Prieto-Diaz and P. Freeman, "Classifying Software for Reusability," *IEEE Software*, Vol. 4, No. 1, Jan. 1987, pp. 6-16.

7. R.G. Lanergan and C.A. Grasso, "Software Engineering with Reusable Designs and Code," *IEEE Trans. Software Eng.*, Vol. SE-10, No. 5, Sept. 1984, pp. 498-501.

8. V.R. Basili and H.D. Mills, "Understanding and Documenting Programs," *IEEE Trans. Software Eng.*, Vol. SE-8, No. 3, May 1982, pp. 270-283.

9. S.D. Conte, H.E. Dunsmore, and V.Y. Shen, *Software Engineering: Metrics and Models*, Benjamin/Cummings, Menlo Park, Calif., 1986.

10. D. Hutchens and V.R. Basili, "System Structure Analysis: Clustering with Data Bindings," *IEEE Trans. Software Eng.*, Vol. SE-11, No. 8, Aug. 1985, pp. 749-757.

11. R.W. Selby, "Empirically Analyzing Software Reuse in a Production Environment," in *Software Reuse: Emerging Technology*, W. Tracz, ed., IEEE Computer Soc. Press, Los Alamitos, Calif., 1988, pp. 176-189.

12. V.R. Basili and H.D. Rombach, "The Tame Project: Towards Improvement-Oriented Software Environments," *IEEE Trans. Software Eng.*, Vol. SE-14, No. 6, June 1988, pp. 758-773.

Victor R. Basili is a professor in the Institute for Advanced Computer Studies and the Computer Science Department at the University of Maryland, where he served as chairman for six years. His research involves measuring and evaluating software development in industrial and government settings. He has consulted with many agencies and organizations, including IBM, GE, GTE, AT&T, Motorola, Boeing, and NASA.

In 1976, Basili cofounded and was a principal investigator in the Software Engineering Laboratory, a joint venture of NASA Goddard Space Flight Center, the University of Maryland, and Computer Sciences Corp. He received the *IEEE Transactions on Software Engineering*'s Outstanding Paper Award in 1982 and the NASA Group Achievement Award in 1989. Basili is an IEEE fellow, a former member of the IEEE Computer Society Board of Governors, and a present Computer Society member.

Gianluigi Caldiera is on the faculty of the Institute for Advanced Computer Studies and coordinates projects on software quality and reusability in the Computer Science Department at the University of Maryland. His research interests are in software engineering, focusing on reusability, productivity, measurement, and quality management. Previously, he was an assistant professor of mathematics at the University of Rome and a lecturer in the Graduate School for Systems Engineering.

Caldiera has worked for the Finsiel Group and has been involved in the ESPRIT program as a project leader and a project reviewer. He received a Laurea degree in mathematics from the University of Rome and is a member of the IEEE Computer Society and the American Society for Quality Control.

SOFTWARE RECLAMATION:
Improving Post-Development Reusability

John W. Bailey and Victor R. Basili

The University of Maryland Department of Computer Science
College Park, Maryland 20742

Abstract

This paper describes part of a multi-year study of software reuse being performed at the University of Maryland. The part of the study which is reported here explores techniques for the transformation of Ada programs which preserve function but which result in program components that are more independent, and presumably therefore, more reusable. Goals for the larger study include a precise specification of the transformation technique and its application in a large development organization. Expected results of the larger study, which are partially covered here, are the identification of reuse promoters and inhibitors both in the problem space and in the solution space, the development of a set of metrics which can be applied to both developing and completed software to reveal the degree of reusability which can be expected of that software, and the development of guidelines for both developers and reviewers of software which can help assure that the developed software will be as reusable as desired.

The advantages of transforming existing software into reusable components, rather than creating reusable components as an independent activity, include: 1) software development organizations often have an archive of previous projects which can yield reusable components, 2) developers of ongoing projects do not need to adjust to new and possibly unproven methods in an attempt to develop reusable components, so no risk or development overhead is introduced, 3) transformation work can be accomplished in parallel with line developments but be separately funded (this is particularly applicable when software is being developed for an outside customer who may not be willing to sustain the additional costs and risks of developing reusable code), 4) the resulting components are guaranteed to be relevant to the application area, and 5) the cost is low and controllable.

Introduction

Broadly defined, software reuse includes more than the repeated use of particular code modules. Other life cycle products such as specifications or test plans can be reused, software development processes such as verification techniques or cost modeling methods are reusable, and even intangible products such as ideas and experience contribute to the total picture of reuse [1,2]. Although process and tool reuse is common practice, life cycle product reuse is still in its infancy. Ultimately, reuse of early lifecycle products might provide the largest payoff. For the near term, however,

gains can be realized and further work can be guided by understanding how software can be developed with a minimum of newly-generated source lines of code.

The work covered in this paper includes a feasibility study and some examples of generalizing, by transforming, software source code after it has been initially developed, in order to improve its reusability. The term software reclamation has been chosen for this activity since it does not amount to the development of but rather to the distillation of existing software. (Reclamation is defined in the dictionary as obtaining something from used products or restoring something to usefulness [3].) By exploring the ability to modify and generalize existing software, characterizations of that software can be expressed which relate to its reusability, which in turn is related to its maintainability and portability. This study includes applying these generalizations to several small example programs, to medium sized programs from different organizations, and to several fairly large programs from a single organization.

Earlier work has examined the principle of software reclamation through generic extraction with small examples. This has revealed the various levels of difficulty which are associated with generalizing various kinds of Ada dependencies. For example, it is easier to generalize a dependency that exists on encapsulated data than on visible data, and it is easier to generalize a dependency on a visible array type than on a visible record type. Following that work, some medium-sized examples of existing software were analyzed for potential generalization. The limited success of these efforts revealed additional guidelines for development as well as limitations of the technique. Summaries of this preceding work appear in the following sections.

Used as data for the current research is Ada software from the NASA Goddard Space Flight Center which was written over the past three years to perform spacecraft simulations. Three programs, each on the order of 100,000 (editor) lines, were studied. Software code reuse at NASA/GSFC has been practiced for many years, originally with Fortran developments, and more recently with Ada. Since transitioning to Ada, management has observed a steadily increasing amount of software reuse. One goal which is introduced here but which will be addressed in more detail in the larger study is the understanding of the nature of the reuse being practiced there and to examine the reasons for the improvement seen with Ada. Another goal of this as well as the larger study is to compare the guidelines derived from the examination of how different programs yield to or resist generalization. Several questions

Reprinted from *Proc. Eighth Nat'l Conf. on Ada Technology*, U.S. Army Communications-Electronics Command, Fort Monmouth, N.J., 1990, pp. 477-480 and pp. 489-499. (Note: Pages 481-488 were intentionally omitted. This omission does not affect the paper's continuity.) Reprinted with authors' permission.

are considered through this comparison, including the universality of guidelines derived from a single program and whether the effect of the application domain, or problem space, on software reusability can be distinguished from the effect of the implementation, or solution space.

Superficially, therefore, this paper describes a technique for generalizing existing Ada software through the use of the generic feature. However, the success and practicality of this technique is greatly affected by the style of the software being transformed. The examination of what characterizations of software are correlated with transformability has led to the derivation of software development and review guidelines. It appears that most, if not all, of the guidelines suggested by this examination are consistent with good programming practices as suggested by other studies.

The Basic Technique

By studying the dependencies among software elements at the code level, a determination can be made of the reusability of those elements in other contexts. For example, if a component of a program uses or depends upon another component, then it would not normally be reusable in another program where that other component was not also present. On the other hand, a component of a software program which does not depend on any other software can be used, in theory at least, in any arbitrary context. This study concentrates only on the theoretical reusability of a component of software, which is defined here as the amount of dependence that exists between that component and other software components. Thus, it is concerned only with the syntax of reusable software. It does not directly address issues of practical reusability, such as whether a reusable component is useful enough to encourage other developers to reuse it instead of redeveloping its function. The goal of the process is to identify and extract the essential functionality from a program so that this extracted essence is not dependent on external declarations, information, or other knowledge. Transformations are needed to derive such components from existing software systems since inter-component dependencies arise naturally from the customary design decomposition and implementation processes used for software development.

Ideal examples of reusable software code components can be defined as those which have no dependencies on other software. Short of complete independence, any dependencies which do exist provide a way of quantifying the reusability of the components. In other words, the reusability of a component can be thought of as inversely proportional to the amount of external dependence required by that component. However, some or all of that dependence may be removable through transformation by generalizing the component. A measure of a component's dependence on its externals which quantifies the difficulty of removing that dependence through transformation and generalization is slightly different from simply measuring the dependence directly, and is more specifically appropriate to this study. The amount of such transformation constitutes a useful indication of the effort to reuse a body of software.

Both the transformation effort and the degree of success with performing the transforms can vary from one example to the next. The identification of guidelines for developers and reviewers was made possible by observing what promoted or impeded the transformations. These guidelines can also help in the selection of reusable or transformable parts from existing

software. Since dependencies among software components can typically be determined from the software design, many of the guidelines apply to the design phase of the life cycle, allowing earlier analysis of reusability and enabling possible corrective action to be taken before a design is implemented. Although the guidelines are written with respect to the development and reuse of systems written in the Ada language, since Ada is the medium for this study, most apply in general to software development in any language.

One measure of the extent of the transformation required is the number of lines of code that need to be added, altered, or deleted [4]. However, some modifications require new constructs to be added to the software while others merely require syntactic adjustments that could be performed automatically. For this reason, a more accurate measure weighs the changes by their difficulty. A component can contain dependencies on externals that are so intractable that removing them would mean also removing all of the useful functionality of the component. Such transformations are not cost-effective. In these cases, either the component in question must be reused in conjunction with one or more of the components on which it depends, or it cannot be generalized into an independently reusable one. Therefore, for any given component, there is a possibility that it contains some dependencies on externals which can be eliminated through transformation and also a possibility that it contains some dependencies which cannot be eliminated.

To guide the transformations, a model is used which distinguishes between software function and the declarations on which that function is performed. In an object-oriented program (for here, a program which uses data abstraction), data declarations and associated functionality are grouped into the same component. This component itself becomes the declaration of another object. This means the function / declaration distinction can be thought of as occurring on multiple levels. The internal data declarations of an object can be distinguished from the construction and access operations supplied to external users of the object, and the object as a whole can be distinguished from its external use which applies additional function (possibly establishing yet another, higher level object). The distinction between functions and objects is more obvious where a program is not object-oriented since declarations are not grouped with their associated functionality, but rather are established globally within the program.

At each level, declarations are seen as application-specific while the functions performed on them are seen as the potentially generalizable and reusable parts of a program. This may appear backwards initially, since data abstractions composed of both declarations and functions are often seen as reusable components. However, for consistency here, functions and declarations within a data abstraction are viewed as separable in the same way as functions which depend on declarations contained in external components are separable from those declarations. In use, the reusable, independent functional components are composed with application-specific declarations to form objects, which can further be composed with other independent functional components to implement an even larger portion of the overall program.

Figure 1 shows one way of representing this. All the ovals are objects. The dark ones are primitives which have predefined operations, such as integer or Boolean. The white ovals represent program-supplied functionality which is composed with their contained objects to form a higher level

478   8th Annual National Conference on Ada Technology 1990

object. The intent of the model is to distinguish this program-specific functionality and to attempt to represent it independently of the objects upon which it acts.

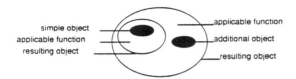

Figure 1.

Some Ada which might be represented as in the above figure might be:

```
package Counter is          -- resulting object
  procedure Reset;          -- applicable function ...
  procedure Increment;
  function Current_Value return Natural;
end Counter;

package body Counter is
  Count : Natural := 0;     -- simple object

  procedure Reset is
  begin
    Count := 0;
  end Reset;
  procedure Increment is
  begin
    Count := Count + 1;
  end Increment;
  function Current_Value return Natural is
  begin
    return Count;
  end Current_Value;
end Counter;


package Max_Count is        -- resulting object
  procedure Reset;          -- applicable function ...
  procedure Increment;
  function Current_Value return Natural;
  function Max return Natural;
end Max_Count;

with Counter;
package body Max_Count is
  Max_Val : Natural := 0;   -- additional object
  procedure Reset is
  begin
    Counter.Reset;
  end Reset;
  procedure Increment is
  begin
    Counter.Increment;
    if Max_Val < Counter.Current_Value then
      Max_Val := Counter.Current_Value;
    end if;
  end Increment;
  function Current_Value return Natural is
  begin
    return Counter.Current_Value;
  end Current_Value;
```

```
  function Max return Natural is
  begin
    return Max_Val;
  end Max;
end Max_Count;
```

In this example, the objects are properly encapsulated, though, they might not have been. If, for example, the simple objects were declared in separate components from their applicable functions, the result could have been the same (although the diagram might look different). In actual practice, Ada programs are developed with a combination of encapsulated object-operation groups as well as separately declared object-operation groups. Often the lowest levels are encapsulated while the higher level and larger objects tend to be separate from their applicable function. Perhaps in the ideal case, all objects would be encapsulated with their applied function since encapsulation usually makes the process of extracting the functionality at a later time easier. This, therefore, becomes one of the guidelines revealed by this model.

If the above example were transformed to separate the functionality from each object, the following set of components might be derived:

```
generic
  type Count_Object is (<>);
package Gen_Counter is      -- resulting object
  procedure Reset;          -- applicable function ...
  procedure Increment;
  function Current_Value return Count_Object;
end Gen_Counter;

package body Gen_Counter is
  Count : Count_Object      -- simple object
        := Count_Object'First;
  procedure Reset is
  begin
    Count := Count_Object'First;
  end Reset;
  procedure Increment is
  begin
    Count := Count_Object'Succ (Count);
  end Increment;
  function Current_Value return Count_Object is
  begin
    return Count;
  end Current_Value;
end Gen_Counter;

generic
  type Count_Object is (<>);
package Gen_Max_Count is    -- resulting object
  procedure Reset;          -- applicable function ...
  procedure Increment;
  function Current_Value return Count_Object;
  function Max return Count_Object;
end Gen_Max_Count;

with Gen_Counter;
package body Gen_Max_Count is
  Max_Val : Count_Object    -- additional object
            := Count_Object'First;
  package Counter is
            new Gen_Counter (Count_Object);
```

```
      procedure Reset is
      begin
        Counter.Reset;
      end Reset;
      procedure Increment is
      begin
        Counter.Increment;
        if Max_Val < Counter.Current_Value then
          Max_Val := Counter.Current_Value;
        end if;
      end Increment;
      function Current_Value return Natural is
      begin
        return Counter.Current_Value;
      end Current_Value;
      function Max return Natural is
      begin
        return Max_Val;
      end Max;
    end Gen_Max_Count;

    with Gen_Max_Count;
    procedure Max_Count_User is
      package Max_Count is
                   new Gen_Max_Count (Natural);
    begin
      Max_Count.Reset;
      Max_Count.Increment;
      ...
    end Max_Count_User;
```

Note that the end user obtains the same functionality that a user of Max_Count has, but the software now allows the primitive object Natural to be supplied externally to the algorithms that will apply to it. Further, the user could have obtained analogous functionality for any discrete type simply by pairing the general object with a different type (using a different generic instantiation).

This model is somewhat analogous to the one used in Smalltalk programming where objects are assembled from other objects plus programmer-supplied specifics. However, it is meant to apply more generally to Ada and other languages that do not have support for dynamic binding and full inheritance, features that are in general unavailable when strong static type checking is required. Instead, Ada offers the generic feature which can be used as shown here to partially offset the constraints imposed by static checking.

Applying this model to existing software means that any lines of code which represent reusable functionality must be parameterized with generic formal parameters in order to make them independent from their surrounding declaration space (if they are not already independent). Generics that are extracted by generalizing existing program units, through the removal of their dependence on external declarations, can then be offered as independently reusable components for other applications.

Unfortunately, declarative dependence is only one of the ways that a program unit can depend on its external environment. Removing the compiler-detectable declarative dependencies by producing a generic unit is no guarantee that the new unit will actually be independent. There can be dependencies on data values that are related to values in neighboring software, or even dependencies on protocols of

operation that are followed at the point where a resource was originally used but which could be violated at a point of later reuse. (An example of this kind of dependency is described in the Measurement section.) To be complete, the transformation process would need to identify and remove these other types of dependence as well as the declarative dependence. Although guidelines have been identified by this study which can reduce the possibility for these other types of dependencies to enter a system, this work only concentrates on mechanisms to measure and remove declarative dependence.

More Examples

In a language with strong static type checking, such as Ada, any information exchanged between communicating program units must be of some type which is available to both units. Since Ada enforces name equivalence of types, where a type name and not just the underlying structure of a type introduces a new and distinct type, the declaration of the type used to pass information between units must be visible to both of those units. The user of a resource, therefore, is constrained to be in the scope of all type declarations used in the interface of that resource. In a language with a fixed set of types this is not a problem since all possible types will be globally available to both the resource and its users. However, in a language which allows user-declared types and enforces strong static type checking of those types, any inter-component communication with such types must be performed in the scope of those programmer-defined declarations. This means that the coupling between two communicating components increases from data coupling to external coupling (or from level two to level five on the traditional seven-point scale of Myers, where level one is the lowest level of coupling) [5].

Consider, for example, project-specific type declarations which often appear at low, commonly visible levels in a system. Resources which build upon those declarations can then be used in turn by higher level application-specific components. If a programmer attempts to reuse those intermediate-level resources in a new context, it is necessary to also reuse the low-level declarations on which they are built. This may not be acceptable, since combining several resources from different original contexts means that the set of low-level type declarations needed can be extensive and not generally compatible. This situation can occur whether or not data is encapsulated with its applicable function, but for clarity, and to contrast with the previous examples, it is shown here with the data and its operations declared separately.

For example, imagine that two existing programs each contain one of the following pairs of compilation units:

```
-- First program contains first pair:
package Vs_1 is
  type Variable_String is
    record
      Data   : String (1..80);
      Length : Natural;
    end record;
  function Variable_String_From_User
                   return Variable_String;
end Vs_1;
```

Note: Page numbers 481-488 were omitted in the original version. This omission does not affect the paper's continuity.

498

```
with Vs_1;
package Pm_1 is
  type Phone_Message is
    record
      From : Vs_1.Variable_String;
      To   : Vs_1.Variable_String;
      Data : Vs_1.Variable_String;
    end record;
  function Phone_Message_From_User
                     return Phone_Message;
end Pm_1;


-- Second program contains second pair:
package Vs_2 is
  type Variable_String is
    record
    - Data   : String (1..250) := (others=>' ');
      Length: Natural := 0;
    end record;
  function Variable_String_From_User
                     return Variable_String;
end Vs_2;

with Vs_2;
package Mm_2 is
  type Mail_Message is
    record
      From    : Vs_2.Variable_String;
      To      : Vs_2.Variable_String;
      Subject : Vs_2.Variable_String;
      Text    : Vs_2.Variable_String;
    end record;
  function Mail_Message_From_User
                     return Mail_Message;
end Mm_2;
```

Now, consider the programmer who is trying to reuse the above declarations in the same program. A reasonable way to combine the use of Mail_Messages with the use of Phone_Messages might seem to be as follows:

```
with Vs_1;
with Pm_1;
with Mm_2;
procedure User is
  Name : Vs_1.Variable_String;
  Pm : Pm_1.Phone_Message :=
             Pm_1.Phone_Message_From_User;
  Mm : Mm_2.Mail_Message :=
             Mm_2.Mail_Message_From_User;
begin
  Name := Pm.To;
  Mm.From := Name;    -- illegal
end User;
```

This will fail to compile, however, since the types Vs_1. Variable_String and Vs_2.Variable_String are distinct and therefore values of one are not assignable to objects of the other (the value of Name is of type Vs_1.Variable_String and the record component Mm.From is of type Vs_2. Variable_String).

In the above example, note that the variable string types were left visible rather than made private to make it seem even more plausible for a programmer to expect that, at least logically, the assignment attempted is reasonable. However,

the incompatibility between the underlying type declarations used by Mail_Message and Phone_Message becomes a problem. One solution might be to use type conversion. However, employing type conversion between elements of the low level variable string types destroys the abstraction for the higher-level units. For instance, the user procedure above could be written as shown below, but exposing the detail of the implementation of the variable strings represents a poor, and possibly dangerous, programming style.

```
with Vs_1;
with Pm_1;
with Mm_2;
procedure Type_Conversion_User is
  Name : Vs_1.Variable_String;
  Pm : Pm_1.Phone_Message :=
             Pm_1.Phone_Message_From_User;
  Mm : Mm_2.Mail_Message :=
             Mm_2.Mail_Message_From_User;
begin
  Name := Pm.To;
  Mm.From.Data (1..80) := Name.Data;
  Mm.From.Length := Name.Length;
end Type_Conversion_User;
```

Notice that we had to be careful to avoid a constraint error at the point of the data assignment. This is one example of how attempts to combine the use of resources which rely on different context declarations is difficult in Ada.

Static type checking, therefore, is a mixed blessing. It prevents many errors from entering a software system which might not otherwise be detected until run time. However, it limits the possible reuse of a module if a specific declaration environment must also be reused. Not only must the reused module be in the scope of those declarations, but so must its users. Further, those users are forced to communicate with that module using the shared external types rather than their own, making the resource master over its users instead of the other way around. The set of types which facilitates communication among the components of a program, therefore, ultimately prevents most, if not all, of the developed algorithms from being easily used in any other program.

This study refers to declarations such as those of the above variable string types as *contexts*, and to components which build upon those declarations and which are in turn used by other components, such as the above Mail_Message and Phone_Message packages, as *resources*. Components which depend on resources are referred to as *users*. The above illustrates the general case of a context-resource-user relationship. It is possible for a component to be both a resource at one level and also a context for a still higher-level resource. The dependencies among these three basic categories of components can be illustrated with a directed graph. Figure 2 shows a graph of the kind of dependency illustrated in the example above.

A resource does not always need full type information about the data it must access in order to accomplish its task. In the above examples, it would be possible for the Mail and Phone message resources to implement their functions via the functions exported from the variable string packages without any further information about the structures of those lower level variable string types. Sometimes, even less knowledge of the structure or functionality of the types being manipulated by a resource is required by that resource for it to accomplish its function.

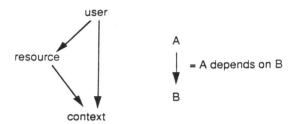

Figure 2.

A common example of a situation where a resource needs no structural or operational information about the objects it manipulates is a simple data base which stores and retrieves data but which does not take advantage of the information contained by that data. It is possible to write or transform such a resource so that the context it requires (i.e., the type of the object to be stored and retrieved) is supplied by the users of that resource. Then, only the essential work of the module needs to remain. This "essence only" principle is the key to the transformations sought. Only the purpose of a module remains, with any details needed to produce the executing code, such as actual type declarations or specific operations on those types, being provided later by the users of the resource. In languages such as Smalltalk which allow dynamic binding, this information is bound at run time. In Ada, where the compiler is obligated to perform all type checking, generics are bound at compilation time, eliminating a major source of run time errors caused by attempting to perform inappropriate operations on an object. Even though they are statically checked, however, Ada generics can often allow a resource to be written so as to free it from depending upon external type definitions.

Using the following arbitrary type declaration and a simplified data store package, one possible transformation is illustrated. First the example is shown before any transformation is applied:

```
-- context:
package Decls is
   type Typ is ...  -- anything but limited private
end Decls;

-- resource:
with Decls;
package Store is
   procedure Put (Obj : in Decls.Typ);
   procedure Get_Last (Obj : out Decls.Typ);
end Store;
```

```
package body Store is
   Local : Decls.Typ;
   procedure Put (Obj : in Decls.Typ) is
   begin
      Local := Obj;
   end Put;
   procedure Get_Last (Obj : out Decls.Typ) is
   begin
      Obj := Local;
   end Get_Last;
end Store;
```

The above resource can be transformed into the following one which has no dependencies on external declarations:

```
-- generalized resource:
generic
   type Typ is private;
package General_Store is
   procedure Put (Obj : in Typ);
   procedure Get_Last (Obj : out Typ);
end General_Store;
```

```
package body General_Store is
   Local : Typ;
   procedure Put (Obj : in Typ) is
   begin
      Local := Obj;
   end Put;
   procedure Get_Last (Obj : out Typ) is
   begin
      Obj := Local;
   end Get_Last;
end General_Store;
```

Note that, by naming the generic formal parameter appropriately, none of the identifiers in the code needed to change, and the expanded names were merely shortened to their simple names. This minimizes the handling required to perform the transformation (although automating the process would make this an unimportant issue). This transformation required the removal of the context clause, the addition of two lines (the generic part) and the shortening of the expanded names. The modification required to convert the package to a theoretically independent one constitutes a reusability measure. A user of the resource in the original form would need to add the following declaration in order to obtain an appropriate instance of the resource:

```
package Store is new General_Store (Decls.Typ);
```

Formal rules for counting program changes have already been proposed and validated [4], and adaptations of these counting rules (such as using a lower handling value for shortening expanded names and a higher one for adding generic formals) are being considered as part of this work.

The earlier example with the variable string types can also be generalized to remove the dependencies between the mail and phone message packages (resources) and the variable string packages (contexts). For example, ignoring the implementations (bodies) of the resources, the following would functionally be equivalent to those examples:

```
-- Contexts, as before:
package Vs_1 is
  type Variable_String is
    record
       Data : String (1..80);
       Len  : Natural;
    end record;
    function Variable_String_From_User
                        return Variable_String;
end Vs_1;

package Vs_2 is
  type Variable_String is
    record
       Data : String (1..250) := (others=>' ');
       Len  : Natural := 0;
    end record;
    function Variable_String_From_User
                        return Variable_String;
end Vs_2;


-- Resources, which no longer depend upon
-- the above context declarations:
generic
  type Component is private;
package Gen_Pm_1 is
  type Phone_Message is
    record
       From : Component;
       To   : Component;
       Data : Component;
    end record;
    function Phone_Message_From_User
                        return Phone_Message;
end Gen_Pm_1;

generic
  type Component is private;
package Gen_Mm_2 is
  type Mail_Message is
    record
       From : Component;
       To   : Component;
       Subj : Component;
       Text : Component;
    end record;
    function Mail_Message_From_User
                        return Mail_Message;
end Gen_Mm_2;
```

Now, the programmer who is trying to reuse the above declarations by combining the use of Mail_Messages with the use of Phone_Messages has another option. Instead of trying to combine both contexts, just one can be chosen (in this case, Vs_2):

```
with Vs_2;
with Gen_Pm_1;
with Gen_Mm_2;
procedure User is
  package Pm_1 is new
               Gen_Pm_1 (Vs_2.Variable_String);
  package Mm_2 is new
               Gen_Mm_2 (Vs_2.Variable_String);
  Name : Vs_2.Variable_String;
```

```
Pm : Pm_1.Phone_Message :=
               Pm_1.Phone_Message_From_User;
Mm : Mm_2.Mail_Message :=
               Mm_2.Mail_Message_From_User;
begin
  Name := Mm.From;
  Pm.To := Name;    -- now OK
end User;
```

An additional complexity is required for this example. The resources must be able to obtain component type values from which to construct mail and phone messages. Although this is not obvious from the specifications only, it can be assumed that such functionality must be available in the body. This can be done by adding a generic formal function parameter to the generic parts, requiring the user to supply an additional parameter to the instantiations as well:

```
generic
  type Component is private;
  with function Component_From_User
         return Component;
                        -- parameterless for simplicity
package Gen_Pm_1 is
  type Phone_Message is
    record
       From : Component;
       To   : Component;
       Data : Component;
    end record;
    function Phone_Message_From_User
                        return Phone_Message;
end Gen_Pm_1;
```

Although the above examples show the context, the resource, and the user as library level units, declaration dependence can occur, and transformations can be applied, in situations where the three components are nested. For example, the resource and user can be co-resident in a declarative area, or the user can contain the resource or vice versa.

This reiterates the earlier claim that, at least for the purpose of this model, it does not matter if the data is encapsulated with its applicable function, it just makes it easier to find if it is. In the programs studied, the lowest level data types, which were often properly encapsulated with their immediately available operations, were used to construct higher level resources specific to the problem being solved. It was unusual for those resources to be written with the same level of encapsulation and independence as the lower level types, and this resulted in the kind of context-resource-user dependencies illustrated above.

For example, in the case of the generalized simple data base, the functionality of the data appears in the resource while the declaration of it appears in the context. The only place where the higher-level object comes into existence is inside the user component, at the point where the instantiation is declared. If desired, an additional transformation can be applied to rectify this problem of the apparent separation of the object from its operations. Instead of leaving the instantiation of the new generic resource up to the client software, an inter.mediate package can be created which combines the visibility of the context declarations with instantiations of the generic resource. This package, then, becomes the direct resource for the client software, introducing a layer of abstraction that was not present in the original (non-general) structure.

For example, the following transformation to the second example above combines the resource General_Store with the context of choice, type Typ from package Decls. The declaration of the package Object performs this service.

```
generic
  type Typ is private;
package General_Store is
  procedure Put (Obj : in Typ);
  procedure Get_Last (Obj : out Typ);
end General_Store;

package Decls is
  type Typ is ...
end Decls;

with Decls;
with General_Store;
package Object is
  subtype Typ is Decls.Typ;
  package Store is new General_Store (Typ);
  procedure Put (Obj : in Typ)
         renames Store.Put;
  procedure Get_Last (Obj : out Typ)
         renames Store.Get_Last;
end Object;

with Object;
procedure Client is
  Item : Object.Typ;
begin
  Object.Put (Item);
  Object.Get_Last (Item);
end Client;
```

Note that no body for package Object is required using the style shown. If it were preferable to leave the implementation of Object flexible, so that users would not need to be recompiled if the context used by the instantiation were to change, the context clauses and the instantiation could be made to appear only in the body of Object. An alternate, admittedly more complex, example is shown here which accomplishes this flexibility:

```
package Object is
  type Typ is private;
  function Initial return Typ;
  procedure Put (Obj : in Typ);
  procedure Get_Last (Obj : in Typ);
private
  type Designated;
  type Typ is access Designated;
end Object;

with Decls;
with General_Store;
package body Object is
```

```
  type Typ is new Decls.Typ;
  function Initial return Typ is
  begin
    return new Designated;
  end Initial;
  package Store is new General_Store (Typ);
  procedure Put (Obj : in Typ) is
  begin
    Store.Put (Obj.all);
  end Put;
  procedure Get_Last (Obj : in Typ) is
  begin
    Store.Get_Last (Obj.all);
  end Get_Last;
end Object;
```

In the alternate example, note that the parameter mode for the Get_Last procedure needed to be changed to allow the reading of the designated object of the actual access parameter. Also, a simple initialization function was supplied to provide the client with a way of passing a non-null access object to the Put and Get_Last procedures. Normally, there would already be initialization and constructor operations, so this additional operation would not be needed. The advantage of this alternative is that the implementation of the type and operations can change without disturbing the client software. However, the first alternative could be changed in a compilation-compatible way, such that any client software would need recompilation but no modification.

It is also possible to provide just an instantiation as a library unit by itself, but this requires the user to acquire independently the visibility to the same context as that instantiation. This solution results in the reconstruction of the original situation, where the instantiation becomes the resource dependent on a context, and the user depends on both. The important difference, however, is that now the resource (the instantiation) is not viewed as a reusable component. It becomes application-specific and can be routinely (potentially automatically) generated from both the generalized reusable resource and the context of choice, while the generic from which the instantiation is produced remains the independent, reusable component. The advantage of this structure lies in the abstraction provided for the user component which is insulated from the complexities of the instantiation of the reusable generic. Since the result is similar to the initial architecture, the overall software architecture can be preserved while utilizing generic resources. The following illustrates this.

```
package Decls is
  type Typ is ...
end Decls;

generic
  type Typ is private;
package General_Store is
  procedure Put (Obj : in Typ);
  procedure Get_Last (Obj : out Typ);
end General_Store;

with Decls;
with General_Store;
package Object is new General_Store(Decls.Typ);
```

```
with Decls;
with Object;
procedure Client is
   Item : Decls.Typ;
begin
   Object.Put (Item);
   Object.Get_Last (Item);
end Client;
```

By modifying the generic resource to "pass through" the generic formal types, the user's reliance on the context can be removed:

```
generic
   type Gen_Typ is private;
package General_Store is
   subtype Typ is Gen_Typ;   -- pass the type through
   procedure Put (Obj : in Typ);
   procedure Get_Last (Obj : out Typ);
end General_Store;

package Decls is
   type Typ is ...
end Decls;

with Decls;
with General_Store;
package Object is new General_Store(Decls.Typ);

with Object;
procedure Client is
   Item : Object.Typ;
begin
   Object.Put (Item);
   Object.Get_Last (Item);
end Client;
```

Measurement

In the above examples, the context components were never modified. Resource components were modified to eliminate their dependence on context components. User components were modified in order to maintain their functionality given the now general resource components, typically by defining generic actual parameter objects and adding an instantiation. In the case of the encapsulated instantiations, an intermediate component was introduced to free the user component of the complexity of the instantiation. It is the ease or difficulty of modifying the resource components that is of primary interest here, and the measurement of this modification effort constitutes a measurement of the reusability of the components. The usability of the generalized resources is also of interest, since some may be difficult to instantiate.

Considering the above examples again, the simple data base resource Store required the removal of the context clause and the creation of a generic part (these being typical modifications for almost all transformations of this kind). In addition, the formal parameter types for the two subprograms were changed to the generic formal private type, causing a change to both the subprogram specification and body. No further changes were required.

```
-- original:
with Decls;
package Store is
   procedure Put (Obj : in Decls.Typ);
   procedure Get_Last (Obj : out Decls.Typ);
end Store;

package body Store is
   Local : Decls.Typ;
   procedure Put (Obj : in Decls.Typ) is
   begin
      Local := Obj;
   end Put;
   procedure Get_Last (Obj : out Decls.Typ) is
   begin
      Obj := Local;
   end Get_Last;
end Store;

-- transformed:
generic
   type Typ is private;                    -- change
package General_Store is
   procedure Put (Obj : in Typ);           -- change
   procedure Get_Last (Obj: out Typ);      -- change
end General_Store;

package body General_Store is
   Local : Typ;
   procedure Put (Obj : in Typ) is         -- change
   begin
      Local := Obj;
   end Put;
   procedure Get_Last (Obj: out Typ) is -- change
   begin
      Obj := Local;
   end Get_Last;
end General_Store;
```

The Phone_Message and Mail_Message resources required the deletion of the context clause, the addition of a generic part consisting of a formal private type parameter and a formal subprogram parameter, and the replacement of three occurrences (or four, in the case of Mail_Message) of the type mark Vs_1.Variable_String with the generic formal type Component.

```
-- original:
with Vs_1;
package Pm_1 is
   type Phone_Message is
      record
         From : Vs_1.Variable_String;
         To   : Vs_1.Variable_String;
         Data : Vs_1.Variable_String;
      end record;
   function Phone_Message_From_User
                             return Phone_Message;
end Pm_1;

-- transformed:
generic
   type Component is private;       -- change
   with function Component_From_User
             return Component;   -- change
```

```
package Gen_Pm_1 is
  type Phone_Message is
    record
      From : Component;          -- change
      To   : Component;          -- change
      Data : Component;          -- change
    end record;
  function Phone_Message_From_User
                    return Phone_Message;
end Gen_Pm_1;
```

Generalizing the bodies of Gen_Pm_1 and Gen_Mm_2 would involve replacing any calls to the Variable_String_From_User functions with calls to the generic formal Component_From_User function. In the case of the simple bodies shown before, this would require three and four simple substitutions, for Gen_Pm_1 and Gen_Mm_2, respectively.

In addition to measuring the reusability of a unit by the amount of transformation required to maximize its independence, reusability can also be gauged by the amount of residual dependency on other units which cannot be eliminated, or which is unreasonably difficult to eliminate, by any of the proposed transformations. For any given unit, therefore, two values can be obtained. The first reveals the number of program changes which would be required to perform any applicable transformations. The second indicates the amount of dependence which would remain in the unit even after it was transformed. The original units in the examples above would score high on the first scale since the handling required for its conversion was negligible, implying that its reusability was already good (i.e., it was already independent or was easy to make independent of external declarations). After the transformation, there remain no latent dependencies, so the transformed generic would receive a perfect reusability score.

Note that the object of any reusability measurement, and therefore, of any transformations, need not be a single Ada unit. If a set of library units were intended to be reused together then the metrics as well as the transformations could be applied to the entire set. Whereas there might be substantial interdependence among the units within the set, it still might be possible to eliminate all dependencies on external declarations.

In the above examples, one reason that the transformation was trivial was that the only operation performed on objects of the external type was assignment (except for the mail and phone message examples). Therefore, it was possible to replace direct visibility to the external type definition with a generic formal private type. A second example illustrates a slightly more difficult transformation which includes more assumptions about the externally declared type. In the following example, indexing and component assignment are used by the resource.

Before transformation:

```
-- context
package Arr is
  type Item_Array is
       array (Integer range <>) of Natural;
end Arr;
```

```
-- resource
with Arr;
procedure Clear (Item : out Arr.Item_Array) is
begin
  for I in Item'Range loop
    Item (I) := 0;
  end loop;
end Clear;
```

```
-- user
with Arr, Clear;
procedure Client is
  X : Arr.Item_Array (1..10);
begin
  Clear (X);
end Client;
```

After transformation:

```
-- context (same)
package Arr is
  type Item_Array is
          array (Integer range <>) of Natural;
end Arr;
```

```
-- generalized resource
generic
  type Component is range <>;
  type Index is range <>;
  type Gen_Array is
          array (Index range <>) of Component;
procedure Gen_Clear (Item : out Gen_Array);
procedure Gen_Clear (Item : out Gen_Array) is
begin
  for I in Item'Range loop
    Item (I) := 0;
  end loop;
end Gen_Clear;
```

```
-- user
with Arr, Gen_Clear;
procedure Client is
  X : Arr.Item_Array (1..10);
  procedure Clear is new Gen_Clear
                    (Natural,
                     Integer,
                     Arr.Item_Array);
begin
  Clear (X);
end Client;
```

The above transformation removes compilation dependencies, and allows the generic procedure to describe its essential function without the visibility of external declarations. As before, an intermediate object could be created to free the user procedure from the chore of instantiating a Clear procedure, which requires visibility to both the context and the resource. However, it also illustrates an important additional kind of dependence which can exist between a resource and its users, namely information dependence.

In the previous example, the literal value 0 is a clue to the presence of information that is not general. Therefore, the following would be an improvement over the transformation shown above:

```
generic
   type Component is range <>;
   type Index is range <>;
   type Gen_Array is
           array (Index range <>) of Component;
   Init_Val : Component := Component'First;
procedure Gen_Clear (Item : out Gen_Array);
procedure Gen_Clear (Item : out Gen_Array) is
begin
   for I in Item'Range loop
     Item (I) := Init_Val;
   end loop;
end Gen_Clear;
```

Note that the last transformation allows the user to supply an initial value, but also provides the lowest value of the component type as a default. An additional refinement would be to make the component type private which would mean that Init_Val could not have a default value. Information dependencies such as the one illustrated here are harder to detect than compilation dependencies. The appearance of literal values in a resource is often an indication of an information dependence.

A third form of dependence, called protocol dependence, has also been identified. This occurs when the user of a resource must obey certain rules to ensure that the resource behaves properly. For example, a stack which is used to buffer information between other users could be implemented in a not-so-abstract fashion by exposing the stack array and top pointer directly. In this case, all users of the stack must follow the same protocol of decrementing the pointer before popping and incrementing after pushing, and not the other way around. Beyond the recognition of it, no additional treatment of this form of dependence between components will appear in this study.

Formalizing the Transformations

The following is a formalization of the objectives of transformations which are needed to remove declaration dependence.

1. Let P represent a program unit.

2. Let D represent the set of n object declarations, $d_1 .. d_n$, directly referenced by P such that d_i is of a type declared externally to P.

3. Let $O_1 .. O_n$ be sets of operations where O_i is the set of operations applied to d_i inside P.

4. P is completely transformable if each operation in each of the sets, $O_1 .. O_n$ can be replaced with a predefined or generic formal operation.

The earlier example transformation is reviewed in the context of these definitions:

1. Let P represent a program unit.
   P = **procedure** Clear (Item : **out** Arr.Item_Array) is ...

2. Let D represent the set of n object declarations, $d_1 .. d_n$, directly referenced by P such that d_i is of a type declared externally to P.
   D = { Arr.Item_Array }

3. Let $O_1 .. O_n$ be sets of operations where O_i is the set of operations applied to d_i inside P.
   O_1 =
   { indexing by integers, integer assignment to components }

4. P is completely transformable if each operation in each of the sets, $O_1 .. O_n$ can be replaced with a predefined or generic formal operation.

Indexing can be obtained through a generic formal array type. Although no constraining operation was used, the formal type could be either constrained or unconstrained since the only declared object is a formal subprogram parameter. Since component assignment is required, the component type must not be limited. Therefore, the following generic formal parts are possible:

```
type Component is range <>;
type Index is range <>;
```

followed by either:

```
type Gen_Array is array (Index) of Component;
```

or:

```
type Gen_Array is
        array (Index range <>) of Component;
```

Notice that some operations can be replaced with generic formal operations more easily than others. For example, direct access of array structures can generally be replaced by making the array type a generic formal type. However, direct access into record structures (using "dot" notation) complicates transformations since this operation must be replaced with a user-defined access function.

Application to External Software

Medium-Sized Projects

To test the feasibility of the transformations proposed, a 6,000-line Ada program written by seven professional programmers was examined for reuse transformation possibilities. The program consisted of six library units, ranging in size from 20 to 2,400 lines. Of the 30 theoretically possible dependencies that could exist among these units, ten were required. Four transformations of the sort described above were made to three of the units. These required an additional 44 lines of code (less than a 1% increase) and reduced the number of dependencies from ten to five, which is the minimum possible with six units. Using one possible program change definition, each transformation required between two and six changes.

A fifth modification was made to detach a nested unit from its parent. This required the addition of 15 lines and resulted in a total of seven units with the minimum six dependencies. Next, two other functions were made independent of the other units. Unlike the previous transformations which were targeted for later reuse, however, these transformations resulted in a net reduction in code since the resulting components were reused at multiple points within this program. Substantial information dependency which would have impaired actual reuse was identified but remained within the units, however.

A second medium-sized project was studied which exhibited such a high degree of mutual dependence between pairs of library units that, instead of selecting smaller units for generalizations, the question of non-hierarchical dependence was studied at a system level. The general conclusion from this was that loops in the dependency structure (where, for example, package A is referenced from package body B and package B is referenced from package body A) make generalization of those components difficult. The program was instead analyzed for possible restructuring to remove as much of the bi-directional dependence as practical. This was partially successful and suggests that this sort of redesign might appropriately precede other reuse analyses.

The NASA Projects

Currently, the research project is examining several spacecraft flight simulation programs from the NASA Goddard Space Flight Center. These programs are each more than 100,000 editor lines of Ada. They have been developed by an organization that originally developed such simulators in Fortran and has been transitioning to the use of Ada over the past several years. Because all the programs are in the same application domain and were developed by the same organization there is considerable opportunity for reuse. In the past, the development organization reported the ability to reuse about 20% of earlier programs when a new program was being developed in Fortran. However, since becoming familiar with Ada, the same organization is now reporting a 70% reuse rate, or better.

After gaining an understanding of the nature of the reuse accomplished in Fortran and later in Ada, and how similar or different reuse in the two languages was, we would like to test several theories about why the Ada reuse has been so much greater. We already know that the reuse is accomplished by modifying earlier components as required, and not, in general, by using existing software verbatim. Because of this reuse mode, one theory we will be testing is that the Ada programs are more reusable simply because they are more understandable.

For the current study, the programs were studied to reveal opportunities to extract generic components which, had they been available when the programs were being developed originally, could have been reused without modification. There is an additional advantage to working with this data, however, since, as mentioned above, the several programs already exhibit significant functional similarities which can be studied for possible generalization. In other words, whereas the initial discussion of generic extraction has focussed on attempts to completely free the essential function of a component from its static declaration context, this data gives examples of similar components in two or more different program contexts and therefore allows us to study the possibility of freeing a component from only its program-specific context and not from any context which remains constant across programs.

This gives rise to the notion of domain-specific generic extraction as opposed to domain-independent generic extraction. Given the problems associated with extracting a completely general component, as examined earlier, a case can be made to generalize away only some of the dependence, leaving the rest in place. The additional problem, then, becomes how to determine what dependence is permissible and what should be removed. The permissible dependence would be common across projects in a certain domain, and would therefore be domain-specific while the dependence to be removed would be the problem-specific context. When reused, then, these components would have their problem-specific context supplied as generic actual parameters.

This is currently a largely manual task, since the programs must be compared to find corresponding functionality and then examined to determine the intersection of that functionality. Interestingly, on the last project the developers themselves have also been devising generic components which are instantiated only one time within that program. This implied to us that some effort was being spent to make components which might be reusable with no, or perhaps only very little, modification in the next project. We have confirmed with the developers that this is in fact the case. By comparing the results of our generalizations with those done by the developers, we find that ours have much more complex generic parts but correspondingly much less dependence on other software. This is a reasonable result, since the developers already have some idea about the context for each reuse of a given generic; what aspects of that context are likely to change from project to project and what aspects are expected to remain constant across several programs. The program-specific context, only, appears in the generic parts of the generics written by the developers, while our generalizations have generic parts which contain declarations of types and operations which apparently do not need to change as long as the problem domain remains the same. In other words, when our generic parts are devised by analyzing only a single instance of a component, we cannot distinguish between program-specific and domain-specific generalizations.

One interesting question we would like to answer is whether we can derive the generic part that makes the most sense within this domain by comparing similar components from different programs and generalizing only on their differences, leaving the software in the intersection of the components unchanged. In this way, a component would be derived which would not be completely independent but, like the developer-written generics, would be sufficiently independent for reuse in the domain. Then, a comparison with the generics developed within the organization would be revealing. If the generics are similar then our process might be useful on other parts of the software that have not yet been generalized by the developers. However, if they differ greatly, it would be useful to characterize that difference and understand what additional knowledge must be used in generalizing the repeated software. Unfortunately, there is not enough reuse of the developer's generics yet to make this final comparison but a project is currently in progress which should supply some of this data.

The following example illustrates the complexity of the generic parts which were required to completely isolate a typical unit from its context. Here, the procedure Check_Header was removed from a package body and generalized to be able to stand alone as a library level generic procedure.

```
generic
    type Time is private;
    type Duration is digits <>;
    with function Enable return Boolean;
    type Hd_Rec_Type is private;
    with procedure Set_Start
        (H : in out Hd_Rec_Type; To : Duration);
    with function Get_Start
        (H : Hd_Rec_Type) return Duration;
    with procedure Set_Stop
        (H : in out Hd_Rec_Type; To : Duration);
    with function Get_Stop
        (H : Hd_Rec_Type) return Duration;
    type Real is digits <>;
    with function Get_Att_Int
        (H : Hd_Rec_Type) return Real;
    with function Conv_Time
        (D_Float : Duration) return Duration;
    Header_Rec : in out Hd_Rec_Type;
    Goesim_Time_Step : in out Duration;
    with function Seconds_Since_1957
        (T : in Time) return Duration;
    with procedure Debug_Write (Output : String);
    with procedure Debug_End_Line;
    type Direct_File_Type is limited private;
    with procedure Direct_Read
        (File : Direct_File_Type);
    with procedure Direct_Get
        (File : in  Direct_File_Type;
         Item : out Hd_Rec_Type);
    with function Image_Of_Base_10
        (Item : Duration) return String;
    with procedure Header_Data_Error;
procedure Check_Header_Generic
    (Simulation_Start_Time : in Time;
     Simulation_Stop_Time  : in Time;
     Simulation_Time_Step  : in Duration;
     History_File : in out Direct_File_Type);
```

The instantiation of this generic part is correspondingly complex:

```
procedure Check_Header_Instance is new
                        Check_Header_Generic
    (Abstract_Calendar.Time,
     Abstract_Calendar.Duration,
     Debug_Enable,
     Attitude_History_Types.Header_Record,
     Set_Start,
     Get_Start,
     Set_Stop,
     Get_Stop,
     Utilities.Read,
     Get_Att_Hist_Out_Int,
```

```
     Converted_Time,
     History_Data.Header_Rec,
     History_Data.Goesim_Time_Step,
     Timer.Seconds_Since_1957,
     Error_Collector.Write,
     Error_Collector.End_Line,
     Direct_Mixed_Io.File_Type,
     Direct_Mixed_Io.Read,
     Get_From_Buffer,
     Image_Of_Base_10,
     Raise_Header_Data_Error);
```

In contrast, a typical generic part on a unit which was developed and delivered as part of the most recent completed project by the developers themselves is shown here:

```
with Css_Types;
generic
    Number_Of_Sensors : Natural :=
        Css_Types.Number_Of_Sensors;
    with function Initialize_Sensor
        return Css_Types.Css_Database_Type is <>;
package Generic_Coarse_Sun_Sensor is
    ...
```

Note that by allowing the visibility of Css_Types, the generic part was simplified. Being unfamiliar with the domain, had we attempted to generalize Coarse_Sun_Sensor by examining only the non-generic version of a corresponding component in another program we would not be able to tell whether the dependence on Css_Types was program-specific or domain-specific. Here, however, the developer leads us to believe that Css_Types is domain-specific while the number of sensors and sensor initialization is program specific.

Guidelines

The manual application of the principles and techniques of generic transformation and extraction has revealed several interesting and intuitively reasonable guidelines relative to the creation and reuse of Ada software. In general, these guidelines appear to be applicable to programs of any size. However, the last guideline in the list, concerning program structure, was the most obvious when dealing with medium to large programs.

• Avoid direct access into record components except in the same declarative region as the record type declaration.

Since there is no generic formal record type in Ada (without dynamic binding such a feature would be impractical) there is no straightforward way to replace record component access with a generic operation. Instead, user-supplied access functions are needed to access the components and the type must be passed as a private type. This is unlike array types for which there are two generic formal types (constrained and unconstrained). This supports the findings of others which assert that direct referencing of non-local record components adversely affects maintainability [6].

• Minimize non-local access to array components.

Although not as difficult in general as removing dependence

on a record type, removing dependence on an array type can be cumbersome.

• Keep direct access to data structures local to their declarations.

This is a stronger conclusion than the previous two, and reinforces the philosophy of using abstract data types in all situations where a data type is available outside its local declarative region. Encapsulated types are far easier to separate as resources than globally declared types since the operations are localized and contained.

• Avoid the use of literal values except as constant value assignments.

Information dependence is almost always associated with the use of a literal value in one unit of software that has some hidden relationship to a literal value in a different unit. If a unit is generalized and extracted for reuse but contains a literal value which indicates a dependence on some assumption about its original context, that unit can fail in unpredictable ways when reused. Conventional wisdom applies here, and it might be reasonable to relax the restriction to allow the use of 0 and 1. However, experience with a considerable amount of software which makes the erroneous assumption that the first index of any string is 1 has shown that even this can lead to problems.

• Avoid mingling resources with application specific contexts.

Although the purpose of the transformations is to separate resources from application specific software regardless of the program structure, certain styles of programming result in programs which can be transformed more easily and completely. By staying conscious of the ultimate goal of separating reusable function from application declarations, whether or not the functionality is initially programmed to be generic, programmers can simplify the eventual transformation of the code.

• Keep interfaces abstract.

Protocol dependencies arise from the exportation of implementation details that should not be present in the interface to a resource. Such an interface is vulnerable because it assumes a usage protocol which does not have to be followed by its users. The bad stack example illustrates what can happen when a resource interface requires the use of implementation details, however even resources with an appropriately abstract interface can export unwanted additional detail which can lead to protocol dependence.

• Avoid direct reference to package Standard.Float

Even when used to define other floating point types, direct reference to Float establishes an implementation dependence that does not occur with anonymous floating point declarations. Especially dangerous is a direct reference to Standard.Long_Float, Standard.Long_Integer, etc., since they may not even compile on different implementations. Some care must also be taken with Integer, Positive, and Natural,

though in general they were not associated with as much dependence as Float. Note that fixed point types in Ada are constructed as needed by the compiler. Perhaps the same philosophy should have been adopted for Float and Integer. Reference to Character and Boolean is not a problem since they are the same on all implementations.

• Avoid the use of 'Address

Even though it is not necessary to be in the scope of package System to use this attribute, it sets up a dependency on System.Address that makes the software non-portable. If this attribute is needed for some low-level programming than it should be encapsulated and never be exposed in the interface to that level.

• Consider the inter-component dependence of a design

By understanding how functionally-equivalent programs can vary in their degree of inter-component dependence, designers and developers can make decisions about how much dependence will be permitted in an evolving system, and how much effort will be applied to limit that dependence. For system developments which are expected to yield reusable components directly, a decision can be made to minimize dependencies from the outset. For developments which are not able to make such an investment in reusability, a decision can be made to allow certain kinds of dependencies to occur. In particular, dependencies which are removable through subsequent transformation might be allowed while those that would be too difficult to remove later might be avoided. A particularly cumbersome type of dependence occurs when two library units reference each other, either directly or indirectly. This should be avoided if at all possible. By making structural decisions explicitly, surprises can be avoided which might otherwise result in unwanted limitations of the developed software.

Acknowledgements

This work was supported in part by the U.S. Army Institute for Research in Management Information and Computer Science under grant AIRMICS-01-4-33267, and NASA under grant NSG-5123. Some of the software analysis was performed using a Rational computer at Rational's eastern regional office in Calverton, Maryland.

References

1. Basili, V. R. and Rombach, H. D. Software Reuse: A Framework. In preparation.

2. Basili, V. R. and Rombach, H. D. The TAME Project: Towards Improvement- Oriented Software Environments. IEEE Transactions on Software Engineering, SE-14, June 1988.

3 Funk & Wagnalls, Standard College Dictionary, New York, 1977.

4. Myers, G. Composite/Structured Design, Van Nostrand Reinhold, New York, 1978.

5. Dunsmore, H.E. and Gannon, J.D. Experimental Investigation of Programming Complexity. In _Proceedings ACM/NBS 16th Annual Tech. Symposium: Systems and Software_, Washington D.C., June 1977.

6. Gannon, J.D., Katz, E. and Basili, V.R. Characterizing Ada Programs: Packages. In _Proceedings Workshop on Software Performance_, Los Alamos National Laboratory, Los Alamos, New Mexico, August 1983.

John W. Bailey is a Ph.D. candidate at the University of Maryland Computer Science Department. He is a part-time employee of Rational and has been consulting and teaching in the areas of Ada and software measurement for seven years. In addition to Ada and software reuse, his interests include music, photography, motorcycling and horse support. Bailey received his M.S. in computer science from the University of Maryland, where he also earned bachelor's and master's degrees in cello performance. He is a member of the ACM.

Victor R. Basili is a professor at the University of Maryland, College Park's Institute for Advanced Computer Studies and Computer Science Department. His research interests include measuring and evaluating software development. He is a founder and principal of the Software Engineering Laboratory, which is a joint venture among NASA, the University of Maryland and Computer Sciences Corporation. Basili received his B.S. in mathematics from Fordham College, an M.S. in mathematics from Syracuse University and a Ph.D. in computer science from the university of Texas at Austin. He is a fellow of the the IEEE Computer Society and is editor-in-chief of _IEEE Transactions on Software Engineering_.

Software reclamation

by E.S. Garnett and J.A. Mariani

One of the major barriers to the introduction of reuse technology into the software development process is the absence of large repositories of reusable components from which manufacturers can build new generations of systems [1, 2]. Owing to the tremendous investment that has been made in developing systems, companies use an evolutionary approach to software development whereby the old version becomes the basis of the next generation. Owing to such costs, companies are understandably reluctant to develop completely new versions from scratch. If software reusability is to emerge as a discipline, then some mechanism whereby components are reclaimed from existing systems and transformed according to reuse criteria must be found. This paper discusses an approach designed to reclaim software components from existing systems and transform them into objects, which we contend are inherently more reusable.

1 Introduction

Reusability throughout the software development process is seen as an important practice in approaching the problems inherent in building large complex software systems. The traditional view of reusability is that of reusing the software components which are found in a library. However, reusability of both the products of the process and the knowledge that was used to produce those products is seen as an important step in reducing costs and constitutes a mature and disciplined method of developing software.

Research into software reusability has shown that most systems are combinations of a few basic patterns, e.g., searching, sorting, traversing, etc. Lanergan [3] and Jones [4] have shown that between 60% and 80% of the software

making up some systems has been implemented previously and is therefore a candidate for reuse. Economic analysis [5] indicates that the cost of software is an exponential function of software size. Reuse of code should decrease complexity, improve quality, and increase programmer productivity.

Reusability as a method of working has been largely unfulfilled ever since McIlroy [6] first espoused the concept of 'mass produced software components'. There are many questions which still have to be answered.

• What are the characteristics of reusable software, and how do we develop software in such a way as to increase its future reusability potential?

• How do we represent reusable components, and, using such a representation, how do we organize the components in such a way as to locate those matching our requirements?

• Once we have found a component which we wish to reuse, how do we help programmers understand the component and help to fit it into a new application?

Another question which has remained largely untouched and which is the theme of this paper is

• How do we re-engineer existing software so that it may be reused in the future?

A major problem facing the software industry in adopting reuse technology is the lack of software components available from which new generations of systems could be developed. Owing to the tremendous investment that has been made in developing systems, companies understandably use an evolutionary approach to software development whereby the old version becomes the basis of the new generation. The costs involved in developing completely new versions from scratch are inhibitive. If software reusability is to emerge as a discipline, then some mechanism whereby components are reclaimed from existing systems and transformed according to reuse criteria must be found. The re-engineering of existing software offers a promising approach to solving this problem.

Re-engineering refers to the identification of components within existing systems possessing reuse potential and qualifying them according to some reuse-oriented specification technique. There are two perspectives to re-engineering software; reverse engineering and reuse re-engineering.

☐ **Reverse engineering** is concerned with the maintenance of badly structured software systems. It involves a reversal of the design process, moving from pure code back to a higher level of abstraction that conveys meaning in a more concise and understandable manner for human perception. This can be used to restructure or document the code.

☐ **Reuse re-engineering** concentrates specifically on the construction of new systems by reusing information from foregoing ones. One technique lies in the conversion of existing software into standard building blocks to form new programs. This approach has been termed 'software reclamation'.

This paper examines the process of software reclamation and describes the implementation of a reclamation system. We address problems such as the nature of software components and how to organise and store components in a library. There are two paradigms that support reuse; the functional model and the object model. It is our belief that the object model offers more potential for reuse and that objects are inherently more reusable across application domains. Therefore, we describe a tool called the Alchemist, which converts existing software into functional building blocks. Another tool, the Prospector, takes these functional building blocks and organises them into an object hierarchy. Finally, other tools support the reuse of these reclaimed components.

2 Paradigms for Reusable Code

Vast quantities of code are produced every year. In a demographic study carried out in 1983, Jones [4] estimated a worldwide total of approximately 6500 million source lines were programmed in that year alone. This arises from two situations.

• Design of new systems that are viewed as solving 'unique' problems. As we have mentioned, this is seldom the case, and much code is duplicated.

• Maintenance of existing systems; required because either bugs have been found in implemented systems or new requirements have been acknowledged.

We argue that it is possible to address both these situations by adopting a code reclamation philosophy. This Section discusses characteristics which promote the reuse of code and describes two paradigms which we believe enable upgrade paths for existing software to be followed and act as a base for the construction of new systems.

It is strongly argued that software has to be specially developed with reusability in mind [7,8]. For software to be reusable, it must exhibit a number of features that directly encourage its use in similar situations. Following the findings of Wood [9], we consider the features detailed below to be important qualities of reusable software. It should be noted that they are not prerequisites for reuse; in fact some of them conflict. However, the more that can be satisfied, the more feasible the practice of reuse becomes.

☐ **Environmental independence.** We require components that can be reused irrespective of the environment from which they were originally captured. Dependencies arise from the referencing of global data and assumptions made about operational usage.

☐ **High cohesion.** We require components that implement a single operation or set of related operations. This allows easy interpretation of their functionality.

☐ **Loose coupling.** We require components that have minimal links to other components. High coupling limits a component's use in isolation by creating an environment which is necessary for its compilation and execution [10].

☐ **Adaptability.** We require components that are adaptable so they can be customised to fit a range of similar situations.

☐ **Understandability.** We require components that are easily understandable so users can quickly interpret functionality.

☐ **Reliability.** We require components that are error-free. This also requires that they react in sensible ways to unexpected situations.

☐ **Portability.** We require components that are not restricted in terms of the software or hardware environment they operate in.

It seems clear that a transformation process is involved to convert existing code into a form that exhibits more reusable properties. What form is appropriate? Sommerville [11] suggests that there are six different classes of reusable code component. Notice that these definitions may not exactly correspond with programming construct meanings.

• **Functions.** These are abstractions over expressions that take as parameters control variables and return a value as a result.

• **Procedures.** These are abstractions over statements. Procedures are dependent on their environment, and execution of a procedure causes some change to that environment.

• **Declaration packages.** These are abstractions over a set of declarations that are relatively poorly supported by encapsulation facilities in most modern programming languages. An obvious exception here is the Ada package construct.

• **Objects.** These are abstractions over variables comprising separate data and function parts.

• **Abstract data types.** These are abstractions over types consisting of a type representation and a set of procedures that apply to objects of that type.

• **Subsystems.** These are abstractions over programs, typically made up of other smaller components.

By comparison of our requirements and those displayed by the

```
int stack[STACKSIZE];                object data int stack[STACKSIZE], stack_pt;
int stack_pt;                        method void push(int value); int pop();
void push(value)                     end;
{
   stack[stack_pt] = value;
   stack_pt + +;
};
int pop()
{
   stack_pt--;
   return (stack[stack_pt]);
};
          (a)                                      (b)
```

Figure 1. Formation of an object — *a* Outline of C code; *b* Stack object.

classes given above, we can decide which class is most appropriate for reusable components. It can be seen that procedures are dependent on their environment and thus fail our independence criteria. Subsystems are conglomerations of smaller components that may not be related, thereby infringing our cohesion criteria. In cases where subsystem components are related, in compilers or database management systems for example, it is always going to make sense to reuse them, rather than write them from scratch. We consider this more a question of standardisation than reusability.

We would also argue that we require a class of component that is well supported by modern programming languages, so components may be made to apply to a number of different languages. This rules out declaration packages, which are poorly supported in most languages. We are left with functions and abstract data types, a common instantiation of which is the object. We will now look at models which describe development in these classes.

2.1 The functional model

The functional model involves the decomposition of monolithic code into functional units that are suitable for component representation within a library. It is a transformation process which attempts to enrich the code with features that are beneficial for reusability. Code is altered in the following ways:

☐ All global references and other side-effects are resolved within functions by capture and positioning in the parameter list. This reduces the coupling between modules and increases environmental independence. Code is more adaptable, since functional operation is governed by parameters, not global data.

☐ Syntactic reliability of the code is ensured by compilation. Code failing this compilation is banned from transformation.

Automatic generation of such functions must take account of the structure of the language in which the source code is

written; therefore a language must be chosen to support functional reuse. In our case, the C language was chosen, because it is one instance of a language that supports functions as the decompositional element in a program. Moreover, we have access to Unix system software and a great deal of development software (used in other projects) that we may use to form our components. The exhaustive analysis of existing source code is the key to the process of reclamation. It is possible to automatically convert this enormous body of software into a large (many thousands) pool of components, generating possibly new combinations of functions and objects. It is hoped that this 'vast' amount of potential components will address the issue of 'small' component catalogues.

2.2 The Object Model

It is possible to utilise other desirable component features by considering an object representation. Here, the building block is an object, consisting of a method set and a data set. A method set can be thought of as a group of functions (plus parameters) which access a fixed set of global variables (the data set). For example, Fig. 1*a* shows a piece of C code concerned with stack manipulation. Transforming to the object model, the functions push( ) and pop( ) become the method set, and the global variables stack [ ] and stack_pt the data set. The stack object is shown in Fig. 1*b*.

The advantages of the object model as a component representation are

• **encapsulation** — data and code are stored as a single representational unit, increasing cohesion by ensuring all information required to use the object is self-contained. Modifications to the code are localised, thus consistency is achieved.

• **information hiding** — a firewall is constructed between the object and users of the object, ensuring access to the data can only be accomplished through the method interface. Code becomes more adaptable, since implementation can now be altered without affecting the user's view of the component.

• **inheritance** — objects exhibit organisational properties, allowing them to be combined into classes, which are objects describing the implementation of sets of similar objects. It is

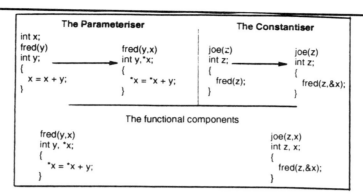

Figure 2. Passes in the Alchemist.

then possible to have one class as a specialisation of another, called a subclass. Only new variables and procedures need to be added to the subclass. All the information and functionality from the generalised class, or superclass, is included automatically, leading to a reduction in code bulk. This is a form of direct reuse.

The novelty of the object model is that, instead of calling functions, programs ask objects to perform operations on themselves. This separates the programs from the physical structure of the objects they handle; specifying not what to do but how to do it. Typically, objects are modelled on real-world entities. When systems required modifications at a future date, it is seldom that brand new entities are to be used, rather that their operation needs minor adjustment. Thus, systems can withstand change better and are more flexible.

Studies examining the desirable characteristics of Ada components [12,13] have concluded that the object is a very appropriate representation for a reusable component. Indeed, work has recently been carried out to produce building blocks that are object-based. Lenz et al. [14] seek to increase the leverage gained when using building blocks, by making them black boxes encapsulating code and a specification of how to use the code for each component. These black boxes resemble Ada packages. Each building block may only be interfaced by specific operations or by a generic creation mechanism. So far, their work has only been applied to the domain of systems programming, but the results do seem to indicate promise.

2.3 Language Support for Building Block Parameters

To program a component as a building block, it is necessary to know what directionality parameters have. Directionality refers to the movement of parameters into a black box or out from a black box. Knowing about directionality can greatly aid retrieval of components, as reusers can classify the parameters they require more explicitly. Some languages, Ada for example, provide language level support for such information. As well as classifying parameters by type, they are also classified as IN, OUT or INOUT, depending on whether they are used solely for input, solely for output or for both input and output. Thus, an Ada declaration of a procedure x with three parameters, a(IN), b(OUT) and c(INOUT), would look like

procedure x (a IN int;b OUT char; c IN OUT char);

Other languages provide similar mechanisms. Pascal classifies parameters as variable or value. A variable parameter indicates that any alterations to the parameter within the function will be remembered on return. A value parameter indicates that any alteration to the parameter while within the function will be discarded on return. In C, information on directionality has to be derived from detailed analysis of functions. All compound data types (for example, arrays and structures) passed as parameters are variables. Singular data types are value parameters, unless specifically denoted otherwise. By syntactical analysis, it is possible to discover the directionality of parameters used within functions.

3 The Software Reclamation System

In this section, we describe the software reclamation system. This consists of the Alchemist and the Prospector.

3.1 The Alchemist Tool

The Alchemist is a syntax analyser capable of turning lead (monolithic C source code) into gold (C functions). We see this as a vital intermediate step in the automatic production of object components. It is a three pass analyser consisting of a parameteriser, constantiser and database lister.

The Parameteriser produces a parameterised C file by manipulating global variable references. All globals are placed in the parameter list of the function. The Parameteriser also takes care of user-defined types declared in C as structures. All structure definitions are examined, and information recorded in database tables on structure name, structure field(s) and type(s), and any instantiations of the structure. The conversion of globals into parameters is relaxed for references (calls) to other functions, so as to allow normal operation of each function. The **Constantiser** ensures that alternations in the actual parameter list are reflected in all formal parameter lists.

The first two passes are iterative, continuing until the file produced by the Constantiser reaches stability. Fig. 2 illustrates this iterative process. The component **fred** is firstly parameterised, which necessitates **joe** being made consistent. This latter process ensures that the call of **fred** has the appropriate syntax, but introduces a global parameter to the function **joe**. Thus, the process iterates once more, finally parameterising **joe** with the global variable **x**.

The **Database Lister** simply takes the C file of functions, splits it into its constituent parts and stores information on it in the database. Every component generated by the Alchemist has a representative within the database. Information stored consists of function name and type, parameter names and types, a list of global reference calls and an indication of which parameters were previously global. The database used is Ingres*, using ESQL as a manipulation language. It is essentially a global name space; different programs will use the same function names for potentially different functions. Therefore, each function has an underlying unique identifier, while retaining its external programmer-given name. We believe that the resultant building block functions are far more applicable to a reuse technology, due to their environmental indifference.

3.2 The Prospector Tool

The Prospector automatically converts from the functional model to the object model (see Fig. 3). An object is formed by the grouping of functions according to commonality of parameter types. This can be justified by the fact that type information can give important clues as to the performance of a function. It indicates the types of objects that identifiers will be used to represent. For example, *int* qualifies an identifier as representing an integer. Thus, if a user requires a representation for a string, the type character array will probably be chosen. The conversion between paradigms is initiated by the user with a simple request. The rest of the process is entirely automatic. The functional database is first scanned for base types. Each one of these types are compared against functions stored. If at least two functions contain the type in their parameter list, they are candidates for an object. Within an object, the grouped functions become the method set which operate on the data set of function parameters; thus if two functions manipulate a character array, they could be methods within an object which has a character array as its data set. Once the base types have been tried, combinations of base types are attempted for every possible combination. A set of component objects is produced. These improve the reuse potential of components by cohesively grouping similar functions together in a single entity. The naming of objects becomes a matter for user intervention. It is necessary to choose a sensible name for the object — this can be aided by presentation of the method set and a manual inspection of the code.

It is possible to apply the same analysis to C structure parameters. These can be treated as base types and merged with functions that utilise structures of the same name to become an instance variable of an object. By considering the synthesis of the individual fields within a structure, it is possible to merge structures with different names but with identical bodies. For example, two structures named STRUCT_X and STRUCT_Y, which both possess field types int and real, can be considered

* Ingres is a trademark of Relational Technologies Inc.

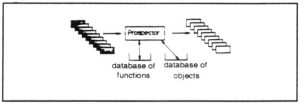

■ C functions
□ C++ objects

Figure 3. The Prospector.

as a single base type and merged during the commonality analysis.

The object-oriented language C++ [15] was chosen to represent the objects, because of its syntactical similarity with C and the accessibility of a C++ compiler. Inheritance is provided by treating each object as a class. The base types thus form the top level of the inheritance hierarchy. Combinations of base types form subclasses; the greater the number of combinations, the lower the level. For example, if the four base types *int, real, char, long* combined to form an object, it would be part of the fourth level in the hierarchy. Objects formed by the Prospector are stored in the INGRES database.

3.3 Encoding More Component Information

The retrieval of components from a database is of crucial importance in any reuse system. The user must be able to specify in detail his requirements for a component, but time is of the essence. For reuse to be attractive, the time taken to discover viable components must be less than the time perceived to create new code. Originally, both models only offered the opportunity of retrieval by parameter types. How could more information be stored about components? Prieto-Diaz and Freeman [16] have developed a facetted classification scheme by capturing details of a components environment. Every component in the library consists of a sextuple of facet terms, three of which describe the internal environment (where the component is executed);

☐ **Function:** the specific primitive function performed by the component — for example, add, input, modify, move, ...
☐ **Object:** the object being manipulated by the component — for example, arrays, files, integers, ...
☐ **Medium:** the entity serving as the locale for the function — for example, bufer, line, screen, ...

and three describing the external environment (where the component is applied);

☐ **System_Type:** the type of system the component can be applied to — for example, assembler, compiler, scheduler, ...
☐ **Functional_ Area:** the application-dependent activities the component can be applied to — for example, accounts, CAD, DB design, ...
☐ **Setting:** where the application is exercised — for example, advertising, auto repair, car dealer, ...

Table 1. Statistical summary of reclaimed software.

	SySL system	England's UT
Files	74	20
Functional components	480	61
Object components	251	50

England's UIT system — Size statistics

	Small 0-20	Medium 21-50	Large 51-150	Very Large 151 +
Size (in loc)				
Number	19	21	13	8
Calls to external functions	0.9	3.6	15.0	47.0
Parameters	2.9	4.4	10.9	10.1
Reuse frequency	1.2	1.7	1.2	1.6

SySL System — Size statistics

	Small 0-20	Medium 21-50	Large 51-150	Very Large 151+
Size (in loc)				
Number	252	151	68	9
Calls to external functions	1.97	5.21	14.94	40.50
Parameters	9.97	2.59	5.30	20.00
Reuse frequency	3.48	2.78	1.84	0.67

It is easy to see how such a facetted scheme can be applied to the functional model. The function facet is given by the name of the component. The object manipulated by the component and the medium of component execution should both be present within the parameter list of a component, along with a number of other external variables. Functional area, system type and setting are all provided by the user, along with files passed to the Alchemist tool. However, in applying this classification to the object model, we are faced with several dilemmas. Since an object is a representation of a number of related entities, it is difficult to associate it with a single function, medium or object facet value. Since constituent methods in an object may be drawn from a number of different functional areas, system types and settings, it is similarly difficult to associate external environment facet values with an object. A solution to this problem is to view each object as an amalgamation of several functions. Links can be created between individual functions and the objects they are members of. Thus, by retrieving functions it is possible to find objects they belong to.

Retrieval from the functional database is now possible

by specifying facet requirements in a template. The reuser simply fills in details on a card provided on the screen, and this information is taken into account, along with type details when retrieval takes place.

4 Preliminary results and experience

In Section two, we presented a list of features which we considered constituted a reusable functional component. Since reusability is a measurement of the ease of reusing a component, what metrics can be applied to show that these features have been improved? Basili and Caldieri [17] have postulated a reusability attributes model which contains several measures that quantify properties of a software component relevant to its potential reuse.

- **Structure** — measured by the number of calls to and the number of links to other components. This is associated with our criteria of environmental independence and loose coupling. The Alchemist operates on the structure of code to eliminate linkages, thereby reducing dependencies between components. However, calls to other components are unaffected.
- **Data bindings measure** — an evaluation of the relationships present between subprograms. If x is a variable and A and B are subprograms, if A assigns x and B references x, the communication path (A,x,B) exists. This provides information on subprogram clustering, a large number of paths indicating that two subprograms belong together as a single component. This matches our principle of high cohesion. This is used by the Prospector to amalgamate common components into objects possessing a maximal data bindings measure.
- **Size** — measured by the number of lines of code. This has implications for our understandability criteria. Basili and Caldieri postulate that a small size is more appropriate, although an exact figure is not stressed. They theorise that the more frequently a component is reused, the more reusabe it is. This gives rise to the reuse frequency measure, calculated by dividing the number of times a component is called in a suite of programs by the total number of calls to all components in that suite. Although we do not directly modify component size (except for parameter list expansion), one byproduct of our work is to discover optimal sizes of reusable C functions. Presumably, there is a size threshold where the number of parameters and number of external calls creates excess complexity and mitigates against reuse. Reuse frequencies can be amassed to calculate if there is a relationship between size and reuse, and if so, to discover the factors that create this relationship.
- **Programming language** — measured by the Halstead language level indicator [18]. This determines whether software is portable across environments. We have no power currently over this.
- **Documentation** — measured by a combination of the language level and a subjective judgement. This has implications for understandability and adaptability.

The Reclamation System has been tested, both with ad hoc

collections of files taken from a variety of sources and complete system software.

In the ad hoc test, five small suites of our colleagues' programs totalling 37 C files were submitted to the Alchemist, from which 64 functional components were generated. The essential component of every C program, the main function, was barred from entrance to the database, as typically it only acts as a guide to the order functions should be called in, and name clash problems would result from its inclusion. Using the Prospector, 34 objects were formed, each possessing several methods. Declared structures were classed as base types for the purposes of the analysis. It was noticeable that the most sensible objects produced contained structure members in their data sets. This is not surprising, since the C structure is an abstract data type which can be designed to model a real-world entity, in the same manner as an object. Structures seem to be ideal candidates for a data set.

Two large complete systems were submitted to the reclamation system, both major parts of the Alvey-sponsored Eclipse project [19]. The SySL system structure language describes the static structure of large software systems, aiding version control and enabling automatic building of the software system from the language description. It comprises 74 C source files, from which 480 functional components were produced. Statistical results are presented in Table 1. Examining SySL components appears to validate Basili and Caldieri's size metrics, and, as we would expect, the size of a component influences the average number of parameters and external calls which creates complexity. The Prospector formed 265 objects, with commonality of structures again forming the most sensible components.

The second complete system is England's user-interface tool [21]. This comprises 20 C source files, from which 61 functional components were produced. Table 1 again presents a statistical summary of the findings. Conversely, the user interface tool structure statistics show no real relationship between size and reuse level, despite the fact that the complexity of the components does increase with size. Fifty object components were generated by the Prospector.

5 Conclusions

This paper has presented a technique known as reclamation, which provides the following benefits:

☐ Automatic upgrading of existing software.
☐ Population of a large (many thousands) component library, which can be utilised as the basis for construction of new software, and used for experimentation into component retrieval tools and reuse support environments.

The identification of appropriate representational media, functions and objects, following analysis of reusable qualities supported by classes of components, enabled conversion tools to be designed for existing code. The Alchemist syntax tool performs a vital intermediate step by decomposing C source files into functional entities. Objects can then be produced from these functions by the Prospector. A facetted classifica-

tion scheme allows components to be catalogued in a library and easily retrieved. Future work will be aimed at enhancing the reclamation system, by automatic discovery of more information on components, and at understanding their operation.

To meet the difficulties currently being faced in the software world, companies must take initiatives to bring the promise of reuse to fulfillment. The work proposed here constitutes an important stimulus which, backed by retrieval research and powerful support environments, brings that promise nearer to fruition.

References

[1] Tracz, W.: "Reusability Comes of Age," *IEEE Software*, 1987, pp. 6-8.
[2] Biggerstaff, T.J. and Richter, C.: "Reusability Framework, Assessment and Directions," *IEEE Software*, 1987, pp. 41-49.
[3] Lanergan, R.C. and Grasso, C.A.: "Software Engineering with Reusable Designs and Code," *IEEE Trans.*, 1984, SE-10, (5), pp. 564-574.
[4] Jones, T.C.: "Reusability in Programming: A Survey of the State of the Art," *IEEE Trans*, 1984, SE-10, (5), pp. 488-494.
[5] Standish, T.A.: "An Essay on Software Reuse," *IEEE Trans.*, 1984, SE-10, (5), pp. 494-497.
[6] McIlroy, M.D., "Mass Produced Software Components," in Buxton, J.R., Naur, P., and Randell, B. (Eds.): *Software Engineering Concepts and Techniques*, Petrocelli/Charter, Brussels, Belgium, 1976, pp. 88-98.
[7] Parnas, D., "Designing Software for Ease of Extension and Contraction," *IEEE Trans*, 1979, SE-5, (2), pp. 128-137.
[8] Batz, J.C., Cohen, P.M., Redwine, S.T., Jr., and Rice, J.R.: "The Application-Specific Task Area," *IEEE Computer*, 1983, 16, (11), pp. 78-85.
[9] Wood, M.: "Software Function Frames: An Approach to the Classification of Reusable Software through Conceptual Dependency," PhD Thesis, University of Strathclyde, UK. January 1989.
[10] St. Dennis, R., Stachour, P. Frankowski, E., and Onuegbe, E.: "Measurable Characteristics of Reusable Ada Software," *Ada Lett.*, 1986, 5, (2), pp. 41-49.
[11] Sommerville, I.: "Software Reuse," ISF Study Paper (ISF/UL/WP/IS-3.1), University of Lancaster, UK, January 1988.
[12] Bott, M.F., Elliot, A.E., and Gautier, R.G.: "Ada Reuse Guidelines — Report," Alvey ECLIPSE Project Report (ECLIPSE/REUSE/DST/ADA_GUIDE/RP), 1985.
[13] Braun, C.L., and Goodenough, J.B.: "Ada Reusability Guidelines," SofTech Report 32 (85-2-208/2 for USAF), 1985.
[14] Lenz, M., Schmid, H.A., and Wolf, P.F.: "Software Reuse through Building Blocks," *IEEE Software*, 1987, 4, (7), pp. 34-42.
[15] Stroustrup, B.: *The C++ Programming Language*, Addison-Wesley, 1986.
[16] Prieto-Diaz, R., and Freeman, P.: "Classifying Software for Reusability," *IEEE Software*, 1987, 4, (1), pp. 6-16.
[17] Basili, R., and Caldieri, V.: "Reusing Existing Software," University of Maryland Internal Paper CS-TR-2116, October 1988.
[18] Conte, C.D., Dunsmore, H.E., and Shen, V.Y.: *Software Engineering Metrics and Models*, Benjamin Cummings, 1986.
[19] Bott, F. (Ed.): *Eclipse — An Integrated Project Support Environment*, Peter Peregrinus, 1989.
[20] Sommerville, I., and Thomson, R.: "SySL — A System to Support Software Evolution," Internal Report CS-SE-6-87, Department of Computing, University of Lancaster, UK, 1987.
[21] England, D.: "A User-Interface Tool," Proc. First European Software Engineering Conf. ESEC87 (Springer-Verlag, 1987).

J.A. Mariani is with, and E.S. Garnett was formerly with, the Dept. of Computing, University of Lancaster, Bailrigg, Lancaster LA1 4YR, UK.
E.S. Garnett is now with Software Sciences Ltd., Deanway Technology Centre, Wilmslow Road, Handforth, Wilmslow, Cheshire SK9 3ET, UK.

Chapter 12

Reverse Engineering
and Design Recovery

Chapter 12
Reverse Engineering and Design Recovery

Purpose

This chapter, along with several other articles reprinted in this book, will help the reader understand the concepts and techniques of reverse engineering and design recovery. Reverse engineering capability is a common feature of today's CASE tools for reengineering. The article, "Getting Back to Requirements Proving to Be a Difficult Task," by M.A. Hanna, reprinted in Chapter 6, gave examples of several commercially available reverse engineering tools. The article, "A Program Understanding Support Environment," by L. Cleveland, also in Chapter 6, discussed the technical ideas, presenting multiple views of source code. In contrast with reverse engineering, full-fledged design recovery[1] is not considered practically feasible yet.[2] Nevertheless, the reader will find in this chapter interesting ideas for approaching the design recovery problem on a small scale.

Papers

In the first paper, "Design Recovery for Maintenance and Reuse," Ted Biggerstaff discusses the conceptual design of a design recovery system. His system, DESIRE, uses design knowledge ("idioms") and domain knowledge to help construct design component abstractions. These abstractions include informal diagrams, informal concepts and relations, design rationales, module refinements, flow information, and control information.

In the next paper, "Recognizing a Program's Design: A Graph-Parsing Approach," Charles Rich and Linda Wills discuss how commonly used program structures, called *clichés*, can be automatically recognized. Their goal is not to mimic human cliché recognition. It is rather to use human knowledge of clichés to improve the cliché recognition of the authors' system, the Recognizer, for finding program plan information. The Recognizer first translates a program into a plan language (the "plan calculus") and then tries to find plans in the translated program.

In the final paper, "Creating Specifications from Code: Reverse-Engineering Techniques," P.T. Breuer and K. Lano use transformation technology to extract descriptions of software functionality and object-oriented classes from source code. They discuss the problem of obtaining specifications from source code and some specific procedures for doing so. They illustrate the procedures with several examples, in Cobol and Fortran. Their approach has a formal foundation, but is easily understandable in this paper.

---

[1] Like large-scale, automatic generation of design rationales for existing code.

[2] T. Corbi, "Program Understanding: Challenge for the 1990s," *IBM Systems Journal,* Vol. 28, No. 2, 1989, pp. 294-306. Reprinted in Chapter 14.

Design Recovery for Maintenance and Reuse

Ted J. Biggerstaff

Microelectronics and Computer Technology Corporation

Software maintenance and harvesting reusable components from software both require that an analyst reconstruct the software's design. Unfortunately, source code does not contain much of the original design information, which must be reconstructed from only the barest of clues. Thus, additional information sources, both human and automated, are required. Further, because the scale of the software is often large (hundreds of thousands of lines of code or more), the analyst also needs some automated support for the understanding process.

Design recovery recreates design abstractions from a combination of code, existing design documentation (if available), personal experience, and general knowledge about problem and application domains. (I use the term "abstraction" in its general sense and specifically not in the abstract-data-type sense. Thus, the abstractions I discuss are generalized structures that contain fewer details than found in the source code. Any reference to ADTs will be explicit.)

The recovered design abstractions must include conventional software engineering representations such as formal specifications, module breakdowns, data

The Desire system helps software engineers understand programs by analyzing code, relying on the analyst's own reasoning, and drawing on a knowledge base of design expectations.

abstractions, dataflows, and program description language. In addition, they must include informal linguistic knowledge about problem domains, application idioms, and the world in general. In short, design recovery must reproduce all of the information required for a person to fully

understand what a program does, how it does it, why it does it, and so forth. Thus, design recovery deals with a far wider range of information than found in conventional software engineering representations or code.

Design recovery occurs across a spectrum of activities from software development to maintenance. The developer of new software spends a great deal of time trying to understand the structure of similar systems and systems components. The software maintainer spends much of his or her time studying a system's structure to understand the nature and effect of a requested change. In each case, the analyst is involved in design recovery. Thus, design recovery is a common, sometimes hidden part of many activities scattered throughout the software life cycle.

A system expert provides one of the most effective ways to recover the design of a foreign system by answering questions, shifting attention quickly to germane areas of the program, interpreting code segments in human (informal) terms, and so forth. An automated system would need access to the same kind of "in-head" expertise. That is, it would need a knowledge base — a *domain model* — that cap-

36

Reprinted from *IEEE Computer*, July 1989, pp. 36-49. ©1989 by The Institute of Electrical and Electronics Engineers, Inc. All rights reserved.

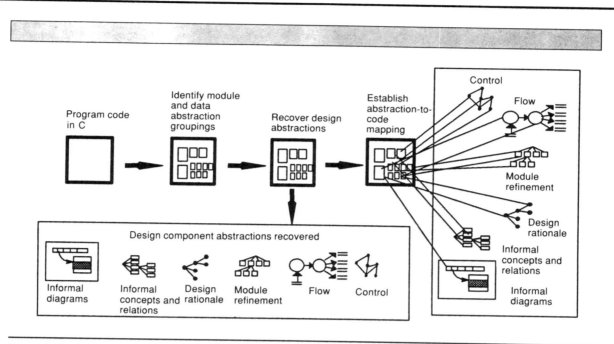

Figure 1. The basic design recovery process.

tures this expertise. The information must be domain oriented, must include more information than the analyst might find in the code alone, and must guide and assist the process of understanding the code. The domain model differentiates design recovery research from such superficially similar efforts as reverse engineering, which automatically abstracts code to a specification level such that the specifications can be modified and revised code can be automatically regenerated. In fact, the domain model is central to the overall success of any attempt to automate portions of the design recovery process.

Design recovery in the broad sense is so inherently unstructured and unpredictable that few tools have been available to help the analyst search through code to find patterns and structures of interest. Exceptions include simple search tools like grep (a pattern searching tool for Unix) and some code analysis facilities in tools like Cscope (an interactive cross-reference tool, also for Unix). Further, there have been few tools to help the software engineer capture, organize, and present the design information once recovered, other than text editors, outliners, and computer-aided software engineering tools.

To show how we might extend the automated assistance available to the software engineer, this article introduces the con-

cept of design recovery, proposes an architecture to implement the concept, illustrates how the architecture operates, describes the progress toward implementing it, and compares this work with other similar work such as reverse engineering and program understanding.

The design recovery process

A key objective of design recovery is to develop structures that will help the software engineer understand a program or system. Understanding is critical to many activities — maintenance, enhancement, reuse, the design of a similar new system, and training, to name a few. This section describes the process of design recovery as it is applied to maintenance and to the population of reuse and recovery libraries. I then outline how a recovery knowledge base (the domain model) can assist in some of the steps of design recovery.

The design recovery process consists of three steps:

Step one: supporting program understanding for maintenance. Figure 1 illustrates the steps of the design recovery process that help a software engineer understand a C program. Other classes of

languages, such as object-oriented languages, require a modest variation of these ideas.

The analyst first looks for large-scale organizational structures such as the subsystem structure, module structure, and important data structures. Next, he or she recovers various useful design structures and expresses them in abstracted forms, such as informal diagrams, informal concepts and relations, design rationale, module structures, flow, and control. In the course of this, the software engineer keeps track of the relationship (the mapping) between the various abstractions and the segments of code that implement them. Now, let us look at the kinds of questions a software engineer asks when trying to understand a system.

What are the modules? Some programming languages formalize the notion of a module and provide constructs to define it, so the module and subsystem structures are easy to determine directly from the source code. For those languages that do not provide constructs, the software engineer must use a combination of human intuition and experience, clues from the source code structures, and some knowledge (expectations) of the conventional organization patterns for applications of the type under consideration.

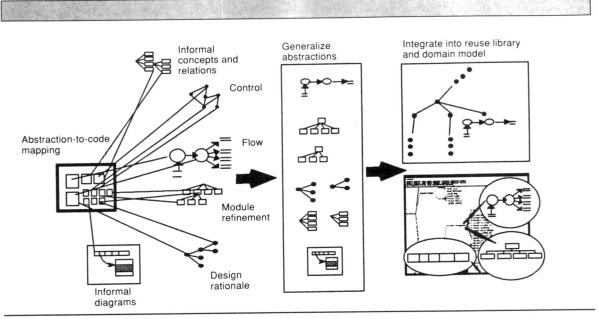

Figure 2. Design recovery extensions supporting reuse library population.

Expectations derived from organizational conventions are powerful and efficient mechanisms for helping the software engineer understand a system. For example, based on their knowledge of typical organizational patterns, experts in the domain of Unix-like multitasking code would expect to find a module that does process management and contains routines for the creation, suspension, and deletion of processes. Of course, such expectations are typically generalizations and, therefore, are only approximations of such multitasking code. Thus, our expectations, drawn from various domains, provide fuzzy patterns to guide our search and analysis of foreign code. But, because of their fuzziness, these patterns can do no more than serve as guides.

In addition to identifying large-scale structures such as modules, we also need to associate the structures with informal semantic concepts. That is, we need to provide semantically rich natural-language abstractions, or *conceptual abstractions*, that represent the essential concept underlying the module. For example, process management would be a good conceptual abstraction to associate with the example module discussed above because the phrase will help the software engineer understand the target system by

referencing his or her existing mental concept and activating a variety of important and powerful expectations.

I will formalize these conceptual abstractions to the point that some measure of intelligent computer processing can be implemented on them. I am not suggesting fully automating the design recovery process; the degree of automation is unlikely to ever go beyond the notion of an assistant that can perform wide-ranging searches and suggest domain-based recovery strategies to the software engineer. However, even these limited capabilities would be quite valuable to an analyst faced with hundreds of thousands of lines of foreign code.

What are the key data items? Among the other first questions an analyst asks are

- What are the important data items?
- What abstract informal concepts do they relate to?
- What are their relations to the modules just identified?

For example, in the multitasking window system example, the analyst might find a process table containing entries that describe the processes currently running under the multitasker. The more experi-

ence the analyst has with multitasking systems, the richer the set of expectations that he or she will have about such a system.

What are the software engineering artifacts? As shown in Figure 1, the understanding process recreates the software engineering-oriented design artifacts and expresses them wherever possible in terms of the module and data abstractions recovered earlier. The specific artifacts captured are determined to some extent by the process model adopted by the programming organization. For example, some companies will use a program description language, dataflow, module refinement, and a simple data dictionary. Others will depend on different design artifact sets. The techniques under investigation at MCC are flexible enough to apply to a broad range of such artifacts.

What are the other informal design abstractions? For the set of abstractions to be really effective, we need other information structures, many of which are not as well defined and formal as the software engineering-oriented design artifacts. For example, design rationale might be useful, perhaps stated in terms of issue-based information systems (IBIS) nets.[1] Further, natural-language prose is unavoidable if we want a really effective model of the design. Similarly, informal diagrams describing abstract views of the target system are often quite useful. Thus, we must expect to recover a wide variety of design artifacts that contain a mixture of formal and informal information.

What is the relation of the design abstractions to the code? After recovering the artifacts, we must preserve the relationships among them. That is, once we determine that a context switch is being performed within some dataflow diagram, we would like to know exactly which chunk of code performs it. Code analysis of a concrete example is often required to answer questions that depend on low-level details abstracted out of the dataflow diagram. Once an engineer establishes this abstraction-to-code link, he or she will have an organized, "in-head" framework (the abstraction) in which to put the code-oriented details and, perhaps more importantly, a set of organized structures to help interpret those details. Thus, the engineer can understand the code in terms of the abstractions in the framework.

Step two: supporting population of reuse and recovery libraries. How might we productively use the recovered design components? Populating the component library of a reuse system is an obvious and valuable use, but that requires further steps to generalize the components to enhance their reusability. Figure 2 illustrates this process. Generalization makes the components applicable to a wider spectrum of applications, but it can require that we factor them to decouple independent design aspects. For example, an independent process-management component might apply far more widely than one that is tightly coupled to window management.

The final step in this process integrates the new abstractions into the reuse library and the recovery knowledge base (the domain model). Thus, we expect to reuse this recovered information to help build similar new components and to recover similar components from other systems.

Step three: applying the results of design recovery. The final step of the process cycle applies the newly populated domain model to design recovery (see Figure 3). The abstract design components stored in the domain model now become the starting point for discovering candidate concrete realizations of themselves in a

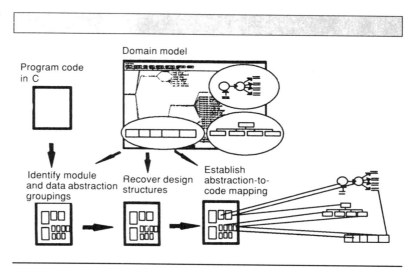

Figure 3. Model-aided design recovery process.

new system's code. Once the software engineer determines that the candidate is truly a concrete realization of the abstract design component, the design recovery system records the finding. For example, domain model information about the expected kinds of functions in the process management example might provide a skeleton for that module and even provide some semantic clues about the names of the various routines in the module.

Of course, the expectations in the domain model will seldom be an exact match of the design structures in the source code, and the software engineer will likely have to edit the design abstraction to synchronize it with the code, but even a partial match reduces the overall work. Further, each significant mismatch provides new expectations that help the domain model grow and evolve.

Distinguishing properties of design recovery

Two key properties distinguish this design recovery model from similar models:

(1) *Use of informal information.* The model exploits multiple kinds of information. Importantly, it uses informal information, which exists outside of the sphere of programming languages and opens a new kind of leverage on the recovery problem — one that exploits a human-oriented, associative style of retrieval and analysis.

(2) *Use of a domain model.* This design recovery model also exploits multiple sources of information. In particular, it uses a domain model to help the software engineer understand and interpret foreign systems. The domain model is a knowledge base of expectations expressed as patterns of program structures, problem domain structures, language structures, naming conventions, and so forth, which provide frameworks for the interpretation of the code. These frameworks can be built on to recreate the design information that is missing from the code as written. Heretofore, such expertise has existed only in the minds of expert software engineers or application domain specialists.

Conceptual abstractions: the use of informal information. Among the information developed by the design recovery process are instances of conceptual abstractions that help the user understand the nature of a design in human terms. That is, the conceptual abstraction instances produced by design recovery must go beyond what can be represented in programming languages. They represent the world not only in rigid formal terms, but also in informal and flexible terms. Such artifacts are not simply optional, informal additions to the formalisms expressed in the programming language, but complementary representations that are necessary and critical to the mental structuring and assimilation of the final design by a software engineer.

Note that I distinguish between the no-

July 1989

39

tion of a conceptual abstraction ("a process management module") and a specific instance of a conceptual abstraction ("the specific process management module in the Unix system"). This distinction is important because each has a distinct role. Conceptual abstractions are implemented in the domain model as object-oriented classes that take an active role in identifying instances of themselves in the code being interpreted. Thus, they represent the set of realizations of that object type in the target code, whereas an instance represents a single, specific realization of that object in the code. The sidebar, "Concepts of object-oriented programming," further clarifies the distinction between class and instance.

If a recovered design contains this addi-

tional kind of entity — the conceptual abstraction instance — how do we identify it? And, what is the character of such an entity?

An instance of a conceptual abstraction has two important properties, one that is structural and one that is semantic or associative. The associative part of the abstraction is represented in the domain model by a "linguistic idiom." The structural part is represented by various kinds of idioms, depending on the kind of information being represented. Introducing associative connections and structural patterns provides a partial formalization for informal conceptual abstractions.

Structural pattern. A conceptual abstraction's first property is its ability to

represent (that is, both hide and relate) some set of lower-level details. For example, a single concept such as "a process management module" can be used in many contexts to represent all of the massive detail that is a process management module, keeping the designer from becoming overwhelmed by the detail. This property is similar to the conventional software-engineering notion of expressing designs as top-down refinement structures. Its function is to describe the successively burgeoning levels of detail in a design. A conceptual abstraction's structure has an additional, operational role as a pattern that defines the kinds of source code structures that would express the abstraction. This pattern is used to search for and identify specific source code structures that are

Concepts of object-oriented programming

The domain model in the Desire design recovery system is strongly related to the concepts of object-oriented programming systems (OOPS), such as Smalltalk,[1] C++,[2] and the Common Lisp Object System (CLOS). Central to OOPS is the concept of a *class*, which is a package of local data items that defines the state of an instance of the class, and a set of functions that manage that state. An *instance* of a class (also called an *object*) is a unique copy of the local data items; to put it another way, it is a specific concrete member of the class. Each data item is called an *instance variable*. The functions of the class are conventionally called *methods*.

An example of a class would be line_segment, which might have instance variables *x*, *y*, and *length* that define the position of the line segment's end point and its length. There might be many specific lines in a drawing, and each would be represented by an instance of the class, that is, a data record containing three values for *x*, *y*, and *length*. The methods of such a class might be named create, destroy, move, rotate, stretch, draw, and so forth. These methods would operate on the instance variables to perform various operations on the line.

To call such a method, we would send a message to an instance of the class. Sending a message is a generalization of the notion of a function call, and it requires at least two pieces of information to perform the invocation: a pointer to an instance (from which the system can determine which class to look in for the method definition) and the name of a method (such as move). The method name is called the *selector*. These two pieces of information uniquely determine the specific method to be called. Some object systems, such as CLOS, provide an optional, special case where additional items can be required, allowing a finer-grained determination of the specific method to be called.

A key concept in OOPS is *inheritance*, which allows us to specify a new class by defining only the differences between it and another class, called its *superclass*. For example, we could specify a class fat_line_segment by declaring it as a *subclass* of line_segment and describing the differences. We would say line_segment is the superclass of fat_line_segment. Suppose this new class has an additional instance variable named *width*, which defines the width of the line to be drawn. Its instance records will contain variables *x*, *y*, and *length*, inherited from line-segment, and the variable *width*, from fat_line_segment's definition. Similarly, we would write a new version of the draw and create methods to accommodate the operational differences between simple line segments and those with width. These new methods would be called whenever the draw or create messages were sent to one of fat_line_segment's instances. When other messages, such as stretch, are sent, the inherited methods from line_segment would be called.

Frames, a slight variation of the concept of classes, come from the field of artificial intelligence. They usually have more built-in conventions for the instance variables (commonly called *slots* in frame systems) than simple OOPS classes do. They therefore have more associated runtime support. Frames systems often include conventions and runtime support for expressing relationships between instance records. For example, semantic net applications often provide frame conventions and built-in facilities that search the frame network for sets of instances that resemble but do not exactly match each other. Such frame conventions and support are often built on top of a conventional OOPS system.

References

1. Adele Goldberg and David Robson, *Smalltalk-80: The Language and Its Implementation*, Addison-Wesley, 1983.

2. Bjarne Stroustrup, "What is Object-Oriented Programming?" *IEEE Software*, May 1988, pp.10-20.

plausible instances of the conceptual abstraction.

Associative connections. A conceptual abstraction's second property is its rich set of informal, natural-language associations that establish its contextual framework for human understanding. That is, the concept of a process management module has semantic connections to other informal, semantic concepts such as context switching, state saving, and multitasking. Each of these concepts allows association of the concept of a process management module with a large body of knowledge that can help an engineer interpret the design of some specific process management module or plan the design of a new one.

These two properties provide clues to the role of conceptual abstractions in dealing with large complex designs. The structural property provides a way to handle lots of detail without being overwhelmed, as well as a way of describing the application patterns one expects to find in programs. In contrast, the associative linguistic property offers a way to deal with partially specified (fuzzy) design objects within the universe of informal, natural language-based semantics. These properties relate to two parallel and complementary models — the software-engineering representation model and the natural-language semantic model.

The importance of informal information. An example will illustrate the importance of the informal aspect of conceptual abstractions. Consider the C function in Figure 4. This is a real function taken from a multitasking window system[2] with the comments removed and meaningful identifiers mapped to semantically empty symbols. What could an analyst tell about the computational intent of this function? Precious little. About all he or she could do is paraphrase the relations expressed in the programming language. For example, the analyst could describe that the function f0001 calls f0002 with arguments that are global arrays (such as g0001) of structures containing some fields (such as s0001 and s0002). Even if the definitions of all of the functions (f0002, f0003, etc.) were available and similarly transformed, the computational intent would remain unclear. What is worse is that, without the informal information, the computational intent of these functions might not be unique. There could be a number of valid interpretations.

The example severs the connection between the artifact and the semantics of the

```
#include <stdio.h>
#include "h0001.h"
#include "h0002.h"
#include "h0003.h"
f0001(a0001)
        unsigned int a0001;
        {
        unsigned int i0001;
        f0002(g0005,d0001,d0002);
        f0002(a0001,d0003,d0002);
        f0003(g0001[a0001].s0001,g0001[a0001].s0002);
        g0006 = a0001;
        i0001 = g0001[a0001].s0003;
        if(!f0004(i0001) && (g0002->g0003)[i0001].s0004 == d0004)
                f0005(i0001);
        }
```

Figure 4. Function with no informal semantic clues.

```
#include <stdio.h>
#include "proc.h"
#include "window.h"
#include "globdefs.h"
change_window(nw)
        unsigned int nw;
        {
        unsigned int pn;
        border_attribute(cwin,NORM_ATTR,INV_ATTR);
        border_attribute(nw,NORMHLIT_ATTR,INV_ATTR);
        move_cursor(wintbl[nw].crow,wintbl[nw].ccol);
        cwin = nw;
        pn = wintbl[nw].pnumb;
        if(!outrange(pn) && (g->proctbl)[pn].procstate == SUSPENDED)
                resume(pn);
        }
```

Figure 5. Function with some informal semantic clues.

problem domain, eliminating associations between the program and our informal knowledge of the world. Interpretation and understanding of the program has become impossible in any deep sense. Thus, we can see that connotation plays an important role in the process by which people deal with, interpret, and understand programs.

It is exactly this kind of semantically impoverished representation that we usually give to automated tools. If people have difficulty dealing with this kind of representation, why should we expect a computer to be more successful?

So what sort of informal information is required to understand the program in a nonsuperficial way? Let us consider a slightly enhanced version of this program. Figure 5 maps the symbolic names back to those used in the original code. Here, the names of the functions are more meaningful and, if the reader understands a bit about multitasking and window systems, he or she can probably make some good

```
#include <stdio.h>
#include "proc.h"
#include "window.h"
#include "globdefs.h"
change_window(nw)            /*Change current window to window nw*/
         unsigned int nw;     /*Number of target window*/
         {
         unsigned int pn;

         /*Restore border of current window to un-highlighted*/
         border_attribute(cwin,NORM_ATTR,INV_ATTR);

         /*Highlight border of new current window*/
         border_attribute(nw,NORMHLIT_ATTR,INV_ATTR);

         /*Move the physical cursor to the new window where the cursor was
         left, and make nw the current window*/
         move_cursor(wintbl[nw].crow,wintbl[nw].ccol);
         cwin = nw;

         /*Resume the process associated with the new window if it is
         suspended.*/
         pn = wintbl[nw].pnumb;
         if(!outrange(pn) && (g->proctbl)[pn].procstate == SUSPENDED)
                  resume(pn);
         }
```

Figure 6. Function with many informal semantic clues.

guesses about the operation. The name of the function suggests that it changes which window is currently active, with the new window probably indicated by the argument nw. Further, we can guess that the function border_attribute alters the visual appearance of the windows' borders, the function move_cursor moves the screen cursor to some position in the new window, and the function resume allows some suspended process to run again (probably the process associated with the new window). The variables similarly come alive with meaning: wintbl is probably the window table and probably has fields ccol and crow that keep track of the cursor (inferred from their use in the call to move_cursor).

By restoring the comments from the original code (see Figure 6), we can corroborate several of our guesses and enhance our understanding of some of the functions and variables.

This exercise should make it clear that the informal linguistic information that the software engineer deals with is not simply supplemental information that can be ignored because automated tools do not use it. Rather, this information is fundamental.

It provides the ability to determine the computational intent of code in a way that is impossible with just the source code denuded of its informal semantics.

If we are to use this informal information in design recovery tools, we must propose a form for it, suggest how that form relates to the formal information captured in program source code or in formal specifications, and propose a set of operations on these structures that implements the design recovery process. To accomplish these goals, we must first analyze the proposed design recovery system in a bit more detail.

A model-based design recovery system

What would a design recovery system look like? Figure 7 is a system-level description of a model-based design recovery system (called Desire) showing some of the sources of information used to recover designs. They include the code of existing systems because such code con-

tains a large amount of important information, but there must be other sources as well. Much design information cannot be formally captured in the program source code because programming languages do not contain the constructs necessary to express information such as the informal conceptual abstractions behind the code. For example, the informal conceptual abstractions behind the change_window function discussed earlier include windows, processes, cursors, and the operations on these entities. And these conceptual abstractions are woven into a rich set of knowledge about the domain that provides clues to understanding the formal source code structures.

Design recovery results in a hypertext web[4] of information that weaves together informal ideas (e.g., the concept of a process), software engineering artifacts (e.g., a dataflow diagram of a process switch), and details of specific examples of these entities as embodied in code (e.g., one specific subroutine for process switching). This web is projected into externalized reports to help the software engineer understand a specific target system and into internalized data structures for use by the Rose reuse system.[3] Since the web is built out of hypertext frames, the design recovered by the Desire system is simply a set of data structures that represent the conceptual abstractions and express the semiformal relationships among them (see sidebar, "Concepts of object-oriented programming").

To understand how this model-based design recovery system works, the nature of the data items in the model, and how those data items are used, consider the following typical design recovery session using the multitasking window system as the application domain. Using the process model of design recovery as a guide, I will first define a set of data objects (called *idioms*) that implement the structural patterns and associative connections of conceptual abstractions. The example idioms codify the domain model's expectations of the entities and structures in a typical multitasking window system running on a personal computer. I will then informally describe how these domain objects behave during the semiautomated recovery of the design of a specific multitasking window system. This scenario is analogous to a nonautomated design recovery performed by an unaided software engineer.

An example. We start to discover the structure of this multitasking window sys-

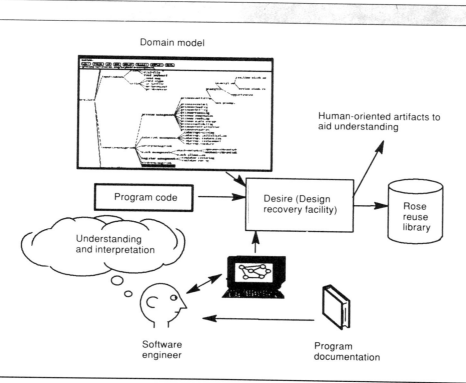

Figure 7. The Desire model-based design recovery system.

tem by looking for key structures, based on our knowledge or expectations of the problem and application domains. A knowledgeable engineer would expect to find a process table, a window table, a window management module, and a process management module, among other structures. (I offer a detailed example of such a system elsewhere.[2])

In Desire's domain model, such expectations are represented by object classes expressed in the Common Lisp Object System (CLOS). In contrast to object classes that *implement* a window management module or a process management module, these domain model classes *operate* on the implementations of window management modules or process management modules. Specifically, domain model objects search for instances of the key structures within the code (perhaps with human help) and bind their instance variables to these key structures, subject to the analyst's approval. An instance of such a domain object represents an occurrence of a concept such as a window management module or a process management module within a specific segment of source code.

The instance variables of that instance point to the segments of code that implement the domain object.

Thus, the first step of recovery is to create a set of instances of the idiomatic structures expected. The engineer examines the domain model, finds an object class describing a multitasking window manager, and creates an instance of that object. As a side-effect, other instances that define the detailed substructure of a multitasking window manager are created as a substructure of this first instance. This structure of instance records represents an architectural overview of a multitasking window manager that might look abstractly like the structure in Figure 8, where the relation on the arcs is the sub-parts relation. Over the course of the design recovery process, the whole set of design details will evolve as a rich substructure beneath this first set of instances. Now let's follow the evolution of that substructure in more detail.

Each of the instances just created can bind to the source code in one of two ways:

(1) It can bind directly to some segment

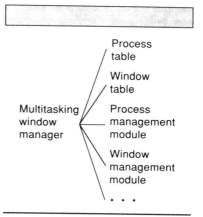

Figure 8. Initial pattern instance records expressing an architectural overview.

of code (associatively).

(2) It can bind indirectly through a subinstance (that is, through a close match of the substructures to the program code).

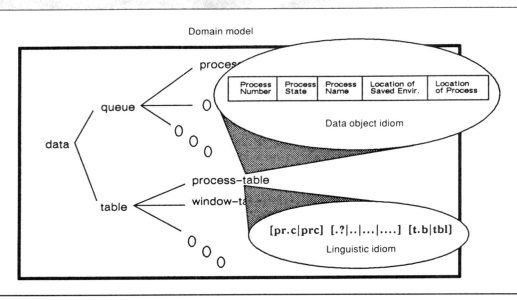

Figure 9. Abstract design idioms within a domain model.

For example, the process table class in Figure 9 contains idioms for both kinds of binding.

Direct binding is implemented via a *linguistic idiom*, which represents the expected linguistic form of a conceptual abstraction such as process table. This idiom might be implemented as a set of regular expression patterns that match the various natural-language forms in source code identifiers or comments. For example, the pattern [pr.c|prc] [.?|..|...|....] [t.b|tbl] defines the linguistic expectations for process table. Of course, we will occasionally encounter an expression of the conceptual abstraction that the existing patterns do not find. The addition of such cases helps the domain model grow and evolve.

How would the recovery system use these patterns? We would seldom want to recklessly search a large system to find all of the associations. Not only would such a search take a large amount of computation time, it also would probably introduce a large number of false positive hits, thereby taking a lot of analyst time to sort out the results. Instead, we would prefer to be more selective and use our knowledge of programs, systems, and domains to focus the search. For example, in the C language we would expect to find the definition of the process table in some header file and so would narrow our initial search to those files. This search might find the chunk of code in Figure 10.

Given this structure as a starting point, the system uses the data object idiom that defines the substructure of a process table and recursively applies the search against the code structure in Figure 10, using the patterns from the classes of each of the subparts of a process table. (Actually, I have simplified this example by ignoring the intervening conceptual structure — the process table entry.) Figure 11 illustrates this recursive step, which binds the fields within the source code definition of the

```
process proctbl[MAXPROCS];          /* Process tbl array */
. . . .
. . . .
typedef struct procentry            /* Process table entry */
    {
    unsigned int savesp;            /* Saved sp register */
    unsigned int savess;            /* Saved ss register */
    unsigned int pspseg;            /* PSP seg addr this proc */
    unsigned int windno;            /* Window number this proc */
    unsigned int procstate;         /* Process state */
    char procname[MAXPNAME+1];      /* Process name */
    int pnum;                       /* Process number for this entry */
    . . . .

    } process;
```

Figure 10. Structure found via search of source code.

44

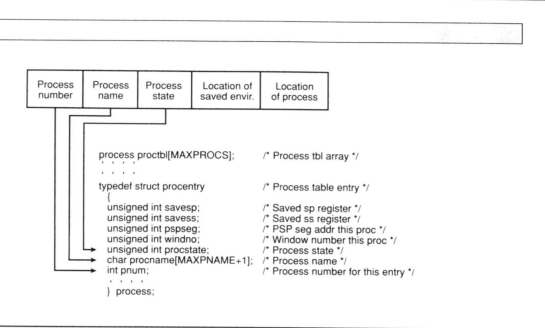

Process number	Process name	Process state	Location of saved envir.	Location of process

```
          process proctbl[MAXPROCS];        /* Process tbl array */

          typedef struct procentry          /* Process table entry */
          {
            unsigned int savesp;            /* Saved sp register */
            unsigned int savess;            /* Saved ss register */
            unsigned int pspseg;            /* PSP seg addr this proc */
            unsigned int windno;            /* Window number this proc */
            unsigned int procstate;         /* Process state */
            char procname[MAXPNAME+1];      /* Process name */
            int pnum;                       /* Process number for this entry */

          } process;
```

Figure 11. Bindings to substructures in source code.

process table to the instance records that define the expectations of those fields.

The recovered design in Figure 8 has now evolved into that in Figure 12, where the dashed lines show the bindings between abstractions and code. Note that the matching of idiom pattern to code is inexact, with some instances of the idiom unbound and some elements of the struct unexplained. We can typically expect an automated aide to produce only partial matches, leaving part of the interpretational work to the software engineer. Thus, the analyst will likely have to specialize (edit) the idiom further to reflect the specific case. However, the partial match provides enormous benefit by focusing the analysis and establishing a broad framework in which to perform the remaining interpretation. The partial match provides a starting point by identifying some of the substructures of the idiomatic form, making completion of the interpretation far simpler than starting from scratch.

So, for data structures in the source code, at least two kinds of information express the key idiomatic features of the source code. The linguistic idiom expresses the natural-language tokens (generalized into search patterns) that we expect to be associated with key data structures. The data object idioms express the substructure relationship within complex data structures. We can exploit structural idioms to discover design structures for the first time (in a top-down manner) as well as to verify associations with large-scale structures discovered earlier (as a bottom-up verification).

This pattern of linguistic and structural design idioms repeats itself when we examine what kinds of structures the domain model must contain to describe the expectations about module structure, dataflow plans, and so forth. For example, in the context of a Unix-like multitasking system, we would expect to find a process management module with routines for

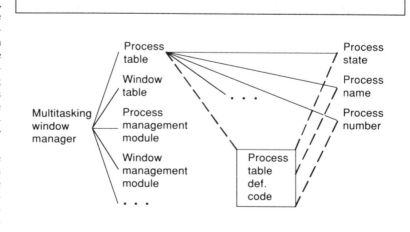

Figure 12. Pattern of instance records with some bindings to code.

creating a process, resuming a process, suspending a process, and so forth. Much as in the data structure idiom, these expectations form an initial framework that might fuzzily match some functions in the code. From here, the software engineer can read and analyze the code and then specialize the domain model patterns to fit the current case. Other artifacts such as dataflow schemas operate in a similar fashion.

Using idioms to guide the search and then act as the skeletal organizing structure for the recovered design offers two important benefits:

(1) The domain model idioms encode expectations as preformed queries, eliminating the need to constantly reenter these

query forms during program analysis.

(2) The system records the resulting design in terms of both informal linguistic abstractions and semiformal software engineering structures.

Desire prototype and current work

MCC has developed a prototype of a design recovery system called Desire Version 1.0. The system is intended to explore only that aspect of design recovery that does not depend on the domain model. Thus, it is an interim system designed to lay the foundation for the full Desire sys-

tem by providing a baseline of facilities to process the information explicitly found in source code.

Figure 13 shows Desire Version 1.0 in operation. The system consists of three major parts: a parser, a set of postprocessing functions, and the PlaneText hypertext system[4] as the presentation engine. The parser processes a set of C files for a given system and produces a set of parse trees. We anticipate the need to use much of the informal linguistic information encoded in variable names, comments, and the like, so the parser must take special care to preserve this information.

A set of postprocessors takes the parse trees as input and produces a dictionary containing information on functions, the

Related work

Commercial reverse engineering tools

A number of reverse engineering tools (closely related to reengineering tools) have appeared on the market recently. These tools solve part of the problem of recovering the design of an existing system. Examples are Cscope, cxref, Bachman/Data Analyst, and Meta's Design/2.0. While these tools find, present, and analyze information in the source code (or in the data dictionary in the case of the Bachman/Data Analyst), they do not reconstruct, capture, and express design abstractions that are not explicitly represented in the source code-related representations. Such design abstractions are a large part of what humans use to understand, modify, adapt, and otherwise deal with systems and programs. The need for and absence of such capabilities should indicate the direction in which these tools will likely evolve, and should be a mandate to push the technology in that direction.

We can loosely classify commercial reverse engineering tools (in the broadest sense of the term "reverse engineering") into the following categories:

- test coverage analyzers;
- debuggers and execution monitors;
- source-to-source translators;
- cross reference facilities;
- code reformatters, pretty printers, and restructurers;
- structure and metric analyzers;
- file comparators; and
- CASE-oriented reverse engineering (and reengineering) tools.

Since these tools are commercial, information about them is limited. Nevertheless, Horton[1] and Aranow[2] provide a short overview plus information on specific products and vendors. In addition, Sneed and Jandrasics[3] describe a prototypical CASE-oriented reverse engineering system.

Related research

In contrast to commercial reverse engineering tools, the tools in the research community come closer to our notion of design recovery. Both sets of tools focus most often on program understanding, but there is a subtle difference in the research goals. Most tools in the area of program understanding have focused on very small-scale problems to achieve precise and complete formal specifications of the source code. Further, they typically have not focused as much on informal information. In contrast, our approach sacrifices formal completeness and precision for scale. In the long run, these two approaches will likely be complementary rather than mutually exclusive, with each providing aspects missing in the other.

Several researchers have been working on the problem of understanding what a program is intended to do.[4-7] Some use information drawn largely from the programming language domain, such as Wills' recognizer.[7] Others incorporate more knowledge from the problem domain. In most cases, the scale of the target programs is quite small — tens or hundreds of lines of code. The most recent Programmer's Apprentice work deals with larger components but does not yet deal with large, industrial sized components.[5]

Most of this work depends on analysis of the low-level, formal details and, therefore, emphasizes a full and exact match of the structure for recognition. The computational load required by such an approach suggests that scaling up to industrial sizes will be quite difficult. People appear to be successful at program recognition because they can attend to a few key features and make tentative, plausible matches based on similarity rather than exactness. Further, most of the time, many of those few key features are informal. Of course, humans supplement such recognition with many other approaches for verification and detailed understanding, but the initial narrowing of attention based on informal, partial clues seems to be critical to handling scale without being overwhelmed by detail.

It seems likely that the understanding and recovery approaches can be productively merged. That is, an initial search strategy based on informal, partial clues, followed by files that contain them, the global data items defined, where they are defined, and where they are used. Informal information, such as that in the comments, is associated with the target program's function definitions and data item definitions. In addition, the postprocessors compute and store the various relationships between these items (such as calls, uses, and depends) in the dictionary.

Once this information is computed, another postprocessor computes a PlaneText web and invokes the PlaneText browser to exhibit the web. PlaneText computes various views that exhibit some relationships (such as calls) and suppresses others. Thus, if the user wants to see a call lattice or the relationship between data items and files, the system can compute each of these as a separate browser view.

The screen dump in Figure 13 suggests some of the prototype's functionality. The prototype provides a set of predefined Prolog queries for computing a variety of questions about the data in the dictionary. These queries include low-level questions such as "What is the set of functions that call function x?" as well as higher-level questions such as "Does any function defined in file A call any function defined in file B?" or "Compute the set of functions that appear to be utility functions." This set of queries is evolving to include a number of complex program analysis functions. Since the user can build on these queries, the question set can be tailored to any specific application domain.

In Figure 13, the user has used one of the predefined Prolog queries to ask for all functions that refer to a piece of data named call_to_times. The browser responds by highlighting all of the functions found by the query. The user inspects the visual design browser and identifies the name of the file (pow2.c) that contains the definition of one of these functions (power). The user then opens a window on that file (lower left-hand corner) and uses Plane-Text's regular expression-based search to find the location of the variable calls_to_times. Of course, as we determine which sequences in the prototype are most useful, we will replace them with a single user command.

the more detailed kind of analysis used in the Programmer's Apprentice, would provide a powerful and scaleable approach to automating more of the program comprehension process. This appears to be the most successful long-term direction for this kind of research.

Other work is more loosely related but nevertheless shares some ideas with our work. Perhaps the overriding theme of this work is the integration of CASE, hypertext (or hypermedia), and knowledge-based technologies. In fact, some of our own work that contributed to our current design-recovery notions (my large-scale reuse[8] and Lubars' Rose[9] system) falls in this class, although the hypertext aspect is largely absent in Rose. The work of Ambras and O'Day[10] and Bigelow[11] shares this theme to a greater or lesser extent, with Bigelow emphasizing hypertext and Ambras and O'Day emphasizing knowledge-based representations. Most of the work in this category is, in principle, able to handle large-scale information bases.

The work by Arango et al.[12] resembles the research reported in the current article. These researchers have solved the problem of scaling up but are not creating the kind of high-level, informal conceptual abstractions that Desire focuses on. Of course, creating such abstractions was not particularly important to Arango et al. because they wanted to port their target program (Draco,[13] in this case) completely automatically from one computing environment to another. From this point of view, their system is more similar to source-to-source translation and restructuring systems than reverse engineering systems of the variety I have discussed.

Abstractly, Arango et al. are also trying to recover designs, but some differences exist between their focus and ours. Their design recovery model focuses more on the structure of the transformations and the operations on transformations than it does on the structure of and operations on the design entities themselves. Our focus is the reverse of this. Further, and perhaps more importantly, their model makes no use of informal information because it is based on a commitment to complete automation. On the other hand, because our model strongly involves people in the design recovery process, we must make heavy use of informal information to help human understanding.

References

1. L. Horton, "Tools are an Alternative to 'Playing Computer'," *Software Magazine*, Jan. 1988, pp 58-67.

2. E. Aranow, "CASE for Existing Systems: Taking Yesterday's Systems into Tomorrow," *System Builder*, Oct./Nov. 1988, pp. 20-29.

3. H.M. Sneed and G. Jandrasics, "Inverse Transformation of Software from Code to Specification," *Proc. Conf. Software Maintenance*, CS Press, Los Alamitos, Calif., Order No. 879, 1988, pp. 102-109.

4. S. Letovsky, "Cognitive Processes in Program Comprehension," *Systems and Software*, No. 7, 1987, pp. 325-339.

5. C. Rich and R. Waters, "The Programmer's Apprentice: A Research Overview," *Computer*, Vol. 21, No. 11, Nov. 1988, pp. 10-25.

6. E. Soloway and W.L. Johnson, "Proust: Knowledge-Based Program Understanding," *IEEE Trans. Software Engineering*, Vol. SE-11, No. 3, Mar. 1985, pp. 267-275.

7. L.M. Wills, "Automated Program Recognition," Tech. Report 904, MIT AI Laboratory, Feb. 1987.

8. T.J. Biggerstaff, "Hypermedia as a Tool to Aid Large-Scale Reuse," Tech. Report, STP-202-87, MCC, 1987, also in *Workshop on Software Reuse*, Rocky Mountain Institute of Software Engineering, Boulder, Col., Oct. 1987.

9. M.D. Lubars, "Wide-Spectrum Support for Software Reusability," Tech. Report, STP-276-87, MCC, 1987, also in *Workshop on Software Reuse*, Rocky Mountain Institute of Software Engineering, Boulder, Col., Oct. 1987.

10. J. Ambras and V. O'Day, "MicroScope: A Knowledge-Based Programming Environment," *IEEE Software*, Vol. 5, No. 3, May, 1988, pp. 50-58.

11. J. Bigelow, "Hypertext and CASE," *IEEE Software*, Vol. 21, No. 3, Mar. 1988, pp. 23-27.

12. G. Arango et al., "Maintenance and Porting of Software by Design Recovery," *Proc. Conf. Software Maintenance*, CS Press, Los Alamitos, Calif., Order No. 648, 1985, pp. 42-49.

13. J.M. Neighbors, "Draco: A Method for Engineering Reusable Software Systems," in *Software Reusability*, T.J. Biggerstaff and A. Perlis, eds., Addison-Wesley, 1989.

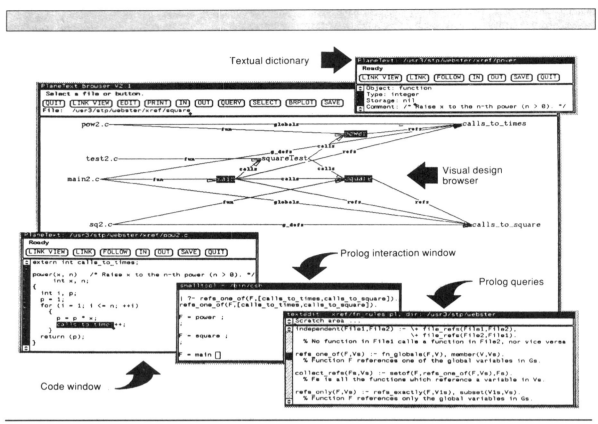

Figure 13. First design recovery prototype: Desire Version 1.0.

Desire Version 1.0 also analyzes the source code and creates a graphical diagram describing its interpretation of the program's module structure. Based on the user's request, this analysis can variously depend on the program's cohesion, its data coupling, and so forth.

As a separate research task, we have used PlaneText[4] to sketch out a domain model drawn from the area of multitasking window systems.[2] This research task uses PlaneText as a simple design aid, and we have not yet integrated the domain model with the Desire Version 1.0 prototype. To do so, we are converting this hypertext design of the domain model into a set of CLOS classes that are the active or implementation form of the domain model. This model bears a strong relationship to the semantic models created with frame languages like KL-One. The primary difference is that the CLOS classes possess more specialized, local behavior. The classes capture

- the *isa* or superclass/subclass lattice of the entities in the domain (e.g., a process-table is a subclass of table);
- the informal patterns for expressing the entities in the domain (e.g., a process might have a variety of abbreviations and synonyms);
- the slots that are to contain the expected substructure of a concept instance (e.g., a queue will have a queue-entry slot);
- restrictions on the slots that constrain what values the slot can have (e.g., a restriction on the class of the value in the slot); and
- methods that provide the entity's behavior (e.g., displaying the concept, searching for possible instances, and binding slots to instances).

A fair amount of work is now aimed at determining what the interface should look like and how it should behave. Specifically, we are working on methods to visually relate the recovered abstract concepts to the portions of the program to which they refer.

More recently, we have begun a series of experiments to refine our notions of search strategies for informal information and to allow fuzzy matches of expectations. We believe that, in addition to the simple search mechanisms described earlier, we will be able to apply ideas from connectionist research[5] to perform some of the fuzzy matches. These searches take advantage of the domain model's structure to allow associative searches that return items based on their indirect associations with the features sought. This part of the research is in an early prototyping stage. □

48

COMPUTER

Acknowledgments

I gratefully acknowledge the work of Keith Andren, Gerry Barksdale, Glenn Bruns, Josiah Hoskins, Peter Marks, Bharat Mitbander, Don Petersen, Dallas Webster, and Mahesh Zarule, who have cast portions of these ideas into working prototypes.

References

1. J. Conklin and M. Begeman, "The Right Tool for the Job," *Byte*, Vol. 13, No. 10, Oct. 1988, pp. 255-266.

2. T.J. Biggerstaff, *Systems Software Tools*, Prentice Hall, 1986.

3. M.D. Lubars, "Wide-Spectrum Support for Software Reusability," Tech. Report, STP-276-87, MCC, 1987, also in *Workshop on Software Reuse*, Rocky Mountain Institute of Software Engineering, Boulder, Col., Oct. 1987.

4. E. Gullichsen et al., "The PlaneTextBook," Tech. Report STP-333-86, MCC, 1986, republished as nonconfidential report STP-206-88, MCC, 1988.

5. J.A. Feldman et al., "Computing with Structured Connectionist Networks," *Comm. ACM*, Vol. 31, No. 2, Feb. 1988.

Ted J. Biggerstaff joined MCC in 1985 as director of design information. He is directing research in design reusability and design recovery. His research interests include software engineering, knowledge-based approaches to reusability and specification, program generation techniques, program development tools, and natural-language processing.

He is the author of *Systems Software Tools* (Prentice Hall, 1986) and coeditor (with Alan Perlis) of a two-volume book titled *Software Reusability* (Addison-Wesley/ACM, 1989) and the September 1984 special issue of the *IEEE Transactions on Software Engineering* that focused on reusability. He also organized one of the first large-scale workshops on reusability (Newport, R.I., 1983).

Biggerstaff received a Boeing Fellowship in 1974. He received the BA degree in physics from the University of Nebraska in 1964, and the MS and PhD degrees in computer science from the University of Washington, Seattle, in 1971 and 1976, respectively. He is a member of ACM, the IEEE Computer Society, and AAAI.

Readers can contact Biggerstaff at Microelectronics and Technology Corporation, 9390 Research Blvd., Kaleido Building II, Austin, TX 78759.

82

Recognizing a Program's Design: A Graph-Parsing Approach

Charles Rich and *Linda M. Wills*, Massachusetts Institute of Technology

Programmers tend to use the same structures over and over. By recognizing these clichés, this prototype can reconstruct a program's design and generate documentation automatically.

An experienced programmer can often reconstruct much of the hierarchy of a program's design by recognizing commonly used data structures and algorithms and knowing how they typically implement higher level abstractions. We call these commonly used programming structures *clichés*. Examples of algorithmic clichés are list enumerations, binary searches, and successive-approximation loops. Examples of data-structure clichés are sorted lists, balanced binary trees, and hash tables.

Psychological experiments[1] have shown that programmers use clichés heavily in many programming tasks. Instead of reasoning from first principles, programmers — like other problem solvers — tend to rely on their experience as much as possible.

In general, a cliché contains both fixed and varying parts. For example, every binary search must include computations to apply the search predicate and divide the remaining search space in half, but the specific search predicate will vary. A cliché may also include constraints that restrict the varying parts. For example, the operation that computes the next approximation in a successive-approximation loop must reduce the error term.

We have built a prototype, the Recognizer, that automatically finds all occurrences of a given set of clichés in a program and builds a hierarchical description of the program in terms of the clichés it finds. So far we have demonstrated the Recognizer only on small Common Lisp programs, but the underlying technology is language-independent.

There are practical and theoretical reasons to automate cliché recognition. From a practical standpoint, automated cliché recognition will ease many software-engineering tasks, including maintenance, documentation, enhancement, optimization, and debugging. From a theoretical standpoint, automated cliché recognition is an ideal problem for studying how to represent and use programming knowledge and experience.

IEEE Software

Difficulties

Our goal is not to mimic the human *process* of cliché recognition. Instead, we want to use human experiential knowledge in the form of clichés to achieve a similar result. Five characteristics of clichés make this difficult:

• Syntactic variation: A programmer can achieve the same net flow of data and control many ways.

• Noncontiguousness: A cliché's parts can be scattered through the program text; they do not necessarily appear in adjacent lines or expressions.

• Implementation variation: An abstraction can be implemented many ways. For example, a hash table's buckets may or may not be sorted.

• Overlapping implementations: Program optimization often merges the implementations of two or more distinct abstractions. Therefore, portions of a program may be part of more than one cliché.

• Unrecognizable code: Not every program is constructed completely of clichés. The recognition system must be able to ignore idiosyncratic code.

Example

How the Recognizer works can be demonstrated by its performance on a simple program that retrieves entries from a hash table, shown in Figure 1a. This program uses three clichés:

• hash table, a data-structure cliché typically used to implement associative retrieval,

• cdr enumeration, the pattern of Car, Cdr, and Null typically used in Lisp to visit each element of a list, and

• linear search, an algorithmic cliché that applies a predicate to a sequence of elements until an element is found that satisfies the predicate, or until there are no more elements.

One way the Recognizer demonstrates

its recognition of the design of the program in Figure 1a is by producing the documentation shown in Figure 1b. The resulting documentation, although stilted, does describe the important design decisions in the program and can help a programmer locate relevant objects in the code (via the identifiers).

One potential benefit of automated cliché recognition is to use such automatically produced documentation to maintain poorly documented or undocumented programs. Automatically produced documentation can be updated whenever the source code changes, solving the pernicious problem of misleading, out-of-date documentation.

Representation shift

The key to the Recognizer's approach is a representation shift: Instead of looking for clichés directly in the source code, the Recognizer first translates the program into a language-independent, graphical representation called the Plan Calculus. The Plan Calculus is a program representation shared by all components of the Programmer's Apprentice,[2-3] an intelligent programming system being developed at the Massachusetts Institute of Technology.

The diagram of the Recognizer architecture in Figure 2 shows the path of the input program in Figure 1a to the documentation in Figure 1b. The program is

```
(DEFUN TABLE-LOOKUP (TABLE KEY)
  (LET ((BUCKET (AREF TABLE (HASH KEY TABLE)))))
    (LOOP
      (IF (NULL BUCKET) (RETURN NIL))
      (LET ((ENTRY (CAR BUCKET)))
       (IF (EQUAL (KEY ENTRY) KEY) (RETURN ENTRY)))
      (SETQ BUCKET (CDR BUCKET)))))
```

(a)

```
TABLE-LOOKUP is an associative retrieval operation.
   If there is an element of the set TABLE with key KEY,
   then that element is returned; otherwise NIL.
   The key function is KEY.
The set TABLE is implemented as a hash table.
   The hashing function is HASH.
A bucket BUCKET of the hash table TABLE is implemented
as a list.
   The elements of the list BUCKET are enumerated.
   Linear search is used to find the first element of the
   list BUCKET whose key is equal to KEY.
```

(b)

Figure 1. (a) The Recognizer, given the Common Lisp program (and an appropriate cliché library) **(b)** automatically produces documentation. Uppercased words in the documentation indicate relevant identifiers in the program.

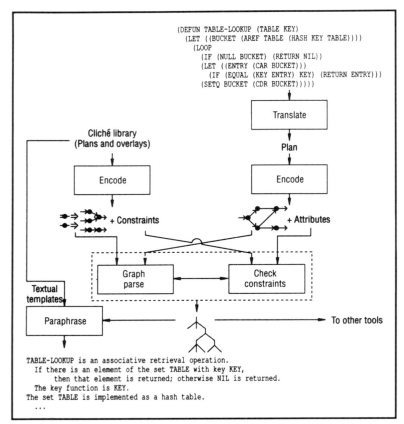

Figure 2. Recognizer architecture. Only the module that translates source code into the Plan Calculus is language-dependent. As part of the Programmer's Apprentice, translators have been written for subsets of Lisp, Fortran, Cobol, and Ada.

first translated into the Plan Calculus and then encoded as a flow graph, as shown in the top right. The flow graph is then parsed with the grammar extracted from the cliché library to produce a design tree. Figure 3 shows the design tree produced

by the Recognizer for the program in Figure 1a.

The system uses this design tree to generate documentation by combining textual templates associated with the recognized clichés, filling in slots with

identifiers taken from the program.

Design trees are the key output of the Recognizer because they can be input to many other tools. For example, the Programmer's Apprentice will include editors, debuggers, optimizers, and other tools that take advantage of design trees to provide more intelligent assistance than purely code-based tools. The Recognizer can be used to produce design trees for existing programs so these tools can be applied.

Plan Calculus. Translating programs into the Plan Calculus helps the Recognizer overcome the difficulties of syntactic variation and noncontiguousness by abstracting away from the details of algorithms that depend only on their expression in code. The Plan Calculus combines the representation properties of flowcharts, dataflow schemas, and abstract data types. Essentially, a *plan* is a hierarchical graph structure composed of boxes, which denote operations and tests, and arrows, which denote control flow and dataflow.

Figure 4a shows two plans in the graphical notation we use for the Plan Calculus. On the left is the plan for an implementation, called hash-table-retrieve, which is a clichéd combination of operations to retrieve an entry from a hash table. It includes three operations: hash, which computes the index of the table that corresponds to the input key, select, which selects the indexed bucket of the table, and retrieve, which applies associative retrieval to the set of entries in the bucket. The solid arrows indicate dataflow constraints between these operations. Because this plan has no conditional structure, there is no control flow, which would be indicated by crosshatch arrows.

On the right side of Figure 4a is the specification for an operation called set-retrieve. When it succeeds, its output is an element of the set whose key is equal to the input key; if there is no such element, the operation fails. We specify preconditions and postconditions such as these in a separate logical language.

Cliché library. In the Programmer's Apprentice, both clichés and individual programs are represented as plans. The rela-

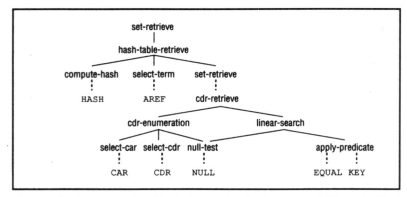

Figure 3. Design tree produced by the Recognizer for the program in Figure 1a. Each nonterminal in the tree is the name of a cliché that has been recognized in the program. The dashed lines at the tree's fringe are links to identifiers in the source code to facilitate documentation generation.

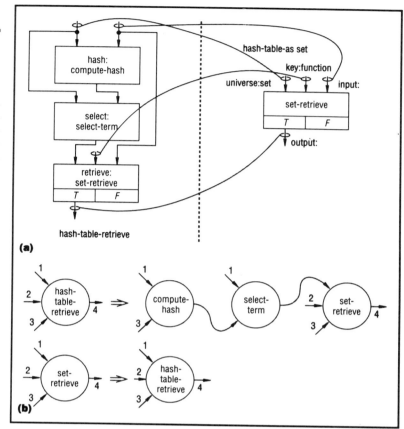

Figure 4. (a) Representation in the Plan Calculus of how associative retrieval can be implemented using a hash table. This overlay is part of the cliché library used to recognize the program in Figure 1a. **(b)** Part of the encoding of the overlay into graph grammar rules (the constraints are not shown).

tionship between a specification cliché and an implementation cliché is represented as an *overlay*. An overlay is composed of two plans and a set of correspondences between their parts, as Figure 4a shows. (Formally, an overlay defines a mapping from instances of one plan to instances of another.)

For example, the overlay in Figure 4a represents the relationship between the set-retrieve specification and the hash-table-retrieve implementation.

The hooked lines crossing the dividing line denote *correspondences*. The set is implemented as a hash table. The input to the hash computation is the input key. The key function of the bucket retrieval is the key function of the overall retrieval. The output of the bucket retrieval is the output of the overall retrieval.

A cliché library may contain different overlays involving the same plans, each one representing a different way to abstract the same implementation or a different way to implement the same specification.

In the Programmer's Apprentice, overlays are used both for program analysis (cliché recognition) and synthesis (design). In program analysis, occurrences of the implementation on the left side of an overlay are replaced by occurrences of the specification on the right; in program synthesis, the opposite happens.

We have compiled an initial library of several hundred plans and overlays in the area of basic programming techniques, such as manipulating arrays, vectors, lists, and sets. About a dozen of these are used to produce the documentation in Figure 1b from the program in Figure 1a.

Graph parsing. Essentially, a plan is a directed graph, and cliché recognition identifies subgraphs and replaces them with more abstract operations. It is therefore natural to view cliché recognition as a graph-parsing problem. Indeed, the heart of the Recognizer is a flow-graph parser developed by Daniel Brotsky. The Recognizer's design trees are derivation trees produced by this parser, as described in the box on p. 88.

To encode a plan as a flow graph, the Recognizer turns the plan's boxes into flow-graph nodes and the plan's dataflow arrows into flow-graph edges. All other information in a plan, such as control flow, preconditions, and postconditions, is encoded in flow-graph attributes. (The resulting graphs are acyclic because the Plan Calculus models iteration by tail-recursion.)

The overlays in the cliché library are similarly encoded as an attribute-graph grammar, a straightforward generalization of attribute-string grammars.

Each plan definition in the library gives rise to a grammar rule. The top rule in Figure 4b encodes the hash-table-retrieve plan in Figure 4a. The left side of this rule is a node with the plan name as its type; the right side of the rule encodes the body of the plan as a flow graph. When the Recognizer uses this rule to parse the flow graph of an input program, it recognizes the hash-table-retrieve cliché.

Each overlay in the cliché library gives rise to a simple grammar rule with one node on each side. The bottom rule in Figure 4b encodes the overlay in Figure 4a. The left side of the grammar rule encodes the right side of the overlay; the right side of the grammar rule encodes the left side of the overlay. The mapping between input and output ports on either side of the grammar rule is computed from the overlay's correspondences. When the Recognizer uses this rule to parse the flow graph of an input program, it reconstructs a programmer's decision to implement set-retrieve by hash-table-retrieve.

We encode the plan for each side of an overlay as a separate grammar rule (instead of a single rule for each overlay) for two reasons. First, there may be plans in the library that are not used in any overlay. Second, some overlays have plans on both sides, while a grammar rule must have a single node on the left side. (The Recognizer handles such overlays by interleaving expansion steps with reduction steps during the parsing process, as detailed by Wills.[4])

86

```
(DEFUN R (L X &AUX B)
  (SETQ B (AREF L (H X L)))
  (PROG (E)
LP (WHEN (NULL B) (RETURN NIL))
   (SETQ E (CAR B))
   (COND ((EQUAL (K E) X) (RETURN E))
         (T (SETQ B (CDR B)))
            (GO LP)))))
```

(a)

```
R is an associative retrieval operation.
  If there is an element of the set L with key X,
    then that element is returned; otherwise NIL.
  The key function is K.
The set L is implemented as a hash table.
  The hashing function is H.
A bucket B of the hash table L is implemented as a list.
  The elements of the list B are enumerated.
  Linear search is used to find the first element of the
    list B whose key is equal to X.
```

(b)

Figure 5. (a) A syntactic variation of the program in Figure 1a and **(b)** the corresponding documentation produced by the Recognizer. The documentation is identical to Figure 1b, except for the names of the identifiers.

```
(DEFUN TABLE-LOOKUP (TABLE KEY)
  (LET ((BUCKET (AREF TABLE (HASH KEY TABLE))))
    (LOOP
      (IF (NULL BUCKET) (RETURN NIL))
      (LET* ((ENTRY (CAR BUCKET)))
            ((Y (KEY ENTRY))))
        (COND ((STRING> Y KEY) (RETURN NIL))
              ((EQUAL Y KEY) (RETURN ENTRY)))
      (SETQ BUCKET (CDR BUCKET)))))
```

(a)

```
TABLE-LOOKUP is an associative retrieval operation.
  If there is an element of the set TABLE with key KEY,
    then that element is returned; otherwise NIL.
  The key function is KEY.
The set TABLE is implemented as a hash table.
  The hashing function is HASH.
A bucket BUCKET of the hash table TABLE is implemented
as a sorted list.
  The elements of the sorted list BUCKET are enumerated.
  The iteration is terminated when an element of the sorted
    list BUCKET is found whose key Y is greater than KEY.
  Linear search is used to find the first element of the
    sorted list BUCKET whose key Y is equal to KEY.
  The sorting relation on keys is STRING>.
```

(b)

Figure 6. (a) An implementation variation of the program in Figure 1a, in which the buckets of the hash table are sorted lists. **(b)** The first seven lines of the documentation are the same as in Figure 1b.

Difficulties revisited

The Recognizer overcomes the five difficulties in automating cliché recognition.

Syntactic variation. Figure 5 shows a table-lookup program that is very different from the one in Figure 1a. Among the differences are the variable names (Table and *L*), control primitives (Loop and Prog), and the syntactic nesting. However, both programs translate into the same plan, so the Recognizer produces an identical design tree (the one in Figure 4) and identical documentation (except identifiers).

This example demonstrates that the Recognizer identifies clichés using only structural information such as control flow, dataflow, and primitive operation types. It does not use any information in the names of variables or procedures. This is both a strength and a limitation.

Noncontiguousness. The Plan Calculus addresses the noncontiguousness problem by explicitly representing dataflow and control flow in programs. For example, the Car, Cdr, and Null steps of the cdr-enumeration cliché are adjacent in the dataflow graph for the program in Figure 1a, even though they are separated by unrelated expressions in the code.

Implementation variation. Figure 6 illustrates the Recognizer's ability to deal with implementation variation. The program in Figure 6a is similar to the program in Figure 1a, except that the buckets of the hash table have been implemented as *sorted* lists. Given the same grammar used in Figure 1, but with the addition of rules that describe the implementation of set-retrieve on sorted lists, the Recognizer produces a design tree (not shown here) that has the same top three levels as Figure 2, but differs in the layers below.

Overlapping implementations. Figures 7 and 8 illustrate the Recognizer's ability to deal with overlapping implementations. The grammar for this example includes rules to find the minimum element of a list (list-min) by enumerating the elements and accumulating the minimum element thus far; it also includes

```
(DEFUN MAX-MIN (L)
  (VALUES (LIST-MAX L) (LIST-MIN L))))

(DEFUN LIST-MAX (L)
  (LET ((MAX MOST-NEGATIVE-FIXNUM))
    (LOOP
      (IF (NULL L) (RETURN MAX))
      (LET ((N (CAR L)))
        (IF (> N MAX) (SETQ MAX N)))
      (SETQ L (CDR L)))))))

(DEFUN LIST-MIN (L)
  (LET ((MIN MOST-POSITIVE-FIXNUM))
    (LOOP
      (IF (NULL L) (RETURN MIN))
      (LET ((N (CAR L)))
        (IF (< N MIN) (SETQ MIN N)))
      (SETQ L (CDR L)))))))
```

Figure 7. An unoptimized Common Lisp program that computes the maximum and minimum elements of a nonempty list of integers.

similar rules to find the maximum element of a list (list-max).

The program in Figure 7 — a simple, inefficient program to compute a list's maximum and minimum elements — could be synthesized straightforwardly from the cliché library by implementing the list-max and list-min specifications separately. (It is inefficient because it enumerates the list twice.)

The optimized version of this program in Figure 8 enumerates the list only once, creating an overlap between the list-max and list-min implementations. The design tree generated for this program shows the overlap in the cdr-enumeration nonterminal, which is shared by the two subtrees of list-max and list-min. In effect, the Recognizer has undone the optimization.

Unrecognizable code. The processing time for Brotsky's parsing algorithm is polynomial in the size of the input and the grammar. This means that if we could guarantee that the input graph can always be derived from the grammar, cliché recognition could be performed very efficiently. Of course, most programs are only partially constructed of clichés, so we extended Brotsky's algorithm in two ways to facilitate partial recognition. Because our extensions amount to computing subgraph isomorphism, the resulting algorithm has exponential worst-case performance.

Our first extension lets the parser ignore indeterminate amounts of unparsable leading and trailing input, so it can recognize clichés in the midst of unrecognizable code. The parser ignores unparsable leading input by starting its read head not only at the leftmost edge of the input flow graph but at every possible intermediate position in the flow graph. It ignores unparsable trailing input simply by allowing parses to complete before the input flow graph is totally scanned.

Our second extension lets the parser recognize low-level clichés, even if it can't reconstruct the higher level design that puts them together. It does this by considering every nonterminal node in the grammar as a possible starting type for a derivation. The design tree in Figure 8 illustrates partial recognition: Because the cliché library contains no single specifica-

tion for computing both list-max and list-min, the design tree does not have a single root. In general, a design tree with multiple roots indicates either that the program's top level is idiosyncratic or that the relevant cliché is not in the library. In this example, it seems reasonable that the library does not include such trivial specification combinations.

For the Recognizer to be a practical maintenance aid, it must be improved and extended several ways.

Extensions. The Recognizer was developed in parallel with — actually, slightly behind — the Plan Calculus. The Recognizer does not now handle data plans or data overlays (facilities in the Plan Calcu-

```
(DEFUN MAX-MIN (L)
  (LET ((MAX MOST-NEGATIVE-FIXNUM)
        (MIN MOST-POSITIVE-FIXNUM))
    (LOOP
      (IF (NULL L) (RETURN (VALUES MAX MIN)))
      (LET ((N (CAR L)))
        (IF (> N MAX) (SETQ MAX N))
        (IF (< N MIN) (SETQ MIN N)))
      (SETQ L (CDR L))))))
```

(a)

(b)

Figure 8. (a) An optimized version of program in Figure 7 and **(b)** design tree produced by the Recognizer. Note the shared occurrence of the cdr-enumeration cliché.

Flow graphs and grammars

A flow graph is a labeled, directed, acyclic graph in which edges connect a node's input and output ports. Node labels identify node types; each node type has a fixed number of input and output ports. Fan-in and fan-out are allowed.

A flow graph is derived from a context-free flow-graph grammar in much the same way a string is derived from a context-free string grammar. Figure A shows a context-free flow-graph grammar, which is a set of rewrite rules, each specifying how a node in a graph may be replaced by a subgraph. The left side of each rule is a single nonterminal node; the right side is a graph that may contain both terminal and nonterminal nodes.

Unlike string grammars, each rule in a flow-graph grammar specifies a mapping (shown by numbers) between the unconnected input and output ports on the left side and unconnected input and output ports on the right side. This mapping determines how the subgraph is connected to the surrounding nodes when it replaces a nonterminal node in a derivation. (For more information on graph grammars in general, see the accounts edited by Hartmut Ehrig.[1])

As with string grammars, it is convenient to abstract a graph derivation sequence as a tree that shows how each nonterminal is expanded, as Figure B shows.

Flow-graph grammars are a natural formalism for encoding various kinds of engineering diagrams, such as electrical circuits or dataflow. Furthermore, polynomial-time algorithms have been implemented for parsing flow graphs based on generalizations of existing string parsing algorithms.[2,3]

References

1. "Graph-Grammars and Their Application to Computer Science," *Lecture Notes In Computer Science Series, Vol. 291*, H. Ehrig et al., eds., Springer-Verlag, New York, Dec. 1986.
2. D.C. Brotsky, "An Algorithm for Parsing Flow Graphs," Tech. Report 704, Artificial Intelligence Lab., Massachusetts Inst. of Technology, Cambridge, Mass., 1984.
3. R. Lutz, Chart Parsing of Flow Graphs, *Proc. 11th Int'l Joint Conf. Artificial Intelligence*, Morgan Kaufman, Los Altos, Calif., 1989, pp. 116-121.

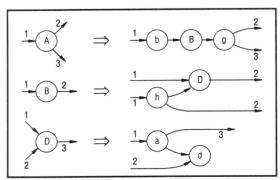

Figure A. A flow-graph grammar.

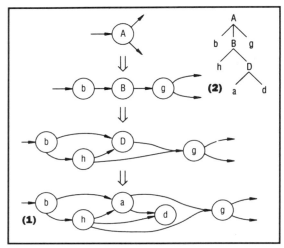

Figure B. (1) A derivation sequence; **(2)** a derivation tree.

lus for language-independent modeling of data structures and data abstraction). Also, the Recognizer's handling of destructive operations (such as modifying an array) is inadequate.

These deficiencies should be relatively easy to correct. We also plan to connect the Recognizer to a new logical reasoning system, developed as part of the Programmer's Apprentice, so it can reason more powerfully about grammar attributes.

Limitations. It is already clear from our experiments with small programs that the exhaustive, purely structural approach used by the Recognizer will not directly scale up to programs of commercial size and complexity: It is too expensive to search for all possible derivations of the input graph from the cliché library.

Other systems use heuristics to prune multiple analyses. For example, Lewis Johnson's Proust[5] pursues the cliché with the greatest number of currently recognized parts. In general, the use of heuristics to prune the search for clichés can lead to missing useful ways of understanding the input program.

Hybrid approach. Another possible way to control the search for clichés is to use the existing documentation, such as comments and mnemonic variable and procedure identifiers. The Recognizer does not now use this information because it is often incomplete and inaccurate. However, this kind of documentation could provide an important independent source of expectations about a program's purpose and design. The Recognizer could then confirm, amend, and complete these expectations by checking them against the code.

Other recognition systems are given a third input, in addition to a program and a cliché library, in the form of a specification (F.J. Lukey's Pudsey[6]), a set of goals (Proust), or a model program that performs the same task (William Murray's Talus[7]). We envisage a hybrid approach to cliché recognition that combines two complementary processes: documentation- and/or specification-driven (top-down) and code-driven (bottom-up). The heuristic top-down process will use documentation or user input to guide the code-driven process by generating expectations. The algorithmic bottom-up process will fill in the gaps in the documentation and verify or reject the expectations.

To design a hybrid recognition system, we first need to conduct additional theoretical and empirical analyses of the complexity of the Recognizer. We are trying to apply the Recognizer to programs at least 10 times larger than the examples in this article.

Learning clichés. One of our long-range goals is to explore how the Recognizer can help automate the task of knowledge acquisition in the Programmer's Apprentice. In particular, we are interested in how the system might automatically learn new clichés.

One idea is to look at programs that use some unfamiliar parts to implement familiar specifications. First, the Recognizer would identify what specifications are implemented by familiar parts of the program. Then, given a top-level specification, it should be possible to identify some lower level specifications that are not accounted for by the recognized program parts. A learning procedure could then reasonably hypothesize that the unrecognizable part of the program is a new cliché for implementing the remaining specifications. Robert Hall has demonstrated a similar learning scheme in the domains of digital circuits and mechanical gears.[8]   ❖

Acknowledgments

We thank Elliot Chikofsky, Richard Waters, Dilip Soni, Howard Reubenstein, Yang Meng Tan, and Scott Wills for their suggestions to improve this article.

Support for this work has been provided in part by the National Science Foundation under grant IRI-8616644, the Defense Advanced Research Projects Agency under Naval Research contract N00014-88-K-0487, IBM, Nynex, and Siemens. The views and conclusions in this article are those of the authors and should not be interpreted as representing the policies, expressed or implied, of these organizations.

References

1. E. Soloway and K. Ehrlich, "Empirical Studies of Programming Knowledge," *IEEE Trans. Software Eng.*, Sept. 1984, pp. 595-609.

2. C. Rich and R.C. Waters, "The Programmer's Apprentice: A Research Overview," *Computer*, Nov. 1988, pp. 10-25.

3. C. Rich and R.C. Waters, *The Programmer's Apprentice*, Addison-Wesley, Reading, Mass., to appear, 1990.

4. L.M. Wills, "Automated Program Recognition: A Feasibility Demonstration," *Artificial Intelligence*, 1990, to appear.

5. W.L. Johnson, *Intention-Based Diagnosis of Novice Programming Errors*, Morgan Kaufmann, Los Altos, Calif., 1986.

6. F.J. Lukey, "Understanding and Debugging Programs," *Int'l J. Man-Machine Studies*, 1980, pp. 189-202.

7. W.R. Murray, "Heuristic and Formal Methods in Automatic Program Debugging," *Proc. Ninth Int't Joint Conf. Artificial Intelligence*, Morgan Kaufman, Los Altos, Calif., 1985, pp. 15-19.

8. R.J. Hall, "Learning by Failing to Explain: Using Partial Explanations to Learn in Incomplete or Intractable Domains," *Machine Learning*, Jan. 1988, pp. 45-77.

Charles Rich is a principal research scientist at the Artificial Intelligence Laboratory of the Massachusetts Institute of Technology. He codirects the Programmer's Apprentice project, which includes the work described in this article. His research interests are knowledge representation and the application of artificial intelligence to engineering problem solving, especially in software engineering.

Rich received a BS in engineering science from the University of Toronto and an MS and PhD in artificial intelligence from MIT. He is a member of ACM, AAAI, and the IEEE Computer Society.

Linda Wills is a PhD candidate at the Artificial Intelligence Laboratory of MIT and a member of the Programmer's Apprentice project. Wills's primary research interest is program understanding. Other interests include intelligent tutoring systems, machine vision, and concurrent computing.

Wills received a BS and MS in computer science from MIT. She is a member of ACM and AAAI.

Address questions about this article to the authors at Artificial Intelligence Laboratory, Massachusetts Institute of Technology, 545 Technology Sq., Cambridge, MA 02139.

SOFTWARE MAINTENANCE: RESEARCH AND PRACTICE, VOL. 3, 145–162 (1991)   145

Creating Specifications from Code: Reverse-engineering Techniques

P. T. BREUER AND K. LANO

Oxford University Computer Laboratory, Programming Research Group, 11 Keble Road, Oxford, U.K.

SUMMARY

Reverse-engineering application codes back to the design and specification stage may entail the recreation of lost information for an application, or the extraction of new information.

We describe techniques which produce *abstractions* in object-oriented and functional notations, thus aiding the comprehension of the essential structure and operations of the application, and providing formal design information which may make the code much more maintainable and certainly more respectable.

The two types of application considered here are (1) data processing applications written in COBOL — of primary importance owing to their predominance in present computing practice — and (2) scientific applications written in FORTRAN. These two require somewhat different abstraction approaches.

KEY WORDS Reverse-engineering Interactive program comprehension Object-oriented specifications Specification normal forms

1. INTRODUCTION

The Programming Research Group at Oxford University is participating in the ESPRIT II project REDO[1] of the 'Maintenance, validation and documentation of software systems'. As part of this project, we have begun to develop automated techniques which can reverse-engineer FORTRAN and COBOL application codes back to the design and specification stage. By agreed convention here, *reverse-engineering* means going all the way back to the design stage from the source code, whereas *inverse-engineering* means going back only as far as the specification. These activities should be distinguished from *de-compilation*, which generally proceeds from machine code (or assembler language) to FORTRAN or COBOL (Ward, 1989). The difference is that these techniques succeed

---

[1] Project no. 2487. Collaborating partners: Lloyd's Register of Shipping (UK), Durham University (UK), Oxford University (UK) and Limerick University (Ire); Centrisa (Sp), CTC (Gr), ITS (Sp), Grumman (Ger), Marconi (UK); Electricité de France (Fr), Delft Hydraulics (Nth).

in putting back the high-level information which is essential to proper maintainability, and de-compilation does not do this. Moreover, because the output of the reverse-engineering process is in a formal notation, the code becomes supported by a formal description which may have been previously lacking. What the formalisms aim to express is the *program functionality*.

1.1. Program functionality

Although many commercial packages generate great reams of documentation and information about the data structures and control flow of a program from the source code or object code, it is the true *functionality* of the code which is the real interest of both clients and maintainers, and this is harder to uncover. We have, however, made considerable progress with both automatic and interactive methods which do just that.

Normally, a maintainer involved in reverse-engineering activities may get some guide to the functionality of a strange application by examining the inputs and outputs of sub-parts, and relating these to the data structure diagrams (JSD, SSADM, etc.) generated for the (in COBOL jargon) *data division* of the application. In plain words, one sees that an A is turned into a B by code segment P just by looking at the lists of data declarations at the head of the code, making sense of the names used, and spotting which are used where. However, the detailed functionality can only be obtained by a statement-by-statement analysis of the *procedure division* — once a precise description has been achieved, further documentation can then be extracted, including natural language explanations connecting the functionality to the problem domain. This must be a methodical procedure if it is to be at all successful, and hence valuable, and we have developed two different regimes which may carry it through.

(1) *Handbook plus reasoning tool.* Code-analysis by hand may be an arduous and error-prone task. Thankfully the regularity and cliché-ridden nature of DP programming at least makes this domain feasible for the application of semi-automated reverse-engineering methods — one can provide the engineer with a powerful reasoning tool and a *handbook* describing how to use it to good effect. In section 2 of this paper we sketch the contents of the 'handbook' with reference to a reasoning tool (Lano, 1990) which has been developed for the purpose by one of us (Lano). An important component of this method is the separation of the code into *objects* and *classes*.

(2) *Automatic tools.* Scientific or real-time applications seem less amenable to patterned methods. The condensation of information in a program is simply too great for the recovery of the design without deep prior knowledge, but in our experience it has always proved possible to unscramble the code as far as a functional specification, even if one does not know what it means in any profound sense. In section 4 of this paper we report on an algorithmic method developed by one of us (Breuer) which generates surprisingly acceptable low-level specifications, and we go on to demonstrate at least one technique which can fully recover the design given such a specification as a starting point. This method generates specifications accessible to the general logic/reasoning tool as the internal part of an object class. The technique

is based on the *simplification* of machine-generated functional specifications to a normal form which has proved itself readily accessible to the human eye and mind.

1.2. The reverse-engineering process

After a year or so of experimentation with both existing tools and those we have built for the purpose, we have discovered a three-stage process in code comprehension — (1) *clean*, (2) *specify*, (3) *simplify* — analogous rather than inverse to the usual compilation process. This is shown in Figure 1.

At first, it may seem surprising that the process does not attempt to reverse each stage of compilation in inverse order. But, even if we were to attempt the special form of reverse-engineering known as decompilation, *stepwise inversion* would be difficult because the final compiler optimization step is not a 1:1 process — it can scramble the code in a way which depends on the surrounding code. A similar process often seems to be at work in a programmer's brain: straightforward concepts become hopelessly scrambled in translation into FORTRAN or COBOL for a variety of reasons, and it is not feasible to attempt to unscramble them directly. Instead, we follow a procedure which *finishes* by normalizing the specification to a standard form, just as a compiler (or programmer?) finishes by optimizing the code produced. The idea is that one is likely to obtain an equivalent, but different, design to the original from scrambled code, and one had then best attempt to convert it to a simple and 'standard' equivalent form, in the hope that this

(a) provides a clear description of the program in a readily understandable format,

(b) provides a solid base for the application of further techniques: reverse-engineering, forward-engineering and documentation.

We use an intermediate language or representation, called *Uniform* (Cahill and Stanley-Smith, 1989), developed for the REDO project, which has a cleaner and simpler semantics than COBOL or FORTRAN. Translating the source languages into a more structured programming language is an essential preparation for the whole process which is elaborated within the '*clean*' stage. Indeed, all our techniques are aimed at representations that have already been *restructured* to some extent to reveal their 'essential structure'. The aim is

Compilation		Inverse-Engineering	
	High-level code		'Dirty' code
• *Precompile*	↓	• *Clean*	↓
	Intermediate code		'Clean' code
• *Compile*	↓	• *Specify*	↓
	Initial machine-code		Initial specification
• *Optimise*	↓	• *Simplify*	↓
	Final machine-code		Final specification

Figure 1. Inverse-engineering is analogous to code compilation

to structure the code so that each line is a meaningful fragment of a program specification — which explains why GOTOs must be replaced; these commands contribute only during execution and tend to hide the real function of the program (examples of programs which use GOTOs to implement loops in obscure ways occur in Ward (1989b) and Linger *et al.* (1990)).

There is scope at all stages for the partial or full application of intelligent human guidance, but it is also possible to conduct the reverse-engineering process entirely automatically. In particular, the '*clean*' (code restructuring) stage can generally be almost entirely automatic. However, the '*specify*' stage is certainly eased by intelligent decisions on the level of detail to be included — for example, that a 'writefile' operation usually also changes the date stamp should often be ignored for the purposes of analysis. Moreover, although there is clearly room for the application of human reasoning in the subsequent '*simplify*' (specification simplification) stage, it often appears satisfactory to let the greater part here be automatic, as described in section 4 (the production of a low-level specification by entirely automated methods) where exactly the detail already present is incorporated, no more and no less. Intelligence seems to consist of knowing just which details to leave out, but, whether intelligence is used or not, in our experiments, we have found that the methods we employ *always* provide a specification which is more readable than the code.

The reverse-engineering process we describe fully supports the object-oriented paradigm — through the construction of classes, objects and processes in terms of which the program functionality can then be expressed. The methods we set out here are also intended to support and use other reverse-engineering processes, such as the derivation of JSD or SSADM diagrams from source code, and the separation of the application into a set of communicating processes.

2. PROGRAM COMPREHENSION STEPS FOR DATA PROCESSING APPLICATIONS

We assume that a structured program has been derived from the given application. This is a program without GOTOs or other 'unclean' constructs, with fully identified inputs and outputs. Then we begin reverse-engineering by reorganizing (1) the data and (2) the code of the program to facilitate analysis, aiming to produce well-defined *objects* and single-function *procedures* respectively.

The final description returned will consist of a set of class definitions, a list of variable declarations using either these classes or the basic types, and a list of descriptions of the functionality of program segments. The methods described in section 4 can be used to further simplify these functional descriptions if necessary, the aim being to extract as much information about the relationships between the program variables as possible. An example follows the description of the technique itself.

2.1. Data organization and abstraction

We have defined a simple syntax for object *classes* (an example is shown in Figure 4), and the aim is to abstract a class of objects from an application code by picking out related program variables and grouping together the operations performed on them as single *actions* on the class. This corresponds to the 'specify' stage of reverse-engineering identified in section 1, and entails a significant amount of logical analysis to find the functionality of each class. The original code can then be amended to contain single *instances* (*objects*) of the class instead of widely separated groups of apparently unconnected statements applied to scattered data. This corresponds to the 'simplify' stage, and further simplifications can be entered as the underlying design of the code becomes clear.

There are certain predefined abstract data types, such as the various forms of *file* in COBOL, and we are looking for *extensions* to these as class abstractions. This is a particular feature of our present approach, because although a multi-level system of definitions of objects could be used, with inheritance (Goguen and Meseguer, 1987), only a single-level system is proposed at present, and each new class has to explicitly list the operations it might otherwise wish to inherit. In the language of OBJ (Goguen and Winkler, 1988), this means we avoid the need to import extra implicit logical *theories* into the context.

The class abstraction process is as follows:

(1) *Identification.* The first step is to collect together those flags and associated data structures in working storage which record important information about the main data structures (files or tables). These flags may record whether a file is empty, or is invalid, or whether the last record read from the file is valid, and so on. The *reverse-engineer* has to then conjecture and assert a relationship between these variables and the main data structure; this will be an *invariant* of the program which is intended to hold true at all significant points in the execution. Checking the validity of this conjecture is actually not a major piece of work since it only requires the examination of a few obviously related statements.

(2) *Assembly.* Taking each target variable f that is of a file or array type, we try to accumulate all the other variables that are logically or conceptually connected with it. We look for operations in the code that change the main structure, such as a read or write to the file, and determine if other variables are updated in nearby (in terms of the control flow) statements, in such a way that the conjectured properties are maintained. For each such subordinate variable x and proposed property θ_x we add x as a local variable of a class F which is intended to extend the declared type of f. We conjoin θ_x to the already known invariants of the structure, and add any operations that change or access this variable and are used in the code to the list of operations. Already discovered operations may need extending to incorporate a side-effect on x which maintains θ_x. We end up with a list of operations ACT and a single logical invariant INV_F which is preserved by each operation in the list and which is *True* after initialization of the local variables x of the class F. Checking these conditions has to be done with the aid of the reasoning tool based on the code-representation language.

(3) *Error detection.* If the checks fail then we either weaken or change the invariant property or conclude that x is not really a component of a structure built on f. In practice there will be imperfections in the correlation between subordinate and main variables, in that the programmer may not update associated variables in line with the main variables when this is in fact logically necessary. If we restrict attention

to the points in the code where these subordinate variables are accessed, however, then we certainly expect a consistent relationship to hold, and if it does not then something is wrong, somewhere — either the reverse-engineer's concept or the original code. If the latter, and we intended to restructure the code at a high level, it is these types of logical flaws that would be the target for correction, and this method of analysis identifies them.

2.2. Code reorganization

The next step is to separate the program into distinct procedures (*process instances*) which perform a single input–output function, possibly on several files or internal data structures, and identify this functionality exactly. We look for two things:

(1) *Process boundaries.* These are obtained by examining the places at which files are opened or closed, when input or output routines cease, or with more work, by examining the pattern of accesses to the structures. We replace where possible the original code statements by the corresponding calls to new objects, as determined by following the procedure in section 2.1 above.

(2) *Functionality.* These code sections (of single functionality) P are then analysed to obtain their *functionality*, either by the methods of section 4, or by postulating that the function they compute is of the form

$$f_P(in_1, \ldots, in_n) = (out_1, \ldots, out_m)$$

where the argument list includes all inputs, and the result list all outputs (this form excludes any undeclared side-effects) and then deriving f_P by using the reasoning tool to find a predicate which expresses the effect of P.

Using a logical reasoning tool in this way is a well-documented procedure (Gries, 1981) and involves working back from the logically last statements of the process, postulating and checking invariants where necessary, aided by heuristics (Breuer and Lano, 1989); (Gries, 1981). Each non-compound statement will have a standard predicate associated with it (i.e. it will be generated automatically by the tool) but loop invariants must be guessed at and then checked. If no simple guess is made by the engineer, the tool just generates a rather uninformative generic statement (but an accurate one!), therefore this is, in principle, an entirely automatic process, but it is far more effective as an interactive progression. The engineer proceeds from outline knowledge about a program to detailed knowledge, using the precision of verification techniques to check and make more precise a growing intuition about the program.

The semantics of the intermediate language used has been given in a precise axiomatic form (Lano, 1989); (Breuer and Lano, 1989), so determining the functionality is simply a matter of applying predetermined rules.

3. EXAMPLE PROGRAM — DATA VALIDATION

The following example is taken from Parkin (1988) and is a structured version of a data validation program — that is to say it has been part-way through the *clean* stage of inverse-engineering, having been treated automatically so far. Here we do a little more cleaning, by hand.

3.1. Data division

The original COBOL program has two input files: table and trans, and two output files, valtrans and error-report, shown in Figure 2. There are also extra constants and flags.

3.2. Procedure division

After preliminary translation (cleaning), the procedure division of the program has four chief paragraphs, process-table, process-tablerec, and also process-trans and process-transrec. These are shown in Figures 3(a)–(d) respectively.

The paragraph process-table (Figure 3(a)) repeatedly executes process-tablerec, counting as it goes. If the final count is over 26, the file table was invalid (too large). Interestingly, the paragraph tests if table is empty by attempting to pull a first record out of it. Failure causes another 'file invalid' report. Of course, pulling a record out ahead of time seems risky, but ... the second paragraph process-tablerec (Figure 3(b)) saves each record in a workspace array ws-tablerec before pulling another out of table. The boolean flag eof-table is maintained to indicate if table has been exhausted or not.

Paragraph process-trans (Figure 3(c)) is called from the paragraph process-table when the array ws-tablerec is filled and table is exhausted. It repeatedly calls the paragraph process-transrec until the file trans is exhausted. Each valid record in the file is transferred by the latter paragraph to a file valtrans. The boolean flag eof-trans shows whether trans has yet been exhausted or not.

The fourth paragraph process-transrec (Figure 3(d)) checks the records it has been passed (from file transrec) for validity according to a number of criteria, and passes the valid records across to the file valtrans. In addition, there are a number of details concerning how the error reports are formed which are omitted here.

It is not at all clear on inspection that the various flags succeed in signalling all the conditions correctly. One could attempt to assert that they do, and check the hypothesis with the reasoning tool, but it pays to attempt to reorganize the code into *objects* first.

```
DATA DIVISION.
FILE SECTION.
FD table LABEL RECORDS OMITTED.                      ! table file !
01 tablerec.
    02 credcde PIC X.
    02 credlim PIC 9(7).
FD trans LABEL RECORDS OMITTED.                      ! trans file !
01 transrecs.
    ...6 fields ...
FD valtrans LABEL RECORDS OMITTED.                   ! valtrans file !
01 valtransrec.
    ...as transrecs ...
FD error-report LABEL RECORDS OMITTED.               ! error-report file !
01 aline ...
```

Figure 2. The data division of the example COBOL program

```
PARAGRAPH process-table                              ! First Paragraph !
BEGIN
   RECEIVE tablerec FROM table;
   IF   AT-END(table)
   THEN WRITE "table file empty";
        HALT
   END  IF;
   eof-table := "F";
   DO   VARYING tablesub FROM 1 BY 1
        UNTIL (eof-table = "T"  ∨  tablesub > 26) :       ! '∨' is 'OR' !
        PERFORM process-tablerec
   END  DO;
   IF   tablesub > 26
   THEN WRITE "table file invalid";
        HALT
   END  IF;
   PERFORM process-trans
END;
```

Figure 3(a). Paragraph process-table

```
PARAGRAPH  process-tablerec                          ! Second Paragraph !
BEGIN
   ws-tablerec(tablesub) := tablerec;
   RECEIVE tablerec FROM table;
   IF  AT-END(table)
   THEN eof-table := "T"
   END  IF
END;
```

Figure 3(b). Paragraph process-trans

```
PARAGRAPH  process-trans                             ! Third Paragraph !
BEGIN
   LINECOUNT := 2;
   SEND report-heading BEFORE 2
       TO error-report;
   eof-trans := "F";
   RECEIVE transrec FROM trans;
   IF   AT-END(trans)
   THEN eof-trans := "T"
   END  IF;
   DO   UNTIL eof-trans = "T" :
        PERFORM process-transrec
   END  DO;
   PERFORM produce-report-footing
END;
```

Figure 3(c). Paragraph process-trans

3.3. Forming objects and classes

We reorganize the data and code of the program to facilitate comprehension. We group together the flags that are used for particular data structures: eof-trans and transrec-valid become local functions of the class transactions of which trans will be an instance. Figure 4 contains the specification of the transactions class, and the paragraph process-transrec

```
PARAGRAPH  process-transrec                                    ! Fourth Paragraph !
BEGIN
    error-line-2  :=  SPACES;
    transrec-valid  :=  "T";
    IF    trans-update-code  ≠  "I"    ∨
          trans-update-code  ≠  "A"    ∨
          trans-update-code  ≠  "D"
    THEN possible-star-col-2  :=  "*";
          transrec-valid  :=  "F"
    END   IF;
    ! many more details of validation tests !
    IF    transrec-valid  =  "T"
    THEN SEND transrec TO valtrans
    ELSE PERFORM produce-error-group
    END   IF;
    RECEIVE transrec FROM trans;
    IF    AT-END(trans)
    THEN eof-trans  :=  "T"
    END   IF;
END;
```

Figure 3(d). Paragraph process-transrec

```
CLASS transactions
OWNS eof-trans, transrec-valid : BOOLEAN;
    contents :  SEQUENCE OF transrecs;
    crec :  transrecs;
USES
    failure-report :  transrecs → error-recs;
INVARIANT
    (eof-trans = "T" ⇔ contents = ⟨ ⟩)    ∧                      ! '∧' is 'AND' !
    (transrec-valid ⇔ (crec.trans-update-code = "I"  ∨
                       crec.trans-update-code = "A"  ∨
                       crec.trans-update-code = "D"  )) ∧
    (                  ... all other validation conditions ...)
OPERATIONS
    RECEIVE _ FROM SELF :       transrecs ! return a  transrecs to a reference !
    AT-END _ OF SELF :          BOOLEAN   ! return a  BOOLEAN into a reference !
    VALID-REC _ OF SELF :       BOOLEAN   ! return a  BOOLEAN into a reference !
    FAIL-REPORT _ OF SELF :     error-recs! return an error report !
ACTIONS
    RECEIVE x FROM SELF   ⟹   ┌──────────────────────────┐
                              │ x  :=  head(contents);   │
                              │ contents  :=  tail(contents); │
                              │ crec  :=  x              │
                              └──────────────────────────┘
    AT-END x OF SELF      ⟹   ┌──────────────┐
                              │ x  :=  eof-trans │
                              └──────────────┘
    VALID-REC x OF SELF   ⟹   ┌────────────────────┐
                              │ x  :=  transrec-valid │
                              └────────────────────┘
    FAIL-REPORT x OF SELF ⟹   ┌─────────────────────────┐
                              │ x  :=  failure-report(crec) │
                              └─────────────────────────┘
END
```

Figure 4. The abstracted class of transactions

has been rewritten using calls to objects of this class in Figure 5. The boxed areas of text (whenever they appear) may contain the mathematical notation of Z specifications (Spivey, 1989).

Of course, we have to establish that the declared invariants of the abstracted classes actually are invariants of the program, in the sense that they hold at every point in the

```
PARAGRAPH process-transrec
BEGIN
    VALID-REC transrec-valid OF trans;              ! check record !
    FAILURE-REPORT error-group FROM trans;          ! record errors !
    IF   transrec-valid = "T"
    THEN SEND transrec TO valtrans
    ELSE SEND error-group TO error-report
    END  IF;
    RECEIVE transrec FROM trans;
    AT-END eof-trans OF trans
END;
```

Figure 5. process-transrec *improved by inserting messages to objects*

execution *between* two statements in the new (after replacement of original operations by new object method calls) code.

The class tables has been abstracted from the program text in a similar way and is shown in Figure 6.

3.4. Forming Processes

There are actually two separate processes in the program, recognizable when one notices the OPEN trans and CLOSE table statements that separate the two distinct phases of the programs operation. The operations of the two processes can as a first approximation be described as functions:

$$readintable(\textbf{table}_{in}) = (\textbf{ws-tablerec}_{out}, \textbf{errors}_{out})$$
$$validatetrans(\textbf{trans}_{in}) = (\textbf{valtrans}_{out}, \textbf{error-report}_{out})$$

The precise definitions depend on the loops in the two paragraphs which process table and trans record-by-record, and build up the outputs. The subscripts serve two purposes: (1) operationally, they can be thought of as designating whether the channel to the file is an *in*put or an *out*put channel, (2) semantically, they distinguish two *associated 'virtual' data structures*, the *stream (sequence) of inputs* received from the file, and the *stream of outputs* written to it. In detail then, we are looking for a function *validatetrans* of one argument, trans$_{in}$: the total sequence of records read from trans. Of the outputs, valtrans$_{out}$ is the total sequence written to valtrans. Using the logical reasoning-tool, we get:

$validatetrans$	::	$\text{seq } transrecs \rightarrow (\text{seq } transrecs, \text{seq } error\text{-}recs)$
$validatetrans(\langle r \rangle)$	=	$(\langle \rangle, \langle \rangle)$
$validatetrans(s ^\frown \langle r \rangle)$	=	$\texttt{if } valid\text{-}rec(last(s))$
		$\texttt{then } (x ^\frown \langle last(s) \rangle, y)$
		$\texttt{else } (x, y ^\frown \langle failure\text{-}report(last(s)) \rangle)$

where *valid-rec(r)* returns true if the record *r* passes all the validation tests, and false otherwise, the definition of this function is extracted directly from the code, as is *failure-report*, by program *slicing*, (Kilpatrick *et al.*, 1988). *Validatetrans* is therefore purely a function on the inputs and outputs as sequences; which is the view of the functionality we are interested in (the '$^\frown$' symbol stands for concatenation of sequences, '$\langle \rangle$' is the empty sequence, and '$\langle r \rangle$' is the singleton sequence of one element).

```
CLASS tables
TYPES
tabrecs    CONSISTS OF [ ! fields of the  table records ! ];
OWNS
    eof-table  :  BOOLEAN;
    contents   :  SEQUENCE OF tabrecs;
USES
    build_table  :  SEQUENCE OF tabrecs  →  tabrec-array
INVARIANT
    (eof-table = "T"    ⇔    contents =<>)
OPERATIONS
    AT-END _ OF SELF :        BOOLEAN ! returns  BOOLEAN to reference !
    RECEIVE _ FROM SELF :     tabrecs ! returns  tabrecs to reference !
    SIZE _ OF SELF :          INTEGER ! returns  INTEGER to reference !
    GET-TABLE _ FROM SELF :   tabrec-array
ACTIONS
    AT-END x OF SELF         ⟹
                                  ┌──────────────────────────────┐
                                  │ x := eof-table               │
                                  └──────────────────────────────┘
    RECEIVE x FROM SELF      ⟹
                                  ┌──────────────────────────────┐
                                  │ x := first(contents);        │
                                  │ contents := tail(contents)   │
                                  └──────────────────────────────┘
    SIZE x OF SELF           ⟹
                                  ┌──────────────────────────────┐
                                  │ x := #contents               │
                                  └──────────────────────────────┘
    GET-TABLE x FROM SELF    ⟹
                                  ┌──────────────────────────────┐
                                  │ x := build_table(contents)   │
                                  └──────────────────────────────┘
END CLASS;
```

Figure 6. The abstracted class tables

The functionality of the process *readintable* can be derived in like manner. It must make use of the abstracted class tables shown in Figure 6 (the subsidiary function *build_table* used to implement the specialised message 'GET-TABLE' is *specified* in Figure 7(a).

The process *readintable* itself can be rewritten in the object-oriented style, using the message-passing constructs defined for tables. This is shown in Figure 7(b). Then, by replacing the message calls by explicit changes-of-state to the objects internal attributes, we can derive the functionality to be that shown in Figure 7(c).

Note that the number of variables accessed within the paragraphs have been reduced, and the functions of these variables are now served by internal attributes of the new objects. Thus the overall scope and visibility of some variables has been reduced, so reducing the complexity of the code under metrics of scope and modularization (Jacob, 1989: Yau and Collofello, 1980).

The process has also enabled us to give more detailed graphical descriptions of the program. For instance, the data diagrams for the original input structures, generated from the DATA DIVISION, are shown on the left in Figure 8, but we now have obtained

```
FUNCTION build_table; SEQUENCE OF tabrecs  →  tabrec-array
WHERE
┌──────────────────────────────────────────────────────────────────────────┐
│ build_table(⟨a⟩)       =   ⟨⟩                                              │
│ build_table(s⌢⟨a⟩)     =   build_table(s) ⊕ {#s ↦ last(s)}, if 27 > #s > 0 │
│ build_table(s⌢⟨a⟩)     =   build_table(s),  otherwise                      │
└──────────────────────────────────────────────────────────────────────────┘
END FUNCTION;
```

Figure 7(a). The specification of the subsidiary function build_table

```
PROCESS readintable(in : tables)
OWNS table-empty : BOOLEAN;   table-size : INTEGER
RETURNS out : tabrec-array;   errors : QUEUE OF STRING
BEGIN
     AT-END table-empty OF in;
     IF table-empty
     THEN SEND "table file empty" TO errors;
     ELSE SIZE table-size OF in;
          IF table-size > 26
          THEN GET-TABLE out FROM in;
               SEND "table file invalid" TO errors;
          ELSE GET-TABLE out FROM in;
          END IF;
     END IF;
END PROCESS
```

Figure 7(b). Process readintable *written using message-passing command style*

```
FUNCTION readintable;   tables  →  (tabrec-array, SEQUENCE OF STRING)
WHERE
```

```
readintable(in)  =   if in.eof-table
                     then (<>, <"table file empty">)
                     else if #in.contents > 26
                          then (build_table(in.contents), <"table file invalid">)
                          else (build_table(in.contents), <>)
```

```
END FUNCTION;
```

Figure 7(c). The functionality of process readintable

a more complete description and logical distinction between cases, so we can generate more complete diagrams, for instance the input file trans can now be seen to have the structure on the right in Figure 8. There are two conceptually distinct cases of records in the trans file, even though they have the same type. Further subcases based on details of the fields of the records can also be specified.

4. FROM CODE TO FUNCTIONAL SPECIFICATIONS

We have also pursued an approach based on the transformation of code into functional specifications, which is generally more suited to scientific and (aspects of) real-time applications. *Specifications* (Breuer, 1990a) consist of a set of

- top-level function definitions of the form '*lhs = rhs*', each guarded by ...

- a predicate defining the valid domain, and each dependent on ...

- a set of lower-level local specifications.

Following the general reverse-engineering scheme laid out in section 1, code is first *cleaned* to remove all but simple conditional branches and subroutine/function calls as control constructs, and then an initial specification is generated *entirely automatically,* using a line-by-line translation mechanism. Many new local variables and sub-blocks are

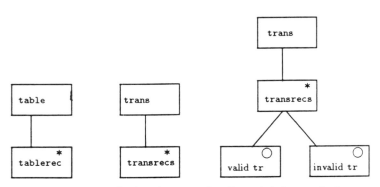

Figure 8(a). Input-file data-diagrams. (b). Expanded diagram for trans

introduced, and needless to say, the output is initially not very 'human-readable', but we have found that the application of a few relatively simple and *automatic* transformations produces a surprisingly acceptable form. This can then serve as the basis for the more strictly supervised transformations employed in equational reasoning, and of which we give an example below.

4.1. Simplifying specifications automatically

The simplifications we use fall neatly into three classes, applied in succession:

- *Promotion:* designated *lhs* entities are promoted to top-level, renaming if necessary (usually function entities are derived from distinct labels in the source code, and therefore already have distinct names).

- *Elimination:* all remaining lower-level entities are eliminated by substituting their specifications in the higher-level specifications which use them.

- *Normalization:* redundancies such as a projection operation applied to a tuple are removed. Specifications with expressions on their *rhs* which consist of disjoint cases are converted instead into guarded specifications and simple expressions. The complete list of twelve Church–Rosser rewrite-rules is given in Breuer (1990a). Because of the Church–Rosser properties, specifications have a unique normal form, and rewrites may be applied in any order until it is achieved.

For example, the following program (part of one of a series of 'challenges' set for us by M. Ward of Durham University):

```
INTEGER STACK s;
INTEGER FUNCTION ra(m, n) RETURNS(n) FROM
BEGIN
        IF (m = 0)
        THEN    IF EMPTY(s)
                THEN    n := n + 1;
                ELSE    RECEIVE m FROM s;
                        n := ra(m - 1, n + 1);
                END IF;
```

```
ELSE    IF (n = 0)
        THEN    n := ra(m − 1, 1);
        ELSE    SEND m TO s;
                n := ra(m, n − 1);
        END IF;
END IF;
END
```

transforms *automatically* to the following normalized specification:

$ra(m, n, \langle \rangle)$	$=$	$n + 1,$	if $(m = 0)$
$ra(m, n, v : s)$	$=$	$ra(v − 1, n + 1, s),$	if $(m = 0)$
$ra(m, n, s)$	$=$	$ra(m − 1, 1, s),$	if $(n = 0)$
$ra(m, n, s)$	$=$	$ra(m, n − 1, m : s),$	otherwise

The 'EMPTY(s)' would translate to an extra guard condition '$...\wedge$EMPTY(s)' on the first line of the specification, but this key-conjunct is intercepted and converted to a pattern-match in which the argument s is replaced by '$\langle \rangle$'.

What is the normal form which the normalization rules lead to? A set of equations in normal form is simply one where

(1) the function definitions appear only at the top level;

(2) no entity is defined twice in the set (this is a rule which is rarely invoked since the source code is usually free from such mislabellings and overloadings);

(3) each equation is in normal form.

A set of equations which together define a single entity is regarded as a single equation. This is what we have in the example for *ra* above. Looking at things this way is an important part of the strategy, because a 'compound equation' of the type shown for *ra* can be represented as a 'simple equation' (for *ra(m,n,s)* in this case), with a single *lhs*, but a *compound expression* on the *rhs*.

A compound *rhs* consists of a *guarded set of several simple expressions*, and we only *print* a simple equation with a compound *rhs* as though it were a compound equation, making top-level guards on the expression look like guards on the components of a compound set of equations instead. The trick is important, because it allows us to normalize equations by normalizing the *compound expressions* on their *rhs* alone. Although the end-result looks as though one could have dealt with *guarded equations* all the way through, the normalization process itself relies inherently on intermediate states in which the expressions and subexpressions are themselves guarded, so it is necessary to deal with these instead. What this means is that a normal 'compound equation' is defined by the concept of a 'normal guarded expression', but a normal compound equation effectively has the following form:

(1) each simple equation of the compound is normal, guarded by a normal simple logical expression, except for the *last* (default) equation, which has no guard;

(2) no guard condition formally implies any earlier guard condition (that is, any above it). This condition applies to pattern-matches too, which are really implicit guard conditions.

A normal simple equation is an equation in which the expression on the *rhs* is a normal simple expression, as in each line of the definition of *ra* above, ignoring the guards. Such expressions are either:

(1) tuples of simple, normal expressions, e.g. (a,b,c);

(2) a function with simple, normal expressions as arguments, e.g. $ra(v - 1, n + 1, s)$;

(3) an atomic expression; a variable or a non-vector constant, e.g. s, or 1;

(4) a *projection* (the ith component, for some i) of a simple normal expression which is not a tuple, e.g. $a[2]$.

Each guard expression is a simple *logical* expression in normal form. This means that it is either:

(1) a disjunction of conjunctive normalized logical expressions, in which no disjunct formally imples any earlier disjunct. The empty disjunction is used to represent *False*;

(2) a conjunction of atomic or negated atomic logical expressions, in which no conjunct is formally implied by any other conjunct. The empty conjunction is used to represent *True*;

(3) (a negation of) an atomic logical expression. That is, a *comparison* via an ($<$, $\leq$, $=$, etc.) between two simple, normal expressions.

Getting down to a normal specification involves the transformation of all alternative forms to intermediates which are more 'nearly' normal. The final normalized specification is a very great improvement over the original code, and clearly sets out the intended functionality, but it does not reveal the design intention.

4.2. Higher equational reasoning

Once a specification has been achieved, we can attempt to eliminate the data structures which appear in it, to obtain a still clearer description. Data structures can implement functionality through their internal constraints, and if we eliminate these structures, then we must render this hidden functionality explicit. In the case of the example above, we first apply a transformation which replaces the stack manipulation by continuation-passing, thus moving into the realm of *higher-order* programming, where functions may be specified as created *dynamically*, as well as at compile-time. We get the specification:

$$
\begin{aligned}
ra(m, n, \langle \rangle) &= ra'(m, n, g) \\
&\quad \text{where } g(n) = n + 1 \\
ra'(m, n, c) &= c(n + 1), &&\text{if } (m = 0) \\
ra'(m, n, c) &= ra'(m - 1, 1, c), &&\text{if } (n = 0) \\
ra'(m, n, c) &= ra'(m, n - 1, c'), &&\text{otherwise} \\
&\quad \text{where } c'(n) = ra'(m - 1, n, c)
\end{aligned}
$$

The general transformation into continuation programming which we have applied here takes the form

$$\text{pattern of equations} \mapsto \text{new pattern of equations}$$

or more exactly:

$$
\begin{aligned}
f(p_0, \langle \rangle) &= g(p_0) \\
f(p_0, v : s) &= f(h(p_0, v), s) \\
f(p_1, s) &= f(k(p_1), l(p_1) : s)
\end{aligned}
\quad \mapsto \quad
\begin{aligned}
f(x, \langle \rangle) &= f'(x, g), \\
f'(p_0, c) &= c(p_0) \\
f'(p_1, c) &= f'(k(p_1), c') \\
&\text{where } c'(x) = f'(h(x, l(p_1)), c)
\end{aligned}
$$

Now, we can argue that all 'reasonable' continuation programs are derived as

$$f(x, c) = c(f_0(x))$$

for some more basic function f_0 (this observation is actually the result of an insight into the nature of computation, as opposed to non-causal processes, obtained in Breuer (1990b)). Applying this reasoning to ra' above the eliminating c' by substituting its definition in the specification above, we get $ra(m, n, \langle \rangle) = ra_0(m, n) + 1$, where

$$
\begin{aligned}
ra_0(m, n) &= n, &&\text{if } (m = 0) \\
ra_0(m, n) &= ra_0(m - 1, 1), &&\text{if } (n = 0) \\
ra_0(m, n) &= ra_0(m - 1, ra_0(m, n - 1)), &&\text{otherwise}
\end{aligned}
$$

which tells us that $ra(m, n, \langle \rangle)$ is essentially the Ackerman function.

These techniques can usefully be applied within the object abstraction technique in the cases that:

(1) a section of code implements a mathematical function on working-storage variables alone; or

(2) a simpler description of a higher-level function (such as *readintable* above) or auxiliary function (such as *build_table* above) may be obtained.

5. OTHER APPROACHES

The preceding sections have described the work being done in reverse-engineering for the REDO consortium at the PRG in Oxford. The other partners include the Centre for Software Maintenance at Durham University, which has collaborated with IBM in the

REFORM project (Ward *et al.*, 1989), aimed at the reverse-engineering of assembly language code into high-level descriptions via an interactive program transformation system.

No method of code comprehension can be entirely automatic, as the work that a maintenance programmer performs in understanding the code is an intelligent activity, involving the understanding of *what* the original programmer has done, *how* this has been achieved from the original design, and *why* a particular direction was chosen (Coleman and Pratt, 1988). All of these are important aspects if changes or enhancements to the code are planned. Systems which support this process by the automated derivation of consequences and checking of hypotheses about the code are a practical possibility in the near future. Work within IBM in reverse-engineering COBOL programs (Linger *et al.*, 1990) has also adopted the approach of restructuring the code to eliminate GOTOs and ALTER GOTO statements before attempting functional abstraction. Their description language is again a simple equational specification language; however, our approach is different in that we use both bottom-up and top-down methods of analysing the code. More ambitious systems, such as the KBSA of Green *et al.* (1986) and the OBJ3/FOOPS based system of Goguen (1989) similarly stress the importance of a precise mathematical language as a means of recording information about an application.

Our reverse-engineering strategy differs also from that described in Zimmer (1990), which similarly aims at producing an object-oriented view of a system to ease comprehensibility and verifiability. We concentrate on data structures, and gathering code up as operations on these data structures, instead of trying to recognize simple operations in the code and attempting to limit the number of program variables involved in these operations. We consider our approach to be more applicable to data-processing programs, whereas Zimmer (1990) is concerned with scientific and numeric programs in FORTRAN. It is clear that a range of styles and strategies of reverse-engineering will need to be developed to deal with the different programming styles that exist.

6. FUTURE DIRECTIONS

Parallelism constructs may be incorporated into our specification language, using symbols such as 'φ' (block) and '|' (non-deterministic choice) on the *rhs* of equations. Specifications would then be normalized to exhibit all alternatives at the top-level only, much as they are already normalized to show all guarded cases at the top only.

We are also investigating the potential for *re-engineering* code through implementing requests for changes in the functionality of the code at a high level (Lano and Haughton, 1990), and then re-implementing, which is a method along the lines suggested by Goguen (1989), and allows for reconfiguration for concurrent execution.

7. SUMMARY

The methods we have described are based on earlier work on the semantics of the language Uniform, and the reverse-engineering of code back into a predicate notation (Breuer and Lano, 1989). After some experience, the multi-level and multi-stage method of data and code abstraction detailed above was adopted. This has the advantage of being consistent with the object-oriented paradigm which was one of the original inspirations behind the Uniform language, and with other work in the REDO project and outside.

References

Breuer. P. T. (1990a). *Inverse Engineering: The First Step*, REDO Document 2487-TN-PRG-1031, Programming Research Group, Oxford University.

Breuer. P. T. (1990b). *Breaking and Building Higher-Order Operating Systems (and some comments on Church's Thesis)*, REDO Document 2487-TN-PRG-1024, Programming Research Group, Oxford University.

Breuer. P. T. and Lano, K. (1989). 'From code to Z specifications', *Z User Workshop 1989*, Springer-Verlag Workshops in Computing, Nicholls J. (Ed.), September 1990, Springer-Verlag, New York.

Cahill. T. and Stanley-Smith. C. (1989). *Uniform: A Language geared to System Description and Transformation*, REDO document 2487-TN-NIL-1002, University of Limerick. Management Systems Group.

Coleman, M. J. and Pratt. S. J. (1988). 'Maintainable software by design', *BCS/IEE Conference on Software Engineering 1988*, Liverpool Polytechnic. IEE, London, pp. 112–121.

Goguen. J. (1989). *Program Renovation*, Programming Research Group, Oxford University.

Goguen. J. and Meseguer, J. (1987). *Unifying Functional, Object-Orientated and Relational Programming with Logical Semantics*, SRI International, CA. USA.

Goguen. J. and Winkler. T. (1988). *Introducing OBJ3*, SRI-CSL-88-9, SRI International. CA, USA.

Green. C., Lukham, D., Balzer, R., Cheatham, T. and Rich, C. (1986). 'Report on a knowledge-based software assistant', *Artificial Intelligence and Software Engineering*. Charles Rich and R. C. Waters (Eds), Morgan Kaufmann, Los Altos, CA. USA.

Gries, D. (1981). *The Science of Programming*, Springer-Verlag, New York.

Jacob. P. (1989). *Software Metrics*, REDO Project Document UL-TN-1020. University of Limerick, November 1989.

Kilpatrick, P., Crooks, D. and Owens, M. (1988). 'Program slicing: a computer aided programming technique'. *Second IEE/BCS Conference: Software Maintenance 88*. University of Liverpool, IEE, London.

Lano, K. (1989). *An Axiomatic Semantics for Uniform*, REDO Document 2487-TN-PRG-1011, Programming Research Group, Oxford University.

Lano, K. (1990). *Generating Verification Conditions for UNIFORM Programs*, REDO Project Document PRG-TN-1039, Programming Research Group.

Lano K. and Haughton, H. (1990). *Integrating Specification, Refinement, and Maintenance*, Programming Research Group Oxford. Submitted to *Software Maintenance: Research and Practice*.

Linger, R. C., Hausler, P. A., Pleszlioch, M. G. and Heruer, A. R. (1990). 'Using function abstraction to understand program behavior'. *IEEE Software*. January, 55–63.

Parkin. A. (1988). *Cobol for Students*. Edward Arnold. London.

Spivey, M. (1989). *Understanding Z*, Cambridge University Press, Cambridge.

Ward. M. (1989). *Transforming a Program Into a Specification*, Centre for Software Maintenance. Durham University, November 1989.

Ward, M., Calliss, F. W. and Munro, M. (1989). 'The maintainer's assistant', *Proceedings of Conference on Software Maintenance 1989*, Miami, Florida. IEEE Computer Society Press, New York, pp. 307–315.

Yau, S. S. and Collofello, J. S. (1980). 'Some stability measures for software maintenance', *IEEE Transactions on Software Engineering*. **SE-6**, 545–552.

Zimmer, J. A. (1990). 'Restructuring for style', *Software — Practice and Experience*. **20**, 365–389.

Chapter 13
Object Recovery

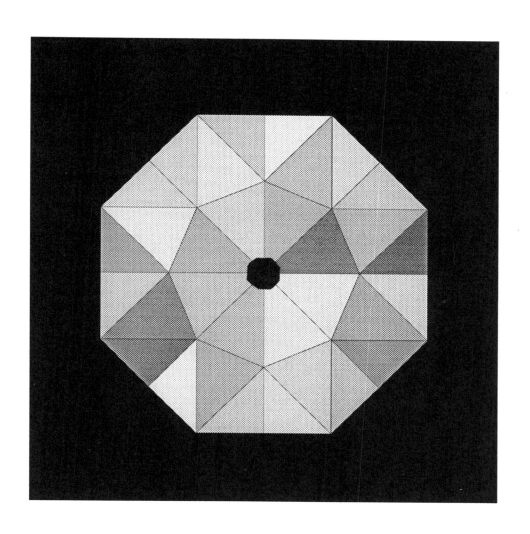

Chapter 13
Object Recovery

Purpose

Of great interest to the reengineering community is extracting object-oriented classes and object instances from non-object-oriented source code. This work is still developing. This chapter presents three papers describing experience with extracting objects from code.

Papers

In the first paper, "Re-engineering of Old Systems to an Object-Oriented Architecture," Ivar Jacobson and Fredrik Lindström describe steps and strategies for migrating from a non-object-oriented to an object-oriented system. They discuss three scenarios: a complete change of implementation with no functionality change, a partial implementation change with no change in functionality, and a change in functionality.

In the next paper, "Saving a Legacy with Objects," Walter Dietrich, Jr., Lee Nackman, and Franklin Gracer describe their experience with taking a legacy system and overlaying an object-oriented interface on it. The legacy system was the Geometric Design Processor (GDP), a solid modeling system written in PL/1 over a fifteen-year period. It consisted of several hundred thousand lines of code. The authors put an object-oriented interface, called the Tiered Geometric Modeling System, over the GDP. The authors feel that the object-oriented interface provides higher productivity for creating new applications.

In the final paper, "Software Reuse in an Industrial Setting: A Case Study," M.F. Dunn and J.C. Knight describe their experience with reimplementing existing software parts with C++ classes. The authors discuss how prospecting ("component search") and domain analysis processes played an important role in finding object classes to recover. The authors' prospecting results are important because the resulting parts showed a high level of reuse. This is significant because *realizing* actual reuse of parts in a repository is more than simply populating the repository with reusable parts.

Re-engineering of old systems to an object-oriented architecture

Ivar Jacobson

Fredrik Lindström

Objective Systems SF AB
Torshamnsgatan 39
BOX 1128
S-164 22 Kista, Sweden
Phone: +46 8 703 45 41
Fax: +46 8 751 30 96

Abstract

Most of our present-day information systems have been in use for a long time. They have been developed using the system development methods, programming tools, data base handlers, etc. that were available when the development work started. Even if the systems are adapted to changed requirements from the surrounding world, the basic structure and the original technical and methodological ties have been retained. Our goal is to show how an object-oriented development method can be used to gradually modernize an old system, i.e re-engineer the system. We do this by showing how three typical cases of re-engineering are related to object-oriented development. The technique is based on experiences from real projects.

1. Introduction

More and more system owners face the following questions: How do you build a model of your system that enables you to reason about modifications? How do you gradually replace parts of the system? How can you integrate a modern programming technique such as object-oriented programming into an existing system? This paper will summarize a technology that will answer these questions.

The basis of our technology is system development using object-oriented technique. The technology implies that occurrences from the application domain are modelled as objects and associations between objects. The resulting system model will be used as a mapping between the occurrences of the application domain and programming elements in the existing system.

Changes in the objects of the application domain can be traced directly to the same objects in the model. Different discussions about changes in the system will therefore be more precise. For example, if a new type of communication protocol shall be used, you can easily identify which program elements in the existing system are candidates for a change.

The technique is founded on two assertions:

1. A change in the application domain is frequently local in the sense that it concerns a behaviour or an occurrence with a clear delimitation.

2. An object-oriented system model can be used to describe a system designed in a non object-oriented manner.

340

It is generally unrealistic to replace an old system by a completely new system; such a change requires too much resources. You must find ways of gradually replacing older system parts without completely losing the investments made so far. Our basic principle is that an old system must be modernized gradually. Figure [1] shows how changes successively can carve out the original system. Eventually, the entire system will be replaced.

The rest of this paper is organized in the following way. First, a presentation of re-engineering, its goals and definitions. Next, we introduce a combination of object-oriented system development and re-engineering. Third, experiences from three projects are presented. Last, a conclusion. Throughout this paper we assume a familiarity of concepts like object, inheritance, encapsulation, analysis, and design.

2. Re-engineering.

All systems have a limited lifetime. Each implemented change erodes the structure which makes the following change more expensive. As time goes on, the cost to implement a change will be too high, and the system will then be unable to support its intended task. This is

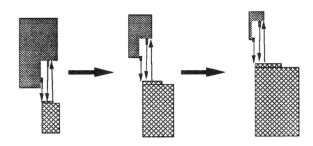

Figure [1]. We gradually want to replace an existing implementation with an object-oriented.

true of all systems, independent of their application domain or technological base.

Before the system reaches this state something must be done. Depending on its position in a "changeability - business value" matrix one of four actions is possible, see figure [2].

We will assume that the old system is difficult to change but has a high business value, in this case we choose to re-engineer the system. A system with a satisfactory degree of changeability or a low business value either does not need the re-engineering investment or is not worth it. What then is "re-engineering"? *Re-engineering is the process of creating an abstract description of a system, reason about a change at the higher abstraction level, and then re-implement the system.* Re-engineering is subsequently defined in terms

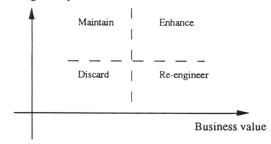

Figure [2]. Decision matrix, what to do with an old system

of relations between different levels of abstraction. Intuitively and similar to (1), this can be expressed with the following formula:

Re-engineering =
Reverse engineering+ Δ + Forward
engineering.

The first element of re-engineering, "Reverse engineering", is the activity of defining a more abstract, and easier to understand, representation of the system.

The second, "Δ" represents change of the system. Changes have two major dimensions, change of functionality and change of implementation technique. The third, "Forward engineering" (i.e normal system development) is the activity of creating a representation that is executeable, e.g. finally a program written in Smalltalk or C. Since the concept of forward engineering is familiar to most readers we will not discuss it further in this section.

341

2.1. Reverse engineering

The goal of reverse engineering is to capture an understanding of the behavior and the structure of the system and be able to communicate this to others. To do this we need at least the three following things:

a) A concrete graph that describes the components of the system and their interrelationship.

b) An abstract graph showing the behavior and the structure of the system.

c) A mapping between the two, i.e how something in the abstract graph relates to the concrete graph and vice versa.

The abstract graph should be free of implementation details. For example, mechanisms for persistent storage or partitioning into processes should not appear on this graph . The concrete graph must, on the other hand, show these details. The mapping between the two should tell us how the ideal world of analysis is implemented the way the concrete graph describes.

2.2. Change

From the perspective of re-engineering we classify changes into two orthogonal dimensions, change of functionality and change of implementation technique. The first is the most common of the two but a change of implementation technique seems to be in increasing demand, see (2) and (3).

A change of functionality comes from a change of the business rules. Thus, modifications of the busines rules results in modifications of the system. Change of functionality doesn't affect how the system is implemented, i.e how the forward engineering is carried out: an end user of a system need never know if the system is implemented with Smalltalk or C.

A new implementation technique of an information management system could mean that the organization will use C++ instead of C, or use an object-oriented database management system instead of a relational one. Needless to say, a change of implementation technique is not an easy process, even if there are tools that can do part of the job automatically.

The dimensions are orthogonal in the sense that it is meaningful to talk about changes in one without changes in the second. We can change the functionality without changing the implementation technique and vice versa. When only part of the system changes its implementation technique it is necessary to enable communication between the two parts. Different languages and operating systems are more or less supportive in this task, a basic functionality that must be supported is that an application can be called on request from another application. (General reasoning about this is found in (4)).

2.3. A small example

Let us consider an invoice system as a small and trivial example to illustrate the process of re-engineering.We assume that the only available description of the system is a number of files of C-code and a database description in SQL. The changes involve both functionality and implementation technique. The change in functionality is that two limitations of the current system have to be removed. It only allows one address per customer and a user can only work with one invoice at the time. The change of implementation technique will be to rewrite part of the system in C++.

The first step, reverse engineering, means that we identify how the components of the system relate to each other and then create a more abstract description of the system. The relationships between components are identified, e.g. the dependencies between the files and the C-functions, the C-functions and the database descriptions, etc. After that, an abstract description (in the sense that we deliberately leave out implementation relevant information) of the system is created, e.g. a dataflow diagram for the C-functions and an entity relationship model of the database description. The process of creating a more abstract description can in theory be repeated as many times as necessary. Practically, it is enough with two levels (design and analysis).

After the first step, we will have an abstract model that shows the business rules of the invoice system and a number of mappings between the different levels of

342

abstraction. Part of the abstract model represents how invoices are regulated by the legal system, other parts represent how the organization that once ordered the system wanted the invoice system to work. The mappings comprise the design decisions that occur when transforming an abstract representation to a concrete one.

The second step, reasoning about the changes in functionality, is done at a more abstract level. Without the abstract model we would have to reason with low-level non-problem domain concepts and make statements like "add one more table that contains the references between customers and addresses". Instead, at the higher level of abstraction, we can say "change the association between the entities Customer and Address".

Next, we redesign the system from the abstract representation to the more concrete representation, i.e forward engineering. In this process we must take the changes of implementation technique into consideration. Since we only change the technique for part of the system we have to answer the question "Where should the border between the old and the new system be"? When we formulate the answer we have to consider what mechanisms there are available that make the communication possible. When implementing the system we also must take all recaptured design decisions into consideration.

To summarize, when we re-engineer a system we need:

a)   A representation of the system "as it is", at some level of abstraction.

b)   A logical representation of the system, at a level that makes it possible to reason about changes in functionality.

c)   A way to capture design decisions, or knowing why the system is implemented the way it is.

d)   A technique that enables two different implementations to communicate.

e)   A technique to delimit the part of the system that we want to explore (without this it is impossible to re-engineer a large sytem)

3.   Different scenarios for re-engineering .

This chapter outlines a combination of object-oriented system development and re-engineering. Since there are many issues involved in the process we introduce the necessary concepts one at the time using three different scenarios. Scenarios that can be combined in a straightforward manner. We will describe re-engineering with:

1.   A complete change of implementation technique and no change in the functionality.

2.   A partial change in implementation technique and no change in functionality.

3.   A change in functionality.

3.1.   Complete re-engineering with no change in functionality.

A complete change of implementation technique will seldom occur for a large system. Nevertheless, we will use the scenario to illustrate part of the re-engineering process, namely reverse engineering and introduce some concepts. Figure [3] shows an overview of the transformation process. In the figure, the rectangles describe different representations of the system. The dark grey represents the existing system, the light grey

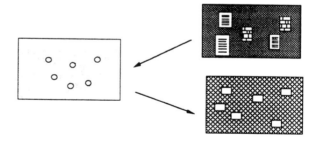

Figure [3]. The figure describes how all of the old system is transformed into an object-oriented implementation.

represents the analysis model, and the middle grey represents the object-oriented implementation, i.e the lighter a rectangle is, the more abstract it is. Rectangles inside the existing system represent the primitive description elements(defined in 3.1.1). Circles inside the analysis model represent analysis objects. Rectangles inside the object-oriented implementation represent design objects.

343

The main steps of the re-engineering process are:

1. Prepare an analysis model. Described in 3.1.1.
2. Map each analysis object to the implementation of the old system. Described in 3.1.2
3. Redesign the system using a forward engineering technique for object-oriented system development. The last step of this re-engineering scenario is to implement the analysis model. This is achieved through a forward engineering process as described in (5).

3.1.1. Prepare an analysis model

The first step, prepare an analysis model, requires that we assimilate the existing information about the system. The existing information has many different forms, e.g. requirements specifications, user operating instructions, maintenance manuals, training manuals, design documentation, source code files, and database schema descriptions. We call them here description elements. An important subset of the description elements is the set of description elements that represent the true system, e.g. source code or documentation that is consistent with the source code, these are called "primitive" description elements.

What is then a primitive description element? Naturally, their nature depends on the quality of the documentation. In the worst case, e.g. when we only trust the source code, their granularity is on the level of methods of a class.

> D is the set of all description elements.
>
> $D_{Primitive}$ is a subset of D, where $D_{Primitive}$ represents a description of the system that is consistent with the source code.

From the set of description elements we prepare an analysis model, see figure [4]. This is done by using the criterias for finding objects that are described in the object-oriented method we use, e.g. see (5), (6), (7), (8). The resulting analysis model can be regarded as a graph, we have a number of analysis objects A_i that are connected to one another with a set of directed edges, E. The edges have different semantics in the

analysis model, but these are ignored at this stage (they all imply some kind of dependency of the terminal object).

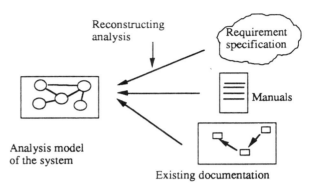

Figure [4]. Preparation of the analysis model.

> The analysis model is represented by a directed graph (A, E, $f(a_i, a_j)$).
>
> A, the nodes, is the set of all analysis objects identified from the description elements, E is the set of all arcs between the nodes, and f is a function that associates an arc with an ordered pair of nodes. The function represents a dependency between the analysis object.

3.1.2. Map each analysis object to the implementation of the old system.

Part of the reverse engineering process is to have a mapping between the analysis model and the system.

We have two constraints on the analysis model:

a) All analysis objects must be motivated by at least one primitive description element. We can express that with is_motivated_by, a mapping from the analysis model to the set of primitive description elements.

> For each analysis object A_i, there must exist at least one element $D_{Prim j}$ such that is_motivated_by($A_i, D_{Prim j}$) exists.

344

b) All edges in the analysis model must be motivated by at least one primitive description element. This is also expressed with is_motivated_by.

> For each edge E_i of the analysis model, there must exist at least one element D_{Prim_j} such that is_motivated_by(E_i, D_{Prim_j}) exists.

Also abstract analysis objects and inheritance associations can be motivated by description elements.

We use the analysis objects, the description elements (both primitive and non-primitive), and the guidance from the experts of the system to map the analysis objects to the implementation of the old system.This is comparable with the normal process of analyzing a system, except for the vast amount of information.

After this step we have a situation as described in figure [5].

3.2. Partial re-engineering with no change in functionality.

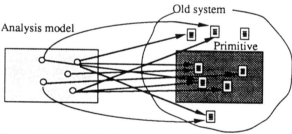

Figure [5] All analysis objects and edges must be motivated by at least one primitive description element. Note that they also can be motivated by non-primitive description elements.

The goal is to make the object-oriented application believe that the whole system consists of objects, the process is visualized in figure [6]. The thick arrows symbolizes the transformations between different levels of abstraction. The thin lines shows the communication between the object-oriented system and the remaining part of the old system.

The main steps of this process are:

1. Identify the part of the system that will be reimplemented using object-oriented technique.
2. Prepare an analysis model of the part to be exchanged and its environment.
3. Map each object to the old implementation of the system .
4. Iterate the previous steps until the interface between the part to be exchanged and the rest of the existing system is acceptable.
5. In parallel:
5.1 Design the new subsystem and its interface to the rest of the old system.
5.2 Modify the old system and add an interface to the new subsystem.
6. Integrate and test the new subsystem and the modified old system.

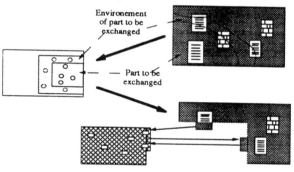

Figure [6]. Part of the system is implemented with an object-oriented technique. The thick arrows symbolizes the transformations between different levels of abstraction. The thin lines shows the communication between the object-oriented system and the remaining part of the old system.

3.2.1. Identify the part of the old system that will be reimplemented using object-oriented technique.

Two subsets of $D_{Primitive}$ are created. The first is D_x, which contains the elements that the new subsystem exchange. The second subset is D_{Env}, which contains the neighbours of D_x. A neighbour is an element that:

a) isn't already included in D_x.
b) is adjacent to elements in D_x in a dependency graph, i.e either a terminal or a initial node.

345

Thus, there must be a graph that shows the dependencies between the primitive description elements. The graph is either implicit, i.e exists in the minds of the technical experts, or explicit, i.e exists in a readable form. In an ideal situation, we would like to have the complete graph. However, due to the size of such a graph we only make it explicit for the part we need to study.

A readable form is always preferable. Although advanced tools and techniques exist, technical experts will always make the task substantially easier.

> A directed graph ($D_{Primitive}$, E_D, $g(D_{Pi}$, D_{Pj})) is created.
>
> $D_{Primitive}$, the nodes, is the set of all primitive description elements, E_D is the set of arcs between the nodes, and g is a function that associates an arc with an ordered pair of nodes. The function represents a dependency between the primitive description elements.

3.2.2. Prepare an analysis model of the part to be exchanged and its environment.

This step is similar to the corresponding step in the previous scenario. The difference is that we only have to concentrate our efforts of understanding the system to a limited part of D. Thus, prepare an analysis model representing the union of D_x and D_{Env}.

3.2.3. Map each analysis object to the implementation of the old system.

We use the function is_motivated_By(x, D_{Pj}) to map the objects and edges of the analysis model to the elements in $D_{Primitive}$. We can then divide the analysis model into two subsets:

a) A_x, which represents the part of the model that definitely will be implemented with the new technique.

b) A_{Env}, analysis objects will serve as wrappers of the old system. They represent objects that A_x is related to.

3.2.4. Evaluate the interface between the part to be exchanged and the remaining part of the old system.

When we have decided what part of the old system that we want to change, we can create an interface between the new and the old system. At this stage, when a better understanding of the old system is reached, it is time to evaluate the interface, i.e we have to examine the partition of $D_{Primitive}$. Through changing the set D_x it is possible to get a set D'_x that, through D'_{Env}, gives a better interface between the old and new subsystems. When we do this we have to repeat the previous steps until we have an interface that is acceptable in terms of implementation cost.

During the evaluation of the interface we must take technical aspects in consideration, e.g. see (9) who describes the technical problems that occurred when an object-oriented language was built on top of an existing system. In general, most of these aspects arises from the problem of communicating the state of one instance between the new and the old subsystem. The basic problem is atomicity of transactions, i.e no intermediate states of the instance should be visible for its clients. As a goal, the cut between the subsystems should be made so that only one of them manages the state of an object and works as a server to the other subsystems. Despite this goal, implementation restrictions may make it unattainable. In that case, we must allow multiple copies of the instance.

3.2.5. Design the new subsystem and its interface to the old system.

The new system is implemented as the object-oriented method prescribes. Objects in A_{Env} are implemented with a set of classes that let the object communicate with the old system, see figure [7].

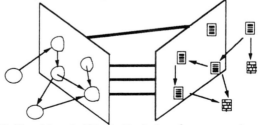

Figure [7]. The objects half-buried in the interface encapsulate the old system.

346

This way, the other objects of the application only sees objects. The objects of A_{Env} behave like objects from the new subsystem and like old software from the old subsystem

Thus, the encapsulation property of objects makes it possible to successively move the plane further and further into the old system. This way it is possible to gradually replace the old system with an object-oriented system.

3.2.6. Modify the old system and add an interface to the new system.

In parallel, we have to modify the old system. All parts that communicate with D_x, i.e. calls procedures or uses data in D_x, are replaced. Instead of their original code, they have to use the interface to the new system. The set D_{Env} contains these parts. Also, we must modify the parts in D_x so that a call or an access to them results in an error. An activation of them means that we have missed redirecting communication meant for the new subsystem.

3.3. Re-engineering with change of functionality.

This scenario is a normal forward engineering process. We add changes in functionality in the analysis model and implement them using the object-oriented technique. The result of this process is described in figure [8].

The main steps of the process are:
1. Change the analysis model according to requirements.
2. Design the system.

Only the first step is described, for a description of the second see (5).

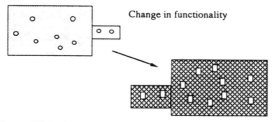

Figure [8] A change of functionality. In this case an addition is depicted.

3.3.1. Change analysis model according to requirements

We change the analysis model in accordance with the requirements on changes in functionality. New objects and edges are added as described in the normal forward engineering process. Objects identified from the old system either are deleted or receive new attributes and edges. Thus, the resulting analysis model can be partitioned into three subgraphs, one that contains all the new objects, one that contains the changed ones, and one that contains the unchanged. We then have three different subsets of the analysis model:

a) A_{New}, which represents the new objects.
b) $A_{\Delta func}$, which represents the elements with a new functionality.
c) $A_{No\Delta func}$, which represents the elements not affected by the change in functionality.

4. Case studies

We have used ObjectOry to re-engineer a number of systems, including two major systems. The first system was a military system for handling spare parts, and the second system was a telecommunication system. One of the others, a traffic control system is also presented.

Our experiences with re-engineering come from using ObjectOry™ (see (5)), an industrial software development process. ObjectOry is a mature object-oriented technique with many important features for supporting the reverse engineering process. Particulary, one unique concept of ObjectOry, use cases, have been an excellent tool for reverse engineering. Briefly, a use case is a sequence of user interactions with the system. Its purpose is to define a typical way of using the system. In the context of reverse engineering, we explore an old system with use cases. That is, together with an expert of the old system, the system analyzer identify a use case. Then, they follow the use case through the existing documentation of the system.

Another important aspect of ObjectOry is the separation of analysis and design. As a result of the projects with re-engineering, our belief in this has been enforced. With an analysis model that clearly, without imp-

347

lementation details, captures the business rules of an organization, it is much easier to understand and change a system. The role of the design model is to capture all the necessary modifications dependent on the implementation environment. Today, all the systems we have reversed or re-engineered have only been documented with at most a design model. They have completely lacked an analysis model.

4.1. Spare part system

The goal of the first project was to demonstrate practically how an object-oriented system development method can be used when designing distributed information systems. The example used for the work was DELTA, a system for redistribution of stock. The system is used by all defence branches in the Swedish Armed Forces. The project was executed on assignment from the Defence Materiel Administration FMV, and our work amounted to about 4 to 5 manyears.

The re-engineering has been done down to class level on a smaller part of the system that concerns spare parts, for example customer orders and redistribution of material between storage places. These functions have been implemented in an object-oriented environment including an object-oriented data base.

We have also specified and implemented the changes required to make the system a geographically distributed system.

The same DELTA system has been used in a parallel study to demonstrate how a conventional, form-based user interface in a terminal environment can be extended with window handling, graphics, and direct manipulation in a personal computer environment.

The main categories of the description elements of the project were:
a)   database schemas
b)   Cobol code
c)   user manuals
d)   interviews with users and technical experts

Before the project had started, the organisation responsible for the system had planned to replace the whole system at once. However, after evaluating the initial results of the project they changed their minds. The effort to replace the whole system was found too large. Instead it was decided that a way of gradual replacement must be found.

4.2.   Telecommunication system

The communication system was reverse engineered in a small project of about 1 manyear. The original work of the system was about 120 manyears and it was developed with an object-based technology. The purpose of the project was to make an analysis model that will be used to restructure the system. After the project, the organisation responsible for the system estimated that a complete reverse engineering process would take about 10 manyears. Due to the understandibility of the analysis model, they also concluded that the model should make it possible to reduce the time to get experienced system engineers from 5 to 2 years.

4.3.   Traffic control system

Basically, the traffic contol system involves three different systems. A resource allocation system, a traffic control system, and a communication system. Historically, the traffic control system was developed first, then the resource allocation system, and last the communication system.

Related to figure [2], the traffic control system is the most difficult to change, closely followed by the resource allocation system. But, the resource allocation system has a high business value and it depends on the traffic control system. Therefore, the company has choosen to re-implement part of the traffic control system and part of the resource allocation system. The communication system is left untouched since its degree of changeability is considered sufficiently high.

348

The project has both a partial change of implementation technique and a change in functionality. To get a complete understanding of the three systems we studied functions that spanned over all of the systems . After that, we created an analysis model and its motivations, see figure [9].

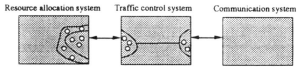

Resource allocation system   Traffic control system   Communication system

Figure [9]. The delimitations and the objects of the trafic control system.

The desired result is found in figure [10]. Part of the resource allocation system and part of the traffic control system will be implemented with object-oriented technology. The change is that the new technology will only be used for a part of the traffic control system, the other part will be left out. Thus, we have to create an interface between the different subsystems and modify them accordingly. On the other hand, the communication system will not be effected by any changes and can be left as it is.

Modified Resource allocation system   New Traffic control system   Unchanged Communication system

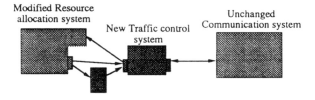

Figure [10]. The desired result of the re-engineering of the resource allocation system.

Based on these projects, we estimate that it requires 1/10 - 1/20 of the total development time of the old system to create an analysis model. That is, if the total development time of a system is 10 manyears, the analysis model takes about 0.5 - 1 manyear to reverse engineer. Of course this figure is uncertain, but we believe that the magnitude is correct.

5. Conclusions

The life span of an information system comprises specification, design and maintenance. The maintenance phase dominates in time and often also with respect to resources. During this phase the system is subjected to a number of changes and additions. The gap between the older technology in the system and the new technology that becomes available increases successively. Changes in the activities of an organization also mean that systems grow old.

Gradually the system approaches a limit where it no longer is cost-efficient or even technically motivated to continue the maintenance. But the cost of enforcing the required changes is usually very high. This poses a serious dilemma for system managers and similar personnel. A possible way out of this dilemma is to define well delimited system parts that are candidates for modernization. Provided this delimitation is made in an efficient manner, replacement can be made with moderate changes in the existing system. This is where re-engineering can help.

We have described a practical method for re-engineering. The method is based on an object-oriented modelling. We have described how the work can be divided into a number of steps from analysis to design and finally design and testing, i.e. the method can be performed in a systematic manner.

We have achieved the following: In a simple manner and with limited efforts you can make a model of an existing system. By means of the model you can reason about where a change can be made, its extent and how it shall be mapped on the existing system. The new model is object-oriented and can serve as a basis for a future development plan. The extensions can be designed as additions outside the existing systems with a minimum of adaptations in the form of interfaces.

Today, we think that the subject of re-engineering is too focused on tools. Despite their importance they are not sufficient. We think it is necessary to change the focus of re-engineering to the complete life-cycle of the system, i.e. try to incorporate re-engineering as a part of a development process, and not as a substitute for it.

349

In the long run, we want to industrilize reenginering techniques so that they will be incorporated as a part of ObjectOry. We belive that Objectory has a good foundation for this. Besides beeing object-oriented, it is based on a mature forward enginering process (see 5). This means that a new system will keep a high degree of changeability.

6. References

(1) J. Chikovsky and J. H. Cross. "Reverse enginee-ring and Design Recovery: A Taxonomy.". IEEE Soft-ware 1990;(January):13-17.

(2) Economist. "How computers can choke compa-nies". 1990 June 9:71-72.

(3) J. Duntemann and C. Marinacci. "New objects for old structures". Byte 1990 April:261-266.

(4) P. Zave. "A Compositional Approach to Multipara-digm Programming". IEEE Software 1989;(Septem-ber):15-25.

(5) I. Jacobson. "Object Oriented Development in an Industrial Environment.". In: Proc. OOPSLA. Orlan-do, Florida.: ACM Press, 1987: 183-191.

(6) P. Coad. *Object-Oriented Analysis.*Englewood Cliffs, New Jersey: Prentice-Hall, 1990:232. (E. Your-don, ed.) Yourdon Press Computing Series

(7) G. Booch. *Object Oriented Design.*Redwood City, California: The Benjamin/Cummings Publishing Com-pany, Inc., 1990:580. (G. Booch, ed.) The Benjamin/Cummings Series in Ada and Software Engineering

(8) R. Wirfs-Brock, B. Wilkerson and L. Wiener. *De-signing Objec-Oriented Software.*Englewood Cliffs, New Jersey: Prentice-Hall, 1990:341.

(9) C. Dietrich, L. R. Nackman and F. Gracer. "Saving a Legacy with objects". In: Proc. OOPSLA. New Or-leans: ACM Press, 1989: 77-83.

350

77

Saving a Legacy with Objects

WALTER C. DIETRICH, JR.
LEE R. NACKMAN
FRANKLIN GRACER

Manufacturing Research Department
IBM Research Division, Thomas J. Watson Research Center
Yorktown Heights, NY 10598

Abstract: Developers of application software must often work with "legacy systems." These are systems that have evolved over many years and are considered irreplaceable, either because it is thought that duplicating their function would be too expensive, or because they are trusted by users. Because of their age, such systems are likely to have been implemented in a conventional language with limited use of data abstraction or encapsulation. The lack of abstraction complicates adding new applications to such systems and the lack of encapsulation impedes modifying the system because applications depend on system internals. We describe our experience providing and using an object-oriented interface to a legacy system.

1. INTRODUCTION

Developers of application software systems must often work with "legacy systems." These are systems that have evolved over many years and are considered irreplaceable, either because re-implementing their function is considered to be too expensive, or because they are trusted by users. Because of their age, such systems are likely to have been implemented in a conventional procedural language with limited use of data abstraction or encapsulation. The lack of abstraction complicates adding new applications to such a system and the lack of encapsulation impedes modifying the system itself because applications come to depend on system internals. We describe in this paper our experience in providing and using an object-oriented programmer's interface to a legacy system.

The legacy system used in our study is the Geometric Design Processor (GDP) [10] [11], a solid modeling system consisting of several hundred thousand lines of PL/I code which has evolved over 15 years. Solid modeling systems provide means for representing, manipulating, and analyzing models of three-dimensional solid objects. They also provide facilities for managing large assemblies of parts, bills of material, dimensions and tolerances, etc. GDP is used routinely in a production environment for the mechanical design of IBM mainframe computers [11].

In a production environment, user requests for new function must be satisfied quickly. This has led to the evolution of many PL/I procedures for creating and manipulating solids, managing data, and interacting with the user. These have been collected and organized into a programming interface. The system described here, the *Tiered Geometric Modeling System (TGMS)*, provides an alternative, object-oriented interface to the GDP programming interface. We believe that such an interface provides a higher-productivity environment for developing new applications.

The overall architecture of *TGMS* is shown in Figure 1. It consists of GDP, interfaced to the interpreter for AML/X (an object-oriented programming language intended for use in design and manufacturing applications [5]), together with some AML/X class definitions. The class definitions constitute the programming environment seen by *TGMS* users.

This paper discusses important issues that arose in *TGMS's* design and implementation, emphasizing the issues that we believe will arise in providing an object-oriented interface to any legacy system. We conclude with a synopsis of *TGMS* user experiences.

2. DESCRIPTION OF THE TIERED GEOMETRIC MODELING SYSTEM

2.1 **Description of the Legacy System:** GDP is an interactive graphic system for modeling three-dimensional objects, especially mechanical parts and assemblies. GDP provides several kinds of simple solids, called *primitives;* primitive types are cuboid (rectangular block), cylinder,

78

cone, hemisphere, translated polygon and rotated polygon (solids of translation and revolution). Complex solids are created by combining solids using set operations (union, intersection, and difference).

Various geometric operations can be performed on solids, such as checking for alignment and interference. Several physical properties (e.g., mass) can also be calculated. A tree is used to represent the structure of the product being modeled. Solids are associated with nodes in the tree: leaf nodes correspond to primitives, internal nodes to combinations of primitives.

GDP is written in PL/1 and runs on IBM mainframe computers, using a variety of graphics workstations. It was written and evolved as a monolithic system, but recently, selected subroutines in GDP were modified and documented to form an application programming interface. The programming interface has several subsets. One subset performs functions required for user interaction, such as pointing and menu display. Another subset allows the programmer to create and manipulate solids.

2.2 **Overview of *TGMS*:** The classes in *TGMS* are designed to be easy to use but powerful. This is achieved by keeping several design goals in mind: orthogonality, conciseness, and compatibility with AML/X. *Orthogonality* means that a single method or subroutine doesn't perform logically separate functions. It usually makes systems easier to learn and use. By *compatibility with*

AML/X, we mean that the semantics of the class should be similar to those of the intrinsic AML/X types. For example, a=b means assign a copy of b to a if a and b are both instances of the same built-in type; it should mean the same if they are both instances of the solid object class. *Conciseness* has the obvious meaning. When dealing with classes that represent mathematical entities, it is possible to design a concise notation that is easy to read by building on our experience with equations and formulas.

TGMS has classes for these low-level geometric entities: point, vector, and transformation matrix [6]. A transformation matrix can be used to represent a translation, a rotation, a change in size (scaling), or a combination of these. The transformation matrix classes have several class methods that create basic transformations such as translations and rotations about the axes. These classes overload the AML/X arithmetic operators so that concise and easily understood expressions can be written using these classes. For example, if point1 is a point, vec1 is a vector, and tmat1 and tmat2 are transformation matrices, point1+vec1 evaluates to the point that results from adding vec1 to point1, point1*tmat1 yields the point that results from applying the transformation matrix tmat1 to point1, and tmat1*tmat2 evaluates to the transformation that would result from applying tmat1 followed by tmat2.

The solid class is used to represent three-dimensional solid objects. As shown in Figure 2, the

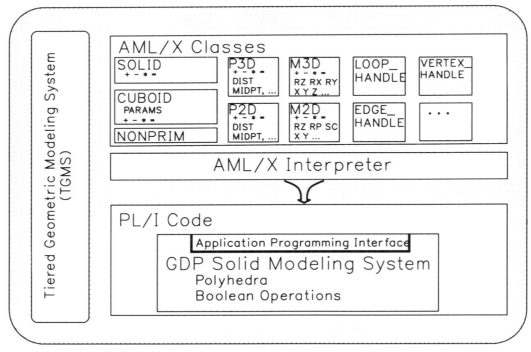

Figure 1. High-level structure of *TGMS*. This figure is based on a figure in [3] copyright (1989). Reprinted by permission of John Wiley & Sons, Ltd.

solid class has subclasses primitive and nonprim.

The primitive class has one subclass for each kind of primitive solid. Instances are created by sending messages to the appropriate classes, giving as arguments the parameters that define the shape, e.g., height and radius for cylinder, polygon and distance for extrusion.

The nonprim class has two subclasses: hull, for solids created by computing the convex hull of a set of points, and boolean_combination, for solids created

by applying union, intersection, or difference (subtraction) to a pair of solids.

Instances of solid can be created by sending messages to the these subclasses. Instances can also be created by using overloaded arithmetic operators to move solids in space, change their size, or perform Boolean operations. For example, evaluating (solid1+solid2)+vec1 results in a new object (of type union) that is the union of solid1 and solid2, trans-

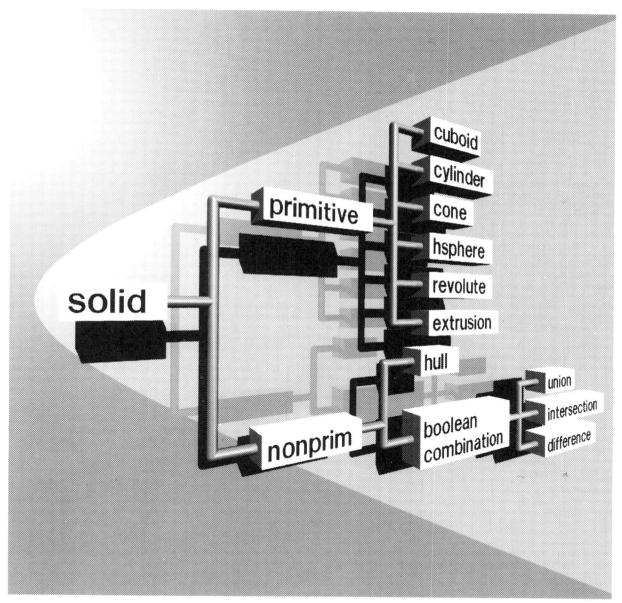

Figure 2. Hierarchical structure of the classes for solid objects. In this rendition, each class's name is closer to the viewer than its subclasses names. This ray-traced image was generated with *TGMS*, using two simulated light sources. (The wall behind the tree contains a shadow of the tree and a reflection of its back.)

lated in the direction and the distance specified by the vector vec1.

Instances can be changed using the assignment operators (=, +=, etc.). The solid class overloads +=, -=, and *= so that operations that modify a solid can be written more concisely. Another advantage of this notation is that using an operator such as += can be more efficient if the modeler's algorithm for the operation can update in place.

The class hierarchy is a natural result of the properties of the different kinds of solids. The primitive subclasses have methods that return creation parameters of their instances, whereas other subclasses do not. The creation parameters of a primitive are the basic data values that, taken together with the primitive's type and its orientation, provide an exact and very concise description of the solid.

TGMS also contains classes that allow the boundaries (faces, edges, vertices, etc.) of solids to be queried. More complete descriptions of all of the classes, with sample programs, appear in [2, 3].

3. DESIGN ISSUES

In designing an object-oriented system, the choice of objects and methods is crucial. The system builder is typically free to make design decisions that result in the most natural metaphor for the system's application domain. Unfortunately, since this is not true when legacy-based object-oriented systems are being developed, a host of new design issues are raised.

Two reasons for implementing an object-oriented system using a legacy system (legacy) are

- the legacy satisfies most of the needs of its users, but a better programming interface is needed for extending or customizing the functions of the legacy, or
- the legacy has code that can be reused to implement (part of) a desired object-oriented system's function.

We built TGMS for both of these reasons.

An important improvement provided by TGMS is to isolate its applications from either modification or replacement of the underlying solid modeler. The GDP programming interface defines data structures and procedures for representing and manipulating solids and lower-level geometric entities. By encapsulating these data structures, TGMS prevents the user from introducing knowledge of the GDP programming interface into new applications. Those GDP functions accessible through the object-oriented interface are also made to appear to be more complete and orthogonal, and thus easier to use.

The second reason for building TGMS resulted from a desire to reuse complex, trusted portions of the GDP code (especially the polyhedral set operations) to implement high-level geometric objects.

Building a single object-oriented system for both reasons requires design compromises. To provide a programming interface for extending GDP's function, the interface must include essentially all of GDP's function,

not just its geometric operations. However, TGMS does not provide access to all of GDP, although most TGMS applications require access to some non-geometric parts of GDP, such as the filing system and the interactive user interface. For example, the GDP model is stored as a tree which is used heavily by GDP applications to aggregate solids and to attach attributes to them. This tree is not exposed by TGMS because more general data structures are simple to implement as classes. This design provides simplicity and generality, but it does not satisfy TGMS applications that need to access the tree (e.g. classes which use models created in GDP sessions.) Therefore, we have had to provide minimal access to GDP's tree despite the loss of simplicity. We believe that one of the most important and difficult aspects of designing a legacy-based object-oriented system is making the trade-off between exposing the legacy's functions and isolating object-oriented applications from changes in the legacy.

This decision is more difficult when the legacy provides an interactive interface as well as a programmer's interface. Should the object-oriented system's end-user interface be based on the same subroutines as the legacy interface? If so, it may be difficult for object-oriented applications to provide the end-user interfaces their users need. For example, GDP's interactive user interface is intended for use by mechanical designers; applications written in TGMS often need to present a very different user interface. Nonetheless, user interfaces for three-dimensional geometry applications usually require various rendering algorithms which are expensive to reimplement. For TGMS, we exposed GDP's interactive interface and also provided programmer access to the subroutines that control the interface (e.g. prompting, menu selection, and viewing and rendering). Thus far, this compromise has been satisfactory.

4. EXTERNAL OBJECT IMPLEMENTATION

TGMS was implemented by writing AML/X classes that call GDP subroutines and refer to its data structures. The code that encapsulates the legacy is called the wrapper. The use of the legacy code is called an external object implementation since we do not directly implement the objects in the object-oriented component. For external object implementations to be successful, several problems must be solved [2].

Interlanguage communication: To build an external object implementation, one needs more than simply the ability to call subroutines in the legacy's language. Since the wrapper depends on data that is internal to the legacy, the inter-language communication mechanism must also preserve the legacy's state when legacy subroutines called from the wrapper return.

Garbage collection: If the legacy does its own garbage collection, it must be prevented from collecting data that is referenced by the wrapper. One way to do this is to ensure that for every pointer in the wrapper that refers to legacy data, there is a corresponding (non-garbage) pointer in the legacy that refers to the same data.

Memory compaction: If the wrapper has pointers to the legacy's data and the legacy does compaction, the legacy may move referenced data without updating the wrapper's pointers. There are two solutions. In the first, pointers in the wrapper refer indirectly to legacy data through a table of pointers in the legacy; it must be possible for the wrapper to access the table in a compaction-invariant way. This solution also solves the garbage-collection problem. An alternate solution is not to use pointers from the wrapper to legacy's data. This solution is used in *TGMS* because GDP has memory compaction but not garbage collection.

If pointers in the legacy can also refer to data in the object-oriented part of the legacy-based object-oriented system, the garbage collection and memory compaction problems can occur in both directions. The same techniques may be used to solve the problems in each direction, but it may be necessary to coordinate the two languages' garbage collectors. In *TGMS*, GDP never refers to the wrapper's data.

Object lifetime synchronization: Generally, if block exit or garbage collection deallocates an object in the wrapper, the corresponding legacy object should be freed or made available for garbage collection. This is only practical if wrapper's language has *destroy methods* [1, 3]. We therefore consider destroy methods to be essential for external object implementations.

Cross-system consistency: The preceding problems are well-defined, concrete, and relatively easy to solve. For external object implementations to be successful, one must also carefully control how the legacy and wrapper interact. *Cross-system invariants* are assertions that relate data in both the legacy and wrapper, for example, "For every instance of class *c* in the wrapper, there is exactly one data block (or structure) of type *d* in the legacy." Even if the wrapper's language does not support assertion checking, cross-system invariants are a useful tool during design and debugging.

Cross-system invariants may be violated if the memory management problems described above are not solved. They may also be violated if interrupts are not taken into consideration during design, as our experience illustrates: When a `solid` instance is deallocated, its destroy method deallocates the corresponding GDP polyhedron. In the AML/X environment, users can interrupt the execution of any method, abort execution of the program, and cause the interpreter to resume the read-eval-print loop. If this is done during execution of a solid's destroy method, the `solid` instance will be deallocated but the GDP polyhedron may not be, depending on when the destroy method was interrupted. Because of this general problem, we have concluded that the semantics of AML/X destroy methods should be changed [1]. This also applies to other languages that have both destroy methods and interrupt handling.

Since the legacy frequently has an attractive end-user interface, it is tempting to allow end-users of the legacy-based object-oriented system to use the legacy interface directly (perhaps in conjunction with one designed specifically for the legacy-based object-oriented system). This is especially true early in the life of a legacy-based object-oriented system, when its function may be more important than its user interface. Unfortunately, it is often possible to violate cross-system invariants through direct use of the legacy's end-user interface. This suggests that legacy-based object-oriented system's should only expose a restricted version of the legacy user interface which only allows data to be queried and displayed, not modified.

Increasing Orthogonality: A design goal for any legacy-based object-oriented system should be to present orthogonal classes. Lack of orthogonality in the legacy makes this difficult to achieve because the wrapper implementers must understand all of the undesired interactions in the legacy. *TGMS* provides a good example of this. The stand-alone version of GDP always keeps the displayed view of the model up-to-date with respect to the actual model, which relieves the user from having to account for differences between the displayed model and the actual model. Unfortunately, some of the modeling subroutines in the first version of the GDP programming interface also updated the display.

Synchronizing the display with the model violates orthogonality because graphics and modeling are different functions. As a practical matter, synchronizing them would make *TGMS* less useful for new solid modeling applications because new high-level operations that require several solid modeling steps would involuntarily update the display several times. This would distract end users (and be inefficient). We could have hidden this non-orthogonality but it would have required us to either know which GDP subroutines caused the display to be updated and under what conditions, or to encapsulate the entire GDP user interface. The first alternative was too complicated and the second was beyond the scope of the project. Partly as a result of our experience, the second version of the GDP programming interface was designed with a clean split between modeling and graphics. This increase in orthogonality was evident in other areas of the programming interface as well, e.g. modeling and input. We believe that building a legacy-based object-oriented system on a legacy that lacks orthogonality requires participation of someone with expertise in the architecture and internals of the legacy.

5. CONCLUSIONS

TGMS came into use at the IBM Thomas J. Watson Research Center in 1986. It has not been tested and documented enough to be a production system, but it has been used to build five different applications. The largest application is WADE, a Workcell Application Development Environment [4]. WADE helps users design and test robotic workcells, and contains classes for equipment

82

found in workcells (e.g., robots, sensors, computers, conveyer belts, feeders) and for concepts related to workcells such as trajectories, events, and programs. Users lay out workcells by creating class instances and positioning them or associating them with other class instances. For example, `robot` instances are created and positioned and `program` instances are created and associated with the robots. Once all of the pieces of equipment are set up and associated with a `workcell` instance, the user can tell the workcell to simulate its execution. Using the kinematics and dynamics of the equipment in the workcell, WADE gives a temporally accurate simulation of the workcell. Because it uses the `solid` class to represent the geometric state of the workcell, visualization, static interference analysis (to make sure parts do or don't touch), and other geometric analyses are easy. WADE contains about 50 classes with about 670 methods.

Two new applications of *TGMS* are in the areas of machine vision and automated machining. Given a solid and a set of features (edges, faces, and vertices), the vision application [8, 9] computes the places where a visual sensor can be positioned to view all of the features without occlusion by the solid. It makes heavy use of the boundary representation classes and the Boolean operations. It is written procedurally and contains about 110 subroutines. The other new application is designed to decide what kind of numerically controlled milling machines are able to create a part, given its solid model. This is the first step in the automated creation of parts from their models. The program, based on an algorithm described in [7], recognizes machining process features using the boundary representation and primitive creation parameters of the model's primitives. It uses an attributed finite state grammar to describe ideal machining process features. The actual features present on a part, which may be different from the ideal features because of feature interaction, are recognized using the grammar. The preliminary implementation is almost complete and contains about 60 subroutines.

TGMS users have found it to be easy to learn, easy to use, and powerful. In the words of Levas and Jayaraman [4],

> The use of a production quality geometric modeling system in [WADE] contributed significantly to the capabilities of the resulting environment. The modeling of the geometric components of the equipment and simulation of many processes such as material removal and sensor based motions are directly attributable to the functionality provided by the underlying modeling system (GDP). The ease of interaction with the modeling system that *TGMS* provided facilitated the system development and user interaction.

We believe that this results from achieving the goals of orthogonality, expressiveness, conciseness, extensibility, and simplicity. Conciseness derives from liberal use of operator overloading and powerful aggregation and

mapping facilities in AML/X. Expressiveness derives from conciseness and from design decisions that made the solid classes consistent with the language.

6. FUTURE WORK

The preceding discussion applies to situations in which one legacy is used as part of an object-oriented system. It should be clear that we are not restricted to one legacy per object-oriented system. Several legacy systems could be integrated to build a very powerful object-oriented environment. An example can be taken from the computer-aided design field. A system for computer design should do many things, including three-dimensional design of components (frames, cables, etc.), analysis of their properties (e.g. strength and resistance), and inspection of electrical connections. We might do this in one object-oriented system using one legacy for solid modeling, another for analysis (a partial differential equation solver) and a third legacy for verifying end-to-end connection of wires.

7. ACKNOWLEDGEMENTS

The idea of building object-oriented systems on top of legacy systems, and of using this as an integrating concept as described in the previous section, arose during discussions among Mark Lavin, Lee Nackman, and Michael Wesley on architectures for computer-assisted design and manufacturing systems. Christine Sundaresan helped design and implement *TGMS*. Jarek Rossignac contributed the low-level geometry classes [6] and was an early user of the system. Anthony Levas and Rangarajan Jayaraman decided to build WADE on *TGMS* before implementation of *TGMS* had even begun. Seeing their system running provided inspiration and helped convince us that we were on the right track. Kostantinos Tarabanis, Roger Tsai, Stephen Byers, and Ramesh Srinivasan, our newest users, helped show us where *TGMS* could be improved and sometimes made the improvements for us.

We thank Michael Karasick and Jarek Rossignac for providing many helpful comments on an early version of this paper. Special thanks go to John Barton for his many insightful comments on this paper.

REFERENCES

1. Atkins, M., and Nackman, L. The Active Deallocation of Objects in Object-Oriented Systems. *Software—Practice and Experience*, 18(11):1073-1089, November 1988.
2. Dietrich Jr., W. C., Nackman, L. R., Sundaresan, C. J., and Gracer, F. TGMS: An Object-Oriented System for Programming Geometry. IBM Thomas J. Watson Research Center, RC 13444, Yorktown Heights, NY. January 1988.

3. Dietrich Jr., W. C., Nackman, L. R., Sundaresan, C. J., and Gracer, F. TGMS: An Object-Oriented System for Programming Geometry. *Software—Practice and Experience*, 19(10), October 1989.

4. Levas, A., and Jayaraman, R. WADE: An Object-Oriented Environment for Modeling and Simulation of Workcell Applications. *IEEE Transactions on Robotics and Automation*, 5(3):324-336, June 1989.

5. Nackman, L. R., Lavin, M. A., Taylor, R. H., Dietrich Jr., W. C., and Grossman, D. D. AML/X: A Programming Language for Design and Manufacturing. *Proc. Fall Joint Computer Conference*, 145-159, November 1986.

6. Rossignac, J. R. AML/X tools for primitive geometric calculations: Points, Vectors, Coordinate Frames, and Linear Transformations. IBM Thomas J. Watson Research Center, RA 189, Yorktown Heights, NY. May 1987.

7. Srinivasan, R., and Ferreira, P. Geometric Models of Machining Processes for Computer-Aided Process Planning. *Geometric Modeling for Product Engineering, selected papers from the IFIP/NSF Workshop on Geometric Modeling*, Rensselaerville, NY, September 1988. To appear

8. Tarabanis, K., and Tsai, R. Y. Viewpoint Planning: The Visibility Constraint. *Proc. of DARPA Image Understanding Workshop*, Palo Alto, California, May 27 1989. To appear

9. Tsai, R. Y., and Tarabanis, K. Sensor Placement Planning. *Proc. Third Machine Vision Workshop*, New Brunswick, New Jersey, April 1989. To appear

10. Wesley, M. A., Lozano-Perez, T., Lieberman, L. I., Lavin, M. A., and Grossman, D. D. A Geometric Modeling System for Automated Mechanical Assembly. *IBM Journal of Research and Development*, 24(1):64-74, January 1980.

11. Wolfe, R., Wesley, M., Kyle Jr., J., Gracer, F., and Fitzgerald, W. Solid modelling for production design. *IBM Journal of Research and Development*, 31(3):277-295, May 1987.

SOFTWARE REUSE IN AN INDUSTRIAL SETTING: A CASE STUDY[†]

Michael F. Dunn   John C. Knight

Department of Computer Science
University of Virginia, Charlottesville, VA 22903

ABSTRACT

This paper is a summary of an ongoing case study of software reuse being carried out by the authors in cooperation with Sperry Marine Incorporated. The goals of the study are to analyze the problems that limit reuse and to seek solutions suitable for industrial application.

To help determine its suitability for use within Sperry Marine, an experimental evaluation of object-oriented development was performed that focused on a specific subsystem domain found in several of Sperry Marine's commercial software products. A reuse library populated with classes written in C++ was prepared, and from this library simple versions of two representative subsystems were built. Measurement of the resulting software showed a very high level of reuse. The development of these experimental subsystems is continuing so as to obtain data on systems that are closer to production-level functionality.

1. INTRODUCTION

This paper is a summary of an ongoing case study of software reuse being carried out by the authors in cooperation with Sperry Marine Incorporated. Sperry Marine manufactures computerized marine electronic systems, both ship based and land based.

The case study is being undertaken in an attempt to answer some of the outstanding questions about software reuse by observation and experimentation in a realistic industrial software development setting. The goals of the study are to analyze the problems that limit reuse and to seek solutions suitable for industrial application. Specifically, the case study is looking for opportunities for software reuse in a particular industrial environment, attempting to determine which reuse techniques that have been described in the literature might be best suited to that environment, and to measure the effectiveness of the selected technique or techniques by experiment. At this point, the emphasis in the study and in this paper is on source text reuse although reuse of other artifacts is being considered.

The reuse of work products from project to project was originally viewed as a promising way to address the difficulties with developing and modifying large systems. However, efficient and practical implementation of large-scale software reuse has proven to be much harder than anticipated. As research on the subject has progressed, it has become clear that this proposed answer to the so-called "software crisis" is fraught with problems of its own. Very little is known, for example, about how to create a set of components that can be used in a variety of different systems with little or no change. Similarly, there are no established techniques for the analysis of existing systems to find pieces of code that can be used in new systems. Finally, no design techniques exist that are specifically intended to take advantage of a set of reusable components.

The case study summarized here proceeded based on the assumption that some technique using component-based reuse was the most likely to succeed[‡]. In the initial phase of the study, a thorough review of the software used in four large existing systems was conducted. This review generated a substantial list of modules likely to yield reusable components. Though not immediately suitable for reuse, these modules will be reengineered to permit their placement in a conventional reuse library. By conventional we mean one in which parts are stored consisting of source code procedures, functions, or other unit of functionality. The review also yielded insight into the mechanics of the code scavenging process, concepts for appropriate support tools, and confidence in the conclusion that existing code can yield reusable components in contrast to some opinions in the literature [2]. The component search is discussed in section 2.

A careful examination of the software designs of the four systems suggested that organizing components as object classes would be a profitable technique for exploiting reuse in the construction of such systems. Work that has been published in this general area includes that of Jette and Smith [4], Meyer [6], and Wybolt [12].

[†] Sponsored in part by Sperry Marine, Inc., of Charlottesville, VA.

[‡] This is in contrast to other reuse techniques such as those based on *application generators* or *application-specific languages* which are less frequently used.

Reprinted from *Proc. Int'l Conf. on Software Engineering*, 1991, pp. 329-338. ©1991 by The Institute of Electrical and Electronics Engineers, Inc. All rights reserved.

In spite of the growing popularity of object-oriented development in the past several years [1], there is still very little literature available detailing experiences with this technique in industrial settings. There is even less data available focusing on object-oriented design as a method for structuring reusable components and the levels of reuse achieved thereby. That which has been published typically discusses fairly obvious and tractable problem domains, such as windowing software and editors.

To begin the process of assessment of object-oriented development as a mechanism for reuse we performed an evaluation experiment. The phases of the experiment were first to select a domain for study, second to perform a domain analysis, third to prepare a reuse library for the domain, and finally to construct and measure two specimen systems in a controlled manner. In section 3, we summarize the domain analysis, and section 4 describes some of the key aspects of the library. A framework for evaluation and a preliminary evaluation of the reuse library based on the construction of the specimen systems is presented in section 5. Finally, section 6 contains our conclusions.

2. COMPONENT SEARCH

The component search had three main goals. The first was to derive an initial set of useful components to form the basis of reusable software libraries, both conventional and object-oriented. The second was to gain insight into the process of comparative source code analysis, and the third goal was to get ideas for tools to make studies of this type easier.

The systems studied were:

- *Adaptive Digital Gyropilot (ADG)*
  The ADG is a shipboard system that provides automatic piloting control.

- *Raster Scan Radar (RASCAR)*
  The RASCAR is a shipboard system that provides a raster-scan radar display of the local region surrounding the ship. It allows simple navigation chart outlines to be superimposed on these radar images.

- *Voyage Management Station (VMS)*
  The VMS is a very complex shipboard system that provides navigation support. Facilities provided include waypoint planning, detailed display of digitized navigation charts, position monitoring of the user's own ship, and display of radar-input images of other ships in the area.

- *Vessel Traffic System (VTS)*
  The VTS is a land-based system that provides support for harbor traffic monitoring. The system allows harbor controllers to see radar-input images of ships in the entire harbor area and their positions relative to each other, to geographical features and hazards, and to designated restricted areas.

SYSTEM	PLATFORM	LINES	MODULES
ADG	M68000	40K	40
RASCAR	M68000	60K	70
VMS	286/386 PC's	125K	150
VTS	286/386 PC's	60K	80

Table 1 - Sizes of Systems Examined

Each of these systems is written in C and is several thousand source lines long, operates in real-time, and uses a multitasking software structure. Some other system characteristics are shown in Table 1.

Searching for reusable components within these systems was achieved by first discussing each system with its developers and then scanning the source text manually in search of recurring processing patterns. The discussions with the developers were organized around an informal list of questions. Despite the informality, several insights were gained. For example, there was agreement by all of the programmers that a more systematic reuse strategy would probably reduce development cycle time, that an informal, "opportunistic" reuse strategy was already being used, and that certain domains, such as device interfaces, would be productive sources of parts.

It became apparent early on that certain semantic patterns were repeated in various places throughout the code. For example, receiving user input from menus or screen icons, drawing icons on the screen, and processing network messages tends to follow the same basic set of steps regardless of in which system it is done. The fact that programs tend to be composed of such semantic patterns has been the topic of much study. Soloway and Ehrlich note that experienced programmers think in terms of plans, or sets of conceptual patterns that help them organize programs in terms of the meaning of a set of statements taken together, rather than focusing on the individual statements themselves [10]. Rich and Waters carry the plan concept further in developing the idea of cliches in their Programmer's Apprentice project [9]. We merely note that we observed exactly the same phenomenon in four large software systems and this suggests the strong potential for reuse.

The first result of this search was the identification of specific functional categories into which reusable components could be grouped. In many cases, specific reusable components themselves were identified. About 140 specific software artifacts ranging in size from single functions to entire modules were identified as good candidates for yielding reusable components. The

330

functional categories of the artifacts found included such areas as data structure manipulation, graphics processing, navigation calculation, and network management. Each artifact is expected to yield several reusable components.

A second result of the component search was the realization that concurrency and exception handling have substantial impact on software structures and they are important factors affecting reuse. The systems examined in this study all employ multitasking with mutual exclusion achieved using semaphores implemented in a proprietary operating system. The implication of this on software reuse is potentially considerable. For example, we note that code which constitutes a critical section in one system might not in another. This raises the question of whether components stored in a reuse library should include synchronization statements just in case, or should omit them and require their placement if necessary by the reuser. We chose to omit the synchronization primitives from the reuse library we prepared but we regard this issue as an open question.

Turning to exception handling, we found that a significant amount of code in the four systems studied is devoted to handling exceptions and undesired events. The C language provides no convenient way for the programmer to specify how an exception should be processed when it occurs; he must provide checks for it at each place it is likely to occur. This sometimes makes for awkward, bulky code with a number of if statements solely devoted to this kind of processing. This constitutes a significant aspect of the code's behavior, and has a major impact on the ease with which code can be understood by the reader. Again, we chose to omit exception handling from the reuse library we prepared, but we regard the systematic treatment of exceptions in reusable code also as an open question.

In describing a similar scavenging effort in the domain of missile software, Carle makes the following statement "Old software is not reusable." [2]. This statement is too general and defeatist in nature to be taken literally. Clearly, old software is reusable, or at least has strong reuse potential if a careful re-engineering effort is undertaken. Even if a particular component cannot be reused verbatim, the analysis embodied in the component often provides a foundation on which to remodel it somewhat to fit the new context. What is needed is a structured way of carrying out this remodeling effort across a broad spectrum of components. We conclude from our scavenging effort that indeed old software can be reusable.

3. DOMAIN ANALYSIS

After the scavenging effort, we decided to experiment with a reuse library based on object classes. Examining the designs of the systems and the results of the scavenging effort suggested that object-oriented design was likely to be an effective technique for reuse. Very

little has been reported on the quantitative benefits and difficulties of using object-oriented design in an industrial setting and so we sought a domain to be the target of study. We chose a domain known as *electronic charts* since software from this domain appears in various forms in many of Sperry Marine's products.

Navigation charts are detailed nautical maps published by various hydrographic services [5]. Their purpose is to provide navigators with visual representations of coastlines, along with as much information as possible for ships to negotiate their way along these coastlines safely. This information includes such features as buoy locations, wrecks and other hazards, shoals, and navigation channels.

Recently, digitized versions of such charts have become available that permit the information previously available only on paper to be presented on color video displays for use in both land- and sea-based marine systems, *i.e.*, electronic charts. Many innovative applications of great value to mariners are made possible by electronic charts such as zoomed and offset views of coastlines, realistic simulations of light house flash rates, real-time motion of one or more ship symbols against a fixed geographic background, real-time motion of the geographic background beneath a fixed ship symbol, real-time display of important information such as position, speed and heading, and automatic update of hazard information by communication networks.

Different applications use electronic charts for vastly different purposes and the domain is surprisingly complex. We summarize the domain analysis [8] as follows:

- *Application Location.*
  Applications tend to be characterized by whether they are land-based or sea-based. A land-based system, for example, does not have to be concerned about voyage planning or track history plotting; a sea-based system does.

- *Data Format.*
  There is a great variety of standards used to describe the information that appears on charts. Every hydrographic organization has its own set of codes to note the various kinds of buoys, land features, and hazards. Applications have to be aware of the source of the charts they will display.

- *Digitizing Semantics.*
  Currently, most charts are digitized into collections of vectors but charts are likely to be represented as bitmaps in future systems to permit the representation of greater detail.

- *Chart Features.*
  Charts are composed of three types of features - polygons composed of line segments that represent irregular shapes such as land masses and shoals,

331

single (x,y) coordinate pairs that represent groups of identical objects such as buoys, and text strings that show sounding depths, label legal boundaries, or identify radar targets.

- *Feature Attributes*
  Each feature has a number of different display attributes associated with it, such as color, fill pattern, line size, and line style. These attributes vary from feature type to feature type but may also vary for different instances of features of the same type.

- *Feature Highlighting.*
  Under various different circumstances, it is desirable to change the display of certain features so as to highlight them, nearby hazards, for example.

- *Chart Motion.*
  It is often necessary to cause the displayed image of chart to move in various different ways. The commonest and simplest of these movements are zooming and recentering; the most complex is motion of the chart in real time.

- *Decluttering.*
  Associated with zooming is a requirement for decluttering in which progressively less detail is displayed as the chart is zoomed out. Decluttering is application dependent and has to be under user control.

- *Overlays.*
  In order to take full advantage of the power of electronic charts, the user has to be able to overlay the chart with additional information. Typical overlays are shown in Table 2.

- *Status Information Display.*
  Many different status items, such as current speed, depth, location, and engine parameters, might need to be displayed. The details of what is displayed and how varies across the domain.

- *Display Window Structure.*
  The window structure used is application dependent. Some applications require the chart to fill the entire display while others require more than one chart to be displayed at a time.

- *Chart Database.*
  Land-based applications require only the chart data associated with the local region, basically a single chart. Sea-based applications require chart data to be available for any geographic region in which the vessel finds itself.

Another important dimension of the electronic chart domain is the ability to automate lengthy and complex distance calculations. Positions and distances can be computed from information available from a chart but the calculations depend on the projection system used, the most common being mercator and transverse mercator.

Extensions to basic calculation include recording and playing back voyage planning, tracking, and other activities.

It is clear that, in general, sea- and land-based systems differ considerably. However, we have noted that this difference increases the variability of other aspects of the domain that appear initially not to depend on whether the application is land- or sea-based. An example of this effect is *feature highlighting*. In a land-based system, the harbor controller might want to highlight ship symbols that are entering a hazardous situation. Ship that are passing too close to each other or to shoals should be highlighted so the controller can issue appropriate warnings. In a sea-based system, the pilot of the ship is concerned about highlighting only for circumstances directly affecting his ship. The underlying rules governing what gets highlighted, and under what circumstances, are very different although the processing necessary to actually highlight a feature might be identical. This difference in perspective between the two system types manifests itself throughout the domain.

4. REUSE LIBRARY

We have prepared a prototype reuse library for use by applications in the electronic charts domain. The components in the library are object classes written in

OVERLAY	CONTENT
Voyage plans	A tracing along a coastline showing planned waypoints.
Track history	A trail showing where a ship has been during a given time period.
Range rings	A set of concentric circles centered on a particular feature.
Grids	Horizontal and vertical lines marking latitude and longitude positions.
Radar targets	Moving symbols showing the positions of other ships in the area.
Ownship symbol	Moving symbol showing the position of the navigator's own ship.
Predicted course	Projection of ship's track over a given period of time.
Restricted areas	Areas designated as off-limits to commercial shipping.

Table 2 - Types of Overlays

332

C++. The library contains 20 classes with a total of 133 methods. It is in no sense novel and was not expected to be since our goal is to assess the reuse performance of a conventional class library. We describe here only some brief examples of components in the library and those aspects of the library's contents that are referred to in later sections.

Two of the more significant classes are:

- *Chart*
  The chart class is the central repository for information about the chart to be displayed. It contains the fundamental projection information used to map the spherical globe to a flat chart. This information is needed to convert real-world (latitude/longitude) coordinates into paper chart coordinates (usually inches), and vice-versa. Data associated with a specific chart is also stored including the actual geographic limits of the chart. The chart class also contains the points defining each feature to be displayed, and data on those features, such as color, fill pattern, line width, and line style.

- *Image*
  The image class associates a specific chart object with a particular window object and as such provides the fundamental mappings between coordinate systems. The image class contains descriptions of the three coordinate systems being used - the real world (latitude/longitude), the chart (inches), and the window (pixels). The image class stores information such as the current extents and current center of the displayed chart, various zoom and offset factors and their defaults, and the chart-to-window transformation. This information permits the image class to implement "special effects", such as zooming and offsetting very elegantly since it knows about all the coordinate systems and thus can manipulate the image correctly irrespective of the source of request. A recentering request, for example, might be in real-world coordinates if it comes from other application software, window coordinates if it comes from the mouse, or chart coordinates if it is based on a chart object.

A window class is provided that control's a window's size and position, assign it to a device, and draw features on it. It operates as one might expect in an object-oriented implementation of a simple windowing system. Other somewhat traditional classes provided facilities such as display hardware management, window manipulation, string and list manipulation, and so on.

Feature is a base class from which more specific display feature types can be derived. New feature types are easily implemented by adding them to the feature inheritance hierarchy (see Figure 1). This hierarchy is a typical example of the use (and extraordinary usefulness) of inheritance in this reuse library.

5. EVALUATION

5.1. An Evaluation Framework

Assessing the performance of a specific approach to reuse is difficult for a number of reasons. First, reuse means different things to different people, but, for comparative purposes, a consistent definition is necessary. Second, even if a definition of reuse were available, it is not possible to draw conclusions based on the evaluation of a simple metric because reuse might be achieved in some situation at an unacceptable cost. Finally, we note that many of the issues of interest are defined typically with phrases such as "the ease of doing something", "the difficulty of doing something", and "the effectiveness of something". Words such as *easy*, *difficult*, and *effective* are extremely nebulous.

In the case study described here, we have defined a framework for the long-term evaluation of the techniques being investigated. The creation of an evaluation framework is a step, but only a step, towards assigning rigorous meaning to the nebulous terms noted above. Although it is too early in the lifecycle of the reuse library we have developed to have sufficient data to draw rigorous conclusions, this framework was established near the beginning of the project to ensure that the right measurements were made from the outset.

The framework is divided into four areas - the initial reuse library development, the use of the reuse library in applications, characterizing necessary change, and object-oriented design and the utility of code scavenging. We can only summarize the framework here, and we do so by listing the key topics we wish to address in each area. More detail is available elsewhere [3].

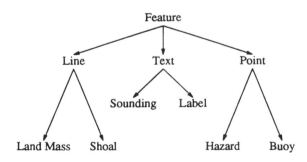

Figure 1 - Inheritance Hierarchy For Feature

333

Initial Reuse Library Development.

The key issues in this area are:

- Identification of the critical design decisions and how are they dealt with. The design decisions that affect the way in which components interact with each other are the most important since they determine how naturally the components can be used in constructing systems. Other design decisions, such as what sort of data structure to use to represent a collection of related elements, can usually be encapsulated in a separate class and modified later if need be.

- The way in which the implementation language support the goals of the design. Some languages are clearly and deliberately more suited to some problem domains, to reuse, and to object-oriented programming than others.

- The total resources required to create the initial reuse library.

Using The Components in Applications.

Once a library has been established, the most important evaluation criterion is the effectiveness of these components in building a specific application or set of applications given their requirements. Effectiveness in this sense is not quantifiable and so we consider a more detailed set of issues, specifically:

- System development effort since this effort is almost always directly proportional to development cost. On average, systems developed using an advocated reuse technique should cost less or the technique has clearly failed. In practice, effort is often taken to be equivalent to source code volume because development effort is difficult to measure, and lines of code acquired from libraries are used as crude reuse measures.

- The effectiveness of the domain analysis. It is important to know whether the library contains the "right" parts and whether they are presented in the "right" way irrespective of the success of the approach in other ways. This can be determined by evaluating how the components are used in specific systems.

- Time and space efficiency, and required levels of reliability or availability. The resulting systems must demonstrate adequate performance in these areas. If they do not, then the reuse technique has failed no matter how well it performs in other ways. Reliability is especially important for electronic charts [7].

VERSION/ PARENT	NEW FACILITY	MODS TO CLASS DATA	MODS TO CLASS METHODS	DESCRIPTION OF NEW CLASSES
1 / 0	Zoom display.	Add current and base zoom factors to Image class.	Add zoom in/out and zoom calc. methods.	
2 / 1	Display shoal and hazard features.	Add shoal and hazard codes to input conversion table.	Modify input method to recognize new codes.	Hazard class derived from feature. New fill pattern and abstract data types.
3 / 2	Color chart display	Add color field to Feature.	Add SetColor and GetColor methods to Feature.	Abstract data types for RGB/X-Windows. Derive new device driver class.
4 / 3	Allow user to choose new chart center.	Add current center value to Image class.	Add ChangeCenter method to Image	

Table 3 - Version Table Example

334

Characterizing Change.

The key issues in this area are:

- The amount of change necessary to use library components to build a new application.

- The amount of change necessary in the library components to accommodate changes in the domain over time.

In order to characterize the ease with which a set of components can be reconfigured to form new system versions, one needs a succinct way of capturing the major functional differences between versions. The method we propose is that of *version tables*. Version tables capture the object and function information of a set of components, and associate it with specific versions of those components. Each version of the components is also associated with a parent version. Thus, if necessary, the programmer can backtrack to previous instances of the system where undesired functionality was not present.

Presenting information in this format allows the programmer to see the order in which versions were derived, and easily check the dependencies between versions. If the different versions of the components involved are maintained under a configuration management system, the programmer can use the version that matches his needs the closest as the base for modifications.

Object-Oriented Design and Code Scavenging.

The central issue here is:

- The ease with which code scavenged from other non-object-oriented systems can be incorporated into an object-oriented reuse library.

Clearly, there is a vast supply of such code available. Note, we are not referring here to the scavenging process itself but to the inclusion of code already located by scavenging. The key issue is the cost of resources required to modify the code, and this cost depends on factors such as the differences in the implementation languages used, the underlying structure of the scavenged code, the tool support available, etc.

As an example of the difficulty, consider that object-oriented languages, particularly C++ [11], allow the programmer to define implicit data initializations to take place automatically when an object is created. This relieves the programmer of the burden of having to explicitly initialize a set of data items every time he or she creates new instances of them. Older code is often peppered with special routines for carrying out these initializations, along with calls to these routines. Automatic initialization does not eliminate the need to create the initialization code, but it does eliminate the need

for the programmer to remember to make calls to this code before using the new data.

5.2. Evaluation Systems

A preliminary evaluation of object-oriented design as a vehicle for reuse was conducted by building a reuse library and implementing two simple but typical systems using the components. One system captures some of the major functional requirements of a land-based system and the other some of the major functional requirements sea-based systems. In no way should these sample systems be construed as fully operational at this stage of the case study. Their purpose is to demonstrate how the components in the reuse library might be used in such systems, and how well the components satisfy the needs of these systems.

Both systems operate with production chart databases and so can display the same information as the production systems. Also, both systems provide simple chart manipulations including zooming, panning, and recentering. Both systems use conventional work stations as their implementation target rather than the ruggedized, special-purpose production hardware.

The specific characteristics of the sea-based system are:

- Provision for the selection of an appropriate chart since sea-based systems move.

- The ability to create a new voyage plan by tracing the required a path on a displayed chart with the mouse. At each planned waypoint, the user clicks a mouse button. The coordinates of each waypoint are stored in a voyage plan object, that can be used for further processing. The voyage plan is shown as a series of line segments overlaying the chart and can be turned on or off.

- The ability to display the real-world latitude/longitude position of any point on the chart. The user positions a cursor with the mouse pointer on any currently displayed point and clicks a mouse button. If two points are selected on a chart, the straight-line distance between them is displayed in nautical miles.

- Update in (simulated) real time the display position of the user's own ship on the chart at some time interval. A completely flexible concurrent software structure is desirable so that the user can perform other chart-based activities while these motion updates are occurring. The current implementation does not have a concurrent structure so the desired flexibility is only partially present.

The specific characteristics of the land-based system are:

335

- Access to only a single chart.

- No provision of user's own-ship and voyage-plan processing functions.

- Provision of processing facilities for radar targets involving monitoring the motion of multiple targets in the field of view of the radar sites placed in the harbor area. New targets can appear at any time, old targets can disappear in various ways, and most of the displayed targets are constantly moving. The sample land-based application simulates radar targeting by reading in a set of target identifiers and corresponding real-world positions (corresponding to a radar scan) every three seconds and updates the displayed targets appropriately.

5.3. Preliminary Evaluation

As noted above, it is too early in the lifecycle of the components we have developed to have sufficient data to draw rigorous conclusions about most of the issues defined in the evaluation framework. In this section, we present some preliminary evaluation data.

Initial Reuse Library Development.

The issue of coordinate system transformations was the most difficult design decision in the project. Three different coordinate systems are used - the display window, the chart itself, and the real world. At issue was the determination of a clean way of transforming points between any two of three coordinate systems at any given time. The main problem was the fact that in order to transform a chart coordinate into a window coordinate and vice-versa, a function has to be created that knows the size of both the chart and the window. It was not clear where such a function could be placed such that it maintained a natural interface to both the chart and the window abstractions. The solution is the image abstraction that associates a particular chart with a particular window. It also implements zooming and offsetting.

A second but minor design problem was ensuring flexibility in the addition of new chart features. The solution was the inheritance hierarchy from the base class Feature that is described in the previous section. New features can be added simply to this hierarchy with minimal disturbance to the existing software.

C++ proved a very effective language vehicle. It has effective data abstraction and encapsulation properties, executes efficiently, and treats classes as first class entities. C++'s function overloading was used extensively also to keep the code consistent.

Using The Components in Applications.

All of the original components from the library were used in creating the sample sea-based system. A number of new classes had to be created, specifically:

- a Voyage Plan class that stores the points entered by the user, and displays the projected track on the chart image when requested,

- an Ownship class that holds current chart coordinate of the user's own ship object. It also holds the user's own ship's track history in a list of points,

- an Ownship Controller that reads a predefined track input and updates the user's own ship symbol on the chart for demonstration purposes.

The main functional modification required to existing classes was the addition of the ability to convert chart coordinates to latitude/longitude points. The changes required were:

- The Chart class required a ChartToLatLon function to invoke conversion function in the Projection class used by this chart.

- The projection class required a new function to perform chart-to-world coordinate conversion.

- The image class required a new PrintLatLon function to print the results of the conversion in a human-readable format. It also required a new Distance function to calculate the nautical mile distance between two points provided in chart coordinates. Also, a WindowToLatLon function was added so the conversion from window to latitude/longitude coordinates could be made directly via the Image object.

Given that there are currently 20 distinct classes in the subsystem, the percentage that required modification was 15%. The rest of the code required for this system was developed from scratch. This included the new overlay classes mentioned above, and code to process input from the mouse using X-Window library calls.

The number of reused lines of code from the library components was about 2600. The new classes and application driver code totaled about 457 lines of code. These estimates are based on simple measurements from the system's .h and .c files.

An informally stated requirement about the subsystem was that it should load and display a given chart in three to five seconds, and zoom an image in one to three seconds. On average when executing on a networked Sun 3/75 workstation, the subsystem can load and display a complete chart in about six seconds and zoom or pan an image in about 1.2 seconds of wall-clock time from the time the request is made.

336

The simple land-based system was able to use all of the components used by the sea-based system without modification. The only additional components that needed to be created were:

- a Target class derived from the Ownship class created in the previous system,
- a Target Controller class that takes in radar input and uses it to create and destroy target symbols as they come into and out of existence, and updates each target as it moves.

The modifications made to the Chart, Projection, and Image components for the sea-based system were used in this system as well. Thus 0% of the classes in the reuse library required modification. About 2710 lines of subsystem code was reused, including development from the previous system. About 420 lines of new code was required to process targets and serve as an application command processor. Again, these estimates are based on the system's .h and .c files.

Characterizing Change.

Table 3 shows a simple version table for the chart subsystem. When using this method, the assumption is that the classes and functions of version 0, the initial version, has been defined in detail. As shown here, the development structure is linear. So version 2 has all the capabilities of version 1, along with the ability to display two new feature types. Version 3 has all of these capabilities, plus it can display charts in color, and so on.

Suppose a hypothetical version 5 is required that requires all of the capabilities of version 2, along with the ability to do overlays. From Table 3, it is clear that this can be achieved by backtracking to version 2 and adding the necessary objects for the required overlays. What is harder is a version that has all the capabilities of version 2, plus the capabilities of version 4, but without the capabilities of version 3. As it turns out, the ability to display color is orthogonal to the ability to choose a new chart center, so this change could be implemented by removing color capabilities from version 4.

We might not be so lucky in all cases, though. Intermediate versions of the subsystem might have capabilities that depend on the existence of other capabilities that we do not want. Care needs to be taken to avoid such dependencies. The ability to display charts in color is a good example of this. It was tempting to modify the monochrome device driver to automatically determine whether it was operating on a monochrome or a color platform, and switch accordingly. But this would mean all subsequent applications would have the ability to do both color and monochrome display. This does not sound bad, but most applications run in color. Including the ability to do both could potentially slow performance somewhat,

and take up extra space. It would certainly make the display driver code more complicated.

It was decided to create a separate color display driver that inherited all of the monochrome features and added processing necessary for color. The programmer can thus choose one driver or the other for a given application. If there is a need to include both capabilities, a simple interface object can be written to determine which driver to use, and instantiate the right class at run-time. Thus color and monochrome are regarded as orthogonal display properties, and are kept separate.

6. CONCLUSION

Although our case study is ongoing, we are able at this point to draw a number of conclusions based on the activities completed so far. From the code scavenging effort, we note first that we observed the same effect of repeated semantic patterns as other authors have reported. We also observed that concurrency and exception handling are important elements of large system designs and that reuse must account for both if it is to succeed. Finally from the code scavenging effort, we can report the location of large amounts of code with reuse potential, and can conclude that, at least in this domain, old software can be reused.

Evaluation of many techniques in software engineering is difficult. Our framework is designed to permit a reasonably precise and complete evaluation as the case study proceeds. In developing the prototype reuse library and building the two specimen systems, we have found great utility in object-oriented design and in the facilities provided by C++. Early indications based on only approximate measurements indicate a high level of reuse is achievable in the domain studied. The effort involved in both building the reuse library and constructing the specimen systems has not been found to be excessive but precise resource comparisons await implementation of production-level demonstration systems.

The case study is continuing with the goal of developing a reuse library and from it demonstration systems with the functionality of production systems. When such systems have been produced, precise comparisons with existing production methods will be possible.

7. ACKNOWLEDGEMENTS

It is a pleasure to acknowledge the very considerable technical support we have received in this project from John Yancey, Steve Scovill, Bruce Carriker, and Michael Berrang. This work was supported in part by Sperry Marine, Incorporated.

337

REFERENCES

[1] G. Booch, "Object-Oriented Development", *IEEE Transactions on Software Engineering*, vol. SE-12, no. 2, February 1986, pp. 211-221.

[2] R. Carle, "Reusable Software Components for Missile Applications", *Proceedings of the Tenth Minnowbrook Workshop on Software Reuse*, Blue Mountain Lake, New York, July 1987.

[3] M.F. Dunn, "Software Reuse in an Industrial Setting: A Case Study", MS Thesis, University of Virginia, August 1990.

[4] C. Jette and R. Smith, "Examples of Reusability in an Object-Oriented Programming Environment", Ted J. Biggerstaff and Alan J. Perlis, editors, ACM Press, 1989, pp. 73-102.

[5] M.C. Lohrenz, "The Digital World Vector Shoreline Database: Current and Future Capabilities", *Proceedings of Symposium '89 - Defense Mapping Agency Systems Center*, Herndon, Virginia, May 1989, pp. 113-122.

[6] B. Meyer, "Reusability: The Case for Object-Oriented Design", *Software Reusability: Applications and Experience*, Ted J. Biggerstaff and Alan J. Perlis, editors, ACM Press, 1989, pp. 1-34.

[7] E.J. Obloy, "The Liability of the Electronic Chartmaker for Negligent Charting - Update", *Proceedings of Symposium '89 - Defense Mapping Agency Systems Center*, Herndon, Virginia, May 1989,

[8] R. Prieto-Diaz, "Domain Analysis: An Introduction", *ACM SIGSOFT*, vol. 15, no. 2, April 1990, pp. 47-54.

[9] C. Rich and R.C. Waters, "The Programmer's Apprentice: A Research Overview", *IEEE Computer*, vol. 21, no. 11, November 1988, pp. 11-25.

[10] E. Soloway and K. Ehrlich, "Empirical Studies of Programming Knowledge", *Software Reusability: Applications and Experience*, Ted J. Biggerstaff and Alan J. Perlis, editors, ACM Press, 1989, pp. 235-267.

[11] Bjarne Stroustrup, *The C++ Programming Language*, Addison-Wesley, 1987.

[12] N. Wybolt, "Experiences with C++ and OOSD", *ACM SIGSOFT*, vol. 15, no. 2, April 1990, pp. 69-86.

338

Chapter 14
Program Understanding

Chapter 14
Program Understanding

Purpose

This chapter discusses techniques for understanding source code and creating models of its operation. The techniques vary from manual code reading to research systems that create models of program behavior based on knowledge of programming patterns. This work is an important complement to the work in design recovery and reverse engineering.

Papers

In the first paper, "Program Understanding: Challenge for the 1990s," Thomas Corbi discusses the activities, theories, and realities of program understanding technology. He addresses the critical role of program understanding in modifying systems, what "old code" is, what activities are involved in program understanding, theories of how people understand programs, and the role of restructuring in improving program understanding. He also explains why full-fledged design recovery (i.e., large-scale, automatic-generation design rationales for existing code) is not presently considered practically feasible.

In the next paper, "Approaches to Program Comprehension," D.J. Robson, K.H. Bennett, B.J.Cornelius, and M. Munro survey several approaches for understanding programs. They discuss program comprehension theories, code reading, program analysis, and "inverse engineering."[1] The paper is a short introduction to program understanding techniques.

In the final paper, "Program Recognition," Dirk Ourston describes several program comprehension approaches, with detailed examples and analyses of the program understanding systems discussed in the first two papers in this chapter.

---

[1]Another term for reverse engineering.

Program understanding: Challenge for the 1990s

by T. A. Corbi

In the Program Understanding Project at IBM's Research Division, work began in late 1986 on tools which could help programmers in two key areas: static analysis (reading the code) and dynamic analysis (running the code). The work is reported in the companion papers by Cleveland and by Pazel in this issue. The history and background which motivated and which led to the start of this research on tools to assist programmers in understanding existing program code is reported here.

"I*f the poor workman hates his tools, the good workman hates poor tools. The work of the workingman is, in a sense, defined by his tool— witness the way in which the tool is so often taken to symbolize the worker: the tri-square for the carpenter, the trowel for the mason, the transit for the surveyor, the camera for the photographer, the hammer for the laborer, and the sickle for the farmer.*

"Working with defective or poorly designed tools, even the finest craftsman is reduced to producing inferior work, and is thereby reduced to being an inferior craftsman. No craftsman, if he aspires to the highest work in his profession, will accept such tools; and no employer, if he appreciates the quality of work, will ask the craftsman to accept them."[1]

Today a variety of motivators are causing corporations to invest in software tools to increase software productivity, including: (1) increased demand for software, (2) limited supply of software engineers, (3) rising expectations of support from software engineers, and (4) reduced hardware costs.[2] A key moti-

vator for software tools in the 1990s will be the result of having software evolve over the previous decades from several-thousand-line, sequential programming systems into multimillion-line, multitasking "business-critical" systems. As the programming systems written in the 1960s and 1970s continue to mature, the focus for software tools will shift from tools that help develop new programming systems to tools that help us understand and enhance aging programming systems.

In the 1970s, the work of Belady and Lehman[3–5] strongly suggested that *all* large programs would undergo significant change during the in-service phase of their life cycle, regardless of the *a priori* intentions of the organization. Clearly, they were right. As an industry, we have continued to grow and change our large software systems to:

- Remove defects
- Address new requirements
- Improve design and/or performance
- Interface to new programs
- Adjust to changes in data structures or formats
- Exploit new hardware and software features

As we extended the lifetimes of our systems by continuing to modify and enhance them, we also

IBM SYSTEMS JOURNAL, VOL 28, NO 2, 1989

increased our already significant data processing investments in them and continued to increase our reliance on them. Software systems have grown to be significant assets in many companies.

However, as we introduce changes and enhancements into our maturing systems, the structure of the systems begins to deteriorate. Modifications alter originally "clean" designs. Fix is made upon fix. Data structures are altered. Members of the original and intervening programming teams disperse. Once current documentation gradually becomes outdated. System erosion takes its toll and key systems steadily become less and less maintainable, being more error prone and increasingly difficult and expensive to modify.

Flaherty's study[6] indicates the effect on productivity of modifying product code as compared to producing new code. His data for the studied System/370 communications, control, and language software show that productivity differences were greater between the ratio of changed source code to total amount of code than productivity differences between the different kinds of product classes—productivity was lowest when changing less than 20 percent of the total code in each product studied. The kind of software seemed to be a less-important factor contributing to lower productivity than did the attribute of changing a small percentage of the total source code of the product.

Clearly, as systems grow older, larger, and more complex, the challenges which will face tomorrow's programming community will be even more difficult than those of today. Even the *Wall Street Journal* stereotypes today's "beeper-carrying" programmer who answers the call when catastrophe strikes:

"He is so vital because the computer software he maintains keeps blowing up, threatening to keep paychecks from being issued or invoices from being mailed. He must repeatedly ride to the rescue night and day because the software, altered repeatedly over the years, has become brittle. Programming problems have simply gotten out of hand.

"Corporate computer programmers, in fact, now spend 80 percent of their time just repairing the software and updating it to keep it running. Developing new applications in this patchwork quilt has become so muddled that many companies can't figure out where all the money is going."[7]

Widespread routinization of computer programming and deskilling and fragmentation of programming work predicted by Kraft[8] has not occurred in the West because of management practices, the introduction of structured programming, and software

Programmers have become part historian, part detective, and part clairvoyant.

production processes. To the contrary, the skills needed to do today's programming job have become much more diverse. To successfully modify some aging programs, programmers have become part historian, part detective, and part clairvoyant. Why?

"Software renewal" or "enhancement" programming is quite different from the kind of idealized software engineering programming taught in university courses as stated by Jones:

"The major difference between new development and enhancement work is the enormous impact that the base system has on key activities. For example, while a new system might start with exploring users' requirements and then move into design, an enhancements project will often force the users' requirements to fit into existing data and structural constraints, and much of the design effort will be devoted to exploring the current programs to find out how and where new features can be added and what their impact will be on existing functions.

"The task of making functional enhancements to existing systems can be likened to the architectural work of adding a new room to an existing building. The design will be severely constrained by the existing structure, and both the architect and the builders must take care not to weaken the existing structure when the additions are made. Although the costs of the new room usually will be lower than the costs of constructing an entirely new building, the costs per square foot may be much higher because of the need to remove existing walls, reroute plumbing and electrical circuits and take special care to avoid disrupting the current site."[9]

The industry is becoming increasingly mired in these kinds of application software "renovation" and maintenance problems. Parikh[10] reports the magnitude of the problem through:

- Results of a survey of 149 managers of Multiple Virtual Storage (MVS) installations with programming staffs ranging from 25–800 programmers indicating that maintenance tasks (program fixes/modifications) represent from 55 to 95 percent of their workload
- Estimates that $30 billion is spent each year on maintenance ($10 billion in the United States) with 50 percent of the data processing budgets of most companies going to maintenance and that 50–80 percent of the time of an estimated one million programmers or programming managers is spent on maintenance
- A Massachusetts Institute of Technology study which indicates that for every $1 allocated for a new development project, $9 will be spent on maintenance for the life cycle of the project

Whereas today's modern design techniques and notations and wider acceptance of reusable software parts may help prevent propagating "old code" to future generations,[11] programmers will need tools to assist in reconstructing and analyzing information in previously developed and modified programs to aid them in debugging, enhancing, modifying, and/or rewriting "old" programs until these approaches take widespread hold in our critical systems.

"Software renewal" tools are needed to reduce the costs of modifying and maintaining large programming systems, to improve our understanding of programs so that we can continue to extend their life and restructure them as needed, and to build bridges from old software to updated software that is improved with new design techniques and notations and reuse technologies.

Just as library and configuration control systems were developed when the volumes of source code and the numbers of programmers working on a system increased, it is inevitable that new tools systems for managing the information about large programming systems will emerge to support long-term software renewal.

Approaches to aging systems

The notion of providing tools for program understanding is not new. Work in the 1970s,[12-16] which grew out of program proving, automatic programming and debugging, and artificial intelligence (AI) efforts, first broached the subject. Researchers stressed how rich program descriptions (assertions, invariants, etc.) could automate error detection and debugging. The difficulty of modeling interesting problem domains and representing programming

---

Positive effects can result from restructuring.

---

knowledge, coupled with the problems of symbolic execution, has inhibited progress. Although there has been some limited success,[17] the lack of fully implemented, robust systems capable of "understanding" and/or debugging a wide range of programs underscores the difficulty of the problem and the shortcomings of these AI-based approaches.

Recognizing the growing "old program" problem present in mature applications, entrepreneurs have transformed this problem into a business opportunity and are marketing code-restructuring tools. A variety of restructuring tools have emerged (see Reference 18 for an examination of restructuring). The restructuring approach to address "old" programs has had mixed success. Although helpful in some cases for cleaning up some modules, restructuring does not appear to help in other cases.

One government study[19] has shown that positive effects can result from restructuring, including some reduced maintenance and testing time, more consistency of style, reduced violations of local coding and structure standards, better learning, and additional structural documentation output from restructuring tools. However, on the negative side, the initial source may not be able to be successfully processed by some restructurers that require modification before restructuring; compile times, load module size, and execution time for the restructured program can increase; human intervention may be required to provide meaningful names for structures introduced by the tool.

Movement and replacement of block commentary is problematic for some restructurers. And, as has

---

**Automatically recapturing a design
from source code
is not considered feasible.**

---

been observed, overall system control and data structures that have eroded over time are not addressed, as indicated by Wendel:

"If you pass an unstructured, unmodular mess through one of these restructuring systems, you end up with at best, a structured, unmodular mess. I personally feel modularity is more important than structured code; I have an easier time dealing with programs with a bunch of GO TOs than one with its control logic spread out over the entire program."[20]

In general, automatically recapturing a design from source code, at the present state of the art, is not considered feasible. But some work is underway and some success has been reported. Sneed et al.[21,22] have been working with a unique set of COBOL tools which can be used to assist in rediscovering information about old code via static analysis, to interactively assist in remodularizing and then restructuring, and finally to generate a new source code representation of the original software. Also, research carried out jointly by CRIAI (Consorzio Campano di Ricerca per l'Informatica e l'Automazione Industriale) and DIS (Dipartimento di Informatica e Sistemistica at the University of Naples) reports that the automatic generation of low-level Jackson or Warnier/Orr documents is totally consistent with COBOL source code.[23]

Both Sneed and CRIAI/DIS agree, however, that determining higher-level design abstractions will require additional knowledge outside of that which can be analyzed directly from the source code.

The experience of IBM's former Federal Systems Division with the aging Federal Aviation Administration's National Airspace System (NAS)[24] seems to indicate that the best way out is to relearn the old software, relying primarily on the source code, to rediscover the module and data structure design, and to use a structured approach[25-27] of formally recording the design in a design language which supports data typing, abstract types, control structures, and data abstraction models.

This process often proved to be iterative (from very detailed design levels to more abstract), but it resulted in a uniform means for understanding and communicating about the original design. The function and state machine models then provided the designer a specification from which, subsequently, to make changes to the source code.

The need to expand "traditional" software engineering techniques to encompass reverse engineering design and to address "software redevelopment" has been recognized elsewhere:

"The principal technical activity of software engineering is moving toward something akin to 'software redevelopment.' Software redevelopment means taking an existing software description (e.g., as expressed in a programming or very high-level language) and transforming it into an efficient, easier-to-maintain realization portable across local computing environments. This redevelopment technology would ideally be applicable to both (1) rapidly assembled system prototypes into production quality systems, and (2) old procrustean software developed 3 to 20 years ago still in use and embedded in ongoing organization routines but increasingly difficult to maintain."[28]

Definitions

Two working definitions are needed before discussing how program understanding relates to software renewal.

First, what is "old" code? It may be the manifestation of age that makes code old. Oldness may come from the lack of familiarity of the current programming team with the part of the system being enhanced. Modern programming practices now accepted as standard may not have been used "way back then" when the code was originally developed. Other key characteristics of old code, which are not necessarily linked to age, are poor design, a constraining design point, use of an obsolete programming language, and/or missing or inaccurate documentation.

Was old code written a week ago or a decade ago? Unfortunately, the answer is that it could be either. Old code is existing code that cannot be easily understood, redesigned, modified, debugged, or rewritten. Why? It has the following attributes:

- Design was done with methods and techniques that do not clearly communicate the program structure, data abstractions, and function abstractions.
- Code was written with a programming language and techniques that do not quickly and clearly communicate the program structure, the program interfaces, data structures and types, and functions of the system.
- Documentation is nonexistent, incomplete, or not current.
- Design and code are not organized in such a way as to be insulated from changing external hardware or software.
- Design was targeted to system constraints that no longer exist.
- Code contains parts where nonstandard or unorthodox coding techniques were used.

Next, what are programmers doing when they are working on old code? The process of working on old code has acquired many names: software renewal, software evolution, program redevelopment, software renovation, "unprogramming," reverse engineering, and software maintenance. I have used the term *software renewal* here because for me that phrase carries more of the notion of enhancement. Today, however, *software maintenance* is still the term most commonly used to describe the process of working on old code, but it has a much wider connotation than just "fixing bugs." Parikh and Zvegintzov define the software maintenance process very broadly:

"... understanding and documenting existing systems; extending existing functions; adding new functions; finding and correcting bugs; answering questions for users and operations staff; rewriting, restructuring, converting, and purging software; managing the software of an operational system, and many other activities that go into running a successful software system."[29]

As defined by the National Bureau of Standards (NBS), "Software maintenance is the performance of those activities required to keep a software system operational and responsive after it is accepted and placed into production."[30] The NBS and others[31-33]

To understand a program, three actions can be taken.

---

generally recognize software maintenance as involving four major kinds of work:

1. Corrective maintenance (20 percent), which acts to correct errors that are uncovered after software is in use, including diagnosis and fixing design, logic, or coding errors
2. Adaptive maintenance (25 percent), which is applied when changes in the external environment precipitate modifications to the software, such as new hardware, operating system changes, peripheral upgrades, etc.
3. Perfective maintenance (50 percent or more), which incorporates enhancements that are requested by the user community, such as changes, insertions, deletions, and modifications
4. Preventive maintenance (5 percent), which improves future maintainability and reliability and provides a basis for future enhancement

The above percentages are based on the Lientz and Swanson study[34] of 487 software development organizations and represent the distribution of the different kinds of software maintenance activities which those authors saw in the surveyed organizations. The numbers are consistent with the Fjeldstad and Hamlen survey[35] of 25 MVS, Virtual System 1 (VS1), and Disk Operating System (DOS) data processing installations and a government study[36] of software maintenance done by the U.S. General Accounting Office in 1981.

Understanding programs: A key activity

With software maintenance defined in this broad sense, studies indicate that "*more than half of the*

programmer's task is in understanding the system."[29]
The Fjeldstad–Hamlen study[35] found that, in making an enhancement, maintenance programmers *studied the original program*

- About three-and-a-half times as long as they studied the documentation
- Just as long as they spent implementing the enhancement

In order to work with old code, today's programmers are forced to spend most of their time studying the only really accurate representation of the system.

To understand a program, three actions can be taken: read about it (e.g., read documentation); read it (e.g., read source code); or run it (e.g., watch execution, get trace data, examine dynamic storage, etc.). Documentation can be excellent or it can be misleading. Studying the dynamic behavior of an executing program can be very useful and can dramatically improve understanding by revealing program characteristics which cannot be assimilated from reading the source code alone. However, the source code is usually the primary source of information.

We all recognize that "understanding" a program is important, but most often it goes unmentioned as an explicit task in most programmer job or task descriptions. Why? The process of understanding a piece of code is not an explicit deliverable in a programming project. Sometimes a junior programmer will have an assignment to "learn this piece of code"—oddly, as if it were a one-time activity.

Experienced programmers who do enhancement programming realize, just as do architects and builders doing a major renovation, that they must repeatedly examine the actual existing structure. Old architectural designs and blueprints may be of some use, but to be certain that a modification will be successful, they must discover or rediscover and assemble detailed pieces of information by going to the site of the structure. In programming, this kind of investigation happens throughout the project:

- While requirements are being examined, lead designers or developers are typically navigating through the existing code base to get a rough idea of the size of the job, the areas of the system that will be impacted, and the knowledge and skills needed by the programming team which does the work.

- As design proceeds from high level to low level, each of the team members repeatedly examines the existing code base to discover how the new function can be grafted onto the existing data structures and into the general control flow and data flow of the existing system.
- Wise designers may "tour" the existing code to get an idea of performance implications that the enhancement may have on various critical paths through the existing system.
- Just before the coding begins, programmers are looking over the "neighborhood" of modules that will be involved in the enhancement. They are planning the detailed packaging—separating the low-level design into pieces which must be implemented by new modules or which can be fit into existing modules. Often, they are building the lists of new and changed modules and macros for the configuration management or library control team who need this information in order to reintegrate the new and changed source code when putting the pieces of the system back together again.
- During the coding phase, programmers are immersed in the old code. Programmers are constantly choosing between courses of action: making very detailed decisions to rewrite or restructure existing code versus decisions to change the existing code by deleting, moving, and adding a few lines here and a few lines there. Understanding the existing programs is also the key to adding new modules: How to interface to existing functions in the old code? How to use the existing data structures properly? How not to cause unwanted side effects?
- A new requirement or two and a few design changes usually come into focus after the programmers have begun their work. These additions must be evaluated as to their potential impact on the system and as to whether or not the proposed changes can be contained in the current schedules and resources. The "old base" and the "new evolving" code under development must be scrutinized to supplement the intuitions of the lead programmers before notifying management of the risks.
- Testers may delve into the code if they are using "white-box" techniques. Sometimes even a technical writer will venture into the source code to clarify something for a publication under revision.
- Debugging, dump reading, and trace analysis constantly require long terminal sessions of "program understanding" in which symptoms are used to postulate causes of an error, or bug. Each hypothesis causes the programmer to explore the existing system to find the source of the bug. When the

problem is found, a more "bounded" exploration is usually required to gather the key information necessary to actually build the fix and insert yet another modification into the system.

Therefore, the program understanding process is a crucial subelement in achieving many of the project

---

> ## The investigation process which programmers undertake when doing software maintenance is akin to idea processing.

---

deliverables: sizings, high-level design, low-level design, build plan, actual code, debugged code, fixes, etc.

Programmers attempt to understand a programming system so that they can make informed decisions about the changes they are making. The literature refers to this "understanding process" as "program comprehension":

"The program comprehension task is a critical one because it is a subtask of debugging, modification, and learning. The programmer is given a program and is asked to study it. We conjecture that the programmer, with the aid of his or her syntactic knowledge of the language, constructs a multileveled internal semantic structure to represent the program. At the highest level the programmer should develop an understanding of what the program does: for example, this program sorts an input tape containing fixed-length records, prints a word frequency dictionary, or parses an arithmetic expression. This high-level comprehension may be accomplished even if low-level details are not fully understood. At lower semantic levels the programmer may recognize familiar sequences of statements or algorithms. Similarly, the programmer may comprehend low-level details without recognizing the overall pattern of operation. The central contention is that programmers develop an internal semantic structure to represent the syntax of the program, but they do not

memorize or comprehend the program in a line-by-line form based on syntax."[37]

The investigation process which programmers undertake when doing software maintenance is akin to *idea processing*, very clearly described by Halasz, Moran, and Trigg:

"The goal of all idea processing tasks is to move from a chaotic collection of unrelated ideas to an integrated, orderly interpretation of the ideas and their interconnections. Analyzing one's business competitors is a prototypical example. The task begins with an analyst extracting scraps of information about competitors from available sources. The collected information must be organized and filed away for subsequent use. More importantly, the collected information needs to be analyzed. The relationships between the various ideas have to be discovered and represented. Multiple analyses should be developed in order to understand the significance of the collected information. Once these analyses are complete, the analyst composes and writes a document or presentation that communicates the discovered information and its significance.

"Idea processing is a convolution of several different activities that can be roughly divided into three phases: acquisition, analysis, and exposition. Acquisition involves the capture or extraction of ideas and information from sources of various sorts, e.g., taking notes from a document or recording the ideas produced during brainstorming. Analysis involves discovering the significance of ideas, in particular, discovering the connections and relationships among ideas. Developing legal arguments based on case research is an example. Exposition involves communicating ideas and analyses in the form of reports, talks, etc."[38]

How do programmers learn to acquire key pieces of information about code, to organize and analyze it, and then to use it to make decisions?

Learning to understand programs

Although software engineering (e.g., applied computer science) appears as a course offering in many university and college computer science departments, software renewal, program comprehension, or enhancement programming are absent. In terms of the skills that are needed as our software assets grow and age, lack of academic training in how to go about understanding programs will be a major inhibitor to programmer productivity in the 1990s:

"... Unfortunately, a review by the author of more than 50 books on programming methodologies revealed almost no citations dealing with the productivity of functional enhancements, except a few minor observations in the context of maintenance.

"The work of functional enhancements to existing software systems is underreported in the software engineering curriculums, too, and very few courses exist in which this kind of programming is even discussed, much less taught effectively."[9]

For other "language" disciplines, classical training includes learning to speak, read, and write. Reading comprehension is a partner with composition and rhetoric. In school, we are required to read and critique various authors. An English education curriculum does not teach basic language skills (programming language syntax and semantics), recommended sentence structures (structured programming), and short stories (algorithms), expecting students to be fully trained, productive copy editors or authors for major publications upon completing the curriculum. Yet, many computer science departments sincerely believe that they are preparing their students to be ready for the workplace.

Unfortunately, most new college graduates entering today's software industry must confront a very considerable learning curve about an existing system before they get to the point where they can begin to try to do design or coding. They have little or no training nor much tool assistance to do this. Acquiring programming comprehension skills has been left largely to on-the-job training while trying to learn about an existing system.[39] Even experienced programmers can have trouble moving to a different project.

The lack of training and tools to help in understanding large, old programming systems also has another negative effect on productivity. It is resulting in a kind of job stagnation throughout the industry which Boehm terms the "Inverse Peter Principle":[40]

"The Inverse Peter Principle: 'People rise to an organizational position in which they become irreplaceable, and get stuck there forever.' This is most often encountered in software maintenance, where a programmer becomes so uniquely expert on the inner complexities and operating rituals of a piece of software that the organization refuses to let the person work on anything else. The usual outcome is for the programmer to leave the organization entirely, leaving an even worse situation."

As a large programming system grows older and older, more and more talented programmers will "get stuck" in accordance with the Inverse Peter Principle. Getting stuck directly impacts attempts by management to maximize project productivity by assigning the most talented programmers to get the next job done. Therefore, a lack of program understanding, training, and tools is a productivity inhibitor for new programmers on a project as well as a career inhibitor for the key project "gurus." As our programming systems grow in age, size, and complexity, these problems will compound, becoming increasingly more acute.

Theories of program understanding

Before we can build tools or begin any training programs, we must go deeper into the question: How do programmers "understand" a system? There are varying cognitive theories as to how a programmer constructs a "multileveled internal semantic representation" which Shneiderman[37] has postulated. Studies have been performed with programmers, and three current theories appear in the literature. Each theory appears plausible:

1. The "bottom up" or "chunking" theory—By reading the code, a programmer essentially iteratively "abstracts" a higher-level understanding of the program by recognizing and then "naming" more and more of the program. This is described in the book edited by Curtis:[41]

   "A process called 'chunking' expands the capacity of the short-term mental workspace. In chunking, several items with similar or related attributes are bound together conceptually to form a unique item. For example, through experience and training programmers are able to build increasingly large chunks based on solution patterns which emerge frequently in solving problems. According to Michael Atwood and Rudy Ramsey (1978),[42] the lines of code in the program listing:

```
      SUM = 0
      DO 10 I = 1, N
      SUM = SUM + X(I)
10    CONTINUE
```

would be fused by an experienced programmer into the chunk 'calculate the sum of array X.' The programmer can now think about working with an array sum, a single entity, rather than the six unique operators and seven unique operands in the four program statements above. When it is necessary to deal with the procedural implementation, the programmer can call from long-term memory these four statements underlying the chunk 'array sum.'

"As programmers mature they observe more algorithmic patterns and build larger chunks. The scope of the concepts that programmers have been able to build into chunks provides one indication of their programming ability. The particular elements chunked together have important implications for educating programmers. Educational materials and exercises should be presented in a way that best allows programmers to build useful chunks."[41]

2. *The "top-down" theory*—This theory proposes that programmers use their own experience and repeatedly try to confirm their expectations on the basis of what they believe the design to be. If they are told that the program they will be working on is a "payroll" system, just hearing that phrase before looking at the code causes them to expect to see certain constructs in the code: a master employee file with names, employee numbers, and salary fields; a timecard or attendance-gathering process; a process for updating salary; a process for deleting or adding employees; various report processors; a check-printing process; various exception-handling mechanisms (vacation, sickness, etc.).

Now, when they pick up the code, they look for where these elements occur and "fill in" their belief of what the design most probably is. If something is missing or is radically different from their expectations (e.g., master file sorted by date of hire), the "surprise" causes some new experience to be stored for the next encounter.

"The major points of the theory can be summarized as follows.

 a. The programming process is one of constructing mappings from a problem domain, possibly through several intermediate domains, into the programming domain.
 b. Comprehending a program involves reconstructing part or all of these mappings.
 c. The reconstruction process is expectation driven by the creation, confirmation, and refinement of hypothesis."[43]

3. *The "opportunistic" theory*—The "opportunistic" theory says that understanding is a mixture

of "top-down" and "bottom-up" strategies. Letovsky[44] believes that understanding a program involves a knowledge base (which represents the expertise and background knowledge a programmer brings to the task), a mental model (which is an encoding of the programmer's current understanding of the program), and an assimilation process:

". . . to direct the understander to turn pages and aim his eyeballs in certain directions, to take in information from the program and documentation text, and to construct the mental model. If we assume that the complete mental model resembles a procedural net, we immediately have a space of possibilities for how the assimilation process constructs it. It could represent the bottom or implementation layer first and build the annotation from the bottom up by recognizing plans. This approach is taken in Brotsky[45] and Shrobe.[46] Alternatively, the understander could represent the specification first and develop possible implementations top down using a planner or automatic programmer, ultimately matching the possible implementations against the code. This approach is used in Johnson–Soloway[17] and Brooks.[43] Our position is that the human understander is best viewed as an opportunistic processor capable of exploiting both bottom-up and top-down cues as they become available . . ."[44]

Which approach to program understanding is correct? As in most attempts to explain human problem-solving behavior, the answer is not clear. Different programmers may be predisposed toward one approach versus another on the basis of their level of experience or familiarity with the code.

". . . The data suggest the representation of the expert is more abstract and contains more general information about what a program does, whereas the representation of the novice is more concrete and contains information about how the program functions . . .

"The results of these experiments do not suggest that expert programmers lost the ability to attend to the details of a program . . . Rather, they suggest that experts have learned that, during comprehension of this type of program, paying attention to the abstract elements of the program is more important than paying attention to low level details . . ."[47]

The same programmer may use different approaches, depending on the kind of task which he or she has been asked to accomplish with respect to under-

Some tasks require more complete understanding; others may involve only a cursory inspection of the code.

standing the code. Some tasks require more complete understanding, whereas others may involve only a cursory inspection of the code. The understander's mental model will change as the process of investigating a piece of code progresses. The result of any investigation may result in a model which is incorrect or incomplete (with uninvestigated parts of the system or vaguely understood pieces) or contains ambiguities (such as multiple conjectures about what the same piece of code might do).

Regardless of which approach is employed, good evidence indicates that the more systematic a programmer is in investigating a program and the more complete the information which is gathered, the more likely the programmer will be successful in performing modifications to that program:

"Understanding how a program is constructed and how it functions are important parts of the task of maintaining or enhancing a computer program. We have analyzed videotaped protocols of experienced programmers as they enhanced a personnel database program. Our analysis suggests that there are two strategies for program understanding, the *systematic* strategy and the *as-needed* strategy. The programmer using the systematic strategy traces data flow and control flow through the program in order to understand global program behavior. The programmer using the as-needed strategy focuses on local program behavior in order to localize study of the program. Our empirical data show that there is a strong relationship between using the systematic approach to acquire knowledge about the program and modifying the program successfully. Programmers who used the systematic approach to study the program con-

structed successful modifications. Programmers who used the systematic strategy gathered *knowledge about the causal interaction of the program's functional components.* Programmers who used the as-needed strategy did not gather such causal knowledge and therefore failed to detect interactions among components of the program."[48]

Although the different theories can give us some ideas as to the cognitive processes in action, the difficulty of comprehending how large, aging programs work is illustrated in the work of Letovsky and Soloway,[49] who identify the problems of recognizing "delocalized plans—that is, programming plans realized by lines scattered in different parts of the program." Their empirical studies show that often a programmer will base a program repair or enhancement on very localized knowledge and partial understanding of the program, and this proves to be error prone, especially when neither the program nor the documentation reveals that specific pieces of code interact with other pieces of code (or data) some "distance" away.

Many large software systems, which were originally written before the software engineering techniques of data encapsulation and information hiding and before programming languages with type enforcement, provide many such opportunities for introducing errors during enhancement because of "widely" delocalized plans which work against large, arbitrarily evolved "control block structures." These baroquely connected pieces of storage, which form the backbone of many major software systems, typically have little or no access control. So, a program provided with an anchor pointer can often traverse areas of the structure that were never intended to be part of the data scope of that program.

Directions for program understanding in the 1990s

At IBM's Research Division, the Program Understanding Project began work in late 1986 on tools that could help programmers in two key areas: static analysis (reading the code) and dynamic analysis (running the code). The work is reported in two papers in this issue: "A program understanding support environment" by Linore Cleveland[50] and "DS-Viewer—An interactive graphical data structure presentation facility" by Donald Pazel.[51]

Cleveland's work focuses on exploiting the workstation multiwindow presentation of static analysis data to give programmers a new way of reading programs. The assumption was a world where there were no listings and that assemblers and compilers put all their internally collected information (symbol table, control flow, data flow, cross reference, etc.) into a structured format which could be accessed from a high-performance workstation.

Pazel's work focuses on exploiting the workstation multiwindow presentation of dynamic data to give programmers a new way of viewing and navigating the dynamic data structures of a program which has

---

Tools and training should encourage development of different systematic investigative approaches.

---

been stopped during execution. The approach was to modify a host-based debugger to interface to a workstation-based presentation tool through which the programmer could explore dynamic data during a debugging session.

We conjecture that combining these static and dynamic data views into a unified tool can provide an experimental base which can be used to observe programmers engaged in complex program understanding tasks. By studying programmers using such a tool, we would hope to add functions which could support systematic investigations that would assist in the interactive rediscovery of design information.

Given the empirical studies elsewhere and what we are beginning to learn from PUNS (Program UNderstanding Support) and DS-Viewer to date, programmer training and tools to assist in understanding existing systems should try to remain neutral in the techniques or functions that are offered and should not favor or force the use of only one way of gathering information about programs. Training and tools should be able to support "top-down," "bottom-up," and "opportunistic" approaches and not impose one theory of investigation on the programmer. The programmer should choose the process and/or tool function which best fits his or her level of expertise and the circumstances of the current assigned task.

Tools and training should show or teach the programmer how to develop strategies which make use of various kinds of basic program information, e.g., control flow, data flow, data declarations and structures, dynamic executions (trace), cross reference, module interface, call graphs, and even documentation. Both should show or assist the programmer in combining these different kinds of information in ways which can support his or her building or confirming hypotheses about the system being investigated.

While remaining flexible, tools and training should encourage development of different systematic investigative approaches so that the programmer can judge the progress and completeness of his or her inquiry on the basis of available data. Obtaining information about the system under study should be made as easy as possible so as not to require excessive effort which might preclude investigating something that could be important to understanding the system.

Tools that require complex query commands should not be used for program understanding, since often the programmer will be diverted from his or her primary purpose and begin struggling with secondary issues such as compound query formation and syntax errors. A good deal of attention to the "human factors" of program understanding tools is required.

Acknowledgments

I would like to thank several people who have contributed to this work. First, Linore Cleveland and Don Pazel, without whose excellent prototyping work all this would have remained just "idea-ware." I would also like to thank Andy Heller and Dr. Daniel Abensour for introducing me to the Research Division; Dr. Bruce Shriver for introducing me to the academic and professional community; Dr. Abraham Peled for believing in the project; Dr. Ashok Malhotra, Bill Harrison, and Vincent Kruskal for their collegial support; George Radin for his advice and counsel; Pat Goldberg for various inspirations; and Dick Butler for understanding the importance of this work.

Cited references

1. Gerald M. Weinberg, *The Psychology of Computer Programming*, Van Nostrand Reinhold, New York (1971).
2. Barry W. Boehm, Maria H. Penedo, E. Don Stuckle, Robert D. Williams, and Arthur B. Pyster, "A software development environment for improving productivity," *IEEE Computer* **17**, No. 6, 30–44 (June 1984).

3. L. A. Belady and M. M. Lehman, "A model of large program development," *IBM Systems Journal* 15, No. 3, 225–252 (1976).

4. M. M. Lehman and F. H. Parr, "Program evolution and its impact on software engineering," *Proceedings of the 2nd International Conference on Software Engineering*, San Francisco, IEEE Society Press (October 1976), pp. 350–357.

5. M. M. Lehman, "Laws of evolution dynamics—Rules and tools for programming management," *Proceedings of the Infotech Conference on Why Software Projects Fail*, London (April 1978), pp. 11/1–11/25.

6. M. J. Flaherty, "Programming process measurement for the System/370," *IBM Systems Journal* 24, No. 2, 172–173 (1985).

7. Paul B. Carroll, "Computer glitch: Patching up software occupies programmers and disables systems," *Wall Street Journal* (January 22, 1988), p. 1.

8. Philip Kraft, *Programmers and Managers: The Routinization of Computer Programming in the United States*, Springer-Verlag, New York (1977).

9. Capers Jones, "How not to measure programming quality" *Computerworld* XX, No. 3, 82 (January 20, 1986).

10. Girish Parikh, "Making the immortal language work," *International Computer Programs Business Software Review* 7, No. 2, 33 (April 1987).

11. Ronald A. Radice and Richard W. Phillips, *Software Engineering: An Industrial Approach, Volume I*, Prentice-Hall, Inc., Englewood Cliffs, NJ (1988), pp. 14–19.

12. I. P. Goldstein, "Summary of MYCROFT: A system for understanding simple picture programs," *Artificial Intelligence* 6, No. 1, 249–288 (1975).

13. S. M. Katz and Z. Manna, "Toward automatic debugging of programs," *SIGPLAN Notices* 10, No. 6, 143–155 (June 1975).

14. G. R. Ruth, "Intelligent program analysis," *Artificial Intelligence* 7, No. 1, 65–87 (1976).

15. S. M. Katz and Z. Manna, "Logical analysis of programs," *Communications of the ACM* 19, No. 4, 188–206 (April 1976).

16. F. J. Lukey, "Understanding and debugging programs," *International Journal of Man-Machine Studies* 12, No. 2, 189–202 (1980).

17. W. L. Johnson and E. Soloway, "PROUST: Knowledge-based program understanding," *Proceedings of Seventh International Conference on Software Engineering*, Orlando, FL (March 1984), pp. 369–380.

18. Robert S. Arnold, Editor, *Tutorial on Software Restructuring*, IEEE Computer Society Press, Washington, DC (1986).

19. *Parallel Test and Evaluation of a Cobol Restructuring Tool*, U.S. General Accounting Office, Washington, DC (September 1987).

20. Irv Wendel, "Software tools of the Pleistocene," *Software Maintenance News* 4, No. 10, 20 (October 1986).

21. H. M. Sneed, "Software renewal: A case study," *IEEE Software* 1, No. 3, 56–63 (July 1984).

22. H. M. Sneed and G. Jandrasics, "Software recycling," *IEEE Conference on Software Maintenance*, Austin, TX (September 1987), pp. 82–90.

23. P. Antonini, P. Benedusi, G. Cantone, and A. Cimitile, "Maintenance and reverse engineering: Low-level design documents production and improvement," *IEEE Conference on Software Maintenance*, Austin, TX (September 1987), pp. 91–100.

24. Robert N. Britcher and James J. Craig, "Using modern design practices to upgrade aging software systems," *IEEE Software* 3, No. 3, 16–24 (May 1986).

25. A. B. Ferrentino and H. D. Mills, "State machines and their semantics in software engineering," *Proceedings of COMP-*

SAC '77 (1977), pp. 242–251.

26. R. C. Linger, H. D. Mills, and B. I. Witt, *Structured Programming Theory and Practice*, Addison-Wesley Publishing Co., Reading, MA (1979).

27. H. D. Mills, D. O'Neill, R. C. Linger, M. Dyer, and R. E. Quinnan, "The management of software engineering," *IBM Systems Journal* 19, No. 4, 414–477 (1980).

28. Walt Scacchi, "Managing software engineering projects: A social analysis," *IEEE Transactions on Software Engineering* SE-10, No. 1, 49–59 (January 1984).

29. Girish Parikh and Nicholas Zvegintzov, Editors, *Tutorial on Software Maintenance*, IEEE Computer Society Press, Silver Spring, MD (1983), p. ix.

30. Roger J. Martin and Wilma M. Osborne, *Guidance on Software Maintenance*, NBS Special Publication 500-106, Computer Science and Technology, U.S. Department of Commerce, National Bureau of Standards, Washington, DC (December 1983), p. 6.

31. E. B. Swanson, "The dimensions of maintenance," *Proceedings of the 2nd International Conference on Software Engineering*, San Francisco, IEEE Society Press (October 1976), pp. 492–497.

32. Roger S. Pressman, *Software Engineering: A Practitioner's Approach*, McGraw-Hill Book Company, Inc., New York (1982), pp. 322–341.

33. James Martin and Carma McClure, *Software Maintenance: The Problem and Its Solutions*, Prentice-Hall, Inc., Englewood Cliffs, NJ (1983), p. 3ff.

34. E. B. Swanson and B. Lientz, *Software Maintenance Management: A Study of the Maintenance of Computer Application Software in 487 Data Processing Organizations*, Addison-Wesley Publishing Co., Reading, MA (1980).

35. R. K. Fjeldstad and W. T. Hamlen, "Application program maintenance study: Report to our respondents," *Proceedings of GUIDE 48*, The Guide Corporation, Philadelphia (1979).

36. *Federal Agencies' Maintenance of Computer Programs: Expensive and Undermanaged*, AFMD-81-25, U.S. General Accounting Office, Washington, DC (February 1981).

37. B. Shneiderman and R. Mayer, "Syntactic/semantic interactions in programmer behavior: A model and experimental results," *International Journal of Computer and Information Sciences* 8, No. 3, 219–238 (1979).

38. F. G. Halasz, T. P. Moran, and R. H. Trigg, "NoteCards in a nutshell," *Conference on Computer Human Interaction and Graphic Interfaces Proceedings*, Toronto (April 1987), pp. 45–52.

39. Carolyn Van Dyke, "Taking 'computer literacy' literally," *Communications of the ACM* 30, No. 5, 366–374 (May 1987).

40. Barry W. Boehm, *Software Engineering Economics*, Prentice-Hall, Inc., Englewood Cliffs, NJ (1981), p. 671.

41. Bill Curtis, Editor, *Human Factors in Software Development*, IEEE Computer Society Press, Washington, DC (1985), p. 7.

42. M. E. Atwood and H. R. Ramsey, *Cognitive Structures in the Comprehension and Memory of Computer Programs: An Investigation of Computer Program Debugging*, U.S. Army Research Institute of Behavioral and Social Sciences, Technical Report TR-78-A21, Alexandria, VA (1978).

43. R. Brooks, "Toward a theory of comprehension of computer programs," *International Journal of Man-Machine Studies* 18, No. 6, 542–554 (1983).

44. Stanley Letovsky, "Cognitive processes in program comprehension," in E. Soloway and S. Iyengar, Editors, *Empirical Studies of Programmers*, Ablex Publishing Corporation, Norwood, NJ (1986), pp. 58–79.

45. Daniel C. Brotsky, *An Algorithm for Parsing Flow Graphs*, Master's thesis, Massachusetts Institute of Technology, Cam-

bridge. MA (March 1984).

46. H. Shrobe. *Dependency Directed Reasoning for Complex Program Understanding.* AI-TR-503. Massachusetts Institute of Technology Artificial Intelligence Lab. Cambridge. MA (1979).

47. B. Adelson. "When novices surpass experts: The difficulty of a task may increase with expertise." *Journal of Experimental Psychology. Learning. and Cognition* 10, No. 3. 483–495 (1984).

48. D. C. Littman. J. Pinto. S. Letovsky. and E. Soloway. "Mental models and software maintenance." in E. Soloway and S. Iyengar. Editors. *Empirical Studies of Programmers.* Ablex Publishing Corporation. Norwood. NJ (1986). pp. 80–98.

49. S. Letovsky and E. Soloway. "Delocalized plans and program comprehension." *IEEE Software* 3, No. 3. 41–49 (May 1986).

50. L. Cleveland. "A program understanding support environment." *IBM Systems Journal* 28, No. 2. 324–344 (1989. this issue).

51. D. Pazel. "DS-Viewer—An interactive graphical data structure presentation facility." *IBM Systems Journal* 28, No. 2. 307–323 (1989. this issue).

Thomas A. Corbi *IBM Data Systems Division. P.O. Box 390. Poughkeepsie. New York 12602.* Mr. Corbi joined the IBM Palo Alto Development Center as a programmer in 1974 after graduating from Yale University. He worked in the General Products Division on text-processing. data management. and database systems. He was a development manager for IMS/VS Fast Path at the IBM Santa Teresa Laboratory in San Jose. California. He joined the Research Division at the Thomas J. Watson Research Center in 1982 and managed the Program Understanding Project from 1986 to 1988. He was also co-program chair of the 1988 IEEE Conference on Software Maintenance (CSM-88). Mr. Corbi is now on assignment to the Data Systems Division. focusing on improving programmer productivity.

Reprint Order No. G321-5360.

J. SYSTEMS SOFTWARE
1991; 14:79–84

Approaches to Program Comprehension

D. J. Robson, K. H. Bennett, B. J. Cornelius, and M. Munro

Centre for Software Maintenance, University of Durham, Durham, UK

Software maintenance is recognized as the most expensive phase of the software life cycle. The maintenance programmer is frequently presented with code with little or no supporting documentation, so that the understanding required to modify the program comes mainly from the code. This paper discusses some of the current approaches to theories of program comprehension and the tools for assisting the maintenance programmer with this problem.

1. INTRODUCTION

In this paper, software maintenance is defined to be any work that is undertaken after delivery of a software system. It has been recognized that software maintenance can consume as much as 70% of the costs during the life cycle of the system [20]. Very little research effort has been put directly into this phase of the life cycle. Research effort has been almost exclusively devoted to the development stage with the aim of reducing the cost of maintenance by using new development techniques. The aim of development methods such as program correctness proofs [13] has been to prove that the code produced is correct with respect to the specifications. This method may or may not be the correct approach to the production of new software, but it ignores the problem of the maintenance of existing software.

Software maintenance has been split into three subtasks, namely corrective, adaptive, and perfective maintenance [39]. Corrective maintenance is defined as that part of the maintenance effort which is devoted to the correction of errors. Adaptive maintenance tasks are the amendments required when the system is moved to a new machine or when changes are made to the external environment in which the system operates. Perfective maintenance is the enhancement of the system to incorporate new tasks which were not previously in the requirements. A survey by Lientz and Swanson

[20] estimated that 65% of the maintenance phase is taken up with perfective maintenance and only 17% is corrective maintenance. New development techniques which are targeted at reducing corrective maintenance are thus missing the most expensive phase of the maintenance activity.

There has also been considerable investment in existing software. It is often not cost effective to throw away existing software and rewrite it with the latest development technique. Thus software continues to evolve. The accompanying system documentation, if any, and requirements may or may not be updated as the program is modified and, if not, then this makes future maintenance more difficult. Thus, future maintenance activity often utilizes the code as the only source of information as to the exact function and behavior of the system.

Understanding the functions and behavior of a system from the code is hence a vital part of the maintenance programmer's task. In the remainder of this paper we describe current approaches to assisting the maintenance programmer in this activity and discuss the requirements for a support system.

2. THEORIES OF PROGRAM COMPREHENSION

It has been estimated that 50–90% of maintenance time is devoted to program comprehension [38]. Even when there is documentation present, one survey [15] has found that the time spent studying the code took up more than three and a half times the amount of time studying the documentation. Littman et al. [23] have identified strategies for program comprehension and have conducted an experiment to investigate the relationship between these strategies and the knowledge acquired. They argue that there are two basic approaches to program comprehension of relatively small programs. First there is the systematic approach, where the maintainer examines the entire program and works out the interactions between various modules. This is completed before any attempt is made to modify the program. The other approach is the as-needed strategy

Address correspondence to David J. Robson, Centre for Software Maintenance, University of Durham, Durham DH1 3LE U.K.

80   J. SYSTEMS SOFTWARE
        1991; 14:79-84

where the maintainer attempts to minimize the amount of study prior to making a modification. Thus, the maintainer tries to locate the section of the program which needs to be modified and then commences the modification. On the small program used in the experiment, it is clear that the systematic approach is superior, but on large programs this approach is not feasible and a possibly adapted as-needed strategy needs to be employed.

Other theories of program comprehension have been proposed. Shneiderman and Mayer [33] argue that comprehension is based on syntactic and semantic knowledge. Syntactic knowledge is the knowledge of the format of various statements in the language concerned. Semantic knowledge consists of more general concepts which are independent of the programming language. This semantic knowledge might be fairly low level and include concepts such as what an if statement does or it may be high level and include various sorting algorithms. The authors argue that comprehension involves applying the syntactic knowledge to develop an internal semantic representation. This internal representation then can be altered or translated into an alternative programming language.

Brooks [8] puts forward a theory of program comprehension which is based on the hypothesis of a mapping between the problem domain and the programming domain. He argues that the developer produces these mappings and the maintainer has to reconstruct them. He views this reconstruction as a bottom-up approach rather than the more usual top-down approach to design. He also argues that the reconstruction of the mappings is an iterative, progressive activity. Thus, a maintainer might start with an initial hypothesis which is adapted as more knowledge of the program is gained. He suggests that the initial hypothesis might be formed from just the name of a particular activity. For instance, an activity with the name ''sort the input'' will immediately give the maintainer some ideas as to the structure of the program. This initial hypothesis could be clarified once the actual sorting algorithm has been determined. Brooks also argues that one of the differences between programmers and their ability to comprehend programs is their domain knowledge. Thus, in order to make comprehension easier, it is important not only to state the requirements but also a history of the decisions that led to those requirements. This history may well contain important clues in the formulation of the correct hypothesis.

Letovsky [21] describes an experiment in which maintenance programmers were given a program to modify and encouraged to think out loud so that their thoughts could be recorded. From the recordings, he focuses on two types of events, namely questions and conjectures, and develops taxonomies of these events. His taxonomy of questions leads him to suggest that a mixture of top-down and bottom-up strategies are employed during comprehension, where the top layer is the specification and the bottom is the implementation. These two layers are connected through various intermediate levels to form the programmer's mental model of the program. He argues that ''the human understander is best viewed as an opportunistic processor capable of exploiting both bottom-up and top-down cues as they become available.''

3. CODE READING

The crudest method of gaining knowledge about a system is to read the code. In the validation phase of the development cycle, this is known as desk checking. It is also often undertaken during code reviews and the debugging stages. Understanding code solely by reading is clearly a function of program size and complexity. Code understanding by reading can be effective, but it is difficult because there is a large amount of information in the code and extracting the required knowledge is far from an easy task.

The design methodology employed can effect readability. Wirth [46], Dijkstra [12] and Naur [28] argue that top-down design results in programs that are readable. Similar claims could no doubt be made for data structured design [16], data flow design [48] and object-oriented design methods [1]. One experiment in this area is described by Woodfield et al. [47] who performed an experiment to measure the effect of modularization techniques on program comprehension. They compared four different techniques, namely monolithic modularization, where there was no modularization at all, functional modularization, where each module corresponded to a functional unit, ''super modularization'', where modules consisted of very small internally cohesive routines, and modularization based on the concept of abstract data types. Their conclusions were that modularization based on abstract data types was significantly easier to comprehend.

Another factor affecting comprehension is the style in which the program is written. If the entire program is written in a consistent manner either by a single programmer or by a team with all the members following a house style, then the program will be easier to comprehend than a similar program which does not have a consistent style. The question then arises as to what is good and bad style. A well known text by Kernighan and Plauger [17] describes various examples of good and bad style.

Experimental evidence has been collected to support some of the well known techniques of good program

Approaches to Program Comprehension

J. SYSTEMS SOFTWARE 81
1991; 14:79–84

style. Schneiderman [32] has investigated the effect of using meaningful identifiers on program comprehension and concluded that, in terms of the syntactic/semantic model described earlier, the effect of meaningful variable names simplifies the conversion from a syntactic to a semantic representation. However, in a small experiment he did not find significant differences in comprehension between a program containing meaningful identifiers and an equivalent one which used non-mnemonic identifiers.

The effect of indentation of program comprehension has been studied by many investigators and a discussion of work in this area is given by Miara et al. [25]. The general conclusion of this work is that indented programs are easier to comprehend. They conducted their own experiments on the effect of levels of indentation and concluded that excessive indentation can slow the rate of comprehension. The optimal level seemed to be between two and four spaces indentation for each new block.

The experiment by Woodfield et al. [47] also investigated the effect of comments on program comprehension. Their conclusion was that comments used in the proper manner can assist in program comprehension. However, their experiment used programs in which indentation had been removed and meaningful identifiers had been replaced by single character identifiers. A previous study by Weissman [45] has shown that there has been no significant difference between commented and uncommented versions when indentation and meaningful identifiers were present. This implies that all indentation, meaningful identifiers and comments are complementary in program comprehension. Van Tassel [41] has given a description of what type of comments should be used at various points within a program.

Basili and Mills [6] have undertaken an interesting experiment in code reading. Their aim was to discover what a program does, as opposed to how it does it and with this restriction they employed some of the techniques of program correctness proofs [13]. For small parts of the program they employed direct cognition, but for medium-sized loops they utilized invariants. They analyzed a small numerical analysis program written in FORTRAN in some detail using these techniques and, though the results were interesting, it is not clear that such an approach would work on large software systems or how this method could be automated.

4. PROGRAM ANALYSIS

In this section some of the techniques and systems which have been developed to automate code reading are described. The advantages of automation when maintaining a large system which none of the maintainers developed is clear. The techniques used can be categorized into either static or dynamic analysis strategies.

Static analysis is the analysis of a program without its execution, and an overview of this topic is given by Fairley [14]. With a static analyzer, it is possible to identify uninitialized variables, departures from some coding standards, code which can never be executed, the frequency of use of statements, and to obtain cross reference information. For the purposes of program comprehension, only some of these features are useful.

Ryder [30] has applied static analysis techniques to develop call graphs of a system which have aided the maintenance programmer's understanding of a system. The work has been extended [31] to produce incremental analysis algorithms which update the local information of a system in response to a change. This avoids the re-analysis of the entire system. Kuhn [18] has done similar work producing a system which extracts information from a C program. His system also extracts an indirect calls matrix and identifies subsystems within the system under analysis. A second system developed by Kuhn [19] obtains cross-reference information from PL/1 programs providing certain coding standards have been followed. Chen and Ramamoorthy [10] have described a C Information Abstractor which stores extracted information in a data base which can then be accessed by the maintainer.

Systems which have been specifically developed to aid understanding have frequently been based on cross referencers. Munro and Robson [27] have described a system which allows the user to submit queries to determine where a variable is used or where a particular procedure is called from. Unlike most simple cross referencers, the system is aware of the scope rules of the target language and can distinguish between different uses of the same name. Some of the ideas from this work have been used to develop a documentation system for recording the knowledge obtained from the source code with the cross-reference information [26]. Cleveland [11] has developed a similar system for extracting knowledge from assembly language programs. The system described presents a window interface to the user and captures both control flow and data flow information. In the paper, Cleveland also distinguishes between soft facts and hard facts. Hard facts are those which are verifiable from an analysis of the program, while soft facts are those which appear to be true, but cannot be verified from the system. Such facts are supplied by the user of the system.

Temin and Rich [40] describe a system which performs dynamic analysis of C programs in order to extract information for the maintenance programmer.

82 J. SYSTEMS SOFTWARE
1991; 14:79–84

With this system, the maintainer can ask questions such as "What will this input do?" and answers are in terms of the output variables. This the authors call forward tracing. They also permit backward tracing in terms of questions such as "What input could have caused this output?" This tracing is implemented by an interpreter. Ambras and O'Day [3] describe a more ambitious system for the dynamic and static analysis of Common Lisp and CommonObjects, which permits different views of the source and performs impact analysis. The system would be able to respond to questions such as "What else must I change if I do this?" It also records a browsing execution history and records this in a knowledge base. The system has been implemented so far only as a prototype for a subset of Common Lisp and CommonObjects.

A different approach to program comprehension is taken by Adam et al. [2]. They have developed an interactive system which manipulates programs and provides transformations of the source code. The system is based on the ideas of symbolic execution [31]. The transformations have to be supplied by the user and it is not clear how the user would discover the correct transformations necessary to simplify the code and hence gain understanding of its function.

5. INVERSE ENGINEERING

Inverse engineering or reverse engineering is the process of obtaining high level representations from source code. Inverse engineering systems should not be confused with restructuring systems which restructure existing systems and produce code in the same language as the original. Inverse engineering systems attempt to screen out the noise which is present in source code representations and provide the maintenance programmer with a more abstract view of the system. They can also be viewed as attempting to recapture design and possibly requirements information. Analysis of the code cannot give a complete picture of the original design [7, 34], because information is lost in the translation of design to code in a similar manner to the information loss after compilation between high-level language code and binary code.

Antonini et al. [4] describe a system which captures low-level design information. From COBOL programs they can produce Jackson structure diagrams or Warnier/Orr design documents. The process is in two stages. First, they use an information abstractor to perform a static analysis of the COBOL code which produces control flow graphs, nesting trees and cross reference lists. These outputs from the first stage are then transformed into either structure charts or Warnier/Orr documents.

Arango et al. [5] describe the transformation-based model or TMM, which can be used to model the maintenance process. The model is based on the Draco paradigm [29] which is a domain modeling approach to software construction. The model assumes that a number of similar software programs are being constructed and that the path from a specification to a piece of code can be represented as a directed acyclic graph. The single root of the graph is the specification and the leaves are executable programs. The nodes in between the root and the leaves represent refinements of the original specification at various levels of abstraction. Different refinements can be applied to any of the specifications, but normally only one path from the root to a leaf is explored. The TMM assumes that when maintenance is taking place the development process is reversed so that instead of proceeding downward towards a leaf, the design is recaptured and hence the movement is upward. The upward movement is continued until a node containing the undesired characteristics and the new desired characteristics is encountered. This node is known as the least common abstraction. Movement then proceeds downward using a different path to a leaf which represents the modified implementation. The difficulty with this approach is the initial upward movement to recapture the design. The paper does not suggest any particular approach but suggests that input could come from various sources as well as the code. These other sources are the maintainer's previous experience, knowledge of the program domain, input from the original designer, and existing documentation. The authors have put their ideas into practice by porting the Draco system itself from one implementation of Lisp to another. The maintenance model is useful, but the central problem of recapturing the design has been avoided.

Soloway has employed the concept of plans to model both development and maintenance [22, 35, 36]. Plans are defined as

"Program fragments that represent stereotypic action sequences in programming, e.g., a running total loop plan, an item search loop plan [35]."

In Soloway's model, programs are composed of program plans that have been modified to suit a particular problem. Plans are implemented using rules of discourse that represent programming conventions such as using variable names that represent their function. Soloway and Ehrlich [36] have shown that rules of discourse are very important in program comprehension by conducting a study of novice and experienced programmers. In programs where the rules of discourse were followed, the experienced programmers were far superior to the novices. However, in programs where

Approaches to Program Comprehension

J. SYSTEMS SOFTWARE 83
1991; 14:79-84

the rules of discourse were not followed, the results of the experienced programmers were not significantly different from the novices. A study by Letovsky and Soloway [22] has shown that experienced programmers have difficulty understanding programs in which plans are delocalized, that is physically scattered within the source code. Soloway and Johnson [37] have described a system named PROUST which recognizes plans in novice programs. The assumption is that the novice program contains bugs and PROUST attempts to analyze the programs by recreating the methods by which they were generated.

PUDSY [24] is a similar system which also attempts program comprehension and the identification of bugs. In the comprehension phase, PUDSY divides groups of statements into chunks and evaluates the input and output assertions for each chunk. PUDSY has a knowledge base of chunks, but if it cannot match a chunk against one in its knowledge base, it undertakes a symbolic execution of the chunk. PUDSY then combines the input and output assertions of the chunks to derive an output assertion for the section of code under analysis. These assertions can then be compared to the original specification which it is assumed is also expressed in terms of an assertion. This approach and Soloway's look promising, but both have been experimental systems which have only been applied to small programs. There is a need to evaluate their effectiveness on larger programs.

Ward [43] has described a different approach to inverse engineering which is based on provable transformations [13, 42]. He describes an internal representation for a program and then applies a series of transformations to simplify the structure of the internal form. These transformations can be applied before comprehension as they have been proved to be correct. In the example in the paper, the transformed internal form is much easier to comprehend than the original source code. The transformed internal form could then be modified in response to a maintenance request and retranslated into an internal form. The author also describes a method of reducing the internal form into a specification. This approach to inverse engineering depends on applying the appropriate transformations in the correct order and this task is currently undertaken by the human maintainer. Developing an algorithm or heuristics for applying the appropriate transformations in the correct order is an interesting research problem.

6. FINAL REMARKS

Program comprehensibility is a vital part of the maintenance process. Current techniques are based on static or dynamic analysis of code or on inverse engineering.

Static and dynamic analyzers can be classified as low-level aids to the comprehension process as they do not assist the maintainer in understanding some of the fundamental characteristics of the program. They are useful in the comprehension of the micro units of the program, for instance in the use of a particular variable within the program, but they give very little assistance in determining the overall design.

The inverse engineering tools can be classified as higher-level aids but they are currently relatively primitive and more work is required in this area. In order to make significant advances in this area, automatic methods of design recapture are required. It is not possible to completely recapture the design, but the difference between the original and the recaptured design, known as the approximation error by Arango et al. [5] should be as small as possible. There is a also a lack of empirical evidence that inverse engineering techniques are as useful as they claim.

Artificial intelligence techniques appear to have made minimal impact in the area of program comprehension. This is surprising, as it would seem a ripe area for exploitation by such techniques. In particular, the development of an intelligent maintenance assistant would be a useful research area. Such ideas [44] have been investigated for the development stage of the life cycle, so there appears to be no reason why such techniques cannot be applied to the maintenance phase.

REFERENCES

1. R. J. Abbot, Program design by informal english descriptions, *Comm. of the ACM*, 26(11), 882-894 (1983).
2. A. Adam, P. Gloess, and J. Laurent, An interactive tool for program manipulation, *Proc. 5th Int. Conf. on Software Engineering*, 1981, pp. 460-468.
3. J. Ambras and V. O'Day, MicroScope: A program analysis system, *Proc. 20th Hawaii Int. Conf. on System Science*, 1987, pp. 71-81.
4. P. Antonini, P. Benedusi, G. Cantone, and A. Cimitile, Maintenance and reverse engineering: Low-level design documents production and improvement, *Proc. Conf. on Software Maintenance, IEEE*, 1987, pp. 91-100.
5. G. Arango, I. Baxter, P. Freeman, and C. Pidgeon, TMM: Software maintenance by transformation, *IEEE Software*, 3(3), 27-39 (1986).
6. V. Basili and H. D. Mills, Understanding and documenting programs, *IEEE Trans. on Software Engineering*, SE-8(3), 270-283 (1982).
7. J. M. Boyle and M. N. Muralidharan, Program reusability through program transformation, *IEEE Trans. on Software Engineering*, SE-10(5), 574-588 (1984).
8. R. Brooks, Towards a theory of the comprehension of computer programs, *Int. J. Man-Machine Studies*, 18, 543-554 (1983).
9. T. E. Cheatam, G. H. Holloway, and J. A. Townley,

84 J. SYSTEMS SOFTWARE
1991; 14:79-84

D. J. Robson et al.

Symbolic evaluation and the analysis of programs, *IEEE Trans. on Software Engineering*, SE-5(4), 402-417 (1979).

10. Y-F Chen and C. V. Ramamoorthy, The C information abstractor, *Proc. COMPSAC 86, IEEE*, 1986, pp. 291-298.

11. L. Cleveland, An environment for understanding programs, *Proc. 21st Hawaii Int. Conf. on System Sciences*, 1988, pp. 500-509.

12. E. W. Dijkstra, A constructive approach to the problem of program correctness, *BIT*, 8, 174-186 (1968).

13. E. W. Dijkstra, *A Discipline of Programming*, Prentice-Hall, Englewood Cliffs, NJ, 1976.

14. R. Fairley, Static analysis and dynamic testing of computer software, *IEEE Computer*, 11(4), 14-23 (1978).

15. R. K. Fjeldstrad and W. T. Hamlen, Application program maintenance study—A report to our respondents, in G. Parikh and N. Zvegintzov (Eds.), *Tutorial on Software Maintenance*, IEEE, 1983.

16. M. Jackson, *Principles of Program Design*, Academic Press, 1975.

17. B. Kernighan and P. Plauger, *Elements of Program Style*, McGRaw-Hill, 1978, 2nd Ed.

18. D. R. Kuhn, Simple tools to automate documentation, *Proc. Conf. on Software Maintenance, IEEE*, 1985, pp. 203-210.

19. D. R. Kuhn, A source code analyzer for maintenance, *Proc. Conf. on Software Maintenance, IEEE*, 1987, pp. 176-180.

20. B. P. Leintz and E. F. Swanson, *Software Maintenance Management*, Addison-Wesley, 1980.

21. S. Letovsky, Cognitive processes in program comprehension, in E. Soloway and S. Iyengar, *Empirical Studies of Programmers*, Ablex, Norwood, NJ, 1986, pp. 58-79.

22. S. Letovsky and E. Soloway, Delocalized plans and program comprehension, *IEEE Software*, 3(3), 41-49 (1986).

23. D. C. Littman, J. Pinto, S. Letozsky, and E. Soloway, Mental models and software maintenance, in E. Soloway and S. Iyengar, *Empirical Studies of Programmers*, Ablex, Norwood, NJ, 1986, pp. 80-98.

24. F. J. Lukey, Understanding and debugging programs, *Int. J. Man-Machine Studies*, 12, 189-202 (1980).

25. R. J. Miara, J. A. Musselman, J. A. Navarro, and B. Shneiderman, Program indentation and comprehensibility, *Comm. of the ACM*, 26(11), 861-867 (1983).

26. M. Munro and J. Foster, A documentation method based on cross-referencing, *Proc. Conf. on Software Maintenance, IEEE*, 1987, pp. 181-185.

27. M. Munro and D. J. Robson, An interactive cross reference tool for use in software maintenance, *Proc. 20th Hawaii Int. Conf. on System Sciences*, 1987, pp. 64-70.

28. P. Naur, An experiment on program development, *BIT*, 12, 347-365 (1972).

29. J. M. Neighbors, The Draco approach to constructing software from reuseable components, *IEEE Trans. on Software Engineering*, SE-10(5), 564-573 (1984).

30. B. G. Ryder, Constructing the call graph of a program, *IEEE Transactions on Software Engineering*, SE-5(3), 216-225 (1979).

31. B. G. Ryder, An application of static program analysis to software maintenance, *Proc. 20th Hawaii Int. Conf. on Systems Sciences*, 1987, pp. 82-91.

32. B. Schneiderman, *Software Psychology*, Winthrop, 1980.

33. B. Shneiderman and R. Mayer, Syntactic/semantic interactions in programming behaviour: A model, *Int. J. Computer and Information Science*, 8(3), 219-238 (1979).

34. H. M. Sneed, Software renewal: A case study, *IEEE Software*, 1(3), 56-63 (1984).

35. E. Soloway, Learning to program = Learning to construct mechanisms and explanations, *Comm. of the ACM*, 29(6), 850-858 (1986).

36. E. Soloway and K. Ehrlich, Empirical studies of programming knowledge, *IEEE Trans. on Software Engineering*, SE-10(5), 595-609 (1984).

37. E. Soloway and W. L. Johnson, PROUST: Knowledge-based program understanding, *IEEE Trans. on Software Engineering*, SE-11(3), 267-275 (1985).

38. T. A. Standish, An essay on software reuse, *IEEE Trans. Software Engineering*, SE-10(5), 494-497 (1984).

39. E. F. Swanson, The dimensions of maintenance, *Proc. of the 2nd Int. Conf. on Software Engineering, IEEE*, 1976, pp. 492-497.

40. A. Temin and E. Rich, Automating the desk analysis of programs, *Proc. 20th Hawaii Int. Conf. on System Sciences*, 1987, pp. 54-63.

41. D. Van Tassel, *Program Style, Design, Efficiency, Debugging and Testing*, Prentice-Hall, 1978, 2nd Ed.

42. M. Ward, Proving Program Refinements and Transformations, D.Phil thesis, 1989, Oxford University, UK.

43. M. Ward, Transforming a program into a specification, *Computer Science Tech. Rep.*, 88/1, 1988, University of Durham, UK.

44. R. C. Waters, The programmer's apprentice: Knowledge based program editing, *IEEE Trans. on Software Engineering*, SE-8(1), 1-12 (1982).

45. L. Weissman, Psychological complexity of computer programs: An experimental methodology, *ACM SIGPLAN Notices*, 9(6), 25-36 (1974).

46. N. Wirth, Program development by stepwise refinement, *Comm. of the ACM*, 14(4), 221-227 (1971).

47. S. N. Woodfield, S. E. Dunsmore, and V. Y. Shen, The effect of modularization and comments on program comprehension, *Proc. 5th Int. Conf. on Software Engineering*, 215-223 (1981).

48. E. Yourdon and L. Constantine, *Structured Design*, Yourdon Press, 1978.

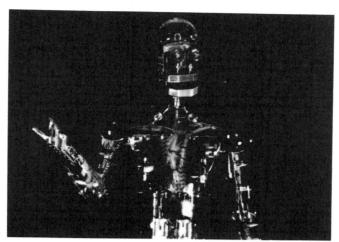

Program Recognition

Dirk Ourston

Lockheed Software Technology Center

Program recognition — a form of program analysis that identifies the reason behind given programs rather than their form or behavior — uses one program to analyze a second program. Analysis programs have existed for many years in the form of compilers, performance monitors, code optimizers, and the like. But program recognition research is relatively new, and applies expert system techniques to discover a given program's purpose.

The need for program recognition is particularly apparent in software maintenance, where programmers must modify unfamiliar programs. For large software systems developed without the aid of modern software engineering techniques, program modification can be virtually impossible. Using automatic program recognition systems, however, would enable maintenance programmers to concentrate on the modifications to be made rather than analyzing in detail the program to be modified.

Program recognition could apply to automatic documentation support. In such applications, a program would produce its own documentation in a specified format. Program recognition would also aid in intelligent query

support, where facts concerning program design are provided to the user. In either case, the issue is understanding; once a program recognition system understands a program, it can enter facts concerning that program into a knowledge base to support many other activities.

Research in program understanding has been quite limited. Lukey designed a theory of program understanding and debugging.[1] Fickas and Brooks developed a system for program understanding based on "description trees" — hierarchical structures, generated by programmers during program design, that analyze the input program during recognition. Lutz[2] is developing a system (resembling MIT's Program Recognizer) that is also based on the "plan calculus" developed at MIT.[3,4]

Other relevant work has been done in intelligent tutoring for computer programmers, in which it is necessary to understand student programs to properly assess student performance and provide guidance.[5] Significant work has been done in automatic program synthesis, taking high-level requirements for a program (an understanding of what a program is to do) and transforming them into operational

Reprinted from *IEEE Expert,* Vol. 4, No. 4, 1989, pp. 36-49. ©1989 by The Institute of Electrical and Electronics Engineers, Inc. All rights reserved.

code.[6] This is the reverse of program recognition, of course, but some techniques have been successfully applied to program recognition (particularly the use of plans).

To explore the issues involved with program recognition, we will review in some detail three systems epitomizing current techniques in program recognition research — the Program Recognizer, Talus, and Proust.

The Program Recognizer

The Program Recognizer, developed by Linda Wills at MIT, recognizes occurrences of stereotyped computational fragments in computer programs.[7] Using the plan calculus developed by Rich, Shrobe, and Waters,[3,8,9,10] it (1) analyzes a program, (2) converts the program plan to a flow graph projection, (3) parses the flow graph projection with a grammar derived from a library of cliches, and (4) checks constraints on the matched flow graph (constraints also derived from the library of cliches). A program cliche, as used here, is a familiar algorithmic program fragment or data structure. A flow graph is a labeled, directed, acyclic graph.[11] In the Program Recognizer, nodes represent operations and edges represent dataflow.

Essentially, the Program Recognizer uses a bottom-up parse of the input program to recognize familiar program parts, and from these builds an understanding of the whole program. The Program Recognizer allows for gaps in understanding the entire program, provided that it recognizes individual cliches.

Using plan calculus. A plan for a program is a graph, with nodes representing operators and edges representing control flow and dataflow. The plan calculus is, theoretically, programming-language independent. Plans are quasi-canonical in the sense that control flow is independent of control constructs associated with a particular programming language. And dataflow is independent of the method used to bind data. For example, Figure 1 shows the plan associated with the function

```
(defun safe-sqrt (a)
    (if (>= a 0)
    (sqrt a))).
```

Crosshatched lines in Figure 1 represent control flow; unmarked lines represent dataflow. The node above the null test represents the predicate for If, illustrating that control flow in the plan is independent of the control operator used (that is, whether it is an If or a Cond) and depends only on actual control logic. Nodes called "splits," which have one incoming control arc and two outgoing arcs, denote control flow branches in plan calculus. Plan calculus is specialized to Lisp in one way: The type of all split nodes is the null test,

since Lisp only tests for null to implement conditional branching. Other languages that use different conditional tests (comparing with a numerical value, as in Fortran) would require different types of split nodes. Joins are nodes having two or more incoming control arcs — control flow and dataflow. Operators specified in the nodes correspond to operators actually implemented in the language.

The current plan calculus used by the Program Recognizer includes representations for loops, but does not include representations for recursive programs. This does not appear to be a deficiency in the plan calculus itself but, instead, seems to be an implementation issue not yet attacked.

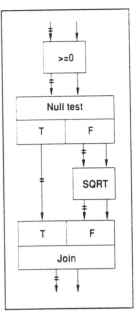

Figure 1. The plan for safe-sqrt (based on Wills).[7]

The flow analyzer. The flow analyzer converts a program in source code into a plan, which occurs in two stages: macro-expansion, followed by control flow and dataflow analysis. In theory, this capability should allow the automatic translation of programs into cliches. However, the generation of cliches for the Program Recognizer was done manually in Wills' thesis research.[7]

Macro-expansion has two purposes: first, to convert the program to a language based on more primitive forms; and second, to replace function calls selectively with in-line code representing the function's actions, thereby eliminating the problem of functional division in program matching. That is, two programs may allocate in entirely different ways the functionality required by the program (through different subfunction allocation) but still achieve exactly the same functionality in the top-level program. Replacing function calls with in-line code causes the programs to look the same — if indeed they are the same. Using more primitive forms simplifies matching through correspondence with the primitive forms used in the cliche library.

The flow analyzer performs control flow and dataflow analysis by symbolic evaluation of the program. Symbolic evaluation follows all possible control paths, converts operations to nodes, and places edges corresponding to dataflow and control flow between operations. Control flow branches are converted to splits, and control flow merges are converted to joins.

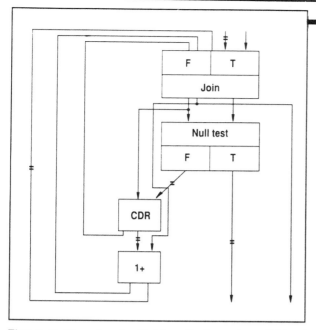

Figure 2. The plan for list length (based on Wills).[7]

The cliche library. Originally developed by Rich[3] to support the Programmer's Apprentice, the cliche library provides a taxonomy of standard computational fragments and data structures represented as plans. Figure 2 depicts a cliche, showing a plan for finding the length of a list.

An example of one form of code corresponding to this cliche follows:

```
(defun list-length (list)
    (do ((counter 0 (1+ counter)))
        ((null list) counter)
        (setq list (cdr list))))
```

Cliches in the cliche library come in two forms — plans, and implementation overlays. Plans pertain to representative algorithms and data structures. Plan nodes can consist of primitive forms (which are irreducible) or nodes corresponding to other plans. Implementation overlays represent alternative ways of expressing the same concept, usually from an abstract into more concrete form; for example, list length is a more concrete form of set cardinality. These considerations are important because grammar rules used to recognize programs are based directly on plan definitions in the cliche library.

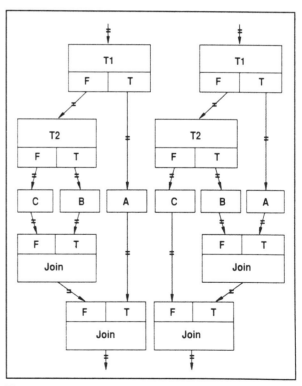

Figure 5. Joins from the left versus joins from the right (based on Wills).[7]

Figure 3. An example of transitivity of control (based on Wills).[7]

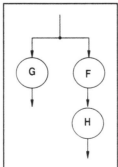

Figure 4. Dataflow for function FGH (based on Wills).[7]

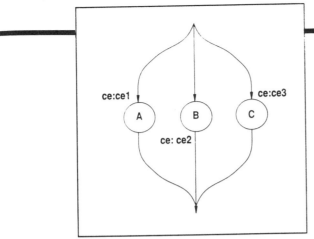

Figure 6. The flow graph equivalent of Figure 5 (based on Wills).[7]

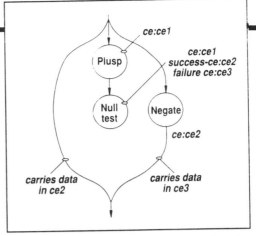

Figure 7. A flow graph with conditionals (based on Wills).[7]

The flow graph representation. Program recognition uses flow graphs, which resemble plans but have some significant differences. For example, control arcs are entirely eliminated from the plans. Instead, each node is annotated with a control environment representing the logical conditions for performing the node's operations. This enables initial program parsing to be based entirely on the dataflow. Then, constraint checking on the control environment is used to verify that program and cliche are actually equivalent. In particular, this simplifies capturing the transitivity of control arcs and the associativity of joins.

The transitivity of control arcs means that, if no data dependency exists between two operators, the order of operators in the control flow graph merely reflects the preference of the program's designer regarding execution order rather than any fundamental constraint on program operation. This is important in program recognition because, in this case, the recognizer wants to associate the same cliche with the target program, regardless of operator order. As an example, consider the program plan shown in Figure 3, corresponding to the following code:

```
(defun FGH (x)
    (let ((z (F x))
    (G x)
    (H z)))
```

Note that G has no data dependency on F and no change in the control environment has occurred between F and H (that is, no splits or joins). Hence, the order of execution between F and G is irrelevant, and the subgraph FH should be recognized as a valid subgraph for FGH. This would not be true if control arcs were explicitly included in the representation, because the order of execution for FGH would be fixed as F, then G, then H. On a purely dataflow basis, FGH would be represented as a fan-out prior to F and G, with a join after H (see Figure 4).

The other issue difficult to capture with plan calculus is join associativity. The two plans in Figure 5 are semantically equivalent, for example, yet they do not match each other structurally. Plan calculus considers these plans as being different. The solution is to remove joins from the plans (replacing them with fan-in arcs) and annotate arcs with the appropriate control environment, as before. Hence, the flow graph depicted in Figure 6 would replace the plans shown in Figure 5.

Therefore, a flow graph is equivalent to a plan that has had the control arcs and join nodes removed and that has had all the remaining nodes (operators) and edges annotated with the required control environment. The system also adds sinks to represent splits (branches) and sources to represent constants in the programs. Figure 7 (taken from Wills[7]) depicts a flow graph containing conditionals and corresponds to the following code:

```
(defun abs-val (x)
    (cond ((plusp x) x)
    (t (negate x))))
```

Finally, the system analyzes loops to specify three control environments: the feedback environment, where control of the loop feeds back to the beginning of the loop; the outside environment, where the loop is entered and to which it will return; and the loop body control environment, the control environment of the first operation reached in the control flow when the loop is entered.

This breaks the cycles in the loop, and loop nodes and edges are annotated in a special way with appropriate control environment information. Currently, the system cannot analyze recursive control structures.

Program parsing. To parse programs, the system attempts to match a flow graph representing a cliche with subgraphs occurring in the program definition. A grammar rule consists of a single node on the left-hand side, with cliche expansion on the right-hand side. For example, Figure 8 shows the grammar rule for the absolute-value cliche. A cliche can also contain cliches (that is, the rule's

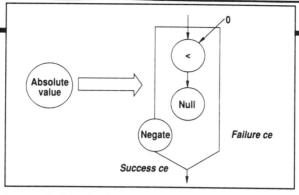

Figure 8. A typical grammar rule (based on Wills).[7]

right-hand side includes other cliches).

The system's parser is based on Brotsky's algorithm, which is Earley's string-parsing algorithm as applied to flow graphs.[11] This algorithm runs in polynomial time, based on the number of nodes in the input graph. From the program to be recognized, the parser scans input nodes and edges exactly once and keeps a list of cliches (called an item list) whose right-hand sides have been at least partially matched by the nodes read thus far. If the right-hand sides contain additional cliches, these are expanded and their nodes added to the item list.

After matching based on the flow graph, the system checks constraints added to the input graph against those that apply to the cliche being matched. If the constraints agree, a successful parse has occurred and the process continues. If not, the cliche is removed from the current item list (as are all cliches that might contain it). Removing cliches from the item list as soon as constraint violations occur eliminates invalid parses early on. Cliches may be reinstated if their right-hand sides are matched by other regions of the input graph.

The Program Recognizer's strengths. Let's analyze the strengths and weaknesses of the Program Recognizer as they relate to program understanding in general, beginning with its strengths:

• **Abstraction capabilities** — The Program Recognizer's use of control flow analysis means that arbitrary ordering decisions in the input program (not affecting control flow) do not affect recognition. In addition, the Program Recognizer's dataflow analysis removes the sensitivity to the order of statement or function calls not affecting program dataflow. For the input program, this creates a canonical representation based on true control flow and dataflow within the program, and not on the actual order of function call statements within the program. The Program Recognizer also provides for implementation overlays that present alternative ways of expressing the same concept (set cardinality, for example) — useful for recognizing similarities between different program types.

• **Recognition capabilities** — To succeed, the Program Recognizer does not require that all program components be recognized.[7] The Program Recognizer will identify components that successfully match cliches, and ignore the rest.

In comparison, Talus recognizes programs deviating significantly from its reference plans — but performance falls off dramatically as deviation increases. Proust must include deviations (bugs) as separate plans.

The Program Recognizer does not require all its reference functions to be present in the input code. But it will not recognize a higher level cliche unless all required lower level cliches are present. For large programs, the Program Recognizer could encounter overlapping cliches: If a given input code segment corresponds to two or more cliches that overlap in the input code (as in Figure 3), which cliches should be selected? The Program Recognize will recognize both — and point this out.

Since the Program Recognizer unravels function calls prior to analyzing programs, it is relatively impervious to the way functions were allocated in input programs. It will recognize elements required by a primitive-level cliche (one not containing other cliches) if they exist in the program. And as long as control flow and dataflow constraints are not violated, the order or separation of statements in the input program will not affect recognition. However, the system will not recognize higher level cliches unless all their lower level cliches occur in the exact order specified.

The Program Recognizer's limitations. In addition to several points already observed above, the Program Recognizer has the following coverage and computational-efficiency limitations:

• **Ease of extension** — Plan calculus provides a method for converting an input program into a plan, but the Program Recognizer requires that grammar rules be manually added whenever it adds a new cliche to the library. The requirement to perform a flow graph analysis manually on a given algorithm (cliche), and then manually transform the flow graph into a set of rewrite rules, limits the Program Recognizer's current range of applicability.

• **Coverage limitations** — The Program Recognizer does not provide coverage for side-effecting operations, full recursion, arbitrary data abstraction, or functional arguments. But it does provide coverage for loops, nested expressions, and programs containing conditionals. The approach to loop analysis should be extensible to recursion in a fairly straightforward way.

• **Computational efficiency** — While Brotsky's algorithm for parsing the input flow graph runs in polynomial time, the Program Recognizer must run the parser at all points in the input program's graph, thereby losing polynomial-time behavior. Prior to flow graph matching, however, we must process the input program to turn it into a flow graph. The reduction to flow graph form requires the program's symbolic evaluation, done by following all logical paths. Dataflow analysis occurs at the level of Lisp primitives, so each Lisp statement may correspond to more than one of these primitives. Flow graph reduction appears to be linear in the input program's number of operations.

Once flow graph reduction is completed, the recognition process requires that the system match all node combinations that could match a rule's right-hand side in number of inputs. Since functions are unraveled in the calling code, no advantage can be taken of the fact that a given function in the input program might correspond directly to a particular cliche. If the input program contained a function *average* that corresponded directly to the cliche *average*, and this function were called many times, the Program Recognizer would require that the function be identified anew each time — a laborious process.

To achieve its power, the Program Recognizer uses a bottom-up approach using every input statement and every primitive operator within an input statement to match every cliche in the cliche library. The Program Recognizer cannot use a top-down approach to scan input programs for clues indicating the presence of higher level cliches, which would limit search space and improve search efficiency.

Talus

To provide automatic program debugging in support of intelligent tutoring, W.R. Murray developed Talus at the University of Texas.[11] Talus' domain is Lisp programs. Designed to analyze programs involving the recursive definition of data structures, Talus permits recursion on data types — list, tree, and number.

Talus' connection with program recognition is that, to support automatic program debugging, Talus must first recognize the input program before it can associate the program with known reference functions. Murray called the program to be recognized the "student's program" and called the program representing the "correct" solution the "reference program."[12] We will call the program to be recognized the "input program" (or "input function," if it is a function being recognized).

Talus separates knowledge representation into three different levels:

(1) **Tasks** are basic programming assignments given to students. Talus has 18 tasks, each at a comparable abstraction level to "write a function returning a list of all the atoms in a tree." Talus assumes that tasks are known prior to their execution.

(2) **Algorithms** are alternative ways of solving tasks.

(3) **Functions** are subelements of algorithms (that is, each algorithm contains one or more functions).

Talus uses four steps to analyze input programs: program simplification, algorithm recognition, bug detection, and bug recognition. Program simplification puts the program in If-Normal form (to be discussed below) and transforms it to a simpler Lisp core dialect. In algorithm recognition, Talus selects the algorithm matching the input program. Once the algorithm is selected, reference algorithm functions are associated with input program functions.

For program recognition, parameters that Talus uses in algorithm recognition are interesting as a clue to the accuracy with which programs can be identified — as are specializations Talus may have made that indicate its domain of applicability.

Using symbolic evaluation, Talus detects bugs to determine differences between input and reference functions — differences that can be accounted for only as incorrect implementations of the input function. Since we are interested in program recognition, we are interested in bug detection as it applies to matching the reference function with a correct input function. In particular, we want to know how much an input function's definition can vary and still match a reference function serving the same purpose.

Once it identifies bugs in the input program, Talus attempts to correct them, using techniques based on theorem proving and other heuristic methods. This article will not detail bug correction because bug correction is not relevant to program recognition.

Program simplification. Talus simplifies programs by (1) transforming them from an extended Lisp dialect to a simpler core dialect, and (2) reducing all conditionals to If-Normal form. Transforming programs to a simpler dialect reduces the number of constructs Talus must consider; for example, a Cond would be changed into an equivalent If set. The use of If-Normal form supports symbolic evaluation by representing the program as a binary tree. The attributes of If-Normal form are

- **The only conditional expression is If;**
- **No If expression will occur as part of another If expression test;** and
- **No If expression occurs inside a function call.**

For If-Normal-form binary trees, nonterminal nodes are conditional tests and terminal nodes are function terminations or recursions. Symbolic evaluation consists of determining a path in the tree from the root to a terminal node. Symbolic evaluation helps Talus find missing or extra conditionals in either the object or reference function.

Algorithm recognition. The key to algorithm recognition in Talus is its use of E-frames — data structures that contain slots representing various program abstractions. Derived from "enumeration frame," E-frames represent abstract properties of the enumeration of recursively defined functions.

To analyze Talus relative to the program recognition problem, we must explore in some detail the definition and use of E-frames because they represent the basic granularity with which Talus accomplishes recognition. In particular, E-frame slots represent program characteristics considered important in program recognition. E-frame slot definitions follow:

• **Function-name** — The name of the function in either the reference library or the student program;
• **Formals** — The formal-variable list for the function;
• **Definition** — The Lisp definition for a data structure;
• **Terminations** — The logical conditions under which a function terminates and the values returned under those conditions;
• **Recursions** — The forms in the function producing recursive calls and the logical conditions required for recursion to occur;
• **Constructions** — How the results of recursive calls are joined to form the answer;
• **Variable-updates** — Updates to formal variables and the logical conditions under which they occur;
• **Variable-data-types** — Constraints on data types for formal variables;
• **Variables-controlling-terminations** — Formal variables used in termination tests;
• **Variables-returned-in-terminations** — Variables used in termination return clauses;
• **Output-data-type** — The type of data structure returned by the function;
• **Side-effects** — An enumeration of side-effecting operations contained in the function;
• **Functions-calling** — A list of functions that call the given function;
• **Function-type** — Which can be recursive, calling (calls other nonprimitive Lisp functions), or simple (calls only primitive Lisp functions);
• **Predicates-called** — Functions used by this function as predicates in conditionals;
• **Constructors-called** — Functions used by this function to return results; and
• **Task-role** — Which can be top (nonrecursive and not called by any other function), main (recursive, and not called by any other function), extra (calls other functions and not top or main), supporting predicate (used in another function's predicate), or supporting constructor (used as a constructor for another function).

Talus uses three steps to recognize algorithms. It performs a best-first search to find the optimum match between reference and input functions, pairs formal variables between corresponding functions, and generates verification conditions to establish the equivalence between paired functions. Failed verification conditions guide · bug detection.

Talus bases its best-first search on a refined version of the A* algorithm.[13,14] Each node in the search space represents a partial mapping between reference functions for a particular algorithm and functions contained in the input program. The best node to expand next is the one with the lowest f score where

$$f[S] = g[S] + h[S]$$

and where S is the node to be expanded, f estimates the quality of the best complete mapping obtained by expanding S, g measures the quality of the mapping in S, and h estimates the cost associated with extending the mapping from S to a complete mapping.

Talus obtains the value of g by computing a penalty for the degree of mismatch between reference functions in S and input functions with which they have been paired. If functions cannot be paired, an additional penalty is assessed.

Talus computes h — the minimum cost associated with extending S to a complete mapping — by calculating the penalty associated with those functions in S that can never be matched with another function of the same role and type (that is, because no other functions of the same role and type remain).

Talus limits the function mappings to be considered by applying the following plausibility constraints:

• **Both functions must have the same function role;**
• **Both functions must be of the same function-type;** and
• **Parent functions for both functions must already have been paired.**

The key to the search process (and to overall algorithm recognition) is the method Talus uses to calculate the degree of match between input and reference functions: Talus compares E-frame slots of the functions being matched, and assigns a weighted score to each slot match. A score of 0 indicates a perfect match. For example, if the recursion slot of the reference function matches that of the input function, a score of 0 is assigned; otherwise, a score of 1 is given.

Weightings indicate the importance of specific factors as discriminants between programs. For example, if the number of formal variables in the input program is less than

> ## In the long term,
> ## program recognition research
> ## must employ
> ## machine-learning techniques.

the number of formal variables in the reference function, the discrepancy is heavily weighted (seven times the difference). This indicates that the reference programs were coded to use the fewest formal variables possible — hence, an input function with fewer formal variables is unlikely to match. Talus' intelligent tutoring input programs (Murray's "student programs"), containing more formal variables, were not weighted as heavily because it was assumed that students might have included extraneous formal variables.

Once Talus determines a best match, it applies solution transforms that reduce differences between matched functions. These transformations represent common variations to algorithms that would otherwise require the storage of multiple algorithms to explain differences. If two recursive functions matched — and the input function had one more formal variable than the reference function — Talus would apply a tail recursion transformation to the reference function, requiring an additional argument. Predicate inversion (for example, testing for nil instead of t) is another transformation example.

Next, Talus uses heuristics to map formal variables between paired functions based on data type and role. These heuristics use the slots variable-data-types, variable-updates, termination-formals, and output-formals. Talus generates all possible mappings and scores them depending on the match between these slot values.

Finally, Talus normalizes reference functions by replacing identifiers in reference functions with those used in input functions. This also involves permuting the reference function's argument list to match the order given in the input function.

Bug detection. In bug detection, Talus determines whether an equivalence exists between input and reference functions, using symbolic evaluation. If none exists, Talus tries to infer which bugs are present in the input program. Symbolic evaluation considers the program in If-Normal form, as a tree — with leaves (terminal nodes) representing function terminations or recursive calls. The system derives conditions required to reach a leaf for input and reference functions, and groups them into cases. Talus then takes cases derived from the reference function, applies them to the input function, and vice versa.

At each node (If test), Talus determines whether conditions for one branch can be derived from the case. If so, Talus continues down the tree until it eventually reaches a leaf node. The associated expression is then returned and symbolically compared with the expression returned from the given case. If a match occurs, the two functions compare for the given case. If not, a bug has been detected.

The only exception occurs when a node is evaluated for which neither branch can be predicted from case conditions. In such situations, Talus follows both paths and returns expressions for both. Because of Talus' orientation to the debugging of student programs, Talus assumes that the input program has an extra (unnecessary) conditional if case splitting occurs in the input (student) program; if case splitting occurs in the reference function, indicating the presence of a bug, Talus assumes the input program is missing a conditional.

After completing case evaluation, Talus checks for functional equivalence between expressions returned, using functional-equivalence-verification conditions. If returned expressions represent recursive calls, Talus uses termination verification conditions to ensure that no infinite loops are entered.

Functional-equivalence-verification conditions test the correspondence between two expressions; for example, (in x (cdr l)) and (in x (car l)) — which, of course, would not be functionally equivalent. Talus has three methods for determining functional equivalence. First, it can test to see if the two expressions could be true simultaneously (the previous expression would fail this test). Second, if functions return lists representing sets, it can test to see if one set is a permutation of the other. Otherwise, it can test to see whether the two objects are equal (that is, that their values are equal). Termination-conditions tests check that arguments to recursive calls diminish according to some measure and to the well-founded LESSP relation.

Since Talus compares programs at the leaf level, it can identify discrepancies at that level — thereby localizing bug detection. Talus uses three methods to perform actual tests for functional equivalence. One method uses the Boyer-Moore theorem prover, which merely invokes the theorem prover to prove that the use of case assumptions proves one of the three forms of functional equivalence. This method, although complete, can be time consuming on other than quite small programs.

The second method invokes a conjecture disprover that binds free variables in the input and reference functions, using stored examples prior to verifying their functional equivalence. The third method, called the counter-example generator, uses heuristics to generate counter examples based on the form of reference and input functions.

Both the conjecture disprover and counter-example generator guarantee that anything they reject is an invalid conjecture (that is, that the programs are not functionally equivalent). But they miss bugs if counter examples have not been generated that test that particular logical condition. Both methods are much faster than the Boyer-Moore theorem prover, however, and are included for that reason. For program recognition, using both of these techniques might cause two programs that are not equivalent to be deemed equivalent (for example, mistaking one program that limits an input variable's range of values for a program that does not).

Talus' strengths. Talus' strengths stem from several sources, which we will discuss individually:

• **Talus allows reference functions to be stored as program code** — Of the three systems reviewed, only Talus allows reference functions to be stored directly as program code. Talus automatically converts reference functions to E-frames, and directly uses the program's code in program-matching functions associated with bug detection. This facilitates the production of reference functions, since they can be viewed as ordinary Lisp programs rather than as flow graphs (as with the Program Recognizer) or plans (as with Proust). This feature is particularly beneficial for automatic documentation because, in theory, existing program libraries can be used as reference functions (subject to limitations discussed in this section).

• **Talus detects localized mismatches automatically** — Talus analyzes a program based on that program's logical structure, and identifies differences between code at the logic tree's lowest level (terminal nodes). Talus thinks of these differences as bugs. In the general program recognition problem, these bugs could represent alternative functionality between the input program and the reference program. Because the differences are extremely localized, this technique would explicitly identify differences between a given reference function and a given input program (that is, "Program x is exactly like reference program y except in the way it computes the average of the count, which is as follows . . . ").

This feature could greatly benefit program description, where small differences between programs can be meaningful. Proust requires explicit plans for typical bugs. The Program Recognizer accounts for bugs as unrecognized regions of code, but does not attempt to localize bugs based on logic flow.

• **Talus represents functions containing functions** — Talus represents functions containing calls to other reference functions. Since most real-world programs operate in this way, this makes Talus more responsive to input programs likely to be encountered in practice. The Program Recognizer provides for cliches containing cliches but, due to its bottom-up parsing method, recognizes these higher level cliches only if all subordinate cliches match perfectly (which seldom occurs in practice). Using heuristics that measure the goodness of the match, Talus matches higher level functions. It does not require a perfect match among subfunctions. If subfunctions mismatch, that mismatch appears as a bug report associated with those subfunctions. Proust does not account for higher level functions at all.

• **Talus recognizes equivalent forms of the same expression** — Under logical conditions applying to the section of code, Talus can recognize whether two expressions will produce the same result. A simple example would be (cons tree nil) <=> (list tree). The Program Recognizer and Proust lack this capability, which gets at the programming variations likely to occur in alternative program implementations. Proust has some stored heuristics — $x + y$ <=> $y + x$, for example — but cannot derive the equivalence of two expressions.

• **Talus derives formal-variable roles** — Talus derives the roles of formal variables in programs it analyzes (termination-formals and output-formals). Extending this concept would make it valuable for program description and for preventing interface mismatches between programs.

Talus' limitations. As is the case with Talus' strengths, the program's limitations result either from theory or from implementation:

• **Talus assumes the task is already known** — This is probably Talus' greatest single limitation at present. For Talus to handle arbitrary input programs, it would require a technique that searched on tasks, since the input program could represent the solution to an arbitrary task. And it would have to use discriminants corresponding to tasks (as current E-frame slots are discriminants for algorithms).

• **Prescribed subfunction definitions** — Talus provides for hierarchical functions — a strength compared to the Program Recognizer and Proust. But Talus is limited in that, for Talus to properly recognize the input program, the input program must allocate its subfunctions exactly as Talus does. Since subfunctions can be allocated in multitudinous ways, this is a serious limitation when dealing with large programs consisting of many subprograms. However, this limitation is one shared by program recognition systems in general.

• **Talus is oriented to recursive programs that update data structures** — To make Talus generally applicable, recognition logic must be extended to account for loops and other program types (for example, scientific calculations involving extensive arithmetical computations and few data structure updates). Although the logic in Talus' actual program comparison can account for arithmetical computations, an examination of E-frame slots used to guide algorithm recognition indicates that algorithm search would be much less effective for other program types. In particular, the slots recursions, variable-updates, variables-

```
DefProgram Rainfall;

DefObject ?Rainfall:DailyRain ObjectClass ScalarMeasurement;

DefGoal Sentinel-Controlled Input Sequence (?Rainfall:DailyRain, 99999);
DefGoal Loop Input Validation(?Rainfall:DailyRain, ?Rainfall:DailyRain<0);
DefGoal Output(Guarded Count(?Rainfall:DailyRain, ?Rainfall:DailyRain>0));
```

Figure 9. An example of a program description.

controlling-terminations, and terminations are based on the assumption that functions involved are recursive — while output-data-type, constructions, and variable-updates assume that the program's purpose is to update data structures.

• **Talus has problems with large programs and imperative programming style** — According to Murray, Talus was designed to debug programs written by students in an introductory Lisp class; its performance degrades when analyzing large programs (the result of various functional decompositions that must be accounted for) or programs written in an imperative style. When dealing with imperative programming style — programs containing PROGs with SETQs, GOTOs, and RETURNS — Talus must convert these programs into equivalent recursive implementations, perform the comparison, identify the bugs, and then reconvert the programs into a similar imperative framework before presenting them to students. With more complex programs, the transformation may incorrectly derive equivalent recursive programs. Or it may fail to transform the edits back to the original program.

• **Talus provides limited data structure definitions** — Talus provides for primitive data types (lists, atoms, and numbers) but not for other commonly used data types (arrays, characters, and streams).

• **Talus' language limitations** — Talus uses a Lisp subset called the extended dialect. Space limitations preclude a complete definition of this subset, but its principal weaknesses (relative to Common Lisp) involve data types and predicates.[15]

Proust

Developed at Yale by W. Lewis Johnson, Proust is a program for debugging Pascal programs. Part of an intelligent tutoring system aimed at novice programming students,[16] Proust uses frames for its knowledge representation and is coded in Lisp. Its unique contribution to automatic program debugging is its attempt to identify programmer intentions in order to correct program bugs.

To analyze a student's program, Proust goes through several steps. It starts by describing the problem to be solved (typically written by the instructor). Proust implements problem descriptions as frames. Slots describe objects the program must manipulate. Other slots list the program's goals, which are put onto an agenda. Proust enters a cycle, selecting (from the agenda) the highest priority goal for expansion, and adding new goals to the agenda as it discovers them.

Goal expansion selects a plan from the plan library— a plan that might be used to implement the goal. When alternative plans are available, Proust uses heuristics to guide plan selection. If plans contain subgoals, Proust adds those subgoals to the agenda for later expansion. Proust's plan matcher matches plans against the input program by matching program identifiers with plan variable names and transforming plan constructs into equivalent forms that may have been used in the input program.

Unresolvable differences between the input program and the plan are passed to the plan difference analyzer for explanation, either as bugs or as unknown programming.

Proust's knowledge representation. How Proust encodes knowledge is key to the strength of its program recognition capability. Knowledge in Proust comprises program descriptions, goals, plans, and object classes:

• **Program descriptions** are a codification of requirements for the problem to be solved. Figure 9 shows a typical program description, an excerpt from the Rainfall problem description (see Johnson,[16] page 136).

Figure 9's use of Rainfall:DailyRain refers to the Rainfall problem and its DailyRain data object. The DefObject statement declares ?Rainfall:DailyRain to be an object of class ScalarMeasurement. The first goal indicates that the program will use a sentinel-controlled input of daily rainfall occurrences; the value used to stop input is 99999. Sentinel-controlled means that, to stop the processing, the program is watching (like a sentinel) for a specific input value. The second goal specifies that the program should contain a loop for input of the daily rainfall and that the loop should validate that the value of the daily rainfall always exceeds zero. The final goal indicates that program output should be a count of daily rainfall occurrences — but only for values greater than zero.

In general, arguments in goal expressions can be data objects, expressions, code, and other goals. Proust uses goals to identify plans that can be used to accomplish those goals. In some cases, goals require the satisfaction of other goals for their success, as in Figure 9's Output(Guarded Count . . .) — where the output goal requires that the Guarded Count goal be satisfactorily achieved first. As a rule, Proust assumes goals for program descriptions to be unordered. But ordering can be imposed on plans by using the "precedes" construct.

• **Goals** are identified in the program description, and indicate the specific attribute the program must have, although such attributes can be implemented in various ways. Figure 10 shows the definition of the Sentinel-Controlled Input Sequence goal.

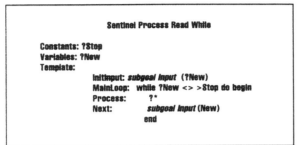

```
Instance-of:      Read & process
Form:             Sentinel-Controlled Input Sequence (?New, ?Stop)
Main segment:     MainLoop
Main variable:    ?New
Name phrase:      "sentinel-controlled loop"
OuterControlPlan: T
Implementations:

                  SENTINEL PROCESS-READ WHILE
                  SENTINEL READ-PROCESS WHILE
                  SENTINEL READ-PROCESS REPEAT
                  SENTINEL PROCESS-READ REPEAT
                  BOGUS YESNO PLAN
                  BOGUS COUNTER-CONTROLLED LOOP
```

Figure 10. The Sentinel-Controlled Input Sequence goal definition.

```
            Sentinel Process Read While

Constants: ?Stop
Variables: ?New
Template:
          InitInput:  subgoal Input (?New)
          MainLoop:   while ?New <> >Stop do begin
          Process:    ?*
          Next:       subgoal Input (New)
                      end
```

Figure 11. An example of a plan.

The InstanceOf slot indicates the goal's class. Currently, only the Read & Process goal class is implemented in Proust.

The main segment slot indicates the most likely place that this goal will appear in the input program. The main variable is the variable bound to the principal quantity that this goal manipulates.

The name phrase is the documentation segment that is associated with the goal. The OuterControlPlan slot indicates whether plans satisfying the goal will determine the program's overall control structure and help Proust determine which goals to expand first (that is, those indicating the program's overall structure).

In addition to the slots shown in Figure 10, other slots are important to Proust's operation. These include (1) ResultVariable, which indicates the variable holding the value generated by the goal (Pascal can have input and output variables), and (2) Compounds, which indicate goals that can be subsumed by a goal. Subsumption occurs when a single plan can simultaneously satisfy two or more goals.

• **Plans** are templates for program fragments that are stereotypical for the operation to be performed. Figure 11 exemplifies a plan used by Proust.

Slots in a plan can consist of the following items: a Pascal statement (see the items in Template), a subgoal to be implemented as one or more statements (see InitInput), and a reference to a component of another plan. The Pascal statements indicate specific Pascal statements that must be present in the input program the plan is attempting to match. Subgoal expressions allow other goals to implement parts of the plan, with the constraint that the code for the plan selected by the subgoal must appear at the same place as the subgoal expression. References to other plan components (not shown in Figure 11) make it possible to interweave plan emplacements by specifying that a particular component of another plan must occur in a specific location in the current plan.

Slot labels indicate the roles of plan components. For example, "Next" indicates a plan component that gets the next value.

Pattern variables are used in plans to match with particular elements of the input program. These elements can be constants, variable names, or pieces of code. Pattern variables are used for code segments when code segments will also be used in part of another plan so that they may be referred to specifically in the other plan.

Proust also permits wildcard pattern matching, signified by ?* or ??. In both cases, wild cards indicate program parts of no concern to the current plan — parts that will eventually be filled in by other plans. The symbol ?* refers to an arbitrary sequence of statements, and ?? refers to exactly one statement.

Plans can also contain slots indicating assertions about the plan. The Prior-Goals slot indicates other goals that must be met before this plan can be activated, whereas the PosteriorGoals slot indicates goals to be added to the agenda after the plan is matched. In effect, these slots control goal-processing order when Proust is executed.

• **Object classes** refer to the way that Proust represents data structures. Figure 12 exemplifies an object class. Object classes and data types differ in that object classes refer to real-world concepts, whereas data types refer to abstract programming concepts. The implementations slot lists implementations known to Proust for this concept. In turn, an implementation object (REAL TRANSACTION AMOUNT, for example) describes the way an object can be realized in Proust's database. Exception conditions limit the range of values for an object type. Plan difference rules indicate which plan difference rules should be applied when, using a plan containing an object of the given type, Proust discovers a plan mismatch.

Principles of operation. Proust proceeds top down to match program requirements and the input program, using a blackboard approach in which items on the blackboard consist of

• **An agenda of goals whose implementation has not been completed;**
• **Plans matched by the program, and the code they match;** and
• **Object descriptions (from the problem descrip-**

Figure 12. An example of an object class.

tion) and an indication of whether or not they have been identified in the program.

Proust operates in a continuous cycle, as follows:

(1) Select a goal from the agenda.

(2) Determine if that goal should be subsumed or unified with other goals already on the agenda.

(3) Expand the goal by identifying implied goals and elaborating the properties of any objects that the goal manipulates.

(4) Retrieve implementation methods for the goal. Implementation methods may correspond to object implementations or to plans.

(5) Attempt to match retrieved plans with the input program. Plan matching may stop because of match errors (which may indicate the presence of bugs), or because the plan contains a subgoal. If an error is indicated, Proust analyzes the error for the presence of bugs. If a subgoal is encountered, Proust adds the subgoal to the agenda and starts a new cycle. If no plan fits the program, Proust begins a new cycle with the goal for the current cycle removed from the agenda.

(6) Choose from among plans if more than one plan matches the current goal. If the current goal is a subgoal of some previous goal, Proust reactivates the previous goal. Otherwise, using an updated goal agenda, Proust continues on the next cycle.

From the agenda, Proust selects goals that have all their contextual information known. Contextual information consists of arguments to the goal and descriptions of where in the input program the goal is likely to apply. If a goal is compound (one containing another goal as an argument), Proust selects the inner goal first. If no goal on the agenda has all its contextual information known, Proust selects from among goals having larger control structures in the program. These are identified by having the Outer-ControlPlan slot marked as *T*. Any time more than one goal qualifies for selection, Proust arbitrarily selects among qualified goals.

If the input program does not fit any plan exactly, Proust invokes plan-difference rules that it uses to (1) identify bugs accounting for the difference, or (2) apply plan transformations that could generate the observed plan differences. In correct programs, plan-difference rules account for minor differences in program structure — differences that might be detected by control flow and dataflow analysis. In buggy programs, plan-difference rules account for minor deviations from plans — deviations associated with such common programming misconcep-

tions as forgetting to initialize loop data. Specific differences between the plan and its implementation trigger plan-difference rules.

Analysis. Before discussing strengths and weaknesses associated with Proust's approach to program recognition, we should identify a Proust facet unimportant to program recognition per se, but quite important to the theory behind Proust; namely, the goal of recognizing the intention behind program implementation.

Because of this goal, Proust must have either alternative plans or plan transformations accounting for every buggy implementation of a Proust plan; it is not sufficient for Proust merely to recognize that a bug has occurred — or even exactly what the bug is. Proust must identify why the bug occurred and associate it with the correct plan that Proust intended to accomplish using a defined deviation or transformation.

Since the space of possible buggy implementations is exponentially large — starting with the possibility of a typographical error (a single incorrect character in an input statement, perhaps) — the impact on a Proust implementation is severe. But the space of a given problem statement's correct implementations, while still large, must be much smaller than the space of buggy programs. Therefore, a Proust version directed toward identifying correct versions of problem statements (that is, the program recognition problem) would be considerably less complex than the current version. Moreover, it would not suffer as drastically from incorrect identification problems associated with the current version.[16]

Proust's strengths. Proust's strengths derive primarily from its knowledge representation, as follows:

• **Top-down template matching** — Based on matching top-level control structure with the input program, prior to completing lower level comparisons, Proust uses an opportunistic approach to program recognition. This depth-first technique minimizes the search space required for successful program identification. Since it operates with goals at each step, Proust can synthesize a solution that is not part of a stored database.

• **Partial recognition** — Since Proust's operation consists of successive refinements to a higher level solution, it recognizes large parts of a program and uses its current plan database to identify localized sections it cannot recognize. Furthermore, its recognition process identifies the program as being associated with a given problem solution, even though it cannot completely identify all parts of the input program.

Proust's limitations. Proust has three basic limitations. It requires a problem description and transformation rules, and it uses templates:

• **Proust requires a problem description** — Like Talus, Proust relies on the fact that the problem to be solved has been specified. Proust then discovers from the alternatives the way that the problem was implemented. Proust's search strategy — the successive decomposition of goals — does not easily extend to the problem of identifying problem descriptions with unknown programs. Proust would have to use a completely new technique to match the problem description with the input program.

• **Proust requires transformation rules** — Proust must explicitly encode equivalences such as $x + y = y + x$. It has no notion of a calculus for programs — a calculus that yields alternative implementations based on first principles. Proust generates each variation of a construct, using a heuristic that must be included in the knowledge base.

• **Proust uses templates** — Proust's use of templates is limiting for two reasons. First, templates place constraints relative to the recognition of equivalence classes. Since programs in Pascal syntax are matched with the template, Proust cannot possibly recognize the equivalence of different implementations (for example, the use of other branching techniques equivalent to an If). Second, templates are tied to Pascal. Therefore, it is impossible to port the program recognition implementation to other languages. Both limitations result from Proust's failure to transform the input program to canonical form when matching against a plan that has also been put into canonical form.

T alus and Proust require program objectives to be specified prior to recognition. The Program Recognizer does not, but its author states that "There are bound to be unrecognizable sections in most large and complex programs."[7] Hence, the Program Recognizer will probably recognize only the program's algorithmic fragments rather than the entire program. All three systems have been tested on small programs only (less than 50 lines) — programs of limited complexity. Yet the Program Recognizer, Talus, and Proust are fairly substantial, comprising several thousand lines of code.

The most promising direction for future research would be to combine the best elements of all programs reviewed in this article. Talus provides strong methods for search, based on program semantics, and provides methods for deducing equivalency between alternative language expressions. On the other hand, the Program Recognizer provides opportunistic techniques for recognizing small algorithmic program fragments. Combining these two methods would use a top-down, bottom-up parse. Identified fragments would be used as clues to program identification (that is, the kind of program involved). Focused search techniques borrowed from Talus would then narrow the search space for the Program Recognizer's grammar. Finally, Talus' functional-equivalence techniques would augment the Program Recognizer's control flow and data-flow analysis techniques.

In the long term, program recognition research must employ machine-learning techniques, because the current theory's major bottleneck is that each system requires a human to devise reference information for comparison; in the Program Recognizer, it is cliches; in Talus, it is E-frames; and in Proust, it is plans. Machine learning's potential is that learners can use a library of programs that perform similar functions. From this, systems will abstract similarities and use them to recognize future programs of the same type.

Program recognition presents a perhaps insurmountable problem, analogous to natural language research in many ways. While computer programs provide a more structured vehicle for conveying thought than does the spoken language, an infinity of possible expressions and a corresponding infinity of possible interpretations exist.

Nevertheless, this is a field worthy of continued research. Recent advances in computer technology, most notably connection machines and neural networks, give reason for optimism that the combinatorial explosion associated with both natural language and program recognition processing may not be an impenetrable barrier.

References

1. F.J. Lukey, "Understanding and Debugging Programs," *Int'l J. Man-Machine Studies,* Vol. 12, 1980, pp. 189-202.

2. R. Lutz, "Program Debugging by Near-Miss Recognition and Symbolic Evaluation," Tech. Report CSRP.044, University of Sussex, UK, 1984.

3. C. Rich, "A Formal Representation for Plans in the Programmer's Apprentice," *Proc. Seventh IJCAI,* Morgan Kaufmann, Palo Alto, Calif., Aug. 1981.

4. R.C. Waters, "KBEmacs: Where's the AI?" *AI Magazine,* Spring 1986.

5. R.G. Farrell, J.R. Anderson, and B.J. Reiser, "An Interactive Computer-Based Tutor for Lisp," *Proc. Nat'l Conf. AI,* 1984.

6. D.R. Barstow, "A Perspective on Automatic Programming," *Proc. Eighth IJCAI,* Morgan Kaufmann, Palo Alto, Calif., 1983.

7. L.M. Wills, *Automated Program Recognition,* master's thesis, MIT, Cambridge, Mass., 1987.

8. C. Rich and H.E. Shrobe, "Initial Report on a Lisp Programmer's Apprentice," *IEEE Trans. Software Engineering,* Nov. 1978, pp. 456-467.

9. C. Rich and R.C. Waters, "Abstraction, Inspection, and Debugging in Programming," Tech. Report AI 634, MIT, Cambridge, Mass., 1981.

10. R.C. Waters, "KBEmacs: A Step Toward the Programmer's Apprentice," Tech. Report AI/TR-753, MIT, Cambridge, Mass., May 1985.

11. D.C. Brotsky, *An Algorithm for Parsing Flow Graphs,* master's thesis, MIT, Cambridge, Mass., 1984.

12. W.R. Murray, *Automatic Program Debugging for Intelligent Tutoring Systems,* doctoral dissertation, University of Texas, Austin, Tex., 1986.

13. P.E. Hart, N.J. Nilsson, and B. Raphael, "A Formal Basis for the Heuristic Determination of Minimum Cost Paths," *IEEE Trans. Systems, Science, and Cybernetics,* July 1968.

14. P.E. Hart, N.J. Nilsson, and B. Raphael, "Correction to 'A Formal Basis for the Heuristic Determination of Minimum Cost Paths,'" *SIGART Newsletter,* Dec. 1972.

15. G.L. Steele, *Common Lisp: The Language,* Digital Press, Boston, Mass., 1984.

16. W.L. Johnson, *Intention-Based Diagnosis of Novice Programming Errors,* Morgan Kaufmann, Palo Alto, Calif., 1986.

Dirk Ourston was a senior staff scientist at the Lockheed Software Technology Center when the work described in this article was completed. At Lockheed, his work centered on AI applications to software development. He was a member of the Express project, which developed an advanced software environment (based on AI techniques) for use in aerospace. Currently completing his PhD in computer science at the University of Texas at Austin, his research focuses on theory revision and extension using hybrid learning techniques. He received his BS in physics (1964) from California State University at Los Angeles and his MS in engineering (1968) from UCLA. He has worked in various technical and managerial positions within the aerospace industry, and has been primarily concerned with developing and testing embedded software systems. He can be reached at the Computer Science Dept., University of Texas, Austin, TX 78712.

Chapter 15
Knowledge-Based
Program Analysis

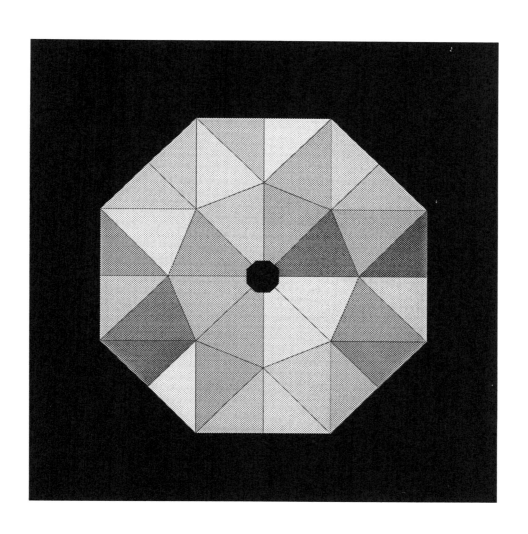

Chapter 15

Knowledge-Based
Program Analysis

Purpose

This chapter discusses knowledge bases and architectures for supporting software reengineering and reverse engineering. Knowledge bases contain information that can support many activities. The technology offers flexibilities that are attractive for reengineering and reverse engineering toolmakers.

Papers

In the first paper, "SRE: A Knowledge-Based Environment for Large-Scale Software Re-engineering Activities," W. Kozaczynski and J.Q. Ning discuss the architecture of a knowledge-based software reengineering system. The knowledge base is implemented in a global object base. The object base is the repository of information about the software object being reengineered. A major emphasis of the system is to support program and system understanding and abstraction.

In the next paper, "A Knowledge-Based Approach to Software System Understanding," W. Kozaczynski, S. Letovsky, and J.Q. Ning elaborate on the knowledge-based software reengineering system architecture described in the previous paper. They describe the types of knowledge needed in the knowledge base, the needed software analysis tools, and the interface functionality available to users. The philosophy of the architecture is that "...software understanding can be best supported by deriving simplified views of the software, using focusing tools that identify semantically meaningful subsets of source code, and graphical and code-oriented presentation tools." The architecture is based on work in implementing two knowledge-based program analysis systems, for assembly code and for Cobol. The system for understanding assembly code has been used successfully at insurance and telecommunications companies.

In the final paper, "Knowledge-Based Program Analysis," Mehdi Harandi and Jim Ning describe the Program Analysis Tool (PAT), a tool that derives functional concepts from source code. The authors define automatic program analysis as "the mechanized process of understanding high-level concepts from program text and the use of those concepts to guide program maintenance." PAT helps programmers find plausible predictions, suggestions, and explanations of a program's function. PAT uses program knowledge and analysis knowledge to recognize plans in programs. The work described is similar to program understanding work, but is included here because of its discussion of the role of knowledge bases.

SRE: A Knowledge-based Environment
for Large-Scale Software Re-engineering Activities

Wojtek Kozaczynski

Center for Strategic Technology Research
Arthur Andersen & Co.
33 W. Monroe Street, Chicago, IL 60603

Jim Q. Ning

Department of Computer Science
University of Illinois at Urbana-Champaign
1304 W. Springfield, Urbana, IL 61801

ABSTRACT

In this paper, we address issues related to the *re-engineering* of large-scale software systems. The key to the software re-engineering activity is the ability to *recover (re-engineer)* "lost" or otherwise unavailable information concerning specification and system design decisions from the information available in the existing system source code. Subsequently, a *forward engineering* step may re-implement and possibly upgrade the existing systems. This paper describes the underlying principles of a knowledge-based Software Re-engineering Environment (SRE) which is intended to provide high-level support to various software maintenance and re-engineering activities.

Introduction

Real world business information systems, Transaction Systems (TS) in particular, are very expensive to maintain. As soon as they are delivered into so-called production, they start going through the continuous process of evolution and modification. This process is dictated by changes to the system environment and/or user requirements.

The system re-engineering activities may vary in type and scope. They may be *corrective, enhancing, adaptive, perfective,* or *pro-active* ([COLL86]). Their scope may range from error correction (system debugging), through program optimization, restructuring, addition or modification of functionality, all the way to system migration (e.g. to a new software/hardware platform) or renovation.

Put aside the extreme cases of system migration and total renovation[1], the rest is simply known as system software maintenance. Although different estimates are circulating among the field practitioners, between 50 and 70% of their time is now spent on keeping the existing systems in relatively good shape. At the same time, a large number of organizations have become critically dependent on the "good health" of those aging systems. Consider, for example, that every state government must maintain a vehicle and driver's license registration system that operates around the clock and is used by a number of public and private agencies. Suppose that some of these systems were written years ago and have almost reached their capacity limits. Yet they must work, regardless of how much it costs to maintain them. The above situation describes what is usually referred to as *software maintenance crisis*.

The main subject of this paper is attacking the difficult problem of re-engineering complex software systems. In particular, we describe a Software Re-engineering Environment (SRE), an intelligent software tool under development at Arthur Andersen and Co. to support the software re-engineering process.

In the next section of this paper, we take a closer look at the software re-engineering issues from the standpoint of system maintainer. Then, we will describe the architecture of SRE and some of its desired functionalities. In addition, we will address system abstraction and understanding, the critical issue in any re-engineering activity. And finally, the current state of SRE implementation and its future capabilities will be described.

Issues In Software Re-engineering

A large TS system contains a complex body of application programs, persistent data elements, and user procedures, all functioning in a given system hardware/software environment. As software engineers, we tend to think of these as the products of a *forward engineering* process — the process of developing a TS from specifications.

---

1. As a matter of fact, both cases should be looked upon as a sequence of smaller and localized system changes used to manage the system migration/renovation risk.

113

Re-engineering those systems, however, is different. The latter process must contain an element of *recovering* the system design (usually not for the whole system but some parts of it) and/or its specification. Unfortunately the system specification and design documentation may be neither complete, reliable, nor even available. The only reliable source of system information is the system itself, its code as the lowest level of the system definition and the system interfaces as the best running model of system behavior.

The typical situation in which system maintainers find themselves is illustrated in Fig. 1. The figure shows the professional skills groups involved in the development and maintenance of a system. In the forward engineering pass, the *users* state their system requirements in a problem domain-specific language. These requirements are analyzed by system *specifiers* (who are usually referred to as systems analysts) and described in a domain independent language. The translation of domain-specific user statements into domain-independent system specification is critically contingent on human creativity.

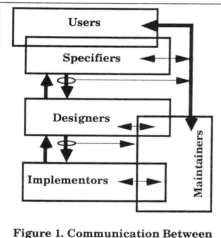

Figure 1. Communication Between System Development and Maintenance Professionals

The system requirement statement is handed over to the *system designers*. The designers produce a single- or multi-level (usually called *logical* or *detailed)* system design. The detailed system design is passed to the *implementors* who write the system code.

In the system development process, the same individual(s) may work as the specifier(s), the designer(s), and the implementor(s). However, this is less likely in large software development projects.

The *system maintainers* are responsible for system modifications. The crucial difficulty of their work is that the change/modification requests that come from the system users are most likely expressed in a very

domain specific language. As shown in Fig. 1, the maintainers may not have access to the current system specifications, the current logical and detailed system design, or the original system developers. Their first objective must be to recover (reverse engineer) the system design and specification using the available system information. As we have pointed out before, the most reliable and available source of system information is usually the system code itself.

A comprehensive approach to system change/modification, regardless of the type and scope of this modification, requires the maintainer to go through a series of software re-engineering steps to accomplish the following objectives:

Identification. User requirements are translated into modification statements described in system terms — the change requirements are identified and reformulated.

System design recovery. The system code and its available documentation are analyzed and the system design decisions are recovered. Any statement which expresses a design decision is a part of the system design. By this definition, a program structure chart, a data base schema, a report layout, a data base constraint, a network topology, a system access constraint, and a system data flow diagram are all parts of the design.

Change and impact analysis. The system design is used to localize system components that need to be changed. If the changes that are introduced into the existing system design are small, an impact analysis is performed. In the case of extensive changes (system renovation, for example), an entirely new design may be produced. This new design may, however, contain parts of the old/recovered design. In either case, the product of this step is a design of the modified system.

Change re-implementation. If the change is relatively small, most of the existing software are reused and only a few are modified. In the case of extensive changes, a large number of existing modules will have to be rewritten.

System validation. The modified system is tested against the new requirement before it is released to production.

We believe that the *design recovery* and the *change/impact analysis* are the two critical steps of re-engineering. Therefore, our initial development of SRE is largely focused on these two issues. Ultimately, an integrated set of specialized tools will be built into it to help software engineer/user to complete the two steps.

The SRE Architecture

The main building blocks of the SRE environment are shown in Fig. 2. The *System Source Information* is the

114

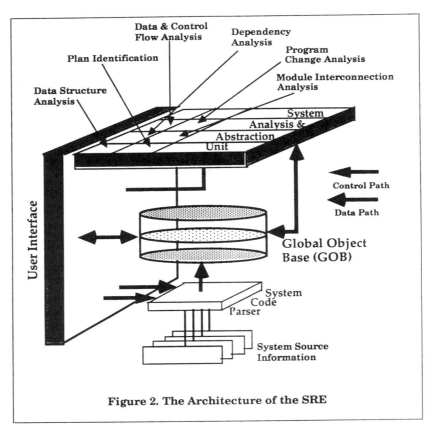

Figure 2. The Architecture of the SRE

input to the environment. It may contain not only the system source programs, but also the JCL statements, the DB schemas, the screen layouts, the report layouts, the conversation descriptions, or any other available system information.

The *System Code Parser* converts the source code into some implementation language independent representation (to be explained in the following section). The parser uses the programming language and implementation-specific knowledge to translate the source information. The low level system information (available facts about system implementation) populate the Global Object Base (GOB).

The GOB is designed to store not only the initial low-level system information, but also the information derived during the process of system analysis and abstraction. The GOB also contains the knowledge required by the analysis and abstraction tools. The GOB is constructed as a central repository for both the analysis knowledge and the system data as well as a vehicle for communication between the components of the environment. More details about the content of the GOB can be found in the next section.

The *System Analysis and Abstraction Unit* is an integrated set of tools that works on different system abstraction levels. These tools are highly specialized modules performing specific tasks. A few examples of what they may do are: control flow analysis, program dependency analysis, program change (ripple effect) analysis, generation of (graphical) program structure representation, symbolic evaluation of program behavior, program/record dependency analysis, "where-used" analysis, etc. All tools use the system facts stored in the GOB. They may either add new facts to the GOB or generate readable representations from the GOB. There are obvious interconnections between the tools. One tool, for instance, may need the services provided by another tool. We assume that the data exchange between the modules is done through the GOB. The flow of control and the resource allocation is organized in a way similar to the *blackboard control flow model* ([NEWM87]) as opposed to the more traditional *thread of control* type models.

The *User Interface* acts as a command driver for the knowledge engineer or the user to control the SRE operation and as a channel to add new system information into the GOB.

115

The above design is based on the assumption that the following services and characteristics must be provided in order to support interactive, full-range, and high-level software maintenance assistance:

- The SRE must support different operation modes:

The browsing mode. The SRE user is allowed to look at the system (or selected parts) from different "perspectives." These perspectives are abstractions of system entities or the abstract representations of relationships/dependencies between these entities. A few examples are: data and control flow graphs, answers to the *where-used* questions, program structure charts, calling hierarchies, program cross-reference tables, logical record dependency diagrams, etc.

The hypothesis verification mode. It has been shown ([LETO86], [PENN86]) that when a software engineer is analyzing a system, he is looking for clues and patterns he can recognize. These focus points help him to form a hypothesis about the function of a particular system component (what it does). Subsequently, he is trying to verify this hypothesis by looking for "things" that must exist in the system in order for the hypothesis to be true. Examples of questions he may ask are: Does this input variable influence this output variable? Is this part of the code reachable? Does this record "update" that record? etc. Some questions, like the first and the second above, may be answered on the basis of a simple dependency analysis. Other questions, like the last one, require knowledge about what it means to update a record. Thus, the system must recognize a record update plan and be able to identify instances of this plan ([HARA88], [RICH81a], [RICH87]).

The concept capturing mode. The SRE user adds his findings to the system knowledge base (the GOB in Fig. 2). These findings become available both to the user and to the SRE tools. The *concept capturing mode* allows incremental buildup of system understanding from the programming language level to the system specification level.

- The SRE must be integrated in the sense that individual tools in the environment should be able to interact with each other. For example, the *Plan Identification* module may need assistance from the *Data & Control Flow Analysis* module. As a result, the user is able to complete different levels of design recovery activities inside a single environment.

- The SRE must be open and expandable. Its architecture should allow easy addition of new tools and functions. It should also allow for customization of existing tools.

- The SRE must accept and represent all the relevant system information. The information should be stored in a central system repository in a uniform representation and be available to the software engineer and different components/tools of the environment.

- The SRE should be able to "learn" from the user. For example, the user wants to know whether one record type "updates" another record type, but SRE does not know the meaning of the update (not an existing concept in the GOB). In this situation, the user (or the knowledge engineer) should be able to specify the update plan and allow the system to add it to its knowledge base.

Software System Abstraction and Understanding

Two major decisions must be made in the context of developing a software re-engineering environment:

1. How to internally represent data and knowledge? That is, how to represent the facts about the system in terms of its components (entities) together with the relationships among the components and the system analysis knowledge in the GOB; and

2. What functionalities to provide? That is, to provide what kind of system analysis services to different re-engineering activities.

Although we would like to concentrate on the first issue in this section, one should keep in mind that, while conceptually different, the above two issues are dependent on each other. On one hand, the internal knowledge representation form may create extra constraints on the types of analysis techniques and tools that can be used. On the other hand, a particular activity on a system component (program restructuring, for example) may produce a specific requirement for the system representation.

The internal system knowledge representation should support various levels of software abstraction. The SRE tools should be able to derive higher level interpretations and abstractions from the system information stored in the GOB. This is a major difference between the traditional software maintenance techniques and the approach we are proposing — the latter emphasize the role that the system abstraction and understanding play in the re-engineering process.

The *understanding* of a software system refers to a more abstract representation constructed from the system source information. The *abstraction* refers to the process that achieves some level of understanding. Observation shows that such understanding and abstraction can happen at very different conceptual levels.

Implementation Language Level

This is the understanding of the system on the level of the programming language(s) used to implement the system. It allows one to abstract away language-specific details of system implementation, identify syntactic entities of the system (program modules, records, files, variables, etc.), and understand how these entities will interact with each other once the system is running. This level of understanding can be achieved automati-

116

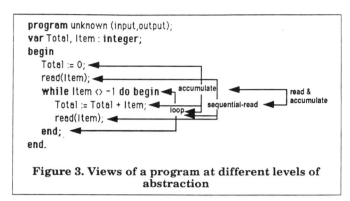

Figure 3. Views of a program at different levels of abstraction

cally. Language compilers and interpreters have the capability of analyzing programs at this level.

Structure Level

This level of system understanding can be achieved by a static analysis of the structural aspects of the system. This *structure-level* system understanding usually reveals details of how execution of a particular system part will influence other parts. More specifically, by inspection of the lexical (physical) structures of the system code, we can come up with the definition of the program control flow, the definition of the program data flow, the module interconnections (or inter-procedural calling relations) definitions, and other *dependency-based* forms of program abstraction. Such understanding was originally developed in building optimizing compilers and data flow machines. Subsequently, it was extended into the program maintenance tools (program restructurers, program structure analyzers, program inspectors, etc.). As a result, there is a variety of techniques available to support system analysis on this level. Some products of the structural system analysis such as control/data flow graphs and interprocedural connection charts (*structure charts* in a limited sense) can be viewed as part of the *detailed system design* produced in software forward engineering terms.

Specification Domain Level

The structure level analysis of a system can help explain the logical relationships among its components, but it tells nothing about their "meaning", the intended functions behind the code. The next system understanding level, the *specification domain level*, associates generic programming interpretations and problem solving heuristics (patterns or plans) with identified system components. Typically individual, otherwise unrelated pieces of the system code are associated with stereotypical implementation patterns of programming constructs, problem solving strategies, abstract data types, and standardized algorithms ([HARA88]). Identified patterns can be further grouped together to facilitate higher level system abstractions.

Take the small Pascal-like program shown in Fig. 3., for example. On the surface, it has a while-type *loop* construct. A higher-level interpretation will view it as a *sequential-read* operation interleaved with an *accumulate* operation. Both operations "share" the *loop* construct and other program components. The most abstract view of the program is a *read&accumulate* algorithm which is built on top of the two lower-level (but non-atomic) operations: *sequential-read* and *accumulate*.

A system analysis tool capable of reasoning about a system on the discussed level should decompose the above program into *logically-related* pieces or modules (as opposed to *physically-related* program procedures or blocks ([LETO86])) and produce a hierarchical generalization/abstraction of its functions (similar to what is shown at the right hand side of Fig. 3.). It should arrive the conclusion that the program *unknown* is sequentially accumulating values from a sequence of items. To simplify the issue, we can think of this abstraction process as the *inverse* of the *stepwise refinement* process in the forward pass of the software design.

Application Domain Level

The *specification domain* level understanding of a system cannot relate the identified programming patterns with the problem domain specific functions of the system. The sample program *unknown* in Fig. 3. could be a part of a *payroll* subsystem which sums up the total amount of the weekly pay checks. The *application domain level* system understanding requires interpretation of the functional behavior of system components expressed in very implementation-independent and problem-domain-specific terms.

The process of recovering the system design and specification can be viewed as *a stepwise reverse synthesis* of all the above four levels of system understanding. As illustrated in Fig. 4., the process starts from the programming language level of analysis of the system source code. The main purpose of this step is to integrate available system information. The information is then expressed in a symbolic form and stored in the system GOB. The information becomes readily available for the next level analysis.

117

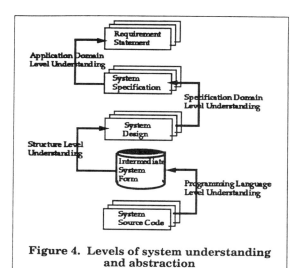

Figure 4. Levels of system understanding and abstraction

The first two levels of system understanding can be automated to some extent. In the next section, we discuss our current position and prospects in automating some aspects of the *specification domain* level understanding of the system. However, as emphasized in a previous section of the paper, the forward transformation from the domain-specific requirements statement into a domain-independent system specification (the inverse of highest level understanding) is critically contingent on human creativity. We do not believe that it is possible to find an artificial substitute for this creativity in the design recovery process.

We have investigated a large number of formalisms for representing knowledge about programs and software systems in general. Among them, the *data base forms* ([WILD87b], [YAU81]) are typical examples of how the implementation language level knowledge is represented. The *dependency-based forms* ([WILD87a], [HORW87], [BIEM85a], [YAU87]) support the structural level understanding of system programs. And finally, the *plan-based* or *intention-based forms* ([HARA88], [JOHN85], [RICH81a]) can capture functionally related concepts and reflect the specification domain level knowledge about system programs.

While each of the above representations has some unique value, none of them standing alone can capture all levels of system abstraction. They must be put into a single framework to achieve this synergetic effect. The *object-oriented* or *frame-based* knowledge representation forms have been used for this purpose ([AMBR88]) and provide certain advantages. We have designed an object-oriented framework with a rich content as the underlying structure of the global data and knowledge base.

Within this framework, all facts about a software system and all the knowledge used to analyze the system are represented by the following categories of objects :

- The objects representing system source information (mainly the source programs). Approximately a dozen classes of program objects have been identified, including: *statements, type descriptors, variables, modules, files, expressions,* etc. Each of these classes may be further specialized through the *isa* hierarchies. Relations among program objects are represented as attribute mappings from the domain object to the range object(s).

- The objects representing information derived through software system analysis. This generally includes data dependency relations, control flow graphs, recognized plan patterns, data type definitions, static program slices, etc. Each type of the derived information has a set of different classes of objects. The control flow graphs, for example, may have *start, process, test, goto,* and *end* as their unique set of classes.

- The objects representing information recorded during the execution of the target system. These may include a succession of values acquired by data objects, side effects, dynamic program slices, and execution time messages.

- The objects capturing the user interactively supplied information during the system analysis process. Specifications, in-line comments, constraints on the data objects, and any other user description of the design decisions fall into this category.

- The objects representing the analysis knowledge. We use objects to define the portion of the software system analysis knowledge that must be represented declaratively. They are mostly inference rules for automatic analysis, recognition, transformation, restructuring, translation, and debugging of system software components.

Because of the size limitation of the paper, we are not able to give an in-depth description of all the GOB objects. Show in Fig. 5. is part of the classification hierarchy of the GOB object classes representing programs written in a third generation programming language such as C, Pascal, or COBOL. Specializations for *descriptor* and the *statement* object classes which represent the type and program statement definitions are omitted from the figure. For example, the *loop* object class is a subclass of the *control-statement* class, which in turn is a subclass of the *statement* class.

The structure of the *loop* object class is shown in Fig. 6. A loop is built of two sequences of statements and a condition. The first sequence of statements, the *u(pper)-part,* is executed before the condition is tested. The second sequence of statements, the *l(ower)-part,* is executed only if the *loop-cond(ition)* evaluates to true. If the loop condition is false, the iteration stops. It is easy to see that the definition of the looping construct provides means for description of *while* and *repeat* loops as well as other types of loops with break-type exits inside the loop bodies.

The counted loop structure is further described by the *counted* subclass of the *loop* class. This subclass con-

118

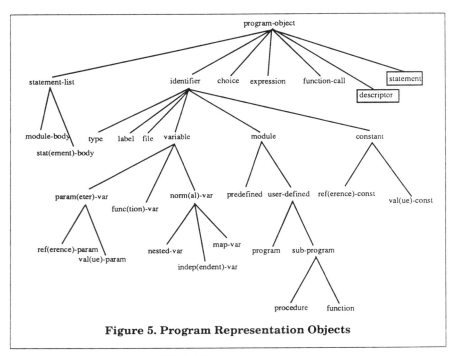

Figure 5. Program Representation Objects

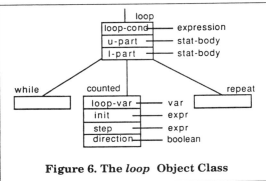

Figure 6. The *loop* Object Class

tains additional loop attributes: the index called *loop-var(iable)*, the *init(ial)* value of the index, the *step* of the index increment/decrement, and the *direction* of the index change. Notice that its termination condition and loop body can be described using the loop-cond and l-part attributes in its superclass.

The object based representation of the programs we have developed is language independent to a large degree. A program written in a standard third generation language such as COBOL can be parsed into this representation and stored in the Program Object Base (POB)[2]. The POB can then be analyzed and additional program abstractions can be derived and incrementally added into the POB.

---

2. POB is a part of the GOB which describes programs.

Implementation and Future Extensions

In this section we give a brief description of the SRE's current implementation status and the directions of the future development of the environment.

We have chosen an object-oriented environment to implement SRE. Within this environment, we represent data, system functions, and analysis rules all uniformly as objects. This choice of object-based representation fits very well into our knowledge-centered architecture of SRE.

A COBOL Analyzer

A prototype COBOL parser has been written. This parser act as a two-way channel (both a *reader* and a *printer*) to complete the translation cycle in both directions. However, a grammar-based parsing is not sufficient to fully bridge the gap between the syntax of the implementation language and our POB program representation. Additional tools to make further abstractions on the parser-generated objects must be constructed. The tools must perform a global and static analysis on both the generated program objects and the source code statements.

Once in the POB, a program becomes available for analysis. In our initial SRE prototype, two kinds of program analysis activities are supported: *"reading"* cross-reference information, and *building dependency relations.*

119

Evidence shows ([LETO86]) that the maintenance programmer is primarily a reader-of-code rather than a writer-of-code and therefore needs strong support for reference-based browsing through the code. He wants to see all places where a variable is used or redefined. Alternatively, he may want to see all calls to a procedure or all procedures called by a segment of the program.

To support *"reading" of cross-reference information,* we have used the knowledge-base browsing capabilities provided by the development environment. It allows one to move from one object to another and view objects in various ways. It is possible to show not only the attributes of an object (which are either values or links to other objects), but also some other object properties such as the sub-class/super-class relations, the next level nodes in the abstract syntax tree of the knowledge base, and the definition/use information of data objects.

Sometimes, the real issue is not how to find the cross reference information, but how to present it to the user in a comprehensive fashion. While it is quite easy to "navigate" through the POB using the system browsing tools, the information presented may not always be intuitive. We have chosen two approaches to improve this: (i) to use the *printing* capabilities of the language parser, and (ii) to preserve the original source code statements and keep them attached to the POB objects.

Dependency-based analysis relies on the structure level understanding of a program. A few examples of the *dependency-based analysis* tools are: the *Dependency Graph Query Interface* ([WILD87a]), which allows one to view the dependencies as a directed graph and answer queries about either direct or indirect relationships between program components; the *Microscope* system ([AMBR88]), which provides *views* of a program from different "dimensions" and conceptual levels so that the user can navigate through a graphical representation of the program's structure and zoom in on details of interest; and other tools ([BIEM85a], [BIEM85b], [YAU87]) that can generate structure graphs (data/control flow graphs, structure charts, etc.) to help understand the logical structures of programs.

In our initial implementation of SRE, we have constructed a prototype control-flow graph generator. It takes a program module object and produces a set of control-flow objects, explicitly representing the control flow links among the components in the program module. At this point the control flow graph, represented as a set of objects, is stored in the POB and can be viewed using the standard browsing capabilities. We are also in the process of developing a data-flow graph generator, a program dependency graph generator ([FERR87]), and a program structure chart generator. We will also build graphical tools that are capable of mapping the internal representations of these dependency graphs into screen layouts which will allow access through on-screen browsing.

An Assembly Language Analyzer

In a more recent experiment, we have constructed an assembly language analysis tool, called SRW (a Software Re-engineering Workbench). It is intended to be a system code translation/upgrading tool capable of: i) uplifting assembly program design, ii) generating equivalent high-level language program frames, and iii) implementing the generated code in a target environment.

The current effort have been focused on the first part. SRW can now load the listing and cross reference table of an assembly language program and create *statement* (for machine instructions and assembly directives) and *symbol* (for program symbols) objects. It can then construct *basic-block* objects from the *statement* objects and generate a control flow graph for the program using basic blocks as its nodes.

The source code, the control flow graph, and a few other representations (e.g. *branching logic graph,* structure chart, etc.) provide multiple views for the original program. It allows user to switch among different representations conveniently. User can "mark" a piece of code and associate comment or design information to it. The tool itself is also able to achieve a limited degree of function-level abstraction. It has a "smart-search" function which matches a library of pre-stored patterns representing the commonly used assembly programming tricks against a user-selected area of code.

But generally speaking, SRW works as a high-level assistant rather than a fully automated tool, helping human maintainers to view the source information in a natural sequence and understand the logical structures of the unstructured code. To achieve this requirement, the current demonstration model of SRW has been built with an icon-based, manu-driven interface on top of a multi-color graphical window environment.

Future Work

The future buildup of the SRE capabilities will be in the direction of improving and constructing: (i) the user interface, (ii) program understanding and design recovery tools, (iii) program decomposition tools, and (iv) system analysis tools.

The need for work in the first direction should be obvious.

The *design recovery* is achievable based on a specification domain level program understanding. A program design recovery tool must be able to recognize certain algorithmic patterns and produce a function-oriented description of the program. PAT ([HARA88]), for example, can automatically paraphrase the intended functional behavior of a program. We have initiated a project to build prototype system understanding and documentation tools based on the *plan-recognition* paradigm.

120

Due to the development of new TS implementation architectures, there is a growing need to support the migration of existing systems into new environments. One of the activities in this migration process is to decompose large software segments into physically smaller but logically more cohesive modules. Some improvement to SRW in this direction have been planned.

Another direction of our work is aimed at extending our analysis scope from program analysis to system analysis. As pointed out at the beginning of the paper, our main concern is the re-engineering of large-scale TSs. These systems usually maintain large data repositories organized as individual files or integrated under a DBMS. One of the difficulties is to recover the underlying system data design ([DAVI85], [NAVA87]). Some data design information is explicitly given in the file layouts. However, the data integrity constraints and the majority of referential integrity constraints can only be recovered by program code analysis. For example, a consistency value test on a field reveals an implementation of a field value constraint. Similarly, two records matched in an update procedure reveals an implementation of a referential integrity rule. Specification-domain level program understanding is a prerequisite for the data design recovery.

There are some other obvious maintenance activities that SRE should ultimately assist, such as *Program Static Slicing/Highlighting* ([WILD87a], [YAU87]), *Source-to-Source Translation* ([WATE86]), and *System Dynamic Testing/Slicing* ([AMBR88]). We will incrementally incorporate any activity that shows practical value in software re-engineering.

Conclusions

As a field of research in Software Engineering, Software Re-engineering has started to attract wide attention in recent years. Part of the reason for this is that the "traditional" software development cycle cannot guarantee the quality of the systems being produced, let alone the more difficult task of migrating systems. There are many functioning systems that have been developed in less than disciplined ways. This is particularly true about systems that have been in production for many years. Surprisingly, current software engineering methodologies give little regard to the issue of adequate maintenance support.

As a result, there is a need to "backtrack" to the system conceptual foundations. That is, to re-engineer the system back through the software life cycle and put it back into production in a better form. The need for *system migration* from one environment to another, *system renovation* to meet new functional requirements, and *system restructuring* to improve *modularity* all call for re-engineering activities.

Although there may be many specific reasons to re-engineer a system, the fundamental objective of re-engi-

neering should not be overlooked — to control and enhance system properties such as: *functionality, efficiency, reliability,* and *capacity.* A system with these qualities contributes the most to the user's productivity.

The SRE presented in the paper is in the early stages of development. The development emphases, at this point, are on its architecture and main functionality. We have presented a knowledge-base centered and object-oriented design, which should provide both the flexibility as well as the extensibility of the environment, as our initial experiment have shown.

Acknowledgements

We would like to thank our CSTaR colleagues for supporting our work and spending time reviewing this paper.

References

[AMBR88] James Ambras, Vicki O'Day, "MicroScope: A Knowledge-Based Programming Environment", *IEEE Software*, May, 1988, pp. 50-58.

[BIEM85a] James M. Bieman, Narayan C. Debnath, "An Analysis of Software Structure Using A Generalized Program Graph", *COMPSAC-85*, Chicago, October 9-11, 1985, pp. 254-259.

[BIEM85b] James M. Bieman, William R. Edwards, "Experimental Evaluation of The Data Dependency Graph for Use in Measuring Software Clarity", *Eighteenth Annual Hawaii International Conference on System Sciences*, 1985, pp. 271-276.

[BROT81] Daniel Brotsky, "Program Understanding through Cliche Recognition", MIT AI Lab, Working Paper 224, December, 1981.

[BUSH85] Eric Bush, "The Automatic Restructuring of Cobol", *IEEE Conference on Software Maintenance*, November, 1985, pp. 35-41.

[COLL86] James S. Collofello, Stephen Bortman, "An Analysis of the Technical Information Necessary to Perform Effective Software Maintenance", *Phoenix Conference on Computers and Communications*, Scottsdale, Arizona, March 26-28, 1986, pp. 420-424.

[DAVI85] K.H. Davis, A.K. Arora, "A Methodology for Translating a Conventional File System into an Entity-Relational Model", *Proc. of The 4th Intern. Conf. on Entity-Relational Approach*, October 1985.

[FERR87] J. Ferrante, K. Ottenstein, J.D. Warren, "The Program Dependence Graph and Its Use in Optimization", *ACM Trans. on Programming Languages and Systems*, Vol. 9, No.3, July 1987.

[HARA83] M.T.Harandi, "An Experimental COBOL Restructuring System", *Software-Practice and Experience*, vol. 13, pp. 825-846.

[HARA88] M.T.Harandi, J.Q.Ning, "PAT: A Knowledge-based Program Analysis Tool", *IEEE Conference on Software Maintenance*, Phoenix, Arizona, October, 1988.

[HOLB87] H.B.Holbrook, S.M.Thebaut, "A Survey of Software Maintenance Tools That Enhance Program Understanding", Software Engineering Research Center (SERC), University of Florida, September, 1987.

[HORW87] Susan Horwitz, Jan Prins, Thomas Reps, "On the Adequacy of Program Dependence Graphs for Representing Programs", University of Wisconsin-Madison, CS Tec. Rep. #699, June, 1987.

121

[HORW87] Susan Horwitz, Jan Prins, Thomas Reps, "Integrating Non-interfering Versions of Programs", University of Wisconsin-Madison, CS Tec. Rep. #690, March, 1987.

[JOHN85] W.Lewis Johnson, Elliot Soloway, "PROUST: Knowledge-Based Program Understanding", *IEEE Trans. on Software Engineering*, SE-11, No. 3, pp. 267-275.

[LETO86] S. Letovsky, E.Soloway, "Delocalized Plans and Program Comprehension", *IEEE Software*, May, 1986, pp. 41-49.

[LETO87] S. Letovsky, J. Pinto, R. Lampert, and E. Soloway, "A Cognitive Analysis of Code Inspection", Empirical Studies of Programmers: Second Workshop, Ablex Publishing Corp., 1987.

[NAVA87] S.B. Navathe, A.M. Awong, "Abstracting Relational and Hierarchical Data with a Semantic Data Model", *Proc. of the 6th Intern. Confr. on Entity-Relatioanl Aproach*, November 1987.

[NEWM87] Richard E. Newman-Wolfe, "Use of Blackboards in Software Project Information Management", SERC, University of Florida, SERC-TR-6-F, November, 1987.

[OTTE84] Karl J. Ottenstein, Linda M. Ottenstein, "The Program Dependence Graph In A Software Development Environment", *SIGPLAN NOTES (USA)*, vol. 19, May, 1984, pp. 177-184.

[PENN86] Nancy Pennington, "Expert Programmer Comprehension of Computer Programs", Center for Decision Research, University of Chicago, N00014-82-K-0759, December 1986.

[RICH81a] Charles Rich, "A Formal Representation for Plans in the Programmer's Apprentice", *Seventh IJCAI conference*, Vancouver, BC, Canada, August, 24-28, 1981, pp. 1044-52.

[RICH81b] Charles Rich, Richard C. Waters, "Abstraction, Inspection, and Debugging in Programming", MIT AI Lab, A.I.Memo No. 643, June, 1981.

[RICH87] Charles Rich, "Inspection Methods in Programming: Cliches and Plans", MIT AI Lab, A.I.Memo No. 1005, December, 1987.

[RYDE88] B.G.Ryder, H.D.Pande, "The Interprocedural Structure of C Programs: An Empirical Study", Laboratory for Computer Science Research, Rutgers University, LCSR-TR-99, February, 1988.

[SEVI87] Rudolph E. Seviora, "Knowledge-Based Program Debugging Systems", *IEEE Software*, vol. 4, no. 3, May, 1987, pp. 20-32.

[SHAP81] Daniel G. Shapiro, "Sniffer: a System that Understands Bugs", MIT AI Lab, A.I. Memo No. 638, June, 1981.

[TAHA88] A.M.Taha, S.M.Thebaut, "Program Change Analysis Using Incremental Data Flow Techniques", SERC, University of Florida, SERC-TR-14-F, 1988.

[WATE86] Richard C. Waters, "Program Translation Via Abstraction and re-implementation", MIT AI Lab, A.I.Memo No. 949, December, 1986.

[WILD87a] Norman Wilde, Brian Nejmeh, "Dependency Analysis: An Aid for Software Maintenance", Software Engineering Research Center, University of Florida, SERC-TR-13-F, September, 1987.

[WILD87b] Norman Wilde, Roger Ogando, Ernest Edge, "Specifications for Prototype Dependency Analysis Tools, Version 3", SERC, University of Florida, SERC-TR-15-F, September, 1987.

[WILD88] Norman Wilde, Scott Liu, Steve Thebaut,"Towards A Maintenance Assistant: Tools and Methodologies for Program Change Analysis", SERC, University of Florida, Progress Report, 1988.

[WILL87] Linda Mary Wills, "Automated Program Recognition", MIT AI Lab, AI-TR-904, February, 1987.

[YAU81] Stephen S. Yau, Paul C. Grabow, "A Model for Representing Programs Using Hierarchical Graphs", *IEEE Trans. on Software Engineering*, SE-7, no. 6, November, 1981, pp. 556-574.

[YAU84] S.S.Yau, J.P.Tsai, "A Graph Description Language for Large-Scale Software Specification in a Maintenance Environment", *COMPSAC-84*, November, 1984, pp. 397-407.

[YAU85] Stephen S. Yau, Jing-Pha Tsai, Robin A. Nicholl, "Knowledge Representation of Software Life-Cycle Information", *COMPSAC-85*, October,1985, pp. 268-277.

[YAU86] Stephen S. Yau, Sying-Syang Liu, "A Knowledge-Based Software Maintenance Environment", *Compsac-86*, October 8-10, 1986, pp. 72-78.

[YAU87] Stephen S. Yau, Jeffery J. Tsai, "Knowledge Representation of Component Interconnection Information for Large-Scale Software *IEEE Trans. on Software Engineering*, SE-13, no. 3, March, 1987, pp. 355-361.

122

A Knowledge-Based Approach to Software System Understanding

Wojtek Kozaczynski, Stanley Letovsky, Jim Ning

Center for Strategic Technology Research, Andersen Consulting
100 South Wacker Drive, Chicago, Illinois 60606, U.S.A.

Abstract

Software understanding is the process of recovering high-level, functionality-oriented information from the source code. This paper presents a knowledge-based approach to supporting understanding-intensive tasks in software maintenance and re-engineering. The approach uses programming language knowledge to parse the source code and analyze its semantics. It uses general programming and application domain knowledge to automate the recognition of functional concepts. Also, a set of presentation, focusing, and editing tools is provided for the user to view and modify the source code and to extract reusable components from it. Two workbench environments that we have recently developed based on this approach are described.

1. Introduction

A central challenge of today's software engineering technology is finding ways to make old software systems more comprehensible. Typically, documentation and formal descriptions of old systems are lacking or obsolete and their structural integrity has been degraded by years of maintenance. For such systems, the source code represents the only completely reliable source of information. This situation creates a need for a technology to automate source code understanding.

This paper describes a knowledge-based approach that provides high-level support for a variety of software understanding tasks. This approach has the advantage of being based on the source code itself, so that what it concludes is true of a system as it is, rather than as it was or should have been. It uses knowledge about source languages, general programming, and application domains to statically infer properties of software systems at several levels of abstraction [KN89]. The structure of the paper is as follows. In Section 2 we identify types of understanding-related questions that may be raised during software maintenance and renovation. Section 3 introduces a set of software understanding and analysis techniques that support answering these questions. Section 4 describes software understanding tools that were developed based on the approach described in Section 3. Finally, Section 5 concludes the paper.

2. Motivation for the Approach

In this section we first consider various tasks in software life cycle that tend to be understanding-intensive. Then, we summarize questions that are likely to be asked while performing these tasks. In the next section, we introduce a set of knowledge-based analysis tools that can be integrated to help in answering these questions.

2.1. Understanding-Intensive Tasks

The life-cycle tasks that demand the greatest ability to understand existing software are the following:

Validation and Verification (V&V): Given a piece of code one must verify that the functional behavior meets its specification. Typically, one needs to know *what* the behavior of the code is, and *where* the specified functionalities are implemented. In formal code reviews, attention is often paid to the behavior of the code in specific situations, leading to questions such as, "What does the code do if a certain condition is true" [LPLS87].

Maintenance: Software maintenance activities may vary in type and scope [CB86], but the need for software understanding always occurs on an as-needed basis [LPLS86]. The maintainer usually wants to obtain minimum information necessary to make a change. Generally

162

Reprinted from *Proc. 6th Annual Knowledge-Based Software Engineering Conference,* 1991, pp. 162-170. ©1991 by The Institute of Electrical and Electronics Engineers, Inc. All rights reserved.

speaking, the maintainers need strong support for code "reading", error detection, and change impact analysis. Questions that arise in maintenance include: "where is some functionality implemented", "what is the function of a code component", and "what are the differences between the original version and the changed version of a program". In bug diagnosis, a common question is "how could a particular condition arise".

Reuse: We can distinguish a number of dimensions or types of reuse. Reuse can occur during maintenance, re-engineering, or in the implementation of new systems. Reuse can occur within a system, between systems, or between a system and a library of reusable components. Reuse can occur at the level of code components or abstract designs. In order to identify reuse opportunities, the typical questions that arise are: "what does a given component do" and, "where is a given functionality implemented".

2.2. Types of Questions

An effective way to support software understanding is to answer different kinds of questions that the user may have. This question-answering model of understanding is supported by empirical studies of the behavior of programmers during understanding-intensive tasks [Let86, LPLS86, Sas90]. Above, we have informally identified some types of questions that arise in understanding. Below, we develop a more systematic description of the important types of questions. Note, that the identification of question types with question words such as *what, when, how,* etc., is heuristic device only. We do not claim that these English words have unique inherent meanings that correspond to our definitions; in fact, the natural meanings of these words appear to be quite flexible and overlapping.

What?: The question *what does <component> do?* asks for a concise functional summary of the behavior of the component. This type of question is frequently asked in program verification and general understanding when a programmer reads through a program and in software reuse when the functionality of a software component has to be known for future reuse.

What-If?: What? questions sometimes may be specialized by providing restrictive conditions that must hold at specified points in the code, giving rise to a type of What-If? question: *what does <component> do under <condition>?* The answer to such a question is similar to the unrestricted What?, but describes only those execution paths where the condition holds. This type of question can be asked in any understanding-intensive tasks.

When?: The question *when does <component> do <behavior>?* relates the behavior of a component to the logical conditions that cause this behavior. Specifically, it asks for the conditions that would cause a specified type of control flow path to occur. When? is thus the inverse of What-If?: the latter maps conditions onto execution paths, while the former maps execution paths onto conditions. When? questions are most commonly asked during V&V and bug diagnosis.

Why?: The question *why does <component> do <behavior>?* asks about the contribution of a component to the system's global behavior. One way to answer such a question is to identify other components of the system that may potentially be affected by this component. Answers to the Why? questions help V&V and general maintenance tasks.

Where?: The question *where does <system> do <behavior>?* initiates a search for system parts that implement a specified system function. This question can be answered by indicating a subset of the system's code. If the target of the question is a reuse library (rather than code), then this question asks the reuse library to return components that possess the specified behavior. Thus, in general, this type of question arises in verification, code reading, and in component recovery and retrieval for reuse.

Difference?: The question *what are the differences between <component-old> and <component-new>?* asks for the effect of a change where *component-new* is a changed version of *component-old*. This question is likely to occur when introducing maintenance changes. In formal inspections, inspectors may try to reconstruct design rationales, i.e., explanations of why functions were implemented in a particular manner [LPLS87]. Such reconstruction can be viewed as a question about the differences between the original and a proposed alternative version. Note that, like What? questions, Difference? questions can also be focused on conditions of interest.

Table 1 summarizes the questions that are most likely to be asked during specific understanding-intensive tasks. In the table, READ, DEBUG, and CHANGE denote code reading, error detection, and change impact analysis tasks of software maintenance.

3. A Knowledge-Based Approach

This section describes the design of a knowledge-based

163

	V&V	READ	DEBUG	CHANGE	REUSE
What?	√	√			√
What-If?	√	√	√	√	√
When?	√		√		
Why?	√	√	√	√	
Where?	√	√			√
Difference?			√	√	

Table 1: Task/Question Map

software understanding system. The architecture of the system is shown in Figure 1. Its major components are described below in the context of how they support answering questions identified in the previous section.

3.1. Central Repository

The central repository contains a *system model*, a *component taxonomy*, and a shared *reuse library*.

System Model: The system model is the abstract internal representation of the analyzed system. The model contains a set of annotated abstract syntax trees (ASTs), each of which represents a separate program module. The annotations of the ASTs contain information about programming semantics, dependence relations [FOW87, HPR88], and functional classifications.

Component Taxonomy: The component taxonomy contains *classification knowledge* that categorizes software components hierarchically. It also contains *recognition knowledge* that can be applied to recognize instances of taxonomy categories. The latter type of knowledge is associated with each taxonomy category and is a set of abstract descriptions specifying how to recognize functionally-related pieces of code. The taxonomy is also used to organize and index the reuse library.

Reuse Library: The reuse library contains software components that can be shared across a system or by multiple systems. The reuse library is structured according to the categories in the component taxonomy. The library may be populated by abstracting components from systems and classifying them (see paragraph 3.5). Components may be retrieved for reuse through the query-by-function

interface (see paragraph 3.3).

3.2. Constructing the System Model

The source code of the analyzed system is represented internally as a forest of annotated ASTs [ASU86]. The annotations are used by the presentation, focusing, and editing tools. This section describes the processes that construct this representation.

Parsing: The first step in the analysis of a software system is the generation of ASTs from the source code. This is done by using a parser automatically generated from a syntax specification of the system's *source language*.

Semantic Interpretation: The semantic interpretation process annotates the ASTs using the language semantic information. We call the knowledge about both the syntax and the seman-tics of a language, a *language model*. The semantic language descriptions define the effects of each AST node on the *environment* (declaration), *store* (state) and *continuation* (control) of a generic execution of the code [All86]. They are specified in the same way for all source languages, so that the subsequent analysis tools need not know about the language idiosyncrasies. The semantic interpretation associates semantic attributes with the ASTs and preserves the syntactic structures of the original programs.

Dependence Analysis: We call data, control, and structure dependencies in the code *dependence relations*. Once the ASTs are annotated with semantic descriptions, dependence analysis can be applied to determine dependence relations. Since the dependence analyzers use only semantic annotations of programs, they can be

164

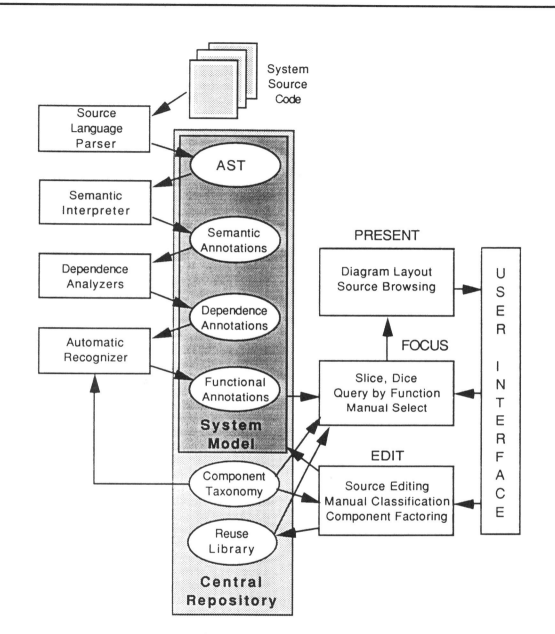

Figure 1: A knowledge-based software understanding system.

built independent of source languages.

Automatic Recognition: Our ideas regarding automatic recognition of software components are elaborated from a body of research conducted over the last decade [Wil87, Let88, Nin89, Har90]. Given a program's annotated AST and a set of category definitions, the automatic recognizer in Figure 1 will try to recognize instances of those categories in the program. The recognizer is implemented as a pattern-matching and reasoning engine that operates on the dependence relations of the AST. The recognition knowledge specified as pattern descriptions is stored in the component taxonomy as part of the central repository. Users can extend the component taxonomy by adding new categories or new pattern descriptions.

165

Recognition of a pattern results in the construction of functional annotations. Functional annotations are classification expressions. The most common format for these expressions is *operation datatype*, for example: *update file-record*, *print dollar-amount*, *invert matrix*, *draw line*, and etc. This style of classification is compatible with object-oriented philosophies of program structure but can be applied to non-object-oriented languages.

3.3. Focusing Tools

Focusing is the process by which the user selects portions of the code for presentation. The system should provide a number of significant capabilities that allow the user to focus attention on code subsets having particular semantic properties. Internally, a focusing region is a subset of the AST nodes. In a typical interaction, the initial focus is set to the entire system code and then narrowed down by application of the focusing tools described below. Sequential applications of focusing tools allows for very precise control over the focusing region.

Some of the focusing techniques described below, such as slicing, forward slicing, and slice differencing, have been studies by earlier researchers [Wei81, HRB88, YL88, HPR89). Other features, such as dicing, inverse dicing, and query-by-function are relatively novel.

Slicer: Program slicing [Wei81] is a method for automatic program decomposition based on flow and data dependence relations. Given a location and a set of variables in a program, a slice finds the minimal executable subset of the code, called a *slice*, that affects the values of the variables at that location. Slicing can be used to understand references associated with data values [LG88] and thus answer Where? questions. It can also be used to find dead code (code not contained in the slices of all the output variables in a program), and to decompose code into fragments that may be reused (or thrown out) separately.

Forward Slicer: A variant of slicing is *forward slicing*, also known as *ripple-effect analysis* [YL88] which finds the minimal subset of the code *affected by* a set of variables at a given location. Forward slicing answers the Why? questions by analyzing forward consequences of changes during program modifications.

Dicer: The notion of *dicing* was introduced as a way to isolate bugs in programs [WL86, LW87]. Our definition of dicing is different: it is a program decomposition technique that identifies the subset of the code executed under specified conditions. Given a program and a logical assertion tied to a control-flow point in the code, a dicer selects the subset of the code that can be executed when the assertion is true. When a program combines multiple functions, it typically contains tests that select between them. Suppose, for example, that an auto insurance system is structured by states (since each state may have a different insurance policy). To retrieve the part that implements policy for the state of Illinois, we could dice modules on condition STATE = 'ILLINOIS'. Another use of a dicer is to identify unreachable code. If we dice on the initial conditions of a program, any parts of the code not selected by the dicer are potentially unreachable. Dicing helps answer What-If? and Where? questions.

Inverse Dicer: We are currently investigating a variation on the idea of dicing, called *inverse dicing*, which identifies the conditions given a description of the code subset. A capability to map program subsets (or more accurately, control flow descriptions) to conditions under which they might be executed is very useful in debugging code that appears to be executing "impossible" paths. It can, therefore, answer When? questions.

Slice Differencer: A slice differencer [HPR89] identifies slices in a program that are changed relative to a variant version of the program. In contrast to a simple *diff* (textual comparison), the slice differencer selects all aspects of the program that are *semantically* influenced by a change, rather than only the syntactical differences.

Query By Function: Query-by-function allows the user to select code subsets based on the functional classifications developed by the automatic recognizer or the manual classification (to be described below). By referring to the taxonomy, the user can either specify a category of interest or examine the categories that have been recognized in a specified region of the code. If a category is specified, the user can further choose particular instances of that category on which to focus. The same query interface can be used to retrieve reusable components from the reuse library, since they are indexed by the same taxonomy which is used to classify code subsets during analysis.

3.4. Presentation Support

There are two basic software presentation forms: graphical form and source code form. Structure charts, data and control flow diagrams, data record layout graphs, control flow graphs, calling hierarchies, and entity-relationship

166

	What?	What-If?	When?	Why?	Where?	Difference?
Slice					√	
Forward Slice				√		
Dice		√			√	
Inverse Dice			√			
Slice Diff.						√
Query By Func.					√	
Presentation	√				√	
Classification	√				√	
Comp. Factoring	√				√	

Table 2: Question/Technique Map

diagrams are examples of effective graphical representations.

Source browsers can be used to present the original, highlighted, or sliced source code. Experiments show that effective presentation support helps user understand and trace programs and thus answer What? and Where? questions.

3.5. Editing Support

Several types of editing support should be provided:

Source Editing: A general-purpose editor allows the user to make arbitrary changes to the source code. At the same time, the system implements certain types of program integrity checking and is able to incrementally update the annotated ASTs after each modification.

Manual Classification: If the automatic recognizer is unable to recognize features of interest, due to its incompleteness or because certain information is not explicit in the code, the user can construct his/her own classifications manually. Manual classification is expressed in the vocabulary of the component taxonomy and functions just like automatic classifications on retrieval. Manual classification can be viewed as a kind of code documentation. However, unlike conventional documentation, it is active in that it can enable further automatic classification. Both automatic classification and manual classification enable the system to answer What? and Where? questions.

Component Factoring: Component factoring is a technique that supports a class of structural modifications that affect modularity, i.e., the organization of the code into modules, procedures, data structures, objects, etc. The following set of high-level editing commands support component factoring:

- **Abstraction:** Converts a code fragment into a parameterized subroutine or function.
- **Folding:** Replaces one or more inline code fragments by calls to a given module.
- **Unfolding:** Replaces a call to a module by an inline expansion of the module - inverse operation of abstraction.
- **Reparameterizing:** Reordering, adding, or removing arguments to/from a given module.

It should be noted, that component factoring described here is not intended to be a general-purpose restructuring technique, but a way of incorporating the understanding gained through analyses into the structure of the source code to improve its comprehensibility. Reuse is another purpose of component factoring. Modularized and parameterized pieces can be more easily reused than fragments embedded in other modules.

Table 2 summarizes techniques described in this section in terms of types of questions that they can address. This table, together with Table 1, establishes our central contention: the tools provided by the system should be useful for answering the key types of questions that occur in understanding-intensive tasks.

167

4. Practical Experience

In Section 3 we gave a general description of a knowledge-based approach to software system understanding. At Andersen Consulting's Center for Strategic Technology Research we have recently developed two knowledge-based software understanding systems that partially implement the described approach. This work has been done as part of the Center's software re-engineering program.

BAL/SRW

BAL/SRW is a knowledge-based software re-engineering workbench developed for recovering the designs from IBM 370 BAL assembler programs. It provides a number of understanding capabilities including presentation and classification supports. In addition, it performs re-engineering functions such as unreachable code elimination and program design editing. It also has some limited slicing and dicing capabilities for identifying logical subroutines and recovering business rules.

Presentation: BAL/SRW can automatically construct control flow graphs from source code and lay them out aesthetically . It also provides a source presentation of the code with which the user may browse the code or cross-reference the variables in the code.

Recognition and Classification: The system has an automatic recognizer that understands stereotypical assembler coding patterns. The user may also manually classify code by associating *clip notes* with code fragments. Clip notes may be formal or informal specifications of the code.

Re-engineering: The system can identify and eliminate regions of code that are unreachable. The program design editor represents the recovered designs of a program as a structure chart. It allows the user to modify the structure chart and associate documentation text with it.

Slicing: In BAL/SRW, slicing is applied to help recognize subroutines implicitly formed by branching and return instructions in the code.

Dicing: Dicing allows the user to create program subsets based on global control conditions.

BAL/SRW has been used on a number of commercial engagements with major insurance and telecommunications companies. The tool has demonstrated satisfactory scalability and practical utility. To given a practical example, the tool was used to recover the design of an interface sub-system between a service order system and a maintenance system. The sub-system consisted of six modules ranging in size from about 700 to 32,000 lines of code and had about 41,000 lines of assembler code in total. A three-person team, using the BAL/SRE, spent only 67 person-days to understand the code and produce a detailed design documentation of the sub-system.

COBOL/SRE

From the functionality point of view, COBOL/SRE (a Software Renovation Environment for COBOL) is an extension of BAL/SRW. In addition to the features supported by BAL/SRW, it also supports syntax-sensitive browsing, calling hierarchy recovery, data model recovery, delocalized concept recognition, and more complete slicing/dicing capabilities.

Presentation: COBOL/SRE can automatically recover and layout control flow, calling hierarchy, and data model graphs from source code. A syntax-sensitive source browser allows to highlight syntactically-related regions of code (in addition to its normal browsing and cross-referencing capabilities).

Recognition and Classification: The automatic recognizer in COBOL/SRE is able to understand delocalized patterns; patterns that break syntactic boundaries but are connected by semantic relations.

Slicing: The user may use the source browser to mark a variable and the slicer will identify all code regions that may potentially affect the value of that variable. Program slices are derived from the data and control dependence analyses [FOW87].

Dicing: The user provides a logical expression, which we call a *dicing condition*, and the dicer will identify the regions of code that can be reached under this condition.

A prototype of COBOL/SRE has been completed and tested on a very large production control system. The size of the system being re-engineered is roughly 2 MLOC. Some of the COBOL modules in this system are over 10 KLOC. This prototype has also been demonstrated at a number of research and industrial settings and received very encouraging feedback. Currently, we are working on producing an industry-strength version of the system.

5. Conclusions

We have described an integrated set of capabilities to support the understanding and maintenance of complex software systems. We claim that software understanding can be best supported by deriving simplified views of

168

software, using focusing tools that identify semantically meaningful subsets of source code, and graphical and code-oriented presentation tools. Maintenance can by supported by partially automating the process of modifying the modular organization of software.

It should be pointed out that the functionalities suggested in this paper are by no means arbitrary choices. They are based upon extensive studies of the requirements set forward by programmers engaged in understanding-intensive tasks, evaluation of existing tools, and our experience in research and development of similar tools.

The described approach requires several types of knowledge:

Knowledge About Program Syntax: This is the syntactic specifications of the source language for parsing and syntax-directed editing.

Knowledge About Program Semantics: This knowledge is associated with the syntactic specification of a language and is a part of the language model. The knowledge is used to annotate the ASTs and support various semantic program analyses.

Classification Knowledge: This knowledge supports classification of software components based on their abstract functions and application areas. It is also used to organize the reuse library.

Recognition Knowledge: This knowledge specifies how to recognize functional patterns in the code that are instances of classification categories representing programming concepts (e.g. search, sort, accumulate, abstract data type definitions, etc.) or application domain concepts (e.g. open an account, update a customer master file, etc.).

The tools we have constructed so far have not achieved a high degree of language independence. This is partially due to the fact that we have been dealing with very specialized source languages. As we move into the re-engineering of more structured languages such as C and Pascal, it will make more sense to construct the analysis tools purely based on a common semantic-oriented language. We are currently evaluating a number of options for the semantic specification language. We are considering such approaches as: attribute grammars based on denotational semantics [All86], a "gray language" that contains all the features of the source languages that we intend to cover, or an intermediate language such as IL used in MALPAS [MAL87] or UNIFORM used in REDO [Kat90].

References

[ASU86] A. V. Aho, R. Sethi, and J. D. Ullman, *Compilers: Principles, Techniques, and Tools.* Addison-Wesley, Reading, Mass., 1986.

[All86] L. Allison, A Practical Introduction to Denotational Semantics, Cambridge University Press, 1986.

[BHW89] Biggerstaff, T., Hoskins, J., and Webster, D., "DESIRE: A System for Design Recovery," *MCC Technical Report*, STP-081-89, April 1989.

[CB86] J. S. Collefellow and S. Bortman, "An analysis of the technical information necessary to perform effective software maintenance," In *Proceedings of the Phoenix Conference on Computers and Communications*, pp. 420-424, Scottsdale, Arizona, March 1986.

[FOW87] J. Ferrante, K. Ottenstein, and J. Warren, "The Program Dependence Graph and its Use in Optimization," *ACM Trans. Programming Languages and Systems.* 9, 3, July 1987, pp.319-349.

[Har90] J. Hartman, *Automatic Control Understanding for Natural Programs*, Ph.D. thesis, University of Texas at Austin, 1990.

[HPR88] S. Horwitz, J. Prins, and T. Reps, "On the Adequacy of Program Dependence Graphs for Representing Programs. *Proceedings of Fifteenth ACM Symposium on Principles of Programming Languages*, 1988, pp. 146-157.

[HPR89] S. Horwitz, J. Prins, and T. Reps, "Integrating Noninterfering Versions of Programs," *ACM Transactions on Programming Languages and Systems*, Vol.11, No.3, July 1989, pp.345-387.

[HRB88] S. Horwitz, T. Reps, and D. Binkley, "Interprocedural Slicing Using Dependence Graphs", *Proceedings of the ACM SIGPLAN 88 Conference on Programming Language Design and Implementation*, July 1988, pp. 35-46.

[Kat90] T. Katsoulakos, "An Overview of the ESPRIT Project REDO Maintenance Validation Documentation of Software Systems," ESPRIT Conference, Brussels, November 1990.

[KN89] W. Kozaczynski and J. Ning, "SRE: A Knowledge-Based Environment for Large-Scale Software Re-engineering Activities," *11th International Conference on Software Engineering*, Pittsburgh, May 1989.

[Let86] S. Letovsky, "Cognitive Processes in Program Comprehension," in *Proceedings of the Conference on Empirical Studies of Programmers*, Washington DC, June 1986.

[Let88] S. Letovsky, *Plan Analysis of Programs*, Ph.D. thesis, Yale University, December 1988.

[LG88] J.R. Lyle, K.B. Gallagher, Using Program Decomposition to Guide Modifications, *Proc. of Conference on Software Maintenance*, Phoenix, Arizona, October 24-27, 1988

[LPLS86] D. Littman, J. Pinto, S. Letovsky, and E. Soloway, "Mental Models and Software Maintenance," in *Empirical Studies of Programmers*, Soloway and Iyengar, Eds., Ablex Publishing Corp., Norwood, N. J., 1986.

[LPLS87] S. Letovsky, J. Pinto, R. Lampert, and E. Soloway, "A Cognitive Analysis of A Code Inspection," in *Empirical Studies of Programmers: Second Workshop*, Olson, Sheppard, and Soloway, Eds., Ablex Publishing Corp., Norwood, N. J., 1987.

[LS86] S. Letovsky and E. Soloway, "Delocalized Plans and

Program Comprehension," *IEEE Software*, May 1986, pp. 41-49.

[LW87] J. Lyle and M. Weiser, "Automatic Program Bug Location by Program Slicing," in *Proceedings of 2nd International Conference on Computers and Applications*, Beijing, China, June 1987, pp. 22-27.

[MAL87] *MALPAS Intermediate Language Manual, IL Version 4.0*, Rex, Thompson & Partners Limited, Surrey, U. K., 1987.

[Nin89] J. Ning, *A Knowledge-Based Approach to Automatic Program Analysis*, Ph.D. thesis, University of Illinois at Urbana-Champaign, October 1989.

[Sas90] W. Sasso, "Empirical Study of Re-Engineering Behavior: Design Recovery by Experienced Professionals," *Software Engineering: Tools, Techniques, Practices*, Vol. 1, No. 1, March 1990.

[Wei81] M. Weiser, "Program Slicing," in *Proceedings of 5th International Conference on Software Engineering*, March 1981.

[WL86] M. Weiser and J. Lyle, "Experiments on Slicing-Based Debugging Tools," in *Empirical Studies of Programmers*, Soloway and Iyengar, Eds., Ablex Publishing Corp., Norwood, N. J., 1986.

[WN87] N. Wilde and B. Nejmeh, "Dependence Analysis: An Aid for Software Maintenance," Software Engineering Research Center, University of Florida, SERC-TR-13-F, September 1987.

[Wil87] L. Wills, *Automated Program Recognition*, Technical Report 904, Master's thesis, MIT AI Lab, February 1987.

[YL88] S. Yau and S. Liu, "Some Approaches to Logical Ripple Effect Analysis," Software Engineering Research Center, University of Florida, SERC-TR-24-F, October 1988.

170

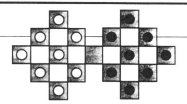

Knowledge-Based Program Analysis

Mehdi T. Harandi and *Jim Q. Ning*, University of Illinois

PAT provides high-level support for program maintenance. It uses an object-oriented framework of programming concepts and a heuristic-based concept-recognition mechanism to understand programs.

Without an adequate understanding of a program's meaning, it is impossible to maintain it effectively. This is especially true for large, complex programs. To modify a program, a programmer usually develops a mental model of its intended function. He then uses this model as a basis when he modifies the intended function or corrects the encoded implementation of the function. However, it is very difficult to construct such a mental model. Without automated support, a large part of the maintenance time is spent trying to understand what is to be maintained.

In this article, automatic program analysis is both the mechanized process of understanding high-level concepts from program text and the use of those concepts to guide program maintenance. The understanding element constructively derives a program's underlying meaning by statically examining its source code without using any specification or execution information.[1,2] Maintenance support offers high-level assistance to the maintainer in documentation, correction, en-

hancement, and other maintenance activities. While high-level support for program maintenance is the goal, program understanding is the means to achieve this goal.

We have realized this notion of automated program analysis in our knowledge-based Program Analysis Tool. PAT uses an object-oriented framework to represent programming concepts and a heuristic-based concept-recognition mechanism to derive high-level functional concepts from the source code.

Program views

Conceptually, you can view a program from different levels of detail. Program understanding transforms a program from a more detailed view into a more abstract view. Based on the abstraction level, we classify program views into four broad categories: implementation-level, structure-level, function-level, and domain-level views.[3,4]

The implementation-level view abstracts away a program's language- and implementation-specific features. To understand a program at this level, you need

0-8186-3272-0/93 $3.00 ©1990 IEEE

knowledge of the language's syntax and semantics and, possibly, some knowledge of the implementation. Typically, an implementation-level view is represented as an abstract syntax tree and a symbol table of program tokens.

The structure-level view further abstracts a program's language-dependent details to reveal its structure from different perspectives. The result is an explicit representation of the dependencies among program components. Examples of structure-level views are dataflow and control-flow graphs, data and control dependency graphs, interprocedural calling relations, ripple-effect graphs, petri nets, structure charts, and other intermediate-to-low-end design graphs. Recently, some effort has been made to generalize these representations to capture all the interesting structural features of programs in a unified representation.[5-7]

The function-level view relates pieces of the program to their functions to reveal the logical (as opposed to the syntactical or structural) relations among them. Each component of a function-level view is an abstract representation of a class of functionally equivalent, but structurally different, implementations.

The domain-level view further abstracts the function-level view by replacing its algorithmic nature with concepts specific to the application domain. For example, in the context of student-record keeping, a program functionally understood as "computing average by summing its inputs divided by the number of inputs" is interpreted as a "grade-point-average computation" routine.

Figure 1 shows how these abstraction categories roughly correspond to the information used in different stages of the development life cycle. While this article's focus is on the function-level view, you can easily extend the methods and tools presented here to deal with domain-level understanding.

Expert's model

Observations show that human experts have a better problem-solving model than previous automatic-program-analysis systems: They can usually comprehend a program efficiently without using a formal method of proof. To understand a program, experts do not exhaustively apply all their knowledge about programming to repeatedly transform the program. Nor do they extract all the information about dataflow and control flow to make abstractions.

An expert views a program not only as a text file of sequenced characters but also as a set of interrelated concepts. He understands a program by learning abstract concepts from it. Initially, he may understand a program only syntactically. Then, discrete, otherwise unrelated low-level concepts may help him recognize higher level concepts until he can comprehend the whole program as a single functional unit.

He uses his programming knowledge to recognize high-level concepts. Typically, this knowledge includes stereotyped code patterns of common programming strategies, data structures, and algorithms. When he sees a concept's stereotyped pattern, he looks for evidence that suggests its existence. This concept-recognition process results in a plausible con-

clusion, rather than a rigorous proof.

Using this heuristic-based knowledge, he skips trivial parts and looks only for things he deems important. He can relate concepts that are not adjacent because all the concepts in his concept base — simple and complex — are equally visible at all times. In the end, he forms a functional model of the program, usually a hierarchical structure that relates all the concepts recognized and rooted in the original concepts. He then uses this model to guide maintenance.

PAT overview

The PAT system, illustrated in Figure 2, is based on the human expert's analysis model. PAT tries to help maintainers answer three questions:

• What does this program do (what high-level concepts does it implement)?

• How are the concepts encoded, in terms of low-level concepts?

• Are the recognized concepts implemented incorrectly?

To do this, the Program Parser first rewrites the program into a set of language-independent objects, called events, and puts them in the Event Base. Using this event set, the Understander recognizes higher level events that represent more function-oriented concepts. The Understander adds these newly recognized

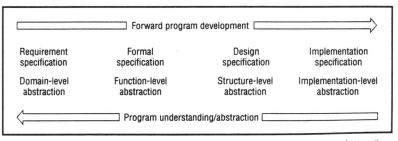

Figure 1. Diagram of forward program development and backward program abstraction.

76

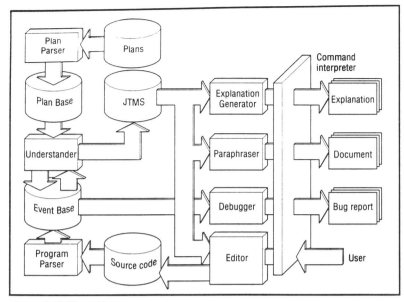

Figure 2. PAT's architecture.

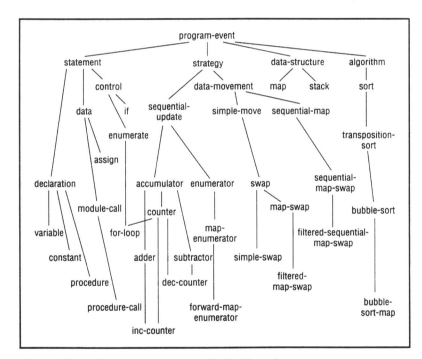

Figure 3. Part of the program event classification hierarchy.

events to the event set and repeats the process until it recognizes no more high-level events. The final event set, presented to the maintainer, answers the first question.

The Understander's main component is a deductive-inference-rule engine. It uses a library of program plans, stored in a plan base, as inference rules to derive new, high-level events. The program plans, which have been parsed by the Plan Parser, contain understanding, paraphrasing, and debugging knowledge. When the Understander generates a new event, it may trigger other rules to fire, causing the derivation of more events.

Discovering new events is of little use without the ability to explain the logical connections among them. To do this, PAT

maintains a justification-based truth-maintenance system to model the understanding process.[8] When the Understander identifies a new event, the JTMS records the result *and* its justifications. The Explanation Generator uses the JTMS to show how high-level events are derived from the low-level events, thus answering the second question.

For example, the Explanation Generator gives the following explanation when an original set of events {$s1$, $s2$, $s3$} causes the recognition of a new set of events {$e1$, $e2$}, where $e1$ is derived from $s1$, $s2$, and $e2$ is derived from $s1$, $s3$, and $e1$:

1. $s1$ is a simple event.
2. $s2$ is a simple event.
3. $s3$ is a simple event.
4. $e1$ is a composite event based on 1 and 2.
5. $e2$ is a composite event based on 1, 3, and 4.

The Paraphraser translates these explanations into natural-language descriptions.

The Debugger examines the final set of recognized events to answer the third question. Each program plan contains knowledge on near-miss implementation patterns that are commonly associated with events that are recognizable by that plan. The Debugger uses this information to identify a possible misimplementation.

Finally, the Editor lets you interactively modify the program; such changes may trigger more inferences, the results of which are updated in the JTMS automatically.

Knowledge representation

PAT represents two types of knowledge explicitly: program knowledge and analysis knowledge. Program knowledge is represented by programming concepts contained in program text. Analysis knowledge embodies information necessary for program analysis and is represented by information contained in program plans.

Program knowledge. In our paradigm, each syntactic or semantic concept contained in a program is expressed in an object-oriented abstract representation, called a program event. Program events are organized in a hierarchy. At the lowest level — the source level — are events representing language constructs like statements and declarations. At a higher level

```
          ...
     38   procedure swap ( var X. Y : integer):
     40   var T : integer:
     43   assign X to T:
     44   assign Y to X:
     45   assign T to Y;
     47   end-procedure;
          ...
    120   proc-call swap (A, B):
          ...

event-class:      SIMPLE-SWAP
interval:         ([0 (120 43 44 45)]   [0 (4 43 44 45)])
external-form:    ((43 44 45) SIMPLE-SWAP A B)
var1:             A₀
var2:             B₀
temp-var:         T₄
```

Figure 4. Event representation of the simple-swap concept.

```
plan   event
    path     event-path-expression
    test     binding-constraints
    text     documentation-information
    miss     near-miss-expression

where the event-path-expression is defined as:

event-path-expression ::= event-specifier | interval-operator {event-path-expression}*
event-specifier       ::= {key} event
interval-operator      ::= c-operator | l-operator
c-operator            ::= c-precede | c-enclose | c-interleave | c-overlap
                          c-contain | c-meet | c-sequential | c-parallel | ...
l-operator            ::= l-precede | l-enclose | l-interleave | l-overlap |
                          l-contain | l-meet | l-sequential | l-parallel | ...
```

Figure 5. Plan-definition syntax.

are events corresponding to common programming patterns and strategies like structure enumerators, accumulating a sequence of values, and counting. Events can also represent data structures or designs like stacks, queues, trees, and their corresponding operations. At an even higher level, events can represent standard algorithms for common problems like mathematical computation algorithms, searching, and sorting.

Whatever it represents, each event is an instance of an event class. Figure 3 shows a partial hierarchy of event classes.

All events have attributes. Each event has an *interval*, which comprises two parts: a control interval and a lexical interval. The control interval determines where the event is in the control path when the code is executed. The lexical interval determines where the event is in the nested hierarchy of the program text. An event also has an external form, for presentation.

Events have an event-class attribute, which denotes their class. We define common attributes in the top-level class (the program-event), and they are inherited by all classes. In addition to inherited attributes, an event may have its own attributes, as Figure 4 shows.

Figure 4 shows a program segment and the event representation of the concept contained in the segment, simple-swap. In Figure 4, the control-interval, [0 (120 43 44 45)], says that this simple-swap event comprises three subevents at locations 43, 44, and 45 and that they are in a module (usually a procedure) that is invoked from location 120. The event at location 120 is part of the main program module. We always assume that the control to the main program is transferred from some imaginary location 0.

The lexical-interval [0 (4 43 44 45)] says that the module that lexically encloses the simple-swap event is numbered 4 (its block number), which is globally declared. The main program module has block number 0.

The local attributes, var1, var2, and temp-var, are variables in the swap operation. Because the value of temp-var should not affect the external behavior of simple-swap, it does not appear in the external-form attribute. Each data object has a sub-script that indicates its declaring block. For example, B_0 says that the data object B is declared globally. We subscript data objects to distinguish multiply declared identifiers in different lexical environments. A language parser and a simple control-flow analyzer determine the attributes of source-level events; the attributes of higher level events are computed from their composing events.

Analysis knowledge. In PAT, knowledge about program understanding, documentation, and debugging is represented as a program plan.

Figure 5 shows the syntax of a plan definition. Understanding knowledge is encoded in the plan's path and test sections. An event-path expression in the path part specifies the lexical and control sequence requirements of a subset of the plan's event patterns. A pattern might match a source-level event, such as an assignment, or it might match a high-level concept, such as an enumerate. An event set is an instance of a plan if it meets the path expression of the plan and any constraints expressed in the test part.

Knowledge to generate documentation is stored in the text part and knowledge to perform near-miss debugging is stored in the miss part.

To understand event-path expressions and interval operators (logical operators we use to define lexical and control sequencing requirements), examine the event-path-expression part of an accumulator plan:

```
plan (accumulator :update-var ?var
    :init-value ?init :update-value ?val
        :update-cond ?cond
            :accumulator-op ?op)
path ( c-precede (assign :var-defined ?var
    :value-used ?init)
    ( c-enclose (enumerator :loop-cond
        ?cond)
        ( key (assign :var-defined ?var
            :value-used (?op ?var ?val)))))
```

In this plan, : denotes an attribute and ?

78

```
...    ...
203  const          N  :  integer = 100;
205  var            A  :  array(1..N, Elem);
...    ...
225  procedure      unknown ();
228      var  S  :  integer;
230      for-loop  K  from  N−1  to  1  do
232          for-loop  J  from  1  to  K  do
233              if  A(J−1) > A(J)  then
234                  assign  A(J)  to  S;
235                  assign  S  to  A(J−1);
236                  assign  A(J−1)  to  A(J)
238              end-if
240          end-for-loop
245      end-for-loop
250  end-procedure;
...    ...
400  proc-call unknown();
...    ...
```

Figure 6. Bubble-sort program.

E_{205}:
event-class:	VAR
interval:	([0 205] [0 205])
name:	A_0
var-type:	array(1..N_0,$Elem_0$)

E_{232}:
event-class:	FOR-LOOP
interval:	([0 (400 232 240)] [0 (45 232 240)])
update-var:	J_0
init-value:	1
final-value:	K_0
direction:	UP
step:	1

E_{233}:
event-class:	IF
interval:	([0 (400 233 238)] [0 (45 233 238)])
if-cond:	$A_0(J_0-1) > A_0(J_0)$

E_{235}:
event-class:	ASSIGN
interval:	([0 (400 235)] [0 (45 235)])
var-defined:	$A_0(J_0-1)$
value-used:	S_{45}

Figure 7. Source-level events generated from the program in Figure 6.

denotes a pattern variable. The path expression specifies two assignment events, one enumerator event (a loop construct), and their variable bindings — a possible component set for an accumulator event.

The path part also requires that ?var be initialized to some value ?init before the loop and the loop-carried assignment events are reached. So an accumulator event is identified only if the initial assignment event precedes the loop event on the control path (c-precede) which, in turn, encloses the second assignment event (c-enclose).

Key events identify important plan components. In this example, the second assignment event is a key; it must be identified first to recognize the accumulator

event. Identifying key events first helps reduce the search space.

Event-path expressions heuristically categorize classes of equivalent event sequences, which may not be lexically adjacent. As long as their relative positions meet the lexical and control requirements expressed by the path, they are recognized as components of a higher level event.

Program analysis

PAT's understanding power comes from a pattern-directed inference engine that uses a plan library. Plans are represented as inference rules that are stored in the plan base.

Plan rules are triggered by events de-

fined in the plan's event-path expression. The control and lexical requirements, extracted from the event-path expression, combined with a plan's binding constraints, govern the firing of a rule. The rule body is always an assertion that declares a new event when the trigger patterns and test conditions are satisfied.

Program understanding is automated as an inference by which new events are inferred from existing ones using the plan rules. Event E matches a trigger pattern P of plan rule R if

• either E and P are in the same event class or P is in a superclass of E; and

• for any attribute A with value $V1$ specified in P, there is an attribute A in E with value $V2$ such that $V1$ and $V2$ are unifiable, given pattern-unification bindings.

The first condition says that a trigger pattern can match with events that are more specific than it is. For example, an array-search pattern could match not only an array-search event but also a linear-array-search event or a binary-array-search event.

The second condition says that P matches E as long as the information in P is subsumed by (not necessarily equal to) the information in E. In defining the plan pattern array-search, for example, you need specify only the attributes containing the array name and the value of the search target. A binary-array-search event will match this pattern, although it may have extra attributes such as the array index pointers.

These conditions guarantee that when a new event is asserted into the event base the inference engine must rerun only those plan rules that are in the same class or in superclasses of the new event. Similarly, when a new rule is added to the plan base, the inference engine will apply the new rule only to events in the same class or subclasses of the rule's class. The JTMS records the results of the inference process.

The reasoning procedure in PAT is less formal than that used in other deduction, transformation, parsing, or graph-matching approaches. A PAT analysis cannot rigorously prove anything because it is a selective inspection, not a total reduction of a program. Our intention is to capture human experts' behavior in program understanding so we can handle programs

P$_{50}$: If there exists a decremental FOR-LOOP event
then there exists a DEC-COUNTER event.

P$_{51}$: If there exists an incremental FOR-LOOP event
then there exists an INC-COUNTER event.

P$_{52}$: If there exists an ASSIGN event from ?Var1 to ?Temp which precedes
an ASSIGN ?Temp to ?Var2 event and another ASSIGN ?Var2 to
?Var1 event on a control path (c-precede)
then there exists a SIMPLE-SWAP(?Var1, ?Var2) event.

P$_{53}$: If there exists a VAR event ?A of type array(?L..?U,?Type)
then there exists a MAP(?A,?L..?U,?Type) event.

P$_{54}$: If there exists a MAP(?A,?L..?U,?Type) and the definition of which
lexically precedes (l-precede) an INC-COUNTER event indexing
through ?A
then there exists a FORWARD-MAP-ENUMERATOR event on ?A.

P$_{55}$: If there exists a SIMPLE-SWAP ?Var1 and ?Var2 event in which ?Var1
and ?Var2 access a MAP(?A,?L..?U,?Type) event
then there exists a MAP-SWAP event.

P$_{56}$: If an IF event lexically enclose c-enclose an MAP-SWAP event
then there exists a GUARDED-MAP-EVENT event.

P$_{57}$: If a FORWARD-MAP-ENUMERATOR event c-encloses an
GUARDED-MAP-SWAP event
then there exists a FILTERED-SEQUENTIAL-MAP-SWAP event.

P$_{58}$: If a DEC-COUNTER event c-encloses an FILTERED-SEQUENTIAL-
MAP-SWAP event
then there exists a BUBBLE-SORT-MAP event.

Figure 8. Plans used in understanding the program in Figure 6.

with missing, extra, or buggy parts, and avoid the combinatorial barriers in the analysis of large programs.

Maintenance support

Based on the final structure of the JTMS net, PAT's Explanation Generator can informally show how the high-level events are derived from the low-level ones. The explanation it provides helps verify the correctness of the conclusions and reveal the functional and logical relations among the program components represented by the recognized events.

Each plan has a text slot that identifies the intended function of the event it is supposed to recognize. This text can be natural-language statements or a formal specification. By tracing the JTMS's net from the top, the PAT Paraphraser generates program documentation using the information in each event's text slot and explanations of how each event is composed of subevents. This documentation helps maintainers find discrepancies between intended and implemented functions.

The miss part of a plan definition contains heuristic knowledge for diagnosing common coding errors in the plan's target event. Typically, a plan's event-path expression is intentionally relaxed so it will recognize correct and buggy patterns as plan instances. The buggy part will be examined only following a successful recognition pass. Allowing near-miss recognition of events may help find very deep bugs that are otherwise very difficult to detect.

The JTMS maintains a network structure that connects the current set of believed events about the program. When a user modifies the program, those changes will be automatically reflected in the JTMS, which relates a modification's effect on the implemented functions directly, making the modification easier to follow.

Example

Figure 6 is a segment of a much larger program written in a Pascal-like language. The maintainer wants to understand only this segment; he does not want to analyze the entire program, so the information provided to PAT is incomplete. The definitions of variables K and J are invisible, we have no idea what the initial value of array A is, and we know nothing about its component's type.

Furthermore, this portion is buggy: To exchange the contents of A(J) and A(J −1) correctly, the assignment at line 236 should occur before the assignment at line 235. Also, the range of looping variable J in the second For loop at line 232 should have been from 2 to K+1, not from 1 to K. Finally, the two indices of A could be substituted by [J, J +1]. This segment also includes noise in the lines indicated by ellipses.

The information we have about this segment is not sufficient to prove formally that the program does a bubble sort, but we can reach such an understanding based on our knowledge of typical bubble-sort implementation patterns. A human expert would assume that array A has been initialized somewhere else before the program control reaches this segment, unless he sees an explicit contradiction.

PAT first parses the segment, recognizing a set of events that represent the program's source-level concepts: events representing each variable and constant definition, an event representing the procedure, six events corresponding to statements in the procedure, and an event representing the call at line 400.

Figure 7 shows four of these events. The interval definitions in Figure 7 indicate that the procedure unknown and the variables J, K, and Elem are declared at block 0 (the global environment) and that the procedure's block number is 45.

After the events are loaded into the event base, the Understander calls the plans from the plan base and tests if their trigger events match the input events. Figure 8 shows the plans used in this example, which are expressed in English to aid comprehension.

Plan P50 is triggered by event E230 (the For loop at line 230) and generates a new event E1001 (dec-counter). Event E232 triggers plan P51, generating E1002. The combination of events E234, E235, and E236 trigger P52 to generate E1003 (simple-swap). Next, E205 triggers P53 to generate event E1004. The combination of E1004 and E1002 triggers P54 to generate E1005. E1003 triggers P55 to generate E1006. P56 is triggered by E233 and E1006 to generate E1007. E1005 and E1007 trigger P57 to generate E1008. Finally, E1001 and E1008 trigger P58 to generate E1009, which is the bubble-sort algorithm.

The JTMS keeps track of the derivation of new events; Figure 9 shows its final structure, annotated with the names of recognized events. Using the text information contained in the recognized

80

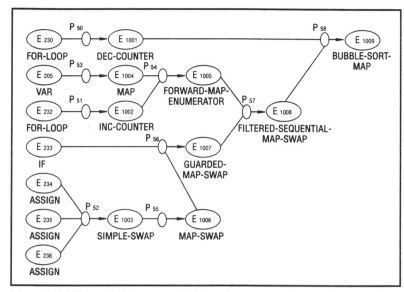

Figure 9. JTMS model of the program in Figure 6.

This program implements a BUBBLE-SORT-MAP event at lines
(205 230 232 233 234 235 236 238 240 245)
which sorts the map A using a bubble sort algorithm.
It consists of
1.   A DEC-COUNTER event at lines (230 245)
      which decrementally changes the value in K from N − 1 to 1.
      It consists of
      1.1 A FOR-LOOP event at lines (230 245).
2.   A FILTERED-SEQUENTIAL-MAP-SWAP event at lines
      (205 232 233 234 235 236 238 240)
      which sequentially switches the adjacent elements in a map A
      if A(J−1) > A(J), indexed by J from 1 to K.
      It consists of
      2.1.   A FORWARD-MAP-ENUMERATOR event at lines (232 240)
              which incrementally enumerates the elements in map A indexed by J
              from 1 to K. It consists of
              2.1.1.   A MAP event named A at line (205)
              which is a mapping from 1..N to Elem.
              It consists of
              2.1.1.1.   A VAR event named A at line (205).
              2.1.2.   An INC-COUNTER event at (232 240)
              which incrementally changes the value in J from 1 to K.
              It consists of
              2.1.2.1.   An FOR-LOOP event at lines (232 240).
      2.2.   A GUARDED-MAP-SWAP event at lines (233 234 235 236 238)
              which switches the values in A(J−1) and A(J) if A(J−1) > A(J).
              It consists of
              2.2.1.   An IF event at lines (233 238).
              2.2.2.   A MAP-SWAP event at lines (234 235 236).
              It consists of
              2.2.2.1.   A SIMPLE-SWAP event at lines (234 235 236)
                          which switches the values in A(J−1) and A(J).
                          It consists of
                          2.2.2.1.1.   An ASSIGN event at line (234).
                          2.2.2.1.2.   An ASSIGN event at line (235).
                          2.2.2.1.3.   An ASSIGN event at line (236).

Figure 10. Paraphrase of the example program.

events, PAT can explain its understanding, as the paraphrase in Figure 10 shows.

As for the two bugs in this segment, without a function-level understanding of the program, we can only point out that the initial value of A(J−1) is not used in each iteration in the inner loop and that J −1 is less than the lower bound of A when J equals 1.

In our paradigm, event-specific debugging information is encoded in the miss part of a plan. For example, in the plan for recognizing the simple-swap event, we intentionally relax the sequencing requirement in its event-path expression, encoding it instead in its miss part. When the Understander recognizes the three assignment events as components of a simple-swap event, it reexamines their control sequence. PAT then determines that
• the three events are intended to accomplish a simple-swap event (they meet the event-path expression) and
• the positions of the last two should be switched (they meet the near-miss expression).

Similarly, when PAT recognizes the bubble-sort-map event, it unifies the 1, N, J−1, and J expressions with the plan's variables, producing the bindings [LowBound 1], [UpBound N], [Index J], [OffSet1 −1], and [OffSet2 0]. If the miss part includes the rules

    If Index runs increasingly
    then The first round of Index values must
      range
        from LowBound − OffSet1 to
          UpBound − OffSet2;
      The last Index value must be
        LowBound − OffSet1.
    else The first round of Index values must
      range
        from UpBound − OffSet2 to
          LowBound − OffSet1;
      The last Index value must be
        UpBound − OffSet2.

PAT can determine that A is indexed incorrectly by J because the first round of J values (when K takes its first value N−1) ranges from 1 to N−1, not from 2 (LowBound − OffSet1) to N (UpBound − OffSet2). Besides, because J runs increasingly, the last J value (when K takes its final value 1) should be 2 (LowBound − OffSet1), not 1.

Experiments with PAT have affirmed our initial expectations. PAT now includes about 100 program-event classes that represent language constructs, coding heuristics, data-structure definitions and operations, and functional coding patterns.

PAT's plan base contains a few dozen plan rules covering value accumulation, structure enumeration, simple mathematical computations, counting, sequential search of ordered and unordered structures, different types of searching, tree traversals, and sorting. For practical applications, we believe PAT will need at least several hundred event classes and plans.

PAT could be improved in several ways. It should be able to incrementally acquire program knowledge by asking an expert for help when it cannot understand a program and by saving the generalized solution for future use. Also, when PAT comes up with a conclusion that an expert rejects, it should know how to modify its knowledge to account for the failure.

PAT is not intended to replace maintenance done by people. Instead, it is a high-level assistant that provides plausible predictions, suggestions, and explanations about a program's function — information that is not easily derived with traditional maintenance tools. ❖

Acknowledgment

This work was supported in part by IBM.

References

1. M.T. Harandi and J.Q. Ning, "PAT: A Knowledge-Based Program-Analysis Tool," *Proc. Conf. Software Maintenance*, CS Press, Los Alamitos, Calif., 1988, pp. 312-318.

2. J.Q. Ning, *A Knowledge-Based Approach to Automatic Program Analysis*, doctoral dissertation, University of Illinois at Urbana-Champaign, Urbana, Ill., 1989.

3. J.Q. Ning and M.T. Harandi, "An Experiment in Automating Code Analysis," *Proc. AAAI Symp. Artificial Intelligence and Software Engineering*, AAAI Press, Stanford, Calif., 1989, pp. 51-53.

4. W. Kozaczynski and J.Q. Ning, "SRE: A Knowledge-Based Environment for Large-Scale Software Reengineering Activities," *Proc. Int'l Conf. Software Eng.*, CS Press, Los Alamitos, Calif, 1989, pp. 113-122.

5. J.M. Bieman and N.C. Debnath, "An Analysis of Software Structure Using a Generalized Program Graph," *Proc. Compsac*, CS Press, Los Alamitos, Calif., 1985, pp. 254-259.

6. N. Wilde, R. Ogando, and E. Edge, "Specification for Prototype Dependency Analysis Tools," Tech. Report SERC-TR-13-F, Software Engineering Research Center, University of Florida, Tallahassee, Fla., 1987.

7. S. Yau and P.C. Grabow, "A Model for Representing Programs Using Hierarchical Graphs," *IEEE Trans. Software Eng.*, Nov. 1981, pp. 556-574.

8. J. Doyle, "A Truth Maintenance System," *Artificial Intelligence*, Vol. 12, 1979, pp. 231-272.

Mehdi T. Harandi is an associate professor of computer science at the University of Illinois at Urbana-Champaign and is director of the university's knowledge-based programming assistant project. His research interests include knowledge-based systems, software specification and design, and AI applications to software development.

Harandi received a PhD in computer science from the University of Manchester, England. He is editor-in-chief of *International Journal of Expert Systems: Research and Applications* and a member of ACM and the IEEE Computer Society.

Jim Q. Ning is an associate scientist at Arthur Andersen and Company's Strategic Technology Research Center. His research interests are forward and reverse engineering, object-oriented methods, knowledge-based systems, and programming knowledge representation.

Ning received a BS in electronics from Beijing Normal University and an MS and PhD in computer science from the University of Illinois, where he did the work reported here.

Address questions about this article to Harandi at Computer Science Dept., University of Illinois, 1304 W. Springfield Ave., Urbana, IL 61801.

Annotated Bibliography

In addition to the papers in this book, the reader will find the following references informative. The list presented here is useful for further reading, but not comprehensive. Omission of any work does not imply that the work is any less significant than those annotated here. Papers that appeared in *Tutorial on Software Restructuring* ([Arnold86]) are preceded by this symbol: ♦.

[Adams91] Adams, N., "Measuring Maintenance Productivity and Quality," *Software Eng.,* Vol. 2, No. 5, July/Aug. 1991, pp. 5-13.
Describes an approach for measuring the productivity of software maintenance effort. The measurement procedure incorporates Sauer's[1] software maintainability index.

[Adams92] Adams, N., "Developing a Software Process Improvement Model," *Software Eng.,* Vol. 2, No. 5, Jan./Feb. 1992, pp. 12-19.
Describes a maintenance process model, part of an inclusive development and maintenance process model. The benefit of such a process model is that the software development portion of the model is more likely to explicitly address maintenance needs. The process model mentioned is more a framework detailing the many issues, such as software quality measurement, to be considered.

♦[Allman82] Allman, E. and Stonebraker, M., "Observations on the Evolution of a Software System," *IEEE Computer,* Vol. 15, No. 6, June 1982, pp. 27-32.
Describes a real-life experience in building and restructuring a database management system. Because the system originated in a university environment with few development and maintenance standards, the system rapidly reached a stage where new maintainers (students) found it difficult to maintain. What followed was a period of reengineering that eventually made the system more understandable and maintenance more controllable. Some valuable insights on what to do correctly the next time conclude the paper.

[Andrews90] Andrews, D.C., "Systems Re-Engineering: A Critical Perspective," *CASE Trends,* July/Aug. 1990, pp. 15-16.
Discusses reengineering as value-added technology. Reengineering can aid in path finding (documentation of the physical design), translating (converting from one platform to another), and enhancing (change of functionality during a technology conversion process).

[Andrews92] Andrews, D.C., and Stalick, S.K., "Business Reengineering," *American Programmer,* Vol. 5, No. 5, May 1992.
Discusses items needed to make business reengineering work. Cultural and managerial changes are needed, as well as technology support. The authors provide a bibliography for further reading.

♦[Arnold82] Arnold, R.S. and Parker, D.A., "The Dimensions of Healthy Maintenance," *Proc. 6th Int'l Conf. on Software Engineering,* Sept. 1982, pp. 10-27.
Discusses the practical application of software metrics to determine problems in software maintenance. This kind of discussion is often omitted when metrics are applied in practice. The paper lists some criteria for maintenance adequacy and shows how these criteria may be used both to detect maintenance problems and to find constructive suggestions for improving maintenance. The implication for this tutorial is that, by creating criteria for software reengineering, the paper's approach can be used to determine where (and if) software should be reengineered. The paper's approach is amplified in [Arnold83].

[Arnold83] Arnold, R.S., *On the Generation and Use of Quantitative Criteria for Assessing Software Maintenance Quality,* PhD dissertation, Univ. of Maryland, 1983. Available as dissertation No. 8402525 from University Microfilms International, 300 N. Zeeb Rd., Ann Arbor, Mich. 48106.
A straightforward approach to applying software metrics during software maintenance. The emphasis is on how measurements can be used to stimulate concrete actions for improving software maintenance. (The technique may also be used during software development.) A detailed example, using software maintenance data from the NASA Goddard Space Flight Center, is given. This work is much expanded from [Arnold82].

[Arnold 84] Arnold, R.S., "A Survey of 24 Techniques for Software Restructuring," *Proc. 2nd Nat'l Conf. on EDP Software Maintenance,* U.S. Professional Development Inst., Silver Spring, Md., 1984, pp. 402-425.
A survey that lays out a range of restructuring techniques and attempts to qualitatively assess their

---

[1]Sauer, F.G., "The Ford Software Maintenance Center," *Proc. Seventh Int'l. Conf. on Software Maintenance and Reeng.,* U.S. Professional Development Institute, Silver Spring, Md., 1990.

relative usefulness. The first known survey paper on software restructuring.

[Arnold86] Arnold, R.S., *Tutorial on Software Restructuring,* IEEE CS Press, Washington, D.C., 1986.

A collection of papers on software restructuring and reengineering. The term "reengineering" was not commonly used in 1986, but many of the papers apply also to reengineering code to improve its maintainability.

[Arnold90] Arnold, R.S., "Heuristics for Salvaging Reusable Parts from Ada Source Code," Tech. Report Ada Reuse Heuristics-90011-N, Software Productivity Consortium, Mar. 1990.

Gives several rules for prospecting for reusable parts from source code. Most of these heuristics can be slightly modified to apply to other languages besides Ada. The heuristics, to be applied, do not require application domain expertise.

[Arnold90] Arnold, R.S., "Software Restructuring: Foundation for Reengineering," *Proc. Reverse Eng. Forum,* Washington Univ., St. Louis, Mo., Apr. 1990.

This presentation argues that understanding software restructuring issues and lessons pays rich dividends in understanding software reengineering technology.

[Arnold90] Arnold, R.S., "Tools for Static Analysis of Ada Source Code," Tech. Report, Ada Static Tools Survey-90015-N, Software Productivity Consortium, June 1990.

This report describes a number of static analysis tools for Ada that can be used in analyzing Ada code. This can facilitate prospecting for reusable part candidates, performing measurements of Ada source code, or creating views of Ada source code.

[Arnold90] Arnold, R.S., "Salvaging Reusable Components from Ada Source Code: A Progress Report," Tech. Report Ada Static Tools Survey-90015-N, Software Productivity Consortium, Sept. 1990.

Reports experience in using static analysis tools to prospect for candidate reuable parts in Ada source code. One lesson learned: use tools with a mature interface to semantic information about Ada source code. Decomposing Ada source code into objects and relationships is best left to specialized generators of such information.

[Arnold91a] Arnold, R.S., "Salvaging Ada Software for Reuse," *Proc. Naval Surface Warfare Center Workshop on Systems Reenineering,* Silver Spring, Maryland, Mar. 1991.

Summarizes the work from the three [Arnold90] technical reports mentioned above.

[Arnold91b] Arnold, R.S., "Risks of Reengineering," *Proc. Reverse Eng. Forum,* Washington Univ., St. Louis, Mo., Apr. 1991.

This presentation categorizes reengineering risks, describes several specific risks in each category, and discusses how to mitigate risk for each of the categories.

[Arnold91c] Arnold, R.S., Koorapaty, S., and Pearce, B., "Criteria for Evaluating Reengineering Technology," Tech. Report SPC-91113-MC, Version 01.00.01, Software Productivity Consortium, June 1991. Available to Software Productivity Consortium member companies only.

This report describes an Analytic Hierarchy Approach to evaluating reengineering technology (tools and services). The report lists seven factors used to evaluate reengineering technology: three that are reengineering-specific and four that are tool-generic. Associated with these factors are over 250 questions to answer. The report applies the framework to several reengineering tools and gives lessons learned.

[Arnold91d] Arnold, R.S., Koorapaty, S., and Marshall, M., "A Reengineering Approach Using Software Salvaging," Tech. Report SPC-91186-MC, Version 01.00.00, Software Productivity Consortium, Dec. 1991. Available to Software Productivity Consortium member companies only.

This report describes a process for reengineering a system with parts salvaged from it. Software parts are salvaged from an existing system. Variations (if any) of similar parts are analyzed and a new reusable part accommodating the variations is designed. The reusable parts are reinserted into the original system and also made available to other systems. The report also describes experience in applying the approach to reengineering two lex- and yacc-based compilers written in Ada.

[Ashcroft71] Ashcroft, E. and Manna, Z., "The Translation of 'goto' Programs into 'While' Programs," *Proc. 1971 IFIP Congress,* North-Holland, Amsterdam, 1971, pp. 250-260.

An early software restructuring paper, significant because of its constructive algorithm for transforming any program into a structured program. "Structure" here is in terms of control structures used by the program. This technique was substantially improved in the book [Linger79] included in this bibliography.

[Bachman88] Bachman, C., "A CASE for Reverse Engineering," *Datamation,* July 1, 1988.

Discusses a framework for forward and reverse engineering. The author is responsible for a CASE toolset that is highly successful in its domain. The toolset successfully incorporates expert system technology. As the author notes, the expert system offers a documentation system that can record, as a system evolves, the design decisions and the explanations for them. This kind of information can be very useful in recovering and maintaining business rules later on.

[Bagnell90] Bagnell, B., "Re-Engineering Software Vendor Applications," white paper, Integral Software, 1990.

Describes experience in using a CASE tool to accomplish data reengineering. The discussion highlights many down-to-earth issues of acquiring and using CASE technology in data reengineering. The author points out that, "Sometime in the near future, software will no longer be delivered as code, but rather in the form of application models." Data reengineering can aid in moving toward "model mode[2]."

[Baker77] Baker, B., "An Algorithm for Structuring Flowgraphs," *Journal of the ACM,* Vol. 24, No. 1, Jan. 1977, pp. 98-120.

Presents an algorithm for structuring programs, based on a graph of the program's control flow. The algorithm was used as a basis for the "STRUCT" tool, available on Unix (trademark of AT&T Bell Laboratories), for rewriting Fortran programs.

[Bartholomew91] Bartholomew, D., "Charles Schwab: Bullish on Reengineering," *Information Week,* July 22, 1991, pp. 12-13.

Discusses one firm's anticipated benefits, and experience with, business process reengineering. One goal of the reengineering is to make the technology be driven by business needs, rather than the business being driven by technology. Recovering a business model from an existing system is important for the reengineering.

[Benander89] Benander, A.C. and Benander, B.A., "An Empirical Study of Cobol Programs via a Style Analyzer: The Benefits of Good Programming Style," *J of Systems and Software,* Vol. 10, 1989, pp. 271-279.

Discusses the use of a Cobol style analyzer to improve the readability of Cobol code.

[Benedusi89] Benedusi, P., Cimitile, A., and De Carlini, U., "A Reverse Engineering Methodology to Reconstruct Hierarchical Dataflow Diagrams for Software Maintenance," *Proc. Conf. on Software Maintenance,* IEEE CS Press, Los Alamitos, Calif., 1989, pp. 180-189.

Discusses in detail a technique for creating dataflow diagrams from source code. The technique is a good example of what many reverse engineering tools do behind the scenes for the user. The language used here is Pascal, but the techniques, suitably modified, will apply to other languages as well.

[Bennett91] Bennett, K., Younger, E., Estdale, J., Khabaza, I., Price, M., van Zuylen, H. (eds.), "Reverse Engineering for Software Maintenance," 2487-TN-WL-1027 Version 0.5 ESPRIT Project 2487, Delft Hydraulics, Research and Development, PO Box 177, 260 0 MH Delft, The Netherlands, Jan. 1991.

An excellent overview of reverse engineering concepts, models, and issues. Covers definitions, processes, methods, and tools. An ESPRIT REDO project technical report.

♦[Bergland81] Bergland, G.D., "A Guided Tour of Program Design Methodologies," *IEEE Computer,* Vol. 14, No. 10, Oct. 1981, pp. 18-37.

An informative discussion of software structure, software design methodologies, and software change. The author believes that "the methodology is the single most important determinant of the life-cycle costs for the resulting software system." Through plausible examples on similar software developed with different design methodologies, the author shows how poor structure may very easily be introduced. Seeing such examples gives clues to how poor software structure may be prevented.

[Berlinger90] Berlinger, S., "Reengineering: Leveraging Your CASE Investment," *American Programmer,* Vol. 3, No. 10, Oct. 1990, pp. 21-26.

Discusses the major ideas behind redevelopment engineering with CASE tools. Redevelopment engineering has three phases: reverse engineering, resystemization, and reengineering. Reverse engineering redocuments existing data structure and functionality. Resystemization changes technology (e.g., system hardware or DBMS) while preserving the system's functionality. Reengineering, the third phase in the author's redevelopment engineering process, uses forward engineering techniques to make system enhancements and generate code.

♦[Berns84] Berns, G.M., "Assessing Software Maintainability." *Comm. of the ACM,* Vol. 27, No. 1, Jan. 1984, pp. 14-23.

Gives a software metric for assessing how difficult a program is to understand. The approach is based on assigning weights (based on usage of programming language constructs) to a program's statements, then summing the weights. The metric is a good example of a software metric whose basic computational framework can be tuned, before being used, to reflect the local views of software maintainability.

[Biggerstaff91] Biggerstaff, T. and Lubars, M., "Recovering and Reusing Software Designs," *American Programmer,* Mar. 1991, pp. 2-11.

Presents a clear conceptual discussion of recovering software design assets. The authors point out that, "...Having a stable, well-understood software asset base is crucial to achieving successful software reuse."

[Bohm66] Bohm, C. and Jacopini, G., "Flow Diagrams, Turing Machines, and Languages with Only Two Formation Rules," *Comm. of the ACM,* Vol. 9, No. 5, May 1966, pp. 366-371.

One of the earliest papers on program restructuring, significant because it showed 'goto' statements are not theoretically necessary for creating arbitrary programs. The proof of this was constructive, and at least one commercially available tool has been created from a refined version of this algorithm.

♦[Brice81] Brice, L., "Existing Computer Applications. Maintain or Redesign: How to Decide?," *Proc. Com-*

[2]Desmond, J., "Towards Model Mode," *Software Magazine,* Dec. 1990, pg. 8.

puter Measurement Group, Dec. 1981, pp. 20-28.

Presents the cost of current maintenance vis-a-vis the cost of restructuring followed by maintenance. Using equations that quantify maintenance costs and restructuring costs, the paper illustrates how a break-even point may be calculated. A break-even point is that point in the future (if ever) when the costs of continued maintenance equal the costs of restructuring plus maintenance. One surprising result of the cost illustrations in this paper is the long calendar times needed to reach the break-even point. The only example given where this is reached still took 13 months from the start of restructuring!

[Brisebois92] Brisebois, R., Abran, A., and Côte, V., "Reengineering Tool Evaluation Indicator," white paper, COGNICASE, 2619, Rue Charlemagne, Montréal, Québec H1W 3S9, Canada, 1992.

This report describes a taxonomy and evaluation framework for comparing reengineering tools. The comparison framework also includes aspects of forward and reverse engineering. Provides an interesting evaluation grid for comparing tools.

♦[Britcher85] Britcher, R. and Craig, J., "Upgrading Aging Software Systems Using Modern Software Engineering Practices: IBM-FSD's Conversion of FAA's National Aerospace System (NAS) en route Stage A Software from 9020's to S/370 Processors," *Proc. Conf. on Software Maintenance,* IEEE CS Press, Los Alamitos, Calif., 1985, pp. 162-170.

Gives a practical application of software restructuring based on mathematical formalisms. The paper describes how 100,000 lines of twenty-year-old software were restructured using the ideas of a state machine data abstraction and function abstraction, standardized internally within IBM/Federal Systems Division.

[Britcher86] Britcher, Robert N. and Craig, J.J., "Using Modern Design Practices to Upgrade Aging Software Systems," *IEEE Software,* Vol. 3, No. 3, May 1986, pp. 16-24.

A revised and expanded version of [Britcher85].

[Brooks75] Brooks, F., *The Mythical Man-Month,* Addison-Wesley, Reading, Mass., 1975.

A software engineering classic, but of interest here because it proposes that maintenance must lead to poor software structure (p.123). An empirical fact perhaps, but not a theoretical necessity.

♦[Brown80] Brown, P.J., "Why Does Software Die?," *Infotech State of the Art Report,* Vol. 8, No. 7, "Life Cycle Management," 1980, pp. 32-45.

Discusses several events that can ruin software structure. These include changes in the model of the outside world on which the software is based, changes to hardware, and software requirements changes. The author surveys several approaches for making software structure more resilient for changes.

♦[Burns81] Burns, K., "Using Automated Techniques

to Improve the Maintainability of Existing Software," *DSSD User's Conf./6—Maintenance,* 1981, pp. 33-39.

Gives a useful approach to systematically restructuring one's code. The approach involves assessing alternatives to restructuring, establishing a maintainability measure to determine hard-to-maintain code and to track restructuring progress, tempering the use of metrics with concern for the payoffs of restructuring certain code portions, automating the restructuring process, accounting for actual costs of restructuring, and estimating restructuring effectiveness.

[Bush85] Bush, E., "The Automatic Restructuring of Cobol," *Proc. Conf. on Software Maintenance,* IEEE CS Press, Los Alamitos, Calif., 1985, pp. 35-41.

Outlines RECODER, a proprietary tool for restructuring the control flow of Cobol programs. The restructuring approach is based on first representing a program's logic as a graph of control flow, successively transforming the graph using proprietary transformations, then using the final control graph to generate the restructured Cobol program. The approach has its historical roots in the work by Bohm and Jacopini (see above). RECODER is now (1992) available from Knowledge-Ware, Atlanta, Ga.

[Bush88] Bush, E., "A Case for Existing Systems," white paper, originally available from Language Technology, Inc., 27 Congress St., Salem, Massachusetts, 01970, 1988.

Points out that the software life cycle deals with the incarnation of business assets. Reengineering helps to "reincarnate" business assets, bringing them from the code level (the "code plane") to the specification and design level (the "design plane"). The paper concludes with lessons learned from applying software restructuring technology.

[Bush90] Bush, E., "Reverse Engineering: What and Why," *American Programmer,* Vol. 3, No. 10, Oct. 1990, pp. 1-7.

Discusses reasons for undertaking reverse engineering. Proposes classifying reverse engineering tools by the level of abstraction of their outputs.

[Calliss88] Calliss, F.W., "Problems with Automatic Restructurers," *SIGPLAN Notices,* Vol. 23, No. 3, Mar. 1988, pp. 13-21.

A response to the comments about restructuring made in [Miller87]. The author discusses some shortcomings of automatic restructuring. For example, he points out that while restructuring may "improve" the form of software by making its constructs more regular, it can reduce understandability because the new form is initially unfamiliar to programmers. He also argues that restructuring can render useless previous embedded comments because these comments depended on their position in the code. Restructurers normally cannot recognize what items that comments refer to, so they have difficulty placing the comments in the restructured code.

[Canfora91] Canfora, G., Cimitile, A., and De Carlini, U., "A Logic-Based Approach to Reverse Engineering Tools Production," *Proc. Conf. on Software Maintenance,* IEEE CS Press, Los Alamitos, Calif., 1991, pp. 83-91.

The authors propose an interesting approach for reverse engineerig source code. First the code is analyzed and intermodular dataflow information extracted. Then the information is translated into a Prolog program dictionary. Finally, questions about the code are answered by posing queries on the Prolog program dictionary. The authors discuss use of the approach with a prototype tool for reverse engineering Pascal software.

[Canning84a] Canning, R. (ed.), "Rejuvenate Your Old Systems," *EDP Analyzer,* Vol. 22, No. 3, Mar. 1984, pp. 1-16.

An excellent account of some practical case studies for restructuring software. This, and its companion article next, are well worth reading.

[Canning84b] Canning, R. (ed.), "Tools to Rejuvenate Your Old Systems," *EDP Analyzer,* Vol. 22, No. 4, Apr. 1984, pp. 1-16.

More insightful case studies.

[Card85] Card, D.N., Page, G.T., and McGarry, F.E., "Criteria for Software Modularization," *Proc. 8th Int'l Conf. on Software Eng.,* IEEE CS Press, Los Alamitos, Calif., 1985, pp. 372-377.

A study of modularization based on empirical measurements. The authors reported that "high-strength modules have a lower fault rate and cost less than low-strength modules." Programmers should write high-strength modules that encompass the entire function.

[Chen89] Chen, Y.-F., "The C Program Database and Its Applications," *Proc. Usenix Conf. Summer '89,* Usenix Association, Berkeley, Calif., 1989.

Gives an overview of the C Information Abstraction system. Discusses the database's conceptual model (object kinds, attributes, and relationships). Also illustrates tools for browsing information in, and information derived from, the database.

[Chen92] Chen, Y.-F., "Incl: A Tool to Analyze Include Files," *Proc. Usenix Conf. Summer '92,* Usenix Association, Berkeley, Calif., 1992.

Describes a tool that analyzes "include" hierarchies to (1) graphically display compilation dependencies, (2) infer what files are not needed to recompile a system, (3) provide ways to remove unused include files. The tool uses the output of the C Information Abstraction system (see the corresponding paper in this tutorial).

[Chikofsky90] Chikofsky, E., "The Database as a Business Road Map," *Database Programming & Design,* May 1990, pp. 62-67.

Discusses how business rules can be inferred from a data model. A business rule defines what, "the information system will allow the business to do." The author gives a detailed example, with specific schemas that show the business rule extraction process involved.

[Chikofsky91] Chikofsky, E., "Realizing Design Recovery with CASE Environments," *Software Eng.,* Nov./Dec. 1991, pp. 5-10.

Discusses how CASE tools can help in finding information artifacts, on which to base corporate evolution, from existing systems. The emphasis with the approach is on recovering the state of the current system and understanding it. Viewed in this way, design recovery poses fewer risks than attempting to recover development rationales from existing software.

[Choi90] Choi, S.C. and Schacci, W. "Extracting and Restructuring the Design of Large Systems," *IEEE Software,* Jan. 1990, pp. 65-71.

This reverse engineering approach "maps the resource exchange among modules, then derives a hierarchical design description using a system restructuring algorithm." The module design of a system is documented with NuMIL, a module interconnection language.

[Cimitile91] Cimitile, A. and De Carlini, U., "Reverse Engineering: Algorithms for Program Graph Production," *Software—Practice and Experience,* Vol. 21, No. 5, May 1991, pp. 519-537.

Presents a general algebraic representation for program modules. This representation is used by algorithms, presented in the paper, for creating graphs of the programs.

[Connell87] Connell, J. and Brice, L., *The Professional User's Guide to Acquiring Software,* "Identifying Systems that Need Rework," Van Nostrand, New York, 1987, Ch. 2.

Describes criteria useful for deciding when to reengineer a system.

[Crawford90] Crawford, M.A., "Improving Cobol Program Maintenance," *Systems Development Management,* Tech. Report 34-09-40, Auerbach Publishers, 1990.

Discusses four areas or techniques for improving existing Cobol code: improving documentation and maintenance, enhancing the code, using a documentation software package, and using an interactive code analyzer. Discusses the use of commercial tools for each activity.

[David92] David, M., "Upper CASE Reverse Engineering—Application Solutions," *CASE OUTLOOK,* Vol. 6, No. 1, Jan.-Feb. 1992, pp. 43-48.

Discusses three situations that may merit reverse engineering, and the applicability of reverse engineering methods and tools to resolving the situations. The situations are: the bad business model, the recently developed system, and the technical upgrade.

[Davis91] Davis, J., "Software Re-engineering: A Beginner's Guide," *CASE Trends,* Summer 1991, pp. 10, 12-13, 15-16.

Discusses issues in selecting reengineering tools. Provides a short list of commercially available tools.

[Davis91] Davis, L., "DB2: Migration without Tears," *Datamation,* May 1, 1991, pp. 67-70.

Gives a process, lessons learned, and tools for assisting in migrating from your current database to IBM's DB2 relational database.

[de Balbine75] de Balbine, G., "Better Manpower Utilization Using Automatic Restructuring," In Parikh, G. (ed.) *Techniques of Program and System Maintenance,* Winthrop, Cambridge, Mass., 1982, pp. 217-233.

This work, originally reported in 1975, describes an automated approach to restructuring Fortran programs. The idea was first to design S-Fortran, a version of Fortran with "structured" constructs. S-Fortran serves "both as a target language for restructured programs and as an implementation language for new programs." A structuring engine, consisting of 30,000 lines of PL/1 code, then restructures a Fortran program into a prettyprinted S-Fortran version, that may be used during maintenance by programmers. The S-Fortran version of a program is compiled by inputting the program to an S-Fortran-to-Fortran preprocessor prior to compilation by the Fortran compiler.

[Desclaux91] Desclaux, C. and Ribault, M., "MACS: Maintenance Assistance Capability for Software A.K.A.D.M.E.," *Proc. Conf. on Software Maintenance,* IEEE CS Press, Los Alamitos, Calif., 1991, pp. 2-12.

Describes a framework for a system to help maintainers understand programs. The areas it seeks to help programmers understand are in-progress applications, factual data, rationale behind design decisions, and the mapping of a domain to programming components. Impact analysis is also available in the framework to help programmers understand interactions between components.

[Desmond90] Desmond, J.,"Software Recycling is Errico's Domain," *Software Magazine,* Nov. 1990, pp. 95-99.

Describes a reengineering service supplier's[3] view of the system reengineering process, along with CASE tools to support the process. The example of reengineering process definition with pictorial flow diagrams, the process steps themselves, and the tools suggested (along with tool selection rationales) are valuable.

[Devanbu92] Devanbu, P. "GENOA—A Customizable, Language- and Front-End Independent Code Analyzer," *Proc. 14th Int'l Conf. on Software Eng.,* ACM Press, New York, pp. 307-317.

Describes an architecture and tool for generating

_____
[3]Steve Errico of Price Waterhouse, Tampa, Florida.

source code analysis tools. Both a front-end language translator and a back-end parse tree analyzer can be generated. The back end analyzer supports queries on parse trees. A subset of the queries are computable in polynomial time.

[Dietrich92] Dietrich, S.W. and Calliss, F.W., "A Conceptual Design for a Code Analysis Knowledge Base," *Journal of Software Maintenance: Research and Practice,* Vol. 4, 1992, pp. 19-36.

Presents a conceptual schema for a modeling intermodule code analysis data in a deductive database. The conceptual schema relationships can be translated into Prolog rules. The Prolog program can then be used to determine if instances of the intermodule relationships occur in a system.

◆[Elshoff82] Elshoff, J.L. and Marcotty, M., "Improving Computer Program Readability to Aid Modification," *Comm. of the ACM,* Vol. 25, No. 8, Aug. 1982, pp. 512-521.

Discusses how programs may be made more readable by manually applying transformations to improve coding style. A useful and instructive battery of code-improving transformations is presented.

[Eliot91] Eliot, L.B., "Overcoming Re-engineering Rigamarole," *CASE Trends,* Summer 1991, pp. 36-37.

Advocates using reengineering tools as part of normal system maintenance, and not just for corporate system overhauls.

◆[Fay85] Fay, S.D. and Holmes, D.G., "Help! I Have to Update an Undocumented Program," *Proc. Conf. on Software Maintenance,* IEEE CS Press, Los Alamitos, Calif., 1985, pp. 194-202.

A practical approach to understanding someone else's code. Whenever possible, code should be understood before it is changed. With down-to-earth advice, the authors describe how up-to-date documentation for old code may be created.

[FCSC81] Federal Conversion Support Center, "Software Improvement—A Needed Process in the Federal Government," Report OSD-81-102, Federal Conversion Support Center, Falls Church, Va., June 3, 1981, 14 pp.

The earliest report in the Federal Conversion Support Center series on software improvement. This short report discusses why software should be improved and what the goals of software improvement should be.

[FCSC83a] Federal Conversion Support Center, "Establishing a Software Engineering Technology (SET)," Report OSD/FCSC-83/014, Federal Conversion Support Center, Falls Church, Va., May 1983, 105 pp.

A description of software engineering practices, standards, guidelines, and tools that would support and be a part of the software improvement process.

[FCSC83b] Federal Conversion Support Center, "The

Software Improvement Process—Its Phases and Tasks," Report OSD/FCSC-83/006, (two parts), Federal Conversion Support Center, Falls Church, Va., July 1983, 229 pp. plus appendices.

A detailed management guide to implementing a software improvement program.

[Fischer91] Fischer, G., Henninger, S., and Redmiles, D., "Cognitive Tools for Locating and Comprehending Software Objects for Reuse," *Proc. 13th Int'l Conf. on Software Eng.*, IEEE CS Press, Los Alamitos, Calif., May 1991, pp. 318-328.

Describes a framework and tools for extracting potentially reusable software objects and understanding them.

[Forte92] Forte, G., "Software Maintenance under the CASE Umbrella," *CASE OUTLOOK,* Vol. 6, No. 1, Jan./Feb. 1992, pp. 7-18.

Consistently looks at the impact of CASE technology in software maintenance, from the perspectives of improvement, enhancement, and asset management. Discusses software maintenance and associated technology relative to reengineering and repository technology.

[Forte92] Forte, G., "Reverse Engineering Tools—For Workstation, PC, and Technical Applications," *CASE Outlook,* Vol. 6, No. 2, March/April 1992, pp. 5-20.

Describes several reverse engineering tools that run on workstations and PCs. Has a helpful list of questions of what to look for when selecting reverse engineering tools.

[Forte92] Forte, G., "Re-Engineering Tools: A Spectrum of Objectives and Capabilities," *CASE Outlook,* Vol. 6, No. 3, May/June 1992, pp. 17-35.

A nice discussion of reengineering tools and their significance, with descriptions of several off-the-shelf tools.

[Gansner88] Gansner, E.R., North, S.C., and Vo, K.P., "DAG—A Program that Draws Directed Graphs," *Software—Practice and Experience,* Vol. 18, No. 11, Nov. 1988, pp. 1047-1062.

Describes an algorithm for reading a list of nodes and edges and computing a layout. The tool is used by the C Information Abstraction system to display graphical output.

[Garner91] Garner, M., "Redevelopment Beats Obliteration," *Insurance & Technology,* Mar., 1991, pp. 6-10.

Advocates reusing code through reengineering, rather than effectively obliterating existing code by ignoring it and redeveloping from scratch.

[Georges91] Georges, M., "Organizational and Technological Framework for Change," *Proc. Spektrum,* Report EY-S0911-2D.G001, Munich, Germany, DECollege (Digital Equipment GmbH), 1991, pp. 1-7.

Discusses the philosophy behind the ESPRIT MACS project for software maintenance. This project supports "maintenance through undestanding" by helping the maintainer understand the why, what, and how of existing software. The author suggests that having design process rationales and nonfunctional requirements are fundamental to understanding an application to be maintained.

[GE91] General Electric, "Environment for Code Re-Engineering (ENCORE) Version 2.0," User Guide, Computer Science Program, General Electric Company, Corporate Research & Development, P.O. Box 8, Schenectady, New York 12301, June 1991.

Documents a tool for Fortran to Ada translation. The tool takes pains to avoid having the Ada look like "Adatran" (i.e., Fortran code structure with Ada syntax).

[Grady87] Grady, R.B., "Measuring and Managing Software Maintenance," *IEEE Software,* Vol. 4, No. 9, Sept. 1987, pp. 35-45.

Describes the application of measurable goals to software maintenance, and how these goals are achieved. Uses measurements and graphs to answer specific questions about software maintenance.

[Grass90] Grass, J.E. and Chen, Y.-F., "The C++ Information Abstractor," *Proc. Second Usenix C++ Conf.,* Usenix Association, Berkeley, Calif., 1990.

Describes the conceptual model used in a tool, like the C Information Abstractor, that can create a relational database containing information about the objects in C++ programs.

[Grass92] Grass, J.E., "Object-Oriented Design Archeology with CIA++," *Computing Systems,* Vol. 5, No. 1, Winter 1992, pp. 5-67.

Describes the use of CIA++ in constructing a working model of an object-oriented program's design.

[GUIDE89] "Application Reengineering," Guide Pub. GPP-208, Guide Int'l Corp., Chicago, 1989.

A good introduction to reengineering, its benefits, and related topics. Has several capsule case studies.

[GUIDE91] GUIDE Reverse Engineering Project, "The Strategic Development of Reverse Engineering Tools," GUIDE Reverse Engineering Project white paper, Mar. 20, 1991.

A good discussion of reverse engineering from a commercial perspective. Focuses on what is needed for, and on processes supporting, reverse engineering.

♦[Harrison82] Harrison, W., Magel, K. Kluczny, R., and DeKock, A., "Applying Software Complexity Metrics to Software Maintenance," *IEEE Computer,* Vol. 15, No. 9, Sept. 1982, pp. 65-79.

Lists 13 software metrics that can be used to measure code level (i.e., intra-module) software structure. The authors point out that, "What is needed is some method of pinpointing the characteristics of a computer program that are difficult to maintain and measuring the degree of their presence (or lack of it)."

[Hartman91a] Hartman, J., "Automatic Control Understanding for Natural Programs", PhD thesis, Dept. of Computer Sciences, Univ. of Texas, Austin, May 1991.

Describes a Cobol restructuring tool, UNPROG, based on bottom-up control concept recognition. The thesis emphasizes finding program plans and using these to guide concept recognition and program restructuring.

[Hartman91b] Hartman, J., "Understanding Natural Programs Using Proper Decomposition," *Proc. 13th Int'l Conf. on Software Eng.,* IEEE CS Press, Los Alamitos, Calif., 1991, pp. 62-73.

This paper discusses UNPROG, a Cobol restructuring tool that develops an understanding of a program and then restructures the program according to that understanding. The understanding in this case corresponds to matches between the program and instances of UNPROG's plan and concept knowledge patterns. The author claims that using plan understanding allows restructuring qualitatively better than more syntactically oriented restructuring techniques.

[Haugh91] Haugh, J.M. (ed.), "State-of-the-Art for Software Recovery/Renewal/Re-engineering," ASEDV Dept., IBM Federal Sector Division (RSD), Houston, Texas, Dec. 1991.

An interesting report that pulls together a large amount of information on reengineering and other topics. The latter half of the report gives short descriptions of many current reengineering tools. It discusses many CASE tools for reengineering and other uses.

[Haughton91] Haughton, H. P. and Lano, K., "Objects Revisited," *Proc. Conf. on Software Maintenance,* IEEE CS Press, Los Alamitos, Calif., 1991, pp. 152-161.

Gives an interesting method, with examples, for extracting objects from non-object-oriented source code. The method starts with identifying abstract data types. Sections of source code are then associated with the data types. Then the objects are expressed formally. The formal object descriptions are then further refined.

[Hazzah89] Hazzah, A., "Everything Is in the Names for Coming 'Capture' Tools," *Software Magazine,* Oct. 1989, pp. 40-50.

One aspect of data reengineering is migrating data from one DBMS to another. This paper describes several tools that can assist with migration. It also describes several other tools, for restructuring, reformatting, and analysis.

[Heiberg90] Heiberg, M.R., "Reverse Engineering: Moving Old Code to the New World," *System Builder,* Aug. 1990.

Describes a four-phase reverse engineering process. The process parts are (1) analyze and select applications or parts to reverse engineer, (2) load the software information into a work database for decomposition, analysis, and data standardization, (3) review and standardize the work database, (4) update the application to use the standardized information in the work database.

[Higgins81] Higgins, D.A., "Structured Maintenance: New Tools for Old Problems," *Computerworld* ("In Depth" section), Vol. XV, No. 24, June 15, 1981.

Concerns how to restructure a program into a structure more easily understood. The idea is, if a program is hard to understand, restructure it into a form more easily understood and then make further restructuring decisions. In this case, the form of the "more easily understood" structure comes from the Warnier-Orr design methodology. This methodology seeks to have a program's structure mirror the structure of the data that the program operates on.

[Houtz83a] Houtz, C., Federal Conversion Support Center, "Guidelines for Planning and Implementing a Software Improvement Program (SIP)," Report OSD/FCSC-83/004, Federal Conversion Support Center, Falls Church, Va., May 1983, 75 pp.

A management-oriented overview for planning a software improvement program. This report is a good summary of the software improvement program.

◆[Houtz83b] Houtz, C., "Software Improvement Program (SIP): Treatment for Software Senility," *Proc. 19th Computer Performance Evaluation Users Group,* National Bureau of Standards Publication 500-104, Oct. 1983, pp. 92-107.

Outlines an ambitious plan for not only improving software at the system and code levels, but also for improving the practices that may have led to poor structure. The paper defines a SIP as a plan to "preserve the value of past software investments as much as possible, and provides an incremental and evolutionary approach to modernizing the existing software to maximize its value, quality, effectiveness, and efficiency." An essential support for the SIP is a local definition of a software engineering technology (SET), a collection of procedures, guidelines, and tools governing the production of software.

[Husmann90] Husmann, H H., "Re-Engineering Economics," Eden Systems, 1990. Also appeared in *System Development,* Feb. 1991.

Discusses portfolio analysis for improving source code. The author uses the concept of expected maintainability to create a maintainability envelope for the software. An envelope is a graphical region delimiting adequate system maintainability bounds. The author uses portfolio analysis to determine if a system's actual maintainability falls within the expected maintainability envelope. He illustrates how measurement can be used to detect sliding maintainability and inspire improvements to it.

[Kapur83] Kapur, G.K., "Software Maintenance,"

Computerworld, ("In Depth" section), Vol. XVII, No. 39, Sept. 26, 1983, pp. ID/13 - ID/22.

This paper presents a software restructuring methodology called a "maintenance reduction plan." The plan involves three phases: a maintenance management audit, a software system audit, and software rehabilitation. The last phase involves (1) improving program format, logic, and documentation, (2) updating all system documentation, and (3) rechecking the quality ratings for program modules to ensure the ratings have improved.

[Kortesoja92a] Kortesoja, A. "Redevelopment Engineering: A Management View," *CASE Trends,* Apr. 1992, pp. 34, 36-37.

Describes the system reengineering process, with emphasis on "re-systematization." Re-systemization is a combination of reverse engineering from source code or data definitions to design or analysis information, then using this information (forward engineering) to redevelop the system. A two-part article.

[Kortesoja92b] Kortesoja, A., "Redevelopment Engineering: A Management View," Part II, *CASE Trends,* May 1992, pp. 54-56.

Continues the discussion of the previous article ([Kortesoja92a]).

[Kozaczynski91] Kozaczynski, W., "A Suzuki Class in Software Reengineering," *IEEE Software,* Vol. 8, No. 1, Jan. 1991, pp. 97-98.

Describes the author's experience in developing a tool to reengineer an assembly code system. The author describes the process of reengineering an old system as "(1) a forward design of what we know and can easily reproduce and (2) an exercise in filling the gaps of details by recovering them from the existing code." To do this, the best of source of design information about old code is still the programmer. The author discusses problems of assembly such as coping with code size and detecting coding tricks (such as packing and unpacking data) in code patterns.

[Jablonowski89] Jablonowski, D. and Guarna, V.A., Jr.,"GMB: A Tool for Manipulating and Animating Graph Structures," *Software—Practice and Experience,* Vol. 19, No. 3, Mar. 1989, pp. 283-301.

Graphs are commonly used to represent information obtained through program decomposition (e.g., abstract syntax trees). Support for graph manipulations is important for reengineering technology. This article describes a graph manager and browser that makes looking at graph-based information much easier. They give many of the technical details behind construction of such environments.

♦ [Lanergan84] Lanergan, R.G. and Grasso, C.A., "Software Engineering with Reusable Designs and Code," *IEEE Trans. on Software Eng.,* Vol. SE-10, No. 5, Nov. 1984, pp. 498-501.

This paper gives a strategy for recognition, defini-

tion, and reuse of functional modules. The paper illustrates the potential economic benefits of restructuring followed by reuse of commonly used software functions.

[Lano91] Lano, K. and Haughton, H., "Extracting Design and Functionality from Code," white paper, from H. Haughton, 1991.

Illustrates an interesting reverse engineering approach using formal transformations. The approach has three phases: (1) transform source code to a more abstract intermediate language, (2) use dataflow diagrams to split the code into single input-output functions, and derive an object class hierarchy, and (3) apply simplifying transformations to the information of (2).

[Lawrence82] Lawrence, M., "An Examination of Evolution Dynamics," *Proc. 6th Int'l Conf. on Software Eng.,* IEEE CS Press, Los Alamitos, Calif., 1982, pp. 188-196.

An independent critique of the five "laws" of software evolution mentioned in [Lehman80]. Software release data from several software systems is presented and analyzed. Except for the first and second laws, little evidence supported the laws. The author suggests a discontinuous model of software evolution to replace the smoothly changing continuous model proposed in [Lehman80].

[Lehman80] Lehman, M.M., "Programs, Life Cycles, and Laws of Software Evolution," *Proc. IEEE,* Vol. 68, No. 9, Sept. 1980, pp. 1060-1076.

An informative article on how programs evolve. Five "laws" of program evolution are presented. The paper has a good practical example on how to decide in which direction a system should evolve.

[Lerner91] Lerner, M., "A Standard Approach to the Process of Re-Engineering Long-Lived Systems," *CASE Trends,* Summer 1991, pp. 18-23.

Advocates using program schematic diagrams, reverse engineered from source code, to make the source code easier to understand and maintain.

[Linger79] Linger, R.C., Mills, H.D., and Witt, R.J., *Structured Programming: Theory and Practice,* Addison-Wesley, Reading, Mass., 1979.

A common problem with restructuring approaches that produce a theoretically "structured" program is that the resulting code is hard to understand. The new program's structure is strange and the correspondence between the new program's code and the old code—especially the documentation—may be obscure.

Chapter 4 of this book concerns code readability as well as code structure for its own sake. A mathematically precise definition of a "structured program" is given. A theorem is given, whose constructive proof shows how to transform an arbitrary program into a structured program. Then the structured program is restructured for readability. The idea is to start with the giant case statement version of a program, a version that can be mechanically generated [Ashcroft71]. Then the case statement is iteratively modified for increased readability. This involves inspecting the cases in the case statement for "islands" of structure, simplifying the case statement by encapsulating the structured islands, and reexamining the program for further simplification.

Chapter 4 is a good place to start for those wanting to build their own tool for restructuring a program's control flow. The IBM Corporation has done this for Cobol programs. The tool is called the Cobol Structuring Facility.

[Liu91] Liu, S.-S., Ogando, R., and Wilde, N., "The Object Finder: A Design Recovery Tool," Software Engineering Research Center, SERC-TR-46-F, Jan. 1991.

Discusses the extraction of "objects" from conventional programming languages. The authors give a framework for object extraction, examples, and related experience.

♦[Lyons81] Lyons, M.J., "Salvaging Your Software Asset (Tools Based Maintenance)," *Proceedings of the National Computer Conf.*, AFIPS Press, Arlington, Va., 1981, Vol. 50, pp. 337-341.

Discusses the use of a Cobol restructuring tool as a way to circumvent totally rewriting poorly structured programs. The tool, Structured Retrofit, is now (1992) available from Compuware, Farmington Hills, Mich.

♦[Maher83] Maher, B. and Sleeman, D.H., "Automatic Program Improvement: Variable Usage Transformations," *ACM Trans. on Programming Languages and Systems*, Vol. 5, No. 2, Apr. 1983, pp. 236-264.

Gives a specific example of a rule-based restructuring system. The improvement strategy is based on first improving the system syntactically by applying syntactic transformation rules (e.g., to delete unreachable code). The system improves the program's usage of variables by applying variable usage rules (e.g., to delete redundant assignments to the same variable). The design of this rule-based restructuring system is simple; the paper clearly reveals implementation details in building a rule-based system for software restructuring. Also of interest is that the system may be used to improve programs in more than one programming language. The set of syntactic transformation rules is easily changed.

[Marsh83] Marsh, R.E., "Application Maintenance: One Shop's Experience and Organization," *Proc. National Computer Conf.*, AFIPS Press, Arlington, Va., 1983, Vol. 52, pp. 145-153.

One of the few papers with any empirical measurements of software restructuring activity. Here restructurings ("preventive maintenance") constituted 2.2 percent of maintenance requests. The effort expended for each restructuring averaged .9 person-days.

♦[Martin84] Martin, R. J. and Osborne, W. M., "System Maintenance vs. System Redesign," Federal Information Processing Standards Publication 106: Guideline on Software Maintenance (Sec. 5), National Bureau of Standards, June 15, 1984, pp. 14-17.

Gives sample symptoms of software that is due for a restructuring audit. The paper suggests that symptoms such as frequent system failures, code over seven years old, code written for previous generation hardware, very large modules, and so on, may imply the need for system redesign. The paper presents a useful checklist of redesign decision factors that the reader may augment for his or her environment.

[McCabe90] McCabe, T.J., "Reverse Engineering, Reusability, Redundancy: The Connection," *American Programmer*, Vol. 3, No. 10, Oct. 1990, pp. 8-13.

Discusses how to find redundant code with metrics and how to use this code to help create reusable parts. Redundant code is prospected with MT™, a tool that displays program control structure. MT™ is available from McCabe & Associates, Columbia, Md.

[McClure92] McClure, C., *The Three Rs of Software Automation: Re-engineering, Repository, Reusability*, Prentice-Hall, Englewood Cliffs, N.J., 1992.

A survey of concepts and issues in the three areas in the title. Designed to give the reader a rapid acquaintance with fundamental ideas. Has many examples of CASE tool outputs.

[Miller87] Miller, J.C. and Strauss III, B.M., "Implications of Automatic Restructuring of Cobol," *SIGPLAN Notices*, Vol. 22, No. 6, June 1987, pp. 76-82.

The authors discuss low-level restructuring issues in Cobol restructuring. The authors argue that restructuring produces more understandable code.

[Moen90] Moen, S., "Drawing Dynamic Trees," *IEEE Software*, July 1990, pp. 21-28.

Discusses a way to simply, efficiently, and flexibly display graphical information.

[Moore86] Moore, J.E., Major, B.H., "Restructuring Scientific Software with Structured Flowcharts," *Proc. Fourth National Software Maintenance Conf.*, May 5-7, 1986, San Francisco, Ca.

Describes a graphical, manual technique that the authors successfully used to restructure Fortran programs. The technique labels the original source code, draws a rough flowchart, translates this to a structured flowchart, and then reorganizes the code according to the structured flowchart.

[Moore90] Moore, T. and Gibson, K., "The Reengineering of Navy Computer Systems," Tech. Report NAVSWC TR 90-216, Naval Surface Warfare Center, Silver Spring, Maryland, Sept. 1990.

A reengineering survey report that defines reengineering processes, establishes reverse engineering guidelines, and lists relevant automated products. The report is an easy-to-follow introduction to reengineering and reverse engineering.

♦[Morgan84] Morgan, H.W., "Evolution of a Software Maintenance Tool," *Proc. Second National Conf. on EDP Software Maintenance,* Silver Spring, Maryland: U.S. Professional Development Institute, 1984, pp. 268-278.

Describes experiences that led to the current versions of a structure recognition aid (Scan/370) and a Cobol restructuring tool (Superstructure). Scan/370, now renamed Scan/Cobol, and Superstructure are available from Computer Data Systems, Inc., Rockville, Maryland.

[Müller90] Müller, H.A., Möhr, J.R., and McDaniel, J.G.,"Applying Software Re-Engineering Techniques to Health Information Systems," Tech. Report DCS-138-IR, Dept. of Computer Science, School of Health Information Science, University of Victoria, Victoria, British Columbia, July 1990. Also appeared in the *Proc. IMIA Working Conf. on Software Engineering in Medical Informatics (SEMI),* Amsterdam, Oct. 8-10, 1990.

Describes the use of a reverse engineering tool, Rigi, to display, analyze, and help reorganize the structure of a health care information system. The extracted intrasystem relationships were module resource flows and program call graphs.

[Müller92] Müller, H.A.,"Spatial and Visual Representation of Software Structures: A Model for Reverse Engineering," Tech. Report TR-74.086, IBM Canada Ltd., Apr. 5, 1992.

An updated report on the use of Rigi, a system and framework for analyzing software system structure, for reverse engineering. The reverse engineering methodology used involves (1) creating resource flow graphs by extracting system components and dependencies, (2) composing subsystem hierarchies on top of the resource flow graphs, (3) computing the interfaces among the constructed subsystems, (4) evaluating the reconstructed subsystems according to software engineering principles, and (5) sequencing related views of the subsystem, for better system understanding, so the views can be played back and forth.

[Olders91] Olders, W.P., "Rule-Based Software Reengineering: Case Studies in the Use of Table Driven Technologies," *Software Eng.,* Mar./Apr. 1991, pp. 13-20.

Shows how reengineering procedural software into table-driven software can make code simpler and easier to develop. An important benefit is that tables capture and make explicit the rules under which code operates. The author illustrates the advantages of table-driven software with case studies from several companies.

[Oman90a] Oman, P.W. and Cook, C.R., "The Book Paradigm for Improved Maintenance," *IEEE Software,* Jan. 1990, pp. 39-45.

Argues that reading source code listings can be more effective if the listings are structured and displayed to look more like a book's organization. Some experimental support is given.

[Oman90b] Oman, P.W., "Maintenance Tools," *IEEE Software,* May 1990, pp. 59-65.

Discusses several tools for visualizing and understanding source code.

[Oman92a] Oman, P., Hagemeister, J., and Ash, D., "A Definition and Taxonomy for Software Maintainability," Tech. Report #91-08, Software Engineering Lab, Univ. of Idaho, Jan. 1992 (revised version).

A well-researched discussion of software maintainability. Presents many hierarchically-organized attributes of software maintainability.

[Oman92b] Oman, P. and Hagemeister, J., "Metrics for Assessing Software Maintainability," Tech. Report #92-01, Software Engineering Lab, Univ. of Idaho, Mar. 1992.

A useful presentation of maintainability metrics. Describes many metrics, along with some mathematical definitions of metrics. This technical report is a good companion report to [Oman92a].

[Parikh84] Parikh, G., "Logical Retrofit May Save Millions of Dollars in Software Maintenance." *Proc. 2nd National Conf. on EDP Software Maintenance,* Silver Spring, Md., U.S. Professional Development Inst., 1984, pp. 427-429.

Suggests restructuring software according to the design techniques created by Jean-Dominique Warnier (see [Warnier78]).

♦[Parnas79] Parnas, D.L., "Designing Software for Ease of Extension and Contraction," *IEEE Trans. on Software Eng.,* Vol. SE-5, No. 2, Mar. 1979, pp. 128-138.

Gives principles for partitioning a system into modules to increase its maintainability. The principles apply equally to repartitioning an existing system. The benefit gained with repartitioning is increased flexibility, which can ease enhancements, reduce errors, and reduce the need for restructuring later on. The paper discusses the issues of (1) identifying functionally independent and complete subsets of requirements, (2) hiding changeable aspects of a design within a module and making module interfaces insensitive to these changes, (3) viewing software as a virtual machine that supplies building block operations for constructing a system, and (4) making precise the virtual machine approach to partitioning by examining the "uses" relation among modules in the system.

♦[Partsch83] Partsch, A. and Steinbruggen, R., "Program Transformation Systems," *Computing Surveys,* Vol. 15, No. 10, Sept. 1983, pp. 199-236.

Rule-based systems for software restructuring originally grew from rule-based systems for automating software development. This paper surveys the latter systems. The wide variety of systems presented attests to the research popularity this area enjoys.

♦[Peercy81] Peercy, D.A., "A Software Maintainability Evaluation Methodology," *IEEE Trans. on Soft-*

ware Eng., Vol. SE-7, No. 4, July 1981, pp. 343-352.

Gives an approach where maintainability is evaluated by reviewing modules answering questionnaires concerning six attributes: modularity, descriptiveness, consistency, simplicity, expandability, and instrumentation. Software maintainability is assessed by using the scores achieved for these attributes.

[Perry81] Perry, W.E., Managing Systems Maintenance. Q.E.D. Information Systems, Wellesley, Mass., 1981.

Appendix A contains a set of qualitative criteria for deciding when to restructure or reengineer software. These can be refashioned as quantitative criteria for use in particular software maintenance environments.

♦[Perry85] Perry, W.E., "Seeking Remedies for Software Spoilage," Government Computer News, GCN Communications Corporation, Silver Spring, Ma., June 7, 1985, p. 23.

Suggests that modifying software also carries with it an engineering support cost. If this cost is not shouldered, the basis for maintaining software quality deteriorates in addition to deterioration of the software structure itself.

[Pfann92] Pfann, P. and Ritsch, H., "A Cobol Restructuring Environment," Tech. Report PSVB-0002-00, IBM Austria, Mar. 1992.

A useful discussion of the role of restructuring from a reengineering process model viewpoint. The report describes several ways where restructuring source code fits in reengineering the code. Illustrates the ideas with an off-the-shelf Cobol restructuring tool.

♦[Philips84] Philips, J.C., "Creating a Baseline for an Undocumented System—Or What Do You Do with Someone Else's Code?" In R.S. Arnold (ed.), Record of the 1983 Software Maintenance Workshop, IEEE CS Press, Los Alamitos, Calif., 1984, pp. 63-64.

Gives a horror story of how a 20,000-line Fortran system was arduously analyzed and redocumented. The paper illustrates that if documentation is allowed to become totally out-of-date, recovering a new documentation baseline can be expensive.

[Pleszkoch90] Pleszkoch, M.G., Hausler, P.A., Hevner, A.R., and Linger, R.C., "Function-Theoretic Principles of Program Understanding," Proc. 23rd Hawaii Int'l Conf. on System Sciences, IEEE CS Press, Los Alamitos, Calif., 1990.

This paper describes a methodology for program abstraction. Program abstraction permits "automatic abstraction of business rules from code to recover precise functional documentation." The authors describe how to systematically derive a program function that describes the mathematical function that a program performs.

[Rajlich1990] Rajlich, V., Damaskinos, N., Linos, P., and Khorshid, W., "VIFOR: A Tool for Software Maintenance," Software—Practice and Experience, Vol. 20, No. 10, Jan. 1990, pp. 67-77.

Describes VIFOR, a tool for maintaining Fortran 77 programs. VIFOR supports editing and displaying programs as source code and graphs. It can reverse engineer program graphs from code, and generate program skeletons from graphs. VIFOR uses a database of information incorporating its own data model for Fortran program information.

[Reiss85] Reiss, S.P., "Pecan: Program Development Systems that Support Multiple Views," IEEE Trans. on Software Eng., Vol. SE-11, No. 3, Mar. 1985, pp. 276-285.

This paper discusses the technical details behind multiple view systems. Multiple view systems are seen frequently in repository-based reengineering and reverse engineering tools. One of the most important issues that Pecan addresses is support for automatic updates of semantic information among views that share the information.

[Reynolds90] R.G. Reynolds and J.C. Esteva, "Learning to Recognize Reusable Software by Induction," white paper, 1990.

In this paper, the authors give several concepts characterizing reusable code, then give software metrics that capture these concepts. Some of the concepts discussed are coupling, cohesion, data structure, control structure, and documentation. They then discuss an approach whereby a recognition system may learn (i.e., build a decision tree) what constitutes a good, reusable code candidate by observing and generalizing from code examples.

[Richardson84] Richardson, G.L., Butler, C.W., and Hodil, E.D., "Mending Crazy Quilt Systems," Datamation, Vol. 30, No. 7, May 15, 1984, pp. 130-142.

Describes "a rational way of managing the software asset and improving the performance of the maintenance dollar." The paper includes (1) a definition of code quality, (2) how poor quality code undergoing maintenance may be located, and (3) the use and economic justification for tools used to improve code documentation.

[Richardson84] Richardson, G.L. and Hodil, E.D., "Redocumentation: Addressing the Maintenance Legacy," Proc. 1984 Nat'l Computer Conf., AFIPS Press, 1984, pp. 203-208.

Describes an approach to allocating reources for software maintenance, and the associated role of automated tools. Maintenance tools should not just be purchased and used. It should be decided quantitatively what parts of the code are good targets for maintenance resource allocation. Illustrates the approach with a case study.

[Rouve92] Rouve, C., "Using Program Analysis Tools to Understand Existing Software," CASE Outlook, Vol. 6, No. 2, March/April 1992, pp. 21-29.

Describes how CASE tools can be used in understanding programs. The article discusses actual tool outputs, for program restructuring, discovering structural defects, dynamic analysis, and transferring program knowledge.

[Sasso90] Sasso, W.C., "An Empirical Study of Reengineering Behavior: Design Recovery by Experienced Professionals," *Software Eng.*, May/June 1990, pp. 13-20.

Discusses the problem of understanding and documenting assembly code. The author describes observations of six programmers who were asked to understand an assembly code program and explain its function to another programmer, who needed to recreate the program in Cobol. The programmers used pseudocode and structure charts as the primary means to create representations of code segments.

[Scandura90] Scandura, J., "Cognitive Approach to Systems Engineering and Re-Engineering: Integrating New Designs with Old Systems," *Journal of Software Maintenance: Research and Practice*, Vol. 2, 1990, pp. 145-156.

Describes an approach to reengineering and a tool, the PRODOC re/NuSys Workbenchä, that supports it. The approach, called CogApp, involves (1) creating a logical design that captures the functionality of the current or planned system, (2) reverse engineering the existing code so that it can be more easily analyzed, and (3) mapping low-level components into high-level design. The paper illustrates the approach with an example.

[Scharenberg91] Scharenberg, M.E. and Dunsmore, H.E., "The Evolution of Classes and Objects During Object-Oriented Design and Programming," *Journal of Object-Oriented Programming*, Jan. 1991, pp. 30-34.

Suggests a five-stage way to characterize how classes and objects can evolve. The stages are "(1) Choose classes describing a five-stage evolution of class hierarchies, (2) Group classes by behavior into abstract objects, (3) Define classes that behave like intelligent agents, (4) Make classes fit into a controlling organization of objects, and (5) Define classes to facilitate interaction." For this tutorial, this approach to creating classes and objects may also figure when extracting classes and objects from non-object oriented source code.

[Schneidewind87] Schneidewind, N.F., "The State of Software Maintenance," *IEEE Transactions on Software Engineering*, Vol. SE-13, No. 3, March 1987, pp. 303-310.

A paper that succinctly describes the technical problems and realities of software maintenance. Discusses a useful sample of the published literature on software maintenance.

[Selfridge90] Selfridge, P.G., "Integrating Code Knowledge with a Software Information System," *Proc. 5th Ann. RADC Knowledge-Based Software Assistant (KBSA) Conf.*, Syracuse, N.Y., Sept. 1990, pp. 183-195.

Describes CODE-BASE, a knowledge base of information about Unix and C code. Users can learn about code by querying CODE-BASE. CODE-BASE also supports the creation of new code concepts that can become part of the knowledge base.

[Sittenauer92] Sittenauer, C., Olsem, M., and Murdock, D., "Software Re-engineering Tools Report," Software Technology Support Center (STSC), Hill Air Force Base, Utah, Apr. 1992.

A useful recent survey of software reengineering tools. The survey is not all-inclusive, but is useful for the tool analyses it does perform. Also contains a model for estimating the cost benefit for reengineering.

♦[Sneed84] Sneed, H.M., "Software Renewal: A Case Study," *IEEE Software*, Vol. 1, No. 3, July 1984, pp. 56-63.

Describes how a 24,000-line PL/1 subsystem was redocumented using automated tools. The tools were critical to the project's success, but the work remained labor intensive. Because of the great effort needed to respecify, redocument, and retest the subsystem, the paper gives a stark example of the relatively great effort needed to recreate up-to-date documentation.

[Sneed88] Sneed, H. and Jandrasics, G., "Inverse Transformation of Software from Code to Specification," *Proc. Conf. on Software Maintenance*, IEEE CS Press, Los Alamitos, Calif., 1988, pp. 102-109.

Describes a process of respecifying, then reconstructing software. Process steps include creating a normalized relational data schema for the modules, translating the schema into an entity relationship specification, then remodularizing and restructuring the software.

[Sneed89] Sneed, H., "The Myth of "Top-Down" Software Development and Its Consequences for Software Maintenance," *Proc. Conf. on Software Maintenance*, IEEE CS Press, Los Alamitos, Calif., 1989, pp. 22-29.

Argues that the top-down approach to constructing software creates software with maintenance problems. Reengineering is needed to resolve the problem.

[Sneed91] Sneed, H., "Bank Application Reengineering & Conversion at the Union Bank of Switzerland," *Proc. Conf.*, IEEE CS Press, Los Alamitos, Calif., 1991, pp. 60-72.

Describes lessons learned from performing a large commercial reengineering project. Testing the reengineered system, among other activities, had to be planned carefully. The project was judged a success by the customer.

[Sneed92] Sneed, H., *Software Sanierung (Reverse unde Reengineering*, Rudolf Müller, Köln, 1992. In German.

A survey of many software reengineering issues and approaches. Discusses several commercial tools as well. The author is one of the world's most experienced software reengineers.

[Sobrinho84] Sobrinho, F.G., "Structural Complexity:

A Basis for Systematic Software Evolution." doctoral dissertation, Univ. of Maryland, 1984. Available from University Microfilms International, 300 N. Zeeb Rd., Ann Arbor, Mich. 48106.

Among other results, this dissertation proposes a way to partition programs into independent sets of programming language statements. The approach features the development of dependency matrices that give the probability that a change in one module will affect another module. The point of the partitioning algorithm is to prepare a matrix that captures a measure of the "similarity" of one module to another that can be used as input to further module clustering algorithms.

♦[Spier76] Spier, M.J., "Software Malpractice—A Distasteful Experience," *Software—Practice and Experience,* Vol. 6, 1976, pp. 293-299.

Shows how an anonymous programmer's optimization, complete with bug, led to computer errors that were extremely difficult to analyze. Ultimately this led to the compiler being used despite known, unsolved bugs. The compiler had become just too widely used for a new (or restructured) compiler to be commissioned. Sometimes the act of unravelling poor structure can uncover bugs that themselves may be too "politically sensitive" to reveal and fix!

♦[Stankovic82] Stankovic, J., "Good System Structure Features: Their Complexity and Execution Time Cost," *IEEE Trans. on Software Eng.,* Vol. SE-8, No. 4, July 1982, pp. 306-318.

Looks at the impact of software structure on performance. Software restructuring can cause software performance to degrade, so techniques for regaining software performance, while still retaining the benefits of good structure for the programmer, are of interest. The paper proposes a technique, called vertical migration, for regaining software performance. The idea is to identify "the control structure and overhead of layered systems for purposes of performance improvement," and then apply automated transformations to perform the improvements. Performance is gained by eliminating unrequired generality present in a layer of a system.

[Tamassia88] Tamassia, R., di Battista, G., and Batini, C., "Automatic Graph Drawing and Readability of Diagrams," *IEEE Trans. on Systems, Man, and Cybernetics,* Vol. 18, No. 1, Jan./Feb. 1988, pp. 61-79.

Display of graphical information is so important for reverse engineering that much study has gone into algorithms for presenting the information in a readable manner. This paper, a classic in its field, describes the technical and esthetic issues confronting those designing display algorithms.

[Travis84] Travis, A.J., "Reengineering Business Systems," IASA Annual Conf., N.Y., May 20-23, 1984. A related paper appeared in the *Proc. 3rd National Conf. on EDP Software Maintenance,* U.S. Professional Development Inst., Silver Spring, Md., 1985.

Perhaps the first paper to use the term "reengineering"

for software improvement. Discusses how restructuring may be used to aid the strategic evolution of an enterprise's data processing capabilities. To reengineer a system, the approach suggests performing bottom-up analysis, to quantitatively assess the code's state; performing top-down planning, to ensure the system is restructured consistent with anticipated enterprise needs; and performing bottom-up implementation, to restructure code in the current system (e.g., migrating a file system-based system to one that uses a database). The approach is implemented for Cobol using the tools PATHVU (for quantitatively assessing the code's state) and STRUCTURED RETROFIT (for restructuring Cobol code). The tools are now (1992) available from Compuware, Farmington Hills, Mich.

[Ulrich89] Ulrich, W., "Developing A Reengineering Strategy," *Bank Systems and Technology,* Sept. 1989.

Points out that computer-aided software engineering (CASE) technology typically revolves around a repository. "Once loaded, this repository represents the existing system in its entirety... ." Reengineering and reverse engineering help load the repository with information from existing systems. The repository becomes the key support for software evolution.

[Ulrich90] Ulrich, W., "An Executive Overview of Redevelopment Engineering," *Quality Data Processing,* Apr. 1990, pp. 21-26.

Presents definitions, motivation, benefits, and strategies for "re-development engineering."

[Ulrich90] Ulrich, W., "From Ugly Legacies to Artistic Beauties," *Software Magazine,* Dec. 1990, pp. 33-45.

A good survey article on the CASE tools and application aspects of applying reengineering in commercial practice. The article discusses reengineering in the context of migrating legacy systems to an integrated CASE-based system.

[Van Sickle92] Van Sickle, L., "Reconstructing Data Integrity Constraints from Source Code," Tech. Report AUS-0792-3, EDS Research, Austin Laboratory, 1601 Rio Grande, Suite 500, Austin, Texas 78701, July 1992.

Describes ongoing work to develop tools for extracting data integrity constraints from Cobol source code for transaction processing applications. Data integrity constraints ensure that data is semantically consistent and meaningful. To find integrity constraints, the author uses a combination of control path analysis, plan recognition, and program verification. Program slicing is used to "reduce the number of statements that must be considered when doing program verification."

[Vo92] Vo, K.-P., and Chen, Y.-F., "Incl: A Tool to Analyze Include Files," *Proc. Summer Usenix Conf.,* June 8-12, 1992.

Discusses a tool that analyzes C and C++ "include" hierarchies. The analysis allows one to show graphically dependencies among files, infer what files are not needed, and indicate how to remove unused include files.

[Von Mayrhauser91] Von Mayrhauser, A., "AMT—The Ada Maintenance Toolchest," *Proceedings Tri-Ada '91,* ACM Press, New York, 1991, pp. 294-299.

This paper succinctly discusses several of the elements of program understanding environments. Even though the author's environment is for Ada code, the ideas apply to understanding code in other languages.

[Ward89] Ward, M., Calliss, F.W., and Munro, M., "The Maintainer's Assistant," *Proc. Conf. on Software Maintenance,* IEEE CS Press, Los Alamitos, Calif., 1989.

This paper describes the general structure of a transformation-based code analysis tool for aiding program understanding. The paper gives two examples of transformational program improvement, for program restructuring and for deriving the specification of a program. The paper uses a theory of transformations developed in: Ward, M., *Proving Program Refinements and Transformations,* doctoral dissertation, Oxford Univ., 1988.

[Warnier78] Warnier, J-D., *Program Modification,* Martinus Nijhoff, Boston, 1978.

Discusses how to modify programs already designed by using Warnier's program design methodology. (Warnier's methodology designs a program to reflect the (hierarchical) structure of the data the program operates on.) Changes to a program are first evaluated as to their impact on input data structure, then the program is modified. Other modification principles are given in case the input data is not affected by a proposed change.

◆[Warren82] Warren, S., "MAP: A Tool for Understanding Software," *Proc. 6th Int'l Conf. on Software Eng.,* IEEE CS Press, Los Alamitos, Calif., Sept. 1982, pp. 28-37.

Some forms of software structure are easier to appreciate by simply extracting and displaying those program parts most relevant to the structure. In this paper, program structure is determined by using tools reflecting different views of the program. Sample views are display of procedures (in a system structure chart) which contain selected program statements; trace of the execution of selected statements; display of possible references or modifications to selected variables; and display of the differences between two versions of a source program. Tools like those available in MAP are becoming increasingly common. (Since publication of this paper, MAP has been renamed and considerably enhanced. It is available as VIA/INSIGHT, from VIASOFT, Phoenix, Arizona.)

[Weinberg82] Weinberg, G., "Worst-First Maintenance," in Parikh, G. (ed.), *Techniques of Program and System Maintenance,* Winthrop, Cambridge, Mass., 1982.

Recommends improving the roughly 20 percent of modules involved in 80 percent of the discovered software problems in a system.

◆[Weinberg83] Weinberg, G., "Kill that code!,"

Infosystems, Aug. 1983, pp. 48-49.

Suggests that very small changes are much more prone to error than larger changes. Why? People may take very small changes less seriously and therefore not think them through or test them as carefully as more "substantial" changes. The paper is a sobering reminder of the fragility of software to even the slightest change.

[Weinman91] Weinman, E.D., "The Promise of Software Reengineering," *Information Week,* April 22, 1991, pp. 32-33, 36, 40.

A brief overview of software reengineering. Gives definitions, benefits, and market possibilities for reengineering. Mentions several commercial reengineering tools and services.

◆[Weiser86] Weiser, M. and Shneiderman, B., "Human Factors of Software Design and Development," in Salvendy, G. (ed.) *Handbook of Human Factors/Ergonomics,* John Wiley and Sons, New York, 1986.

Surveys the research on the effects of software structure on programmer performance. The paper considers a wide range of issues, from methods for inferring whether software structure impacts programmer performance, to what aspects of programming style positively influence programmers, to how software quality and productivity may be evaluated with software metrics. From a practical viewpoint, the work supplies a rich source of ideas for software structure—information which, for example, can be helpful in deciding one's local definition of software structure standards.

[Weizman92] Weizman, D., "Integration by Re-Engineering," *CASE OUTLOOK,* Vol. 6, No. 1, Jan./Feb. 1992, pp. 27-32.

Describes a reengineering approach where the target system architecture is distributed. The desktop workstation is the primary delivery platform.

[Wild90] Wild, C., Maly, K. and Liu, L., "Decision-Based-Support-Paradigm: A New Method to Structure Source Code," *Proc. Conf. on Software Maintenance,* IEEE CS Press, Los Alamitos, Calif., 1990, pp. 218-229.

Describes an approach to documentation that captures the decisions made in producing software. The decision structure is linked to products affected by the decisions. Maintainers use the decision structure to help understand the rationale behind pieces of source code. A hypertext-based prototype tool supporting the approach is described.

◆[Wolberg83] Wolberg, J.R., "Conversion Economics," in J. Wolberg, *Conversion of Computer Software,* Prentice-Hall, Englewood Cliffs, N.J., 1983, ch. 2, pp. 39-59.

Software restructuring is a typical first step in preparing a system for conversion. In a sense, restructuring the software converts the software to run on a new virtual machine that makes the software's operations easier to understand and therefore easier to convert. Studying the economics of software conversion can be helpful in calculating software restructuring costs. Such economics are discussed in this paper. Among other valuable results, the paper compares cost equations for software redesign, reprogramming, and conversion.

[Workman91] Workman, D.A., "REENEW: A Reengineering Environment and Workbench," white paper, Univ. of Central Florida, Dept. of Computer Science, Orlando, Fla., 1991.

Describes GRIP (Graphical Interactive Programming), a forward development environment that was extended to support reengineering. GRIP supports a variety of views of programs, such as a structure view, control view, and data view.

♦ [Yau80] Yau, S.S., and Collofello, J., "Some Stability Measures for Software Maintenance," *IEEE Trans. on Software Engineering,* Vol. SE-6, No. 6, Nov. 1980, pp. 545-552.

Presents a measure of the logical stability of a program. Software stability is "the resistance to the amplification of changes in the program." The more stable the program, the more software changes can be confined to one or a few modules.

[Yourdon75] Yourdon, E., *Techniques of Program Structure and Design,* Prentice-Hall, Englewood Cliffs, N.J., 1975.

Presents the control-flow restructuring techniques of the boolean variable approach and the duplication of coding approach. An example of the Ashcroft-Manna giant case statement approach (see reference above)—called the state variable approach by Yourdon—is also presented.

[Yourdon89] Yourdon, E., "Re-3, Part 2: Re-engineering, Restructuring, and Reverse Engineering," *American Programmer,* Vol. 2, No. 6, June 1989, pp. 3-12.

Provides several reengineering product vignettes. The vignettes will introduce the reader to typical reengineering tool capabilities. He starts with one pointed example of the possible difficulties in getting information about tools in a highly competitive reengineering market. He then discusses how reengineering capabilities have been added to CASE tools that were originally

forward engineering-oriented. He then discusses several tools available from Language Technology, Inc.[4] Included in this discussion is the concept of portfolio analysis and how software assets can assume various representations during their life cycles.

[Yu91] Yu, D., "A View on Three R's (3Rs): Reuse, Reengineering, and Reverse-engineering," *SIGSOFT Software Engineering Notes,* Vol. 16, No. 3, July 1991, p. 69.

Suggests that understanding the fundamental concepts behind reuse, reengineering and reverse engineering—the "3Rs"—will help one understand their relationships. The author points out that goal-oriented transformations often underlie reverse engineering and reengineering. A flow diagram figure in the paper helps to relate the 3Rs to supporting repository technology.

[Zimmer90] Zimmer, J.A. "Restructuring for Style," *Software—Practice and Experience,* Vol. 20, No. 4, Apr. 1990, pp. 365-389.

Describes a style for restructuring the source code of a program. The style emphasizes making invariants true throughout a program, and reducing potential data cobwebs. A data cobweb occurs between two data items when "a modification in the meaning or use of one might necessitate a modification in the meaning or use of the other because of program structure." The author illustrates the approach in detail to restructure a Fortran program.

[Zvegintzov92] Zvegintzov, N., "On Reverse Engineering, Reengineering, and Conversion," *Software Management News,* Vol. 10, Nos. 7/8, July/August 1992, pp. 8-12, 14-25.

Summarizes the state of commercial technology for reengineering, conversion, and reverse engineering. Discusses terminology and some industry trends. Has a good list of currently available services and tools for software reengineering.

---

[4]Language Technology, Inc. was acquired in 1991 by KnowledgeWare, Atlanta, Ga.

About the Author

Robert S. Arnold is principal of Software Evolution Technology (SEVTEC) in Herndon, Virginia. Arnold has been project manager at the Software Productivity Consortium's Reengineering Project in Herndon, Virginia. He has worked at MITRE Corporation and the IBM San Jose Research Laboratory. He is the author of the *Tutorial on Software Restructuring,* published by the IEEE Computer Society Press in 1986.

His research and practical interests include reengineering, reverse engineering, impact analysis, repository and bridge technology, maintenance, and reengineering for reuse.

Arnold received a BA "with highest distinction" in mathematics and computer studies from Northwestern University in 1975, an MS in computer science from Carnegie Mellon University in 1977, and a PhD in computer science from the University of Maryland in 1983. He is a member of the IEEE Computer Society. He can be reached at Software Evolution Technology, 12613 Rock Ridge Road, Herndon, VA 22070; telephone/fax (703) 450-6791, e-mail r.arnold@compmail.com.